India at her best
2020-22
COMBINED EDITION

First published in 2021 by Hachette India
(Registered name: Hachette Book Publishing India Pvt. Ltd)
An Hachette UK company
www.hachetteindia.com

This edition published in 2022

1

On account of the COVID-19 pandemic and the copyright owner's decision about the best time to publish the book so that it can easily reach its readers, this volume for continuity is a combined edition covering selections from entries for the 2020 and 2021 editions, but to restore the sequence of annual publishing it has been titled 2020–22. The entries ongoing now for the 2022 edition (for which the entry cut-off date was 31 May 2021) and those for the 2023 edition (with the cut-off date as 31 May 2022) will be featured in the 2023 edition, which (assuming no further disruptions) is planned for publication in end-2022.

Information in the book has been updated to 31 March 2021, except in the *Business and Economy, Combating COVID-19, States and Union Territories* and *Sports* chapters, where select information relates to later dates.

All Wikipedia Commons photographs and those from similar sources have been accessed between 1 June 2019 and 20 March 2021 and their copyright status confirmed between 31 March and 10 April 2021. Shafali Verma's image (on the back cover) was sourced and its copyright status confirmed on 1 July 2021. 2021. Images of Indian Museum (p. 145) and farmers' protest (p. 190) were sourced and their copyright status confirmed in March 2022. Any later additional notifications relating to such photographs or changes made in the copyright status of such photographs after this date cannot be considered legally valid or applicable for this book in all versions, and are not legally binding. Some photos in *The Natural World* chapter are extralimital.

All maps in this work are pictorial representations, not to scale, and are not meant to represent exact political boundaries. They are for general illustration only, and are not intended to be used for reference purposes or reproduction elsewhere.
It is clarified that the representation of a particular theme or data set across regions with colour demarcations do not reflect political boundaries. It is also reiterated that such pictorial maps do not either represent or contradict India's national sovereignty, jurisdiction or the recognition of political regions as mandated by the Surveyor General of India for maps showing political boundaries.

Old place names (such as Madras, Calcutta and Bombay) may have been used to retain the historicity of the information as well as avoid confusion with earlier Presidencies and Provinces of the same name.

All efforts have been made to verify the copyright ownership of photographs as well as the correctness of the information included in this edition. Any omissions are unintentional and regretted, and, following written communication, will be rectified in the next edition.

Hardback edition ISBN 978-93-88322-98-0
Paperback edition ISBN 978-93-91028-74-9
Ebook edition ISBN 978-93-88322-99-7

Hachette Book Publishing India Pvt. Ltd
4th & 5th Floors, Corporate Centre
Plot No. 94, Sector 44, Gurugram 122003, India

Designed and typeset
by Syed Salahuddin

Printed and bound in India
by Manipal Technologies Limited, Manipal

Dear Readers,

Welcome to a new decade of excellence with the *Limca Book of Records.*

In a remarkable way, this celebratory edition of 30 completed years of the book coincides with the brand commemorating 50 years since its inception in 1971. Once again, in this iconic book of Indian milestones, we are thrilled to witness the achievements of Indians from all walks of life and all parts of the country. With its small but stellar beginnings in 1990, the *Limca Book of Records* has grown each year, and this edition too shares with you a superb selection of outstanding records.

We are living in exceptional times, experiencing the most surreal situations and fighting for survival amidst a global pandemic. Unthinkable and unprecedented as it may be, it is deeply inspiring to see that people have achieved so much even in these testing times. It truly marks the resilience and strength of humankind in the face of challenges.

This special edition also reflects the many dimensions of India's battle against the virus, and respectfully applauds COVID-19 warriors and front-line workers as well as innovators and altruists in a special section. A few of the highlights are the Vande Bharat mission that became the world's largest repatriation exercise, while Noccarc Robotics, a start-up led by Nikhil Kurele and Harshit Rathore, developed low-cost portable ventilators; Bharat Biotech in collaboration with the Indian Council for Medical Research developed Covaxin while the Serum Institute of India developed Covishield, both vaccines that join the gallery of accomplishments on display in the *Limca Book of Records.*

What makes this year's cover truly special is that it celebrates people who look beyond themselves and their immediate surroundings, to focus on our unique blue planet. The book showcases several such protectors of the earth, who steered sustainability campaigns, drew attention to waste management, and undertook recycling and other environment-friendly missions. From the most massive plog run in Bengaluru, Karnataka, where 6,518 participants collected 6.5 tonnes of plastic waste, to Sasmita Lenka, who won the United Nations Asia Environmental Enforcement Award 2020, and from a one-of-its-kind plastic-free B.Y.O.C. (Bring Your Own Container) store to inaugurating the country's first wilderness park, these green warriors have set records in one of the most relevant fields today.

We have much more to be proud of in every area, with an incredible range of records that stand testimony to the spirit of human endeavour and perseverance against all odds. A few record holders who shine brilliantly among the brightest are Ngangom Bala Devi, who not only became the first Indian woman footballer to sign a professional contract overseas but also the first to actually score in a professional European football league match, and Praveen Kumar, a battle casualty of the 2008 Mumbai terror attacks, who became the first differently-abled triathlon athlete to win the Ironman title. Many more such fascinating feats and incredible triumphs are waiting to be discovered on the ever-continuing journey of the *Limca Book of Records.*

In fulfilling its mandate to bring the best of India to you, the *Limca Book of Records* 2020–22 has added on befitting photographs, friendly infographics and easy-to-scan charts to present to you a comprehensive chronicle of our country's many remarkable facets and successes. We are always inspired by our record holders and welcome our readers to share with us their views and, of course, their records.

Stay well, stay healthy, and stay with us.

***LBR* Marketing Team**
Coca-Cola India

EDITOR EMERITUS
Vijaya Ghose

HACHETTE INDIA *LBR* EDITORIAL TEAM (FOR THIS EDITION)
Editor: Vatsala Kaul Banerjee
Project Executive: Shubhali Chopra,
Editorial Assistant: Debomitra Ghosh

CONSULTANTS

ADVENTURE
Ajeet Bajaj

BUSINESS and ECONOMY
Rajiv Nagpal

CINEMA
Diptakirti Chaudhuri

COMMUNITY DEVELOPMENT and NATURE
Usha Rai

EDUCATION
Dr Alpana Neogy

MEMORY
Squadron Leader Jayasimha Ravirala

THE HUMAN STORY
Vijaya Ghose

SPORTS
Chief Coordinator: Athletics, Badminton, Football, Hockey, Squash: **Novy Kapadia**

Archery, Basketball, Boxing, Cue Sports, Gymnastics, Wrestling, Kabaddi, Powerlifting, Weightlifting, General Sports: **Suresh Kumar Lau**

Chess, Golf, Table Tennis: **Rakesh Rao**

Shooting, Tennis: **Kamesh Srinivasan**

Swimming: **Meenakshi Pahuja**

Cricket: **Vimal Kumar**

Statistics: **Hariprasad Chattopadhyay**

SPECIAL CONTRIBUTOR
Amrit Menon, Wildlife Trust of India

LAST DATE FOR NEW ENTRIES (COMPLETE WITH DOCUMENTATION) FOR THE *LIMCA BOOK OF RECORDS* 2023 EDITION: 31 MAY 2022

Please see the Rules and Guidelines section for details.
Limca Book of Records does not have any branch offices or representatives.

General and Sales enquiries: **sales@hachetteindia.com**

Dear Readers,

We have been waiting eagerly to bring this edition to you, but the pandemic prevented us from doing so thus far. COVID-19 has caused death and devastation on an unimaginable scale in India and around the world, and it continues to lurk, and loom up menacingly again and again. As the virus continues to threaten and rage and kill, we have – just like you – tried to adjust to the new normal and move forward. For what is the spirit of this book if not to rise to challenges and leap to victory!

That is why, as a tribute to the courageous and the enterprising everywhere, we are proud to bring you this special edition that marks over 30 completed years of the *Limca Book of Records,* a veritable archive of the incredible achievements and irrepressible essence of India and its people.

Each edition is preceded by a whole year of exciting news – old records are outperformed and new ones are achieved to set a higher bar to surpass. Each record is marked by uniqueness – in its concept, originality, and a variety of markers such as endurance, courage, teamwork, or the degree of the risk taken – and the sheer perseverance that every such endeavour demands.

It's difficult not to be impressed by the range and diversity of the records attempted and attained by the record holders featured in this edition. They come from all corners of our country, having braved unpredictable rivers and high seas, built the smallest objects and the largest sculptures, discovered amazing things and phenomena, set up centres of faith and headquarters of industry, performed medical marvels, and won gold, silver and bronze medals for the nation in super-competitive sports. They have written, danced, drawn, painted, run, jumped, constructed, governed, acted, directed...the list of their feats is both engrossing and laudatory. From leaders in their fields to common men and women driven by unusual ambition and equally outstanding dedication, these tenacious champions of excellence are truly inspiring.

Our heartfelt congratulations – and gratitude – to those of you who have made it into this edition of the book. Your determination and diligence are the very reason that the *Limca Book of Records* has been going strong for more than three full decades.

As in earlier years, we have filled this edition with not just the most enthralling records but also extra-special information, including the Super 30 and Record Rewind features, to whet the appetite of knowledge buffs, quizzers, fact-collectors and anyone who wishes to be inspired.

And as always, for those who could not be featured in the book this time, there's always the next edition. Please do read our revised and updated Rules and Guidelines carefully as we try each year to make the parameters for records sharper, more exact and clearly understood for others to be able to set new ones. We look forward to fresh superlatives from around the country and welcome your participation. It is your continuing enthusiasm and your constant passion to be the best you can be that makes this book what it is, and our nation a proud one.

Vatsala Kaul Banerjee
Editor, *Limca Book of Records*

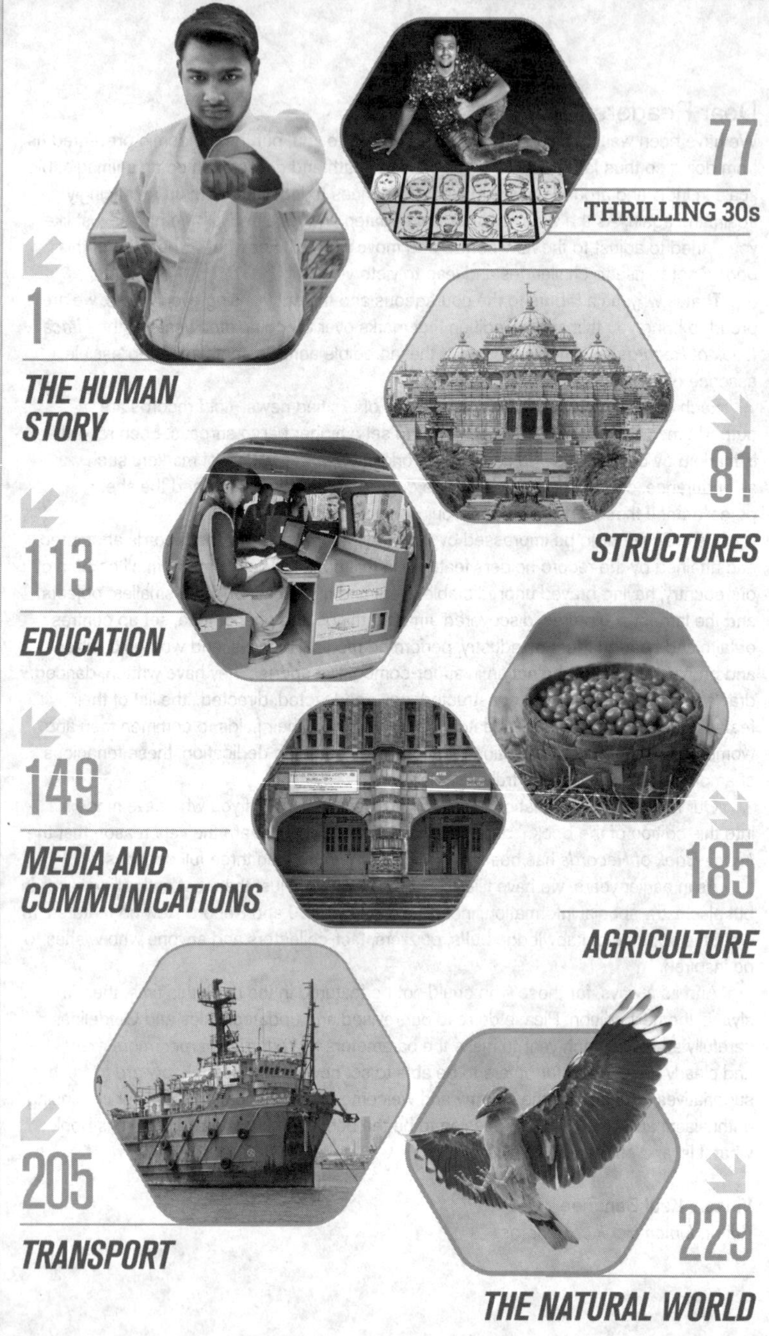

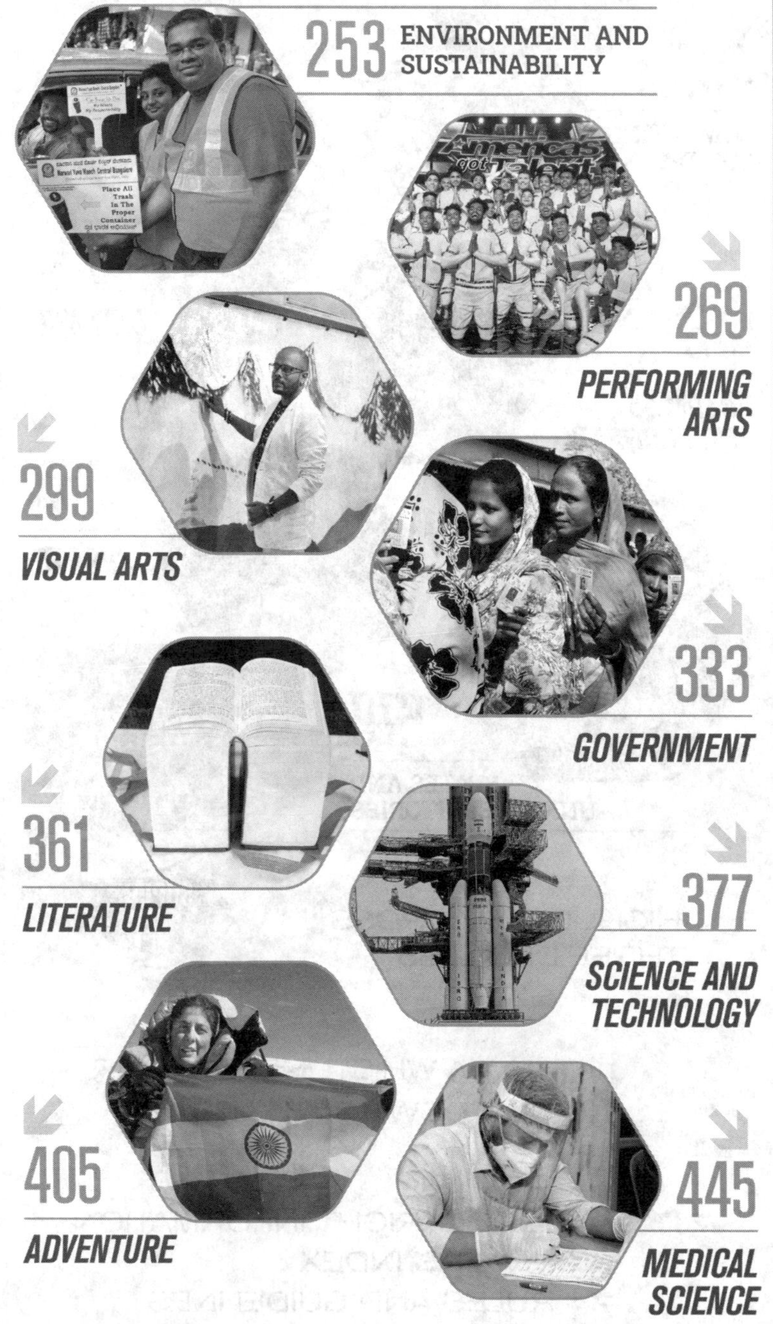
Place All
Trash
In The
Proper
Container

SUPER
30

30

THE HUMAN STORY

MEMORY

First winner of the Mental Calculation World Championship

Neelakanta Bhanu Prakash (b. 13 October 1999) from Hyderabad, Telangana, became the first Indian gold medallist at the Mental Calculation World Championship at Mind Sports Olympiad (MSO) held in London, UK, on 15 August 2020. He beat 29 contenders from 13 countries by a margin of 65 points.

Fastest solving of mirror cube while blindfolded

Mohammed Aiman Koli (b. 1 August 2004) from Mumbai, Maharashtra, solved a mirror cube (3 x 3), blindfolded, in 1 min. 0.8 sec. on 26 December 2017 at Veermata Jijabai Technological Institute, Mumbai, Maharashtra.

Fastest solving of cubes

Vipin (b. 21 February 2003), a student of Abacus Champs Academy, New Delhi, solved a 2 x 2 Rubik's cube and a 3 x 3 Rubik's cube (25 times each) in 10 mins 36 secs on 27 May 2019.

Fastest identification of all elements of the periodic table

Jag Prasad Bhattarai (b. 27 July 1980) from Dehradun, Uttarakhand, identified all 118 elements of the periodic table by looking at the atomic numbers arranged in random order in 1 min. 30 secs on 19 February 2019 at the Choice Coaching Institute, Kaulagarh, Dehradun.

Fastest to arrange all elements of the periodic table in order

Meenakshi Agrawal (b. 5 March 1975) from Delhi NCR arranged all the 118 elements of the periodic table in order in 2 mins 49 secs on 27 September 2019 at the Press Club of India, New Delhi.

Fastest to recall 2,500 digits of pi

Vimosh Venugopal (b. 23 May 1984) from Thrissur, Kerala, recalled 2,500 digits of the value of pi correctly in 12 mins 18 secs 90 microseconds on 27 October 2019 at Hotel Joys Palace, Thrissur.

Most Rubik's cubes solved – 5 mins

Peram Madhumitha (b. 23 May 2007) from Kamareddy, Telangana, successfully solved 20 Rubik's cubes (3 x 3) in 5 mins on 23 May 2020 at Hotel Hamsa, Kamareddy.

Meenakshi Agrawal

Vimosh Venugopal

Peram Madhumitha

Most Rubik's cubes solved – 15 mins

S.P. Shankar (b. 1 March 2011) from Hyderabad, Telangana, correctly solved 49 Rubik's cubes (3 x 3) in 15 mins on 19 September 2020 at his residence.

Most Rubik's cubes solved – 1 hour

Satya Sudhai Kolipaka (b. 20 February 2011) from Hyderabad, Telangana, solved 93 scrambled Rubik's cubes (3 x 3) in 1 hr on 23 July 2019 in Hyderabad, Telangana.

Satya Sudhai Kolipaka

Most binary numbers memorized – 5 mins

Peram Madhumitha (b. 23 May 2007) from Kamareddy, Telangana, successfully recited 300 binary numbers in 5 mins on 10 June 2020 at Hotel Hamsa, Kamareddy.

Most number of national anthems sung by an individual

Yathaarth Murthy (b. 23 February 2006) from Bengaluru, Karnataka, can sing the national anthems of 260 countries, as on 31 May 2019. He learnt all the anthems in a span of three years and five months.

Most dinosaur names recalled – 1 min.

Padmanabhan Nair (b. 13 September 2014) from Alleppey, Kerala, correctly recalled the names of 41 different dinosaurs in 1 min. on 2 September 2020 at the Indian Cultural Centre, Doha, Qatar.

Most days of the week identified from dates (1600–2100) – 5 mins

Shaurya Sarda (b. 22 August 2013) from New Delhi correctly identified 95 days of the week from dates between 1600 and 2100 in 5 mins on 15 September 2020 at Sardar Patel Vidyalaya, New Delhi.

Shraddha Garg

Shraddha Garg (b. 18 October 1997) from Neemuch, Madhya Pradesh, solved the addition of 5 rows of 25-digit numbers and doubled the answer 10 times in 2 mins 40 secs on 17 October 2017.

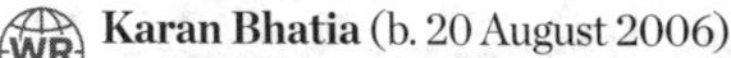

WR **Karan Bhatia** (b. 20 August 2006)

1. Solved the addition of 2,500 rows of 1-digit numbers flashing at 0.6 sec. intervals on Flash Anzan.
2. Solved two consecutive tasks of the addition of 1,100 rows of 1-digit numbers flashing at 0.27 sec. intervals on Flash Anzan.

Hitanshi Bedi

Hitanshi Bedi (b. 19 October 2006) from New Delhi recalled all the multiplication tables from 10 to 99 (till 10 times) in 5 mins 32 secs on 27 May 2019 *orally*.

ABACUS CHAMPS ACADEMY

On 25 and 27 May 2019, students of Abacus Champs Academy, New Delhi, performed the following records and their calculations were 100 per cent accurate. The participants were mentored and coached by Davinder Singh – chief mentor, and Ravinder Kaur – teachers' head.

Harshit Goyal

Harshit Goyal (b. 27 June 2006)

1. Solved the addition of 900 rows of 2-digit numbers flashing at 0.3 sec. intervals on Flash Anzan.
2. Solved four consecutive tasks of addition of 450 rows of 2-digit numbers flashing at 0.3 sec. intervals on Flash Anzan.

Harshit Goyal (b. 27 June 2006)

1. Solved three consecutive tasks of addition of 2,000 rows of 1-digit numbers flashing at 0.8 sec. intervals on Flash Anzan.
2. Solved three consecutive tasks of addition of 800 rows of 2-digit numbers flashing at 0.7 sec. intervals on Flash Anzan.

Suraj Chakraborty

Suraj Chakraborty (b. 30 May 2005)

1. Solved the addition of 10 rows of 5-digit numbers flashing at 0.6 sec. intervals on Flash Anzan.
2. Solved the addition of a 4-digit number to itself (56 steps) *orally* in 1 min.
3. Solved the addition of 130 rows of 4-digit numbers flashing at 1.5 sec. intervals on Flash Anzan.
4. Solved two consecutive tasks of addition of 65 rows of 5-digit numbers flashing at 1.5 secs. intervals on Flash Anzan.
5. Solved three consecutive tasks of addition of 110 rows of 3-digit numbers flashing at 0.5 sec. intervals on Flash Anzan.

Naman Singla (b. 5 May 2007) solved three consecutive tasks of addition of 800 rows of 2-digit numbers flashing at 0.7 sec. intervals on Flash Anzan.

Shreya Gupta (b. 22 January 2007) solved the addition of 10 rows of 2-digit numbers (42 sums) in 5 mins by *writing*.

Yuvraj Manchanda (b. 16 December 2005)

1. Solved the addition of 120 rows of 2-digit numbers in 1 min. by *listening*.
2. Solved the addition of 120 rows of 2-digit numbers flashing at 0.23 sec. intervals on Flash Anzan.

Yuvraj Manchanda (b. 16 December 2005) solved the addition of 80 rows of 3-digit numbers in 1 min. by *listening*.

Yuvraj Manchanda

Manik Dhiman

Naman Karthik

Aaryaman Singh

Manik Dhiman (b. 20 June 2005)

1. Solved seven consecutive tasks of addition of 400 rows of 1-digit numbers flashing at 0.3 sec. intervals on Flash Anzan.
2. Solved the addition of 150 rows of 1-digit numbers flashing at 0.2 sec. intervals on Flash Anzan.

Manik Dhiman (b. 20 June 2005) solved six consecutive tasks of addition of 60 rows of 1-digit numbers flashing at 0.16 sec. intervals on Flash Anzan.

Naman Karthik (b. 27 November 2008) solved seven consecutive tasks of addition of 400 rows of 1-digit numbers flashing at 0.3 sec. intervals on Flash Anzan.

Aaryaman Singh (b. 30 July 2007) calculated the square root of 4-digit numbers (56 sums) in 1 min. by *writing*.

Ujjwal Goyal (b. 27 April 2009) calculated the cube root of 7-digit numbers (47 sums) in 1 min. by *writing*.

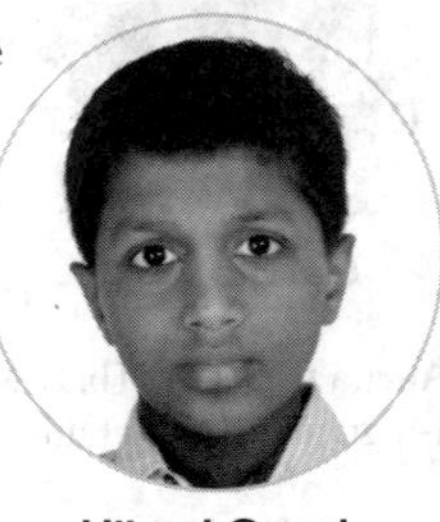

Ujjwal Goyal

Chaitanya Choudhary (b. 29 December 2006) calculated the cube root of 7-digit numbers (60 sums) in 1 min. by *writing*.

Aarahan Gupta (b. 31 May 2009)

1. Solved the addition of 450 rows of 3-digit numbers flashing at 1 sec. intervals on Flash Anzan.
2. Solved four consecutive tasks of addition of 35 rows of 4-digit numbers in 1 min. by *listening*.

Harjas Kaur (b. 18 July 2006) solved the addition of 2 rows of 10-digit numbers (5 sums) in 5 mins by *listening*.

TRENDZ ABACUS, KOTA, RAJASTHAN

During 23–26 May 2019, students of Trendz Abacus, Kota, performed the following records with 100 per cent accuracy:

Aryan Gupta (b. 10 October 2007)

1. Solved 34 tasks of addition of 3 rows of 9-digit numbers in 5 mins.

2. Solved 30 tasks of addition of 4 rows of 8-digit numbers in 5 mins.
3. Solved nine tasks of addition of 4 rows of 7-digit numbers in 1 min.
4. Solved 42 tasks of addition of 4 rows of 6-digit numbers in 5 mins.
5. Solved 10 tasks of addition of 4 rows of 6-digit numbers in 1 min.
6. Solved 32 tasks of addition of 5 rows of 6-digit numbers in 5 mins.
7. Solved 41 tasks of addition of 5 rows of 5-digit numbers in 5 mins.
8. Solved five tasks of addition of 10 rows of 4-digit numbers in 1 min.
9. Solved 61 tasks of addition of 4 rows of 4-digit numbers in 5 mins.
10. Solved nine tasks of division of 4-digit numbers by 2-digit numbers in 1 min.
11. Solved 40 tasks of division of 4-digit numbers by 2-digit numbers in 5 mins.
12. Solved 66 tasks of multiplication of a 1-digit number by a 1-digit number by a 1-digit number in 1 min.
13. Solved 200 tasks of multiplication of a 1-digit number by a 1-digit number by a 1-digit number in 5 mins.

Garvita Raj (b. 10 October 2008)

1. Solved eight tasks of addition of 3-digit numbers flashing at 1.4 sec. intervals on Flash Anzan.
2. Solved 13 tasks of addition of 4 rows of 3-digit numbers in 1 min.

Garvita Raj

Aarna Bhargava

Vandan Nyati

Aarna Bhargava (b. 17 May 2007) solved eight tasks of addition of 20 rows of 1-digit numbers in 1 min.

Vandan Nyati (b. 18 October 2008) solved four tasks of addition of 4-digit numbers flashing at 1.5 sec. intervals on Flash Anzan.

Radhika Maheshwari (b. 21 August 2005)

1. Solved two tasks of multiplication of a 30-digit number by a 1-digit number in 1 min.
2. Solved four tasks of multiplication of a 20-digit number by a 1-digit number in 1 min.
3. Solved 35 tasks of multiplication of a 6-digit number by a 2-digit number in 5 mins.
4. Solved nine tasks of multiplication of a 6-digit number by a 2-digit number in 1 min.
5. Solved 29 tasks of multiplication of a 5-digit number by a 3-digit number in 5 mins.
6. Solved 49 tasks of multiplication of a 5-digit number by a 2-digit number in 5 mins.

7. Solved 12 tasks of multiplication of a 5-digit number by a 2-digit number in 1 min.
8. Solved nine tasks of multiplication of a 5-digit number by a 3-digit number in 1 min.
9. Solved nine tasks of multiplication of a 4-digit number by a 3-digit number in 1 min.
10. Solved 68 tasks of multiplication of a 4-digit number by a 2-digit number in 5 mins.
11. Solved 15 tasks of multiplication of a 4-digit number by a 2-digit number in 1 min.
12. Solved 55 tasks of multiplication of a 3-digit number by a 3-digit number in 5 mins.
13. Solved 91 tasks of multiplication of a 3-digit number by a 2-digit number in 5 mins.
14. Solved 18 tasks of multiplication of a 3-digit number by a 2-digit number in 1 min.
15. Solved 145 tasks of multiplication of a 2-digit number by a 2-digit number in 5 mins.
16. Solved 12 tasks of calculating the square of randomly selected 3-digit numbers in 1 min.
17. Solved one task of addition of 10 rows of 15-digit numbers in 1 min.
18. Solved five tasks of addition of 4 rows of 10-digit numbers in 1 min.
19. Solved 77 tasks of addition of 4 rows of 3-digit numbers in 5 mins.
20. Solved 20 tasks of division of 5-digit numbers by 2-digit numbers in 5 mins.
21. Solved 15 tasks of division of 4-digit numbers by 2-digit numbers in 1 min.

Aanya Gupta (b. 11 May 2006)

1. Solved eight tasks of addition of 30 rows of 3-digit numbers in 5 mins.
2. Solved 63 tasks of addition of 4 rows of 3-digit numbers in 5 mins.
3. Solved 15 tasks of addition of 4 rows of 3-digit numbers in 1 min.
4. Solved 31 tasks of addition of 15 rows of 2-digit numbers in 5 mins.
5. Solved 17 tasks of addition of 50 rows of 3-digit numbers in 5 mins.
6. Solved nine tasks of addition of 2 rows of 1-digit numbers in 1 min.

Aanya Gupta

Hitansh Khandelwal (b. 15 January 2006)

1. Solved five tasks of multiplication of a 20-digit number by a 1-digit number in 1 min.
2. Solved four tasks of multiplication of a 17-digit number by a 1-digit number in 1 min.
3. Solved six tasks of division of a 10-digit number by a 1-digit number in 1 min.
4. Solved nine tasks of multiplication of a 9-digit number by a 1-digit number in 1 min.

Hitansh Khandelwal

5. Solved 11 tasks of multiplication of an 8-digit number by a 1-digit number in 1 min.
6. Solved 13 tasks of multiplication of a 7-digit number by a 1-digit number in 1 min.
7. Solved 28 tasks of division of a 4-digit number by a 2-digit number in 5 mins.
8. Solved 13 tasks of calculating the sum of the squares of 3-digit numbers in 1 min.
9. Solved eight tasks of the addition of 3-digit numbers flashing at 1.04 sec. intervals on Flash Anzan.
10. Solved two tasks of addition of 20 rows of 2-digit numbers with decimal in 1 min.

Nehal Nyati

Bhavya Dadhich

Nehal Nyati (b. 10 August 2008)

1. Solved five tasks of addition of 5 rows of 8-digit numbers in 1 min.
2. Solved 20 tasks of addition of 5 rows of 8-digit numbers in 5 mins.
3. Solved six tasks of addition of 10 rows of 1-digit numbers with decimal in 1 min.

Bhavya Dadhich (b. 11 November 2005)

1. Solved one task of addition of 10 rows of 20-digit numbers in 1 min.
2. Solved one task of addition of 10 rows of 15-digit numbers in 1 min.
3. Solved five tasks of addition of 10 rows of 15-digit numbers in 5 mins.
4. Solved four tasks of addition of 5 rows of 10-digit numbers in 1 min.
5. Solved two tasks of addition of 10 rows of 10-digit numbers in 1 min.
6. Solved nine tasks of addition of 10 rows of 10-digit numbers in 5 mins.
7. Solved nine tasks of addition of 11 rows of 10-digit numbers in 5 mins.
8. Solved 17 tasks of addition of 5 rows of 10-digit numbers in 5 mins.
9. Solved 10 tasks of addition of 10 rows of 9-digit numbers in 5 mins.

Record Rewind

Fastest to memorize a deck of playing cards

1996

Rajiv Kumar from Palampur, Himachal Pradesh, demonstrated his memory skills with a pack of shuffled playing cards. He took approximately 4 mins to memorize the cards and 5 mins 45 secs to recall them with only 4 errors on 5 August 1995.

2014

Saswat Satapathy (b. 2 July 1997), a class 10 student of Delhi Public School, RK Puram, New Delhi, recalled the sequence of a deck of 52 cards in 56 secs at the Indian National Memory Championship in Hyderabad, Telangana, on The Human Story 28 October 2012.

10. Solved five tasks of addition of 5 rows of 9-digit numbers in 1 min.
11. Solved 11 tasks of addition of 10 rows of 8-digit numbers in 5 mins.
12. Solved 23 tasks of addition of 6 rows of 6-digit numbers in 5 mins.
13. Solved five tasks of addition of 6 rows of 6-digit numbers in 1 min.
14. Solved seven tasks of addition of 15 rows of 2-digit numbers in 1 min.
15. Solved four tasks of addition of 20 rows of 2-digit numbers with decimal in 1 min.
16. Solved 104 tasks of calculating the sum of the squares of 3-digit numbers in 5 mins.
17. Solved nine tasks of multiplication of a 5-digit number by a 4-digit number in 5 mins.

Chahat Panjwani

Chahat Panjwani (b. 19 March 2007)

1. Solved 28 tasks of addition of 10 rows of 2-digit numbers with decimal in 5 mins.
2. Solved six tasks of addition of 10 rows of 2-digit numbers with decimal in 1 min.
3. Solved 54 tasks of the addition of 10 rows of 1-digit numbers with decimal in 5 mins.

Anshul Yadav

Anshul Yadav (b. 10 July 2006)

1. Solved one task of addition of 2 rows of 100-digit numbers in 1 min.
2. Solved 31 tasks of addition of 2 rows of 50-digit numbers in 1 min.
3. Solved 19 tasks of addition of 2 rows of 9-digit numbers in 1 min.
4. Solved 27 tasks of addition of 2 rows of 7-digit numbers in 1 min.
5. Solved 36 tasks of addition of 2 rows of 5-digit numbers in 1 min.

Ishita Goyal

Ishita Goyal (b. 12 December 2005)

1. Solved one task of addition of 3 rows of 50-digit numbers in 1 min.
2. Solved two tasks of addition of 2 rows of 50-digit numbers in 1 min.
3. Solved eight tasks of addition of 3 rows of 30-digit numbers in 5 mins.
4. Solved two tasks of addition of 3 rows of 30-digit numbers in 1 min.
5. Solved two tasks of addition of 3 rows of 20-digit numbers in 1 min.
6. Solved 32 tasks of addition of 20 rows of 1-digit numbers in 1 min.

Hardik Singh

Hardik Singh (b. 31 March 2005)

1. Solved eight tasks of calculating the ratio of 4-digit numbers: 3-digit numbers in 1 min.

2. Solved 38 tasks of calculating ratio of 4-digit numbers : 3-digit numbers in 5 mins.

Abhilakshya Arora (b. 9 February 2007)

Abhilakshya Arora

1. Solved 47 tasks of calculating the cube root of 12-digit numbers in 5 mins.
2. Solved 12 tasks of calculating the cube root of 12-digit numbers in 1 min.
3. Solved 37 tasks of calculating the cube root of 9-digit numbers in 1 min.
4. Solved 146 tasks of calculating the cube roots of 9-digit numbers in 5 mins.
5. Solved seven tasks of calculating the square roots of 4-digit numbers selected randomly in 1 min.
6. Solved 29 tasks of multiplication of a 2-digit number by a 2-digit number in 1 min.
7. Solved 107 tasks of addition and subtraction of 2 rows of 2-digit numbers in 1 min.
8. Solved 381 tasks of addition and subtraction of 2 rows of 2-digit numbers in 5 mins.
9. Solved 104 tasks of addition and subtraction of 4 rows of 1-digit numbers in 1 min.

Mudrika Garg (b. 14 August 2007)

Mudrika Garg

1. Solved 10 tasks of multiplication of a 6-digit number by a 6-digit number in 6 mins 0.8 sec.
2. Solved seven tasks of multiplication of a 4-digit number by a 4-digit number in 1 min.
3. Solved 10 tasks of multiplication of a 3-digit number by a 3-digit number in 1 min. 0.07 sec.
4. Solved 15 tasks of multiplication of a 3-digit number by a 3-digit number in 1 min.
5. Solved 19 tasks of calculating the cube roots of 9-digit numbers in 1 min.
6. Solved 93 tasks of calculating the cube of every number from 1 to 93 in 1 min.
7. Solved 44 tasks of calculating the cube of 2-digit numbers selected randomly in 1 min.
8. Solved 101 tasks of calculating the square of 2-digit numbers selected randomly in 1 min.
9. Solved 12 tasks of division of 6-digit numbers by 1-digit numbers in 1 min.
10. Orally recalled all the multiplication tables from 11 to 99 in 6 mins 35 secs.

Deepak Nagar (b. 27 August 2004)

Deepak Nagar

1. Solved five tasks of multiplication of a 50-digit number by a 1-digit number in 5 mins.
2. Solved one task of multiplication of a 50-digit number by a 1-digit number in 1 min.

3. Solved two tasks of multiplication of a 40-digit number by a 1-digit number in 1 min.
4. Solved three tasks of multiplication of a 25-digit number by a 1-digit number in 1 min.
5. Solved two tasks of division of a 20-digit number by a 1-digit number in 1 min.
6. Solved 11 tasks of addition of 3 rows of 8-digit numbers in 1 min.
7. Solved 28 tasks of addition of 2 rows of 6-digit numbers in 1 min.
8. Solved 14 tasks of addition of 3 rows of 6-digit numbers in 1 min.

Kanishk Chaurisiya (b. 25 September 2005)

Kanishk Chaurisiya

1. Solved 74 tasks of multiplication of a 5-digit number by a 1-digit number in 5 mins.
2. Solved six tasks of addition of 3 rows of 50-digit numbers in 5 mins.
3. Solved 38 tasks of addition of 3 rows of 10-digit numbers in 5 mins.
4. Solved nine tasks of addition of 3 rows of 10-digit numbers in 1 min.
5. Solved 10 tasks of addition of 3 rows of 9-digit numbers in 1 min.

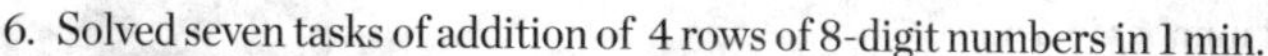

6. Solved seven tasks of addition of 4 rows of 8-digit numbers in 1 min.
7. Solved 50 tasks of addition of 3 rows of 7-digit numbers in 5 mins.
8. Solved 13 tasks of addition of 3 rows of 7-digit numbers in 1 min.
9. Solved 60 tasks of addition of 3 rows of 6-digit numbers in 5 mins.
10. Solved 82 tasks of addition of 3 rows of 5-digit numbers in 5 mins.
11. Solved 21 tasks of addition of 3 rows of 5-digit numbers in 1 min.
12. Solved 103 tasks of addition of 2 rows of 5-digit numbers in 5 mins.
13. Solved one task of division of a 25-digit number by a 1-digit number in 1 min.

Vaibhav Garg (b. 12 December 2005)

Vaibhav Garg

1. Solved 14 tasks of addition of 20 rows of 2-digit numbers in 5 mins.
2. Solved four tasks of addition of 20 rows of 2-digit numbers in 1 min.
3. Solved 126 tasks of calculating the squares of 2-digit numbers selected randomly in 1 min.

Parth Garg (b. 15 Jun 2007)

Parth Garg

1. Solved five tasks of addition of 5 rows of 7-digit numbers in 1 min.
2. Solved nine tasks of addition of 5 rows of 5-digit numbers in 1 min.
3. Solved 24 tasks of multiplication of a 1-digit number by a 1-digit number by a 1-digit number in 1 min.

Hetansh Patira (b. 5 November 2004)

1. Solved 151 tasks of calculating the cube root of 6-digit numbers in 1 min.

2. Solved 20 tasks of calculating the square root of 6-digit numbers in 1 min.
3. Solved 160 tasks of calculating the square root of 4-digit numbers in 1 min.
4. Solved 314 tasks of calculating the square root of 4-digit numbers in 5 mins.
5. Solved 176 tasks of multiplication of a 1-digit number by a 1-digit number in 1 min.
6. Solved 53 tasks of multiplication of a 1-digit number by a 1-digit number by a 1-digit number in 1 min.
7. Solved 60 tasks of calculating the 6th root of given numbers in 5 mins.
8. Solved 14 tasks of calculating the 6th root of given numbers in 1 min.
9. Solved 113 tasks of calculating the 5th root of given numbers in 5 mins.
10. Solved 29 tasks of calculating the 5th root of given numbers in 1 min.
11. Solved 88 tasks of calculating the 4th root of given numbers in 5 mins.
12. Solved 21 tasks of calculating the 4th root of given numbers in 1 min.

Hetansh Patira

Mahi Jhamb (b. 30 April 2005)

1. Solved six tasks of division of a 25-digit number by a 1-digit number in 5 mins.
2. Solved seven tasks of division of a 9-digit number by a 1-digit number in 1 min.
3. Solved nine tasks of division of an 8-digit number by a 1-digit number in 1 min.
4. Solved 124 tasks of addition of 2 rows of 3-digit numbers in 5 mins.

Mahi Jhamb

Nandini Garg (b. 25 August 2004)

1. Solved four tasks of addition of 10 rows of 20-digit numbers in 5 mins.
2. Solved one task of addition of 10 rows of 20-digit numbers in 1 min.
3. Solved two tasks of addition of 11 rows of 10-digit numbers in 1 min.
4. Solved 10 tasks of addition of 10 rows of 10-digit numbers in 6 mins 0.6 sec.
5. Solved two tasks of addition of 10 rows of 10-digit numbers in 1 min.
6. Solved 11 tasks of addition of 10 rows of 7-digit numbers in 5 mins.
7. Solved 15 tasks of addition of 10 rows of 6-digit numbers in 5 mins.
8. Solved three tasks of multiplication of a 10-digit number by a 10-digit number in 5 mins.
9. Solved three tasks of multiplication of a 9-digit number by a 9-digit number in 5 mins.
10. Solved one task of multiplication of a 9-digit number by a 9-digit number in 1 min.
11. Solved 10 tasks of multiplication of an 8-digit number by an 8-digit number in 13 mins 40 secs.

Nandini Garg

12. Solved three tasks of multiplication of an 8-digit number by an 8-digit number in 5 mins.
13. Solved one task of multiplication of an 8-digit number by an 8-digit number in 1 min.
14. Solved 500 tasks of addition of 1-digit numbers flashing at 0.5 sec. intervals on Flash Anzan.
15. Solved 300 tasks of addition of 1-digit numbers flashing at 0.4 sec. intervals on Flash Anzan.

Yuvanjay Bhadoriya (b. 1 October 2003)

1. Solved 53 tasks of addition of 2 rows of 2-digit numbers with decimal in 1 min.
2. Solved the addition of recurring 1-digit numbers (176 steps) in 1 min.
3. Solved the subtraction of recurring 1-digit numbers (94 steps) in 1 min.
4. Orally recalled all 95 prime numbers between 1 and 500 in 1 min.
5. Orally recalled all the multiplication tables from 2 to 9 (10 steps) in 16.12 secs.

Yuvanjay Bhadoriya

Parth Mittal (b. 25 December 2005)

1. Solved two tasks of addition of 3 rows of 20-digit numbers in 1 min.
2. Solved six tasks of addition of 8 rows of 3-digit numbers in 1 min.
3. Solved 24 tasks of addition of 10 rows of 3-digit numbers with decimal in 5 mins.
4. Solved four tasks of addition of 10 rows of 3-digit numbers with decimal in 1 min.

Parth Mittal

SUPER 30

SHAKUNTALA DEVI: FASTER THAN A CALCULATOR

Shakuntala Devi (1929–2013), born in Bangalore (now Bengaluru, Karnataka), was a mathematician and writer, exceptionally gifted in mental calculation and memory. A child prodigy, her talents were recognized when she was only three years old. She travelled to several countries, demonstrating her arithmetic abilities and placed India on the world map in this field. On 18 June 1980, she correctly multiplied two 13-digit numbers in just 28 seconds! The numbers – 7,686,369,774,970 and 2,465,099,745,779 were randomly selected by the computer department of Imperial College, London, UK. Interestingly, the certificate for the unbroken record was given posthumously after a gap of 40 years, a day before her eponymous biopic was released on Amazon Prime Video on 31 July 2020.

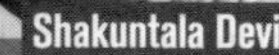

Shakuntala Devi

5. Solved three tasks of addition of 8 rows of 3-digit numbers with decimal in 1 min.
6. Solved four tasks of addition of 15 rows of 2-digit numbers with decimal in 1 min.
7. Solved three tasks of addition of 50 rows of 1-digit numbers with decimal in 1 min.
8. Solved 100 tasks of addition of 6 rows of 1-digit numbers with decimal in 5 mins.

There are 43,252,003,274,489,856,000 possible ways to arrange a standard 3 x 3 x 3 Rubik's cube.

Vedant Mangal (b. 2 September 2005)

1. Solved 13 tasks of addition of 4 rows of 3-digit numbers in 1 min.
2. Solved 166 tasks of addition of 4 rows of 1-digit numbers with decimal in 5 mins.

Vedant Mangal

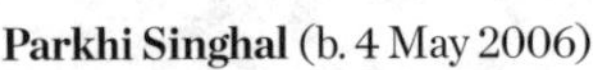

Parkhi Singhal (b. 4 May 2006)

1. Solved 20 tasks of addition of 5 rows of 7-digit numbers in 5 mins.
2. Solved 18 tasks of addition of 20 rows of 2-digit numbers with decimal in 5 mins.
3. Solved 37 tasks of addition of 6 rows of 1-digit numbers in 1 min.
4. Solved 23 tasks of addition of 10 rows of 1-digit numbers with decimal in 1 min.

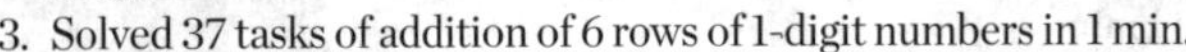

YOGA

Longest *upavishta konasana**

J. Sree Vaishnavi (b. 16 March 2009) from Muscat, Oman, performed *upavishta konasana* (wide-angle seated forward-bend pose) for 26 mins 39 secs on 19 April 2019 at the Indian Embassy auditorium, Oman.

Longest *uttana padasana**

K.S. Naga Adithi Karupakala Sandeep (b. 26 July 2013) from Chintamani, Karnataka, performed *uttana padasana* (raised legs pose) for 4 mins from 9:15 a.m. to 9:19 a.m. on 12 May 2019 at Sri Vasavi Temple, Chintamani.

Longest *bhoomasana**

Naga Shreeshyl Karupakala Sandeep (b. 13 November 2007) from Chintamani, Karnataka, performed *bhoomasana* (a split pose) on two chairs placed at 45 cm (1 ft 5.7 in.) height for 5 mins 55 secs on 12 May 2019 at Sri Vasavi Temple, Chintamani, Karnataka.

Longest *parshva poorna dhanurasana*

Amrutha Anand (b. 13 July 1991) from Chidambaram, Tamil Nadu, performed

* The rules regarding the age of participants have been modified. Please see Rules and Guidelines.

Longest *parshva poorna dhanurasana*

parshva poorna dhanurasana (full side bow pose) for 15 mins 10 secs, starting at 2:00 p.m., on 2 March 2019 at the Great Wall of China, Beijing.

WR Longest *setu bandhasana*

Prof. Dr S. Ramesh Babu (b. 12 February 1957) from Bengaluru, Karnataka, performed *setu bandhasana* (bridge pose) for 24 mins from 8:00 a.m. to 8:24 a.m. on 9 July 2019 at Vidyanjali Academy for Learning, Bengaluru.

Longest *paschimottanasana*

Virendra Vikram Singh (b. 2 December 1954) from Balrampur, Uttar Pradesh, performed *paschimottanasana* (seated forward bend pose) for 40 mins non-stop from 9:00 a.m. to 9:40 a.m. on 19 May 2020 at Neel Bagh Palace, Balrampur.

Longest *supta padangushthasana*

Virendra Vikram Singh (b. 2 December 1954) from Balrampur, Uttar Pradesh, performed *supta padangushthasana* (reclining hand to big toe pose) for 20 mins from 9:50 a.m. to 10:10 a.m. on 19 May 2020 at Late Maharaj Dharmendra Prasad Singh Memorial, Balrampur.

Most Participants Performing 108 Surya Namaskars Simultaneously – Single Venue**

'Yoga with Chetna', a yoga event organized by Yoga with Chetna, Arti Saluke Foundation, 'Landspeaks' and Vinay Gandecha, had 800 participants performing 108 surya namaskars on 16 June 2019. The event held at Country Club in Andheri, Mumbai, Maharashtra, lasted for 45 mins between 6:00 a.m. and 7:15 a.m. Of the 800 participants, only seven could not complete the 108 surya namaskars.

** This is a one-time category. Further and future claims for this category will not be accepted.

Longest *ashtavakrasana*

Adesh Motiramji Karnase (b. 9 April 1997) from Gurugram, Haryana, performed *ashtavakrasana* (eight-angle pose) for 1 min. 4 secs on 10 June 2020 in Morshi, Maharashtra.

Longest *vishvamitrasana*

Nitin Mohanrao Prajapat (b. 2 April 1996) from Gurugram, Haryana, performed *vishvamitrasana* for 1 min. 13 secs on 10 June 2020 in Morshi, Maharashtra.

Longest *ekapada shirshasana*

Virendra Vikram Singh (b. 2 December 1954) from Balrampur, Uttar Pradesh, performed *ekapada shirshasana* (foot behind the head pose) for 10 mins from 10:00 a.m. to 10:10 a.m. on 20 February 2019 at M.L.K. PG College, Balrampur.

Longest *Hanumanasana*

Dr Narendra Kumar Sharma (b. 30 March 1978) from Jaipur, Rajasthan, performed *Hanumanasana* (monkey pose) for 23 mins 36 secs on 22 June 2020 in Malviya Nagar, Jaipur.

Most yoga poses on a BMX bike

Khiv Raj Gurjar (b. 1 July 1952) from Jodhpur, Rajasthan, performed 62 power yoga postures on a BMX bike in 10 mins on 26 January 2019 at the Shri Dadasaheb Rawal Stadium, Dhule, Maharashtra.

Most people performing *setu bandhasana*

Art of Living and Department of Tourism, Government of Puducherry, organized *setu bandhasana* (bridge pose) for 3 mins with 1,682 participants on 6 January 2019 at Indira Gandhi Stadium, Puducherry.

Record Rewind

Longest *shirshasana*

2014

Rushikesh Jagannathrao Bingewar (b. 10 April 1986) from Nanded, Maharashtra, performed the longest *shirshasana* without any support continuously for 1 hr 2 mins at Hotel City Pride on 10 April 2013.

2020

Rakesh Chandra Singh Patel from Kanpur, Uttar Pradesh, performed the *shirshasana* for 3 hrs 30 mins during a yoga day event on 21 June 2017.

Marathon surya namaskars

Abhishek Arora (b. 18 May 2000) from Saharanpur, Uttar Pradesh, performed 5,469 non-stop surya namaskars in 24 hrs 10 mins from 6:10 p.m. on 4 March to 6:20 p.m. on 5 March 2020 at Live Young Fitness Club, Saharanpur. He took 15 breaks adding up to 1 hr 9 mins 45 secs. The performance time was 23 hrs 15 secs.

Most people performing 151 surya namaskars simultaneously – single venue**

'Yoga with Chetna' by Model Town Residents Association, 'Landspeaks' and Vinay Gandecha, conducted 151 non-stop surya namaskars with 660 participants on Youth Day at Chacha Nehru Park, Mumbai, Maharashtra, on 12 January 2020.

** This is a one-time category. Further and future claims for this category will not be accepted.

The event started at 7:00 a.m. and ended by 8:00 a.m. The final count of successful participants was 620.

Most *naukasanas* – 1 hr

Prof. Dr S. Ramesh Babu (b. 12 February 1957) from Bengaluru, Karnataka, performed 652 non-stop *naukasanas* (boat pose) for 1 hr from 7:30 a.m. to 8:30 a.m. on 14 April 2019 at Prof. Satish Dhawan Park, Bengaluru.

Most *kapalbhati* strokes – 1 hr

Sunil Baban Bhujbal (b. 16 January 1965) from Mumbai, Maharashtra, performed 14,500 *kapalbhati* strokes in 1 hr from 7:25 a.m. to 8:25 a.m. on 18 May 2019 at Yoga Vidya Niketan, Damle Yoga Kendra.

PHYSICAL FEATS

Most half-knuckle push-ups

Ashif Khan (b. 30 September 1990) from Gurugram, Haryana, did 145 half-knuckle push-ups in 1 min. from 12:05 p.m. to 12:06 p.m. on 23 May 2019 at H2O Fitness gym, Gurugram.

Most spiderman knuckle push-ups*

Aman Khan (b. 9 September 2002) from Pratapgarh, Uttar Pradesh, performed 73 spiderman knuckle push-ups in 1 min. from 9:50 a.m. to 9:51 a.m. on 5 December 2019 at Stadium Multipurpose Hall, Pratapgarh.

Most contortion push-ups

Rajendra Bishnoi (b. 5 November 1995) from Bikaner, Rajasthan, performed 132 unique contortion push-ups in 1 min. on 17 March 2019 at Swargiya Shri Balasaheb Thackeray Maidan, Mumbai.

Most two-finger push-ups – both arms

Arya Rishabh Rameshchandra (b. 26 September 1997) from Ahmedabad, Gujarat, performed 65 two-finger push-ups (index and middle finger) in 1 min. on 19 May 2019 at I-Can Gym, Ahmedabad.

Most two-finger push-ups – both arms

Most diamond push-ups

Most diamond push-ups
V. Kaliraj (b. 3 October 1996) from Virudhunagar, Tamil Nadu, did 112 diamond push-ups in 1 min. on 26 May 2019 at D'Pearl Sport Academy, Ramapuran, Chennai.

Most clap push-ups
Jatin Goel (b. 10 April 1994) from Gurugram, Haryana, performed 85 clap push-ups in 1 min. from 12:05 p.m. to 12:06 p.m. on 10 May 2019 at H2O Fitness gym, Gurugram.

Most bicycle crunches – woman
Sunita Chhabra (b. 3 May 1972) from Jaipur, Rajasthan, performed 88 bicycle crunches in 1 min. from 7:32 p.m. to 7:33 p.m. on 18 February 2020 at the office of JVP Media Group, Jaipur.

Most abdominal crunches
Mohit Bhardwaj (b. 29 March 1988) from Gurugram, Haryana, performed 108 abdominal crunches in 1 min. from 12:06 p.m. to 12:07 p.m. on 23 May 2019 at H2O Fitness gym, Gurugram.

Most abdominal sit-ups – woman
Shreya Bhardwaj (b. 21 October 1999) performed 85 abdominal sit-ups in 1 min. from 12:05 p.m. to 12:06 p.m. on 23 May 2019 at H2O Fitness gym, Gurugram.

Most squats – woman
Priyanka Prasher (b. 14 February 1986) from Gurugram, Haryana, performed 97 squats in 1 min. from 12:09 p.m. to 12:10 p.m. on 10 May 2019 at H2O Fitness gym, Gurugram.

Most pistol squats – alternating legs
Shivam (b. 5 October 2000) from Lucknow, Uttar Pradesh, performed 45 pistol squats in 1 min. using legs alternately on 4 September 2019 at his residence.

Most jump squats
Himanshu Jadon (b. 28 November 1993) from Gurugram, Haryana, performed 82 jump squats in 1 min. from 12:05 p.m. to 12:06 p.m. on 28 May 2019 at H2O Fitness gym, Gurugram.

Most jumping jacks
Venkata Sairam Reddy Pulusu (b. 11 April 1988) from Hyderabad, Telangana, performed 127 jumping jacks in 1 min. from 12:05 p.m. to 12:06 p.m. on 23 May 2019 at H2O Fitness gym, Gurugram.

Most jumping jacks – woman
Richa Maheshwari (b. 23 September 1988) from New Delhi performed 115 jumping jacks in 1 min. from 12:07 p.m. to 12:08 p.m. on 25 May 2019 at H2O Fitness gym, Gurugram.

Most people performing jumping jacks simultaneously*
The Wajra O'Force Empowerment Foundation and Shree Sarkhej Kelavni Mandal, Ahmedabad, Gujarat, organized an event with 2,988 students performing jumping jacks simultaneously for 1 min. on 11 October 2019 at Shree Sarkhej Kelavni Mandal School. The event celebrated the Fit India movement.

Most burpees – woman
Ankita Nagpal (b. 2 January 1994) from Gurugram, Haryana, performed 48 burpees in 1 min. from 12:05 p.m. to 12:06 p.m. on 23 May 2019 at H2O Fitness gym, Gurugram.

Most ab wheel rolls
Nitin Mudgal (b. 5 October 1989) from Gurugram, Haryana, performed 35 ab wheel rolls in 1 min. from 12:05 p.m. to 12:06 p.m. on 28 April 2019 at H2O Fitness gym, Gurugram.

Record Rewind

Most two-thumb push-ups in 1 min.

2006

Samad Memon from Boisar, Palghar District, Maharashtra, did 45 push-ups in 1 min. using only thumbs on 12 June 2006. He kept his elbow at a 90-degree angle.

2019

Harpreet Singh (b. 4 October 1975) from Kapurthala District, Punjab, performed 69 two-thumb push-ups in 1 min. at the Lyallpur Khalsa College for Women on 17 April 2017.

Most reverse dips
Ankush Gurjar (b. 12 September 1992) from Gurugram, Haryana, performed 137 reverse dips in 1 min. from 12:06 p.m. to 12:07 p.m. on 4 May 2019 at H2O Fitness gym, Gurugram.

Most parallel dips
Ashish Lohia (b. 10 July 1998) from Gurugram, Haryana, performed 75 parallel dips in 1 min. from 12:05 p.m. to 12:06 p.m. on 28 May 2019 at H2O Fitness gym in Gurugram.

Most full-contact knee strikes – one leg
M.A. Murtoza (b. 9 January 1979) from Gurugram, Haryana, performed 101 full-contact knee strikes using only one leg in 1 min. from 6:40 p.m. to 6:41 p.m. on 30 May 2019 at Jitender Behl Park, Gurugram.

* The rules regarding the age of participants have been modified. Please see Rules and Guidelines.

Most full-contact alternate elbow strikes – woman
Ponnapalli Srilekha (b. 24 May 1996) from Hyderabad, Telangana, performed 144 full-contact alternate elbow strikes in 1 min. on 24 October 2019 at Fresh Living Apartments, Hyderabad.

Most Chudan-Zuki (karate punches)
Rohit Bhore (b. 29 September 1998) from Thane, Maharashtra, performed 217 Chudan-Zuki (karate punches) in 1 min. from 10:30 a.m. to 10:31 a.m. on 15 January 2020 at his residence.

Most Chudan-Zuki (karate punches)

Most nunchaku rotations – both hands
John Paul Kodiyath Rajan (b. 14 May 1986) from Thrissur, Kerala, performed 134 nunchaku rotations, while blindfolded, using both hands, in 1 min. on 28 May 2019 at Othayi, Malappuram District, Kerala.

Most skips over a 10 m rope

Most skips – over a 10 m rope
Akasha B. Jogaraddi (b. 10 May 1999) from Dharwad, Karnataka, performed 40 skips over a 10 m rope in 1 min. from 8:45 a.m. to 8:46 a.m. on 12 December 2019 at S.D.M. Engineering College, Dharwad.

Most lunges – 1 hr
Kapil Arora (b. 28 September 1975) from Mumbai, Maharashtra, performed 948 lunges in 1 hr between 8:16 a.m. and 9:16 a.m. on 28 June 2020 at his residence.

Most hops – one leg – 1 hr
Mohamed Rizwan T.K. (b. 22 July 1996) from Thanjavur, Tamil Nadu, performed 8,013 hops on one leg in 1 hr between 4:32 p.m. and 5:32 p.m. on 11 March 2020 at his residence.

Longest plank
Abhishek Sihag (b. 15 August 1997) from Sikar, Rajasthan, performed the longest plank for 8 hrs 5 mins from 6:51 a.m. to 2:56 p.m. at the Railway Community Centre, Sikar, on 1 January 2019.

Longest handstand – both arms*
Manish Kothari (b. 6 February 2004) from Jaipur, Rajasthan, stood ramrod straight on his hands with legs fully upright for 1 min. 22 secs on 7 May 2019 at the Jhalana office of *Rajasthan Patrika*.

* The rules regarding the age of participants have been modified. Please see Rules and Guidelines.

Longest sumo squat balancing

Saurabh Kumar Pathak (b. 16 January 1990) from Greater Noida, Uttar Pradesh, performed sumo squat balancing for 20 mins 23 secs on 3 May 2019 in Greater Noida.

Longest slalom wave boarding*/**

Tiluck Keisam (b. 3 January 2008) from New Delhi performed the longest slalom wave boarding by covering 3,880 cones (3.88 km) in 40 laps on 20 May 2019 at the Siri Fort Sports Complex, New Delhi.

Marathon nunchaku performance

Yugraj Singh Kaleka (b. 26 October 1992) from Kharar, Punjab, conducted a 37 hrs 10 mins non-stop nunchaku performance at Leo Gym, Kharar, from 4:20 a.m. on 7 December 2018 till 5:30 p.m. on 8 December 2018. He didn't take any breaks during the event.

Most *urumi* strokes within a minute – both hands

Harikrishnan S. (b. 26 July 1995) from Alappuzha, Kerala, performed 230 strokes using two *urumi*s (flexible sword) with both hands in 37 secs on 19 September 2018 at Ekaveera Kalaripayatu Academy, Alappuzha. The length of the sword was 160 cm (5 ft 2.9 in.).

Longest duration balancing on a glass

Abdul Samad (b. 5 January 1974) from Balaramapuram, Kerala, balanced himself on top of a glass for 1 min. 49 secs on 24 March 2019 at Manavatty Auditorium, Balaramapuram. He used a tea glass, a stool and a cloth in between to prevent the glass from slipping.

Juggling a football on knee most times

Aman Singh (b. 26 November 1999) from Muzaffarnagar, Uttar Pradesh, juggled a football with both knees 123 times in 1 min. on 23 December 2017 at Vidya Knowledge Park, Meerut, Uttar Pradesh.

Juggling a football on knees most times in 1 min.

ENDEAVOUR

Running 365 days**

Samarjit Banik (b. 14 November 1974) from Guwahati, Assam, who has had two major operations (an open-heart surgery and the other for kidney stone removal) ran 11.95 km every day for 365 days from 1 April 2018 till 31 March 2019. He ran a total of 363.45 km every month and a total of 4,361.51 km in a year.

Longest *padayatra***

Awadh Bihari Lal, managing director of Yuva Jagriti International Jan Jagran Anterved Sewa Sansthan, Lucknow, Uttar Pradesh, launched a *padayatra*

** This is a one-time category. Further and future claims for this category will not be accepted.

No Challenge Too Tough

Vanitha Balasubramanian Iyer

Vanitha Balasubramanian Iyer from Navi Mumbai, Maharashtra, won the 2019 National Award for 'Best Employee with Hearing Impairment', presented by the Union Ministry of Social Justice and Empowerment in Delhi on 3 December, celebrated as International Day for Persons with Disabilities. Hearing-impaired since birth, she is a trained lip-reader and currently works at New India Assurance Company Ltd. A graduate with a degree in engineering, she also has a black belt in karate, which she obtained when she was eight years old. A trained Bharatanatyam dancer, she was also a child artiste in the award-winning Tamil-language film, *Malli*. She won the Role Model (women) for Persons with Disabilities award from the Ministry of Social Justice and Empowerment in 2013.

that began on 30 July 1980 from Kanniyakumari with 20 members. Covering 40 km in a day, the members walked 390,000 km through 10 countries (India, Nepal, Afghanistan, Bangladesh, Pakistan, Myanmar, Thailand, Pakistan, Bhutan and China). They concluded the *padayatra* on 15 May 2018 at Pithoragarh, Uttarakhand.

Non-stop running
Lihas Ashwin Trivedi (b. 26 October 1969) from Ahmedabad, Gujarat, ran continuously, covering a distance of 278.2 km on a 400 m track, for 50 hours starting at 6:00 a.m. on 16 November and finishing at 8:00 a.m. on 18 November 2019 at Rajpath Club Ltd, Ahmedabad.

Non-stop running

Longest distance covered while skipping with a rope of over 10 m**
Prof. Dr S. Ramesh Babu (b. 12 February 1957) from Bengaluru, Karnataka, used a 10.82 m (35 ft 5.9 in.) long skipping rope and skip-ran for a distance of 100 m with 12 skips in 22.1 secs on 23 December 2019 in Tatanagar, Bengaluru.

SKILLS

Fastest to form the English alphabet on Rubik's cubes while blindfolded
Affan Kutty (b. 10 August 2005) from Thane, Mumbai, formed all 26 letters of the English alphabet from A to Z, while blindfolded, on 7 x 7 Rubik's cubes on 30 May 2020 at Noori Garden, Mumbai, in 5 mins 6 secs 55 microseconds. Each letter was formed on all six sides of the Rubik's cube.

Peacock artwork while blindfolded**
Abhishek Kumar Chouhan (b. 15 July 1993) from Patiala, Punjab, made a peacock from 20 long blades of grass, while blindfolded, in 17 mins on 12 December 2018.

* The rules regarding the age of participants have been modified. Please see Rules and Guidelines.

Vintage car model made with currency notes**

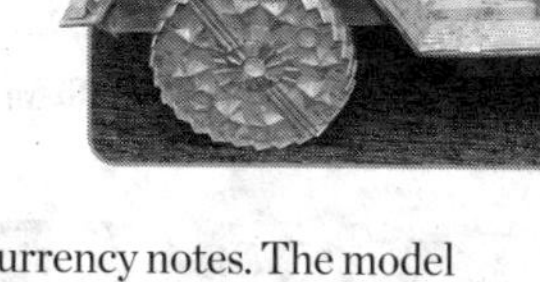

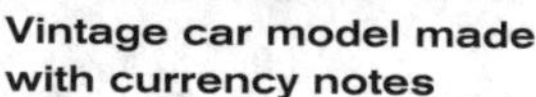

Vintage car model made with currency notes

Noman Haji (b. 25 July 1951) from Chennai, Tamil Nadu, designed a 1.22 m x 0.61 m (4 ft x 2 ft) vintage car model with ₹5 currency notes. The model weighs 15 kg and was made in three months from November 2017 to January 2018.

Walking on hands*/**

Manish Kothari (b. 6 February 2004) from Jaipur, Rajasthan, walked on his hands, covering a distance of 72 m (236 ft) in 155 steps in 1 min. 5 secs on 28 May 2019 at Central Park, Jaipur.

Non-stop inline skating with hula hoop*/**

Stuti Kishor Kulkarni (b. 29 July 2010) from Hubli, Karnataka, did non-stop inline skating while performing hula-hoop spins on 27 October 2018 at Indira Glass House Skating Rink, Hubli. She performed 2,500 hula-hoop rotations in 42 mins 12 secs.

Most body rotations in *padmasana* posture*/**

Anamika Kothari (b. 18 March 2002) from Jaipur, Rajasthan, rotated her body 50 times in the *padmasana* posture (lotus pose) in 1 min. 5 secs on 7 May 2019 at the Jhalana office of *Rajasthan Patrika.* She placed one hand on her mother's foot and the other hand on her father's foot while performing this.

Most knee hula-hoop spins*

Tharun R.S. (b. 11 September 2003) from Chennai, Tamil Nadu, performed 188 knee hula-hoop spins in 1 min. on 3 May 2019 at his residence.

One-handed hula-hoop rotations*

Janani R.S. (b. 25 January 2009) from Chennai, Tamil Nadu, performed 166 hula-hoop rotations in 1 min. on 3 May 2019 at her residence with her right hand.

Skipping on football most times*

Bipasha Baishnab (b. 11 February 2005) from North 24 Parganas, West Bengal, skipped on a football 90 times in 1 min. on 23 June 2017 at the Guma Renesa Club auditorium.

Longest slow-cycle balancing

Bharath Kumar Urs (b. 8 February 1983) from Bengaluru, Karnataka, performed slow-cycle balancing for 43 mins within a radius of 5 cm (2 in.) on 15 May 2019.

Most ball hits against a wall

Meena Ganesan (b. 17 June 1977) from Bengaluru, Karnataka, hit a ball against a

** This is a one-time category. Further and future claims for this category will not be accepted.

Coin Stacking

Shripad Krishnarao Vaidya (b. 5 May 1969) from Nagpur, Maharashtra, holds the record for performing the coin-stacking feats listed below. He does not use glue or adhesive to make his structures with coins.

Tallest spirally stacked coin tower: 1,894 coins (₹1, ₹2, ₹5 and ₹10) were stacked to make a 51 cm tall spiral coin tower in 8 hrs on 15 September 2019.

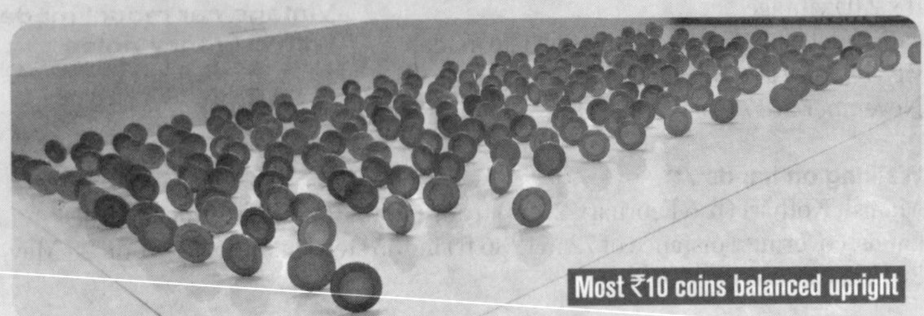

Most ₹10 coins balanced upright

 **Most stacked coins on hand:** 561 coins of ₹10, ₹2 and ₹1 were stacked on his left hand for 50 secs on 28 July 2018. The 15 cm (6 in.) high structure was made in 2 hrs.

 **Most ₹10 coins balanced upright:** 244 coins were balanced upright on a plane surface by Vaidya in 6 hrs on 9 February 2018.

Coin tower between joint of thumb and index finger:** 162 coins of ₹10 were stacked to build a coin tower on the opisthenar (back of the hand) between the knuckle of the thumb and index finger. Measuring 9.2 cm (3.62 in.) in height, the structure was completed in 1 hr 30 mins on 29 September 2019.

Hanging bridge of coins on lower arm:** 68 coins of ₹10 were stacked on his left lower arm to form a hanging bridge of coins with two pillars stacked vertically in 1 hr on 29 September 2019.

Most coins stacked on the edge of vertical palm:** 44 coins of ₹10 were stacked on the edge of his vertical palm in 30 mins on 29 September 2019.

wall with a tennis racquet non-stop 1,347 times in 15 mins 45 secs from a distance of 0.91 m (2 ft 11.8 in.) on 6 December 2017 at her residence.

Longest duration of non-stop hitting of a dangling cricket ball

Dr Arjun Anand Shirsath (b. 19 March 1977) from Ahmednagar, Maharashtra, knocked a dangling cricket ball with a 1.83 m (6 ft) cord length non-stop 10,332 times, using a bat, for 4 hrs 34 mins 35 secs on 24 April 2020.

Walking on hands with football between legs*/**

Manish Kothari (b. 6 February 2004) from Jaipur, Rajasthan, walked on his hands with a football between his legs, covering 71 m (232 ft 11.2 in.) in 152 steps during a summer camp in 1 min.11 secs on 24 May 2019 at Amritam Health Resort, Jaipur.

Retro walking**

Dinesh Kumar Agarwal (b. 1 March 1951) from Mumbai, Maharashtra, walked

* The rules regarding the age of participants have been modified. Please see Rules and Guidelines.

Most coins stacked on bicep:** 32 coins of ₹10 were stacked one at a time to make a 5.4 cm (2.13 in.) high tower on his left-arm bicep in 2 mins 16 secs on 22 September 2019.

Art structures with stacked coins:** Coin-stacking representing the 17 Sustainable Development Goals (SDGs) declared by the United Nations were created from 9 December 2019 to 20 January 2020. It took him 69 hours to assemble 18 coin-art structures. A total of 27,648 coins of value ₹1, ₹2, ₹5, ₹10 were stacked to make the sculptures.

No Poverty: 1,201 coins stacked in 4 hrs
Zero Hunger: 1,589 coins stacked in 6 hrs
Good Health and Well-being: 970 coins stacked in 3 hrs
Quality Education: 1,496 coins stacked in 3 hrs
Gender Equality: 1,531 coins stacked in 3 hrs
Clean Water and Sanitation: 1,659 coins stacked in 4 hrs
Affordable and Clean Energy: 1,579 coins stacked in 5 hrs
Decent Work and Economic Growth: 1,900 coins stacked in 5 hrs
Industry, Innovation and Infrastructure: 1,699 coins stacked in 4 hrs
Reduced Inequalities: 1,327 coins stacked in 3 hrs
Sustainable Cities and Communities: 1,840 coins stacked in 3 hrs
Sustainable Consumption and Production: 1,823 coins stacked in 5 hrs
Climate Action: 1,398 coins stacked in 3 hrs
Life below Water: 1,576 coins stacked in 3 hrs
Life on Land: 1,338 coins stacked in 3 hrs
Peace, Justice and Strong Institutions: 1,732 coins stacked in 5 hrs
Partnerships for the Goals: 1,599 coins stacked in 4 hrs
SDGs: 1,391 coins stacked in 3 hrs

5,000 steps backwards in 28 mins 22 secs on 4 February 2019 in Andheri East, Mumbai.

Highest jump with both legs**

Harish C.S. (b. 30 January 1999) from Coimbatore, Tamil Nadu, jumped with both legs simultaneously 35 times to a height of 76 cm (2 ft 5.9 in.), holding a bamboo stick in both hands at Siva Guru Silambam Academy on 12 May 2019.

Longest time balancing a hockey stick on the middle finger

Arun Kumar Kannan Murthy (b. 15 September 1985) from Kachipuram, Tamil Nadu, balanced an on-field hockey stick on his middle finger for 3 hrs 11 mins 50 secs on 18 August 2019 at Neat Trust , Vellore.

Most football rolls from eye to eye

Satish Kasi (b. 19 December 1990) from Bengaluru, Karnataka, performed 164

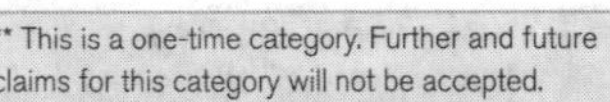
** This is a one-time category. Further and future claims for this category will not be accepted.

football rolls from eye to eye in 1 min. from 9:36 a.m. to 9:37 a.m. on 16 May 2019 at Sree Kanteerava Stadium, Bengaluru. He shifts the football from eye to eye while balancing the ball on the forehead.

Longest time balancing a hockey stick on the little finger
Gagandeep Singh (b. 25 November 1998) from Fatehgarh Sahib, Punjab, balanced a hockey stick weighing 660 g on his little finger for 1 hr from 4:00 p.m. to 5:00 p.m. on 10 May 2019 in Sirhind–Fatehgarh.

Most football rolls from eye to eye

Balancing a hockey stick on the little finger

MOST

Most tie knots tied – 1 minute
Dr Deepak M. Sharma (b. 2 June 1967) from Ahmedabad, Gujarat, knotted a tie around the neck seven times in 1 min. on 12 February 2020 at a stage performance in Surat.

Most handwritten pages
Dr Sukant Gupta (b. 24 May 1967) from Chandigarh, has been maintaining a handwritten log called 'Current International Affairs' since 20 March 1990. As of 31 May 2020, the log in his own handwriting ran into 36,485 pages. Since 1 September 1992 he has also been maintaining an index for easy reference, which has gone up to 9,604 pages. The total number of pages are 46,089, all handwritten on foolscap paper.

Most letters received by post**
Sadanand Paul (b. 5 March 1975) from Katihar, Bihar, has received 56,711 letters by India Post since 1983. He had 29,812 postcards and 26,899 letters in envelopes and inland letters up to 31 May 2019.

Most signatures in a book**
Swarnlata Vishwafool (b. 25 February 1983) from Katihar, Bihar, received 50,791 signatures by celebrities, friends and relatives in her 70-page poetry book, *Ye Udas Chehare*.

Most decorated car**
K. Viswanathan (b. 4 May 1962) from Lodi Colony, New Delhi, won the most decorated car award for the 12th time on 22 October 2017 at the 17th Family Mega Car Rally. The car was decorated by him along with his son V. Vignesh.

** This is a one-time category. Further and future claims for this category will not be accepted.

Most internationally travelled couple

Sujoy Kumar Mitra (b. 8 July 1983) and his wife Sharmistha Dey (b. 2 May 1986) have travelled to 133 countries together in 7 years 202 days from 9 December 2011 to 28 June 2019 by utilizing airline and hotel credit card points.

Most varieties of samosas

Most varieties of samosa

The faculty of hospitality, GNA University, Phagwara, Punjab, led by Chef Varinder Singh Rana, prepared 406 varieties of samosas using 217 ingredients in 2 hrs on 26 October 2018. The varieties included dry-fruit samosa, egg samosa and beetroot samosa, among other flavours.

Most varieties of flavoured rasgulla

A team of 10 chefs and 20 students of Chandigarh University, Ghauran, Punjab, led by Chef Dev Raj, prepared 720 varieties of rasgullas at the campus on 14 August 2018. The flavours included mango, apple, green chilli, lemon and mint, among others.

Most varieties of canapés

Most varieties of canapés

The School of Hospitality Management, IMS Unison University, Dehradun, Uttarakhand, assembled 351 varieties of canapés, in 2 hrs 30 mins from 10:30 a.m. to 1:00 p.m. at their campus on 24 April 2019. The canapés were prepared by the 'Fantastic 34' team and the event was anchored by Abhay Chamoli.

Most varieties of cakes made and displayed

Bakersville India Pvt. Ltd executed the largest display of cakes at the Bombay Exhibition Centre, Mumbai, Maharashtra. A team of 15 chefs made and displayed 598 cakes from 9:00 a.m. on 19 September to 8:15 a.m. on 20 September 2019. The cakes were kept on display during 20–22 September. All the cakes were unduplicated in design and flavour.

Record Rewind

Most grapes fitted in mouth

2013

Dinesh Shivnath Upadhyaya (b. 16 January 1976) from Mumbai, Maharashtra, fitted 80 seedless grapes in his mouth for 30 secs live at the TV9 Mumbai News studio in Andheri on 8 April 2012.

2019

Dinesh Shivnath Upadhyaya (b. 16 January 1976) from Mumbai, Maharashtra, fitted 94 grapes in 3 mins 47 secs at the PFR office, Goregaon, on 16 February 2018.

Most varieties of besan *chillas*

Sandeep Lohani, principal, St Soldier Institute of Hotel Management, Jalandhar, Punjab, along with five faculty members and 30 students, prepared 389 besan *chillas* with various toppings in 1 hr 25 mins from 10:55 a.m. to 12:20 p.m. on 27 March 2019.

Most *batata vadas* fried

Satyendra Arun Jog (b. 10 December 1975), a chef from Mumbai, Maharashtra, made 25,101 *batata vadas*, a popular Maharashtrian snack. The event was completed in 10 hrs 22 mins at Dombivli Gymkhana, Thane, on 28 December 2019, with the help of 25 assistants. Jog had the main job of dropping the spice-mixed mashed potato ball coated with gram-flour batter in the hot oil in the karahi.

Most dishes made – 1 hr – solo**

Santhosh M. P. (b. 21 August 1958) from Kottayam, Kerala, cooked 33 dishes between 3:00 p.m. and 3:58 p.m. on 27 May 2018. He prepared eight non-vegetarian and 25 vegetarian dishes. The event was organized by Vyapari Vyavasayi Ekopana Samiti, Vaikom, and held at Vattathara Resident Hall. He had two assistants, Dikku Santhosh and Seem Dinesh, to arrange and garnish the items.

Most patents granted to an individual

Sachin Gangadhar Lokapur (b. 11 October 1986) from Sangli, Maharashtra, was granted 45 Indian patents, including one trademark and one copyright, by the Patent Office, Government of India, from 2009 to 2019. The inventions include a digital micro-imaging adaptor, a digital oral inhaler and an LED panel for microscopes, among others.

Most patents filed in a day – group**

Prof. Dr Harish Umashankar Tiwari (b. 19 August 1971) and Amruta Tiwari (b. 18 January 1975) filed 14 patents in a single day at Indian Patent and Trade Marks Office, Mumbai, Maharashtra, on 22 November 2019. Both worked on the inventions for more than a year.

Most patents filed in a day – solo**

Dr Shirish Yograj Khedikar (b. 11 October 1984) from Bhandara, Maharashtra, a scientist working at the India Meteorological Department, Pune, filed 10 patents in a single day for his various innovative sensors and devices on 30 March 2020 at the Office of Controller General of Patents, Designs and Trade Marks, New Delhi.

** This is a one-time category. Further and future claims for this category will not be accepted.

Most towels used

Welspun India Ltd created a record for most towels used at a single platform, using 9,000 towels as giveaways with a reusability of 135,000 times at the Kumbh Mela 2019 at Prayagraj, Uttar Pradesh. The company distributed 3,000 towels (in three batches, thus totalling 9,000 towels) to pilgrims visiting the Mela. The towels were then dry-cleaned and reused during the course of 45 days.

Most greeting cards made in 24 hours**

Dr Anshuja Rushikesh Kimmatkar (b. 1 October 1977) from Nagpur, Maharashtra, made 502 greeting cards by hand, each measuring 17 cm × 10 cm (6.6 in. x 3.9 in.) in 24 hrs from 8:00 a.m. on 19 April to 8:00 a.m. on 20 April 2020. She used multimedia painting and waste materials like dry flowers, tags, rangoli, buttons, safety pins, broken pieces of glass, balloons, earbuds, needle and syringes, and seeds for decoration. She took 45 mins of break time.

Most mannequins displayed

Most mannequins displayed

The MBO Store owned by Jay Patadiaa in Parel, Mumbai, Maharashtra displayed 72 mannequins in 42.36 sq. m (456 sq. ft) on 5 June 2017. There were shelves of mannequins sporting T-shirts and other men's apparel.

Most pocket cartoons on farmers**

Lahu Bhivraj Kale (b. 29 October 1970) from Pune, Maharashtra, has been publishing pocket cartoons on the life of farmers in a single newspaper, *Agrowon* (from the Sakal Group), since 2007. By January 2019 the number of pocket cartoons was 4,341.

Most Baby Births on New Year's Day

According to a release by UNICEF, India recorded the highest baby births on New Year's Day on 1 January 2021. An estimated 371,504 babies were born on the day globally and India contributed to the figure with 59,995 births. It was followed by China (35,615) and Nigeria (21,439). Fiji was projected to have the first baby of 2021 and USA recorded the last baby birth on 1 January 2021. Previously India also held the same record for 2020 with 67,385 births.

Most designs with currency notes**

Nishant Choudhary (b. 5 August 1979) from Jaipur, Rajasthan, has created 111 designs of Mahatma Gandhi wearing various headgear, using ₹10 currency notes, since 16 June 2009.

Most eyebrows threaded**

Pratiksha Sanjay Bharati (b. 9 July 1980) from Ambarnath, Maharashtra, threaded 62 pairs of eyebrows in 1 hr from 4:31 p.m. to 5:31 p.m. on 9 December 2018.

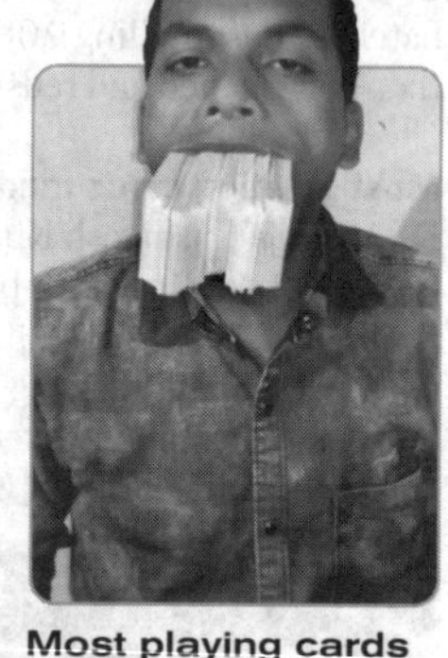

Most playing cards fitted in mouth

Most playing cards fitted in the mouth

Manoj Kumar Maharana (b. 15 May 1994) from Bhabarada, Ganjam District, Odisha, fitted 265 playing cards vertically in the mouth and kept them for 1 min. on 22 January 2018.

Most faces painted – 1 hr – group

G. H. Raisoni College of Engineering (GHRCE), Nagpur, Maharashtra, organized a face-painting event with the theme 'Save Tigers' on 18 February 2019. Together, 381 painters (340 students and 41 teachers) painted 1,686 faces in 1 hr from 9:00 a.m. to 10:00 a.m. at the campus.

FASTEST

Fastest to pocket 100 centre-cut carom pawns**

Prof. Dr S. Ramesh Babu (b. 12 February 1957) from Bengaluru, Karnataka, has achieved the fastest time to pocket 100 centre-cut carom pawns in 5 mins at his residence on 12 February 2020. The overall average striking speed was 21 pawns per minute.

Fastest to pocket 100 centre-cut carom pawns

Fastest to make 500 sandwiches – group

CT Institute of Hotel Management (CTIHM) Shahpur, Jalandhar, Punjab, celebrated the 550th birth anniversary of Guru Nanak Dev (30 November) with 500 students and 30 chefs preparing 500 different types of vegetable sandwiches in 3 mins 39 secs on 15 October 2019. The components of the 6-inch-thick sandwiches were bread, fillings like fruits, nuts, pastas, cheese, dairy products and vegetables, and dressings like mayonnaise, Thousand Island and tandoori, among others. The sandwiches were distributed among underserved children and students.

Fastest fruit slicing

Prof. Dr S. Ramesh Babu (b. 12 February 1957) from Bengaluru, Karnataka, sliced 12 bananas into 350 slivers in 1 min. on 11 August 2018 at Auroville.

** This is a one-time category. Further and future claims for this category will not be accepted.

Fastest slicing of vegetables while blindfolded

Vimal Radheshyam Rajoriya (b. 1 June 1992) from Palghar, Maharashtra, sliced a carrot, while blindfolded, into 92 slivers in 30 secs and a 1-inch cucumber into 32 thin slivers in 10.33 secs on 28 May 2019 at Al-Ramniy Hotel, Palghar.

Fastest slicing of vegetables while blindfolded

Fastest double throwball rally

Prof. Dr S. Ramesh Babu (b. 12 February 1957) and M. Suresh (b. 13 July 1969) from Bengaluru, Karnataka, using two Cosco throwballs, simultaneously threw them at each other in 86 rallies in 1 min. on 8 June 2019 at Akai Public School, Bengaluru.

Top: Fastest double throwball rally

Below: Fastest lighting of diyas

Fastest lighting of diyas – group

The NSHM Faculty of Hospitality and Tourism, Durgapur, West Bengal, with the help of 200 participants, lit 21,328 diyas in 13 mins 22 secs at the NSHM Knowledge Campus on 25 January 2019. The event was organized by the

students, teachers and management of the college, teachers and students from neighbouring schools, eminent members of society and underprivileged children.

Fastest assembling of cycles

Hindustan Petroleum Corporation Ltd organized the 'Velocipede Challenge', where 313 participants simultaneously assembled 60 bicycles from different segregated components in 45 mins at the Yuvantage 3.0 Grand Finale on 7 January 2019 at Ramoji Film City, Hyderabad.

SMALLEST

Smallest rugby stadium model

Shaminder Singh (b. 13 January 1976) from Coventry, UK, constructed a model of the Ricoh Arena rugby stadium, 122 cm (48 in.) long, 76 cm (29.9 in.) wide and 41 cm (16.1 in.) high, with 45,000 toothpicks. He worked on the model for a total of 900 hours over six months between 1 September 2017 and 2 March 2018.

Smallest rugby stadium model

Smallest microwave oven

Salvendar Ghansheed Baba (b. 21 October 1999) from Vijayawada, Andhra Pradesh, made the smallest microwave oven, 80 mm (3.15 in.) long, 35 mm (1.38 in.) wide and 40 mm (1.57 in.) high in 15 days, from 11 to 25 December 2018. He used plywood cardboard, green and orange LED lights of 3 volts, 1,000-ohm resistor, small wires, Nichrome wire, aluminium foil, Fevicol glue, a small switch, a design sticker, a 3.7 volt phone battery and a connecting pin to make the oven.

Smallest microwave oven

Smallest functioning guitar

Smallest functioning guitar

Prakash Chandra Upadhyay (b. 25 May 1973) from Haldwani, Uttarakhand, made the smallest functioning guitar, measuring 3 cm (1.2 in.) in length, using sandalwood, copper wire, aluminium and iron pins on 29 April 2020. He took 4 hrs 30 mins to make it. The sound of the guitar is audible with audio speakers.

Smallest spinning wheel

Gaya Prasad Agarwal (b. 9 October 1976) from Jaipur, Rajasthan, made the smallest spinning wheel (charkha) in 18 days between 12 and 30 January 2018. The spinning wheel, made of metal, is 5.10 mm (0.20 in.) long , 3.81 mm (0.15 in.) wide and 3.16 mm (0.12 in.) high.

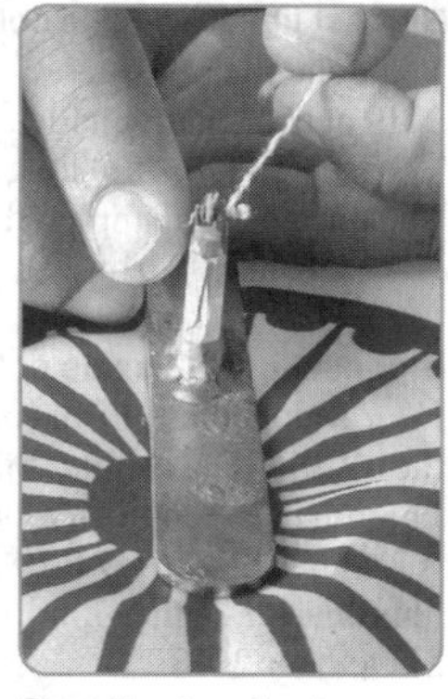

Smallest spinning wheel

BIGGEST

Biggest postcard

Suresh Kumar (b. 2 January 1980) from Marthandam, Kanniyakumari, Tamil Nadu, made the biggest replica of an India Post postcard using plywood. The postcard measured 3.65 m (11 ft 11.7 in.) long, 2.44 m (8 ft) wide and 18 mm (0.71 in.) thick. Balakrishna Matriculation Higher Secondary School, Vadakkankulam, got 1,686 students to sign the card. The card was made in two weeks from 15 April to 1 May 2019.

Biggest Dharma Chakra

The Buddhist Forum, Yamunanagar, Haryana, made the biggest Dharma Chakra (Ashoka Chakra) with mild steel in 240 days between 25 February and 22 October 2018. Created by Dr Satyadeep Neil Gauri and Sidhartha Gauri, the structure weighs 6 tonnes and has a diameter of 9.14 m (29 ft 11.8 in.).

Biggest steel charkha

District Administration, Wardha, Maharashtra, Sevagram Ashram Pratishthan and Sir J. J. School of Arts, Mumbai, unveiled the biggest functional mild-steel charkha on 2 October 2018. It is 9.75 m (31 ft 11.8 in.) long, 3.45 m (11 ft 3.83 in.) wide, 5.64 m (18 ft 6 in.) high and weighs 5.5 tonnes. It was built in 21 days from 11 September to 1 October 2018 (both days included).

Biggest steel charkha

Biggest jigsaw puzzle solved – group

Vodafone Idea Business Services created the largest jigsaw puzzle on 17 January 2019 at the Vodafone Idea office in Peninsula Towers, Mumbai, Maharashtra. The 6 m (19 ft 8.2 in.) long and 3.96 m (12 ft 11.9 in.) wide jigsaw had 912 pieces. The puzzle was completed by 264 employees from 18 cities in 3 hrs 20 mins from 9:45 a.m. to 1:05 p.m.

Biggest jigsaw puzzle solved – solo

Heer Kalpakbhai Doshi (b. 10 March 2006) from Rajkot, Gujarat, completed the 32,256 Ravensburger jigsaw puzzle titled 'New York City Window' in 3 years 1 month between 18 October 2015 and 18 November 2018. The finished puzzle is 5.44 m x 1.92 m (17 ft 10 in. x 6 ft 3.59 in.) in area. LED lamps were used to illuminate it from behind. Celebrations started on 12 October and ended on 21 October 2018.

Biggest jigsaw puzzle solved – solo

Biggest handmade newspaper

Students of Vidya Vihar Central School, Thrissur, Kerala, made a newspaper, *Vidya Times,* which had 6,000 pages, weighed 70 kg and was 55 cm (1 ft 9.6 in.) high. Each page was 80 cm (2 ft 7.6 in.) long and 50 cm (1 ft 8 in.) wide. A total of 1,000 students from classes 5 to 11 prepared it as a three-month project from 1 November 2018 to 8 February 2019.

Biggest Jaipur blue-pottery plate

Leela Bodria, proprietor of Neerja International Inc., based in Jaipur, Rajasthan, involved nine craftsmen to make a Jaipur blue-pottery plate 76 cm (30 in.) in diameter on 16 May 2017. The plate weighed 12 kg and was made in 50 days.

Biggest Jaipur blue-pottery plate

Biggest desk calendar

Revati Ravi Sonar (b. 19 December 2000) from Pandharpur, Maharashtra, received the biggest desk calendar as a gift from her brother, Omkar Ravi Sonar, on 19 December 2018. The area of the calendar is 6.503 sq. m (70 sq. ft) and it is 3.048 m (10 ft) wide and 2.134 m (7 ft) high. The flex calendar has seven pages.

Biggest traditional lamp

Dr Braj Kishore Shukla (b. 3 June 1970) from Gandhinagar, Gujarat, created the biggest traditional lamp to spread the message of humanity. The 10.97 m (35 ft 11.8 in.) tall stainless steel lamp, with a bowl 4.8 m (15 ft 8.98 in.) in diameter, weighed 3,000 kg. Named the 'Lamp of Humanity', it has solar panels and was installed at the Sabarmati waterfront in Ahmedabad, Gujarat, on 25 September 2018. It has five flames, with four side flames representing Truth, Justice, Honesty and Compassion, and the central flame symbolizes Humanity.

Biggest *chandmala* (decorative hanging)

JSW Cement and Ekdalia Evergreen Club Puja Committee from Kolkata, West Bengal, inaugurated the largest *chandmala*, an initiative to support and revive the shola and *chandmala* art of Kolkata. Hanging from a five-storeyed building, the 9.75 m (32 ft) *chandmala* had three discs, each with a diameter of 2.43 m (8 ft). Each disc had three layers made of an iron structure, plywood, shola and thermocol.

LARGEST

Largest wall clock

Nisha Jayesh Chheda (b. 16 June 1977) from Mumbai, Maharashtra, conceptualized and designed the largest wall clock, which was executed by Vipul Panchal, Saikrishna Vasam, Jayesh L. Chheda, Saachi J. Chheda and Digvijay Singh. The 1.8 m (5 ft 10.8 in.) diameter clock was made using plywood, acrylic, stainless steel nuts, moulds and colours. The clock was made in 49 days from 15 January 2019 to 4 March 2019.

Largest compilation of maths formulae**

Kislay Sharma (b. 25 February 1991) from Patna,

Record Rewind

Biggest envelope

2014

Garima Angel (b. 24 January 1991) from Agra, Uttar Pradesh, made and displayed the biggest envelope, 14.51 m (47 ft 7 in.) long and 9.86 m (32 ft 4.1 in.) wide, at the Agra College main campus on 24 November 2012. She used 3,500 chart papers weighing 50 kg. Preparation for the envelope took 38 days while the work of cutting and sealing took 10 days (total 48 days). The message on the cover was 'Save Taj Mahal and Polluted Yamuna'.

2017

WR Jagadeesh Pillai from Varanasi, Uttar Pradesh, made the biggest envelope measuring 25.55 m (83 ft 9 in.) in length and 14.4 m (47 ft 2 in.) in width, on 19 February 2017. The envelope was made to spread awareness about industrial waste.

** This is a one-time category. Further and future claims for this category will not be accepted.

Bihar, has the largest compilation of mathematics formulae, totalling 5,067 up to 3 June 2020, a collection he began in 2014. They range from high-school to postgraduate levels. All formulae have been arranged topic-wise.

Largest painting using non-traditional art media

Largest painting using non-traditional art media

Aadipudi Devisri (b. 23 August 2005) from Ongole, Prakasam District, Andhra Pradesh, made a portrait of Mahatma Gandhi with coffee powder (post-expiry-date) and water. The 156.5 sq. m (1,684.6 sq. ft) portrait was made in 32 hrs 48 mins at the M.H.R. Function Hall, Ongole, between 7 and 9 May 2019.

Largest human representation of a text

Rotary Club of Mapuca, Rotarian Ajay Menon and Nishita Pednekar of Rotaract District 3170, organized the largest human representation of a text with 962 people on 23 February 2019 at Peddem Sports Complex, Mapusa, Goa. Students from various schools in Mapusa stood in an undivided line holding one placard with one letter of the alphabet to make the largest human presentation of a text. The attempt was completed in 2 hrs 15 mins from 9:00 a.m. to 11:15 a.m.

Largest sanitary pad

MyPadBank, an NGO in Bareilly, Uttar Pradesh, made the largest sanitary pad, 6.7 m (21 ft 11.7 in.) long and 3.35 m (10 ft 11.8 in.) wide, using 1,720 'NIINE Sanitary Pads' at Gandhi Udyan Ground, Bareilly, on 23 December 2018. Chitransh Saxena, Utkarsh Saxena, Shilpi Saxena, Saher Choudhry, Anil K. Razz, Rashi Udit, Yash Vajpai, Emmanuel Singh, Ajayank, Ana Khan, Jennifer Lal, Aishwarya Lal, Shilpi Jaiswal, Sunidhi Malick and Amaan Siddiqui participated in the event.

Largest collective reading – single theme – multiple venues**

The former governor of Madhya Pradesh, Lalji Tandon, organized a collective reading of Gandhian literature, conducted by 4,427 educational institutions of 51 districts, which culminated on the 150th birth anniversary of Gandhiji on 2 October 2019. As many as 548,506 students participated and read books written by Mahatma Gandhi. From 3,898 schools, 440,077 students of classes 9 to 12 read *Hind Swaraj* between 25 September and 2 October 2019. From 599 colleges and 30 universities, 108,429 students read *Hind Swaraj* and *My Experiments with Truth* on 2 October 2019. The activity of 'Collective Reading of Gandhian Literature', organized throughout Madhya Pradesh, was supported by the Raj Bhavan, Bhopal.

** This is a one-time category. Further and future claims for this category will not be accepted.

SUPER 30

UNBREAKABLE AND UNSHAKEABLE

While we celebrate the breaking of one record by another, there is a selection of records that have stood the test of decades. These records have either not been surpassed or have been updated over the years by the same record holder. Here's a glimpse of the unbroken records from the 1990s.

Year	Record Holder	Record Category	Measurement
1992	Atiya Kindergarten School, Hyderabad (now in Telangana)	Largest slate/ blackboard	3.14 m (10 ft 4 in.) long, 2.13 m (6 ft 11.8 in.) wide
1992	Textile exhibition, Pragati Maidan, New Delhi	Largest paisley	18.58 sq. m (200 sq. ft)
1994	Jatinder Mahajan, Damtal, Himachal Pradesh	Largest collection of antique coins	18,000 (1994) to 70,607 (1999)
1996	Raju Umamaheshwar, Coimbatore, Tamil Nadu	Largest collection of crosswords	467,987 (1990) to 714,881 (2019)
1998	Shoppers Stop, Mumbai	Largest friendship band	970 m (3,182 ft 4.9 in.)

Largest broom

Ashok Kumar Bairwa (b. 1 August 1994) from Sawai Madhopur, Rajasthan, made a 20.11 m (65 ft 11.7 in.) long broom, along with Mangilal Rathor, Vinod Kumar, Sukhdev and Pannalal. He sourced bamboo, palm leaves, waste materials and rope in 15 days and the finishing work was done in 6 hrs from 7:00 p.m. to 1:00 a.m. during 8–9 April 2019.

Largest broom

Largest insurance agent meet

SBI Life Insurance, Chennai, Tamil Nadu, conducted an insurance agents' meet with 7,048 Regional Level Life Mitras from 9:00 a.m. to 6:00 p.m. on 20 November 2019 at the Trade Centre.

Largest plumbing event

The Indian Plumbing Skills Council conducted the Plumbing Skills Mahotsav at the Thyagaraj Sports Complex, New Delhi, from 9:00 a.m. to 5:00 p.m. on 3 February 2019 with 10,000 plumbers participating in it.

Largest plumbing event

Largest walkathon – multiple venues

The Public Works Department of Maharashtra and Maharashtra Motor Vehicle Department, along with CASI Global and CSR Diary, organized Maha Walkathon 2018, a 2 km walk in 503 different locations across several states simultaneously with a total of 507,367 participants on 18 November 2018. The duration of the walk was 30 mins and it was flagged off by Chandrakant Dada Patil and Prof. Paresh Sheth.

Largest photo exhibition – single personality**

Manmohan Agarwal (b. 16 December 1975) and Nishant Choudhary (b. 5 August 1979) from Jaipur, Rajasthan, organized the largest exhibition with 197,610 photographs of Prime Minister Narendra Modi on 17 September 2018 at Triton Mall, Jaipur, in association with the Government Senior Secondary School, Laxman Dungri. They gathered the photos in six months from Facebook, Google and other sources with nine volunteers from Garima Foundation.

Largest photo exhibition – single personality

Largest doll display in a home**

M.P. Kavitha Ananth (b. 11 June 1965) from Secunderabad, Telangana, put up a display of 1,520 dolls on three floors as part of observing 'Bommala Koluvu',

** This is a one-time category. Further and future claims for this category will not be accepted.

Largest doll display in a home

the traditional custom of arranging dolls during Diwali in Telangana and Andhra Pradesh. Her display during Diwali 2018 had nine steps of big dolls, nine steps of small dolls and a unique arrangement of 85 scenes from epics such as the Ramayana, the *Bhagavata Purana* and the Mahabharata, showing the entire story of Rama and Krishna.

Largest Indian flag mosaic – group**

The Aorta Foundation organized 5,000 children from government schools to write individual postcards by hand to service personnel at Siachen, thanking them for their invaluable service to the nation, at Gnana Bodhini High School, Bengaluru, Karnataka, on 26 January 2020. The postcards carried a thank-you note on the back, and on the front each postcard was in one colour of the national flag – saffron, white or green. When put together they formed the Indian national flag, measuring 13.7 m x 9.14 m (45 ft x 30 ft).

Largest birthday celebration – multiple venues

Largest birthday celebration – multiple venues

Atul Bakery, Surat, Gujarat, organized the largest birthday celebrations at multiple venues in south Gujarat on 17 September 2019 to honour Prime Minister Narendra Modi on his birthday. A total of 14,623 children participated in the celebrations across 215 locations.

Largest same birthday celebrations

Atul Bakery in Surat, Gujarat, organized a gathering of 711 people who shared the same birthday with Prime Minister Narendra Modi on 17 September 2018 at the Surat International Exhibition and Convention Centre (SIECC), to honour the prime minister.

WR Largest serving of chips

Chandresh Himmatlal Bayad (b. 3 September 1985) of Helly & Chilly Foods, Ahmedabad, Gujarat, cooked the largest serving of potato chips, weighing 659 kg, at Rifle Club, Ahmedabad, on 22 September 2018. It was prepared in 9 hrs from 10:00 a.m. to 7:00 p.m. with 2,080 kg of potatoes. The chips were distributed to visitors, media persons, Roti Bank, Food Bank and people with disabilities.

WR Largest moulded potato chip

Chandresh Himmatlal Bayad (b. 3 September 1985) of Helly & Chilly Foods, Ahmedabad, Gujarat, cooked the largest moulded potato chip, weighing 11 kg, at Rifle Club, Ahmedabad, on 7 October 2018. The potato fry was 291 cm (9 ft 6.567 in.) long, 6.4 cm (3.30 in.) wide and 6.2 cm (2.4 in.) thick. It was made in 3 hrs from 4:30 p.m. to 7:30 p.m. with five other persons.

Largest chocolate fall

Windsor Chocolatier created the largest chocolate fall with milk chocolate between 21 June and 28 June 2019. Headed by Rhea Gupta, the 2.84 m (9 ft 3.8 in.) high and 4.90 m (16 ft 1 in.) wide fall was made by 12 people.

Largest chocolate wall

Windsor Chocolatier created the largest chocolate wall, which was 5.23 m (17 ft 2 in.) in length, 2.29 m (7 ft 6 in.) in height, 0.15 m (6 in.) wide and weighed 1,050 kg. The chocolate wall was made between 3 March and 20 March 2020. They used dark chocolate, white chocolate and chocolate colours for their attempt. The chocolate wall was initiated by Rhea Gupta and involved five persons.

Largest chocolate fall

Largest momo

Jackie's Chinese Restaurant, Vasant Kunj, New Delhi, made the largest steamed chicken momo, weighing 78.24 kg and measuring 1.52 m (4 ft 11.8 in.) in diameter on 25 March 2019 at the restaurant. It took 3 hrs from 12:30 p.m. to 3:30 p.m. to make it.

Largest bean salad

The Tamil Nadu Chamber Foundation and Chef M.S. Rajmohan (b. 28 September 1985) from Madurai, Tamil Nadu, made bean salad weighing 1,121.6 kg at IDA

Scudder Trade Centre auditorium, Madurai, on 15 August 2018. The salad was made by 20 professional chefs and 64 student chefs in 19 hrs on the sidelines of Vibrant Tamil Nadu – the Global Food Expo Summit 2018.

Largest *kaju katli*

Kanti Sweets from Bengaluru, Karnataka, made the largest *kaju katli* (a sweet made with cashew nuts), measuring 3.3 m x 2.1 m x 0.2 m (10 ft 9.9 in. x 6 ft 10.6 in. x 7.87 in.) and weighing 1,051 kg, at Ganakallu Village on 15 January 2020. A total of 540 kg of ground cashew nuts, 486 kg of sugar, ghee and silver foil were used. Twelve people were involved in the preparation that took 5 hrs.

Largest *kaju katli*

WR Largest thali – dimension and dishes

The PCTE Group of Institutes – Hotel Management, and Travel and Tourism College, Ludhiana, Punjab, put together the largest Indian traditional-style thali called Atulniya Bharat. The wooden thali, which was 2.44 m (8 ft) in diameter, had 270 authentic dishes prepared from the cuisines of all the 28 states and eight Union Territories of India and three add-on dishes – a variety of sweets, chutneys and *shorba* (soup). From the starters to the desserts, the items were served in 270 steel bowls and glasses. The participants were chefs Anirban and Sumit, and Kayamudin along with 220 students and the faculty of PCTE. The preparation of all the dishes took 5 hrs from 6:00 a.m. to 11:00 a.m. on 14 August 2019 at PCTE College, Crimson Banquet Hall, Campus 2.

LONGEST

Longest *mandua* yule log

The Institute of Hotel Management, Dehradun, Uttarakhand, prepared a 19.35 m (63 ft 5 in.) long *mandua* yule log with 20 students and seven faculty members in 11 hrs from 8:00 a.m. to 7:00 p.m. on 16 October 2018. The yule log was prepared using *mandua* atta, refined oil, jam, eggs, cream and desiccated coconut. The *mandua* yule log was unveiled at 10:00 a.m. on 17 October 2018.

Longest necklace

The students and team members of the International School of Design, Kolkata,

West Bengal, in association with Shree Jeen Education Centre, made a 36 m (118 ft 1.3 in.) long necklace on the concept of *kasu mala*, a traditional piece of jewellery from Kerala. It was made using wooden ply, metal loops, gold and silver paint, green plastic and glass stones, brooches, copper coins, pearly plastic balls and diyas between 16 September and 13 October 2018.

Longest hair

Akanksha Yadav (b. 21 January 1988) from Thane, Maharashtra, has the longest hair, which is 3.01 m (9 ft 10.5 in.) long.

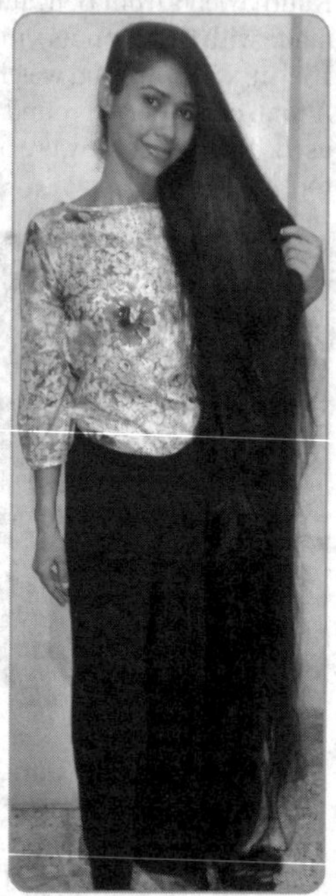

Longest hair

Longest *taali*

Suresh Fashion Jewellery, based in Marthandam, Tamil Nadu, made the longest and heaviest *taali* (marriage symbol) on 10 May 2019. The *taali* was 1.219 m (4 ft) long and weighed 2,412 kg.

Longest joint-family gathering**

The SK family, located in Gujarat and Maharashtra, has been hosting joint family get-togethers for 40 years during Diwali by spending a few days in various locations every year. Their first trip organized in 1979 had only 30 members. By 2018, the number of members participating in the get-togethers had gone up to 120.

Longest continuous *antakshari* stage show

Mithakshari – the single longest continuous *antakshari* stage show – was conducted by Dipesh Mehta at Mahaveer School, Jaipur, Rajasthan, for 13 hrs 41 mins on 28 July 2019 from 9:30 a.m. to 11:11 p.m. It was coordinated by Mahendra Girdharwal from the Jain Social Group International Federation (JSGIF). The participating groups were the Jain Social Groups (JSG – 33 groups) and the Sangini Group (six groups). There were 39 teams with four participants each, totalling to 156 participants.

Longest soap-wrapper chain

Sharmistha Chakraborty (b. 24 March 1987) from Kolkata, West Bengal, made the longest toilet-soap-wrapper chain measuring 159 m (521 ft 7.8 in.) with 2,019 packets of Nirma soap. Each soap-cake wrapper was 7.87 cm (3.1 in.) long and 5.08 cm (2 in.) wide. She joined the wrappers as a chain in 2 hrs from 6:00 p.m. to 8:00 p.m. on 10 January 2019.

WR **Longest paper chain**

Pavitra Patro (b. 29 September 1981) from Ahmedabad, Gujarat, made the longest paper chain, measuring 924.88 m (3,034 ft 4 in.), at the Statue of Unity, Kevadia, Gujarat, on 19 May 2019. He made the paper chain in 13 hrs 44 mins from 6:31 a.m. to 8:15 p.m.

** This is a one-time category. Further and future claims for this category will not be accepted.

Longest and largest human chain

The Government of Bihar, as part of its 'Jan Jeevan Hariyali' campaign, organized an 18,034 km long human chain with 5.16 crore (51,600,000) people on 19 January 2020. It took seven helicopters and over 100 drones to take aerial images of the human chain. The event championed the cause of environment conservation along with other social causes.

Longest charcuterie platter

Spectra, a restaurant at The Leela Ambience Gurugram Hotel and Residences, Gurugram, Haryana, displayed a 9.448 m (31 ft) long and 30 cm (11.8 in.) wide Christmas charcuterie platter on 24 December 2018. It had a variety of cheeses, meats, compotes, crudités, sandwiches, canapés, truffles and chocolates, among other dishes.

Longest charcuterie platter

Longest service at the Siachen Glacier

Hon. Capt. Perma Nand – JC-121569K (b. 7 July 1945), who retired from the Indian Army Corps of EME had the longest service at Siachen Glacier from 12 December 1987 to 16 May 1989 (around 18 months) in temperatures between –25 °C and –50 °C.

Longest bill

Sanjay Dodrajka (b. 28 January 1972) from New Delhi ordered 420 burgers from the Burger King outlet in Dhaula Kuan for children of MCD School, Nangal Punya, New Delhi on 7 December 2019. As a result, Sanjay got a 12 ft (144 in.) long bill.

TALLEST

Tallest fibreglass bottle

Dabur India Ltd's Pudin Hara (an ayurvedic medicine for indigestion) created the tallest fibreglass bottle filled with diluted Pudin Hara at Nauchandi Mela Ground in Meerut, Uttar Pradesh, on 30 May 2019. The bottle was 1.83 m (6 ft) tall and 61 cm (2 ft) wide, with a capacity of 400 litres. It was made in 15 days between 15 May and 30 May 2019.

Tallest man-made Christmas tree

Delhi International Airport Ltd, New Delhi, commissioned India's tallest man-made Christmas tree, 30.7 m (101 ft) tall (including the 2.4 m (8 ft) star on top).

The tree itself was 28.3 m (93 ft) tall. It had over 16,000 Christmas ornaments and 60,000 pine twigs as decoration. The 12-tonne installation was made in 23 days by a team of 80 members from Karmic Events India and inaugurated on 23 December 2019.

Tallest man-made Christmas tree

COLLECTIONS

Electrical lamps and tubes
Ajit Kesarinath Chaudhari (b. 5 July 1946) from Pune, Maharashtra, has 10,546 electrical lamps and tubes including a 2.44 m (8 ft) long tube light. The oldest lamp is manufactured by Thomas Alva Edison's company in the 19th century.

Ludo tokens
Tatsamyak Manu (b. 31 December 1994) from Katihar, Bihar, has a collection of 6,400 ludo tokens and 400 dice, a hobby he has pursued since 2012.

A–Z audio cassettes of debutant actors
Ninad Jadhav (b. 11 July 1977) from Barkuhi, Chhindwara District, Madhya Pradesh, has the largest A–Z collection of 211 audio cassettes of 214 movies.

Audio cassettes

Live recordings of music
Parameshwar Mangalam Harihari (b. 4 July 1945) from Mumbai, Maharashtra, has a collection of 23,080 recordings of live Indian classical concerts, including both Hindustani and Carnatic, as on 9 October 2017.

Mukesh's songs
Mukul Kapoor (b. 19 August 1964) from Ajmer, Rajasthan, has the largest

collection of playback singer Mukesh Chand Mathur's songs, including memorabilia. The collection, started in March 1990, includes 1,188 film songs, 65 non-film songs, 78 regional-language songs, 15 bhajans and 13 parts of the Ramayana.

Audio cassettes of songs featured on one actor

Ninad Jadhav (b. 11 July 1977) from Barkuhi, Chhindwara District, Madhya Pradesh, has a collection of 104 audio cassettes of songs featuring actor Mithun Chakraborty on screen.

Amitabh Bachchan memorabilia

Mohan Rajgopal Iyer (b. 12 February 1963) from Nagpur, Maharashtra, an ardent admirer of superstar Amitabh Bachchan, has a collection of his photographs, articles, press clippings, filmography, correspondences and articles from the Internet. The total number of items were 8,650 up to 31 May 2019.

Sridevi press clippings

Anuradha Gupta (b. 30 May 1968) from New Delhi has a collection of 1,270 press clippings about late actor Sridevi from newspapers and magazines in many languages starting from 24 February 2018.

Cinema clips (Hindi)

Swarnlata Vishwafool (b. 25 February 1983) from Katihar, Bihar, has collected 100,147 clippings related to Hindi cinema from various Hindi newspapers from 1998 to 2019.

A–Z cinema books

Ninad Jadhav (b. 11 July 1977) from Barkuhi, Chhindwara District, Madhya Pradesh, has a collection of A–Z Indian cinema books, a hobby he started in 2007. It comprises 107 books on Indian cinema some of which are old and rare. Published in Hindi, English, Bengali and Marathi, most of the books are on the Kapoor family (Raj, Shammi, Shashi, Rishi and others) and Mithun Chakraborty. The rarest book is Raj Kapoor's *Fabulous Showman* and the oldest is *Shalimar*. Some of the books have been signed by the authors.

A–Z cinema books

Record Rewind

Largest collection of stickers

2008

Dishant Garg (b. 23 January 1991) from Delhi had various types of stickers - 2,076 with singles and 2,762 duplicated. He had divided them into 3D and PVC, plastic and holograms.

2015

Nidhi Bansal (b. 6 June 1989) from Fatehgarh Sahib, Punjab, had collected 103,800 stickers, a hobby since 2007. She had categorized her collection into subjects like smiley faces, flowers, footballs, birds, trains and cartoons, among others.

Chitra Kathayen comics

Ninad Jadhav (b. 11 July 1977) from Barkuhi, Chhindwara District, Madhya Pradesh, has the largest collection of Hindi-film *Chitra Kathayen,* numbering 123, a collection since 1997. Most of the comics feature Mithun Chakraborty, Dimple Kapadia, Madhuri Dixit, Vinod Khanna, Rajesh Khanna, Shah Rukh Khan and Navin Nischol. All *Chitra Kathayen* are from Diamond Comics. Amit Jain from Berasia, Bhopal, an ardent fan of Amitabh Bachchan, helped Ninad build this collection.

Film stars' print ads

Anuradha Gupta (b. 30 May 1968) from New Delhi has accumulated 1,727 print media advertisements with endorsements by movie stars since May 2018.

Ties

Dr Deepak M. Sharma (b. 2 June 1967) from Ahmedabad, Gujarat, has a collection of 4,589 ties including 2,611 theme-based ones.

T-shirts with one brand's logo

Nishant Choudhary (b. 5 August 1979) from Jaipur, Rajasthan, has 61 T-shirts, all with the Mi logo in different colours, a collection he built from 29 November 2018 to 29 May 2019.

Airmail envelopes

Jinesh Joseph (b. 8 April 1984) from Bengaluru, Karnataka, has a collection of 1,858 airmail envelopes from 338 regions including recognized countries, disputed territories and autonomous republics. He receives the newly released stamps through post office web-shops or online shops and affixes them on a custom-made airmail envelope with his address on it. He then posts them back with instructions on how to send them back to him.

Postcards

Sayam Sanjay Bagmar (b. 7 September 2000) from Gadag, Karnataka, has postcards addressed to him, sent from 185 different countries and territories. His collection began in 2013.

Autographed pencil sketches

Sharad Bhaskar Patil (b. 29 April 1981) from Mumbai, Maharashtra, has a collection of 268 autographed pencil sketches made by him in six years. The sketches are autographed by celebrities from Maharashtra in the field of art, cinema, politics and sports.

Aircraft models

Aircraft models

Vikram Rajkumar Tirkannad (b. 13 April 1980) from Chennai, Tamil Nadu, has collected 719 models of aircraft over the last 38 years. The first model in his collection was an Air India Boeing 747. The largest are the Airways Concorde and a Jet Airways Boeing 737-800 Winglet, both measuring 0.6 m (2 ft). The smallest is the Air India ATR 42-320 measuring only 6 cm (2.36 in.).

Autographed books

Tatsamyak Manu (b. 31 December 1994) from Katihar, Bihar, has 3,247 autographed books of writers, a hobby started in 2005. He has autographed books of Chetan Bhagat, Khushwant Singh, Anand Kumar and Kunal Narayan, among others.

Autographs of Indian Olympians

Nitin Jain (b. 6 January 1977) from Haridwar, Uttarakhand, has autographs of all 15 Indian Olympic medal winners in individual sports, including rare ones of Norman Pritchard and K.D. Jadhav, a collection he started in 2010.

Autographs of Arjuna Award winners

Somu Choudhury (b. 16 November 1992) from New Delhi has a collection, built over the last three years, of more than 100 autographs of Arjuna Award winners.

Autographed Photographs

Yogiraj Sarvesh Soni (b. 3 November 1972) from Nashik, Maharashtra, has the largest collection of autographed photographs of VVIPs of the world, a hobby since 1991. By 30 May 2019, his collection had grown to 51,336 autographs – 14,050 Indian and 37,286 foreign celebrities from 231 countries. He has autographed photographs of presidents, prime ministers, Governor Generals, kings, queens, heads of states and freedom fighters, among others.

Autographs of astronauts

Deepak Sharma (b. 8 November 1985) from Moradabad, Uttar Pradesh, has the largest collection of 1,018 unduplicated, autographed photographs of 335 astronauts since November 2000. His collection includes famous astronauts like Rakesh Sharma, Sunita Williams, Raja Chari, Valentina Tereshkova, Alexey Leonov, Edgar Mitchell, Charles Duke and Jack R. Lousma, among others.

Autographs of royals

Ajay Kumar Agarawala (b. 17 October 1973) from Sambalpur, Odisha, has 87 autographed photographs of royalty – kings, queens, crown princes and princesses – from 11 erstwhile Indian princely states as well as from Iran, Nepal and Pakistan, a collection started in 2011.

Crosswords – Hindi

Swarnlata Vishwafool (b. 25 February 1983) from Katihar, Bihar, has 581,002 Hindi crossword clippings from newspapers of which 258,105 are solved and 322,897 are unsolved.

Crosswords

Raju Umamaheswar from Coimbatore, Tamil Nadu, has a collection of solved and unsolved crosswords, a hobby pursued since 1991. By 31 May 2019, he had 169,350 solved crosswords, with 545,531 unsolved ones. He solves them every day and marks them with the date, time and location, creating a detailed diary of his work. He also has memorabilia related to crosswords, such as pens, beer mugs, reference books and dictionaries, in printed and in digital versions.

WR **Sudoku**

K.S. Rao (b. 10 August 1940) from Hyderabad has collected sudoku puzzles since 2009 and the collection had grown to 10,545 puzzles by June 2020.

Sudoku clippings

Archana Kumari (b. 3 February 1986) from Katihar, Bihar, has collected 13,175 newspaper clippings of sudoku puzzles, a hobby since 2011.

Erasers

Khushboo Marda Malani (b. 10 March 1980) from Delhi has a collection of 19,095 erasers (14,065 different types and 5,030 duplicates) from more than 25 countries up to 31 May 2020. They are of different shapes, sizes and colours, and categorized into prominent individuals, sports, animals, food items, transportation and currencies, among others.

Register covers

Dr Kanika Gupta (b. 7 December 1993) from New Delhi has collected 4,162 register covers since 2011. She has categorized them into themes including historical, personalities, monuments, sports, vehicles, environment and schools.

Wood-finish fountain pens

Dr Sunil Gupta (b. 26 November 1964) from Jaipur, Rajasthan, has a collection of 638 wood-finish fountain pens, a hobby he started in 1982. His collection has no duplicates and all the pens are in working condition. They are made of materials like metal, plastic, ebonite and sandalwood, among others.

WR Ganeshas (handmade)

Rama Satish Shah (b. 8 November 1961) from Mumbai, Maharashtra, has made 454,500th Ganesha idols in 20 years from March 2000 to 31 May 2020. The washable Ganesha idols have all been made by hand without using any block or mould.

Free gifts

Vishav Gupta (b. 10 September 1962) and Vishal Gupta (b. 10 September 1964) from Chandigarh have been collecting free gifts since 1992, starting with a tonic bottle and a lunch box. By 30 June 2020, their collection had grown to a staggering 91,050 articles. They have three rooms stacked with these 'free gifts', worth an estimated value of ₹7 lakh or more.

CDs pasted with Ganesha images (handmade)

Ayushi Shrivastava (b. 29 September 1995) from Bhopal, Madhya Pradesh, has a collection of 5,001 old and scrap CDs, which she covered with Ganesha images to turn them into art pieces. She started this venture from 1 January 2018 and completed it on 1 January 2020.

Hair clips

Sana Fathima (b. 24 October 2014) from Pudukkottai, Tamil Nadu, has 1,200 hair clips, a collection from 24 October 2017 to 24 March 2018.

Handwritten SMS**

Hemlata Ramchand Bhatia (b. 5 November 1939) from Mumbai, Maharashtra, has written down 120,000 text messages in 76 diaries from 11 May 2005 to 31 May 2019. As soon as she sends or receives a message, she transcribes it in a diary along with the date, name and time.

Hair clips

Hanuman Chalisas

Parveen Gupta (b. 29 April 1969) from New Delhi has been collecting *Hanuman Chalisa*s, a hobby he started 28 years ago. By 31 May 2019, he had 317 kinds of *Hanuman Chalisa*s. His collection includes two metal *Chalisa*s, in silver and brass, and another in Braille.

Panchangs

Shubhangi Apte (b. 25 April 1955) from Raipur, Chhattisgarh, has a *panchang* or *panchagam* collection, which was started in 1998. Since then she has collected 278 *panchang*s of many languages and traditions like Gujarati, Sindhi, Chinese, Bengali, Odia, Marathi, Punjabi, Tamil, Malayalam and Telugu, among others. She has a 100-year Odia *panchang* covering 1935 to 2035.

** This is a one-time category. Further and future claims for this category will not be accepted.

Jokes – Hindi
Swarnlata Vishwafool (b. 25 February 1983) from Katihar, Bihar, has collected 10,147 Hindi jokes from different newspapers from 2000 to 2019.

Quotations
Gulnar Sultanali Fazal (b. 9 May 1960) from Mombasa, Kenya, has a collection of 88,073 quotations and proverbs (up to 31 May 2019).

Quotations – Hindi
Archana Kumari (b. 3 February 1986) from Katihar, Bihar, has a collection of 107,108 Hindi quotations, a collection since 1998.

Key ring with caricatures (handmade)
Sanjeev Kumar Jain (b. 13 May 1960) from Dehradun, Uttarakhand, has a collection of 921 handmade key rings (up to June 2019) with caricatures of Indian and world personalities, including Bollywood stars, sportsmen and prime ministers, among others. His collection began in October 2017.

Key rings with caricatures

Key rings (handmade)
Rakesh Vaid (b. 7 September 1953) from Delhi is a collector of key rings since 1979. His collection has 47,700 key rings (till 31 May 2019). He not only has unusual shapes and sizes but also handmade ones in the shape of India Gate, a swimming pool and a gramophone. He also makes key rings using precision-work tools.

Knives and other pointed objects
Anupam Kamal (b. 1 April 1967) from Delhi has been collecting knives and other pointed objects since he was five years old. Ranging from ancient to modern, his licensed collection of 800 unduplicated objects spans over 90 manufacturers from 42 countries and six continents, and includes *karambits*, boot knives, khukris, kirpans, swords, daggers, folding knives, and tactical and military knives, among others.

Knives and other pointed objects

Matchboxes and labels
Sunil Kumar Bhatt (b. 27 September 1968) from Bhopal, Madhya Pradesh, has an unduplicated collection of 35,000 matchboxes and labels from 126 countries. Pursuing this hobby since 1982 he has held exhibitions twice a year, called 'Own My Collection', since 2011. His collection has been exhibited across the country with the latest (101st) one on 26 January 2020. The only international one (78th) was held in Sweden.

Matchboxes and labels

Matchboxes with political party symbols
Alok Mehrotra (b. 16 October 1970) from Kanpur, Uttar Pradesh, has 1,575 matchboxes with symbols of 64 political parties, a collection he built during 2016–17.

Napkins
Parveen Gupta (b. 29 April 1969), his wife Anuradha Gupta (b. 30 May 1968) and daughter Dr Kanika Gupta (b. 7 December 1993) from New Delhi have collected 12,246 commercial and 9,325 non-commercial paper napkins from countries like Romania, Egypt, Slovakia, the UK, the USA, the UAE, Germany, Australia, Switzerland and India, among others. They started their collection in 2014.

Napkins

Hindi-language newspapers
Dr Ashok Pandey 'Gulshan' (b. 25 June 1963) from Bahraich, Uttar Pradesh, has a collection of 12,634 different Hindi newspapers under 655 titles from Indian states, and Nepal, China and Thailand, all received by India Post in Uttar Pradesh since 1990. He has bound volumes alphabetically as Daily,

Record Rewind

Largest collection of playing cards

1990

Kishor Gordhandas from Bombay (now Mumbai), Maharashtra, had a collection of over 2,500 sets of playing cards. Gordhandas, a mining engineer, who started his collection in 1991, had cards of all sizes, shapes and types on all kinds of themes. The collection also included rare Indian traditional cards like the Ganjifa of Orissa (now Odisha).

2016

Aditi Shailesh Agarwal (b. 27 July 1979) from Ahmedabad, Gujarat, has 6,000 sets of Indian and foreign playing cards, the largest such collection, which she started when she was 15 years old. The collection varies in theme, form, size, shape and material. Aditi has a card deck that was used for a code during the First World War and a celebrity collection on Lady Diana, George Bush, Nelson Mandela, and Bollywood stars like Amitabh Bachchan, Madhuri Dixit, Shah Rukh Khan and others.

Tri-weekly, Biweekly, Weekly, Fortnightly, Monthly, Bimonthly, Tri-monthly and Annual Special Issues.

Foreign-language newspapers
Shashanka Sekhar Dash (b. 1 July 1978) from Jajpur, Odisha, has a collection of 981 newspapers in 63 languages from 102 countries. Started in 2005, his collection has newspapers from countries like Lesotho, Seychelles, Peru, Palestine, East Timor and Papua New Guinea, and in languages like Estonian, Yakut, Tok Pisin, Tetum, Hebrew, Dari and Pashto.

Newspaper editorials
Om Prakash Gupta (b. 5 January 1941) from Delhi has a collection of 4,285 editorials of *Navbharat Times* since 1 January 2003. He has 43 files with 100 editorials by date in each file.

Sequential same-date newspaper
Akanksha Jain (b. 20 July 1994) from Vadodara, Gujarat, has the longest unbroken sequential collection of the same-date newspaper, *The Times of India*, dated 20 July for 16 years, right from 1994 to 2009.

Mahatma Gandhi's 150th birth anniversary newspapers
Shiju Thomas (b. 25 February 1976) from Bengaluru, Karnataka, has the largest collection of Mahatma Gandhi's 150th birth anniversary newspapers, dated 2 October 2019. His collection comprises 603 newspapers, which includes 301 newspapers with different titles and 302 newspapers with different place editions in 17 Indian languages. The collection includes weekly, fortnightly and monthly publications.

Newspaper clippings on Atal Bihari Vajpayee
Anuradha Gupta (b. 30 May 1968) from New Delhi has collected 612 newspaper clippings of former prime minister Atal

Bihari Vajpayee. The clippings are in many languages including Hindi, English, Marathi, Gujarati, Tamil and Telugu.

Newspaper clippings – Hindi

Sadanand Paul (b. 5 March 1975) from Katihar, Bihar, has the largest collection of Hindi newspaper cuttings from more than 70 Hindi newspapers. The number of newspaper cuttings was 805,150 by 31 May 2019.

Magazine covers with Prime Minister Narendra Modi

Anuradha Gupta (b. 30 May 1968) from New Delhi has collected 317 different magazines in various languages with Prime Minister Narendra Modi on the cover. The collection began in 2017.

Nokia handsets

Jayesh Umesh Kale (b. 13 April 1985) from Thane, Maharashtra, has a collection of 1,600 Nokia handsets, a hobby he started in 2013. All the mobile handsets are in working condition.

Nokia handsets

Models of owls

Ramesh Kumar Bhatia (b. 27 March 1948) from Mumbai, Maharashtra, has a collection of 351 owl models (up to 31 May 2020) since 2013. The models of owls are from different countries including India, Bhutan, China, New Zealand, Australia, Iceland, Uzbekistan and Morocco, among others.

Dinosaur toys and books

Kaveer Punit Kamdar (b. 23 January 2016) from Mumbai, Maharashtra, has the largest collection of dinosaur toys and books, amounting to over 300 items.

Owl-shaped jewellery

Dr Prashant Laxman Wagh (b. 16 June 1978) from Nashik, Maharashtra, has a collection of owl-shaped jewellery, which he started in 2016. He has 717 items in his collection – 478 pendants, 129 brooches, 62 earrings and 48 rings. He also has 11 owl-shaped unique watch pendants. The jewellery is made of materials like zinc alloy, stainless steel, rhinestone, synthetic turquoise stone and semi-precious metals, among others.

Owl-shaped jewellery

Hotel key cards

Prachi Kagzi (b. 26 August 1980) from Mumbai, Maharashtra, has a hotel key card collection that she started in 2007 with her husband, and the number had grown to 120 by 30 June 2018.

Railway items

Vimlesh Chandra (b. 8 August 1969) from Ahmedabad, Gujarat, has a collection of 50 coffee-table books on different zones of the Indian Railways, national and international railway books numbering 200, and 0.1 million railway and science magazines collected from 1978 to April 2019. His collection also has all annual reports, yearbooks and railway timetables from 1990 to April 2019.

Seers

Ranjeet Kumar Jha (b. 26 January 1989) from Bhopal, Madhya Pradesh, has 201 'seer' or 'ser' (old Indian measure of weight) of spherical shape from different Indian princely states such as Bhopal, Gwalior, Mewar, Agra, Rajkot and Indore. The weights carry different state seals with different values in different languages. The collection was started on 28 May 2015.

Waste-to-wonder miniature models

Devendra Prakash Tiwari (b. 18 November 1961) from Bhopal, Madhya Pradesh, has a collection of over 250 miniature models, all made with scrap materials, a hobby since childhood. All models are up to 38 cm (1 ft 2.9 in.) in size and the themes include space sciences, earthmovers, means of transport, war equipment, musical and photography equipment and more.

Waste-to-wonder miniature models

Water-bottle wrappers

Anuradha Gupta (b. 30 May 1968) from New Delhi has a collection of wrappers of water bottles, containers and glasses. By 31 May 2019 she had 3,102 wrappers from India and other countries, including Germany, Pakistan, France, Japan, Brazil, Qatar, Saudi Arabia and Malaysia.

Unique cycles

Unique cycles

Sanat Rath (b. 21 January 1985) from Bhubaneswar, Odisha, owns eight unique cycles including a fat bike, a tandem bicycle, a folding bike, a road bike, a penny-farthing, a unicycle, a chopper and a recumbent trike.

Headgear

Ananta N. Joshi (b. 20 February 1968) from Kalyan, Maharashtra, has a collection of caps, turbans and armoury, a hobby he started in August 1975. His headgear collection had a total of 2,850 items till 31 May 2019 including pagris, cowboy hats and medieval helmets.

Headgear collection

Soap wrappers (alphabetical)

Jayadevan Rajagopala (b. 29 April 1953) from Thrissur, Kerala, has 1,840 unique bath-soap wrappers, a collection spanning more than 30 years. No two covers are the same in his collection, although the same brand might have more than one cover.

Walking sticks

Capt. Satish Kumar Minocha (b. 2 May 1942) from Kolkata, West Bengal, has a collection of 75 walking sticks, each different in colour, shape, design and material. He makes all his walking sticks on his own without any help.

CURRENCY, COINS AND STAMPS

Commemorative coins

Mitesh Dilipkumar Dave (b. 20 March 1989) from Morbi, Gujarat, has 394 commemorative coins, a collection started in 1999. By 24 December 2019, his collection included coins featuring Bhagat Singh, Jawaharlal Nehru, Dr B.R. Ambedkar, Loknayak Jayaprakash Narayan, Rabindranath Tagore, Lal Bahadur Shastri, the First War of Independence, the Air Force Platinum Jubilee, the Parliamentary Union Conference and Subhas Chandra Bose's birth centenary, among others.

Commemorative coins from most countries

Abhisarth Gupta (b. 1 December 1996) from Jhansi, Uttar Pradesh, has 2,907 commemorative coins from 165 countries, a collection he started in 2017.

₹100 commemorative coins

Sanjeev Kumar Jain (b. 13 May 1960) and Nidhi Jain (b. 23 June 1963) from Dehradun, Uttarakhand, have a collection of 57 commemorative coins of ₹100 issued by various mints from 1980 to 2019.

₹100 commemorative coins

₹5 commemorative coins

Sanjeev Kumar Jain (b. 13 May 1960) and Nidhi Jain (b. 23 June 1963) from Dehradun, Uttarakhand, have 70 commemorative coins of ₹5, a collection from 1984 to 2019.

Coins featuring Queen Elizabeth II from most countries

Dina Nath (b. 19 July 1947) from Delhi has 75 coins featuring Queen Elizabeth II from 45 countries, a collection since 2007. He also has a collection of coins with images of horse riders from 50 countries. These include images of Queen Elizabeth II on horseback on her coronation and wedding anniversaries, army generals, warriors and other riders on horseback in war scenes, victory processions and equestrian sports.

Indian coins from foreign mints

Amit Belwal (b. 18 March 2000) from Chaubattia, Uttarakhand, has a collection of 19 Indian coins minted in 10 mints from seven foreign countries during 1985–2001: Canada (4), Slovakia (4), South Korea (3), Russia (3), the United Kingdom (3), Mexico (1) and South Africa (1).

One-paisa coins

Deepali Gupta (b. 15 December 1986) from Faridabad, Haryana, has a collection of 20 varieties of one-paisa coins, issued by the Government of India from 1943 to 1972. Her collection includes all one-paisa coins including one with three holes in the centre, one with a four-horse symbol and two coins struck in bronze, among many others.

Same year and denomination (₹1)

Vinay Bhanawat (b. 9 February 1957) from Udaipur, Rajasthan, has a collection of 60,300 coins of ₹1 of the same year, i.e., 2016.

Bimetallic coins

Nishant Choudhary (b. 5 August 1979) from Jaipur, Rajasthan, has 5,879 bimetallic coins, a collection he started in 2018.

Coins of denomination of 10 from most countries

Abhijit Biswas (b. 14 December 1985) from Bilaspur, Chhattisgarh, has a collection of foreign coins of the denomination of 10 from 193 countries and sovereign states of the world, with 353 different kinds of coins. His collection also features coins from 45 erstwhile countries.

Coins of denomination of 1 from most countries

Dr Johnson Nayankara (b. 1 August 1961) from Thrissur, Kerala, has a collection of coins of the denomination of 1 from 175 different countries, a collection he started in 2009. Among them, 10 coins are from erstwhile countries.

Coins of denomination of 1

Odd-shaped coins

Hari Mohan Purwar (b. 26 January 1951) from Jalaun, Uttar Pradesh, has 732 odd-shaped coins, all unduplicated (as on 5 May 2020), a collection since January 2010. They are of various materials like plastic, wood, porcelain, glass and metal. They are in many shapes too: hexagonal, pentagonal, decagonal, serrated, holed, car, bike, animals, guitar and maps of countries, among others. Some are 3D and embossed with gemstones.

₹2 currency notes

Rajendra Chandulal Shah (b. 8 February 1953) from Pune, Maharashtra, has collected 15,235 currency notes of ₹2 denomination. He began his collection in 1980 and has arranged the notes year-wise, signature-wise, inset-wise, prefix-wise and number-wise. These notes, which were printed in four different parts of the country, were discontinued in 1994.

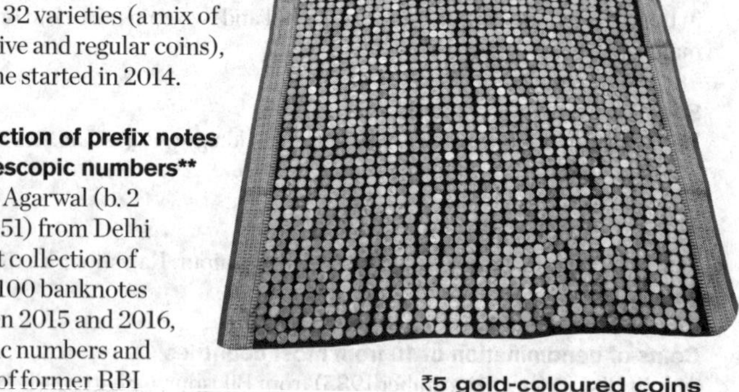

₹5 gold-coloured coins

₹5 gold-coloured coins
Gandikota Lahari (b. 28 April 2006) from Tirupati, Andhra Pradesh, has a collection of 2,035 gold-coloured coins of ₹5 in 32 varieties (a mix of commemorative and regular coins), a collection she started in 2014.

Largest collection of prefix notes of ₹100 – telescopic numbers**
Vinod Kumar Agarwal (b. 2 September 1951) from Delhi has the largest collection of serial prefix ₹100 banknotes issued between 2015 and 2016, with telescopic numbers and the signature of former RBI governor Raghuram G. Rajan. He has 1,960 such notes in his collection.

Currency notes of denomination of 1 from most countries
Sudhir Lunawat (b. 12 November 1986) from Bikaner, Rajasthan, has a collection of currency notes of the denomination of 1 from 110 different countries. He started his collection in 2018.

Pair of same-serial currency notes
Jasvinder Singh (b. 1 February 1966) from New Delhi has 8,159 pairs of the same serial number of Indian currency notes in the denominations of ₹1 (4,379 notes), ₹2 (1,268 notes), ₹5 (4,058 notes), ₹10 (6,070 notes) , ₹20 (493 notes), ₹50 (24 notes) and ₹100 (26 notes).

Banknotes featuring Queen Elizabeth II
Shiv Chander Sablok (b. 29 September 1984) from Ludhiana, Punjab, has the largest collection of currency notes featuring Queen Elizabeth II from 24 Commonwealth countries with 67 different currency notes, a collection he started in 1998.

₹10 currency notes ending in 786
Vinay Bhanawat (b. 9 February 1957) from Udaipur, Rajasthan, has a collection of 99,000 currency notes of ₹10 denomination ending in 786, a collection since 2008. His collection also has notes, all ending in 786, from countries like Singapore, Bahrain, Portugal, Myanmar and Germany.

Postage stamps
Dr Jawahar Verhomai Israni (b. 22 August 1943) from Delhi has a collection of 51,682 postage stamps, all singles, from 237 countries, a hobby he started in 1948. The collection includes different themes such as leaders, colleges, poets, statues, sculptures, dances, birds, animals, cats, butterflies, ships, dams, flags, sports, bikes and the Olympics, among others.

** This is a one-time category. Further and future claims for this category will not be accepted.

Joint-issue stamps and stationery
Dhaval Rashmikant Kalathia (b. 12 August 1981) from Ahmedabad, Gujarat, has 650 joint-issue stamps and stationery, a collection since 2012. It includes 135 dual cancellations, 50 leaflets/cards and 70 packs/folders.

Stamps from 711 regions
Pratyush Srivastava (b. 29 October 1984) and his wife Pallavi (b. 6 December 1988), from Pune, Maharashtra, have collected stamps from 711 countries/territories/issuing authorities, a collection since 1992.

Stamps (biggest)
Yashoda Devi (b. 25 May 1949) from Katihar, Bihar, has a collection of the biggest India Post stamps, 9 cm x 4 cm (3.54 in. x 1.57 in.) to 6 cm x 4 cm (2.36 in. x 1.57 in.). Having started in 2017, she had 25 such stamps up to 31 May 2019.

Largest triptych se-tenant postal stamp
Deepak Sharma (b. 8 November 1985) from Moradabad, Uttar Pradesh, possesses the largest triptych se-tenant postal stamp, 18 cm x 3 cm (7.09 in. x 1.18 in.), issued in China on 20 August 2016. Valued at 6 yuan, it depicts the Great Wall of China. A triptych stamp is a set of three panels hinged together to make a complete picture.

Stamps featuring Queen Elizabeth II
Abhishek Meena (b. 15 June 1987) from Chhattisgarh has 2,368 stamps featuring Queen Elizabeth II, a collection since 1999. He has stamps from 13 regions – the United Kingdom, Hong Kong Special Administrative Region of the People's Republic of China, Isle of Man, Wales, Canada, Australia, New Zealand, Singapore, Gibraltar, Guernsey Island, Newfoundland and Labrador, British Antarctic Territory and Tristan da Cunha Islands.

Queen Elizabeth II stamps

Postal stamps featuring astronauts
Deepak Sharma (b. 8 November 1985) from Moradabad, Uttar Pradesh, has a collection of 250 commemorative postal stamps featuring astronauts, issued by various countries, a collection since November 2017.

Bollywood philately
Anuradha Gupta (b. 30 May 1968) from New Delhi has collected 361 philatelic items like FDCs, miniature sheets, postcards and stamps on the theme 'Indian cinema' since January 2015.

Record Rewind

Largest collection of stamps featuring Mahatma Gandhi

2001

Nandini Sur specialized in collecting stamps exclusively on Mahatma Gandhi and had so far collected 171 unduplicated stamps. The collection of stamps on Gandhi was not just from India but from 71 other countries that have honoured him.

2020

Rajeshkumar Mukundbhai Thakkar (b. 20 October 1960) from Gandhinagar, Gujarat, has a collection of 854 Gandhi stamps.

Gandhi philatelic items

Rajeshkumar Mukundbhai Thakkar (b. 20 October 1960) from Gandhinagar, Gujarat, has 5,439 philatelic items on Mahatma Gandhi from 110 countries, including 854 Gandhi stamps. His collection from 1969 includes 1,100 postal stationery, 1,300 special covers and 771 First Day Covers (FDCs), among others.

Gandhi philatelic items

Heritage stamps

Yashoda Devi (b. 25 May 1949) from Katihar, Bihar, has 110 heritage stamps of India Post, a collection since 1980.

Philatelic items from service organizations

Sudhir Jain (b. 7 October 1954) from Satna, Madhya Pradesh, has 1,793 different philatelic items (stamps, special covers, special cancellations, postal stationery) issued from 158 countries on the Rotary International and Lions International service organizations. He started his collection in 1968. The Rotary International collection has 714 different stamps and 227 different philatelic items from 135 countries. The Lions International items include 158 different stamps and 694 different philatelic items from 83 countries.

Stamps featuring freedom fighters

Yashoda Devi (b. 25 May 1949) from Katihar, Bihar, has 66 stamps featuring freedom fighters, issued by India Post (till 31 May 2019).

A Collector's Guide to Definitive Stamps

Definitive stamps are used for day-to-day mailing. They are of different denominations from 25 paise upwards. Special stamps issued annually to mark specific occasions are termed special definitive stamps. India has the largest postal network in the world and our list of definitive and special definitive stamps is fascinating. Here's a glimpse into such stamps issued from 1991 to 2009.

Definitive Stamps

Date of Issue	Name of the Stamp	Denomination (in ₹)
30 January 1991	Mahatma Gandhi	₹1
4 April 1994	Sanchi Stupa	₹5
11 July 1994	Family Welfare	75 paise; ₹1
18 February 1995	Oil Conservation	₹1
19 November 1995	Communal Harmony	₹2
21 September 1998	Pulse Polio Immunization	₹3
30 April 2000	Leopard Cat	₹5
	Tigers, Sundarbans Biosphere Reserve	₹10
20 July 2000	Blackbuck	25 paise
	Nilgiri Tahr	₹50
	Saras Crane	₹1
	Smooth Indian Otter	₹3
30 October 2000	Paradise Fly Catcher	₹50
20 November 2000	Butterfly	₹15
	Amaltas	₹20
20 September 2001	Painted Stork	₹4
20 July 2002	Smooth Indian Otter	₹3
16 August 2002	Rose	₹2
1 December 2008	Jawaharlal Nehru	25 paise
	Mahatma Gandhi	₹1
	Dr B.R. Ambedkar	₹2
	Satyajit Ray	₹3
	Homi Jahangir Bhabha	₹4
	Indira Gandhi	₹5
	Rajiv Gandhi	₹5
	J.R.D. Tata	₹15
	Mother Teresa	₹20
11 May 2009	E.V. Ramaswamy	50 paise
	C.V. Raman	₹10
	Rukmini Devi Arundale	₹50

Special Definitive Stamps

Date of Issue	Name of the Stamp	Denomination
30 October 2000	Sardar Vallabhbhai Patel	₹2
23 January 2001	Netaji Subhas Chandra Bose	₹1
14 April 2001	Dr B.R. Ambedkar	₹3

Stamps of smallest value

Kali Prasad Paul (b. 10 January 1947) from Katihar, Bihar, has 78 varieties of small-value stamps of which 18 are of 20 paise, six of 25 and 50 paise, 26 types of ₹1 and 22 types of ₹2, among others, in a collection that began in 1962.

Gommateshwara philatelic items

Sanjeev Kumar Jain (b. 13 May 1960) and Nidhi Jain (b. 23 June 1963) from Dehradun, Uttarakhand, have a collection of 111 philatelic items on Gommateshwara or Lord Bahubali. They began this collection in 1981.

Gommateshwara philatelic items

₹5 stamps

Kali Prasad Paul (b. 10 January 1947) from Katihar, Bihar, has collected 177 varieties of ₹5 India postage stamps, a collection he began in 1962.

Commemorative stamps

Kali Prasad Paul (b. 10 January 1947) from Katihar, Bihar, has collected 166 commemorative postage stamps since 1962.

Postal items on mountains

Dr Kamal Mohanani (b. 18 September 1954) from Vadodara, Gujarat, has 3,519 postal stamps, miniature sheets and First Day Covers, among other postal items, related to mountains and people living there, a collection since 1997. The smallest stamp is a 1 cm x 1 cm (0.39 in. x 0.39 in.) stamp from Romania.

Postal items on mountains

First Day Covers of a person

Satish Laxman Chaphekar (b. 5 February 1957) from Thane, Maharashtra, has collected 241 First Day Covers featuring iconic cricketer Sachin Tendulkar, published by India Post. Tendulkar scored an unbeaten 241 not out against Australia in Sydney in 2004.

First Day Covers featuring Sachin Tendulkar

Autographed FDCs on astronauts

Deepak Sharma (b. 8 November 1985) from Moradabad, Uttar Pradesh, has the largest collection of 110 unduplicated autographed First Day Covers of 100 astronauts, a collection since November 2014. It includes autographs of famous astronauts such as Rakesh Sharma, Valentina Tereshkova, Alexey Leonov, Naoko Yamazaki, Anatoly Solovyev, Helen Sharman, Gerald P. Carr and many more.

Biggest order for My Stamp – single day

Dr Guinness Madasamy (b. 20 November 1974) from Idukki, Kerala, a marketing executive at India Post, procured 2,083 sheets of My Stamp, a bulk order of ₹5 lakh from Kerala State Financial Enterprises (KSFE), Kerala, in a single day on 25 October 2019. 'My Stamp' is the brand name for personalized sheets of postage stamps of India Post. There were 12 stamps on each sheet.

Science and technology philatelic covers

Gunvant Narrottamdas Shah (b. 20 January 1950) from Mumbai, Maharashtra, has 4,138 philatelic covers exclusively on the theme of science and technology. It is a unique collection depicting STEM education, i.e., science, technology, engineering and mathematics. It includes stamps, miniature sheets and sheetlets on subjects such as environment, nuclear science, medicine, space, agriculture and water, among others.

THIS AND THAT

A–Z chocolate flavours

Aanandana Garg (b. 30 January 1987) from Mumbai, Maharashtra, created 26 chocolate flavours named A–Z in 17 mins 53 secs at her residence on 3 March 2019. Each piece weighed 6 g and measured 2 cm x 2 cm x 1.5 cm (0.79 in. x 0.79 in. x 0.59 in.). Each letter represented a flavour like 'A for almond chocolate', 'B for butterscotch chocolate', 'C for cherry chocolate', and so on.

Frame embossed with coins

Avdhesh Kumar Bhargava (b. 15 July 1971) from Kannauj, Uttar Pradesh, made a 1.37 m (4 ft 6 in.) long and 0.76 m (2 ft 6 in.) wide frame of Vaishno Devi and embossed it with coins. He used 1,196 coins of ₹5 and 415 coins of ₹10 and made the frame in five days from 15 to 19 May 2019.

Upside-down cycle

Amjad Pasha (b. 21 May 1976) from Gajwel in Siddipet District, Telangana, made an unusual cycle named Telangana Wonder Cycle. Amjad rides the 2.13 m (7 ft) cycle, upside down, body down, feet up! He has made another 4.57 m (15 ft) tall cycle that can be driven from the high seat. Apart from the two cycles, he has made small working vehicles – 35 motorcycles, two tractors, three autorickshaws and 51 tiny cycles.

Upside-down cycle

All teeth intact

Aura Yadav (b. 27 January 2011) from Pune, Maharashtra, still retains all her milk teeth. This was confirmed through X-ray.

Jacket made of kite sticks

Shankar Singh (b. 15 August 1959) from Jaipur, Rajasthan, made a wooden jacket using kite sticks. It is 1.06 m (3 ft 5.7 in.) long and 0.53 m (1 ft 8.8 in.) wide. Made using kite sticks, watercolours, brush, Fevicol adhesive and Touchwood (chemical for water resistance), the jacket has the names of all Indian presidents, prime ministers, chief ministers of all states, lieutenant governors of Union Territories (who held office between 15 August 1947 and July 2018) handwritten on it. This unique jacket was made in six months between 8 January 2018 and 5 July 2018.

Jacket made of kite sticks

Unique wedding
Anand Bansfore (b. 29 July 1985) from Solapur, Maharashtra, and Akshaya Arote (b. 8 April 1993) from Ahmednagar, Maharashtra, got married by reading the Preamble to the Constitution of India in the presence of orphans on 26 January 2016.

Waistcoat made of guitar plectrums

Waistcoat made of guitar plectrums
Vikas Sikharam (b. 6 July 1992) from Bengaluru, Karnataka, made a waistcoat using 1,080 guitar plectrums and sticks, using sticking tape, on 14 January 2020. The waistcoat, which weighs 500 gm, is 75 cm (2 ft 5.5 in.) long and 62 cm (2 ft 0.41 in.) wide. The total width is 124 cm (4 ft 0.8 in.). He took 9 hrs to complete the waistcoat.

Daily SMS to same 151 people**
Sadanand Paul (b. 5 March 1975) from Katihar, Bihar, has been sending non-stop messages from his mobile phone to 151 people including family members and friends since 5 March 2014. He had sent 316,055 messages till 31 May 2019.

Good luck wishes for ICC World Cup 2019
Field executives of Zydus Healthcare Ltd ran the VIVA INDIA campaign and reached out to 8,000 medical fraternity (cardiologists and diabetologists) from across India to sign 70 cricket bats, wishing good luck to the Indian cricket team for the ICC World Cup 2019.

Longest non-stop speech relay
KGiSL Educational Institutions, Coimbatore, Tamil Nadu, organized a speech relay with 431 participants from 6:16 a.m. on 22 December 2018 to 7:37 a.m. on 23 December 2018 at the KGiSL campus auditorium, Coimbatore. The event was concluded in 25 hrs 21 mins, with each participant speaking for 1–31 mins.

'Hum Fit Toh HP Fit' Challenge

Hindustan Petroleum Corporation Ltd organized the 'Hum Fit Toh HP Fit' Challenge, (#HFTHPF2018), with 7,968 participants (their employees and their spouses) from all over India between 1 September and 30 September 2018. GOQii, the fitness partner, tracked the distance and number of steps covered by the participants. The participants covered 1,403,788 km and a total of 2,035,449,557 steps.

Highest Christmas Star
Jaimon Joseph (b. 6 May 1973) from Kottayam, Kerala, erected the highest Christmas star at St Antony's Church, Poozhikkol, at a height of 33.22 m (108 ft 11.8 in.). Fixing the star took three days from 20 to 23 December 2019. The star was measured by Amal Jyothi College of Engineering by Leica Total Station.

Highest Xmas star

Handwritten postcards for a single cause
The Times of India launched 'Kolkata Once More, Phirey Esho Kolkata' campaign, inviting residents to send postcards. Stapled on the newspapers, 135,000 postcards were distributed across the city. A total of 50,000 letters were received (30,000 handwritten and 20,000 digital) from the Kolkata General Post Office. The campaign extended from 1 November 2018 to 31 March 2019. Kiran Kumari, Konark Panday, Debayuti Karan, Badal Rag, Sunando Sarkar and Sanjeev Bhargava were involved in the campaign.

Crocheted flag

Crocheted flag
Minu Bhatia (b. 10 July 1978) from Calgary, Canada, crocheted a large Canadian flag with wool, measuring 74.32 sq. m (800 sq. ft – 20 ft x 40 ft) and weighing 59 kg. The flag was displayed at the Genesis Centre on 12 July 2018 and later on 31 August 2018 at Prairie Winds Park in Calgary.

COMMUNITY DEVELOPMENT

Largest Swachh Bharat pledgethon**
The Rashtriya Military School (RMS), Dholpur, Rajasthan, organized the largest Swachh Bharat Pledgethon at the Rakesh Sharma Stadium on 2 October 2018, in association with Ganityoga. RMS Dholpur collected 37,449 pledges from school

** This is a one-time category. Further and future claims for this category will not be accepted.

students and staff members on a pre-printed khadi fabric of 20 cm x 20 cm (7.8 in. x 7.8 in.). The students dipped their hands in colour and stamped them on the cloth to show individual commitment.

Most sanitary pads distributed – multiple days**

Nischay Foundation from Jamshedpur, Jharkhand, distributed sanitary pads to 5,240 girls from 120 villages of East Singhbhum District during the lockdown imposed due to the COVID-19 pandemic. For 50 days from 12 April 2020 to 31 May 2020, around 20 volunteers walked and cycled to the villages making doorstep deliveries. The Sanitary Pad Relief Campaign was launched with the support of 400 donors and 20 'pad human volunteers' under the leadership of Tarun Kumar, founder-secretary of the foundation.

Longest candle-lighting relay

The longest candle-lighting relay was held on 16 February 2019 at Government Senior Secondary School, Dhawa, Jodhpur, to create awareness about saving and educating the girl child, and for universal peace. The event, organized by the school principal Sheela Asopa along with the Rajasthan Education Service Association Principal (RESA-P), had 550 participants. The relay lasted 1 hr 45 mins.

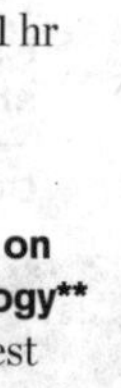

Longest candle-lighting relay

Largest campaign on Gandhian ideology**

The world's largest campaign on Gandhian thought and philosophy was held by the Bihar State Literacy Mission to mark the centenary of the Champaran Satyagraha in 1917. The campaign lasted a year from 2017 to 2018 with 46,000 literacy workers distributing pamphlets and folders on Gandhian philosophy to 15 million households across the state.

Largest shoe donation

INC.5 Shoes Pvt. Ltd in Mumbai, Maharashtra, distributed 5,000 pairs of shoes to women, girls and the underprivileged in Mumbai and Navi Mumbai between 10:00 a.m. and 5:00 p.m. on 15 March 2019.

Largest rally against drug usage**

Nomads on Wheels Riding Club, Ludhiana, Punjab, organized a 'Say No to Drugs' rally from 4:00 p.m. to 8:00 p.m. from Barnala Automobiles till KPJ Banquet Hall, Ludhiana, on 24 March 2019. It saw the participation of 300 people on 200 motorcycles (with pillion riders) while teams of doctors from Christian

** This is a one-time category. Further and future claims for this category will not be accepted.

Medical College, Ludhiana, spoke on the effects of drugs. The Environmentalist Foundation of India (E.F.I.), an NGO based in Ludhiana, organized a *nukkad natak* on the same topic.

Largest health marathon for women**

The Vama Wellness Centre for Women organized a health marathon for women from lower- and middle-income strata for 49 days from 19 January to 8 March 2019 in Surat and its outskirts, including Dang District, Gujarat. During this, as many as 13,544 adolescent girls were educated about age-related health concerns like menstruation, diet and fitness, and 1,839 women were scanned for cancer with sonography and cervical pap smear. Free tests were conducted for 15,383 women for anaemia, diabetes and blood pressure.

Largest run for a social cause – multiple venues

Shudh Plus Hygiene Products organized Run4Niine, the largest run to create awareness on menstruation, on International Women's Day on 8 March 2019. Organized in 531 cities with 222,269 participants across age groups and genders, the run varied from 2 km to 6 km. Talks on menstrual hygiene were also organized by the Federation of Obstetric and Gynaecological Societies of India (FOGSI) and others. The event, flagged off by actor Akshay Kumar, was supported by the Junior Chambers International, Rotary and Lions clubs, Niine Foundation, UN Women, WaterAid and other NGOs.

Largest run for a social cause

Largest signature campaign**

The Akhil Bharatiya Terapanth Kanya Mandal (girls wing of the Akhil Bharatiya Terapanth Mahila Mandal), Nagaur, Rajasthan, conducted a 'Say No to Littering in Public' signature campaign across 16 states of India as well as Biratnagar and Kathmandu, Nepal. They collected 301,955 signatures in 53 days from 11 August to 2 October 2018. The campaign covered 107 cities and

Floral Tricolour Made by the Visually Challenged

Twenty-five visually challenged schoolchildren celebrated the 73rd Independence Day by making a 9 ft x 15 ft (135 sq. ft/12.54 sq. m) tricolour with flowers under the supervision of Sumeet Patil from Shreerang Charitable Trust in 1 hr from 11:00 a.m. to 12 noon at the Omkar Blind and Special School, Mumbai, Maharashtra, on 13 August 2019.

towns in Andhra Pradesh, Assam, Bihar, Chhattisgarh, Delhi, Gujarat, Haryana, Karnataka, Madhya Pradesh, Maharashtra, Odisha, Punjab, Rajasthan, Tamil Nadu, Telangana and West Bengal, besides Nepal.

Most selfies for the empowerment of women**

The police department of Bilaspur, Chhattisgarh, led by Superintendent of Police Arif A. Shaikh, launched a campaign 'Rakhi with Khaki' during which police personnel took 50,033 selfies with girls and women of the city in 10 hrs on 25 August 2018. This initiative reached out to women and girls to empower them to fight exploitation and abuse. Fifty groups of 10 students each and 100 police personnel fanned out across 200 schools and 15 colleges, besides railway stations, bus stands and markets for the campaign.

Most selfies for the empowerment of women

Longest awareness campaign for a social cause – group**

Ajay Oli and Kartikaa Thapliyal of the Ghanshyam Oli Child Welfare Society undertook the *Unmukti* campaign, a 25-day journey covering 3,200 km, to create awareness against child beggars and child labour. They started on 4 May 2019 from Pithoragarh, Uttarakhand, and travelled to Yamunotri, Gangotri, Rudraprayag, Kedarnath, Badrinath and Joshimath on vehicles and on foot. They reached out to thousands of people and collected *bheek nahi denge* pledges from 10,000 people.

Largest awareness camp – multiple days – multiple venues**

Zydus Healthcare Limited, Mumbai, Maharashtra, manufacturers of FOL-XT, conducted the largest nutrition awareness campaign among 51,320 pregnant

** This is a one-time category. Further and future claims for this category will not be accepted.

First Dog with a Pacemaker

A seven-and-a-half-year-old cocker spaniel, Khushi, has become the first dog in the country to be fitted with a customized paediatric pacemaker on 15 December 2019. Khushi's heart was functioning at 4 per cent of its capacity when its owner, Alka Kumar from Gurugram, Haryana, decided to opt for a pacemaker for the pooch. It was fitted after a surgery lasting for an hour and a half at the Max Vets Hospital, Greater Kailash, Delhi, by Dr Bhanu Dev Sharma and Dr Kunal Dev Sharma, the interventional cardiology team for small animals. Since this was the first surgery of its kind in India, the paediatric pacemaker was imported and vets in India and abroad were consulted. A representative of the National Heart Institute (for humans) was also present at the surgery. A monitoring device was used to keep the vets updated about her post-operative progress. Khushi recovered fully and is back home and going for her usual walks.

women, focusing on folic acid levels for preventing congenital birth defects and ensuring the good health of mother and child. During 8–19 April 2019, a team of 2,000 gynaecologists and nutritionists studied the dietary pattern of the selected women and advised them. The campaign was conducted in Mumbai, Pune, Indore, Hyderabad, Bengaluru, Chennai, Lucknow, Patna, Delhi and Ahmedabad.

Longest distance travelled for social awareness – two-wheeler – solo
Pramod Laxman Mahajan (b. 11 July 1953) from Sangli, Maharashtra, a member of the Rebirth Foundation, Pune, undertook an expedition to promote organ donation. A kidney donor himself, he started the Bharat Organ Yatra on his motorcycle from Pune, Maharashtra, on 21 October 2018, covered 12,655 km and returned to Pune on 25 January 2019. The journey covered 69 cities in 19 states.

Most child marriages annulled in consecutive years**
Dr Kriti Bharti, rehabilitation psychologist and managing trustee of Saarthi Trust, has had four child marriages annulled in three consecutive years in the family courts of Jodhpur and Ajmer on the day of Akshay Tritiya when normally mass marriages take place across Rajasthan. While two of the child marriages were annulled in 2015 in Jodhpur, one was annulled in 2016 in the family court of Jodhpur, and the fourth was annulled in 2017 in Ajmer family court. Some of the cases resolved included 10-month-old babies and children up to five-year-olds. The 2015 child marriages were also annulled in the fastest time – just three days. The Saarthi Trust counsels parents as well as children and helps to assure them education, livelihood, shelter and rehabilitation.

Most half-marathon–distance runs for a cause
Sandeep Kumar Rana, a professional engineer, promoted 'no honking' by running 31 half-marathon–distance runs over 31 consecutive days in Panipat

and Gurugram, Haryana, and Delhi, from 20 September to 20 October 2019. On all days he wore a T-shirt that carried the 'no-honking' logo. Wanting to lead by example and create awareness about noise pollution due to unnecessary blowing of horn by vehicles, Sandeep has stopped honking while driving since 2011. The dates and timing of the runs were maintained by Garmin Ltd.

Honouring 2,018 mothers on Mother's Day**
International Mother's Day was celebrated in Guntur, Andhra Pradesh, on 13 May 2018 by honouring 2,018 mothers (58 of them over 100 years old) with as many daughters simultaneously cutting a 615 m (2,017 ft 8.6 in.) long cake, weighing 2,018 kg, at the Venkateswara Vignan Mandiram, Guntur. The celebrations began at 8:00 a.m. and ended at 4:00 p.m.

Honouring 2,018 mothers

Biggest slogan writing competition on road safety**
The Western India Automobile Association organized a drawing and slogan writing contest on the theme of road safety for 5,000 children (classes 1 to 12) at the Smt. Sulochanadevi Singhania School, Thane, Maharashtra, on 13 February 2019. Vivek Phansalkar, police commissioner of Thane, spoke to the students on the importance of road safety.

Biggest dance workshop for the differently abled**
A three-day dance workshop was held for 60 hearing-impaired and speech-impaired students (between eight and 21 years of age) at the School for Deaf-Mutes, Ahmedabad, Gujarat, by Priyanki Patel. The classes were held for two hours every day from 28 to 30 December 2018.

Former chairman of Wipro, Azim Premji, was the most generous philanthropist in India, having donated ₹ 7,904 crore in 2020, according to the EdelGive Hurun India Philanthropy List.

Longest road safety campaign**
Jaypee Palace Hotel, Agra, Uttar Pradesh, conducted the longest road safety campaign on 16 January 2019. A human chain of 350 hotel employees, assisted by students of the hotel's training centre, displayed messages on 2,000 handmade chart papers across 2 km from Amar Hotel to the Circuit House in Agra for four hours from 11:00 a.m. to 3:00 p.m. Commuters on the road were asked to pledge

** This is a one-time category. Further and future claims for this category will not be accepted.

that they would not drink and drive, and would respect traffic rules.

Longest cycle ride by the differently abled for awareness

Popat Jaywant Khopade (b. 30 June 1969) with 40 per cent disability, cycled 1,784 km in 44 days from Raireshwar Fort, Pune, to Rajghat, Delhi. He started on 3 December 2017 and completed his journey on 15 January 2018, spreading the message of saving the environment and keeping India clean.

Longest cycle ride by the visually challenged for awareness

Gyanam Ganga Indian Scouts and Guides Fellowship Guild organized the longest cycle ride by the visually challenged on tandem bicycles with escorts from India Gate, Delhi, to the Gateway of India, Mumbai. A total of 38 cyclists including 27 visually challenged participants and 11 escorts cycled 1,700 km through six states and met many people. The ride was undertaken to spread awareness about disabilities. The four main cyclists were Dr Rajesh Shukla, Fatema Manthalkar, Anjana Shah and Jayant Jadhav. The awareness drive developed the confidence of the visually challenged participants while sensitizing other riders and autorickshaw drivers to the presence of physically challenged people on the road.

Record Rewind

Most benches donated

2008

The Ghanshyamdas Saraf Trust from Mumbai, Maharashtra, installed 14,795 benches in public places in Mumbai, Maharashtra, between 2003 and May 2007.

2020

The Ghanshyamdas Saraf Trust, Mumbai, Maharashtra, donated and placed 21,467 three-seater benches at various public places in and around Mumbai as a service to the community.

Longest distance covered for awareness – gearless bicycle – group

Grameen Sneh Foundation, Dwarka, New Delhi, organized and supported a cycle ride by four people across five states and 14 districts to create awareness about cancer. Led by Havildar (retd) K. Ganjanam of Army Air Defence and accompanied by an ambulance, the cyclists – Kumar Aman, Premjeet Singh and Vicky Kumar – covered 1,561.4 km in 23 days between 2 and 25 December 2018. They started from Gopalpur, Odisha, and travelled through Telangana, Andhra Pradesh, Karnataka and Maharashtra, ending their journey in Pune, Maharashtra. En route, they interacted with students from 46 schools and colleges, and people in many villages.

Most food donated in a single day – multiple venues

The ISKCON Temple in Dwarka, Delhi, under the chairmanship of Pradyumna Priya Das, in coordination with the district magistrate of south-west Delhi, Rahul Singh, cooked and distributed food to migrant labourers and other needy persons during the lockdown. Beginning in the third week of March 2020 with 5,000 meals a day, they increased the meals to 10,000 and subsequently 100,000 a day.

On 6 May 2020 they distributed the maximum number of meals – 511,600 to as many people in 24 hours across 241 locations of the capital. Food was served in the morning and evening. The food was transported in sanitized e-rickshaws, vans and autorickshaws, and the process was monitored by CCTV, GPS and drone cameras.

Most food packets distributed among the poor

Swami Sunil Das Prabhakaran, chairman of the Muthalamada Charitable Trust in Palakkad, Kerala, has been distributing 1,000 food packets every day to the poor since 1992. He distributed nine million food packets and 70 million litres of drinking water to the poor up to September 2018.

Feeding the sick**

Zeeshan Majeed from Kolkata, West Bengal, gave home-cooked food for 50 consecutive Sundays from 20 May 2018 to 28 April 2019 to the patients coming to government hospitals in the city. Food is prepared for 150 people every Sunday. He fed 7,500 people during the period.

Most rangoli kits distributed to celebrate 'Nari Shakti'**

Shubhangi Apte from Raipur, Chhattisgarh, distributed 900 rangoli kits to girls in government primary and middle schools of the city on 21 September 2017 to celebrate Nari Shakti (woman power). The event was organized as a part of her mission to promote Indian culture under the Swachh Bharat Abhiyan.

** This is a one-time category. Further and future claims for this category will not be accepted.

Asia Game Changer Award 2020 Served to Chef Vikas Khanna

Vikas Khanna

Michelin-star chef Vikas Khanna was awarded the Asia Game Changer Award 2020 in a virtual ceremony held on 22 October 2020. Khanna's humanitarian efforts to feed millions in India through his food distribution drive titled #FeedIndia, during the COVID-19 lockdown and after, while being in New York, USA, earned him the honour. The initiative distributed 35 million meals (including dry ration) as well as hygiene products and essentials. Among the six winners, he was the only Indian award winner in 2020. Previous Indian winners include social activist and entrepreneur Madhav Chavan, former banker Chanda Kochhar, British-American actor of Indian origin – Aasif Mandvi, interior designer Kiran Bir Sethi, IPS officer Chhaya Sharma, and Indian-American business executive and former CEO of PepsiCo Indra Nooyi.

Most housewarming ceremonies**

Housewarming (*griha pravesh*) ceremonies were held simultaneously in 300,000 homes across 13 districts of Andhra Pradesh on 5 July 2018. The Andhra Pradesh State Housing Corporation Ltd worked over nine months to construct these houses for weaker sections in rural and urban areas. The function was inaugurated by Chief Minister Y.S. Jagan Mohan Reddy at Vijayawada.

Biggest Human-chain Shape Formation by Differently-abled Children

As many as 710 special children from Surat, Gujarat, formed a 37 m x 40 m (121 ft x 131 ft) human kite at the Ashirwad Estate, Surat, on 11 January 2019. The human kite was formed in 5 hrs from 8:00 a.m. to 1:00 p.m. and the children stood in pairs on the chalked line of the kite structure drawn on the ground. The event was organized by media house Sandesh Ltd.

Most free funeral services

Prakash Keval Gidwani, a social activist from Mumbai, Maharashtra, has helped in the cremation of over 2,250 unclaimed bodies in Mumbai. These mainly include accident victims and over 250 deceased due to COVID-19. Due to his consistent efforts since 2008, he was also able to lobby with the Brihanmumbai Municipal Corporation and get wood free of cost for the disposal of these bodies in 86 crematoriums. During the pandemic he was issued a Corona Warrior (CW) identity card by the Versova police and a CW certificate from MLA Dr Bharti Lavekar.

Most paintings donated

Rakhee S. Shah from Mumbai, Maharashtra, has donated 717 of her paintings over the last 10 years to hospitals, cancer centres and NGOs in the UK, the USA, Canada, New Zealand, Australia, Belgium and France. She has also participated in the Marie Curie Cancer Care charity and auction at the prestigious Royal Academy of Arts, London, UK.

Most eye donation pledges in a year**

The Akhil Bhartiya Terapanth Yuvak Parishad, a youth NGO, with its network of 340 branches and 40,000 members motivated pledges for eye donations, through camps and personal contact. In 2019, they achieved the most pledges of 750 eye donations across India, with the highest number from Assam. The Eye Bank Association of India has registered this as the largest donation made in a year by an organization. Assam accounts for over two-thirds of eye donations in the country, followed by West Bengal, Gujarat and Delhi.

Most people taking anti-tobacco pledge**

The Government of Rajasthan, along with the National Tobacco Control Programme, conducted the biggest anti-tobacco campaign on 30 June 2019 across schools, colleges, healthcare institutions, *anganwadis*, police stations and government departments across 33 districts, during which 11,398 people took a pledge to not use tobacco or other intoxicants. The campaign, which began at 10:00 a.m. and ended at 11:30 a.m., was led by Dr Samit Sharma, the director of the State National Health Programme.

Most dentures donated – single day

The Sindhi Forum Coimbatore, Tamil Nadu, in association with A.B. Shetty Dental College and RVS Dental College, prepared and delivered 149 dentures to needy patients free of cost in a single day. Called 'Gift a Smile', the event was held on 23 June 2019 with 200 doctors, dental interns and 100 volunteers. Initially, 600 patients were screened over three months. After teeth extraction and medical intervention, finally 149 were selected for the gift of a smile. The programme began at 6:30 a.m. and concluded at 10:45 p.m.

Most *godhris* made and donated

Mr Jagjivan Jethva, 73, a retired schoolteacher, stitched 3,200 *godhris* (baby blankets made with many layers of soft cloth) from June 2016 to January 2020 and donated them to the Kranti Jyoti Phule Hospital in Borivali, Mumbai, Maharashtra, for use for newborns in the maternity ward. Living across from the hospital, he would drop in to give biscuits and cloth for children and noticed that their bed linen was often stained. Deciding to make *godhris* and donate them, he bought a sewing machine and

Most *godhris* made and donated

** This is a one-time category. Further and future claims for this category will not be accepted.

polished his tailoring skills. He is known as Godhri Uncle at the hospital, and cloth shops in Borivali happily give him their leftover cloth pieces. He stitches five to six *godhris* every day.

Most sanitary napkins distributed
The District Water and Sanitation Mission, Zilla Parishad, Sindhudurg, Maharashtra, distributed 400,242 sanitary napkins to married women and adolescent girls in 3 hrs on 24 January 2019 under its Utkarsha programme.

Most truckers educated on road safety**
Magma Foundation, Kolkata, West Bengal, educated 153,068 truck drivers on road safety and petroleum conservation across 310 locations in 14 states between 11 December 2015 and 27 March 2019. The event was supported by the Petroleum Conservation Research Association.

Promoting the girl child**
The District Task Force of the Beti Bachao Beti Padhao (BBBP) Scheme at Mandi, Himachal Pradesh, organized the biggest Kanya Poojan (worship of the girl child) of 1,008 girls between four to 10 years of age at Seri Manch of Mandi for 1 hr 30 mins on 9 March 2019, as part of its campaign.

Most hair donated to charity – group
'Eight Inches of Compassion', a camp for hair donation, was held at Bharathamatha Higher Secondary School, Palakkad, Kerala, in which 322 students, teachers, alumni and well-wishers donated 10.02 kg of hair for making wigs for cancer patients in 30 mins on 8 December 2018. Each person gave 8 inches of hair, which was made into 10 wigs and distributed by the district medical officer to patients identified by the Palliative Care Unit, Palakkad, on 2 February 2019.

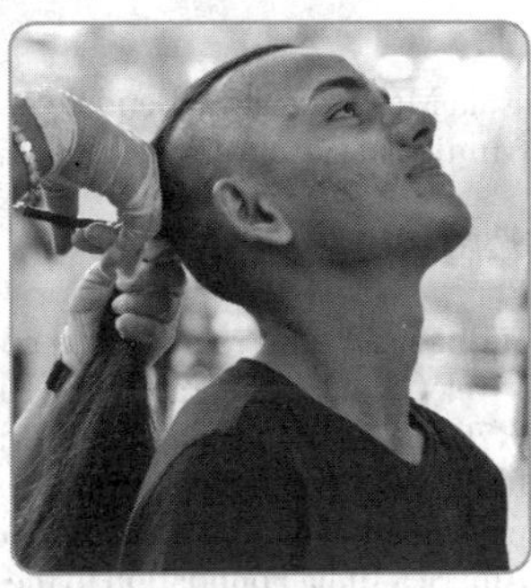
Most hair donated

Most tourist destinations cleaned
The Indian Institute of Tourism and Travel Management, Gwalior, Madhya Pradesh, conducted clean-up campaigns, and created awareness on keeping tourist and pilgrim destinations clean in 450 cities in two phases from September 2017 to March 2018 and July 2018 to March 2019. The cities were selected on the basis of the domestic tourist footfall they receive. The campaign addressed 45 billion domestic tourists, 22.5 billion school and college students, and 27,000 tourism stakeholders through workshops.

Most walls painted
Under the Swachh Bharat Abhiyan, 500 walls of Jalgaon city, Maharashtra, were scrubbed clean, whitewashed and painted under the theme 'Swachh Shahar, Sundar Shahar' by 70 students and seven teachers. They completed the work of painting the walls over a time period of 50 hrs between 9:00 a.m. on 8 January and 7:00 p.m. on 12 January 2019. The event was jointly organized by Ojaswini

Hope, Wrought by Hand

Social entrepreneurs Lakshmi Menon and Gopinath Parayil gave Kerala a handmade doll named Chekutty, which became a symbol of hope to 600 weavers. The weavers in Chendamangalam, Ernakulam, Kerala, thought they had lost their source of livelihood when the floods in August 2018 destroyed their units, raw material and stock. Chekutty dolls were made from the garments that were soiled in the floods. From each sari 360 dolls were made and each doll was sold at ₹25, thereby taking up the value of the sari to ₹9,000.

Kala Mahavidyalaya, Bendale Mahila Mahavidyalaya, School of Design, and the Municipal Corporation, Jalgaon, Maharashtra.

ONLINE FEATS

Highest amount raised for a social cause – online
Vivek Chandrakant Patel from Richmond, Virginia, USA, raised US $1.05 million (₹70,880,803) in 11 days for the families of Pulwama martyrs. One of the highest fundraisers conducted through a social media platform, this initiative had the participation of 26,000 NRI donors. The amount was transferred through the America India Foundation to the Bharat Ke Veer Trust of the Central Reserve Police Force. Vijay Kumar, deputy inspector general, CRPF, and nodal officer of Bharat Ke Veer, thanked Patel and the Team Pulwama Fundraisers, which included Aditya Singh, Mugdha Gangopadhyay, Amit Kha, Abhishek Singh and others.

Longest lesson – online
Manish Raghav (b. 28 April 1983) from Lucknow, Uttar Pradesh, conducted an English lesson online, which lasted 12 hours from 7:00 a.m. to 7:50 p.m. on 29 April 2020, from his residence. He took a 10-minute break after every two hours. The total break time was 50 mins. There were six batches in all, with 30 students in each batch.

Longest non-stop speech relay – online
Vivek Education Society, Mumbai, Maharashtra, organized a non-stop speech relay event online with 155 participants between 10:00 a.m. to 3:40 p.m. on 2 October 2019. The theme of the speech relay in 21 languages was 'Mohan to Mahatma', the journey and ideologies of Mahatma Gandhi.

THRILLING 30s

THRILLING 30s

Limca Book of Records has completed 30 years of publishing. It has been a stunning journey of chronicling the many awe-inspiring achievements of our country and its people. To mark this milestone, we had invited applications for a special section with a '30s' theme. Here are the top achievers from among those who participated in these one-time categories.

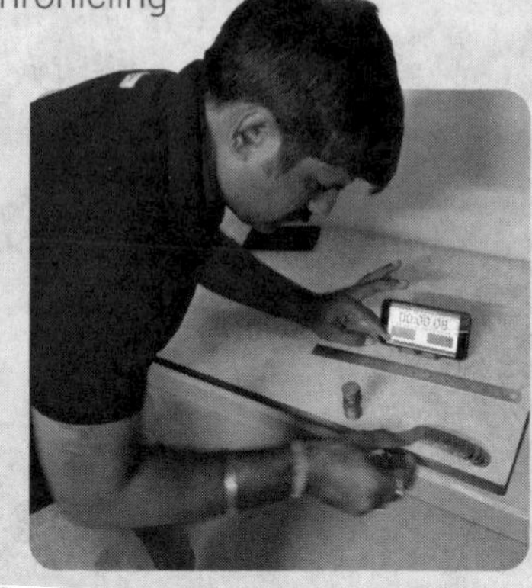

Most coins stacked in a tower in 30 secs

Most push-ups in 30 secs

Most sit-ups in 30 secs

Most coins stacked in a tower (₹1 coins) 30 secs
Pawan Sharma (b. 8 January 1977) from Surat, Gujarat, stacked 44 coins in 30 secs, starting at 9:21 p.m.

Most push-ups 30 secs
Keshav Kumar (b. 20 July 2000) from Jaspur, Uttarakhand, performed 50 two-arm push-ups in 30 secs, starting at 5:30 p.m.

Most sit-ups 30 secs
Ruchika Gupta (b. 29 January 1989) from Chennai,

Tamil Nadu, performed 12 sit-ups in 30 secs, beginning at 9:49 a.m. on 28 June 2020.

Most jumping jacks 30 secs
Mohamed Rizwan T.K. (b. 22 July 1996) from Thanjavur, Tamil Nadu, performed 70 jumping jacks in 30 secs, beginning at 5:25 p.m. on 29 June 2020.

Most portraits made 30 mins
Pradheesh Kumar (b. 6 April 2000) from Udupi, Karnataka, made 30 portraits in 30 mins from 3:36 p.m. to 4:06 p.m. on 20 June 2020.

Most portraits made in 30 mins

In 30 Seconds...

1. We think up to 25 thoughts.
2. We blink up to 6 times.
3. Our heart beats up to 36 times.
4. Our blood travels 7 km around the body.
5. 129 babies are born around the world.
6. 29 aeroplanes take off in the world.
7. 282 new websites are created globally.
8. 101,736,111 emails are sent in the world.
9. 1,320 lightning strikes hit Earth.
10. A bee flaps its wings 8,100 times.

Note: Figures are approximate and sourced from the public domain.

Most squats 30 secs
Shajan Samuel (b. 13 August 1974) from Pune, Maharashtra, performed 24 squats in 30 secs, starting at 6:25 a.m.

Most crunches 30 secs
Nitin Arora (b. 18 March 1977) from Ghaziabad, Uttar Pradesh, performed 58 crunches in 30 secs, starting at 5:20 p.m.

Most crunches 30 mins
Nitin Arora (b. 18 March 1977) from Ghaziabad, Uttar Pradesh, performed 2,710 crunches in 30 mins from 6:00 p.m. to 6:30 p.m.

Most times Rubik's cubes solved 30 mins
Amev Singh Bagga (b. 25 October 2007) from Hyderabad, Telangana,

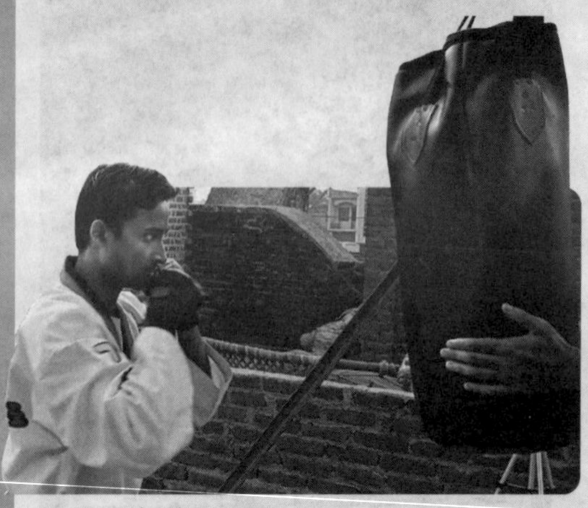
Most punches in 30 secs

solved 89 Rubik's cubes (3 x 3) in 30 mins.

Most punches 30 secs
Ankush Rana (b. 20 May 1999) from Gurugram, Haryana, performed 165 jab punches in 30 secs, starting at 9:00 a.m.

Most photographs clicked 30 mins
Sandeep Kumar Srivastava (b. 7 November 1983) from Gorakhpur, Uttar Pradesh, clicked 303 unduplicated photographs in 30 mins from 9:38 a.m. to 10:08 a.m. on 15 March 2020. He clicked images of the various statues and idols at the Gorakhnath Temple, the architecture of the temple, and its garden. He used a Nikon D3500 camera for his record.

In 30 Minutes...

1. **8,640,000** new stars are created.
2. **1,770** weddings take place in the world.
3. **180,000,000** reactions take place in a human cell.
4. **3,240** people die in the world.
5. **1,620,000,000** WhatsApp messages are sent around the world.
6. **845,001,000** Facebook 'likes' are generated around the world.
7. **298,800** rainforest trees are felled in the world.
8. **150** earthquakes occur on Earth.
9. **1,672,710** barrels of oil are used around the world.
10. **11,310** litres of blood is pumped by the human heart.

Note: Figures are approximate and sourced from the public domain.

Most photographs clicked in 30 mins

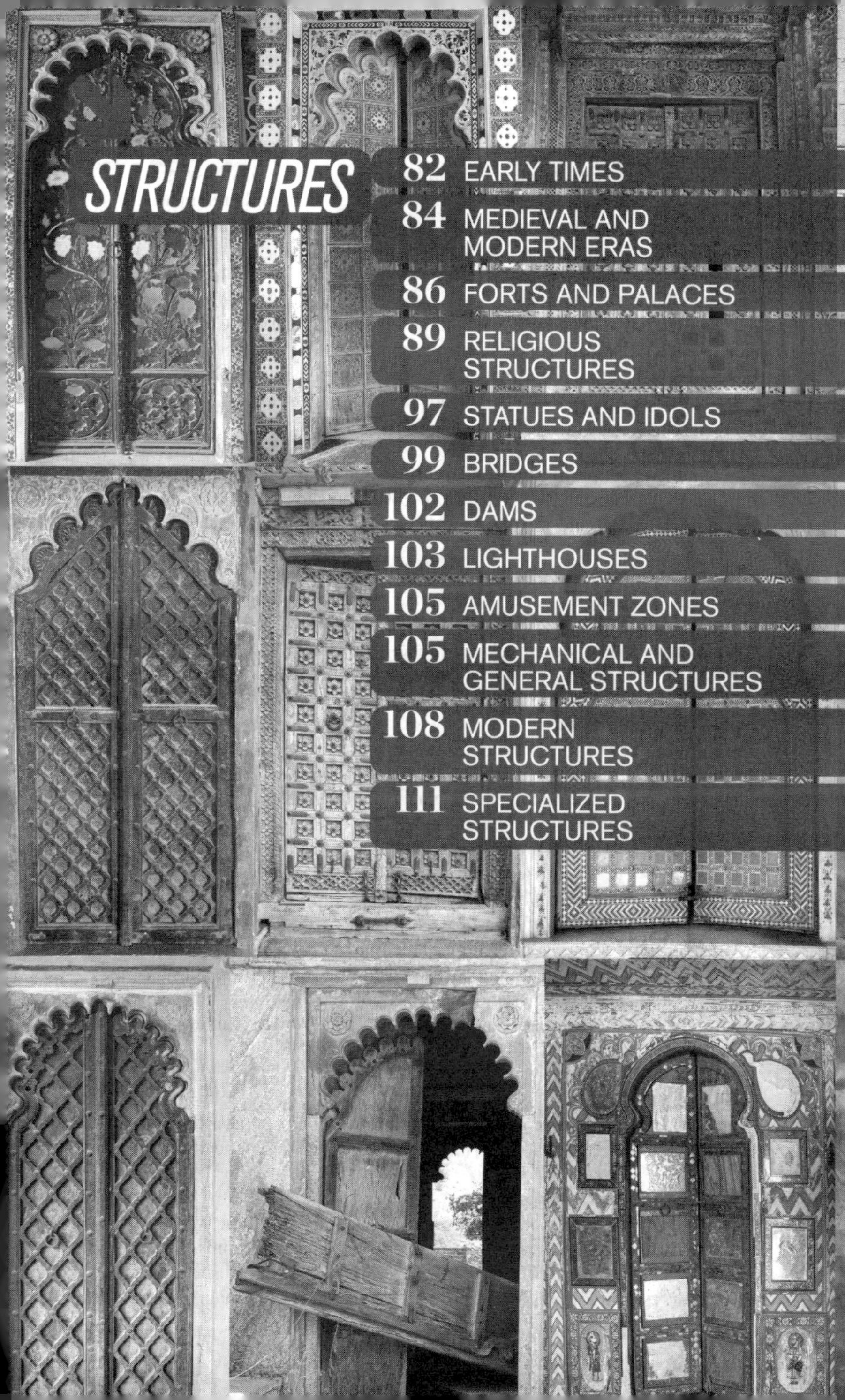

STRUCTURES

EARLY TIMES

Earliest structures

The oldest structures excavated in Koldihwa in Allahabad (now Prayagraj) District, Uttar Pradesh, date to the first half of the seventh millennium BCE. Archaeological evidence has indicated that the site had circular huts made of timber posts and thatch, and a cattle pen.

Earliest village settlement

A 4,000-year-old village settlement of the Chalcolithic period (Copper Age), along with remnants of subsequent Iron Age occupation, was unearthed at Balathal near Udaipur, Rajasthan. It included a massive mud rampart. It is the oldest village settlement in India outside of Harappan sites.

Earliest known fortified city

The remains of rubble masonry and mud bricks, dug up at the Harappan site of Kalibangan in Rajasthan, dated to 3000–2500 BCE, show that it was a fortified city with a stone citadel, and surrounded by a massive rampart of mud bricks.

Earliest *stambha*

The oldest surviving examples of the *stambha* or pillar belong to the period of Emperor Ashoka (r. c. 268 to 232 BCE). The best known is the pillar and its edict at Sarnath near Varanasi, Uttar Pradesh, ordered by him 26 years after his coronation, to convey to his subjects the teachings of the Buddhist scriptures.

Earliest open-air theatre

The third century BCE brick structure at Nagarjunakonda in Guntur District, Andhra Pradesh – found to be similar to ancient Greek and Roman amphitheatres – has a pit with tiers on all four sides, which could seat at least 1,000 spectators. It encloses a rectangular room of 16.5 m x 13.7 m (54 ft 1.5 in. x 44 ft 11.4 in.). The structure has good acoustic properties.

Earliest comprehensive works on architecture

The *Manasara* ('Essence of Measurement') is the earliest known comprehensive treatise on architecture. Written around the third century BCE, it has 70 chapters on topics such as the measurement of sacred edifices and statues, rules for selecting the sites for temples and houses, orientation of temples and layout of city streets. Another treatise on housing architecture from the same period is the *Mayamata,* authored by the 'divine' architect Maya.

First architect

Maha Govinda, mentioned in the Buddhist work *Dhammapada*, is the first architect on record, who designed many north Indian cities in the fifth century BCE.

Earliest extensive drainage system

The Harappan towns of Lothal in Gujarat and Mohenjo-Daro (now in Pakistan), with rectangular houses, chessboard streets, brick-lined bathrooms, drainage pipes and cesspits, are unique in the ancient world. The toilets were flushed with water chutes carrying dirty water away to covered street drains. The main sewer, about

1.5 m (4 ft 11 in.) deep and 91 cm (2 ft 11.8 in.) across, connected to north–south and east–west sewers.

Ancient hydraulic engineering

A first century BCE site in Singraur (Sringaverapura) near Allahabad (now Prayagraj), Uttar Pradesh, revealed the remains of a large rectangular brick tank, a unique example of ancient hydraulic engineering. Water from the River Ganga was brought through a feeding channel into a silting chamber, from which clean water flowed into a main tank.

Oldest rust-free iron pillar

The iron pillar in the Qutub (Minar) complex in Delhi has stood strong since the fifth century CE when it was erected by King Chandra Varman. A solid iron shaft, 7.32 m (24 ft) high, it has six lines in Sanskrit inscribed on it.

Oldest man-made lake

Sudarshan Lake at the foot of Girnar Hills in Junagadh District, Gujarat, was built during the reign of Chandragupta Maurya (c. 321–297 BCE), according to the epigraph engraved on the Ashokan pillar a kilometre from the lake. It was restored by Emperor Ashoka around 273 BCE. Now the lake has shrunk due to silt and debris.

Only swastika-shaped well

A 1,200-year-old well at Thiruvellarai near Manachanallur in Tiruchirappalli District, Tamil Nadu, is shaped like a swastika, with steps on four sides. It was dug by Pallava ruler Dantivarman in c. 800 CE. It was later developed and built in the form of a swastika by Alambakathu Vijayanallulan Thambi Kamban Arayan.

Only natural arch

The Silathoranam, a 7.62 m x 3.05 m (25 ft x 10 ft) natural arch at the Tirumala Hills, about 1 km north of the Venkateswara Temple in Tirumala town in Tirupati, Andhra Pradesh, is the only one of its kind in Asia. It is also a notified National Geo-heritage Monument.

SUPER 30

INTACH: KEEPING HERITAGE INTACT

The Indian National Trust for Art and Cultural Heritage (INTACH), a non-profit charitable organization, was founded in 1984 in New Delhi. Started with the aim of heritage awareness and conservation in India, INTACH is now recognized as one of the world's largest heritage organizations, with over 209 chapters across the country. In the past 30 years, INTACH has been operating through divisions such as Natural Heritage, Architectural Heritage, and Intangible Cultural Heritage, among others. In 2007, the United Nations (UN) awarded INTACH a special consultative status with the UN Economic and Social Council. The INTACH Heritage Academy was established in 2012 and it rolled out a first of its kind full-time postgraduate diploma in heritage studies in April 2018. The course offers a blend of archaeology, conservation and management.

Largest stupa

The Great Stupa at Sanchi in Madhya Pradesh, built with bricks by Emperor Ashoka between 273 and 232 BCE, was later enlarged and enclosed within another stone stupa. In its present form, the stupa now has a diameter of 37 m (121 ft 5 in.) and a height of 16 m (52 ft 6 in.).

Deepest step well

Chand Baori, a step well located at Abhaneri in Jaipur, Rajasthan, is the deepest step well in India, extending to 30 m (98 ft 5 in.) down from the ground. It is also considered to be the largest ancient step well in the country and among the oldest wells in the world. The oldest parts of the step well were constructed in the eighth century by King Chanda and the upper storeys were built during the reign of the Mughals in the 18th century. The step well has 13 levels and 3,500 narrow steps. The temperature at the bottom of the well remains 5–6°C lower than the temperature at its surface.

MEDIEVAL AND MODERN ERAS

First garden tomb

The tomb of Sikandar Lodi of the Lodi dynasty (r. 1489–1517) is located in Lodi Garden near Lodi Road in New Delhi and was built during 1517–18 by his son Ibrahim Lodi.

Earliest known monumental tomb

The Sultan Garhi tomb in Delhi was built over a *garhi* (cave) in 1231 for Prince Nasiruddin Mahmud by his father Iltutmish, the third sultan of the Slave dynasty, who ruled in Delhi (r. 1210–36). The octagonal tomb is like a fortress with a courtyard-like layout, uncommon for a tomb.

WR Tallest brick minaret

The Qutub Minar in Delhi, which is constructed in fluted sandstone carved with verses from the Quran, is 72 m (236 ft) high with 379 steps inside leading to the top. It is a tapering tower of five storeys, with a base diameter of 14.3 m (47 ft), which reduces to 2.74 m (9 ft) at the top. Its construction began under Qutbuddin Aibak in 1193 CE and his successor Iltutmish added three storeys. Firuz Shah Tughlaq completed the last storey in 1383 CE.

There are 40 UNESCO World Heritage Sites in India: 32 cultural sites, 7 natural sites and 1 of mixed criteria.

Largest silver article

A 1.8 m (5 ft 11 in.) tall silver jug at the City Palace in Jaipur, Rajasthan, was made for the maharaja of Jaipur to store drinking water during his visit to England in 1901 for the coronation of King Edward VII.

WR Largest corbelled cornice dome

The Gol Gumbaz, built in 1659 in the tomb complex of the Adil Shahi sultans at Bijapur in Karnataka, has a dome that measures 42 m (137 ft 9.5 in.) in diameter. Its corbelled cornice (the ornamental projection crowning a building) projects over 3 m (9 ft 10 in.) and is the largest of its kind in the world.

Longest corridor

The corridor in the Ramanathaswamy Temple in Rameswaram, Tamil Nadu, which is dated to the 17th century, is 1,220 m (4,002 ft) long. Though it has 1,212 sculpted and painted pillars, it is popularly known as the 'corridor with a thousand pillars'.

Ramanathaswamy Temple, Rameswaram, Tamil Nadu: longest corridor

Largest vaulted hall

The Bara Imambara in Lucknow, Uttar Pradesh, is not only India's but also Asia's largest hall without any external support of wood, iron or stone beams. The hall measures 49.4 m x 16.2 m (162 ft x 53 ft 2 in.). The ceiling is more than 15 m (49 ft 2.5 in.) high.

Largest bas-relief

The 'Descent of the Ganges' bas-relief, also known as 'Arjuna's Penance', in Mamallapuram in Chengalpattu District, Tamil Nadu, is 27 m (88 ft 7 in.) long and 9 m (29 ft 6 in.) high. Created during the Pallava period in the seventh century CE, it features over 30 large and small sculptures of animals, humans, sages and gods.

Largest maze

The Bhul-bhulaiya, which is a set of passages on the top terrace of the Bara Imambara building in Lucknow, Uttar Pradesh, is a labyrinth of over 1,000 interconnected passages that can be approached through a narrow flight of steps but seem to lead nowhere. These passages reduced the load on the walls, which support the massive 4.88 m (16 ft) thick roof with an estimated weight of about 20,000 tonnes.

Oldest British inscription

The Fort St George cemetery in Chennai, Tamil Nadu, has a tombstone belonging to one Elizabeth Baker, dating back to 1632.

FORTS AND PALACES

Oldest fort

The Kalinjar Fort in Banda District of Uttar Pradesh has several temples dating to the rule of the Gupta dynasty from the third to the fifth centuries. Built on a hill at one end of the Vindhya mountain range, at 367 m (1,204 ft), the fort was used by many of Bundelkhand's ruling dynasties, including the Chandela dynasty of Rajputs in the 10th century, and the Solankis of Rewa.

Oldest palace site excavated

Kumrahar in Patna, Bihar, dating to 250 BCE, is said to be one of Emperor Ashoka's palaces. The remains of the columns at the site indicate that the palace had an 84-pillar hall, originally made of wood.

 **The Agra Fort is said to have been built by around**  **1,400,000 workers in**  **eight years.**

Fort on three hills

Gingee Fort, about 100 km from Chennai, Tamil Nadu, is built on three hills – Krishnagiri, Chandragiri and Rajagiri – forming a triangle. Together they form a fort complex, each with its own citadel. The fort walls are 13 km long and the hills are connected by walls enclosing an area of around 11 sq. km. Built by the Chola dynasty in the ninth century CE, the fort was modified in Vijayanagar times.

Oldest extant marble structure

The white marble structure over Hoshang Shah Ghori's tomb, built by his son, at Mandu, Dhar District, Madhya Pradesh, is the oldest extant marble structure known.

Fort with largest metal ordnance

The Bijapur Fort in Bijapur District, Karnataka, houses the famous bell-metal cannon Malik-e-Maidan ('lord of the battlefield'), the largest piece of medieval bell-metal ordnance, which is 4.45 m (14 ft 7 in.) long, with a diameter of 1.5 m (4 ft 11 in.). It weighs 55 tonnes and has a bore of 0.71 m (2 ft 4 in.) from which an iron ball of over a tonne could be fired.

Only fort in a tiger reserve

The 'forest fort' of Ranthambore, a classical *vana durg*, is located in the Ranthambore National Park, Sawai Madhopur District, Rajasthan. Built between 944 and 1110 by a Chauhan ruler whose name is disputed, it towers over the park from atop a hill.

Only palace facade

Hawa Mahal ('the palace of winds') in Jaipur, Rajasthan, has a facade built on to a wall of the main palace compound. Royal ladies seated in its 953 niches and windows could look down at the street below.

Only surviving mud fort

Gaur citadel in Malda District, West Bengal, once led into a *mahi durg* (mud fort) of dynasties including the Guptas and the Palas. Its ramparts – which are 9.65 km (31,660 ft) long, 9.14 m (30 ft) high and 54.86 m (180 ft) thick at the base – are now in ruins. It was hidden by a dense jungle.

Undefeated marine fort

Jaṇjira Fort is a *jala durg* (sea fort) near Murud Village in Raigad District, Maharashtra. It is said to be the only standing undefeated fort along the western coast of India, despite attacks by the Dutch and British East India Companies. It was built by Malik Ambar, an Abyssinian minister of the Nizam Shahi dynasty. Built at the end of the 17th century, the fort is almost entirely intact.

Only palace with a bird sanctuary

The Bharatpur Palace in Rajasthan houses the Keoladeo Ghana National Park (earlier Bharatpur Bird Sanctuary) within its site. It is the only nature reserve in India whose owner, the maharaja of Bharatpur, augmented the water supply in 1760 with an irrigation canal to create the habitat that became a stopover for the migratory Siberian crane. It was converted into a bird sanctuary in 1956 and a national park in 1981.

Highest gateway

Buland Darwaza, the highest gateway in India, is 53.5 m (175 ft 6 in.) high. It was built by Mughal emperor Akbar (r. 1550–1605) at Fatehpur Sikri,

UNESCO WORLD HERIAGE SITES: THE SPLENDID 17

The United Nations Educational, Scientific and Cultural Organization (UNESCO) World Heritage Sites are important places of cultural or natural heritage across the world. There are 38 World Heritage Sites located in India, which include 30 cultural sites, seven natural sites and one mixed-criteria site. After the addition of 14 sites till 1989, seventeen more sites have been added to the list in the past 30 years. Here are the valuable additions:

1. Humayun's Tomb, Delhi
2. Qutub Minar and its Monuments, Delhi
3. Mountain Railways of India (the Darjeeling Himalayan Railway, West Bengal; the Nilgiri Mountain Railway, Tamil Nadu; and the Kalka–Shimla Railway, Haryana and Himachal Pradesh)
4. Mahabodhi Temple Complex at Bodhgaya, Bihar
5. Rock Shelters of Bhimbetka, Madhya Pradesh
6. Chhatrapati Shivaji Maharaj Terminus (formerly Victoria Terminus), Mumbai, Maharashtra
7. Red Fort Complex, Delhi
8. The Jantar Mantar, Delhi
9. Hill Forts of Rajasthan (Chittorgarh, Kumbhalgarh, Sawai Madhopur, Jhalawar; Jaipur and Jaisalmer)
10. Rani Ki Vav ('The Queen's Step Well'), Gujarat
11. Archaeological Site of Nalanda Mahavihara, Bihar
12. The Architectural Work of Le Corbusier, Chandigarh
13. The Historic City of Ahmedabad, Gujarat
14. The Victorian and Art Deco Ensembles of Mumbai, Maharashtra
15. Jaipur, Rajasthan
16. Kakatiya Rudreshwara (Ramappa) Temple, Telangana
17. Dholavira, Gujarat

about 40 km from Agra in Uttar Pradesh, and commemorated his conquest of Ranthambore Fort and Khandesh.

Longest time to build a mausoleum

The Taj Mahal, one of the Seven Wonders of the World, was built by Mughal emperor Shah Jahan (r. 1627–58) as a mausoleum for his wife Mumtaz Mahal, on the banks of the River Yamuna in Agra, Uttar Pradesh. It is said to have taken 22,000 workmen 22 years (1631–53) to complete it. It is built on a 29 sq. m (312 sq. ft) marble platform on a sandstone base.

Palace with the largest chandelier

The durbar hall of Jai Vilas Mahal of Gwalior, Madhya Pradesh, has two chandeliers, each 12.5 m (41 ft) high and weighing 3.5 tonnes. It is said that three (or eight!) elephants were hoisted to the roof (or suspended from it!) to make sure it would withstand the weight of the chandeliers.

Oldest medieval amphitheatre

The Rang Ghar, about 3 km from Sivasagar in Assam, was built during the reign of Swargadeo Rudra Singha (r. 1696–1714) with bamboo and wood. It was rebuilt in brick by Swargadeo Pramatta Singha during 1744–50. It was the royal sports pavilion where Ahom kings watched cockfights and bullfights.

Longest fortification wall

A 36 km (118,110 ft) long fortification wall was built by Rana Kumbha (r. 1433–68) along the Aravallis in Rajasthan to protect his kingdom of Mewar. It enclosed 34 fortresses. At its widest sections, the wall is 15 m (49 ft) thick, and has stone-brick masonry and decorative flourishes along the top.

Palace with a thousand doors

Hazar Duari ('thousand doors'), the palace of Nizam Humayun Khan (r. 1824–38) in the Kila Nizamat premises in Murshidabad, West Bengal, has 1,000 doors, of which 100 are false. It was designed by Scottish architect Duncan McLeod.

First restoration of a fort

In 1986, Aman Nath, a designer, and Francis Wacziarg, a former French diplomat, along with businessmen O.P. Jain and L. Poddar, bought the 15th-century ruins of the Neemrana Fort, built by local chieftain Nimola Meo, on the Delhi–Jaipur highway. They restored it and opened it as a hotel with 12 rooms in 1991.

RELIGIOUS STRUCTURES

Earliest extant structural temple

A third century BCE circular brick-and-timber shrine excavated at Bairat (now Viratnagar) in Jaipur District, Rajasthan, is considered to be the earliest surviving structural temple. The shrine, with a diameter of 8.23 m (27 ft), was built with lime-plastered panels of brickwork alternating with 26 octagonal wooden pillars. The shrine, portico and a 2 m (6 ft 6.7 in.) wide ambulatory were enclosed in a rectangular compound that measures 305 m x 21 m (1,000 ft 7.8 in. x 68 ft 10.7 in.).

Earliest extant Hindu temples

The Gupta period temples in Sanchi and Tigawa near Jabalpur in Madhya Pradesh belong to the fifth century CE. The Kankali Devi Temple in Tigawa is well preserved.

Earliest temple with a shikhara

The earliest known extant temple with a rudimentary shikhara or pinnacle is the Vishnu Dashavatara Temple, belonging to the Gupta period (320–550 CE), at Deogarh in Jhansi District, Uttar Pradesh. It is one of the earliest to draw on the stories of Rama and Krishna to decorate the panels.

WR Earliest Buddhist monument

A stupa, which was estimated to be 2,500 years old, was excavated in 1898 in Piprahwa in Siddharthnagar District, Uttar Pradesh, by British colonial engineer and landowner W.C. Peppe. The solid brickwork stupa was 7 m (23 ft) high and its cupola measured 35 m (114 ft 10 in.) in diameter. Most of the other surviving stupas are from the reign of Emperor Ashoka (c. 273 to 232 BCE).

A Pillar that Hangs from the Ceiling of a Temple

The Veerabhadra or Lepakshi Temple is a 16th-century temple located in Anantapur District, Andhra Pradesh. It has 70 stone pillars among which one 6.09 m (20 ft) granite pillar hangs from the ceiling, defying gravity. In 1910, a British engineer, Hamilton, tried to pull it down, considering it an architectural irregularity. He made one corner of the pillar touch the ground, but this disturbed the very foundations of the temple. According to the Archaeological Survey of India, the pillar was built in this manner to provide stability to the roof.

Biggest queue complex
The Vaikuntham queue complex at the Venkateswara Temple complex, Tirumala, Tirupati, Andhra Pradesh, permits the free flow of nearly 35,000 pilgrims daily. It has a two-tier seating gallery, two corridors and amenities at the ground level within a semicircular length of 238 m (781 ft). A new complex was added later for *sarvadarshan* or free entry of devotees.

Biggest bathing tank
The Brahma Sarovar at Thanesar in Kurukshetra District, Haryana, is 1,370 m x 762 m (4,495 ft x 2,500 ft) and attracts thousands of pilgrims during solar eclipses. The ancient water reservoir finds mention in the Mahabharata.

Biggest temple bell
The 110-year-old bronze bell at Tirumala Devaswom, Kochi, Kerala, is more than 1.8 m (5 ft 11 in.) high and weighs over 3 tonnes. The bell is suspended from a huge wooden frame that rests over four massive granite pillars.

The Vithala Temple complex at Hampi, Karnataka, has 56 musical pillars, which when struck, emit unique musical tones.

Biggest temple lamp
A lamp with 1,000 wicks placed in the Chettikulangara Devi Temple in Alappuzha District, Kerala, is made from 1,500 kg of gunmetal. It is 3.3 m (10 ft 10 in.) high and has 13 tiers like the branches of a banyan. The lowest rung is 2.1 m (6 ft 10.7 in.) in circumference and holds 101 wicks. The topmost is over a metre wide and holds 53 wicks.

Only leaning temple
Built in the 17th century by Baliar Singh of the Chauhan dynasty, the 10.6 m (34 ft 9 in.) tall Shiva Temple at Huma, a village on the banks of the River Mahanadi in Sambalpur District, Odisha, leans at an angle of 13.8 degrees. Its

smaller shrines, bull pillar and *Shivalinga*, all lean at different angles and in different directions.

Only Nataraja temple

The Thillai Nataraja Temple, located in Chidambaram in Cuddalore District, Tamil Nadu, was built by a succession of kings and devotees between the 10th and the 17th centuries CE. The temple is unique because Shiva is worshipped here not as a lingam but as Nataraja, the Lord of Dance. The temple has four gopurams (monumental entrance towers) carved with 108 dance postures described in the *Natyashastra*, the ancient Hindu text on the performing arts.

Thillai Nataraja Temple: only Nataraja temple

Only rat temple

The 575-year-old temple of Karni Devi (believed to be one of the incarnations of Goddess Durga) houses a large number of rats called *kaba*, believed to be the offspring of the presiding deity. Located at Deshnok, 35 km from Bikaner, Rajasthan, this temple is devoted to the 'holy' rats, which have the run of the place.

Only temple with an apsidal sanctum

The Durga Temple at Aihole in Bagalkot District, Karnataka, is a peripheral structure with a semicircular *garbhagriha* (sanctum sanctorum). The 18 m (59 ft) long and 11 m (36 ft) wide temple has a 7 m (23 ft) verandah. The flat roof, 9 m (29 ft 6 in.) above the ground, is surmounted by a gopuram. The temple is built on an earlier Buddhist *chaitya* hall.

WR **Richest Hindu temple**

The Sree Padmanabhaswamy Temple in Thiruvananthapuram, Kerala, is a Hindu temple dedicated to Lord Vishnu. Its idol is made up of 12,008 *salagramas* (a fossilized shell used as a symbol of the god Vishnu) that build up the reclining Lord. The temple's treasure has valuable objects including a gold throne, crowns, coins, statues, ornaments, diamonds and other precious stones donated to the deity over several thousand years, and stored by various dynasties. In July 2011, the existence of six vaults was revealed, of which five reportedly housed over a trillion rupees worth of treasure.

Largest sun temple

Built by Narasimha Deva I in 1200 CE, the Sun Temple at Konark in Odisha represents a huge solar chariot with 12 pairs of ornamental wheels, drawn by seven horses rearing up to the east. The original temple consisted of a sanctum sanctorum with a lofty curvilinear shikhara, a 34.14 m (112 ft) long and 38.4 m (126 ft) high *jagmohana* (assembly hall), and a dance hall. Along with many subsidiary structures, the Sun Temple, which is now the largest extant sun temple, was enclosed within a compound wall 264 m (866 ft) long and 165 m (541 ft) wide, with three gates.

Heaviest and highest single-stone shikhara

The 80-tonne single-piece granite shikhara atop the Brihadisvara Temple at Thanjavur, Tamil Nadu, is the largest and heaviest single-stone object on top of any temple in the world, and is a marvel of engineering. The temple was constructed from 1004 CE, during the reign of Rajaraja Chola, to 1009 CE. It is the world's first temple built with granite. Its *vimana* (a pyramidal tower built over the central shrine of a temple) is also the highest, at 66 m (216 ft 6 in.).

Tallest temple tower

The 13-storey Sri Ranganathaswamy Temple, built between 1982 and 1987 at Srirangam in Tiruchirappalli District, Tamil Nadu, has a 72 m (236 ft) high *rajagopuram* (main gateway).

Largest collection of temples

There are as many as 1,000 Jain temples and 12,000 idols in the Shatrunjai Hills of Palitana in Bhavnagar District of Gujarat.

Largest comprehensive Hindu temple

The Swaminarayan Akshardham Temple in Delhi is the world's largest comprehensive Hindu temple. It is 109 m (357 ft 7 in.) long, 96 m (315 ft) wide and 43 m (141 ft) high, and stands in a complex covering 8,021.4 sq. m (86,341 sq. ft). This ornately hand-carved stone temple was built without structural steel over five years by 11,000 artisans and volunteers.

Swaminarayan Akshardham Temple, Delhi: largest comprehensive Hindu temple

Most sculptures in a temple

The Meenakshi Sundareswar Temple in Madurai, Tamil Nadu, has over 30 million sculptures in its shrines, halls and colonnades. It covers an area of 243 m x 228 m (797 ft x 748 ft).

Oldest yogini temple

The Chausath Jogini Temple at Hirapur, around 20 km from Bhubaneswar, Odisha, is the earliest extant yogini temple, dated to the ninth century CE. Its inner diameter is 7.6 m (25 ft) and outer circumference is 27 m (88 ft 7 in.). In the middle of the enclosure is a rectangular open mandap 2.8 m x 2.4 m (9 ft 2 in. x 7 ft 10 in.). The niches in the inner enclosure feature images of yoginis and the outer surface has nine images of Katyayani, one of the nine forms of the Hindu goddess Parvati.

Only quadrangular yogini temple

The 10th-century Chausath Yogini Temple at the famous Khajuraho complex in Madhya Pradesh is the only quadrangular yogini temple in the country. Built entirely of coarse granite, the temple stands on a terrace that is 7.6 m (25 ft) high and has peripheral shrines.

Maharashtra has the highest number of architects registered with the Council of Architecture in India, with 25,992 architects registered.

Largest cave temple complex

The cave temples in Ellora in Aurangabad District, Maharashtra, were built between the fifth and 10th centuries CE. There are 12 Buddhist, 17 Hindu and five Jain cave temples and monasteries. The Kailasa or Kailasanatha Temple in cave 16 is the world's largest single monolithic rock excavation.

Oldest church

St Thomas's Church, located in Palayoor in Thrissur District of Kerala, is dated to 52 CE. According to tradition, it was established by St Thomas. It was rebuilt in the 17th century by the Reverend Fenichi. The original altar remains.

Largest church

The 76.2 m x 55 m (250 ft x 180 ft 5 in.) Se Cathedral at Old Goa, around 10 km from Panaji, is the largest in India. It was constructed between 1562 and 1619, and consecrated in 1640. It had two towers, but one collapsed in 1776 and was not rebuilt.

Tallest church

The Gothic-style Basilica of Our Lady of Dolours, known locally as Puthanpally, is a minor basilica of the Syro-Malabar Catholic Church in Thrissur, Kerala. Its construction started in 1929. Its two front towers are 45 m (147 ft 8 in.) tall and the central tower is 79 m (259 ft 2 in.) tall.

Oldest active synagogue

The Paradesi Synagogue in Mattancherry in Kochi, Kerala, was built by the

Record Rewind

Largest mosque

1991

The Masjid-i-Jahan Numa, commonly known as the Jama Masjid, in Delhi was built by Mughal emperor Shah Jahan (r. 1628–58). It was completed in 1656 with 5,000 persons working over six years. The name means 'the mosque commanding a view of the world'. The courtyard of the mosque can accommodate 25,000 worshippers. The Jama Masjid houses several relics including a copy of the Quran written on deerskin.

2020

The Taj-ul-Masjid or Taj-ul-Masajid in Bhopal, Madhya Pradesh, was built by Sultan Shah Jahan Begum between 1868 and 1901. Constructed over decades, the mosque was completed in 1985 by Maulana Sayed Hashmat Ali Sahab and Allama Mohammad Imran Khan Nadwi Azhari. Its name means 'The Crown of Mosques' and it has an interior area of 23,000 sq. m (250,000 sq. ft). The mosque is made of red stone and can accommodate 175,000 worshippers.

descendants of the European Jews in 1568 CE. The synagogue is also the first one that is known to have been built in a Commonwealth country.

Largest synagogue

Located on Moledina Street, in Pune, Maharashtra, the Ohel David Synagogue is a 30 m (98 ft 5 in.) high tower, built in the Gothic style with a spire and four giant clocks. Its foundation was laid on 5 November 1863 by David Sassoon, the leader of the Jewish community in Bombay (now Mumbai), Maharashtra, and it was completed in five years. The interior is 19.4 m (63 ft 7.7 in.) long, 13.75 m (45 ft 1 in.) wide and 9.4 m (30 ft 10 in.) high.

Earliest mosques

- The Cheraman Jama Masjid in Kodungallur, Thrissur District, Kerala, is said to have been built in 629 CE.
- The Adhai Din Ka Jhonpra in Ajmer District, Rajasthan, was one of the earliest examples of an Indo-Islamic mosque. It was commissioned by (the later Delhi sultan) Qutbuddin Aibak in 1192 CE, on the orders of Muhammad Ghori. It was built reportedly from the remains of dismantled temples, according to the Archaeological Survey of India.

First single-aisle mosque

The Bara Gumbad Mosque, a single-aisle mosque in Delhi's Lodi Garden, was constructed by Sikandar Lodi in 1494.

Only mosque in marble

Moti Masjid, built by Mughal emperor Aurangzeb during 1659–60 within the Red Fort in Delhi, is made entirely of marble.

Only shaking minarets

At the Sidi Bashir Mosque in Ahmedabad, Gujarat, the two minarets, which are three storeys high and have carved balconies, are known as the *jhulta* or shaking minarets. Dated to 1452 CE, the mosque is believed to have been built either by Sidi Bashir, a slave of Sultan Ahmed Shah, or by Malik Sarang, a noble in the court of Sultan Mahmud Begada. The shaking of either minaret results in the other minaret vibrating too after a few seconds, a fact that was first observed in the 19th century by an Englishman and Sanskrit scholar, Monier M. Williams. At present, one of these minarets has been partly taken down to prevent it from falling over.

First revolving minaret

The minaret of the 55-year-old Masjid-e-Chini Ki Burj also known as the Chhoti Masjid, located in Jaipur, Rajasthan, was the first revolving minaret in India. The 10-tonne dome of the 30.5 m (100 ft) high minaret, with a 3 m (9 ft 10 in.) diameter, completed one round in a minute, running on a 1.5 HP motor.

First Baha'i house of worship

The Baha'i House of Worship or 'Lotus Temple' in Kalkaji in New Delhi, the first such structure in Asia, is built on 26 acres (10.52 hectares) of land. Built between 1980 and 1986, it is designed as a blossoming lotus: the main structure has three folds of nine concrete petals, each covered with Grecian marble. The temple rises to 35 m (114 ft 10 in.) and is surrounded by several pools of water.

Highest gurdwara

The gurdwara at Hemkund–Lokpal in Chamoli District, Uttarakhand, at a height of 4,328.16 m (14,200 ft) above the mean sea level, finds mention in the Guru Granth Sahib and in Guru Gobind Singh's memoir, *Bachittar* (or *Bichittar*) *Natak*.

Highest monastery

The Tangyud Monastery at Komic Village near Hikkim in Spiti Valley, Himachal Pradesh, is India's highest monastery at an altitude of around 4572 m (15,000 ft). Built like a fortified castle, it lies on the edge of Kibber Wildlife Sanctuary.

Largest chaitya hall

The Karla Caves near Lonavala, Maharashtra, house the largest known chaitya (Buddhist prayer hall) cave. Its dimensions are 37 m x 14 m x 14 m (121 ft 5 in. x 46 ft x 46 ft).

WR Tallest hollow stone structure

The Global Vipassana Pagoda at Gorai in Mumbai, Maharashtra, is one of the largest structures enshrining the relics of the Buddha, donated by the Sri Lankan government and the Mahabodhi Society, Bodhgaya, Bihar. Inaugurated on 8 February 2009, it contains the largest and tallest pillar-less hollow stone pagoda in the world. The height of the dome is 29 m (95 ft 1.7 in.) and the height of the building is 96.12 m (315 ft 4.2 in.) It took around 11 years and 2.5 million tonnes of stone to complete it.

Largest monastery

The largest Buddhist monastery, and a functioning one, in India is located in the city of Tawang in Arunachal Pradesh. The three-storey structure spread over 140 sq. m (1,507 sq. ft) has 65 residential buildings that can house up to 450 lamas. This monastery's Tibetan name – Galden Namgey Lhatse – translates as 'celestial paradise on a clear night'.

Largest Bird Sculpture

Jatayu, the largest bird sculpture in the world, is located at the Jatayu Earth's Center (also known as Jatayu Rock or Jatayu Nature Park) in Chadayamangalam, Kollam, Kerala. The sculpture, conceptualized and built by sculptor and film-maker Rajiv Anchal, is 60.96 m (200 ft) long, 45.72 m (150 ft) wide and 21.34 m (70 ft) high. Taking 10 years to construct, it is built on a rock called Jatayupara, believed to be the spot where the divine bird Jatayu, mentioned in the Ramayana, fell after a courageous confrontation with Ravana when he was carrying away Sita forcibly. It houses a digital museum and a multidimensional theatre, making it a 'functional' sculpture. With a utility space of 1,393.5 sq. m (15,000 sq. ft), the sculpture is a tribute to the safety and honour of women.

Largest tent structure

The largest permanent tent structure stood at the Osho International Commune in Pune, Maharashtra. Oval in shape – with a 62.75 m (205 ft 10 in.) major axis and a 32.8 m (107 ft 7 in.) minor axis – it had a floor area of 1,582 sq. m (17,029 sq. ft). The roof, 3.9 m (12 ft 9.5 in.) high, was a free-spanning, tensile structure on a three-hinged steel arch covering 45.5 m (149 ft 3 in.). It used nylon-reinforced PVC material, weighing 1,990 kg.

STATUES AND IDOLS

WR **Tallest statue**

A 182 m (597 ft) 'Statue of Unity' of Sardar Vallabhbhai Patel, inaugurated on 31 October 2018, stands on Sadhu Bet river island in the River Narmada near Rajpipla, Gujarat. Designed by sculptor Ram V. Sutar, it took nearly four years to build and cost an estimated ₹29.89 billion (2,989 crore).

WR **Tallest monolithic statue**

The Gommateshwara statue at Shravanabelagola, Karnataka, is the world's tallest monolithic statue. Dedicated to Bahubali and venerated by the Jains, it is 17.37 m (57 ft) high. It was carved from a single block of granite rock and weighs 80 tonnes. It was built between 978 and 993 CE by Chavundaraya, a minister of the Western Ganga dynasty. The Mahamastakabhisheka festival is celebrated here every 12 years.

WR **Largest bust**

Inaugurated on 24 February 2017, the 34.1 m (112 ft) tall 'Adiyogi' Lord Shiva steel statue located in Coimbatore, Tamil Nadu, at the Isha Yoga Centre, has been funded by the Isha Foundation, founded by Sadhguru Jaggi Vasudev. Built over eight months, the structure weighs a reported 500 tonnes. Its height signifies the 112 chakras in the human system to explore the 112 dimensions of life.

India has the second highest number of statues of over 30 m (98.4 ft) in the world, with 25 of them; China has 34.

Largest Nandi statue

Nandi is the sacred bull and Lord Shiva's vehicle in Hindu mythology. The Nandi statue, about 200 m (656 ft) from the Veerabhadra Temple at Lepakshi Village in Anantapur District, Andhra Pradesh, is 4.57 m (15 ft) tall and 8.23 m (27 ft) long, and is carved out of a single piece of granite.

Largest *Shivalinga*

Located in Bhojpur, on the outskirts of the city of Bhopal in Madhya Pradesh, the Bhojeshwar Temple, built by Raja Bhoj (r. 1010–53 CE), houses the largest *Shivalinga*, 5.5 m (18 ft) high and 2.5 m (8 ft 2 in.) in circumference.

WR **Tallest Hanuman statue**

The Hanuman statue at the Manav Bharti University, Solan, Himachal Pradesh, is the tallest Hanuman statue in the world. The construction of the

SUPER 30

DR B.V. DOSHI: ARCHITECT EXTRAORDINAIRE

A pioneer of modernist architecture in India, Dr Balkrishna Vithaldas Doshi (b. 26 August 1927) has catalysed architectural evolution in India. Besides having worked with influential architects such as Le Corbusier and Louis Kahn, Doshi is a Fellow of the Royal Institute of British Architects and received the Padma Bhushan award in 2020. The founder director of the School of Architecture, Ahmedabad (1962–72), he was the first Indian architect to receive the prestigious Pritzker Architecture Prize in 2018. Besides his role in establishing the globally renowned Vastu-Shilpa Foundation for Studies and Research in Environmental Design, Doshi's remarkable works include IIM-Bangalore (Karnataka), NIFT Delhi, Amdavad Ni Gufa (Ahmedabad, Gujarat), the National Institute of Fashion Technology (Delhi) and the Aranya Low Cost Housing Project in Indore (Madhya Pradesh), which was awarded the Aga Khan Award for Architecture in 2019. He made a cameo appearance as himself in the 2015 Tamil language film, *O Kadhal Kanmani*.

Dr B.V. Doshi

47.3 m (155 ft 2 in.) high statue was completed in four years from March 2015 to March 2019. The statue was constructed by the Manav Bharti Foundation.

WR Tallest *Shivalinga*

The tallest *Shivalinga* in the world was created by Maheswaram Sri Sivaparvathi Temple Trust, Thiruvananthapuram, Kerala. The *Shivalinga* measures 33.85 m (111 ft) and was constructed in six years and one day between 31 December 2012 and 31 December 2018.

WR Tallest Shani Dev statue

The Shani Dev Sewa Samiti, Shani Dham, Jammu, built and installed the world's tallest Shani Dev statue, which is 11.88 m (39 ft) high, including its 1.83 m (6 ft) base, in Jourian Village, Akhnoor District, Jammu and Kashmir. It weighs around 2,100 kg.

Tallest Ganesha Idol

A 6 m (19 ft 8 in.) high and 3.35 m (11 ft) wide Ganesha, weighing 190 tonnes and carved out of a single block of stone, was installed at the Mundhi Vinayagar Temple at Puliakulam, Coimbatore District, Tamil Nadu. Its *abhisheka* ritual needs 3 litres of oil and is performed using a ladder.

Tallest Durga structure

Nuruddin Ahmed from Bishnupur Village in Chirang District, Assam, built the tallest Durga structure, measuring 30 m x 14.5 m x 8 m (98 ft 5 in. x 47 ft 7 in. x 26 ft 3 in.), using only bamboo materials (including 5,000 bamboo sticks). No

India Shines at the World Architecture Festival 2019

The World Architecture Festival (WAF), an annual awards function organized for the architecture and development industry, was held from 4 to 6 December 2019 in Amsterdam, Netherlands. Out of 550 shortlisted candidates from around the world, the School of Planning and Architecture, Bhopal, Madhya Pradesh, won the ROCKWOOL Student Charrette award for 'AMSA, Bridging the Disharmony – A Case of Fishing Community, Penthakata Village, Puri, Odisha' while architectural firms – Charged Voids and Studio Lotus – were highly commended for their design for a student hostel in Mohali, Punjab, and the Krushi Bhavan in Bhubaneswar, Odisha, respectively.

Krushi Bhavan, Bhubaneswar

other material was used except cotton cloth as rope. It was made to promote the bamboo sector in Assam.

Tallest Buddha statue

A 31.4 m (103 ft) high statue of the Buddha, dedicated to the Dalai Lama, is situated in Clement Town Monastery, the highest Mindrolling monastery in the world, in Dehradun District, Uttarakhand. A large Tibetan community lives in Clement Town.

BRIDGES

First iron bridge

The first iron bridge was built by Jessop & Company Limited in 1815 over the River Gomti in Lucknow in Uttar Pradesh. Designed by engineer Rennie, it was made at Butterfly Iron Works, England, for the nawab of Oudh (now Awadh).

First cable-stayed road bridge

The Akkar Bridge in Jorethang, over the River Rangit in Sikkim, is an all-concrete, cable-stayed road bridge built in 1988. It spans a 1.5 km (4,921 ft) wide and nearly 20 m (65 ft 7 in.) deep valley. The bridge consists of two 77 m (252 ft 7 in.) symmetrical spans supported from a single central pylon. With 17 pairs of cable stays, the 55 m (180 ft) high pylon supports the decking 21 m (69 ft) above the riverbed.

Longest cable-stayed bridge

The Vidyasagar Setu in Kolkata, West Bengal, more popularly known as the second Hooghly Bridge, is over 1 km long and is made of steel and reinforced concrete. Holding this up are 152 cables sheathed in high-density plastic. Work on the bridge began in 1977 and it was declared open for traffic and pedestrians in 1992.

Longest balanced cantilever bridge

The 3,015 m (9,892 ft) road bridge across the River Brahmaputra at Tezpur,

Record Rewind

Longest sea bridge

1990

The Annai Indira Gandhi bridge connecting the island of Rameswaram with Mandapam in Tamil Nadu was India's longest bridge across the open sea. The 2.34 km long bridge has a 115.21 m (378 ft) span and a vertical clearance of about 18 m (59 ft) above high tide level. It was inaugurated on 2 October 1988.

2020

The Bandra-Worli Sea Link (also known as the Rajiv Gandhi Sea Link), the longest sea bridge in India, is 5.6 km (18,373 ft) long. It connects Bandra in the western suburbs of Mumbai to Worli in south Mumbai, across Mahim Bay. This cable-stayed bridge, which carries eight lanes of traffic, was inaugurated on 30 June 2009.

Assam, called Kolia Bhomora Setu, is the longest bridge that has been provided with a central suspended span of 15 m (49 ft 2.5 in.) length due to its geographical location in a seismic zone. The bridge consists of 24 spans of 120 m (393 ft 8 in.) each and two shore spans of 67.5 m (221 ft 5 in.) each. This bridge, with a carriageway of 7.5 m (24 ft 7 in.) width, was constructed between October 1981 and April 1987.

WR Longest Bailey bridge

The 182.8 m (600 ft) long suspension bridge over the River Chubi in Wokha, Nagaland, connects the Mokokchung District and the Dimapur District of Nagaland.

Biggest cantilever bridge

Howrah Bridge (or Rabindra Setu) is India's biggest cantilever bridge. It spans the River Hooghly in Kolkata, West Bengal, and is 457 m (1,499 ft) long. It was completed in 1943.

Only bascule bridge

The only bascule bridge in India is at Khidirpur in Kolkata, West Bengal. Operated by the Kolkata Port Trust, it is built in two halves, each of which goes up to allow ships to pass through. The bridge has a span of about 35 m (114 ft 10 in.) and was built by Wagner Biro AG, Austria. It was commissioned on 5 November 1966, and replaced a swing bridge built in 1892.

Highest Bailey bridge

The highest Bailey bridge in the country is at a height of 5,602 m (18,380 ft) at Khardung La in Ladakh. The 30 m (98 ft 5 in.) long bridge rests on ice. It consists of square diamond-braced panels that can be assembled on approach and then pushed or pinned together at the corners to form a girder. It was designed and built by Lieutenant Colonel S.G. Vombatkere of the Border Roads Organization in August 1982.

Longest bridge over water

The Bhupen Hazarika Setu or Dhola–Sadiya Bridge, connecting Dhola and Sadiya in Dibrugarh District and Lakhimpur District, respectively, in Assam, is the longest bridge over water. The 9.15 km (30,020 ft) long bridge on the River

Highest Rail Bridge

The highest rail bridge in the world is being built over the River Chenab in Jammu and Kashmir, and it is planned to be higher than the height of the Eiffel Tower. Built at a height of 359 m (1,177 ft 10 in.) from the surface of the river, this bridge is 1,315 m (4,314 ft 3.6 in.) long. The cost of building it is estimated to be `11 billion (1,100 crore). Connecting Bakkal and Kauri in Reasi District, it is being constructed using 24,000 tonnes of blast-proof steel. Being built in collaboration by the Indian Railways and the Defence Research and Development Organization (DRDO), the bridge is expected to be completed by December 2022.

Brahmaputra was inaugurated on 26 May 2017 by Prime Minister Narendra Modi. It is named after Bhupen Hazarika, a well-known Assamese musician and film-maker who died in 2011.

Tallest bridge
The 64 m (210 ft) high Panval Nadi viaduct near Ratnagiri, Maharashtra, is the tallest bridge in the country.

Highest suspension bridge
At 4,144 m (13,596 ft) above sea level, Chicham Bridge is built over a deep gorge and connects Kibber and Chicham in Laul and Spiti District in Himachal Pradesh.

 **Pamban Bridge, India's first sea bridge, was opened on 24 February 1914 in Tamil Nadu.**

Busiest bridge
With nearly 60,000 vehicles a day and countless pedestrians, Howrah Bridge, also called Rabindra Setu, in Kolkata, West Bengal, is the country's busiest bridge.

Longest road-and-rail bridge
The 4.940 km (16,207 ft) long Bogibeel Bridge on the River Brahmaputra, between Dhemaji and Dibrugarh Districts, Assam, is the longest road-and-rail bridge. Started in April 2002, it was completed in December 2018. It has a double-line 1.676 m (5 ft 6 in.) broad-gauge railway on the lower deck and a three-lane road on the upper one. It is India's first bridge with fully welded steel–concrete support beams to bear earthquakes of magnitudes up to 7 on the Richter scale.

DAMS

Earliest canal system
Canal systems have existed since the pre-Harappan era (around 2500 BCE). Excavations at Dholavira in Gujarat have revealed ingenious systems for diverting water from seasonal nullahs.

Earliest dam and canal
The earliest dam discovered was built on Sudarshan Lake in Junagadh (then Girinagar) in Gujarat. It dates to 326 BCE.

Longest canal
The Indira Gandhi Canal or Rajasthan Canal, which starts in Punjab and ends in Rajasthan, is 959 km (3,146,325 ft) long, and the world's second longest canal. Its schemes include 6,308 km of distributary canals.

Indira Gandhi Canal, Rajasthan: longest canal

Oldest extant dam
The Grand Anicut Dam, also called Kallanai Dam, built on the River Kaveri, 24 km from Tiruchirappalli in Tamil Nadu, is the oldest extant dam. The masonry dam, built in the second century CE by the Chola king Karikalan, is 330 m (1,083 ft) long, 5.49 m (18 ft) high and 12–18 m (39–59 ft) wide. The dam was remodelled, repaired and fitted with sluice gates during 1899–1902. For centuries, it has irrigated over a million acres of land.

Oldest cement masonry dam
The Khadakwasla Dam on the River Mutha, 20 km from Pune in Maharashtra, was built on the suggestion of Colonel Fife of the Royal Engineers and civil engineer N.G.K. Murti. It was started in 1869 and completed in 1879. The dam has since been rebuilt.

Longest ancient dam
The 16 km (52,493 ft) long Veeranam embankment dam in Cuddalore District, Tamil Nadu, was built in 1037 CE and is still in use.

First hydroelectric project

Shivanasamudra in Chamarajanagar District, Karnataka, opened in 1902 and involved the harnessing of the Kaveri Falls to supply electrical energy to run the machinery at the Kolar goldfields. The power station still functions.

Longest breakwater

The V.O. Chidambaranar Port (earlier Tuticorin Port) North Breakwater in Tamil Nadu is the longest at 4.14 km (13,583 ft).

Largest water reservoir

Indirasagar Dam is a multipurpose project on the River Narmada in the East Nimar District of Madhya Pradesh. The reservoir has a capacity of 12.2 billion cubic metre (9,890,701 acre-ft) and, in terms of water storage, stands as the largest reservoir in India.

Largest river dam

The Sardar Sarovar Dam is a gravity dam on the River Narmada near Navagam in Surat District, Gujarat. One of 30 dams planned on the River Narmada, it is the largest such structure to be built and among the largest dams in the world. Four Indian states – Gujarat, Madhya Pradesh, Maharashtra and Rajasthan – receive water and electricity supplied from the dam.

WR Largest barrage

The Farakka Barrage on the River Ganga was opened in 1972 to help maintain navigable depths in Kolkata Port. Its length of 2,245 m (7,365 ft 6 in.) contains 108 gated bays of 18 m (59 ft) and two 8 m (26 ft) fish locks.

Highest earth-fill dam

The Pong Dam, also known as the Beas Dam, is an earth-fill embankment dam on the River Beas in Himachal Pradesh and the highest of its type at 133 m (436 ft 4 in.). Maharana Pratap Sagar Lake, created by the dam, is a bird sanctuary.

LIGHTHOUSES

Oldest lighthouses

In 1766, two signal houses were built, one on Old Woman's Island (now part of Colaba) and the other at Malabar Point, in Bombay (Mumbai), Maharashtra. The former was replaced by the first proper lighthouse built during 1768–71. This had a height of 45.72 m (150 ft) and a beam range of seven leagues (around 34 km) seaward in clear weather. It was repaired in 1828 and 1853, but stopped operating when Prongs Lighthouse was installed in 1874.

Tallest lighthouse

The Jakhau Lighthouse in Gujarat is the tallest at 46 m (151 ft). It was established in 1957 and the present tower was built in 1965. Located on the main quay of Jakhau, a fishing port in western Kachchh, the lighthouse has a range of 33 km.

Oldest functional lighthouses

- The lighthouse built in 1821 on Sagar Island, at the mouth of the River Hooghly

First unmanned lighthouse, near Thalassery, Kerala

in West Bengal, was renovated in 1911. Its elevation from the mean sea level is 26 m (85 ft 4 in.) and the tower is 25 m (82 ft) high. Its flashing light has a range of 31 km in clear weather.

- The Prongs Lighthouse in the Colaba area in Bombay (now Mumbai), Maharashtra, was built in 1874 by Thomas Ormiston. Its beam range is 30 km and it is still operational. Its height is 41 m (135 ft) and range is 43 km.

First unmanned lighthouse
Near Thalassery (earlier Tellicherry) in Kannur District, Kerala, stands the first unmanned lighthouse. It was built in 1835 and renovated in 1924. It is at an altitude of 27 m (89 ft) from the mean sea level and its range is 8 km.

Tallest lighthouse from the mean sea level
The tallest lighthouse from the mean sea level is at Dolphin's Nose at Visakhapatnam, Andhra Pradesh. Its masonry tower rises 19 m (62 ft 4 in.) from ground level and it has an elevation of 173 m (567 ft 7 in.), which is 192 m (630 ft) from the mean sea level.

Lighthouse farthest from shore
The lighthouse farthest from the seashore is on the Vengurla rocks, 20 km from Vengurla in the Sindhudurg District of Maharashtra.

AMUSEMENT ZONES

First amusement park

Appu Ghar at Pragati Maidan, New Delhi, was the first family entertainment centre in India, opened at the same time when the the 1982 Asian Games were organized in Delhi. It was named after the Games' mascot – Appu the elephant. Shutting down in 2008, it reopened in Gurugram, Haryana, with projects in The Great India Place mall and Worlds of Wonder amusement and water-theme park in Noida, as well as at Metro Walk and Adventure Island in Rohini, Delhi.

Largest amusement park

Spread over 138 acres (56 hectares), Imagica is located off the Mumbai–Pune Expressway at Khopoli, Maharashtra. It has India's largest theme park, a water park, India's largest snow park, and first theme park hotel. It also features the longest, tallest and fastest roller coaster, 40.2 m (132 ft) high with over 853.4 m (2,800 ft) of track length and a speed of 120 km/hr. It also has 'I for India', the country's first simulation ride and India's longest flume ride of 470 m (1,542 ft).

WR Largest adventure park

The world's largest adventure park was opened by the Indian Air Force Station, Bagdogra, Darjeeling District, West Bengal, under the aegis of the Eastern Air Command, Indian Air Force, and the Directorate of Adventure Sports in August 2018. Spread over 860 acres (348 hectares), the park at the Bagdogra Air Force Station has 62 land, air and water adventure sports, like skydiving, parasailing and rappelling.

First indoor amusement play station

Funky Orbit at Ansal Plaza mall on Khel Gaon Marg in New Delhi was launched on 15 June 2000 by Panoramic Entertainment Pvt. Ltd. The multi-tiered play station had an 8.53 m (28 ft) long curly slide and a ball pool.

First marine amusement park

In 1998, Dolphin City was set up by Amusements and Picnic Resorts Private Limited in Chennai, Tamil Nadu, with three performing dolphins and a performing sea lion show. Following the death of the performing dolphins, the marine amusement park featured sea lion performances, underwater viewing and leisure boating.

First water park

Shanku's Water Park on the Ahmedabad–Mahesana Highway in Gujarat was launched by Shankarbhai Chaudhary in 1993, on a 75-acre (30.35-hectare) campus. It introduced a giant 15.24 m (50 ft) speed slide that ended in a shallow water pool, a spiral ride, a wave pool that simulated sea waves, and a kids' corner.

MECHANICAL AND GENERAL STRUCTURES

First elevator

The first elevator was installed at Raj Bhavan, in Calcutta (now Kolkata, West Bengal) in 1892. It used Otis's first design of an electric lift.

Not Just a Washroom

The Light Box – Restroom for Women is a toilet block measuring 9 m x 3 m (29 ft 6 in. x 9 ft 10 in.) in Thane, Maharashtra, built by architect Rohan Chavan in 2016. Containing four female-only toilets located around the trunk of a tree, it has a central courtyard designed to be a place for women to rest and socialize, and is monitored by CCTV cameras and security guards. The initiative gets its name from the light that filters in through its transparent roof and shipping-container like appearance. While there are two stalls arranged at one end of the building with a washbasin, the other end has a nursing room and a toilet for seniors and the differently abled. Commissioned by Agasti, a non-profit organization that works to improve public access to toilets in urban areas, the space also includes a vending machine for female hygiene products, mobile phone charging points and a panic alarm system. Plans are being made for the socializing area to become a place for informal exhibitions, lectures and educational campaigns, and to also house a cash machine, all within a safe space.

First hand-operated crane
The first hand-operated crane was built by Jessop & Company in 1850. The 5-tonne crane was installed at the then Calcutta Port Customs in Bengal.

First houseboat
The first houseboat, which was named *Victory*, was built in 1888 and stationed at the Dal Lake in Srinagar, Jammu and Kashmir.

First floating restaurant
The first floating restaurant was built at Sirhind, Punjab, on the Bhakra Canal in 1979. The eight-room air-conditioned restaurant was part of a tourist complex.

First revolving restaurant
Neelkanth Patang at Ahmedabad, Gujarat, was the first revolving restaurant at 67.4 m (221 ft) above ground level. Opened in 1984, it has a 90-minute rotation, which unfolds a view of the old and new city of Ahmedabad.

First space-frame concrete structure
The first space-frame structure in reinforced concrete was the Hall of Nations at the Trade Fair Authority of India exhibition grounds in Pragati Maidan, New Delhi. Built during 1971–72, the then path-breaking hall structure offered an uninterrupted exhibition area of 6,700 sq. m (72,118 sq. ft) in a 82 m x 82 m x 27 m (269 ft x 269 ft x 88 ft 7 in.) pyramid supported at eight points. The hall has since been razed in the rebuilding of the Pragati Maidan complex.

Largest official residence
The Rashtrapati Bhavan in New Delhi, the official residence of the president of India, has 340 rooms, 18 staircases, 74 lobbies, 37 salons, 1 km of corridors, 37 fountains and 190 acres (76.9 hectares) of gardens. The residence covers 50 acres (20.2 hectares) of a 330-acre (133.5-hectare) estate.

Largest auditorium
The Sri Shanmukhananda Hall, inaugurated on 22 August 1963 in Bombay (now Mumbai), Maharashtra, has a total capacity of 3,012 seats. The ground floor seats 1,552, the first balcony 896 and the second balcony 564 people. The stage has a depth and width of 16 m (52 ft) each and a height of 6.4 m (21 ft).

Largest table
The teakwood table in the Banquet Hall at the president's residence, Rashtrapati Bhavan in Delhi can seat 104 people.

Largest cooking vessel
The original *badi deg* (big vessel), christened Deg-i-Chittor-Kusba or the 'Chittor-conquering vessel', said to be presented by the Mughal emperor Akbar to the dargah of Khwaja Moinuddin Chishti in Ajmer, Rajasthan, could hold 4,000 kg of food at a time, enough for 12,000 people.

Largest retractable roof
Kunta International Ltd, Noida, designed, built, installed and commissioned an electrically driven retractable roof on a reusable structure on the presidential dais on Rajpath, New Delhi, for Republic Day 2018. Made of steel and polycarbonate sheets with inbuilt sensors, it was 30.5 m (100 ft) wide and 6.4 m (21 ft) deep.

Record Rewind

Largest glasshouse

1993
The glass-covered hall at the Lalbagh Botanical Gardens in Bengaluru, Karnataka, occupies 2,787 sq. m (30,000 sq. ft). The garden was commissioned by Hyder Ali (r. 1761-1782), the ruler of Mysore (now Mysuru), and later completed by his son Tipu Sultan.

2020
A glass-covered hall in Davangere, Karnataka, completed in 2018, covers 7,334 sq. m (78,945 sq. ft). The glasshouse houses a horticultural information centre as well as a botanical garden.

Largest cinema multiplex
Mayajaal in Kanathur in Chennai, Tamil Nadu, has the largest movie multiplex with 16 screens and a seating capacity of 2,600. It is part of an entertainment centre that houses a shopping mall, a sports complex and a resort.

Longest conveyor
The longest single-belt international conveyor stretches from near Shella, East Khasi Hills District, Meghalaya, in India to a cement factory at Chhatak in Sylhet

now Sunamganj District) District, Bangladesh. It is about 17 km long (7 km in India and 10 km in Bangladesh) and conveys limestone and shale at 960 tonnes/hr. The conveyor was engineered by AUMUND France and Larsen & Toubro, and installed on-site by Beltpro. Its rollers are unusually designed to deal with both horizontal and vertical terrain curves.

WR Most names engraved on a monument

India Gate in Delhi carries the names of 13,516 British and Indian soldiers of the British Indian Army, who died during 1914–21 at various fronts of the First World War and the Third Anglo-Afghan War. This constitutes the largest number of names inscribed on a monument. Designed by architect Edwin Lutyens, the arch was completed in 1921. It is 42.3 m (139 ft) high and 9.1 m (30 ft) wide.

Longest underground pipeline

The Hazira–Bijapur–Jagdishpur (HBJ) gas pipeline was India's first cross-country gas pipeline. This project by GAIL (India) Ltd began in 1986 to supply gas to fertilizer plants in Uttar Pradesh. The first phase, consisting of a non-branched 1,750 km grid, was later expanded to supply gas for industrial and domestic use in Rajasthan, Haryana and the National Capital Territory (NCT). This extended the grid length to 3,474 km.

The first skyscraper

Usha Kiran, a 80 m (260 ft) high apartment building of 26 storeys in Bombay (now Mumbai), Maharashtra, was the pioneer of high-rise buildings in India. It was built between 1964 and 1967.

Tallest chimney

The 275.2 m (903 ft) high chimney of the Reliance Dahanu Thermal Power Station in Dahanu in the Palghar District of Maharashtra is India's tallest RCC chimney. The base diameter of the chimney is 7 m (23 ft).

Oldest ice-skating rink

The ice-skating rink near Lakkar Bazaar in Shimla, Himachal Pradesh, was founded in 1920 by one Mr Blessington. Initially out of bounds for Indians during British rule, it is now managed by the Shimla Ice-skating Club and is open for skating between the winter months of December and February.

MODERN STRUCTURES

First concrete building

The Golconde dormitory at Sri Aurobindo Ashram in Pondicherry (now Puducherry) was designed by Czech-American architect Antonin Raymond (1888–1976) and completed in 1948. All its features evolved from a thorough study of the local climatic conditions and the needs of the occupants of the building.

First rock garden

In 1958, Nek Chand, a government road construction worker, discovered an unused place on the outskirts of Chandigarh, which he eventually transformed into a fantasy rock garden with his incredible structures made from scrap. The garden

TOP 10 TALLEST SKYSCRAPERS*

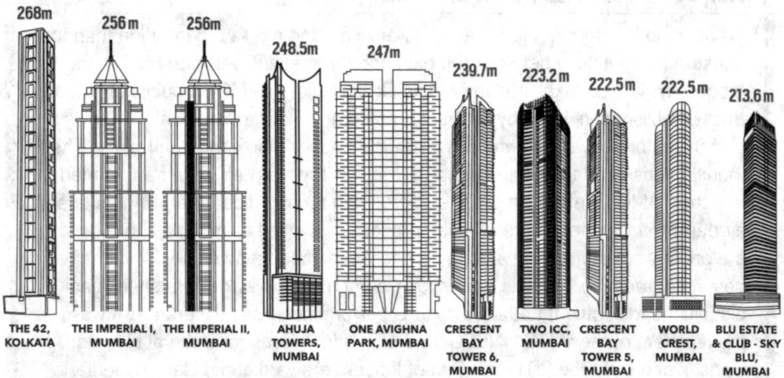

*Completed; Source: Council of Tall Buildings and Urban Habitat (http://www.ctbuh.org); Data accessed on 27 August 2020

comprises 12 acres (4.86 hectares) of sculptures, waterbodies, plants, a stage and a nursery.

First underground market
Palika Bazaar, the first fully air-conditioned underground market at Connaught Place (now Rajiv Chowk) in New Delhi, was set up in 1978.

First permanent crafts market
Dilli Haat in Delhi opened in 1994 with 62 stalls selling handicrafts from all over the country, and 25 food stalls.

The Chowdiah Memorial Hall in Bengaluru, Karnataka, is built in a shape resembling a 7-stringed violin.

First all-steel building
The ICICI headquarters in Mumbai, Maharashtra, designed by Raja Aederi and built in 1995, have a superstructure area of 39,948 sq. m (430,000 sq. ft) with two-level basements of 21,368 sq. m (230,000 sq. ft) and a structural area of 14,000 sq. m (150,700 sq. ft).

WR **Largest bathing complex**
The bathing complex at Shirdi in Nashik District, Maharashtra, built and maintained by Sulabh International for the Shirdi Saibaba Trust, has 120 toilets, 108 bathing cubicles, 28 special toilets and six dressing rooms, besides urinals, to serve 30,000 persons a day.

Tallest building
'The 42', a residential project constructed in Kolkata, West Bengal, is the tallest building in the country at the height of 268 m (879 ft 3 in.). It has 65 floors and was completed in 2019.

LAMO CENTRE: BUILDING ON HERITAGE

What could be more fitting for an alternative art and media organization than to construct a continuity between the past and the present, between history and modernity! The Ladakh Arts and Media Organization (LAMO), a public charitable trust established in 1996 by Monisha Ahmed and Ravina Aggarwal, did just that by restoring two 17th-century historical houses below the Leh Palace. The Munshi house and the Gyaoo house in the Old Town of Leh were transformed into the LAMO Centre's art galleries, screening room, office, library and an open-air performance site. The restoration process preserved as much as possible of the original structure while adding on necessary modern amenities. The centre hosts programmes, projects, workshops, artist residencies, performances and exhibitions to spotlight Ladakh's culture, performing arts and literature. It was the recipient of the 2018 UNESCO Asia-Pacific Awards for Cultural Heritage Conservation and the 2019 'Project of Influence' award at the Best in Heritage conference in Dubrovnik, Croatia.

First Indian to win the Pritzker Architecture Prize
Dr Balkrishna Vithaldas Doshi (b. 26 August 1927), the renowned architect, won the famed Pritzker Architecture Prize on 12 March 2018, making him the first Indian to do so in the award's 40-year history. The Pritzker Prize is referred to as the Nobel Prize in architecture.

Tallest escalator
The Janakpuri West metro station on the Magenta line of the Delhi Metro has India's tallest escalator, which is 15.6 m (51 ft 2 in.) high.

First honorary doctorate in architecture
Joseph Allen Stein, a US-born architect who came to India in 1952, was conferred an honorary doctorate, the first in architecture, by Anna University, Chennai, Tamil Nadu, in September 1999.

SPECIALIZED STRUCTURES

WR Oldest slide

The rock-cut slide at Mamallapuram in Chengalpattu District, Tamil Nadu, is believed to be the world's oldest children's slide.

Most elaborate step well

The Rani Ki Vav ('queen's step well') at Patan, Gujarat, was built by Rani Udayamati, the queen of Bhimadeva I (r. 1022– 64 CE) of the Chalukya dynasty, in memory of her husband. It measures 65 m x 20 m (213 ft 3 in. x 65 ft 7 in.) and is over 28 m (91 ft 10 in.) deep. Originally, more than 800 sculptures decorated it. It currently features on the ₹100 currency note.

First eco-hotel

Asia's first certified eco-friendly hotel, The Orchid, opened in Mumbai, Maharashtra, in 1997.

Poovar Island Resort, Kerala: first floating cottages

First floating cottages

Kabeer Khader and M.R. Narayanan's Floatels India in 1999 launched 20 floating cottages at Poovar Island Resort in Thiruvananthapuram District, Kerala. Designed by architect N. Mahesh, they are built on laminated ferro-cement platforms, with techniques used in building fibreglass boats.

First igloo cafe

India's first cafe in the shape of an igloo opened in Gulmarg, Jammu and Kashmir, on 24 January 2021, at an altitude of 2,650 m (8,694 ft) in the Pir Panjal range of the Himalayas. A part of the Kolahoi Green Group of Hotels and Resorts, the igloo cafe is a 4.5 m (14 ft 9.17 in.) high structure that was completed by a team of 20 members in 15 days and has a diameter of 7.3 m (23 ft 11.4 in.). Accommodating four tables and around 16 people at a time, this is currently Asia's biggest igloo cafe.

Largest underground aquarium

The Bagh-e-Bahu Aquarium at the Baghe-Bahu Garden that surrounds Bahu Fort in Jammu in Jammu and Kashmir, is the largest underground aquarium in India. At more than 220 m (721 ft 9 in.) in length, this fish-shaped aquarium has 24 caves with 13 smaller caves containing freshwater fish, besides those with saltwater fish species.

Largest cricket stadium

The Narendra Modi Stadium (earlier known as the Sardar Patel Stadium) in Ahmedabad, Gujarat, is the largest cricket stadium in the world. Inaugurated on 24 February 2020 after its reconstruction and expansion, the stadium now has the capacity to seat over 132,000 people at a time. It was originally constructed in 1983.

Largest planetarium

Birla Planetarium in Calcutta (now Kolkata, West Bengal), built in 1962, has an inner diameter of 33 m (108 ft 3 in.). It seats around 700 people.

Largest dome

The World Peace Monument is located at the Maharashtra Institute of Technology (MIT)'s World Peace University (MIT-WPU) campus at Loni Kalbhor near Pune, Maharashtra. At a height of 29 m (95 ft), the world's biggest pillar-less dome is built on top of the World Peace Prayer Hall and Library and has a diameter of 48.7 m (160 ft), compared with the Vatican's Dome's 42.5 m (139 ft 5 in.). Completed in 2018, the dome has a bell hanging from the centre.

The Gulmarg Gondola ticket centre

Highest and longest ropeway

The Gulmarg Gondola, a gondola lift that covers 2,540 m (8,333 ft), is a joint venture of the Jammu and Kashmir government and French firm Pomagalski S.A. Its first stage transfers people from Gulmarg at 2,600 m (8,530 ft) to Kongdori station in Kongdori Valley. The second stage goes to 3,747 m (12,293 ft) on Kongdori Mountain.

Longest river ropeway

A 1.8 km (5,906 ft) long ropeway was opened in August 2020 across the River Brahmaputra in Guwahati, Assam. It connects the southern part of the city to the northern part, cutting down travel time from an hour to eight minutes.

Longest railway tunnel

The 11.21 km long Pir Panjal or Banihal Railway Tunnel is the longest transportation tunnel in India. It connects Bichleri Valley, Banihal, to Qazigund in the Kashmir Valley. The first train here was flagged off on 26 June 2013.

EDUCATION

LITERACY

First state/UT with 100 per cent literacy
On 18 April 1991, also the 81st birthday of Dr Malcolm S. Adiseshiah, the doyen of adult education in India, Kerala was declared cent per cent literate.

First 100 per cent literate district
In 1990, Ernakulam, Kerala, with a population of three million then, became the first completely literate district in the country, with a literacy rate of 98.34 per cent in the age group of 5–60 years.

First national education council
The All India Council for Secondary Education (AICSE) was set up in 1955.

State/UT with the highest literacy rate
Kerala, with 96.2 per cent, has the highest rate of literacy among all states, according to the 75th round of the National Sample Survey (NSS) conducted from July 2017 to June 2018.

State/UT with the lowest literacy rate
Andhra Pradesh, with 66.4 per cent, has the lowest rate of literacy among all states, according to the 75th round of the National Sample Survey.

State/UT with highest/lowest female literacy rate
The female literacy rate in Kerala was 95.2 per cent while Rajasthan recorded 57.6 per cent, according to the 75th round of the National Sample Survey.

State/UT with the highest percentage of graduates
Out of a total of around 68 million graduates in the country, Chandigarh, with 24.65 per cent, has the highest percentage of its population as graduates, according to the 2011 Census of India.

A School that Takes Plastic as Fees

The Akshar Foundation School, founded by Parmita Sarma and Mazin Mukhtar in 2016 in Guwahati, Assam, aims to use innovative teaching methods, and build a bridge between conventional academics and vocational training. Initially started with only 20 students, this school has an inventive fee scheme – plastic! Seeing heaps of plastic waste being burned to keep warm during winter in the surrounding areas, Sarma and Mukhtar asked their students to pay their fees in plastic found in and around their houses. Along with spreading awareness in the community about the hazards of burning plastic waste, the school now has around 100 students whose 'fees' are processed into eco-bricks at their recycling centre.

State/UT with the lowest percentage of graduates

Assam has the lowest percentage of graduate population, with only 4.83 per cent as per Census 2011.

Oldest woman to top a literacy programme

Karthiyani Amma, a 96-year-old woman from Alappuzha District, Kerala, scored 98 per cent in *Aksharalaksham* ('Lakh Letter' programme), a project conducted under the Kerala Literacy Programme, which tests reading, writing and basic arithmetic skills.

SCHOOLS

Earliest schools for girls

- St Thomas School for Girls, which was founded in 1789 for the English-speaking community of Calcutta (now Kolkata, West Bengal), was the first girls-only school in India.
- John Elliot Drinkwater Bethune (1801–51) established Calcutta Female School, the first school for girls, with the help of Raja Dakshinaranjan Mukhopadhyay, Ramgopal Ghosh and Pandit Madan Mohan Tarkalankar in 1849. Bethune was the Law member of the Governor General's Council and became the President of the Council of Education. It was maintained from his private funds.
- The Church Missionary Society opened the first boarding school for girls in Tirunelveli, Tamil Nadu, in 1821.

Oldest extant school

St Mary's Church Charity School, now called St George's School, was established in 1715 in the vestry of St Mary's Church, Fort St George, Madras (now Chennai, Tamil Nadu). The school began with 30 students, and the Reverend W. Stevenson as the principal.

First school for the hearing-impaired

Established in 1893, the Calcutta Deaf and Dumb School in Bengal (now in Kolkata, West Bengal) was the first school for the hearing-impaired.

Oldest extant institute for the blind

The Institute for the Blind – Andh Vidyalaya – was established in Lahore (now in Pakistan) in 1939 and shifted to Delhi after Independence in 1947.

First minister of education

Independent India's first minister of education was Maulana Abul Kalam Azad (1888–1958) during 1947–58. Besides establishing the first Indian Institute of Technology (IIT), the Indian Institute of Science (IISc), the School of Planning and Architecture (SPA) and the University Grants Commission (UGC), he set up key cultural and literary organizations – the Sangeet Natak Akademi, the Lalit Kala Akademi, the Sahitya Akademi and the Indian Council for Cultural Relations.

First Indian school abroad

The Indian High School, Dubai, set up in 1957, was the first Indian educational institution abroad.

First to score 100 per cent in Indian School Certificate (ISC) class 12 exam
Dewang Kumar Agarwal, a science student from La Martiniere for Boys, Kolkata, West Bengal, became one of the two students who scored 100 per cent marks in the ISC class 12 exams in the results declared on 7 May 2019. Vibha Swaminathan, a student of humanities from Mallya Aditi International School, Bengaluru, Karnataka, was the other student to score full marks.

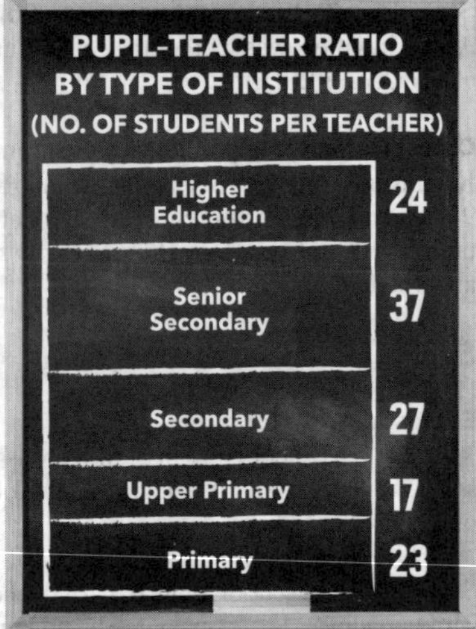

Source: *Educational Statistics at a Glance,* Ministry of Human Resource Development 2018

Largest kindergarten
The Naval KG School in Old Navy Nagar, Colaba, Mumbai, Maharashtra, has two classes – lower KG and upper KG. On an average, the student strength for these two has been over 1,000 in the past years.

Largest chain of government schools
The Kendriya Vidyalaya Sangathan, an autonomous body under the Ministry of Human Resource Development, Government of India, since 15 December 1963, administers 1,245 schools, including three abroad, with 1,388,899 students, as of December 2020.

WR **Largest open school**
Established as an autonomous institution under the Ministry of Human Resource Development in 1989, the National Institute of Open Schooling has a cumulative enrolment of 2.71 million students, as well as 6,222 accredited study centres in India and abroad.

WR **Largest school by student strength within a city**
The City Montessori School in Lucknow, Uttar Pradesh, has more than 20 campuses and 55,000 enrolled students.

Largest free boarding school for tribal children
Established in April 1993, the Kalinga Institute of Social Sciences (KISS) in Bhubaneswar, Odisha, provides free schooling and boarding to 30,000 tribal children from more than 62 different tribes of India.

Only school for grandmothers
Ajibainchi Shala, a school in Fangane Village in Thane, Maharashtra, has 30 students – all grandmothers – aged between 60 and 90 years, who could not go to school when they were young. At Ajibainchi Shala, they receive elementary education, i.e., learning the Marathi alphabet, nursery rhymes and basic maths.

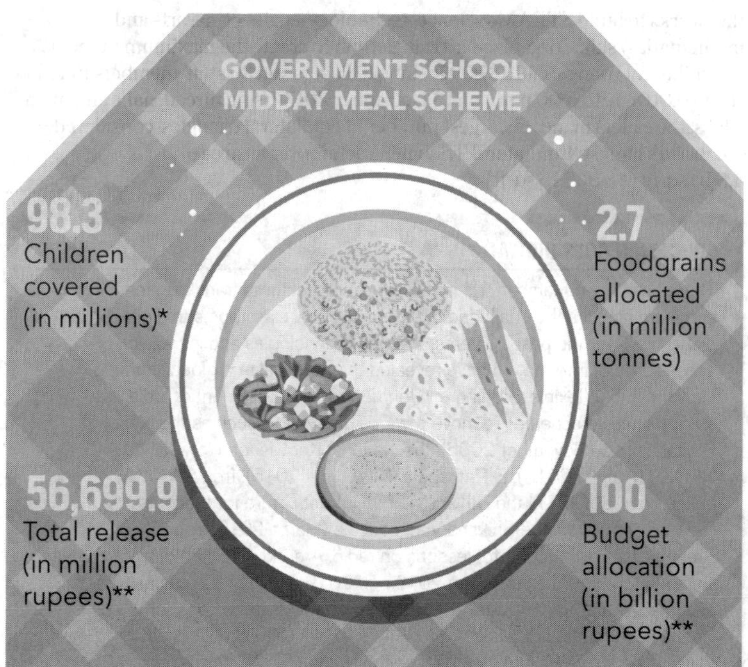

*Project Approval Board approval for 2017–18 **Release as on 11 November 2017; Source: *Educational Statistics at a Glance*, Ministry of Human Resource Development 2018, Government of India

First solar-powered school

Sri Aurobindo International Centre for Education in White Town, Puducherry, became India's first fully solar-powered educational institute in 2014. It was set up in 1943 by Mirra Alfassa, the spiritual collaborator of Sri Aurobindo.

Largest cultural education programme

Routes 2 Roots, a non-governmental voluntary organization, launched VIRSA (derived from *virasat*, meaning heritage), a digital learning programme for performing arts, in 2016. It enables children to learn from reputed gurus and teachers through live daily interactive classes. It reaches 20,000 schools and over two crore (20 million) children, free of cost, in over 150 cities in India and abroad.

Largest school science fair – single venue – single day

Science World, a science club formed by science communicators, in Prayagraj, Uttar Pradesh, in collaboration with Shri Mahaprabhu Public School, organized a science fair on 14 December 2019 at Delhi Public School, Prayagraj, in which 4,272 students of classes 6–12, coming from more than 35 schools, participated.

WR **Largest Equilateral Triangle Fractal**

The Rashtriya Military School in Dholpur, Rajasthan, with technical support, training and methodology provided by Ganityoga, an organization that works to build STEAM (science, technology, engineering, arts and mathematics) skills, organized a Trianglethon to create the maximum number of equilateral triangles – 1,187,097 – by 320 cadets and 30 staff members in 12 hrs (from 6:00 a.m. to 6:00 p.m.) on 13 December 2017. Using thread, nails and metal sticks, the cadets made the largest number of equilateral triangles, considered the world's largest 'Equilateral Triangle Fractal', over an area of 4,540 sq. m (48,868.15 sq. ft).

SUPER 30

EDUCATION GOES DIGITAL

There have been many efforts in the education sector to transform teaching and learning from the chalk and duster of physical classrooms to digital online platforms. Over the past 30 years, evolving technologies and increasing accessibility of information have revealed the potential of a global learning platform and a flexible learning environment. The Government of India has started multiple schemes to move towards digitization, such as the National Digital Library (November 2006), the National Knowledge Network (2010), NROER (August 2013), E-Pathshala (November 2015), free SWAYAM online courses (2017) the DIKSHA digital infrastructure for teachers (September 2017), the Shiksha Vani podcast (March 2019) and SWAYAM Prabha Channels (2020) for lessons on radio. Around 4,450 edtech start-ups were launched in India between 2014 and 2019. The COVID-19 pandemic hastened virtual learning, and schools with the requisite facilities turned online. Kerala became the first state to move its entire public-school education to the digital platform on12 October 2020 with around 45,000 classrooms and 11,000 labs. While IT accessibility remains a hurdle to full digitization, India is moving forward on this path.

Happiness Enters in the Curriculum

Launched in July 2018, 'happiness class' curriculums have made their way into government schools across Delhi. One of the flagship schemes of the Delhi government in the education sector, the course for this class has been designed to develop skills such as self-awareness, mindfulness, critical thinking and effective communication in students, and to help them deal with situations they face. It was India's low ranking of 133 among 155 nations in the global rankings of the World Happiness Report 2018 that led to happiness classes being introduced from nursery to class VIII.

Largest school science fair – multiple venues – single day
More than 22,500 students from 637 upper primary schools of Bastar District, Chhattisgarh, conducted more than 35,000 scientific experiments at 116 centres on 18 January 2017. Called Bastar Vigyan Mela, the annual event was organized by the Department of Education, Bastar District. The students demonstrated scientific activities based on their curriculum and displayed innovative science models.

Largest collection of societal teaching aids
Dr Mihir Kumar Panda from Baleshwar, Odisha, has designed, researched and constructed over 10,000 societal teaching aids and innovations with the sole purpose of popularizing scientific thinking among children and adults across the fields of agriculture, education, technology and environmental development. These aids are funded from his own savings and are stored in his personal laboratory.

HIGHER EDUCATION

First steps
The first educational policy in colonial India was articulated in an 1854 dispatch sent by Sir Charles Wood to the then Governor General Dalhousie. Sir Charles's suggested policy stressed the adoption of vernacular languages in local primary schools, Anglo-vernacular language in high schools and English-medium education in colleges.

First Sanskrit university
The Sampurnanand Sanskrit Vishwavidyalaya in Varanasi, Uttar Pradesh, was the first Sanskrit university in India and is said to have been established in 1791 as a Sanskrit college during Company rule. It has 628 affiliated colleges across India.

Computer Classrooms in Cars

Launched in September 2018, Project Surya Kiran set out to make education accessible and affordable for underprivileged rural children in Ranchi, Jharkhand. Led by entrepreneur Sanwill Srivastava and his education empowerment organization – Edimpact – the project turns Maruti Suzuki EECO cars into solar-powered mobile computer labs, where students can learn information and communication technology (ICT) skills. Lessons include learning the basics of operating a computer, working with Windows 10 and Microsoft Office (Word, Excel, PowerPoint), Internet browsing, emails, cashless transactions and cybersecurity. The project also has plans to provide basic governmental services to rural citizens, like UID (Unique Identification/ Aadhaar) registration, PAN (Permanent Account Number) registration, certificates, applications, and printing of results. Now expanded to Bihar, Meghalaya and Karnataka, the mobile computer labs have helped over 4,000 students by travelling to various locations within villages and conducting lessons.

First modern university
William Carey, a British Christian missionary, opened the first missionary college at Serampore, Bengal (now Srirampur, Hooghly District, West Bengal) in 1818. It was granted the status of a university in 1829.

First modern college
The first college to offer modern education in India was the Hindu College of Calcutta, Bengal (now Kolkata, West Bengal), established in 1817. Scottish watchmaker and philanthropist David Hare was its first principal. It was renamed Presidency College in 1855 and then rechristened the Presidency University on 7 July 2010.

First university act
The Indian Universities Act, 1904, was the first set of educational reforms, which stipulated that universities should offer more teaching and research opportunities, and exert more control over affiliated colleges.

Longest functioning ancient university
Nalanda Mahavihara, located about 95 km south-east of present-day Patna in Bihar, functioned uninterrupted as a university from the Buddha's time in the sixth century BCE up to the 13th century CE, when it was destroyed by Muhammad bin

Bakhtiyar Khilji. The university's curriculum then included many subjects such as logic, medicine, metaphysics, grammar and the sciences. In an effort to emulate the ancient centre of learning, Nalanda University, an exclusively postgraduate and doctoral institution, was started in 2014 in Rajgir, Bihar.

First intermediate colleges
The University of Punjab (now in Chandigarh) and the University of Allahabad (now in Prayagraj, Uttar Pradesh) were the first to establish intermediate colleges, offering two-year courses between high school and a degree college, in 1917, as proposed by the Sadler Commission.

First five universities
The universities of Calcutta (now University of Calcutta), Madras (now University of Madras) and Bombay (now University of Mumbai), which were modelled on London University, were established in 1857 as non-teaching examining bodies. The universities of Punjab (now University of the Punjab in Lahore, Pakistan) in 1881 and Allahabad (now Prayagraj, Uttar Pradesh) in 1887 followed after several years.

India was ranked 115 among 167 countries in education in 2020, according to the Legatum Prosperity Index.

First five residential universities
In 1915, the Banaras Hindu University (BHU) was established as a teaching and residential university, followed by the Universities of Mysore (1916), Patna (1917) and Osmania (1918), and Aligarh Muslim University (1920).

First college for women
The Bethune School of Calcutta (now Kolkata, West Bengal), set up in 1849, was reorganised after it merged with Banga Mahila Vidyalaya. In 1879, Bethune College classes started with one student, Kadambini Bose.

First women's university
The Shreemati Nathibai Damodar Thackersey (SNDT) Women's University was established in Pune, Maharashtra, by D.K. Karve (its first principal) on 5 July 1916. Dr R.P. Paranjpye was its first vice chancellor.

First college alumni association
Dr William Miller, principal of Madras Christian College, Madras (now Chennai, Tamil Nadu) formed the first alumni association in 1891.

First school of mines
The Indian School of Mines – now renamed the Indian Institute of Technology – in Dhanbad, Jharkhand, opened in 1926.

First institute to teach modern architecture
The first course in architecture can be traced to the founding of a draftsman's class at the Sir J.J. School (estab. 1856) of Arts, Bombay (now Mumbai, Maharashtra)

in 1896. In 1913, the course was reorganized, and an independent Department of Architecture was formed.

First department of library science

The Department of Library Science in Delhi University was the first teaching department in the country set up to teach library science. It was the first to start a one-year postgraduate diploma in library science in 1947. The advance course leading to a Master of Library Science (MLibSc) degree was started in 1948, along with provision for research programmes for PhD degrees.

First department of linguistics

The department of linguistics at the Deccan College Postgraduate and Research Institute, Pune, Maharashtra, was founded by Prof. S.M. Katre in 1939. Known as the Department of Indo-European Linguistics during 1939–56, it was a research division. The linguistics course for the Master of Arts degree began in 1958.

First technical university for women

The Indira Gandhi Delhi Technical University for Women (IGDTUW), New Delhi, was founded in 1998.

First IIT

The first Indian Institute of Technology (IIT) was established in 1951 at Kharagpur, West Bengal, at the site of the Hijli Detention Camp. There are 23 approved IITs in India currently.

First metro technology institute

The Institute of Metro and Rail Technology (IMRT) opened in October 2013 in Hyderabad, Telangana. It offers short- and long-term courses to design, build and manage modern rail systems.

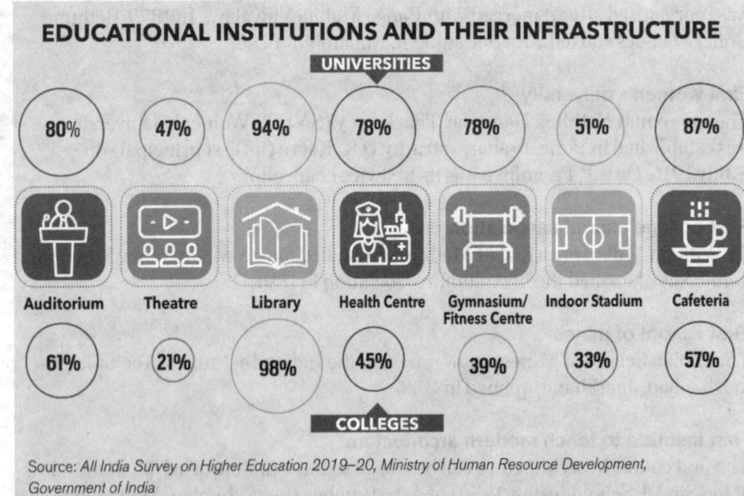

Source: *All India Survey on Higher Education 2019–20, Ministry of Human Resource Development, Government of India*

IIT-Roorkee: first technical university

First technical university
The Thomason College of Engineering, established in 1847 at Roorkee (now in Uttarakhand), was India's first technical university. Its civil engineering department is the oldest one. It is now the Indian Institute of Technology (IIT), Roorkee.

First railway university
The National Rail and Transport University was inaugurated by Prime Minister Narendra Modi on 5 September in 2018 at the Pratap Vilas Palace in Vadodara, Gujarat. This university provides education and training in the latest technological applications related to the railways, such as radio frequency identification, artificial intelligence and satellite-based tracking. It offers a BBA degree in transportation management, a BSc degree in transportation technology, and BTech degrees in rail infrastructural engineering, rail systems and communication engineering.

Record Rewind

Oldest to obtain a PhD

1992

Ghulam Abbas Dalal from Bombay (now Mumbai, Maharashtra) submitted a thesis in Persian when he was 86 years old.

2020

Nonagenarian Paul S. Soromoni was awarded a doctorate in February 2017 by Serampore College (University) in Srirampur, West Bengal, at the age of ninety.

First college of nursing
The Christian Medical College and Hospital, Vellore, is a private educational institute that includes a network of primary, secondary and tertiary care hospitals in and around Vellore, Tamil Nadu. It was started in 1902 by Dr Ida Scudder, a third-generation American missionary in India. In 1903, she began training women compounders at CMC – and started the first school of nursing at CMC – in 1909.

First medical college
William Bentinck (Governor General of India during 1828–35) founded Calcutta Medical College in Calcutta (now Kolkata, West Bengal) on 28 January 1835.

First veterinary research institute
Established in 1889, the Indian Veterinary Research Institute (IVRI) at Izatnagar in Bareilly District, Uttar Pradesh, is India's premier advanced research facility

in the field of veterinary medicine and allied branches. IVRI is currently under the Indian Council of Agricultural Research, New Delhi, and has six regional campuses for graduate, postgraduate and diploma courses.

First AIIMS

The first All India Institute of Medical Sciences (AIIMS) was established in Delhi in 1956 and functions under the Ministry of Health and Family Welfare, Government of India. AIIMS, Delhi, has many firsts to its credit including the first successful cardiac transplant (*See chapter on 'Medical Sciences'*). Currently, there are 15 campuses for AIIMS across the country.

First college of veterinary science

The first college of veterinary science was established at Lahore (now in Pakistan) in 1882. Before this, lectures in veterinary science were given to civilians at the Agricultural College at Saidapet, Madras (now Chennai, Tamil Nadu) and at the College of Sciences in Poona (now Pune, Maharashtra).

First school of industrial arts

The first School of Industrial Arts, established in 1854 at Calcutta, Bengal (now Kolkata, West Bengal), was run by the Industrial Arts Society. The School of Industrial Arts in Madras (now Chennai, Tamil Nadu), opened later that year.

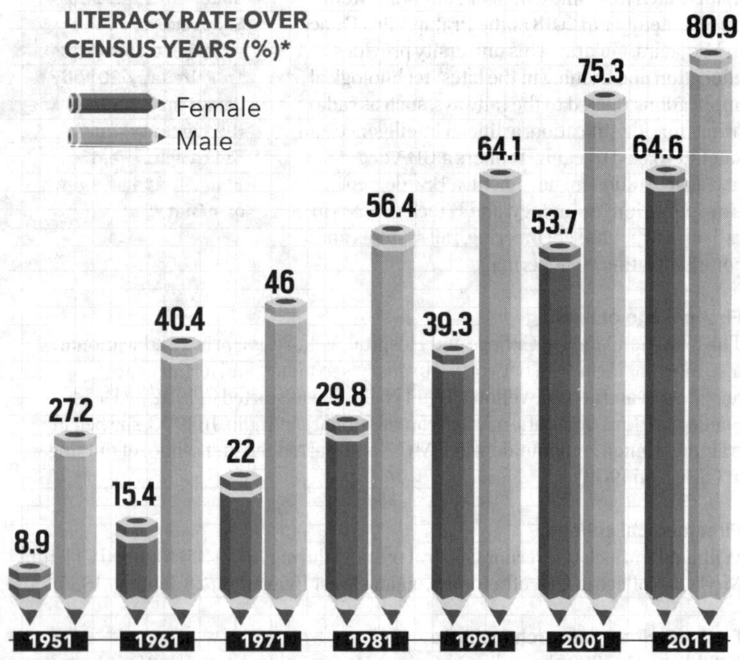

*1951–71: Age group: Five years and above, 1981–2011; Age group: Seven years and above; Source: Office of the Registrar General and Census Commissioner, India

First statistical institute

The Indian Statistical Institute (ISI) was established in 1931 in Calcutta, Bengal (now Kolkata, West Bengal), by scientist and statistician P.C. Mahalanobis.

First university of fisheries and ocean studies

The College of Fisheries in Panangad, Cochin (now Kochi), Kerala, established in 1979, was a constituent college of the Kerala Agricultural University. The Kerala Legislative Assembly passed a bill on 30 December 2010, seeking to establish the Kerala University of Fisheries and Ocean Studies (KUFOS) with its headquarters at the College of Fisheries. It is the first university dedicated to the study of fisheries and allied disciplines.

First institute of oceanography

The National Institute of Oceanography, founded on 1 January 1966, is an autonomous research organization that undertakes scientific research and studies of special oceanographic features of the northern Indian Ocean. The institute has its main campus in Dona Paula, Goa, and regional centres have been set up in Mumbai, Kochi and Visakhapatnam.

First institute for population sciences

The Institute for Population Sciences in Bombay (now Mumbai), Maharashtra, earlier known as the Demographic Training and Research Centre, was established in 1956 to prepare students for administrative, teaching, research and consultancy careers in population sciences.

First university for the study of outer space

The Indian Institute of Space Science and Technology (IIST) in Thiruvananthapuram, Kerala, is the first university in Asia to be solely dedicated to the study and research of outer space. was set up by the Indian Space Research Organization (ISRO) under the Department of Space, Government of India, in 2007. The institute offers undergraduate, postgraduate and doctorate programmes with a focus on space science, space technology, geoinformatics, earth system sciences and their applications.

First gemmological institute

The Gemmological Institute of India (GII), a non-profit public institution founded by the Gem and Jewellery Exporters Association, was established in Bombay (now Mumbai), Maharashtra, in 1971 to promote the scientific knowledge of gemmology.

Oldest institute for oriental studies

The Asiatic Society, Calcutta, Bengal (now Kolkata, West Bengal) was founded by Sir William Jones, a Sanskrit scholar and judge at the Supreme Court, Calcutta, on 15 January 1784. Its logo depicted the face of Sir William Jones.

First institute of mass communication

The first institute to provide a formal education in mass communication was the Indian Institute of Mass Communication (IIMC). Set up by the Government of India in 1965, it is now located in the JNU (Jawaharlal Nehru University) campus in New Delhi. In 1966, it was made an autonomous institution under the Ministry of Information and Broadcasting and offers courses related to different media.

First department of English
English was first introduced as a subject in Delhi College, New Delhi, in 1828.

Oldest school of art
Sir J.J. School of Art in Bombay (now Mumbai, Maharashtra), was founded by Sir Jamsetjee Jeejeebhoy in 1833.

First department of sociology
The University of Bombay (now University of Mumbai, Maharashtra) set up the first department of sociology in 1919.

First home science college
Lady Irwin College, established in 1932 in New Delhi, was the country's first home science college.

First institute of fashion technology
The Ministry of Textiles, Government of India, set up the National Institute of Fashion Technology (NIFT) in Delhi on 24 August 1987 to provide professional human resources for the textile industry. There are currently 17 NIFT campuses in the country.

First cartoonists' institute
Fifteen Indian cartoonists, under the noted cartoonist B.V. Ramamurthy of the *Deccan Herald*, established a charitable organization called the Indian Institute of

Burning the Midnight Oil: Abhyas Gali, Mumbai's 'Study Street'

Tucked away near Poddar Hospital in Mumbai, Maharashtra, is a peaceful street that goes by the name of Abhyas Gali ('practice alley'). Also called Padhai Gali ('study alley'), it is said to have been around since 1920 as a haven for students, and was originally a part of Sudam Kali Ahire Marg. Armed with books and stationery, students are seen taking a spot and starting on their night of undisturbed studies. Considered to be responsible for shaping the career of thousands of students, the street is equipped with bright lights, clean benches, and motivational art painted by Misaal Mumbai, an initiative led by artist Rouble Nagi.

Cartoonists in Bangalore (now Bengaluru), Karnataka, in December 2000. It aims to offer a common platform for Indian cartoonists.

First institute for studying footwear design

The Footwear Design and Development Institute (FDDI), set up in 1986 at Noida, Uttar Pradesh, trains students in footwear technology, computer-aided designing and pattern making.

First law university

The National Law School of India University (NLSIU) in Bangalore (now Bengaluru), Karnataka, was established on 29 August 1987. Currently, there are 23 such national law universities in India.

First exclusive photography institute

The Light and Life Academy in Ootacamund (Ooty, now Udhagamandalam), Tamil Nadu, was established in 1998, supported by Kodak India; Eastman Kodak, USA, Lakshmi Machine Works, Coimbatore, Kerala; Calumet, USA; Photoquip India Limited and ZenTask, India; and Gretag Imaging, Switzerland.

Indian Institute of Management (IIM) Calcutta: first national institute of management

First national institute of management

The Indian Institute of Management Calcutta (now in Kolkata, West Bengal) was established for the pursuit of postgraduate studies in management on 17 November 1961 by the Government of India, in collaboration with the MIT Sloan School of Management, USA, the Government of West Bengal, the Ford Foundation, and several Indian industries.

Ranjitsinh Disale Wins the Global Teacher Prize 2020

He turned a decrepit school building into a centre of learning, translated the textbooks into the students' mother tongue and embedded them with unique QR codes directed to audio and video content, thus starting the QR-coded textbook revolution in India. No wonder then that Ranjitsinh Disale from Zilla Parishad Primary School in Paritewadi, Solapur District, Maharashtra, was announced the winner of the Global Teacher Prize 2020 on 3 December 2020 for his efforts to promote education for girls. From over 12,000 nominations from 140 countries, besides Disale, two others from India – citizenship teacher Shuvajit Payne from Shiksha Niketan Barefoot College in Rajasthan and computer science teacher Vineeta Garg from SRDAV Public School in Delhi – were in the top 50 shortlist for the prize. Worth $1 million (₹76,172,500 approx.), the Global Teacher Prize was set up by the Varkey Foundation, UK, in partnership with UNESCO in 2015 to recognize one exceptional teacher for his/her outstanding contribution to the profession and to emphasize the importance of teachers in society. Marking a first in the award's six-year history, Disale shared half the award money with the other nine finalists.

Ranjitsinh Disale

First model-training school
Catwalk, set up in Bombay (now Mumbai), Maharashtra, in 1990 by leading model Lubna Adams, was the first training school in India for fashion models.

First college of physical education
The YMCA College of Physical Education in Madras (now Chennai, Tamil Nadu), established in 1920 by Harry Crowe Buck of Pennsylvania, USA, was Asia's first college for physical education. It is now affiliated to the Tamil Nadu Physical Education and Sports University, and is considered a pioneer in the promotion of sports for persons with disabilities.

First radio jockey training academy
The Academy of Broadcasting in Chandigarh, set up in July 2003, was the first academy for training radio jockeys.

First yoga university
The Bihar Yoga Bharati in Munger, Bihar, an institute for advanced studies in yoga, set up in 1964, was the first of its kind in Asia.

First finishing school for women
Former actor Anooradha Patel set up The Orchid, India's first finishing school for women, in 1987 in Bombay (now Mumbai), Maharashtra. She is currently the director of the Dynamic Training Academy, offering courses in grooming and personality development.

First university for the disabled
The Jagadguru Rambhadracharya Handicapped University in Chitrakoot, Uttar

Pradesh, was established as a private university on 27 September 2001 to provide higher and professional education only to persons with disabilities in four categories: the visually impaired, the hearing-impaired, the mobility-impaired and the mentally impaired, as defined in the Persons with Disability Act, 1995.

First national institute for the visually impaired

The National Institute for the Visually Impaired was established in Dehradun, Uttarakhand, in 1979.

First college for the hearing-challenged

The St Louis Institute for the Deaf and Blind in Madras (now Chennai), Tamil Nadu, which opened on 8 September 1993, was the first college for the hearing-impaired in the country. It is affiliated to the University of Madras and offers a BCom degree in Tamil and English mediums, and a BCA degree in the English medium.

State/UT with the highest student enrolment in higher educational institutions

Uttar Pradesh has the highest student enrolment in the country with 6,469,367 students enrolled in higher education. It is followed by Maharashtra with 4,230,326 students and Tamil Nadu with 3,414,196 students in the year 2018–19 as per the AISHE (All India Survey on Higher Education) report 2019.

First military school

The Prince of Wales Royal Indian Military College in Dehradun, Uttarakhand, now called the Rashtriya Indian Military College (RIMC), was inaugurated on 13 March 1922 by Prince Edward VIII, the Prince of Wales, to provide training to Indian boys to become officers in the armed forces.

First university with undergraduate and postgraduate courses for army personnel

In December 2017, Jamia Millia Islamia, Delhi, became the first university in India to offer undergraduate and postgraduate programmes for army personnel through its Centre for Distance and Open Learning. Originally established at Aligarh in

Record Rewind

Most postgraduate degrees

2007

Dr C.D. Dwivedi from Jamshedpur, Jharkhand, had 15 postgraduate degrees. He acquired his first postgraduate degree in English literature from Agra University in 1954. His latest master's degree was obtained in 2006.

2020

Anil Kumar Yadav (b. 4 June 1968) from Chandigarh has obtained 21 postgraduate degrees, awarded to him by 12 different universities in India, spread across nine states and Union Territories. His first postgraduate degree was in sociology from Annamalai University, Tamil Nadu, in 1995. His latest degree was an MA (political science) from the University of North Bengal, West Bengal, in March 2019.

Eleven Chairs Established in Honour of Women Scientists

The establishment of 11 chairs in the names of women scientists at science institutes across the country was announced on 28 February 2019, which is also observed as National Science Day, by women and child development minister, Smriti Irani. Aiming to honour their contribution in the field of science, inspire women and encourage the participation of young girts in STEM (science, technology, engineering and mathematics), the initiative features the names of India's foremost women scientists, both contemporary and from the past, including cytogeneticist Archana Sharma (1932–2008), botanist Janaki Ammal (1897–1984), organic scientist Darshan Ranganatham (1941–2001), chemist Asima Chatterjee (1917–2006), doctor Kadambini Ganguly (1861–1923), anthropologist Iravati Karve (1905–70), meteorologist Anna Mani (1918–2001), engineer Rajeshwari Chatterjee (1922–2010), mathematician Raman Parimala (b. 21 November 1948), physicist Bibha Chowdhuri (1913–91) and biomedical researcher Kamal Ranadive (1917–2001).

Kadambini Ganguly

the United Provinces in 1920, Jamia Millia Islamia became a central university in 1988.

First defence academy

The National Defence Academy at Khadakwasla, Maharashtra, was opened on 16 January 1955, to give its students a military orientation to join any of the three services of the Indian armed forces.

First university to offer free education to transgender students

In a unique initiative, Manonmaniam Sundaranar University (MSU), Tirunelveli District, Tamil Nadu, made all its study courses free for transgender students from the academic year 2017–18 onwards. Its aim is to help improve the economic well-being of the transgender community.

First woman Indian resident to be elected to the Royal Society

Dr Gagandeep Kang, a clinical scientist working in India as a professor in the Department of Gastrointestinal Science at the Christian Medical College in Vellore, Tamil Nadu, and formerly the executive director of the Translational Health Science and Technology Institute in Faridabad, Haryana, was elected to the fellowship of the Royal Society of London in 2019. Dr Kang is a leading medical researcher of viral infections in children in the country and the testing of rotaviral vaccines.

First university only for tribal students

The Kalinga Institute of Social Sciences, founded by Achyuta Samanta in Bhubaneswar, Odisha, became India's first exclusively tribal university when it was granted university status by the Ministry of Human Resources in 2017. It admits only tribal students and is the only known university in the world to do so. Seven new innovative departments are being introduced in the first phase to provide an impetus to research tribal studies. Nearly 37,000 students are imparted free education from grade one to the postgraduate level.

Oldest course in pharmacy

Education in pharmacy is among the oldest in modern education on the Indian subcontinent. The Portuguese introduced the first pharmacy course along with a medical course in 1842 at an old Portuguese school known as 'Escola Medica de Goa'. It was renamed the Goa College of Pharmacy in 1963 and moved to its current premises, a former Portuguese school in Panaji. The course was upgraded to a full-fledged degree course (BPharm) under the University of Bombay (now University of Mumbai), Maharashtra. The college is now affiliated to Goa University and is run by the Government of Goa.

First correspondence courses

The University of Delhi introduced non-formal education in 1962 with its first correspondence course.

First course in oncology

In 1984, the Adyar Cancer Institute, Madras (now Chennai), Tamil Nadu, started a full-time three-year super-speciality course in medical oncology.

First course in artificial intelligence

IIT Hyderabad in Telangana has become the first Indian institute to offer a full-fledged course in artificial intelligence (AI). India is the second country to offer a BTech in AI, after the USA.

 **In India, there are 16 universities exclusively for women.**

First government institute to offer a course in scuba-diving

Goa University became the first government institute to offer a course in scuba-diving in 2012.

First postgraduate degree

Calcutta University in Calcutta, Bengal (now Kolkata, West Bengal), conferred the first postgraduate degree (MA) in India in 1862.

First to obtain a PhD in library science

In 1957, the University of Delhi awarded the first PhD in library science to D.B. Krishna Rao for his study on 'Facet analysis and depth of agriculture classification' under Dr S.R. Ranganathan and Dr S. Dasgupta.

First engineer

Nilmani Mitra (1828–94) is considered the first Indian to obtain an engineering degree, from the Roorkee Engineering College (now IIT-Roorkee), Uttarakhand. A civil engineer, he built many famous mansions in 19th-century Calcutta, besides the Sadharan Brahmo Samaj and the Indian Association for the Cultivation of Science buildings.

Most postgraduate degrees obtained by a woman
Vandana Agrawal (b. 12 November 1954) from Alwar, Rajasthan, has 10 MA degrees, the highest number of postgraduate degrees attained by a woman in India.

First Indian to receive a PhD from a foreign university
Agostino Lourenco of Margao, Goa, is considered to have received his PhD in chemistry in Paris, France, in 1860.

First woman doctor
Kadambini Ganguly née Bose obtained the Graduate of Bengal Medical College degree to become the first woman doctor in 1888.

First woman vice chancellor
Hansa Jivraj Mehta (1897–1995) set a benchmark when she became the vice chancellor of the Maharaja Sayajirao University of Baroda, Vadodara, Gujarat in 1949.

Oldest to clear NEET (PG)
- Sixty-four-year-old Dr (Col) Rita Dadwal passed the NEET (PG) 2018 examinations and enrolled in an MD in the anaesthesiology course at Dr Rajendra Prasad Medical College in Kangra, Himachal Pradesh. After retiring from the armed forces, she worked as an administrator in civil hospitals in the state.
- Sixty-four-year-old Jay Kishore Pradhan cleared the NEET 2020 examinations and enrolled for an MBBS course at the Veer Surendra Sai University of Technology, Odisha. He is a retired banker.

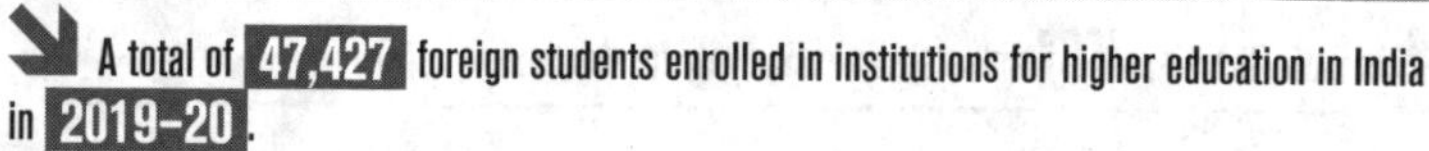
A total of **47,427** foreign students enrolled in institutions for higher education in India in **2019–20**.

Oldest to become a matriculate
Kirit Mahiji Makwana (b. 16 April 1959), then a housekeeper at the Willingdon Sports Club, Haji Ali, Bombay (now Mumbai), Maharashtra, passed the SSC examination held by the Maharashtra State Board of Secondary and Higher Education in March 2008, at the age of 48 years.

Oldest to graduate
Govind Laxman Parulekar (b. 26 April 1928) completed his BA degree from Yashwantrao Chavan Maharashtra Open University, Nashik, Maharashtra, in November 2006 at 76 years of age and his LLB from the University of Mumbai in May 2014, to become the oldest double graduate at 86 years 1 month.

Oldest woman to obtain a PhD
Mandakini Krishneshwar Dravid (b. 19 July 1927) from Pune, Maharashtra, completed her PhD in the field of social work from Pune University in April 2008, at 81 years of age.

Oldest person to obtain a DLitt
Narayan Lal Kankar was 86 years old when he was awarded his DLitt in Sanskrit, which he had completed in 2011, by the University of Rajasthan on 7 July 2015, thereby becoming the oldest Indian to be awarded the degree.

First gender-neutral hostel
On 5 April 2018, the administration of the Tata Institute of Social Sciences (TISS) in Mumbai, Maharashtra, earmarked the ground floor of the existing girls hostel (Hostel IV) with its 10 two-seater rooms to accommodate gender non-conforming students of the institute. The hostel is a culmination of a long-standing campaign by the Queer Collective, which is an informal student body that advocates a safe space for LGBTQ+ students. Seventeen gender-neutral students moved into the hostel after this initiative was introduced.

First gender-neutral certificate
The National Academy of Legal Studies and Research (NALSAR), Hyderabad, Telangana, issued the first gender-neutral graduation certificate in June 2015.

First Indian vice chancellor
In 1890, Gurudas Banerjee became the vice chancellor of Calcutta University, Bengal (now West Bengal).

First women graduates
Kadambini Ganguly and Chandramukhi Basu passed the BA examination from Calcutta University (now in Kolkata, West Bengal) in 1883.

30

Record Rewind

Oldest to obtain a postgraduate degree

1992

K.K. Kapoor of Kanpur, Uttar Pradesh, obtained an MD in the pharmacology discipline of medical sciences at the age of 70 from Medical College, Kanpur.

2020

Raj Kumar Vaish (b. 1 April 1920) enrolled for an MA in economics from Nalanda Open University, Bihar, in September 2015, 77 years after graduating from Agra University in 1938. He completed his postgraduation when he was 98 years old.

First woman Bachelor of Medicine
Anandibai Joshi was the first Indian woman to obtain a Bachelor of Medicine degree in 1886 from the University of Philadelphia in the USA, but she did not practise medicine.

First woman law graduate
Cornelia Sorabji (b. 1866) graduated in law from the University of Bombay (now University of Mumbai) in 1894.

First woman to obtain a PhD
Sita Poovaiah of Coorg (now Kodagu, Karnataka) obtained a doctorate in dance from the University of Bombay (now University of Mumbai) in the 1940s.

First woman engineer
A. Lalitha (b. 1919) qualified as an electrical engineer from the College of Engineering, Guindy (CEG), University of Madras (now in Chennai, Tamil Nadu) in 1937.

Longest-serving college principal
Dr Rajendra Prasad, who served as the principal of Ramjas College, University of Delhi, from July 1985 to February 2017, was the longest-serving principal, with 31 years of service.

First to pass Indian Medical Service examination
Surjo Kumar Chakraborty (1826–74), MRCS, was the first Indian to pass the Indian Medical Service (IMS) examination in 1855. He subsequently became the first Indian professor of Materia Medica at Calcutta Medical College in the second half of the 19th century. He was the first Indian to pass this exam in January 1855.

First to be elected to the Royal Society of London
Ardaseer Cursetjee Wadia, a Parsi shipbuilder and engineer from the Wadia shipbuilding family, was the first Indian elected to the Royal Society of London in 1841.

First transgender principal
Dr Manabi Bandyopadhyay was the first transgender person to become principal of the Krishnanagar Women's College in Nadia District, West Bengal, on 9 June 2015.

Dr Manabi Bandyopadhyay: first transgender principal

Youngest chancellor
Dileep K. Nair became the youngest chancellor of a university in the country when he took office at the North East Frontier Technical University (NEFTU) in Arunachal Pradesh in April 2017. He was 38 years old at the time.

First student with cerebral palsy to complete a BHMS degree
In April 2015, Shivam Sharma (b. 7 September 1991) became the first cerebral palsy (75 per cent permanent disability) student to complete the Bachelor of Homoeopathic Medicine and Surgery (BHMS) degree. He was a student of the Homoeopathic Medical College and Hospital, Chandigarh, affiliated to Punjab University.

Only Hebrew teacher
Dr Khurshid Imam, assistant professor of Hebrew at the Centre for Arabic

MILESTONES IN EDUCATION

1961

The National Council of Educational Research and Training (NCERT) was formed to establish a common national system of education.

1968

The first National Education Policy (NEP)

The first policy was proposed for a National School System to provide compulsory education to all students up to 14 years.

1986

New National Education Policy

This policy set out to remove disparities and equalize educational opportunities.

1992

NEP 1986 was modified in 1992. It envisaged a common all-India entrance examination for admission to professional and technical programmes.

1995

The Midday Meal scheme was launched.

2001

The National Council for Teacher Education (NCTE) Regulations, 2001, came into force to determine the minimum qualifications for recruitment of teachers in schools.

2009

The Right of Children to Free and Compulsory Education Act or Right to Education Act (RTE) laid down the modalities for the education for children of 6–14 years under Article 21A of the Indian Constitution. The Act came into force on 1 April 2010.

2020

National Education Policy 2020 (NEP 2020)

Providing a comprehensive structure for elementary and higher education, the policy was approved by the Union Cabinet of India on 29 July 2020 and has replaced NEP 1986.

and African Studies, School of Language, Literature and Culture Studies at the Jawaharlal Nehru University (JNU), New Delhi, is the only teacher of Hebrew to hold a tenured position in Indian academia.

Longest-running event by an institute

The 91st edition of Regatta took place at the Boat Club of the College of Engineering, Pune, Maharashtra, on 10 March 2019 on the River Mula. As many as 300 students participated in water sports like rowing, kayaking and canoeing. The first edition was held in 1928.

First use of virtual reality in academics

Arvind Malik (b. 15 August 1980), an assistant professor at the PES Institute of Technology and Management, Shivamogga, Karnataka, conducted the first classes utilizing virtual reality for MBA students (third semester) on 'Consumer Behaviour', at the institute campus, on 28 October 2016.

WR Largest open university

The Indira Gandhi National Open University (IGNOU) at Maidan Garhi, New Delhi, has the distinction of being the largest open university in the world, serving more than three million enrolled students through its 21 schools of studies, and a network of 67 regional centres, around 2,667 learner support centres and 29 overseas partner institutions.

WR First satellite for education

The world's first satellite dedicated to education, called the EDUSAT GSAT-3, was launched by the Indian Space Research Organization on 20 September 2004 from the Satish Dhawan Space Centre at Sriharikota, Andhra Pradesh. Then the heaviest satellite launched by an indigenously made rocket, it uses the virtual classroom concept to facilitate long-distance education, specifically in remote villages and areas without good technical institutes, besides adult literacy and teacher training programmes.

Men make up the majority of the total number of teachers in India, at 57.8%. Female teachers account for 42.2% of the total.

First college for sanitation workers

The Harpic World Toilet College, located in Aurangabad in Maharashtra, was established in August 2018. It is the first of its kind in the country and has trained more than 3,200 sanitation workers. It trains workers in the required skills and also makes them aware of the occupational hazards related to the job. It is run by British consumer goods company Reckitt Benckiser.

Attaining 100 per cent in JEE Main 2017

Kalpit Veerval (b. 22 April 1999), the son of a compounder in a government hospital and a schoolteacher in Udaipur, Rajasthan, was the first ever candidate to top the Joint Entrance Examination (JEE) Main 2017 for IITs and other engineering colleges in the country, with a score of 360 out of 360. The 17-year-old was ranked first both in the general category and the SC/ST/OBC category.

First dedicated educational centres for disability studies

- The first Centre for Disability Studies in a central university was inaugurated by the then Mizoram chief minister Lalthanhawla on 5 July 2018 at Mizoram University in the state's capital Aizawl. It was set up by the Department of Empowerment of Persons with Disabilities, under the Ministry of Social Justice and Empowerment, Government of India. The centre offers short-term courses as well as postgraduate diploma courses in a subject related to disability, besides undertaking research projects on related themes. It also plans to introduce ID cards for differently abled people, to facilitate them in education, health and political engagement.
- In 2006, the Centre for Disability Studies and Action, Tata Institute of Social Sciences (TISS), Mumbai, Maharashtra, was the first-of-its-kind centre established in a deemed university set-up with a postgraduate programme in disability studies and action in social work.

First educational crowd-funding platform

In 2017, Edudharma, a volunteer team based in Coimbatore, Tamil Nadu, initiated the first crowd-funding platform in India to provide access to affordable and good-quality education to hundreds of deserving underprivileged children. Donors were given access to the students' achievements as well as academic records, thus assuring them that their money would reach the right beneficiary.

ARCHIVES AND LIBRARIES

First library

Christian missionaries at Serampore, Bengal (now Srirampur, West Bengal) set up their first library (later the William Carey Library) in 1800, which became the hub of their educational activities. The Reverend John Fountain, sent to India in 1796 to assist William Carey, a missionary, was its first librarian.

First human library

The first human library was conducted for two hours on 26 June 2016 at Indore, Madhya Pradesh, by founder and organizer Amrita Goel. In human libraries, a person (a 'human book') tells the person who has selected him or her a story (a unique personal experience), usually for 20–30 mins.

First toy library in a school

On the occasion of former prime minister Atal Bihari Vajpayee's birth anniversary (25 December), the Atal Toy Library was inaugurated at the South Delhi Municipal Corporation (SDMC) School in Sector 9, R.K. Puram, New Delhi, on 26 December 2016, to promote toys as tools of learning. Its collection of toys can be borrowed by around 300 underprivileged children at a time.

First online Braille library

Launched in 2012 by the National Institute for the Visually Handicapped (NIVH), Dehradun, Uttarakhand, to commemorate the birth anniversary of Louis Braille on 4 January, the online Braille library provides access to 12,000 books in 10 languages in a user-friendly format. The library can be accessed at *http://nivh.gov.in/index.php/national-braille-library.*

SUPER 30

INSPIRATION ON THE BOARD

Beula Gabriel: A teacher by profession, Beula Gabriel started St Joseph's Secondary School in Hyderabad, Andhra Pradesh (now in Telangana), in 1993 – a school where first-generation schoolgoers like the children of domestic help, rickshaw pullers, labourers and watchmen, often denied education in other schools, are welcomed. Acclaimed as an exceptional educator, Gabriel even sold her home to sustain the school when funds were low. The school currently has an enrolment of 300 students from kindergarten to class ten.

Geeta Dharmarajan: A writer and social entrepreneur, Geeta Dharmarajan founded the non-profit organization, Katha, in 1988 to work with underprivileged children across the country and remains its president today. With a career spanning more than three decades, she has been an influential force in children's education and literature and is responsible for inculcating the joy of reading among children, and providing entrepreneurship-, income-generation– and skills-based training to women. Her work at Katha has impacted more than 10,000,000 children, 39,000 youth, 47,000 women, 1,000 schools, and 2,000 low-income communities in India. Honoured with the Padma Shri award in 2012 for her contribution to education and literature, Dharmarajan has over 48 published books and 450 articles in leading newspapers and magazines to her name. In 1988, she started a magazine called Tamasha! for the underserved communities, and now has nearly 1 lakh (0.1 million) grassroots volunteers and advocates working for Katha, including a team of around 8,000 writers, translators, illustrators, and photographers.

Sanjit 'Bunker' Roy: After attending the Doon School (1956–61) and St Stephen's College (1962–67), Roy was so moved by the Bihar famine in 1965 that he worked as an unskilled labourer digging wells for five years in the Ajmer District of Rajasthan. Exposed to the rich traditional knowledge, skills and wisdom of the rural poor, he started the Barefoot College in 1972, following Mahatma Gandhi's style of working. He established the first and only fully solar-electrified college in rural India to serve the rural poor. The college is known for training 885 illiterate rural women living in 410 non-electrified villages from 94 of the least developed countries of the world, and solar-electrifying 40,000 houses. Roy was awarded the Padma Shri in 1986 and recognized by *Time* magazine in 2010 as one of the 100 most influential people in the world. He received an honorary degree from Princeton University, USA, in 2017.

Dr Mithu Alur: The founder chairperson of The Spastic Society of India in 1972 – now rechristened ADAPT (Able Disabled All People Together) – Dr Mithu Alur is an educator, writer and disability rights activist known for her work for inclusive education for children with disabilities. Instrumental in guiding government policy for people with disabilities, Alur established the National Resource Centre for Inclusion (NRCI), in Mumbai, Maharashtra, in 1999 to include disabled children from special schools into normal schools. She has six books on inclusive education to her name, and a Padma Shri, which she received in 1989.

First pet library

The library at the Birla Industrial and Technological Museum, Kolkata, allows you to take pets home in much the same way you borrow books. The library began in 2009 to instil affection for animals among the young.

First operational digital library network

DELNET is the first operational digital library network in the country. It was started as a project of the India International Centre in 1988 and registered as a society in 1992. 'Library network' refers to an interconnected platform of a group of libraries with the common objective to acquire and develop the unique collection of each and to avoid duplication of material.

First classical library

The mission of the Murty Classical Library of India is to present the pre-modern classics of Indian literature from the past two millennia, a part of world literature's treasured heritage, to a new generation. It began publishing classics in January 2015. The original Indic text, in the appropriate script, is accompanied by a modern English translation on the opposite page. The library was established through a generous grant from Rohan Murty, the son of Infosys co-founder N.R. Narayana Murty and social worker and author Sudha Murty.

Biggest public library system

The Delhi Public Library, started as a UNESCO project in 1951 by the Government of India, is the biggest public library system in India and reportedly the busiest set of public libraries in South Asia. The library network consists of a central library, three branch libraries, 20 sub-branch libraries, one community library, eight resettlement colony libraries, one Braille library, 100 mobile library service points (including 25 Braille mobile library points) and 33 deposit stations in the Union Territory of Delhi and the NCR. It has a collection of over 1.8 million books in English and other Indian languages.

Only underground library

Almost 128 km from Jaisalmer, Rajasthan, in Bhadriya Village in Jaisalmer District, is an underground library 16 ft (4.87 m) below ground level. Above this library is a temple of Devi Bhadariya Mata. The library can seat 4,000 persons and is maintained by the trustees of the temple. As many as 900,000 books are lined up in 562 shelves with glass shutters. The library was started by Harbansh Singh Nirmal, who was an avid reader and more popularly known as Bhadariya Maharaj. The books were collected from all over the world since 1998, and many thousands were gifted to him. The books are mostly in Hindi, and their subjects range from science and astronomy to astrology and history, besides a number of classic Indian texts, atlases and dictionaries.

Largest university library

The Maulana Azad Library, the central library of Aligarh Muslim University in Aligarh, is the largest university library in Asia. The current seven-floor library houses about 1,400,000 books, periodicals, pamphlets, 43,000 e-journals and manuscripts, paintings and photographs. It was inaugurated by Jawaharlal Nehru, the first prime minister of India, in 1960.

Only bookshop-cum-library on a lake

Gulshan Books, a bookshop-cum-library set up in May 2016, has a reading room, a café and over 80,000 books. Located on Nehru Park Island on the Dal Lake in Srinagar, Jammu and Kashmir, it can be reached by a shikara.

Largest film archives

The National Film Archives were set up in 1964 in Poona (now Pune), Maharashtra, as a media unit of the Ministry of Information and Broadcasting, Government of India. In addition to more than 100,000 films, it has 157,687 photographs, 23,748 film posters, 14,210 song booklets, over 100,000 press clippings and more.

Oldest and largest library

The National Library in Kolkata, West Bengal, has more than 2.6 million books and arrangement for seating around 1,700 readers. The Calcutta Public Library (established in 1836) was merged with the Imperial Library (established in 1891) in 1903. In 1953, it was inaugurated as the National Library with B.S. Kesavan as the first librarian.

A first-of-its-kind tram library

A specially designed tram library to run along Kolkata's College Street route was inaugurated on 1 October 2020. The tramcar has free Wi-Fi to help passengers read e-books while they travel. A boon for bibliophiles and students, the library has books and magazines, including those on competitive examinations such as the civil services, WBCS (West Bengal Civil Services), GMAT (Graduate Management Admission Test) and GRE (Graduate Record Examinations). The Kolkata tram library gives a new dimension to the city's electric tram service which has been in existence since 1902.

First transgender resources library

The country's first transgender library was opened as part of the transgender resource centre in Viswanathapuram, Madurai, Tamil Nadu, in 2016. The centre focuses on providing materials to help people become aware of the non-binary gender and ambisexual people in the country.

Library with the most comprehensive collection of ancient manuscripts

The Raza Library at Hamid Manzil Qila in Rampur, Uttar Pradesh, houses the most comprehensive collection of ancient manuscripts from South Asia. This treasure trove of Indo-Islamic culture was founded in 1774 by Nawab Faizullah Khan of the erstwhile princely state of Rampur. It has a collection of 17,000 manuscripts, 3,000 works of Islamic calligraphy, 5,000 miniature paintings, astronomical instruments, nearly 1,500 gold, silver and copper coins from fifth century BCE to the 19th century, and rare illustrated works in Arabic and Persian.

Library of Tibetan works and archives

The Library of Tibetan Works and Archives in Dharamshala, Himachal Pradesh, is one of the most important libraries and institutions of Tibetan Buddhist works in the world. Inaugurated by the Dalai Lama on 11 June 1970, it contains manuscripts and archives related to Tibetan history, politics, culture and art, relocated from

Tibet in 1959. There are over 80,000 Tibetan Buddhist manuscripts, books and documents, and over 600 *thangka*s (painting on cotton or silk appliqué, usually depicting a Buddhist deity, scene or mandala) as well as statues and other artefacts of Buddhist heritage.

First boat library

The Young Readers' Boat Library was set up on a boat by the West Bengal Transport Corporation in collaboration with a heritage bookstore! It was launched on 26 January 2021, and houses a collection of over 500 titles in English and Bengali. The boat library conducts three-hour ferries on the River Hooghly, starting from Millenium Park to Belur Math Jetty and back. It also offers free Wi-Fi facilities and various readership activities, and conducts three trips on all weekdays. The ride is priced at ₹100 for adults and ₹50 for children.

Largest collection of educational brochures

David K.M. (b. 11 May 1960) from Kannur in Kerala has collected 7,524 educational brochures from institutions in India and 69 other countries from across the world.

MUSEUMS

First public museum in a university

Established in 1937, the Ashutosh Museum of Indian Art, located in the main campus of the University of Calcutta, West Bengal, is the first public museum in any university in India. It is named after Sir Ashutosh Mookerjee, the great educationist, who introduced the study of Indology – including Indian art and archaeology – at the university level, and was the vice chancellor of the university from 1906 to 1914 and 1921 to 1923. The museum houses more than 25,000 sculptures, paintings, folk-art objects, textiles and terracotta items, among other artefacts from various phases of Indian art, with special emphasis on the art of Bengal.

First museum of textiles

The Calico Museum of Textiles in Ahmedabad, Gujarat, was set up by Gautam Sarabhai, chairman of Calico Mills, in 1949, at the suggestion of the pioneering art historian and philosopher, Dr Ananda Coomaraswamy. The museum has a comprehensive collection of Indian textiles. The foundation of modern Indian textile studies was laid here and the catalogues of the Calico Museum textile collection are an indispensable reference.

First railway museum

Inaugurated by Kamlapati Tripathi, the then minister of railways, in 1 February 1977, the Rail Transport Museum at Chanakyapuri, New Delhi, was the first rail museum in India. it was renamed the National Rail Museum in 1995 and features historical exhibits and artefacts related to the history of rail transport in India.

First museum of sexual health

Located at Kamathipura in Mumbai, Maharashtra, Antarang – Sex Health Information Art Gallery – or Antarang Museum, was an unusual museum dedicated to educating people about the human body, sexuality and HIV/AIDS. It was founded in 2002 by the municipal corporation of Greater Mumbai

(Brihanmumbai Municipal Corporation), Mumbai Aids Control and Dr Prakash Sarang, following an increase in AIDS cases. It housed a visual display of the reproductive process, safe-sex exhibits and information about sexually transmitted diseases. Twenty sculptures educated visitors about the human form, HIV/AIDS and other related sexual health topics. In 2007, it was shut down with the plan of moving it elsewhere.

First Partition museum

The Arts and Cultural Heritage Trust, set up on 24 October 2016 in Amritsar, Punjab, is the world's first museum on Partition of India. Housed in a restored portion of the Town Hall, it is dedicated to Partition of the subcontinent in 1947. The museum commemorates Partition's victims, its survivors and its legacy. On display are photographs, clothes, utensils and other memorabilia of the time.

First museum themed on Partition

First national museum of Indian cinema

The country's first National Museum of Indian Cinema (NMIC) was inaugurated in Mumbai, Maharashtra, in January 2019. Conceived in 1997, it has been designed by the National Council of Science Museums and implemented by the Films Division, under the Ministry of Information and Broadcasting, Government of India. It is placed in a period 19th-century heritage bungalow called Gulshan Mahal, and extends to another new high-technology five-floor building with two mezzanine floors. On display are projectors, recording equipment, cameras, archival posters of old films, and biographies of actors and other film personalities, all comprehensively displaying the cinematic heritage of India.

First heritage transport museum

Opened on 7 December 2013, the Heritage Transport Museum at Tauru, Nuh District, Haryana, has a rich collection of 2,500 objects, including howdahs, bullock carts, palanquins, a 1924 Ford, vintage scooters, a 1946 Piper aircraft, transport toys from the 1920s to now, and other related artefacts.

First kite museum

A museum dedicated to the rarest kites in the world is housed in Ahmedabad, a city popular for its annual International Kite Festival. Established in 1985, the museum was the brainchild of Bhanu Shah, who donated his rare collection of over 50 years to the Ahmedabad Municipal Corporation. The second such museum in the world, this one is located in the basement of Sanskar Kendra and boasts of kites of many shapes and sizes, with some that measure up to 6.7 m x 4.81 m (22 ft x 16 ft).

First underground museum

India's first underground museum opened in the Rashtrapati Bhavan on 2 October 2016. The museum showcases a collection of artefacts associated with each of the past presidents of India, including their personal belongings and vehicles, with a range of materials showcasing the history of India's freedom struggle. It also has facilities for virtual-reality presentations and multiscreen projections for story narration. The museum showcases more than 2,000 artefacts in a sprawling 12,077.39 sq. m (130,000 sq. ft) space.

The first museum on Netaji Subhas Chandra Bose was inaugurated on 23 January 2019 at the Red Fort complex in Delhi.

First museum of toilets

WR The Sulabh International Museum of Toilets at Mahavir Enclave in New Delhi, the only museum in the world dedicated to toilets, has 300 objects with a mix of originals, models and photographs. The museum traces 4,500 years of the history of toilets.

First election museum

Inaugurated in 2016, the Election Museum, located in the office premises of the chief electoral officer at Kashmiri Gate, Delhi, depicts the election journey of the largest democracy in the world. The four sections – library, audio-visual, photo gallery, and electoral management – display more than 200 archived photographs, maps, artefacts and references. Possibly the largest of its kind in the world, the museum showcases the electoral journey of India since the first general election in 1952.

First insect museum

An insect museum was unveiled by Tamil Nadu chief minister Edappadi K. Palaniswami, at the Tamil Nadu Agricultural University in Coimbatore, Tamil Nadu, in March 2018. Covering 621.61 sq. m (6,691 sq. ft), the museum displays insect specimens from since the early 20th century. It has live butterflies in a natural setting, termite mounds, bee species and insect-eating plants, along with images, videos and models of their behaviour and habitats.

First interactive museum of music

The Indian Music Experience (IME), established in 2018 in Bengaluru, Karnataka, is a rare museum that offers an interactive musical journey during which the visitor is encouraged to touch and feel instruments on display to create one's own music. IME features a Sound Garden with 10 playable musical sculptures. It also houses exhibit galleries, which showcase touchscreens, musical instruments, small theatres and audio-video kiosks as well as a Learning Centre that offers music classes and workshops on a regular basis.

First wax museum
Madame Tussauds Delhi, located in the vintage Regal Theatre in Connaught Place, New Delhi, was part of the famed international chain of wax museums, the first of which opened in London in 1835. Set up in December 2017, the Delhi wax museum had on display over 40 life-size wax sculptures of political leaders, and celebrities from sports and music, Bollywood and Hollywood. The 23rd location for the Tussaud museums, it shut down in December 2020.

WR **First museum of utensils**
Vechaar (Vishalla Environmental Centre for Heritage of Art, Architecture and Research), a museum that archives heritage utensils, including more than 5,400 pots, pans, serving vessels, nutcrackers and other utensils, is housed in a village-like complex called Vishalla in Ahmedabad, Gujarat. The museum was set up in April 1981 by its collector and owner, Surendra C. Patel, and anthropologist Jyotindra Jain.

First culinary arts museum
Michelin-starred Indian chef Vikas Khanna opened India's first living culinary museum, the Museum of Culinary Arts, at his alma mater, Welcomgroup Graduate School of Hotel Administration in Manipal, Karnataka, in April 2018. Over 2,000 utensils, objects and artefacts collected from all over India and dating back hundreds of years are housed in the museum, which is the shape of a giant pot (similar to the ones found at Harappan sites). It is spread over more than 25,000 sq. ft (2,322 sq. m), as a part of the new Department of Culinary Arts.

First dinosaur museum and park
The Dinosaur Museum Park, situated in Raiyoli Village in Balanisor Taluka in Gujarat's Mahisagar District, was inaugurated in June 2019 by Chief Minister Vijay Rupani. With an enhanced version of the Dinosaur Museum already existing there, the facility is equipped with modern technology like 3D projection, virtual-reality presentations, interactive kiosks and life-size dinosaur replicas. The 10 galleries of the museum exhibit dinosaur remains and fossil records from the area as well as other regions of Gujarat and India, and communicate the history of these dinosaurs (such as the *Rajasaurus narmadensis*) from their origin to extinction.

First science museum
The first science museum was set up by the industrialist Ghanshyam Das Birla at BITS (Birla Institute of Technology and Science), Pilani, Jhunjuhunu District, Rajasthan, in 1954. Located in a hall (185 sq. m/1,991 sq. ft area) of the Tower Building, it depicts the industries and business enterprises of the Birla family. It is the only museum of industry and technology located inside a university campus.

First Gandhi digital multimedia museum
The Eternal Gandhi Multimedia Museum, set up at Gandhi Smriti, Delhi, is a state-of-the-art digital museum that takes visitors through Mahatma Gandhi's life and philosophy with visual and audio inputs. It was inaugurated on 14 April 2005.

The Indian Museum in Kolkata, photographed in 1905

Largest chain of science museums

The National Council of Science Museums (NCSM), under the Ministry of Culture, Government of India, is the largest chain of science centres/museums under a single administrative umbrella in the world. There are, at present, 24 science centres or museums and an R&D laboratory and training centre of NCSM, located in different states in India.

Largest and oldest museum

The Indian Museum in Kolkata, West Bengal, one of the oldest museums in the world, founded by the Asiatic Society of Bengal in 1814 has rare collections of antiques, armour and ornaments, fossils, skeletons, mummies and Mughal paintings. Its founder curator was Nathaniel Wallich, a Danish botanist.

QUIZZES

First live quiz on TV

Neil O'Brien, called the 'father of quizzing', brought the concept of quizzes to India in 1967, after watching them on TV in England in the 1960s. He moderated the Eddie Hyde Memorial Quiz Contest 1967 in the small parish hall of the Church of Christ the King in Calcutta (now Kolkata, West Bengal) before an audience of 40 people. The open live quiz had four teams with members from all walks of life.

First winners at the International Physics Olympiad

Five boys – Lay Jain and Pawan Goyal from Kota, Bhaskar Gupta from Mumbai, Nishant Abhangi from Rajkot and Siddharth Tiwary from Kolkata – were selected by the Homi Bhabha Centre for Science Education after a rigorous selection process to represent India at the 49th International Physics Olympiad (IPhO) in

Lisbon, Portugal. India has been participating in the IPhO since 1998 and for the first time in 20 years, all the five participating Indian students bagged gold medals.

First quiz show on radio

On 12 April 1972, the *Cadbury Bournvita Quiz Contest* for high-school students became the first English quiz show to be broadcast on radio (Vividh Bharati) in India. It became one of India's famous quiz contests. It ran for over a decade and was later revived as a television quiz in June 1992. The original quizmaster on the radio show was Hamid Sayani, a prominent broadcast personality.

First national TV quizmaster

Raman Kumar was the first quizmaster on national television. He hosted *Mashoor Mahal* during 1985–86 in the quiz genre, featuring famous personalities.

First quiz in Antarctica

Walnut Knowledge Solutions (WKS), a Bengaluru-based education company, organized a quiz in the Antarctic Ocean in the Aurora Lounge on the ship MV *Ocean Endeavour* on 18 March 2016.

Online quiz running for 15 years without a break

Rajeev Kondapalli (b. 19 January 1976) from Secunderabad, Telangana, has been posting *Biz Quizzard*, an online weekly quiz on business, every Sunday since 21 March 2004. It has now crossed 16 years without missing a single week till date. The questions are posted on Quinkie, a Yahoo! Group site as well as his blog with the URL: *www.bizquizzard.blogspot.com.*

Kaun Banega Crorepati, the popular quiz show hosted by Amitabh Bachchan, has aired 12 seasons, completing 857 episodes in 2020.

Most participants in an online quiz – single day

An e-quiz based on the theme 'Atmanirbhar Bharat: Strengthen the Future', organized by the School of Entrepreneurship Skills, Bharatiya Skill Development University in Jaipur, Rajasthan, and conducted in association with The Employers Association of Rajasthan and the Global Foundation for Skill Development and Entrepreneurship, attracted 5,058 participants on 1 June 2020. The purpose of this quiz was to disseminate knowledge about the Atmanirbhar Bharat Abhiyan or Self-Reliant movement initiated by Prime Minister Narendra Modi.

Longest-running open quiz

Instituted in 1992 in Chennai, Tamil Nadu, by the Landmark Bookstores, the annual Landmark Quiz is the longest-running open quiz in the country. A preliminary round of about 40 questions that come up on a screen is held due to the huge turnout. The quiz is hosted by Dr Navin Jayakumar and his team (which includes his mother) since its inception, with the exception of 2006 when Derek O'Brien was the quizmaster.

Most participants in an online quiz –multiple days

An online quiz competition on World Environment Day was organized from

Indian-origin Teen Wins USA's Jeopardy! Teen Tournament 2019

Avi Gupta, an Indian-American teenager, won the top title at the 2019 edition of the Teen Tournament of Jeopardy!, one of the most-watched individual quizzes in the USA, on 28 June 2019. Featuring a total of 15 students, this is an American television game show that hosts trivia quizzes on general knowledge with clues in the form of answers, and responses in the form of questions. A high-school senior from Catlin Gabel School in Portland, Oregon, Avi Gupta walked away with a grand prize of $100,000 (approximately ₹7,618,000) from the tournament. In second place was Ryan Presler, an eighth grader from Sioux Falls, South Dakota, followed by Lucas Miner, a high-school junior from Miami.

5 June 2020 to 15 June 2020, under the aegis of the National Service Scheme, Bangabasi Morning College, Kolkata, West Bengal. A total of 13,582 participants participated from 21 countries, viz, India, Afghanistan, Algeria, Bangladesh, Bhutan, Canada, China, the Czech Republic, Ethiopia, Indonesia, Iraq, Malaysia, Morocco, Myanmar, Nepal, Nigeria, Pakistan, the Philippines, Saudi Arabia, South Africa and Sri Lanka. On an average 1,358.2 participants took part in it every day.

WR Longest-running school quiz

The *Bournvita Quiz Contest* was a weekly televised show that started in 1992 as the first televised school quiz in India. Anchored by Derek O'Brien, it ran continuously on Zee TV till 2001, after which it moved to the TV channel Sony, followed by Colors. Now, it is conducted in a mobile app format.

Longest-running televised quiz

Prashnottari, a twice-a-week (previously fortnightly) quiz, with participants from schools, colleges and a general live TV audience, was first telecast on Prasar

Bharati's Jaipur Doordarshan Kendra on 23 July 1993. Hosted by former IAS officer Dr Mahendra Surana since it began, it continued without break on the same channel, completing 900 episodes on 15 March 2020.

Largest quiz at one location

Aqua Regia: The Science Quiz is the Annual All-India Inter-School Science Quiz, open to school students of classes 8 to 10. Conducted by TIME (Triumphant Institute of Management Education), it is the largest quiz held at one location. By 2015, as many as 1.6 million students participated in it. Preliminary rounds are conducted in the form of written tests for participating teams in various cities. These are followed by regional finals and national finals. The entire national circuit takes more than three months to complete.

School quiz with the maximum participation

The Haryana Police organized an hour-long state-level quiz competition on 8 November 2016 on the theme of road safety. As many as 2,447,744 students participated in it.

Longest-running state-level quiz

Initiated in 1986 by Vijaya Bank, Karnataka's oldest quiz competition, titled VGenUth Quiz Contest (now called the Baroda Champ Annual Quiz Contest) is open to all high-school students across Karnataka. Its 34th edition was held on 2 February 2020 in Bengaluru, in which more than 400 students from over 200 schools participated in the competition. Eight teams made it to the final round during which quizmaster Giri Balasubramaniam quizzed the students on various topics and fields including general knowledge, finance, history, pop culture, literature, language, technology and other facts from around the world.

First online quiz for overseas youth

In July 2018, the Government of India launched *Bharat Ko Janiye* Quiz (Know India Quiz), an online quiz organized to generate an interest in India among people between 15 and 35 years, who live abroad. It is held for three different categories of participants: Non-resident Indians (NRIs), persons of Indian origin (PIOs) and foreign nationals. The three finalists from each category are invited to a 15-day tour of India. The top three winners from each category received gold, silver and bronze medals, respectively, at the Pravasi Bharatiya Divas Convention in January 2019 at Varanasi, Uttar Pradesh.

Only quiz conducted on each continent

Walnut Knowledge Solutions, Bengaluru, Karnataka, has conducted at least one quiz on each of the conventionally accepted seven continents. Five quizmasters conducted the seven quizzes on MV *Ocean Endeavour* (Antarctica on 18 March 2016); at Building Tomorrow, Kampala, Uganda (Africa on 25 April 2017); at Massachusetts Institute of Technology (MIT), USA (North America on 12 August 2017); at the Centre for Law and Policy Research, Bengaluru, Karnataka, India (Asia on 28 September 2018); at the Hertie School of Governance, Berlin, Germany (Europe on 5 May 2018); at the International School Nido de Aguilas, Santiago, Chile (South America on 19 December 2017); and at Deakin University, Melbourne (Australia on 13 December 2018).

MEDIA AND COMMUNICATIONS

PRINT

First printing press
The first printing press came to India accidentally, in 1556, when the patriarch designate of Abyssinia (now Ethiopia, Africa) broke his journey at Goa and later died there. The printing press was left behind. The printers were a Spaniard called Joao de Bustamante and his Indian assistant, whose name is not known.

First paper-making machine
William Carey (1761–1834), a British Christian missionary, translator, social reformer and cultural anthropologist, who founded the Serampore College and University in Bengal, first set up a paper-making machine in Calcutta (now Kolkata), West Bengal in 1830.

First lithographic printing
Lithographic printing was introduced by the Calcutta Art Studio in 1878 in Calcutta (now Kolkata), West Bengal.

First multilingual press
A multilingual press for all the main local Indian languages was first set up in Serampore, Bengal (now Srirampur, Hooghly District,) West Bengal in 1800 by Christian missionaries.

Earliest type
The first types in any Indian language were cast in Goa in 1577 by Joao Goncalves, assisted by Father Pero Luis, who was a Tamil Jesuit priest.

According to the Indian Readership Survey (IRS), newspaper readership in the country grew from 407 million readers in 2017 to 425 million at the end of March 2019.

First typewriters
The first typewriters were imported into India in 1896.

First indigenous typewriters
- Godrej & Boyce Manufacturing Company Ltd manufactured India's first manual typewriter in 1955. It was designed and created entirely by Indian engineers.
- Blackwood India Ltd in Calcutta (now Kolkata), West Bengal, set up in 1960 and renamed J.K. Business Machines in 1961, were the first makers of portable typewriters in India.
- The first indigenous electronic typewriters were manufactured by Hindustan Teleprinters Ltd in 1975.

First press regulation
The Censorship of Press Act of 1799 was the first regulation with an element of censorship to enforce wartime restrictions on the press. All news was scrutinized by a special security administration unit, in order to prevent information leaks

Digging up Old News

Copies of the *National Herald* and *The Economic Times*, possibly from a crashed Air India Boeing 707 flight, were found by Timothee Mottin in July 2020. The items were found from the melting French glacier of Bossons on the Mont Blanc mountain range in the French Alps. The flight had crashed on 24 January 1966, claiming 177 lives. The recovered newspapers carry headlines about the election of Indira Gandhi as India's first woman prime minister in January 1966. Mottin, a café owner near the site, added the newspapers to his display of discoveries for customers.

during the Carnatic Wars, fought between the French East India Company and the British East India Company in India.

First newsprint factory
The first paper mill in India to manufacture newsprint was a factory at Nepanagar, Burhanpur District, Madhya Pradesh, set up in January 1955.

WR First news agency to supply news in Urdu
On 5 June 1992, the United News of India (UNI) became the first agency in the world to supply Urdu news. It remains the only agency to do so.

First news agency
The Press Trust of India (PTI), which is a non-profit-sharing cooperative of Indian newspapers, was established on 27 August 1947. It took over the Associated Press of India and the Indian operations of Reuters, and provided news, photographs, features and infographics from February 1949 onwards.

First vernacular paper
Samachar Darpan was published in Bengali from Serampore, Bengal (now Srirampur, Hooghly District), West Bengal, by William Carey and John Clark Marshman from May 1818. Marshman was a British journalist, historian and publisher of the *Friend of India* from which *The Statesman* newspaper descended.

First newspaper
Hicky's Bengal Gazette or the *Original Calcutta General Advertiser*, India's and Asia's first newspaper, was launched on 29 June 1780 by James Augustus Hicky, an Irishman.

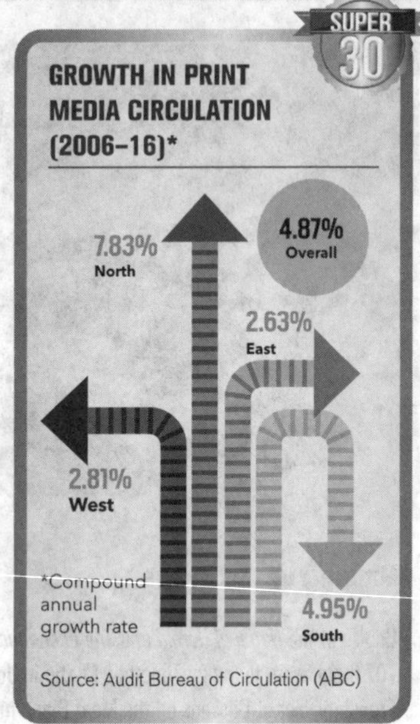

First non-English newspaper
In 1794, the Reverend Harutyun Shmavonyan edited and published *Azdarar* in the Armenian script in Madras (now Chennai), Tamil Nadu. This was the first Armenian journal in the world and the first non-English one in India.

The only handwritten newspaper
The Musalman, the oldest Urdu-language daily newspaper, published in Chennai, Tamil Nadu, is the only handwritten newspaper in the world. It is a four-page evening paper handwritten by four calligraphers or *katibs*, and printed. Established in 1927 by Syed Azmatulla, it has not missed a single day's publication. The paper has correspondents all over India and sells at 75 paise a copy to around 25,000 subscribers.

First Hindi newspaper
Banaras Akhbar began in 1845, under the editorship of Govind Narayan Thatte, as the first Hindi newspaper.

First newspaper for the visually impaired
Swagat Thorat's *Sparshdnyan*, launched in February 2008, is India's first newspaper for the visually challenged. Its name means 'knowledge by touch', and it is published in Marathi on the 1st and 15th of every month.

First financial daily
The Economic Times, India's first financial daily, was launched by the Times of India Group in March 1961. Like the London-based *Financial Times*, it too was printed on salmon-pink paper.

First daily with an international edition
In February 1994, India's global newspaper, *The Asian Age*, was launched simultaneously from Delhi, Mumbai and London. It has a Kolkata edition too.

First magazine in Hindi
Saraswati, India's first Hindi monthly magazine, was first published in January 1900. Its founder was the well-known printer and publisher Chintamani Ghosh and it was published by the Indian Press, which was based in Allahabad (now Prayagraj), Uttar Pradesh.

First newspaper run entirely by women

Khabar Lahariya is India's first newspaper entirely staffed, edited and published by women. The eight-page rural weekly in Hindi is sold in 600 villages in its print form and on multiple digital platforms. It was launched in 2002 in Chitrakoot District, Uttar Pradesh. In 2009, it was the recipient of the UNESCO King Sejong Literary Prize for its contribution to literacy.

First women's magazine in English

The Indian Ladies' Magazine was first published in English in 1901 by Kamala Satthianadhan in Madras (now Chennai), Tamil Nadu.

First women's magazine in an Indian language

Masik Patrika in Bengali, published from Calcutta, Bengal (now Kolkata), West Bengal, in 1854, was the first women's magazine in an Indian language.

First magazine for the visually challenged

White Print is the first lifestyle magazine in English in India for visually challenged people. It was launched in May 2013 by Upasana Makati, a former communications student from the University of Ottawa, Canada. This 64-page monthly, printed at the National Association for the Blind, Mumbai, Maharashtra, and circulated across India, features articles about sports, politics, culture, fashion and technology, besides short stories and reader contributions. *White Print* has also released Braille-tactile alphabet books in Braille, both in English and Hindi, called 'Tactabet'.

heritage site open to tourists

Sacred Games, Lust St...

...ace begins for intern...

MONDAY, SEPTEMBER 2, 2019

THE HINDU

INDIA'S NATIONAL NEWSPAPER SINCE 1878

MUMBAI
CITY EDITION
18 pages • ₹10.00

Russia is helping India in 4-5 critical areas of Gaganyaan
page 10

Security presence in J&K will come down in coming days: Jaishankar
page 11; editorial: page 8

At least 7 dead as gunman hijacks truck and opens fire in Texas
page 12

Bumrah's hat-trick and six-wicket haul bundles out West Indies
page 16

Assam to move SC for NRC reverification in select districts

"Technical flaws" may have caused exclusion of Bengali Hindu refugees: Minister

Kulbhushan to meet Indian officials today

Five States to g... new Governo...

Arif Mohammed Khan sent...

Raj Bhavan bound

The Hindu: first newspaper to be published in colour

First newspaper to be printed in colour

The Hindu, with its headquarters in Madras (now Chennai), Tamil Nadu, began as a weekly in 1878 and turned into a daily in 1889. A family-run newspaper, it was the first to be printed in colour in 1940. It was also the first Indian newspaper to own aeroplanes to distribute newspapers (1963), and the first newspaper to digitize and be available online (1995).

First feminist journal

Manushi, founded in 1978 in Delhi, and edited by Madhu Kishwar, was the first feminist journal in the country.

Record Rewind

State/UT with most published newspapers

1991

Uttar Pradesh with a total of 3,324 publications was the state with the highest number of newspaper publications.

2020

Uttar Pradesh with 5,360 publications is the state with the most newspaper publications.

First vernacular periodical
Digdarshan, a Bengali monthly, first appeared in April 1818.

First Indian publication in the USA
India Abroad, the first Indian weekly in the USA, was launched by Gopal Raju, an India-born American publisher and editor, in 1970. It focused on news for the Indian diaspora.

First letters to the editor column
The letters to the editor column was introduced in the biweekly magazine *Calcutta Journal*, published in 1878 in Bengal (now West Bengal).

Multi-edition daily with the largest readership
Dainik Jagran, which has its headquarters in Kanpur, Uttar Pradesh, leads with 37 editions across 11 states and a readership of 68,667,000 (2019 Q4; IRS).

Daily (and Hindi daily) with the largest readership
Dainik Jagran, which is headquartered in Kanpur, Uttar Pradesh, has a readership of 68,667,000 (2019 Q4; IRS).

State/UT with the most Indian-language publications
Delhi leads among all states and UTs in publications in the maximum number of Indian languages, with publications in as many as 18 languages. It is followed by Maharashtra, with publications in 16 languages. Karnataka and Tamil Nadu come after that with publications in 12 languages each.

English daily with the largest readership
The Times of India, headquartered in Mumbai, Maharashtra, has a recorded readership of 17,344,000 (2019 Q4; IRS).

State/UT with the most publications
Uttar Pradesh, with 17,992 publications, leads with the maximum number of publications in India. It is followed by Maharashtra with 16,241 publications and Rajasthan with 5,744 of them.

Most circulated government publication
Employment News, an English weekly that is published from New Delhi by the Publications Division, Ministry of Information and Broadcasting, Government of India, has the highest circulation of 239,498 among government publications (as of 2019).

Largest read regional-language daily

Malayala Manorama, with its headquarters in Kottayam, Kerala, has a readership of 17,763,000 (2019 Q4; IRS).

Most read English magazine

India Today, a weekly published from Noida, Uttar Pradesh, by the India Today Group, has a readership of 9,493,000 (2019 Q4; IRS).

Most read Hindi magazine

India Today (Hindi), a weekly published from Noida, Uttar Pradesh, by the India Today Group, has a total readership of 6,641,000 (2019 Q4; IRS).

Most read magazine in a regional language

Vanitha, a Malayalam fortnightly magazine, published from Kottayam, Kerala, by the Malayala Manorama Group, has a readership of 5,886,000 (2019 Q4; IRS).

State/UT with most publications in a single language

Uttar Pradesh, with 4,806 publications in Hindi, leads among all states and UTs with the most publications in a single language (Hindi). It is followed by Madhya Pradesh with 3,096 Hindi-language publications, and Uttarakhand with 1,795 publications.

First Indian-origin journalist to win the Pulitzer Prize

Gobind Behari Lal, a science journalist in the USA, won the Pulitzer Prize in 1937.

Longest-running Indian women's magazine

Femina, started in July 1959 with Irene Talyarkhan as its first editor, continues to be published. It is now owned by Worldwide Media, a joint venture of BBC Worldwide and the Times Group. It was also the first lifestyle magazine of the country in English, and now has the highest circulation in its category (108,560 in August 2019).

Oldest children's magazine

Chandamama, founded by Telugu film-makers B. Nagi Reddy and Aluri Chakrapani was launched in July 1947 in Telugu. It was edited by Kodavatiganti Kutumba Rao. The magazine ceased publication in 1998. In 2007, it was acquired by Geodesic Ltd, which planned to digitize it. Its last edition came out in March 2013 and since then its status is unknown. In its heyday, *Chandamama* was published in 13 languages and had a readership of approximately 200,000 across the country.

Chandamama: **oldest children's magazine**

Oldest extant newspaper – regional language

The *Bombay Samachar*, now titled *Mumbai Samachar*, is the oldest continuously published newspaper in any language in India, and continues to be published. Launched on 1 July 1822 by Fardoonjee Marazban (1787–1847), the daily is published in both Gujarati and English. Marazban, who was from Bombay (now Mumbai), Maharashtra, was a printer and a newspaper editor. He established vernacular journalism in India and initiated the production of Gujarati types.

Oldest extant newspaper – English

The Times of India began on 3 November 1838 as a biweekly, initially called *Bombay Times and Journal of Commerce*. It was renamed *The Times of India* in 1850, with J.E. Brennan as its editor.

Longest career as a journalist

B.P. Sharma, a journalist from Jammu and Kashmir, who died in 2005 at the age of 97, was an active journalist for over 70 years. He established the Jammu station of Radio Kashmir (All India Radio) and was its first director. He also worked with the news agency Reuters, *The Times of India*, *Hindustan Times* and *The Tribune*. Later, he served as the principal information officer of Jammu and Kashmir.

Longest spell as editor

Tushar Kanti Ghosh (1898–1994) was editor of the *Amrita Bazar Patrika*, based in Kolkata, West Bengal, for 64 years. He had founded the newspaper in 1928.

Longest letter to the editor

Vinod Chandrashekhar Dixit (b. 1 December 1964) from Ahmedabad, Gujarat, wrote the longest letter to the editor on the topic 'As Taj Stands for Beauty, Modi Stands for Duty', which was published in *Free Press*, Ahmedabad, Gujarat. Its word count was 2,796 and it was published on 15 June 2019.

Most letters to the editor

Vinod Chandrashekhar Dixit (b. 1 December 1964) from Ahmedabad, Gujarat, has written the most number of letters to the editor in the span of a year. He wrote a total of 1,769 letters between 1 April 2016 and 31 March 2017, and they were published in different newspapers and magazines.

Most articles published in a year

Vinod Chandrashekhar Dixit (b. 1 December 1964) from Ahmedabad, Gujarat, holds the record for publishing the most number of articles in newspapers and magazines in a year. The total number of articles published by him between May 2019 and April 2020 was 742.

Articles published in most continents*

Pitamber Kaushik (b. 12 March 1998) from Bokaro, Jharkhand, has published articles in six continents. The articles were published in *Cape Times*, South Africa (Africa); *The Hindu*, India (Asia); *The Brussels Times*, Brussels (Europe); *Papua New Guinea Post-Courier*, Papua New Guinea (Oceania); *Andean Air Mail* and *Peruvian Times*, Peru (South America); and *The Independent Utah*, USA (North America).

*This is a one-time category. Further and future claims for this category will not be accepted.

Most pages in a newspaper supplement

Kannada daily *Vijayavani*'s Mysuru edition brought out a special issue with 320 pages in 10 volumes on 25 March 2020. This supplement was dedicated to Shri Mayakara Madappa, a social reformer and spiritual leader of the 16th century. The newspaper was sold at a price of ₹4.

RADIO

First private radio station

On 10 September 1935, Akashvani Mysore, a private radio station, was set up in what is present-day Karnataka by Dr M.V. Gopalaswamy, professor of psychology and principal of the Maharaja's College, at his residence.

Largest media organization

All India Radio (AIR) today reaches almost the entire population across the length and breadth of the country and nearly 92 per cent of the total area, embracing socio-economically and culturally diverse people. It broadcasts in 23 languages and 179 dialects. Programmes of its External Services Division are broadcast in 11 Indian and 16 foreign languages.

First direct relay

A historic occasion, the first direct relay coincided with India's 'freedom at midnight' from British colonial rule. The ceremonies for the transfer of power from Britain to an independent India on the night of 14–15 August 1947 at the Central Hall of the Parliament House in Delhi was relayed by AIR.

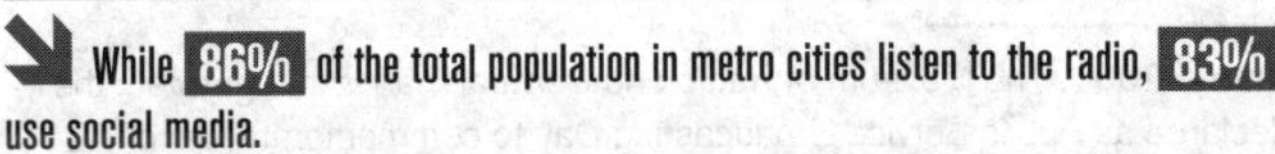
While 86% of the total population in metro cities listen to the radio, 83% use social media.

First Frequency Modulation (FM) service

- AIR inaugurated the first ever FM service from Madras (now Chennai), Tamil Nadu, on 23 July 1977.
- Delhi started an FM stereo station on 19 March 1988.

First private FM broadcaster

Times FM from The Times Group commenced operations in 1993 from Ahmedabad, Gujarat. It ran till June 1998 and was relaunched as Radio Mirchi in 2000. Over the years, Radio Mirchi has expanded its presence across 63 cities in India and multiple stations in the UAE and the USA.

First private FM station

Radio City Bangalore, based in Bengaluru in Karnataka, started on 3 July 2001, as India's first private radio station, after the Government of India opened up the FM broadcasting industry to private competition.

First sponsored programme

A musical programme, *Saridon Ke Saathi*, sponsored by Saridon was aired on 3 May 1970 on the Mumbai–Pune–Nagpur network.

ALL INDIA RADIO: THE VOICE OF THE NATION

All India Radio (AIR) has a legacy of over nine decades, commencing its broadcasting operations in 1927. It has touched millions of lives and its signature tune summons deep nostalgia. In a celebration of the past three decades, here is a timeline of AIR's milestones in the same period.

2 March 1990: 100th AIR station is commissioned at Warangal, Andhra Pradesh.

1 April 1993: 150th AIR station is commissioned at Berhampur, Orissa (now Odisha).

28 September 1994: Four 500kW superpower short-wave transmitters is set up in Bangalore (now Bengaluru), Karnataka, making it one of the world's biggest transmitting centres.

31 October 1994: 175th AIR station is commissioned at Nashik, Maharashtra.

2 May 1996: AIR online information services is launched.

13 January 1997: Audio-on-demand Internet service is started.

25 February 1998: AIR 'News on Telephone' and AIR 'Live on Internet' services \ are launched.

1 September 2001: Infotainment channels, known as FM-II, are launched in Delhi, Mumbai, Kolkata and Chennai.

12 November 2001: The Museum of Radio and Doordarshan is inaugurated; the date is declared as Public Service Broadcasting Day to commemorate Gandhiji's only visit to AIR in 1947.

First news bulletin

On 19 January 1936, AIR aired its first news bulletin. The Central News Organization (CNO) was formed in August 1937. AIR came under the Department of Information and Broadcasting four years later.

First national programme of talks

On 29 July 1953, AIR aired the first national programme of talks in English.

First cricket commentary

On 1 January 1936, Bertie Meyer provided commentary for a match between the All-India XI and the maharaja of Patiala's Australian XI, from Bombay (now Mumbai) station, Maharashtra, from 12:46 p.m. to 1:00 p.m.

First broadcasting service

The Madras Presidency Radio Club, under the stewardship of C.V. Krishnaswamy Chetty, started a broadcasting service in 1924, using a tiny 40-watt transmitter with an effective range of only 8 km.

27 February 2002: First digital satellite home service is launched.

July 2002: AIR completes 75 years of broadcasting.

26 January 2004: Bhasha Bharati channel is launched in Delhi.

2005: A special project to digitize all archival recordings is completed. It was started in 2001.

May 2008: SMS service for national news headlines is launched from Delhi.

16 January 2009: The first digital radio transmission in short-wave band is carried out by using DRM (Digital Radio Mondiale) technology to improve the quality of reception and the coverage.

May 2010: AIR's two entries win seven prizes in different categories at the International Radio Festival of Iran, held in Tehran.

2012: The first National Community Radio Awards presented during the second national conference (*sammelan*).

31 December 2015: AIR network grows to 414 stations and 602 transmitters.

February 2016: The website www.prasarbharatiarchives.co.in is launched in order to promote the sales of material from the archives of both Akashvani and Doordarshan.

28 September 2018: AIR streaming services are launched on Amazon's Alexa.

4 July 2020: *Sanskrit Saptahiki*, the first weekly news show in Sanskrit is launched; AIR network now has 482 stations and 653 transmitters.

First national programme of plays
On 15 August 1956, AIR first aired a play that was broadcast countrywide.

First national programme of music
AIR broadcast its first national music programme on 20 July 1952 with sitar maestro Pandit Ravi Shankar as the music conductor.

First phone-in programme
Phone-in programmes were introduced on 10 January 1993 at AIR, Delhi.

First radio *sangeet sammelan*
All India Radio held its first Radio *Sangeet Sammelan* (festival of music on the radio) in 1954.

First relay between radio stations
On 18 January 1939, an inter-station relay took place between Delhi and Bombay (now Mumbai), Maharashtra.

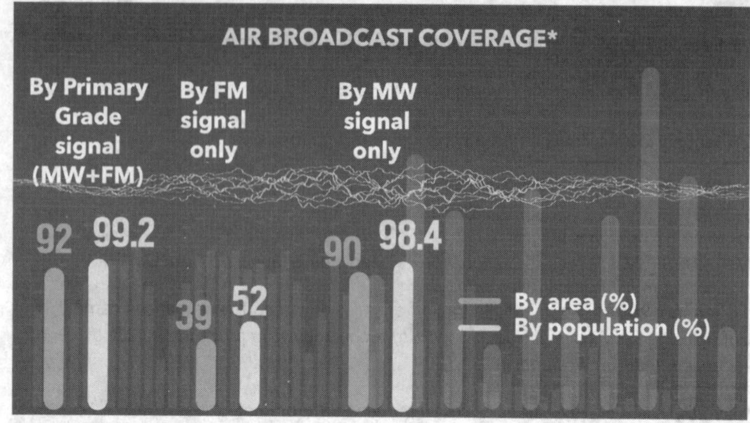

*As per installed capacity (as on 1 April 2019); Source: All India Radio

First broadcast

In June 1923, the Radio Club of Bombay made the first ever broadcast in the country from Bombay (now Mumbai), Maharashtra. This was followed by the setting up of the Calcutta Radio Club in West Bengal around five months later.

First broadcasting company

The Indian Broadcasting Company (IBC) was set up in Bombay (now Mumbai), Maharashtra, on 23 July 1927, with a medium-wave transmitter that had a range of 50 km.

WR **Highest radio station**

The Himbotingla station of AIR in Ladakh, located at an altitude of 4,053.84 m (13,300 ft) above the mean sea level, is the highest radio station in the world. The 10 kW, high-power transmitters were inaugurated on 25 September 2021.

First controller of broadcasting

Lionel Fielden took over as the first controller of broadcasting for the Indian State Broadcasting Service (ISBS) on 30 August 1935. A senior BBC producer, he spent five years in India, establishing a countrywide radio service. On 8 June 1936, the ISBS was renamed All India Radio.

Most commercial radio programmes anchored

The legendary radio announcer and programme anchor Ameen Sayani started his broadcasting career in 1951. During his career, he compèred more than 10,000 commercial radio programmes, and voiced 12,000 spots and jingles. He produced more than 38,920 publicity programmes for feature films.

Longest running commentary

Melville de Mellow's running commentary on the last journey of Mahatma Gandhi on 31 January 1948, a day after his assassination, lasted for more than seven continuous hours.

Longest running DX (digital transformation) Net broadcast on ham radio

Muthuvama Sanil Deep (b. 17 January 1959) from Kozhikode, Kerala, operates the longest running broadcast DX Net on Ham radio. The network was started on 27 November 1988 on 7085 kHz at 8:30 a.m. He has been single-handedly operating the network from 1990 till date. The network operates from 8:30 p.m. to 9:30 p.m. on Sundays where he shares information regarding radio channels across the world. His radio network also disseminates vital updates during natural disasters. His individual call sign is VU3 SIO.

Top FM Broadcaster

Radio Mirchi is heard by over 40 million people across the country. It led in 25 cities in India, including the top six metros – Delhi (42.9 lakh/4.29 million), Mumbai (34.6 lakh/ 3.46 million), Pune (16.3 lakh/1.63 million), Kolkata (9.6 lakh/0.96 million), Hyderabad (7.6 lakh/0.76 million) and Ahmedabad (7.6 lakh/0.76 million), by the end of 2019.

Reception from most number of radio stations

Jose Jacob, assistant director at the National Institute of Amateur Radio in Hyderabad, Telangana, has collected certificates for achieving reception from 132 radio stations of All India Radio. His first certificate of reception from All India Radio was in 1976, when he was 17 years old. In 42 years, he has achieved reception from 132 radio stations ranging from short-wave and medium-wave to FM.

TELEVISION

First telecast

The first experimental telecast was carried out in Delhi on 15 September 1959 from a makeshift studio with the help of a single transmitter of 500W, which carried signals up to 25 km for an operational time of an hour a day. The studio was relocated to Rajpath for the first live telecast of the Republic Day parade in 1960.

First national telecast

Doordarshan started nationwide telecasts on 15 August 1982 from its TV studio in Mandi House in New Delhi.

First simultaneous tele-broadcast

Om Namah Shivay, directed by Dheeraj Kumar, was the first tele-serial to be telecast and broadcast at the same time on television and radio, respectively, from March 1999.

First colour TVs

In 1982, the year India hosted the Asiad (Asian Games), colour TVs were introduced in India.

First colour transmission

An experimental telecast was conducted from the

PERMITTED TV CHANNELS: NEWS VERSUS NON-NEWS

Source: Annual Report 2020–21, Ministry of Information and Broadcasting, Government of India

Madras TV station (in present-day Chennai, Tamil Nadu) on 18 July 1980 for one hour. It was transmitted to Delhi viewers.

First programme for rural areas

Krishi Darshan, a TV programme aimed at disseminating useful information on farming to rural areas and agricultural communities, started on 26 January 1967 on DD National and still continues on the channel as well as on DD Kisan. It is considered to be the longest-running non-fiction TV series.

First TV station to get a second channel and multi-channels

Delhi was the first TV station to get a second channel on 17 September 1984. Doordarshan introduced five new channels on 15 August 1993 via Insat-1B.

First satellite linkage

The first satellite linkage experiment was launched on 1 August 1975 in six states in the country for one year. Later, satellite channels were available for the first time in 1991 to a select few who had access to the powerful dish antennas in embassies and five-star hotels.

First central production centre

Set up in 1989 at the Siri Fort Complex, New Delhi, the Central Production Centre began with two large studios equipped with modern facilities to produce high-quality, well-researched programmes.

First private producer of national news

In February 1995, New Delhi Television Ltd (NDTV) became the first private producer of national news with the show titled 'The News Tonight', which was hosted by Prannoy Roy at 8:00 p.m. They were the first private broadcasters for news on Doordarshan.

Bringing the Magsaysay Home

On 2 August 2019, TV journalist Ravish Kumar was awarded Asia's highest honour, the Ramon Magsaysay Award for 2019. The 44-year-old senior executive editor of NDTV India was the second Indian journalist to win this award; Amitabha Chowdhury, an investigative journalist with Bengali daily *Jugantar*, received it in 1961. Born in Jitwarpur Village, Bihar, Ravish Kumar joined NDTV in 1996 as a field reporter. His programme Prime Time deals with under-reported problems of common people, the primary reason quoted for the award being given to him.

Ravish Kumar

First private channel
Zee TV, the first private television channel in the country, was launched in October 1992 in collaboration with Star TV and Zee Telefilms Limited.

First private satellite channel
Aaj Tak was the first private satellite channel permitted in 2000.

First 24-hour news channel
Star News, India's first 24-hour news channel, started on 3 February 1998, with news updates every hour from 6:00 a.m.

First business channel
Asia Business News International (ABNI), a 24/7 business channel, was launched on 14 February 1996 by the Hinduja Group in collaboration with Asia Business News (ABN) and TV18.

First infotainment channel
DD-3, Doordarshan's channel for infotainment, was launched on 14 November 1995.

First teleshopping programme
Shopping through TV was introduced on 1 January 1995, with an hour-long home- shopping programme on Doordarshan's Metro channel in Delhi.

First serial
Teesra Rasta was the first fiction serial telecast from Doordarshan Kendra, Delhi, starting from 2 May 1962.

First video film
Teri Meri Kahani, the first video film, was produced by B.R. Chopra in 1981.

First telefilm
Satyajit Ray's *Sadgati* was telecast on the national network on 13 April 1981. This 52-min. telefilm was based on Munshi Premchand's short story. Produced by Doordarshan, it starred well-known actors, such as Om Puri and Smita Patil.

First major TV series produced
Doordarshan produced the first major TV series, *Ramayan* and *Mahabharat*.

First telefilm in sign language
Nishabda Kanasugalu, a five-episode serial about a deaf girl, produced in Kannada by Ivan Nigli, was telecast from 8 January 1995 by Doordarshan Kendra, Bangalore (now Bengaluru), Karnataka.

First soap opera on Indian TV
Hum Log was the first soap opera on television in India. Its 154 episodes were telecast between 7 July 1984 and 17 December 1985.

First sci-fi serial
Space City Sigma, produced by Studio Ifekt, was telecast from 21 May 1989.

First Indian animation serial
Featuring Ghayab, the do-gooder ghost, *Ghayab Aya* was the first fully 'made-in-India' serialized animation film telecast on Doordarshan in 1986. The animator-director was the well-known painter-illustrator Suddhasattwa Basu.

First director general of Doordarshan
P.V. Krishnamoorthy became the first director general of Doordarshan on 1 April 1976, the day Doordarshan and AIR were each given separate status.

First newsreader
Doordarshan began a five-minute news bulletin in 1965 with Pratima Puri as the first TV newsreader.

First high-definition channel
The first high-definition (HD) channel was introduced in India by Discovery Communications in March 2010.

First DTH service
Launched on 2 October 2013, Dish TV was the first DTH (Direct-to-Home) service in India.

Tallest TV tower
The tallest TV tower in India is located in Rameswaram, Tamil Nadu. The height of the tower is 323 m (1,060 ft). The tower was built in 1995 and is used by Doordarshan for television broadcasting. It is made of reinforced cement concrete and the mast is of lattice steel.

Most watched daily soap

Anupamaa, starring Rupali Ganguly and Sudhanshu Panday, is the most watched daily soap in India, according to the Broadcast Audience Research Council (BARC) between 21 and 27 October 2021. It was followed by *Taarak Mehta Ka Ooltah Chashma* and *Kaun Banega Crorepati* 13.

POST AND PHILATELY

MAIL VOLUME* (IN CRORE)

Total	510.27
Premium products**	54.65
Registered	19.30
Unregistered	446.66

*2019–20; ** Speed Post and Express Parcel Post; Source: Annual Report 2020–21, Department of Posts

Earliest postal communication

- In India, the earliest evidence of a systematic mail service is found during the reign of Chandragupta Maurya (r. 321–297 BCE), who ruled from Magadha (now in southern Bihar). In his empire, confidential reports were dispatched from the emperor to the outlying provinces, and from the provinces back to the ruler.
- The first recorded mention of a postal service was made by Ziauddin Barani, who wrote that Alauddin Khilji (r. 1296–1316) organized a regular foot-runner service, called *harkara,* as early as 1296. These *harkara*s carried a baton with bells and ran across allotted territory, carrying mail in a relay system with the runners changing every mile.
- Sikandar Lodi (r. 1488–1518) of the Lodi dynasty set up small posts across his kingdom and sent two firmans or orders daily to his armies.
- Babur (r. 1483–1530), the founder of the Mughal Empire, set up horse couriers from his capital at Agra up to Kabul, maintaining a regular 'postal' system.

Birds and animals as carriers of mail

- **Bullock mail:** Between 1846 and 1904, bullock carts were used along the Grand Trunk Road between Allahabad (now Prayagraj), Uttar Pradesh, and Delhi to deliver mail. By 1875, as many as 41 government bullock 'trains' operated in the north-west provinces and Punjab. With the coming of the railways, bullock routes were used less and the last line from Ambala in Haryana to Simla (now Shimla) in Himachal Pradesh was shut down in October 1904.
- **Camel post office:** A mobile post office on camelback was started at Mithariya, Bikaner District, Rajasthan, on 27 October 1977. The postmaster here was given a special allowance for maintaining the camel. The office was later converted into a stationary post office.
- **Pigeon post:** Pigeons were used as messengers by the Odisha Police till 2004. The force then had a strength of around 900 homing pigeons.

Postal communication under British rule

- The first superintendent of post offices was appointed in Allahabad (now Prayagraj,) Uttar Pradesh, in 1870.
- British India became the first non-founding member of the General Postal Union in 1876.

First mail by steamboat

In 1828, mail was sent by a steamboat service between Calcutta (now Kolkata, West Bengal) and Allahabad (now Prayagraj), Uttar Pradesh, along 1,266 km of the River Ganga, the earliest instance of mail delivery by steamer in Asia.

First postal training centre

Established on 2 April 1951, the postal training centre at Saharanpur, Uttar Pradesh, was the first training centre in Asia, set up exclusively for postal and telegraph personnel.

First pigeongram

The first pigeongram in India was carried from Asansol to Calcutta (now Kolkata) on 18 February 1931 in Bengal (now West Bengal), with 42 homing pigeons carrying missives over 212.43 km. There were 21 military and 21 civilian pigeons, two of which were named Amy Johnson and Akash Ranee, carrying messages for Lady Ezra and David Ezra respectively.

The Express Mail Service (EMS) of India Post has an existing network in 106 countries as per its annual report 2020–21.

WR **First ship-to-shore pigeongram**

The world's first 'ship to shore' pigeongram was released by the postmaster genera of Calcutta in Bengal (now Kolkata), West Bengal, on 27 December 1933 from the ship *Sarbajaya* for Tangra.

First electronic Indian Postal Order

On 22 March 2013, the first electronic Indian Postal Order (E-IPO) was introduced for Indian nationals living abroad. On 14 February 2014, the service was also extended to all Indian citizens.

WR **Largest postal network**

With a network of 156,600 post offices, the Indian Department of Posts has the world's largest postal network as recorded in 2020.

Longest time taken for domestic delivery

A postcard sent from Lucknow, Uttar Pradesh, on 18 May 1981 to a trading company at Raja Darwaza, Varanasi, Uttar Pradesh, reached its destination after over seven years on 1 December 1988.

First postcard

The Postal and Telecommunications Department issued the first postcard on 1 July 1879.

LEAVING THEIR MARK: STAMPS ISSUED FEATURING OUTSTANDING WOMEN (1990–2020)

Year	Number of Stamps	Names
1991	1	Mahadevi Verma
1993	1	Nargis Dutt
1994	1	Rani Rashmoni
1996	4	Kasturba Gandhi – Kasturba Trust, Saint Alphonsa, Ahilyabai Holkar and Rani Gaidinliu
1997	1	Rukmini Lakshmipathi
1998	2	Aruna Asaf Ali and Savitribai Phule
1999	2	Jijabai and Arati Gupta (Saha)
2000	1	Vijaya Lakshmi Pandit
2001	1	Vijaya Raje Scindia
2002	3	Chandraprabha Saikiani, Kanika Bandyopadhyay and Matangini Hazra
2003	1	Allah Jilai Bai
2004	1	Neerja Bhanot
2005	2	M.S. Subbulakshmi and Dr T.S. Soundram
2008	5	Saint Alphonsa, Madhubala, Rani Velu Nachiyar, Thillayiyadi Valliammai and Violet Alva
2009	2	Jeanne Jugan and Dineshnandini Dalmia
2010	3	Kranti Trivedi, Veenai Dhanammal and Thanjavur Balasaraswati
2011	7	Leela Naidu, Savithari, Nutan, Meena Kumari, Kanan Devi, Devika Rani and Subhadra Joshi
2014	2	D.K. Pattammal and Gangubai Hangal
2016	3	Mother Teresa, Shamshad Begum and Geeta Dutt
2017	1	Aatukuri Molla
2018	1	M.L. Vasanthakumari

First value payable post service

Sending inland parcels by value payable post (VPP) was introduced in India from 1 December 1877, on demand from the traders' community of Calcutta (now Kolkata), West Bengal.

First window delivery of letters

The Madras GPO (now in Chennai, Tamil Nadu) began the window delivery of letters from 1 June 1786 in the then Fort St George Square.

First hot-air balloon carrying mail

A special postal cover was carried in a hot-air balloon carrier of India Post from Sakthi Mills Ground, Pollachi in Coimbatore District, Tamil Nadu, to the postmaster of Kovipalayam, Pollachi, on 3 January 2016.

In India, one post office serves **8,605** people on average.

First post office

The East India Company set up its first post office in Calcutta, Bengal (now Kolkata), West Bengal, in 1727. It was later merged with the General Post Office, Kolkata. The building was designed in 1864 by Walter B. Grenville, a consultant architect. In one end of the building is the Philatelic Bureau.

Oldest traced postal receipt

B.K. Prakash of Kasaragod (earlier Kasargod), Kerala, found a postal receipt in Kannada, dated 29 March 1826, belonging to his great-grandfather Devappa of Pallikere Village. It proved the delivery of a registered petition to him from Kasaragod District P.O. to the Kasaragod Taluk *tehsildar*, 20 km away, at a postal price of one anna.

First postmen

Postmen or delivery peons were first engaged on a security bond with a specific responsibility, as part of postal reforms carried out in Bengal in 1840. They were dressed in uniform and wore badges supplied by post offices. They were allowed to earn baksheesh of 2 pies (1 pie = 1/192 of a rupee) on each letter delivered, in addition to the collection of postage due to the post office.

Highest post office

The highest post office in India is located at an altitude of 4,440 m (14,567 ft) in Hikkim Village in Spiti Valley, Himachal Pradesh. For around 35 years since the post office opened on 5 November 1983, Rinchen Chhering has been the postmaster. The village is home to around 160 residents with no mobile phone or Internet connection, and the post office is shut for six months in winter because of snow. There is no motorable road to the village.

First Indian postmaster general

- **Male:** Rai Bahadur Saligram became the first Indian postmaster general for the north-western provinces in 1881.
- **Female:** Sushila Chaurasia, who was born in Bijapur, Karnataka, in 1923,

became the first woman to become postmaster general in the country. She assumed charge of the Madhya Pradesh circle on 24 May 1979.

First woman postal inspector

R. Santhakumari from the Thiruvananthapuram postal division, Kerala, passed the inspector's examination in 1968 to become the first woman postal inspector.

First postwoman

K. Padmakshy Amma, who worked in the Thiruvananthapuram postal division in Kerala, joined service on 19 February 1959 as the country's first postwoman.

First aircraft of India Post

India Post launched a dedicated freight aircraft – a Boeing 737-200 with a capacity of 15 tonnes, leased from Air India – to carry Speed Post, mail and parcels to the north-east. It made its maiden flight from Kolkata, West Bengal, to Guwahati, Assam, on 29 August 2007.

First letter by airmail

The first airmail letter was introduced in the country in November 1944. Priced at six annas, the airmail letter was called an 'aerogramme' and could be sent to the UK and other countries under the British Empire.

First insured mail service

The system of insurance post for letters and parcels, which was then called the 'insured mail service', was introduced on 1 January 1878.

First all-woman post office

- Avinashilingam Home Science College post office at Coimbatore, Tamil Nadu, which opened in January 1966, was the first all-woman post office in India.
- A post office, which started functioning at Manoramaganj in Indore, Madhya Pradesh, on 31 March 1976, is also fully run only by women employees.

First express mail service

Speed Post was introduced by the Government of India on 1 August 1986, connecting seven cities in the country, and five other countries to India.

First dead letter office

A post office for undelivered, unclaimed letters and letters with incomplete addresses was set up during 1834–37 in Benson Town in Bangalore (now Bengaluru), Karnataka. It was also called a Returned Letter Office.

First post office savings bank account

The post office savings bank, which started on 1 April 1882, introduced the then revolutionary concept of banking with a post office instead of a bank, which had been the usual method of keeping one's savings.

First computerized registration centre

The first computerized registration centre (CRC) was opened in June 1996 at the Market Road wing of the New Delhi General Post Office (or GPO).

Record Rewind

Stamps from most countries in honour of a person

1991

More than 80 stamps in honour of Gandhiji had been issued from 42 countries.

2019

Stamps in honour of Mahatma Gandhi had been issued from over 150 countries up to 2019.

First floating post office

The Floating Post Office, located on a shikara at Dal Lake, Srinagar, Jammu and Kashmir, is the world's first and only floating post office. It was inaugurated in 2011 and housed a philately museum and a souvenir shop, and also offered Internet facility along with international phone calls.

First mobile post office

On 1 November 2011, the Department of Post launched the Post Office on Wheels initiative with its first mobile van running in Pune, Maharashtra. The van worked from 8:00 a.m. to 8:00 p.m. daily covering 30 locations in a week, stopping at each location for two hours. The van offered all types of postal service including e-enabled services, selling postcards, opening a new savings account and selling postal life insurance among others. The service was recently resumed during the Lockdown in 2020 to deliver pension and provide mobile services in states like Kerala and Uttar Pradesh.

First drive-in post office

A drive-in post office was inaugurated on 11 November 1975 in Pune, Maharashtra.

First online post office

The Head Post Office located at Sansad Marg, New Delhi, became fully computerized on 24 June 1998.

First Indian post office outside India

Set up in 1983, the first Indian post office outside Indian territory was located at the scientific base of Dakshin Gangotri, Antarctica, during the third Indian expedition to Antarctica and became operational on 24 February 1984. On 26 January 1988, the Dakshin Gangotri P.O. was set up under the Department of Post in north Goa. Scientist G. Sudhakar Rao, a member of the Seventh Indian Scientific Expedition to Antarctica in 1987, was appointed its first honorary postmaster. Reports say that in the first year, 10,000 letters were posted and cancelled here. Dakshin Gangotri was decommissioned in 1990.

A stamp depicting the Dakshin Gangotri Post Office

First letter boxes

A great reform in the history of Indian post took place in October 1854 with the introduction of letter boxes located away from post offices.

First parcel service

Originally known as Bhangy post, parcel service was introduced on 2 December 1884. Its name came from the *bhangy* or bamboo stick with parcels on either end that the parcel carriers balanced on their shoulders.

First registered mail service

The first mention of a system of registration being adopted by a post office to secure the safety of coins or documents in transit was found in an advertisement published on 20 February 1795. Actual registered post was introduced in Bombay Presidency on 1 November 1849 with a postal notice on 16 October 1849. In Bengal, it was established at Calcutta GPO on 1 January 1851 and later at Madras GPO. The fee was eight annas for registering a letter.

First automatic mail processing centre (AMPC)

The first AMPC was launched at the Mumbai GPO, Maharashtra, on 29 April 1993, and a second one was established at Chennai, Tamil Nadu, in October 1995.

WR First airmail

India became the first country in the world to send mail by plane when 6,500 letters and postcards were flown from Allahabad to Naini (a distance of only 18 km!) in Uttar Pradesh in a Humber-Sommer biplane by Henri Pequet on 18 February 1911. A pictorial postmark showing the aeroplane was used.

First stamp

The Scinde Dawk (Provincial), India's first half-anna stamp, was issued with the help of Edward Lees Coffey, the postmaster of Karachi on 1 July 1852 in Scinde District, Karachi (now in Pakistan). It was embossed on circular red wafers used as seals on letters, with the East India Company emblem and the legend Scinde District Dawk around the circumference. It was Asia's first ever adhesive stamp. It was withdrawn in 1854.

First letter to post office in space

According to reports in 1992, Reagan Jones sent a letter from Vandiperiyar P.O. to the Russian consul general in Chennai, Tamil Nadu, who further sent it on to Moscow, Russia. Using radio waves, Moscow sent the message – greetings for space scientists – to the post office in space.

Longest-serving postmaster

Brother K.V.S.J. Peter, who received a Padma Shri in 1983, was the longest-serving postmaster, for 68 years. He took charge of the Shenbaganur post office in Dindigul District, Tamil Nadu, on 12 September 1913, and was in service till 8 February 1982.

Largest post office

With an area of 11,148 sq. m (120,000 sq. ft), India's busiest and biggest post office

Mumbai General Post Office: the largest in the country

is the Mumbai General Post Office. With 101 business counters, it caters to more than 50,000 address sites and handles 25,000 customers every day.

Earliest official stamps

India issued stamps in 1866 and the State of Hyderabad issued stamps in 1873. The stamps had 'service', 'official' or '*sarkari*' over-stamped.

First state to issue a stamp (pre-1947)

Kathiawar state in Saurashtra (later Gujarat) issued a one-anna stamp in November 1864 with the inscription 'Saurashtra Post 1864–65'.

First Indian stamp featuring a woman

The Indian saints and poets series, issued on 1 October 1952, featured Mirabai, the 16th-century bhakti poet-saint.

First stamp of independent India

A 3.5-anna stamp with the inscription 'Jai Hind' was issued on 21 November 1947.

First sportsperson on a stamp

A stamp that portrayed pioneering cricketer Sir Ranjitsinhji Vibhaji Jadeja (1872–1933) was issued on 27 September 1973. He was the first Indian to play Test cricket for England.

PHILATELY STATISTICS*

*2019–20; Source: *Annual Report 2020–21, Department of Posts*

First aromatic stamp

India introduced its first aromatic stamp, a ₹15 stamp fragrant with the scent of sandalwood, in 2006.

Only living persons on Indian stamps

Only eight persons have been featured on stamps in their lifetime: social reformer Dr D.K. Karve (1958); statesman and scholar Dr M. Visvesvaraya (1960); India's first president Dr Rajendra Prasad (1962); second president Dr S. Radhakrishnan (1967); fourth president V.V. Giri (1974); Mother Teresa (1980); former prime minister Rajiv Gandhi (1985); and cricketing legend Sachin Tendulkar (2013).

First differently shaped stamps

- **Polygonal:** The four-anna indigo-and-red stamp of India, issued on 15 October 1854, was polygonal, with the top and side panels raised from the main frame, which was slightly curved.
- **Circular:** The earliest circular stamp was the Scinde Dawk, though only the first printing was circular in the true sense since the later versions were issued on sheets that were usually cut square. It was the first circular stamp issued in Asia. Later, the states of Indore (1889) and Jammu and Kashmir (1866–78) issued similar circular stamps.
- **Oval:** The half-anna red stamp, issued by the Indian state of Bhor (now in Maharashtra) in 1879, was oval in a horizontal format. It was imperforate and had to be cut out.
- **Triangular:** Stamps of this shape were issued on 10 October 1985 by the Border Roads Organization.
- **Diamond-shaped:** Depicting Raja Rammohun Roy, these stamps were issued on 27 September 1964.
- **Trimmed:** These revenue stamps, reissued for postal use in 1866, had their inscriptions cut off at the top and bottom.
- **Octagonal:** A set of six octagon-shaped commemorative stamps to mark the 150th birth anniversary of Mahatma Gandhi was released on 2 October 2019 for the first time.

A diamond-shaped stamp featuring social reformer Rammohun Roy

First customization of stamps

Initially introduced in India during the World Philatelic Exhibition 'INDIPEX-2011', 'My Stamp' is the scheme for personalized sheets of postage stamps of India Post. Such a sheet has a thumbnail image, e.g., the customer's photograph, logos of institutions, artwork, famous tourist places, historical cities, heritage buildings and wildlife, among others, on a selected template sheet featuring postage stamps. The facility is available for both non-corporate and corporate entities.

First stamp to be jointly issued with another country

India and erstwhile USSR issued a set of two stamps on the Festival of India in the USSR, which was held in August 1990. Both countries issued the stamp with the same design.

Social activist Henry Dunant of Switzerland: first foreigner on an Indian stamp

First foreigner on a stamp (post-1947)
Henry (also Henri) Dunant featured on a 15-paisa Red Cross centenary stamp issued on 8 May 1963. A Swiss businessman and social activist, he co-founded the International Red Cross and was the first recipient of the Nobel Peace Prize.

First centenary stamp
A commemorative stamp was issued on 1 October 1954 to celebrate the first centenary of Indian postage stamps.

First all-India stamps
Called the 'Independence series', these three stamps featured the Indian flag (3.5 annas), the Lion Capital of Ashoka (1.5 annas) and an aircraft (12-annas). The Indian flag, the first stamp of independent India, which was released on 21 November 1947, was meant for foreign correspondence. The Ashoka Pillar capital on the second stamp depicted the national emblem of India and this stamp was for domestic use. The third stamp, showing a Douglas DC-4 aircraft, was intended for use on foreign airmail.

 India Post has **1,000** ATMs operational across the country.

First commemorative stamps
A set of six stamps was issued on 9 February 1931 on the laying of the foundation of New Delhi as the new capital of India. These were the first pictorial stamps depicting the important landmarks of the city.

First private printing of commemorative stamps
A set of four stamps on Mahatma Gandhi was first printed by Courvoisier, who was a Swiss printer, and issued in 1948.

First autograph-inscribed stamp
A stamp issued on 7 May 1961 to commemorate the birth centenary of Nobel laureate Rabindranath Tagore had his signature inscribed on it.

First one-rupee charity stamp
The first charity stamps were issued on 26 January 1950. Three 'Healthy India' charity stamps were brought out in denominations of one anna, four annas and one rupee.

First stamp designer (pre-Independence)
Captain H.E.L. Thuillier, the deputy surveyor general of India, who was then stationed in Calcutta, Bengal (now Kolkata, West Bengal), designed the first

lithographic stamps, which were issued in 1854 and said to be engraved by an artist called Munirooddin.

First miniature sheet

To commemorate the India International Philatelic Exhibition 1973 in Delhi, a miniature sheet with a face value of ₹4.65 was issued on 14 November 1973.

First philatelic society

The Philatelic Society of India, the country's first philatelic society, was formed in Bombay (now Mumbai), Maharashtra, on 6 March 1897.

First stamp featuring wildlife

The first Indian stamp depicting an animal was released in 1962, and it was a 15-paisa stamp showing the Indian rhinoceros. Next year, five more such stamps came out, featuring the Indian gaur (10 paise), the red panda (15 paise), the Indian elephant (30 paise), the Bengal tiger (50 paise) and the Asiatic lion (one rupee).

First Indian president of Federation Internationale de Philatelie (FIP)

Late D.N. Jatia, a reputed philatelist, was elected president at the 59th Congress of the FIP in London, UK, on 14 May 1990.

First Indian to design a stamp for the United Nations

Dipok Dey (b. 1938) of Calcutta (now Kolkata), West Bengal, was the first Indian to design a stamp for the UN. This stamp, based on the theme of 'Child Survival', was designed in 1985.

Largest philatelic bureau

Mumbai General Post Office Philatelic Bureau in Maharashtra, also an international philatelic bureau, is the largest in the country.

First national philatelic museum

The National Philatelic Museum of India was established in New Delhi on 6 July 1968. It has large collections of postage stamps printed and issued by India and former princely states of India, early essays, proofs and colour trials, Indian stamps used abroad, early Indian postcards, postal stationery and other thematic collections. It also has a philatelic bureau and postal objects such as postboxes from Victorian times.

First philatelic exhibition

The Philatelic Society of Bengal held an exhibition of postage stamps at the art gallery of the Government School of Art (now renamed the Government College of Art and Craft) in Calcutta, Bengal (now Kolkata), West Bengal, in December 1894.

First international stamp exhibition

'India 80' was the first international stamp exhibition held in Asia under the patronage of the Federation Internationale de Philatelie (FIP), held from 25 January 1980 to 3 February 1980.

TELECOM

Last money order

In April 2015, India Post discontinued the traditional money order service, which was more than a century old.

Last telegram

Inda's 163-year-old telegram service ended at 11:45 p.m. on 14 July 2013. Its last message was booked at the Central Telegraph Office, Janpath, New Delhi, by Ashwani Mishra, who sent telegrams to Congress leader Rahul Gandhi and the director general of DD news S.M. Khan.

First Indian radio telegraphy company

The Indian Radio Telegraphy Co. was established in 1923, which ushered in the era of wireless telegraphy.

First submarine cable link

Madras (now Chennai), Tamil Nadu, was linked to Penang, Malaysia, in 1886 with a submarine telegraph cable.

First fibre-optic link

India's first fibre-optic link was made in 1979 when Hindustan Cables Ltd's office at Shivaji Nagar, Pune, Maharashtra, was linked to the Cotton Telephone Exchange, a distance of 4 km.

First Indo-European telegraph line

The first independent double line of telegraph from London, UK, to Karachi (now in Pakistan) via Tehran, Iran, which was undertaken by M/s Siemens and Co., was opened for operations on 31 January 1870.

COMPOSITION OF TELEPHONE SUBSCRIBERS* (WIRELESS+WIRELINE)

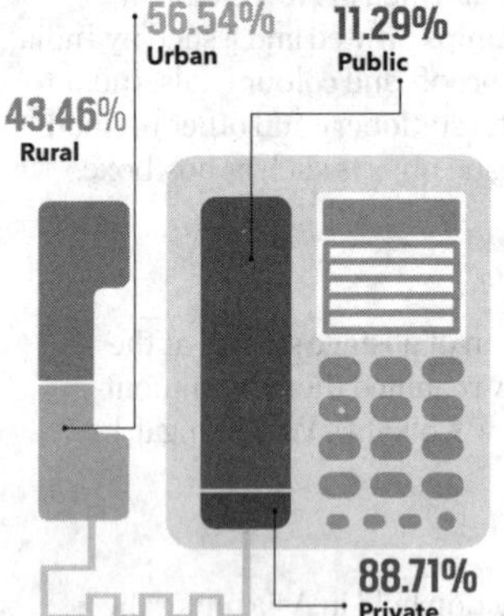

*2018–19; Source: Telecom Regulatory Authority of India, Annual Report 2018–19

First director general of the telegraph service

Sir William O'Shaughnessy was appointed as chief superintendent of telegraphs in 1857 in colonial India.

First manufacturer of telephones

- A telecommunication maintenance and repair shop was set up at Alipore, Calcutta (now Kolkata), West Bengal, in 1860. Manufacture of minor components needed for the Baudot Telegraph and Line stores was initiated at the P&T workshop in 1913.
- The Indian Telephone Industries Ltd was established at Doorvaninagar near Bangalore (now Bengaluru), Karnataka, in July 1948 for manufacturing automatic and carrier equipment. The local assembly

First STD service

The facility for subscriber trunk dialling (STD) was first started between Lucknow and Kanpur in Uttar Pradesh on 26 November 1960.

First ISD service

The Arvi earth station for satellite communication, set up in 1971 in Arvi near Poona (now Pune), Maharashtra, marked the introduction of the first operator-dialled service to international subscribers. The first intercontinental telephone exchange was commissioned in 1973 and the first international subscriber dialling (ISD) telephone service was introduced between Bombay (now Mumbai), Maharashtra, and London, UK, in 1976.

SUPER 30

BSNL: CONNECTING INDIA

Possibly the oldest communication establishment in the country, Bharat Sanchar Nigam Limited (BSNL) is a telecom company with its headquarters in New Delhi. It was formally incorporated on 1 October 2000 by the Ministry of Communications, Government of India. The BSNL landline was introduced in the early 1990s and was then the only fixed wireline service in the country. It still is the largest wireline telecommunication network in India, holding 60 per cent of the market share. Ranking fourth in terms of wireless services, BSNL offers a wide range of services, including mobile, landline, Internet, broadband, fibre and wing services.

On 24 October 2019, BSNL and Mahanagar Telephone Nigam Limited (MTNL), another government undertaking, were merged. As of September 2020, BSNL has 126.73 million (12.673 crore) subscribers for its wireless and wireline services and 31.36 million (3.136 crore) subscribers for its Internet services.

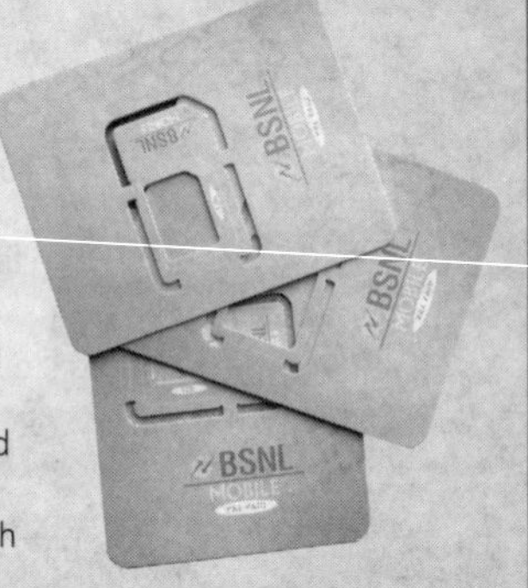

BSNL also provided telegraph services for 160 years in India since 1858, and stopped doing it in July 2013. In its place, it started a web-based messaging system in 2010 through 182 telegraph offices across India.

of phones from imported parts began in 1948 and the first phone off-the-line was produced on 26 January 1949.

- The first telephone with indigenous components was made in 1951.

First known use of SOS signal

On 1 November 1977, the duty operator in the astral wireless station at Ennore, near Madras (now Chennai), Tamil Nadu, received a weak SOS call from a cargo ship in the Bay of Bengal; its engine room was on fire. The call was acknowledged and rescue ships reached in an hour.

First radio phone link

On 1 May 1933, Sir Samuel Hoare, Secretary of State for India, spoke from London, UK, to Sir Frederick Sykes, governor of Bombay, on radio phone, thus establishing a communication network between Britain and India.

First push-button telephone

The first Indian firm to manufacture electronic push-button phone answering machines was Bharti Telecom Ltd. It was also the first Indian company to launch cordless phones that were called 'Beetel'.

First automatic telephone exchange

The first automatic telephone system in the country was commissioned at Simla (now Shimla), Himachal Pradesh, in 1914. The exchange had 400 working lines and another 300 lines in reserve.

First call using a mobile phone

On 31 July 1995, the then Union telecom minister Sukh Ram and the then chief minister of West Bengal Jyoti Basu spoke to each other using hand-held mobile phones, over Modi Telstra's MobileNet service.

First Internet telephony service

On 25 July 2018, government-owned Bharat Sanchar Nigam Limited (BSNL) launched India's first Internet telephony service that allows users to dial any phone number in India through its mobile app.

First SMS provider

Hutchison Max offered a global text messaging service (SMS) in Indian in 2001.

First circle launch

In 1996, Bharti Mobile Ltd, which was a joint venture of Bharti Enterprises with Telia Company of Sweden, launched Airtel, the first to provide services in a circle (outside metros) in Himachal Pradesh.

First cellular operators' association

The Cellular Operators Association of India (COAI), Delhi, was set up in 1995.

First national/international roaming service

On 12 September 1997, the Department of Telecommunications (DoT), Ministry of Communications, Government of India, cleared a national automatic roaming facility for cellular operators in Delhi, Mumbai, Calcutta (now Kolkata) and Chennai. International roaming facility was approved on 12 January 1998.

First carrier to demonstrate 5G service capability

Bharti Airtel became the first carrier to successfully demonstrate live 5G service over a commercial network on 28 January 2021 in Hyderabad, Telangana. Capable of delivering 10x speed, 10x latency (the time it takes for data to pass from one point on a network to another) and 100x concurrency (the execution of multiple instruction sequences at the same time) in comparison with existing technologies, the carrier will be able to switch to 5G after government approval.

Service area with largest access subscriber base

Uttar Pradesh (East), with 98.14 million (9.814 crore) wireless and wireline subscribers, has the largest subscriber base (September 2020).

First net fax service

Satyamfax, launched by Satyam Infoway on 25 April 2000 at Chennai, Tamil Nadu, in technical association with Singapore Telecom, was the first to provide fax to fax, web to fax, email to fax, and PC desktop to fax services.

First telephone exchange

In 1881, the Government of India licensed the Oriental Telephone Company to set

Record Rewind

Fastest Internet speed

1995

VSNL'S Gateway Internet Access Service provided a speed plan of 128 Kbps for an annual charge of up to ₹30 lakh. The cheapest plan offered a speed of 9.6 Kbps for ₹5,000 a year.

2019

In 2019, the average broadband download speed in India was 34.07 Mbps. This translates to 34,070 Kbps.

up telephone exchanges in Calcutta (now Kolkata), Bombay (now Mumbai), Madras (now Chennai), and Karachi (now in Pakistan). A 50-line exchange was set up in Calcutta in 1881 as one of the oldest exchanges in the world. It was set up only five years after the invention of the telephone.

First cellular service

Modi Telstra, a joint-venture company of the B.K. Modi Group and the Telstra Corporation of Australia, inaugurated the first commercial cellular service in India on 23 August 1995. The network was constructed by Telecommunication Engineering Centre and the Modi Telstra team.

Mobile tower at the highest altitude

Installed by BSNL with the help of the Indian Army's Trishul Signallers, the highest mobile tower is located at 4,877 m (16,000 ft) in Chongtash in Ladakh. With this tower, even the remotest regions of Ladakh are connected by a communication link.

Largest wireline service provider

BSNL was the leading operator in wireline service, with 7.74 million (77.4 lakh) subscribers and 38.55 per cent of the market share as in September 2020

Largest wireless service provider

Reliance Jio was the leading wireless service provider with 404.13 million subscribers, followed by Bharti Airtel with 326.61 million subscribers, up to September 2020.

Highest teledensity state/UT

Delhi had 273.14 per cent teledensity (number of fixed (landline) telephone connections per 100 people in a specified area) up to 30 September 2020.

Highest number of rural subscribers

Reliance Jio has 170.08 million rural subscribers, which amounts to 32.43 per cent of total rural subscribers.

INTERNET, SOCIAL MEDIA AND APPS

First private Internet service provider (ISP)

Satyam Infoway (Sify) became the country's first private Internet service provider company on 22 November 1998.

First provider of Internet services

Videsh Sanchar Nigam Limited (VSNL), under DoT, Ministry of

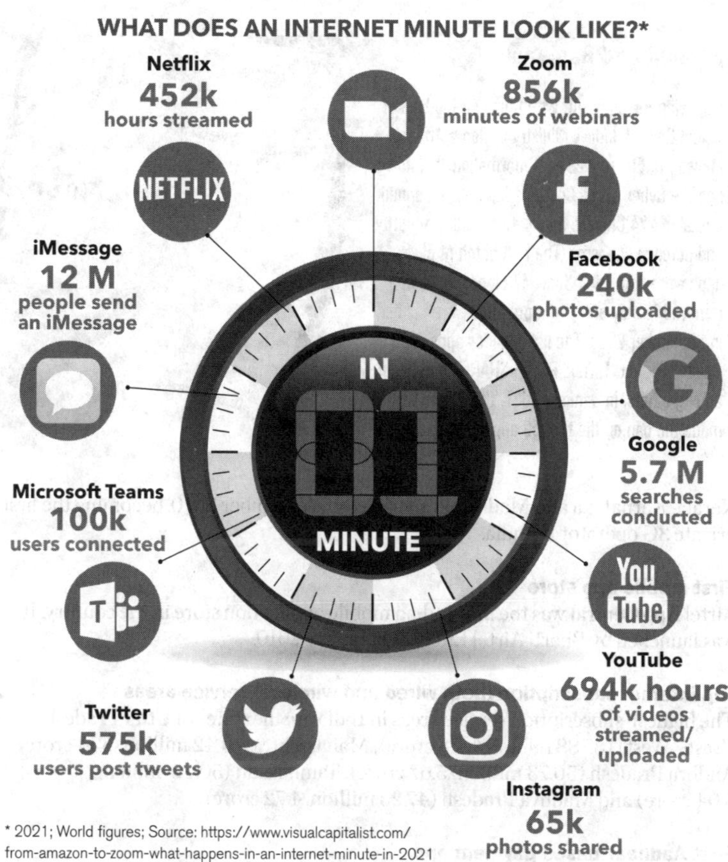

* 2021; World figures; Source: https://www.visualcapitalist.com/from-amazon-to-zoom-what-happens-in-an-internet-minute-in-2021

Telecommunications, Government of India, was the first provider of Internet services in the country. It was launched on 15 August 1995.

First free email service

Conceived by Sabeer Bhatia (and colleague Jack Smith), Hotmail was the first free email service that took the whole world by storm in 1996. Bhatia was a Bengaluru-born Indian-American businessman and led Hotmail as its president and CEO, until its eventual acquisition by Microsoft in 1998.

First 3G operators

- The public sector telecom service provider Mahanagar Telephone Nigam Limited (MTNL) first provided 3G mobile service in parts of Delhi on 11 December 2008.
- Tata Docomo launched its 3G mobile service in many states – Rajasthan, Uttar Pradesh (West), Gujarat, Maharashtra (except Mumbai), Haryana, Punjab,

Banned and Banished

Following the stand-off with China on the Line of Actual Control, India's Ministry of Home Affairs, Ministry of Electronics and Information Technology and the Cyber Crime Coordination Centre banned a total of 224 Chinese applications, citing security and defence concerns. The first batch of 59 apps were banned in June, 47 clone apps were removed in July and 118 more apps were banned in September 2020. The list includes apps such as Baidu, WeChat, TikTok, PUBG, SHAREit and Shein, among others. In January 2021, the government made the ban on the first 59 apps permanent.

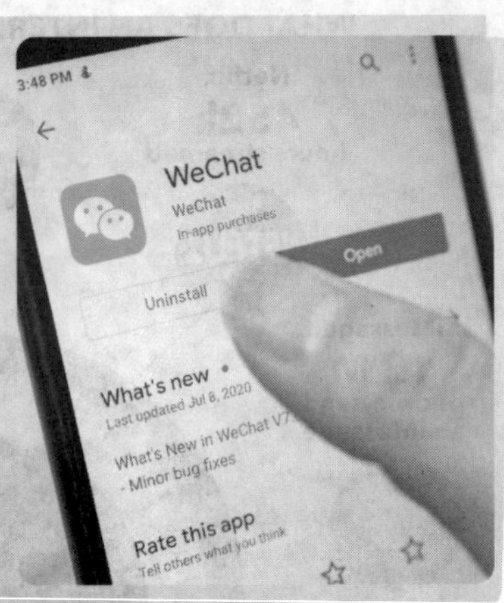

Kerala, Karnataka and Madhya Pradesh – on 5 November 2010, becoming the first private 3G operator in India.

First mobile app store

Airtel App Central was the first Indian mobile application store in the country. It was launched by Bharti Airtel Ltd on 9 February 2010.

Top Internet subscription (both wired and wireless) service areas

The highest-subscription service areas in India are the states of Uttar Pradesh (East+ West) (87.88 million/8.78 crore), Maharashtra (61.42 million/6.14 crore), Andhra Pradesh (56.73 million/5.67 crore), Tamil Nadu (50.42 million/ 5.04 crore) and Madhya Pradesh (47.23 million/4.72 crore).

First Aadhaar-based payment app

The Government of India launched Bharat Interface for Money (BHIM) app, an Aadhaar-based mobile app for digital payments, on 30 December 2016.

TOP 5 POPULAR APPS (DIFFERENT SEGMENTS)*

	Segment	Application
1	Gaming	Carrom Pool
2	Finance	Google Pay Tez
3	Retail	Amazon
4	Video Streaming	Mx Player
5	Social	Helo – Share Your Life

*2020; Source: Year-on-year growth; State of Mobile 2020, App Annie

WR **Largest WhatsApp user base in the world**
India remained WhatsApp's biggest market with 400 million (40 crore) monthly active users, who exchange around 60 billion (6,000 crore) messages daily (July 2019). The country has been the biggest market for WhatsApp since November 2015.

Most viewed Indian video on YouTube
Phonics Song with two words, an alphabet learning video by ChuChu TV has garnered 4,348,214,171 views on YouTube as on 14 December 2021. The video was posted on 7 March 2014.

Highest data consumption
India has the highest data consumption of 11 Gb/month per user on an average.

Most popular mobile operating system
The favourite mobile operating system in India is Android with 62 per cent usage; next is Windows with 19.4 per cent usage.

WR **Largest Facebook user base**
With 310 million (31 crore) active users, India emerged as Facebook's largest country audience in July 2020.

WR **Most number of mobile app downloads**
India had the most number of mobile app downloads on the Apple iOS Appstore as well as on Google Playstore in the second quarter of 2020 with 7 billion (700 crore). It is followed by USA with 3.75 billion (375 crore.) and Brazil with 3 billion (300 crore).

Most popular browser
The most popular browser in India is Google Chrome, with a share of 51.91 per cent among all.

Fastest 4G service provider
Vodafone Idea Ltd is the provider of the fastest 4G network in the country with a download speed of 13.74 Mbps and an upload speed of 6.19 Mbps. It is followed by Bharti Airtel and Reliance Jio.

Most popular search engine
Google, with a user base of 93.4 per cent, is the favourite search engine in India.

Most downloaded mobile application
Aarogya Setu, a COVID-19 contact-tracing app launched and mandated by the Government of India has become the most downloaded application in India and the seventh most downloaded application in the world. It recorded 127.6 million (12.76 crore) installations up till July 2020.

WR **First and only 4G, all Internet protocol network**
Reliance Jio, which revolutionized the mobile Internet market in India when it rolled out 4G services in 2016, is the only network in the world to rely

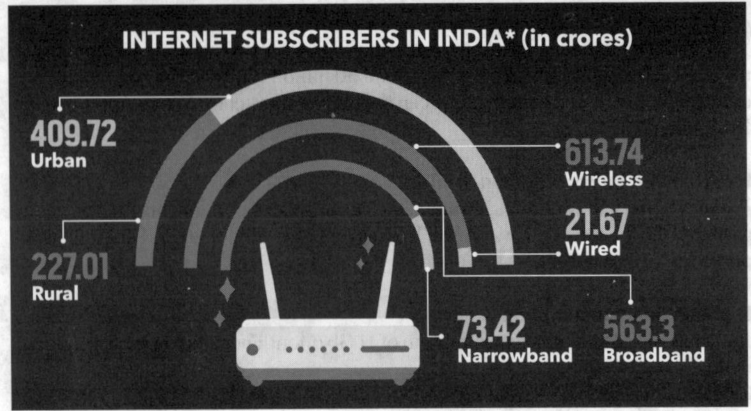

*2019; Figures in crores; Source: Telecom Regulatory Authority of India (TRAI)

solely on 4G LTE (Long-Term Evolution) network, based on Internet telephony, without the backing of the legacy 3G/2G services.

Most subscribed YouTube channel

T-Series, a music record label and film production company, became the first YouTube channel in the world to reach 100 million subscribers in May 2019. As of January 2021, it had 169 million (16.9 crore) subscribers.

Highest concurrent video viewership

In the nail-biting ICC Cricket World Cup 2019 semi-final between India and New Zealand, Hotstar scaled a new global peak in concurrent viewership, with 25.3 million (2.53 crore) users tuning in to the video-streaming platform during the 49th over on 10 July 2019. This surpassed the platform's earlier peak of 15.6 million (1.56 crore), which it had recorded on 16 June 2019 during the India–Pakistan match. That game had also attracted a cumulative single-day reach of 100 million (10 crore). The ICC Cricket World Cup was streamed across six languages: English, Hindi, Bengali, Tamil, Telugu and Kannada.

Most Internet shutdowns

India recorded the highest number of Internet shutdowns in the world in 2020. With 109 instances, out of a global total of 155, India topped the list for the third consecutive year in a report released by Access Now, a digital rights and privacy organization. India was followed by Yemen (six), Ethiopia (four) and Jordan (three). The reasons for the Internet shutdowns include political instability, protests, religious holidays, cheating in exams and communal violence.

Largest social network penetration

India is the world's second largest market with 349.97 million (34.997 crore) users in 2020. While there are many apps available to the Indian public, YouTube leads with an 82 per cent market penetration. It is closely followed by Facebook (76 per cent), WhatsApp (70 per cent), Instagram (64 per cent) and Facebook Messenger (53 per cent), according to the 2019 Q3 figures.

AGRICULTURE

HISTORY AND RESEARCH

Earliest cotton cultivation

The earliest evidence for cotton production comes from the Harappan civilization (2500–1700 BCE). The first sample of cotton material, discovered by archaeologist Daya Ram Sahni during 1921–22, was a small fragment of cotton from Mohenjo-Daro (now in Pakistan), clinging to the side of a vase and dyed red with madder pigment (*Rubia tinctorum*).

Earliest irrigation

Evidence of irrigation on agricultural land in the Indian subcontinent dates back to the Chalcolithic period (3000–1000 BCE). The Inamgaon area of Maharashtra has a prehistoric mud embankment structure with a stone foundation. This was connected to the River Ghod by a number of channels. Floodwater was used effectively to irrigate the surrounding regions by storing it and then distributing it during the dry months.

Earliest ploughed field

Archaeologists B.B. Lal and B.K. Thapar of the Archaeological Survey of India (ASI) found a ploughed field dated to c. 2450–2300 BCE during excavations at Kalibangan in Pilibangan Tehsil in Hanumangarh District, Rajasthan.

First famine commission

The Famine Commission set up in 1880 with Sir Edward Buck as its secretary and provincial agencies under his guidance, was the first famine commission in the country. It was a forerunner of the later Ministry of Food and Agriculture of the government after India became independent.

By August 2020, India had 19 operational Mega Food Parks that linked agricultural production to the market by bringing together farmers, processors and retailers.

First agricultural research institute

The Imperial Agricultural Research Institute, established in 1905 at Pusa, Samastipur District, Bihar, was India's first agricultural research institute. After the building was damaged in an earthquake in 1934, the institute was shifted to New Delhi in 1936. It is now known as the Indian Agricultural Research Institute (IARI) and is the oldest agricultural institute in India.

First agricultural society

William Carey, a British Christian missionary, social reformer, translator and anthropologist, founded the Agri-Horticultural Society of India in September 1820 in Calcutta (now Kolkata, West Bengal) to help disseminate scientific information among the people.

First society of soil sciences

The Indian Society of Soil Sciences was formed on 22 December 1934 in Calcutta (now Kolkata, West Bengal) with 28 members, and it was formally inaugurated on 3 January 1935 at the Presidency College (now Presidency University). Sir Bryce

The Low-down on Locusts

In April 2020, India witnessed an invasion by swarms of desert locusts, the biggest such attack in nearly three decades. The swarms originated in East Africa and came to India from across Pakistan. The states affected by locusts included Rajasthan, Madhya Pradesh, Uttar Pradesh, Maharashtra, Punjab, Haryana, Gujarat and Delhi NCR. In a first, the authorities used drones and civil aviation planes to spray pesticides to control the attack. Desert locusts are migratory pests that can eat up to double their weight in a single day. A single square kilometre of a swarm contains up to 40–80 million adult locusts that can, in a day, eat as much as around 35,000 people can. They are a major threat to food security and the rural economy.

C. Burt, the then agricultural commissioner in the Imperial (now Indian) Council of Agricultural Research (ICAR), was its first president and Prof. J.N. Mukherjee, its first secretary.

First pollen cryobank

The first pollen cryobank (frost bank) was established in 1983 at the Indian Institute of Horticultural Research, Bangalore (now Bengaluru), Karnataka, to conserve genetic biodiversity among plants and to support the work of crop breeders.

First agricultural university

The G.B. (Govind Ballabh) Pant University of Agriculture and Technology (GBPUA&T), also known as Pantnagar University, was the first agricultural university in India. It was inaugurated on 17 November 1960 as the Uttar Pradesh Agricultural University (UPAU). Later, in 1972, its name was changed to Govind Ballabh Pant University of Agriculture and Technology after the first chief minister of Uttar Pradesh and Bharat Ratna recipient Pandit Govind Ballabh Pant.

First spices research institute

The regional station for spice research, set up at Kozhikode, Kerala, in 1975, which later evolved into the Indian Institute of Spices Research in 1986, is the apex research organization for spices in the country.

WR Largest groundwater irrigation system

India is the country with the largest groundwater irrigation system in the world, with 39 million hectares (96.4 million acres) of land under this kind of irrigation. Besides groundwater, India's irrigation depends on canals from rivers, well-based systems, tanks and other rainwater harvesting. About two-thirds of farmland still depends on the monsoon.

Research institute located at the highest altitude
The Defence Institute of High Altitude Research (DIHAR), situated at 3,505 m (11,499 ft) in Leh, Ladakh, is a laboratory of the Defence Research Development Organization (DRDO). It was established in 1962 to help Indian defence troops as well as farmers of the region with appropriate agro-animal technologies.

WR Only research centre for tropical tuber crops
The Central Tuber Crops Research Institute at Sreekariyam in Thiruvananthapuram District, Kerala, is the only institute in the world dedicated to research on tropical tuber crops. It was established in 1963.

WR Oldest desert locust control programme
The Locust Warning Organization (LWO) established in 1939 in Karachi (now in Pakistan) by the British is the oldest locust control programme in the world. In 1946, the LWO moved to Delhi under the Directorate of Plant Protection, Quarantine and Storage, Ministry of Agriculture and Farmers' Welfare, Government of India. It surveys locust populations and issues regular bulletins to the farming community.

WR Only weed research centre
The Directorate of Weed Science Research (DWSR), Jabalpur, Madhya Pradesh, set up as the National Research Centre for Weed Science on 22 April 1989, is the only one in the world for weed management research.

Tocklai Experimental Station: oldest tea research station

WR Oldest tea research station
Set up in 1911, the Tocklai Experimental Station in Jorhat, Assam, is the world's oldest and largest tea research station. Its many contributions include the invention of tea machinery and the development of 30 vegetative clones. The transfer of innovative technology to its member estates is carried out through its advisory network that covers 1,076 tea estates occupying 341,049 hectares (842,750.4 acres) of land spread over the Brahmaputra Valley, the Barak Valley, Tripura, the Dooars, Darjeeling and the Terai areas. Tocklai has its regional R&D centre at Nagrakata in Jalpaiguri District, West Bengal.

AWARDS AND HONOURS

First Indian scientist to receive the Ramon Magsaysay award
Geneticist Dr M.S. Swaminathan received the Ramon Magsaysay award in 1971 for community leadership, becoming the first Indian scientist to do so. Known as

the 'Father of the Green Revolution' for his leading role in food self-sufficiency in India, he was the director of the Indian Agricultural Research Institute (IARI) in Delhi at the time. Dr Swaminathan advocates environmentally sustainable agriculture as well as preservation of biodiversity, culminating in what he has termed an 'evergreen' revolution.

First Indian Fellow of the Royal Society

Dr Benjamin Peary Pal, the first director of the Indian Council of Agricultural Research (ICAR), was also the first Indian agricultural scientist to become a Fellow of the Royal Society of London, UK, while in office, in 1972. He was also awarded the top national civilian awards: the Padma Shri (1959), the Padma Bhushan (1968) and the Padma Vibhushan (1987).

First winner of the World Food Prize

So far, eight Indians have won the World Food Prize. This global award is given to outstanding individuals who have advanced human development by improving the quality, quantity or availability of food in the world. The first Indian winner of this award was Dr M.S. Swaminathan in 1987, and the most recent was Dr Rattan Lal, an India-born British scientist from the USA, in 2020.

First Indian president of the International Society of Soil Sciences

Dr J.S. Kanwar was elected president of the International Society of Soil Sciences for the period 1978–82. The Society was founded in 1924, mainly by European agro-pedologists interested in establishing standardized methods of soil analysis.

Record Rewind

Employment in the agricultural sector

1991

Employment of people in agriculture in India was 63.05 per cent of total employment in 1991.

2019

Employment of people in agriculture in India was 43.21 per cent of the total employment in 2019.

GENERAL

Biggest farm loan waiver

The then Maharashtra chief minister Devendra Fadnavis announced a farm loan waiver of ₹340 billion (34,000 crore) in June 2017. This unprecedented waiver was intended to provide relief to 8.9 million (89 lakh) farmers in the state.

First agricultural theme park

N.K. Kurian, a civil engineer is the person behind Mango Meadows, India's first man-made agriculture-themed park spread on 12 hectares (29.65 acres) of land, in Kottayam, Kerala. Work on the park began in 2004 and it was opened to the public in December 2016. With saplings and seeds collected from 15 countries, currently the park has 4,500 species of plants, including 1,900 medicinal plants, 700 trees and 900 flowering plants.

Farm Law Reforms

The liberalization reforms in 1991 opened up opportunities for Indian business and industry. Three decades later, the Lok Sabha approved three agricultural reform bills on 17 September 2020 and the Rajya Sabha did so on 20 September. President Ram Nath Kovind gave his assent on 27 September amid protests by farmers' associations. These farm laws were: the Farmers' Produce Trade and Commerce (Promotion and Facilitation) Act, 2020; the Farmers (Empowerment and Protection) Agreement on Price Assurance and Farm Services Act, 2020; and the Essential Commodities (Amendment) Act, 2020. The most widespread protests against these laws took place in Punjab, Haryana and western Uttar Pradesh for over a year and three months. The laws were later repealed and the Farm Laws Repeal Bill was passed by both houses of the Parliament on 29 November 2021.

First village to use aquaponics

Cherai, a small coastal village on Vypin island, Ernakulam District, Kerala, has used aquaponics on a large scale since 2016. Many residents grow a variety of chemical-free foods, employing aquaponics, which is a revolutionary technology that has plants growing in aquatic mediums and deriving nutrition from the waste produced by the fish introduced in the water.

First fruit train

A train exclusively carrying fruit – 980 tonnes of locally grown bananas – was flagged off from Tadipatri railway station in Anantapur District, Andhra Pradesh, to the Jawaharlal Nehru Port in Mumbai, Maharashtra, on 31 January 2020. The train was laden with 43 refrigerator containers of bananas that had been despatched for export to international markets.

Largest all-India farmer interaction programme*

The Bank of Baroda organized the largest farmer interaction programme across India during 1–16 October 2018. Through their network of 3,989 branches, they organized 8,018 *choupal*s with 238,974 participants, 1,621 Kisan Melas (farmers' fairs), 310 literacy camps and 339 health camps for animals, fields and farmers. The event connected 255,587 farmers and celebrated the contribution of farmers to the overall development of the country.

First State/UT to enact a law on contract farming

Tamil Nadu became the first state to pass a law on contract farming after the Agricultural Produce and Livestock Contract Farming and Services (Promotion and Facilitation) Act was passed in February 2019. Contract farming enables

*This is a one-time category. Further and future claims for this category will not be accepted.

more transparency and legally safeguards the interests of farmers, producer companies and purchasers. The Act covers the produce of agriculture, sericulture, horticulture, apiculture, animal husbandry and forest activities.

First fully organic state

Sikkim was declared India's first fully organic state on 18 January 2016. It has succeeded in converting around 75,000 hectares (185,329 acres) of its agricultural land to certified organic land by implementing organic practices as per the guidelines of the National Programme for Organic Production.

First state/UT to regulate crops

Telangana has become the first state in the country that will stipulate for its farmers when and how much of which crops to grow. From the beginning of the kharif season in 2020, the state decided to regulate the cropping pattern with the help of a detailed cropping map and a seed regulation authority. The emphasis is to drive supply according to the market demand.

FARMLANDS AND PRINCIPAL CROPS

Largest single farm

The Central State Farm at Suratgarh in Rajasthan, with an area of 6,296 hectares (15,557.8 acres), is said to be the largest farm in Asia.

Largest average farm holdings in a state/UT

Nagaland has the largest farm holdings, with 5.06 hectares (12.5 acres) as the average size of an operational unit as per the 2015–16 Agricultural Census.

Smallest average farm holdings in a state/UT

The average size of an operational farm in Kerala is 0.18 hectares (0.4 acres) as per the 2015–16 Agricultural Census.

WR First hybrid Basmati rice

The IARI, New Delhi, developed and released RH-10 in 2001, the first hybrid superfine-grained aromatic rice in the world. The optimum yield of this variety of rice, with typical Basmati traits, is 7 tonnes/hectare.

WR First pigeon pea hybrid *(arhar)*

The International Crops Research Institute for Semi-Arid Tropics (ICRISAT) released the world's first hybrid pigeon pea, ICPH-8, in 1991. This variety recorded a yield potential of 2,057 kg/hectare.

Only transgenic crop approved for commercial cultivation

Bt cotton is the only transgenic crop approved for commercial cultivation in India by the Genetic Engineering Appraisal Committee (GEAC). The GEAC has also approved confined field trials of 20 GM (genetically modified) crops, viz., cotton, mustard, brinjal, okra, sorghum, groundnut, maize, potato, tomato, chickpea, pigeon pea, banana, castor, papaya, watermelon, sugar cane, wheat, rice, rubber tree and Indian wormwood, for generation of bio-safety data from both private and public sector institutions.

First cotton hybrid
The first commercial cotton hybrid in India, named H-4 or Sankar-4, was developed at Gujarat Agricultural University in 1970 by agricultural scientist Dr Chandrakant T. Patel.

First tobacco variety
Chatham, a flue-cured Virginia variety of tobacco, with a cured leaf yield potential of 1,100 kg/hectare was released in 1950 at the Clinical Trials Registry-India in Rajahmundry, Andhra Pradesh,

First tea estate
In 1837, the British East India Company set up the first tea estate at Chabua in Dibrugarh District, Assam. Now the estate is owned by Amalgamated Plantations Private Ltd. The first Tea Committee in India was set up in 1834 by the then Governor General of India, William Bentinck.

REGION-WISE DISTRIBUTION OF CROP STORAGE CAPACITY

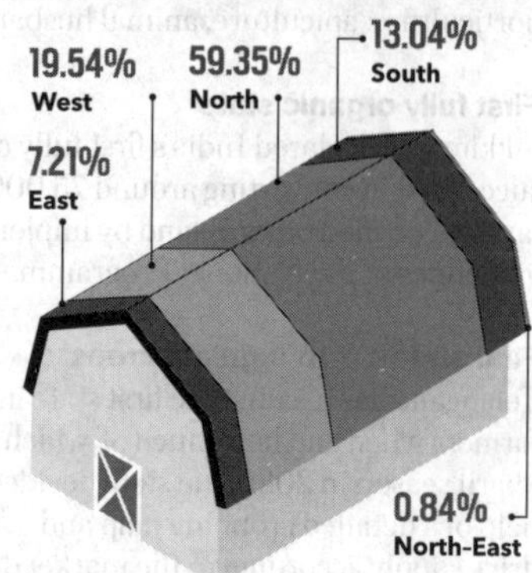

Source: *Agricultural Statistics at a Glance 2020*, Directorate of Economics and Statistics, Government of India

State/UT with maximum cold storage capacity
Uttar Pradesh has 14,176,062 tonnes of cold storage capacity.

Coffee: From Araku to Paris

Launched in 2001 as a livelihood project for tribal people by the Naandi Foundation, an NGO, Araku coffee first made its debut in Paris, France, through a flagship store opened in 2017. Grown in Araku Valley, Andhra Pradesh, by 25,000 tribal farmers across 720 villages, it was started by Anand Mahindra, Manoj Kumar and two other trustees of the Naandi Foundation. Called Araku Originals, the coffee launched its first online sale in India in February 2019 with four customized variants: Signature, Selection, Micro Climate and Grand Reserve. Benefiting from the region's unique environment, biodynamic agriculture (an alternative system of synthetics-free farming, which factors in the rhythms of the day and the year, along with phases of the moon, and so on) and the involvement of the world's top coffee experts, the Naandi Foundation plans to open cafés in Bengaluru and Mumbai next. They won the gold medal for the best coffee pod in the Prix Epicures OR 2018 Award in Paris.

TOP 10 COUNTRIES BY NUMBER OF ORGANIC PRODUCERS*

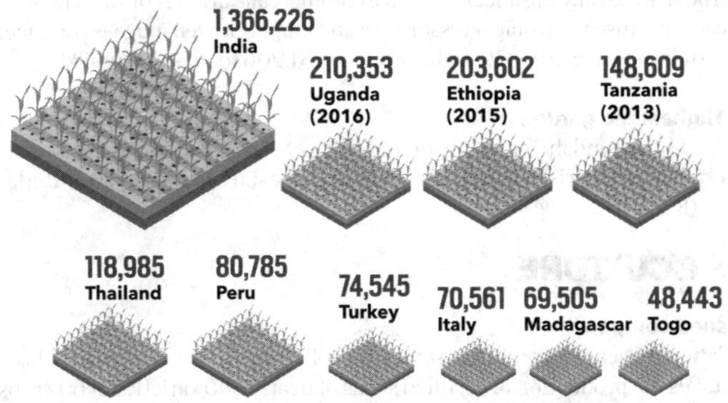

*2019; Source: *The World of Organic Agriculture Statistics and Emerging Trends 2021*, Research Institute of Organic Agriculture (FiBL) and International Federation of Organic Agriculture Movements (IFOAM)

WR Tallest paddy

Tanaji Nikam, a farmer in Vannur Village in Kolhapur, Maharashtra, grew a paddy plant 2.8 m (9 ft 2 in.) tall in 2005 using organic manure.

Tallest sugar cane

Vedant Rajendra Yadav (b. 28 January 1998) from Fursungi Village in Pune District, Maharashtra, grew a sugar cane plant that was 12.2 m (40 ft) in height in January 2019. The plant was 2.5 years old and had 120 internodes.

Tallest jowar

Dodda Ramachandra Reddy (b. 20 January 1951) from Peddapalli, Karimnagar District, Telangana, grew a jowar plant that was 5.3 m (17 ft 4 in.) high. It took 161 days to grow to this height.

WR Largest number of organic producers in the world

According to the World of Organic Agriculture Report 2020, India has the largest number of organic producers in the world. With 1,149,371 certified organic producers, the country is home to more than 41.04 per cent of the total number of organic producers (2.8 million) worldwide. However, when it comes to the total area under certified organic cultivation, India only has 1.94 per cent of its entire agricultural area under organic cultivation.

Largest ploidy series in a crop plant

A team at the ICAR-Indian Grassland and Fodder Research Institute (IGFRI) in Jhansi, Uttar Pradesh, generated the world's largest ploidy series in a crop plant from a single progenitor in the fodder crop guinea grass. From a tetraploid (4x) plant with 2n=32 chromosomes, they developed offspring with ploidies 3x, 4x, 5x, 6x, 7x, 8x, 9x and 11x. The team led by Dr Pankaj Kaushal included Dr A.K. Roy, Dr D.R. Malaviya, Dr K.K. Dwivedi, Dr M. Chakraborti, Dr A. Radhakrishna, Sharmishtha Paul and Saurabh Saxena.

Only producer of five commercial silk varieties

India is the only producer of all five commercial varieties of silk, viz., mulberry, oak tussore, tropical tussore, *eri* and *muga*. Golden muga is produced only in India. During 2018–19, India produced 31,906 tonnes of raw silk.

Highest tea garden

The Korakundah Tea Estate of the United Nilgiri Tea Estates Co. Ltd, near Coonoor in the Nilgiris in Tamil Nadu, has its highest tea garden at an altitude of 2,471 m (8,107 ft).

HORTICULTURE

First seed company

The National Seeds Corporation, set up in 1963 by the Government of India, undertakes the production of certified seeds of nearly 600 varieties of 60 crops through its 8,000 registered seed growers.

Hottest chilli

The *bhut jolokia*, or 'ghost chilli', is the hottest chilli in India. Rated at 1,041,427 Scoville heat units (SHUs), this variety is cultivated in the north-eastern states of Arunachal Pradesh, Assam, Nagaland and Manipur.

First vanilla cultivation

The first cultivation centres of vanilla were set up more than a century ago at the Kallar Fruit Research Station, Thiruvananthapuram District, and the Ambalavayal Horticultural Research Station, Wayanad District, Kerala.

First non-narcotic poppy

Sujata, a poppy variety developed in 1998 at the Central Institute of Medicinal and Aromatic Plants, Lucknow, Uttar Pradesh, was the first poppy variety free of opium and opium alkaloids.

Highest vineyard

At 1,585 m (5,200 ft) above the mean sea level, Kookkal Vineyards (Domaine

TOP 5 STATES WITH THE HIGHEST AREA UNDER HORTICULTURE CROPS*

	State	Area (in '000 Ha)
1	Karnataka	2,362.84
2	Uttar Pradesh	2,282.40
3	Madhya Pradesh	2,106.23
4	West Bengal	1,972.09
5	Maharashtra	1,858.83

* 2019–20; Third advance estimates; Source: *Agricultural Statistics at a Glance 2020*, Directorate of Economics and Statistics, Government of India

ALL INDIA PRODUCTIVITY OF HORTICULTURE CROPS

Year	Fruits	Vegetables	Flowers, Aromatic and Medicinal	Plantation Crops	Spices	Total*
1991–92	9.96%	10.47%	No data	3.26%	0.95%	7.56%
2001–02	10.72%	14.40%	5.05%	3.25%	1.17%	8.79%
2011–12	11.40%	17.39%	2.92%	4.57%	1.85%	11.07%
2017–18	14.96%	17.97%	3.49%	4.83%	2.09%	12.25%

1991–2018; Source: *Horticulture Statistics at a Glance 2018,* Ministry of Agriculture and Farmers' Welfare, Government of India; *The total is not the cumulative total of entries listed but also includes any other horticulture item not included in this table.

Kookkal) at Kookkal Village, near Udhagamandalam, Tamil Nadu, are the highest commercial-scale vineyards in the country.

Tallest papaya plant

Jhantu Paul from Kolkata, West Bengal, owns the tallest papaya tree (*Carica papaya*) measuring 14.07 m (46 ft 2 in.) as verified on 22 January 2017.

Heaviest jackfruit

Kaithakkoli Kurichiya's family found a jackfruit weighing 57.9 kg in their compound in Thallappuzha, Wayanad District, Kerala, in May 2020. The jackfruit was 67 cm (26 in.) long, with a circumference of 1.35 m (4 ft 5 in.).

The agriculture sector employs 80 per cent of India's economically active women. Of them 33 per cent comprise the agricultural workforce and 48 per cent are self-employed farmers.

First coconut hybrids

Researchers at the Coconut Research Station, now called the Central Plantation Crops Research Institute (CPCRI), Kasaragod, Kerala, produced the first coconut hybrids between the tall and dwarf palms in 1932, with two to three times more nuts than in each of the parent palms.

First mustard hybrid

In 2008, NRC Sankar Sarson (NRCHB 506), an Indian mustard hybrid, was developed by a team of scientists led by Dr K.H. Singh at the National Research Centre on Rapeseed-Mustard (NRCRM; now Directorate of Rapeseed Mustard Research) in Bharatpur, Rajasthan.

Longest and biggest coconut

Dr Dilip Kumar Vitthaldas Patil, a senior scientist at the Central Institute for Cotton Research, Nagpur, Maharashtra, has preserved for 12 years, the largest and biggest coconut (and the longest preserved) seen in India. Dr Patil found this giant coconut in a farm in Pilicode Village, Kasaragod District, Kerala. Even in its dried state, the coconut is 27 cm (10.6 in.) horizontally, 67.5 cm (26.57 in.) long

Breaking Ground with Asafoetida

In a first, *hing* (asafoetida) will now be cultivated in India. Until now, India imported all its asafoetida. The first seedling was planted in Kwaring Village of Lahaul Valley, Himachal Pradesh, on 15 October 2020. The farmers were supported by agro-technology developed by the Palampur-based Institute of Himalayan Bioresource Technology (IHBT) under the aegis of the Council of Scientific and Industrial Research (CSIR). They introduced six accessions of seeds from Iran, sourced by the National Bureau of Plant Genetic Resources (NBPGR), New Delhi, and set up its production protocol for cultivation. IHBT also organized demonstrations and training for farmers to cultivate it on a commercial scale. Only one species *(Ferula asafoetida)* is used to produce the spice.

(technically known as equatorial length) as against normal green coconuts, which are 14 to 20 cm (5.5 to 7.87 in.) horizontally and 25 to 45 cm (9.8 to 17.7 in.) long. In its dried state this coconut weighs 1,450 g against an average of 300–500 g.

First onion hybrid

The world's first onion hybrid was developed at the Indian Agricultural Research Institute, New Delhi, in March 2002 with a potential of increasing yield by 20 per cent.

First castor hybrid

The Castor and Mustard Research Station in Sardarkrushinagar in Banaskantha District, Gujarat, developed the first castor hybrid named GCH 3 and released it in 1968–69 on a commercial scale. GCH 7, released in 2006, has the highest potential productivity (3,000 kg/hectare) in India.

Largest producer, exporter and consumer of spices

India is the largest producer, exporter and consumer of spices and spice products. The total production of spices during 2018–19 was 9.22 tonnes from an area of 3.89 million hectares.

Largest producer of coconuts

India produces 34.73 per cent of the global production of coconuts. As per 2017–18 reports, the area and production of coconuts in the country is 2.10 million hectares and 23,798 million nuts, respectively. The four southern states of Kerala, Tamil Nadu, Karnataka and Andhra Pradesh account for 89.02 per cent of the coconut area and 93.05 per cent of the coconut production in the country.

Largest producer of mangoes

According to the first estimates for 2018–19, India's mango production stood at 22,352.87 tonnes. Andhra Pradesh turned out to be the top mango-producing state with the production of 5,001,740 tonnes of mangoes. India is also the top producer of guava, papaya, banana, lemon and lime in the world, making it the second largest global fruit producer.

ANIMAL HUSBANDRY

Early vet research

Research on animal healthcare began with the setting up of the Imperial Bacteriological Laboratory at Poona (now Pune), Maharashtra, on 9 December 1889, with Dr Alfred Lingard as the first bacteriologist in 1890. It was moved to Mukteshwar, Uttarakhand, in 1895. The Indian Veterinary Research Institute (IVRI) later began in 1913 at Izatnagar, Bareilly District, Uttar Pradesh.

First veterinary surgeon

William Moorcroft (1767–1825), a Britisher who was appointed veterinary surgeon in 1808 at the Pusa Stud Farm, Bihar, is the first one on record in India.

Only camel farm

The National Research Centre on Camel (NRCC), also a camel-breeding farm, was set up in Bikaner, Rajasthan, in 1957 for conducting scientific research on camels. The centre aims to study ways of optimizing the working capacity of camels. It is the only camel farm in the country.

First dairy research institute

Established in 1923 as the Imperial Dairy Institute of Animal Husbandry and Dairying in Bangalore (now Bengaluru), Karnataka, it was renamed National Dairy Research Institute (NDRI) after Independence. In 1955, its headquarters were shifted to Karnal, Haryana. It undertakes research, teaching and extension activities in dairy development.

The period from 2012 to 2019 saw a growth of 4.82 per cent in total livestock in India.

Largest dairy development programme

Project Operation Flood, launched in 1970 by the National Dairy Development Board (NDDB) and led by Dr Verghese Kurien, general manager and later chairman, AMUL, Chairman – NDDB and Institute of Rural Management (IRMA), Anand, Gujarat, involved forming a National Milk Grid that connected milk producers to consumers in over 700 towns and cities in India.

Top milk-producing country

India has led the world in milk production since 1997. Milk production in the country increased from 176.3 million tonnes during 2017–18 to 187.7 million tonnes during 2018–19. The top milk-producing states are Uttar Pradesh, Rajasthan, Madhya Pradesh, Andhra Pradesh and Gujarat.

First frozen semen bank for bulls

The first frozen semen bank for bulls was established in 1963 in Mattupatti,

SUPER 30

AMRITA PATEL: SHINING IN THE 'MILKY' WAY

A renowned businesswoman and environmentalist, Amrita Patel (b. 1943) has made a stellar contribution in the cooperative dairy sector. She joined Amul in 1965 and trained under Dr Verghese Kurien, known as the pioneer of the White Revolution. After four decades of working in the dairy industry, she served as the chairperson of the National Dairy Development Board from 1998 to 2014. During her tenure, she led 'Operation Flood', the world's biggest dairy development programme that transformed India from being a milk-deficient country to its largest producer in the world. For her work in this sector, she has received the Borlaug Award (1991), the title of the World Dairy Expo's International Person of the Year (1997), the Indian Dairy Association Fellowship, the Padma Bhushan (2001), the Indira Gandhi Paryavaran Puraskar (2005) and the Mahindra Samriddhi Krishi Shiromani Samman (Lifetime Achievement Award (2016), among others.

Amrita Patel

Kerala, with Indo-Swiss collaboration, with the objective of evolving a new breed of cattle adapted to the local environment. The bank dealt with the collection, processing, storage and transportation of the semen of bull breeds.

First artificial insemination in bulls
Artificial insemination was successfully attempted for the first time in 1939 by Sampath Kumaran, who crossed the Indian Hallikar breed with Holstein Friesian bulls.

First calf cloned from frozen semen
In July 2014, a male cloned calf named Rajat was produced by the National Dairy Research Institute (NDRI), Karnal, Haryana, using a donor cell from the frozen semen of a highly ranked Murrah buffalo bull. This was the first time when frozen semen was used for cloning a farm animal.

First lamb from frozen embryo
Scientists at the Central Sheep and Wool Research Institute in Avikanagar in Tonk District, Rajasthan, implanted a cryo-preserved Bharat Merino embryo into a Kheri surrogate ewe, which birthed a lamb on 20 January 1999.

Most piglets in a single litter
An artificial insemination field project by scientists at the National Research Centre on Pig in Guwahati, Assam, achieved the largest litter size of 19 piglets in a single delivery in 2012.

First cloned pashmina goat
Noori, the first cloned pashmina goat, was born at the Faculty of Veterinary Sciences and Animal Husbandry, Sher-e-Kashmir University of Agricultural

Sciences and Technology, Srinagar, Jammu and Kashmir, on 9 March 2012. With a birthweight of 1.3 kg, she was produced by a team headed by Dr Riaz Ahmad Shah, using somatic cell nuclear transfer technique.

First test-tube yak calf

The world's first test-tube yak calf named Norgayal, a male yak calf weighing 19 kg, was born at the Nyukmadung farm of the National Research Centre on Yak (NRCY), Dirang Dzong, West Kameng District, Arunachal Pradesh, on 15 July 2013.

First and largest cattle farm

The District Livestock Farm in Hosur in Krishnagiri District, Tamil Nadu, which is spread over 664 hectares (1,641 acres), is India's and Asia's largest cattle farm. A horse-rearing centre during British rule in the 19th century, it was given over to the Agricultural Department of India in Madras (now Tamil Nadu) in 1924 to be run as a cattle-breeding station. Its mandate was to maintain pure native milk breeds, such as the Red Sindhi, and to conduct research on cattle.

Heaviest and highest-priced bull

In March 2018, Haryana's first Murrah Ratan Award was won by a buffalo called Shahenshah, which weighed between 1,100 and 1,200 kg and was owned by Narender Singh from Didwari Village, Panipat, Haryana.

State with the most veterinary institutions

Rajasthan leads Indian states and UTs with 7,897 veterinary institutions (as on 31 March 2018).

Record Rewind

Largest livestock population

1991

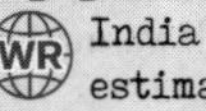

India had an estimated population of 92,453,000 heads of cattle, the highest number of livestock in the world (according to the 1982 census).

2019

India had the largest population of livestock, with an estimated 535,800,000 heads of cattle, making up as much as 31 per cent of the world's livestock population.

Highest stud farm

The Zanskar Pony Breeding and Training Centre at Partapur in Nubra Block, Ladakh, is located at 3,146 m (10,321 ft) above the mean sea level.

First cross-bred cow

The first cross-bred cow breed in India, called Taylor, was named after an Englishman, William Taylor, who started cattle cross-breeding in Patna, Bihar, in the mid-19th century.

Heaviest goat

Asif Ali from Bhopal, Madhya Pradesh, reared the heaviest goat named King on his R.K. Goat Farm. King weighed 171 kg on 25 July 2019.

First cloned buffalo

On 6 February 2009, a team of six scientists – S.K. Singla, M.S. Chauhan, R.S. Manik, P. Palta, R.A. Shah and A. George – all from the Animal Biotechnology Centre at the National Dairy Research Institute (NDRI) in Karnal, Haryana, produced the first female water buffalo calf in the world by cloning from a year-old buffalo of the Murrah breed. Although the calf died five days later, the team of scientists succeeded in testing the cloning and other technologies that helped them achieve one of their objectives of getting the desired gender of the cloned animal.

First cloned female buffalo by hand-guided technique

In June 2014, scientists of the National Dairy Research Institute (NDRI) in Karnal, Haryana, produced the world's first female cloned buffalo calf through 'hand-guided' cloning, using a donor cell from the ear of a high-yielding Murrah buffalo. The calf was named Lalima.

First buffalo-milk powder

The Kaira District Cooperative Milk Producers Union (Amul Dairy), Anand, Gujarat, produced whole and skimmed milk powder from buffalo milk in 1955. It was also the first in the world to commercially produce cheese and baby food from buffalo milk in 1960.

Oldest cow

Ruby, a cow owned by Dr Dipa Panjuani of Pune, Maharashtra, crossed 35 years in 2017. It was milking till six months before it turned 32 years old.

POULTRY AND FISHERIES

First broiler chicken variety

B-77, the first broiler variety of chicken, was released by the IVRI in Izatnagar in Bareilly District, Uttar Pradesh, in 1977.

First transgenic rohu fish

During 2004–05, a team of scientists led by Dr T.J. Pandian at the Madurai Kamaraj University, Madurai, Tamil Nadu, developed a genetically modified rohu fish that could grow 6–7 times faster than a normal one.

First deep-sea fishing station

The Deep-Sea Fishing Station, Mumbai, Maharashtra, was set up in October 1946. It was renamed the Exploratory Fisheries Project (EFP) in 1974 when it systematically surveyed the coastal and offshore waters up to a depth of 70 m (230 ft). Engaged in oceanic surveys of Exclusive Economic Zones, it was renamed the Fishery Survey of India in 1979.

Top shrimp-producing state/UT

Andhra Pradesh led with 570,840 tonnes, followed by West Bengal with 80,400 tonnes, in 2018–19.

First pearl culture

The first cultured pearls, using the Akoya pearl oyster, were produced in 1973 at the Tuticorin Research Centre at the Central Marine Fisheries Research Institute (CMFRI) in Thoothukudi, Tamil Nadu, in collaboration with the Tamil Nadu State Fisheries Department.

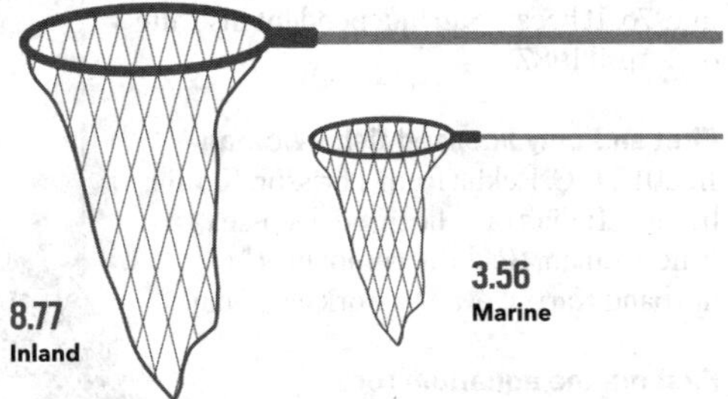

*2017–18; Source: *Basic Animal Husbandry and Fisheries Statistics 2018 Report*, Department of Animal Husbandry and Dairying, Government of India

Biggest hen egg
A hen at the Dev Research and Breeding Farms of Sukhbir Singh of Ramrai Khera in Jind, Haryana, laid an egg weighing 167 g on 28 September 2014. It was 8.35 cm (3.3 in.) long and 5 cm (2 in.) wide.

Oldest fisheries research institutes
The oldest fisheries research institutes are the Central Marine Fisheries Research Institute (CMFRI), established in 1947, and the Central Inland Capture Fisheries Research Institute (CICFRI), also set up in 1947 under the name of Central Inland Fisheries Research Institute (CIFRI) in Calcutta (now Kolkata, West Bengal).

Largest poultry company
Suguna Foods Private Limited, which achieved a sales turnover of over ₹8,700 crore (87 billion) during 2019–20, is the largest broiler chicken company in India. The company, headquartered in Coimbatore, Tamil Nadu, ranks among the top ten poultry enterprises worldwide and has its operations in 18 states in India, covering about 39,000 farmers from over 8,000 villages. Its products and services include hatcheries, feed mills, processing plants, value-added eggs, and broiler and frozen chicken.

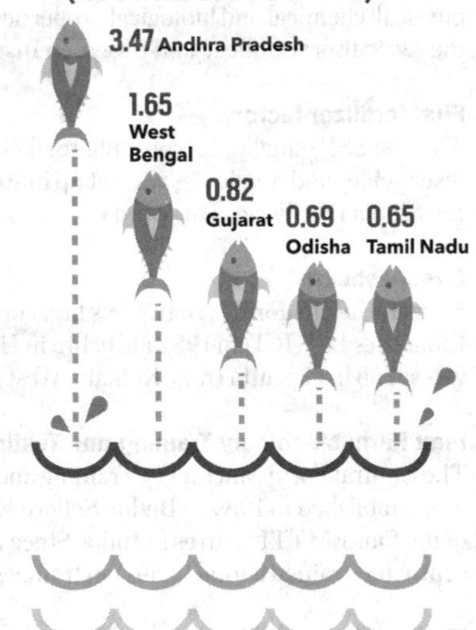

*2017–18; Source: *Basic Animal Husbandry and Fisheries Statistics 2018 Report*, Department of Animal Husbandry and Dairying, Government of India

First research institute for freshwater aquaculture
The Central Institute of Freshwater Aquaculture, Bhubaneswar, Odisha, began in the Pond Culture Division of the Central Inland Fisheries Research Institute, at Cuttack, Odisha, in 1949. The division

was later upgraded as the Freshwater Aquaculture Research and Training Centre in 1976. It became an independent institute on 1 April 1987.

First and only licensed fisherwoman

In 2017, K.C. Rekha from Thrissur, Kerala, became India's only licensed deep-sea fisherwoman. Rekha accompanies her husband Karthikeyan to work every day.

K.C. Rekha: first and only licensed fisherwoman

First marine aquarium for ornamental fish

An aquarium for ornamental fish breeding and multiplication was established in 1998 in Vizhinjam near Kovalam in Kerala.

FERTILIZERS, PESTICIDES AND MACHINERY

First biocontrol agents

The ladybird beetle of Australia was introduced in 1898 to control mealy bugs on fruit crops.

Earliest soil treatment experiments

The earliest methods to find out the effects of inorganic fertilizers on the soil – its physical, chemical and biological properties vis-à-vis crop yields – were started at the Agricultural College and Research Institute, Coimbatore, Tamil Nadu, in 1909.

First fertilizer factory

The first SSP (single superphosphate) factory that produced fertilizer mixtures, insecticides and fungicides was set up in 1906 in Ranipet District in Tamil Nadu by East India Distilleries Parry Ltd.

First pesticide

Benzene hexachloride (BHC) was first commercialized by the Imperial Chemical Industries Ltd (ICI) in 1952 at Rishra in Hooghly District, West Bengal. A factory was set up in Calcutta (now Kolkata, West Bengal).

First Farm Machinery Training and Testing Institute

The Central Farm Machinery Training and Testing Institute (FMTTI), which was established in 1959 in Budni, Sehore District, Madhya Pradesh, was the first of the four FMTTI centres in India. Since its inception and up to March 2020, the centre has trained a total of 69,056 trainees from all over the country.

First synthetic pesticide

DDT (Dichlorodiphenyltrichloroethane) was introduced in 1946 for vector control and used in agriculture in 1948. Its use was banned in May 1989.

	Name and Service	Founders	Funding (₹ Crores)
	TOP 5 FUNDED AGRICULTURAL START-UPS		
1	Ninjacart: Fresh produce supply chain	Sharath Loganathan, Thirukumaran Nagarajan, Vasudevan Chinnathambi, Kartheeswaran K.K., Ashutosh Vikram and Sachin Jose	265.5
2	Agrostar: Agronomy advice, service and input producs	Shardul Sheth and Sitanshu Sheth	205.06
3	Stellapps: Optimizing the dairy supply chain	Ranjith Mukundan, Ravishankar G. Shiroor, Praveen Nale, Ramakrishna Adukuri and Venkatesh Seshasayee	106.33
4	Jumbotail: Food and grocery ecosystem	S. Karthik Venkateswaran and Ashish Jhina	68.35
5	Cropin: Software-service-based solutions to agribusinesses	Krishna Kumar, Kunal Prasad and Chittaranjan Jena	60.76

*2018; Source: *Agritech in India: Emerging Trends in 2019*, National Association of Software and Services Companies (NASSCOM)

First neem biocide

The first neem-based biocide was tested and commissioned by the National Tree Growers Cooperative Federation during 1997–98.

State/UT with the highest use of pesticides

Maharashtra was the highest consumer of both chemical (11,746 tonnes) and bio-pesticides (1,164 tonnes) in 2018–19.

State/UT with the highest use of fertilizers (NPK) per unit area

With a consumption of 289.24 kg per hectare, Puducherry is the largest consumer of fertilizers (NPK: nitrogen, phosphorus and potassium) in 2016–17.

First use of lift irrigation

In 1926, an experimental lift irrigation system on 1,012 hectares (2,500 acres) of wasteland was started in the Rachna Doab region of Gangapur Village in Punjab (now in Pakistan) by Sir Ganga Ram, a member of the Regional Commission on Agriculture.

First agri-plane

Hindustan Aeronautics Ltd's HA-31 Basant monoplane was built in 1972 for agricultural needs. Its use was discontinued in 1980.

First semi-autonomous tractor

In April 2018, Mahindra and Mahindra Ltd rolled out a high-tech tractor, the Pack 1. This is an 'intelligent' tractor with a driver-assist system. Mahindra is validating the Pack 2 driverless version.

Earliest use of tractors

Sardar Sir Jogendra Singh (1877–1946) experimented with steam tractors for wasteland reclamation in 1914 at Aira estate in Lakhimpur, Uttar Pradesh, and at Iqbal Nagar (now in Pakistan) in Punjab.

A steam tractor: one of the earliest farm machines

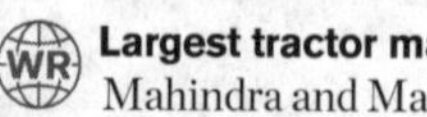

Largest tractor market

Mahindra and Mahindra Limited is the largest-selling tractor brand in India, with domestic sales of 291,901 units for the financial year ended March 2020. The total domestic sales in the same period were at 709,000 units.

First natural farming state

In June 2018, the Government of Andhra Pradesh launched a plan to move six million farms/farmers cultivating eight million hectares (19.8 million acres) of land from traditional chemical farming to zero-budget natural farming by 2024, to make the state the country's first 100 per cent 'natural farming' one, following UN sustainable development goals. Led by Rythu Sadhikara Samstha (RySS) and supported by the Sustainable India Finance Facility, a partnership between UN Environment, BNP Paribas and the World Agroforestry Centre, it promotes regenerative farming, soil biodiversity and livelihoods for smallholder farmers.

There are 82 fertilizer quality control testing laboratories including four central ones in the country.

Farm equipment with largest market share

Tractors have the biggest share of the farm machinery market in India, at 80 per cent. In 2018–19, overall tractor sales were 878,476 units with exports of 92,095 units.

State/UT with most tractor exports

Maharashtra with exports worth ₹1,382.96 crore (13.8296 billion) is the state with the most tractor exports in the year 2019–20. It was followed by Punjab with exports valued at ₹1,323.48 crore (13.2348 billion) and Tamil Nadu with exports worth ₹1,159.9 crore (11.599 billion).

State/UT with most registered Custom Hiring Centres (CHC)

Punjab has the most CHC's registered on the FARMS app, developed by the Ministry of Agriculture and Farmers' Welfare. Punjab leads with 10,586 registered centres, followed by Andhra Pradesh (8,455) and Telangana (6,566). The app was launched in September 2019 as 'CHC Farm Machinery', and was recently revised and renamed with the acronym 'FARMS' app (Farm Machinery Solutions app). It is available on Google Playstore.

TRANSPORT

AIR

First flight

On 18 February 1911, Henri Pequet flew a Humber-Sommer biplane carrying mail from Allahabad (now Prayagraj), Uttar Pradesh, to Naini Junction, about 10 km away. Proper civil aviation, however, began on 15 October 1932, when a 2,092 km long flight of the aircraft D.H. *Puss Moth,* flown by aviator and industrialist J.R.D Tata, under Tata Air Services, a division of Tata Sons, delivered mail from Drigh Road Aerodrome in Karachi (now in Pakistan) to Juhu Aerodrome in Bombay (now Mumbai, Maharashtra) and then continued to Madras (now Chennai).

First pilot licence

Jehangir Ratanji Dadabhoy (J.R.D) Tata, an aviator, entrepreneur and chairman of Tata Group, became the first licensed pilot in India when he received his pilot licence No. 1 in 1929.

First airline

Tata Airlines, set up by pioneering industrialist J.R.D. Tata soon after he piloted India's maiden civil flight in 1932, was later converted into a public company in 1946 under the name Air-India Ltd, with him as its chairman. In March 1953, it was raised to be a public corporation and became today's Air India.

First airfield

The grass aerodrome at Juhu in Bombay (now Mumbai), Maharashtra, opened in 1932. It was the base for Tata Airlines.

First aircraft designer

S.V. Setty, an assistant engineer with the Public Works Department, Mysore (now Mysuru), Karnataka, in 1911–12, designed, piloted and helped manufacture planes at Avro (a British company). With an eight-cylinder engine, the Avro biplane had a 9.76 m (32 ft) span and weighed 362.8 kg without a pilot or passenger. The plane touched a speed of around 72–80 km/hr.

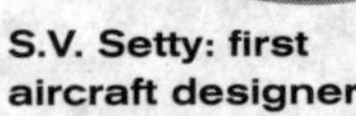

S.V. Setty: first aircraft designer

First helicopter school

Hindustan Aeronautics Ltd (HAL), based in Bangalore (now Bengaluru), Karnataka, established a training school on 1 May 2000 for potential aviators to obtain commercial as well as private helicopter pilot licences.

First flying club

The Aero Club was established in Bombay (now Mumbai), Maharashtra, by industrial magnate Sir Victor Sassoon in 1928. In September 1929, it was affiliated to the Royal Aero Club, UK. It was recognized by the Government of India as the coordinating body for flying clubs in India, and in 1948, it was affiliated to the Federation Aeronautique Internationale.

First aeronautical society
On 17 December 1948, the Aeronautical Society of India was inaugurated at Bangalore (now Bengaluru), Karnataka, to promote advancement in the field of aeronautics, and dissemination of knowledge about aeronautical science and aircraft engineering.

First radio plane
The twin-engine de Havilland DH-89 Dragon Rapide, which was on the Karachi–Bombay–Colombo route, was equipped with wireless transmission facilities on 1 December 1937.

First cargo service
An air cargo service started on 21 May 1927, between Calcutta (now Kolkata), West Bengal, and Bagdogra in Darjeeling District of West Bengal, by West Bengal Air Transport, operated for only a week.

India has Air Service Agreements with 115 countries. This allows international commercial air transport services between two nations.

First air ticket booking office
The first air ticket booking office was opened in 1939 in a building in the Churchgate Reclamation area in Bombay (now Mumbai), Maharashtra. The space now houses the Asiatic Department Store.

First air freight service
Air Freight Pvt. Ltd was set up in 1945 as handling agents for Tata Airlines and Air-India International. It was also the first air cargo clearing agent.

First international flight
Malabar Princess (a Lockheed L-749 Super Constellation) of the Air-India International Corporation, with Captain K.R. Guzder in command, flew from Bombay (now Mumbai), Maharashtra, to London, UK, via Cairo, Egypt, and Geneva, Switzerland, on 8 June 1948, carrying 35 passengers.

First crash
On 17 July 1950, a DC-3 aircraft was recorded to have crashed near Pathankot, Punjab, tragically killing all 22 passengers.

First indigenously assembled plane
The first HS-748 was assembled at the Aircraft Manufacturing Depot, Kanpur, Uttar Pradesh, and delivered to Indian Airlines on 27 June 1967.

First indigenous aircraft
- The Hindustan Trainer-2, built by Hindustan Aeronautics Ltd (HAL), Bangalore (now Bengaluru), Karnataka, made its maiden flight in August 1951. Meant for military use, it was also used by flying schools.
- *Swati*, a two-seater trainer for flying club pilots, was designed and built at Bharat Heavy Electricals Ltd (BHEL), Haridwar, Uttar Pradesh (now in

Uttarakhand), by the Directorate General of Civil Aviation (DGCA). Its maiden flight was in November 1990 at Delhi.

First all-jet carrier

In 1962, Air India became the world's first all-jet carrier when it replaced Super Constellation planes with a fleet of Boeing 707s.

First indigenous helicopter

The advanced light helicopter (ALH) was built at HAL, Bangalore (now Bengaluru), Karnataka, in 1992. The ALH was used both in defence and civil operations.

First Boeing 737-900 aircraft

Jet Airways acquired the first Boeing 737-900 aircraft in May 2003. Longest among the Boeing 737 family, the aircraft can seat 177–190 passengers and has a maximum flight range of 5,084 km. In 2018, Jet Airways took the delivery of the first 150 Boeing 737 MAX aeroplanes, becoming the first Indian carrier to fly the new variant.

First jet

Air India entered the jet age on 20 April 1960, when its Boeing 707 *Gauri Shankar* flew to London, UK. Soon after, on 14 May 1960, it flew to New York, USA. With this, India became the first Asian country to operate a transatlantic flight. The aircraft was written off after a landing accident at Bombay (now Mumbai, Maharashtra) on 22 June 1982.

First air taxi

India's first air taxi service started at Chandigarh Airport on 14 January 2021 under the UDAN-RCS (Regional Connectivity Scheme) of the Central government. With the capacity to seat a pilot and three passengers, the

SUPER 30

AIR INDIA: THE SKY HAS NO LIMITS

Founded by J.R.D. Tata on 15 October 1932 as Tata Airlines, Air India became a government-owned enterprise in 1953, operating a fleet of aircraft serving 102 domestic and international destinations. It started its operations in 1946, became the world's first all-jet airline in 1962, and is now the largest international carrier out of India and has its headquarters and primary hub in Delhi (Indira Gandhi International Airport, New Delhi). The airline was also featured in *Guinness World Records*, for evacuating more than 111,000 Indian expatriates from Amman, Jordan, to Mumbai, Maharashtra, by operating 488 flights from 13 August to 11 October 1990 (59 days), during the First Gulf War. On 8 October 2021, the Tata Conglomerate won the bid to acquire Air India.

daily flight was 45-minute long and it plied on the Chandigarh–Hisar route at a cost of ₹1,755 per seat.

First air varsity

The Central Training Establishment in Hyderabad (now in Telangana), an independent training centre of Indian Airlines Ltd, was upgraded to a deemed university in 1997. The centre is equipped with infrastructure and training facilities for courses in civil aviation.

First air traffic control system

A state-of-the-art Air Traffic Control (ATC) system, supported by Raytheon flight data and equipped with radar-processing hardware, was installed at the Indira Gandhi International Airport (IGIA), New Delhi, on 14 January 1999. This new system provided three-dimensional radial, bearing and height information regarding the location and situation of any aircraft within a range of 250 nautical miles.

First airport to instal a body scanner

The first full-body scanner system was installed on a trial basis at Terminal 1D of the Indira Gandhi International Airport, New Delhi, on 10 April 2010. Initially it was used only on volunteering passengers and the scanning process took less than a minute. The system, called SmartCheck, was built by American Science and Engineering (AS&E) and used the X-ray backscatter technology.

First airport to install waste recycling machines

The Rajiv Gandhi International Airport (RGIA) in Hyderabad, Telangana, became the first airport in the country to instal waste recycling machines, launched as a pilot project in October 2017. Operated by GMR Hyderabad International Airport Ltd (GHIAL), the airport has equipment to crush and recycle plastic PET (polyethylene terephthalate) bottles, steel or aluminium cans and plastic bags into reusable raw material. These 'Swachh Bharat Recycling Machines' were designed and created by Mumbai-based company Wild West Media, and can be used to manufacture upcycled goods like bags, wallets and denim. Passengers may either make a donation or claim a discount coupon in return for submitting their empty plastic products. RGIA is also the first airport to have its own composting plant, which processes the food waste generated at the airport.

Highest commercial airport

Kushok Bakula Rimpochee Airport (or Leh airport) in Leh, Ladakh, is the highest commercial airport at 3, 256 m (10,682 ft) above the mean sea level. The airport is named after Kushok Bakula Rinpoche, whose Spituk Monastery is very close to the airfield. The Indian Air Force handed over the airport to the Airport Authority of India in 2016.

Largest passenger airport terminal

On 3 July 2010, Terminal 3 of Indira Gandhi International Airport, New Delhi, became India's and South Asia's largest aviation hub, with the capacity to handle more than 40 million (four crore) passengers a year. The airport handled over 69.23 million (6.923 crore) passengers in 2018–19.

First fully solar-powered airport

The Cochin International Airport in Kochi, Kerala, became the first airport in the world to run completely on solar power on 18 August 2015. The solar plant installed at the airport has 46,000 solar panels and can produce 50,000 to 60,000 units of electricity every day. This airport won the coveted Champion of Earth Prize, awarded by the United Nations, in 2018.

First Boeing 787 Dreamliner

The Boeing 787 Dreamliner, a fuel-efficient aircraft that can carry up to 290 passengers and fly 15,750 km at a stretch, touched down for the first time at the Indira Gandhi International Airport, New Delhi, on 13 July 2011.

Boeing 787 Dreamliner

Oldest fleet

Founded in 1932, Air India has a fleet size of 125 aircraft (excluding subsidiaries), with an average age of 8.2 years, making it the oldest fleet in India. The airline has its headquarters in New Delhi.

Oldest to obtain a commercial pilot's licence

Captain Rajagopal Nagarajan (b. 25 April 1962) from Coimbatore, Tamil Nadu, joined the commercial pilot's course after retiring from the Indian Air Force. He obtained the commercial pilot's licence (CPL) from the Civil Aviation Authority, Philippines, at 48 years on 11 December 2009, becoming the oldest to do so.

Highest airfield

The Daulat Beg Oldi airstrip in Ladakh, at an altitude of 5,065 m (16,617 ft), is the highest airfield in the world. The Indian Air Force landed a C-130J Super Hercules aircraft at this airfield, reactivating it in 2013.

Most flights taken in a year

Ganesh Kumar Sukumaran Nair, managing director of Ayoki Fabricon Private Ltd in Pune, Maharashtra, set a record by taking a total of 234 flights from 1 January to 31 December 2018. Of these flights, 149 were on domestic routes and 85 were to international destinations.

Most air freight traffic

Indira Gandhi International Airport, New Delhi, handled 1,042,950 tonnes of freight traffic during 2018–19, followed by Chhatrapati Shivaji Maharaj International Airport in Mumbai, Maharashtra, which handled 963,460 thousand tonnes during the same period.

Highest number of women pilots

In a report released by Air Line Pilots Association, International (ALPA)

➔ FLYING HIGH

First woman to obtain a pilot's licence
Urmila K. Parekh became the first woman to obtain a pilot's licence in 1930.

First woman Airbus pilot
On 14 May 1987, Durba Banerjee became the first woman to co-pilot a flight– Airbus A300 – on the Calcutta–New Delhi–Calcutta (now Kolkata, West Bengal) route.

First woman Airbus commander
WR Captain Indraani Singh *(in pic)*, who joined Indian Airlines in April 1986, was the first Asian woman to fly the Airbus A320 in 1989 and became the world's first woman commander of the wide-bodied Airbus A300 in August 1996.

First woman commercial pilot
The first woman commercial pilot was Prem Mathur for Deccan Airways in 1951.

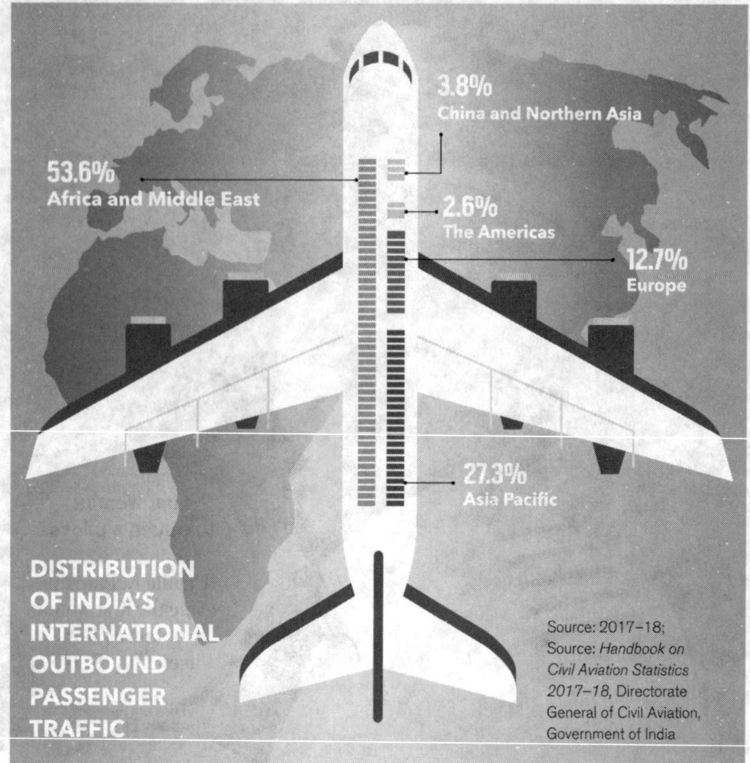

in 2018, India leads the charts in the number of female pilots among all countries. Around 13 per cent of the pilots in the country are women whereas the global average is only 5 per cent. This means that out of every eight flights in India, one is flown by a woman. Airlines such as IndiGo, SpiceJet and Air India have the highest recruitment numbers of women pilots.

Longest length of runways

The Indira Gandhi International Airport, New Delhi, has the longest stretch of airport runways in the country, with a length of 4,430 m (14,534 ft).

First woman chief executive officer of an airline

Harpreet A. De Singh was appointed as the chief executive officer (CEO) of Allaince Air, a regional subsidiary of Air India, on 30 October 2020. Previously the executive director for flight safety at Air India, she became the first woman CEO of an airline. She was also the first woman pilot to be selected by Air India in 1988.

Longest direct-route flight with an all-woman cockpit crew

Air India's flight AI-176 made history on 11 January 2021 when an all-woman cockpit crew flew a distance of 16,000 km from San Francisco, California, USA, to Bengaluru, Karnataka. The flight departed on 9 January 2021 and was flown by four pilots – Captain Zoya Aggarwal, Captain Papagari Thanmai, Captain Shivani Manhas and Captain Akansha Sonaware. The longest commercial flight to be operated by an Indian airline and the longest flight entering India, its flying time was 17 hours and its route remarkably included flying over the North Pole.

Largest passenger airline

IndiGo, a low-cost airline with its headquarters in Gurugram, Haryana, is the largest passenger airline in India by passengers carried and fleet size. Since its inception in August 2006, it has grown from one plane to a fleet of 280 aircrafts. It is also the largest individual Asian low-cost carrier in terms of jet fleet size and passengers carried, and the sixth largest in Asia, with more than 61 million passengers annually.

RAIL AND METRO

First rail construction company

R.M. Stephenson, a British railway engineer, formed the East Indian Railway (EIR) Company in 1844 for the construction of railways. In a contract signed on 17 August 1849, the EIR and the Great Indian Peninsula (GIP) Railway Company, England, were authorized to construct and operate railway lines at Calcutta (now Kolkata), West Bengal, and Bombay (now Mumbai), Maharashtra.

First passenger train

India's first passenger train chugged away from Bori Bunder (later renamed Victoria Terminus, and then Chhatrapati Shivaji Maharaj Terminus) station in Bombay (now Mumbai) to Thane, Maharashtra, on 16 April 1853. It was pulled by three locomotives named Sindh, Sultan and Sahib, and carried 400 passengers in 14 railway carriages. This historic journey, which was about 1 hr 15 mins long, was flagged off with a 21-gun salute.

First indigenous railway carriages

The first railway coaches made in India were built by two coach-building firms in Calcutta (now Kolkata), West Bengal: Steward and Company, and Seton and Company. John Hodgson was the chief engineer of the East Indian Railway then, and the coaches were employed for the first train journey from Howrah to Hooghly in West Bengal on 15 August 1854.

Record Rewind

Fastest train

1991

Shatabdi Express between New Delhi and Bhopal was the fastest train with a maximum speed of 140 km per hour. It covered a distance of 194 km from New Delhi to Agra Cantonment, Uttar Pradesh, in 1 hr 50 mins. The Shatabdi Express also covered the longest distance with the least stops.

2020

The fastest train in India is the Vande Bharat Express or Train 18, which reached a top speed of 180 km/hr during test runs. Its current operating speed is 130 km/hr and it reportedly has a potential speed of 200 km/hr. It runs between Delhi and Agra, Uttar Pradesh.

First Railway Restaurant on Wheels

The Indian Railways' Eastern Railway zone launched its first restaurant on wheels on 26 February 2020 at Asansol, West Bengal, by converting two overage MEMU (Mainline Electric Multiple Unit) coaches into an eating joint for railway users as well as the general public. Inaugurated by Babul Supriyo, minister of state for environment, forest and climate change, the restaurant has been divided into a tea and snacks outlet called 'Chai-Chun' and 'Wow Bhojan', a fine-dining restaurant for breakfast, lunch and dinner. The initiative is expected to generate non-fare revenue of around ₹50 lakh per annum. (5 million) by 2025.

First double-decker train

India's first double-decker train was the Flying Ranee, a superfast train that runs between Mumbai Central and Surat station. It began operating in 1906, was halted in 1939 due to the Second World War, and resumed in 1950 as a daily service train.

First double-decker coaches

The Bombay, Baroda and Central India (BB&CI) Railway Company in Bombay (now Mumbai), Maharashtra, introduced the first double-decker coaches in 1862. These coaches had a seating capacity of 120 to 150 on the lower deck and 70 on the upper one.

First tramway company

The Calcutta Tramway Company was registered in London, UK, in 1880. The Government of West Bengal nationalized it in 1976.

First tramcars

A horse-drawn tramcar ran on a 3.8 km route between Sealdah and Armenian Ghat Street in Calcutta (now Kolkata), West Bengal, on 24 February 1873.

First superfast train

The Rajdhani Express, commissioned on 1 March 1969, runs between New Delhi and Howrah, West Bengal. It has an average speed of 130 km/hr.

First air-conditioned train

Prior to 1936, some coaches on the Bombay, Baroda and Central India (BB&CI) Railway Company, Bombay (now Mumbai, Maharashtra), had double walls lined with lead-zinc sheets filled with ice. The Frontier Mail (now renamed the Golden Temple Mail, which runs between Mumbai and Amritsar) was the first train to get air-conditioned (AC) coaches in 1934.

First deluxe train
The first deluxe train, the Deccan Queen, began between Victoria Terminus, Bombay (now Chhatrapati Shivaji Maharaj Terminus, Mumbai) and Poona (now Pune), Maharashtra, on 1 June 1930. It had 61 first-class, 156 second-class and 19 attendants' seats.

First electric train
The first electric train operated on the Harbour branch of the Great Indian Peninsula Railway from Victoria Terminus (now Chhatrapati Shivaji Maharaj Terminus) to Kurla in Bombay (now Mumbai), Maharashtra, over 16 km, on 3 February 1925.

First locomotive factory
The first locomotive factory in India was set up at Chittaranjan in Paschim Bardhaman District, West Bengal, in 1950. The first diesel locomotive, with an imported engine, was manufactured at the Varanasi Diesel Locomotive Works, Varanasi, Uttar Pradesh, on 4 January 1964.

First green corridor
The Manamadurai–Rameswaram stretch of the Southern Railway was inaugurated as India's first green corridor in July 2016, by installing bio-toilets in 150 coaches of 13 pairs of express and passenger trains on the 114 km long train route. Developed by Indian Railways and the Defence Research and Development Organization, the toilets have zero human-waste discharge.

Indian Railways installed 49,487 bio-toilets in 14,916 coaches between 2019 and 2020.

First Vistadome trains
A special seven-coach Vistadome passenger train was introduced on the Visakhapatnam–Araku route in Andhra Pradesh on 16 April 2017 by the Indian Railways. It has features such as see-through glass on all sides, glass roofs, LED lights, a GPS-based information system and an observation lounge that offers its passengers panoramic views throughout the journey.

WR **Most locomotives produced in a year**
The Chittaranjan Locomotive Works in present-day Paschim Bardhaman District, West Bengal, produced 431 locomotives in the financial year 2019–20. They surpassed their own record of 402 locomotives produced in 2018–19.

WR **Most coaches produced in a year**
The Integral Coach Factory, located at Perambur in Chennai, Tamil Nadu, manufactured 4,166 railway passenger coaches in 2019–20.

WR **Oldest steam engine**
The Fairy Queen, or the East Indian Railway Nr. 22, has the world's oldest working steam engine. This train started running in 1855 but was stopped in 1908. It was restored in 1997 by Perambur Loco Works in Perambur in Chennai, Tamil

Record Rewind

Longest network of electrified railway tracks

1991
Indian Railways had 9,968 cumulative electrified route kilometres (Rkm).

2020
Indian Railways have 934,319 cumulative electrified route kilometres.

Nadu. In July 1977, this heritage train resumed its route between Delhi and Alwar, Rajasthan, and it still runs occasionally.

First woman train driver

Surekha Yadav Bhosale was the first woman to drive an Indian Railways train in 1988. She drove the first 'Ladies Special' local train, which started in April 2000 in Mumbai, Maharashtra. She was the first woman to join the Indian Railways as a trainee assistant driver in 1986. She also became Asia's first woman train driver in 2011, driving the Deccan Queen from Pune to Chhatrapati Shivaji Maharaj Terminus in Mumbai.

First stations

Bori Bunder, Byculla, Sion and Thane stations on the Bori Bunder–Thane line in Maharashtra, were the first railway stations built at the time of the inaugural run of the first passenger train from Bori Bunder to Thane in 1853.

Only Railway Station Listed as a UNESCO World Heritage Site

The first train was flagged off on 16 April 1853 from Bori Bunder (now Chhatrapati Shivaji Maharaj Terminus) in Mumbai, Maharashtra. The station is one of the busiest railway stations in India, and the only one declared as a UNESCO World Heritage Site. The building, featuring a Victorian Gothic style of architecture, was designed and constructed by draughtsman Axel Herman and architect Frederick William Stevens in 1888.

Station with most platforms

Howrah Junction, West Bengal, serves around one million passengers every day. It has 23 platforms, making it the station with the most platforms in India.

Busiest railway station

Kanpur Central, Uttar Pradesh, is the busiest railway station in India in terms of the frequency of trains. As many as 230 trains pass through the station daily. This station also holds the record for the largest interlocking route system in the world.

WR Station with the longest platform

On 6 October 2013, Gorakhpur railway station in Uttar Pradesh became the station with the world's longest railway platform, which measures 1,366.42 m (4,483 ft).

First public–private partnership railway station

Habibganj railway station in Bhopal, Madhya Pradesh, is the first railway station to be built under a public–private partnership to make it at par with international standards. The work of its redevelopment began in partnership with Bansal Group on 9 June 2017. It lies on the main Jhansi–Bhopal–Itarsi route. The plan includes airport-like facilities, such as shopping complexes, forex kiosks and eateries, among others, making it the first of its kind in the country.

WR Longest rails manufactured

The Bhilai Steel Plant, the largest plant of the Steel Authority of India Ltd (SAIL), became the only rail maker in the world capable of producing 260 m (853 ft) long rails, on 23 February 2005. It first manufactures 65 m (213 ft) long rails, which are welded together to form the 260 m tracks for high-speed trains.

Longest train route

The Dibrugarh–Kanniyakumari Vivek Express has the longest train route on the Indian Railways network, and the ninth longest in the world. It joins Dibrugarh in Assam to Kanniyakumari in Tamil Nadu, covering 4,286 km, while halting at 56 stations along the route. It starts at 11:05 p.m. and reaches at 9:50 a.m. on the fifth day, with a scheduled journey time of 82 hrs 5 mins.

Longest rail tunnel

The Pir Panjal railway tunnel or the Banihal railway tunnel, is 11.215 km (36,795 ft) long. Located in the Pir Panjal range of the Himalayas in Jammu and Kashmir, it opened in 2013.

First fully solar-powered railway station

Guwahati railway station in Assam is India's first fully solar-powered station. Commissioned in 2017, the project has 2,352 solar panels on the roof . This solar project aims to make the railways environmentally responsible and reduce their carbon footprint. The panels have an average power generation capacity of 2,048 kWh per day.

First metro

A 16.3 km underground mass rapid transit system in the country was inaugurated on 24 October 1984 in Calcutta (now Kolkata), West Bengal, between Dum Dum and Tollygunge. The carrying capacity of this metro was 1.73 million passengers a day. The trains for the metro system were manufactured at the Integral Coach Factory, Perambur, Madras (now Chennai), Tamil Nadu, during 1981–82.

First corporatized train

The Indian Railways launched the Tejas Express, India's first corporatized train, on 4 October 2019. The physical infrastructure is owned and run by the Indian Railway Catering and Tourism Corporation (IRCTC), a subsidiary of the Indian Railways, while the services provided on board are outsourced to private contractors. These services include catering, housekeeping, ticketing and refund, among others. The train shuttles between Lucknow and New Delhi, and has only two halts – Kanpur and Ghaziabad. Running all week, except Tuesdays, it is contracted under the public-private–partnership model.

Fastest construction of an underground metro station*

The Lucknow Metro Rail Corporation (LMRC) completed the construction of the Chaudhary Charan Singh Airport (CCS Airport) metro station in 19 months and 10 days, making it the fastest ever constructed metro station. They started the work on 13 July 2017 and completed on 22 February 2019. The metro station is part of the 22.87 km long North–South corridor. They obtained the certification from the commissioner of metro rail safety for the commencement of commercial operations on 23 February 2019.

First to buy a Delhi Metro Smart Card and travel using it

Anil Marwah, with his son Ankit Marwah, became the first passenger to buy a Delhi Metro Smart Card and travel on all the then existing lines of the Delhi Metro when it commenced on 25 December 2002.

Deepest metro tunnel

Delhi Metro Rail Corporation (DMRC) completed a metro tunnel at a depth of 45 m (147 ft 7 in.), and 20–25 m (65 ft 7 in.–82 ft) on 30 April 2009. The 1,556 m (5,105 ft) long tunnel below the underground Rajiv Chowk metro station in New Delhi is part of the 22.7 km (74,475 ft) long Airport Express Line.

Deepest metro station

The Hauz Khas station on the Magenta Line and the Yellow Line of the Delhi Metro is the deepest metro station at a depth of 32 m (105 ft).

Largest metro network

The Delhi Metro, set up by the Delhi Metro Rail Corporation (DMRC, spread across 296 km, is the largest metro rail network in the country in terms of both route length and ridership.

First underwater metro

India's first underwater metro, connecting the two main terminals, the Howrah station and the Sealdah station. was completed in February 2020 in Kolkata, West Bengal, below the River Hooghly. Of the 16.6 km long east–west stretch, 520 m will be under the riverbed. The tunnels are built more than 33 m below the riverbed.

First 'driverless' metro

The Magenta Line in the Delhi Metro became the first 'driverless' metro line in India. The 12.64 km long line, started operations on 25 December 2017, and connected Kalkaji Mandir, New Delhi, to Botanical Garden, Noida, while halting at nine stations. The line was extended by 24.34 km to Janakpuri West in May 2018. Initially, it was run by an operator, with high levels of automation based on the Communication Based Train Control technology, and is planned to be 'driverless' in future.

ROAD

First state transport system

- In June 1932, the Nizam's State Railways Transport Department (NSRTD), Hyderabad (now in Telangana), set up a road transport service on a 24 km route, with 27 buses operating through three depots. Each bus could seat as many as 25 passengers.

- The first state-controlled road transport system in the country was introduced on 31 July 1948 by the Calcutta State Transport Corporation, headquartered in Calcutta (now Kolkata), West Bengal.

First highway

Lord William Bentinck, Governor General of India (1828–35), began metalling work on the 2,400 km long historic Grand Trunk Road from Calcutta (now Kolkata), West Bengal, to Peshawar (now in Pakistan) and beyond. During his tenure, the first steps were taken to build a metalled road from Calcutta (now Kolkata), West Bengal, to Delhi.

First regular public transport

The first regular long-distance public road transport was introduced between Aligarh and Kanpur in Uttar Pradesh in November 1841.

First mail cart service

In 1845, mail bullock carts were running between Calcutta (now Kolkata), West Bengal, and Lahore (now in Pakistan), and from Bombay (now Mumbai), Maharashtra, to Surat, Gujarat. Bullocks were replaced by horses in 1850 and companies were formed to run this service. First among these was the Inland Transport Company of Tanti Mai in Kanpur in Uttar Pradesh.

First traffic police

The Traffic Department of Calcutta Police in Calcutta (now Kolkata), West Bengal, came into force in 1874 with 17 sepoys in its ranks.

Earliest route

In 1926, the Brihanmumbai (then Bombay) Electricity Supply and Transport (BEST) purchased motor buses, choosing two points to try them out. The route covered present-day Afghan Church to Crawford Market through Dadar tram terminus, King's Circle, Opera House, Lal Bagh and Arthur Road in Mumbai, Maharashtra.

First car

The first motor car was reportedly imported in 1892 by the then maharaja of Patiala in Punjab. It was a De Dion Bouton car.

SUPER 30

THE 'FLYOVERS MAN' OF INDIA

Nitin Jairam Gadkari, a senior leader of the Bhartiya Janata Party (BJP), is the current minister for road transport and highways and the minister of micro, small and medium enterprises in the Government of India. Known as the 'flyovers man', he has been instrumental in constructing roads, expressways and flyovers during his tenure as the Public Works Department minister of Maharashtra (1996–99), including India's first six-lane concrete, high-speed expressway, the Mumbai–Pune Expressway. As the minister of road transport and highways and minister of shipping from 2014 to 2019, he has been responsible for the increase of pace in road creation in the country from an estimated rate of 2 km/day in his first year to 30 km/day by the end of 2018.

Nitin Jairam Gadkari

Sign of the Times

In order to promote gender equality, female-figure signs were installed at a traffic junction in the Dadar area of Mumbai, Maharashtra, by the Brihanmumbai Municipal Corporation (BMC) in August 2020. With plans made to change road signs and pedestrian signals at 13 junctions on Cadell Road (a 4.5 km arterial stretch in Mumbai's Dadar and Mahim), it is part of a broader urban initiative known as 'Culture Spine' that aims to improve the footpath and gardens from Siddhivinayak Temple to Mahim in Mumbai, Maharashtra.

First trolley bus

Twelve trolley buses were imported to replace tramcars on the Gowalia Tank–Mazagon route in Bombay (now Mumbai), Maharashtra, on 11 June 1962. They were withdrawn in March 1971 in favour of buses.

First zero-emission electric car

REVAi, the environment-friendly electric car, is manufactured by the Reva Electric Car Company, Bengaluru, Karnataka, a joint venture formed by Amerigon Inc. of California, USA, and the Maini Group of Industries based in Bengaluru, Karnataka. This eco-friendly car was first flagged off from New Delhi in March 1998 and sold worldwide by 2011 in 26 countries. It was acquired by Indian conglomerate Mahindra & Mahindra in May 2010 and the company launched the electric hatchback e2o in 2013.

First motor bus

The motor bus was introduced in Bombay (now Mumbai), Maharashtra, on the Afghan Church–Crawford Market route on 15 July 1926. With a cruising speed of 20 km/hr, it carried 24 passengers, with two to three standing ones. Twenty-six buses were bought for ₹12,000 each.

First stainless-steel bus

The first bus made of stainless steel was built at the Maharashtra State Road Transport Corporation workshop in Aurangabad, Maharashtra. It was inaugurated on the Bombay (now Mumbai)–Ratnagiri route, Maharashtra, on 12 February 1988.

First Indian car manufacturers

Hindustan Motors Ltd, registered in 1942 to manufacture vehicles, was followed by Premier Automobiles (1944) and Standard Motor Products of India Ltd (1948). The first Indian-built car, Hindustan 10, not fully indigenous but identical to the series M10 HP Morris, rolled out of the factory in 1946.

ROAD ACCIDENTS BY TYPES OF TRAFFIC RULE VIOLATIONS*

TOTAL NUMBER OF ACCIDENTS: 4 67,044

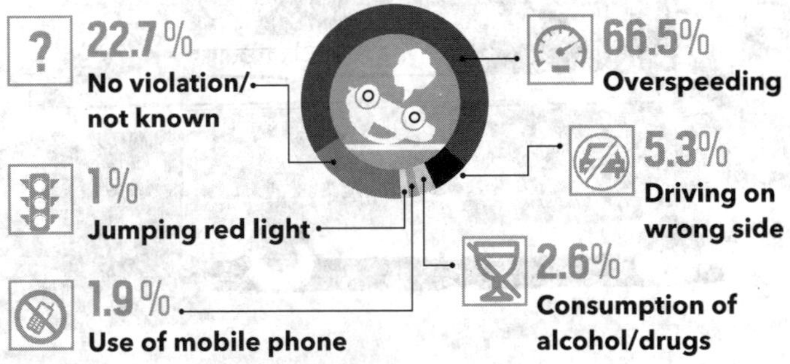

TOTAL NUMBER OF PERSONS KILLED: 151,417

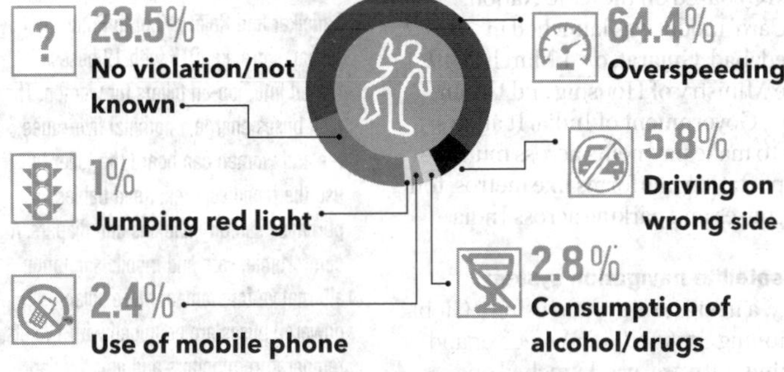

TOTAL NUMBER OF PERSONS INJURED: 469,418

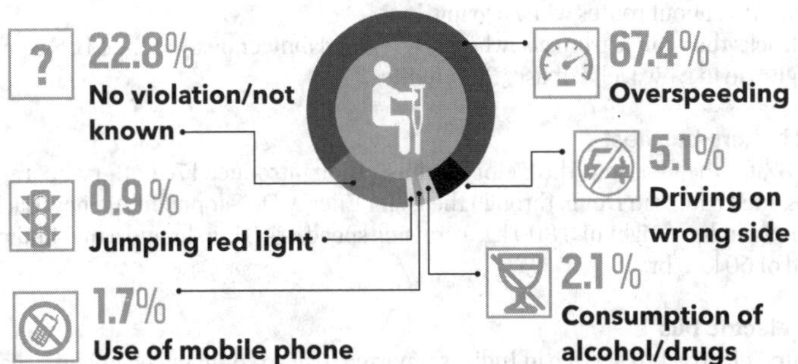

*2017; Percentages may not add up to 100 due to rounding off at source; Source: Road Accidents in India – 2018, Ministry of Road Transport and Highways, Government of India

Hop-on Toilets on Wheels

The Ti (Marathi for 'her') Toilet project was launched by entrepreneurs Ulka Sadalkar and Rajeev Kher in Pune, Maharashtra, in 2016 with 12 buses turned into hop-on toilets for women. The pink buses charge a nominal five-rupee fee and women can board the toilet to use the facilities, breastfeed babies, or purchase sanitary napkins and diapers. A comfortable, safe and mobile sanitation alternative for women, these solar-powered buses are equipped with TV sets, temperature monitors and an attendant. The duo plan to open 1,000 such toilets across India by 2025.

First indigenous payment eco-system for transport
The National Common Mobility Card (NCMC) based on the 'One Nation, One Card' model was launched in Ahmedabad, Gujarat, on 4 March 2019, by the Ministry of Housing and Urban Affairs, Government of India. It allows users to make payments across multiple transportation platforms like metros, toll taxes, buses and parking across India.

First satellite navigation system
Sanjay, a navigation system using a Global Positioning System (GPS) receiver and mapping software, was launched on 15 February 1999 in New Delhi. Having installed it in the vehicle, the user could access Delhi's road map and get vocal information about routes while driving. It also tracks the vehicle from elsewhere. Developed indigenously at the I.B. Saxena Design Lab in New Delhi, it uses 24 satellites.

First battery-bus fleet
In 1987, for the first time, the Delhi administration introduced 76 battery-operated buses on 11 routes in Delhi, through the Delhi Energy Development Agency. Each bus had a laden weight of 3,800 kg, a cruising speed of 40 km/hr and a maximum speed of 60 km/hr.

First electric bus
The first electric bus service in India is reported to have commenced in Himachal Pradesh for Rohtang Pass, near Manali, at an altitude of 3,962.4 m (13,000 ft). The bus has been developed by Goldstone Infratech and the Automobile Research

Association of India. It has the capacity to carry 30 passengers and can run 200 km on fully charged batteries.

First electric cabs

Nagpur in Maharashtra is India's first city to have an electric mass mobility system. It has a fleet of 200 electric vehicles including taxis, buses, e-rickshaws and autorickshaws, owned by cab aggregator Ola. This multimodal electric vehicle project, the first of its kind in India, was inaugurated on 26 May 2017.

First CNG autos

Bajaj Auto Ltd launched the first of its Compressed Natural Gas (CNG) autorickshaws in Delhi on 29 May 2000. With a 3-kg CNG tank and a standby 3-litre petrol tank, it is powered by a 175 cc, four-stroke single overhead camshaft engine that gives 50 km per kg of CNG and meets the Bharat-II emission norms.

First fully electrical SUV

Hyundai launched India's first fully electric SUV, the Kona Electric, on 9 July 2019. The eco-friendly vehicle can cover approximately 452 km on a single charge and was introduced with four drive modes – Eco, Eco+, Comfort and Sport.

First 3D smart traffic lights

Students of Chitkara University in Rajpura, Punjab, designed the first 3D smart traffic lights in India, which were piloted by the Mohali Traffic Police on 2 August 2019. The new system, which is called 'Intelights', employs 3D technology and sensors to manipulate the green and red lights based on the actual number of cars that are present at the signal. This smart system of traffic lights has been installed at Quark City near Airport Road in Mohali to enhance cost- and time-effective traffic management.

WR Highest filling station

The Indian Oil Corporation Ltd operates a filling station at Kaza, Spiti Valley, Himachal Pradesh, at an elevation of about 3,740 m (12,270 ft) above the mean sea level.

Kaza filling station: world's highest filling station

Record Rewind

State/UT with the largest fleet of buses

1991

Delhi had nearly 14,000 buses on its roads. While a large number belonged to the government-owned Delhi Transport Corporation (DTC), many were owned by private operators of buses and minibuses.

2020

Tamil Nadu State Transport Corporation (TNSTC) has a fleet of 22,000 buses. It is the largest government-owned bus transport corporation in the country (2019).

First Advanced Traffic Control system

The Delhi Police installed the first Advanced Traffic Control system at 47 intersections of the capital city in April 2000. The intelligent sensors in this high-tech system are equipped to assess the volume of traffic at each intersection and control the traffic light system accordingly.

Shortest highway

National Highway 327 B, located in West Bengal, is the shortest highway in India. Only 1.2 km long, it starts from its junction with NH-327 near Panitanki in Darjeeling District, connecting Mechi Bridge and terminating at the Indo-Nepal border.

Largest road network

India has a total road length of approximately 3,300,000 km, the second largest road network in the world, after the USA.

Largest automotive company

Tata Motors Limited (earlier Tata Engineering and Locomotive Company), founded in 1945 and headquartered in Bombay (now Mumbai), Maharashtra, is the largest automotive company with a portfolio of cars, sports vehicles, buses, trucks and defence vehicles. Their consolidated net revenue for the fiscal year 2020 was ₹2,61,068 crore (₹ 2,610.68 billion).

WR **Highest highway**

The 490 km long Manali–Leh highway has an average elevation of more than 4,000 m (13,123 ft). Its highest elevation is 5,328 m (17,480 ft) at Tanglang La in Ladakh.

Most bituminous concrete poured – single day

Travelling over an approximate linear distance of 18,701 km, Hyderabad-based IJM (India) Infrastructure Ltd (IJMII) poured 15,656 metric tonnes (6,068.217 cu m) of bituminous concrete in 20 hrs 40 mins on 25 February 2021. The laying of the 26.82 km Solapur–Bijapur single lane of the four-lane NH-13 between Maharashtra and Karnataka was implemented under the National Highway Authority of India.

WR **Longest highway tunnel**

Atal Tunnel, a 9.2 km long tunnel on the Manali–Leh highway was inaugurated on 3 October 2020. It cuts down the distance between Manali and Leh by 46 km and reduces travel time by four hours. Equipped with CCTVs and fire hydrants, the tunnel is the only one in India to have an emergency exit tunnel inside.

WATER

Earliest representation of ships

A rectangular seal portraying a vessel with a sharply upturned prow and stem was unearthed in an archaeological excavation at Mohenjo-Daro (now in Pakistan). It was dated to 3000 BCE.

Earliest compass

According to the *Bombay Gazetteer*, Vol. XIII, Part II, Appendix A, a crude forerunner of the modern magnetic compass, the Matsya Yantra, was used around the fifth century CE. It featured an iron fish that floated in a vessel of oil, and pointed north.

Oldest ship

- Training ship HMS *Foudroyant* (*Trincomalee*), was built at the Bombay docks (now in Mumbai, Maharashtra) in 1817 and is now a museum ship in Hartlepool, UK. The *Trincomalee* carried 46 guns and displaced 1,065 tonnes.
- MV *Safeena* of Ellon Hinengo Ltd, Port Blair, Andaman and Nicobar Islands, built at the government dockyard in Rangoon (now Yangon), Myanmar, in 1942, is the oldest passenger ship.

First steamboat

The steamboat *Diana* was built in India in 1819 by Jessop & Co. Ltd in Calcutta (now Kolkata), West Bengal, and launched on 12 July 1823.

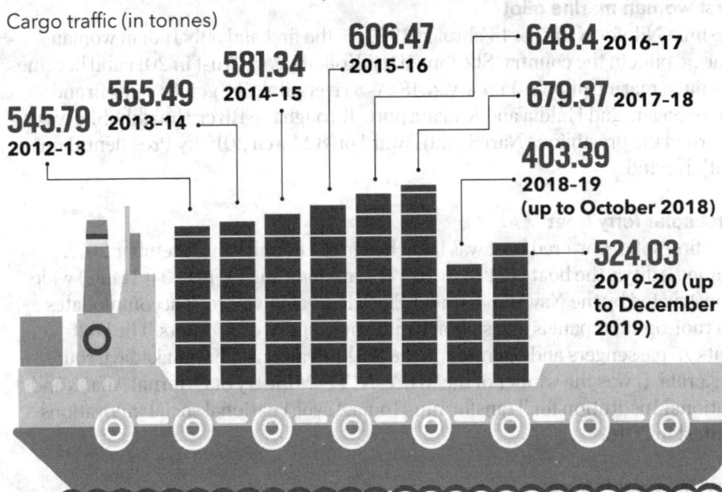

Source: Ministry of Shipping 2017 – *Year of Consolidation Report*, Press Information Bureau Release and Annual Report 2019–20

Oldest known dockyard

Substantial remains of the Harappan civilization have been discovered at Lothal near the Gulf of Cambay (now Khambhat) in Gujarat. Built in 2300 BCE, the dock is a long, rectangular tank, 218 m x 37 m (715 ft x 121 ft), and about 16 km from its nearest seaport. It bears testimony to the knowledge of the Harappans as boats docked at Lothal till the 1850s.

First ship to sail from India

The first ship carrying the flag of an Indian Shipping Company, SS *Loyalty* of the Scindia Steam Navigation Company, sailed with a full complement of passengers from Bombay (now Mumbai), Maharashtra, to the British Isles. A hospital ship, *Loyalty* was bought on 17 February 1919 and converted to a passenger vessel. The day, 5 April, on which it undertook this voyage in 1919, is now observed as National Maritime Day.

First diesel engine ship

MV *Dwarka*, a modern D-Class passenger and cargo ship of the British India Steam Navigation Company, entered service in 1947. Weighing 4,851 gross tonnes, it was 121.6 m (399 ft) long and 16.8 m (55 ft) wide. It had a service speed of 13.5 knots.

 **The number of sea vessels registered under the Indian flag was 1,429 in 2019.**

First shipping company

Freedom fighter V.O. Chidambaram Pillai established the Swadeshi Shipping Company at Tuticorin (Thoothukudi), Tamil Nadu, in 1906.

First woman marine pilot

Reshma Nilofer Naha (b. 4 February 1989) is the first and only Indian woman marine pilot in the country. She joined the Kolkata Port Trust in 2011 and became a trained marine pilot in January 2018. As a river pilot, she guides ships in and out of Sagar, and Haldia and Kolkata ports through the River Hooghly. She was awarded the prestigious Nari Shakti Award on 8 March 2019 by President Ram Nath Kovind.

First solar ferry boat

The first solar-powered boat was launched in the country in December 2017. Named Aditya, the boat is 21.18 m (69 ft 7 in.) long and 7.0 m (22 ft 11 inc.) wide. Constructed by the NavAlt Solar and Electric Boats Pvt. Ltd, it accommodates 78 rooftop solar panels and sails at a maximum speed of 7.5 knots. The boat seats 75 passengers and operates on the 2.5 km Vaikom–Thavanakadavu route in Kerala. It was the winner of the MEA–NITI (Ministry of External Affairs and National Institution for Transforming India Aayog) national social innovations contest in 2016.

First hovercraft ferry

A diesel hovercraft service began between Surat and Ghogha Port in Gujarat on 10 December 1992, linking the two ports, 55 nautical miles apart, in two hours.

First overseas cargo service

On 3 February 1948, a continental line for an overseas cargo service between India and European countries was inaugurated by the Scindia Steam Navigation Company, with the sailing of the SS *Jalabala* cargo steamship from Bombay (now Mumbai), Maharashtra.

Oldest port

Calcutta Port, Bengal (now Kolkata Port, West Bengal), built by the East India Company and operating since 1870, is the oldest operating port.

First corporatized port

Ennore Port (now Kamarajar Port Ltd) on the Coromandel Coast, Chennai, Tamil Nadu, is the first Indian port that is a public company in India and a corporatized port since 1999.

First private sector port

Pipavav Port in Gujarat, which was inaugurated in November 1996, has three dry cargo berths built as a single-length jetty of 725 m (2,379 ft), and a liquid cargo berth.

Largest private port in India

Mundra Port in the Gulf of Kachchh, Gujarat, run by Adani Ports and Special Economic Zone Ltd (APSEZ), with its headquarters in Ahmedabad, is India's largest private port. It crossed the mark of 100 million tonnes of cargo handling in 2016, overtaking the government-owned Jawaharlal Nehru Port Trust near Mumbai, Maharashtra, as India's largest container port by capacity. Mundra Port is also India's biggest commercial port by volume handled.

Largest covered dock

Hindustan Shipyard houses the largest covered dock at Visakhapatnam in Andhra Pradesh. The dock measures 240 m x 53 m x 11.25 m (787 ft x 174 ft x 37 ft) with an intermediate twin gate and undocking draft of 8 m (26 ft). It can accommodate ships of up to 80,000 deadweight tonnage.

First indigenous hovercraft

A twin-engine, air-cushioned hovercraft, manufactured in 1987 by the Scientific Instrument Co. Ltd, Allahabad (now Prayagraj), Uttar Pradesh, had a 55 HP thrust engine for propulsion and an 8 HP engine for lift, with a payload capacity of 500 kg and a speed of 45 km/hr.

First superfast catamaran service

A superfast catamaran service between Bombay (now Mumbai), Maharashtra, and Goa became operational from 14 November 1994. The 40 m long, 400-seater, twin-hull luxury catamaran was imported by Damania Shipping Ltd from Norway. It moved at 40 knots, covering 225 nautical miles in 6 hrs 30 mins.

First roll-on–roll-off (Ro–Ro) ferry service

The first phase of the roll-on–roll-off ferry service began on 22 October 2017 between Ghogha Port and Dahej in Gujarat. The first of its kind in India, the 31 km service reduces the travel time between the two towns from 7–8 hours to just over an hour. It can carry 1,000 passengers and 150 vehicles.

First passenger-and-cargo vessel
MV *Andamans,* which had a 2,420 deadweight tonnage, was built at the Hindustan Shipyard in Visakhapatnam, Andhra Pradesh, in 1957.

Only ship design and research centre
The National Ship Design and Research Centre (NSDRC) at Visakhapatnam, Andhra Pradesh, functions under the administrative control of the Ministry of Surface Transport, Government of India. It was completed in April 1993 with help from the Netherlands.

Oldest shipping company
The Scindia Steam Navigation Company was started by Narottam Morarji, Walchand Hirachand, Lallubhai Samaldas and Kilachand Devchand on 27 March 1919.

SUPER 30

SHIPPING CORPORATION OF INDIA: FORMING LINKS ACROSS THE SEAS

Established in 1961 after the consolidation of the Eastern Shipping Corporation and the Western Shipping Corporation, the Shipping Corporation of India (SCI) is a public sector undertaking (PSU) that operates and manages vessels in both national and international services. Honoured with Navratna status by the Government of India on 1 August 2008, SCI initially started with 19 vessels and has now become the largest shipping company in the country, with 80 ships. The Government of India approved the privatization of SCI on 21 November 2019.

THE NATURAL WORLD

PHYSICAL FEATURES

Longest land mountain range

The Himalayan range is the loftiest and most rugged mountain barrier in Asia. Out of the 7,300 mountain peaks in the world, 96 are in the Himalaya–Karakoram range. The range stretches over 2,500 km and varies from around 500 km in width in Jammu and Kashmir to around 200 km in Arunachal Pradesh. Some of the higher ranges are composed of 600-million-year-old Precambrian rocks.

Highest peak

Kangchenjunga, with its base partly in India and partly in Nepal, stands at 8,586 m (28,169 ft). Yalung Kang (also on the India–Nepal border) is second at 8,505 m (27,903 ft) and Nanda Devi comes third at 7,816 m (25,643 ft).

Largest glacier

Siachen Glacier, near the India–Pakistan border, is India's largest glacier. It is 75.6 km long and 2–8 km wide. It is also the second longest glacier in the non-polar regions of the earth.

Only cold desert

Ladakh, located at an average altitude of 4,878 m (16,004 ft), is the only cold desert in India.

Longest river

The 2,525 km long River Ganga is the longest river in the country. Its source is in the western Himalayas in Uttarakhand, from where the river flows south and east through the Gangetic Plain and Bangladesh, finally merging into the Bay of Bengal.

There are 41 waterfalls in India ranging from 85 m (279 ft) to 455 m (1,493 ft) in height.

Largest river system

Of the total river discharge in India, 65 per cent is from the Himalayan group of rivers. The Rivers Ganga, Indus and Brahmaputra are part of this river system.

WR Largest delta

The triangular land mass formed by the River Hooghly, the Rivers Ganga–Padma–Meghna combined, and the Bay of Bengal is called the Bengal Delta. Two-thirds of this 57,000 sq. km delta is in Bangladesh and the rest lies in West Bengal, India.

Largest catchment area

The Ganga–Brahmaputra–Meghna system is the biggest river system with a catchment area of 272 million acres (110 million hectares), more than 43 per cent of the catchment area of all the major rivers of the Indian subcontinent.

Largest crater

The Lonar meteorite crater in the Buldhana District of Maharashtra is India's

SUPER 30

CAVING IN THE ABODE OF THE CLOUDS

Founded by B.D. Kharpan Daly in 1990, the Meghalaya Adventurers' Association (MAA) is responsible for researching and mapping caves from October to March every year in Shillong, Meghalaya. With the help of European speleologists, cavers from India, speleology experts from other regions of the world, the Indian Army and the Indian Navy, the MAA has been carrying out regular explorations to bring the scientific and cultural value of caves into focus. The MAA's members are part of 'Caving in the Abode of the Clouds', an annual expedition that brings together 30 to 40 cavers from all over the world, eager to explore and discover the natural and archaeological heritage in the caves of Meghalaya. The team from MAA has discovered more than 1,700 caves since they started, including Krem Puri, the world's longest sandstone cave, near Laitsohum village in the East Khasi Hills District.

largest and the world's third largest meteoric crater. It measures 1,800 m (5,906 ft) across and is 170 m (558 ft) deep. It is estimated that the crater was formed 50,000 years ago by a meteorite that was around 100 m (328 ft) in diameter, weighed a million tonnes, and was travelling at a speed of around 90,000 km per hour.

Largest freshwater lake
Wular Lake, India's largest freshwater lake, has an area of 260 sq. km. It is in Bandipora, Jammu and Kashmir.

Largest brackish-water lagoon
Chilika Lake in Odisha has an area of around 1,100 sq. km.

Largest cave
Amarnath Cave, about 44 km from Pahalgam in Jammu and Kashmir, is a popular pilgrimage. It is a natural cave at a height of 3,800 m (12,467 ft). The cave is 50 m (164 ft) wide and 25 m (82 ft) high. A remarkable stalagmite in the cave is worshipped as a *Shivalinga.*

Largest desert
The Thar Desert stretches over an area of about 200,000 sq. km in India and spreads over four states: Punjab, Haryana, Gujarat and Rajasthan. It is interspersed with hillocks, gravel plains, salt marshes and lakes.

WR **Largest island – freshwater**
The island of Majuli, with an area of 352 sq. km, on the River Brahmaputra in Assam, is the largest freshwater island in the world.

Last Major Free-flowing River of Peninsular India

The 124 km long River Aghanashini in Karnataka is the last remaining free-flowing river of peninsular India. While the other rivers have been dammed or diverted into channels, the Aghanashini originates in the town of Sirsi, Uttar Kannada District, and flows to the Arabian Sea at Kumta in the same district. The river's survival and its unobstructed flow can be attributed to the residents of the region who protest against any projects that are proposed and have endeavoured to keep it as it is.

Largest island – ocean

The island of Middle Andaman (1,523 sq. km) in the Andaman and Nicobar Islands is the largest ocean island in India.

Largest meteorite shower

On 14 July 1860, a heavy meteorite shower fell at Dharamshala (32°14′N, 76°28′E) in Kangra District, Himachal Pradesh. It consisted of many stones, the largest of which weighed 150 kg.

Highest waterfall

Kunchikal Falls in Nidagodu Village near Masthikatte in Shivamogga District of Karnataka falls down a total height of 455 m (1,493 ft), making it the highest waterfall in India.

Minimum rainfall area

Jaisalmer in Rajasthan receives an average rainfall of only about 200 mm (around 7.87 in.) in a year.

Maximum rainfall

Mawsynram, a village in the East Khasi Hills District, Meghalaya, about 65 km from Shillong, gets an average mean annual rainfall of 11,873 mm (467 in.) in about 147 days in a year. Earlier the record for the highest average rainfall was held by Cherrapunji (now Sohra) in the same district.

Highest temperature

On 19 May 2016, India recorded its highest ever temperature – 51°C – in Phalodi town in Jodhpur District in Rajasthan.

Highest surface salinity

The surface salinity in the Gulf of Kachchh, off the coast of Gujarat, varies from a maximum of 45.5 psu (practical salinity units), which is equivalent to parts per thousand, near the head of the gulf to 36.6 psu at the mouth.

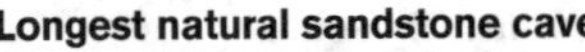

Longest natural sandstone cave

The world's longest sandstone cave, with a length of about 24.58 km, Krem Puri in East Khasi Hills District, Meghalaya, is also known for its dinosaur fossils from 66–76 million years ago. Krem Puri is 6 km longer than the previous record holder – Venezuela's 18.2 km long Cueva Del Saman sandstone cave in Edo Zulia.

Lowest temperature

The lowest temperature recorded in Dras, Ladakh, was –60°C on 9 January 1995, making it the coldest inhabited place in India.

Lowest surface salinity

Salinity near the surface in the northern Bay of Bengal can be as low as 31 psu, because the bay receives freshwater as rain as well as run-off from the Rivers Ganga, Brahmaputra, Irrawaddy and others.

Only active volcano

Barren Island, which lies 110 km north-east of Port Blair in the Andaman and Nicobar Islands, is India's only active volcano. On 10 April 1991, it blew up after nearly two centuries. It had last erupted in 1803.

FOSSILS

Oldest dinosaur fossil discovery

The first dinosaur fossils in India were discovered by a British palaeontologist, W.H. Sleeman, in Jabalpur, Madhya Pradesh, in 1828. The specimens were lost in 1877 and found in 2013 in the office of the Geological Survey of India, Kolkata, West Bengal.

MAMMALS

Oldest living mammal

One of the oldest living mammals is the Indian one-horned rhinoceros (*Rhinoceros unicornis*). The Indian and Javan rhinoceroses first appeared in the fossil record of Asia 1.6–3.3 million years ago, though the species may have diverged much earlier, around 11.7 million years ago.

Smallest mammal

- *Land:* The white-toothed pygmy shrew (*Suncus etruscus*), which has a head-and-body length of 3–5.5 cm (1.18–2.17 in.) and a tail length of 2.5–3.2 cm (0.98–1.26 in.), is the smallest Indian land mammal by weight, weighing around 1.8 g. This shrew can be found across the Indian subcontinent, except in Jammu and Kashmir, and arid areas of Gujarat and Rajasthan.
- *Water:* The smallest water mammal in the country is the finless porpoise (*Neophocaena phocaenoides*), which is only 1.2–2 cm (0.47–0.79 in.) long. It is found in the waters of peninsular India.

Fastest mammal

- *Land:* The blackbuck (*Antilope cervicapra*), which is native to India, can run at a speed of up to 80 km per hour. It is found from Rajasthan to Punjab, and up to

Odisha in the east and Tamil Nadu in the south.

• *Water:* The 2–2.5 m (6 ft 6 in.–8 ft 2 in.) long-beaked common dolphin (*Delphinus capensis*), found off the coast of peninsular India, swims at 30 knots or 55.5 km per hour.

The blackbuck: fastest land mammal

Largest land mammal

The adult Asian elephant found in India (*Elephas maximus indicus*) belongs to the species of the largest land mammal *Elephas maximus.* An adult bull elephant averages 2.74 m (9 ft) in height at the shoulder and weighs around 4.5 tonnes. The female elephant or cow measures 2.35 m (7 ft 8.5 in.) at the shoulder and weighs around 3 tonnes. Elephants are found in four clusters in the plains of north, south, east and central India, and in the north-east.

Slowest mammal

• *Land:* The Bengal slow loris (*Nycticebus bengalensis*), which measures around 30–40 cm (11 ft 10 in.–15 ft 9 in.), is the slowest land mammal in the country. It is found in Assam.

• *Water:* The slowest mammal in water is the 3.2 m (10 ft 6 in.) long dugong or sea cow (*Dugong dugon*), found in the Gulf of Kachchh, off the Malabar Coast and in the Andaman Islands.

Largest litter

The Indian mole rat (*Bandicota bengalensis*), found in most plains and forests, is known to have litters of more than 12 young ones at a time.

Fastest breeders

The Indian mole rat is the fastest-breeding mammal. The males mature in 58 days after birth and females in 90–100 days. Females have an average count of 11.32 pregnancies a year with a total break of 32.3 days in between. The female may produce as many as 70 young ones a year.

Slowest breeders

The elephant's main breeding season is the summer and when the monsoon begins. Only one calf is born at a time and at intervals of three years.

Longest-lived

• Human beings are the longest living mammals.

Record Rewind

Population of tigers in India

1990

The estimated number of tigers in the country was 3,500.

2018

The estimated number of tigers in the country was 2,967.

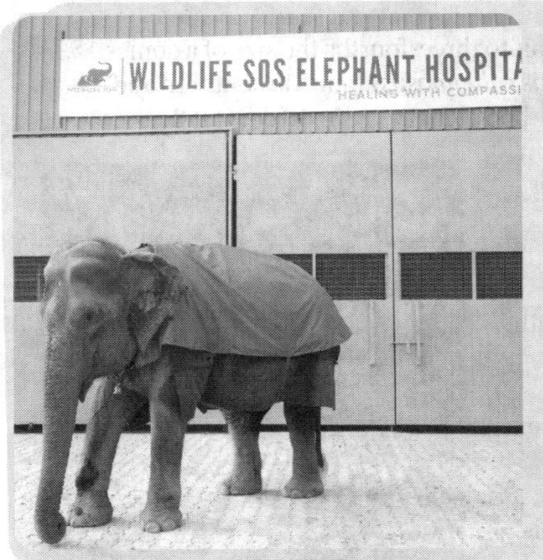

First Hospital for Elephants

In November 2018, India's first hospital for elephants opened in Mathura, Uttar Pradesh. Located on the bank of the River Yamuna, close to an elephant conservation and care centre run by Wildlife SOS, the hospital provides facilities such as wireless digital X-ray, thermal imaging, ultrasonography and quarantine areas for the pachyderms. The facility aims to check the declining population of elephants in the country, which reached 27,312 in 2017, down from estimates of 29,391–30,711 elephants in 2012.

- The average lifespan of a blue whale (*Balaenoptera musculus*) is 80–90 years.
- The Indian elephant follows with an average lifespan of around 60 years, but they can live up to 80–90 years.

Primate with the longest tail
The tail of the common langur measures an average of around 1 m (3 ft 3.4 in.).

Longest gestation
The elephant has a gestation period of about 20 months.

Shortest gestation
Rodents have a gestation period averaging a month.

The only apes
The western hoolock gibbon (*Hoolock hoolock*) and the eastern hoolock gibbon (*Hoolock leuconedys*) are the only ape species found in India, and they are the tallest primates too. Their average height, standing on hind legs, is about 0.9 m (3 ft).

WR The only camels that swim
The Kharai camels from Kachchh, Gujarat, are the only ones of their kind in the world that can swim. They live with nomadic camel herders, who are indigenous to the region. The camels have padded hooves that help them navigate wet and salty coastal land and they can swim up to three kilometres.

Only herbivorous marine mammals
Dugongs and manatees form the only group of herbivorous marine mammals. They are found in the Gulf of Mannar and the Palk Bay, where seagrass meadows provide them food. Highly endangered, dugongs are also found in the Gulf of Kachchh and near the Andaman Islands. They are 1 m to 3 m (3 ft 3 in. to 9 ft 10 in.) long and weigh around 400 kg.

Smallest feline

The world's smallest cat, about half to three-fourths the size of a domestic cat, is the rusty spotted cat *(Prionailurus rubiginosus)* found in southern and central India. The male has a head-and-body length of 35–48 cm (1 ft 2 in.–1 ft 7 in.) and the tail measures 15–30 cm (5.9–11.8 in.). It weighs about 1.5–1.6 kg (male) and 1.1–1.5 kg (female).

Snow leopard: feline found at the highest altitudes

Largest/heaviest feline

Male tigers have a head-and- body length of 3.55–4.2 m (11 ft 7 in.–13 ft 9 in.). Females have a head-and- body length of 2.4–2.65 m (7 ft 10 in.–8 ft 8 in.). The height at shoulder is around 90–110 cm (35–43 in.). The average weight of males is 175–260 kg and for females, it is 100–160 kg.

Feline found at highest altitude

The snow leopard (*Panthera uncia*) is found at around 3,650–3,960 m (12,000–13,000 ft) in the Himalayan mountains.

BIRDS

Largest round nests

The nests made by the megapodes (*Megapodius nicobariensis*) reach a height of 1.5 m (4 ft 11 in.) and have a circumference of 10 m (32 ft 10 in.).

Smallest and lightest

The Nilgiri flowerpecker (*Dicaeum concolor*) is only 7 cm (2.7 in.) long and weighs around 4.5 g.

Longest claws

The hind claw of the bronze-winged jacana (*Metopidius indicus*) measures around 6.5–7 cm (2.5–2.7 in.) long. Its leg (tarsus) is 6.5–6.8 cm (2.5–2.6 in.) in length.

Tallest flying bird

The sarus crane (*Grus antigone antigone*) is the world's tallest bird, standing 1.52 m (5 ft) tall. This greyish crane with a red head is common around the jheels of northern and central India. Of the 14–15 species of cranes in the world, six are found in India.

Smallest egg

The average size of the egg of the scarlet-backed flowerpecker (*Dicaeum cruentatum*) is 14 mm x 10.3 mm (0.5 in. x 0.4 in.).

Largest egg

The average size of the sarus crane's egg is 10.4 cm (4 in.) x 6.4 cm (2.5 in.).

Longest beak
The beaks of the rosy pelican (*Pelecanus onocrotalus*) and the Dalmatian pelican (*Pelecanus crispus*) are 43–45 cm (1 ft 4.9 in.–1 ft 5.7 in.) long.

Slowest
The Eurasian woodcock (*Scolopax rusticola*) flies at a speed of around 8 km per hour.

Swiftest/fastest dive
The peregrine falcon (*Falco peregrinus*) reaches speeds of over 320 km per hour. It can dive at a speed of up to 360 km per hour – faster than a moving racing car.

Peregrine falcon: swiftest dive

Shortest legs
The crested tree swift (*Hemiprocne coronata*) has around 7–9 mm (0.27 –0.35 in.) long legs.

Longest legs
The legs (tarsus) of the sarus crane (*Grus antigone antigone*) measure 31–35 cm (1 ft 0.2 in.–1 ft 1.7 in.), making them the longest among birds.

SUPER 30

VIJAY CAVALE: PIONEER OF MODERN BIRD PHOTOGRAPHY

Vijay Cavale

The avid birdwatcher who put India on the world map with his photographs in the late 1990s, Vijay Cavale (1961–2020) from Bengaluru, Karnataka, was a pioneer of modern bird photography. Starting when most impressive bird images were from other countries, he set a new bar for wildlife enthusiasts and photographers. Co-founder of the Wildlife Preservation Group (WILPEG) in 1984, he worked closely with the state forest department to organize tree plantation drives and educational camps for schoolchildren for a decade before the group disbanded.

Eager to showcase India's avian life across the world, Cavale created India Nature Watch, the first free online forum for Indian photographers, as well as the Oriental Bird Images (OBI), an ongoing repository of bird photographs from the 'oriental' region. Cavale's immense knowledge of birds and their behaviours attracted visitors and students keen to learn the tricks and tips used by him in his photography expeditions.

A Unique Election for a Bird

Wardha city in Maharashtra conducted an unusual election to choose its favourite bird. Held online and through ballot paper by Bahar Nature Foundation and the Wardha Municipal Council, the polling process began on 23 June 2018 and took 54 days. From the 51,267 votes polled by the city, the winner was declared, by ornithologist Maruti Chittampalli, to be the electric-blue Indian roller with 29,835 votes.

Smallest wingspan
The Nilgiri flowerpecker (*Dicaeum concolor*) male has a wingspan of 43–48 mm (1.69–1.89 in.). The female has an even smaller wingspan of 42–45 mm (1.65–1.77 in.).

Largest wingspan
The bearded vulture (*Gypaetus barbatus*) or the lammergeier, found along the lower Himalayas in Jammu and Kashmir, Himachal Pradesh, Uttarakhand, Sikkim, Assam and Arunachal Pradesh, has a wingspan of 2.31–2.83 m (7 ft 7 in. –9 ft 3 in.).

Rarest birds
Possibly, the rarest bird is the critically endangered Jerdon's courser (*Rhinoptilus bitorquatus*). The Nicobar megapode (*Megapodius nicobariensis*) or Nicobar scrub fowl, found in the Nicobar Islands, is also one of the rarest of Indian birds.

Mysuru and Kerala Make Their Own Bird Atlases

Mysuru, Karnataka, now has a bird atlas with 192 species mapped, laboriously compiled over three years (2014–16) with the help of 60 avid birders using binoculars and cameras. They divided the city into 33 square cells of 2.2 km x 2.2 km and collected information on birds in the winter. A step ahead is Kerala, with its own bird atlas mapped across seasons over five years (2015–20) by over 1,000 volunteers guided by the Kerala Agricultural University in Vellanikkara, Thrissur, and Bird Count India, an informal partnership of organizations and groups that work to augment knowledge of bird distribution and populations. This project was undertaken on a larger scale, by dividing the state into 6.6 km x 6.6 km cells and assigning volunteer groups to record bird species. Used for predicting the distribution of bird communities over the next 25 years under different climate and land use change scenarios, the atlases are invaluable resources to conserve birds and their habitats.

Smallest bat
The Indian pygmy bat (*Pipistrellus tenuis*) has a head-and-body length of 3.3–4.5 cm (1.3–1.8 in.). Its tail is 3.5 cm (1.37 in.) and forearm is 2.5–3 cm (1.0–1.2 in.) long.

The skipper (family Hesperiidae), with more than 223 species, is the most commonly found butterfly in India.

Largest bat
The large flying fox (*Pteropus vampyrus*) is the largest bat at 19.8–30 cm (7.8–11.8 in.), and is found in the Himalayas and peninsular India.

Rarest bat
Salim Ali's fruit bat (*Latidens salimalii*) found in southern India, and named after the famous ornithologist Salim Ali, is one of the rarest bats in India.

First bird hospital
The Charity Birds' Hospital in Chandni Chowk, Delhi, caters to about 20,000 birds a year and is the only exclusive hospital for birds in the country.

Only breeding ground for flamingos
The only known breeding ground in India for the lesser and greater flamingos is the Rann of Kachchh in Gujarat. Thousands of flamingos nest every year in the seasonal marshes of both the Great Rann and the Little Rann of Kachchh.

Most intricate nest
The weaver bird species, like the baya (*Ploceus philippinus*), makes the most intricate nests. Shaped like the pipe of a snake charmer, the nests have many chambers.

BUTTERFLIES

Smallest
The grass jewel (*Freyeria trochylus*) butterfly has a wingspan of only 1.5 cm (0.6 in.).

Largest moth
The Indian atlas moth (*Attacus atlas*) is possibly the largest in the world. The average length of males is 16.7–27.1 cm (6.57 -10.67 in.) and females are 14.2–26.2 cm (5.59–10.31 in.) long.

Record Rewind

Biggest butterfly

1990

The South Indian representation of the southern birdwing (*Troides minos*) has a wingspan of up to 19 cm (7.5 in.). It is found across the western peninsula from Mumbai to the Malabar Coast.

2020

The female of the golden birdwing (*Troides aeacus*) species has a wingspan of 19.4 cm (7.6 in.) and was recorded seen in Didihat, Uttarakhand. The male is much smaller with a wingspan of 10.6 cm (4.2 in.).

Butterfly at highest altitude

The blue Apollo *(Parnassius hardwickii)* is found at altitudes of 4,267–4,876 m (14,000–16,000 ft) in the Green Lake area at the base of Mt Kangchenjunga. This bluish white butterfly, with orange spots, has a wingspan of 4.5 cm (1.8 in.).

AMPHIBIANS

Smallest frogs

In February 2017, Indian scientists found seven new endemic species of *Nyctibatrachus*, or night frogs, which make insect-like calls. Four species of these nocturnal amphibians, including Vijayan's night frog *(Nyctibatrachus pulivijayani)*, were found in the Agasthyamala Biosphere Reserve (ranging across many districts in Tamil Nadu and Kerala). They all measure around 12.2–15.4 mm (0.5–0.6 in.).

Largest frog

The Indian bull frog (*Hoplobatrachus tigerinus*), found all over the country, can grow up to 15 cm (5.9 in.). Some weigh as much as 1 kg.

Flying frog

The Malabar gliding frog *(Rhacophorus malabaricus)*, found in Karnataka and the Wayanad District of Kerala, glides from the top of a tree to the base of another using its concave body and webbed feet as a parachute.

Rarest frog

The black, narrow-mouthed Malabar frog or Kerala Hills frog (*Melanobatrachus indicus*), found in the Annamalai Hills of the Western Ghats, inhabits moist evergreen forests at 1,220 m (4,000 ft) and is considered one of the rarest frogs in the country.

First discovery of the purple frog

The purple frog (*Nasikabatrachus sahyadrensis*), also known as pignose frog, was first discovered in October 2003 in the Idukki District of Kerala by S.D. Biju

Rare Indian Frog Goes Straight from Eggs to Froglets

Last seen in 1874, the white-spotted bush frog (*Raorchestes chalazodes*#) was thought to be extinct. In 2010, it was found again, after more than 130 years, in the wet evergreen forests of the Western Ghats. Seshadri K.S., one of its 'rediscoverers', and his colleagues at the National University of Singapore and the Indian Institute of Science, Bengaluru, Karnataka, observed an unusual breeding behaviour in it. The frog bred in hollow, living shoots of bamboo, with the father looking after the eggs, which hatched directly into froglets. This mode of reproduction is called direct development, where eggs do not go through the water-requiring tadpole stage.

#The taxonomic status of *Raorchestes chalazodes* is currently subject to review and may be updated upon further research.

from the Tropical Botanic Garden and Research Institute in Palode, Kerala, and Franky Bossuyt from the Vrije Universiteit Brussel (Free University of Brussels), Belgium. Found in the Western Ghats, the purple frog remains underground most of the year except for 2–3 weeks in the monsoon.

REPTILES

LIZARDS

Largest lizard

The water monitor (*Varanus salvator*) reaches a length of 2.5 m (8 ft 2 in.) and can weigh up to 14 kg. It is a carnivorous lizard of the Sundarbans, Odisha and the Andaman Islands. Land monitor lizards (*Varanus bengalensis*) also grow to 61–175 cm (24 in.–69 in.) from snout to tail end.

Longest tongue

The chameleon's tongue is three-fourths the length of the body (30 cm/11.8 in.) and has a viscid club-shaped tip. It can flick out its tongue and catch prey in 1/25th of a second.

Longest tail in relation to body

The long-tailed grass lacertid (*Takydromus sexlineatus khasiensis*) measures only 5 cm (2 in.), but its tail is 35 cm (13.7 in.) long – a ratio of 1:7. It is found in the Khasi Hills of Meghalaya.

Only flying lizards

Norvill's flying lizard (*Draco norvillii*), found in north-east India, and the Indian flying lizard (*Draco dussumieri*) from the Western Ghats and South India are endemic to India. Their average length is 23 cm (9 in.) and they can glide through the air for around 17 m (55 ft 9 in.).

Only legless lizard

The Asian glass lizard or Burmese glass lizard (*Ophisaurus gracilis*) is found at altitudes of 820–1,500 m (2,690–4,920 ft) in Darjeeling, West Bengal, and the Khasi Hills, Meghalaya. It crawls and uses its tongue in a snake-like fashion.

GECKOS

Smallest gecko

A 4 cm (1.6 in.) Persian sand dwarf gecko (*Tropiocolotes persicus*), also called the dwarf or pygmy gecko, was recorded in Rajasthan in 2011.

Largest gecko

The *Hemidactylus frenatus* or the common house gecko, found in Bihar, Bengal and north-east India, grows to around 34 cm (13.4 in.) in length. It feeds on insects, rats, birds and small snakes.

'Flying' gecko

The gliding gecko *(Ptychozoon kuhli)*, found in the Nicobar Islands and north-east

India, can glide over 13 m (43 ft). It has skin flaps on the side of its head, body and tail, which help it glide when the animal launches into the air.

Rarest gecko

The golden hill gecko (*Calodactylodes avreus*), found in the Tirumala Hills of Andhra Pradesh, is a very rare species. Its body is golden yellow with brown spots.

CROCODILES

Shortest crocodile

The mugger crocodile (*Crocodylus palustris*), found in streams, is only 3 m (9 ft 10 in.) long. It is found almost all over India except at higher altitudes such as in the Himalayan mountains.

Heaviest crocodile

The estuarine or saltwater crocodile (*Crocodylus porosus*) is the heaviest reptile in the country. The adult male crocodile may weigh around 1,000–1,300 kg while adult females weigh around 76–100 kg.

Longest crocodile

The estuarine or saltwater crocodile grows to a recorded length of 7 m (23 ft). It is found in tidal estuaries, marine swamps and coastal waters in and around the Sundarbans, Odisha, and the Andaman and Nicobar Islands.

First known white crocodile

- Gori, an albino white crocodile, was artificially hatched at the Bhitarkanika Dangamal Crocodile Research Centre in Odisha on 26 June 1975.
- In 2018, forest officials sighted 12 albino crocodiles in Bhitarkanika National Park and its nearby areas during the annual reptile census.

Rarest crocodile

The rarest of the three crocodile species found in India, the gharial (*Gavialus gangeticus*) grows to 6.25 m (20 ft 6 in.) and is the only living member of family Gavialidae in India. The surviving population is found in the tributaries of the River Ganga – Girwa (Uttar Pradesh), Son (Madhya Pradesh), Ramganga (Uttarakhand),

The gharial: rarest of Indian crocodiles

Gandak (Bihar), Chambal (Uttar Pradesh, Madhya Pradesh and Rajasthan) – and Mahanadi (Odisha). it is classified as critically endangered by the International Union for the Conservation of Nature (IUCN).

First/largest crocodile bank

The Madras Crocodile Bank Trust and Centre for Herpetology, 40 km off Madras (now Chennai, Tamil Nadu) was founded in 1976 by the legendary naturalist Romulus Whitaker, and had over 8,000 crocodiles of 10 different species.

SNAKES

Longest sea snake

The yellow sea snake (*Hydrophis spiralis*) grows to a length of 1.8 m (6 ft). Specimens up to 3 m (10 ft) are not uncommon. It is found both in the Bay of Bengal and the Arabian Sea.

WR **Longest snake**

The reticulated python (*Python reticulatus*) is the longest snake in the world. It is found in the Nicobar Islands. The average length is between 3 and 6 m (10 and 20 ft). While the reticulated python prefers small mammals, it can take large animals up to the size of a full-grown wild boar.

Only snake that builds a nest

The king cobra (*Ophiophagus hannah*), found in the Western Ghats, parts of north India, the east, the north-east and the Andaman Islands, builds a 30 cm (11.8 in.) nest by scraping leaves together.

SUPER 30

ROMULUS WHITAKER: THE SNAKE MAN OF INDIA

Legendary herpetologist and wildlife conservationist, Romulus Earl Whitaker (b. 23 May 1943) founded India's first reptile park – the Madras Snake Park Trust (now Chennai Snake Park) in the Guindy National Park campus in Tamil Nadu – in 1972 to protect and study snake species of India. The project was conceived to help the Irula tribe (who were skilled in catching snakes), offering them work in extracting snake venom used for antivenom drugs. Four years later, he worked to establish the Madras Crocodile Bank Trust and Centre for Herpetology (40 km off Chennai) to breed crocodile species on the brink of extinction. Among co-founding many organizations, in 2005, he founded the Agumbe Rainforest Research Station in Karnataka to study king cobras. The author of several scientific articles and books on reptiles, Whitaker received the Padma Shri in 2018 for his efforts in wildlife conservation. In honour of his long and distinguished career working with reptiles, a non-venomous species of Indian boa found in south-western coastal India was named *Eryx whitakeri*.

Romulus Whitaker

Only 'flying' snake
The ornate flying snake (*Chrysopelea ornata*) is capable of gliding by launching itself from height. An instance of this species gliding for a distance of 50 m (164 ft) has been recorded. This snake inhabits the hilly forests of the south-west and the north-east, besides the Andaman Islands.

Fastest snake
Rat snakes and bronze-back tree snakes can reach a speed of 10 km per hour.

Loudest hiss
Russell's viper (*Daboia russelii*) hisses the loudest from among all Indian snakes – nearly as loud as the hiss of a pressure cooker.

Only snake with heat sensors
The pit viper (subfamily Crotalinae), found in the hilly parts of India, is able to locate warm-blooded prey using two heat sensors between its nostrils and eyes.

Snake at the highest altitude
No other species of snake has been found at an altitude higher than the Himalayan pit viper (*Gloydius himalayanus*). Herpetologist Frank Wall (1868–1950), who lived in Sri Lanka and India, claimed to have seen one at an altitude of 3,658 m (12,000 ft) in Kashmir and one was captured at the foot of the glacier at Dharamshala at an altitude of 4,877 m (16,000 ft).

TORTOISES AND TURTLES

Largest rookery
The 12 km long sandy beach in the Gahirmatha region of Odisha is one of the largest rookeries for marine sea turtles. In February–March, olive ridley turtles (*Lepidochelys olivacea*) come out here in hundreds of thousands to mate and nest. The olive ridley is one of the seven endangered species of turtles in the world due to the disturbance and destruction of their habitat.

Largest terrapin
The Batagur terrapin (*Batagur baska*), found in the river estuaries of the Sundarbans, West Bengal, is the largest terrapin and a critically endangered species. The carapace of this terrapin is 59 cm (23 in.) long.

Largest turtle
The leatherback sea turtle (*Dermochelys coriacea*) has a shell length averaging 2.5 m (8 ft) and weighs 700 kg. It feeds mainly on jellyfish.

Smallest tortoise
The Indian star tortoise (*Geochelone elegans*) grows to a length of only around 15 cm (5.9 in.).

The Indian star tortoise: the smallest tortoise

Smallest carapace
The Cochin cane forest turtle (*Vijayachelys silvatica*) has a carapace that is 13 cm (5.1 in.) long.

Rarest freshwater turtle
India's rarest freshwater turtle is possibly the Assam leaf turtle (*Cyclemys dentata),* found in the hill streams of Assam. It grows to a length of around 24 cm (9.4 in.).

FISH AND MOLLUSCS

Oldest freshwater fish
Fossil remains of the Dipnoi subclass of fish or lungfish (*Ceratodus agassiz*) were found in the Maleri beds of the Godavari Valley in the late Triassic period (237–201.3 million years ago). The genus *Ceratodus* evolved in the northern hemisphere in the early Triassic period (251–247 million years ago).

Lightest/smallest fish
The dwarf pygmy goby (*Pandaka pygmaea*) is 1 cm (0.39 in.) long and weighs 4–5 mg.

Only fish with suction plates
The remora or suckerfish (family Echeneidae) can swim, but is usually found attached to sharks, turtles, dolphins and even ships. The first dorsal fin is modified into a suction apparatus, and the erection of the plate where the fish joins its host creates a vacuum, enabling the fish to stay attached.

Heaviest fish
The whale shark *(Rhincodon typus)* is the largest and heaviest shark in India, weighing up to 60 tonnes.

Only fish without a bony skeleton
Sharks (and their relatives, the guitar fish and swordfish) do not have a bony skeleton. They have cartilage or gristle. They are predominantly marine fish with a few freshwater representatives.

Only anadromous fish
Hilsa (*Tenualosa ilisha*) is India's only anadromous fish, which migrates from sea or estuarine waters up rivers for breeding. This fish is found mostly in the Gangetic estuary.

Only male fish producing young
Seahorses (Genus *Hippocampus*) are predominantly marine. The male fish carries a kangaroo-like pouch in its belly. The female passes her eggs to this pouch where the father incubates them. The young are thus born from the father.

WR **Largest subterranean fish**
A fish measuring around 45 cm (17.7 in.) was discovered by Daniel Harries, a biologist from Heriot Watt University in Edinburgh, UK, in a cave in Meghalaya in February 2019.

Shortest-lived fish
Small fish such as the *Pandaka pygmaea*, and of the families Oreichthys and Gambusia (such as mosquito fish), live hardly for a year.

Longest-lived fish
The common carp is said to live in sheltered ponds for over 50 years if left alone.

Largest clam
The giant clam (*Tridacna gigas*) grows to 1 m (3 ft 3.4 in.) long and weighs over 100 kg. This clam has been exploited throughout its Asia-Pacific range, but is fortunately plentiful in the coral reefs of the Andaman and Nicobar Islands.

PLANTS

Oldest plant fossils
Fossils, which are 1.6 billion years old and appear to contain red algae, were found embedded in mats of cyanobacteria in phosphate-rich sedimentary rocks in Chitrakoot in central India, in May 2017. Until this discovery, the oldest known red algae were 1.2 billion years old.

Longest-lived tree species
The banyan tree (*Ficus benghalensis*), found in most parts of India, lives for more than 250 years.

Fastest-maturing trees
The eucalyptus and the subabul (*Leucaena leucocephala*) trees mature very fast and are both ready for cutting in 6–7 years.

The eucalyptus: one of the fastest-maturing trees

Tallest trees
The fir (*Abies pindrow*) and deodar (*Cedrus deodara*) grow to an average height of 76.2 m (250 ft).

Biggest tree trunk
The deodar (*Cedrus deodara*) found in Jammu and Kashmir, Himachal Pradesh and Uttarakhand, have trunks with a circumference of around 12 m (39 ft 4 in.) or more.

Largest hollow tree
A baobab or monkey-bread tree (*Adansonia digitata*), which is a species of African origin, stands amid the ruins of the eastern part of the historic Golconda Fort near Hyderabad, Telangana. Reportedly, its 3.3 sq. m (35.5 sq. ft) hollow can comfortably fit in 10–12 people.

Largest tree canopy
A banyan tree identified in Anantapur District of Andhra Pradesh in 1988 by freelance photographer 'Regret Iyer' and K.S. Ramakrishna from Bangalore (now Bengaluru, Karnataka) has a canopy covering 2.1 hectares (5.19 acres) and is believed to be over 600 years old.

Record Rewind

National parks in India

1990
There were 72 national parks in India, covering up to an area of 43,360.22 sq. km.

2020
There are 105 national parks in the country, covering an area of 50,735.99 sq. km.

Tallest flower
- The gigantic Himalayan rhubarb (*Rheum nobile*) grows 0.9–1.2 m (3–4 ft) long. It is found even at 4,268 m (14,000 ft) in the Himalayan ranges.
- The corpse flower (*Amorphophallus titanum*) or 'titan arum', though not a native species, is the tallest flower (2.4 m/7 ft 10 in.) in India, and the largest by diameter (more than 1 m/3 ft 3.3 in.).

Longest creeper
The elephant creeper (*Argyreia nervosa*) grows to a length of 1.5 km, making it the longest creeper in the country and one of the longest in the world.

Largest family of plants
Family Poaceae is the largest in the country, represented by as many as 263 genera and 1,291 species. Poaceae or Gramineae is a ubiquitous family of monocotyledonous flowering plants known as grasses. The Poaceae family includes cereal grasses, bamboos and grasses of natural grasslands as well as of cultivated lawns and pastures.

Plants at the highest altitude
- The *Ermania himalayensis* grows at 6,000 m (19,685 ft) in the Himalayas.
- *Christolea himalayensis*, a herb usually about 10–15 cm (3.9–5.9 in.) tall, is found at 5,000–6,000 m (16,404–19,685 ft).

Rare flowering
Found in southern and eastern India, the talipot palm (*Corypha umbraculifera*) flowers once in 25–80 years and then dies.

Largest leaf
The leaf of the water lily (*Victoria amazonica*) may measure up to 1.5 m (5 ft) in diameter.

Heaviest fruit
The jackfruit tree (*Artocarpus heterophyllus*) is planted (but also grows wild) in the Western Ghats and elsewhere in India. The tree bears fruit of enormous size – weighing up to 40 kg.

Heaviest wood
Anjan (*Hardwickia binata*) wood is the heaviest, with a specific gravity of 0.61–0.73.

Lightest wood
Balsa (*Ochroma lagopus*) has a specific gravity of 0.12 to 0.15.

FIGHTING THE GOOD FIGHT

The contradictions between development and conservation, and consumerism and sustainability never cease. As habitat destruction continues to push more species to extinction, here are a few front liners helping to protect them.

WWF India
World Wildlife Fund India was established as a charitable trust in 1969 in Bombay (now Mumbai, Maharashtra). It works with many groups and institutions across different sections of society in its mission of conserving biodiversity, sustainably using natural resources, and maintaining ecosystems and ecosystem services for the survival of wildlife and the people depending on them. While its Forest and Biodiversity Conservation Division works to promote and enhance conservation of forest ecosystems, its Environmental Education Programme strengthens nature conservation and environmental protection. Launched in 2013, the Education for Sustainable Development Programme includes a trainer kit with materials in six languages for teachers and educational bodies responsible for the curriculum in nature conservation.

Wildlife SOS
Established in 1995 with the aim of rescuing and rehabilitating wildlife in distress, and preserving India's natural heritage, Wildlife SOS (WSOS) started with a small group of individuals and is currently one of the largest non-profit wildlife organizations in South Asia. Founded by Kartick Satyanarayan and Geeta Seshamani to address the abusive practice of 'dancing' bears, the organization is now responsible for taking action against animal cruelty, rescuing wildlife in distress, working to resolve man–animal conflicts, conducting scientific research

Tallest bamboo/grass

The tallest bamboo (*Dendrocalamus giganteus*), known as dragon bamboo, is found in Assam and West Bengal. It grows up to 40 m (130 ft) with a diameter of around 20–25 cm (8–10 in.).

CONSERVING NATURE

Oldest zoos

- Raja Rajendra Mallick Bahadur started the Marble Palace Aviary and Zoo in Calcutta (now Kolkata, West Bengal) in 1854 specifically for the education and entertainment of the public.
- The Thiruvananthapuram Zoological Gardens in Kerala is said to have been set up by Maharaja Swathi Thirunal in 1859. Spread over 30 acres (12 hectares), it is the oldest extant zoo.

Oldest botanical gardens

The Acharya Jagadish Chandra Bose Indian Botanic Garden was established in 1787 in Shibpur, Howrah, near Kolkata in West Bengal, with about 12,000 living plants and 2.5 million dried plant specimens in the

SUPER 30

and conservation studies, training enforcement officers as well as educating the public about the need for habitat protection. Wildlife SOS also works towards curbing the illegal trade and poaching of wildlife and its products while also providing sustainable alternative livelihoods for communities dependent on wildlife. A 24-hour animal rescue helpline with a team trained to perform emergency rescue operations of wild animals was started in 1998 in Delhi, Gujarat and Uttar Pradesh, and now responds to nearly 300 rescue calls a month.

Wildlife Trust of India

The Wildlife Trust of India (WTI) is a leading Indian nature conservation organization committed to the service of nature. Launched with a three-member team in a room in South Delhi in 1998, it is now run by 120 professionals, all driven by their love for wildlife. WTI's strategic approach to wildlife conservation is expressed in nine overarching concepts: Wild Aid, Enforcement and Law, Species Recovery, Protected Area Recovery, Wild Rescue, Conflict Mitigation, Wild Lands, Natural Heritage Campaigns and Right of Passage. Measuring its impact in very tangible terms, the organization has saved more than 48,000 animal lives* ranging from turtles to tigers and whale sharks; sensitized more than 24 lakh (2.4 million) children to nature conservation through campaigns; saved over 2,000 elephants from train hits by working with local forest departments and Indian Railways; helped secure over 2.5 crore (25 million) hectares of habitat for wildlife (including tripling the area of Manas National Park through policy interventions); trained more than 18,000 front-line wildlife staff of over 150 Protected Areas; provided ex gratia assurance to more than 30,000 front-line forest staff against death or injury on duty; assisted enforcement authorities to initiate nearly 250 operations against illegal wildlife trade; and enabled over 19,000 families to adopt green livelihoods to reduce dependency on forests.

**Figures are rounded off till December 2020*

herbarium, from all over the world. The gardens cover 276.75 acres (112 hectares) in 25 sections.

First conservation organization

The Indian Board for Wildlife (IBWL), with S. Dharmakumar Sinhji as its vice chairman, was set up in 1952 by the Government of India with. It was replaced by the National Board for Wildlife (NBWL) in September 2003.

First marine reserve

The Marine National Park and Sanctuary in Jamnagar District, Gujarat, forms the first marine reserve of India. Including Pirotan Island and other islands, it was given the status of a national park in 1980, and is rich in corals, octopuses, giant snails, sponges, crabs, lobsters and fish.

Largest zoological park

Arignar Anna Zoological Park at Vandalur near Chennai, Tamil Nadu, is the largest zoological park in South Asia. Spread over 602 hectares (1,487.57 acres), it has more than 100 species of birds, 50 species of mammals and 20 species of reptiles.

First wildlife magazine

Indian Wildlife was published by Jim Corbett in the 1930s.

First virtual herbarium

Since February 2017, a virtual digital herbarium of specimens preserved in the Kerala Forest Research Institute at Peechi in Thrissur District, Kerala, can be accessed at the URL *http://kfriherbarium.in*.

Highest national park

The Kangchenjunga Biosphere Reserve or the Khangchendzonga National Park in Sikkim is the highest national park at 8,585 m (28,166 ft) above the mean sea level.

Oldest NGO engaged in conservation and biodiversity research

On 15 September 1883, eight men established the Bombay Natural History Society at the then Victoria and Albert Museum (now Bhau Daji Lad Museum) in Bombay (now Mumbai, Maharashtra) to exchange information on natural history and exhibit interesting specimens. They were E.H. Aitken, Dr G.A. Maconochie, Dr D. MacDonald, J. C. Anderson, Colonel C. Swinhoe, J. Johnston, Dr Atmaram Pandurang and Dr Sakharam Arjun, along with H.M. Phipson.

State/UT with most national parks

Madhya Pradesh leads with 10 national parks, with 365,725 sq. km dedicated to them. Andaman and Nicobar Islands follow with nine national parks across 115,394 sq. km.

State/UT with most wildlife sanctuaries

Andaman and Nicobar Islands have 96 wildlife sanctuaries (389.39 sq. km) and Maharashtra has 46 (7,592.3 sq. km).

First national park
Jim Corbett National Park (earlier Hailey National Park and then Ramganga National Park), established in 1936, stretches over 521 sq. km across the two hill districts of Pauri Garhwal and Nainital, Uttarakhand, and is home to around 110 tree species, 50 species of mammals, 580 bird species and 25 species of reptiles. It was the first to come under the Project Tiger initiative. The elevation of the park ranges from 400 m to 1,200 m ((1,300 ft to 4,000 ft).

WR Largest camera trap tiger census
India's tiger census of 2018 became the largest camera trap wildlife survey in the world. Camera traps (outdoor photographic devices fitted with motion sensors that start recording when an animal passes by) were placed in 26,838 locations across 141 different sites and surveyed an effective area of 121,337 sq. km as part of the survey. Individual tigers (excluding cubs), which were identified using stripe pattern recognition software from the photographs clicked by camera traps, numbered 2,461 by this method.

GARDENING

Tallest rose plant
Arunsinh Solanki grew a rose plant 11.88 m (39 ft) tall at his home in Godhra in Gujarat, as recorded on 13 May 2019.

Tallest prickly amaranth plant
In August 2017, T. Damodar and his wife Shobha T. Damodar from Belagavi, Karnataka, grew the tallest prickly amaranth plant (*Amaranthus spinosus*), which measured 4.03 m (13 ft 3 in.) in height. Normally this plant grows to a height of 0.3 m to 2.43 m (1–8 ft).

Discovery of New Indian Orchid Species

Among Indian scientists, Dr A.N. Rao, former director of the Centre for Orchid Gene Conservation of the Eastern Himalayas in Hengbung, Senapati District, Manipur, has discovered the most new orchid species, totalling thirty-five, all from the north-eastern Himalayas. While 20 are his individual finds, fifteen of them were discovered with other scientists. With rampant destruction of forests, many orchid species are becoming extinct, and the discovery of new species is proving to be crucial.

Representational Image

Tallest bougainvillea

Prof. Dr Ramesh Babu (b. 12 February 1957) has grown a 10.33 m (33 ft 11 in.) tall *Bougainvillea spectabilis* in his garden in Bengaluru, Karnataka. The over 16-year-old bougainvillea with white blossoms had a spread of 6.09 m (20 ft) and the girth at its base was 0.2 m (7.8 in.) as on 29 January 2020. Normally, the bougainvillea grows to an average height of 6.09 m (20 ft).

WR Tallest coriander plant

Dalbir Maan (b. 1 June 1982) grew a 2.28 m (7 ft 6 in.) coriander plant at his home in Melbourne, Australia, as recorded on 18 November 2020.

Biggest lemon

K. Mohanchandran from Kothanur, Bengaluru, Karnataka, grew a lemon measuring 28 cm x 14 cm (11 in. x 5.5 in.) in his garden. The lemon had a circumference of 49 cm (19.2 in.) and weighed 2.365 kg on 22 February 2020.

Longest mango leaf

A mango tree with a leaf measuring 61 cm (2 ft) was found at the primary school of Budapur in Varanasi, Uttar Pradesh, by Dr Bhola Vishwakarma, one of the schoolteachers, on 30 October 2018.

Largest taro leaf

A taro (*Colocasia esculenta*) leaf measuring 76.0 cm x 64.5 cm (2 ft 5.9 in. x 2 ft 1.39 in.) was found and cultivated in Boudhgarh, Boudh District, Odisha, by Jayaram Rana on 7 January 2020.

Tallest drumstick tree

Prof. Dr Ramesh Babu from Bengaluru, Karnataka, has the tallest drumstick tree (*Moringa oleifera*) growing in his residential garden. On 20 June 2019, the 11-year-old tree was 8.2 m (26 ft 11 in.) tall with a spread of 3.66 m (12 ft) and a base girth of 47.6 cm (1 ft 6.74 in.) The average height of a drumstick tree is 6.1 m (20 ft).

Longest mango leaf

WR Tallest musk mallow plant

A.K. Narayanan from Thrissur, Kerala, had a three-year-old musk mallow plant, 2.74 m (9 ft) tall as in June 2016, in his garden.

WR Tallest *jamun* tree

Prof. Dr Ramesh Babu from Bengaluru, Karnataka, has the tallest *jamun* tree (*Syzygium cumini*) in his garden. On 20 June 2019, the 15-year-old tree was 11.9 m (39 ft) tall with a spread of 6 m (20 ft) and a base girth of 1.04 m (41 in.) The average height of a jamun tree is 9.1–10.6 m (30–35 ft).

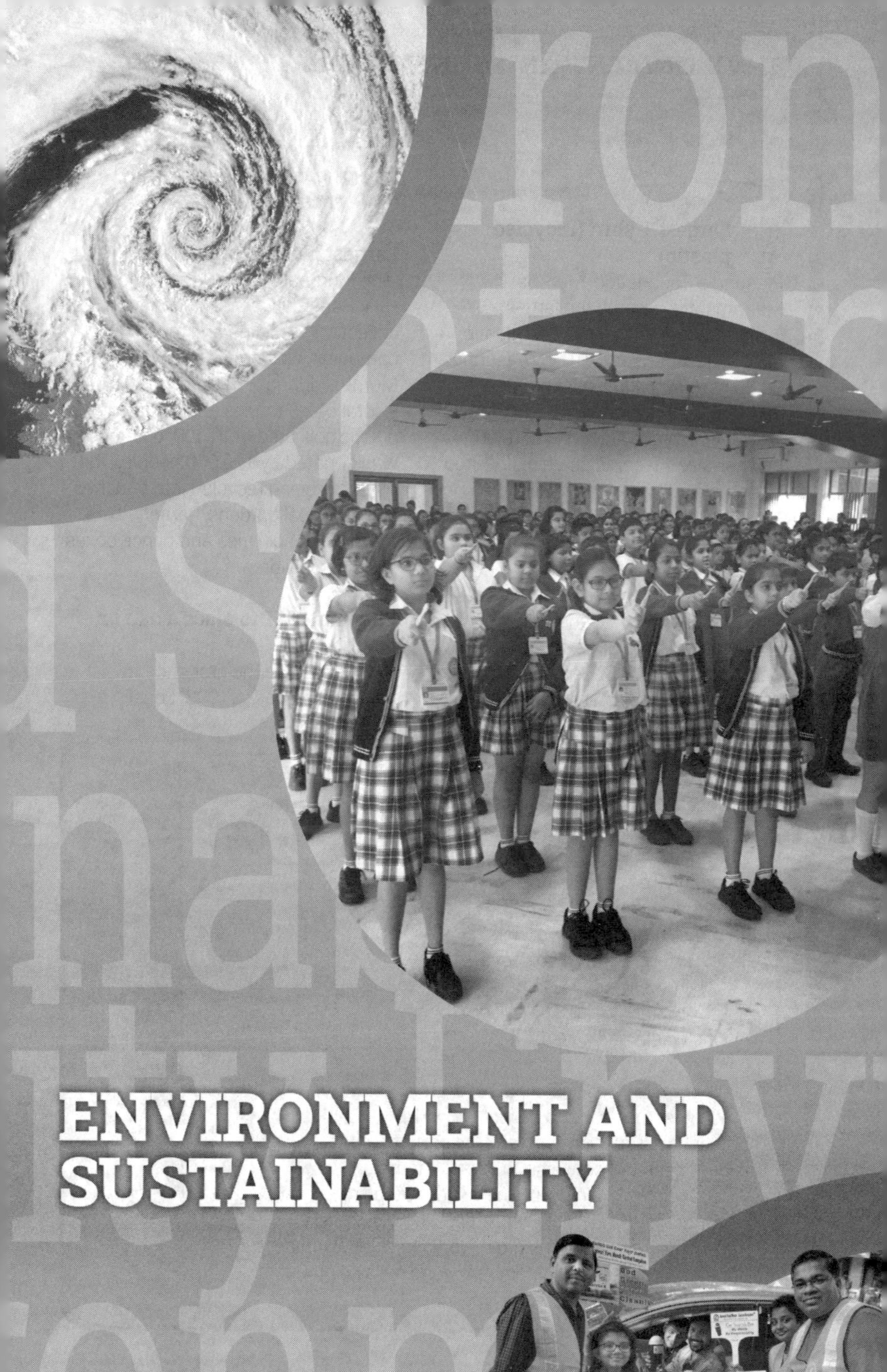
ENVIRONMENT AND SUSTAINABILITY
Place All Trash In The Proper Container

'No' to Plastic

Largest T-shirt (recycled plastic)

Plastindia Foundation, Mumbai, Maharashtra, created the largest T-shirt from 200,000 recycled plastic bottles on 5 January 2018. Measuring 98.86 m (324 ft 4 in.) in length and 69.77 m (228 ft 11 in.) in width, the T-shirt was broken down into 10,000 normal-sized T-shirts, to be distributed after the event.

First plastic-free conference by doctors

The annual conference of the Association of Physicians (Rajasthan chapter) was a garbage-free event held during 22–23 December 2018 at Mayo College, Ajmer, Rajasthan. Wood, glass, ceramic, metal, paper and cloth were used instead of plastic for dining, decoration, gifting and other conference proceedings.

Largest plastic recyclothon

'The Mumbai Plastic Recyclothon – Ek Baar Phir', a plastic donation, collection, recycling and reuse campaign, was organized by Project Mumbai during 2–8 October 2019. A total of 2.8 tonnes (2,800 kg) of plastic collected from 500 locations was donated by 125,000 people. The plastic is being recycled into benches for municipal gardens, garbage bins for housing societies and pencil boxes for schoolchildren.

First state/UT to place a ban on plastic bags

Sikkim became the first state to ban plastic bags in 1998. Local

Reverse Vending Machines

Founded by Dinesh Parikh, Aditya Parikh and Sachin Sharma in 2013, GEM Enviro Management Pvt. Ltd is a scrap management company that collects and recycles polyethylene terephthalate (PET) plastic items into consumer products such as bags, T-shirts, furniture and soft toys. By 2019, this Delhi-based start-up had helped recycle approximately 1 lakh (0.1 million) tonnes of plastic waste and saved 1.4 lakh (0.14 million) carbon dioxide emissions by transforming plastic waste. They installed 10 reverse vending machines (machines to collect waste PET bottles) at Gurugram, Haryana, as part of their pilot project and now plan to install another 25 in Delhi NCR. While obtaining most of their raw materials from factories, offices, hotels, motels and institutes, the organization works to raise awareness about environmental sustainability and sells its products under its brand called 'Being Responsible'.

Kulhads All the Way

Current Indian railway minister, Piyush Goyal, announced the replacement of plastic cups with *kulhads* for all railway stations on 29 November 2020. This green catering initiative has already been implemented in over 400 railway stations and a complete shift to these terracotta cups will contribute to the vision of a plastic-free India. The use of *kulhads* is more hygienic and eco-friendly, and generates jobs too.

communities in Yuksom Village were upset by the harmful impact of plastics on the environment and formed the Khangchendzonga Conservation Committee (KCC), which banned plastic bags and bottles in 1996 and collected around 800 kg of plastic waste from trails and trek routes. Encouraged by their success, the state government announced a statewide ban on plastic bags on 4 June 1998.

Students pledging to replace plastic toothbrushes with eco-friendly bamboo ones

Most participants simultaneously pledging to replace plastic toothbrushes with eco-friendly ones

As part of a recycling movement championship, 'Vital Waste', organized by Redivivus Recyclers Pvt. Ltd, 1,800 school students bought recycling kits and raised toothbrushes in salutation as they pledged to recycle waste and work towards environment sustainability. The event took place on 'Vital Waste Day' on 16 January 2020 at 11:00 a.m. They pledged to replace plastic toothbrushes with eco-friendly bamboo toothbrushes.

First 'garbage café'

The Garbage Café in Ambikapur, Surguja District, Chhattisgarh, has

India generates 25,940 tonnes of plastic waste every day. This is as much as the weight of 9,000 Asian elephants.

Bring Your Own Container to this Grocery Store

The '7 to 9 Green Store' in Kolenchery, Kerala, was opened by Bittu John with the aim to reduce plastic usage and promote sustainable living. The store is based on the B.Y.O.C. concept – 'Bring Your Own Container'! Customers are encouraged to bring containers and carry back the products they purchase in loose quantities. In case you don't, cotton bags, glass bottles and paper bags are available at the store at nominal prices. Started in 2019, the store offers an encouraging 2 per cent discount to all customers who bring their own container.

a unique system! Here, one can get meals in exchange for plastic waste. Established in October 2019, by the Ambikapur Municipal Corporation (AMC), the café aims to make the district plastic-free. The café weighs the amount of plastic waste and food is bartered in exchange. The collected plastic is later sent to the municipal corporation for disposal. Cafés with similar concepts also came up in Dwarka, New Delhi (January 2020) and Dahod District, Gujarat (February 2020).

Clean-up Campaigns

Plog run with most participants

The biggest plog run (combining jogging with picking up litter – from Swedish *plockaupp*) was organized on Gandhi Jayanti on 2 October 2018 from 55 locations of Bengaluru, Karnataka, and 6.5 tonnes (6,500 kg) of plastic waste, including bottles and litter, was collected by 6,518 participants in four hours from 7:00 a.m. to 11:00 a.m. The participants, representing five organizations – BBMP (Bruhat Bengaluru Mahanagara Palike); Go Native,; Namma Nimma Cycle Foundation, Let's Be the Change, United Way Bengaluru – and an individual, Ramakrishna Ganesh, created awareness on urban cleanliness by proper disposal of waste, especially plastic.

Mumbai's clean-up campaign for waterbodies*

Project Mumbai, a not-for-profit organization from Mumbai, Maharashtra, organized the biggest cleaning up of waterbodies during 1–2 and 5 June 2019 as part of their World Environment Day celebrations. Called 'Jallosh – Clean Coasts', the campaign attracted 5,000 volunteers, who collected 20 tonnes (20,000

*This is a one-time category. Further and future claims for this category will not be accepted.

kg) of waste from three rivers, eight beachfronts and four mangrove points/areas across Mumbai.

Most waste collected – 15 mins

The Good Quest Foundation, Bengaluru, Karnataka, organized a garbage-free, plastic-free, healthy India programme, called 'Namma Vision 150', to commemorate Mahatma Gandhi's 150th birth anniversary year, on 30 November 2019. The event saw 36,800 students and volunteers picking up 765 kg of plastic waste from around 170 school campuses of the city in 15 mins. Suresh Kumar, the state minister for primary and secondary education and labour, was a guest at one of the venues and several bureaucrats, academicians and city corporation workers motivated the students to work for a green and clean India.

Most waste recycled from a gathering – non-biodegradable and organic combined

Bhopal Municipal Corporation, the Government of Madhya Pradesh, the Tablighi Ijtema organizing committee and 2,200 Swachhata Mitras organized a zero-waste event during 22–25 November 2019. The gathering of around 15 lakh (1.5 million) people generated 6,250 kg of non-biodegradable waste and 12,285 kg of organic waste. With the help of 3,000 volunteers, along with the use of mobile composting vans, the non-biodegradable waste was collected and recycled. The organic waste was processed into 3,870 kg of compost. Around 500 kg of biogas was processed from it, and 31 lakh (3.1 million) litres of waste water was treated and released into waterbodies.

First Beach to Receive the 'Blue Flag' Certification

Chandrabhaga Beach in Odisha became Asia's first beach to get the prestigious Blue Flag certification on 5 June 2018. The Blue Flag certifies beaches on 33 stringent criteria based on environmental, educational, water quality, services, and accessibility and safety standards, among others. It is accorded by the Foundation for Environmental Education (FEE), Copenhagen, Denmark. In 2020, eight beaches from India were certified with the Blue Flag in a single attempt – an achievement exclusive to India. The latest certified beaches are – Ghoghla (Dadra and Nagar Haveli and Daman and Diu), Shivrajpur (Dwarka, Gujarat), Kasarkod and Padubidri (Karnataka), Kappad (Kerala), Rushikonda (Andhra Pradesh), Radhanagar (Andaman and Nicobar Islands) and Golden Beach (Puri, Odisha).

Most Car Dustbins Distributed

The All India Marwari Yuva Manch, based in Delhi, distributed 105,000 mini portable dustbins for cars at traffic signals and other places free of charge to encourage people to not litter streets. The 11-month long campaign was carried out by 750 volunteers from 26 April 2019 to 31 March 2020 under the Swachh Bharat Abhiyan. They beat their previous record of distributing 65,500 car dustbins from 26 May 2018 to 26 April 2019 at Noida and Bengaluru, among other cities.

Waste Not...

Tallest scrap-metal structure – group

A group of 120 students, training to be fitters, welders, electricians, plumbers and painters at the Government ITI in Berhampur, Ganjam District, Odisha, created the tallest scrap metal structure, a 21.33 m (70 ft) tall guitar, over a period of three months from 17 July 2019. The 'Best out of waste' mission sought to integrate skill development with waste management in an eco-friendly manner. The guitar is exhibited at the open-air Scrap Sculpture Museum of the ITI, along with 10 other smaller sculptures, also all created from waste.

Tallest scrap-metal structure – solo

Sandeep Pisalkar from Vadodara, Gujarat, created a replica of the iconic

Sparkling It Up!

Sparkle, a start-up that manufactures sanitary pads using discarded banana stems, was launched in 2017 by Chirag and Hetal Virani, a couple from Surat, Gujarat. With a mechanical engineering background, Chirag developed a machine to manufacture these pads that can biodegrade within 140 days while Hetal worked to make the pads affordable for a wide user base. With a view to making these pads more accessible, the Viranis plan to launch their new product at a relatively more affordable ₹9.99 each. The start-up also donates one sanitary napkin for each napkin sold under its initiative called, 'Buy One, Give One', and works with NGOs and schools to create awareness about menstrual health and hygiene.

India's total municipal solid waste is estimated to reach an annual weight of 165 billion kg by 2030.

Eiffel Tower, measuring 21.33 m (70 ft) in height, with 40 tonnes a(4,000 kg) of automobile scrap. The three levels of the structure were created separately and then assembled with the help of a crane. The material used included petrol tanks from trucks, C-channels, angles and clutch plates. It was exhibited at the Waste to Wonder Park, New Delhi, in February 2019.

Largest jute bag

The largest jute bag, measuring in 30.68 m (100 ft 8 in.) length and 24.87 m (81 ft 7 in.) in width, was made by Chaitali Das and Rakshak Foundation in Kolkata, West Bengal, on 7 January 2021.

Only Indian city to win C40 Cities Bloomberg Philanthropies award

Kolkata, West Bengal, was the only Indian city in the list of seven winners for the 2019 edition of the C40 Cities Bloomberg Philanthropies award. The theme was 'The Future We Want' and Kolkata was awarded 'The Future We Want Relies on Green Mobility' for its low-carbon commute transition projects making up the city's Green Mobility plans, at the C40 World Mayors Summit held in October at Copenhagen, Denmark.

Green Growth

Most trees planted – single day*

The Department of Forests and Wildlife, Uttar Pradesh, planted 258,747,661 saplings in one day, 5 July 2020, with the participation of various departments of the state as well as the general public. Starting at 5:55 a.m., the plantation work at selected plantation sites in all 75 districts concluded at 6:00 p.m. Almost five million people were deployed for the mammoth task and the saplings were collected from the forest nurseries that had started work for the 2020 plantation a whole year in advance. In all some 44.27 crore (442.7 million) saplings were raised for the event in 1,760 nurseries.

Largest airport nursery

The country's largest airport nursery was inaugurated on 5 June 2020, celebrated as World Environment Day. Spread over more than 37,161.22 sq. m (400,000 sq. ft) near Indira Gandhi International Airport, New Delhi, the nursery has, in each plantation season, lakhs of air-purifying plants – white fig *(Ficus infectoria)*, golden shower *(Cassia fistula)*, Indian Pulai *(Alstonia scholaris)*, gulmohar *(Delonix regia)* and many more. At this picturesque attraction for passengers, the temperature and humidity is managed by a digitally controlled cooling fan and pad facility along with an automatic fogging and irrigation system.

Most trees planted – 1 hour

The District Collectorate of Dehradun,

*This record attempt was made while observing COVID-19 social distancing guidelines and safety protocols.

Forest Officer Receives Environmental Honour from the United Nations

Sasmita Lenka, a forest officer from Odisha, won the United Nations' Asia Environmental Enforcement Award 2020, thus becoming the first Indian woman to receive this honour. A divisional officer from Athgarh, Cuttack District, she won the accolade in the 'Gender Leadership and Impact' category for her work in destroying international pangolin-smuggling rackets found to be operating in Athgarh and Khuntuni. These pangolins were being supplied to China, Vietnam and Myanmar. She also conducted multiple awareness programmes regarding the illegal trade of pangolins among locals so that they report back to the authorities with information. Now posted as a deputy conservator of forests in the Bhubaneswar District headquarters, Lenka manages a team of 92 members.

Uttarakhand, planted a record 351,253 saplings in 1 hour, from 9:00 a.m. to 10:00 a.m. on 16 July 2020 to celebrate Harela, the harvesting season. The plantation work was planned meticulously with a nodal officer in charge of each village, municipal ward and forest range, and was overseen by 1,096 people. The pits were dug in advance and the sapling to be planted placed alongside with a person standing ready next to it. Trivendra Singh Rawat, the then chief minister of Uttarakhand, planted the first sapling at Asthal Village of Raipur Block. Nurseries of the forest department, the horticulture department and self-help groups provided the saplings.

Silver Jubilee Celebrations of Neem Trees

The 25th birthday of three neem trees was celebrated with the cutting of a cake and the trees being decorated by the Azad market residents at the marketplace at Piplani, Bhopal, Madhya Pradesh, on 21 June 2019. Shopkeeper Sudheer Kumar Pandya had planted the trees in 1994 to help provide shade and clean air in the market. As people realized the importance of the trees, on their 10th anniversary they began the celebrations and simultaneously began planting more trees. The silver jubilee was a special one with shopkeepers and the BHEL administration supporting the event.

GREENING THE WORLD

According to satellite data from NASA, USA, India has been the second largest contributor in making the world a greener place in the last two decades.

The data tabulated from 2000 to 2017 from the Moderate Resolution Imaging Spectroradiometer on NASA's Terra and Aqua satellites suggests that both China and India have contributed largely to the global greening effort. India's greenery can be divided into croplands (82 per cent) and forests (4.4 per cent). The change in leaf area is around 6.5 per cent per decade for India whereas the global average is 2.3 per cent. Contributing, with China, to about one-third of the green area, India has come a long way in its journey for a sustainable environment.

Most trees gifted in a year

'Treeman' Deepak Ramesh Gaur (b. 2 April 1976) from Gurugram, Haryana, has improved on his earlier record of gifting saplings and encouraging people to go green. Between 31 March 2018 and 31 March 2019, he gifted 1.5 lakh (1,50,000) trees, bringing the overall number to 6.5 lakh (6,50,000).

Most trees planted – in a quarter

The Maharashtra Forest Department, with the support of individual volunteers, planted 351,376,361 seedlings across the state between 1 July and 30 September 2019. The plantation work was done by 951,963.5 million people at 23,986.8 million plantation sites. To integrate the work of the forest department, the government hosted a Plantation Monitoring Information System (PMIS) and captured the plantation data of forest and non-forest agencies. The department's call centre, Hello Forest 1926, was made available to the people and greening organizations to register their plantation achievements.

Most saplings distributed – single day

The Department of Environment, Forest and Climate Change and the Department of Tourism, Government of Uttar Pradesh, along with the District Administration, Prayagraj, Uttar Pradesh, distributed 76,824 saplings on 9 August 2019. This was part of their larger campaign for tree plantation.

Most plants cultivated – in a quarter

Rahul Mahajan from Chandigarh, with

Aarey Forests Receive Protection

The Aarey Forest, also known as Aarey Milk Colony, is an unclassified forest area in the urban landscape of Mumbai, Maharashtra. The colony was established in 1949 to cater to the dairy requirements of the city. It occupies a total area of 16 sq. km and houses 27 hamlets within its bounds. Protests to 'Save Aarey' started when the Bombay High court granted the Mumbai Metro Rail Corporation clearance to cut trees in order to build a car shed. After protests and urging from citizens, on 11 October 2020, Chief Minister Uddhav Thackeray announced that 800 acres (323.75 hectares) of Aarey Colony would be declared a reserve forest.

the support of DSP (Jails), Amandeep Singh, and the inmates of Burail Jail, cultivated 1.5 lakh (150,000) seedlings of 10 varieties of flowers between 1 January and 15 March 2020. He distributed them free to resident welfare associations, schools, colleges, government institutions and religious places. The inmates were engaged in making the beds, planting the seeds and nurturing the seedlings.

First winner of the Indira Priyadarshini Vriksha Mitra (IPVM) award

The IPVM awards are given by the Ministry of Environment, Forest and Climate Change, Government of India, to individuals and organizations doing pioneering and groundbreaking work in afforestation and wasteland development projects. The first recipients were U. Veerakumar (Tamil Nadu), Social Forestry Department (Junagarh, Kalahandi District, Odisha), women's self-help groups (within Binodpur–Baikunthapur Forests Protection Committee under the Raidighi Range of the 24 Parganas Division, West Bengal) and the Jalgrahan Institution (Dungarpur, Rajasthan) in 2006.

First forest healing centre

India's first forest healing centre was inaugurated on 7 March 2021 in Ranikhet, Uttarakhand. Spread across an area of around 13 acres (5.26 hectares), it was developed by the research wing of the Uttarakhand Forest Department as a space where visitors can take walks, hug trees and engage in calming activities like meditation and sky-gazing. The centre draws inspiration from the Japanese therapy of forest bathing (*shinrin-yoku*) and ancient Indian traditions.

Wildlife Warriors

Most sparrow homes built

Shri Labhubhai Trivedi Institute of Engineering and Technology, Rajkot, Gujarat, under the Swachh Survekshan of the Rajkot Municipality, transformed 10,051 discarded red clay *garba* pots from nearby temples into beautiful homes for sparrows in 17 hrs 49 mins on 20 October 2018.

Most birds and animals rescued individual

Yogender Kumar (b. 6 January 1971), head warden of Tihar Central Jail, social activist and honorary member of the Animal Welfare Board of India, has saved 500 injured birds and animals by treating them himself or sending them to the Sanjay Gandhi Bird Care Centre and Hospital. He spends 10 per cent of his earnings on the care of birds and animals.

Most eco-awareness camps

People for Animals (PFA) in Angul, Odisha, organized 260 snake awareness camps in five districts of the state – Angul, Dhenkanal, Cuttack, Bhubaneswar and Puri – during 2018–19. They educated people on the kinds of snakes found in India, and how to treat snake bite.

First wilderness park

The Konda Gorre Wilderness Park was inaugurated at Lalgadi Malakpet close to the Karimnagar Highway near Hyderabad, Telangana, on 27 November 2020. The park will focus on biodiversity conservation and rewilding of the area. Named after the *chousingha*, a four-horned antelope locally called *konda gorre*, the forest area covers 2,635 acres (1,066.35 ha), of which this urban park is a part. The project has been undertaken by the Telangana State Forest Development Corporation (TSFDC), which plans to build cycling and jogging tracks, cafés, nature trails and campsites here.

Most butterflies nurtured

Prachi Singh (b. 29 November 1989), a chartered accountant by profession and a lepidopterist by inclination, has been nurturing 580 butterflies at her home in Faridabad, Haryana, over the past 16 years. In 2018,

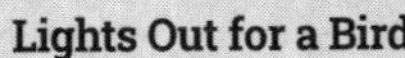

Representational image

Lights Out for a Bird

Pothakudi Village in Sivaganga District of Tamil Nadu went without street lights for over a month till the three eggs of an by founder Naman Gupta, Indian robin (*Copsychus fulicatus*) in a nest in the community's common switchboard were hatched. The board had the switches for all 35 street lights of the village, but when college student A. Karuppuraja saw a bird filling the box with straw and leaves, he looked inside and found three greenish blue spotted eggs there. After circulating the information on a WhatsApp group, a collective decision was taken not to disturb the robin till the eggs were hatched.

SUPER 30

ROBIN BANERJEE: A LIFE AMONG WILDLIFE

Dr Robin Banerjee (1908–2003) from Golaghat, Assam, was an environmentalist, film-maker, painter and photographer. A veteran of the Second World War, he settled down near the Kaziranga National Park after his first visit there. His documentary on the park brought attention to its natural richness and diversity, and he went on to establish the Kaziranga Wildlife Society, an NGO that works towards securing the interests of the park. He went on to film 32 documentaries on wildlife in India and won many accolades and awards, including the Padma Shri (1971), the R.G. Baruah Award (2001), and honorary doctorates from Assam Agricultural University (1991) and Dibrugarh University (1994). In 2009, his house was converted to a museum housing a collection of his films, photographs, paintings and natural history items. Christened Uncle Robin's Museum, it is now a popular tourist spot showcasing the rich legacy left behind by him.

she led the butterfly census for the Faridabad region, conducted by the Conservation Education Centre of the Bombay Natural History Society. Her 2019 record was for nurturing 550 butterflies.

Longest-running parrot rescue programme

Dharmendra Shah (b. 1 May 1975) from Bhopal, Madhya Pradesh, has been releasing captive parrots for the last 20 years from 19 March 1999, rescuing over 20,000 birds. He buys the parrots from bird markets, and goes from home to home, persuading parrot owners to release the winged creature. Inspired by his mother, he calls his initiative Mission Pankh (wings). His focus has been parrots and he is particularly concerned about those species that he claims may go extinct. He has written stories on releasing the caged birds and has several video films on YouTube promoting Mission Pankh.

First green village

Khonoma Village, located in the Sechu-Zubza Subdivision of Kohima District, Nagaland, has become the country's first 'green village'. The first steps in this direction were taken by setting up the Khonoma Nature Conservation and Tragopan Sanctuary in 1998, leading to a ban on hunting in a 20 sq. km area. Ecological studies suggest that the village has 250 plant species, 204 species of trees, 45 varieties of orchids and 19 varieties of bamboo. The fauna includes 25 varieties of snakes, six kinds of lizards, 11 types of amphibians and 196 bird species, including Blyth's tragopan which is categorized as vulnerable on the Red List of the IUCN.

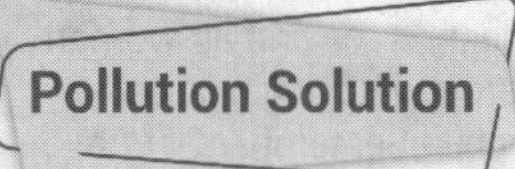

Pollution Solution

Winners of the Champions of the Earth Award

Tulsi Tanti, chairman and managing director of the wind turbine manufacturer Suzlon Energy Ltd, was the first Indian recipient of the Champions of the Earth award in 2009 in the entrepreneurial vision category. Since then, India has won five more awards. The latest recipients of the awards were Prime Minister Narendra Modi for policy leadership and the fully solar-powered Cochin International Airport for entrepreneurial vision in 2018. The award is given by the United Nations Environment Programme.

Most cigarette waste collected and recycled in a year

Code Effort Pvt. Ltd, established in 2018 by founder Naman Gupta, collected the most cigarette waste, amounting to a total of 10,000 kg, from across India in the financial year 2019–20 and recycled 40 per cent of it to create colourful bolsters, cushions, soft toys for children, handicrafts like key chains, and mosquito repellents using organic manure. They employ trained and semi-skilled women at their factory in Noida, Uttar Pradesh. Founder Naman Gupta's aim was to clean the environment of the toxicity generated by non-biodegradable cigarette butts, which have cellulose acetate that takes 10 years to decompose.

5 MOST POLLUTED CITIES*

	Location	Average Pollution Score – 2017	Average Pollution Score – 2018	Average Pollution Score – 2019
1	Ghaziabad, Uttar Pradesh	144.6	135.2	110.2
2	New Delhi	108.2	113.5	98.6
3	Noida, Uttar Pradesh	134.0	123.6	97.7
4	Gurugram, Haryana	145.6	135.8	93.1
5	Greater Noida, Uttar Pradesh	No data	No data	91.1

*2017 to 2019; Source: World Air Quality Index, IQ Air. Scores ranging from 55.5 to 150.4 are considered unhealthy. The unit of the score is $\mu g/m^3$.

Renewable Recycling

Longest distance travelled for awareness – bicycle – group

A team of eight cyclists showed that it is possible to save fuel by cycling long distances. They travelled 2,160 km from Kishore Sagar in Kota, Rajasthan, to Arambol Beach in Goa in 12 days. Nikhil Pal Singh, Shashikant Sonawane, Shubham Mamliwad, Pratik Nalawade, Tushar Bhoite, Girish Sharma, Ravindra Kumar and Surya Pratap Singh Adhikari set out at 3:00 p.m. on 15 August 2018 from Kota and reached Goa on 27 August 2018 at 4:00 p.m.

Longest distance travelled for awareness – two-wheeler – solo

Nand Kishore Verma (b. 2 November 1967), founder of the Neela Jahan Foundation, and his teammate travelled a distance of 1,787 km across 20 districts of Uttar Pradesh and Bihar on motorcycles from 5 June 2018 to 15 June 2018 to spread awareness among people about conserving water.

Largest single rooftop solar plant

On 17 May 2016, a rooftop solar power plant was inaugurated at the Dera Baba Jaimal Singh (Radha Soami sect) premises at Beas, Amritsar District, Punjab. Spread over 42 acres (17 ha), the plant is the largest single rooftop facility and can generate 11.5 MW of electricity. The solar panels are laid over 82 acres (33.18 hectares) on eight rooftops and the project is planned for producing electricity to cater to the demands of 8,000 households.

First women's organic carpet-making unit

Mandira Utsav in Nai Bazaar, Bhadohi, Uttar Pradesh, is the first all-woman organic carpet-weaving unit in India. Begun in September 2017 by Gurugram-based Sushanto Mittra, it is recognized by the Indian Institute of Carpet Technology, Bhadohi. Carpets made here were displayed at the international fair 'Pure London' in February 2019.

WR **First solar-heated tent**

Considered to be the first in the world, a 10-seater portable tent that can be heated using solar panels was built by engineer and innovator Sonam Wangchuk along with the Himalayan Institute of Alternatives of Ladakh (HIAL) for the Indian Army. Built in four weeks at a cost of ₹5 lakh (0.5 million), the tent weighs less than 30 kg and was specifically developed for Indian soldiers and army personnel serving in areas with temperatures as low as −140°C.

Biggest rally of electric vehicles

A rally of 500 battery-operated two-wheelers by Tunwal E-Vehicle India Pvt. Ltd was held at Gandhinagar, Gujarat, from 7:30 a.m. to 9:00 a.m.

Marking presence at the United Nations Young Leaders for SDGs, Class of 2020

Udit Singhal (b. 28 December 2001) from New Delhi was selected as one of the 17 Young Leaders for Sustainable Development Goals (SDGs) in the class of 2020 by the Office of the Secretary General's Envoy on Youth of the United Nations. Founder of Glass2Sand, a glass recycling ecosystem that was launched in 2019, Udit pitched the project and succeeded in receiving a grant from the New Zealand high commissioner. His project has so far converted over 14,000 glass bottles into more than 8,400 kg of high-grade silica sand. The Young Leaders (aged 18–29) represent the diverse voices of the world and help mobilize support for the accomplishment of SDGs.

Udit Singhal

Karnataka Creates Green Index to Rate Development

In the face of climate change, Karnataka is the first state in India to introduce a Green Index as an essential ingredient of its policies and guidelines. Developed by the Environmental Management and Policy Research Institute (EMPRI) and the Indian Institute of Science (IISc), Bengaluru, the index has been divided into four classes: dark green (maximum attention to conservation measures), light green (some mention of measures), orange (limited pollution) and red (no mention at all, maximum pollution). Based on environment-friendly measures such as emission reduction and reforestation, a scorecard with 0–5 ranking has been created after assessment, and the points obtained will impact the release of funds from the state government to the departments. Twenty government departments including agriculture, animal husbandry and forests, among others, have introduced the index.

on 3 March 2019. The vehicles, driven mostly by students, covered 22 km to highlight the reduction of air pollution with e-vehicles.

First country to have a cooling action plan

The India Cooling Action Plan (ICAP) is the first cooling action plan in the world. It addresses cooling requirements across all sectors to reduce direct and indirect emissions. ICAP aims to balance socio-economic and environmental needs while reducing refrigerant transition and cooling demand, enhancing energy efficiency and evolving better technology options.

Most sustainable aluminium company

Hindalco Industries, which is headquartered in Mumbai, Maharashtra, the metals flagship of the Aditya Birla Group, is recognized as an industry leader, according to the S&P Dow Jones Sustainability Indices' (DJSI's) Corporate Sustainability Assessment (CSA) rankings 2020. With a score of 75, Hindalco is at the top in the category where the average score was 51. In a first, Hindalco collaborated with cement manufacturers and replaced mined resources with red mud. It was the only Indian company to register as an industry leader in the 61 industries that were ranked.

Most cloth diapers changed simultaneously – 1 hour

Superbottoms.com India, an eco-friendly cloth diaper company headquartered in Mumbai, Maharashtra, organized an event in which diapers of 426 babies were changed by as many adults simultaneously in 1 hour from 10:30 a.m. to 11:30 a.m. across 11 cities. The event focused on eco-friendly washable cloth diapers that can be reused up to 300 times.

Climate Care

Worst Natural Disasters in India in 2020

	The Disaster	Areas Affected	Estimated Damage (in ₹ crore/million)
1	Cyclone Amphan	West Bengal, Odisha, Andaman Islands	94,966.49/949,664.9
2	Kerala Floods	Kerala	19,000.00/190,000.00
3	Cyclone Nisagra	Maharashtra	6,000.00/60,000.00
4	Hyderabad Floods	Hyderabad, Telangana	5,000.00/50,000.00
5	Cyclone Nivar	Tamil Nadu, Puducherry, Andhra Pradesh	4,000.00/40,000.00

India's Preparedness for Climate-based Disasters

The Global Climate Risk Index 2021 (CRI) placed India at the seventh spot among countries most vulnerable to weather change–related disasters in 2019. This vulnerability index was based on fatalities and economic loss. India topped the charts with the most fatalities (2,267) and the most severe economic losses (₹50,263.2 crore/502,632 million). Although India's rank improved from five in CRI 2020 to seven in CRI 2021, India now has to propel its efforts towards sustainability with dedicated and inventive measures.

PERFORMING ARTS

DANCE

Earliest scriptural mention of dancers

The first known textual mention of dancers can be traced back to the Rig Veda (composed between c. 1500 and 1200 BCE), which has references to mythical apsaras (divine dancers) in the story of the celestial dancer Urvashi and the mortal king Pururava.

Earliest known treatise on the performing arts

The *Natyashastra,* said to be the work of Bharata Muni, is dated variously between the second and third centuries BCE and the fourth and fifth centuries CE. It is the earliest known treatise on the performing arts. The *Natyashastra* has 37 chapters with 5,569 slokas. It is the basis of classical Indian dance, music and drama, and is often referred to as the fifth Veda.

Earliest evidence of formalized dancing

The statuette of a dancing girl from Mohenjo-Daro in the Indus Valley that dates to 2500 BCE, is the earliest evidence of formal dance.

Earliest sculptures of Odissi

Sculptures depicting dancers in the Jain cave temples of Khandagiri and Udayagiri, such as the Machapuri and Hathigumpha caves (second century BCE) in present-day Odisha, show the existence of a dance form in the region, in which the dance of the *maharis* (devadasis) formed a ritual during worship in temples. Hundreds of figures depicting dance movements are carved on the walls of the Parashurameshwara, Kapileshwara, Brahmeshwara, Mukteshwara, Rajarani and Lingaraj Temples in Bhubaneswar, Puri and Konark in Odisha, displaying the complete complex vocabulary of Odissi.

---

5 dance forms of India are on UNESCO's list of the Intangible Cultural Heritage of Humanity.

Earliest text to mention Odissi

Odissi has been traced to a dance form that prevailed in present-day Odisha and Bihar in ancient times in a region referred to as Odhra-Magadha in the *Natyashastra.* The dance was performed by devadasis (female temple dancers) called *maharis* and male temple acolytes called *gotipuas*. It is also mentioned in Maheswar Mahapatra's *Abhinaya Chandrika* (15th–16th century CE). This dance form, which includes the *tandava* style and the *lasya* style, has its own repertoire, costumes, music and grammar.

Oldest surviving dance drama form

Mudiyettu from Kerala, now incorporated in Kathakali, is the oldest extant dance drama form, traced back to the ninth century CE.

First known dance drama form

In the early 17th century, Manaveda Raja, Zamorin of Calicut (now Kozhikode), Kerala, was inspired by Jayadeva's *Gita Govinda* to compose the *Krishna Geeti*

SUPER 30

BOOGIE WOOGIE BOO!: THAT'S DANCE FOR YOU

Taking off in 1996, Boogie Woogie was an iconic TV show of the decade. It was one of the first dance reality programmes in the country and ran for seven seasons on Sony Entertainment Television between 1996 to 2014. Predominantly judged by actor and TV host Jaaved Jaaferi, Naved Jafri (director and producer of the show) and actor Ravi Behl, it had various themes for dance performances and led to many spin-off championship series. Running for almost two decades in the last 30 years, the highly popular show, which became a biweekly weekend offering in the later seasons, set the benchmark and the trend for the many dance reality shows that followed it.

Ravi Behl (*left*), Jaaved Jaaferi (*centre*) and Naved Jafri (right) on the sets of *Boogie Woogie*

in Sanskrit. He set it to a new dance drama form known as Krishnanattam – 'the dance of Krishna'. It combined ancient theatre traditions such as Kutiyattam, ritual performances like Theyyam and folk dances like Kaikottikali.

First modern translation of the *Natyashastra*

In 1950, Manmohan Ghosh translated the *Natyashastra* into English for the Asiatic Society. This was the first successful attempt at translating the definitive text on Indian performing arts.

First English periodical on Carnatic music and dance

Sruti, first published in October 1983 in Madras (now Chennai), Tamil Nadu, by P.N. Sundaresan and edited by N. Pattabhiraman, garnered 30,000 readers in its very first year. This was the first known English periodical on Carnatic music and dance.

First revivalist dance school

The Kerala Kalamandalam in Trichur (now Thrissur), Kerala, was founded in 1930 by the poet Vallathol Narayana Menon to re-establish Kathakali as a major regional theatre art and to revive Mohiniattam, a classical dance form from Kerala. These art forms flourished briefly under Maharaja Swathi Thirunal in the 19th century and then languished, until they were revived by Vallathol Narayana Menon.

First dance schools

- Santiniketan, which was founded in 1901 in Bolpur, Birbhum District, Bengal (now West Bengal) by Rabindranath Tagore, had a department of dance to which he invited gurus from regions as far-flung as Manipur and Kerala to live on the campus and teach their dance forms to students. Santiniketan, which later evolved

PADMA AWARD WINNERS 2020–21		
Padma Shri		
2020	Guru Shashadhar Acharya	Seraikela Chhau dance
2020	Indira P.P. Bora	Sattriya dance
2020	Purushottam Dadheech	Kathak
2020	Vajira Chitrasena	Sri Lankan traditional dance
2020	Utsav Charan Das	Odissi Chaiti Ghoda dance
2021	I. Wayan Dibia	Balinese dance
2021	Kanaka Raju	Gussadi dance
2021	Matha B. Manjamma Jogati	Jogati Nritya, Janapada songs
2021	Radhe Shyam Barle	Panthi folk dance and art
2021	Ramachandra Manjhi	Naach performances

into the Visva-Bharati University, now has an institute of dance, drama and music, called the Sangit Bhavan.

- Kalakshetra, a premier school for classical dance, was established in 1936 at Adyar, Madras (now Chennai), Tamil Nadu, by Indian classical dancer Rukmini Devi Arundale. Initially called the International Academy of Arts, it was renamed Kalakshetra on the suggestion of Sanskrit and Tamil scholar Pandit P.S. Subrahmanya Sastri. Its first dance production was titled Kutrala Kuravanji.

First classical dance to be revived

Odissi was rediscovered by dancer Indrani Rehman, who then popularized it abroad in the early 1940s, though it was recognized as a classical dance form only from the 1960s.

First modern work on dance

The book titled *Classical Indian Dance in Literature and the Arts* by scholar Dr Kapila Vatsyayan, published in 1968 by the country's premier institution of dance and music, the Sangeet Natak Akademi, was the first definitive modern work on dance, written in English. Dr Vatsyayan received the Sangeet Natak Akademi fellowship in 1970.

First national dance seminar

The Sangeet Natak Akademi held the first national seminar on dance from 30 March to 7 April 1958. Dr P.V. Rajammar was the Akademi's chairman then. The seminar's inaugural dance was performed by leading Kathak exponent Pandit Shambhu Maharaj.

First campaign for revival of Bharatanatyam

E. Krishna Iyer, a lawyer based in Madras (now Chennai), Tamil Nadu, was the first to fight the anti-nautch campaigns of the 1920s by learning the dance

First Transgender to Receive a Padma Shri

Narthaki Nataraj, a member of the transgender community and a well-known Bharatanatyam dancer, created history by becoming the first transperson to win the prestigious Padma Shri award. President Ram Nath Kovind presented the award to her in 2019. Nataraj specializes in the Thanjavur-based Nayaka Bhava tradition and has trained for 15 years with her guru, Thanjavur Kittappa Pillai. She has received acclaim both nationally and internationally. Earlier, in 2011, she was the first transgender person to receive the Sangeet Natak Akademi Award too.

Narthaki Nataraj

form Bharatanatyam in 1926 from the famous Natesa Iyer from Melattur, Kerala. For six years, he lectured and wrote for his cause, and presented devadasis in public performances outside of temples. Finally, it was with T. Balasaraswati's dance performance at the All-India Music Conference in Varanasi, Uttar Pradesh, in 1935, that the dance became accepted as a respectable art form.

First Kuchipudi dance couple to receive the Padma Shri

Raja and Radha Reddy were the first couple to receive the Padma Shri award, for a single cause, individually and together, in 1984. Widely travelled, they were responsible for popularizing the Kuchipudi form of dance in India and abroad. They also won the Padma Bhushan in 2000.

First woman to perform Chhau

Sonal Mansingh, the well-known exponent of Kuchipudi, was the first woman to learn the Chhau dance form. It is a semi-classical dance with martial, tribal and folk origins, and is found in three styles drawing their names from the region where they are traditionally performed.

First Sangeet Natak Akademi award winners for dance

T. Balasaraswati and Shambhu Maharaj won the first Sangeet Natak Akademi awards for dance in 1955 for their contribution to Bharatanatyam and Kathak, respectively. The awards were instituted in 1952 to honour performing artistes.

First Sangeet Natak Akademi award for creative dance

Dance pioneer Uday Shankar was the first to be honoured by the Sangeet Natak Akademi with an award for creative dance in 1960. Two years later, he received the Sangeet Natak Akademi fellowship. In 1971, he became the first modern dancer to receive the Padma Vibhushan.

First Kuchipudi solo

Vedantam Lakshminarayana Shastri performed the first solo recital in the traditional dance drama form of Kuchipudi. He learnt the dance form from Sri Vempati Venkatanarayana. He also introduced the popular *tarangam*, during which the dancers have to balance themselves on the edges of a thali.

V. Unbeatable Dances to the Top of *America's Got Talent!*

V. Unbeatable, a dance group from Mumbai, Maharashtra, won the top title in the 15th season of *America's Got Talent: The Champions*, a televised American talent show, on 18 February 2020. The group is led by Om Prakash Chauhan who ran away from Masinagaon Village in Uttar Pradesh to escape poverty and seek opportunity, and created this troupe with children like himself, from slums near Naigaon. The 29 dancers won prize money amounting to $1 million at their final performance with drummer Travis Barker. After local events and dance shows across India, they first appeared on *America's Got Talent* in 2019 and were placed fourth. The 'V' in the group's name honours Vikas Gupta, the co-founder of the group, who died in 2014 in an accident while performing a stunt.

First ballet film

Classical–folk fusion guru Uday Shankar's film *Kalpana,* which was released in 1948, used the ballet form for a major part of its narration, making it the country's first ballet film.

First known Kathak teacher

Pandit Birju Maharaj (b. 1938) is the first known Kathak teacher. Born in Lucknow, Uttar Pradesh, to Shri Achhan Maharaj, a Kathak exponent, he has been the popular face of the dance form globally. He was invited to teach Kathak at the age of 13 at Sangeet Bharati, and later at the Bharatiya Kala Kendra, New Delhi. He received the Sangeet Natak Akademi award in 1966 and the Padma Vibhushan in 1986.

First dance theatre form recognized by UNESCO: Kutiyattam

Kutiyattam, a traditional Sanskrit performing art form originating in Kerala, is recognized by UNESCO as a 'Masterpiece of the Oral and Intangible Heritage of Humanity'. It is considered to be at least 2,000 years old and the oldest living theatre tradition globally. UNESCO usually considers only monuments and heritage sites, and this was the first art form recognized for its exceptional value. Mizhavu, a large percussion instrument, is the primary musical instrument that accompanies Kutiyattam. Considered to be sacred, Kutiyattam was traditionally performed only in temple theatres, called *koothambalam*.

First to win an international dance competition

Madame Menaka (1899–1947), whose real name was Leila Sokhey, was the first Indian to win an international dance competition, at the Berlin Dance Olympiad in July 1936. A pioneering choreographer and dancer, she set up a dance company in Bombay (now Mumbai), Maharashtra, to produce dance dramas on Indian themes. Her troupe, which featured on two days, performed Menaka's original ballet, *Deva Vijay Nritya,* and won the first three individual prizes, along with the first prize in the competition.

First celebrity dance competition

Ten famous television couples participated in the first ever celebrity dance competition, *Nach Baliye*, on TV channel Star One. The show premiered on 11 October 2005. The judges were choreographer Saroj Khan, film-maker Farhan Akhtar and VJ-and-model Malaika Arora Khan. TV stars Sachin and Supriya Pilgaonkar were the first winners of the contest.

First Indian–European fusion

Versatile dancer Uday Shankar (1900–77), who was born in Udaipur, Rajasthan, is known as the father of modern dance in India. He combined European theatrical dance techniques with the classical and folk-dance forms of India. He danced with Anna Pavlova, the Russian ballerina, during the 1920s and created *Hindu Wedding* as well as the duet *Radha and Krishna*, which was included in Pavlova's performance *Oriental Impressions*. In 1971, he was awarded the Padma Vibhushan, the second highest civilian award in India.

WR Thickest make-up

The *chutti*, used in Kathakali, is a three-dimensional mask-like attachment made of rice paste and paper, which may extend to 15 cm (6 in.) from the face. It is the thickest make-up used in any dance form in the world.

WR Dance performance at the highest altitude

Shruti Gupta (b. 15 August 1987) from Solan, Himachal Pradesh, performed Kathak in freezing conditions at an altitude of 5,602 m (18,379 ft), at Khardung La, Ladakh, on 27 October 2016. The 20-minute performance, attended by Indian Army and Indo-Tibetan Border Police (ITBP) officers, was dedicated to the armed forces.

Record Rewind

Marathon performance of Bharatanatyam

1990

K.R.S. Prasanna performed Bharatanatyam non-stop for 24 hours at the Gokhale Institute of Public Affairs in Bangalore (now Bengaluru), Karnataka.

2004

T. Sangeedha, a dance student from Pondicherry (now Puducherry), performed Bharatanatyam continuously for 60 hours 10 minutes at Gandhi Thidal, Pondicherry, from 9:00 a.m. on 1 June 2003 to 9:10 p.m. on 3 June 2003.

Oldest recipient of President's Award

Asan Chandu Panikkar (1873–1969), a pioneer of 20th-century Kathakali, received the President's Award in 1958 at 84 years. He danced at the award ceremony, in front of the then prime minister Jawaharlal Nehru and the then president Dr Rajendra Prasad.

Only extant pre-Vedic dances

Bhutam and Theyyam are ritual dances of Karnataka and Kerala, respectively. The dancers represent local gods and ancestral spirits, based on a pre-Vedic belief system.

Record Rewind

Marathon performance of Kuchipudi

1990

Sarala Kumari from Hyderabad (now in Telangana) danced for 24 hours, beginning her performance at 6:30 p.m. on 1 February 1985.

2020

Sivala Vijaya Durga from Visakhapatnam, Andhra Pradesh, performed a 50-hour Kuchipudi dance from 9:08 a.m. on 28 December 2001 to 11:09 a.m. on 30 December 2001. It was held at Dr B.R. Ambedkar Assembly Hall, Andhra University, Visakhapatnam. She took a 15-minute break after every 8 hours of performance and a 30-second pause between songs.

Oldest to perform Bharatanatyam *arangetram*

Bakulaben Ramanlal Patel (b. 26 October 1944) from Surat, Gujarat, performed her Bharatanatyam *arangetram* for 2 hrs 30 mins between 2: 45 p.m. and 5: 45 p.m. on 12 October 2019. The 74-year-old artiste performed at the Rang Bhavan, Jeevan Bharati School, in Surat.

Only pan-Indian dance text

Jayadeva's Sanskrit book of verse, the *Gita Govinda* (12th century CE), has been choreographed in all major Indian dance styles. It is sung in both Hindustani and Carnatic modes, and has been translated into many European languages.

Only dance form varied in three states

Chhau, the classical folk dance with martial overtones, has three versions based on the regions it is performed in – as Seraikela Chhau in Jharkhand (masked), Mayurbhanj Chhau in Odisha and Purulia Chhau in West Bengal.

Only dance drama performed only by women

Kuravanji, a form of musical play popular at the beginning of the 18th century, was meant only for devadasis and was performed at the annual festivals of some temples in Tamil Nadu.

Only Asthana Nartaki

In 1978, Bharatanatyam exponent Yamini Krishnamurthy was awarded the title of 'Asthana Nartaki', meaning 'resident dancer' of Lord Venkateswara Temple, Tirupati, Andhra Pradesh.

Only classical dancer with an artificial foot

Accomplished Bharatanatyam dancer Sudha Chandran, who lost a leg in a car crash in 1981, resumed her dancing career with a prosthetic Jaipur Foot in 1984. She was rehabilitated by Dr P.K. Sethi of the Sawai Man Singh Hospital in Jaipur, Rajasthan.

Only Persianized classical dance

Kathak is a classical dance form that derives its name from the female professional storytellers or *kathikas* who recited verses from the Ramayana and the Mahabharata, along with explanatory gestures, appropriate choreography and music, as a part of a system of ritualistic worship. This dance form, with its fast and intricate movements, attracted the attention of the Mughal rulers. Over time, the dance form split into two main schools: 'Temple Kathak', with its emphasis on *bhava* (or emotion), and a court dance or 'Darbari Kathak', with its focus on rhythmic display.

Largest Charadakuthi Kolkali ensemble*

Shenoy Smaraka Government Higher Secondary School and Mahadeva Gramam Kolkali Sangham, under the leadership of Gurukal K. Sivakumar, organized the largest Charadakuthi Kolkali performance with 212 participants at the school in Kannur, Kerala, on 29 December 2019. It lasted for 20 mins. The inner circle was made up of 42 participants while 64 were in the middle circle, and the outer circle had 106 participants.

Largest Margamkali ensemble

Largest Margamkali ensemble*

Syro Malabar Cultural Association–Kuwait, organized the largest Margamkali performance with 870 participants on 7 February 2020 at the Amateur Athletic Stadium, Kaifan, Kuwait. The performance lasted for 26 mins 30 secs. Margamkali, an Indian group dance that traces its roots to Kerala, is practised by the Saint Thomas Christians, a community of Syrian Christians from Kerala.

Largest arts festival

Soorya Festival, organized annually by the Soorya Stage and Film Society, Thiruvananthapuram, Kerala, is the largest of its kind in India, both in terms of membership and the number of activities. The festival is held across 111 days between September and January each year. The 30,000-plus members of Soorya Society, founded in 1978, conduct around 200 programmes annually.

*The rules regarding the age of participants have been modified. Please *see* Rules and Guidelines.

Largest Bharatanatyam ensemble

The Department of Tourism, Government of Tamil Nadu, organized the largest Bharatanatyam ensemble with 10,176 dancers on 8 February 2020. The event, Sathir 10000, which based the dance on the famous Tamil text *Thirukkural*, was held at S.I.V.E.T College in Chennai, Tamil Nadu.

Marathon performance of Ottanthullal

Jaimon V.J. (b. 10 February 1974) from Kottayam, Kerala, performed a non-stop marathon session of Ottanthullal, a dance drama form, depicting 10 stories in 12 hrs from 5:00 a.m. to 6:45 p.m. on 12 May 2019 at the Karippadavathu Temple, Uzhavoor, Kerala. The break time was 1 hr 45 mins.

MUSIC

First raga

The first raga is believed to be the Carnatic Mayamalavagowla (equivalent to the Hindustani raga Bhairavi) that Purandara Dasa (c. 1484–c. 1565), the bhakti poet and musician, also known as Adi Guru, used as the teaching scale. Called Adi Raga, it is said to have emanated from Lord Shiva.

Earliest ballad singing

Both Vedic and epic literature mentions minstrels singing *akhyanas* (texts narrated by professional storytellers), sung to the veena, in the *marga* style of singing. While the Vedas mentions both instrumental music and *akhyana* recitation in yagnas, the Ramayana (400 BCE to 200 CE) also has several references to the singing of ballads.

Earliest form of classical song

The Dhrupad, originally called Dhruvapada, was the prevailing mode of music until medieval times. Though this form traces its roots to the *Natyashastra*, it was developed by Swami Haridas and the legendary singer Tansen in the 15th century.

Only multilingual classical songs

Manipravalam *kritis* are songs in the Carnatic tradition in which two or even three languages are used and the lines sung alternately in these languages, which include Tamil and Sanskrit.

Earliest Prakrit (popular) songs

The *Natyashastra* mentions *dhruvas*, i.e., songs of five different kinds that were an integral part of drama. These songs indicate the context, place and people in a scene. *Dhruvas* were originally in Prakrit and were mostly sung by a choir.

Earliest reference to musical performances

The grammarian Panini (c. fourth century BCE) in his comments on *nritya* (dancing) mentions composers of sutras on dancing. The *Pali Pitaka* (c. 300 BCE) mentions two disciples of Gautama Buddha attending one such recital.

First medieval treatise on music

The Chalukyan king, Someshvara III, who ruled in the Karnataka region in the 12th century CE, wrote the *Manasollasa*, an encyclopaedic work in Sanskrit on a variety of topics, including music, with 2,500 verses dedicated to the topic. The music section, one of the largest sections in the book, is considered the earliest treatise on music. Other well-known works on music from the period are the *Sangitaratnakara* by Sarangadeva, chief accountant of King Soddhala (r. 1210–1247 CE) of the Yadava dynasty, and a Jain work, *Sangita Samaya Sara*, by Parsvadeva (c. 13th century).

Earliest form of music

The Rig Veda has references to *saman* hymns, the earliest form of music in India. *Saman* singing is also mentioned in the *Brahmanas* as well as the Upanishads, and features as a part of spiritual observances and exercises.

Earliest musical notes

The Sama Veda, which is believed to date to c. 1200–1000 BCE, mentions seven musical notes in *saman* singing, viz., Krushta, Prathama, Dvitiya, Tritiya, Chaturtha, Mandra/Panchama and Antya/Atisvara.

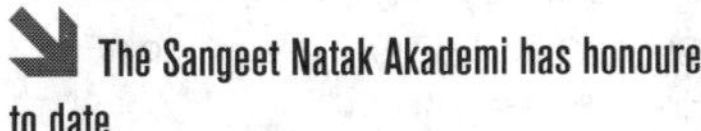

The Sangeet Natak Akademi has honoured 154 eminent artistes as Akademi Fellows to date.

Earliest mention of raga

The term 'raga' in its modern connotation appears first in the classical Sanskrit text *Brihaddeshi* by Matanga (c. eighth century CE). It is described as 'a combination of tones which, with beautiful illuminating graces, pleases people'.

First to standardize music

Purandara Dasa (1484–1564) is revered as Sangeet Pitamaha ('grandfather of music'). He standardized Carnatic music for teaching, besides classifying 35 types of tala. He pioneered a musical notation system that is still being used.

Early treatises on Carnatic music

- Rama Amatya, a royal composer at the court of King Ramaraja of Vijayanagar, gave the first detailed exposition of the Carnatic system of music in his text titled *Swaramela Kalanidhi,* around 1550 BCE. He described the first collection of ragas.
- The *Ragavibodha,* an important work on Carnatic music, was written by Somanatha, a famous scholar and poet, in 1609. It is written in masterly couplets in the Arya metre.
- Another work of the same period, the *Chaturdandi Prakashika* by Pandit Venkatamakhi gives the basis of the present-day Carnatic system of music and its raga classification.

Most prolific composer

Purandara Dasa (1484–1564), the philosopher – saint and bhakti poet, is credited with as many as 475,000 compositions.

Earliest royal composers of ragas

- Maharaja Swathi Thirunal (r. 1813–46), the ruler of the erstwhile princely state of Travancore (now in Kerala), created more than 400 classical compositions in

INDI-POP: THE SOUND OF THE 1990S

The notes of the 1990s were dominated by artistes and pop albums independent from soundtracks for Indian cinema, including Bollywood. 'Hindi' pop music had begun to be popular across the Indian subcontinent in the early1980s, with the albums of Pakistani brother–sister duo Nazia and Zohaib Hassan, produced by Biddu, while artistes such as Remo Fernandes had already released several albums in English. Channel [V], which debuted in 1994, helped to bring indigenous talent to the fore with its inclusion of Indi-pop along with Western music, a model that MTV too followed when it returned to India after a hiatus. In the early 2000s, the line between Indi-pop and Indian cinema music began to get blurred, the independent genre faced rising competition from film music, and many pop singers stopped releasing albums and began singing for movies. Here's a look at a selection of the stars of the Indi-pop era and their songs:

- Suneeta Rao: '*Pari Hoon Main*' (1991), '*Chhoti Chhoti Baatein*' (1997)
- Bally Sagoo: '*Mera Lawng Gwacha*' (1991), '*Chura Liya*' (1994)
- Malkit Singh: '*Tootak Tootak Tootiyan*' (1990), '*Gur Naalo Ishq Mitha*' (1991)
- Baba Sehgal: '*Thanda Thanda Pani*' (1992)
- Alisha Chinai: '*Bombay Girl*' (1994), '*Made in India*' (1995)
- Suchitra Krishnamoorthi: '*Dole Dole*' (1995)
- Daler Mehndi: '*Bolo Ta Ra Ra Ra*' (1995), '*Ho Jayegi Balle Balle*' (1997), '*Tunak Tunak Tun*' (1998)
- Apache Indian: '*Chock There*', '*Don Raja*' (1993)
- Colonial Cousins: '*Krishna*' (1996), '*The Way We Do It*' (1998)

both the Carnatic and Hindustani modes.

- The 25th maharaja of Mysore (now Mysuru), Karnataka, Jayachamaraja Wodeyar, who ruled from 1940 to 1950, was a 20th-century scholar, patron of arts, philosopher and an accomplished pianist. He composed 94 songs under his signature Sri Vidya and invented many new ragas.

The trinity of Carnatic music

The three prolific 18th-century composers – Thyagaraja, Muthuswamy Dikshitar and Syama Sastri – are known as the Trinity of Carnatic music as the music system is based centrally on compositions attributed to them. The compositions of Syama Sastri are known for their intricate rhythmic patterns, those of Thyagaraja for the blend of emotion and melody, and those of Dikshitar for their depiction of melodic beauty and variety.

First codifier of Carnatic concert format

Ariyakudi Ramanuja Iyengar (1890–1967) was the architect of modern concert Carnatic music. He pioneered the transition of the Carnatic concert from temples and courts to modern concert halls, codifying and adapting its format, order and duration. He introduced the largest number of compositions from the trinity of Thyagaraja, Muthuswamy Dikshitar and Syama Sastri to the concert repertoire,

- Remo Fernandes: '*Politicians Don't Know to Rock 'n' Roll*', '*Everybody Wants to*' (1992), '*O Meri Munni*' (1998)
- Mehnaz Hoosein: '*Miss India*' (1996), '*Mausam*' (1999)
- Anaida: '*Oova Oova*' (1996)
- Anamika Grover: '*Kahin Karta Hoga Woh Mera Intezar*' (1996)
- Shubha Mudgal: '*Ali More Angana*' (1996), '*Ab Ke Sawan*' (1999)
- Shaan and Sagarika: '*Naujawan*' (1996)
- Amitabh Bachchan: '*Eer Beer Phatte*' (1997)
- Euphoria: '*Dhoom*' (1998)
- Falguni Pathak: '*Yaad Piya Ki Aane Lagi*' (1998)
- Lucky Ali: '*O Sanam*' (1996), '*Teri Yaadein Aati Hain*' (1998)
- Raageshwari: '*Duniya*' (1997)
- Shweta Shetty: '*Johnny Joker*' (1993), '*Deewane To Deewane Hain*' (1998)
- Silk Route: '*Dooba Dooba*' (1998)
- Shankar Mahadevan: '*Breathless*' (1998)
- Sonu Nigam: '*Tu…*' (1998)
- Mika: '*Saawan Mein Lag Gayi Aag*' (1998)
- Kamaal Khan: '*O Oh Jaane Jaana*' (1998)
- Aryans: '*Aankhon Mein Tera Hi Chehra*' (1999)
- Bombay Vikings: '*Kya Soorat Hai*' (1999)
- Jasbir Jassi: '*Dil Le Gayi*' (1998), '*Kudi Kudi*' (1999)
- Sukhbir: '*Ishq Tera Tadpave*' (1999)

new pallavis (opening phrase of a song), the order of *tukkadas* (composition played towards the end of a Carnatic concert), and padams (other songs) that follow the main item of *ragam-thanam*-pallavi.

First fusion melody

The 14th century saw the introduction of Persian models into Indian music. Amir Khusrau (1253–1325), the famous singer at the court of Alauddin Khilji (r. 1296–1316) introduced the qawwali mode of singing, a mixture of Persian and Indian music. He also introduced the sitar, a modification of the veena.

Oldest gharana

The Gwalior gharana was founded in the 16th century by Nathan Khan Pir Bakhsh.

Oldest *sabha* for dance and music

- Sri Parthasarathy Swami Sabha at Triplicane, Madras (now Chennai,) Tamil Nadu, was established in 1900.
- The Bangalore Gayana Sabha, Bangalore (now Bengaluru), Karnataka, set up on 5 August 1905, is the second oldest private cultural organization with programmes in dance and music.

Oldest musical instrument

A lithophone (stone chimes comparable to a xylophone), around 3,000–4,000 years old, was identified by German archaeologists in Sankarjang Village in Angul District, Odisha. All the 20 similar-shaped polished basalt stones found possibly formed fragments of a lithophone, with excellent acoustic quality, as the edges were ground thin to achieve a specific pitch.

Oldest South Indian stringed instrument

The *yazh*, a seven-stringed lute is mentioned in Tamil Sangam literature (first to fourth century CE), making it the oldest south Indian stringed instrument known.

Oldest known percussion instrument

The ghatam or mud pot, still in vogue in Carnatic concerts, is mentioned in the Ramayana. It was used in folk music for centuries and later elevated to concert status by maestro Palani Krishna Iyer (1876–1908). This tradition continued with maestros such as Kodandarama Iyer and T.H. 'Vikku' Vinayakram, who popularized it.

First mention of the drum

The *Mahajanaka Jataka* (c. second century BCE) mentions the drum, along with horns, gongs and cymbals. Two ancient Tamil books – *Purananuru* and *Pattupattu* (c. 100–200 CE) – mention the drum as occupying a position of great honour in the musical tradition of India.

Earliest musical instruments

Drums came into being during the Vedic period. The earliest drums included the *dundubhi* and *adambara*, ordinary drums; *bhumi dundubhi*, an earth drum made by digging a hole in the ground and covering it with hide; and *vanaspati*, a wooden drum. Early stringed instruments included the *skanda veena* and *karkari*, ordinary lutes; *vana*, a lute with a hundred strings; and the veena (similar to the present-day one). Wind instruments included the *tunava*, a wooden flute; the *nadi*, a reed flute; and *bakura*, whose shape is unknown.

First three-in-one classical instrument

The *mridanga veenai*, a stand-up instrument that is framed in wood and played sitting on a chair, was invented by Audanoor P. Haridass, who demonstrated it on 23 September 1984 at the Purasawalkam Arts Academy, Madras (now Chennai), Tamil Nadu. Played with bamboo sticks, it not only reproduces the sounds of percussion and strings, but also simulates the sound of cymbals used in *natuvangam* (rhythmic sound play) and the tinkle of *gajjai* (ankle bells).

Earliest use of the Carnatic veena

Govinda Dikshitar modified the Saraswati veena into the Carnatic veena to enable the playing of all ragas. He was a minister of King Raghunatha Naik of Thanjavur (r. 1614–32 CE), Tamil Nadu, and carried this out during his reign.

First Indian performer at the Royal Albert Hall

The first Indian singer to perform at the iconic venue, the Royal Albert Hall, in London, UK, was Bollywood playback singer Lata Mangeshkar, who gave a performance at the venue in 1974. Other Indians who have also performed

ON THE RECORD

First recorded song
Sashi Mukhi of Classic Theatre in Calcutta (now Kolkata, West Bengal) recorded the first song '*Kanha Jeevan Dhan*' in 1902, from the play *Srikrishna* on a 22.86 cm (9 in.), one-sided disc made by the Gramophone and Typewriter Ltd.

First singer to be recorded on gramophone
Gauhar Jaan (1873–1930) was selected to sing when Fred Ginsberg decided to introduce the gramophone in India with the first disc being cut in Calcutta (now Kolkata), West Bengal, in 1902. She attended the recording session for a sum of ₹3,000.

First gramophone record
Indian music was first produced on a gramophone record in 1898 at the Beliaghata factory of the Gramophone and Typewriter Ltd. In July 1908, the production of disc records was started at the Sealdah factory located on Beliaghata Road, Calcutta (now Kolkata), West Bengal. In 1928, the Sealdah factory was closed and building work commenced at the new factory on Jessore Road, Dum Dum, Calcutta.

First gramophone company
On 7 July 1901, J. Watson Harrod opened a branch of the Gramophone Company Ltd at Calcutta (now Kolkata), West Bengal, which was further developed by T.W. Gainsberg. In 1908, the first factory to process and press records, was set up in Beliaghata, Calcutta.

First voices recorded on gramophone
The voices of Dr Harnamdas and Ahmed were recorded by the Gramophone Company in 1899 in London, UK. They sang songs based on the Ramayana and recited the *aayat*s of the Quran for the recordings.

India's Only Gramophone Museum

Discs and Machines – Sunny's Gramophone Museum and Records' Archive in Kottayam, Kerala, is a unique repository of around 110,000 records and more than 260 gramophones. Owner Sunny Matthew has been collecting them for the last 32 years and opened the museum to public on 25 January 2015. A copy of the first recorded song in India is also on display here. The museum may be visited by appointment.

First Winner of 'The World's Best' Talent Competition

Lydian Nadhaswaram, a child prodigy who plays the piano, won the global talent contest, 'The World's Best', in 2019. Hailing from Chennai, Tamil Nadu, he spent four years at A.R. Rahman's KM Music Conservatory. He played at an astonishing speed of 280 beats per minute and then increased it to 325 beats per minute. The thirteen-year-old pianist took home US $1,000,000 as the cash prize.

Lydian Nadhaswaram

here included Pandit Ravi Shankar, Hariprasad Chaurasia, Shreya Ghoshal and Anoushka Shankar, among others.

First electronic instruments

- The first electronic tala aid called talometer was invented by M.G. Raj Narayan of Bangalore (now Bengaluru), Karnataka, in June 1978. It helps musicians to get a precise, unerring and continuous course of cycles in all the talas.
- The first electronic tanpura was also developed by M.G. Raj Narayan in December 1979. This innovative box-like device had knobs for fine tuning. Nine years after this, he developed the first electronic tabla, designed to produce the actual sounds of a tabla as played in a live performance.

First duo to introduce *jugalbandi*

Pandit Ravi Shankar and Ustad Ali Akbar Khan formed the first musical duo to introduce instrumental duets popularly known as *jugalbandi*. Shankar and Khan performed the *jugalbandi* for the first time at the debut performance of the former in 1939, with Shankar playing the sitar and Khan playing the sarod. The duo was also among the first to popularize Indian classical music abroad.

First harp player

Meagan Pandian from Mumbai, Maharashtra, is the first harp player from India and the first Indian harpist to participate in A.R. Rahman's concerts. She received the 'Young Musician of the Year' award from the Olga and Jules Craen Foundation in 2014.

First use of *shehnai* in Hindustani classical music

The *shehnai*, like the *sundari* and *surnayi,* was originally a folk instrument that was played on festive occasions. It was Bharat Ratna–winner Ustad Bismillah Khan (1916–2006) who brought it into the realm of classical music, on par with other classical instruments.

First woman instrumentalist

Renowned sarod player Sharan Rani Backliwal (1929–2008), was a leading exponent of Hindustani instrumental music and the first female instrumentalist to give a public recital, in the 1930s. She trained sarod maestros Baba Allauddin Khan and Ustad Ali Akbar Khan. Popularly known as Sarod Rani, she was given the Sahitya Kala Parishad award and the Sangeet Natak Akademi award for classical Hindustani instrumental music in 1974. She received the Padma Shri in 1968.

Sarod player Sharan Rani Backliwal *(centre)*: first woman instrumentalist

First woman *nadaswaram* player
Madurai M.S. Ponnuthayi from Madurai, Tamil Nadu, was the first professional woman player of the *nadaswaram*, long considered a male bastion. Born into a family of musicians, she was introduced to the instrument by her father. After receiving training under Natesa Pillai, she gave her first performance at the age of nine in the 1940s.

First woman *shehnai* player
Bageswari Gamar was crowned 'Shehnai Queen' at Chandigarh in 1983, the year she made her debut. A disciple of Ustad Bismillah Khan, she recorded a *jugalbandi* with the maestro, besides releasing solo cassettes. She represented India at the Bharat Mahotsav in Russia in 1988.

First woman ghatam player
Sukanya Ramgopal (b. 13 June 1957) from Bangalore (now Bengaluru), Karnataka, became the first woman to play the ghatam in the Carnatic music tradition. Born in Mayiladuthurai, Tamil Nadu, she began training in the instrument at the age of 12 years, under the guidance of T.R. Harihara Sharma and later under T.H. 'Vikku' Vinayakram. Among many of her innovations are the 'Ghata Tarang', a melody created out of six ghatams, and the 'Sthree Taal Tarang', an all-woman percussion ensemble, experiments that have taken her to stages across India and abroad. She received the Sangeet Natak Akademi Award in 2014.

First female professional saxophone players
Sisters M.S. Lavanya and M.S. Subbalaxmi from Chennai, Tamil Nadu, have given a new dimension to Carnatic music by playing ragas on the saxophone. Daughters of mridangam exponent M.R. Sainath, the duo, called the 'Saxophone Sisters', learnt the instrument from Padma Shri award-winner Dr Kadri Gopinath. They have performed at venues such as the Soorya Festival in Thiruvananthapuram, Kerala, the Sri Thyagaraja Festival at Thiruvaiyaru, Tamil Nadu, and the Malleswaram Sangeetha Sabha, Bengaluru, Karnataka. They have also performed at the 'One City One World Festival' in Nottingham and the Bath International Music Festival in the UK.

First to perform at the UN
M.S. Subbulakshmi (1916–2004) was the first Indian to perform at the United Nations (UN) in a concert at the UN General Assembly on UN Day, 23 October 1966. She received the Padma Bhushan in 1954, the Padma Vibhushan in 1975,

and became the first musician to be awarded the Bharat Ratna in 1998. Subbulakshmi was also the first Indian musician to receive the Ramon Magsaysay Award for Public Service in 1974.

M.S. Subbulakshmi: first to perform at the UN

First foreign concert tour by a woman instrumentalist

According to a report in *Amrita Bazar Patrika*, dated 11 September 1912, Satyabala Devi, an 18-year-old Bengali girl, had gone to America in the summer of 1911 to play the veena. The article stated that she was the first Indian woman to have gone abroad to perform in an instrumental music concert and it was declared a great success.

First music school

Pandit Vishnu Digambar Paluskar (1872–1931) set up the Gandharva Mahavidyalaya – India's first known music school – in Lahore (now in Pakistan) on 5 May 1901. It was run on public donations and funds raised by his concerts. Another branch was opened in Bombay (now Mumbai), Maharashtra, by Pandit Vishnu Digambar Paluskar in September 1908, and Pandit Vinayakrao Patwardhan started a branch in Poona (now Pune), Maharashtra, on 8 May 1932. Later, the Lahore school was shifted to Bombay after Independence in 1947.

First to perform at an international jazz festival

Brahma Naad, a jazz band, became the first Indian band to perform at the Festival International de Jazz de Montreal in Montreal, Canada, in 2010. The band, which was founded by Louiz Banks, India's best-known jazz performer, had his son Gino on drums, Tony Lakatos on saxophone, Joe Alvares as the lead vocalist, Shelden D'Silva on bass, Bala Bhaskaran on the Carnatic violin and Sameera Koppikar as the Indian vocalist. The band played a fusion of Indian classical music and jazz.

WR Most recorded artiste

Asha Bhosle is the most recorded artiste in the history of music. Having begun her career in 1948 with the Hindi film *Chunariya*, she had recorded 11,000 solo, duet and chorus songs by 2011. In a career spanning more than six decades, she has sung in over 20 Indian and foreign languages. She received the Dadasaheb Phalke Award in 2000 and the Padma Vibhushan in 2008. She was also the first Indian singer to be nominated for the Grammy Awards.

First set of records

Renowned businessman H. Bose's Talking Machine Hall, a recording shop in Calcutta (now Kolkata), West Bengal, released the first set of phonograph records on 19 March 1906. The set featured eight songs by Rabindranath Tagore and four by D.L. Roy.

First recorded music

In the 1930s, an organization called Shining Star Society recorded sets of discs with mythological themes. A mix of music and dialogue, the sets ran into several records. A 10-disc *Ramayana* by Saraswati Stores was very popular, followed by other drama sets: *Tukaram* (four discs), *Purandara Dasa* (five discs), *Siruthondar* (three discs) and *Thirugnana Sambandhar* (four discs). Their recording was supervised by the Katcheri set pioneer, Thuraiyur Rajagopala Sharma.

First compact disc

Pankaj Udhas's album titled *Shagufta* was the first to be formally released in a compact disc (CD) format by Music India in December 1987.

First fusion album

Violinist Yehudi Menuhin and sitar maestro Pandit Ravi Shankar collaborated on a double album called *West Meets East,* which was released in Britain in January 1967, where both played Western and Indian classical pieces alternately.

WR First portable digital audio player

Carvaan, by Saregama India Ltd, is the world's first portable digital audio player with over 5,000 inbuilt songs. The songs are categorized based on singers, lyricists, music composers and moods. Using a jog dial, music stations can be selected, from Kishore Kumar classics and R.D. Burman's hits to timeless love songs and soulful Sufi tracks. Carvaan can function as an FM radio, and also has Bluetooth and USB features.

First Asian to win the Golden Reel Award

Resul Pookutty was the first Asian to win the 63rd American Motion Picture Sound Editor's Golden Reel Award in 2016 for best sound for the documentary *India's Daughter.* A sound designer, editor and mixer who works in Hollywood and Indian cinema, he also won the Academy Award (Oscar) in 2009 for best sound mixing for the movie *Slumdog Millionaire,* along with Richard Pryke and Ian Tapp. He was awarded the Padma Shri in 2010 and the National Film Award for best audiography in the same year.

First all-woman Hindustani–Carnatic music band

Tabla soloist Anuradha Pal from Mumbai, Maharashtra, founded Stree Shakti, the first all-woman Hindustani–Carnatic music band, in 1996. It performed in India as well as other countries, including at international festivals such as BBC Music Live and Rhythm Sticks.

Gaana: Music App with More Than a Million Active Monthly Users

Gaana, a leading music streaming application, became the first in the country to have a user base of 150 million (15 crore) active monthly users in December 2019. Launched in April 2010, the service features a catalogue of Indian music across 21 languages, including Hindi, Assamese, Urdu, English and Punjabi, among others. The application has features like personalized playlists, Gaana Video and Artist Dashboard. It also introduced an in-app voice assistant, sing-along lyrics and instant downloads.

Grammy Award for the Best World Music Album

Music composer and tabla player Sandeep Das won a Grammy Award for the Best World Music Album in 2017 for his collaboration with Yo-Yo Ma and The Silk Road Ensemble on the album *Sing Me Home*.

Only Indian to win both an Oscar and a Grammy Award

Composer and singer A.R. Rahman won two Grammys following his Oscar wins for the soundtrack of Danny Boyle's *Slumdog Millionaire*, becoming the first Indian to win an individual Grammy. He won the first Grammy in the Best Compilation Soundtrack for a Motion Picture category. The second was for the song '*Jai Ho*' in the Best Motion Picture Song category for the same in 2009.

First Grammy Award–winning Indian percussionist

T.H. 'Vikku' Vinayakram was the first Indian percussionist to win the Grammy Award in 1991. He won it for his participation in *Planet Drum* by Mickey Hart. Vinayakram, well-known for playing the ghatam and popularizing Carnatic music, was honoured with the Padma Shri in 2002 and with the Padma Bhushan in 2014. He also won the Sangeet Natak Akademi fellowship in 2012.

A.R. Rahman has won the National Award for Best Music Direction 6 times, the most by an individual.

First Indo-jazz (fusion) albums

Indo-jazz came into its own in India in the 1970s with Shakti, a group formed by jazz guitarist John McLaughlin, along with L. Shankar on the electric double violin (which he invented), Zakir Hussain on tabla and T.H. 'Vikku' Vinayakram on the ghatam.

First whistling LP

An album of Carnatic and Hindustani ragas entirely whistled by Siva Prasad from Hyderabad (now in Telangana) was released on 15 June 1985.

First Indian band on MTV

Rana Banerjee and Sanjoy Sengupta's band, Extinct, was the first Indian group to be featured on MTV Asia, in September 1993.

First all-girl pop music band

Channel [V], through a nationwide hunt from 12 January 2001 across 10 cities, handpicked five girls – Pratichi Mohapatra, Mahua Kamat, Neha Bhasin, Anoushka Manchanda and Seema – to constitute India's first customized all-girl band, Viva. It disbanded in 2003.

First female rapper

Taran Kaur Dhillon (b. 29 July 1979) aka Hard Kaur was the first female rapper of Indian origin. A British citizen of Indian origin, she topped the UK charts with her song, '*Ek Glassy*' in 2007. Her first solo album *Supawoman*, released the same year, had 11 tracks. She marked her Bollywood debut with the title track (which she co-wrote) of the film *Johnny Gaddaar* (2007).

First differently abled DJ
Varun Khullar aka DJ Aamish from New Delhi is the first differently abled professional disc jockey (DJ) in India. He began his career in May 2017 and is currently a resident DJ with Kitty Su, New Delhi, a part of Lalit Group and Hotels. He has performed at festivals like Time Out 72 and Greeshma Utsav.

India's only music director couple
Samir and Mana Raval from Ahmedabad, Gujarat, are India's first and only music director couple, having composed music for more than 100 songs in 35 feature films in Gujarati and Hindi. Having started with music direction for *Teenagers Gang*, a Gujarati film, in 2013, the couple continues to compose music for Hindi and other films, and TV serials and jingles.

First virtual music festival
Sunburn Home Festival, a two-day virtual music festival, was organized from 11 to 12 July 2020. The festival featured a line-up of international stars such as Bassjackers, Vini Vici and Ummet Ozcan, among others. The highlight of the event was the application of extended reality (XR) technology offering a mixed reality and holistic environment, also used for the first time.

Longest *ravanhatha*
Praveen Singh Rathore along with Shiv Pal Ram, Sugana Ram and Manwari from Jodhpur, Rajasthan, made the longest *ravanhatha*, a folk string instrument of Rajasthan. The *ravanhatha*, measuring 224 cm (7 ft 4.19 in.), was made in two weeks at Bhakrasani, Jodhpur, using bamboo, mango wood, goat leather, bull horn, iron, cotton threads, plastic threads, *baval* (babul) wood, *ghungroo* (bells) and fabric.

Record Rewind

Marathon violin recital

1990
Carimella Gopalakrishna from Hyderabad (now in Telangana) played the violin non-stop for 30 hours during 21-22 December 1986.

2005
L. Athira Krishna (b. 14 July 1987) performed a 32-hour non-stop violin recital in Thiruvananthapuram, Kerala. The event was organized by the Soorya Stage and Film Society from 9:15 a.m. on 10 November to 6:00 p.m. on 11 November 2003.

WR Longest innings as a conductor
Western music maestro Zubin Mehta (b. 29 April 1936) from Bombay (now Mumbai), Maharashtra, spent over 13 years as the music director and principal conductor of the New York Philharmonic Orchestra from 1978 to 1991. Currently, he is the music director of the Israel Philharmonic Orchestra.

Marathon flute performance
Ananthakrishnan S.R., a flautist from Thiruvananthapuram, Kerala, played the flute for 33 hrs 36 mins, from 6:30 a.m. on 13 July to 6:30 p.m. on 14 July 2017 in Thrissur, Kerala, with a total break time of 2 hrs 24 mins.

Marathon qawwali performance

WR

Haji Mohammad Idris and Mohammad Ilyas, known as the Qutbi brothers of Dargah Hazrat Qutbuddin, performed Sufi qawwali for 12 hrs. They began at 9:00 p.m. on 12 November 2016 and ended at 9:00 a.m. on 13 November 2016 at the Sangeet Natak Akademi in Delhi. Sixteen singers accompanied them.

Marathon duet singing

Venkatesh and Sangeetha Rajeshkumar from Chennai, Tamil Nadu, sang duets together for 28 hours at the Akshaya Mahalakshmi Mahal, Chennai, Tamil Nadu, during 28–29 January 2017. They sang 342 Tamil film songs from around 4:00 a.m. on 28 January and ended by 12:30 p.m. the next day. The total break time was 4 hrs 30 mins.

Marathon Carnatic vocal performance

Sajna Sudheer (b. 1 August 1984) from Thiruvananthapuram, Kerala, performed a marathon Carnatic vocal recital for 37 hrs 50 mins at the Ganesham Natakakalari of Soorya Stage and Film Society. She began her performance at 3:15 a.m. on 21 January 2019 and ended at 9:15 p.m. on 22 January 2019, with a total break time of 4 hrs 10 mins.

Sajna Sudheer: Carnatic vocal marathon

Most people playing the harmonica together

Hindustan Petroleum Corporation Ltd, as part of its mega festival – Yuvantage BLITZ during 6–7 January 2019 – set a record for most people playing the harmonica simultaneously. The music was played by 457 of the company's employees on their harmonicas for 6 mins 17 secs on 6 January 2019 at Ramoji Film City, Hyderabad, Telangana.

Largest folk artiste gathering

Ranga Samsthana organized the largest folk artiste gathering in an event called the – 'Kannada Geet Mala', with 1,112 *bhavageethe* singers singing together at the Samsa Open Air Theatre, Bengaluru, Karnataka, on 10 January 2017. The performance was led by Bandlahalli Vijayakumar, a folk artiste and *bhavageethe* virtuoso from Bengaluru.

Songs sung in most languages in a single concert*

Rahath Malladi (b. 14 May 2003) from Vijayawada, Andhra Pradesh, has sung songs in most languages in a single concert. He sang 105 songs in 105 languages in a concert lasting 7 hrs 13 mins on 6 January 2018 at Sri Rama Function Place, Vijayawada. The languages included Telugu, Mandarin, Dogri, Sanskrit, Swahili, Bengali, Marathi and French.

*The rules regarding the age group of participants have been changed. Please see Rules and Guidelines.

PADMA AWARD WINNERS 2020-21		
Padma Vibhushan		
	Chhannulal Mishra (2020)	Hindustani classical singer
	S.P. Balasubrahmanyam (2021)	Musician; playback singer
Padma Bhushan		
	Ajoy Chakrabarty (2020)	Hindustani classical vocalist
	K.N. Shantakumari Chithra (2021)	Carnatic, devotional, playback singer
Padma Shri		
2020	Kalee Shabi Mahaboob and Sheik Mahaboob Subani	*Nadaswaram* players
2020	Lalitha Chidambram and Saroja Chidambram	Carnatic singers, known as the 'Bombay Sisters'
2020	Madan Singh Chauhan	Folk and Sufi singer
2020	Madhu Mansuri Hasmukh	Sambalpuri lyricist and composer
2020	Manilal Nag	Sitar player
2021	Mitrabhanu Gountia	Nagpuri Lok Sangeet
2021	Suresh Wadkar	Odia songs; playback singing
2021	Ustad Anwar Khan Manganiyar	Rajasthani folk music
2021	Annavarapu Rama Swamy	Classical violinist, Carnatic musician
2021	Damodaran Kaithapram	Carnatic musician
2021	Dulal Manki	Jhumar singer; Assamese folk singer
2021	Gopiram Bargayn Burabhakat	Sattriya traditional musician
2021	Gulfam Ahmed	Sarod and Afghani rabab player
2021	('Bombay') Jayashri Ramnath	Classical singer
2021	Lakha Khan	Sindhi sarangi player
2021	Mahesh and Naresh Kanodia	Singers and musicians
2021	Nidumolu Sumathi	Percussionist (mainly mridangam)
2021	Rewben Mashan	Tangkhul Naga folklore through songs
2021	Sanjida Khatun	Musicologist

Most events in a single day

Pernod Ricard India Pvt. Ltd organized 104 musical events on a single day – 29 November 2019. These events were held in different venues across 27 cities in the country, including Delhi, Mumbai, Pune, Chennai, Visakhapatnam and Chandigarh, among others. Titled, 'Play for a Cause', this campaign raised awareness on issues such as pollution, nature, plastic use, and meals for the underprivileged. Bands and artistes including Perfect Strangers (Bengaluru), Parikrama (Gurugram), Ankur Tiwari and the Ghalat Family (Mumbai), Cherry Singh (Chandigarh) and Usha Uthup (Kolkata), among others, performed at these events.

THEATRE

Oldest extant play

Palm-leaf fragments belonging to the Kushana period (around first century CE) feature a nine-act Buddhist play by Ashvaghosha, the court poet of king Kanishka, titled *x*, which is the earliest extant play. It follows all the rules for drama laid down in the *Natyashastra.*

Oldest cave theatre

The cave theatres at Sita Bengra and Jogimara in the Surguja District of Chhattisgarh are estimated to be around 3,000 years old. Sita Bengra, which pre-dates the Lomas Rishi caves of the Mauryan period (322–187 BCE), was chiefly used for dance and dramas.

Early dramatic references

There are references to drama, dancing, music and acting in the Ramayana, the Mahabharata and the Puranas. Buddhist and Jain texts mention that monks were forbidden to watch dramatic performances. Panini (c. fourth century BCE) mentions dramatic works in his *Ashtadhyayi*. Patanjali (variously dated from 2nd century BCE to 4th century CE), describes the conditions of dramatic performers. Kautilya also refers to music, dance and drama in the *Arthashastra*.

SUPER 30

GIRISH KARNAD: MANY FACETS, MANY ROLES

Girish Karnad

A man of numerous talents, Girish Karnad (1938–2019), born in Matheran, Maharashtra, was a celebrated playwright, besides being an award-winning actor, director and screenwriter in Hindi and Kannada films. He also served as the director of the Film and Television Institute of India (1974–75), the chairman of the Sangeet Natak Akademi (1988–93), and the director of the Nehru Centre and minister of culture in the Indian high commission, London, UK (2000–03). His plays in Kannada were profusely translated and his accomplishments in theatre are highly lauded. Ever since the early 1960s, his work was deeply rooted in the country. In 1990, his play *Taledanda* (Death by Beheading) was an iconoclastic play that used Veerashaivism as the backdrop to bring out the political undercurrents of that time. His other works after 1990 include – *Agni Mattu Male* (The Fire and the Rain, 1995), *Tipu Sultan Kanda Kanasu* (The Dreams of Tipu Sultan, 1997), *Odakalu Bimba* (A Heap of Broken Dreams, 2006), *Maduve Album* (2006), *Flowers* (2012), *Benda Kaalu on Toast* (2012) and *Rakshasa Tangadi* (2018). He received the Padma Bhushan (1992), The Kannada Sahitya Parishat Award (1992), The Sahitya Akademi Award (1994), The Jnanpith Award (1998) and the Kalidas Samman (1998) for his contributions to literature.

Earliest plays

• Patanjali mentions plays such as *Kamavadha, Balibandhan* and *Sariputra-prakarana* in his text *Mahabhashya* (c. 3rd century BCE).

• Bharata also mentions plays such as *Devasura Sangrama, Amrita Manthana* and *Tripuradaha* in his *Natyashastra.*

• *Uparupakas* (secondary dramas) are found in the Rig Veda in the form of dialogue hymns. The most famous one tells the story of Pururava and Urvashi. Eighteen such *uparupakas* are mentioned in the *Sahitya Darpana,* a book on rhetoric and dramaturgy from the 14th century, authored by Pandit Vishwanath Kaviraj. These plays pre-date even the *Natyashastra. Uparupakas* were probably enacted before the public on royal occasions and temple festivals.

 **Pune city's first 'black box' theatre, called 'The Box' was opened on 5 November 2020.**

Early political plays

Mrichchhakatika by Shudraka (dated between third and fifth century CE) and Vishakhadatta's *Mudrarakshasa* (dated between late fourth and eighth century CE), both depict clashes between different powers, political intrigue, espionage and counterespionage. They are considered to be the first plays with political themes.

Origins of social theatre

The folk theatre form of Bhavai in Gujarat is said to have been introduced in the early 15th century by Asaita Thakar, a brahmin of the Andichya clan. Legend goes that Asaita, after being ostracized for saving a lower-caste girl from dacoits, composed playlets attacking social injustice and the caste system.

Earliest playwright

Bhasa (third to fourth century CE) of the Chola times is believed to be the earliest playwright. Well-known plays by him include *Abhisheka, Swapnavasavadattam* and *Pratimanatakam*.

Earliest street plays

Therukoothu, a theatre form originating during 200 BCE– 200 CE, in ancient Tamilakam, literally means 'street play'. It was performed on streets on an improvised stage with very few props and hardly any special costumes. Themes were taken from the epics. Therukoothu as well as other forms of street plays like Pallu, Kuravanji and Nandi Natakam are still performed in south India.

Oldest children's theatre

Children's Little Theatre, the oldest children's theatre in the country, was founded in Calcutta (now Kolkata), West Bengal, by Samar Chatterjee (1908–86) in May 1951. It included dance, drama, music and puppetry.

First modern Indian plays (translations)

Gerasim Lebedev, a Russian adventurer, founded the first European-style proscenium drama theatre in Calcutta (now Kolkata), West Bengal, in 1795, helped by local intellectuals. Along with his Bengali tutor, Goloknath Das, he presented the plays *The Disguise* and *Love Is the Best Doctor* on 7 November

1795. These English comedies, translated into Bengali, were the first urban theatrical performances.

First foreign translation of a Sanskrit play
Kalidasa's *Abhijnana Shakuntalam* was translated into German in 1791 by revolutionary Georg Forster and into English by Anglo-Welsh philologist Sir William Jones in 1795.

First protest play
Nil Darpan, a play in Bengali about the plight of indigo farmers, was written by Dinabandhu Mitra in 1860. The play was banned by the British authorities.

Marathon street play performance

Marathon *nukkad natak* performance
The Mayaar Group of the Bhopal School of Social Sciences in Bhopal, Madhya Pradesh, organized a street-play marathon to celebrate Mahatma Gandhi's 150th birth anniversary. A record was set with a team of 17 members performing 151 street plays from 5:00 a.m. on 3 March 2019 to 3:56 a.m. on 4 March 2019 at different locations in the city. The performance time added up to 21 hrs 34 mins, with a break time of 2 hrs 26 mins. The plays conveyed the messages and importance of the Swachh Bharat Mission of the Government of India.

First dramatic club
The first dramatic club was the Parsi Natak Mandali established in 1853 in Bombay (now Mumbai), Maharashtra. They performed their first play *Roostum Zabooli and Sohrab* that year, followed by *King Afrasiab and Rustom Pehlvan* and *Padshah Faredun*. Other Parsi theatre clubs were the Elphinstone, established in 1860, and the Victoria, established in 1867. These drama clubs inspired Gujarati theatre.

First public theatre hall

The Star Theatre in Calcutta (now Kolkata), West Bengal, was inaugurated on 21 July 1883 with the play *Daksha Yajna*. Among the first to produce plays here was acclaimed playwright, novelist, theatre director and actor Girish Chandra Ghosh. The theatre shifted to its present site on Bidhan Sarani in 1888 and now mainly functions as a cinema hall with plays also being staged.

First commercial theatre

The first commercial Parsi theatre, started by Pestonji Framji in 1870, was the first aimed at commercialized mass entertainment, while dealing with social problems. Though based in Bombay (now Mumbai), Maharashtra, the theatre company travelled widely all over north India.

First and only play on Broadway and West End

The Ramayana by Gopal Sharman, enacted in a one-woman tour de force by Jalabala Vaidya, was played at the Barbizon Plaza Theatre, Manhattan, New York, in February 1975. The play was also performed at other venues, such as the Smithsonian Institution, Washington DC, and the United Nations headquarters, New York, USA, and Sedler's Wells Theatre, London, UK.

First full-fledged opera

The Fakir of Benares, an Indo-French opera was staged at the Siri Fort Auditorium, New Delhi, on 27 February 2002. The opera was directed by Muzaffar Ali while his wife Meera Ali designed the costumes.

Only national institute for theatre training

The National School of Drama (NSD), set up by the Sangeet Natak Akademi in 1959, became autonomous in 1975.

First opera in English by an Indian

Well-known author Vikram Seth's *Arion and the Dolphin*, which premiered in the UK in June 1994, was the first opera written in English by an Indian. Commissioned by the English National Opera, it was performed at the 964-seat drill shed of HMS *Drake*, a high-security naval base. The opera was directed by Rebecca Meitlis.

Only village to preserve 'Gamaka' storytelling

On the bank of the River Tunga, near Shivamogga in Karnataka, lies Hosahalli,

Record Rewind

Most performances of a play in a single day

1990

Kalyanathil Galatta by the Tamil playwright Radhu (Radhakrishnan) was staged eight times on the same stage in one day in Madras (now Chennai), Tamil Nadu, from 8: 00 a.m. to 10:00 p.m. on 10 April 1988.

2017

The play *Yugpurush - Mahatma's Mahatma* holds the record for the most number of performances of a play in one day. On 26 March 2017, ten shows were performed at eight venues in five cities, viz., Jaipur, Kolkata, Mumbai, Palghar and Valsad.

First Indian Theatre Festival to Travel Abroad

The Qadir Ali Baig theatre festival, held annually in Hyderabad, Telangana, took place in Dubai, UAE, in 2019, marking the first time a local theatre festival was held in another country. Founded in 2005 by theatre personality and advertisement and documentary film-maker Mohammed Ali Baig, it celebrates the rich contributions of his father Qadir Ali Baig. The festival presented two acclaimed plays – *Quli: Dilon Ka Shahzaada* and *Under an Oak Tree* – as part of the 14th year showcase and the 35th death anniversary of the legend. The plays were staged at Taj Dubai, UAE, on 20 April and the festival headed to Mountbatten Hall, London, UK, on 12 June 2019.

a village that preserves and promotes the ancient art of storytelling known as Gamaka or *kavya vachana*. This form consists of *vachana* (recitation) and *vyakhyana* (explanation), traced back to the times of the Ramayana.

Play performed in most languages – single day

Yugpurush – Mahatma's Mahatma, a two-hour play based on the relationship between Mahatma Gandhi and his spiritual guide, Shrimad Rajchandra-ji, was performed in five languages, viz., English, Hindi, Bengali, Gujarati and Tamil, on 11 August 2017. It was organized by the Shrimad Rajchandra Mission in Dharampur, Valsad District, Gujarat, as one of the 808 performances for the 150th birth anniversary celebrations of Shrimad Rajchandra-ji.

WR Most theatrical performances

The Gujarati stage actor Pransukhlal Nayak (1910–89) had 22,455 theatrical performances to his credit by December 1986. He had played 241 roles in stage productions in a career he started at the age of nine.

WR Longest play*

The Mayaar Group of the Bhopal School of Social Sciences, Bhopal, Madhya Pradesh, organized the longest play, titled *Katha-e-Hind: The Journey of India*, which lasted for 48 hrs 29 mins 6 secs. Sixty artistes performed from 12:47 p.m. on 29 February 2020 to 1:16 p.m. on 2 March 2020. The play depicted the history of India from the Harappan civilization to the country's independence.

*The rules regarding the age group of participants have been changed. Please see Rules and Guidelines.

FIRST PLAYS IN DIFFERENT INDIAN LANGUAGES	
Language	**Play**
Assamese	*Ramanavami* (1857) by Gunabhiram Barua
Bengali	*Kalpanik Rang Badal Ba Saaj Badal* (1795) – first adaptation from another language; *Vidyasundar* (1835) – first original
Chattisgarhi	*Charandas Chor* (1975) by Habib Tanvir
Dogri	*Bawa Jito* (1948) by Ramnath Shastri
English	*The Persecuted* (1837) by Krishna Mohan Banerjee
Gujarati	*Lakshmi* (1850) by Dalpatram
Hindi	*Prabodha Chandrodaya* by Krishnamishra Yati (c. 13th century), translated from the Sanskrit by Maharaja Jaswant Singh of Jodhpur in the18th century
Kannada	*Mitravinda Govinda* (1696) by Singanarya
Marathi	*Thorle Madhavrao Peshwe* (1860) by Vinayak Janardan Keertane
Odia	*Babaji* (1877) by Jaganmohan Lala
Punjabi	*Dulhan* (1914) by I.C. Nanda
Rajasthani	*Kesar Vilas* (1900) by Shiv Chandra Bharatiya
Urdu	*Raja Gopichand Aur Julundhar* (1853) by Bhodaji Lad; *Inder Sabha* (1853) by Mian Agha Hasan Amanat

Asia's biggest theatre festival
Bharat Rang Mahotsav, the annual theatre festival of the National School of Drama (NSD), is the biggest theatre festival in Asia. Established in 1999, the Bharat Rang Mahotsav includes theatre groups from around the world. The 20th edition of the Bharat Rang Mahotsav concluded in February 2019 and featured 111 national and international acts including folk theatre, plays by groups invited for this, and plays by NSD students.

Most performances as a personality – stage and screen
Deepak Madhukant Antani (b. 20 August 1964) from Ahmedabad, Gujarat, is a professional actor who has performed the most times as Mahatma Gandhi on screen and stage. His maiden venture enacting the role of the Mahatma was on 20 June 2000 in *Sardar Patel*, a play written by him for Sardar Vallabhbhai Patel's 125th birth anniversary celebrations. As a Gandhi lookalike he has

PADMA AWARD WINNERS 2020–21		
Padma Shri		
2020	Dalavai Chalapathi Rao	Shadow leather puppetry
2020	Daya Prakash Sinha	Theatre
2020	Moozhikkal Pankajakshi	Nokkuvidhya Pavakalli puppetry
2020	Sarita Joshi	Theatre, film and TV
2020	Yadla Gopalarao	Padya Natakam
2021	Yazdi Naoshirwan Karanjia	Parsi theatre
2021	K.K. Ramachandra Pulavar	Puppet theatre
2021	K. Kesavasamy	Puppet theatre
2021	Parshuram Atmaram Gangavane	Chitrakathi storytelling
2021	Peter Brook	English theatre direction
2021	Subbu Arumugam	Villupattu theatre art

performed in one advertisement, two feature films, 21 short films, one TV serial, 190 stage plays, three documentaries, four voice-overs and a 200 km *padyatra* completed in nine days.

Most performances as a character – (mythological) stage
V.S. Narayanan (b. 20 November 1943) from Bombay (now Mumbai), Maharashtra, has been performing the role of Hanuman for the annual Ramnavami festival held by the Mulund Bhajana Samaj, Mumbai, annually since 1967. He has performed every year for the last 53 years.

Longest-serving director of NSD
Ebrahim Alkazi (1925–2020) served as the director of the National School of Drama (NSD) for the longest period. He was appointed in 1962 as the second director of NSD and left the post in 1977.

First Marathi musical
Shakuntala was staged as a Sangeet play on 31 October 1880 by Balwant Pandurang 'Annasaheb' Kirloskar and his Kirloskar Natak Mandali. Written in Marathi, it featured simple songs. This format was followed by Marathi stage in the musical drama genre called Sangeet plays. It attracted giants like Bal Gandharva (Narayanrao Rajahansa) and Keshavrao Bhonsle.

First recipient of the Kalidas Samman (theatre)
Shombhu Mitra (1915–1997) from Kolkata, West Bengal, was the first recipient of the Kalidas Samman for his contribution to Bengali theatre.

VISUAL ARTS

CINEMA

PIONEERS

First film shot in India

Coconut Fair is said to be the first short film shot in India in 1897 by an unknown foreign photographer. Shortly after, another 'film' made in India, a short dancing scene from the Bengali opera, *The Flower of Persia*, was exhibited at the Star Theatre, Calcutta (now Kolkata, West Bengal) on 9 February 1898.

First films exhibited

The first screening of six short films, by France's famed Lumière Brothers, Louis and Auguste, was held on 7 July 1896. They were: *Entry of Cinematographe, Arrival of a Train, Sea Bath, Workers Leaving the Factory, A Demolition* and *Ladies and Soldiers on Wheels.*

First film shot by an Indian

H. S. Bhatavadekar was the first to import a Riley camera from the UK and shoot two short films – *The Wrestlers,* which featured a wrestling match, and *Man and Monkey,* which was about a juggler training his monkeys – both released in November 1899.

First box-office hit

Dadasaheb Phalke's *Lanka Dahan* (1917), which ran for 23 weeks, was India's first box-office hit. It is on record that the money collected at the ticket counters had to be transported in bullock carts protected by armed guards!

First indigenous feature film

Dadasaheb Phalke's silent feature film *Raja Harishchandra* was released at the Coronation Theatre in Bombay (now Mumbai, Maharashtra) on 3 May 1913. It was a fully Indian venture and was shown along with four imported short films, together making up a 90-minute show. It ran for 23 days and was screened again later at multiple venues.

***Raja Harishchandra*: first indigenous feature film**

First talkie

Alam Ara, made in Hindustani by Ardeshir Irani and released on 14 March 1931 in Bombay (now Mumbai, Maharashtra), became India's first talkie feature. The first talkie stars were Master Vithal as hero, Zubeida as heroine, Prithviraj Kapoor in a supporting role and W.M. Khan as a singing fakir. The first music directors were Pirojshah Mistry and B. Irani. It was a costume fantasy with seven songs. The film reel was 3,048 m (10,000 ft) long and it ran for seven weeks.

First female actor of the talkies

After silent performances in 36 movies, Zubeida Begum acted in the first Indian talkie *Alam Ara* (1931).

Rajinikanth and a League of Extraordinary Gentlemen

REAL NAME: Shivaji Rao Gaekwad

QUALIFICATIONS: Studied till pre-university course PUC (Class 12); enrolled into an acting course at the Madras Film Institute (now Adyar Film Institute or M.G.R. Government Film and Television Training Institute, Chennai, Tamil Nadu).

PROFESSION BEFORE MOVIES: Bus conductor with Bangalore Transport Service.

K. Balachander

- Mentor who spotted him when he was doing plays and learning acting.
- Gave him a break in movies including his debut film (*Apoorva Raagangal*, 1975) and first major role (*Anthuleni Katha*,1976).
- Produced some of his biggest hits including *Muthu*,1995.

Kamal Haasan

- Considered to be his biggest rival in Tamil cinema but also someone Rajinikanth admires for his acting.
- Both acted in several hit films together in Tamil and Hindi.

Amitabh Bachchan

- Co-star of Rajinikanth's first Hindi film, *Andhaa Kaanoon* (1983) and several hit films thereafter; good friend and admirer.
- Several of Bachchan's Hindi films were remade in Tamil, starring Rajinikanth, which went on to become huge hits in Tamil (e.g., *Billa, Thee* and *Mr Bharath*).

Dhanush

- A huge star and acclaimed actor of Tamil cinema, Dhanush was Rajinikanth's son-in-law, married to his elder daughter, Aishwarya. Dhanush and Aishwarya announced their separation in January 2022.
- Yet to act with his father-in-law, he has produced Pa. Ranjith's *Kaala: Karikaalan* (2018), starring Rajinikanth.

S. Shankar

- Collaborator in the later phase of Rajinikanth's career; first joint venture was *Sivaji: The Boss* (2007), a massive hit.
- Director and creator of the *Enthiran/Robot* franchise; both films of the franchise are marvels of visual effects and among the most expensive and biggest hits of Indian cinema.

First experiment of colour films

The very first colour venture was by Madan Theatres of Calcutta (now Kolkata, West Bengal) in 1932. Their talkie feature *Bilwamangal* was sent abroad for printing. The Prabhat Company under V. Shantaram tried a colour-processed film, *Sairandhri*, which was sent to Germany for printing. The results of both were unfit for viewing.

First woman film-maker

Fatma Begum was the first woman to produce, direct and script a film in the silent era. She formed Fatma Film Corporation and made *Bulbule Paristan* in 1926.

SUPER 30

NATIONAL FILM AWARDS

The National Film Awards were instituted in 1954. In the last 30 years of our journey, we have chronicled the many winners of these awards.

In 1990

Dadasaheb Phalke Award: Akkineni Nageswara Rao
Film and Screenplay: *Marupakkam* (Tamil), directed by K. S. Sethumadhavan
Director: Tapan Sinha for *Ek Doctor Ki Maut* (Hindi)
Actor: Amitabh Bachchan for *Agneepath* (Hindi)
Actress: Vijayashanthi for *Karthavyam* (Telugu)
Music Direction: Hridaynath Mangeshkar for *Lekin...* (Hindi)
Lyrics: Gulzar for *Lekin...* (Hindi)
Popular Film Providing Wholesome Entertainment: *Ghayal* (Hindi), directed by Rajkumar Santoshi
Costume Design: Bhanu Athaiya for *Lekin…* (Hindi)
Film Critic: Shoma A. Chatterjee

In 2021

Dadasaheb Phalke Award: Rajinikanth
Feature Film: *Marakkar: Lion of the Arabian Sea* (Malayalam), directed by Priyadarshan
Screenplay (original): Kaushik Ganguly for *Jyeshthoputro* (Bengali)
Screenplay (adapted): Srijit Mukherji for *Gumnaami* (Bengali)
Dialogues: Vivek Ranjan Agnihotri for *The Tashkent Files* (Hindi)
Direction: Sanjay Puran Singh Chauhan for *Bahattar Hoorain* (Hindi)
Best Actor (Male): Manoj Bajpayee for *Bhonsle* (Hindi); Dhanush for *Asuran* (Tamil)
Best Actor (Female): Kangana Ranaut for *Panga* and *Manikarnika: The Queen of Jhansi* (both Hindi)
Music Direction: D. Imman for *Viswasam* (Tamil)
Background Score: Prabuddha Banerjee for *Jyeshthoputro* (Bengali)
Lyrics: Prabha Varma for *Kolaambi* (Malayalam)
Popular Film Providing Wholesome Entertainment: *Maharishi* (Telugu), directed by Vamshi Paidipally
Costume Design: Sujith Sudhakaran and V. Sai for *Marakkar: Lion of the Arabian Sea* (Malayalam)
Film Critic: Sohini Chattopadhyay

Gulzar: winner for best lyrics (1990)

TOP-GROSSING FILMS OF THE 2010s

Here is a look at the most successful Indian films between 2010 and 2020 – the highest earners at the global box office!

Year	Film	Original Language	Director	Worldwide gross (million ₹)*	Main Draw and Markets
2010	*Enthiran*	Tamil	S. Shankar	2,890	Rajinikanth and Shankar's collaboration with eye-popping special effects drew crowds all over India, thanks to language dubs.
2011	*Don 2*	Hindi	Farhan Akhtar	2,800	The sequel of the remake of a 1970s classic, this SRK-starrer was a craze all over the world.
2012	*Ek Tha Tiger*	Hindi	Kabir Khan	3,344	Salman Khan starred in a spy thriller and the film collected an astounding amount in India and abroad.
2013	*Dhoom 3*	Hindi	Vijay Krishna Acharya	5,892	The third film of a popular franchise that charmed Indians and NRIs across the world.
2014	*PK*	Hindi	Rajkumar Hirani	8,320	Box-office magic with Aamir Khan hitting the jackpot in China (besides India, of course).
2015	*Bajrangi Bhaijaan*	Hindi	Kabir Khan	9,691	A star vehicle for Salman Khan, which did exceptional business in China, the Middle East, North America and even Pakistan.
2016	*Dangal*	Hindi	Nitesh Tiwari	20,240	This Aamir Khan–starrer was very successful in India and even more so in China, making it the highest grossing Indian film of all times.
2017	*Baahubali 2: The Conclusion*	Telugu	S.S. Rajamouli	18,100	This sequel to the mythological drama, *Baahubali* (2015) was dubbed in multiple languages and created a passionate following all over.
2018	*2.0*	Tamil	S. Shankar	8,000	The sequel to *Enthiran* (2010), by the same director (S. Shankar) and actor (Rajinikanth), which did extremely well in India and overseas.
2019	*War*	Hindi	Siddharth Anand	4,755	This spy thriller combined typical Bollywood masala with eye-popping action, made tonnes of money in double-quick time, breaking records all the way.

*Figures have been rounded off to the nearest whole number.

LANGUAGE

First Indian film in English

Ardeshir Irani's *Noor Jahan*, directed by Ezra Mir in 1931, starring Mazhar Khan, Nayampally, Mubarak and Vimala was given an English version a year later for foreign markets.

First film in multilingual versions

J.B.H. Wadia's *Court Dancer* (*Raj Nartaki*), directed by Madhu Bose and featuring Sadhana Bose and Prithviraj Kapoor, was shot in Hindi, Bengali and English in 1941.

Music scores in most languages

Composer Bappi Lahiri has scored music in eight languages: Hindi, Bengali, Telugu, Tamil, Kannada, Malayalam, Punjabi and English. One of them was for the film *Lal Darja* in Bengali, which won the 1996 National Award and was produced by his wife, Chitrani Lahiri, and Dulal Roy.

Films edited in most languages/dialects
A. Sreekar Prasad (b. 12 March 1963) from Chennai, Tamil Nadu, has edited films in 17 languages: English, Hindi, Tamil, Telugu, Malayalam, Kannada, Odia, Assamese, Bengali, Punjabi, Nepali, Marathi, Sinhalese, Karbi, Mishing, Bodo and Pangchenpa.

A. Sreekar Prasad: editor of films in most languages/ dialects

FIRSTS

First cinemascope films
- Guru Dutt made *Kaagaz Ke Phool* in 1959 in black-and-white Cinemascope.
- Mahesh Kaul made *Pyar Ki Pyaas* in Cinemascope and colour in 1961.

First film in 70 mm
- The first Indian film in 70 mm (using the blowing-up method) was director Pachchi's *Around the World*, starring Raj Kapoor and Rajshri, in 1967. It was in Technicolor and had stereophonic sound.
- G.P. Sippy's *Sholay* in 1975 was shot on the 70 mm format in India, along with stereophonic soundtrack, the four channels of which could be connected to amplifiers in theatres. Those not equipped for it were provided flat (35 mm) single-track prints.

FILM CELEBRITIES WHO LEFT US

- **Rishi Kapoor** (1952–2020): Scion of Kapoor family went from teen heart-throb to romantic hero to offbeat character artiste over a nearly five-decade-long career in which he was part of some of Hindi cinema's most memorable films.
- **Sushant Singh Rajput** (1986–2020): Came from television and became a top star with both box-office hits and critically acclaimed films to his name. His promising career was cut short by his death.

Sushant Singh Rajput

- **Basu Chatterjee** (1927–2020): Doyen of 'middle of the road' cinema, he brought stories of regular, middle-class people to the silver screen and was hugely successful with films like *Rajnigandha*, *Chhoti Si Baat*, *Khatta Meetha* and *Baton Baton Mein*.
- **Saroj Khan** (1948–2020): Probably Bollywood's best-known choreographer, she played an important role in the careers of dancing divas like Sridevi and Madhuri Dixit in the 1980s and '90s.
- **Bhanu Athaiya** (1929–2020): India's first Oscar-winner in an individual capacity, she won the Best Costume Designer award for *Gandhi* but had a durable and memorable career in Bollywood, being responsible for some of the most iconic costumes from the 1960s to the early 2000s.

• Tarachand Barjatya's *Maine Pyar Kiya* (1989) was made in Cinemascope with a new system of four-track magnetic stereophonic sound. This could be fitted in theatres. Later, mobile equipment was provided for the stereophonic effect in small towns and touring cinemas.

First film serial

Rama Banvas (The Exile of Rama) was made by Patankar Friends and Company,

SPOTLIGHT ON BIOPICS

The first Indian film – *Raja Harishchandra* – was (sort of) a biopic! Biopics have always been a popular source of stories for cinema, and famous historical figures like Mahatma Gandhi, Jawaharlal Nehru, Bhagat Singh and Netaji Subhas Chandra Bose have been the subject of several biopics made in different languages.

Bhagat Singh had the honour of having three biopics releasing in the same year (2002): *The Legend of Bhagat Singh; 23rd March 1931: Shaheed; and Shaheed-e-Azam.*

In recent years, the rush for biopics has only increased and Hindi cinema has seen a wide range of characters being portrayed on screen. Here is a selection of the films and their subjects:

2017

■ *'Ek Thi Rani Aisi Bhi:* The personal journey of 'Rajmata' Vijayraje Scindia of Gwalior during the time of India's political integration and after ■ *Sachin: A Billion Dreams*: Sachin Tendulkar, cricketer par excellence ■ *Daddy*: Gangster Arun Gawli ■ *Haseena Parkar*: The sister of underworld mobster and alleged terrorist, Dawood Ibrahim.

2018

■ *Pad Man:* Arunachalam Muruganantham, a social entrepreneur who invented low-cost sanitary pads ■ *Omerta:* Global terrorist Ahmed Omar Saeed Sheikh (who was released in exchange for the passengers of the hijacked flight IC 814) ■ *Sanju:* Bollywood superstar Sanjay Dutt ■ *Soorma:* Indian hockey player Sandeep Singh who came back to the team after recovering from paralysis ■ *Manto:* Urdu author Saadat Hasan Manto.

2019

■ *The Accidental Prime Minister:* Former prime minister Manmohan Singh ■ *Thackeray:* Politician and founder of the Shiv Sena, Bal Thackeray ■ *Manikarnika: The Queen of Jhansi*: One of India's first freedom fighters ■ *Kesari:* Havildar Ishar Singh, who led 20 men in the Battle of Sargarhi ■ *PM Narendra Modi:* Narendra Modi, the 14th prime minister of India ■ *Super 30:* Mathematician and educator, Anand Kumar.

2020

■ *Tanhaji:* Maratha warrior Tanhaji Maulsare ■ *Shakuntala Devi:* The human calculator, a globally renowned mathematician ■ *Gunjan Saxena: The Kargil Girl:* Gunjan Saxena, ex-IAF pilot who participated in the Kargil war ■ *Soorarai Pottru:* Pioneer of low-cost aviation in India, Captain Gopinath ■ *Chhapaak:* Acid-attack survivor, Laxmi Agarwal

Record Rewind

Longest running films

1990

G. P. Sippy's *Sholay* ran for five-and-a-half years from 1975 in a combined run of regular and special shows at a theatre in Bombay (now Mumbai), Maharashtra.

2020

Yash Raj Films' *Dilwale Dulhania Le Jayenge (DDLJ)* is still running at Mumbai's Maratha Mandir theatre – twenty-five years after the film premiered there. The single show at 11:30 a.m. is the result of an arrangement between Yash Raj and the theatre, which agreed to run the film there for (what seems like) eternity. But even before the arrangement, *DDLJ* ran to semi-packed houses for over two decades, making it the longest running film in the world.

and released on 14 September 1918. It was shown in four parts, each running for a period of a few weeks.

First one-actor, one-set film

Sunil Dutt made *Yaadein* in 1964, the first experiment of its kind in the world with only one actor (himself) emoting on only one set. In 2005, Kannada film *Shanthi* became the second movie with a single actor to be released.

First adult film

Social Evil, a docudrama, was made by the Social Purity League of Bombay (now Mumbai, Maharashtra) in 1929 to provide information about sex problems. It was also the first sex educational film. It was shown free of cost and was the first film given the label 'For Adults Only'.

First use of surround sound

Khuda Gawah (1992), when screened in big cities, used stereophonic four-track sound with special gadgets fitted into theatre walls and ceilings. This gave the impression of sound surrounding the audience, to give more impact to scenes of fights, horse rides and the Afghan game of buzkashi, among others.

First animated film

Directed by R.C. Boral, *On a Moonlit Night* (1934) was the first Indian animated film with a soundtrack.

First 3D film

My Dear Kuttichathan (1994), produced by M.C. Punoos and directed by his son, Jijo, was the first Indian 3D film.

First cinema hall

Elphinstone Picture Palace was started by J.F. Madan in Calcutta (now Kolkata, West Bengal) in 1905. It was renamed Minerva and later called Chaplin Cinema. This piece of history was demolished in 2013 by the Kolkata Municipal Corporation (which owned it).

First studio

Khan Bahadur Ardeshir Irani (1886–1969) started his first studio – Star Films – in 1920.

Soumitra Chatterjee (1935–2020)

Soumitra Chatterjee

Once described as Satyajit Ray's 'one-man stock company', Chatterjee had as impressive a body of work with other film-makers as he had with Ray. He debuted as Apu in *Apur Sansar* and immediately became a star for his portrayal of the legendary character from Bengali literature. In a career spanning seven decades, Chatterjee played diverse roles in Bengali films, and critical acclaim and international recognition for them made him one of Indian cinema's best-known faces globally. A popular star of several superhit romantic comedies, he also played Feluda, the popular detective created by Ray. Along with cinema, he acted in theatre, often writing and directing the plays, many of which are classics of Indian theatre. Beyond acting, he wrote and recited poetry, edited journals, hosted radio shows and even painted in watercolour – making him an icon in his hometown Kolkata.

Notable films: *Apur Sansar* (1959), *Jhinder Bondi* (1961), *Saat Paake Bandha* (1963), *Charulata* (1964), *Akash Kusum* (1965), *Teen Bhubaner Parey* (1969), *Aranyer Din Ratri* (1970), *Sonar Kella* (1971), *Kony* (1984), *Wheelchair* (1994), *Asukh* (1999), *Podokkhep* (2006), *Belaseshe* (2015), *Ahalya* (short film) (2015)

First censor boards

- The first film censor boards were set up in Bombay (now Mumbai), Calcutta (now Kolkata) and Madras (now Chennai) in 1920.
- Film censorship was centralized under a central board, the Central Board of Film Certification (CBFC) in Bombay (now Mumbai), Maharashtra, in 1951.

INTERNATIONAL

First Academy Award

Bhanu Athaiya (1929–2020) became the first Indian to win an Academy Award (Oscar) in 1983, for designing the costumes for the acclaimed film *Gandhi* (1982), directed by Sir Richard Attenborough.

First to act in a Hollywood film

The first Indian actor to feature in a role that was credited in a Hollywood movie was Dastagir, who was also known as 'Sabu' in the film world. He hailed from the princely state of Mysore (now Mysuru, Karnataka). He acted in Robert Flaherty's film *Elephant Boy* (1937). His other films include *The Thief of Baghdad* (1940) and *Jungle Book* (1942).

First foreign film award

The film *Seeta* (1934) by East India Films Co., Calcutta (now Kolkata, West Bengal), which was directed by Debaki Bose, was the first film from India to win the gold medal at the Third International Exhibition of Cinematographic Art in Venice, Italy, in 1935.

PERFORMANCE

First woman stunt actor

Nadia, India's legendary woman stunt actor, has been described as 'Zorro, Tarzan and John Wayne rolled into one'. Born Mary Evans, she swung from chandeliers, jumped from moving trains and performed many other incredible stunts that earned her the title of 'Fearless Nadia'. Her best-known film is the 1935 hit, *Hunterwali*.

A poster of *Hunterwali* featuring Nadia: first woman stunt actor

Roles in most number of films

Manorama, a popular Tamil heroine of the 1950s and '60s, who subsequently became a character actor, acted in more than 1,000 films. Her first film was *Malayitta Mangai* (1958).

Most films as a lead

Prem Nazir, born Abdul Kadar in Chirayinkeezhu, Kerala, played the lead role in as many as 600 films. He has starred in Malayalam, Tamil, Kannada and Telugu films, and has co-starred with at least 85 female actors.

Maximum roles in a single film

- Harish Raj enacted 16 roles in the Kannada film *Shri Sathyanarayana*, which released on 11 March 2016. He essayed the role of the lead character named Sathyanarayana as well as 15 other cameo roles with screen time ranging from one to five minutes for each.
- Priyanka Chopra played 12 roles (one for each sign of the zodiac) in Ashutosh Gowariker's *What's Your Rashee?* (2009).
- Kamal Haasan played 10 roles in K.S. Ravikumar's *Dasavathaaram* (2008), including one as former US president George W. Bush.

And the Emmy Goes to...

Delhi Crime released on Netflix in 2019 and became the first Indian programme to win an International Emmy. The fictionalized crime drama series depicting the aftermath of the Delhi gang rape in 2012, stars Shefali Shah, Rasika Dugal, Adil Hussain, Rajesh Tailang, Avijit Dutt, Gopal Dutt, Jaya Bhattacharya, Denzil Smith and Yashaswini Dayama in pivotal roles. The seven-episode show was the winner for the Best Drama Series award at the 48th International Emmy Awards, held virtually in 2020. *Four More Shots Please* (Amazon Prime Video, 2019) was nominated for the International Emmy for Best Comedy and actor Arjun Mathur was nominated for the International Emmy for Best Performance by an Actor for his role as Karan Mehta in *Made in Heaven* (Amazon Prime Video, 2019).

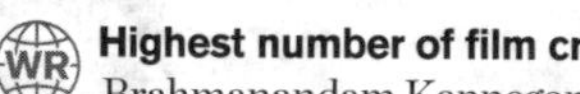

Highest number of film credits

Brahmanandam Kanneganti, a well-known comedian of Telugu cinema, has received credits for acting in 1,146 films. He achieved this feat over an acting career of more than 30 years and he is still going strong.

Highest-earning actor

Forbes magazine placed Akshay Kumar sixth on its list of the 'World's Highest-Paid Actors of 2020', with estimated earnings of US $48.5 million (₹356.97 crore), making him the country's highest-earning actor. His earnings include remuneration for films (ranging from US $5 to 10 million – around ₹35.58 to 71.17 crore), endorsement deals and appearance fees. Kumar was also the only Indian, placed 52nd, on the 'Forbes Celebrity 100' list for 2020.

OTT Platforms: Watch This Space

Netflix streamed its first Indian original series, *Sacred Games* (2018), with A-list stars like Nawazuddin Siddiqui and Saif Ali Khan in lead roles, forever blurring the line between cinema and TV. Netflix's rival Amazon Prime Video's first Indian original was *Inside Edge* (2017), a large-canvas thriller about a T20 league, combining cricket, politics, sex, crime and Bollywood. The promise of creative freedom due to less stringent censorship, a global audience, freedom in deciding duration and format – all this and more have drawn pretty much every major film-maker to streaming platforms. In the last three years, almost every major TV network and production house in India has launched its own streaming service. With the global pandemic shutting down movie theatres across the country, streaming services received a fresh boost with a slew of major films going direct-to-streaming and triggering off a head-to-head battle with cinemas. Every major language saw the release of at least one major star vehicle, many even coinciding with the festival weekends like Independence Day, Eid, Diwali and Christmas. As theatres reopen and mega blockbusters return to the big screen, their battle with the streaming services will get more exciting. Keep watching!

Film	Platform	Language	Director	Cast
Gulabo Sitabo	Amazon Prime Video	Hindi	Shoojit Sircar	Amitabh Bachchan, Ayushmann Khurrana
Dil Bechara	Disney + Hotstar	Hindi	Mukesh Chhabra	Sushant Singh Rajput, Sanjana Sanghi
Shakuntala Devi	Amazon Prime Video	Hindi	Anu Menon	Vidya Balan, Sanya Malhotra, Jisshu Sengupta
Gunjan Saxena: The Kargil Girl	Netflix	Hindi	Sharan Sharma	Janhvi Kapoor, Pankaj Tripathi, Angad Bedi
Sadak 2	Disney + Hotstar	Hindi	Mahesh Bhatt	Sanjay Dutt, Alia Bhatt, Aditya Roy Kapur
Sufiyum Sujatayum	Amazon Prime Video	Malayalam	Naranipuzha Shanavas	Jayasurya, Aditi Rao Hydari
Soorrai Pottru	Amazon Prime Video	Tamil	Sudha Kongara	Suriya, Aparna Balamurali, Paresh Rawal
Laxmii	Disney + Hotstar	Hindi	Raghava Lawrence	Akshay Kumar, Kiara Advani
Ludo	Netflix	Hindi	Anurag Basu	Abhishek Bachchan, Rajkummar Rao, Pankaj Tripathi, Fatima Sana Sheikh

SUPER 30

THE KHANS: 30 YEARS OF BOLLYWOOD'S TRIUMVIRATE

Between 1988 and 1989, two superhit films and one TV serial with a cult following announced the arrivals of three future megastars. *Qayamat Se Qayamat Tak*, *Maine Pyar Kiya* and *Fauji* were not the first on-screen appearances of Aamir Khan, Salman Khan and Shah Rukh Khan respectively, but they sealed their stardom. It took SRK three more years to hit the big screen (with *Deewana*), but it was almost as if people were expecting him. Just as Amitabh Bachchan brought in the 'Angry Young Man' to counter the romantic wave unleashed by Rajesh Khanna, these three stars brought romance back to Bollywood – making chocolate-

THREE DECADES THREE KHANS

The chart shows their continuing magic at the box office. In the years from 1988 to 2019, twenty-three of India's top-grossing films have starred one of them. The years of release not shown indicate that the top-grossing film in those years was not a Khan-starrer.

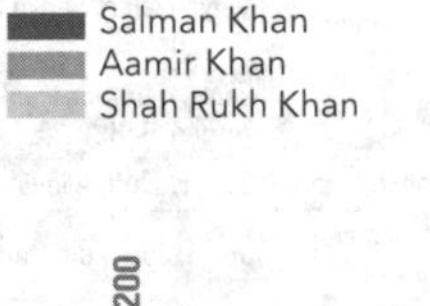

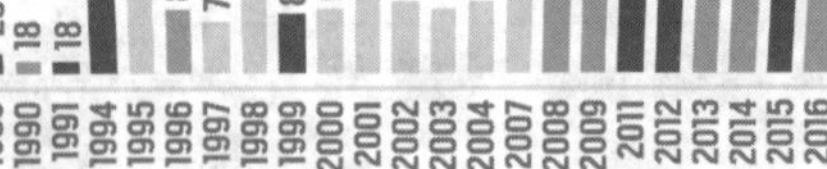

Year indicates year of release for period 1988–2019. Figures in ₹crore

box heroes and teenybopper romances popular again.

While all of them started with a similar lover-boy image, their appeals soon diverged. SRK created a splash as a crazed lover (in *Baazigar* and *Darr*) but soon became the dutiful lover with an international appeal (*Dilwale Dulhania Le Jayenge* and *Dil To Pagal Hai*), which continued well into the 2010s. When Salman's brawny-romantic image turned stale, he became a masala-action hero who created box-office records with every film (*Wanted*, *Dabangg*, the Tiger franchise, *Sultan*). Aamir Khan started slow but brought a seismic change in the industry when he refused to work in more than one film at a time, and all the stars eventually followed suit. This led to both box-office bonanzas as well as great reviews. At the end of 2020, he had three critically acclaimed films (*Dangal*, *Secret Superstar* and *PK*) in the five top-grossing Indian films of all time.

Beyond box-office success, the three Khans have been cultural prime movers in India, influencing fashion and expressions apart from driving popular discourse. With interests in film production, sports and TV, they are far from being done.

Irrfan Khan (1967–2020)

In one of his last interviews, Soumitra Chatterjee expressed his willingness to work in Hindi films – which he had avoided all his life – if he had a co-actor like Irrfan. It was a compliment Khan would have cherished had he not passed away so early.

Irrfan Khan made his debut with a small part in Mira Nair's *Salaam Bombay!* (1988) but did not make it big immediately. He was initially noticed for his roles in TV shows like *Chandrakanta, Banegi Apni Baat* and *Bharat Ek Khoj*. His breakthrough came in an international production, Asif Kapadia's

Irrfan Khan

The Warrior, soon making him one of India's crossover stars. He acted in blockbusters like *Slumdog Millionaire* (2008), *The Amazing Spiderman* (2012), *Jurassic World* (2012) and *Life of Pi* (2015) besides arthouse classics like *The Namesake* (2006) and *The Darjeeling Limited* (2007). His Hindi film career was as impressive with offbeat films like *Maqbool* (2004), *The Lunchbox* (2012), *Paan Singh Tomar* (2013) and *Hindi Medium* (2017) becoming sleeper hits thanks to his enigmatic presence. Irrfan had the endearing quality of being identifiable in all his roles – be it in films, advertisements or music videos – making him one of the most-liked stars of Hindi cinema, which became abundantly evident in the outpouring of grief on social media on his untimely demise.

Record Rewind

Oscars tally

1990

Bhanu Athaiya shared the award for Best Costume Design with John Molle for Richard Attenborough's biopic *Gandhi* in 1982, becoming the first Indian to win an Oscar award.

2020

Danny Boyle's *Slumdog Millionaire* got three Indians on the Oscar podium: Gulzar and A.R. Rahman for Best Original Song ('Jai Ho'), A.R. Rahman for Best Original Score and Resul Pookutty for Best Sound Design.

Satyajit Ray was awarded an honorary Oscar in 1992, for his lifelong contributions to world cinema. He received the trophy from his hospital bed.

Oldest debut actor in a film

Ninety-three-year-old Chinnakrishnan Kaliyaperumal from Ariyalur, Tamil Nadu, acted as the lead in the Tamil short (20-minute) film, *93* Not Out* (2016), directed by engineer-turned-film-maker Arudra Saravanakumar. It is the story of an old man who, after a pacemaker implant, has the desire to ride a cycle and to buy a book, and how he finally achieves it at the age of ninety-three. The film has won several awards, besides a jury mention at the Dada Saheb Phalke film festival 2017, and has been showcased at national and international film festivals.

WR Most pairings

Actors Prem Nazir and Sheila paired together in 107 films and hold a world record for the highest number of movies done together. An interesting comparison is with the Hollywood husband–wife pair of Charles Bronson and Jill Ireland, who starred together in 15 films.

LENGTH

Films with longest footage

- Vithalbhai Jhaveri's documentary on Mahatma Gandhi, *Mahatma: Life of Gandhi, 1869–1948* (1968), was 5 hrs 30 mins long, and was broken up into many segments for general screening.
- Gemini's *Chandralekha* in 1948, the first big Hindi film from south India, ran for over 3 hrs.
- R.K. Films' productions *Sangam* (1964) and *Mera Naam Joker* (1970) were the first to be run with two intervals.

Longest film title

The Telugu film *Shree Shree Rajadhiraja Shree Shree Madana Kamaraja Shree Shree Vilasa Raja Shree Shree Madhubana Raja Shree Shree Krishnadeva Donga Raja*, with a title comprising 20 words in 118 characters (excluding spaces) was released in Chennai, Tamil Nadu, in December 1994.

Shortest film title

Kannada director Upendra's film *A* (1998), a runaway blockbuster, was a psychological romance and the first film to have a single letter of the alphabet as the title. This record has been emulated by director Shankar's Tamil film *I* (2015).

Most episodic films in a single feature film

BSB Films, a film-making company from Jaipur, Rajasthan, made a Hindi-language film, *Prabhu Mahaveer Ki Divyavani* under their banner. The film features 23 episodic films as part of it, the highest in a single feature film. The film has a total duration of 157 mins and 27 secs. However, the release of the film was delayed due to the COVID-19 pandemic.

WR **Shortest film**

Pamarthi Sivanaga Rao (b. 28 May 1978) from Vijaywada, Andhra Pradesh, released the shortest film, *The Farmer*, with a total duration of nine seconds. The first three seconds cover the CBFC certificate, making the actual time of the film to be six seconds. The film was released in five theatres on 7 February 2020 under the banner of Siva Arts Creations.

MUSIC

Maximum songs recorded in a day

In 1993, playback singer Kumar Sanu recorded 28 songs in a single day at the Musicians Studio in the Juhu area in Mumbai, Maharashtra. The session was made for Sterling Records and Cassettes and the chief recordist was Vishram More, who was on the machines for 24 hours.

WR **Most number of songs in a Hindi film**

Madan Theatre's film *Indra Sabha*, made in 1932, featured 71 songs.

S.P. Balasubrahmanyam (1946–2020)

Usually referred to as SPB, S.P. Balasubrahmanyam was one of India's best-loved singers, popular across four south Indian languages and Hindi. He won six National Awards (for best male playback) in four different languages, the number of awards being second only to K.J. Yesudas and the number of languages second to none. Balasubrahmanyam was already a popular singer in the south with several awards to his credit when he broke into Hindi cinema with *Ek Duuje Ke Liye* (1981). His career continued unabated across film industries and he was the voice for stars as diverse as Kamal Haasan and Salman Khan. His partnerships with composers Ilaiyaraaja and A.R. Rahman were legendary and yielded many hits. He is one of the claimants for the record of the highest number of playback songs recorded. While it has not been possible to verify the exact number of songs, their longevity and popularity is evident. Beyond singing, he was also seen in short acting roles and was much in demand as a dubbing artiste.

National Award-winning films: *Sankarabharanam* (1979, Telugu), *Ek Duuje Ke Liye* (1981, Hindi), *Saagara Sangamam* (1983, Telugu), *Rudraveena* (1988, Telugu), *Sangeetha Sagara Ganayogi Panchakshara Gavai* (1995, Kannada) and *Minsara Kanavu* (1996, Tamil)

S.P. Balasubrahmanyam

Most Tickets Booked in Advance

BookMyShow, a ticket-booking app, saw a record sale of advance tickets when it sold over 1,000,000 tickets online in a day. The tickets for Marvel's *Avengers: Endgame* were booked in a manic frenzy as soon as they were available on 22 April 2019. The sale averaged about 18 tickets per second!

Most prolific lyricist
Shitala Pande, who is better known as Sameer, holds the world record for writing lyrics for the most number of songs. Starting in 1983 with the Hindi film *Bekhabar*, he had written lyrics for over 3,500 songs for Hindi and Bhojpuri films by 15 December 2015. He has also written lyrics for music albums. He has done the highest number of films (146) with the music director duo Anand–Milind, writing around 899 songs for them.

MAKERS

Most film-making aspects handled
Narasimha Raju (b. 4 March 1955) from Bengaluru, Karnataka, handled 18 segments of film-making for Kannada film, *The Fire* (2017). He was credited for direction, story, screenplay, dialogues, fight, stunt, direction of cinematography, editing, special effects, grading, DI (digital intermediate), sound, dubbing, voice dubbing, BGM (background music) placing, rerecording, poster design and acting in the film. The 113-minute film participated in the 10th Bengaluru International Film Festival from 22 February to 1 March 2018.

Largest film city/studio
Ramoji Film City in Hyderabad, Telangana, spread over a little more than 2,000 acres 810 hectares), is the largest film city/studio in the world. It has sound stages and permanent sets ranging from railway stations and temples to gardens and residential streets, among others. It is also a tourist attraction because of its unique cinema-like experience.

Tallest film cut-out
The world's tallest cut-out – 65.5 m (215 ft) high – advertised a film in Thiruttani town, Tiruvallur District, Tamil Nadu. It featured actor Suriya (in a folded *veshti,* holding a flaming torch) to promote his film *Nandha Gopalan Kumaran (NGK)* in 2019.

Most films produced
Well-known director and producer of Telugu films, Dr D. Ramanaidu holds the record of having produced 110 films (including 11 dubbed films) in six languages over a span of 36 years. He started his career with *Anuragam* in 1963.

Most expensive film produced
Directed by S. Shankar, *2.0* (2018) is a sequel to *Enthiran* (2010). Starring the

legendary Rajinikanth and Bollywood star Akshay Kumar in leading roles, the movie was made on an estimated budget of ₹540 crore (5,400 million). It was made in three languages (Tamil, Telugu and Hindi) and two formats – 3D and 2D.

First Indian winner of the Legion d'Honneur

Satyajit Ray is the only Indian film personality to be awarded the Commandeur level of France's highest civilian award, the Legion d'Honneur on 2 February 1989 – one of only two film-makers in the world to have received it. He is also the only film-maker to receive the Magsaysay Award.

SUPER 30

THE SAGA OF THE STAR KIDS

One of the entries in the 1990 edition of the *Limca Book of Records* was for the largest film family: 'Veteran actor Prithviraj Kapoor's family tree forms the biggest clan of actors in filmdom. The youngest name in that entry was Sanjana Kapoor, who had just taken baby steps in the film industry with a leading role in *Hero Hiralal* (1988). In the next 30 years, three Kapoor kids – Karisma, Kareena and Ranbir – entered Bollywood with resounding success. The year 1989 was also the time when *Filmfare* instituted two awards for the best debutants, male and female. This award has been a roll-call of filmi families, with their scions entering Bollywood. Till 2020, ten out of 31 female award winners and a whopping 18 out of 27 male award winners have been from film families. Also, every variation and combination of family relationships have been awarded:

- Father–daughter: Saif Ali Khan (1994) and Sara Ali Khan (2019)
- Mother–son: Bhagyashree (1990) and Abhimanyu Dassani (2020)
- Siblings: Akshaye Khanna (1998) and Rahul Khanna (2000)
- Step-siblings: Bobby Deol (1996) and Esha Deol (2003); Shahid Kapoor (2004) and Ishan Khatter (2019)
- Cousins: Kareena Kapoor (2001) and Ranbir Kapoor (2008); Priyanka Chopra (2004) and Parineeti Chopra (2012)

Uncle–nephew: Aamir Khan (1989) and Imran Khan (2009)

Star kids are a part of the industry since the 1940s, when Prithviraj Kapoor's son, Raj, became India's youngest producer by raising money independently. The surname would have helped, but the senior Kapoor did not help his son financially.

As more star children did well, more began to enter the industry with varying degrees of success. The1980s were particularly busy with big-ticket launches featuring Kumar Gaurav, Sunny Deol and Sanjay Dutt, among others. The decade also saw the launch of three directors from major film families: Sooraj Barjatya (grandson of Tarachand Barjatya and son of Rajkumar Barjatya), Aditya Chopra (son of Yash Chopra) and Karan Johar (son of Yash Johar).

In recent times, star kids have come under fire for nepotism – for instance, nepotism was said to be a major reason behind actor Sushant Singh Rajput's death, allegedly by suicide. Large groups on social media threatened to boycott films with star kids and trailers featuring them received an avalanche of 'dislikes'. Whether this 'click-tivism' will actually translate into a real drop in viewership of films starring star kids remains to be seen.

Maximum feature films directed

Dr Dasari Narayana Rao, who completed his 100th directorial venture *Lankeswarudu* (1989) in Telugu, has directed the most films. Among women, Vijaya Nirmala has directed 35 films in Telugu and Tamil.

WR Largest film poster

Global United Media Co. Ltd, in collaboration with Impresario Event Management (I) Ltd, unveiled a 75.28 m (247 ft) long and 63.39 m (208 ft) wide poster of *Baahubali,* to mark the launch of the film's Malayalam audio, at the Sacred Heart College football field in Thevara, Kochi, Kerala, on 27 June 2015. The poster, designed by the director of the movie, S.S. Rajamouli, and made by Sign Maker Digital Solution at Vyttila, Kochi, took 30 hrs to print.

Maximum screens

Tubelight, Salman Khan's film, directed by Kabir Khan (2017), beat S.S. Rajamouli's *Baahubali 2: The Conclusion* (2017) by releasing on the maximum number of screens worldwide: 1,200 screens abroad, 100 more screens than *Baahubali 2* (with 1,100 screens).

Maximum horror films produced

The seven Ramsay brothers made more than 30 horror films on low budgets, of which the well-known ones are *Purana Mandir* (1984), *Veerana* (1988) and *Purani Haveli* (1989).

WR Largest producer of feature films

The Indian film industry is a front runner when it comes to producing feature films. India produced a whopping 1,986 feature films, in over 20 languages and varied genres in 2016 alone. The numbers have been increasing regularly over the years and tower over and above those of any other country by at least 1,000 more films.

PHOTOGRAPHY

First photo exhibition

The first All-India Photographic Exhibition was organized by the Photographic Society of India in Bombay (now Mumbai, Maharashtra) in 1856. The exhibition was inaugurated by the then Governor General of India, Lord Canning.

First use of the daguerreotype

Within a year of its first use in England, the daguerreotype (early photography process using an iodine-sensitized silvered plate and mercury vapour) was used in Calcutta (now Kolkata, West Bengal) in January 1840. They were brought to document India's architecture and landscape.

First commercial photographer

Lala Deen Dayal of Hyderabad, the 'photographer of kings', is India's best-known photographer from the British times. His career began in the mid-1870s and he went on to set up studios in three cities in three different states – Indore (Madhya Pradesh), Bombay (now Mumbai, Maharashtra) and Hyderabad (Telangana).

He was appointed as the photographer to the viceroy of India in 1885. His lens captured India's rich culture, architecture and landscapes.

Earliest recorded commercial album

A gilded and bound album of a hundred photographs of Indian buildings, scenery, races, costumes and bazaar incidents was sold for ₹12 in Bombay (now Mumbai, Maharashtra) in 1884. It used to be a popular souvenir among the British.

Earliest commercial studio

Bourne and Shepherd was well known for its studio portraits of the ruling classes, both Indian and British. Its photographers attended royal events, state visits and the imperial durbars of 1877, 1903 and 1911. When India gained Independence, Bourne and Shepherd was bought over by Indian proprietors, who operated under the same name in Calcutta (now Kolkata, West Bengal). The studio was closed down on 20 April 2016 after 176 years of operations.

 **Early digital cameras in the 1970s weighed around** 

kg.

Earliest book on photography

Pagoda Hallibee written by R.B. Gakley in 1859 was the first book on photography published in India.

Oldest extant portrait studio

Sir Victor Sassoon, who was passionate about photography and constructed many public buildings in Bombay (now Mumbai, Maharashtra), set up Hamilton Studios in the E.D. Sassoon Building, which he owned, in 1928. Photography sessions at these studios were held by appointment, and the rich and famous personalities of Bombay were seen coming for quick and glamorous shoots. Currently, the studios are run by Ajita Madhavji and can be found on Ballard Estate.

First woman photographer

Homai Vyarawalla (1913–2012), born into a priestly family in Navsari, Gujarat, in December 1913, was the first Indian woman photojournalist to document Indian life. Her very first photographs were published in *Bombay Chronicle* in 1936. She and her husband even covered wartime activities for *The Illustrated Weekly of India* and the Far Eastern Bureau of the British Information Service. *Life* and *Time* magazines also featured her photographs of the Indian independence movement.

Homai Vyarawalla: first woman photographer

First Kodak Express outlet

Established in 1978, Skylab was the first colour lab in suburban Bombay (now Mumbai), Maharashtra. Initially the lab catered to advertising agencies, but gradually the focus shifted to providing a photo colour lab and studio for amateurs and ordinary people.

First personal studio
Maharaja Sawai Man Singh of Jaipur was a 19th-century amateur photographer. Thousands of photo-plates of his work were discovered in the 1980s in the storerooms of the City Palace, the royal residence in Jaipur. He recorded the life of the people in his state.

First photo film–manufacturing company
Hindustan Photo Films Manufacturing Co. (HPF), a public sector unit, was set up in 1960 at Ooty (now Udhagamandalam), Tamil Nadu, to make photosensitive materials for the Indian film industry, still photography and X-ray films for medical and industrial use. It introduced the Indu brand of raw film.

World Photography Day is observed on 19 August every year.

First course in photography
The first photography course began in Elphinstone College, Bombay (now Mumbai, Maharashtra) in 1855. The J.J. School of Art, Bombay, and the Madras School of Art, Madras (now Chennai, Tamil Nadu), began similar courses around the same time.

First PhD in photography
Tulika Sahu, a student of the Government Arts and Crafts College, Lucknow, Uttar Pradesh, was the first woman to be awarded a PhD in photography. On 10 February 2015, she was declared eligible to receive her doctoral degree by the University of Lucknow for her research work on 'The pictorial movement in photography vis-à-vis painting between the late 19th and the early 20th century'.

Largest photography show
In August 2005, as many as 2,500 images by 250 Indian photographers were showcased in 'The Incredible Moment' exhibition. The aim of this fund-raiser for People for Animals was to change the way people look at photographs. It was organized in association with *The Times of India*. Photographers whose works were up for sale included Raghu Rai, Atul Kasbekar and Pablo Bartholomew.

NATIONAL PHOTOGRAPHY AWARDS 2019

Award Category	Award Winner
Lifetime Achievement	Ashok Dilwali
Professional Photographer of the Year	S.L. Shanth Kumar
Amateur Photographer of the Year	Gurdeep Dhiman
Special Mention (Professional)	Arun Sreedhar, P.V. Sunderrao, Kailash Mittal, Mihir Singh and Ranita Roy
Special Mention (Amateur)	V. Ravi Kumar, S. Neelima, Manish Jaisi, Mahesh Balasaheb Lonkar and Avijit Datta

First photographic society

The Bombay Photographic Society was founded in October 1854 with British Captain Harry J. Barr, as its first president. It had more than 200 people as members, many of them Indian. Divisions in Madras (now Tamil Nadu) and Bengal (now West Bengal) followed in 1856.

WR **Largest camera museum**

The Museo Camera Centre for the Photographic Arts, Gurugram, Haryana, houses more than 2,500 cameras, which is the world's largest collection of vintage and other cameras on display. Inaugurated on 27 September 2019, it is spread over 1672.2 sq. m (18,000 sq. ft) of built-up space and can accommodate up to 200 visitors at a time. It is a collaboration between acclaimed photographer Aditya Arya and the Municipal Corporation of Gurugram.

Largest private collection of images from India

Well-known theatre personality Ebrahim Alkazi (1925–2020) had the largest personal collection of more than 40,000 photographs from India, partly housed at the research and library facility at Sepia International in New York, USA, and the rest in London and New Delhi. A large part comprises 19th-century images from the subcontinent. The photographs are stored in albums, photographically illustrated books and as images.

Ebrahim Alkazi: held the largest private collection of images from India

Largest unit for photo production/distribution

The Photo Division of the Ministry of Information and Broadcasting, Government of India, provides photographs to media units, and Central and state government departments. In the year 2019–20, it acquired 259,757digital images in-house and supplied 13,212 digital prints.

Most people in a selfie

During Ragam, the annual cultural festival at the National Institute of Technology Calicut (NITC) in Kozhikode, Kerala, actor Sreenath Bhasi clicked a selfie, with a camera mounted on a selfie stick, at the Open Air Theatre on the campus, with 2,151 students on 26 March 2015.

Highly Commended Photo: Wildlife Photographer of the Year

Aishwarya Sridhar's photograph titled *Lights of Passion* won the Highly Commended award at the Wildlife Photographer of the Year 2020, announced on 13 October 2020. The awards are developed and produced by the Natural History Museum in London, UK. Sridhar, a 23-year-old from Panvel, Maharashtra, is the first Indian woman to win this award. Her image of an indigenous plum tree, shot against the verdant backdrop of Bhandardara, Maharashtra, depicts the golden glow reflected on a tree from the bioluminescence of fireflies. She took 27 images over a 24-second exposure and combined them.

BUT FIRST, LET ME TAKE A SELFIE

Selfies took the world by storm and have captured the rapt attention of people. Thirty years ago, no one could have imagined the present scenario. We have come a long way from painstaking self-portraits or timed photographs to digital selfies, which are just a click away. Self-photographs with ordinary cameras were popular in Japan and East Asia since the 1990s, but the first known use of the term 'selfie' was in 2002 on the Australian Internet. India, unfortunately, leads the world charts for the most selfie-related deaths and accidents. Researchers from the All India Institute of Medical Sciences (AIIMS) in 2018 found in a study titled 'Selfies: A Boon or Bane?' that about half of the 259 reported selfie deaths and accidents between 2011 and 2017 occurred in India. Most of these 'killfies' were caused by drowning, being hit by a train or car, or falling from a height. Many such cases go unreported too as 'death by selfie' isn't recognized as an official cause of death.

Marathon photography – models

Photographer Vivek Ashok Somani (b. 7 August 1995) from Surat, Gujarat, successfully conducted a marathon photo shoot on 12 May 2019. He clicked 11,076 photographs in 15 hrs 55 mins. Using a Nikon D5300 camera, and an 18–55 mm lens, he photographed 70 models at Future Dance Studio, Surat.

Marathon photography – city/structures

Hariohm N. Gurjar from Vadodara, Gujarat, set out to document his city's various dimensions at 7:00 a.m. on 14 March 2014. He travelled 95 km in the city, shooting for 13 hrs. He captured 3,555 unduplicated images of people, architecture, markets, monuments and more.

WR **Largest collection of cameras**

Dilish Parekh, a photojournalist from Mumbai, Maharashtra, has a collection of 4,425 cameras, some dating back to 1906. It includes brands such as Leica, Nikon, Kodak, Canon, Hasselblad and Royal Mail Postage, and types such as watch, binocular and button cameras. He began the collection in 1977 with 600 cameras gifted by his grandfather.

Longest negative

The negative of the group photograph of the ninth Lok Sabha, comprising 500 members is 1.8 m (6 ft) long and 0.3 m (1 ft) wide. The camera used by 75-year-old Agya Ram Dutta was also unique. The 1925 Kodak circuit camera revolved from one side of the frame to the other so that a person sitting on one side of the group could run to the other side and be shot twice in one frame.

Longest photograph

India's longest single-frame colour photograph is 2.7 m x 0.58 m (9 ft x 1 ft 10 in.). It captures 117 elected members of the Punjab Vidhan Sabha with Governor S. Nath and Chief Minister Beant Singh. Tejbans Singh Janhar shot the photo using a Swedish Hasselblad camera, with an interchangeable German glass lens. The

First Permanent Photo Exhibition in Space

WR Dr Hersh Chadha (b. 27 November 1957) is the first person to organize a permanent photo-exhibition in space on the International Space Station (ISS). Five images of different flowers were sent to the ISS on 16 October 2016 with the ISS 49/50 team. The purpose of this was to help the astronauts staying in space for months to remain connected with nature. On 1 March 2017, Dr Chadha was honoured by the Yuri Gagarin Cosmonaut Training Centre, Russia, for this.

contact print was magnified 3,500 times using a special enlarger to project the picture on a wall.

Most-travelled photographer

Benoy K. Behl, art historian and photographer, covered 1,193,949 km to document the Buddhist and Hindu art heritage of Indian and Asian monuments from April 2001 to April 2020. He has documented the Buddhist heritage of 20 regions in 18 countries, and delivered 579 lectures in 225 universities, museums and cultural institutions in 34 countries. He has made 145 documentary films on Indian art and cultural history. His exhibitions have been held in 325 major cultural institutions in 74 countries. He has taken more than 53,000 photographs of monuments and art heritage in India and across the world.

AWARDS AND HONOURS

First Indian fellow of the British Photographic Society

Sir Prodyot Coomar Tagore (1873–1942), a prominent landowner of the time in Calcutta (now Kolkata, West Bengal), was an art collector besides being a keen photographer. He was the first Indian to be elected a Fellow of the British Photographic Society in 1896. He had a studio in his Tagore Castle home and exhibited his works. He was the founder and first president of the Academy of Fine Arts, Calcutta.

First winner of the Wildlife Photographer of the Year title

The Wildlife Photographer of the Year, organized by the Natural History Museum, London, UK, is one of the most famed contests in the world. Rajesh Bedi became the first Indian to win the grand title in 1986 for his photograph of the Asiatic black bear.

First Asian to win the International Photography Awards

Sharad Haksar from Chennai, Tamil Nadu, won gold, silver, two bronzes and

21 nominations in the International Photography Awards 2004. India finished fourth behind the USA, the UK and Canada that year.

First winner of the Académie des Beaux-Arts Photography Award – William Klein

Raghu Rai won the first-ever Académie des Beaux-Arts Photography Award – William Klein (Fine Arts Academy award for Photography). He was named the laureate and was awarded the prize at the Palais de l'Institut de France on 30 October 2019. The award carries a prize money of 120,000 euros (approximately ₹10.79 crore). It was instated in honour of William Klein, a celebrated America-born French photographer and film-maker.

First winners of the Pulitzer Prize for feature photography

- Anushree Fadnavis and Adnan Abidi were part of the Reuters team that won in the 'Breaking News Photography' category of the Pulitzer Prize for photography in 2020, for their work on the Hong Kong protests.
- Dar Yasin, Mukhtar Khan and Channi Anand from Associated Press won in the 'Feature Photography' category of the Pulitzer Prize for photography in 2020 for their coverage of Jammu and Kashmir.

PAINTING AND CRAFT

FIRSTS

Earliest paintings discovered

Painted pottery, mostly in fragments, excavated at Mohenjo-Daro, Chanhu-daro, Harappa and other places in the Indus Valley, are dated to 3000–2250 BCE.

Earliest rock paintings

The largest and the oldest collection of rock paintings in India is at Bhimbetka near Bhopal, Madhya Pradesh. The paintings have been found in more than 700 rock shelters, dated to 30,000 years ago, depict people's everyday lives such as hunting, dancing and decoration of bodies.

Oldest extant murals

Two 1,000-year-old Chola paintings, which were unearthed at the Brihadisvara Temple in Thanjavur, Tamil Nadu, are believed to be the oldest existing mural paintings. They depict two women who are watching a procession from a balcony.

Earliest use of tempera method

The Ajanta Caves are rock-cut Buddhist cave monuments in Aurangabad, Maharashtra, dating back from the second century BCE to about 650 CE. The paintings in these caves used the tempera method. A rough mud plaster containing some organic matter like cow dung and animal hair was first pressed on the surface of the rocks and then a coat of fine lime plaster was laid over it. It was allowed to dry thoroughly before applying colour. The scenes represented in these caves are mostly from Buddhist texts and events from the Buddha's life.

First Mughal illuminated manuscript

Emperor Humayun engaged Mir Sayyid Ali and a group of painters to paint the

'*Dastan-i-Amir*' (the story of Amir Hamza), which featured as many as 1,375 miniatures painted on cotton cloth in the Persian Safavid style.

First painting gallery

Maharaja Ram Singh, a 19th-century king of Jaipur, built a unique hall displayed with paintings, called the Ram Vilas, in the garden of the Ram Niwas Bagh Palace. The walls of this hall were covered with imitations of several Greek, Roman, Persian and Chinese paintings.

First realist painter

Raja Ravi Varma (1848–1906) from the princely state of Travancore (now in Kerala) painted themes mainly from Indian mythology and legends in the realistic style of the West, making him the first realist painter in India and the pioneer of a new movement in Indian art. In 1904, the then viceroy Lord Curzon bestowed the Kaisar-i-Hind Gold Medal on him.

First fine arts exhibition

The first fine arts exhibition was held in the Public Library, Calcutta (now Kolkata, West Bengal), on 1 February 1831, by the Brush Club, with paintings drawn by foreign artists in India.

First modern art school

The Mechanical Institute was founded by Frederik Corbyn and Tarapada Chakrabarty in Calcutta (now Kolkata, West Bengal) on 2 February 1839. First named 'Society for the Promotion of Industrial Art', it was finally called the School of Industrial Art on 16 August 1854. It held its first exhibition from 22 January to 3 February 1855.

First auction of contemporary Indian paintings abroad

Sotheby's hosted the first ever auction of contemporary Indian paintings in New York on 12 June 1995. The 38 artists whose works were displayed included Jogen Chowdhury, M.F. Husain, Arpita Singh, Ganesh Pyne, S.H. Raza and Jamini Roy.

First academy for visual arts

The Lalit Kala Akademi, which was established in Delhi in 1954, started its work by organizing national exhibitions of contemporary Indian art. It also gives awards and honours, conducts Triennale-India (a global art show) and a Rashtriya Kala Mela (national art fair), where artists from across the country come together to present their work.

First art summit

The first India Art Summit was held at Pragati Maidan, New Delhi, during 22–24 August 2008. The 34 exhibition galleries exhibited over 550 artworks and sold more than half of them. The summit was brought to India by Hanmer MS&L Communications Pvt. Ltd.

First art bank

The Art Bank, set up in 2007 and started by curator Adishwar Puri, primarily for novice collectors apprehensive of making bad choices, now has corporations and government institutions, banks and hospitals as clients. The artists who register benefit by receiving 50 per cent of the rental value of the work.

First artists' village

The Cholamandal Artists' Village at Injambakkam, Madras (now Chennai), Tamil Nadu, was established in May 1966 by K.C.S. Paniker, then principal of the Madras College of Arts and Crafts, to help talented young artists develop their work. He had already founded the Artists' Handicrafts Association in 1964, with around 40 artist members. They held an exhibition of their work, especially batiks, and bought the land at Injambakkam to build a community of artists.

First cartoon gallery

The Indian Institute of Cartoonists opened its 186 sq. m (2,000 sq. ft) gallery, the Indian Cartoon Gallery, at Midford House, Bangalore (now Bengaluru), Karnataka, on 16 August 2007. It has a seminar hall, a library and a cartoon bibliography from across the world.

First officially recognized female graffiti artist

Kajal Singh from New Delhi, who goes by the moniker 'Dizy', is the first recognized female graffiti artist from India. Her art form includes the use of bright colours and different font styles that instantly pop out. Besides India, she has left her signature in countries like Germany, China, the USA, Russia and Indonesia, among others. She was part of the Indo-German Hip-Hop Urban Art Project (2012), Each One Teach One (2013), 25 Years of the Berlin Wall (2014), Hip-Hop Cultural Exchange (2015) and On The Run Exhibition (2016). She was honoured as the 'First Lady' of graffiti in India by the Ministry of Women and Child Development, Government of India, on 20 January 2018.

Kajal Singh: first officially recognized female graffiti artist

LARGEST, LONGEST AND MARATHON ARTWORK

Largest collage – group

Forty-four students and three teachers from Christ University, Bengaluru, Karnataka, created the largest collage on 2 March 2018. The collage, which measured 85.34 m x 9.14 m (280 ft x 30 ft), was made in 2 hrs 12 mins.

Largest quilling artwork – solo

Dr Jiji S. Deepak from Thrissur, Kerala, created a 6.71 m x 3.66 m (22 ft x 12 ft) artwork, using the paper-quilling technique. It took him 45 hrs 10 mins over a period of nine days. The artwork is based on the theme 'Mother Earth'.

Largest doodle art – group

Students from the NIFT- TEA College of Knitwear Fashion, Coimbatore, Tamil Nadu, created a doodle artwork measuring 89 sq. m (960 sq. ft),

India's First Public Art District

The Lodhi Art District in New Delhi, inaugurated by the Central Public Works Department on 1 March 2019, is the first public art district in the country. Conceptualized and realized by the St+Art India Foundation, a not-for-profit that works on art projects in open spaces, the artistic transformation of the district began in 2015. The area was chosen for its unique characteristics of being non-gated and green, with large pavements, low traffic and large walls, and therefore ideal for creating a public space open for all. With the support of the local community, and civic and cultural bodies, more than 50 artists of 23 nationalities have reimagined the area's facades by creating murals that bring the viewer into a contemporary urban art museum. A total of 56 walls with an area of approximately 16,310 sq. m (175,565 sq. ft) have been painted by the artists. This was followed by the Mahim (East) art district in Mumbai, Maharashtra; the Maqta art district in Hyderabad, Telangana; and the Panjim (Panaji) art district in Goa.

Largest Zentangle Art

Twenty-five students from the NIFT-TEA College of Knitwear Fashion, Tiruppur, Tamil Nadu, created the largest Zentangle artwork measuring 185.8 sq. m (2,000 sq. ft), with 'Make In India' as its theme. The students completed the artwork in 34 hrs during 17–18 August 2018.

depicting the historical development of the Tiruppur cluster, over 36 hrs during 14–15 July 2016.

Largest Rubik's cube mosaic*
On 3 February 2019, R City Mall, Mumbai, Maharashtra, created a Rubik's Cube mosaic in its premises, using 24,000 cubes. The mosaic was made by 23 college students in 11 hrs 15 mins. It measured a total of 65 sq. m (700 sq. ft).

Largest pencil drawing – solo
Megha Harsha (b. 12 July 1992) from Bikaner, Rajasthan, created the largest pencil drawing by an individual. The artwork measured 455.21 sq. m (4,900 sq. ft) and was completed in 86 hours over the course of 17 days from 16 October to 1 November 2019 at Bikaner Boys School, Bikaner. The artwork created awareness regarding the United Nations' Sustainable Development Goals (SDGs) related to climate change, safety of women and pollution, among others.

Largest pencil portrait – solo
Aman Gulati from Lakhimpur, Uttar Pradesh, created the largest pencil portrait, which measured 410.25 sq. m (4,416 sq. ft). The portrait of Mahatma Gandhi

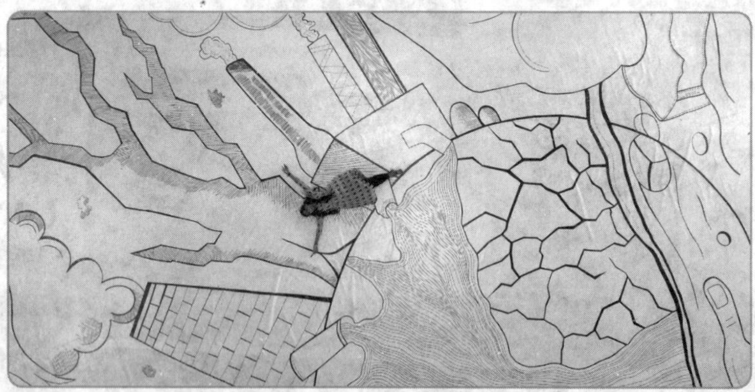

Megha Harsha: artist of the largest pencil drawing – solo

*This is a one-time category. Further and future claims for this category will not be accepted.

was completed on 2 October 2019 to mark the celebration of Gandhiji's 150th birth anniversary.

Largest Phad painting - solo*

Abhishek Joshi (b. 30 April 1975) from Shahpura, Bhilwara district, Rajasthan, made the largest traditional Phad painting on a handmade canvas measuring 2.6 sq. m (27 sq. ft). It took 18 months, from 23 March 2017 to 25 September 2018, to complete the painting using natural stone colours. It depicts the glorious history of Mewar. Abhishek, who has held many exhibitions and workshops and won several awards, comes from a family of Phad painters of Shahpura, dating back to the 10th century.

Largest Warli painting – solo

Mihir Mahendra Walavalkar (b. 5 May 1995) from Mumbai, Maharashtra, created a 245.2 sq. m (2,640 sq. ft) piece of Warli art in 70 hrs 43 mins over three days at the Joggers Park, Thakur Complex. He started his painting on 5 May 2019 and finished on 8 May 2019.

Largest Warli painting – solo

Largest graffiti wall

As a part of the Bharat Ka Benz Yatra, an initiative by Daimler India Commercial Vehicles Pvt. Ltd and their brand, Bharat Benz, a graffiti wall measuring 947.58 sq. m (10, 200 sq. ft or 1,700 ft x 6 ft), was spray-painted and written on with markers by more than 3,000 drivers, helpers, mechanics and fleet owners over 38 days. The endeavour was undertaken to spread awareness about road safety among drivers and other stakeholders.

Marathon pencil-art session

Dinesh K. Gupta (b. 22 May 1978) from Mumbai, Maharashtra, completed 201 drawings in a marathon pencil-art session, starting at noon on 5 April 2019 and ending at noon on 6 April 2019. Using 6B pencils, he sketched famous people, natural sceneries, religious figures and still life on A3 sheets. The event took place at Dr Babasaheb Ambedkar Art Gallery, Kalyan, Maharashtra. The total break time was 1 hr 50 mins.

Largest wall painting –single wall – solo

NIFT-TEA College of Knitwear Fashion, Tiruppur, Tamil Nadu, created a wall painting measuring 46.82 sq. m (504 sq. ft) in 250 hrs over 25 days in the college premises. The painting was made by R. Sanjay Kumar for the college. He started his painting on 17 June 2020 and finished on 11 July 2020.

Largest easel

Rajasekharan Parameswaran from Kanniyakumari District, Tamil Nadu, built an easel, 17.22 m (56 ft 6 in.) high and 9.45 m (31 ft) wide, on which he painted a 7.62 m (25 ft) high and 15.24 m (50 ft) wide artwork of E.M.S. Namboodiripad, Kerala's first chief minister. He completed it in five days in April 2008 and it took two months to set it up near Neyyattinkara (Thiruvananthapuram–Kanniyakumari NH47).

Longest strip of cartoons – solo*

Rajasekaran K. (b. 26 April 1989) from Tamil Nadu completed a 352.46 sq. m (3,794 sq. ft) drawing of cartoon characters at the Main Convention Centre, L&T Construction, Manapakkam, Chennai, Tamil Nadu, from 8:00 a.m. on 22 April 2019 to 5:45 p.m. on 26 April 2019. It took him 75 hrs 51 mins to complete the artwork. He sketched and coloured 1,153 cartoons of Cartoon Network characters like Tom and Jerry, The Powerpuff Girls and The Flintstones, among others.

Rajasekaran K.: artist of the longest cartoon strip

Largest art competition – multiple venues

Sakal Media Pvt. Ltd organized the largest drawing and painting competition at several locations across Maharashtra and Goa on 16 December 2018. The Sakal Chitrakala Spardha (held annually for the last 33 years) took place at 2,000 locations between 9:00 a.m. to 12:30 p.m. and 763,264 students from classes 1 to 10 participated. The painting centres were schools across the districts of Pune, Satara, Ahmednagar, Nanded, Mumbai, Nagpur, Akola, Jalgaon, Kolhapur, Solapur and Nashik, besides the state of Goa.

*This is a one-time category. Further and future claims for this category will not be accepted.

SUPER 30

SUDARSAN PATTNAIK: MARKING PERMANENCE IN SAND

Born in Odisha, Sudarsan Pattnaik is a world-renowned sand artist. Pioneering the art form in the country, he began charting his career in the early 1990s and in 1994, set up the Sudarsan Sand Art Institute in Puri, Odisha. Having represented India in over 60 international championships and festivals around the world, he has made an indelible mark for himself and the country. Most of his artworks are made on the Puri Beach and he has graced the pages of many editions of the *Limca Book of Records* with his artwork. At the helm of this artform, he has been appreciated and awarded all over the world. He has created awareness about world peace, climate change, pollution and landmark global events through his artwork and was awarded the Padma Shri in 2014.

Here's a look at Pattnaik's sand sculptures over the years.

- *Top right*: The tallest sandcastle (48 ft 9 in./14.86 m tall) to symbolize the message of world peace (2017);
- *Right*: The largest sand turtle (55 ft/16.76 m long and 30 ft/ 9.14 m wide) to create awareness about the impact of plastic pollution in oceans (2018).

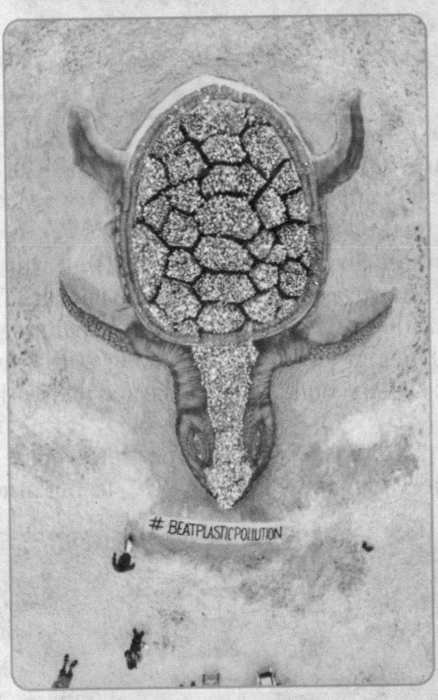

Largest sand artwork

Sudarsan Pattnaik (b. 15 April 1977) from Puri, Odisha, created the largest sand artwork, measuring 557.42 sq. m (6,000 sq. ft), at Puri Beach, Odisha, on 24 December 2020, to create awareness about mask usage during the COVID-19 pandemic.

Largest sand artwork

Sandeep Sinha: artist of the largest oil painting – solo

Largest oil painting – solo

Sandeep Sinha (b. 6 January1982), an artist from Pune, Maharashtra, made an oil-on-canvas painting titled 'HiMakhan'. The artwork measures 48.78 sq. m (525.06 sq. ft) and is a single-scene painting of the Himalayas. He began in August 2018 and completed it by October 2018. It was exhibited at the Raja Ravi Varma Art Gallery, Pune. Sinha dedicated this work to acid attack survivors.

Largest acrylic painting – portrait – solo

Rajeev Ranjan (b. 1 March 1977) from Purnea, Bihar, who is popularly known as

Largest acrylic painting – portrait – solo

Rajeev Raj, created a painting of former prime minister Atal Bihari Vajpayee with acrylic paints on canvas. He began painting on 3 December 2018 at 4:43 p.m. and completed the artwork at 11:18 p.m. on 4 December 2018 at the Vidya Vihar Residential School. He took 31 hrs 17 mins and used 225 pieces of canvas, each 0.762 m x 0.762 m (2.5 ft x 2.5 ft). The artwork covered a total area of 130.6 sq. m (1,406 sq. ft).

Marathon sand painting

Neha Umak (b. 22 December 1990) from Thane, Maharashtra, completed 133 pieces of sand painting artwork in 24 hrs 47 mins 19 secs from 9:16 a.m. on 30 June 2019 to 10:05 a.m. on 1 July 2019 at Kundan Talent Academy, Thane. The total break time was 1 hr 37 mins 40 secs. The artworks were a mix of portraits and sceneries.

Record Rewind

Highest price at an auction for an Indian piece of art

1990

A five-headed statue of Shiva fetched a record £319,000 (approx. ₹88.5 lakh/8.85 million) at a Sotheby's, London, UK, auction in January 1989.

2017

Vasudeo S. Gaitonde (1924-2001) was regarded as India's leading abstract painter. An untitled painting by him was sold for ₹209.3 million (20.93 crore) in December 2015 at a Christie's auction in Mumbai, Maharashtra. The oil-on-canvas painting was bought by an anonymous buyer and is the most expensive Indian painting sold since 1965.

***(Left):* Artworks from marathon sand painting**

Largest Traditional Floor-Art Portrait – Solo

Saundarya Bansod (b. 29 October 2006) from Ahmednagar, Maharashtra, created the largest traditional floor art portrait measuring 41,487 sq. m (446,562 sq. ft). It depicts the image of Chhatrapati Shivaji Maharaj. The artwork was completed in 30 days, starting on 26 January 2019 and ending on 25 February 2019.

Marathon acrylic painting
Ramita Bhaduri (b. 27 September 1971) from Nazir Bagan, Kolkata, West Bengal, completed 213 artworks, using acrylic paints in 24 hrs from 4:05 p.m. on 5 June 2018 to 7:35 p.m. on 6 June 2018. The total break time was 3 hrs 30 mins.

Largest natural colours painting – solo
Sangeeta Gupta (b. 25 May 1958) from New Delhi, created a painting using natural indigo titled, 'Aadiyogi Shiv – A Journey in Cosmic Indigo'. The artwork measures 169.15 sq. m (1,820.78 sq. ft) and is painted on *khadidar* fabric. She began the artwork on 25 February 2020 and completed it on 4 March 2020 at the Shilpi Sansthan, Rataliya Village, Jaipur, Rajasthan. The artwork was made to create awareness for sustainable living, using natural colours and dyes.

Largest origami artwork – widest – solo
Radhika Chintalapati, an artist from Hyderabad, Telangana, created a butterfly with nine folds in 15 mins at Glendale International School on 21 February 2019.

Marathon sculpture-making
Ramita Bhaduri (b. 27 September 1971) from Nazir Bagan, Kolkata, West Bengal, completed a marathon sculpture-making session during 29–30 April 2019, using clay and cement. She logged 15 hrs of sculpting and 3 hrs break time (30 mins after every 3 hrs), making 29 sculptures in all. The average dimensions were 30.48 cm x 30.48 cm x 33.02 cm (12 in. x 12 in. x 13 in.) for standing figures, 25.4 cm x 25.48 cm x 38.1 cm (10 in. x 12 in. x 15 in.) for lying down ones and 25.4 cm x 25.4 cm x 25.48 cm (10 in. x 10 in. x 12 in.) for sitting figures.

GOVERNMENT

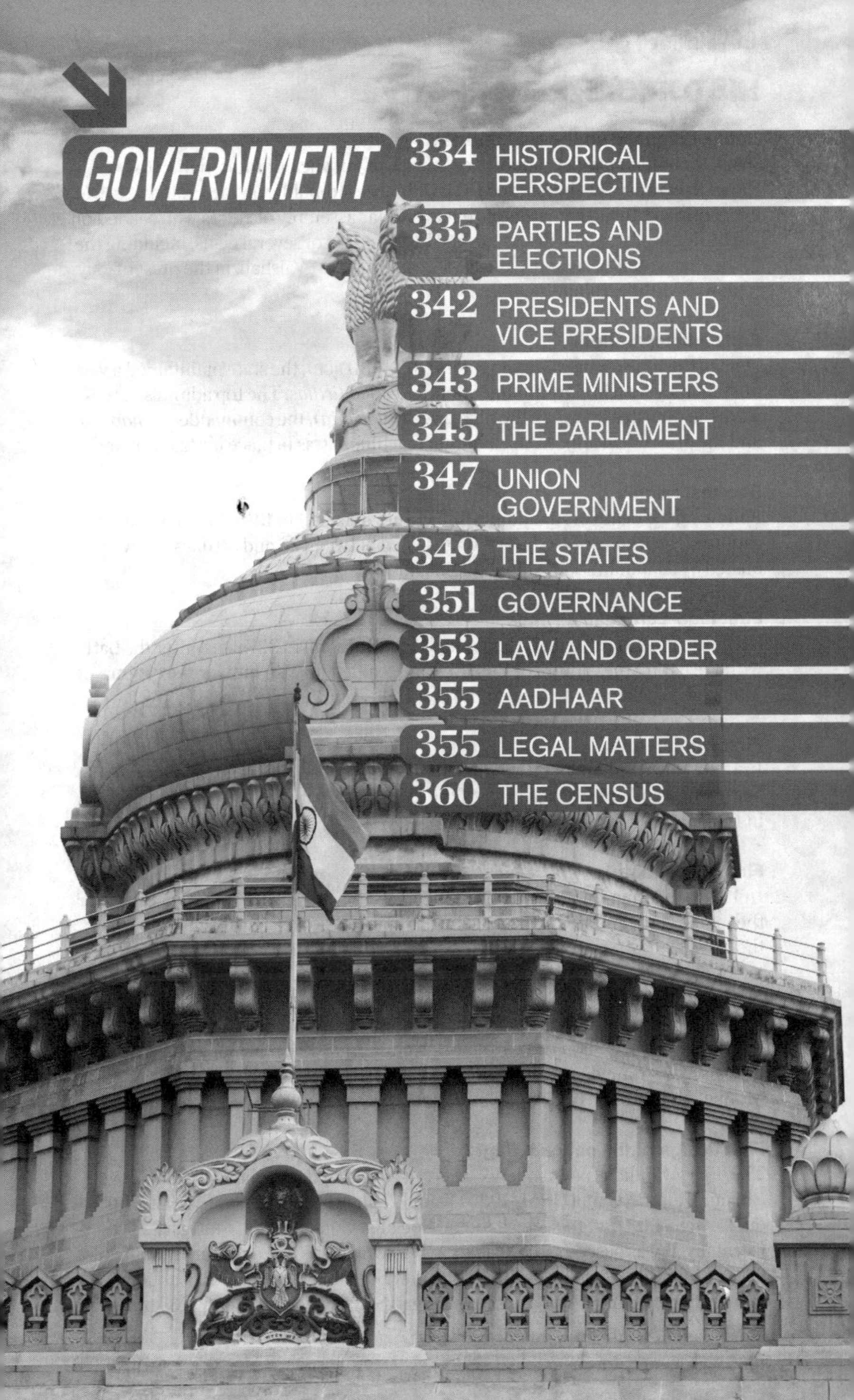

HISTORICAL PERSPECTIVE

Earliest republic on the subcontinent

Vrijji, a *mahajanapada* ('republic' or 'kingdom') of ancient India, dating to the sixth century BCE, is believed to be the earliest republic on the Indian subcontinent. It had no monarch, but a popular assembly of elders who carried on the business of state. Vrijji was formed by the union of several clans, including the Lichchhavis, Jnatrikas and Videhas. Its capital was at Vaishali, in the present-day region of Mithila, Bihar.

Early administration

During the time of the Mauryan rulers (322–180 BCE), the state maintained a vast bureaucracy with important functionaries called *tirtha*s. The top administrators were the minister (*mantri*), the high priest (*purohita*), the commander (*senapati*) and the prince (*yuvaraja*). An elaborate machinery was in place for taxation too.

Shortest reign

Following the death of Alauddin Khilji (Khilji dynasty) in 1316, Malik Kafur captured the throne of Delhi. His reign lasted between 25 and 30 days. He was ousted by Alauddin's son, Shihabuddin Omar.

First Indo-European alliance

Chandragupta Maurya met Alexander III of Macedon in 327 BCE – after the battle with Porus and the capture of Punjab – and teamed up with him for the capture of Magadha in what may be termed the first Indo–European treaty.

First woman ruler

In 1236, Razia Sultan of the Mamluk dynasty ascended the Delhi throne, making her the first and only female ruler of the Delhi Sultanate and the first woman ruler in India.

First satyagraha

In 1917, Mahatma Gandhi organized the first satyagraha in Champaran, Bihar, for the indigo cultivators, to protest against British laws governing the cultivation of the plant.

First colonial rule

Colonial rule in India took seed with the establishment of the first European trading centre in Quilon (now Kollam), Kerala, in 1502 by the Portuguese. Dom Francisco de Almeida was appointed the first Portuguese viceroy in India by King Manuel I of Portugal in 1505.

First design of the national flag

The 'Flag of Indian Independence' was raised by freedom fighter Bhikhaiji (or Bhikaji) Rustam Cama (1861–1936) from Bombay (now Mumbai, Maharashtra) on 22 August 1907 at the International Socialist Conference in Stuttgart, Germany. It was based on the 'Calcutta flag', which was one of the first unofficial flags of India, designed by Sachindra Prasad Bose and Hemchandra Kanungo, and hoisted on 7 August 1906 at Parsi Bagan Square, Calcutta (now Kolkata, West

Bengal). Cama's flag featured three colours: the top band was green, the middle one was saffron and the bottom one was red. The upper band had eight lotuses, symbolizing the eight provinces of British India. The middle band had the words *Vande Mataram* in Devanagari script, and the lower band had a crescent and a sun, representing Islam and Hinduism, respectively. The flag went through many versions before its present form.

Longest colonial rule

Goa, Daman and Diu were under colonial rule for the longest period in Indian history – over 450 years. For over a decade after the British had left India, the Portuguese ruled these pockets as 'Estado da India Portuguesa' (the Portuguese State of India). They were liberated by the Indian Army on 19 December 1961.

First War of Independence

The country's First War of Independence, which British historians called the Sepoy Mutiny or the Revolt of 1857, was the first organized fight against the colonial rulers, and an important milestone in the long struggle for independence.

First rendition of the national song

'*Vande Mataram*', India's national song, composed by Bankim Chandra Chatterjee and published for the first time in his work *Anandamath,* was first sung at the Indian National Congress session in 1896 in Calcutta (now Kolkata, West Bengal).

First rendition of the national anthem

'*Jana Gana Mana*', India's national anthem composed by Rabindranath Tagore, was sung for the first time on 27 December 1911 at the Calcutta (now Kolkata, West Bengal) session of the Indian National Congress. The song was formally adopted in its Hindi version by the Constituent Assembly as India's national anthem on 24 January 1950.

First Republic Day parade

India became an independent nation on 15 August 1947, and declared itself a sovereign and democratic republic with the promulgation of the Constitution of India on 26 January 1950. The first Republic Day parade was held five years later in 1955 at Rajpath, which became its permanent venue.

PARTIES AND ELECTIONS

First political organization

The first political organization was the Zamindari Association of Calcutta (now Kolkata, West Bengal). Formally launched in 1838, it was a body of landlords, which changed its name to Landholders' Association shortly after its inception. Its principal organizers were Radhakanta Deb and Prasanna Kumar Tagore. Set up to defend the landlords against the so-called pro-peasant policies of the government, it became defunct in 1851.

Oldest political party

Allan Octavian Hume, a member of the Imperial Civil Service, initiated the events that led to the formation of the first political party in India. Speaking out against

British policies in India, in 1883, he exhorted Calcutta University graduates to form their own national political movement. This led to the first session of the Indian National Congress in Bombay (now Mumbai, Maharashtra) in 1885.

A.O. Hume: one of the founders of the first political party

First party constitution

The first constitution of the Indian National Congress was drawn up in 1908, after the split in the party between the moderates and the extremists in the 1907 session held in Surat, Gujarat.

First woman president of the Indian National Congress

British socialist and women's rights activist Annie Besant, who was elected president of the Indian National Congress in 1917, was the first woman to head the party.

First communist party

According to the Communist Party of India (Marxist), M.N. Roy, Virendranath Chattopadhyay and Abani Mukherjee set up a communist party in Tashkent, Uzbekistan, in 1920. However, the Communist Party of India goes by the belief that the first communist party in India was established by Satyabhakta, a left-wing Congressman, in Kanpur, Uttar Pradesh, in December 1925.

First woman to address a session of the Indian National Congress

Kadambini Ganguly, who was the first Indian woman doctor, was the first woman to address an open session of the Indian National Congress held in Calcutta (now Kolkata, West Bengal) in 1901, when she moved the vote of thanks.

Longest-serving president of the Indian National Congress

Sonia Gandhi, the Italian-born Indian politician and wife of former Indian prime minister Rajiv Gandhi, is the longest-serving president of the Indian National Congress. She headed the party from 1998 to 2017. She was named the president again in August 2019. With her at the helm, the Congress-led United Progressive Alliance (UPA) was victorious in the 2004 and 2009 general elections.

First Political Party to Host a Digital Conclave

The Telugu Desam Party (TDP), a regional political party active in Andhra Pradesh and Telangana, became the first political party in the country to organize a digital political conclave on 27 and 28 May 2020 amid the COVID-19 lockdown. Called the Digital Mahanadu 2020, the party's annual meeting was kicked off at their headquarters in Mangalagiri, Andhra Pradesh, with a flag hoisting followed by a videoconference with around 14,000 party cadre and leaders. Mahanadu, the birth anniversary of the party's founder president N.T. Rama Rao, is organized on 28 May every year since 1982. The party also celebrated and honoured Chandrababu Naidu for 25 years of service as the party president.

First chief election commissioner

Sukumar Sen (1898–1963) was India's first chief election commissioner from 21 March 1950 to 19 December 1958. Under his leadership, the Election Commission of India conducted India's first two general elections during 1951–52 and 1957. He also administered the first parliamentary elections in Sudan in 1953.

First general election

India went to the polls as a free country for the first time during 1951–52, with 314 constituencies with one seat, 86 constituencies with two seats, and one with three seats. There were also two nominated Anglo-Indian members. The Election Commission of India recognized 14 political parties as multi-state parties and 39 parties as state parties. Voting was based on the 'balloting system', i.e., casting votes in ballot boxes allotted to the respective candidates.

Longest tenure as chief election commissioner

K.V.K. Sundaram, India's second chief election commissioner, served for eight years, nine months and 11 days, from 20 December 1958 to 30 September 1967.

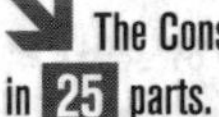

The Constitution of India is the world's longest written constitution, with 448 articles in 25 parts.

Shortest tenure as chief election commissioner

V.S. Ramadevi, India's first woman chief election commissioner (acting), held the post of chief election commissioner for 17 days from 26 November 1990 to 12 December 1990.

First use of single ballot paper and single ballot box

The general election of 1962 introduced the single ballot paper system, in which the voter had to mark one choice from the candidates and drop the paper in a ballot box. Earlier, during the 1951–52 and 1957 Lok Sabha elections, there were separate ballot boxes for each candidate with his/her name and party symbol on them.

First use of indelible ink

Indelible ink was used for the first time in the third Lok Sabha elections in 1962. Mysore Paints and Varnish Limited, based in Mysore (now Mysuru), Karnataka, was authorized to manufacture the ink. This continues to date.

First electronic voting machines

Electronic voting machines (EVMs) were used for the first time in the assembly by-elections in Kerala in April 1982. The machines were introduced by the Electronics Corporation of India Ltd (ECIL).

First app launched for voter vigil

For the first time in elections, an application called 'cVIGIL' was launched for citizens to report any malpractice or violation of the model code of conduct before or during elections. This Android-only app includes a combination of live photo/video and time-stamping with auto-location. A government official is bound to respond within 100 minutes. Launched in July 2018, the app was rolled out across India before the 2019 Lok Sabha election.

First 'Others' category of voters
A third gender category of voters, called 'Others', was introduced in the electoral rolls in 2014. As many as 28,314 voters enrolled in this category in 2014 and 38,970 voters in 2019.

First teenage vote
The 61st amendment of the Constitution of India in 1989 lowered the voting age for election to the Lok Sabha and the state legislative assemblies from 21 years to 18 years. As a result, 35.7 million voters in the age group of 18–21 years voted.

First NOTA option
The 2014 general elections were the first to offer Indian voters the option of 'None of the Above' (NOTA), also known as the 'against all' or a 'scratch' vote internationally. The NOTA option provides a neutral vote to those electors who do not wish to vote for any candidate on the electoral ballot. Around 1.04 per cent of voters polled NOTA in the 2019 elections.

Record Rewind

Women members in the Lok Sabha

1991

The 1991 general election saw 36 women members in the Lok Sabha, which was 7 per cent of the total number of seats.

2019

The 2019 election saw the highest number of women Lok Sabha members. They won 78 seats, making up 14.6 per cent of the total seats.

First woman to be elected to a legislative body
Indian women were allowed to vote and be elected in the provincial legislatures for the first time in 1926. Following this, the Indian Women's Association (IWA) put forward candidates and Dr Muthulakshmi Reddy became the first woman to be elected to an Indian legislative Council. Indian women won the right to full franchise in 1952 and voted in the first general election in 1951–52.

Highest voter turnout in the Lok Sabha general election
The 2019 general election had the largest voter turnout to date with 613,136,854 voters, constituting 67.1 per cent of the total electorate.

Lowest voter turnout in the Lok Sabha general election
In the 1951–52 general election, only 44.87 per cent of the electorate was recorded as having cast their votes.

Most female candidates in a Lok Sabha general election
The 2019 general election registered 723 female candidates.

Most women elected in a Lok Sabha general election
Seventy-eight women were elected in the 2019 Lok Sabha general election, making it the election with the highest number of successful female candidates.

LOK SABHA ELECTION 2019

The most expensive election

WR The 2019 Lok Sabha election was estimated to be the most expensive election in the world. An estimated ₹55,000 crore (550 billion) was spent during the elections, according to a report by the Centre for Media Studies.

First transgender election ambassador

Gauri Sawant, a transgender activist from Mumbai, Maharashtra, was appointed as the first transgender election ambassador in the country.

Voter-verifiable paper audit trail in all constituencies for the first time

The Election Commission of India set up the voter-verifiable paper audit trail or VVPAT system in all constituencies in 2019. The VVPAT prints a slip with the serial number, name and symbol of the candidate for whom the vote was cast.

First EVMs/ postal ballot papers with photographs of candidates

For the first time in the history of elections in India, the EVMs/postal ballot papers carried the photographs of all the candidates in the constituency. This was done to enable the voters to identify the political leaders and to avoid confusion between candidates with similar names.

EVM FOR FAIR ELECTIONS

First conceived in 1977 by the Election Commission of India (ECI), the Electronic Voting Machine (EVM) was developed and demonstrated by the Electronics Corporation of India Ltd (ECIL) in 1980. Acting as a replacement for paper ballots and manual voting, EVMs were used for the first time in the assembly by-elections in Kerala in 1982. Introduced in Indian elections between 1998 and 2001 in a phased manner, EVMs, which are portable and have reportedly 275 safety protocols to make them tamper-proof, have been used in all general and state assembly elections in India since 2014. Manufactured by Bharat Electronics Limited, Bengaluru, Karnataka, and ECIL, Hyderabad, Telangana, EVMs have reduced electoral fraud and made elections fairer. To date, more than 315 crore (3.15 billion) votes have been cast on EVMs.

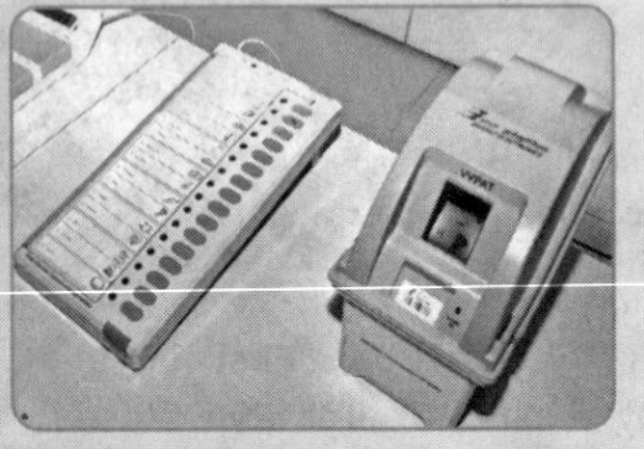

Fewest women elected in a general election
Only 19 women were elected in the 1977 general election, which was the least ever in the history of general elections.

Most independent candidates elected in a general election
In the history of Indian elections, independent candidates had the most successful run in the 1957 general election, winning 42 seats.

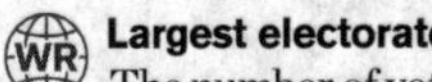

Largest electorate
The number of voters in the 2019 general election was 908,722,153, making India the largest (most populous) democracy in the world.

State/UT with the largest electorate
Uttar Pradesh had the largest electorate in the 2019 general election, with 145,858,999 eligible voters.

An Electronic Voting Machine (EVM) can record a maximum of 2,000 votes.

State/UT with the smallest electorate
The Union Territory of Lakshadweep had the smallest electorate in the 2019 general election, comprising a total of 55,057 eligible voters. The UT also holds the record for being the constituency with the smallest electorate in the country

State/UT with the largest voter turnout
Madhya Pradesh had the largest voter turnout in terms of percentage of the total number of voters in the 2019 general election, with a turnout of 71.2 per cent. In terms of number of voters, Uttar Pradesh, with 86,481,398 voters, led all states.

State/UT with the smallest voter turnout

In terms of percentage turnout, Jammu and Kashmir had the smallest voter turnout in the 2019 general election, with 29.39 per cent of the total number of voters turning out to vote. In terms of the number of voters, Lakshadweep, with 47,009 voters, registered the smallest voter turnout. It was also the constituency with the smallest voter turnout in numbers.

Most independent candidates in a general election

The 1996 general election had 10,636 independent candidates, the highest ever so far.

Fewest independent candidates elected in a general election

Only three of the 3,235 independent candidates in the 2014 general election were successful, the lowest win by independents in the history of general elections in India.

Oldest winning candidate

Bharatiya Janata Party (BJP) leader Lal Krishna (L.K.) Advani was 86 years old when he won the Gandhinagar seat in Gujarat in the 2014 general elections.

Youngest winning candidate

Biju Janata Dal (BJD) member Chandrani Murmu was only 25 years old when she contested and won the Keonjhar seat in Odisha in the 2019 general election.

Largest voter ID distribution camp

The district administration of Allahabad (now Prayagraj), Uttar Pradesh, led by District Magistrate Sanjay Kumar and Chief Development Officer Andra Vamsi,

India's Re-entry in the UN Security Council

India will sit in the 15-nation United Nations Security Council (UNSC) for the 2021–22 term as a non-permanent member – the eighth time that the country has had a seat on this powerful forum. It started its tenure on 1 January 2021. Being the only candidate for the lone seat from the Asia-Pacific grouping, India was elected as one of five non-permanent members in the UNSC on 17 June 2020, when the 193-member General Assembly held its elections. Each year, the General Assembly elects five non-permanent members (out of 10) for a two-year term and the 2021–22 term is critical for India as it will see the country's efforts to seek a permanent membership of the Security Council. India was previously elected as a non-permanent member of the Council for the years 1950–51, 1967–68, 1972–73, 1977–78, 1984–85, 1991–92 and 2011–12. Under the new voting arrangements due to COVID-19, the elections of non-permanent members to the UNSC were held without a physical meeting, for the first time.

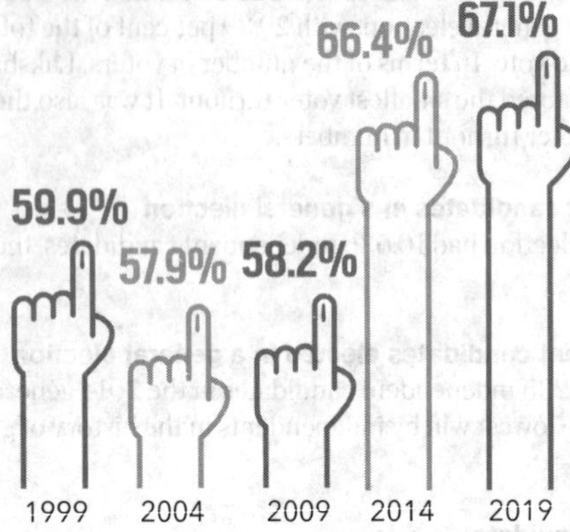

conducted the largest ever voter ID distribution camp on 16 February 2017, distributing 12,594 voter ID cards in one hour. The distribution event took place from 11:00 a.m. to 12:00 noon at the Parade Ground in the city.

Highest polling station

The polling station at Tashigang in Spiti Valley, Himachal Pradesh, situated at an altitude of 4,650 m (15,256 ft), is the highest polling station in the world. It has around 49 registered voters. On 19 May 2019, the poll registered 70 votes as 34 local officials obtained special permissions to vote at Tashigang.

PRESIDENTS AND VICE PRESIDENTS

First presidential election

The first presidential election in the country was held in 1962 when former vice president Dr S. Radhakrishnan (1888–1975) became the president of India. He held the post till 1967.

First vice president

Dr S. Radhakrishnan was vice president of India during 1952–62. He also had the longest tenure as vice president, that of 10 years, a record he shares with Hamid Ansari, who was in office from 11 August 2007 to 11 August 2017.

First woman president of India

Pratibha Patil (in office: 25 July 2007–25 July 2012) became the first woman to be appointed the president of India. Earlier, Pratibha Patil had held the office of governor of Rajasthan during 2004–07. She was affiliated with the Congress party.

Oldest vice president to assume office

Bhairon Singh Shekhawat (1923–2010) became vice president on 19 August 2002, when he was 79 years of age – the oldest vice president of India to date.

Shortest tenure as president

Dr Zakir Hussain (1897–1969), who was the third president of India, held the office of president from 13 May 1967 until his death, for a little less than two years, making his tenure the shortest for a president in Indian history. Dr Hussain was also the first to die in harness.

Dr Zakir Hussain: shortest tenure as president

Longest tenure as president

Dr Rajendra Prasad (1884–1963), a lawyer and freedom fighter, was appointed as the first president of India on 26 January 1950, a post he occupied for 12 years, three months and 18 days until 13 May 1962.

Oldest to become president

On 25 July 1997, K.R. Narayanan (1920–2005) assumed the office of president of India when he was 76 years and 271 days old, making him the oldest president to assume office.

Most presidents from a state

With three presidents to date, Tamil Nadu is the state that has given the country the most number of presidents. They are: S. Radhakrishnan, R. Venkataraman and A.P.J. Abdul Kalam.

- Dr S. Radhakrishnan, the first vice president and second president of India, held the position as president during 1962–67.
- R. Venkataraman, the eighth president of India, held office during 1987–92.
- A.P.J. Abdul Kalam, the eleventh president of India, held the presidential office during 2002–07.

Youngest to become president

Neelam Sanjiva Reddy (1913–96) assumed the office of president of India on 25 July 1977 at the age of 64 years and 67 days, the youngest to hold the position. His tenure was until 25 July 1982.

Shortest tenure as vice president

V.V. Giri (1894–1980) was vice president for two years during 1967–69, making his tenure the shortest for a vice president. He was elevated to the post of (acting) president on 24 August 1969. following the death of Dr Zakir Husain.

PRIME MINISTERS

First prime minister

Jawaharlal Nehru became the first prime minister of India on 15 August 1947. Previously, he had headed the interim government as prime minister, starting 2 September 1946. He served as prime minister until he died in 1964.

First and only woman prime minister

Indira Gandhi, the first and only woman to become prime minister of India, was in office from 1966 until 1977. She was re-elected in 1980 and her second tenure lasted four years, until her assassination in 1984.

Legion of Merit for Prime Minister Modi

Former US President Donald Trump presented Prime Minister Narendra Modi with the prestigious Legion of Merit award on 21 December 2020, for his leadership in elevating the strategic partnership between the two countries and helping India to emerge as a global power. Given by the US president to heads of state or government for exceptionally meritorious service, the Legion of Merit was received by India's ambassador to the USA, Taranjit Singh Sandhu, on behalf of the Indian prime minister.

First death in harness

- Jawaharlal Nehru, the first prime minister of India, passed away on 27 May 1964, after serving the office for 17 years. He was the first prime minister of India to die in harness.
- Jawaharlal Nehru's successor, Lal Bahadur Shastri, died at Tashkent, Uzbekistan, on 11 January 1966. He was the first prime minister of India to die in harness abroad.
- Indira Gandhi was the first prime minister to be assassinated while in office, on 31 October 1984.

First resignation

Morarji Ranchhodji Desai (1896–1995) was the first prime minister of India to resign from the office. He assumed office on 24 March 1977 and resigned from his post on 28 July 1979, following a split in the Janata Party, which he was heading at the time.

Oldest to become prime minister

Morarji Ranchhodji Desai, who had been a freedom fighter during India's struggle for independence, assumed the prime ministerial office at the age of 81 years and 24 days on 24 March 1977, making him the oldest prime minister of India to date. Earlier he had held many offices, such as those of minister of home affairs, deputy prime minister and finance minister.

Youngest to become prime minister

Rajiv Gandhi assumed office on 31 October 1984, when he was 40 years and 72 days, following the assassination of his mother, Prime Minister Indira Gandhi.

Shortest tenure as prime minister

- Chaudhary Charan Singh (1902–87) was prime minister for 171 days from 28 July 1979 to 14 January 1980, making him the shortest-tenured prime minister on record.
- Gulzari Lal Nanda had two shorter tenures as acting prime minister, once from 27 May to 9 June 1964, after Jawaharlal Nehru's death, and again from 11 to 24 January 1966, following Lal Bahadur Shastri's demise.

First deputy prime minister

Sardar Vallabhbhai Patel was sworn in as the first deputy prime minister of India on 15 August 1947 in the first cabinet of independent India, which was headed by the then prime minister Jawaharlal Nehru.

THE PARLIAMENT

First session of Parliament

The first session of Parliament in free India was held on 13 May 1952 with Jawaharlal Nehru as prime minister and Dr Rajendra Prasad as president.

First Speaker of the Lok Sabha

Freedom fighter 'Dadasaheb' G.V. Mavalankar was the first Speaker of the Lok Sabha, holding the post from 15 May 1952 to 27 February 1956.

First deputy Speaker of the Lok Sabha

On 30 May 1952, Madabhushi Ananthasayanam Ayyangar was elected as Lok Sabha's deputy Speaker.

First visually impaired Member of Parliament

Sadhan Chandra Gupta (1917–2015), an Indian lawyer and politician, became the first blind member of Parliament (MP) in 1953. He later served as the advocate general of West Bengal. Gupta was elected to the Lok Sabha from the Calcutta (now Kolkata, West Bengal) South-east constituency in a 1953 by-election on a Communist Party of India (CPI) ticket.

Longest term as Speaker

Balram Jakhar served as Speaker from 1980 to 1989, for eight years and 329 days in two terms, becoming the Speaker with the longest tenure.

First representative in the British House of Commons

The 'Grand Old Man of India', Dadabhai Naoroji, was the first non-white member of the British House of Commons, when he was elected as a Liberal Party member of Parliament in London from Central Finsbury in July 1892, by a bare majority of three votes. He held the position till 1895.

Longest tenure as Rajya Sabha chairman

Dr S. Radhakrishnan, the second president and first vice president of India, had the longest tenure as chairman of the Rajya Sabha, from 1952 to 1962.

First Woman Candidate in Mizoram – 2019 Lok Sabha Election

Lalthlamuani

For the first time in the history of the Lok Sabha elections in Mizoram, a woman candidate filed her nomination for the single seat in the state. Lalthlamuani, a 63-year-old independent candidate, is the leader of the Chhinlung Israel People Convention, an NGO to unite the people of the Chhinlung tribe. She decided to contest the election after receiving a 'signal from God'. Lalthlamuani got 1,975 votes, and though she lost, she still made a mark. She was also a candidate in the 2018 legislative assembly election in the Aizawl South-I constituency, where she got 69 votes.

Shortest term as Speaker

Neelam Sanjiva Reddy was Lok Sabha Speaker from 26 March to 13 July 1977, thus serving the shortest term as Speaker. He was the sixth president of India, from 1977 to 1982.

First woman Secretary General of Rajya Sabha

V.S. Ramadevi was the first woman to be appointed as the Secretary General of the Rajya Sabha on 1 July 1993, for three years. She was also acting chief election commissioner for some time in 1990.

Shortest Lok Sabha term

The 12th Lok Sabha lasted from 10 March 1998 to 26 April 1999, a duration of around 13 months, due to the withdrawal of support by the All India Anna Dravida Munnetra Kazhagam (AIADMK) to the National Democratic Alliance (NDA) government led by Atal Bihari Vajpayee.

First couple in Parliament

Joachim and Violet Alva from Karnataka were the first couple in Parliament. While Violet was elected to the Rajya Sabha in 1952, Joachim became a Lok Sabha member in the same year.

First state legislative assembly

The maharaja of Travancore, Sree Moolam Thirunal Rama Varma, constituted an eight-member assembly in March 1888. A bicameral system was introduced on 28 October 1932 by King Chithira Thirunal Balarama Varma, who abolished the existing council and set up the Sree Moolam Assembly (Lower House) and the Sree Chitra State Council (Upper House).

First woman legislator

Dr S. Muthulakshmi Reddy was a social worker, educationist and physician, with many firsts to her credit. In 1926, she became the first woman legislator (Madras Legislative Council member) and in 1930, by way of the All India Women's Conference, pushed through the Child Marriage Restraint Act. She was also the first woman alderman of the Madras Corporation in 1937.

Shortest session of state legislative assembly

There was a one-minute session of the Rajasthan Legislative Assembly from 11:00 a.m. to 11:01 a.m. on 14 August 1972, the shortest session of a legislative assembly on record.

First Lok Sabha dissolution

The fifth Lok Sabha was dissolved by Indira Gandhi in 1971, the first time in the history of the Indian Parliament. The second Lok Sabha dissolution came in 1979 under Charan Singh, and the third was the ninth Lok Sabha on 6 March 1991 under Chandra Shekhar.

First hung Parliament

A hung parliament is a situation where no single political party has an absolute majority of seats in the Parliament. For the first time in nine general elections,

Indian-origin US Vice President's Long List of Firsts

Kamala Devi Harris (b. 20 October 1964) was announced as the vice president elect of the USA alongside president-elect Joe Biden on 7 November 2020. Having broken through many barriers in her career, she is USA's first female vice president, the first highest-ranking female elected official, the first African American and first South Asian American vice president in history. The daughter of an Indian mother – Shyamala Gopalan Harris – and Jamaican father – Donald Harris, Harris is from Oakland, California, and was the 27th District Attorney of San Francisco (2004–11) as well as the 32nd Attorney General of California (2011–17). A member of the Democratic Party, Harris assumed office with Biden on 20 January 2021.

India's electorate did not give a decisive verdict in 1989. The Congress (I) was ousted in the north and the ruling regional parties were similarly ousted in the south.

Lok Sabha with highest average age
The average age of the elected MPs in the current 17th Lok Sabha is 54 years, making it the Lok Sabha with the highest average age in the history of the Indian Parliament.

Lok Sabha with lowest average age
The first Lok Sabha (1952–57) had the lowest average age of 46.5 years.

Maximum bills passed in a year
The Parliament passed 118 bills in 1976, which is the highest number of bills ever passed by it in a single year.

UNION GOVERNMENT

First non-Congress government
The Janata Party, led by Jayaprakash Narayan, overthrew the Indira Gandhi government in the 1977 general election to form the first non-Congress government in the history of independent India. Morarji Desai was appointed prime minister of the government formed by the Janata Party.

First woman cabinet minister
Vijaya Lakshmi Pandit was elected to the provincial legislature of the United Provinces as minister for local government and health in 1937, making her the first woman cabinet minister. Later, she was president of the United Nations General Assembly from September 1953 to September 1954.

First electoral win by an Indian party
In the elections held under the provisions of the Government of India Act, 1935, the Indian National Congress formed governments in seven states, in addition to a

coalition ministry in Assam. They lasted till October–November 1939, after which they unanimously resigned in protest against the inclusion of Indians in the Second World War.

First woman full-term finance minister

Nirmala Sitharaman became the first woman to be a full-fledged finance minister of India on 31 May 2019. She is the second woman finance minister after former prime minister Indira Gandhi, who held the finance ministerial office for some time while she was prime minister during 1970–71. Sitharaman was also the first woman minister with defence as her sole portfolio from 2014 to 2019.

First Union minister to die in harness

Sardar Vallabhbhai Patel, India's first home minister and first deputy prime minister, who died on 15 December 1950, was the first Union minister to die while in office.

SUPER 30

UNION MINISTRIES: CHANGES FROM THE 1990s

The Government of India exercises its executive authority through a number of government ministries or departments of state. Ministries such as those of agriculture and farmers' welfare, commerce and industry, and finance, among others, were established by the government since 1942, while some were set up later. The Ministry of Science and Technology was established only in 1971. The Ministry of Social Justice and Empowerment, and the Ministry of Women and Child Development were set up as late as 1985. Here's a look at the ministries set up since 1990 – some of these were departments under other ministries, or were named differently earlier.

- Ministry of Chemicals and Fertilizers (1991)
- Ministry of New and Renewable Energy (1992)
- Ministry of Power (1992)
- Ministry of Statistics and Programme Implementation (1999)
- Ministry of Tourism (1999)
- Ministry of Tribal Affairs (1999)
- Ministry of Youth Affairs and Sports (2000)
- Ministry for Development of North Eastern Region (2003)
- Ministry of Panchayati Raj (2004)
- Ministry of Earth Sciences (2006)
- Ministry of Minority Affairs (2006)
- Ministry of Micro, Small and Medium Enterprises (2007)
- Ministry of Skill Development and Entrepreneurship (2014)
- Ministry of AYUSH (2014)
- Ministry of Planning (2014)
- Ministry of Communications (2016)
- Ministry of Electronics and Information Technology (2016)
- Ministry of Housing and Urban Affairs (2017)
- Ministry of Jal Shakti (2019)
- Ministry of Animal Husbandry, Dairying and Fisheries (2019)

Party with most votes
The Congress (I) secured a record 115,221,078 votes (78.5 per cent of the total votes) and won 412 out of the 513 parliamentary seats in the elections held in December 1984. This is the largest victory margin of any political party on record.

First Union minister to resign
Dr Shyama Prasad Mookerjee resigned from the Union cabinet on 19 April 1950. After leaving the Nehru government and the Congress party, he founded the Bharatiya Jana Sangh in 1951.

Longest-serving cabinet minister
Jagjivan Ram was a Union minister for over 28 years from 15 August 1947 to 25 July 1979 with a break from 31 August 1963 to 24 January 1966. Some of the portfolios held by him included the Ministry of Labour, the Ministry of Defence, and the Ministry of Transport and Communications.

Shortest tenure of a cabinet minister
Justice H.R. Khanna was in office as the minister for law and justice in the Charan Singh ministry for five days from 30 July to 3 August 1979.

TOP 5 STATES WITH MOST WOMEN CANDIDATES IN THE 2019 LOK SABHA ELECTION

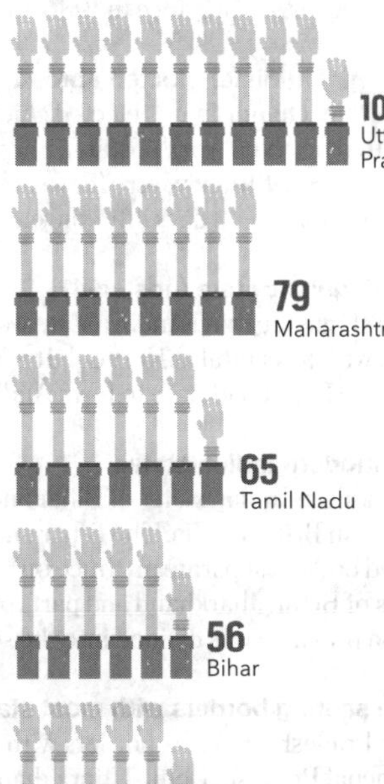

Source: Participation of Women Candidates in Polls, Lok Sabha Election 2019, Election Commission of India

First use of Hindi at UN
Atal Bihari Vajpayee (1924–2018) made a speech in Hindi at the United Nations (UN) in 1977 when he was foreign minister, the first to do so. It was translated into English by an Indian diplomat. Vajpayee spoke again in Hindi in 1978. He later became the tenth prime minister of India in 1996 for 13 days, and then again from 1998 to 2004.

First Union cabinet of independent India (15 August 1947)

THE STATES

First linguistic state (pre-1947)
The Orissa (now Odisha) province that was formed as a result of the division of the Bihar and Orissa province in 1936, was the first to be formed on a linguistic basis.

First chief minister elected abroad
M.G. Ramachandran was elected chief minister of Tamil Nadu while he was admitted in a New York hospital. His nomination papers for the Andipatti assembly constituency were flown in from the USA and he was elected in absentia. He was sworn in 43 days after the election on 10 February 1985.

First linguistic state (post-1947)
The Telugu-speaking Andhra state was carved out of Madras state on 1 October 1953, with its capital at Kurnool. It was later merged with the Telugu-speaking areas of Hyderabad state to form Andhra Pradesh on 1 November 1956.

First modern Indian states
The modern Indian states of Bihar and Orissa (now Odisha) were the first to be formed in British India. The Bihar and Orissa province of Bengal Presidency was carved out as a separate province on 1 April 1912, which included the present-day states of Bihar, Jharkhand and parts of Odisha. On 1 April 1936, the then Bihar and Orissa province was divided into the separate provinces of Bihar and Orissa.

State sharing borders with most states
Uttar Pradesh shares its borders with nine Indian states – Rajasthan, Haryana, Himachal Pradesh, Delhi, Uttarakhand, Bihar, Madhya Pradesh, Jharkhand and Chhattisgarh.

State with the largest area
With an area of 342,239 sq. km, Rajasthan is the largest state. It covers around 10.4 per cent of India's total area.

State with the smallest area
Goa is India's smallest state with a total area of 3,702 sq. km.

State with the longest coastline
Gujarat has the longest coastline of 1,214.7 km, followed by Andhra Pradesh with a coastal length of 973.7 km.

State with longest international border
West Bengal shares a 2,216.7 km long border with Bangladesh, making it the state with the longest international border.

Shortest term as chief minister
- Jagdambika Pal was chief minister of Uttar Pradesh for one day – on 21 February 1998.
- Harish Rawat's second term as chief minister of Uttarakhand lasted a day – 21 April 2016.

Youngest state

Telangana was formed on 2 June 2014, after its separation from the state of Andhra Pradesh.

First woman chief minister

India's first woman chief minister was freedom fighter Sucheta Kripalani (1908–74). She was the chief minister of Uttar Pradesh (1963 to 1967).

First state under president's Rule

President's Rule was imposed on Punjab from 20 July 1951 to 17 July 1952. The proclamation came after the resignation of the Congress ministry headed by Dr Gopichand Bhargava.

WR First elected communist government in power

On 5 April 1957, the Communist Party of India in Kerala formed the first communist government in the world to come to power by voting. It was led by E.M.S. Namboodiripad. It was dismissed by the Centre in 1959.

First 'film star' chief minister

M.G. Ramachandran or 'MGR' was the first film star to become chief minister when he assumed office in Tamil Nadu on 4 July 1977.

Oldest chief minister

Mizoram's chief minister Zoramthanga (b. 13 July 1944) is the oldest serving chief minister of a state.

Most chief ministers in a year

Haryana had four chief ministers in nine months from November 1989 to July 1990: Devi Lal (November 1989), Om Prakash Chautala (December 1989), Banarsi Das Gupta (May 1990) and Hukam Singh (July 1990).

Youngest chief minister

- M.O. Hasan Farook Maricar, three-time chief minister of Pondicherry (now Puducherry), was the youngest chief minister when he came to power in 1967 at 29 years. He died in office in 2012 as Governor of Kerala.
- Pema Khandu, elected as chief minister of Arunachal Pradesh in 2016 at the age of 38 years, is the youngest serving chief minister of a state.

Chief minister with longest tenure and most consecutive terms

Pawan Kumar Chamling (former chief minister of Sikkim) has been India's longest-serving chief minister, having served in that post for five terms from 12 December 1994 to 26 May 2019 (24 years, 165 days). He is the second longest-tenured chief minister after Jyoti Basu of West Bengal, who held office from 1 June 1977 to 6 November 2000 (23 years, 137 days) to have served for such a long tenure.

GOVERNANCE

First Indian in the Imperial Civil Service

Satyendranath Tagore, elder brother of Rabindranath Tagore, was the first Indian to join the service in 1863. He was recruited into the Covenanted Civil Service (later named the Imperial Civil Service). His first posting was in the Bombay Presidency (which included parts of present-day Maharashtra, Gujarat and Sindh).

First member of the Viceroy's Executive Council
Satyendra Prasanna Sinha, or First Baron Sinha (1863–1928), was a prominent lawyer and statesman. In 1909, he was honoured with an appointment as a law member to the Viceroy's Executive Council under Lord Minto.

Satyendra Prasanna Sinha: first member of the Viceroy's Executive Council

First Indians in the Privy Council
K.G. Puta and Syed Hussain Bilgrami were admitted to the Privy Council of India in 1907. It was the supreme appellate authority in British India, with advisers to the British monarchy.

First municipalities
Municipal corporations for civic amenities were set up first between 1880 and 1884, when Lord Rippon was the viceroy of India.

First Public Service Commission
The Public Service Commission was first constituted under the chairmanship of Sir Charles Umpherston Aitchison, governor of Punjab, in 1926.

First panchayats
Panchayats were first established in villages under the Panchayat Act in 1912, but with little success. It was in 1952 that a new Panchayat Act revived the system.

First woman ambassador
Vijaya Lakshmi Pandit, the sister of India's first prime minister, Jawaharlal Nehru, was India's first woman ambassador, to the erstwhile USSR from 1947 to 1949. She also served as ambassador to the USA and Mexico (1949–51) and in Ireland (1955–61). She held a post in the cabinet in pre-Independence India, the first Indian woman to do so. Her longest tenure was in London, as high commissioner to the UK, serving from 1954 to 1961. Her last posting as ambassador was in Spain. She served as governor of Maharashtra from 1962 to 1964 and as member of the Lok Sabha from 1964 to 1968.

First woman career diplomat
Chonira Belliappa Muthamma from Coorg (now Kodagu), Karnataka, qualified for the Indian Civil Service and joined the foreign service in 1949. She served in France, the UK and Burma (now Myanmar), and later as ambassador to Hungary and Ghana.

First woman IAS officer
Anna Rajam George (b. 17 July 1927) from Calicut (now Kozhikode), Kerala, was the first woman to qualify for the Indian Administrative Service (IAS) in 1950. She was posted as a subdivisional officer in a small town in Tamil Nadu in 1951.

First woman mayor
Tara Cherian (1913–2000) was appointed mayor of Madras (now Chennai, Tamil Nadu) in 1957. She received the Padma Bhushan in 1967.

First woman sarpanch
Chhavi Rajawat, the first woman sarpanch (head of the village panchayat) in India, looks after Soda, a village in Tonk District, Rajasthan. She assumed office in February 2010 at the age of 30 years. She is an alumna of Rishi Valley School, Madanapalle, Andhra Pradesh; Mayo College Girls' School, Ajmer, Rajasthan; and Lady Shri Ram College, New Delhi. She also holds an MBA from Balaji Institute of Modern Management, Pune, Maharashtra. She left her corporate job to work in rural India.

Youngest governor
Swaraj Kaushal was appointed governor of Mizoram in February 1990 when he was 37 years and seven months old.

Youngest sarpanch
Anant Parag Khadilkar, the youngest sarpanch in India, secured the post in Nagargao Sattari Village in Goa in 2017 when he was only 21 years old. He was then a graduate in commerce.

Record Rewind

Number of states and Union Territories

1990
There were 24 states and seven Union Territories in India.

2020
There are 28 states and eight Union Territories in India.

Youngest mayor
Arya Rajendran (b. 12 January 1999), the Left Democratic Front councillor from the Mudavanmugal ward, became the mayor of Thiruvananthapuram Corporation, Kerala, in December 2020 when she was 21 years old.

Youngest woman sarpanch
Twenty-one-year-old Asruni Khan was elected as the sarpanch of Chulhera Village in Bharatpur District, Rajasthan, in January 2020.

LAW AND ORDER

First Indian sheriff
Manockjee Rustomjee, a Parsi businessman and judge from Bombay (now Mumbai, Maharashtra), was appointed as the sheriff of Calcutta (now Kolkata, West Bengal) in 1873, the first Indian to be appointed to the position.

Largest self-defence training programme
The self-defence wing of the Special Police Unit for Women and Children (Delhi Police) imparted self-defence training from 1 January 2018 to 31 December 2018 to school/college-going girls, working women and housewives. The programme

consisted of more than 325,081 girls and women from Delhi in 1,526 training sessions comprising 15 days' training during summer/winter camps and 10 days' training in other self-defence training camps of two hours every day.

First all-woman police station

The first all-woman police station in the country was started in October 1973 at Calicut (now Kozhikode) in Kerala. Sub-inspector Padmini was in charge of it.

WR **First fingerprint bureau**

The first fingerprint bureau in the world was set up in Calcutta (now Kolkata, West Bengal) in June 1897. A murder case in 1898 in Jalpaiguri is reported to be among the first in which the culprit was incriminated on the basis of dactyloscopy, which is the science of fingerprint identification.

First forensic science laboratory

In 1853, the Government Examiners' Laboratory was set up in Calcutta (now Kolkata, West Bengal), followed by labs in Madras (now Chennai, Tamil Nadu), Bombay (now Mumbai, Maharashtra), Lahore (now in Pakistan) and Agra, Uttar Pradesh. Currently, there are seven central forensic science labs in India, viz., Hyderabad, Kolkata, Chandigarh, New Delhi, Guwahati, Bhopal and Pune.

First Indian director of the Intelligence Bureau

T.G. Sanjeevi Pillai took over as the first Indian director of the Intelligence Bureau, Ministry of Home Affairs, from Sir N.P.A. Smith in April 1947 and held office till July 1950.

First open prison

The first open prison in India, Durgapura Open Camp, was started in Rajasthan in 1956 by the then governor, Dr Sampurnanand, in the Government Agriculture and Research Centre campus at Jaipur. Prisoners who had spent six years behind bars could live with their families and go out in the day to earn.

First Police Act

The Police Act of 1861 led to the creation of a police service. This Act introduced a uniform system that was applicable to entire British India.

First police dog squad

The Madras City Police Dog Squad, now called the Chennai City Police Dog Squad, was started in 1952 by a sub-inspector of police, Kanniah Naidu, in Chennai, Tamil Nadu. It was the first police dog squad in India.

High court with the most judges

Allahabad High Court has the largest sanctioned strength of 160 judges, but has never held its full complement. As on 1 November 2020, it had fifty-nine permanent judges and 41 additional judges

First woman winner of Sena Medal

Bimla Devi of the 88th Mahila Battalion of the Central Reserve Police Force was on duty at Elephant Pass in Sri Lanka on 31 August 1988, when she recovered

1,200 detonators from a Sri Lankan woman while checking passengers, which led to the capture of many militants. She was awarded the Sena Medal.

Largest prison complex

Tihar Prisons, which started with the Central Jail in 1958, now includes nine central jails, apart from a district jail at Rohini, New Delhi, making it the largest prison complex in Asia. Starting with a capacity of 1,273 prisoners, it now houses 15,468 prisoners against the sanctioned capacity of 10,026 prisoners.

First transgender sub-inspector

India's first transgender sub-inspector, K. Prithika Yashini, joined the Tamil Nadu Police force on 2 April 2017. She was posted to Dharmapuri District in Tamil Nadu after a legal battle that ended with the Madras High Court ruling in her favour.

K. Prithika Yashini: first transgender sub-inspector

First woman IPS officer

Kiran Bedi (b. 9 June 1949) was the first woman to join the Indian Police Service (IPS) on 16 July 1972. She retired in 2007 and was later the lieutenant governor of Puducherry (May 2016–February 2021).

Biggest cryptocurrency crime

India's biggest cryptocurrency crime involving US $300 million through a multi-level bitcoin marketing scam allegedly perpetrated by Amit Bhardwaj, director of Gain Bitcoin, was registered in Pune, Maharashtra. The victims allegedly claimed that the bitcoin investment company duped them into investing in bitcoins for higher returns. Bhardwaj had allegedly fled India and was traced to Bangkok, Thailand, before his arrest at Delhi airport in April 2018.

AADHAAR

State/UT with least Aadhaar coverage

Assam, with a low saturation percentage of 22.5 per cent, has the lowest Aadhaar saturation among all states and Union Territories in India, on the basis of total projected population.

State/UT with maximum Aadhaar coverage

Delhi, with an Aadhaar saturation percentage of 116.4 per cent, has the maximum Aadhaar coverage. The saturation percentage is calculated as a percentage of the number of Aadhaar cards assigned, upon the total projected population for the year.

LEGAL MATTERS

First British Indian Code

The East India Company's proposal for separate civil and criminal courts in districts on 15 August 1772 in Calcutta (now Kolkata, West Bengal) was the first British Indian Code.

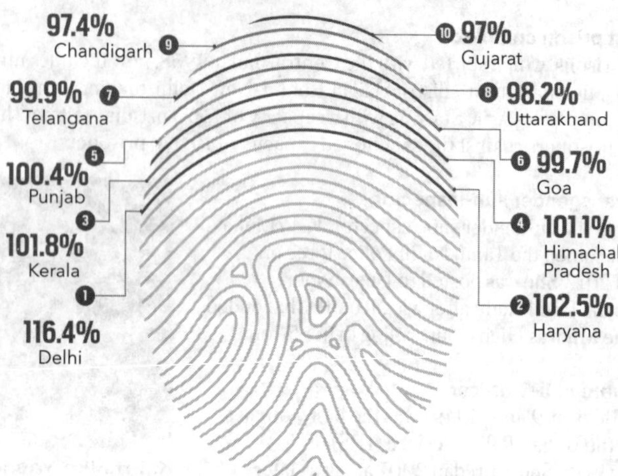

*Coverage percentage exceeds 100 due to the population figures being projections; Source: Unique Identification Authority of India, 31 May 2020

First Penal Code
The Indian Penal Code (IPC) and the Criminal Procedure Code (CrPC), which were introduced in Bengal in 1862, were drafted on the recommendations of the first Law Commission of India set up in 1834, chaired by British historian and politician Thomas Babington Macaulay.

First woman advocate
Cornelia Sorabji (1866–1954) was the first woman to graduate in law in 1894. However, law being a male bastion then, she was enrolled in the Allahabad High Court Bar only in 1923.

First barrister-at-law
Gyanendramohan Tagore (1826–90) passed the barrister-at-law examination from Lincoln's Inn in England on 21 June 1862, becoming the first Indian to do so. In November 1865, he was enrolled into Calcutta High Court in Bengal Presidency (now in Kolkata, West Bengal) as the first Indian barrister.

First public prosecutor
S. Subramania Iyer (1842–1924), jurist and freedom fighter, was appointed public prosecutor at Madras (now Chennai, Tamil Nadu) in 1887.

First high court judge
Shambhunath Pandit, a Kashmiri domiciled in Calcutta (now Kolkata, West Bengal), was appointed judge at the Calcutta High Court on 2 February 1863. His tenure ended in 1867.

First woman chief justice

Justice Leila Seth (1930–2017) was appointed the chief justice of Himachal Pradesh on 5 August 1991, becoming India's first woman chief justice of a state high court.

First woman judge of the Supreme Court

Meera Sahib Fathima Beevi (b. April 1927) was appointed judge of the Supreme Court in October 1989, the first Indian woman and only the second in the world to hold such a position.

First chief justice of India

India's first chief justice was Justice Sir Harilal J. Kania (1890–1951), who held the position from 26 January 1950 to 6 November 1951.

First Indian president of the International Court of Justice

Dr Nagendra Singh (1914–88) was the first Indian president of the International Court of Justice, serving from 1985 to 1988. He was also the first Indian to be a judge of the court. He received the Padma Vibhushan in 1973.

First woman judicial officer

Anna Chandy (1905–96), a member of the Travancore Legislative Council during 1923–24, graduated in law in 1930 and was appointed munsif by the erstwhile state of Travancore in 1937. She became a district and sessions judge in 1948, and a judge of the Kerala High Court in 1959.

SUPER 30

WOMEN JUDGES OF THE SUPREME COURT OF INDIA

Female representation in Indian courts has been an issue of recent discussion. Of the 627 judges functioning across high courts, only 66 are women.There are only four women among the 33 currently presiding Supreme Court judges. Only eight women judges (including the three currently incumbent) have been appointed to the Supreme Court of India since its inception 70 years ago. They are:

1. Fathima Beevi (in office: 6 October 1989–29 April 1992)
2. Sujata Manohar (in office: 8 November 1994–27 Aug. 1999)
3. Ruma Pal (in office: 28 January 2000–2 June 2006)
4. Gyan Sudha Misra (in office: 30 April 2010–27 April 2014)
5. Ranjana Desai (in office:13 September 2011–29 Oct. 2014)
6. R. Banumathi (in office:13 August 2014–19 July 2020)
7. Indu Malhotra (in office: 27 April 2018–13 March 2021)
8. Indira Banerjee (in office since 7 August 2018)
9. Hima Kohli (in office since 31 August 2021)
10. Bela Trivedi (in office since 31 August 2021)
11. B.V. Nagarathna (in office since 31 August 2021)

Justice Indira Banerjee

First Indian woman on the United Nations law board
Neeru Chadha, an international law expert, became the first Indian to be appointed to the International Tribunal for the Law of the Sea (ITLOS), being elected to the UN body in June 2017.

First citizen to have a 'no caste, no religion' certificate
M.A. Sneha Parthibaraja, a lawyer from Tirupattur, Tamil Nadu, became the first Indian citizen to win the right to not have a caste or religion on 5 February 2021. She was granted the certificate after a nine-year-long court battle.

First visually challenged Indian Administrative Service officer
In October 2019, Pranjal Patil (b. 1 April 1988) from Ulhas Nagar in Mumbai, Maharashtra, became India's first visually challenged IAS officer, posted as the sub-collector of Thiruvananthapuram, Kerala. Born with weak eyesight, Patil lost her vision at the age of six. A postgraduate in international relations from Jawaharlal Nehru University, New Delhi, she achieved the 773rd rank in

LANDMARK JUDGEMENTS BY THE SUPREME COURT (DURING 2019–20)

Parties Involved	Verdict	Date of Verdict
B.K. Pavitra v. Union of India	Upheld the validity of Karnataka's 2018 reservation law, which granted reservation in promotion to employees belonging to the SC and ST categories.	10 May 2019
D.A.V. College Trust and Management Society and Others v. Director of Public Instructions and Others	NGOs that are substantially financed, directly or indirectly, by government funds will fall within the ambit of public authority under the Right to Information (RTI) Act, 2005.	17 September 2019
M. Siddiq v. Mahant Suresh Das and Others (Ayodhya dispute)	The land title was given to the construction of the Ram Temple and the State was directed to grant the Sunni Waqf Board an alternative site at Ayodhya for the building of a mosque.	9 November 2019
Anuradha Bhasin v. Union of India	Internet services come under freedom of speech and expression and an undefined restriction would be illegal. The orders for Internet shutdown must satisfy the tests of necessity and proportionality.	10 January 2020
Mukesh Kumar and Another v. The State of Uttarakhand and Others	States are not bound to provide reservation in government appointments and promotions, and this rests on their discretion.	7 February 2020

Virtual Hearings: The Future of Indian Courtrooms

The Supreme Court of India stepped into virtual mode to hear cases on 23 March 2020 to manage the caseload amid the COVID-19 crisis across the country, and discourage overcrowding by lawyers and litigants on its premises. While the judges heard the cases from their residential offices, the lawyers argued from their chambers at home through videoconferencing, a process made possible by the court's registry that shared a digital link of the virtual courtroom hearings with the lawyers so that proceedings could be accessed on their laptops or mobile phones. This move provided access to litigants in remote locations and to people with disabilities.

the Union Public Services Commission (UPSC) Civil Services Examination conducted by the UPSC in her first attempt in 2016. In her second attempt in 2017, she secured the 124th rank.

First transgender lawyer

Sathyasri Sharmila, a lawyer in the Bar Council of Tamil Nadu and Puducherry, is the first transgender lawyer in India. Although she completed her education in 2007, she enrolled as an advocate after the NALSA (National Legal Services Authority of India) judgment of 2014, which recognized the third gender.

First transgender judge

Joyita Mondal Mahi, India's first transgender judge, was appointed as a judge in the Lok Adalat in West Bengal in 2017. She was 29 years old at the time.

Oldest Civic Body

The Greater Chennai Corporation, Tamil Nadu, was inaugurated under a royal charter issued by King James II of England, on 29 September 1688, as the Corporation of Madras. It is the oldest civic body in the country and the second oldest in the world.

Oldest high court

The Calcutta High Court, established on 1 July 1862, under the Indian High Courts Act, 1861, is the oldest high court in India. It also has jurisdiction over West Bengal, and the Union Territory of the Andaman and Nicobar Islands. Its building was designed by British architect Walter Granville, who based it on the Cloth Hall at Ypres in Belgium. The seat of the high court is Kolkata. It also has a permanent circuit bench in Port Blair, the capital of the Andaman and Nicobar Islands. It has a sanctioned strength of 72 judges. Thottathil B. Radhakrishnan is its current serving chief justice.

Record Rewind

State with highest number of reported crimes

1991

Uttar Pradesh had 164,751 cases of reported crimes, followed by Maharashtra, with 161,200 cases in 1987.

2020

Uttar Pradesh had 628,578 cases of reported crimes, followed by Maharashtra, with 509,443 cases in 2019.

THE CENSUS

First census

The first all-India census was conducted in 1872 in British India. However, the first regular census in the country was conducted in 1881, and then every ten years. The last census was conducted in 2011. The census is conducted by the registrar general and census commissioner under the Ministry of Home Affairs, Government of India.

Most populated state

Uttar Pradesh is India's most populated state, with a population of 199,812,341.

Most populated Union Territory

Delhi is India's most populated Union Territory with a population of 16,787,941.

Least populated state

Sikkim is India's least populated state, with 610,577 persons.

Least populated Union Territory

Lakshadweep, with a population of 64,473, emerged as the least populated Union Territory.

Most densely populated state

Bihar has a population density of 1,106 persons per sq. km, making it the most densely populated state in India.

Most densely populated Union Territory

The national capital Delhi, with a population density of 11,320 persons per sq. km, is the most densely populated UT.

Least densely populated state

Arunachal Pradesh, with a population density of 17 persons per sq. km, is the least densely populated state in India.

Least densely populated Union Territory

Andaman and Nicobar Islands have a population density of 46 persons per sq. km, making it the least densely populated UT.

Longest service as a governmental census officer

K. Narender Reddy, a retired statistical officer from Nizamabad, now in Telangana, served in five population censuses in 1971, 1981, 1991, 2001 and 2011. He was honoured by both the Central and state governments for his work.

State with highest sex ratio

Kerala has the highest sex ratio among states, with 1,084 females per 1,000 males.

State with lowest sex ratio

Haryana has a sex ratio of 879 females per 1,000 males, making it the state with the lowest sex ratio.

LITERATURE

BOOKS

Oldest living language
Tamil, which belongs to the Dravidian group of languages, is the oldest living language of India. *Tholkappiyam,* the oldest known work in Tamil, is a work on Tamil grammar. It has been dated to between the second century BCE and the fifth century CE.

Oldest manuscript
The oldest manuscript among contemporary Indian languages is that of a bilingual Tulu–Greek comedy titled *Sariti,* currently housed at the Bodleian Library at Oxford, UK. The manuscript dates to the first century.

Oldest surviving book
The oldest surviving Indian book is the Tamil work *Christiya Vanakkam,* a revised edition of the *Doctrina Christiana*. It was first published in 1560 in Goa, and followed by its Tamil version published in 1564.

Earliest known grammar text
The Sanskrit grammar treatise *Ashtadhyayi,* which was composed around 500 BCE by Panini, a grammarian, is said to be the earliest formalized book on Sanskrit grammar. It contains 4,000 precise rules of grammar in as many sutras expounding an array of topics such as syntax, root derivatives and moods.

First known printed book
The first known printed book in India, titled *Conclusoes e Outras Coisas,* was printed in Portuguese in Goa by Joao de Bustamante, a Christian missionary.

Earliest known anthology
Therigatha, the ninth book of the *Khuddaka Nikaya,* is the earliest known anthology. This Buddhist scripture, written in Pali, consists of short poems recited by the early members of the Buddhist sangha. It has 73 poems, which are organized into 16 chapters, and the text comprises 522 stanzas.

Earliest known Tamil work
Tholkappiyam, a treatise on the grammar of the Tamil language, which has been dated to between the second century BCE and the fifth century CE, is the earliest extant work in Tamil. The authorship is loosely attributed to the sage Tholkappiyar.

Earliest known Malayalam work
Samkshepa Vedartham, a catechism book by the Reverend Clement Pianius, was printed in movable type in Rome in 1772.

Earliest original Odia work
Lavanyavati, the first Odia epic, was an original work featuring the love story of a prince of Karnataka and a princess of Sri Lanka, by Upendra Bhanja (1680–1720), who belonged to a ruling feudatory family in Ghumsar in Bhanjanagar in present-day Odisha. Called '*Kavi Samrat*', he is said to have written many books.

Sahitya Akademi Goes Online

Since its inception in 1954, the Sahitya Akademi (National Academy of Letters), India's premier literary institution supported by the Government of India, decided to sell its books online for the first time in 2019. In collaboration with the Ministry of Culture, the online sale was launched via Amazon.com on 20 January 2020 with the aim of increasing the institution's readership reach. Books and ebooks published in 24 Indian languages were included in the sale with the Akademi selling a range of 10 English titles and 50 Tamil ones, including *Myths, Legends and Literary Antiquities* by Manoj Das, *History of Indian English Literature* by M.K. Naik, and *Tales of Tomorrow* by Rana Nayar, among others.

Earliest known Kannada works

- The earliest extant work in Kannada, the second oldest living language in India, is the *Kavirajamarga*, which was written (possibly in parts) by a Rashtrakuta king – Nrupatunga Amoghavarsha I (r. 814–78 CE). It is a work on the rhetoric, poetics and grammar of Kannada.
- The Kannada prose work titled *Vaddaradhane* (sixth to ninth century CE), which is believed to be written by Shivakotiacharya, consists of inspiring stories of 19 great Jain saints.

Earliest known Marathi works

- *Viveka Sindhu* was written by Mukundraj (1128–1200 CE) in Marathi verse, and preached Advaita bhakti. Mukundraj was a follower of Adi Shankaracharya's philosophy of Advaita or 'non-dualism', which inspired him to write this religious composition.
- *Leela Charitra* by Mahim Bhat is a biography of Chakradhara, a 13th-century saint who founded the Mahanubhava sect and socio-religious movement. The work contains more than a hundred stories on the subject.

Earliest known Gujarati works

- The earliest work in Gujarati prose was *Balavabodha*, written by Tarunaprabha and dated to 1355 CE.
- *Prithvichandra Charita,* written by Manikyasundara in 1422 CE, is a great example of old Gujarati prose, and said to be reminiscent of Banabhatta's *Kadambari*.

Earliest known Telugu work

The first printed prose work in Telugu, which was a part of the New Testament, was translated by the Reverend Benjamin Schultze in the early 18th century.

Earliest English work

Cavelly Venkata Boriah's *Account of the Jains*, published in 1809, is the first extant evidence of Indian writing in English.

Madhuri Vijay Sweeps Literary Awards

Madhuri Vijay won four major literary prizes for her account of Kashmir's deep tragedies in her debut novel, *The Far Field* (2019). A teacher by profession and a graduate of Iowa's Writers' Workshop, this Bengaluru-born, US-based writer wrote about a young woman's search for a lost figure from her childhood and a journey that carries her from Bengaluru to Kashmir on the brink of conflict in the 1990s. The recipient of the Pushcart Prize 2019 (an American literary award), Madhuri won the Crossword Book Award (Jury) for Fiction 2019, the Tata Literature Live First Book Award 2019 and the JCB Prize for Literature 2019.

Madhuri Vijay

First known printed books in local languages

- **Assamese**: An early translation of the New Testament, titled *Dharmapustak*, printed by the Serampore Mission Press, Serampore, Bengal (now Srirampur, West Bengal), in 1813.
- **Bengali**: *Regulations for the Administration of Justice in the Courts of Dewanee Adaulat*, popularly known as the Regulation Impey Code, published by the East India Company's Press, Calcutta (now Kolkata, West Bengal), in 1792.
- **Devanagari/Hindi**: *Grammar of Sanskrit* and *Grammar of the Hindustani Language*, published by the Chronicle Press, Calcutta (now Kolkata, West Bengal), in 1796.
- **Dogri**: *Valmiki Ramayana*, published by Sri Saraswati Press, Jammu and Kashmir, in 1858.
- **Gujarati**: *Dabestan-e-Mazaheb*, the Gujarati translation of a Persian book, published by Fardoonjee Marazban in Bombay (now Mumbai, Maharashtra), in 1815.
- **Kannada**: *A Grammar of the Karnatic Language* by William Meckerell, published from the Serampore Mission Press, Serampore, Bengal (now Srirampur, West Bengal), in 1820.
- **Konkani:** *Doutrina Crista*, printed at the Society of Jesus Press, Goa, in 1556.
- **Maithili**: *Krishna Janma*, edited by Grierson, published by Vidyapati Press, Laherisarai, Bihar, in 1936.
- **Malayalam**: *The Bible*, printed at the Courier Press, Bombay (now Mumbai, Maharashtra), in 1811.
- **Odia**: A translation of the New Testament by Pandit Mrityunjaya Vidyalankar, printed at the Serampore Mission Press, Serampore, Bengal (now Srirampur, West Bengal) in 1807.
- **Tamil**: *A Book of Prayers*, published by the Society of Jesus Press, Goa, around 1560.
- **Telugu**: *A Grammar of Telugu*, printed at the Serampore Mission Press, Serampore, Bengal (now Srirampur, West Bengal), in 1813.
- **Urdu**: Hallhead's Urdu translation of Kannada laws, published by Honourable Company Press in Calcutta (now Kolkata, West Bengal) in 1792.

Longest novel

Avakasikal, written by M.K. Menon in Malayalam, runs into 3,958 pages, in four volumes, making it the longest novel in any Indian language. He received the Sahitya Akademi Award in 1981 and the Vayalar Award in 1983 for the novel.

WR Largest scripture

A special edition of the Bhagavadgita at the ISKCON temple in New Delhi is the world's largest scripture. The book measures 2.8 m x 2 m (9 ft 2.2 in. x 6 ft 6.7 in.) and has 670 pages. Weighing 800 kg, it was printed in Milan, Italy, on YUPO synthetic paper, making it untearable and waterproof. It was unveiled on 26 February 2019.

Only Shakespeare folio

A rare copy of Shakespeare's First Folio (1623) was found at the Mahatma Gandhi Central Library, University of Roorkee (now IIT-Roorkee) in Uttar Pradesh. The 900-page volume titled *Mr William Shakespeare's Comedies, Histories and Tragedies* was found in an old trunk in the librarian's office. It contains 36 of Shakespeare's 37 plays.

Smallest book

B. Jameela of Madras (now Chennai, Tamil Nadu) had a copy of the Quran, which is 27 mm (1.06 in.) long, 19 mm (0.74 in.) wide and 10 mm (0.39 in.) thick, and weighed only 4.4 g.

WR Thickest book

Shree HaricharitramrutSagar, which was published by Swami Gyanjivandasji, is the thickest book. It is 49.6 cm (19.52 in.) thick, and measures 21.9 cm (8.62 in.) in length and 14.4 cm (5.67 in.) in width. The book was launched on 2 February 2020 at the Shree Swaminarayan Temple in Botad city, Botad District, Gujarat.

***Shree HaricharitramrutSagar*: thickest book**

Most translated Indian work

The most translated Indian work is the Bhagavadgita, which is an integral part of the Mahabharata. The Bhagavadgita was first translated into English in 1785 by British typographer and founder of the Asiatic Society, Charles Wilkins. Since then, it has been translated into as many as 55 languages.

Shortest title of a book

First Step Publishing, a publishing house based in Mumbai, Maharashtra, launched an anthology titled *I* on 25 May 2014. The book contains 15 short stories (14 short stories and a foreword also in the form of a story) written by 15 authors, all based on the topic 'I'. The authors of the short stories are from India, South Africa and the UK. The book's cover features the word 'I' in 10 languages – five Indian and five other foreign ones.

SUPER 30

A SUITABLE BOY AWAITS A SUITABLE SEQUEL

First published in May 1993, *A Suitable Boy* by Vikram Seth is a landmark novel in Indian writing in English – one that has contributed immensely to the literary culture of India. Counted among the longest novels in English – it reportedly took Seth nearly eight years to complete it – the saga makes up more than 1,000 pages with over 590,000 words. Set in newly independent India, the novel explores love, social hierarchies, conflicts and changes, familial relationships, and the post-Partition political scenario, among other themes. It won the Commonwealth Writer's Prize for Best Book (1994) and was included in BBC's 2019 list of '100 Novels That Shaped Our World'. In 2020, a six-part TV drama miniseries, adapted from the book by Andrew Davies and directed by Mira Nair for BBC One, was streamed on Netflix. A 'jump' sequel, *A Suitable Girl*, is keenly anticipated.

Vikram Seth

Longest title of a book – English

Dr Vangeepuram Sreenathachary of Mahbubnagar, Telangana, has written a book with the longest known title. The book, *Handy Crystals, A Quiver of Smile...* is about the origin and etymology of 108 idioms, proverbs, phrases and words. The title consists of 1,086 words (5,633 characters). This bilingual (English and Telugu) book was released at the Sri Shirdi Sai Baba Sansthan, Hyderabad, Telangana, on 27 September 2009.

Largest sales for a children's book – hardback

Harry Potter and the Cursed Child (Parts One and Two) is the official script book for the play of the same name written by J.K. Rowling, John Tiffany and Jack Thorne. It is the eighth story published in the Harry Potter book series. Released in India by Hachette India, Gurugram, Haryana, in July 2016, it sold 259,537 print copies (as of October 2017), making it the largest-selling children's book in India.

Largest sales on release for a fiction title – hardback

Dan Brown is a bestselling American author of thrillers. His book *Origin* was the fifth in his Robert Langdon series, following *Angels & Demons, The Da Vinci Code, The Lost Symbol* and *Inferno*. It was released in India on 3 October 2017 by Penguin Random House, with an initial subscription of 125,000 copies, breaking all records in the fiction hardback category.

Largest-selling bilingual dictionary

The English–English–Malayalam Dictionary by T. Ramalingam Pillai was first published in May 1983. Published by DC Books, based in Kottayam, Kerala, it is in its 55th impression now. As on September 2019, around 2.4 million copies had been sold.

Largest lifetime sales – hardback

The Secret by Rhonda Byrne, published by Simon and Schuster, USA, in 2006, is a bestselling self-help book, based on the pseudoscientific 'law of attraction', which claims that a person's thoughts can change the world directly. The book has sold over 700,000 copies in India and has also been translated into 50 languages.

Largest adult non-fiction seller – hardback

Cricket legend Sachin Tendulkar's autobiography, *Playing It My Way*, which he co-authored with Boria Majumdar, was published in India by Hachette India, Gurugram, Haryana, and released on 6 November 2014. It broke all previous records in the adult non-fiction (hardback) category with 150,289 copies confirmed on order subscriptions.

Anthology in most languages

An international multilingual anthology of poetry, titled *Amaravati Poetic Prism 2019*, edited by Padmaja Iyengar–Paddy and published by the Cultural Centre of Vijayawada and Amaravati, Andhra Pradesh, features 1,303 poems in 120 Indian and foreign languages, contributed by poets from across India and the world.

First Indian poet in English

Henry Louis Vivian Derozio (b. 18 April 1809), assistant headmaster of Hindu College, Calcutta (now Presidency University, Kolkata, West Bengal), is considered to be the first Indian poet who wrote in English. The poems that he submitted to the newspaper *India Gazette* under the pseudonym 'Juvenis' were published as a collection in 1827. The second edition of the collection was released in the following year and included his most famous poem, 'The Fakeer of Jungheera', which featured aspects of life in colonial India.

First pseudonym

'Sujatha' was the pseudonym of the popular Tamil author S. Rangarajan (1935–2008), who wrote more than 100 novels, 250 short stories, ten books on science, ten stage plays and a volume of poems.
He was a regular contributor to

India's First Sign Language Dictionary

Bridging the gap for the deaf and speech-disabled communities, *The Indian Sign Language Dictionary*, a first-of-its-kind book, was launched on 23 March 2018. Developed by the Delhi-based Indian Sign Language Research and Training Centre (ISLRTC), it contains 3,000 words in Hindi and English, and their corresponding graphic representations. It is available in both print and video formats. In an effort to bring uniformity to the various sign languages used across the country, the book divides the words into five categories – Everyday, Legal, Academic, Medical and Technical Terms.

topical columns in Tamil periodicals such as *Ananda Vikatan*, *Kumudam* and *Kalki*. He served for a brief period as the editor of *Kumudam*, and also wrote screenplays and dialogues for Tamil movies.

BOOK SELLING AND PUBLISHING

First book fair

The First International Book Fair opened at New Delhi's Pragati Maidan on 18 March 1972 during the International Book Year. Around a hundred Indian publishers took part, displaying about 10,000 books in English and local Indian languages. Foreign participants included those from the USSR, the USA, France, New Zealand, Turkey and Sri Lanka.

First book café

The first book café was opened in India in 1991. The Full Circle Bookstore and Turtle Café in Delhi were among the first book cafés in India.

Biggest retail bookstore chain – high street

Crossword Bookstores Ltd, a wholly owned subsidiary of Shoppers Stop Ltd, is the largest high-street bookstore chain in India. Established in October 1992, the company had 84 stores, including franchises, across India in December 2019, including in Mumbai, Bengaluru, Ahmedabad, Gurugram, Delhi, Kolkata, Chennai, Pune, Nashik, Vadodara, Jaipur, Bhopal, Kanpur, Panaji, Thrissur, Kottayam, Thiruvananthapuram, Siliguri, Lucknow, Kohima, Ghaziabad, Raipur and Hyderabad.

Largest bookstore

Sapna Book House in Gandhinagar, Bengaluru, Karnataka, was started in 1967 by Suresh C. Shah. Spread over 3,716 sq. m (40,000 sq. ft), it has more than 220,000 titles covering many genres and topics. Sapna Book House has four more branches in Bengaluru and Mysuru – adding up to retail space of about 9,290.3 sq. m (100,000 sq. ft).

India's First Book Village

Bilhar, located in Satara District of Maharashtra, was identified as the first book village in India on 4 May 2017. Known as 'Pustakanch Gaav', the village has genre-specific libraries in 25 locations, housing more than 15,000 books, mostly in Marathi. The village is decorated with murals, paintings and artworks on the theme of books. The aim of the initiative is to share a passion for books and an appetite for knowledge.

Further south, the Bappuji Smaraka Vayanasala and the Kerala State Library Council turned Perumkulam in Thiruvananthapuram District, Kerala, into a village of books, as announced by Jnanpith Award winner M.T. Vasudevan Nair in June 2019. Ten boxes with 50 books each were set up for anyone to take books from and replace with others.

Oldest bookshop
Higginbothams, the oldest bookshop in the country, was opened in 1844 by Abel Joshua Higginbotham in Madras (now Chennai, Tamil Nadu). It has a subscription division that helps educational institutions, corporate bodies and professionals to get journals and periodicals from more than 3,000 publishing houses abroad.

Largest book market
College Street in Kolkata, West Bengal, is the venue of the largest book market in the country and possibly the largest used-books market in the world. Known locally as *boi para* (the neighbourhood of books), this 1.5 km long street sees a large number of book lovers and buyers every day. The street suffered major damage due to cyclone Amphan in May 2020, but crowd funding efforts and the resilience of he shopkeepers brought it back in business soon.

Most travel bookstores
Wheeler (A.H. Wheeler and Co. Pvt. Ltd) owns a bookstore chain co-founded by Emile Moreau and T.K. Banerjee in Allahabad (now Prayagraj, Uttar Pradesh) in 1877, with around 900 popular bookshops selling magazines and books at as many as 264 railway stations.

First literary agency
Neville Tuli of Osian, Rajasthan, set up the first professional agency for authors on 9 April 2007. The first author they signed on was Omair Ahmad on 1 June 2007. The literary agency was a division of Osian's Connoisseurs of Art Pvt. Ltd.

First independent publisher
The first Indian publisher to set up a press was Gangakishor Bhattacharya in 1821 in Calcutta (now Kolkata, West Bengal), a former employee of the Serampore Press, Serampore, Bengal (now Srirampur, West Bengal). He published 18th-century ballads in Bengali and adaptations from classics.

Record Rewind

Longest title of a book - regional language

2013
Jayakumar Jaiji from Kollam District, Kerala, wrote a book in Malayalam with the longest title of 1,147 words. Titled *Sukhakaramya Jeevitham...*, it was about achieving a good life and was published by Future Media Books, Kollum, in February 2012.

2020
Ravi Vasant Sonar from Maharashtra wrote a poetry book in Marathi, titled *Sakhisobati Kshanvaividhyanchi Gumphan...*, with the longest title of 1,057 words and 6,076 characters. It was published on 1 January 2017 by Shivpradnya Prakashan Publication, Maharashtra.

First feminist publishing house
Kali for Women, a not-for-profit trust, publishing a wide variety of books by women and on women, was started in 1984 by Urvashi Butalia and Ritu Menon in New Delhi.

I for Instapoetry

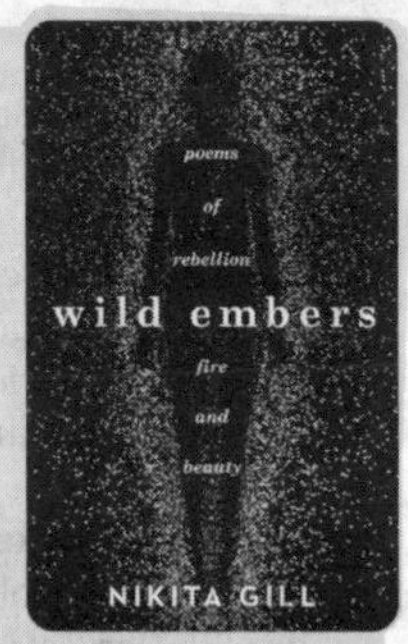

Instagram, a picture-sharing social media service, has provided a platform for poets across the world. Popularly known as 'Instapoets', they share short and relatable poems that appeal to the millennial mindset for their accessibility and aesthetic. Rupi Kaur (@Rupikaur), an Indian-born Canadian poet, was one of the first to harness the potential of Instapoetry, with published works such as *Milk and Honey* (2014) and *The Sun and Her Flowers* (2017). Other well-known Indian Instapoets include Nikita Gill (@Nikita_gill), Arunoday Singh (@Sufisoul), Chhaya Dabas (@baatein), Pratishtha Khattar (@_paradoxandmetaphors_) and Karuna Ezara Parikh (@Ezarawrites), among others.

Largest trade publishing house

Penguin Random House India is the subcontinent's largest English-language trade publisher. It publishes more than 250 new titles every year and has an active backlist of 3,000 titles.

According to a Nielsen survey in July 2020, 9% of respondents preferred Indian authors, 26% preferred international ones and 65% liked both equally.

Largest literary publisher

DC Books in Kottayam, Kerala, started in 1974 by Dominic Chacko Kizhakemuri, is considered the publishing hub of south India. The translation programme of DC Books is considered to be the largest in India. It publishes around 1,400 books in a year (2019).

AWARDS AND HONOURS

First Sahitya Akademi Bhasha Samman Award

The Bhasha Samman Awards are given annually for contribution towards the development of a language. The first of these awards were given in 1996 to:

- Dharikshan Mishra for Bhojpuri.
- Bansi Ram Sharma and M.R. Thakur for Pahari (Himachali).
- K. Jathappa Rai and Mandara Keshava Bhat for Tulu (Karnataka).
- Chandra Kanta Murasingh for Kokborok (Tripura).

First recipients of the Sahitya Akademi Award

- Makhanlal Chaturvedi (1889–1968), a Hindi poet, was the first person to receive this award for *Him Tarangini* (Hindi) in 1955.
- The Punjabi poet and writer Amrita Pritam (1919–2005) received the award in 1956, the year after its inception, for *Sunehre* (Punjabi), a collection of poems.

First recipients of the Jnanpith Award

The Jnanpith Award is presented annually by the Bharatiya Jnanpith to an Indian author for his/her contribution to literature.

LIT FESTS

First virtual literary festival
LitFest X, organized between 23 October and 1 November 2015 was the country's first virtual literary festival. The event used multiple platforms like YouTube, Google Hangouts, Facebook and Twitter to present the interactive sessions to readers.

First children's literary festival
Co-founded by Swati Roy, Jo Williams and Venkatesh M. in 2008, Bookaroo was the first children's literary festival in India, with its first edition held in New Delhi.

Largest literary festival
The Jaipur Literature Festival, founded in 2006, is an annual literary festival in Jaipur, Rajasthan, which brings together some of the most prominent thinkers and writers from across the world, every January. The festival directors are authors Namita Gokhale and William Dalrymple, and it has been produced by Sanjoy Roy of Teamwork Arts since 2008.

First Comic Con
The Annual Indian Comic Convention was organized for the first time on 19 February 2011 by Twenty Onwards Media at Dilli Haat. Fifty publishers participated in it, bringing together writers, gamers, cosplayers, games and films.

TOP 10 FRONT-LIST TITLES* 2020

	TITLE	AUTHOR	VOLUME
ADULT FICTION	*ONE ARRANGED MURDER*	CHETAN BHAGAT	121,054
	LEGEND OF SUHELDEV: THE KING WHO SAVED INDIA	AMISH	40,647
	STORIES WE NEVER TELL	SAVI SHARMA	29,506
	THE VAULT OF VISHNU	ASHWIN SANGHI	20,474
	A SECOND CHANCE	SUDEEP NAGARKAR	9,066
	WHEN LOVE CAME CALLING	PREETI SHENOY	6,769
	HIDDEN IN PLAIN SIGHT	JEFFREY ARCHER	5,312
	ONE DAY, LIFE WILL CHANGE: A STORY OF LOVE AND INSPIRATION TO WIN LIFE WHEN IT HITS YOU HARD	SARANYA UMAKANTHAN	3,755
	CROSS YOUR HEART, TAKE MY NAME	NOVONEEL CHAKRABORTY	3,473
	SHUGGIE BAIN (WINNER OF THE 2020 BOOKER PRIZE)	DOUGLAS STUART	3,364
ADULT NON-FICTION	*THINK LIKE A MONK*	JAY SHETTY	123,224
	DEATH; AN INSIDE STORY: A BOOK FOR ALL THOSE WHO SHALL DIE	SADHGURU	104,941
	12-WEEK FITNESS PROJECT	RUJUTA DIWEKAR	47,203
	THE PSYCHOLOGY OF MONEY	MORGAN HOUSEL	18,103
	A PROMISED LAND	BARACK OBAMA	17,690
	EATING IN THE AGE OF DIETING	RUJUTA DIWEKAR	10,872
	WHY NOT ME? A FEELING OF MILLIONS	ANUBHAV AGRAWAL	10,663
	THE ARCHER	PAULO COELHO	9,689
	THE INDIA WAY: STRATEGIES FOR AN UNCERTAIN WORLD	S. JAISHANKAR	9,645
	LET ME SAY IT NOW	RAKESH MARIA	8,855
CHILDREN'S FICTION	*DIARY OF A WIMPY KID: THE DEEP END*	JEFF KINNEY	17,599
	THE TRIALS OF APOLLO: THE TOWER OF NERO	RICK RIORDAN	8,980
	ROWLEY JEFFERSON'S AWESOME FRIENDLY ADVENTURE	JEFF KINNEY	6,845
	MIDNIGHT SUN	STEPHANIE MEYER	5,839
	GRANDPARENTS' BAG OF STORIES	SUDHA MURTY	3,658
	THE ICKABOG	J.K. ROWLING	2,763
	THE BATTLE FOR CRYSTAL CASTLE	GERONIMO STILTON	1,790
	THE JOURNEY THROUGH TIME: TIME WARP	GERONIMO STILTON	1,589
	DOG MAN: CRIME AND PUNISHMENT	DEV PILKEY	1,527
	THE LAST HOURS: THE CHAIN OF GOLD	CASSANDRA CLARE	1,412

CHILDREN'S NON-FICTION	TITLE	AUTHOR	VOLUME
	INDIA'S SPACE ADVENTURE	BIMAN BASU	1,697
	THE CONSTITUTION OF INDIA FOR CHILDREN	SUBHADRA SEN GUPTA	1,550
	THE INCREDIBLE HISTORY OF THE INDIAN OCEAN	SANJEEV SANYAL	1,217
	UNLOCKING THE UNIVERSE	STEPHEN HAWKING AND LUCY HAWKING	968
	6 SECRETS SMART STUDENTS DON'T TELL YOU	CHANDAN DESHMUKH	882
	WOW!: SECRETS OF THE OCEANS: ENCYCLOPEDIA IN AUGMENTED REALITY	DREAMLAND PUBLICATIONS	758
	INDIA IN SPACE	HARPERCOLLINS PUBLISHERS INDIA	680
	WOW!: ANIMALS: ENCYCLOPEDIA IN AUGMENTED REALITY	DREAMLAND PUBLICATIONS	657
	SCIENCE PUZZLES FOR CLEVER KIDS: OVER 100 STEM EXERCISES TO EXERCISE YOUR MIND	GARETH MOORE, CHRIS DICKASON AND DAMARA STRONG	379
	CANDID TALES: INDIA ON A MOTORCYCLE	ADITHI RAO	314

* Titles published between 1 January and 31 December 2020. Data sourced from Nielsen BookScan retail panel market and © Nielsen BookScan. Volume indicates the number of copies sold.
NOTE: Nielsen BookScan is the world's first continuous retail sales monitoring service for print books, based on electronic point-of-sale data collected directly from tills and despatch systems. It is the most comprehensive book sales tracking system in India. While it does not claim to have full market coverage, it is still the best representative collated data available in the country, covering the mix of channels, i.e., national and regional chain bookstores, independent bookstores and online players.

- Ashapurna Devi (1909–95), Bengali novelist and poet, was the first woman author to receive the Jnanpith Award in 1976 for her novel *Pratham Pratishruti* (which was published in 1965), the first of a trilogy that included *Subarnalata* and *Bakul Katha*.
- G. Sankara Kurup (1901–78), the Malayalam poet, was the recipient of the first Jnanpith Award in 1965, the year of its inception, for his anthology of poems, titled *Odakkuzhal*.

Most prolific translator – published literary works
Prof. Bibek Debroy, an economist, policymaker and author, has translated into English, the *Mahabharata* (2.25 million words), *Harivamsha* (160,000 words, published in 2016), the *Valmiki Ramayana* (0.5 million words, published in 2017) and the *Bhagavata Purana* (0.5 million words, published in December 2018). He is the third person (after Kisari Mohan Ganguli [1883 to 1895]), and Manmatha Nath Dutt [1895 to 1905]) to translate the unabridged version of the Mahabharata into English. His translation was published in 10 volumes (2010–14), and a box set released in 2015 by Penguin Random House India.

First Indian citizen to win the Booker Prize
Arundhati Roy (b. 24 November 1961) won the prestigious Booker Prize in 1997 for her first novel, *The God of Small Things*.
- Two other Indian-origin authors had won the Prize before her – Salman

First Indian Writer in English to Win the Jnanpith Award

Amitav Ghosh

Amitav Ghosh (b. 11 July 1956), a renowned contemporary literary figure, became the first Indian writer in English to be given the Jnanpith Award on 12 June 2019 at the 54th Jnanpith Awards (2018) in New Delhi. He was chosen for his contribution to the enrichment of Indian literature. His most famous works include *The Shadow Lines*, *The Glass Palace*, *The Circle of Reason* and The Ibis Trilogy (*Sea of Poppies*, *River of Smoke* and *Flood of Fire*), among others. His works have been translated into more than 30 languages.

Rushdie for his novel *Midnight's Children* in 1981 and Sir V.S. Naipaul for *In a Free State* in 1971 (he also won the Nobel Prize in literature in 2001).

- Kiran Desai won the laurel for her novel, *The Inheritance of Loss,* in 2006.
- Aravind Adiga won the Booker Prize in 2008 for his novel, *The White Tiger*.

First Indian winner of the Commonwealth Writers' Prize

Author Nayantara Sahgal (b. 10 May 1927) won the Commonwealth Writers' Prize for Best Book in 1987, for her novel *Plans for Departure.*

First Indian winner of the Neustadt Prize

The Neustadt International Prize (given for an author's body of work) is one of the few international prizes for which poets, novelists and playwrights are all eligible. Raja Rao was the first Indian to win it in 1988. Indian-Canadian writer Rohinton Mistry won the prize in 2012.

The Jnanpith Awards, given annually for the best literary works in the 22 Scheduled Languages of India, have been awarded 60 times up to 2019.

First Indian winner of the Ondaatje Prize

Sports journalist Rahul Bhattacharya's *The Sly Company of People Who Care* won the Royal Society of Literature Ondaatje Prize 2012. It also won the Hindu Literary Prize (2011) and was the Kirkus Fiction Book of the Year in the USA.

First Indian recipient of the UNESCO International Book Reading Award

Dina Nath Malhotra started Hind Pocket Books and became a book consultant to UNESCO in 1971, before being awarded the Book Reading Award. His son Shekhar Malhotra later started Full Circle publishing house and bookshop in New Delhi.

First Sahitya Akademi Fellowship

Former Indian president and eminent scholar Dr S. Radhakrishnan (1888–1975) was the first to receive this honour in 1968 for his contribution to Indian thought and universal humanism. The first woman to be elected Fellow of the Akademi was the poet Mahadevi Varma in 1979.

BOOKED FOR AN AWARD

The past three decades have seen a steady rise in the spread and recognition of outstanding Indian writing in English on the global platform, notching up awards and prizes for noteworthy works. Indian and Indian-origin writers have won the Man Booker Prize three times (1997, 2006 and 2008), the DSC Prize for South Asian Literature six times (2013, 2014, 2015, 2016, 2018 and 2019), the Pulitzer Prize for Non-fiction once (2000), the Pulitzer Prize for Fiction once (2000), the Neustadt International Prize once (2012), the Ondaatje Prize once (2012) and the Newbery Medal once (2019) all in the years between 1990 and 2020.

First winner of Grinzane Cavour award

Anita Desai won the lifetime achievement award of the Grinzane Cavour Prize in Piedmont, Italy, on 18 July 2005.

First Indian winner of Newbery Medal

- Dhan Gopal Mukerji (1890–1936), who was born in a village near Calcutta (now Kolkata, West Bengal) and later went to the USA, was the first Indian winner of the Newbery Medal for his novel, *Gay-Neck, the Story of a Pigeon*, in 1928.
- The most recent winner of the award is Indian-origin writer Veera Hiranandani for her work *The Night Diary* in 2019.

First to win the DSC Prize for South Asian Literature

Poet and novelist Jeet Thayil won the DSC Prize for South Asian Literature 2013 for his novel *Narcopolis* (Faber & Faber).

First Indian winner of the Pulitzer Prize – literature

Jhumpa Lahiri's *Interpreter of Maladies* (Mariner Books/ Houghton Mifflin) won the Pulitzer Prize for Fiction in 2000.

A Titanic Text in Titanium

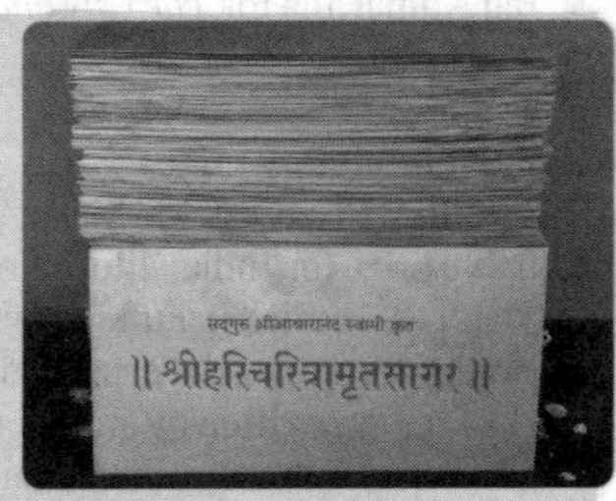

Shree HaricharitramrutSagar, a sacred text of the Swaminarayan sect, was inscribed into a manuscript made of titanium plates to preserve it for posterity. The original book was written by Shree Adharanand Swami around 200 years ago and the same manuscript is engraved on the titanium plates. It consists of 12,404 lustrous silver-coloured 'pages', weighs 778 kg, and contains 102,564 *doha*s and *chaupai*s, 29 cantos and 2,409 *tarang*s. The original manuscript was scanned to digitize the pages and later inscribed on to the plates using laser technology. Swami Gyanjivandasji (Kundaldham) engraved the manuscript from 24 May 2015 to 7 July 2018. Shree Swaminarayan Mandir, Karelibaug, Vadodara, Gujarat, then dedicated it to the Shree Swaminarayan Temple, Vadtal, Kheda District, Gujarat, on 20 November 2018.

AWARD WINNERS (2019–20)	
Award/Prize	**Winner**
Jnanpith Award	Akkitham Achuthan Namboothiri – Malayalam (2019)
DSC Prize for South Asian Literature	Amitabha Bagchi for *Half the Night Is Gone* (2019)
JCB Prize for Literature	• Madhuri Vijay for *The Far Field* (2019) • S. Hareesh for *Moustache* (2020)
Kamaladevi Chhatopadhyay NIF Book Prize	• Ornit Shani for *How India Became Democratic* (2019) • Amit Ahuja for *Mobilizing the Marginalized* and Jairam Ramesh for *A Chequered Brilliance* (2020)
Hindu Literary Prize	• Mirza Waheed for *Tell Her Everything* (Fiction – 2019) • Santanu Das for *India, Empire, and First World War Culture: Writings, Images and Songs* (Non-fiction – 2019)

First winners of the Rabindranath Tagore Literary Prize

The Rabindranath Tagore Literary Prize, started in 2018, is awarded annually for valuable contributions to literature and poetry.

- Kabir (awarded posthumously) for *One Hundred Poems of Kabir* in 2018.
- Rana Dasgupta for *Solo* (2010) in 2019.
- Raj Kamal Jha for *The City and the Sea* (2019) in 2020.

Highest monetary prize

- The JCB Prize, established in 2018, is the most valuable prize for Indian literature, amounting to ₹25 lakh (2.5 million). Funded by JCB, a British manufacturing firm, the prize is given to the best work of fiction written by an Indian citizen in English or translated from any other language into English. While two of the four JCB nomination spots are reserved for translations, each of the five shortlisted books is awarded ₹1 lakh (0.1 million) and a separate prize of ₹5 lakh (0.5 million) is given if the winning entry is a translation. Mita Kapur now serves as its literary director.
- The richest prize for non-fiction writing is the New India Foundation Prize, valued at ₹15 lakh (1.5 million).

Mita Kapur, literary director, JCB prize

SCIENCE AND TECHNOLOGY

FORMAL SCIENCES

MATHEMATICS

Earliest mention of mathematical series

Arithmetic and geometric series were mentioned in Vedic literature as early as 2000 BCE. They are mentioned in the *Taittiriya Samhita* and in the *Panchavimsa Brahmana*.

Earliest treatise on geometry

The *Shulba Sutras* are the earliest known treatises that are related to geometry. Dating to the Vedic period, these texts are focused on the measurement and the building of altars. Baudhayana, who lived around 800 BCE, wrote the first *Shulba Sutra*.

Earliest use of irrational numbers

The use of irrational numbers dates back to the *Shulba Sutras* (c. first millennium BCE).

First mention of geometry

In the first millennium BCE, Apastamba, the founder of a Vedic school, propounded practical geometry for the construction of sacrificial altars, which describes acute, obtuse and right angles.

Earliest magic squares

The oldest magic square that can be dated in India occurs in polymath Varahamihira's encyclopaedic work, the *Brihat-Samhita* (c. 550 CE). He used a modified 4 x 4 magic square to indicate combinations and quantities of ingredients for making perfumes.

Use of sines and cosines in place of chords

In a significant contribution to trigonometry, Indian mathematicians changed the use of chords to sines and cosines, making the system much more convenient and the various theorems on triangles much neater. Starting with the *Arya-siddhanta* (c. fourth century CE), Aryabhata used a simple table for sines. Varahamihira gave the first clear statements of $\sin^2 A$ and $\sin^2 A + \cos^2 A$.

Srinivasa Ramanujan: The Man Who Knew Infinity

Srinivasa Iyengar Ramanujan (1887–1920), born in Erode, Madras Presidency (now in Tamil Nadu), is known for mathematical analysis, number theory, infinite series and continued fractions. In his short life, Ramanujan independently compiled exemplary work such as the Ramanujan prime, the Ramanujan theta function, partition formulae and mock theta functions. His work has been analysed and studied for decades as a source of new mathematical ideas. *The Man Who Knew Infinity*. a 2015 British biopic about him, starring Dev Patel, was based on the 1991 book of the same name by Robert Kanigel.

Srinivasa Ramanujan

First to discover Kuttaka

Aryabhata was the first mathematician who solved the equation ax + by = c, where x and y are unknown quantities and a, b and c are known quantities with integer values. The solution to this equation is known as 'Kuttaka' (or 'pulverizer') because it involves a process of continued division. It is now more popularly known around the world as the 'Diophantine equation', after a Greek mathematician.

Earliest mention of the decimal system

Medhatithi, who lived around the ninth or tenth century CE, was the first to propound the concept of counting numbers in multiples of 10 and stated very high numerals in a systematic manner.

Earliest use of the decimal system

A Gupta inscription from 448 CE found in Allahabad (now Prayagraj) District, Uttar Pradesh, indicates that the decimal system was known in India at the beginning of the fifth century CE.

Invention of algebra

Aryabhata (476–550 CE) from Kusumapura (Pataliputra) in Bihar is credited with the invention of algebra. He was also the first to approximate the value of pi to 3.14159, which is accepted today.

First to understand 'zero'

- Brahmagupta (c. 598–c. 668 CE) was the first mathematician to treat zero as a number and present its mathematical operations.
- Bhaskara I (c. 600 – c. 680) was the first mathematician to understand the properties of both zero and infinity, and to state that any number divided by zero equals infinity.

First Study of Infinite Series

Founded in the 14th century by Madhava of Sangamagrama (c. 1340–c. 1425), who is said to have been born in present-day Irinjalakuda in Thrissur District, Kerala, the Kerala school of astronomy and mathematics (or the Kerala school) was responsible for notable contributions to the study of infinite series, trigonometry, geometry, algebra and calculus. The foundations for calculus laid by Madhava were further developed by his successors at the Kerala school, with many results

Record Rewind

Fastest human calculations

1991

Shankuntala Devi of Bengaluru, Karnataka, was the only person in the world to calculate faster than a computer. Her record was for successfully multiplying two randomly selected 13-digit numbers in 28 seconds, at Imperial College London, UK, on 18 June 1980.

2020

20-year old Neelakantha Bhanu Prakash (b. 13 October 1999) became the fastest human calculator in the world after winning the gold for India in the Mental Calculation World Championship at Mind Sports Olympiad (MSO) in September 2020.

A New Definition of Kilogram

In May 2019, India adopted the new definition of kilogram, one that is no longer defined by the platinum-iridium cylinder called Le Grand K. The new kg is defined based on the Kibble balance, which uses Planck's constant, one of the most important quantities in physics, to measure the mass of an object using a precisely measured electromagnetic force. The extra accuracy will help scientists, but there will be no change for the common person.

that would later be repeated in Europe, including the infinite series for circular and trigonometric functions.

Earliest solution of the Brahmagupta–Bhaskara equation
Brahmagupta had nearly solved the indeterminate equation that is now referred to as the Pell equation. Bhaskara II (c. 1114–1185) had improved upon the solution long before Western mathematicians solved it. In Sanskrit, this equation is known as *varga prakriti* or the equation of the multiplied square.

Garga, a sage belonging to the Vedic period, is known to have enumerated 27 Indian constellations or nakshatras.

First textbook on arithmetic
Ganita Sara Sangraha, written by the great mathematician Mahavira in 850 CE, is the first known textbook on arithmetic. The subject matter and its arrangement is said to be practically the same as that in present-day textbooks. It only lacks a chapter on decimals.

WR **Discovery of differential calculus**
Bhaskara II (c. 1114–1185), said to have been born in Bijapur (now Vijayapura) in Karnataka, conducted mathematical operations that showed he had invented calculus long before Isaac Newton and Gottfried Leibniz, who are considered its pioneers. He used calculus to determine the area and volume of a sphere and the daily motion of planets.

First to give the Gregory series
In 1502, Keḷallur Nilakantha Somayaji (1444–1545 CE) from Tirur in present-day Malappuram District, Kerala, devised the *Tantrasangraha* equation employed to give the approximate value of Π or pi (3.14159...). This is known today as the 'Gregory series' after it appeared in the works of later mathematicians James Gregory (1638–75) and Gottfried Leibniz (1646–1716).

Discovery of the Kaprekar Constant
D.R. Kaprekar (1905–81) discovered in 1946 what is now known as the 'Kaprekar Constant' in mathematics. This is a constant (6174) that arises when one takes a four-digit number with at least two different digits and forms the largest and

smallest numbers using its digits, and then subtracts the smaller one from the larger one. Continuing with this, one will always arrive at the number 6174.

WR Biggest sundial

The Samrat Yantra built by Sawai Jai Singh II, ruler of the kingdom of Amber in Rajasthan, in 1728 CE at Jaipur, Rajasthan, is the biggest sundial in the world. Its gnomon rises to 22.6 m (74 ft).

Invention of the Mahalanobis distance

Pioneering statistician P.C. Mahalanobis (1893–1972) invented statistical tools such as the Mahalanobis distance and fractile graphical analysis in 1936. He was the first statistician to be elected a Fellow of the Royal Society, UK, in 1945.

First mathematical society

The Indian Mathematical Society (IMS) was the oldest organization in India devoted to the promotion of the study of and research in mathematics. With its headquarters in Pune, Maharashtra, it was founded by V. Ramaswamy Aiyer in April 1907. The society's first president was Dr B. Hanumantha Rao.

First to propose a theory on infinite dimensional representations

India-born American mathematician-physicist Harish Chandra (1923–83) created a theory for infinite dimensional representations in 1947, which first appeared in quantum mechanics when it was necessary to analyse the effect of symmetries on the motions of particles and waves.

PHYSICAL SCIENCES

ASTRONOMY

Earliest observation of the Pole Star

Ancient astronomers Ashwalayana and Patanjali recorded observing the Pole Star (or *dhruvatara*) in c. 1300 BCE.

The first astronomers

- Lagadha, who lived around 900 BCE near Srinagar, Jammu and Kashmir, was the first to systematize astronomy, the first to complete a text – *Vedanga Jyotisha* or *Jyotishavedanga* – on astronomy and the first to work out simple formulae to derive unknown quantities from known ones.
- Aryabhata (476–550 CE) was the first astronomer to deduce that the earth is round and that it rotates on its own axis, causing day and night.

First manual on the astrolabe

The astrolabe is an instrument for measuring the altitude of stars. Mahendra Suri (c. 1340–1400), an astronomer, wrote a manual on the astrolabe in Sanskrit while under the patronage of ruler Firuz Shah Tughlaq of the Tughlaq dynasty.

First known record of an astrolabe

The Yantraraja, which was 276 mm (10.87 in.) in diameter, was designed and built in Ahmedabad, Gujarat, in 1607 for astronomer Damodara during the reign of the Mughal ruler Jahangir.

Evolution of the universe

Kapila, who lived around the eighth or seventh century BCE, was the first to give a theory of the evolution of the universe. According to his Samkhya philosophy, the present universe evolved from an unmanifested, undifferentiated, infinite and eternal primordial ground state called *prakriti*.

WR First chain of observatories

About a century after European astronomers had verified Polish scientist Nicolaus Copernicus's theory that the sun was at the centre of the universe, Sawai Jai Singh II (1686–1743), maharaja of the kingdom of Amber in Rajasthan, was the first in the world to build a chain of astronomical observatories, in Mathura, Varanasi, Delhi and Jaipur, from 1719 to 1737.

First modern catalogue of stars

The Madras or Taylor catalogue was made by T.G. Taylor, astronomer to the British East India Company, in 1844. The catalogue contained the positions of 11,015 stars, based on his observations of the night sky in Madras (now Chennai), Tamil Nadu.

First astronomical observatory

On 5 December 1786, William Petrie, an officer of the East India Company, made the first astronomical observations to calculate the latitude and longitude of the Masulipatnam Fort from his private observatory. This observatory on the terrace of his residence was fitted with an astronomical clock, a transit instrument and two or three telescopes. The first modern astronomical observatory, the Nizamia Observatory, was set up more than a century later in Hyderabad (now in Telangana) in 1908 by the Nizam's administration.

First to observe a nova

Radha Gobinda Chandra (1878–1975) from Jessore (now in Bangladesh) was the first Indian astronomer to observe a nova. A nova is a transient astronomical event that causes the sudden appearance of a bright and seemingly 'new' star that slowly fades over weeks or months. He sighted the nova in the Aquila constellation on 7 June 1918. A pioneer of observational astronomy in Bengal (now West Bengal), Chandra was one of the first international members of the American Association of Variable Star Observers.

Discovery of the Bappu–Wilson effect

Indian astronomer M.K.V. Bappu (1927–82), in collaboration with Colin C. Wilson at Mount Wilson and Palomar Observatories, USA, discovered a relationship between the luminosity of particular types of stars and their spectral characteristics. Known as the 'Bappu–Wilson effect', this helps determine the luminosity and distance of these types of stars and was discovered in 1957.

Rings of Uranus discovered

Prof. J.C. Bhattacharya and Sri Kuppuswamy from the Indian Institute of Astrophysics, Bangalore (now Bengaluru), Karnataka, discovered the rings of planet Uranus in 1976 at the Vainu Bappu Observatory in Kavalur, Tamil Nadu. Around the same time, US astronomer James Elliot and his team, aboard the airborne Kuiper Observatory, discovered the same rings during an occultation of a star by the planet.

Discovery of solar radio burst

In 1958, Prof. Govind Swarup (b. 1929) and A. Maxwell discovered a burst, called 'type U solar radio burst'. A pioneer of radio astronomy, Swarup was behind the concept, design and installation of the Ooty Radio Telescope near present-day Udhagamandalam, Tamil Nadu, and the Giant Metrewave Radio Telescope (GMRT) near Poona (now Pune) in Maharashtra.

M.P. Birla Planetarium, Kolkata: oldest planetarium

Oldest planetarium

The M.P. Birla Planetarium at Calcutta (now Kolkata), West Bengal, was set up on 29 September 1962 by the Birla Education Trust. The planetarium coordinates the activities of the Amateur Astronomers Association, which include telescope fabrication, astrophotography and organizing skywatching sessions.

Discovery of the variability of stars

In 1958, astrophysicist K.D. Abhyankar (1928–2007), professor of astronomy at the Osmania University in Hyderabad (now in Telangana), discovered the variability of two types of stars, called dwarf cepheid and the short period eclipsing binary BD-18 3477.

First university to teach astronomy

Osmania University, based in Hyderabad (now in Telangana), was the first educational institution in the country to start teaching astronomy and astrophysics at postgraduate and research levels in 1959. The Astronomical Society of India was also registered in Hyderabad, in 1972.

Largest optical telescope

The Vainu Bappu telescope of 2.34 m (7 ft 8 in.) diameter at Kavalur, Tamil Nadu, is the largest in Asia. It was built indigenously (including the mirror) in 1986 by the Indian Institute of Astrophysics, Bangalore (now Bengaluru), Karnataka.

Record Rewind

Number of planetariums

1993

There were 23 planetariums in India.

2017

There were 55 planetariums in the country.

First discovery of an asteroid

R. Rajamohan (b. 1944), associate professor at the Indian Institute of Astrophysics, Bangalore (now Bengaluru), Karnataka, and his team discovered an asteroid (No. 4130) in 1988, through the optical telescope at Kavalur, Tamil Nadu.

Highest astronomical observatory

Established in 2001, the Indian Astronomical Observatory, under the aegis of the Indian Institute of Astrophysics, Bangalore (now Bengaluru), Karnataka, is located in Hanle (at Digaparatsari located atop Mt Saraswati) in Ladakh. It has the world's second highest optical telescope at 4,500 m (14,764 ft) above the mean sea level.

First woman president of the Astronomical Society of India

In 2019, the Astronomical Society of India elected its first woman president, Dr G.C. Anupama, a senior professor and dean at the Indian Institute of Astrophysics in Bengaluru, Karnataka. She has projects such as the Himalayan Telescope at the Hanle Observatory in Ladakh to her credit and is a member of an international team setting up a 30 m telescope (TMT) in Hawaii, USA.

First robotic telescope

India's first robotic telescope became functional on the night of 12 June 2018 at Hanle, Ladakh. It is the first one designed to observe dynamic or transient events in the universe. GROWTH-India, the facility at Hanle, is part of a multi-country collaborative initiative, known as the 'Global Relay of Observatories Watching Transients Happen' (GROWTH), to observe transient events in the universe.

PHYSICS

Earliest atomistic theory

Kanada, an ancient natural scientist and philosopher, who lived between the sixth and second centuries BCE, composed the *Vaisheshika Sutra,* a text in which he explored the relationship between cause and effect for the first time in relation to physics and philosophy.

First wireless demonstration

In 1894, scientist Jagadish Chandra Bose (1858–1937) at Presidency College, Calcutta, Bengal (now Presidency University, Kolkata, West Bengal), demonstrated the transmission of radio waves before Italian inventor Guglielmo Marconi did it in Europe, using very short radio waves or 'microwaves'.

First solar heater

Pandit Sri Krishna Joshi from Almora, who lived in Allahabad (now Prayagraj),

First Global Science Exhibition

A mega science exhibition in India, 'Vigyan Samagam', began in May 2019 and travelled for 11 months across major cities, spreading information about India's participation in and contribution to global research projects, including the Large Hadron Collider at CERN (European Organization for Nuclear Research) and the India-based Neutrino Observatory. It was organized by the Department of Science and Technology and the Department of Atomic Energy, Government of India, along with the National Council for Science Museums.

Uttar Pradesh, invented an apparatus for utilizing solar heat as a substitute for fire, named 'Bhanu Taap'. Also called the 'heliotherm', it was patented in 1900 and awarded a gold medal at the Industrial Exhibition of Calcutta (now Kolkata), West Bengal, in 1901.

Discovery of bosons

In the late 1920s, Nobel Prize-winner Albert Einstein and Indian scientist Satyendra Nath Bose worked together on the Bose–Einstein equations, which pointed to a state of matter comprising particles, now known as 'bosons'. As researchers at the Joint Institute of Laboratory Astrophysics, Colorado, USA, they cooled thousands of atoms of rubidium to create the 'Bose–Einstein condensate'.

Discovery of the 'Krishnan effect'

In the 1930s, Indian experimental physicist Rappal Sangameswaran Krishnan (1911–99) from the Indian Institute of Science (IISc), Bangalore (now Bengaluru), Karnataka, discovered the 'Krishnan effect' – a new optical effect in the scattering of light. This led to the discovery of the presence of large clusters of molecules in liquid mixtures, glasses and colloidal solutions. It also helps in assessing the size of the scattering particles.

Discovery of mesons

Indian nuclear physicist Dr Homi Jehangir Bhabha and German physicist Dr Walter Heinrich Heitler presented the 'Cascade Theory of Electron Showers', called the 'Bhabha–Heitler Cascade Theory' in 1937 in Cambridge, UK, which explains the process of electron showers in cosmic rays. Bhabha recognized heavy electron particles in cosmic rays, which he named 'mesons'.

First molecular distillation unit

Major General Sir Singh Sokhey of Haffkine Institute, in Bombay (now Mumbai), Maharashtra, installed the first molecular distillation unit in India to separate vitamin A from shark liver oil in the early 1940s. He was also the first Indian scientist to receive the Lenin Peace Prize in 1947.

First Nobel Prize in physics
Sir Chandrasekhara Venkata Raman (1888–1970) from Tiruchirappalli, Madras Presidency (now Tamil Nadu), won the 1930 Nobel Prize in physics for his groundbreaking work in the field of the scattering of light, or the 'Raman effect'.

New method for thermal conductivity
Suresh Chand Jain (1926–2009), former director of the Solid State Physics Laboratory and Defence Research and Development Organization (DRDO), developed a new method known as the Jain–Krishnan method in 1952, which is now a standard method for measuring the thermal conductivity of solids at high temperatures.

In June 2018, scientists from the Physical Research Laboratory in Ahmedabad, Gujarat, discovered a planet that is 600 light years away.

Inventing optical fibre
Narinder Kapary from the Imperial College, University of London, UK, invented the optical fibre in 1955. This is a thin and long fibre of glass through which light can travel without hindrance, whether it is bent or not. Optical fibres have a wide variety of applications in a range of fields, including medicine, computers, communications and the automotive industry.

WR **First double radio source**
Mrinal Kumar Dasgupta from the Institute of Radio Physics and Electronics, Calcutta (now Kolkata), West Bengal, discovered the first double radio source Cygnus A in 1953 in collaboration with R.C. Jennison at the Jodrell Bank Experimental Station in Cheshire, UK.

First nuclear reactor
Apsara, the first Asian research reactor, at the Bhabha Atomic Research Centre (BARC) in Bombay (now Mumbai), Maharashtra, went critical in 1956.

Discovery of helium isotope in cosmic rays
Dr K.M.V. Apparao (b. 1933), a scientist at the Tata Institute of Fundamental Research in Bombay (now Mumbai), Maharashtra, discovered an isotope of helium in cosmic rays, the energetic particles that fall down on Earth like a continuous rain from outer space, in 1961.

First carbon dioxide laser
Chandra Kumar Naranbhai Patel (b. 1938), an Indian-origin scientist in the USA, invented the powerful carbon dioxide laser in 1963, which resulted in making lasers a valuable tool in scientific research.

Discovery of quantum Zeno paradox
Indian theoretical physicists Baidyanath Misra and E.C.G. Sudarshan, then conducting research at the University of Texas at Austin, USA, discovered the quantum Zeno effect (or paradox) in 1977. It is the quantum mechanical analogue of the proverbial adage 'a watched kettle never boils'. In 1989, the paradox was

experimentally proven – 'Under continuous measurement, an unstable atomic nucleus that normally decays, was found not to decay.'

First semiconductor laser

The Bhabha Atomic Research Centre, Bombay (now Mumbai), Maharashtra, developed a semiconductor laser in 1965.

First nuclear implosion

On 18 May 1974, India imploded its first nuclear device at Pokhran in Rajasthan. The test, which was conducted at a depth of 107 m (351 ft), yielded 12 kilo tonnes and produced a 47 m (154 ft) wide and 10 m (33 ft) deep crater.

First prediction of hot superconductors

S.N. Ekbote and A.V. Narlikar from the National Physical Laboratory (NPL), New Delhi, were the first scientists to predict the presence of 'hot' superconductors based on their new theory of superconductivity formulated in 1981, which challenged the then accepted Nobel Prize–winning theory.

First to measure ozone in the atmosphere

In 1985, M. Vivekananda and R.S. Arora from the Raman Research Institute, Bangalore (now Bengaluru), Karnataka, first measured the density and height distribution of ozone in the atmosphere over Bangalore by a simple ground-based technique using radio waves.

Only nuclear safety institute

With the inauguration of the Safety Research Institute at Kalpakkam, Tamil Nadu, on 20 February 1999, India became the second country after France to have such a facility.

First synchrotron radiation facility

The first synchrotron radiation facility in India was INDUS-1, set up in 2002. An advanced, indigenously built nuclear particle accelerator, it is part of the Centre for Advanced Technology at Indore, Madhya Pradesh.

First advanced heavy water reactor

In 2016, the Bhabha Atomic Research Centre (BARC) in Mumbai, Maharashtra, designed an Advanced Heavy Water Reactor that uses thorium instead of uranium as fuel. It was the centrepiece of India's nuclear power programme.

CHEMISTRY

First chemistry department

Chemistry was first taught as a subject in 1872–73 at Presidency College, Calcutta, Bengal (now Presidency University, Kolkata, West Bengal). Postgraduate courses were introduced in 1886. In 1889, chemist Prafulla Chandra Ray (1861–1944) set up the first organized laboratory here for research.

First heavy chemicals company

Behramji Sorabji Lalkaka (1880–1957) started the Pioneer Magnesia Works Ltd in 1915 at Kharagodha in the Little Rann of Kachchh, Gujarat, for the manufacture of magnesium chloride, the import of which was stopped from Germany due to the First World War. Magnesium chloride is used in a variety of ways in the chemical industry.

First chemicals company

In 1892, Prafulla Chandra Ray set up the Bengal Chemicals and Pharmaceutical Works Ltd at Calcutta (now Kolkata), West Bengal, using locally available materials, which led to the production of many chemicals and medicines indigenously. He was also the first person to synthesize ammonium nitrite (NH_4NO_2) in its pure form.

Discovery of the isomerism of thiosulphuric acid

Prof. Priyada Ranjan Ray (1888–1982), director, Indian Association for the Cultivation of Science, Calcutta (now Kolkata), West Bengal, established for the first time the isomerism (compounds that have the same molecular formulae but different molecular structures) of thiosulphuric acid.

Aditya: first tokamak

First tokamak

The first Indian tokamak – essentially a magnetic bottle that can maintain conditions present inside the sun wherein enormous energy from nuclear fusion reactions is produced – named Aditya, was set up at the Institute for Plasma Research, Gandhinagar, Gujarat, in 1986.

Discoveries in terpene chemistry

Dr Sukh Dev (b. 1923) from the Indian Institute of Technology-Delhi, discovered many new fundamental types of terpenoids, a class of naturally occurring organic compounds found in plants.

Discovery of phosphocreatine

In 1927, Dr Yellapragada Subbarow (1895–1948) from Bhimavaram, Madras Presidency (now in Andhra Pradesh), who went on to study at Harvard University,

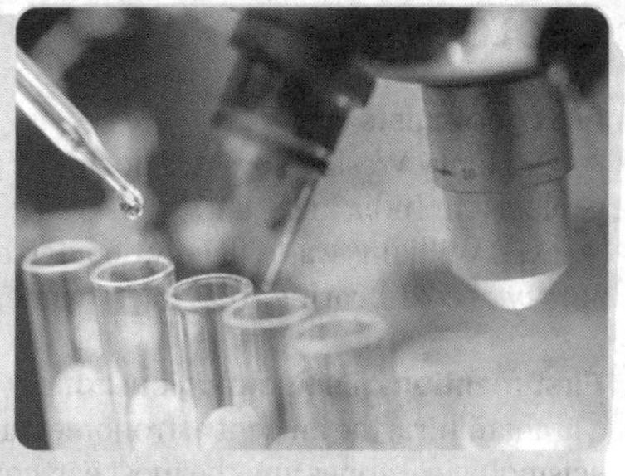

Thinner than a Sheet of Paper

In 2018, scientists at the Indian Institute of Technology-Gandhinagar, Gujarat, reported having developed a material that is just one nanometre thick, which is 100,000 times thinner than a sheet of paper. These nanosheets, made of boron atoms, are created by dissolving a boride compound in water and letting it crystallize for a specific duration. Now they are working towards utilizing these nanosheets to develop next-generation batteries and nanocatalysts.

USA, and Cyrus H. Fiske of the same university, discovered the function of adenosine triphosphate, an organic phosphorous compound, as an energy source in the human cell, connected with the chemical mechanism of muscle contraction. He also discovered methotrexate (still used in chemotherapy) and diethylcarbamazine (DEC), which is used for effectively treating filariasis).

First observation of spontaneous fission
Prof. Shyamadas Chatterjee (1909–95) from the Indian Physical Society in Calcutta (now Kolkata), West Bengal, first observed spontaneous fission – the splitting of a heavy nucleus on its own in uranium – in 1940, almost at the same time when scientists in Western countries reported its discovery.

The Royal Society of Chemistry in 2011 honoured the life and work of Prafulla Chandra Ray with the first ever Chemical Landmark Plaque awarded to anyone outside Europe.

Largest scientific and industrial research organization
The Council of Scientific and Industrial Research (CSIR), which was set up in 1942, is India's largest research and development organization for scientific and industrial research for economic and environmental development.

First chain of national laboratories
Indian scientist and professor of chemistry Sir S.S. Bhatnagar proposed the setting up of national laboratories for research in individual fields and the Council of Scientific and Industrial Research (CSIR) approved five premier national laboratories. First among these were the National Physical Laboratory founded in 1947 in Delhi and the National Chemical Laboratory in Poona (now Pune), Maharashtra, in 1950.

Discovery of tetracycline
Tetracycline, a life-saving drug, was discovered and developed in 1948 by a research group headed by Dr Yellapragada Subbarow at the Lederle Laboratories in New York, USA. An anti-plague drug, it helped save many lives in the 1994 plague epidemic in Surat, Gujarat.

GEOLOGY

First geologists

- Dr Henry Wesley Voysey, a doctor by profession, became the first professional geologist in India in 1818.
- D.H. Williams was officially deputed by the British rulers to undertake the survey of coal-bearing areas in erstwhile Bengal in 1836.

First mention of seismological zones

Varahamihira, the ancient astronomer and scientist, was the first to mention seismological zones and the most earthquake-prone areas in his treatise *Brihat-Samhita* (c. 550 CE).

First geomagnetic observatory

The Colaba Geomagnetic Observatory in Bombay (now Mumbai), Maharashtra, was the first geomagnetic observatory to be set up in pre-Independence India. It was established in 1846 by the scientists of the East India Company to study the earth's magnetic field by using geomagnetic instruments.

Discovery of iron ore deposits

Pramatha Nath Bose discovered the first iron ore deposit in Mayurbhanj region in present-day Odisha, in 1904, paving the way for the modern iron industry.

First official Indian geologist

Pramatha Nath Bose is considered to be the first official Indian

SUPER 30

SUDIPTA SENGUPTA: TRAILBLAZING GEOLOGIST

Even though the Government of India established the Geological Survey of India (GSI) in 1851 and the first geology department emerged at the Presidency College, Calcutta (now Presidency University, Kolkata, West Bengal) in 1892, women did not enter the field until much later. Sudipta Sengupta, a professor in structural geology at Jadavpur University, Kolkata, West Bengal, was one of the first Indian women scientists – along with marine biologist and oceanographer Aditi Pant – to set foot on Antarctica in 1983, and again in 1989, where she conducted pioneering geological studies in the Schirmacher Hills.

Sudipta Sengupta

A Fellow of the Indian National Science Academy, Sengupta worked as a geologist with the GSI during 1970–73 and was awarded the Shanti Swarup Bhatnagar Prize for Science and Technology (1991), one of the highest Indian science awards, for her contributions to earth, atmosphere, ocean and planetary sciences. With many papers published in Indian and international journals to her name, Prof. Sengupta's work has covered studying the formation and deformation of rocks, and has used the results to compose what is called the 'story of a region'. She was honoured with the National Mineral Award in 1997 and the Antarctic Award in 2001.

geologist. He joined the Geological Survey of India (GSI) as an officer in 1880. He is known to have mapped the Vindhya Range as well as the igneous rocks of Raipur and Balaghat areas of what was then the Central Province.

First course in geology

Geology as a degree course leading to postgraduation was started at the Presidency College, Calcutta, Bengal (now Presidency University, Kolkata, West Bengal), for the first time in the country in 1892.

First president of the International Geological Congress

Dr D.N. Wadia, president of the 22nd International Geological Congress, which was held in New Delhi in 1964, was the first and only Indian to become president of the International Geological Congress.

Discovery of vanadium

Abani Kumar Dey and J.A. Dunn discovered a new vanadium-bearing mineral in the Singhbhum–Mayurbhanj area, in present-day Jharkhand and Odisha, in the 1930s and called this mineral coulsonite (composition FeV_2O_4), the main source of vanadium in India. It is of strategic importance for making special steels. Abani Dey was the recipient of the First National Mineral Award in 1968.

Vanadium ore

Largest mineral explorer

The Mineral Exploration Corporation Ltd, established in October 1972, is a public sector company with its corporate office at Nagpur, Maharashtra, and regional offices at Kolkata, Hyderabad, Ranchi, Jaipur and Nagpur. Its functions include mineral targeting, deposit assessment and mine development under the Ministry of Mines, Government of India.

First dinosaur fossils

The Geological Survey of India (GSI) discovered dinosaur bone fossils from the Lameta formation of the late Cretaceous age (145 to 66 million years ago) at Raiyoli near Balasinor in the Kheda District, Gujarat, in 1981. Dinosaur egg clutches were also found at the site in 1982. Both the eggs and bones are preserved at the Indian Museum in Calcutta (now Kolkata), West Bengal.

WR **Periodicity of geomagnetic reversals**

J.G. Negi and R.R. Tewari from the National Geophysical Research Institute, Hyderabad (now in Telangana), put forward, in 1983, the theory that the flipping of the earth's magnetic field, i.e., the North Pole becoming the South Pole and vice versa, is related to variations in the gravitational force of the earth. They found that the frequency with which the earth's magnetic field flips is directly correlated to the periodicity of the orbit of the sun.

First megafossil from the Himalayas

In 1984, R.N. Lakhanpal, a scientist at the Birbal Sahni Institute of Palaeosciences, Lucknow, Uttar Pradesh, and his team discovered a leaf of the temperate palm *Trachycarpus*, the first definite megafossil record of the Miocene period (23 million to 5.3 million years ago) in Ladakh in the Himalayas.

First aeromagnetic survey of groundwater and minerals

The first aeromagnetic groundwater and minerals survey was undertaken as a collaboration between the Indian and Australian governments in March 1993.

First geoscientific data centre

The Geological Survey of India (GSI) set up a geoscientific data centre at Calcutta, Bengal (now Kolkata), West Bengal, on 3 November 1998. It is the largest repository of knowledge on earth sciences in Asia, Australia and Africa.

First underwater mining system

The National Institute of Ocean Technology, Chennai, Tamil Nadu, in collaboration with the University of Siegen, Germany, devised an underwater mining vehicle called the crawler, which extracts mineral-rich polymetallic nodules from the ocean floor. The mining system consists of the crawler, cutter and slurry pump. Mounted on board the ship ORV *Sagar Kanya*, its first test was conducted successfully on 14 March 2000 near Tuticorin (now Thoothukudi), Tamil Nadu.

OCEAN STUDIES

First course in oceanography

The first postgraduate course in oceanography was introduced in 1948 at Andhra University in Visakhapatnam in Andhra Pradesh.

First marine research institute

In 1974, the Central Marine Fisheries Research Institute was established at Mandapam in Ramanathapuram District, Tamil Nadu.

First oceanographic research vessel

RV *Gaveshani*, commissioned on 1 December 1975, was the first oceanographic research vessel. It carried teams of scientific personnel on various marine expeditions that could last from a few days to months.

Highest wave

Scientists on board the ship RV *Gaveshani* of the National Institute of Oceanography recorded a wave 13 m (42 ft 7.8 in.) high in the Arabian Sea off the coast of Goa in June 1979.

First Antarctic expedition

Dr S.Z. Qasim, director, National Institute of Oceanography, Goa, reached Antarctica on 9 January 1982. The 21-member team left Mormugao harbour, Goa, on 6 December 1981 on a Norwegian ship, MV *Polar Circle*, and returned on 21 February 1982. During the expedition, the team built Dakshin Gangotri, the first Indian scientific research base station in the Queen Maud Land area in .Antarctica,

First women on Antarctica

Structural geologist Sudipta Sengupta, and marine biologist and oceanographer

Aditi Pant were the first Indian women to visit Antarctica, during the third Indian expedition to Antarctica from 3 December 1983 to 25 March 1984. The expeditions aimed to study atmospheric, biological, earth, chemical, and medical sciences in the region.

LIFE SCIENCES

BIOLOGY

Oldest biological fossils

Fossils of three-billion-year-old photosynthetic blue-green algae of the Archaean era (4 billion to 2.5 billion years ago) were discovered at Kashia in Orissa (now Odisha) in 1998 by scientists of the Birbal Sahni Institute of Palaeosciences in Lucknow, Uttar Pradesh. The latest find includes 1.6-billion-year-old red algae fossils in the Chitrakoot region of central India.

Discovery of earliest multicellular organisms

In October 1998, Pradip K. Bose, a professor at Jadavpur University, Calcutta (now Kolkata), West Bengal, found a site close to Churhat town in Sidhi District, Madhya Pradesh, where multicellular organisms with body fluid existed around 1.1 billion years ago. He discovered tracks on sandstone rock left by wormlike creatures about half a centimetre thick, while burrowing through the sea floor ages ago. This was the first evidence of macroscopic animals in India.

WR First zoologist

Rama Brahma Sanyal (1850–1908) joined the Calcutta Zoological Gardens in Calcutta (now Kolkata), West Bengal, in 1876. He wrote scientific papers on birds and sea snakes, and books on zoology.

First methane plant

Biomethane was first put to use in India in 1857 when a methane plant was installed in a colony near Bombay (now Mumbai), Maharashtra.

MANAV: A Citizen Science–based Human Atlas Project

In May 2019, the Department of Biotechnology, under the Ministry of Science and Technology, Government of India, launched MANAV, a project that aims to create a human atlas by mapping every cell, tissue and organ of the human body. The project's vision is to put together the scattered bits of human biological data in public databases, to pinpoint gaps and attain a holistic understanding of how changes at the molecular level affect the human organs and body. To be executed by two collaborating institutes in Pune, Maharashtra – the Indian Institute of Science Education and Research, and the National Centre of Cell Sciences – it will find application in disease modelling, drug discovery and personalized healthcare.

First anther culture

S.C. Maheswari and Sipra Mukherjee from Delhi discovered the anther culture technique in 1967, in which anthers (part of a stamen that contains pollen, in a plant) were placed on a synthetic culture medium.

Discovery of gymnosperms

In 1948, Birbal Sahni (1891–1949) discovered Pentoxyleae (gymnosperms), a plant group that belonged to the Jurassic period (208 to 145 million years ago).

First synthesis of a workable gene

India-born US resident Dr Har Gobind Khorana (1922–2011), using off-the-shelf chemicals, synthesized a total gene of the simple microbe *Escherichia coli* (which lives in the intestines of humans and animals) in 1976. He was awarded the Nobel Prize for physiology or medicine in 1968 for discovering the genetic code, which opened up the possibility of producing DNA in a laboratory. He shared the prize with US scientists Robert W. Holley and Marshall W. Nirenberg.

Discovery of seminal plasmin

Pushpa M. Bhargava and E.S.R. Reddy from the Regional Research Laboratory, Hyderabad (now in Telangana), discovered the protein seminal plasmin in the seminal fluid of a bull in 1979. This is a potent antimicrobial agent active on a wide range of micro-organisms, such as yeast.

Discovery of the cholera exotoxin

S.C. Seal from the All India Institute of Hygiene and Public Health, Calcutta, (now Kolkata), West Bengal, discovered cholera exotoxin in the early 1940s. The vaccine based on this helped in the eradication of cholera epidemics in India.

First to extract insulin from a plant

In the early 1980s, Pushpa Khanna, professor at the University of Rajasthan, Jaipur, was the first to extract an insulin-like substance from bitter gourd. That substance is an active ingredient called polypeptide-P, which lowers blood sugar in the body. Insulin is currently extracted from animal pancreas for the treatment of diabetes.

First national gene bank

R.S. Paroda, director general of the Indian Council of Agricultural Research, Delhi, established the first National Gene Bank in Delhi in 1985.

First bamboo tissue culture

A.F. Mascarenhas, R.S. Nadgauda and V.A. Parasharami from the National Chemical Laboratory in Pune, Maharashtra, worked to produce a tissue culture of bamboo in 1990.

First biocentre

The M.S. Swaminathan Foundation, Chennai, Tamil Nadu, opened a biocentre in Pillayarkuppam Village in Pondicherry (now Puducherry) on 10 April 1999. This centre functions as a demonstration, training, information dissemination and service unit for sustainable food security.

LALJI SINGH: PIONEER OF DNA FINGERPRINTING

Lalji Singh

An Indian scientist from Jaunpur, Uttar Pradesh, Lalji Singh (1947–2017) was instrumental in bringing DNA fingerprinting into the mainstream in India in the 1990s. Responsible for founding various institutes and laboratories in the country, including the Centre for DNA Fingerprinting and Diagnostics in 1995, the Laboratory for the Conservation of Endangered Species (LaCONES) in 1998, and the Genome Foundation (for diagnosis and treatment of genetic disorders, especially those affecting underprivileged, rural people) in 2004, Singh was highly regarded for his contributions in the areas of molecular basis of sex determination, wildlife conservation, silkworm genome analysis, population genetics and ancient DNA studies. While he was serving as the director of the Centre for Cellular and Molecular Biology (CCMB), Hyderabad (now in Telangana), from 1998 to 2009, Singh was honoured with the Padma Shri award in 2004 for his contribution to Indian science and technology. The 25th vice chancellor of Banaras Hindu University (BHU) and the chairman of the Board of Governors of the Indian Institute of Technology-Varanasi (2011–14), Singh also published more than 200 research papers during his career.

First clone of hepatitis E virus

Dr S.K. Panda, professor of pathology, and his support team of scientists at the All India Institute of Medical Sciences (AIIMS), New Delhi, genetically engineered a clone of the hepatitis E virus in 1996.

First biologist to win the Linnean Medal

In 2018, Dr Kamaljit Bawa, president of the Ashoka Trust for Research in Ecology and the Environment (ATREE), and distinguished professor of biology at the University of Massachusetts, Boston, USA, was awarded the Linnean Medal for his pioneering research in the field of conservation biology. He researched biodiversity, the evolution of tropical plants, deforestation and non-timber forest products in Central America, the Western Ghats and the Himalayas.

First to isolate insulin-blocking enzyme

In 2013, India-born Kanwal Gambhir from Harvard University, USA, and his co-workers isolated an insulin-blocking enzyme. As insulin controls sugar levels in blood, this discovery had far-reaching implications in the control of diabetes, cardiovascular diseases and cancer.

Human organ regeneration

In 2001, Dr Balakrishna Ganpatrao Matapurkar from Maulana Azad Medical College, New Delhi, was granted US Patent No. 6227202 (from 1995) for enabling regeneration of mammalian organs in the body at the site of old and diseased organs. He used unique stem cells in the body to regenerate organs like the uterus, urethra and ureters in animals, and large tendons in the human abdomen.

INTERDISCIPLINARY AND APPLIED SCIENCES

COMPUTERS

First indigenous chip

The Graphics and Intelligence-based Script Technology (GIST), developed by the Centre for Development of Advanced Computing (C-DAC), hit the market in the 1990s. While it was designed especially for land records departments based in different climatic zones, where protection from dust and other vagaries is not always available, it was also used by industries and public information systems.

First analogue computer

Biswaranjan Nag (1932–2004), former professor of radio physics and electronics at the Institute for Radio Physics and Electronics (IRPE), Calcutta (now Kolkata), West Bengal, built the first indigenous analogue computer (also called a differential analyser) in 1957.

First indigenous computer

HEC-2M, the first fully India-made computer, was installed in Calcutta (now Kolkata), West Bengal, in 1955. In 1964, the first indigenous computer, ISIJU-1, was developed by the Jadavpur University and the Indian Statistical Institute, Calcutta (now Kolkata), West Bengal.

First indigenous palmtop computer

In 1995, a team of engineers working for Signals and Systems India Private Ltd, headquartered in Gurugram, Haryana, built the country's first indigenous palmtop computer suitable for a variety of industrial and field applications.

First computer centre for the visually disabled

The Blind Relief Association School in New Delhi started a computer centre in 1996 to help the visually disabled who know how to type and have a fair knowledge of English. Students were trained in all aspects of computers including multimedia to help them access text sources such as the *Encyclopaedia Britannica.* They could also access newspapers or other books, which were first scanned and put on the hard disk. Once scanned, the page was read out by the machine in a clear tone. It could also give a printout in Braille.

First Indian to obtain a PhD in computer science

Dr Raj Reddy (b. 13 June 1937), the dean of the School of Computer Science, Carnegie Mellon University, Pittsburgh, USA, was the first Indian with a PhD in computer science, which he obtained in 1966 from Stanford University, USA. He was also the first person of Asian origin to receive the Association for Computing Machinery (ACM) Turing Award, in 1994, then the highest award in computer science, for his work in the field of artificial intelligence.

SUPER MACHINES

Fastest Supercomputer

- In January 2018, India unveiled Pratyush and Mihir, an array of computers that raised India's supercomputing profile. They are able to output a peak power of 6.8 petaflops (one petaflop is a million billion floating-point operations per second) across two sites – the Indian Institute of Tropical Meteorology, Pune, Maharashtra, and the National Centre for Medium Range Weather Forecast, Noida, Uttar Pradesh. The combination is dedicated to weather and climate research.
- A high-performance computing–artificial intelligence (HPC–AI) supercomputer, established under the National Supercomputing Mission (NSM), PARAM Siddhi–AI, was conceived by C-DAC, Pune, Maharashtra, and developed jointly with the support of the Department of Science and Technology, Ministry of Electronics and Information Technology, Government of India. Able to output a peak power of 6.5 petaflops, the supercomputer is expected to jump-start research efforts in areas such as healthcare, agricultural technology, cybersecurity, robotics and more. In November 2020, PARAM Siddhi-AI ranked 63rd among the most powerful supercomputers in the world.

First indigenous supercomputer

Developed by C-DAC in Pune, Maharashtra, in 1991, PARAM 8000 was capable of one billion calculations per second. The then director of C-DAC, Dr Vijay P. Bhatkar, under whom this project was conducted, is considered the architect of India's national initiative in supercomputing.

First supercomputer

On 25 March 1989, the Supercomputer Cray XMP-14 was installed as a key facility at the National Centre for Medium Range Weather Forecasting, New Delhi, to facilitate medium-range weather forecasting and agrometeorology programmes.

First powerful indigenous supercomputer

PARAM 10000, also developed by C-DAC under Dr Vijay P. Bhatkar's directorship, in 1998, was the first powerful indigenous supercomputer, capable of 100 billion calculations per second. It is housed at the National PARAM Supercomputing Facility (NPSF) at C-DAC, Pune.

First to invent a new and speedy algorithm

In 1984, India-born mathematician Dr Narendra Karmarkar from Bell Laboratories in New Jersey. USA, introduced a new algorithm, called 'Karmarkar's algorithm', which solved linear programming efficiently, and helped computers find solutions to simultaneous inequalities very quickly. It solved problems 50 to 100 times faster than the methods known at the time.

First Super Fab Lab

The first super fab lab (fabrication laboratory) of the country was inaugurated via remote control from the Government Polytechnic College, Palakkad, Kerala, on 25 January 2020. Located at the Integrated Startup Complex of the Kerala Startup Mission (KSUM), Kalamassery, Kochi, the lab offers digital fabrication and computation, and was launched in collaboration with MIT (Massachusetts Institute of Technology, USA). The brainchild of Dr Neil Gershenfeld, director of the MIT Centre for Bits and Atoms, it aims to enable researchers, innovators and developers to do things beyond the purview of the existing fab labs of the country.

SUPER 30

THE DIGI-LOG

Computers began to be used in India in the 1950s, and the first Department of Electronics (DoE), Government of India, was set up in1970. By 1979, Indian companies began to make minicomputers. Developments caught speed with the use of computers and computer applications in the 1982 Asian Games. In 1984, as prime minister, Rajiv Gandhi initiated the liberalization of the computer industry with N. Seshagiri of the DoE as adviser. The Indian Railways' reservation system was the first to be computerized in 1986 and a National Supercomputer Centre was established at IISc, Bangalore (now Bengaluru). In 1991, the production and Import of computers was liberalized and, in 1995, Videsh Sanchar Nigam Ltd (VSNL) launched the first commercial Internet service. Former prime minister Atal Bihari Vajpayee set up a National Task Force on information technology (IT) in1998 to promote India as an IT and software superpower. In 2006, the National e-Governance Plan rolled out to make all government services available electronically. By 2010, IT contributed 6.5 per cent of the gross domestic product (GDP). In 2015, the Ministry of Electronics and IT announced a National Supercomputing Mission to install 73 indigenous supercomputers by 2022. The Digital India campaign was launched in July 2015 by Prime Minister Narendra Modi to deliver government services digitally with enhanced online infrastructure, Internet connectivity and universal digital literacy, including in rural areas. A National Statistical Office (NSO) survey in 2018 reported that 23.4 per cent of urban and 4.4 per cent of rural households owned a computer, showing that equal, easy digital access is still work in progress.

First smallest multimedia notebook

In 1997, Bangalore–Ncore Technology's multimedia sub-notebook computer called the Yantra, which weighed just 2.1 kg, was the lightest laptop in the world. The Yantra occupied less than half of a briefcase, had a CD-ROM, a built-in sound blaster, two PCMCIA (Personal Computer Memory Card International Association) card slots and a small yet powerful battery built to last for more than three years.

First powerful commercial computer

In 2001, Tata Consultancy Services (TCS) commissioned the 64-bit z-Series e-Server from IBM to become the first organization in South Asia to adopt the then latest technology being used in mainframe computing.

METALLURGY

Earliest zinc artefact

An artefact (No. 4189) containing 6.04 per cent zinc was found at the Harappan site of Lothal (dated to 2200–1500 BCE) in Gujarat. It indicated that the Harappan people could generate temperatures of above 1,000°C required for zinc metallurgy.

Earliest copper kiln

A copper smelting kiln, 35 cm (13.8 in.) high with an 18 cm (7 in.) rim diameter and 10 cm (3.9 in.) base diameter, was discovered at the Harappan site of Lothal (2200–1500 BCE) in Gujarat. Lothal copper was found to be very pure.

Earliest use of iron

Around 1000 BCE, iron was used in eastern Punjab, western Uttar Pradesh and Rajasthan. Excavations show that iron weapons such as arrowheads and spearheads were commonly used in western Uttar Pradesh from about 800 BCE. Iron is called *shyama* or *krishna ayas* (black/dark metal) in later Vedic texts.

First metallurgist to work with plutonium

Dr P.R. Roy, a scientist and director at the Bhabha Atomic Research Centre (BARC), Bombay (now Mumbai), Maharashtra, was the first Indian metallurgist to handle plutonium. He played a crucial role in India's first nuclear implosion at Pokhran, Rajasthan, in 1974.

First manufacture of steel

Indian smiths manufactured crucible steel, known as 'wootz', which was exported to many countries in medieval times. Indian craftsmen were known around the world at the time for their steel swords. After the British banned the production of weapons following the First War of Independence in 1857, wootz technology was lost.

New class of quasicrystals

In 1985, P. Ramachandra Rao and G.V.S. Sastry from the National Metallurgical Laboratory, Jamshedpur, now in Jharkhand, discovered a new class of quasicrystals composed of aluminium, manganese and zinc metals.

Earliest iron furnace

An iron furnace was found at Pandu Rajar Dhibi in Burdwan (later Bardhaman District), West Bengal, and was dated to 1100–800 BCE.

SPACE

First space venture

Launched from the base in Thumba near Trivandrum (now Thiruvananthapuram), Kerala, on 21 November 1963, a Nike-Apache rocket supplied by NASA kick-started the Indian space programme. Parts of this first sounding rocket launched by India were transported to the Thumba base on the carrier of a bicycle! St Mary Magdalene Church in Thumba is a preferred site for rocket launches because of its proximity to the magnetic Equator. Quite fittingly, the church houses the Vikram Sarabhai Space Centre (VSSC) space museum.

First Indian space organization

India's space programme took off in 1972 with the Department of Space, Government of India, executing projects in space sciences, technology and activities through the Indian Space Research Organization (ISRO), with its headquarters in Bangalore (now Bengaluru), Karnataka.

Record Rewind

Number of Indian satellites launched to date

1991

16 Indian satellites had been launched by the Indian Space Research Organization (ISRO) by this time.

2020

111 Indian satellites had been launched by ISRO up to 2020.

First satellite centre

ISRO's Satellite Centre (ISAC), established in 1972, conducts research in satellite technology. Aryabhata, the first Indian satellite, Bhaskara I and II, and Rohini and APPLE satellites, were all designed and built at ISAC. The spacecraft of the Indian Remote Sensing satellite series and the Stretched Rohini satellite series were also designed at ISAC.

First weather-cum-communications satellite

Indian National Satellite INSAT-1A, launched on 10 April 1982 on an American Delta-3920 launch vehicle, was India's first satellite employed for meteorological observations over India and the Indian Ocean, as well as for domestic telecommunications, including nationwide direct TV broadcasting, TV programme distribution and meteorological data distribution.

First in space

- **Squadron Leader Rakesh Sharma** (b. 13 January 1949), then an Indian Air Force pilot, flew aboard spacecraft Soyuz T-11, launched on 2 April 1984, as part of the Intercosmos programme and spent over seven days orbiting Earth. He was the first Indian person to travel to space.

ISRO Launches Highest-Resolution Imaging Satellite

CARTOSAT-3, considered to be India's highest-resolution civilian satellite to date, was successfully launched into space along with 13 nano US satellites by ISRO on 27 November 2019. Weighing 1,625 kg, the observation satellite lifted off from the Satish Dhawan Space Centre, SHAR (Sriharikota High Altitude Range), Sriharikota, Andhra Pradesh. It is an advanced imaging and mapping satellite with a mission life of five years and a panchromatic resolution of 0.25 m.

- **Dr Kalpana Chawla** (1962–2003), an American cosmonaut who was born in Karnal, Haryana, was the first woman of Indian origin in space. She zoomed into orbit aboard space shuttle Columbia on 19 November 1997 on a 16-day scientific mission, along with five fellow astronauts, and returned to Cape Canaveral on 5 December 1997. In 2003, Chawla was one of the seven crew members who died in the space shuttle Columbia disaster when it disintegrated during its re-entry into Earth's atmosphere.

First remote-sensing mission

IRS-1A, the first of a series of indigenous state-of-the-art remote-sensing satellites, was launched into a polar sun-synchronous orbit on 17 March 1988 from the Soviet Cosmodrome at Baikonur. It carried two cameras, LISS-I and LISS-II, with a swathe width of 140 km during each pass over India.

First indigenous satellite series

Designed and built by ISRO, INSAT-2A was launched by the Ariane launch vehicle from Kourou, French Guiana, on 10 July 1992. INSAT-2B was also launched by Ariane on 23 July 1993. INSAT-2C, the third in this series of satellites, was launched on 7 December 1995 and put into operation in February 1996.

First indigenous satellite launcher

The PSLV-D3, developed by ISRO, hoisted a 930 kg Indian Remote Sensing satellite (IRS-P3) into an orbit of 807 km from Earth, 17 minutes after it shot into space on 21 March 1996.

First flight of PSLV

With a lift-off weight of 294 tonnes, the 44.4 m (145 ft 8 in.) tall Polar Satellite Launch Vehicle (PSLV) is a four-stage vehicle that employs two solid and liquid propellant stages each. The first operational flight of PSLV took place on 29 September 1997, putting the satellite IRS-1D into a polar sun-synchronous orbit, from ISRO's SHAR (Sriharikota High Altitude Range) centre in Sriharikota, Andhra Pradesh.

First oceanographic satellite

IRS-P4 (Oceansat), the first satellite built for ocean applications, was launched into a polar sun-synchronous orbit, 720 km high, by the PSLV from SHAR, Sriharikota, Andhra Pradesh, on 26 May 1999. A 1,050 kg satellite measuring 2.8 m x 1.98 m x 2.57 m (9 ft 2 in. x 6 ft 6 in. x 8 ft 5 in.), the IRS-P4 orbited the earth in 99.31 mins. It completed its mission on 8 August 2010.

First flight of GSLV

India's first Geosynchronous Satellite Launch Vehicle (GSLV-D1) blasted off from the Satish Dhawan Space Centre, SHAR, Sriharikota, Andhra Pradesh, at IST 15:43 hrs on 18 April 2001. The giant three-stage vehicle carried a 1,540 kg experimental communication satellite, GSAT-1, to be placed in the geosynchronous transfer orbit.

First lunar probe

Chandrayaan-1 was India's first lunar probe. It was launched by ISRO, using a PSLV-XL rocket on 22 October 2008 from Satish Dhawan Space Centre, SHAR, Sriharikota, Andhra Pradesh. It operated until August 2009. The mission included a lunar orbiter and an impactor.

First university for the study of and research on outer space

The Indian Institute of Space Science and Technology (IIST), located at Valiamala in Thiruvananthapuram, Kerala, was inaugurated on 14 September 2007 by G. Madhavan Nair, the then chairman of ISRO. A government-aided institute and deemed university, it is the first in Asia to be dedicated to the study of and research on outer space. It was set up by ISRO with former Indian president A.P.J. Abdul Kalam as its first chancellor. The university offers engineering undergraduate, postgraduate and doctorate programmes, focusing on space science, technology and their applications.

'Vyommitra': ISRO's Friend in Space

As a prelude to India's first manned mission – Gaganyaan – the Indian Space Research Organization unveiled a robot named Vyommitra on 22 January 2020. A combination of two Sanskrit words – *vyom* (space) and *mitra* (friend), it is a prototype half-humanoid robot that can communicate with astronauts, recognize them and also respond to their queries. A 'friend in the sky', the female-human-looking robot can only move sideways and forward, and will interact with the environment-control life-support system as part of a study by ISRO to see how real astronauts might respond to living outside Earth in controlled zero-gravity conditions. The launch of Gaganyaan has been postponed to the end of 2023.

First Mission to Land a Rover on the Moon

ISRO's plan to land on the moon with the ambitious Chandrayaan-2 mission, which included an orbiter, a lander and a rover, would have been the first-ever mission in the world to land a rover near the unexplored lunar south pole. Chandrayaan-2 was launched on 22 July 2019 and was expected to land on the moon on 7 September 2019. However, communication with the Vikram lander was lost when it was just 2.1 km away from the moon's surface. The orbiter, where 95 per cent of the experiments are placed, was not affected. Debris from the Vikram lander was located on the moon's surface by NASA's Lunar Reconnaissance Orbiter (LRO) camera on 3 December 2019. Located about 750 m (2,460 ft) north-west of the main crash site, the debris was initially spotted by Shanmuga Subramanian, a mechanical engineer from Chennai, Tamil Nadu, who then contacted the American space agency.

First interplanetary mission

On 5 November 2013, PSLV-C25, the 25th flight of PSLV (Polar Satellite Launch Vehicle) launched Mangalyaan, the Mars Orbiter Mission (MOM) spacecraft, from SHAR, Sriharikota, Andhra Pradesh. Under the aegis of ISRO, the mission was conducted to observe the physical features of Mars and the Martian atmosphere. With this mission, ISRO became the fourth space agency in the world to reach Mars. India is the first Asian nation to reach the Mars orbit, and the first nation in the world to do so in its first attempt.

WR Smallest spacecraft launched

On 23 June 2017, the world's smallest spacecraft, Sprites, was launched by ISRO's PSLV rocket and placed in the low-earth orbit. The 3.5 cm x 3.5 cm (1.38 in. x 1.38 in.) space probe weighs just 4 g and runs on sunlight.

First dedicated commercial satellite mission

India's Polar Satellite Launch Vehicle PSLV-C51 successfully launched the satellite Amazonia-1, developed by Brazil, along with 18 co-passenger private satellites, from SHAR, Sriharikota, Andhra Pradesh, on 28 February 2021. The first dedicated commercial mission of NewSpace India Limited (NSIL), under the Department of Space, Government of India, it was part of space reforms aimed at increasing the participation of private companies in the space sector. The co-passenger satellites included four from Indian National Space Promotion and Authorization Centre (IN-SPACe) and 14 from NSIL.

First private satellite launched

Exseed SAT-1, built by Exseed Space Innovations Private Ltd, founded by scientists Kris Nair and Asshar Farhan, became the first private Indian satellite to be launched in space. The amateur (ham) radio satellite hitched a ride on the Elon Musk–led company SpaceX's Falcon 9 rocket on 4 December 2018.

Heaviest satellite launched

GSAT-11, weighing 5,854 kg and laying claim to being the heaviest Indian satellite ever launched, was sent up into space on 5 December 2018 from the Ariane Launch Complex at Kourou in French Guiana. The satellite is expected to help boost communication services across India.

WR Lightest satellite in orbit

Kalamsat-V2 was launched by ISRO on 24 January 2019 from the Satish Dhawan Space Centre, SHAR, Sriharikota, Andhra Pradesh. Weighing only 1.26 kg, it is said to be the world's lightest satellite to be put into orbit. It was made by students belonging to Space Kidz India, a Chennai-based organization that designs innovative educational concepts. The satellite will also serve as a communications device for ham radio transmission, which is a form of wireless communication used by amateurs for non-commercial activities. It took six days to make and cost around ₹12 lakh (1.2 million).

Kalamsat-V2: lightest satellite in orbit

Most satellites launched in a single mission

ISRO launched an unprecedented 104 satellites, including India's earth observation satellite, on a single rocket from the spaceport in SHAR, Sriharikota, Andhra Pradesh, on 15 February 2017 . Elon Musk's SpaceX broke this world record by launching 143 satellites on a single rocket on 24 January 2021.

ADVENTURE

AERO SPORTS

Highest hot-air balloon take-off

Indradhanush, the hot-air balloon of the Ballooning Club of India, piloted by the then club president, Vishwa Bandhu Gupta, along with pilot R.K. Wason, took off from the Kushok Bakula Rimpochee Airport (3,310.7 m/10,862 ft) in Leh, Ladakh, on 29 September 1988.

Youngest paramotor pilot

Ravi Kanabar (b. 21 June 1994) from Gujarat became the youngest paramotor pilot at 20 years. He earned his pilot licence (No. 139) on 8 January 2015 from the Federation Aeronautique Internationale, Switzerland, which was issued by the Aero Club of India.

First international paramotor medallist

- Appasaheb Bhimraj Dhus (b. 26 December 1970) from Maharashtra is the first Indian to win international medals in paramotor games. He won a gold medal in the Pure Economy Task category of the World Paramotor Championship Test Event at Lopburi, Thailand, held from 28 April to 7 May 2017.
- In the same event, Captain Prafulla Raj Singh won a silver medal in the Pure Navigation Task category.

Longest paramotor expedition

The Indian Air Force paramotor team, with Wing Commander M.P.S. Solanki as their leader, conducted a circumnavigation-of-India expedition called 'Pradakshina', covering 10,041.7 km in 53 days from 3 February to 26 March 2016. Flagged off from the air force station in Kalaikunda, West Bengal, the team flew along the periphery of the country before returning to Kalaikunda. They followed a clockwise route along the eastern and western coasts and the north-western and eastern regions, covering an average of 218.3 km per day.

Highest skydive landing

Wing Commander Jai Kishan from the Indian Air Force jumped off an aircraft at 6,401 m (21,000 ft) and landed at Kalapathar Plateau, 5,242 m (17,198 ft) above the mean sea level in the foothills of Mt Everest, on 28 October 2009.

Most skydiving jumps

Rajkumar Balakrishnan (b. 1 April 1977) from Theni, Tamil Nadu, started making skydiving jumps in February 2006 and completed his 10,000th jump on 23 March 2018.

Most hours logged in free fall

Rajkumar Balakrishnan (b. 1 April 1977) from Theni, Tamil Nadu, has logged a total of 84 hours in free fall while skydiving, up to 6 July 2018.

First woman skydiver

Rachel Thomas (b. 9 August 1955) from Chittaranjan, West Bengal, was the first Indian woman to skydive, from 2,133.6 m (7,000 ft) over the North Pole on 20 April 2002, to commemorate 150 years of the Indian Railways. An employee of the Indian Railways, Thomas was also the first woman to represent the country in a skydiving competition in 1987. She was honoured with the Padma Shri in 2005.

Youngest skydiver

Krish Shanghvi (b. 19 July 2003) from Mumbai, Maharashtra, became the world's youngest skydiver when he jumped off a plane from an altitude of 3,048 m (10,000 ft) at Mossel Bay, South Africa, on 22 May 2012.

Oldest woman skydiver

Intrepid skydiver Savita Vinayak Padmawar (b. 7 November 1952) from Yavatmal, Maharashtra, is the oldest Indian woman skydiver. She skydived from an altitude of 4,572 m (15,000 ft) at St Kilda Beach in Melbourne, Australia, on 26 December 2017.

First differently abled skydiver in Asia

Major Devender Pal Singh (b. 13 September 1973) from Gurugram, Haryana, is the first differently abled skydiver in Asia. A war-injured amputee veteran, Major Singh skydived from an altitude of 2,743.2 m (9,000 ft) at the military cantonment in Nashik, Maharashtra, on 28 March 2019.

Major D.P. Singh: first differently abled skydiver in Asia

Highest flight

Megha Jain (b. 21 September 1988) from New Delhi made the highest flight in an MiG-29 fighter jet, touching 18,400 m (60,367 ft 5 in.) at a top speed of 1,850 km/hr over Sokol Airbase in Nizhny Novgorod, Russia, on 16 February 2017.

Longest motor glider flight

Captain Surendra Prasad Sinha (b. 26 July 1968), director, Flying Operations, Civil Aviation Department, Government of Jharkhand, flew a Sinus 912 VT-GEE two-seater aircraft for 1,098.24 km in eight flying hours, making it the longest motor glider flight in the country. Along with his co-pilot Captain Anil Gill, he took off from Karnal in Haryana on 13 March 2014 and reached Ranchi, Jharkhand, the next day.

First Indian woman to skydive over seven continents

Shital Mahajan (b. 19 September 1982) from Pune, Maharashtra, completed 705 skydives across seven continents during 2017–18, adding to her skydive at Skydiver Empuriabrava in Spain (Europe) in 2014. She skydived at Skydive Go Fly at Boituva in Brazil (South America); Skydive Utti in Sky Dance Skydiving Center, USA (North America); Sydney Skydivers in Sydney (Australia); Patriot Hill, Antarctica (Antarctica); Skydive Pretoria, Johannesburg, South Africa (Africa) and Skydive Pattaya, Thailand (Asia), taking the total to seven continents.

Microlight aircraft flight

- **First**: Flying at a cruising speed of 56 km/hr on a 90 kg tricycle-shaped aircraft,

Lieutenant Anil Kumar Yadav covered 3,000 km from Jaisalmer, Rajasthan, to Calcutta (now Kolkata), West Bengal, in 31 days from 21 September 1994.

- **Fastest**: Squadron Leader B.K. Das flew a microlight aircraft from Jaisalmer, Rajasthan, to Dibrugarh, Assam, covering 3,250 km during 1–23 February 1999.

Most podium finishes in FAI F3M Championship

Harshil Virendra Mane (b. 3 March 1999) from Pune, Maharashtra, has six international podium finishes in the FAI F3M category championship of aeromodelling, the highest number by an Indian. He is also the first aeromodeller representing India in international championships including the World Cups conducted by the Federation Aeronautique Internationale (FAI).

Harshil Virendra Mane: aeromodelling champion

First jump from a microlight

Wing Commander U.K. Palat skydived from a powered hang-glider piloted by Captain K.A. Vasan from 8,000 ft at 7:40 a.m. on 18 October 1999 in Bangalore (now Bengaluru), Karnataka.

Longest cross-country microlight expedition

The Cross India Air Expedition 2011, organized by the Indian Air Force, covered 7,600 km in 80 hrs 15 mins over 19 days. Wing Commander Akhilesh Chauhan piloted the two-seater microlight, while Squadron Leader Asha Vashisht, Squadron Leader N.D. Gholba and Sergeant M.P. Singh joined him as co-pilots at different stages of the journey. The flight took off from Air Force Station, Hindon, Ghaziabad, Uttar Pradesh, on 8 February 2011, proceeded to Udhampur, Jammu and Kashmir, and traversed the length of the country, flying over Delhi, Jodhpur (Rajasthan), Vadodara (Gujarat), Pune (Maharashtra), Bangalore (now Bengaluru, Karnataka), Sulur (Tamil Nadu) and Thiruvananthapuram (Kerala), returning to Hindon by the same route on 27 February 2011.

First aerial world circumnavigation in a single-engine plane

Ravinder K. Bansal (b. 26 February 1949) from Clarence, New York, USA, undertook an aerial circumnavigation in a Cessna 400 and flew solo, covering 36 cities over 20,959 nautical miles. He started from Buffalo, New York, USA, on 4 July 2017 and returned on 20 August 2017. The expedition was undertaken to raise funds for the Rotary Ambala Cancer and General Hospital.

Most microlight expeditions

Mountain Eagles, the Indian Army microlight formation flying team, based at Army Adventure Nodal Centre (Microlight and Powered Hang-Gliding), Mhow, Madhya Pradesh, conducted three expeditions in 13 months from February 2015.

The first, with seven aircraft, covered 1,800 km in 10 flying days between 13 and 26 February 2015. In the second one, commemorating the golden jubilee of the India–Pakistan war in 1965, three microlights covered 3,050 km in 10 flying days from 5 to 14 September 2015. The third one, at the 15th reunion of the Corps of Signals, was from 9 to 17 February 2016, with six aircraft covering 1,500 km in nine flying days. The core team remained the same in all three expeditions.

First paraglide from a high cliff

Anand Munje (b. 7 November 1956) from Kitty Hawk Ground School, Pune, Maharashtra, launched a flight from the 1,646 m (5,400 ft) high Kalsubai Peak, part of the Western Ghats in Maharashtra, on 25 February 1997. The flight covered 4 km in 11 mins.

First to paraglide with a prosthetic leg

Lieutenant Colonel Dharamdatt Goel (b. 14 August 1976) from Pune, Maharashtra, successfully performed solo paragliding on 19 October 2013 at Al-Hilal, Himachal Pradesh, thereby becoming the first Indian with a prosthetic leg to paraglide. He performed the paraglider flight from an altitude of 2,400 m (7,874 ft) and for 25 mins.

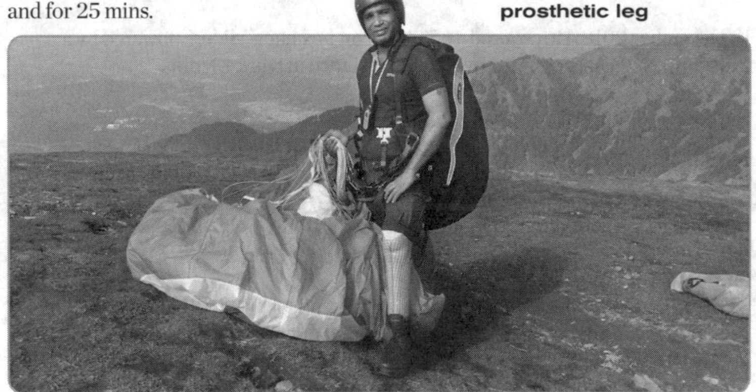

Lieutenant Colonel Dharamdatt Goel: first to paraglide with a prosthetic leg

First visually impaired person to paraglide

Divyanshu Ganatra, who lost his eyesight due to glaucoma at 19 years, performed a solo paraglider flight over Kamshet near Pune, Maharashtra, on 30 April 2014. The flight up to 213.36 m (700 ft) lasted 1 min 30 secs.

First at the Mantar Paragliding XC Open Championship

Prakash Chand Thakur won the first prize at the Mantar Paragliding XC Open Championship, organized by the Asian Continental Paragliding Association in Mantar, Indonesia, from 18 to 24 July 2017.

Longest harness hang-glider flight

Havildar Sanjeev Kumar from the Indian Army Hang Gliding Team, completed the longest harness hang- glider flight from Suratgarh to Barmer, Rajasthan, on

First to complete a BASE jump during day and night

Mayank Nagpal (b. 21 September 1983) from New Delhi became the first Indian to complete a BASE (Building, Antenna, Span and Earth) jump from all four platforms, during both day and night. For the World BASE number, he jumped from Perrine Bridge, USA (5 September 2014), a cliff called Crooked Stick in Idaho, USA (11 September 2014), a mobile antenna in Gua Damai Xtreme Park, Malaysia (6 October 2015), and an under-construction building in Delhi, India (31 December 2016). For the Night BASE number he jumped from Perrine Bridge, USA (7 September 2014), an antenna in Idaho, USA (on 8 September 2014), an under-construction building in Delhi (26 June 2017) and Gua Damai Cliff, Malaysia (28 September 2018).

12 December 2018. He covered 465.33 km on Fox hang-gliders powered by a Mosquito NRG harness. He covered the distance in 8 hrs 43 mins.

Highest and longest wingsuit flight

Lieutenant Colonel Satyendra Verma (b. 24 August 1969), a retired Indian Army officer, on 31 March 2018, jumped from 5,913.12 m (19,400 ft) using a hot-air balloon platform at Phalodi, Rajasthan. He flew in his wingsuit for 4 mins, covering 10 km across the Jodhpur desert in this time.

First BASE jump

- Lieutenant Colonel Satyendra Verma (b. 24 August 1969), then an officer of the Indian Army from the Corps of Signals, carried out a BASE jump from the 137.16 m (450 ft) high deck of the Pitampura TV Tower, New Delhi, on 29 October 2010. This feat was part of the centenary celebrations of the Corps of Signals and the silver jubilee of the Army Adventure Wing.
- Archana Sardana (b. 1 April 1972) from Visakhapatnam, Andhra Pradesh, is India's first female BASE jumper. She performed 25 BASE jumps off a 122 m (400 ft) high bridge above a canyon in Utah, USA, on 13 July 2010.

First balloon bungee jump

Major M.K. Yadav jumped from a hot-air balloon, which was at a height of 3,310.73 m (10,862 ft) over Leh, Ladakh, on 18 August 1995.

First Asian triple amputee to complete a bungee jump

Tinkesh Kaushik (b. 21 June 1993) from Jhajjar, Haryana, became the first Asian triple amputee to bungee from the world's highest canyon swing. He performed the jump from a height of 160 m (525 ft) at The Last Resort, Kathmandu, Nepal, on 25 November 2018.

Daring Dives

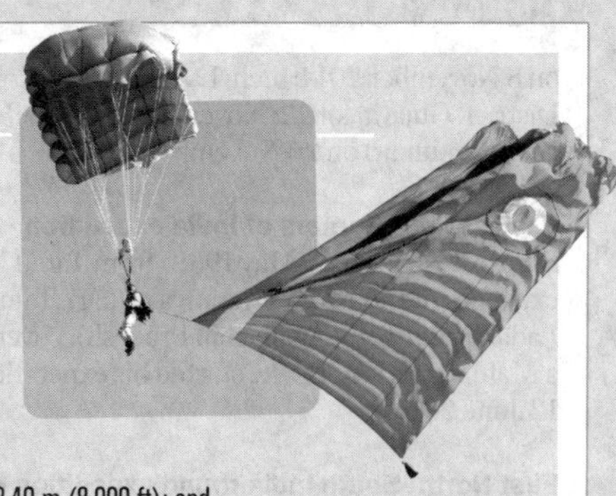

Wing Commander Gajanand Yadava of the Indian Air Force (IAF) created four national records in the field of wingsuit skydive jumping in 2019 in Agra, Uttar Pradesh:
1. First wingsuit skydive jump from high-speed aircraft (An-32);
2. Highest wingsuit jump from an altitude of 7,437.12 m (24,400 ft);
3. First to do a night wingsuit jump from 2,438.40 m (8,000 ft); and
4. The only jumper to undertake high-altitude night-time wingsuit jump from 3,657.60 m (12,000 ft), where he opened the chute at 914.40 m (3,000 ft) after doing wingsuit flying for 2,743.2 m (9,000 ft).

Part of the IAF's skydiving team Akashganga and a parachute jump instructor, Wing Commander Yadava has taken more than 2,900 jumps till date and was awarded the Tenzing Norgay National Adventure Award 2019 in the air adventure category.

Highest BASE jump
Mayank Nagpal (b. 21 September 1983) from New Delhi, performed the highest BASE jump from the 3,080 m (10,105 ft) high point of Eiger Mountain in the Bernese Alps in Switzerland on 24 July 2019.

Lowest BASE jump
Lieutenant Commander Mahesh V. Birajdar from the Indian Navy performed the lowest BASE jump from a 116 m (380 ft 6 in.) high span over a river in the Solang Valley, Himachal Pradesh, on 30 January 2011.

Highest bungee jump – woman
Sudhalakshmi Thanigai Arasu (b. 2 July 1965) performed a 220 m (721 ft 9 in.) high bungee jump at Diga Verzasca, Switzerland, on 13 August 2010.

ROAD EXPEDITIONS

FOUR-WHEELER

First all-India expedition – group
Arun Kumar Basra and Kamaljit Singh Virdi from Rapid Action India completed an all-India car expedition in their Fiat Padmini, covering 15,179 km in 19 days 19 hrs 5 mins. They were flagged off from Delhi on 5 January 1998 and returned on 25 January 1998.

First Four Corners of India expedition – solo
Dr S.S. Chaudhari (b. 7 March 1962) from Jalgaon, Maharashtra, completed a solo drive connecting the four corners of India, covering 13,834 km in 26 days 22 hrs 15 mins. Driving a Maruti SX4 car, he set out from Kanniyakumari, Tamil Nadu, on 30 October 2014. He reached Tezu, Lohit District, Arunachal Pradesh,

on 8 November 2014; Leh, Ladakh, on 16 November 2014; Koteshwar, Kachchh District, Gujarat, on 22 November 2014; and concluded the expedition at Kanniyakumari on 26 November 2014.

Fastest Four Corners of India expedition – solo
Suresh Joseph (b. 14 May 1958) from Tamil Nadu successfully completed the four extremes of India tour (Kanniyakumari, Tamil Nadu; Koteshwar, Gujarat; Leh, Ladakh; and Tezu, Arunachal Pradesh), covering 13,214 km in 403 hrs. Driving a Mahindra XUV500, he started his expedition on 7 May 2015 and ended it on 12 June 2015.

First North–South India round expedition – solo
Suresh Joseph (b. 14 May 1958) from Tamil Nadu is the first person to complete the trailblazing North–South expedition India round trip and, in the process, breaking the record of the fastest North–South solo expedition in 2012. He started his expedition from Kanniyakumari, Tamil Nadu, on 2 July 2012 and reached Leh, Ladakh, on 7 July 2012, covering 3,811 km in 129 hrs 30 mins. Four days later, he was back on the trip, taking off from Leh on 11 July 2012. He reached Kanniyakumari on 15 July 2012. He drove a Maruti Swift car for the journey.

The Mana Pass on the Indo-China border, at an altitude of 5,610 m (18,406 ft), is one of the highest vehicle-accessible passes in the world.

Fastest North–South expedition – solo
Saroj Sinha (b. 11 May 1979) from Bengaluru, Karnataka, completed the fastest North–South expedition in a Jeep Compass, across 3,832.7 km in 63 hrs 34 mins, starting from Leh, Ladakh, on 3 July 2019 and reaching Kanniyakumari, Tamil Nadu, on 5 July 2019. The total riding time was 61 hrs 38 mins and the total break time was 1 hour 56 mins.

Fastest North–South expedition – group
Vinu Kurian Jacob, Josin Baby and Joe Jacob from Kerala set a record for the fastest North–South India group expedition, covering 3,888 km in 52 hrs 58 mins. Driving a Honda Amaze car, the trio started from Leh, Ladakh, on 5 October 2014, reaching Kanniyakumari, Tamil Nadu, on 7 October 2014.

First trans-Himalayan expedition – solo
Suresh Joseph (b. 14 May 1958) from Tamil Nadu set out in a Ford Endeavour to create a new record for a trans-Himalayan solo trip, which he accomplished in 18 days 13 hrs 15 mins. Starting his journey from Jammu in Jammu and Kashmir on 21 August 2015, he reached Tezu in Arunachal Pradesh on 8 September 2015. Joseph covered 5,845 km across nine Indian states, Nepal and Bhutan, and crossed altitudes of up to 2,554.2 m (8,380 ft).

First West–East India round expedition – solo
Daljit Singh Matharoo (b. 29 September 1986) completed a solo West–East–West India expedition, covering 7,715 km in 217 hrs 25 mins. He broke the record for the fastest solo East–West India expedition by covering 3,832 km in 94 hrs 44 mins.

He started in his Maruti Zen car from Koteshwar, Kachchh District, Gujarat, on 27 April 2018, and reached Tezu, Arunachal Pradesh, on 1 May 2018. He started back on 1 May 2018 and reached Koteshwar on 6 May 2018.

Fastest East–West India expedition – group

Apurba Kumar Deka (b. 27 March 1975), Animesh Deka (b. 15 January 1982) and Md Zillur Rahman (b. 2 December 1975) from Guwahati, Assam, completed the fastest East–West India expedition from Tezu, Arunachal Pradesh, to Koteshwar, Gujarat, covering 3,771.4 km in 70 hrs 52 mins. The team drove a Renault Duster car, starting their journey on 27 October 2015 and ending the expedition on 30 October 2015.

Fastest East–West India expedition by a differently abled person – solo

Eric Paul (b. 14 January 1988), a wheelchair-bound paraplegic from Rohini, New Delhi, completed the East–West India solo expedition in a hand-controlled Maruti Swift, covering 3,697 km in 4 days 18 hrs 55 mins. He started from Tezu, Arunachal Pradesh, on 30 November 2017 at 4:13 a.m., reaching Koteshwar, Gujarat, at 11:43 p.m. on 4 December 2017.

Eric Paul: fastest to complete East–West India solo expedition by a differently abled person

Longest journey within a country – solo

Shashi Kapila (b. 3 November 1942) from New Delhi completed the longest journey in a Honda Mobilio car, covering 8,227 km in 105 hrs 15 mins. He started from Delhi at 6:00 a.m. on 12 November 2016 and reached back at 12:28 p.m. on 22 November 2016. The farthest location he travelled to was Kanniyakumari.

Longest journey within a country – group

A two-member team of Sagar Thakar (b. 30 June 1982) and Kanak Barsadia (b. 14 February 1984) from Surat, Gujarat, completed the longest journey in a Maruti Swift Dzire car, covering 60,830 km in 82 days. They set off from Bardoli, Gujarat, on 20 March 2017 and reached back on 12 June 2017.

Longest distance travelled across countries – solo

Hitendra Sharma (b. 11 January 1978) from Gwalior, Madhya Pradesh, successfully undertook a solo expedition by road, covering 30,195 km across

11 Asian countries in a Honda Amaze car in 92 days. Starting from Gwalior in Madhya Pradesh, India, on 10 February 2017, he reached Bangladesh, driving through India, Myanmar, Thailand, Laos, Vietnam, Cambodia, Malaysia, Singapore, Bhutan and Nepal, and returned to India on 21 May 2017.

TWO-WHEELER (MOTORCYCLE)

Fastest All-India expedition – solo

Prashant Kumar (b. 14 July 1987) from Bengaluru, Karnataka, completed the all-India expedition on 7 November 2019 on his Triumph Tiger XCA 800 bike, covering 16,305 km in 23 days 9 hrs 46 mins. He started from Hyderabad, Telangana, on 15 October 2019 and returned on 7 November 2019, travelling through the then 29 states and five Union Territories.

Prashant Kumar: fastest to complete all-India expedition – solo

Fastest East–West India expedition – solo

Dr S.T. Thomas (b. 8 January 1987) from Tamil Nadu covered 3,729 km from Tezu, Arunachal Pradesh, to Koteshwar, Gujarat, in 68 hrs 18 mins to set a new record in the East–West India two-wheeler expedition category. He started his journey on his Honda CBR 250R bike on 20 March 2016 and concluded the expedition on 23 March 2016.

Vishvesh Dhirendrakumar Mehta: fastest to complete Four Corners of India expedition – solo

Fastest Four Corners of India expedition – solo

Vishvesh Dhirendrakumar Mehta (b. 10 June 1980) from Jamnagar, Gujarat, completed the fastest solo expedition connecting the four extremes of India, covering 11,217 km in 313 hrs 51 mins. Riding a Royal Enfield Classic 350, he set out from Koteshwar, Gujarat, on 21 May 2019 and returned to Koteshwar (covering Kanniyakumari, Tamil Nadu; Leh, Ladakh; and Tezu, Arunachal Pradesh) on 8 June 2019. His break time was 113 hrs.

Fastest North–South India expedition – solo

Sridhar Ramulu Chidumalla (b. 2 January 1978) from Mumbai, Maharashtra, completed the fastest North–South solo expedition on a Royal Enfield motorcycle, covering 3,849 km in 74 hrs 45 mins. He started from Leh, Ladakh, on 25 June 2018 and reached Kanniyakumari, Tamil Nadu, on 28 June 2018.

Fastest Golden Quadrilateral (GQ) expedition – solo

Souvig Sarkar (b. 22 October 1986) from Mumbai, Maharashtra, completed the GQ solo motorcycling expedition, covering 5,962.09 km in 87 hrs 42 mins on a Triumph Street Triple RS motorcycle, between 18 and 22 October 2019.

Fastest North–South India expedition – group

Ajay Rana (b. 23 November 1996) and Vishal Pundir (b. 10 November 1998) covered 3,963 km from Leh, Ladakh, to Kanniyakumari, Tamil Nadu, in 87 hrs 3 mins to set a new record in the North–South India two-wheeler (group) expedition category. They started on two Royal Enfield motorcycles on 2 June 2018 and reached Kanniyakumari on 5 June 2018.

First North–South India round expedition by a differently abled person – solo

Vadivel Baluchamy (b. 14 June 1990), an amputee from Madurai, Tamil Nadu, completed the first North–South solo round expedition by a differently abled person, covering 9,136 km in 576 hrs 23 mins. He started on a Royal Enfield Classic 350 bike from Kanniyakumari on 30 August 2018 at 4:25 p.m. and travelled to Leh, Ladakh. He returned to Kanniyakumari on 22 September at 8:18 p.m.

Fastest GQ expedition – group

The Brotherhood of Tourers, a team of six motorcycling enthusiasts from Mumbai, Maharashtra, covered 6,011 km in 118 hrs 35 mins. The team members – Eshan Banodkar, Dheeraj Landge, Aalesh Lade, Gyanesh Yadav, Brian Monteiro and Sudeep N.S. – started the journey from Mumbai on 22 September 2015 and travelled anticlockwise via Bengaluru, Chennai, Kolkata and Delhi, and returned to Mumbai on 27 September 2015.

Fastest GQ expedition by a differently abled person – solo

Vadivel Baluchamy (b. 14 June 1990), an amputee, completed the fastest GQ expedition by a differently abled person, covering 6,723 km in 14 days 9 hrs and 30 mins. He started on a Royal Enfield Classic 350 bike from Chennai, Tamil Nadu, on 25 September 2017 and travelled to Kolkata, Delhi and Mumbai, returning to Chennai on 9 October 2017.

Record Rewind

Riding a motorcycle while standing

1993

Ganesh Gurjar stood on a Suzuki motorcycle and rode it from Rajsamand, Rajasthan, to New Delhi, covering 700 km in 28 hrs 45 mins. He began his journey on 14 November 1992 and completed it on 16 November at 12.45 p.m.

2018

Inspector Ashish Bhargava (b. 4 September 1985) of the Border Security Force (BSF) began the longest continuous ride, standing on a motorcycle seat on 16 April 2018 at 11:23 a.m. He covered 80.5 km in 2 hrs 21 mins 16 secs at the R.K. Wadhwa Parade Ground, 25 Bn BSF Chhawla Camp, Delhi.

Longest journey within the country – solo

Krishanu Kona (b. 27 September 1991) from Delhi travelled 50,338 km on his motorcycle in 224 days to set the record for the longest motorcycle journey in India. He started on a Bajaj Pulsar NS200 bike on 30 August 2015 from Delhi and returned on 9 April 2016.

Longest distance covered within the country by a differently abled person – solo

Mahinder Singh Raghuwanshi (b. 2 October 1987), an amputee with 70 per cent disability, and a prosthetic limb, covered 5,331.5 km on an Enfield Bullet 350 bike in 17 days. He started from his hometown Mhow, Madhya Pradesh, on 3 June 2016, and went up to Khardung La (5,359 m/17,582 ft) in Leh, Ladakh, returning to Mhow on 19 June 2016.

Most passes covered – group

A team of eight members: team leader Colonel Rajesh W. Adhau (b. 3 December 1972), deputy team leader Colonel Saurabh Bhardwaj (b. 20 February 1974), and Major Sashikant (b. 15 June 1982), Major Mahesh Mahto (b. 14 August 1977), Captain Karanvir Singh Sidhu (b. 28 February 1990), Havildar Vinayak Dhamale (b. 27 July 1985), Lance Naik Pintu Das (b. 4 April 1988) and Lance Naik Deepak Kumar Singh (b. 14 January 1986) of the Army Medical Corps (AMC) Motorcycle Expedition crossed eight of the highest Himalayan passes at Khardung La (5,359 m/17,582 ft), Saser La (5,411 m/17,753 ft), Wari La (5,312 m/17,428 ft), Chang La (5,360 m/17,585 ft), Marsimek La (5,582 m/18,314 ft), Kaksang La (5,438 m/17,841 ft), Photi La (5,524 m/18,123 ft) and Tanglang La (5,328 m/17,480 ft), in that order, between 31 August 2019 and 5 September 2019. They covered 1,505 km in their expedition to commemorate the 20th year of the Kargil war and the 55th biennial conference of the AMC.

First to cross Umling La pass – solo

Pallavi Fauzdar (b. 20 December 1979) from Delhi was the first to cross Umling La pass on 4 August 2017 at 3:16 p.m. It is the highest motorable pass in the world, situated at an altitude of 5,882.64 m (19,300 ft) above sea level. On her expedition, she even named the Bonni La pass, situated at an altitude of 5,083 m (16,677 ft), which was unnamed before.

Pallavi Fauzdar: first to cross Umling La pass – solo

WR Most people on a moving motorcycle

On 19 November 2017, the Tornadoes Despatch Rider team of the Army Service Corps put 58 men on a single 500 cc Royal Enfield motorcycle driven by Subedar Rampal Yadav for 1.2 km at the Yelahanka Air Force Station in Bengaluru, Karnataka. The previous world record of 56 men was created in

2010 by the Corps of Signals, also of the Indian Army. The Tornadoes were led by Major Bunny Sharma. The Tornadoes hold 19 world and national records since their inception in 1982, with Colonel C.N. Rao and Captain J.P. Verma as their first leaders.

Largest rally (less than 100 km) by woman riders – multiple venues

The largest two-wheeler rally by only women riders was organized by the Akhil Bharatiya Terapanth Mahila Mandal on 8 March 2020, International Women's Day. As many as 6,205 women rode distances ranging from 1.5 to 10 km at various locations like Udaipur, Ahmedabad, Balotra, Surat and Delhi, among others. The rally was held as part of their 'I Respect' campaign to emphasize the need for women to respect one another for their choices in careers, family and other life decisions.

Akhil Bharatiya Terapanth Mahila Mandal: largest rally (less than 100 km) by women riders - multiple venues

Highest motorable pass

Umling La Top, Ladakh, at an altitude of 5,883 m (19,300 ft) is the highest motorable pass in the world. The 86 km long road connects Chisumle and Demchok villages to Leh.

Largest moving human pyramid – women

A team of Central Reserve Police Force (CRPF) women personnel, the first such all-woman motorcycling team, has shown their daredevilry many times, starting with their first performance at the CRPF's diamond jubilee at India Gate, New Delhi, on 2 November 2014. Titled 'Desh Ke Rakshak', a total of 37 women personnel of the CRPF formed a human pyramid on nine Enfield Bullet 350 motorcycles. They covered 100 m at a speed of 25 km per hour. They completed the ride without any belt, harness or other supporting equipment.

Longest non-stop motorcycle ride standing backwards – group

Constable Ravinder Minde (b. 20 June 1987) and Inspector Awadesh Kumar Singh (b. 19 April 1980) of the Border Security Force (BSF) completed the longest motorcycle standing backwards, covering 64.3 km in 2 hrs 10 mins 57 secs at 7:32 a.m. on 24 October 2018 at the R.K. Wadhwa Parade Ground, 25 Bn BSF Chhawla Camp, New Delhi. They did not use any harness, belt or other supporting equipment.

Longest non-stop motorcycle standing on footrest – solo

H.C. Rampal Singh (b. 12 November 1977) of the Border Security Force (BSF) performed the longest standing-on-footrest bike ride on 22 October 2018 at 9:14 a.m. He covered 77.6 km in 2 hrs 11 mins 5 secs at the R.K. Wadhwa Parade Ground, 25 Bn BSF Chhawla Camp, New Delhi. He did not use any harness, belt or other supporting equipment.

Three-bike human pyramid

Thirty-six personnel of the Border Security Force (BSF) formed a human pyramid on three motorcycles on 13 April 2018. The human pyramid covered a distance of 1 km in 55.52 secs, setting a new record. They began riding at 9:39 a.m. on the Najafgarh–Dauralla Shaheed Rao Laxmi Chand Marg, New Delhi. They completed the ride without any belt, harness or other supporting equipment.

Longest non-stop motorcycle ride standing on seat bracket – group

Two teams of the Border Security Force (BSF) successfully completed the longest motorcycle ride while standing on the seat bracket simultaneously. One team comprised Constable Sunil Yadav (b. 1 November 1983) and Constable Jasvir Kumar (b. 25 April 1992), and the other team had Constable Arjun Singh (b. 20 June 1980) and Constable Arvind (b. 5 March 1997). One member rode the motorcycle while carrying the other member on his shoulders. Both teams covered 19.85 km in 41 mins 12 secs on 24 October 2018 at the R.K. Wadhwa Parade Ground, 25 Bn BSF Chhawla Camp, New Delhi. They did not use any belt, harness or other supporting equipment.

Longest motorcycle ride while standing on seat bracket – group

Longest non-stop bike ride on a ladder

H.C. Durvesh Babu (b. 10 August 1979) of the Border Security Force successfully completed a continuous ride, standing on a ladder of 5.3 m (17 ft 4 in.) height fitted on a motorcycle. He began his ride on 24 April 2018 at 9:25 p.m. at the R.K. Wadhwa Parade Ground, 25 Bn BSF Chhawla Camp, New Delhi. He rode for 10 hrs 34 mins 27 secs without any belt, harness or other supporting equipment.

Longest non-stop bike ride on a pole

Inspector Awadesh Kumar Singh (b. 19 April 1980) of the Border Security Force performed a continuous ride on a 5.3 m (17 ft 4 in.) high pole fitted on a motorcycle, for 10 hrs 34 mins 27 secs. He started riding on 24 April 2018 at 9:25 p.m. at the R.K. Wadhwa Parade Ground, 25 Bn BSF Chhawla Camp, New Delhi. He did not use any belts, harness or supporting equipment.

THE HIMALAYAN ODYSSEY: A BIKER'S DREAM

The Royal Enfield's Himalayan Odyssey is a 15-day annual biking trip to and back from Khardung La, one of the world's highest motorable passes, in Leh, Ladakh, 5,359 m (17,582 ft) above sea level. Held in 2005 for the first time, the event saw a participation of 46 bikers from across the country, who came from all walks of life and belonged to varying age groups between 19 and 57 years. Crossing an expanse of 2,066 km under extreme terrain and weather conditions, the riders navigate through stretches of pristine landscape and rock-strewn pathways to reach their destination and back on this journey. The 16th edition of the Himalayan Odyssey was flagged off on 4 July 2019 from Chandigarh and witnessed 60 riders from India and abroad. An All-women Himalayan Odyssey was launched in July 2016 for women riders from across the world.

Longest motorcycle ride hands-free standing backwards – solo

Constable Ravinder Minde (b. 20 June 1987) of the Border Security Force, covered 106.1 km of back-riding while standing on a motorcycle. He completed the ride in 4 hrs 17 mins on 16 April 2018 at the R.K. Wadhwa Parade Ground, 25 Bn BSF Chhawla Camp, New Delhi, without any belts, harness or other supporting equipment.

TWO-WHEELER (BICYCLE)

Largest bicycling marathon

Organized by Vodafone India, the second edition of the Vodafone Cycling Marathon held in Bengaluru, Karnataka, on 1 March 2015, attracted 6,123 cyclists. The event was held under four different categories: Champion Race (60 km), Passion Race (40 km), Green Ride (20 km) and Fashion Ride (5 km). It was conducted under the aegis of the Cycle Federation of India, supported by Bengaluru City Traffic Police. Around 5,000 cyclists took part in the first edition of this marathon.

Oldest Super Randonneuse

Ela Ghose (b. 8 April 1961) successfully completed 4 brevets organized by Noida Randonneurs and Delhi Randonneurs (a part of Audax India Randonneurs) under the aegis of Audax Club Parisien of France, and earned the title of

Super Randonneuse in the 2018–19 season. A randonneuring event is called a randonnée or brevet, and a rider who has completed a 200 km event is called a randonneur. The Super Randonneur/Randonneuse title is awarded on the completion of a series of 4 brevets within a single (cycling) year, i.e., November 2018–October 2019. The 4 brevets cover 200 km (completed within 13.5 hrs), 300 km (completed within 20 hrs), 400 km (completed within 27 hrs) and 600 km (completed within 40 hrs).

Saurabh Bharat Zagade: fastest North–South expedition – gearless – solo

Fastest North–South expedition – gearless – solo
Saurabh Bharat Zagade (b. 28 October 1996) from Pune, Maharashtra, completed a solo North–South India expedition on a normal (gearless) bicycle, covering a distance of 3,440 km in 14 days 7 hrs. He started from Dharmal, Jammu and Kashmir, at 6:25 a.m. on 15 April 2019 and reached Kanniyakumari, Tamil Nadu, at 1:25 p.m. on 29 April 2019.

Fastest North–South expedition – geared – solo
Nimesh Mansukhbhai Jivrajani (b. 11 February 1980) from Bhavnagar, Gujarat, completed a solo North–South India expedition on a geared bicycle, covering 3,400 km in 14 days 16 hrs 15 mins. He started from Jammu, Jammu and Kashmir, at 5:40 a.m. on 24 December 2018 and reached Kanniyakumari, Tamil Nadu, at 10:00 p.m. on 7 January 2019.

Fastest North–South expedition – gearless – group
Ashwani Kumar Singh (b. 14 August 1995) from Deoria, Uttar Pradesh, and Akash Yadav (b. 1 February 1990) from Azamgarh, Uttar Pradesh, completed the fastest North–South India tour by cycle, covering 4,197 km in 14 days 15 hrs 37 mins. The duo started from Leh, Ladakh, on 13 June 2016 and reached Kanniyakumari, Tamil Nadu, on 27 June 2016.

Fastest East–West expedition – geared – solo
Naresh Kumar Rajendran (b. 3 June 1992) from Vellore, Tamil Nadu, completed the fastest East–West solo expedition in a geared bicycle by covering 3,613 km in 10 days 8 hrs 57 mins. He started from Tezu, Arunachal Pradesh, at 4:00 a.m. on 5 December 2018 and ended at Koteshwar, Gujarat, at 12:57 p.m. on 15 December 2018.

Longest distance covered within the country – geared – solo
Karan Singh Jagawat (b. 1 March 1948) covered a distance of 20,948 km on his geared cycle in 178 days. He started his journey on 23 April 2017 from Jaipur, Rajasthan, and returned to Jaipur on 18 October 2017. He travelled through

Koteshwar, Gujarat; Tezu, Arunachal Pradesh; Khardung La, Ladakh; and Kanniyakumari, Tamil Nadu.

Md Soyab Ansari: fastest to complete GQ expedition – geared – solo

Most passes covered – solo

Sumit Patil (b. 25 April 1985) from Alibaug, Maharashtra, pedalled through six Himalayan passes, covering 517 km in 71 hrs 28 mins. Starting from Manali, Himachal Pradesh, on 16 September 2015, he reached Khardung La (5,359 m/ 17,582 ft) on 19 September 2015. He covered Rohtang La (3,978 m/ 13,051 ft), Baralacha La (4,892 m/ 16,050 ft), Nakee La (4,739 m/ 15,548 ft), Lachunga La (5,059 m/ 16,598 ft) and Tanglang La (5,328 m/17,480 ft).

Fastest Golden Quadrilateral (GQ) expedition – geared – solo

Md Soyab Ansari (b. 4 June 1994) from Jagdishpur, Bihar, completed the GQ solo expedition, covering a distance of 6,726.47 km in 20 days 58 mins 24 secs on his bicycle. The total break time was 25 hrs 44 mins. He started his expedition on 7 January 2019 from Bengaluru, Karnataka, and concluded it on 21 February 2019 at Hosur, Bengaluru, Karnataka.

First tandem bicycling

Ashok N. Bhanushali (b. 21 May 1974) from Mumbai, Maharashtra, and

Fastest Asian to Cycle across the World

Vedangi Kulkarni (b. 1998) from Pune, Maharashtra, became the fastest Asian to cycle across the world. She started her expedition from Perth, Australia, in July 2018 and reached Kolkata, West Bengal, on 23 December 2018. She crossed a distance of 29,000 km in 159 days, pedalling up to 300 km every day. She covered 14 countries during the expedition including New Zealand, Canada, Iceland, Portugal, Spain, France, Belgium, Germany, Denmark, Sweden, Finland and Russia. During her ride she endured temperatures ranging between –20°C and 37°C.

Record Rewind

Longest distance within the country – cycling – solo

1992

Twenty-five-year-old Madhukar Sharma cycled from Delhi to Khardung La (2,500 km) over four months and 8 days, finishing on 1 September 1988.

2018

Lieutenant Colonel Vishal Ahlawat from Delhi covered 25,338 km within India by bicycle in three months and 16 days, starting on 15 August 2018 and finishing on 1 December 2018.

Dr Meera Velankar (b. 11 December 1975) from Bengaluru, Karnataka, completed India's first 300 km brevet ride on a tandem bicycle. The feat was part of an event organized by Surat Randonneurs on 10 July 2016. The duo started the ride from M.T.B. College, Surat, Gujarat, and covered a distance of 309 km in 17 hrs 36 mins.

Longest tandem bicycling – women

Sheetal Bambulkar (b. 27 October 1978) from Mumbai, Maharashtra, and Dr Meera Velankar (b. 11 December 1975) from Bengaluru, Karnataka, completed a tandem cycling brevet ride of 206 km in 12 hrs 27 mins in Vadodara, Gujarat, on 20 December 2015.

All-India tour on a mono-wheeler

Subrata Chakraborty (b. 5 November 1976) from Kolkata, West Bengal, completed an all-India solo expedition on a monocycle, covering 10,500 km in 256 days. He started his journey from Raj Bhavan, Kolkata, on 8 September 2000 and returned to Kolkata on 21 May 2001. He passed through 17 states of the country, viz., West Bengal, Odisha, Andhra Pradesh, Tamil Nadu, Kerala, Karnataka, Goa, Maharashtra, Gujarat, Rajasthan, Haryana, Delhi, Uttar Pradesh, Madhya Pradesh, Bihar, Assam and Arunachal Pradesh.

WATER SPORTS

First sail down the River Ganga

Captain P.P. Sabharwal and Captain S.N. Dubey completed the first sail down the River Ganga in a racing craft from Chandi Ghat at Haridwar, Uttarakhand, to Kolkata, West Bengal, from 26 to 28 July 1960. The total distance they covered was 1,931.23 km.

First circumnavigation of the globe by a differently abled sailor

Major Ashok Kumar Singh, a permanent member of the INS *Trishna* crew and winner of the National Adventure Award in 1994, went around the globe in 1985. It was the longest journey undertaken by a differently abled person.

First circumnavigation of the globe – group

On 28 September 1985, a group of 10 sappers, led by Colonel T.P.S. Chowdhury, set off on INS *Trishna*, for a 55,000 km odyssey in an 11.3 m (37 ft) long, 10.5 tonne fibreglass yacht. They sailed from Mumbai, Maharashtra, to Maldives and Mauritius, and then to St Helena Island. Crossing the Equator for the second time, they sailed into the Port of Belem in Brazil, then through the Panama Canal towards the Galapagos Islands, the Polynesian Islands and Bali, and reached Mumbai on 10 January 1987.

First sailing expedition on the River Brahmaputra and longest on any Indian river

Sixty NCC cadets of Assam undertook a 220 km long sailing expedition on the capricious River Brahmaputra in three whaler boats of the NCC naval units, with safety and support vessels provided by the Indian Army Eastern Command. The maiden expedition named 'Lachit-1' was flagged off at Biswanath Chariali, Assam, by Major General Bipin Bakshi and flagged in at Pandu Port, Guwahati, on 16 October 2019 by handing over the flag to Assam's chief minister Sarbananda Sonowal.

First sailing expedition on the River Brahmaputra; and longest on any Indian river

First circumnavigation – woman – solo

On 15 October 1988, Ujwala Rai became not only the first Indian woman, but also the first Asian one, to sail around the world after a 17-month voyage in *Jaykus III*, a 9.75 m (32 ft) Vancouver-class sailboat.

First circumnavigation – man – solo

Commander Dilip Donde of the Indian Navy completed a solo circumnavigation of the globe in 276 days. He covered 21,600 nautical miles sailing on INSV *Mhadei*, a 17 m (56 ft) long sailing boat fitted with high-tech navigation and communication equipment. He embarked on the voyage on 19 August 2009. On return, his boat touched base at Sunk Rock Lighthouse at Mumbai harbour on 22 May 2010. The expedition was part of the Indian Navy's 'Sagar Parikrama' project.

First catamaran sailing expedition

A team of sailors from the Artillery Water Sports Association, Hyderabad, Telangana, completed the Sarvatra Sailing Expedition, a 1,364 km long marine voyage along the eastern coast of India. The longest such expedition in the country, it was launched from Marina Beach, Chennai, Tamil Nadu, on 18 December 2011 and culminated at Gopalpur, Odisha, on 3 January 2012. They also set records of sailing 153 km non-stop in a day on 21 December 2011 and of 15 hours of non-stop sailing on 31 December 2011.

Longest social campaign through an adventure sport
The National Mission for Clean Ganga, operated under the Department of Water Resources, River Development and Ganga Rejuvenation, Ministry of Jal Shakti, Government of India, organized the Ganga Aamantran Abhiyaan – a river-rafting and kayaking expedition on the River Ganga, conducted between 10 October and 12 November 2019 with a team of nine members. The expedition started from Devprayag and culminated at Ganga Sagar after covering 2,500 km. They spread the message of water conservation and river rejuvenation.

First deep-bounce dive
Commodore Vimal Kumar of the Indian Navy was the first person to dive to a depth of 160 m in a diving bell in the Black Sea in 1970. He explored the bottom of the sea for about 10 mins. After surfacing, he underwent a decompression schedule for 10 hrs.

First saturation dive
Commodore Vimal Kumar of the Indian Navy conducted the first saturation dive in May 1985 in a decompression chamber, using a mix of helium and oxygen, on INHS *Ashvini* in Mumbai, Maharashtra. Pratap Singh and T. Vinod Rao were pressurized to a depth of 67 m (219 ft 10 in.) on 16 May 1985 and stayed in saturation for six days.

Most stand-up paddle-boarding
Kumaran M. (b. 2 March 1981) from Chennai, Tamil Nadu, had completed stand-up paddle-boarding on 19 different waterbodies, including 17 in India and one each in Sri Lanka and Malaysia, as on 30 June 2016.

Longest stand-up paddle-boarding – group
Sri Krishnan (b. 31 July 1991) and Siddharth C. (b. 6 July 1992) from Chennai, Tamil Nadu, accomplished the longest stand-up paddle-boarding in the open sea, covering 31 km in the Bay of Bengal on 15 April 2016. They started at Kovalam Beach, Kerala, and paddled to reach Marina Beach, Tamil Nadu, covering the distance in 6 hrs 27 mins.

First surfing and stand-up paddle competition
The Surfing Federation of India, with the Kerala Tourism Department, organized Spice Coast Open, India's first official national surfing and stand-up paddle (SUP) competition at Kovalam Beach, Kerala, from 3 to 5 May 2013. The three-day event had more than 100 participants in surfing contests under five categories and SUP races under two.

Youngest junior master scuba-diver
Scuba-diver Adithya Srinivasan (b. 6 April 2007) from Chennai, Tamil Nadu, became the youngest junior master scuba-diver certified by the Professional Association of Diving Instructors (PADI) on 7 April 2019. Adithya performed his qualifying 13.4 m (44 ft) dive in the Bay of Bengal off the coast of Puducherry.

First junior master scuba-diver
Twelve-year-old Jashan Nilesh Shah (b. 15 August 2000) from Surat, Gujarat,

K FOR KAYAKING

Longest kayaking – solo

Kaustubh Kisan Khade (b. 17 January 1987) from Mumbai, Maharashtra, completed the west coast expedition from Dwarka, Gujarat, to Kanniyakumari, Tamil Nadu, from 17 November 2016 to 7 February 2017. He paddled 1,845 km in 83 days.

Longest kayaking – group

Tarun K. Roy and Brij Mohan Bisht from New Delhi completed the Himalaya-to-Ocean Ganga Expedition from Rishikesh, Uttarakhand, to Ganga Sagar Island in the Bay of Bengal from 5 January to 19 March 2003. They paddled 2,443 km in 74 days.

MANDIP SINGH SOIN: MAKING MOLEHILLS OUT OF MOUNTAINS

Mandip Singh Soin's (b. 9 March 1957) initial foray into adventure was when he became a part of the first public school boys' expedition to the Black Peak (6,387 m/20,954 ft), Uttarakhand, at the age of fifteen. Inspired by his father's tales of jumping off planes as a paratrooper in the Indian Army, Soin found himself undertaking early adventures of rock climbing, trekking and mountaineering while growing up. With a master's degree in history from St Stephen's College, Delhi University, he turned his passion into a career and started Ibex Expeditions, an award-winning adventure travel company, in early 1979. A mountaineer, explorer, environmentalist and Fellow of the Royal Geographical Society, UK, Soin has been part of many first Indian mountaineering ascents and explorations (Mount Meru in 1986, the French and Swiss Alps, Italian Dolomites, Wales and Scotland) and has travelled to over 45 countries and all seven continents. Through Ibex Expeditions, he pioneered unique journeys, such as the crossing of the Thar desert on camelback from Jaisalmer to the Rann of Kachchh in 1986 and the frozen river (Chadar) trek on the River Zanskar in 1994, now famous for paving the way for winter tourism in Ladakh. The first and only Indian to receive the Ness Award by the Royal Geographical

Tandem skydiving *(below)* in New Zealand (1994)

qualified as a junior master scuba-diver, certified by the Professional Association of Diving Instructors (PADI) on 25 March 2013, becoming the first Indian to do so. He also became the first junior rescue diver of PADI on the same day.

Marathon windsurfing

Rahul Rastogi from Hyderabad, Telangana, was the first Asian to windsurf 400 km from Kavaratti, Lakshadweep, to Kozhikode, Kerala. He started on 22 April 1988 and completed the marathon three days later. His average windsurfing timing was 14 hrs a day.

First canoeing expedition

Sheo Shankar Gope and Ravindra Kumar Bhuyan were team leaders of a canoeing expedition that started from Kolkata, West Bengal, on 6 July 1991. They paddled upstream on the Ganga and sailed a distance of 2,000 km, touching Bhagalpur, Mokama, Patna, Allahabad (now Prayagraj) and Etawah, reaching Delhi on 25 September 1991.

Yachting at the highest altitude

Captain Gautama Dutta from Mumbai, Maharashtra, carted his laser boat to an altitude of 5,460 m (17,913 ft) at Devtal Lake, Uttarakhand, and yachted there on 18 September 1993.

Society, UK, in 1992, Soin was also the recipient of the Tenzing Norgay Adventure Award for Lifetime Achievement in 2012, and has climbed, trekked, skydived and been a part of several diverse adventures in India and abroad over the last four decades. Responsible for launching India' s first international ecotourism expedition to the Andaman and Nicobar Islands in 2002, Ibex Expeditions continues to be a member of many juries for best environmental practices in tourism while Soin's contribution to the cause is his participation in adventure task forces and committees for the Government of India and state governments.

Reaching the summit of Monch, Swiss Alps (2002)

Joining the ranks of past award winners like Jeff Bezos and Robert Swan in 2015, he became the only Indian to be honoured with the Citation of Merit from the Explorers' Club, USA, for his outstanding work in mountaineering and an unmatched spirit of adventure and exploration spanning six continents. Also the founder president of the Ecotourism Society of India (now the Responsible Tourism Society of India), Soin has delivered over 250 lectures in schools, colleges and institutions across the globe. He is joined by his wife, Anita Singh Soin, an artist, poet and writer, in creating Ibex experiences for people who choose to explore the outdoors in an ecologically responsible way.

Swimming at the highest altitude

Petty officer R.L. Sharma and leading seaman Dhani Ram swam a distance of 4,746 m (15,571 ft) across the breadth of Kedartal, a glacial lake at an altitude of 4,750 m (15,584 ft) in Uttarakhand, on 25 September 1995.

WR First and youngest Asian woman to swim in Antarctic waters

Bhakti Sharma (b. 30 November 1989) from Udaipur, Rajasthan, is the first Asian woman and the youngest in the world to set a record in open swimming in Antarctic waters. She swam 2.3 km in 41 hrs 14 mins, in temperatures of around 1°C, breaking the record of L. Cox (USA) and L. Pugh (Britain). She was awarded the Tenzing Norgay National Adventure Award in 2010.

First woman to cross the English Channel – solo

Arati Saha (b. 24 September 1940) from West Bengal became the first Indian woman to cross the English Channel on 29 September 1959. She swam from Cape Gris Nez, France, to Sandgate, England, in 16 hrs 20 mins.

First to swim the English Channel thrice – solo

● **Men:** Taranath Narayan Shenoy (b. 1958) from Maharashtra became the first person to cross the English Channel thrice in 1985. Deaf and nearly blind, he had previously swum across the channel in 1983 and 1984.

● **Women:** Rashmi Sharma (b. 1988) from Kolkata, West Bengal, became the first woman to cross the English Channel thrice in 2009. She had previously swum across the channel in 2006 and 2007.

First sailing expedition around the Indian peninsula

Alok Kumar Yadav (b. 20 June 1984) from EME Sailing Association completed the first sailing expedition around the Indian peninsula. He started from Haldia, West Bengal, along the east coast on 21 October 2018 and reached Porbandar, Gujarat, on the west coast on 1 December 2018. He covered a distance of 4,597 nautical miles in 41 days.

Alok Kumar Yadav *(middle)*: first sailing expedition around the Indian peninsula

Oldest to cross English Channel

Srikaanth Viswanathan (b. 15 July 1972) from Bengaluru, Karnataka, crossed the English Channel on 21 July 2018, at the age of 46, becoming the oldest Indian to do so. He started swimming at 5:00 a.m. and completed the crossing at 7:07 p.m., crossing the channel in 14 hrs 7 mins.

Youngest in the world and first Asian to complete the Ocean's Seven challenge

Rohan Dattatrey More (b. 30 October 1985) from Pune, Maharashtra, at the age of 32, became the world's youngest swimmer to complete the Ocean's Seven challenge on 9 February 2018 when he swam across the Cook Strait between North and South Islands of New Zealand in 8 hrs 37 mins. He is the first Asian swimmer and the ninth in the world to complete the difficult open-water swimming challenge that includes the English Channel, the North Channel, the Molokai Channel, the Catalina Channel, the Tsugaru Channel, the Strait of Gibraltar and the Cook Strait.

First Asian woman to swim across the seven seas

Bula Chowdhury (b. 2 January 1970) from West Bengal was the first Asian woman to swim across seven seas in the world: the Arctic Ocean, the North Atlantic Ocean, the South Atlantic Ocean, the Indian Ocean, the North Pacific Ocean, the South Pacific Ocean and the Antarctic Ocean. She crossed the English Channel twice in 1989 and 1999, and in 2005 she became the first woman to swim across sea channels off five continents. She received the Arjuna Award in 1990 and the Padma Shri in 2008.

Fastest Asian swimmer to cross Gibraltar Strait

Shubham Dhananjay Vanmali (b. 20 December 1995) from Mumbai, Maharashtra, became the fastest Asian swimmer to cross the Strait of Gibraltar, completing 16.7 km from Isla de Tarifa in Spain to Point Cires in Morocco in 3 hrs 16 mins on 14 August 2014. Earlier, Vanmali had also swum the English Channel (England–France), crossing the channel in 12 hrs 42 mins on 4 August 2014 and the 35 km long stretch from Dharamtar to the Gateway of India in Mumbai, Maharashtra, in 8 hrs 1 min. 17 secs on 21 January 2014.

The length of a standard stand-up board is 3–3.3 m (9 ft 10 in.–10 ft- 10 in.).

First backstroke swimming across the Strait of Gibraltar without neoprene

Tejesh Vishnu Parsekar (b. 30 May 1990) from Mumbai, Maharashtra, became the first Indian and second in the world (since 1928) to successfully complete backstroke swimming across the Strait of Gibraltar from Isla de Tarifa, Spain, to Perejil Island near Morocco on 16 August 2010. He was the first in the world to complete it without neoprene (protective suit). He covered 19. 4 km in 5 hrs 21 mins.

King of Gibraltar

B. R. Ghadge of Mumbai Police, Maharashtra, crossed the shark-infested and freezing Strait of Gibraltar (Spain–Morocco) four times. He was conferred the title 'King of Gibraltar' by the Gibraltar Strait Association in August 2002 as he completed the fourth feat in 6 hrs 10 mins on 2 August 2002. He was the first Indian to cross the 26 km long Toroneos Gulf, Greece, in 10 hrs 43 mins on 20 July 2002.

First to complete the Triple Crown

Taranath Narayan Shenoy (b. 1958) from Maharashtra became the world's second swimmer and the first Indian to complete the Triple Crown of Open Water

Water Sports for the Police Force

The 19th All India Police Water Sports Championship was held from 12 December 2019 to 16 December 2019 at Bhojtal Lake in Bhopal, Madhya Pradesh (MP). Organized by MP Police, it was a four-day event where teams competed in three fields – kayaking, rowing and canoeing. While the Indo-Tibetan Border Police (ITBP) dominated the rowing event with 22 points, it was the Border Security Force (BSF) that led the way in kayaking with 49 points, along with the Central Reserve Police Force (CRPF) making its mark in canoeing with 38 points.

Swimming when he crossed the 32.2 km long Catalina Channel (or San Pedro Channel, separating Santa Catalina Island from the southern California mainland, USA) on 25 August 1987. Deaf and nearly blind, he had previously swum the 20 Bridges Swim (a 45.9 km circumnavigation of Manhattan Island, New York City, USA) on 9 August 1987 and the English Channel on 18 August 1983.

First to complete the Round-Trip Angel Island marathon

Shubham Dhananjay Vanmali (b. 20 December 1995) from Mumbai, Maharashtra, was the first Indian to complete the Round-Trip Angel Island marathon swimming. He completed the 16.1 km marathon swim in 10 hrs in San Francisco, USA, on 24 May 2018. He is also the youngest male swimmer and 12th in the world to complete this challenging bay-water swim marathon.

First Indian woman to swim Strait of Gibraltar

Aarti Pradhan from Maharashtra became the first Indian woman to swim the Strait of Gibraltar in 1988. She covered the distance of 22.2 km in 7 hrs 17 mins from Isla de Tarifa, Spain, to Morocco. She received the Arjuna Award in 1988.

Srikaanth Viswanathan: oldest to complete the Triple Crown

Oldest to complete the Triple Crown

Srikaanth Viswanathan (b. 15 July 1972) from Bengaluru, Karnataka, at the age of 47, completed the 20 Bridges Swim in New York City, USA, in 8 hrs 7 mins on 31 August 2019, becoming the oldest Indian to complete the Triple Crown of Open Water Swimming. He had previously swum across the English Channel (14 hrs 7 mins) on 21 July 2018 and the Catalina Channel (13 hrs 4 mins) on 16 August 2019.

Youngest to complete the Triple Crown

Prabhat Raju Koli (b. 27 July 1999) from Mumbai, Maharashtra, at the age of 17 years, became the youngest Indian to complete the Triple Crown of Open Water Swimming when he completed the 20 Bridges Swim in New York City, USA, on 25 June 2017 in 8 hrs 5 mins. He had previously swum the Catalina Channel on 8 August 2016 in 10 hrs 30 mins and the English Channel on 20 September 2015 in 13 hrs 14 mins.

Longest open-sea swimming by a paraplegic

M.S.A. Shaikh (b. 17 July 1986) from Mumbai, Maharashtra, a paraplegic with 100 per cent disability due to a spinal cord injury, participated in open-sea swimming from Sinquerim to Baga and back to Candolim Beach, Goa, on 8 April 2017 at the UMOJA #BeachFest 2017. He completed the 8 km swim in 4 hrs 4 mins.

WR Long-distance swimming by a paraplegic woman

Deepa Malik (b. 30 September 1970) is an Indian athlete from New Delhi. She swam against the current in the River Yamuna at Allahabad (now Prayagraj), Uttar Pradesh, covering a distance of 1 km in 35 mins 36 secs on 15 June 2008. She received the Khel Ratna in 2019.

WR Youngest to swim the Molokai Channel

Prabhat Raju Koli (b. 27 July 1999) from Maharashtra became the youngest Asian to swim the Molokai Channel at the age of 17 years and seven months. He swam 14 km from Molokai to Oahu, Hawaii, USA, in 17 hrs 22 mins. He also swam across the North (Irish) Channel too on 4 August 2018 to become the youngest swimmer in the world to complete this challenge. Besides, he is the youngest Asian Triple Crown achiever in open-water swimming as recognized by the World Open Water Swimming Association.

First expedition on the River Beas

A team of 13 people from Atal Bihari Vajpayee Institute of Mountaineering and Allied Sports (ABVIMAS), Manali, Himachal Pradesh, was the first to raft across the length of the River Beas from 23 to 26 October 2019. Led by Colonel Neeraj Rana, the director of ABVIMAS, the 230 km long rafting expedition was undertaken with two rafts and three kayaks from Manali to Dehra Gopipur Bridge at Pong Dam.

First expedition on the River Beas

First rafting event in the country

The Indo-USA Upper Ganga Rafting Expedition in 1984 was the first rafting expedition in India led by American Ken Warren and Avinash Kohli. The expedition rafted sections of the Rivers Bhagirathi and Alaknanda till Devprayag, and the River Ganga from Devprayag to Rishikesh in Uttarakhand.

Longest white-water rafting expedition

Aqua Scullers, the nine-member rafting team of the Indian Air Force, successfully completed the longest white-water rafting expedition on the River Ganga, covering over 3,000 km from Gangotri in Uttarakhand to Ganga Sagar in West Bengal in 16 days from 19 October to 4 November 2013. The first such expedition undertaken by the Indian Air Force, it included the Himalayan portion of the river from Gangotri (3,049 m/10,003 ft) to Haridwar (295 m/968 ft), one of the world's most challenging white-water stretches with Grade IV–V rapids.

Non-stop rafting expedition

Eight members of the Bihar Adventure Foundation, led by Sanjay Kumar Dutta, set off on a non-stop rafting expedition on the River Ganga. They began from Haridwar, Uttarakhand, on 29 October 1991 and covered 2,400 km in 621 hrs, ending at Calcutta (now Kolkata), West Bengal, on 24 November 1991.

Deepest underwater cycling – ocean – solo

Nishant K. Patel (b. 15 February 1982) from Mumbai, Maharashtra, successfully attempted underwater cycling at a depth of 32.7 m (107 ft 3 in.) on 25 October 2016. He covered a distance of 100 m in 6 mins 47 secs in the Bay of Bengal off Puducherry coast. He used a Firefox Vortex 20 cycle and tied weights of 5 kg in the front and 2 kg in the back of the cycle to avoid floating. He had a 12-litre (200 bar) air tank attached for breathing support.

MARATHONS

Longest distance covered while running – single day

Ullas Narayana from Bengaluru, Karnataka, ran 250.3 km in 24 hours on 1 December 2018, becoming the first to cover this distance in a day. He completed the non-stop run at the 2018 International Association of Ultra Running (IAU) 24-Hour Asia and Oceania Championships in Taipei, Taiwan.

First to complete Grand-to-Grand Ultramarathon

Arpita Maitra (b. 31 October 1978) from Kolkata, West Bengal, became the first Indian to successfully complete the Grand-to-Grand Ultra (G2G) marathon, a gruelling week-long foot race from the Grand Canyon to the Grand Staircase in the USA, in which she covered the 273 km route in 76 hrs 21 mins 43 secs in six stages from 22 to 28 September 2013.

First 4 Deserts Grand Slam winner

Atul Patki (b. 8 November 1965), a US citizen of Indian origin, completed the 4 Deserts Ultramarathons Series on 8 November 2014. He became the first Indian to complete all four 250 km events in one calendar year.

Longest cross-country run

Long-distance runner Raj Vadgama (b. 18 June 1967) from Mumbai, Maharashtra, successfully undertook 'Bharathon 10,000', a unique run across 70 cities in 17 states of India to spread the message of unity. He covered a distance of 9,902 km from 15 August 2014 to 26 January 2015, making it the first and longest such self-supported cross-country run. He ran 60 km a day for 165 days.

	Year	Name	Race	Time Taken
1	2015	Uma Chigurupati	Women's half-marathon	21:36:43
2	2015	Krishna Chigurupati	Men's half-marathon	20:59:38
3	2018	Pushpa Chandra	Women's marathon	45:55:27
4	2020	Aditya Raj	Men's marathon	36:47:36

INDIANS AT THE WORLD MARATHON CHALLENGE

Longest relay race

As part of its golden jubilee celebrations, while also paying tribute to former president A.P.J. Abdul Kalam, the Border Security Force (BSF) Sector Headquarters in West Bengal organized the BSF Golden Jubilee Baton Relay Race 2015. The event saw 1,785 BSF jawans in commando uniform cover a distance of 174.2 km in relay format in 8 hrs 55 mins 36 secs on 24 August 2015.

WR First to complete all Six World Marathons

Siddhartha Ghosh (b. 21 February 1975) from Kolkata, West Bengal, was the first person to complete all Six World Marathons in one calendar year during 2013. He is also the first recipient of the Six Star World Marathon certificate and has received the Six Star World Marathon certificate five times consecutively from 2012 to 2016. The World Marathon Majors consist of six races annually across cities and are accredited by the International Association of Athletics Federations.

First to complete the 7 Emirates Run

M.A. Shaikh (b. 29 September 1974) from Mumbai, Maharashtra, became the first Indian to successfully complete the 7 Emirates Run, an ultramarathon across all seven emirates of the United Arab Emirates (UAE). He covered a distance of 575 km in 12 days from 21 November to 2 December 2014.

Starting in 2012, the annual Ladakh Marathon is held at an altitude of 3,505–5,370 m (11,500–17,618 ft) in Leh, Ladakh.

First to complete the Golden Quadrilateral (GQ) run

Michelle Kakade (b. 9 October 1968), a long-distance runner from Pune, Maharashtra, became the first person to cover the Golden Quadrilateral on foot. The GQ is a highway network connecting Mumbai, Delhi, Kolkata and Chennai. She covered 5,968.4 km in 193 days, 1 hr 9 mins from 21 October 2015 to 1 May 2016.

First to complete the World Marathon Challenge – full marathon

Aditya Raj (b. 22 June 1983) from Gurugram, Haryana, became the first Indian to complete the World Marathon Challenge in 2020, in which runners travel across the globe, completing seven marathons (each 42.2 km) in seven days on seven continents. Starting on 6 February 2020 in Novo, Antarctica, Raj travelled to Cape Town in Africa, Perth in Australia, Dubai in Asia, Madrid in Europe and Brazil in South America, finishing his seventh marathon in Miami, North America, on 12 February 2020. His total running time was 36 hours 47 minutes 36 seconds.

First Ultraman triathlete

Arunaabh Shah (b. 11 August 1990) from Delhi completed the Ultraman Triathlon (a 10 km swim, 421.1 km of cycling and an 84.3 km run) in Australia on 16 May 2016. He is the first Indian to do so in Ultraman's 33-year-long history.

First Ironman triathlon

The first Indian Ironman triathlon was held in Goa with over 1,000 participants on 20 October 2019. Considered the most prestigious endurance triathlon event worldwide, the race included 1.9 km of swimming, 90 km of cycling and 21.1 km of running, which were all done sequentially in a single day. Bishworjit Singh Saikhom from Pune, Maharashtra, completed the triathlon in 4 hrs 42 mins 44 seconds, securing the first place.

Praveen Kumar: first differently abled Ironman

First differently abled Ironman

Praveen Kumar (b. 17 July 1985) from New Delhi became India's first differently abled Ironman on 17 November 2018 in the Ironman event organized in Langkawi, Malaysia. He completed a 3.86 km long swim in 1 hr 36 mins 7 secs, 180 km of cycling in 7 hrs 49 mins 50 secs and a 42 km long run in 5 hrs 40 mins 55 secs. Kumar is a battle-casualty soldier who was injured during the terrorist attack in Mumbai, Maharashtra, in November 2008.

Most half-marathons by an individual

Adil S. Nargolwala (b. 31 August 1969) from Gurugram, Haryana, completed his 164th half-marathon, the most by an individual, at the Ironman Virtual Club 5 70.3 (miles/113 km) race on 1 May 2020. These half-marathons were conducted at venues both in India and abroad, and included road as well as trail events. He had also completed at least one marathon in each of the seven continents by 15 January 2019.

Most half-marathons in a year

Vijay Boddupalli (b. 1 September 1988) from Chennai, Tamil Nadu, completed 17 half-marathons, the most by an individual in a year, from 1 June 2017 to 31 May 2018. The 17th half-marathon was completed at the H20 Run on 22 April 2018. The half-marathons were conducted across seven states in India.

Most full marathons in a year

Sivabalan Pandian (b. 21 September 1958) from Mumbai, Maharashtra, completed 114 full marathons, the most by an individual in a year, from 6 January to 31 December 2019. These full marathons were conducted at venues both within India and abroad. The count also includes 14 ultramarathons.

Most ultramarathons in a year

Sivabalan Pandian (b. 21 September 1958) from Mumbai, Maharashtra, has run and completed 18 ultramarathons in a year from 16 June 2018 to 23 December 2018.

Most triathlons completed in a year

Adil S. Nargolwala (b. 31 August 1969) from Gurugram, Haryana, completed the most triathlon races in a year in 2019. He completed the Triathlon Sprint at the Delhi International Triathlon 2019, the Triathlon Olympics at the New Delhi Triathlon Championship, the Ironman 70.3 (miles/113 km) in Kazakhstan, the Ironman at Sweden and the Ultramarathon at the Ultraman India Race.

Most visually impaired athletes completing marathons

Six visually impaired athletes – Nandeesh J., Sunita N.D., Renuka Rajput, Kavya Ramesh, Ajay and Mala Kolkar – ran a full marathon in 7 hrs 21 mins on 21 October 2018 at Sree Kanteerava Outdoor Stadium, Bengaluru, Karnataka. Helped by guide runners, the students, who were from the Samarthanam Trust for the Disabled, Bengaluru, Karnataka, were led by their coach, Bhumika Patel.

First to finish the Ultraman World Championship

Gaurav Makkar (b. 26 November 1979) from Gurugram, Haryana, became the first Indian to finish the Ultraman World Championship. The championship is a

Gaurav Makkar: first to complete the Ultraman World Championship

three-day, 515 km multi-sport race held annually in Hawaii, USA. He completed a 10 km swim (in 4 hrs 24 mins), a 421 km bicycle ride (in 16 hrs 20 mins) and an 84 km run (in 8 hrs 56 mins) during 23–25 November 2018. He also completed the Ultraman Florida 2018 during 16–18 February 2018, thereby completing two Ultraman races, the most by an individual in a year.

Oldest marathoner

WR Fauja Singh (b. 1 April 1911) of Indian origin, residing in the UK, is the world's oldest marathon runner. He completed the London Marathon, covering a distance of 42.16 km in 6 hrs 2 mins on 22 April 2012. His marathon record, for age 90-plus, was 5 hrs 40 mins at the Toronto Waterfront Marathon held in Canada in 2013.

Only Asian to complete Ironman triathlons in six continents

Kaustubh Radkar has completed the Ironman triathlon in six continents between March 2014 and November 2016, and is the only Asian to do so. He has completed 25 Ironman triathlons since he ran his first triathlon in 2008.

Most half-marathons organized in a single day – multiple venues

The Indian Air Force organized half-marathons simultaneously across 100 air force stations as part of the centenary celebrations of the Marshal of the Indian Air Force Arjan Singh on 14 April 2019. The marathon began at 5:30 a.m. and concluded at 9:30 a.m., and saw the participation of 12,600 air force officers. The marathon distance was 21 km and it was conducted in three age categories: below 35 years; between 35 and 45 years; and 45 years and above. Marshal of the Indian Air Force Arjan Singh was the first and only officer of the Indian Air Force to hold a five-star rank.

Fastest at Badwater Ultramarathon

Brij Mohan Sharma (b. 1 January 1974) of the Indian Navy, from Mumbai, Maharashtra, is the fastest Indian at the Badwater Ultramarathon, one of the world's toughest foot races, held in California, USA, from 18 to 20 July 2016. He completed the 217 km run in 40 hrs 47 mins.

MOUNTAIN ADVENTURES

First club

The Himalayan Club was founded in February 1928 in the room of Field Marshal Sir William Birdwood, then commander-in-chief of the British Indian Army.

First mountaineering institute

The first Himalayan Mountaineering Institute at Darjeeling, West Bengal, was formed in 1954 by the then prime minister Jawaharlal Nehru, along with Major Nandu Jayal of the Corps of Engineers of the Indian Army, who was the first director.

First to walk the Siachen Glacier

Siachen Glacier, lying along India's border with China, is about 700 sq. km in area and situated at an altitude touching 5,753 m (18,875 ft) above the mean sea level. Under Indian Army protection since 1984, it is the highest battlefield in the world. In 1984, Captain (now Colonel) Ashok Pratap Tanwar became the first person to cover the entire glacier on foot. Appointed as the official photographer of a military formation, he walked the length and breadth of the 76 km long and 3–5 km broad glacier.

First mountaineering expedition

In 1951, Gurdial Guru Singh from Dehradun, Uttarakhand, led an expedition to the 7,120 m (23,360 ft) high Trishul 1 Peak in the Garhwal Himalayas, Uttarakhand.

Trishul: a group of three Himalayan mountain peaks

First to complete the Seven Summit challenge

Mastan Babu Malli (3 September 1974–24 March 2015) was an Indian mountaineer best known for his 2006 world-record– creating feat of climbing each continent's highest peak in the shortest period at the time – a total of 172 days – with the first climb on 19 January 2006 and the seventh on 10 July 2006. This feat made him the fastest Seven Summiteer in the world by 2006, and the first Indian and South Asian to climb the Seven Summits.

New Height for Mt Everest

The world's highest peak now has a revised height of 8,848.86 m (29,031 ft 8 in.), about 86 cm (2 ft 10 in.) more than the previous measurement done by the Survey of India in 1954. Mt Everest stands on the border between China and Nepal and is climbed by mountaineers from both sides. Jointly announced by Nepal and China on 8 December 2020, the recalculation was carried out due to various debates regarding the height of the mountain over the years.

AJEET AND DEEYA BAJAJ: LIKE FATHER, LIKE DAUGHTER

There is almost no adventure activity that has not been mastered by adventurer and explorer Ajeet Bajaj (b.19 September 1965). The first in the country to complete the polar trilogy in skiing (North Pole, South Pole and across the Greenland Ice Sheet), Bajaj is also the first Asian to have rafted and kayaked across some of the most challenging rivers in the world. In his career spanning 30 years, Bajaj has been instrumental in changing the landscape of adventure tourism in India. A bronze medallist at the National Games for kayaking, he bagged one silver and two bronze medals for India in international rafting championships. Turning his passion into profession, he started Snow Leopard Adventures, an adventure tourism company, in 1990. Honoured with the Padma Shri award in 2012, he has also been inducted into the Hall of Fame by the Adventure Tour Operators Association of India (ATOAI) for his contribution to the growth of adventure tourism in India.

An avid mountaineer, proficient downhill and cross-country skier as well as a white-water and sea kayaker, Deeya Bajaj (b. 9 March 1994) followed her father's footsteps into the world of adventure from a very young age. In May 2011, at 17 years, she was the youngest to undertake the Trans-Greenland Skiing expedition. Completing her advanced course in mountaineering from the Nehru Institute of Mountaineering, Uttarkashi, Uttarakhand, in 2012, Deeya went on to become an instructor for cross-country skiing and white-water kayaking at Cornell University, New York, where she studied in 2016. A rescue diver certified by the Professional Association of Diving Instructors (PADI), she is closely associated with the cause of female empowerment in India.

In 2008, Ajeet and Deeya (the youngest member of the team at 14 years) undertook their first expedition together when they took part in a sea kayaking expedition along the west coast of Greenland. The duo then skied from the west to

Most Himalayan summits

Sange Sherpa from Darjeeling, West Bengal, has six summits to his credit, which include Mt Everest thrice, Aqtash in 1993, Jaloni in 1994 and Nanda Devi in 2000. He is the only person in the world to climb Mt Everest from three faces: from South Col in 1992, North Col in 1996 and Kangshung face in 1999. He received the National Adventure Award in 1998.

First to summit the Volcanic Seven and youngest to climb both the Seven Summits and Volcanic Seven summits

At 34 years, Satyarup Siddhanta (b. 29 April 1983) from Bengaluru, Karnataka, completed the Volcanic Seven Summits (Messner list) on 15 December 2017 becoming the first Indian to do so. The Volcanic Seven Summits include Mt Kilimanjaro (5,895 m/19,341 ft – Africa), Mt Ojos del Salado (6,893 m/ 22,615 ft – South America), Mt Elbrus (5,642 m/18,510 ft – Europe), Mt Damavand (5,628 m/18,465 ft – Asia), Mt Giluwe (4,367 m/14,327 ft Australasia), Mt Pico de Orizaba (5,610 m/18,406 ft – North America) and Mt Sidley (4,181–4,285 m/13,717–14,058 ft – Antarctica). He also completed the Seven Summits challenge in on 15 January 2019, becoming the youngest Indian to climb both the Volcanic Seven Summits and Seven Summits.

Deeya Bajaj (*left*) and Ajeet Bajaj at the summit of Mt Vinson, Antarctica (2019)

the east coast of Greenland in May 2011, covering 550 km in 21 days, which made Deeya, then seventeen, the youngest in the world to undertake the expedition at the time. The first Indians to ski across the Greenland Ice Sheet, they were also the first to traverse Mt Elbrus (5,642 m/18,510 ft), the highest mountain in Europe, along with Rohit Kapur, from the north side to the summit and descend from the south side, in July 2012.

On 16 May 2018, Ajeet and Deeya became the first Indian father–daughter duo to scale Mt Everest (and that too from the harder north side of Tibet). With a message that any girl, given the right opportunities, can reach the highest of summits, Ajeet and Deeya Bajaj had successfully climbed six of the Seven Summits (the highest mountain on each continent) by April 2020.

Satyarup Siddhanta: first to scale the Volcanic Seven

Vikas Shukla

First Indian to Summit the Three Highest Peaks of South America

Vikas Shukla (b. 6 December 1989) from Bhusawal, Maharashtra, is the first Indian to summit the three highest peaks of South America. He scaled Mt Aconcagua (6,961 m/ 22,838 ft) on 16 February 2019; Mt Pissis (6,793 m/ 22,287 ft) on 24 February 2019; and Mt Ojos del Salado (6,893 m/22,615 ft) on 1 March 2019.

Oldest to climb the Seven Summits

Ankur Bahl (b. 25 January 1961) from Haryana, at 57 years, became the oldest to complete the Messner list of the Seven Summit challenge in 2018, which involves the summiting of the highest mountains in each continent, which include Mt Kilimanjaro (5,895 m/19,341 ft – Africa), Mt Elbrus (5,642 m/18,510 ft – Europe), Mt Denali/McKinley (6,194 m /20,322 ft – North America), Mt Aconcagua (6,961 m/22,838 ft – South America), Mt Everest (8,848.86 m/ 29,031 ft 8 in. – Asia), Mt Kosciuszko (2,228 m/ 7,310 feet – Australia) and Mt Vinson (4,897 m/16,066 – Antarctica).

First woman to scale Mt Everest

Bachendri Pal (b. 24 May 1954) became the first Indian woman to reach the summit of Mt Everest in 1984.

First to summit four unscaled peaks above 6,000 m

A team of eight mountaineers from the Nehru Institute of Mountaineering, in collaboration with Uttarakhand Tourism Development Board, summited four unscaled and unnamed peaks in the Gangotri region of the Garhwal Himalayas

Bachendri Pal: first Indian woman to summit Mt Everest

in 8 days between 9 October and 16 October 2018. The team, led by Colonel Amit Bisht, SM, scaled peaks 6,566 m (21,542 ft), 6,557 m (21,512 ft), 6,126 m (20,098 ft) and 6,086 m (19,967 ft) high.

First to summit Mt Everest without supplemental oxygen
Phu Dorjee was the first to summit Mt Everest (then measured at 8,848m/ 29,028 ft) without supplemental oxygen on 9 May 1984 through the South-east Ridge route. He was part of the third Everest expedition led by Captain M.S. Kohli in 1965. Dorjee died in 1987 on the Kangchenjunga Expedition of the Assam Rifles.

Oldest at Mt Everest
S.C. Negi (b. 8 March 1950), additional deputy inspector general of the Border Security Force, became the oldest to scale Mt Everest on 24 May 2006.

WR **Youngest girl on Mt Everest**
Malavath Purna (b. 10 June 2000) is a mountaineer from Nizamabad District, Telangana. On 25 May 2014, she scaled the highest peak of Mt Everest. Then just 13 years and 11 months old, Purna became the youngest girl in the world to scale the Everest.

Most on Mt Everest in a single day
On the 50th anniversary of the first Indian expedition to Mt Everest in 1959, the Nehru Institute of Mountaineering (NIM) Everest Expedition 2009 put 10 Indian climbers atop Mt Everest on 21 May 2009. The expedition started from Kathmandu on 8 April 2009.

Oldest woman to scale Mt Everest
Sangeeta Sindhi (b. 9 February 1965) from Gurugram, Haryana, became the oldest Indian woman to summit Mt Everest on 19 May 2018 at the age of 53 years.

Sangeeta Sindhi: oldest woman to summit Mt Everest

Fastest scaling of Mt Everest

Kazi Sherpa climbed Mt Everest in 20 hrs 24 mins in 1998, breaking the earlier record of 22 hrs 29 mins.

First twins to summit Mt Everest

Tashi Malik and Nungshi Malik (b. 21 June 1991) from Dehradun, Uttarakhand, became the first twin sisters to summit the Everest on 19 May 2013. The duo accomplished it as members of the Seven Summit International Everest Expedition 2013, led by Satyabrata Dam.

Highest rappelling

Shalom Adventures, Maharashtra, a team of nine, rappelled 548.64 m (1,800 ft), at Konkan Kada in Harishchandragad, Maharashtra, on 19 December 2013. The team of Miron Benny Joseph, Avinash A. Rao, Shreyas Popat, Jayant R. Deo, Krishna Kuya, B.K. Shukla, Sunil Gupta, Debdut Pramanik and Romila Sil set another record of covering 335.28 m (1,100 ft) at a stretch, where Miron Benny Joseph was the fastest to rappel 335.28 m (1,100 ft) in 2 mins 38 secs.

TREKKING

Oldest trekker

Gopal Vasudev Lele (b. 8 March 1932) from Pune, Maharashtra, is a man with a long and enduring passion for trekking. Then 81 years of age, Lele made a week-long trek to Rupin Pass (4,680 m/15,354 ft) in Himachal Pradesh from 21 to 28 September 2013. He completed a 70-degree climb. Lele had completed 20 treks since 1972.

Fastest Everest Base Camp trek by a differently abled person

Mahinder Singh Raghuwanshi (b. 2 October 1987) completed the longest trekking in Nepal, with a prosthetic leg, to the Everest Base Camp from an altitude of 2,859.9 m to 5,642.7 m (9,383 ft to 18,513 ft). He started his trek on 28 April 2018 and ended it on 11 May 2018, covering 150 km in 14 days. He started his trek from Lukla, Nepal, and covered Kala Patthar (5,550 m/(18,209 ft), Cho La (5,368 m/17,612 ft), Gokyo (4,790 m/15,715 ft), Renjo La (5,360 m/17,585 ft) and Everest Base Camp (5364 m/17,598 ft). He was accompanied by a friend and a guide.

First women's team to complete Snowman Trek

A team of 11 women led by iconic Indian mountaineer Bachendri Pal successfully completed the Snowman Trek in Bhutan, considered one of the toughest in the world. Starting at Paro Valley on 4 June 2011, the trek was completed at Sephu Village on 27 June 2011. It involved crossing 11 high mountain passes and other difficult terrain. This expedition was sponsored by the Tata Steel Adventure Foundation in Jamshedpur, Jharkhand.

Longest desert trek – group

The 22nd battalion of the Mahar Regiment, part of the Golden Katar Division of the Indian Army, successfully completed the 'Golden Katar Desert Trek 2017–18'. A ten-member team of soldiers trekked 700 km through the Thar Desert, Rajasthan, in 21 days from 22 December 2017 to 12 January 2018. The arduous

Green Passport for Trekking Enthusiasts in Karnataka

In an effort to prevent illegal trekking in forests and to encourage tourism, the Tourism and Forest Departments in Bengaluru, Karnataka, have implemented the Passport Adventure Initiative, a rule that requires all trekkers to carry a green passport when going into forest areas. Bearing a stamp for every trek completed, the passport can be obtained at the local forest department office and acts as an identification document, equipped with a unique identification number for the trekker. Launched in December 2017, the initiative has now grown, prompting officials to make green passports mandatory on many trekking routes in Karnataka.

journey on foot through the Great Indian Desert began from Bakhasar, Barmer District, and concluded in Gajjewala, Bikaner District, Rajasthan.

THE POLES

First at the Arctic

Sharat Kumar Roy (1897–1962) was the first to reach the Arctic as a member of the Rawson–Macmillan Arctic Expedition in 1927.

First at Antarctica

Meher Moos (b. 1944) from Maharashtra was the first woman to set foot on the icy continent of Antarctica way back in 1976, long before any of the scientific expeditions went there.

Youngest at the Arctic

Seventeen-year-old Shailendra Sinha and his instructor Mandip Singh Soin reached the Eureka Base Camp in the Canadian Arctic on 22 April 1989. His adventure was part of 'Ice Walk 1989', led by the polar explorer Robert Swan.

First to reach North Pole by surface

Dr M.R. Shetty from Bangalore (now Bengaluru), Karnataka, reached the North Pole by surface on 5 August 2001 with a 100-strong team, by *Yamal*, a nuclear-powered ice-breaking ship, starting from Longyearbyen, Svalbard's administrative centre in Norway, on 1 August 2001.

First organization to reach 'three' poles

Indian Navy teams have been to three poles: Mt Everest, the vertical pole, in 2004; the Geographic South Pole in 2006; and the North Pole in 2008. Commander Satyabrata Dam and two POMAs (petty officer medical assistants) Vikas Kumar and Rakesh Kumar were the first to reach all three poles.

Colonel J.K. Bajaj: first at the Geographic South Pole

Youngest at the poles

Malaika Vaz (b. 13 April 1997) from Panaji, Goa, travelled to both the polar regions as a member of the educational expedition, 'Students On Ice' (SOI). Malaika first went to Antarctica from 27 December 2011 to 10 January 2012, and then to the Arctic from 29 July to 13 August 2012. She is a windsurfer, sailor and scuba-diver.

First at the Geographic South Pole

On 17 January 1989, Colonel J.K. Bajaj became the first Indian to reach the Geographic South Pole at 22:15 hrs (GMT). He was the only Indian in this 11-member international expedition that skied over 1,200 km in 50 days to the Geographic South Pole. The five-nation expedition was organized by Mountain Travel, USA, and the International Adventure Network, Canada.

First route recce to the South Pole

Major Anand Swaroop and Captain R.R. Bhat of the Corps of Engineers of the Indian Army were the first to recce the route from the Maitri base, Antarctica, to the Polar/Antarctic Plateau in 2000.

Longest stay in Antarctica

Shaik Mastan (b. 12 February 1968) from Gudavalli Village, Guntur District, Andhra Pradesh, had the longest uninterrupted stay of 490 days in Antarctica at the Indian Antarctic research station, Bharati, from 16 November 2011 to 19 March 2013. He was a member of the 35th Indian expedition to Antarctica.

First to ski to the North Pole

Ajeet Bajaj is the first Indian to ski to the North Pole and complete the polar trilogy, which entails skiing to the North Pole and South Pole, and crossing the Greenland Ice Sheet. He started his ski expedition to the North Pole from the Russian Arctic Polar Research Station called Barneo and reached the North Pole on 26 April 2006, along with three other skiers.

MEDICAL SCIENCES

GENERAL

Earliest treatise on medicine

The Atharva Veda (1500 –1200 BCE), is the earliest known treatise on diseases and medicine.

First Persian text on medicine

Ma'dan-i-Shifa-i-Sikandar Shahi was the first Persian text on the Unani and Ayurvedic systems of medicine, authored by Hakim Bahwa bin Khwas Khan during 1512–13 CE. It was printed in 1987 by Naval Kishore Press in Lucknow, Uttar Pradesh.

WR Largest healthcare scheme

Ayushman Bharat Yojana, as it is commonly known, announced as a universal healthcare plan by the Government of India in February 2018, is the largest healthcare scheme in the world. Aimed at providing free healthcare access to around 0.5 billion (50 crore)) people in the country, the Ayushman Bharat Pradhan Mantri Jan Arogya Yojana (AB-PMJAY) was launched in September 2018. A paperless and cashless scheme, it involves e-cards being issued to beneficiaries and health insurance cover of up to ₹500,000 per family per year.

The total number of licensed blood banks in the country was 3,263 in November 2019.

WR Largest survey sample

India's Annual Health Survey (AHS) is the first nationwide survey initiative to provide district-level fertility and mortality statistics. Begun with a baseline study in 2010–11 and a sample of 18.2 million people (3.6 million households), the survey is conducted in all 284 districts in eight Empowered Action Group (EAG) states, viz., Madhya Pradesh, Jharkhand, Bihar, Uttar Pradesh, Chhattisgarh, Uttarakhand, Odisha and Rajasthan. It reports vital indicators such as total crude birth and death rates, sex ratios (at birth, 0–4 and all ages) and mortality rates (maternal, infant, neonatal and under-five), separated by urban/rural and male/female data.

FERTILITY, CHILDBIRTH AND BABIES

First IVF baby

Baby Harsha was born to Mani and Shyami Chawda on 6 August 1986 by the in vitro fertilization and embryo transfer (IVF-ET) method. This technique was used after three years of research by Dr Indira Hinduja of King Edward Memorial Hospital and Seth Gordhandas Sunderdas Medical College, Bombay (now Mumbai), Maharashtra.

WR Oldest IVF mother

On 12 October 2019, seventy-five-year-old Prabha Devi became the oldest woman to give birth, after conceiving through IVF. She delivered a baby girl, weighing 680 g, prematurely by caesarean section performed at Kinker Hospital, Kota, Rajasthan.

First GIFT twins
The first twins, both of them male, born through the gamete intra-fallopian transfer (GIFT) technology, were born to Renuka and Vijay Thakkar on 5 September 1990 in Bombay (now Mumbai), Maharashtra.

First woman to give birth after a uterine transplant
Meenakshi Valand from Bharuch District, Gujarat, became the first Indian woman to deliver a baby after undergoing a uterine transplant on 19 October 2018 at Galaxy Care Hospital, Pune, Maharashtra.

Heaviest baby at birth
On 26 May 2016, Nandini, a 20-year-old mother, gave birth to a baby girl by caesarean section at a hospital in Hassan, Karnataka. The baby, whose birth weight was 6.8 kg, was reported to have been the heaviest one ever born in the country. The heaviest baby boy, who weighed 6.7 kg, is recorded to have been born in November 2015.

Record Rewind

Lightest baby

1991

A baby girl born to Madhu Jain at the Jawaharlal Nehru Hospital in Ajmer, Rajasthan, on 1 April 1989, weighed just 500 g. Dr S.P. Chaudhary and her team saved the prematurely born baby through neonatal care and she was discharged from the hospital when she was two months old.

2018

Nitika and Saurabh Ajmani from Chhattisgarh had a baby girl at Rainbow Children's Hospital in Hyderabad, Telangana, on 27 February 2018. Born at 25 weeks and weighing 375 g at birth, she was the lightest baby in South-East Asia. Named Cherry by the doctors, she measured 26 cm (10.2 in.) - the size of an adult palm.

MEDICAL INSTITUTIONS AND LABORATORIES

First hospital
The first modern hospital was established at Fort St George, Madras (now Chennai, Tamil Nadu), in 1664.

Oldest eye hospital
The Madras Eye Infirmary in Madras (now Chennai, Tamil Nadu) was set up in 1819. It is recorded to be the oldest eye hospital in India and Asia. It was renamed as the Government Ophthalmic Hospital in 1886, and is currently called the Regional Institute of Ophthalmology and Government Ophthalmic Hospital. It is locally referred to as the Ezhumbur Kanaaspatiri.

First governmental family planning programme
India was the first country in the world to have government-sponsored family planning programmes to control the population, in 1952. The first private family planning clinic was opened even earlier in Mysore (now Mysuru, Karnataka) in 1930.

First medical college

Medical College (later renamed Medical College Kolkata) in Calcutta, Bengal (now Kolkata), West Bengal, set up on 28 January 1835, was the first medical college to be established in India.

First homoeopathic college

Dr L. Salzar from Austria began homoeopathic education in India in 1867. He influenced Dr P.C. Majumdar and Dr B.L. Bhaduri in Bengal, and in 1878, Dr Majumdar, with Dr D.N. Roy, Dr B.N. Banerjee and Dr Younan, set up the Calcutta Homoeopathic Medical College (now Kolkata), West Bengal, which was India's first homoeopathic college.

First homoeopathic company

M. Bhattacharya and Company Pvt. Ltd in Calcutta, Bengal (now Kolkata), West Bengal, was set up in 1889 by Mahesh Chandra Bhattacharya from Comilla (now in Bangladesh), for making homoeopathic medicines.

First college of nursing

Christian Medical College and Hospital (CMCH), Vellore, Tamil Nadu, set up the first college of nursing in India in 1946.

First organized medical service

The Indian Medical Service was the formal collective name for the top echelon of the East India Company's and British Indian Army's medical service from the early 1800s up to 1896. Categorized into three divisions – Bengal Medical Service, Madras Medical Service and Bombay Medical Service – in January 1897, these three services were combined into a single service under government control.

First dental college

Dr Rafiuddin Ahmed, the 'father of modern dentistry' in India, founded the Calcutta Dental College in Calcutta (now Kolkata), West Bengal, in 1920. By 1928, it was a well-known institution for scientific dental education in India.

First blood bank

Upendranath Brahmachari (1873–1946) set up a blood bank at Calcutta, Bengal (now Kolkata), West Bengal, in September 1939.

Upendranath Brahmachari: the founder of India's first blood bank

First medical school to offer oncology degrees

The Adyar Cancer Institute in Chennai, Tamil Nadu, is a non-profit cancer treatment and research centre set up in 1954 under the leadership of Dr Muthulakshmi Reddy. It was the first medical school in India to offer degrees in various sub-specialities of oncology, recognized by the Medical Council of India.

First centre for cancer rehabilitation

Dr Darab Jehangir Jussawala (1915–99) was a medical and surgical oncologist, medical writer, and director of Tata Memorial Centre in Bombay (now Mumbai),

STATEWISE DISTRIBUTION OF BLOOD BANKS IN INDIA*

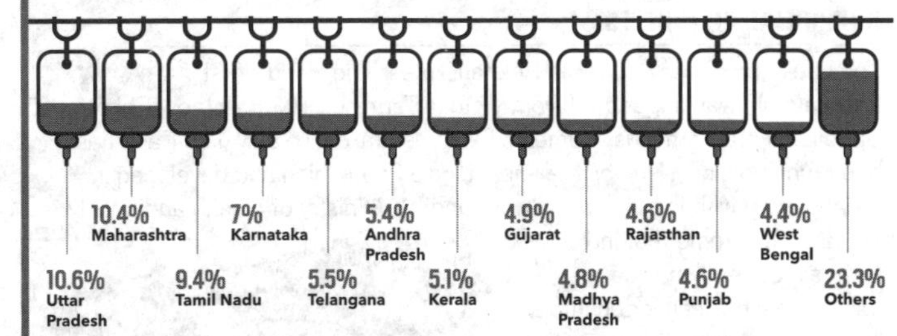

Percentage	State
10.6%	Uttar Pradesh
10.4%	Maharashtra
9.4%	Tamil Nadu
7%	Karnataka
5.5%	Telangana
5.4%	Andhra Pradesh
5.1%	Kerala
4.9%	Gujarat
4.8%	Madhya Pradesh
4.6%	Rajasthan
4.6%	Punjab
4.4%	West Bengal
23.3%	Others

*2019; Source: Central Drugs Standard Control Organization (CDSCO), Ministry of Health and Family Welfare (2019), Government of India

Maharashtra. Jussawala was the co-founder of the Indian Cancer Society with Naval Tata in 1951 and set up the Indian Cancer Rehabilitation Centre in Parel, Bombay, in 1956, which was the first such centre in India.

First online clinic
Homoeopath Dr Mukesh Batra set up Dr Batra's Positive Health Clinic in Bombay (now Mumbai), Maharashtra, in 1982, which now has 230 clinics across 122 cities in India, Bangladesh, Dubai and the UK. He went online in 1997, which made him the first online medical consultant in the country.

First corporate hospital
Apollo Hospitals, founded by Dr Prathap C. Reddy in Madras (now Chennai), Tamil Nadu, in 1983, was the first corporate hospital in India.

First biotechnology department
Dr Indira Nath set up the first department of medical biotechnology at the All India Institute of Medical Sciences (AIIMS), New Delhi, for teaching and research in 1986.

First medical laser facility
India's first medical laser to destroy tumours with minimal blood loss was set up at the K.B. Bhabha Hospital in Bombay (now Mumbai), Maharashtra, in October 1993.

First sperm bank
Dr Aniruddha Malpani and Dr Anjali Malpani from Bombay (now Mumbai), Maharashtra, opened a sperm bank in 1990 to help infertile patients. It also has facilities for storing sperm of people who may be critically ill, for implantation at a later date.

First breast milk bank
Dr Armida Fernandez pioneered the establishment of Asia's first human milk bank at the Lokmanya Tilak Municipal General Hospital in Bombay (now Mumbai), Maharashtra, in November 1989.

SUPER 30

A HOSPITAL ON WHEELS

The Lifeline Express or Jeevan Rekha Express, the world's first hospital train was flagged off from Victoria Terminus, Bombay (now Chhatrapati Shivaji Maharaj Terminus, Mumbai), Maharashtra, on 16 July 1991 and has been running since. Run by the Impact India Foundation and developed in collaboration with the Indian Railways and the Ministry of Health and Family Welfare, Government of India, this train currently has seven railway coaches converted into a 'hospital' with a modern operation theatre. It is also equipped with a cancer diagnostic centre and a sterilization room. Since it is a mobile hospital, each piece of large equipment has been anchored to the floor.

First tribal medical college
A tribal medical college was founded in Attapadi, Kerala, in 1993 with Achappan, a physician of the Kurichya tribe, as principal. Traditional knowledge of medicinal plants here has reportedly cured many people of diseases such as asthma, jaundice and blood pressure.

First low-vision rehabilitation centre
L.V. Prasad Eye Institute, Hyderabad (now in Telangana), opened the Meera and L.B. Deshpande Centre for Sight Enhancement on 18 February 1997, to provide complete low-vision rehabilitation for patients by restoring optimal physical, psychological and social functioning.

First hormone replacement therapy clinic
A hormone replacement therapy (HRT) clinic was started by Urvashi P. Jha in March 1993 at the P.D. Hinduja National Hospital in Bombay (now Mumbai), Maharashtra, to deal with aspects of menopause.

First endoscopy lab
The first fully equipped endoscopy centre was established at the Bhatia General Hospital in Bombay (now Mumbai), Maharashtra, in October 1994. An endoscopy is performed to examine the interior of a hollow organ.

First indigenously developed vaccine
Rotavac, a rotavirus vaccine, was India's first indigenously developed vaccine, launched in 2015. Rotavirus is the most common cause of serious (often fatal) diarrhoea in children.

First department of minimal access surgery
Dr Pradeep Kumar Chowbey from Sir Ganga Ram Hospital, New Delhi, set up the

first dedicated department of minimal access surgery (MAS) in Asian in 1995 and has trained nearly 1,000 doctors in laparoscopy in India and abroad.

First liver clinic

The first liver clinic opened at Sir Ganga Ram Hospital, Delhi, in 2002 for treating patients with liver diseases.

First hospital with a stealth neuro-navigation system

The Sri Sathya Sai Institute of Higher Medical Sciences, Whitefield, Bangalore (now Bengaluru), Karnataka, set up in 2001, is the first in India and second in the world to acquire a stealth neuro-navigation system (for image-guided surgeries), which is one of the cutting-edge technologies in precision neurosurgery.

First hospital with a rooftop helipad

The eleven-storey Lakeshore Hospital and Research Centre, Kochi, Kerala, is the first super-speciality hospital in the country to have air, water and road ambulance services at its doorstep. Inaugurated in January 2003, this hospital with state-of-the-art medical services, has a helipad on its roof to facilitate heli-lifting of critically ill patients from airports in Kerala.

The Union budget 2021 proposed increasing public healthcare spending to 2.5% from the current 1.15% of India's gross domestic product (GDP).

First rural medical college

Kasturba Health Society's Mahatma Gandhi Institute of Medical Sciences (MGIMS) in Sevagram, Maharashtra, was India's first rural medical college. It was founded by Dr Sushila Nayar in 1969 and was affiliated to the Maharashtra University of Health Sciences.

WR Largest vaccine company

The Serum Institute of India in Pune, Maharashtra, founded by Cyrus Poonawalla in 1966, is the world's largest vaccine-making company by the number of doses produced and sold globally, with 1.2 billion vaccine doses supplied yearly to 147 countries.

First institute of advanced virology

The first Institute of Advanced Virology was inaugurated by the chief minister of Kerala, Pinarayi Vijayan, in February 2019 at Thiruvananthapuram, Kerala. It is affiliated to the Global Virus Network (GVN), which has 45 centres of excellence in more than 29 countries.

AIIMS: A hub of medical firsts

The All India Institute of Medical Sciences (AIIMS) is a public hospital and medical research university and hospital based in New Delhi. Established in 1956, it operates autonomously under the Ministry of Health and Family Welfare. It was:

- The first to start a medical toxicology lab in a medical college in 1986.
- The first to develop a DNA profiling lab in a medical college in 1990.

- The first Indian centre to perform a successful cardiac transplant in 1994.
- India's first minimally invasive surgery training centre.
- The first in the public sector to have an in vitro fertilization (IVF) facility, in February 2008.

First government-run department for disorders of sex development
The Postgraduate Institute of Medical Education and Research (PGIMER), Chandigarh, in July 2019, established the country's first government-run facility for children with disorders of sex development (DSD). The facility provides diagnosis of genetic and hormonal issues, surgical correction and psychological support for such children. Around 200 children per year can now be treated here.

PUBLICATIONS

First to win a Pulitzer Prize for a health/medicine-related publication
Indian-origin American oncologist Siddhartha Mukherjee won the Pulitzer for General Non-fiction in 2011 for *The Emperor of All Maladies: A Biography of Cancer*, published in 2010 by Scribner, USA. The book was acclaimed as one of the 100 most influential books of the last 100 years by *Time* magazine and one of the 100 best works of non-fiction by the *New York Times Magazine*.

Prolific writer on toxicology
Prof. (Dr) Pawan K. Gupta, an acclaimed toxicologist with more than 50 years of experience of teaching and research management in toxicology, published 1,616 pages of medical documents in print form (in books and book chapters) and blogs in one year (2018) through international agencies such as Academia Press and Springer, USA.

DOCTORS

Father of plastic surgery
Sushruta is considered the 'father of plastic surgery'. He is believed to have lived around the sixth century BCE and pioneered the advancement of medicine in ancient India. His teaching of anatomy, pathophysiology and therapeutic strategies, featured in his *Sushruta Samhita*, were far ahead of his time.

First mention of leprosy
Susannah C.J. Kearns and June E. Nash, in an article for the *Encyclopaedia Britannic*a (2008), stated that the first mention of leprosy is described in the Indian medical treatise *Sushruta Samhita* (c. sixth century BCE). However, *The Oxford Illustrated Companion to Medicine* holds that the mention of leprosy, as well as ritualistic cures for it, was described in the *Atharva Veda* (1500–1200 BCE), written before the *Sushruta Samhita*.

First doctors
- The first students to qualify as doctors were Bholanath Basu, Gopal Chandra Sheel, Dwarakanath Basu and Surajit Chakrabarti in 1839.
- Kadambini Ganguly (1861–1923) was the first South Asian female physician trained in Western medicine to graduate in South Asia in 1888 from the Calcutta

Medical College (now Medical College Kolkata, Kolkata, West Bengal).

First psychosurgeon

M.S. Govindaswamy (1904–62) was the first psychiatrist to start psychosurgery in India. He combined psychological, medical, psychiatric and nursing aspects for holistic treatment of patients.

First neurosurgeons

- Dr Jacob Chandy (1910–2007) started the department of neurology and neurosurgery in 1949 at Christian Medical College and Hospital, Vellore, Tamil Nadu. He initiated the first training programmes in neurosurgery in 1958 and in neurology in 1962.
- Dr Subramanian Kalyanaraman (b. 1 January 1934) from Tiruchirappalli, Tamil Nadu, was the first Indian to receive a PhD in neurosurgery from the Royal College of Edinburgh, Scotland, in 1964.
- Dr Thanjavur Santhanakrishna Kanaka (1932 –2018) was the first female neurosurgeon in Asia. She was also the first neurosurgeon in India to perform chronic electrode implants in the brain, having performed deep brain stimulation as early as in 1975.

GAP IN REQUIREMENT AND AVAILABILITY OF MENTAL HEALTH STAFF IN INDIA*

Requirement | Availability

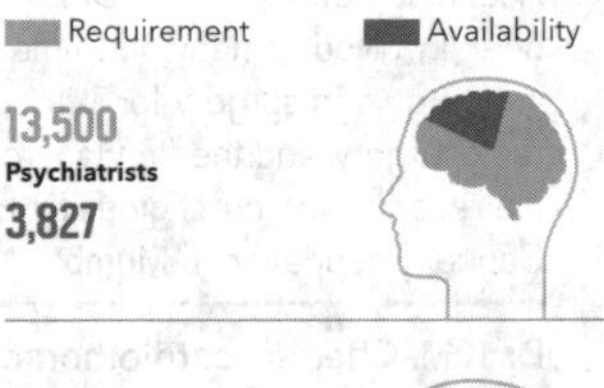

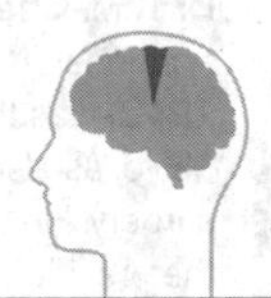

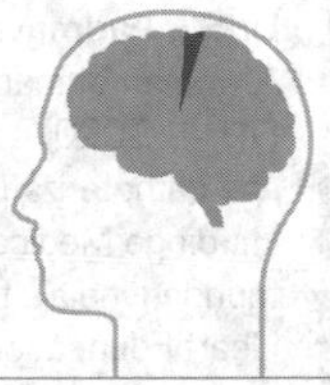

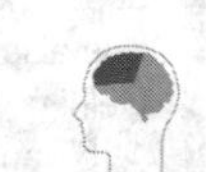

*2015; Source: Ministry of Health and Family Welfare (2017), Government of India

First woman doctor to receive the Sword of Honour

Medical Cadet Shikha Awasthi became the first woman doctor to receive the Sword of Honour for overall excellence at the passing-out parade of the 45th course of the Armed Forces Medical College (AFMC) on 18 March 2011. She also became the first graduate of AFMC to receive three top honours awarded by the college – the Sword of Honour, the President's Gold Medal and the Kalinga Trophy for academic excellence.

First woman surgeon general

Mary Poonen Lukose (1886–1976) from Kerala graduated from the University of Madras (now in Chennai), Tamil Nadu, in 1909 and studied medicine in the UK. She became the first woman surgeon general of India in 1938 and was awarded the Padma Shri in 1975.

First woman aerospace doctor

Dr Parvathi Gopal from Bengaluru, Karnataka, joined the Institute of Aerospace Medicine in the Department of High Altitude Physiology in 1992. Her field of

SUPER 30

TRAILBLAZERS IN MEDICINE

Dr B.K. Misra, neurosurgeon

A leading neurosurgeon, Dr B.K. Misra (b. 18 January 1953) has been involved in many first-time surgeries in India, including the world's first image-guided surgery for intracranial aneurysms, South Asia's first gamma knife radiosurgery, and the first laparoscopic spine surgery and awake craniotomy. He received the prestigious Dr B.C. Roy Award and has co-founded the Konark Cancer Foundation in Mumbai, Maharashtra.

Dr K.M. Cherian, cardiothoracic surgeon

A pioneer in cardiothoracic surgery, Dr Kotturathu Mammen Cherian (b. 8 March 1942) was the first in the country to perform a coronary artery bypass surgery in 1975, as also the the first heart–lung transplant and the first paediatric cardiac surgery. He was awarded the Padma Shri in 1991 and was honorary surgeon to the president of India from 1990 to 1993.

Dr S.I. Padmavati, cardiologist

Dr S.I. Padmavati

A woman of many firsts, Dr S.I. Padmavati (1917–2020) established the first cardiology clinic and catheterization lab in India in 1953-54 at Lady Hardinge Medical College, Delhi. In1962, she founded India's first heart foundation, the All India Heart Foundation, and set up India's first cardiology department at Delhi's G.B. Pant Hospital in 1967. She also started the National Heart Institute, New Delhi in 1981, and was its director. She was awarded the Padma Bhushan in 1967 and the Padma Vibhushan in 1992. She became the oldest Fellow of the European Society of Cardiology, in 2007, at 90 years. She died in August 2020 in Delhi., at 103 years, due to COVID-19.

work included research and treatment to determine whether a fighter pilot is medically and mentally fit to fly.

Discovery of feeding centre in the hypothalamus

Prof. Bal Krishan Anand (1917–2007) was a famous physiologist and pharmacologist, born in Lahore (now in Pakistan). He was credited with the discovery of the 'feeding' centre in the hypothalamus in 1951 and regarded as the founder of modern neurophysiology in India.

First Lasker Award

Rustom Jal Vakil (1911–74) was the first Indian to receive the International Albert Lasker Award of the American Public Health Association in 1957 for the discovery of 'reserpine' extracted from the *sarpagandha* plant, used in the Ayurvedic system to cure hypertension.

Most innovations by a medical professional

Dr Pankaj Garg (b. 27 December 1972), a colorectal surgeon from Panchkula,

New Tool Developed for Autism Screening

Prof. Priti Arun and Prof. Bir Singh Chavan from the Department of Psychiatry, Government Medical College and Hospital, Chandigarh, have designed the Chandigarh Autism Screening Instrument (CASI) – a questionnaire-based tool to help community health workers in the initial screening for autism. Formulated in 2018 in Hindi, it helps in the early identification of autistic spectrum conditions, which are often misdiagnosed as mental disabilities and attention deficit hyperactivity disorder (ADHD).

Haryana, has 16 innovations in the medical field to his name. Consisting of seven surgery procedures and nine treatment concepts, these innovations have been published in various national and international surgical journals from April 2015 to May 2019.

First doctor-to-doctor online chat session
A doctor-centric portal, with the URL – *www.ranbaxyfordoctors.com,* hosted a discussion on 'Current trends in management of cardiac arrhythmia' on 28 August 2000, where 69 doctors chatted online. The discussion was moderated by Prof. (Dr) K.K. Sethi, the director of interventional cardiology and cardiac arrhythmia services at Sir Ganga Ram Hospital in New Delhi.

HEALTH CHECK-UPS AND SCREENING CAMPS

Most people screened – multiple venues
Lions Club International District 323 H-2, under the leadership of District Governor Mohinder K. Aggarwal and District Activity Chairperson Dr Sanjay Vora, organized a vision screening camp in 2015 in which 140,388 students were screened from 7:00 a.m. to 7:00 p.m. in 13 districts of Maharashtra on 8 October (World Sight Day).

Most people screened – single venue
An eye check-up camp organized by Netra Kumbh on 26 February 2019, at Prayagraj, Uttar Pradesh, from 8:00 a.m. to 5:00 p.m., saw a record visit of 6,660 people. The check-ups were done by ophthalmologists and optometrists from accredited hospitals from across India. Free spectacles were also distributed to many visitors.

MEDICINE AND SURGERY

Earliest cataract surgery
Ancient Indian physician Sushruta (c. sixth century BCE) had diagnosed that

Record Rewind

State with the most registered medical practitioners

1991

Maharashtra had 37,394 registered doctors out of an all-India total of 306,966.

2020

Maharashtra, with 179,783 registered doctors out of an all-india total of 1,201,354, had the most registered medical practitioners.

cataract was a disease of the eye lens, characterized by its opacity resulting in impaired vision, and had prescribed surgery as the only remedy. It was performed with a curved needle used to loosen the lens and push the cataract out of the field of vision. The eye would later be soaked with warm butter and then bandaged.

First medical symposium

The Vedic sage Bharadwaja, who is believed to have founded of the Indian Ayurvedic system of medicine, presided over the first-ever symposium on medicinal plants in the seventh century BCE, possibly in the Himalayan region.

First conference

The first medical conference, inaugurated by the then viceroy of colonial India, Lord Elgin, was held in Calcutta, Bengal (now Kolkata), West Bengal, between 24 and 29 December 1894.

First international homoeopathic congress

The first International Homoeopathic Congress in India was held in 1967. It was organized and presided over by the renowned homoeopathic doctor Diwan Harish Chand. All the earlier ones, commencing from 1876, had been held in Europe and North America.

First separation of conjoined twins

Dr J. Dalal, paediatrics and neonatology specialist, surgically separated a set of conjoined twins (also known as Siamese twins) born to one Mrs Kambli on 11 August 1962 at Bhatia Hospital, Bombay (now Mumbai), Maharashtra.

First open-heart surgery

Dr Reeve H. Betts, an American missionary, founded the first department of thoracic and cardiovascular surgery in 1948 at the Christian Medical College and Hospital, Vellore, Tamil Nadu, with cardiac surgical work beginning in 1950. Along with Dr N. Gopinath, he performed the first successful open-heart surgery here on a 12-year-old patient, Beulah, on 6 July 1959.

Christian Medical College and Hospital's many firsts

Christian Medical College and Hospital (CMCH), Vellore, Tamil Nadu, is a private educational and research institute, which includes a network of primary, secondary and tertiary care hospitals. Founded in 1900 by an American missionary, Dr Ida S. Scudder, CMCH has many firsts to its credit:

- First reconstructive surgery for leprosy in the world (1948).
- First department of neurological sciences (1948).

- First successful open-heart surgery in India (1961).
- First kidney transplant in India (1971).
- First virology department (1978).
- First bone marrow transplant (1986).
- First successful ABO incompatible (organ donated by a donor of a different blood type) kidney transplant (2009).

First heart-shrink surgery

Dr Naresh Trehan (b. 12 August 1946), a cardiovascular and cardiothoracic surgeon, performed the first successful heart-shrink surgery in India, which was also the first in Asia, with his team of cardiac surgeons, on a 50-year-old patient, Mani Ram Gurera, at the Escorts Heart Institute and Research Centre, New Delhi, on 21 May 1996.

First bloodless breast surgery

Doctors at the Dr B.R. Ambedkar Institute Rotary Cancer Hospital, AIIMS, New Delhi, carried out a major bloodless breast cancer surgery in September 1998, using ultrasonic waves.

First laser surgery on trachea

Dr Deepak Talwar, a leading pulmonologist, and his team at the Metro Hospital and Heart Institute, Noida, Uttar Pradesh, successfully opened up the lower part

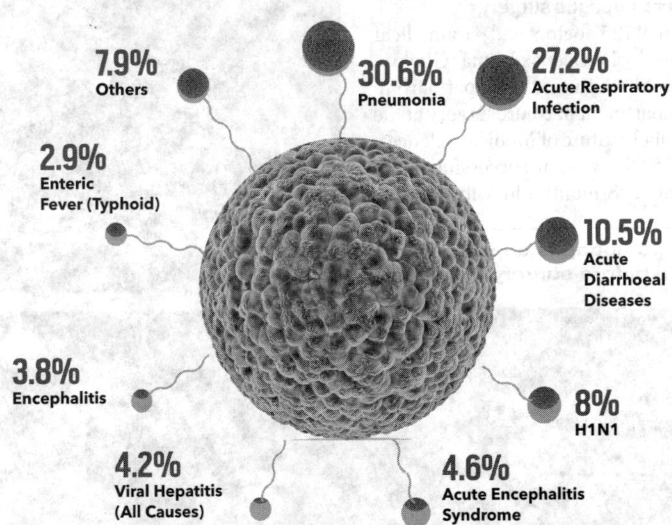

*2018; percentages may not add up to 100 due to rounding off of figures in the source data. Source: National Health Profile (2019), Central Bureau of Health Intelligence, Directorate General of Health Services, Ministry of Health and Family Welfare, Government of India

of a patient's windpipe. which had narrowed to 0.5 cm (0.2 in.) from the usual circumference of 2 cm (0.79 in.), in 1998. This was the first such surgery in India performed using laser technology.

First global telecast of surgery
On 11 June 1998, a team of doctors, led by leading cardiovascular and cardiothoracic surgeon Dr Naresh Trehan, operated upon six patients with heart ailments at the Escorts Heart Institute and Research Centre, New Delhi. The procedure was beamed live to 200 cardiac specialists and 1,000 delegates in San Francisco, USA. The back-end support was provided by the Medical Products Group at Hewlett-Packard.

India has **23,582** government hospitals with a capacity of **710,761** beds.

First cochlear implant
Dr Sandra Desa Souza was the first woman surgeon to perform a cochlear implant surgery in the human ear to treat complete deafness. The surgery was performed at Jaslok Hospital, Bombay (now Mumbai), Maharashtra, in November 1987.

First video-assisted heart surgery
Video-assisted thoracic surgery (VATS) was used for the first time in heart surgery at the B.M. Birla Heart Research Centre, Calcutta (now Kolkata), West Bengal, on several children, suffering from a congenital heart disease called patent ductus arteriosus (PDA), in August 1994.

First craniopagus surgery
A team of 125 doctors and paramedical staff, led by Dr Deepak Kumar Gupta and Dr Ashok Kumar Mahapatra from the Department of Neurosurgery at the All India Institute of Medical Sciences (AIIMS), New Delhi, successfully separated 28-month-old twins Jagga

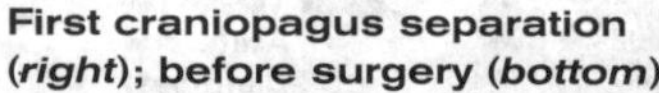

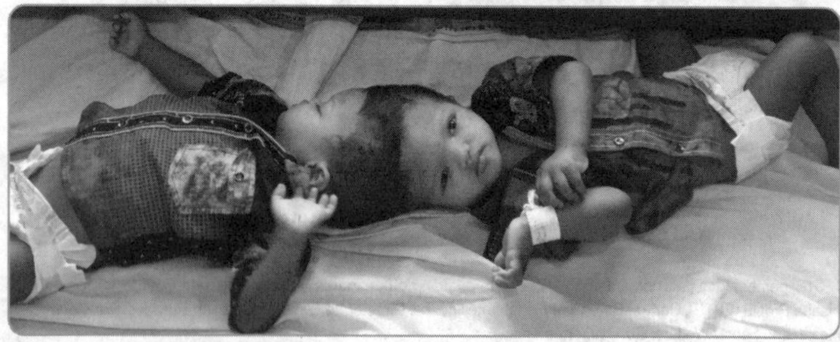

First craniopagus separation (*right*); before surgery (*bottom*)

SUPER 30

SAYING GOODBYE TO SPECTACLES AND LENSES

Providing an alternative to spectacles and contact lenses, LASIK is a laser eye surgery performed by ophthalmologists for the correction of eye disorders. This vision-correcting surgery in its modern form came into the country in the 1990s, and its convenience and painlessness made it popular.

From a handful of centres in 1995 to thousands in 2020, LASIK surgery has proven to be a safe and effective procedure in India, with a huge potential to help millions of patients. The surgery is completed in a matter of 15 to 20 minutes. With favourable results, patients undergoing LASIK surgery do not need to use spectacles or contact lenses as much, or at all.

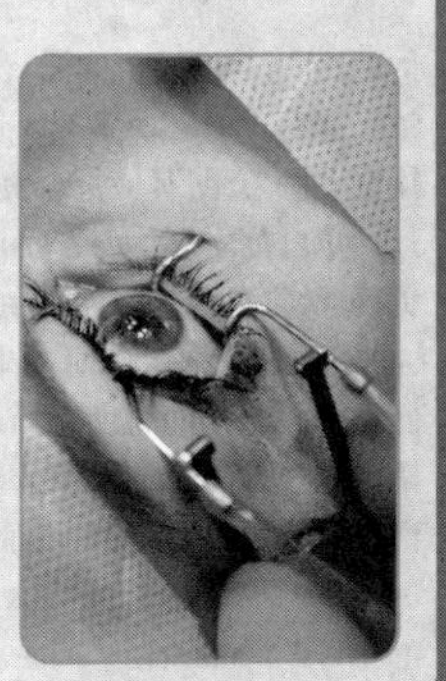

and Kalia, who were joined at the cranium. The twins belong to Milipada Village in Odisha. The complex surgery was conducted in two stages, on 28 August 2017 (25 hrs long) and 25 October 2017 (20 hrs long).

First Maze III operation

A heart surgery to cure arterial fibrillation (fast and irregular heartbeat) was performed for the first time in India by Dr Amit Banerjee, cardiothoracic surgeon, on 25-year-old Kiran Bir at the Govind Ballabh Pant Hospital, New Delhi, on 25 August 1994. Dr Banerjee conceived and successfully performed this surgery.

First coronary artery bypass surgery

Dr K.M. Cherian performed India's first successful coronary artery bypass surgery in 1975. He has pioneered several transplants at the Madras Medical Mission and Institute of Cardiovascular Diseases in Chennai, Tamil Nadu.

First bi-ventricular pacemaker

Prof. Kewal Kishan Talwar, cardiologist and former chairman of the Medical Council of India, New Delhi, and Dr T.S. Kler of Escorts Heart Institute and Research Centre, New Delhi, implanted bi-ventricular pacemakers on end-stage heart-disease patients on 8 May 2000 in two separate surgeries. This pacemaker ensures that all chambers of the heart contract and expand simultaneously.

Pioneering cataract removal

Cataract (diseased and opaque lens of the eye) surgery was normally done through a 10–12 mm incision until 15 August 1998 when Dr Amar Agarwal pioneered the technique called Phakonit, in which a cataract was removed through a 0.9 mm incision at Dr Agarwal's Eye Hospital, Chennai, Tamil Nadu. This technique has now been adopted all over the world.

Smallest medical robot

The smallest medical robot measuring 120 nm (one nanometre is one-billionth of

Highest Number of Live Births (Triplets) following Laparoscopic Myomectomy

In a first, K. Sudha, then 30 years old, a resident of Sullurpeta, Andhra Pradesh, conceived triplets following a laparoscopic myomectomy. Dr Kaliki Hymavathi *(seen in pic: second from left, in a later photo with the triplets)* removed the tumour from Sudha's uterus and later successfully delivered the triplets by caesarean section on 9 September 2015 at Narayana Medical College and Hospital, Nellore, Andhra Pradesh. Managing a triplet pregnancy with an operative scar in the uterus is a high-risk case, making it a noteworthy achievement.

a metre) was created by Soutik Betal, a doctoral research student from India, at the University of Texas, San Antonio, Texas, USA, on 10 November 2016. Capable of being remotely controlled electromagnetically and of interacting with biological cells, these robots may be used to advance research in cell-based therapy and for direct medication to cells for treating cancers and Alzheimer's disease.

TRANSPLANTS

First successful thumb transplant

Dr Tapeshwar Anand and Dr Mohan Das were part of a team of specialists who performed a 12-hr limb transplant surgery on a seven-hour-old baby Amy, at St Bart's Hospital, London, UK, on 24 March 2001. Her twin sister's thumb was transplanted on the hand of Amy (born thumbless) after the sister died at birth.

First successful liver transplant

The first successful liver transplant was performed at the Stanley Medical College in Chennai, Tamil Nadu, on 19 January 1996. It was the third transplant, the first two having been performed at Apollo Hospitals, Chennai, and AIIMS, New Delhi, respectively. In both cases, the patients died within a few days.

First liver re-transplant

On 9 January 2008, Dr A.S. Soin, head of liver transplant at Sir Ganga Ram Hospital, New Delhi, led a team of doctors to perform the first liver re-transplant surgery. The patient, Suman Kapoor, had undergone the first transplant a year and a half before.

First womb transplant

Doctors at Galaxy Care Hospital, Pune, Maharashtra, successfully conducted India's first womb transplant on 18 May 2017 by transferring a woman's uterus to her 21-year-old daughter, who was unable to conceive. The procedure, which took 9 hrs using the laparoscopic technique, was performed by a team of 12 doctors.

First successful heart transplant

A team of doctors led by Dr P. Venugopal at the All India Institute of Medical Sciences (AIIMS), New Delhi, performed a successful heart transplant operation in 5 hrs on 3 August 1994.

First paediatric heart transplant

On 14 June 1997, an 11-year-old boy underwent a successful heart transplant at the Institute of Cardiovascular Diseases, Madras Medical Mission, Chennai, Tamil Nadu. The surgery took three-and-a-half hours.

First kidney transplant with a tumour-bearing kidney

Dr Priyadarshi Ranjan of Fortis Hospital, Mohali, Punjab, on 28 July 2018, harvested a tumour-bearing kidney from Rosy Sharma, removed the tumour (3.7 cm x 2.9 cm/1.45 in. x 1.14 in.), reconstructed the kidney and successfully transplanted it in her husband, who was suffering from kidney failure.

MEDICAL MARVELS

First scalp replantation

A completely avulsed scalp was microsurgically replanted on Gurkripal Singh by Dr Abraham Thomas and Dr Jaychandran of Christian Medical College and Hospital, Ludhiana, Punjab, in March 1985.

First double (liver and kidney) transplant

Ganesh Nehru became the first recipient of a liver from his maternal uncle Mohan Ram and a kidney from his mother Hemlata simultaneously. The double transplant lasted 18 hrs on 17 April 2007, and involved 50 doctors and paramedics, besides intricate coordination between three operating theatres at Sir Ganga Ram Hospital, New Delhi. Dr A.S. Soin was the transplant surgeon in charge of the case.

First caesarean section on a comatose woman

B. Ramdevi from Telangana, pregnant with her second child, went into coma for 36 hrs at the Kakatiya Hospital, Secunderabad (now in Telangana) due to a cerebral haemorrhage. Dr P.S. Sugunakar Raju conducted a high-risk caesarean section on her on 1 April 2014. The mother came out of the coma gradually and was discharged from the hospital after 18 days.

Most triplets in a row

Chenai Kirkoo, a 35-year-old from Majuli District, Assam, delivered triplets for the third time in a row, in a rural hospital on 19 January 1988.

Most twins in a row

Ujiben Barvad, then 30 years old, a shepherdess in Munjka Village, Gujarat, birthed twins for a third successive time in March 1988.

Oldest to undergo hip surgery

- A team of doctors at PGI, Chandigarh, performed a hip replacement surgery on a 110-year-old woman (age based on her Aadhaar card), Manjauki, on 8 January 2020. The team comprised Prof. Vijay G. Goni, Dr Tanvir Samra, Dr Deepak,

Dr Karan, Dr Pradeep and Dr Sumeet.

- Ram Lal, a 105-year-old patient, was the oldest to undergo a bipolar replacement of the right hip when he sustained a fracture around the hip joint. The surgery was carried out under Dr Sujoy Kumar Bhattacharjee, director, joint replacement surgery, at Metro Heart Institute with Multispeciality Hospital in Faridabad, Haryana, on 23 March 2018. The operation lasted 2 hrs 52 mins.

Oldest woman to deliver twins
Seventy-four-year-old Mangayamma Yaramati gave birth to a pair of twin girls on 5 September 2019 at the Ahalya Hospital, Guntur, Andhra Pradesh. Dr Sankayalla Uma Shankar delivered the babies through caesarean section. The twins were conceived through IVF and were the first children of the couple.

Largest small-intestinal tumour removed
A tumour measuring 21 cm x 19 cm x 13 cm (8.26 in. x 7.48 in. x 5.11 in.) was removed from the small intestine of a patient by Dr Karthik Babu Perumalla at Ramesh Sanghamitra Hospital, Ongole, Andhra Pradesh. The surgery was conducted on 1 March 2019 from 11:00 a.m. to 4:00 p.m. The CT scan and biopsy reports confirmed the size of the tumour.

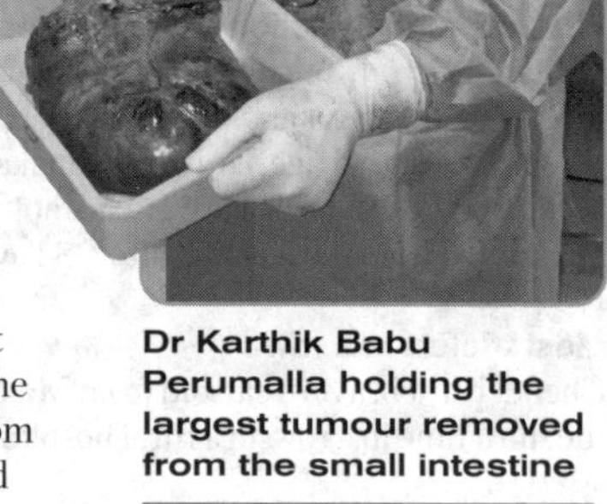

Dr Karthik Babu Perumalla holding the largest tumour removed from the small intestine

Longest object removed from the brain
Dr Rahul Prakash Modgi, neurosurgeon, and Dr Rajendra Gawatre, anaesthesiologist, operated on Pallavi Vijay Shelke, 17, at Shri Saibaba Hospital, Shirdi, Maharashtra, on 29 December 2012. They removed a 12 cm (4.72 in.) long iron rod, weighing 47 g, from her right fronto-temporo-parietal region.

Largest breast tumour removed
The largest breast tumour recorded, which measured 41 cm x 39 cm x 37 cm (16.14 in. x 15.35 in. x 14.56 in.), was removed from a patient by Dr Vikas Jain at the B.J. Hospital, Gondia, Maharashtra. The surgery was conducted on 25 July 2019 from 3:30 p.m. to 6:00 p.m. The tumour weighed 5.6 kg after it was removed.

Largest urinary bladder stone removed
Dr D.C. Patel operated on Maheshbhai Patel, a 49-year-old suffering from blocked urine, at Shree Sainath Surgical and Maternity Hospital, Dharampur, Gujarat, on 6 April 2017. Dr Patel removed a bladder stone 15 cm x 12 cm x 10 cm (5.90 in. x 4.72 in. x 3.93 in.) and weighing 1.365 kg. He was assisted by Dr Hemant Patel and Dr Nital Patel.

Friendly Neighbourhood Clinics

Last-mile healthcare has had an optimistic start with Mohalla Clinics. These primary health centres in New Delhi offer basic health services such as medicines, diagnostics and consultation, all free of cost. Under this Aam Aadmi Party government initiative, which started in 2015, as many as 450 such clinics had been set up across the city by 2020. Each clinic is estimated to serve 10,000 to 15,000 people within a radius of 5 km and 70–100 patients visit a Mohalla Clinic every day on average. In a country with very low health insurance coverage, the free healthcare services offered by Mohalla Clinics reduce the financial burden on low-income households. This project was commended as a model for scaling up universal health coverage in urban areas of India and the world, and delivering good results in accessible and affordable primary healthcare. It has been reported that other states and UTs, including Telangana, Karnataka, Rajasthan, Madhya Pradesh, Jharkhand, Jammu and Kashmir and Maharashtra, have plans for a similar network of centres based on the Mohalla Clinics.

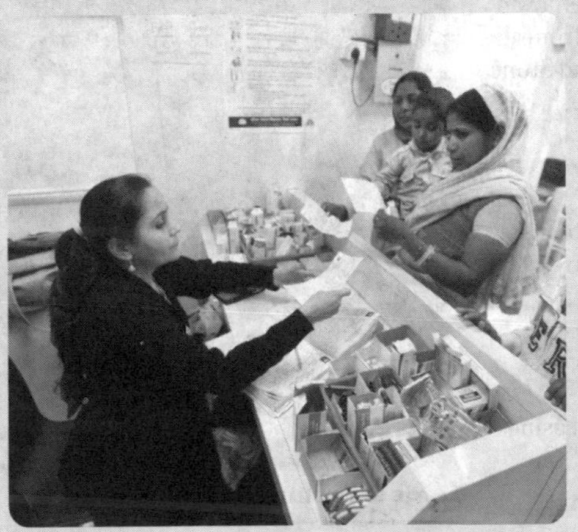

WR Heaviest ovarian tumour removed

The world's heaviest ovarian tumour, weighing 50 kg, was removed on 18 August 2020, at the Indraprastha Apollo Hospitals, New Delhi, from a 52-year-old patient, by a team of surgeons led by Dr Arun Prasad. The surgery lasted for three-and-a-half hours.

Longest foreign body removed

Dr Sanjay Kolte, urologist and kidney transplant surgeon at Sparsh Urology and Kidney Hospital, Dhantoli, Maharashtra, removed a 154 cm (5 ft 0.6 in.) long soft electric wire from the urinary bladder of a patient by percutaneous cystoscopy extraction of foreign body surgery on 28 August 2012.

WR Heaviest brain tumour removed

A brain tumour weighing 1.8 kg, recorded as the heaviest brain tumour in the world, was removed by a team of surgeons on 14 February 2018, at the B.Y.L. Nair Hospital in Mumbai, Maharashtra, from a 31-year-old patient. The surgery lasted 7 hrs.

Largest overjet jaw correction*

An overjet is a discrepancy in the upper and lower front teeth, and surgical

* This is a one-time category. Further and future record claims for this category will not be accepted.

correction is advised for an overjet greater than 9–12 mm. Dr Abhishek Kshetrapal from Kota, Rajasthan, defied this limit by successfully and non-surgically correcting an overjet measuring 20 mm, on a 16-year-old, by fixed orthodontic treatment using tads, over a course of 45 months.

Largest kidney stone removed
Dr Hemendra Shah at R.G. Stone Urological Research Institute, Mumbai, Maharashtra, removed a 13 cm (5.11 in.) wide kidney stone from a patient on 18 February 2004.

Largest urethral calculus removed
Dr Neeraj Kumar Agrawal removed a 5.6 cm (2.2 in.) long stone from a patient at Neeraj Lifecare and Stone Centre, Bareilly, Uttar Pradesh, on 21 August 2019.

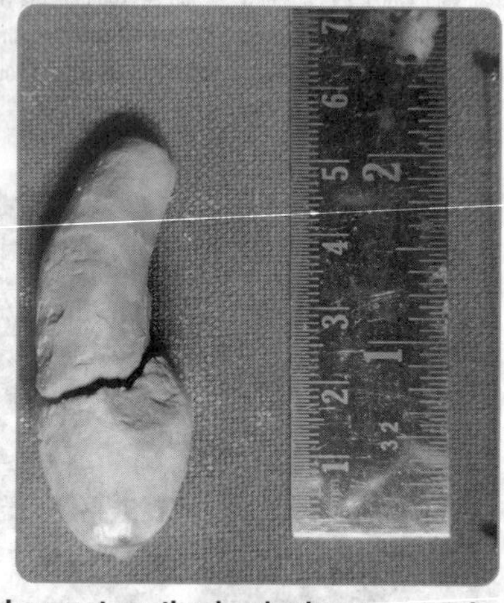

Largest urethral calculus removed

Longest fistula removed
A 110 cm (43.30 in.) long fistula was removed from a patient by Dr Ashwin Porwal at Healing Hands Clinic, Pune, Maharashtra, on 10 May 2019. The surgery was conducted from 3:00 p.m. to 7:00 p.m. and was performed using the distal laser proximal ligation (DLPL) technique.

Largest bone tumour removed
Dr B.K.S. Sanjay, professor and head of orthopaedic surgery, Himalayan Institute of Medicine, Dehradun, Uttarakhand, removed a malignant bone tumour (chondrosarcoma) of the right femur, weighing 16.5 kg, from 35-year-old Naresh Kumar of Haridwar, Uttarakhand, on 10 June 2002. The tumour was 45 cm (17.71 in.) in length and 30 cm (11.81 in.) in width, with a circumference of 97 cm (38.19 in.) and a volume of 14,135 cubic cm.

Largest liver cystic tumour
Dr N. Bheerappa from the department of surgical gastroenterology at the Nizam's Institute of Medical Sciences, Hyderabad, Telangana, successfully removed the largest known cystic liver tumour (mucinous cystic neoplasm) in 2017. The 24-year-old female patient was operated on for a tumour measuring 40 cm x 28 cm x 15 cm (15.74 in. x 11.02 in. x 5.90 in.).

Largest thoracic tumour removed
The largest thoracic tumour was removed by a team of surgeons in December 2019 at the BLK Super Speciality Hospital, New Delhi, from a 54-year-old international patient from Tuvalu. The tumour, which measured 12 cm x 10 cm (4.72 in. x 3.93 in.), was removed through robotic intervention in a minimally invasive surgical procedure.

Largest meningo-myelocele removed

On 13 June 2016, Dr Sandeep Vaishya (b. 8 July 1965), director of neurosurgery, conducted the surgical removal of the largest case of meningo-myelocele, 60 cm x 50 cm (23.62 in. x 19.69 in.) with an overall circumference of 90 cm (35.43 in.). The surgery was carried out at Fortis Memorial Research Institute, Gurugram, Haryana. The patient was Gurdeep Singh from Patiala, Punjab.

Longest hairball removed from stomach

Dr Keyur Bhatt, surgical gastroenterologist at Surat Institute of Digestive Sciences (SIDS), Gujarat, removed a 149.86 cm (59 in.) long hairball from the stomach of a patient on 26 October 2017.

Youngest to undergo endoscopic surgery

On 25 August 2013, Dr Pradip Uppal, an ENT surgeon (otolaryngologist) from Thane city in Maharashtra, removed pus from the eye of a 29-day-old baby named Hrishikesh Pandey (b. 27 July 2013) using nasal endoscopy.

Surgery on heaviest woman

Forty-two-year-old Amita Rajani, weighing 300 kg, underwent bariatric surgery performed by Dr Shashank Shah at Dr Shah's hospital in Pune, Maharashtra, in 2015. She was bedridden for eight years before the surgery and had multiple risk factors such as kidney failure, diabetes and low oxygen levels. She lost 214 kg due to the surgery.

Heaviest kidney removed

Dr Puvvada Sandeep and three other doctors from his team at Ramaiah Medical College, Bengaluru, Karnataka, removed a kidney weighing 7.72 kg on 21 November 2019. Containing 3.12 litres of fluid, it was removed from a 53-year-old patient suffering from bilateral adult polycystic kidney disease (APKD) and chronic kidney disease.

WR Surgery on world's heaviest teenager

Mihir Jain, then 14 years old, became the world's heaviest teenager to undergo bariatric surgery. He weighed 237 kg at the time of the surgery, with a BMI of 92 kg/sq. m. The surgery was performed by Dr Pradeep Kumar Chowbey at Max Hospital, Saket, New Delhi, and a team of six doctors in 2 hrs 20 mins in July 2018.

Record Rewind

Largest kidney operated on

2000

Dr A.K. Hemal, Dr S.N. Wadhwa and their team from the department of Urology, AIIMS, New Delhi, removed a non-functional kidney measuring 25 cm x 20 cm x 20 cm (9.84 in. x 7.87 in. x 7.87 in.), containing five litres of fluid, by laparoscopic nephrectomy in a unique operation with no incision, on 3 June 1996.

2018

A kidney measuring 40.5 cm x 22 cm x 12.5 cm (15.94 in. x 8.66 in. x 4.92 in.) and weighing 6.24 kg was removed by Dr Niket Kantilal Shah at Wanless Hospital, Miraj, Maharashtra, on 23 June 2017. It was removed from a 50-year-old patient suffering from adult polycystic kidney disease (APKD).

A Step towards Universal Health Coverage in India

The National Health Stack (NHS), an integrated digital infrastructure proposed by Government of India's think tank – NITI Aayog, and built to make the health insurance system transparent and healthy, is the country's first healthcare information system for use across public and private sectors. Launched in 2020, it is a single source of health data, providing a coverage and claims platform and a federated personal health records framework for patients, medical researchers and other stakeholders. Its building blocks are an architectural document called the National Digital Health Blueprint (NDHB), and the National Digital Health Mission (NDHM), a specialized organization to oversee the implementation of the countrywide scheme.

WR Most teeth removed

In July 2019, doctors at the Saveetha Dental College and Hospital, Chennai, Tamil Nadu, removed 526 teeth from a boy's mouth in a five-hour long surgery. Five surgeons and seven pathologists were engaged in surgery to remove a 4 cm x 3 cm (1.57 in. x 1.18 in.) tumour from the lower right side of his jaw, after which they spotted the teeth there. Though some were tiny particles, the doctors said they had the properties of teeth.

Most items removed from stomach

- In July 2017, at least 150 needles and nails were removed from the stomach of 56-year-old Badrilal, a Bundi resident, at a hospital in Faridabad, Haryana.
- In 2019, doctors led by surgeon Dr Anil Saini at the Bundi Government Hospital, Bundi, Rajasthan, removed 116 iron nails, a long wire and an iron pellet from the stomach of a 42-year-old man, Bhola Shankar, in 1.5 hrs.

COMBATING COVID-19
Warriors against the Pandemic
Aarogya Setu

Timeline Of COVID-19 in 2020

The last time India faced a pandemic was in 2009 when the first case of swine flu (a highly contagious respiratory infection), caused by the H1N1 virus, was found on 16 May in Hyderabad, now in Telangana. Declared to be over in August 2010 by the World Health Organization (WHO), the virus had claimed lives of more than 2,744 people across the country.

Just over a decade later, India – and the rest of the world – faces a new pandemic: COVID-19, an infectious disease caused by the most recently discovered coronavirus. Unknown to the general population before the outbreak of the disease began in Wuhan, China, the new virus can be transmitted when one comes in contact with aerosols or droplets containing the virus. The first case in India was reported on 30 January 2020 and the 'first wave' of COVID-19 swept the country in March 2020. The 'second wave' began in March 2021 and turned out to be deadlier than the first due to mutations and variants of the virus.

14 April 3 May

Lockdown 2.0
The lockdown is extended till 3 May 2020, after a review of the outbreak conditions and observations on 14 April 2020.

1 16 May

Lockdown 3.0 (zonewise restrictions)
The Ministry of Health and Family Welfare decides on restrictions according to risk profiles – red zones are hotspots, orange zones are areas with limited cases and green zones are areas with zero confirmed cases to date or no confirmed case in the preceding 21 days.

17 31 May

Lockdown 4.0
The governments of states and Union Territories (UTs) are given powers to delineate red, green and orange zones. Interstate movement of passenger vehicles and buses is allowed with the mutual consent of states and UTs.

8 June

Unlock 1.0 (phased reopening begins)
Religious places, places of worship, hotels, restaurants and hospitality services as well as shops inside shopping malls are opened.

2 July

India's first plasma bank opens at the Institute of Liver and Biliary Sciences (ILBS) in Delhi.

17 July

India reaches 10 lakh (1 million) recorded cases of COVID-19.

First COVID case in India

Originating from Wuhan, China, the first case of the coronavirus pandemic in India is reported in Kerala when a third-year medical student from Wuhan University tests positive for coronavirus after she returns home during her semester holidays.

30 January

31 January

India airlifts citizens from China

A special Air India flight is sent to evacuate a large number of Indians stranded in China's COVID-19–hit Wuhan city.

COVID-19 declared a pandemic

The World Health Organization (WHO) declares the Novel Coronavirus Disease 2019 (COVID-19) outbreak as a pandemic and reiterates the call to countries to take immediate action and scale up their response to detect, treat and reduce its transmission to save people's lives.

11 March

12 March

India's first COVID-19 fatality

Health officials in the country report the first COVID-19 death when a 76-year-old man dies in Karnataka.

15 March

India records 100 confirmed COVID-19 cases.

22 March

Janata curfew

A 14-hour Janata curfew is announced where all markets and establishments, except those dealing in essential goods and services, are closed for the day to help check the spread of COVID-19.

25 March

Lockdown 1.0

Prime Minister Narendra Modi announces a 21-day nationwide lockdown after consulting health experts and WHO in order to mitigate the spread of the disease.

30 March

India records 100 confirmed recoveries.

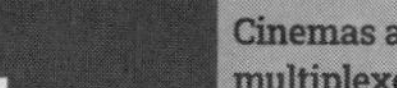

6 September

First COVID-19 reinfection case in the country

A 27-year-old woman tests positive for COVID-19 for the second time in Bengaluru, Karnataka.

7 September

India registers the world's second highest number of active/recorded cases after the USA; metro services resume in New Delhi.

1 October

Cinemas and multiplexes are allowed to open to 50 per cent capacity.

19 December

India's COVID-19 tally crosses 1 crore (10 million).

21 December

India suspends flights to the UK where a new strain of COVID-19 has emerged.

The new Delta variant of the virus, first identified in India in October 2020, has been declared as the fastest transmitting strain of the coronavirus by the WHO. Officially known as B.1.617.2, the variant is believed to be the driving force behind the second wave in India and elsewhere. Scientists have expressed concern about a Delta Plus (B.1.617.2.1) variant as of June 2021.

Milestones, Victories and Triumphs

First dedicated hospital
Reliance Industries Ltd (RIL) set up India's first dedicated COVID-19 hospital in a span of two weeks on 23 March 2020 in Mumbai, Maharashtra. This facility at Seven Hills Hospital is a 100-bedded centre for COVID-19 patients, and has been set up by Sir H.N. Reliance Foundation Hospital, in collaboration with the Brihanmumbai Municipal Corporation (BMC). With all beds equipped with biomedical equipment such as ventilators and pacemakers, among others, the facility includes a negative-pressure room that helps in preventing cross-contamination and infection.

First indigenous testing kit
A Pune-based diagnostic firm, Mylab Discovery, developed the country's first testing kit under virologist and research and development chief, Minal Dakhave Bhosale. The kit, which was named Patho Detect, was developed in just six weeks and reached the market on 26 March 2020. It gave the diagnosis in two-and-a-half hours compared to the six to seven hours taken by imported testing kits.

First drive-through testing facility
The country's first drive-through COVID-19 testing facility was opened on 6 April 2020 in Delhi by Dr Arjun Dang of Dr Dangs Labs in order to ensure maximum safety and minimum exposure to both the patients and the sample collectors. People were advised to first fill an online form on the website of the testing centre, pay for the test on digital platforms and book a slot. Advised to drive to the facility close to their allotted time, people could provide the healthcare professionals with the required samples and drive away in less than 30 minutes. The test cost ₹4,500 and reports were made available online within 36 hours.

First state to start pool testing
With the increase in the number of COVID-19 patients, the Uttar Pradesh government decided to start pool testing (testing several samples at a time) of COVID-19 samples on 13 April 2020. In order

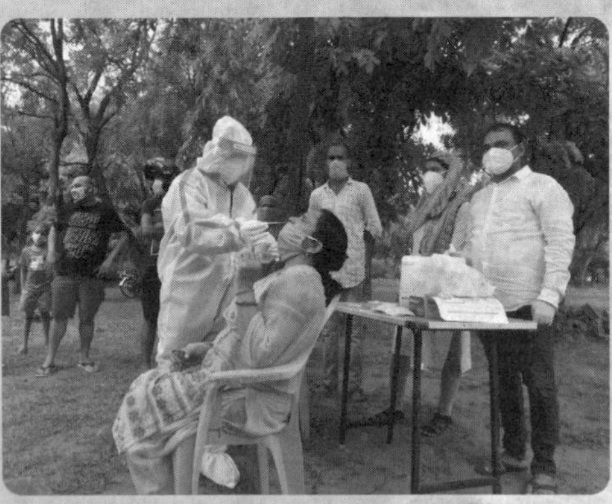

to help maximize the testing of samples on a daily basis, the Indian Council of Medical Research (ICMR) gave permission for pool testing to the state health department.

First sanitizing tunnel

A walk-through mass sanitizing tunnel was set up by the Western Railway station of Ahmedabad, Gujarat, on 8 April 2020 to ensure the safety of staff and passengers. The 6 m (20 ft) long tunnel was fitted with a sensor to start fogging with WHO-approved sanitizer as soon as a person approached it. With the capacity of disinfecting 25–30 people in a minute, the tunnel's system converts the sanitizer mixture into vapour and forms a uniform layer over the surface to be sanitized.

Most handmade masks made in a day

Nitika Singh Gaur (b. 11 February 1991) from Jhansi, Uttar Pradesh, stitched 50 masks a day, taking 3 mins 45 secs to make each reusable cotton mask, on 29 March 2020. She distributed them free of cost.

Most portable handwashing units installed

Under the Wash on Wheels programme, Jal Seva Charitable Foundation (WaterAid India) installed 500 portable handwashing units in as many autorickshaws in Sant Ravidas Nagar District, Bhadohi, Uttar Pradesh, from 14 to 25 July 2020 to prevent and contain the spread of COVID-19.

Largest repatriation exercise

An initiative launched by the Government of India, the 'Vande Bharat' mission was carried out to bring back Indians stranded in various parts of the world due to the restrictions imposed on air travel. Being pegged as the largest repatriation exercise in history, it was open to an Overseas Citizen of India (OCI) card holder, or any Indian who holds the citizenship of a foreign country, a valid visa of more than one year of that country or a Green Card, in accordance with the guidelines issued by the Ministry of External Affairs (MEA). Operating 64 flights to 12 countries from 7 May to 13 May 2020, Air India brought back around 15,000 Indians with the first two flights carrying 363 Indians from the Gulf to Kochi, Kerala. Carried out in 11 phases, Air India (including Air India Express and Air India Group) repatriated 2,113,972 inbound passengers on 13,997 flights and flew out 1,516,428 passengers on 13,989 outbound flights by 4 July 2021.

Largest evacuation by the Indian Navy

An evacuation operation by the Indian Navy was launched on 8 May

2020 as part of Operation Samudra Setu for the Vande Bharat Mission – India's efforts to get its citizens back to their homeland. The largest evacuation in naval history, it sent out four naval ships, INS *Jalashwa*, INS *Airavat*, INS *Shardul* and INS *Magar* to bring back about 3,992 Indians. With disembarkation ports in Kerala, Tamil Nadu and Gujarat, the mission was undertaken along with the Ministries of Defence, External Affairs, Home Affairs, and Health and Family welfare, as well as other agencies and state governments.

Empty roads in Pune, Maharashtra, during lockdown

Largest lockdown

Around 1.3 billion people across India were asked by the Government of India to stay home for 21 days, starting 24 March 2020, making it the world's largest lockdown ever. While designated red and orange zones with high risk of infection, had to limit movement to emergencies and essential goods and services, rules were eased in green zones with no confirmed COVID-19 cases. The lockdown was extended thrice up to 31 May, with a few relaxations.

Largest temporary hospital

By 9 July 2020, the Indian Army had established a temporary 1,000-bed hospital in Delhi for COVID-19 patients, under the guidance of CEO (Operations), Major General S.S. Bhatia. Built by the Defence Research and Development Organization (DRDO) and Tata Sons Pvt. Ltd, it was manned by personnel from the Armed Forces Medical Services. It offered 250 ICU and 750 acute-care ward beds, with facilities for oxygen supply.

First to culture the UK COVID-19

India became the first country in the world to successfully isolate and culture the variant strain of COVID-19 that emerged in the UK. It was cultured at the National Institute of Virology, Pune, Maharashtra, from clinical samples collected from people returning from the UK. ICMR announced the achievement on 2 January 2021.

India vaccinated 294,639,111 (29.4 crore) people by 23 June 2021.

Words and Meanings of an Unprecedented Year

The Oxford Languages Word of the Year campaign in 2020 turned out to be different from previous years as it had to adapt, much like people across the world, to an entirely changed environment. The *Words of an Unprecedented Year* report explored the changes and development that the English language went through because of the COVID-19 pandemic. Here are a few examples:

ANTI-MASKER A person who opposes wearing a face mask.

ANTI-VAXXER A person who is opposed to vaccination.

BC Before COVID-19 or before Coronavirus.

BUBBLE (during an outbreak of an infectious disease) A restricted group of people whose members are allowed to be in close proximity when maintaining a physical distance is otherwise required.

CIRCUIT BREAKER A short period of lockdown intended to inhibit the spread of an infectious disease.

COMMUNITY TRANSMISSION The spread or transmission of an infectious disease or pathogen between members of a community, especially as a result of casual contact.

CORONAVIRUS (specifically) The virus responsible for an outbreak of a serious respiratory disease in humans, especially the major pandemic beginning in 2019.

COVID-19 A short form of CoronaVirus Disease 2019, an acute respiratory illness in humans caused by a coronavirus, a virus that is capable of producing severe symptoms and death, especially in the elderly and other people with certain underlying health conditions.

COVIDIOT (depreciative) A person who disobeys guidelines designed to prevent the spread of COVID-19.

FLATTEN THE CURVE To take measures designed to reduce the rate at which infection spreads during an epidemic, with the aim of lowering the peak daily number of new cases and extending the period over which new cases occur.

HYGIENE THEATRE Cleaning practices that give the illusion of sanitization without reducing the risk of infection.

INFODEMIC A proliferation of diverse, often unsubstantiated, information relating to a crisis, controversy, or event, that disseminates rapidly and uncontrollably through news, online and social media, and is regarded as intensifying public speculation or anxiety.

LOCKDOWN A state of isolation, containment, or restricted access, usually instituted for security purposes or as a public health measure; the imposition of this state.

PANDEMIC A disease which is epidemic over a very large area and affects a large proportion of a population; an outbreak of such a disease.

PPE Personal protective (or protection) equipment; clothing and equipment designed to provide the wearer or user protection against hazardous substances or environments, or to prevent transmission of infectious diseases.

R NUMBER Reproduction number, the average number of cases of an infectious disease arising by transmission from a single infected individual.

RONA (informal) Coronavirus; COVID-19.

SANNY (chiefly Australian) Short form for hand sanitizer.

Innovations in a Pandemic

In the wake of the COVID-19 outbreak, technology that was only being used as a support system came to stand and be counted at the forefront of this health crisis. Online health consultation solutions, which were resisted earlier, started being accepted by doctors and patients alike. Governments were aided by start-ups to help get the word out to the masses. For instance, Yellow Messenger, an AI-based virtual assistance provider developed by Raghavendra Kumar Ravinutala and Jaya Kishore Reddy in Bengaluru, Karnataka, in partnership with Facebook Messenger, was appointed by the National Health Authority of India to provide chatbots to several state governments, including Madhya Pradesh, Punjab and Rajasthan, to assist with citizen engagement over WhatsApp and Facebook Messenger. Here's a glimpse of some of the leading innovations during the pandemic:

Low-cost portable ventilators made in 82 days

With the aim to help the elderly and underserved get access to medical services amid the COVID-19 crisis, Noccarc Robotics, a start-up led by Nikhil Kurele and Harshit Rathore, developed a low-cost portable ventilator in a record time of 82 days. Significantly cheaper than the ones available in the market, this ventilator was made at a cost of ₹3.5 lakh (350,000) per unit with indigenous components. Started from the Startup Incubation and Innovation Centre, IIT- Kanpur, Noccarc aimed to control the device and display critical information through a 10-inch

SELF-ISOLATE To undertake self-imposed isolation for a period of time, typically in one's own home, in order to avoid catching or transmitting an infectious disease, or as one of a number of public health measures designed to inhibit its spread.

SOCIAL DISTANCING Action or practice of maintaining a certain physical distance from, or limiting physical contact with, another person or people (especially family and friends) in order to avoid catching or transmitting an infectious disease, or as one of a number of public health measures designed to inhibit its spread.

SUPERSPREADER An individual infected with a (pathogenic) microorganism who transmits it to an unusually large number of other individuals.

UNMUTE To turn on (a microphone/audio on an electronic device), especially after having turned it off.

WORKATION A working vacation; a holiday during which one also works.

touchscreen connected to the ventilator. With a battery backup of eight hours, the V310 was launched on 27 June 2020 and saw an increase of around 25 per cent in demand during the second wave in 2021.

Toaster-sized ventilator helps hospitals in fighting the virus

A toaster-sized device, initially created to help the poor, the AgVa ventilator proved to be useful during the COVID-19 pandemic that swept through the nation. Developed by Dr Deepak Agrawal, a neurosurgeon, and Prof. Diwakar Vaish, a robot scientist, in 2017, it is priced at around ₹1.5 lakh (150,000) and is an affordable option to a conventional ventilator that can cost more than ₹7 lakh (700,000). As it is lightweight and portable, and operates on low power, it helps move less critical patients back home. As India's need increased, the production of this 3.5 kg oxygenation machine went up to 20,000 per month with the help of automobile manufacturer Maruti Suzuki.

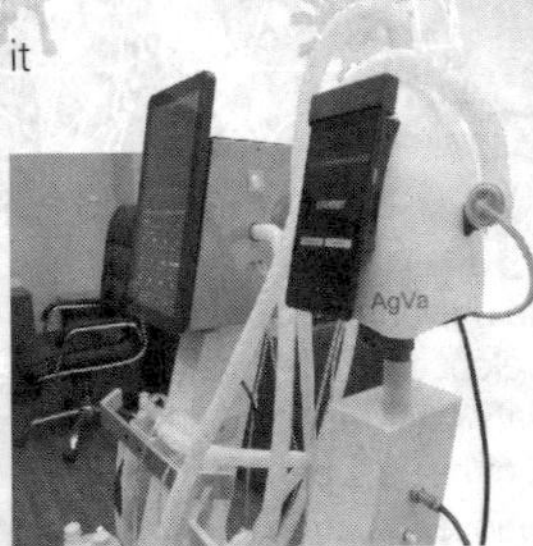

Tap-water technology to combat COVID-19

Shashi Rajan and Debayan Saha, the founders of PerSapien, a team of scientists, engineers, medical professionals and designers who use science for meaningful inventions, realized quickly that the formulation of an effective vaccine or medication for COVID-19 would take time. Choosing to focus on bridging the existing gap in sanitization instead, the duo used their knowledge of fundamental physics and came up with the Airlens Minus Corona technology that uses tap water and electricity to kill the virus. Developed in May 2020 by scientists at PerSapien, the technology was also tested by the Indian Council of Medical Research (ICMR) and proved to be successful in inactivating and destroying the virus. It is currently installed in Narayana Hospital, West Bengal, and GMR Airport, Hyderabad, Telangana.

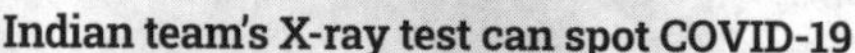

Indian team's X-ray test can spot COVID-19

In collaboration with Balasubramanian Raman, a professor from IIT-Roorkee and his students, a team of Indian medical scientists in Kyoto, Japan, developed an AI-based software that uses X-ray to detect cases of COVID-19 and predict the same in asymptomatic patients. An economical option that does not need invasive swabs, it acts as a surveillance tool for authorities to predict who should be tested for confirmation. Led by Kyoto-based medical scientist Namasivayam Ganesh Pandian and his student Vinodh Joseph, the software facilitates rapid screening (100 images in 3.63 seconds) with an accuracy of 99.69 per cent.

Indian Railways' mobile doctor booths

A system that allows doctors to examine patients without direct physical contact, 'Charak' is a mobile booth designed by the West Central Railway's Coach Rehabilitation Workshop (CRWS), Bhopal, Madhya Pradesh. Initially made using a toilet from one of the old train coaches, these booths facilitate zero-contact check-ups and also ensure the safety of the medical professionals, including doctors. In this booth, which has a back entrance and a glass exterior in front, doctors can sit comfortably on a specially designed chair and examine patients through two openings covered with protective gear.

IIT-Delhi start-up develops masks that can be reused up to 50 times

Among the many companies that stepped up to help prevent the spread of the COVID-19 virus, Nanosafe Solutions, a start-up, developed 'NSafe+ masks' that can be reused up to 50 times. The anti-microbial, water repellent NSafe+ mask has three layers to filter the air and is claimed to be 99.2 per cent efficient for bacterial filtration. A part of the Foundation for Innovation and Technology

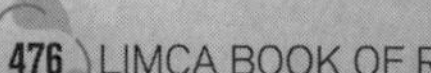

Transfer (FITT) at IIT-Delhi, the company is led by founder and CEO Dr Anasuya Roy and aimed to make around 5 lakh (500,000) masks in a month.

Fastest application to reach 50 million downloads

In order to spread awareness about COVID-19 and to connect health services to the people of India, Aarogya Setu, a tracking app, was launched by the Government of India on 2 April 2020. Developed by the National Informatics Centre, Ministry of Electronics and IT, the app helps track COVID-19 cases by using the smartphone's GPS system and Bluetooth to determine if a person has been in an infected area or within six feet of an infected person. It reached 50 million users in a record time of 13 days, making it the fastest and most downloaded app in the world then.

First remote health-monitoring system

The All India Institute of Medical Sciences (AIIMS), Rishikesh, Uttarakhand, in partnership with Bharat Electronics Limited (BEL) set up India's first remote health monitoring system. The system allowed doctors to monitor the body temperature and oxygen level of patients remotely through a website and mobile app, reducing the risk of exposure to healthcare workers. Suspected COVID-19 patients or those quarantined in hospitals or at home could enrol themselves with AIIMS, Rishikesh in order to receive a kit to monitor their health parameters, such as pulse rate, oxygen saturation and respiration rate.

Robots help India fight the good fight

Based in Kochi, Kerala, Asimov Robotics (part of the Kerala Startup Mission) developed a robot in March 2020 that was deployed in hospitals to ease the pressure on the medical staff and to minimize risk to healthcare workers. The three-wheeled KARMI-Bot, made in 15 days by a team of seven people, can carry food, medical and clinical consumables

IIT-Bombay researchers patent a smart stethoscope

A 'digital stethoscope' that can listen to heartbeats from a distance and record them was developed by a team at IIT-Bombay (IIT-B) in Mumbai, Maharashtra. Consisting of a tube connected to two earpieces that transmit sound from the body and eliminate background noise, this patented device, called AyuLynk, works to minimize the risk of healthcare professionals contracting COVID-19 from patients, and has the ability to store and share a patient's heartbeat wirelessly. As part of a start-up called 'AyuDevice', the team sent 1,000 such stethoscopes to hospitals and healthcare centres across the country through IIT-B's technology business incubator. Developed with clinical inputs from Dr Nambiraj Konar at Reliance Hospital and Dr Lancelot Pinto at P.D. Hinduja Hospital, it can translate sounds into electric signals to be displayed on a smartphone or laptop.

as well as navigate freely in the hospitals. It can also collect trash disposed of by patients, perform disinfection, and enable video calls between doctors and patients.

In April 2020, the Industrial Training Institute (ITI) in Cuttack, Odisha, developed two low-cost robots – CO-BOT and NIGA-BOT, to protect health workers from COVID-19 and reduce the need for PPE. While CO-BOT is a service robot that can move on wheels in hospitals to carry food, water and medicines to patients, NIGA-BOT is a telepresence robot that can be used for surveillance (to monitor the health of patients) and teleconsultation by doctors (who can interact with patients remotely through live video streaming).

Indian consumer robot maker Milagrow launched four humanoid robots in July 2020 to help in the country's fight against the pandemic by reducing human contact. Called RoboDiCaprio, RoboJulia, RoboNano and RoboElf, the humanoid robots have been specifically designed to cater to hotels, hospitals, restaurants and corporate offices.

1. **RoboDiCaprio**, the guest relations robot, is 155 cm (5 ft) tall and equipped with advanced sensors to sense human presence in proximity. Possessing face recognition capabilities, it can be used for business consulting, greeting visitors, reservations, advertising and patrolling.
2. **RoboJulia**, the serving robot, is designed to deliver meals to guest-designated tables, explain the menu as well as give restaurant information. It can take fast turns and has an emergency stop feature.
3. **RoboElf** is a service assistant that can be deployed in various locations such as metros, banks and shopping malls. Already deployed at AIIMS, New Delhi, and Sir H.N. Reliance Foundation Hospital and Research Centre in Mumbai, Maharashtra, the robot's latest version has a business management system that can collect and manage data from other robots so that the users can better run their businesses.
4. **RoboNano** is a personal assistant robot equipped with Amazon's Alexa Voice Service with features such as voice assistance, smart-home control and remote surveillance. With 50 sensors to avoid objects in its way, the robot can recognize voices and knows when someone enters the room.

Flying Friends

Drone start-ups such as Garuda Aerospace, ideaForge, Marut and Indian Robotics Solutions (IRS) have been working with the Indian government to check the spread of COVID-19 in different ways.

Founded in 2016, Chennai-based Garuda Aerospace started using unmanned aerial vehicles (UAVs) to disinfect around 3.28 million sq. km of area across India to prevent the spread of COVID-19. Called **Corona Killer**

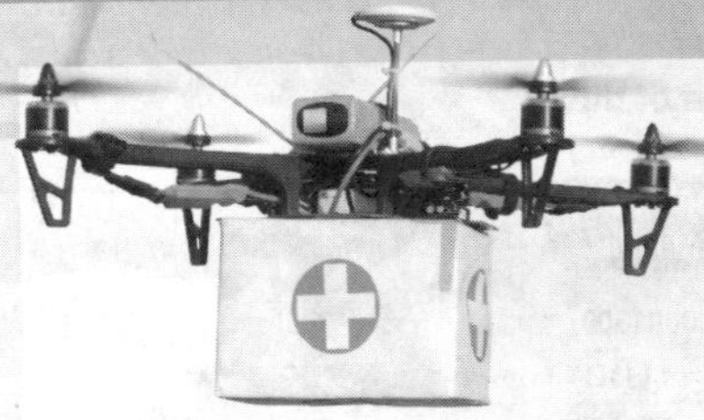

(CK), these UAVs helped in the sanitization of crowded locations such as markets, metro stations, airports, schools and hospitals.

Headquartered in Mumbai, Maharashtra, ideaForge is engaged in security surveillance and helped the police in monitoring social distancing across cities. Their drones were deployed to provide real-time intelligence to the command and control centre, local patrol vans and ground forces to help prevent theft and other unlawful activities.

Marut Dronetech, a Hyderabad-based company, worked with the Telangana government by deploying drones that sprayed disinfectants across eight districts. Public monitoring and warning drones were also fitted with cameras and speakers to aid in monitoring the situation and delivering critical medical supplies.

In order to target personal and mass detection, Indian Robotics Solutions (IRS) developed land thermal detection headgear, known as **Thermal Corona Combat Headgear** (TCCH) as well as the **Thermal Corona Combat Drone.** While a person wearing TCCH would be able to thermally scan elevated body temperature (a possible symptom of the infection) of individuals from a safe distance of 10–15 m, the drone can be used to monitor temperature, see real-time images, and disinfect and sanitize areas. It has a loudspeaker for giving instructions besides a medical box to carry medical essentials.

How We Survived

India at the forefront of vaccine exports

India was expected to fulfil 70 per cent of the world's COVID-19 vaccine needs and two vaccines (Serum Institute of India–Oxford–AstraZeneca Covishield vaccine and Bharat Biotech–ICMR Covaxin) were being exported. By mid-February 2021, India had supplied 16.7 million doses of Covishield to 20 countries. This included nearly 6.3 million doses given for free to 13 countries including Bangladesh, Myanmar, Bhutan, Nepal, Afghanistan, Sri Lanka, Bahrain, Oman, Barbados and Dominica. About 10 million more doses were supplied on a commercial basis to seven countries including Brazil, Morocco and South Africa. The MEA also cleared the supply of 24 million doses on a commercial basis to 25 countries including Saudi Arabia, Brazil, Morocco, Myanmar, Nepal, Nicaragua and Mauritius.

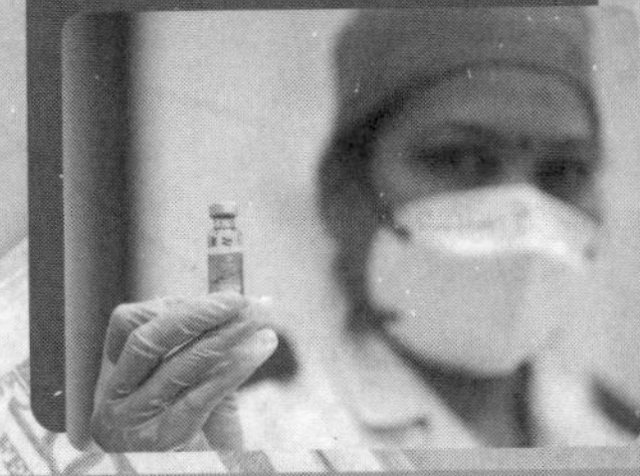

COMBATING COVID-19

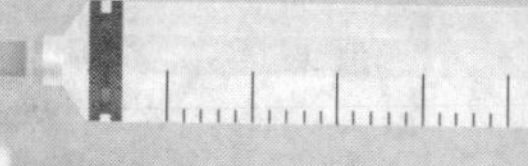

Who was vaccinated in the first phase of the vaccine rollout?

Priority Population Segment	No. of Beneficiaries in lakhs/millions
Healthcare Workers	3,000 (300)
MBBS doctors	11 (1.1)
Nurses	15 (1.5)
Frontline workers	210 (21)
Municipal workers, public transport drivers	150 (15)
Police and armed forces	60 (6)
People above 50 yrs	2,600 (260)
People below 50 yrs but with co-morbidities (estimates)	120 (12)

From 1 May 2021, the vaccination programme was opened to all citizens above 18 years.

Source: Credit Suisse

As of 24 June 2021, there were 643,194 active cases in India while 28,994,855 had been discharged and 390,660 lives were lost to the virus.

FLATTENING THE CURVE

India successfully limited the rate of growth of daily new COVID-19 cases after September 2020 with movement restrictions and medical facilitation. This infographic covers the first wave from 1 March 2020 to 17 February 2021.

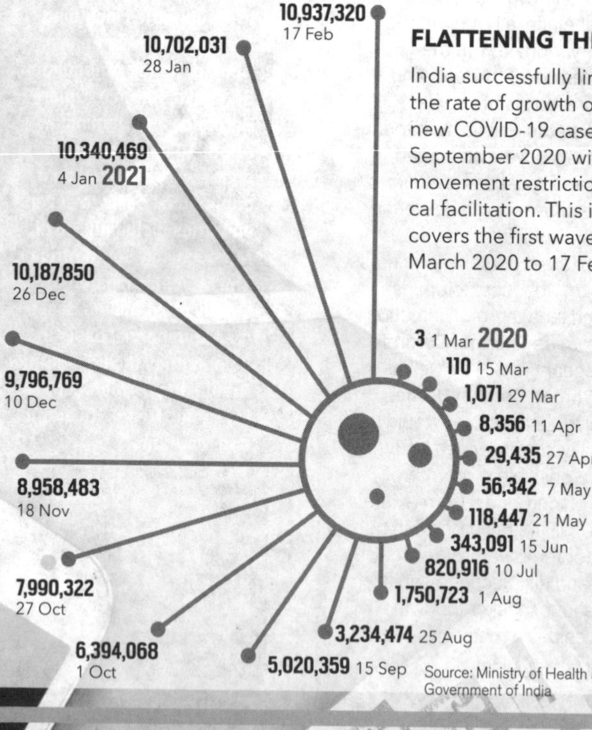

3 1 Mar **2020**
110 15 Mar
1,071 29 Mar
8,356 11 Apr
29,435 27 Apr
56,342 7 May
118,447 21 May
343,091 15 Jun
820,916 10 Jul
1,750,723 1 Aug
3,234,474 25 Aug
5,020,359 15 Sep
6,394,068 1 Oct
7,990,322 27 Oct
8,958,483 18 Nov
9,796,769 10 Dec
10,187,850 26 Dec
10,340,469 4 Jan **2021**
10,702,031 28 Jan
10,937,320 17 Feb

Source: Ministry of Health and Family Welfare, Government of India

COVID-19 vaccines in India

To vaccinate people across the country in a phased manner, the Indian government approved two vaccines on 3 January 2020 – Covaxin, developed by Bharat Biotech in collaboration with ICMR and the National Institute of Virology (NIV), and the Oxford–AstraZeneca vaccine – Covishield – manufactured by the Serum Institute of India. They are scientifically formed with safe materials that cannot cause illness among the recipients on their own (dead coronavirus and harmless adenovirus respectively). As reported by Credit Suisse, the number of doses needed to vaccinate the adult population of India is estimated at 1.7 billion. Sputnik V, developed in Russia and distributed by Dr Reddy's Laboratories in India was approved in April 2021.

The second-wave surge

In March 2021, active COVID-19 cases in India shot up drastically, indicating the second wave. With rampant and deadlier transmission, this wave put a considerable strain on the already pressured healthcare system. A new variant of the virus, now termed the Delta variant, emerged as the primary mutation that led to the spike in cases. It caused severe respiratory problems, diagnostic failure and increased transmissibility. The country witnessed a sharp rise in fatalities owing in part to an increased demand and acute shortage of oxygen resources (cylinders and concentrators). As India's daily active cases and deaths shot up, many states and UTs imposed curfews and lockdowns to break the chain of transmission. By June 2021, these restrictions were relaxed gradually. As the second wave recedes, taking pressure off the healthcare infrastructure, India still leads the global tally for active COVID-19 cases. On 2 July 2021, India reported a grim total of approximately 400,312 fatalities owing to the pandemic. Roughly a half of these were reported during the second wave.

The ASHA line of defence

Part of the first line of defence against the pandemic, more than 10 lakh (1 million) Accredited Social Health Activist (ASHA) workers were called on to act as an interface between the community and the public health system, and provide healthcare support services. A dangerous assignment, their work included visiting the communities, ensuring that people did not break their quarantine, bringing medicines and supplies, and taking care of the palliative needs of those who had tested positive.

5 MOST AFFECTED STATES (AS ON 23 JUNE 2021)

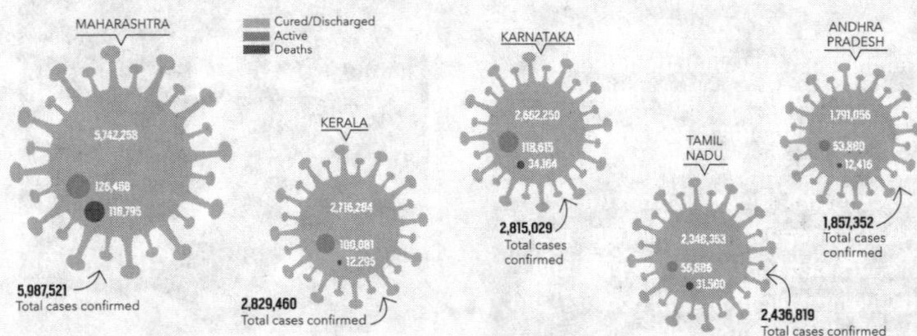

Source: Ministry of Health and Family Welfare

Care and Compassion during the Pandemic

Into the virtual world

With people all over the country and the world under lockdowns, communication over phone and video calls became the next best thing for social interaction. Since the crisis hit, people started connecting in new social ways in the virtual world, whether it be work-related meetings, hosting reunions with friends, playing games such as ludo for hours on end, and even getting married over video.

Healthcare volunteers trained for COVID-19

The New Delhi District Administration, with the support of the Delhi Medical Council, trained 12,000 *swasthyadoots* or community-based healthcare workers to reduce the burden on doctors and medical professionals during the COVID-19 pandemic. The 17 days of training from 27 June to 14 July 2020 covered the human anatomy, vital monitoring and pulse oximeter, and the use of thermal scanners and digital blood-pressure measuring instruments. Selected from the resident population, volunteers were also trained for record-keeping and telecommunication with doctors, and psychological counselling.

Free distribution of bird feeders

Sunny Amitbhai Shah from Ahmedabad, Gujarat, designed colourful bird feeders from 15 kg oil tins and distributed 120 such feeders free of cost in order to beautify gardens, and inspire people to provide water and grains to birds during the pandemic. His mission for helping thirsty birds during summer took about a month from 25 May to 27 June 2020, an undertaking in which he was assisted by Hemraj Padhiyar, Malav Shodhan, Ashani Shah and Kavmil Gandhi, among others. The feeder has five sections: the central part for holding water and the four sides for holding grain.

DEFENCE

ARMY

PERSONNEL

First Indian commander-in-chief

General (later field marshal in 1986) K.M. Cariappa (1899–1993) took over from the British commander-in-chief (C-in-C), General Sir Roy Bucher, on 15 January 1949 and held office till 14 January 1953. The only other C-in-C was General M. Rajendra Sinhji Jadeja, who took over as the first chief of army staff (CoAS) in April 1955, after which the post of C-in-C was abolished.

First field marshal

S.H.F.J. (Sam) Manekshaw, the then general, became field marshal in 1973. He was honoured with the Padma Bhushan in 1968 and the Padma Vibhushan in 1972.

First chief of integrated defence staff

On 1 October 2001, Lieutenant General Pankaj Joshi was appointed the first chief of integrated defence staff (CIDS) in the country, reporting to General Sundararajan Padmanabhan, chairman of the Chief of Staff Committee at the time.

First commissioned officer

Major General K. Bhagwati Singh (ID I-O-No. 1) passed out of the Indian Military Academy (IMA) in 1934 along with his batchmate (and later field marshal) Sam Manekshaw.

First women in the army

The first batch of 25 women outside the Army Medical Corps (AMC) was commissioned in the Indian Army on 6 March 1993 at the Officers Training Academy in Madras (now Chennai), Tamil Nadu. They were inducted into non-combat departments, such as supply, legal, education and logistics.

First chief of defence staff

On 31 December 2019, after demitting office as chief of army staff, General Bipin

New Rule for Service Medals

The protocol to wear medals is laid down in Defence Services Regulation, Regulations for the Army (Revised Edition) 1987. On 11 July 2019, the Ceremonial and Welfare Directorate Adjutant General's Branch of the army passed an order, which allowed the next of kin, including the spouse, children and parents, of deceased decorated soldiers, to wear the medals won by their relative, on the right side of the chest on civilian clothes during homage ceremonies at war memorials, cemeteries and funerals. This is a gesture to honour the services of such soldiers.

Rawat (1958–2021) took over as India's first chief of defence staff (CDS), serving as a tri-services chief and principal military adviser to the defence minister on all matters related to the army, navy and air force. He also headed the Department of Military Affairs created within the Ministry of Defence.

First woman lieutenant general

Dr Punita Arora from Saharanpur, Uttar Pradesh, was promoted to the rank of lieutenant general on 1 September 2004. She was the first woman in any of the four services (army, navy, air force and coast guard) to reach a three-star rank.

First woman to lead the Army Day parade

On 15 January 2019, Lieutenant Bhavana Kasturi of the Army Service Corps (ASC) led a contingent of 144 men at the 71st Army Day parade. The ASC is responsible for logistic support and its contingent was participating in the Army Day parade after 23 years.

Lieutenant Bhavana Kasturi (*in front*): first woman to lead the Army Day parade

First woman parade adjutant

Captain Tania Shergil of the Corps of Signals became the first woman parade adjutant for the Army Day parade in Delhi Cantonment on 15 January and the Republic Day parade on 26 January 2020 down Rajpath. A fourth-generation army professional and a graduate in electronics and communications, she was commissioned into the army in March 2017 after training at the Officer Training Academy, Chennai, Tamil Nadu.

First woman to lead the Daredevils act

Captain Shikha Surabhi led the Daredevils motorcycle display team of the army in a feat that had 33 men riding nine motorcycles in a pyramid formation. Captain Surabhi, on a 350 cc Royal Enfield, saluted the guests while riding a bike during the Republic Day parade in 2019. The team, part of the army's Corps of Signals, holds 24 world records. The entire Daredevils contingent was led by Major Manpreet Singh on that day.

First women in Military Police

On 25 April 2019, the Indian Army issued a formal notification inviting women applicants for the post of soldier – general duty. This was the first time that the army opened its ranks to women for personnel below officer rank (PBOR). The soldiers were to be inducted into the Corps of Military Police (CMP) to investigate offences like theft, molestation and rape. Their portfolio also included assisting civil police and the prevention of breach of regulations by army personnel.

MEDALS AND HONOURS

First Victoria Cross

The first Indian to be awarded the Victoria Cross was Sepoy (later Subedar) Khuda Dad Khan of the 129 Baluchis, on 31 October 1914, for gallantry at Hollebeke, Belgium, in the First World War.

Youngest to receive the Victoria Cross

At nineteen, Sepoy Kamal Ram of the Royal Indian Army was the youngest Indian to receive the Victoria Cross in 1944. Born in Bholupura Village of Karauli District, Rajasthan, he was with the 3rd Battalion of the 8th Punjab Regiment during the Second World War.

First George Cross

Havildar Nandlal Thapa of Gurkha Rifles received the George Cross in 1935 for exceptional courage and devotion to duty. He was about 32 years old at the time, and was serving in the 2nd Battalion of the 8th Gurkha Rifles.

First prisoner of war and first Kirti Chakra recipient

Flying Officer Ulrich Anthony D'Cruz, whose aircraft was shot down by ground fire on 1 December 1947 in the 1947–48 Kashmir war, was taken prisoner by Pathan tribesmen and later by the Pakistan Army, and released after a year. He was awarded the Kirti Chakra in 1952 for bravery during captivity.

First Param Vir Chakra

Major Somnath Sharma, heading a detachment of the Kumaon Regiment at Badgam, Jammu and Kashmir, laid down his life in the effort to save Srinagar city and airport from a Pakistani attack during the Kashmir operations in 1947. He received the award posthumously in 1950.

First Ashok Chakra

Naik Nar Bahadur Thapa of 5 Gurkha Rifles was awarded the Ashok Chakra Class

India's Gift to Bangladesh

The Indian Army gifted 20 military horses and 10 mine detection dogs, trained by the Remount and Veterinary Corps, to the Bangladesh Army in November 2020. Personnel from the Bangladesh Army were also trained in handling and training the equines and canines. The delegation of the Indian Army was led by Major General Narinder Singh Khroud, chief of staff of Brahmastra Corps, and the Bangladesh Army was led by Major General Mohammad Humayun Kabir, commanding the Jessore-based division. Brigadier J.S. Cheema from the Indian high commission in Dhaka was also present at the ceremony, which was held at the Petrapole–Benapole Integrated Check Post on the India–Bangladesh border. The gesture was made in an endeavour to strengthen the ties between the two armies and the two nations.

I (now Ashok Chakra). On 15 September 1948, during the Hyderabad police action, as the No. 2 Platoon of the A Company came under fire on the banks of the River Tungabhadra, he dashed across the 100-yard open ground and single-handedly silenced the gun crew.

India is among the top five troop contributors to UN missions, with a deployment of 6,000 personnel.

First Republic Day commander and first army officer to receive the Padma Bhushan

The first Republic Day parade, featuring interservice contingents from the army, navy, air force and police forces, was held on 26 January 1950, and was commanded by Brigadier (later Lieutenant General) Joginder Singh Dhillon, a Bengal Sapper. On 24 November 1965, he was awarded the Padma Bhushan, becoming the first Indian Army officer to receive it.

First Indian peacekeeper to win the United Nations Military Gender Advocate Award

Major Suman Gawani, an Indian Army officer, was awarded the UN Military Gender Advocate of the Year award on 29 May 2020 in a virtual ceremony, becoming the first Indian peacekeeper to receive the honour. She previously served as a peacekeeper in a UN mission in South Sudan (UNMISS) in 2019.

UNITS

First artillery company

- The first artillery company was raised temporarily in 1748 in colonial India with Indian troops, and was called the Gun Lascars.
- A company of Bombay Artillery, which still exists as 5 Bombay Mountain Battery, was raised on 28 September 1827, which is celebrated as Gunners' Day.

First artillery unit

On 15 January 1935, A Field Brigade (now 1 Field Regiment SP), with four batteries of horse-drawn guns, was raised at Bangalore (now Bengaluru, Karnataka). This date was adopted by the Regiment of Artillery as its birthday.

First administrative unit

The Army Service Corps (ASC) was established in 1748 when Stringer Lawrence, commander-in-chief in India, appointed Robert Clive as commissary. It was formally set up in 1760 in the Bengal, Madras and Bombay Presidencies, and became a formal Supply and Transport Corps in 1901. The ASC was the oldest administrative component of the East India Company and was then known as the Commissariat.

Oldest infantry brigade

5 Mountain Brigade was raised in September 1939. Deployed in the Along sector of Arunachal Pradesh, its area of responsibility comprises a frontage of more than 460 km.

Rajnath Singh *(left)* and Suh Wook

Indo-Korean Friendship Park Inaugurated

To commemorate the contribution of the Indian peacekeeping forces during the Korean War of 1950–53, a Indo-Korean Friendship Park was inaugurated on 26 March 2021. It was jointly inaugurated by Defence Minister Rajnath Singh and the Minister of National Defence of South Korea, Suh Wook, at Delhi Cantonment.

Oldest infantry unit
Raised on 4 August 1768, the 1 Maratha Light Infantry or Jangi Paltan is the only unit that does not hang captured enemy flags upside down in its mess. It is also the only unit that was in constant battle for 20 years after it was raised, and in this duration it earned 18 battle honours and five theatre honours.

First cavalry unit
The first Indian cavalry unit was raised in 1787 as 5 Regiment of Madras Native Cavalry. It became 1 Regiment in 1788 under Major Tonyn. Renamed 26 Light Cavalry in 1903, it was amalgamated with 30 Lancers in 1922 and became the 8th Light Cavalry.

First cavalry regiment
The first cavalry regiment before Independence, the Scinde Horse, was raised in 1838 as the Scinde Irregular Horse by Captain Ward in Hyderabad (in Sind, now in Pakistan) under the command of Captain John Jacob. It last paraded its horses in April 1938 at Rawalpindi (now in Pakistan).

First rifle regiment
The rifle regiment as a tactical unit was introduced in 1841 and the first such unit was the 4 Bombay Native Infantry, which till 1947 was 1 Battalion of Rajputana Rifles and is now 3 Guard. They were issued Enfield muzzle-loaders and 577 bullets.

Oldest field army
The Southern Command, headquartered in Poona (now Pune), Maharashtra, was raised on 1 April 1895. As India's oldest field army, it has participated in many operations, including humanitarian assistance and disaster relief missions.

First tri-services affiliation
Bengal Sappers has been affiliated with the Indian Navy and Indian Air Force since 2002. Originally known as the Bengal Sappers and Miners, and headquartered in Roorkee (now in Uttarakhand), it has won 80 battle honours and 11 theatre honours.

First Special Operations Division
India's first Special Operations Division was announced on 15 May 2019. At its peak, this tri-services division will have around 3,000 commandos from the Indian

Army's special forces, the Indian Air Force's Garud force and the Indian Navy's Marcos commando units. The raising is the first step for counterterrorism operations. Major General A.K. Dhingra, from the 1 Para Special Forces Regiment, is the first chief of the division.

EQUIPMENT

First gun foundry

The Board of Ordnance was constituted in April 1775, but it took 27 years to establish a factory at Cossipore in Calcutta (now Kolkata, West Bengal) on 18 March 1802 as the Gun Carriage Agency. In 1830, it was renamed the Gun Foundry and, in 1905, this name was changed to the Gun and Shell Factory. This is the first ordnance factory to have received ISO 9001: 2000 certification.

First and oldest extant armament checker

The Proof and Experimental Establishment in Chandipur in present-day Odisha, called the Proof Department, was set up on 7 November 1895. It has been associated with major armament developments. Included under the Defence Research and Development Organization (DRDO) in 1958, it had Lieutenant Colonel B.N. Mitra as its first Indian director.

First rifle factory

A rifle factory, set up at Ichhapore, Bengal (now Ishapore, West Bengal), began production on 20 September 1904. It produced the .303-inch Bolt action rifles in large quantities for the First and Second World Wars.

Record Rewind

Most decorated regiment

1991

The Sikh Regiment had to its credit the highest number of gallantry awards: two Ashoka Chakras, 14 Maha Vir Chakras and 58 Vir Chakras, among other decorations.

2020

The Sikh Regiment has to its credit the highest number of gallantry awards, i.e., 1,652. These include two Param Vir Chakras, eight Maha Vir Chakras, 64 Vir Chakras, and four Ashok Chakras, among other decorations.

Earliest tanks

The first three tanks of the Indian Army were two varieties of Medium-D tanks brought in 1920 before Indian independence. Fifty Vickers Mk II-B light tanks were acquired for use in India in 1933.

First indigenous tank

The first military tank that was made in India, named Vijayanta, rolled out of the assembly line on 12 December 1965 at the Heavy Vehicles Factory in Avadi in Madras (now Chennai, Tamil Nadu). It entered service on 29 December 1965.

First flying spy

Unmanned aerial vehicles (UAVs) were used first in the Kargil conflict in 1999 to detect the movement of enemy troops and locate bunkers. UAVs were brought in

First Original Martial Tune

'Shankhnaad' (the call of the conch shell), a military tune eulogizing the valour of Mahar soldiers, was played officially for the first time at the Republic Day parade in 2019. It is the first original martial tune of India and is based on Indian classical music. It has been composed by Brigadier Vivek Sohal (retd) and Dr (Mrs) Tanuja Nafde.

to counter Pakistan's Gultari guns and the US-made AN/TPQ-36-37 gun-locating radars.

First indigenous armoured personnel carrier

In 1987, the first BMP-2 infantry fighting vehicle, Sarath, was assembled at the ordnance factory at Shankarapally, Andhra Pradesh (now in Telangana), from Soviet-supplied components. Sarath went indigenous in 1991.

First indigenous training simulator

On 20 February 2002, the Simulator Development Division, Secunderabad (now in Telangana), introduced the aiming training simulator (ATS) for infantry combat vehicles.

First indigenous revolver

In 2002, the research and development wing of the Ishapore Rifle Factory in Barrackpore, near Kolkata in West Bengal, after 24 months of research, developed

First E-Cars for the Army

On 1 July 2019, the Indian Army launched e-cars (or electric cars) for its staff in New Delhi. The cars were launched with help from Energy Efficiency Services Ltd (EESL), a joint venture of Central PSUs under the Ministry of Power. This initiative is in keeping with government policies to protect the environment. The first batch of 10 e-cars was flagged off by the Quartermaster General, Lieutenant General Gopal R. These electric cars not only cut down on emissions that harm the environment but are also more economical and efficient.

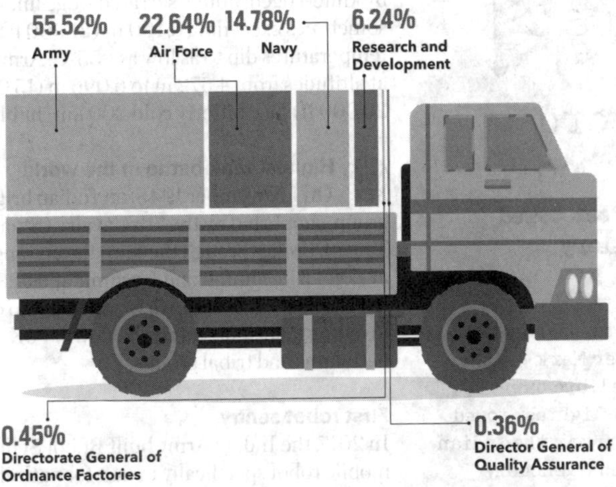

Source: *Annual Report 2018–19*, Ministry of Defence, Government of India; percentages may not add up to 100 due to rounding off at source.

a low-cost and high-tech revolver, which weighs barely 380 g. The .22-in. automatic had a range of 20 m (65 ft 7 in.).

Longest-range nuclear missile

On 26 December 2016, India successfully test-fired Agni-V, a surface-to-surface nuclear-capable missile with the longest range, from Abdul Kalam Island off the Odisha coast. Designed and developed by DRDO, this 17 m (55 ft 9 in.) long missile can carry a nuclear warhead of about 1.5 tonnes reportedly over 5,000–8,000 km. India is the sixth country after France, China, Russia, the USA and the UK to have a missile with a range of over 5,000 km.

First bulletproof helmets

In July 2017, the army obtained bulletproof helmets for the first time. The 1.2 kg to 1.4 kg lightweight helmets are being made in Kanpur, Uttar Pradesh, by MKU Systems, which is manufacturing them for the Indian Army for the first time. It has earlier manufactured them for the UN and the North Atlantic Treaty Organization (NATO) forces.

First indigenously manufactured bulletproof vests

Shantanu Bhowmik, professor at the Department of Aerospace Engineering at the School of Engineering, Amrita University, Coimbatore, Tamil Nadu, designed the first indigenous bulletproof vest for the armed forces in 2017. The 20-layer vest, made with indigenous ultramodern lightweight thermoplastic technology, is being developed in collaboration with DRDO. The vest is effective up to a temperature of 57°C and weighs 1.5 kg compared to the earlier jacket, which weighed 15 kg.

Record Rewind

Lightest towed artillery

1994

The 75 mm pack gun/ howitzer Mark 1 with a 24-calibre barrel was the lightest towed artillery in the Indian Army. Indigenously designed by Brigadier Gurdial Singh, it could be carried on mules or jeeps, or slung under helicopters. It had a striking range of 11 km.

2018

On 18 May 2017, the Indian Army received the first batch of two M-777 A-2 ultralight howitzers (ULH) from the USA. These ULHs, with a maximum range of 30 km, manufactured by BAE Systems, were test-fired in Pokhran, Rajasthan. The 155 mm, 39-calibre guns are equipped to fire Indian ammunition.

Highest battleground

Siachen is a 76.8 km river of ice abutted by knife-edged, fluted, serrated ridge lines, sometimes exceeding 6,400 m (21,000 ft) where temperatures dip to as low as −55°C. Army posts at altitudes from 4,572 m to 6,096 m (15,000 ft to 20,000 ft) face bitterly cold 200 km/hr blizzards.

Highest tank battle in the world

On 1 November 1948, an Indian brigade group, supported by the 7th Cavalry (Stuart Tanks), broke through the Himalayan range at Zoji La in Jammu and Kashmir at 3,528 m (11,575 ft) in order to drive out a group of invading Pakistanis intermixed with PoK battalions and tribal groups.

First robot sentry

In 2017, the Indian Army built Robot Sentry, a mobile robot specifically meant for patrolling and surveillance applications in urban campuses of the army. Another robot, the Snake, has 14 active joints for lateral undulation, sidewinding and rolling. These help the robot to navigate difficult passages.

First Dhanush guns

On 26 March 2019, the Ordnance Factory Board handed over the first batch of Dhanush, the first indigenous 155 mm, 45-calibre artillery gun, to the Central Ordnance Depot, Jabalpur, Madhya Pradesh. Dhanush is the first indigenous artillery gun in this calibre. The medium-calibre towed guns, indigenized to 81 per cent, will be deployed along the China and Pakistan borders.

First indigenous sniper rifles

SSS Defence, a major defence manufacturer based in Bengaluru, Karnataka, has developed the country's first indigenous sniper rifle prototypes with 7.62 mm x 51 mm calibre and .338 Lapua magnum platforms. The barrel length ranges from 20 to 24 inches based on use environments and specific missions.

OPERATIONS

First heli-lifted battalion

The First Guards (2 Punjab), raised in 1762 as 10 Battalion of the Coastal Sepoys and redesignated 18 times since, was heli-lifted during the counter-insurgency operations in Nagaland during 1969–70.

First heli-borne operations

In 1971, the Indian Army used helicopters to capture the 7,000-strong Sylhet garrison in East Pakistan (now Bangladesh). The 5 Gurkha Rifles (Frontier Force), which were led by Major M.M. Malik, landed with the first sortie of seven helicopters at Mirpara on the banks of the River Surma.

First para-regiment in action

The 17 Para Field Regiment supported operations at Tangail in Bangladesh in 1971 by sending 49 Para Field Battery, a sub-unit of the regiment along with 2 Para.

First use of air cavalry

In May 2018, during Exercise Vijay Prahar in the Mahajan Firing Range near Suratgarh, Rajasthan, Indian troops worked on the first use of the concept of air cavalry unleashed by the US Army in Vietnam during 1955–73. In these operations, weaponized attack helicopters carried out combined action against the 'enemy' in coordination with tanks and mechanized ground forces, while conventionally helicopters are called in only when ground forces cannot neutralize ground targets. This requires very precise coordination but speeds up the operation.

GENERAL

First army veterinary school

A veterinary school was started at Kirkee in Poona (now Pune) District, Maharashtra, in 1862, for officers and men of artillery, cavalry and mounted police. Similar schools also came up in Hapur (1877, now in Uttar Pradesh), Lahore (1882, now in Pakistan), Ambala (1889, now in Haryana) and Simla (1891, now Shimla in Himachal Pradesh).

First military dog school

The War Dog Training School was opened in 1959 at the Indian Army Remount and Veterinary Corps Centre and School (now RVC Centre and School) in Meerut, Uttar Pradesh. Training for avalanche rescue operations began here in September 1976.

First military intelligence school

Opened in Karachi (now in Pakistan) on 20 January 1945, the first military intelligence school moved to Mhow (Dr Ambedkar Nagar) in Madhya Pradesh, and was renamed the Intelligence Corps Training School and Depot. On 29 February 1984, its name was changed to Military Intelligence Training School and Depot.

First board of ordnance

The Board of Ordnance was set up in 1775 at Fort William, Calcutta (now Kolkata, West Bengal). Currently, the Indian Ordnance Factories organization – a set of 41 ordnance factories under the aegis of its corporate headquarters, the Ordnance

Highest Jump by a Dog

Known for its agility and the power to negotiate any obstacles, the Mudhol hound – a native Indian dog breed, trained in the army – created a new record. Tiger, an army dog, upon showing great promise, was put into the regimen of high jumps. Having a flair for running, apart from enjoying his agility jumps and raised hurdles, he cleared a 165 cm (5 ft 5 in.) high jump in 2018, the highest by a dog. This talent among dogs is an asset to the army in situations such as a hostage crisis, housebreaking drills, or scaling hurdles and walls, when required.

Factory Board (OFB), Kolkata – has more than 200 years of experience in the development and marketing of a range of land, sea and air defence systems. At present, the OFB has nine training institutes, three regional marketing centres and four regional controllers of safety under it.

First counter-insurgency school
The Counter-Insurgency and Jungle Warfare School was established at Mynkre, Meghalaya, in 1967. It was relocated to Vairengte in Mizoram on 1 May 1970.

First high-altitude warfare school
Instituted as a formation ski school at Gulmarg, Jammu and Kashmir, the High Altitude Warfare School came into being on 8 April 1962. The courses at this institute include those on skiing and mountaineering.

Longest bridge built during war
The Indo-Pakistan war in 1971, termed the Sappers War, saw the construction of a 421.8 m (1,384 ft) composite bridge across River Madhumati in East Pakistan (now Bangladesh) in a matter of 34 hours. It was the longest 'war' bridge to be constructed by India after the Second World War and the longest operational bridge constructed during a war involving India.

First nuclear shelter
The Defence Research and Development Organization (DRDO), the Pune-based research and development laboratory, introduced an integrated battlefield shelter for all three services in 2002 to withstand nuclear or chemical strikes for up to 96 hours. The portable shelter, 28 m (91 ft 10 in.) long and with a diameter of 2.5 m (8 ft 2 in.), had chemical toilets, water tanks, pumps for sewage disposal and two power generators. It could accommodate 30 people and could be used as a command post, an observation post and a communication centre.

First National War Memorial
The armed forces first proposed a National War Memorial way back in 1960. On 25 February 2019, the memorial, designed by the Chennai-based WeBe Design Lab, led by Yogesh Chandrahasan, was inaugurated near India Gate, New Delhi.

MAJOR OPERATIONS OF THE INDIAN ARMY: LAST THREE DECADES

Here's a glimpse of the important military and humanitarian operations of the Indian Army between 1990 and 2020:

Operation	Type
Operation Rakshak – **1990** onwards	Counter-insurgency
Operation Rhino – **1990:** Assam	Counter-insurgency
Operation Golden Bird – **1995:** India and Myanmar	Counter-insurgency
Kargil War/Operation Vijay – **1999:** Jammu and Kashmir (now Ladakh)	Counter-insurgency
Operation Parakram – **2001:** Punjab, and Jammu and Kashmir	Counter-insurgency
Operation Sarp Vinash – **2003:** Jammu and Kashmir	Counter-insurgency
Operations Ganga Prahar and Surya Hope – **2013:** Uttarakhand	Flood rescue and relief
Operation All Out – **2015:** Jammu and Kashmir	Counter-insurgency/ terrorism
Operation Maitri – **2015:** Nepal	Earthquake rescue and relief
Operation Dhangu Suraksha – **2016:** Punjab	Counter-insurgency
Operation Sahyog – **2018:** Kerala	Flood rescue and relief
Operation Randori Behak – **2020:** Jammu and Kashmir	Counter-insurgency
Operation Namaste – **2020**	Pan-army to tackle COVID-19 exigencies

Covering over 40 acres (16.2 hectares), it has names of Indian soldiers martyred in 1947–48 (Kashmir), 1961 (Goa), 1962 (China), 1965 and 1971 (Pakistan), 1987 (Siachen), 1987–88 (Sri Lanka), 1999 (Kargil) and other operations. It has concentric circles, with the Amar Chakra (Circle of Immortality) and an Eternal Flame in the centre. Around it are the Veerta Chakra (Circle of Bravery), a gallery depicting iconic battles and the Rakshak Chakra (Circle of Protection). The circles represent the *chakravyuh* or traditional Indian war formation. The Param Yodha Sthal has busts of 21 recipients of the Param Vir Chakra.

First Indian dog breed in active duty

The Indian Army began to use dogs for active duty in 1959, the preferred breeds being the Labrador retriever, the Great Swiss Mountain dogs and the German

Oldest Known US Aircraft Wreckage Recovered

On 30 March 2019, the Indian Army recovered a wreckage of a Second World War vintage US Air Force aircraft in Arunachal Pradesh's Roing District. The army was told about it by a group of trekkers. Thereafter, a 12-member army patrol and a representative of the local police went ahead to look for it, scouring more than 30 km of difficult terrain. The wreckage was covered by thick undergrowth and buried under 1.5 m (5 ft) of snow. Over 400 American soldiers are believed to have gone missing during the Second World War while aircraft tried to cross the treacherous region. The wreckage will provide important information about the war.

shepherd. In 2017, the Remount and Veterinary Corps introduced the first Indian breed, the Mudhol hound (or caravan hound), a sight hound used as a hunting hound first in Central Asia and later in the Deccan region, especially Karnataka. It is known for its courage, incredible speed and loyalty.

First Bactrian camels join the army

The double-humped Bactrian camel is native to high-altitude cold deserts and comfortable in such environs. Since February 2017, this camel was put through its paces at the Defence Institute of High Altitude Research (DIHAR), a DRDO laboratory in Leh, Ladakh. Bactrian camels are used to patrol the Line of Actual Control (LAC) in Ladakh and carry loads for the army.

Biggest mountain assault exercise

On 7 October 2019, the Indian Army and Indian Air Force began Exercise Him Vijay about 100 km on the Indian side from the Line of Actual Control in Arunachal Pradesh. It was held in two phases. The first phase ended on 10 October, while the next phase was during 20–24 October. The exercise was held to test mobility, communication and coordination of a vast body of fast-moving troops in difficult terrain to be prepared for a quick and short war. Three battle groups, with about 4,000 soldiers each, participated. With some special forces, they practised mobilization, mountain assault and air assault. Helicopters and craft like the C-17, C-130J Super Hercules and An-32 transferred equipment and personnel to heights of up to 4,572 m (15,000 ft). The exercise checked the preparedness of the new Integrated Battle Groups.

First win at International Scout Masters Competition

Held in India for the first time, the host Indian Army team, trained by Southern Command, won the Fifth Army International Scout Masters Competition (ISMC). Part of the International Army Games, was held at Jaisalmer Military Station, Rajasthan, during 6–14 August 2019 and included five stages of competitions. Participants included teams from the armies of Armenia, Belarus,

DEFENCE EXERCISES (2018–19)

Year and Venue	Name	National/ International
ARMY		
August 2018, Jaisalmer, Rajasthan	Army International Scout Masters Competition	International: eight countries
September 2018, Pune, Maharashtra	MILEX-18	National
November 2018, Mizoram	Ex Dharma Guardian 2018	International: Japan
March 2019, Pune, Maharashtra	Africa–India Field Training Exercise (AFINDEX-19)	International: 17 African nations
8–11 April 2019, Babina Military Station, Madhya Pradesh	Bold Kurukshetra- 2019	International: Singapore
31 August–13 September, Pithoragarh, Uttar Pradesh	KAZIND-2019	International: Singapore
NAVY		
June–July 2018, Andhra Pradesh	Coordinated Patrol (CORPAT) Exercise	International: Bangladesh
January 2019, Coastline and Exclusive Economic Zone of India	Sea Vigil	International: eight countries
AIR FORCE		
March 2018, Southern Air Command, multiple venues	Exercise Samvedna (Humanitarian Assistance and Disaster Relief)	International: Bangladesh, Sri Lanka, the UAE and Myanmar
April 2018, Pakistan and China border	Gaganshakti-2018	National: Indian Army, Indian Air Force and Indian Navy
July–August 2018, Australia	Exercise Pitch Black- 2018	International: Royal Australian Air Force

China, India, Kazakhstan, Russia, Sudan and Uzbekistan. Uzbekistan won the runners-up trophy while Russia was adjudged second runners-up.

Longest bridge on the River Indus

Beginning in early 2019, the Indian Army completed the longest bridge over the River Indus in Leh, Ladakh, in just 40 days, one of the fastest feats in bridge-making in its category. The 79.25 m (260 ft) long cable suspension bridge was named Maitri Bridge to signify the camaraderie between the army and local people. It was inaugurated by war veterans of operations from 1947–48, 1962, 1971 and 1999 in the Ladakh region. It was built by the Corps of Engineers under the XIV Corps (Fire and Fury Corps).

Largest training academy

On 8 June 2019, a total of 459 gentleman cadets passed out of the Indian Military Academy (IMA) at Dehradun, Uttarakhand. Of these, 382 were from India. The rest were from friendly foreign countries including Afghanistan, Bhutan, Maldives, Fiji, Mauritius, Papua New Guinea, Tonga, Lesotho and Tajikistan. With this batch of cadets graduating into officers, the IMA became the largest training organization in India. It has an alumni strength of 61,536 officers. This batch had the highest number, 72, of gentleman cadets from Uttar Pradesh.

First virtual camp

The NCC directorates from different states and regions organized a virtual camp – 'Ek Bharat Shreshtha Bharat'. The NCC Directorates of Maharashtra and Uttarakhand organized the first of these during 6–11 July 2020. Fifty cadets participated in the online camp while ensuring social distancing norms. The camp aimed to aid national integration among NCC cadets.

NAVY

PERSONNEL

First naval pilot

Lieutenant Y.N. Singh of the Royal Indian Navy was deputed to England in 1941 for basic training and later to Canada where he obtained his wings in 1944 before serving in the escort carriers of the Royal Navy in the Second World War.

First commander-in-chief

- The first commander-in-chief of the Royal Indian Navy was Admiral Sir Edward Parry in August 1948.
- Rear Admiral I.T.S. Hall was the first post-Independence commander-in-chief of the Royal Indian Navy. The word 'Royal' was dropped on 26 January 1950.

First chief of naval staff

- Admiral Sir Mark Pizey was the first chief of naval staff in 1955.
- The first Indian chief of naval staff was Vice Admiral R.D. Katari in 1958.

First four-star admiral

Admiral A.K. Chatterji (1914–2001) became a four-star admiral on 1 March 1968. He joined the Royal Indian Marines as a cadet in 1933 and became chief of naval staff in 1966.

First woman maritime reconnaissance pilot

Shubhangi Swaroop became the first woman pilot in the navy who was trained to fly maritime reconnaissance aircraft in 2017. Three other women cadets – Astha Segal, Roopa A. and Sakthi Maya S. – passed out with her in the first batch of women officers from the Indian Naval Academy, Ezhimala, Kerala, on 22 November 2017, and were inducted into the naval armament inspection (NAI) branch. The Indian Navy had inducted its first woman officer in 1991. Its aviation branch had women working as air traffic control officers and as observers in aircraft.

First woman pilot of naval aircraft

On 2 December 2019, 24-year-old Sub-lieutenant Shivangi graduated with two other trainee officers from the Seventh Dornier Conversion Course (DOCC) at Kochi, Kerala. Originally from Muzaffarpur, Bihar, this Short Service Commission pilot entry scheme officer was commissioned into the Indian Navy in June 2018 and underwent a year of flying training at the Air Force Academy (AFA), Dundigal, Telangana, and Indian Naval Air Squadron (INAS) 550 and INS *Garuda* in Kochi. During training, she flew aircraft such as Pilatus PC 7 Mk II, Basic Trainer at AFA before the Dornier Conversion Course.

The Indian Navy had 696 women employees as recorded on 22 March 2021.

First woman sailor

Commissioned on 13 July 1992, Lieutenant Tanuja Chaturvedi of the Logistics Cadre was a Short Service Commission officer up to 12 July 1999.

First woman officers as 'Observers'

Sub-lieutenant Kumudini Tyagi and Sub-lieutenant Riti Singh graduated as 'Observers' (airborne technicians) in the Indian Navy's stream of helicopters to be deployed on warships for short- or long-term missions. They were awarded their wings in a graduation ceremony held at INS *Garuda* on 21 September 2020.

UNITS

First navy air squadron

On 17 June 1959, the Fleet Requirement Unit was commissioned as the Indian Naval Air Squadron 550. INS *Vikrant*, formerly HMS *Hercules*, joined the Indian Navy on 16 February 1961 as the first aircraft carrier and saw action during the Goa liberation struggle in December 1961. The squadron completed 60 years of service in 2019. It has flown 14 types of aircraft, starting with Sealands to the Dornier maritime reconnaissance aircraft flown currently.

First unmanned aerial vehicle squadron

The navy's first unmanned aerial vehicle (UAV) squadron, intended to patrol the seas, was commissioned on 6 January 2006, with 12 UAVs from Israel. The Intensive Flying and Training Units were based in Kochi, Kerala.

Only training command

The Southern Naval Command is the only training command of the Indian Navy. It was augmented by INS *Magar,* which arrived at Kochi, Kerala, on 10 April 2018 to join the first Training Squadron for sea training of officers.

First exclusive naval base

INS *Kadamba,* inaugurated on 31 May 2005 near Karwar in Karnataka, is

India's third operational naval base after Mumbai and Visakhapatnam, and the first under the sole control of the navy. Signifying another first, the inauguration was read out in Sanskrit. Sanctioned in 1985 as Project Seabird, its foundation stone was laid in 1986.

EQUIPMENT

First diesel engine ship

Hugh Lindsay, a 411-tonne steamship of the Bombay Marine Corps, left Bombay (now Mumbai), Maharashtra, on 20 March 1830 and reached the Suez Canal after 21 days, averaging just over 6 knots.

First cruiser and flagship

HMS *Achilles*, a 7,030-tonne battleship, formerly of the Royal Navy, was commissioned as HMIS *Delhi* on 5 July 1948 in England, and became the first cruiser and flagship of the Indian Navy. It arrived at Bombay (now Mumbai, Maharashtra) on 15 September 1948. HMIS *Delhi* (renamed INS *Delhi*) was 169.1 m (554 ft 9 in.) long and 16.77 m (55 ft) across its beam, with a maximum speed of 32 knots. Its armaments included six 152 mm guns, eight 102 mm guns, fifteen 40 mm guns, four anti-aircraft three-pounders and eight torpedo tubes.

The Indian Navy had developed 23 major equipment/systems and over 4,500 components indigenously for their ships and submarines by 1 January 2021.

First missile boat

INS *Vinash*, a Soviet OSA 1 commissioned on 21 January 1971, was fitted with four SS-N-2A surface-to-surface missiles and four 30 mm guns. With a complement of 30 crew, it could reach speeds exceeding 35 knots.

First submarine depot ship

INS *Amba*, an ex-Soviet Ugra-class ship with a displacement of 6,750 tonnes, is a submarine tender and was commissioned on 28 December 1968. INS *Amba* has two cranes (6 tonnes and 10 tonnes) and it can accommodate 750 personnel.

First indigenous patrol boat

Godavari-class frigate INS *Ajay*, commissioned on 21 September 1960, is a front-line warship equipped with missiles, guns and anti-submarine equipment, as well as early warning navigation and electronic warfare systems. Built by Garden Reach Shipbuilders & Engineers (GRSE) Ltd, it could carry two Sea King helicopters.

First submarine base

On 19 May 1971, INS *Virbahu*, the Indian Navy's first submarine base, was commissioned near Visakhapatnam, Andhra Pradesh.

First submarine rescue ship

INS *Nistar* was converted from a fleet minesweeper to a submarine rescue ship and commissioned on 29 March 1971. An ex-Soviet Valday-class ship, it features a diving bell, a recompression chamber, two rescue chambers and a lift of 10 tonnes.

First indigenous submarine

INS *Shalki,* the first of SSK Type-1500 submarines, built at Mazagon Dock Ltd, Bombay (now Mumbai), Maharashtra, was commissioned in February 1992. It has a displacement of 1,450 tonnes and carries 14 AEG SUT torpedoes.

First nuclear submarine

INS *Chakra,* the navy's first nuclear-powered submarine belonging to the Victor 1 SSN class had a speed of 32 knots and a dive displacement of 5,000 tonnes. It carried 90 sailors. On lease from the USSR, it was commissioned on 3 February 1988 and sent back in 1991.

First missile corvette

INS *Kora,* the first indigenously built missile corvette, was commissioned on 10 August 1998. Capable of operating in nuclear, biological and chemical confrontation zones, it had a displacement of 1,300 tonnes and an overall length of 91.16 m (299 ft). INS *Kora* had two indigenous fuel-efficient diesel engines and could touch 26 knots. Equipped with a helipad for advanced light helicopters and Chetaks, it had a complement of 11 officers and 110 sailors.

INS *Kora*: first missile corvette

First indigenous modern warship

INS *Nilgiri,* which was commissioned on 3 June 1972, was the first modern warship built at Mazagon Dock Ltd, Mumbai, Maharashtra. INS *Nilgiri,* based on the British Leander-class frigates, had a hangar with a telescopic extension to take Alouette III helicopters. It was decommissioned on 31 May 1996.

First ocean minesweepers

INS *Pondicherry* and INS *Porbandar,* built at the Isora Yard, Leningrad, Russia, were given to the Indian Navy in 1978. These Natya-1-class sweepers have steel hulls with active mine detection sonars.

First dedicated cadet training ship

INS *Tir* (A86), named after HMIS *Tir,* a River-class frigate of the Royal Indian Navy that had served in the Second World War as HMS *Bann* (K256), was the first dedicated cadet-training ship built at Mazagon Dock Ltd. It was the senior ship of the First Training Squadron under the Southern Naval Command. Commissioned on 21 February 1986, it carried a complement of 120 cadets and 20 instructors.

First anti-ship missile

On 2 March 2017, the first anti-ship missile was fired from an indigenously built Kalvari-class submarine, the first in a series of Scorpene-class submarines being built in India. The submarine was stationed in the Arabian Sea and the missile successfully hit a surface target.

First fast attacker

INFAC-T-80 (Indian Navy's extra-fast attack craft), commissioned at the Naval Dockyard in Mumbai, Maharashtra, on 24 June 1998, was the first fast-attack high-speed vessel and the first of an Indo-Israeli defence project. This aluminium-hull vessel could sustain 45 knots and it was the smallest ship in the Indian Navy.

First multi-warships

INS *Talwar* was launched in May 2000, INS *Trishul* in November 2000 and INS *Tabar* in May 2001. These Talwar-class guided missile frigates were designed and built by Russia.

First indigenous fleet replenishment tanker

INS *Aditya*, built by GRSE, Kolkata, West Bengal, was commissioned at Visakhapatnam, Andhra Pradesh, on 3 April 2000. Manned by 16 officers and 140 sailors, the 172 m (564 ft) long fleet tanker has a deadweight tonnage of 1,700. It can touch a speed of 24 knots with an endurance of 10,000 nautical miles, and load six ships simultaneously on the high seas. It also carries a Sea King helicopter. Captain Vimal Narayan was the first commanding officer of the ship.

First Integrated Automatic Aviation Meteorological System

On 28 March 2017, the then chief of naval staff, Admiral Sunil Lanba, inaugurated the first Integrated Automatic Aviation Meteorological System (IAAMS) at INS *Rajali* (informally also known as the Arakkonam naval air station) in Tamil Nadu. The IAAMS has been established with the objective of modernizing the meteorological infrastructure and aviation safety of the nine naval air stations of the Indian Navy through automated monitoring of weather.

First Aircraft Carrier Dry Dock

On 28 September 2019, the first aircraft carrier dry dock was inaugurated at the Naval Dockyard in Mumbai, Maharashtra. The largest dry dock of the Indian Navy, it can accommodate INS *Vikramaditya* (IAC-I), the indigenous aircraft carrier under construction at Cochin Shipyard Ltd and ships with a tonnage of up to 90,000 tonnes. Started in 2010, the completed dock is 281 m (921 ft 11 in.) long, 45 m (147 ft 8 in.) wide and 17 m (55 ft 9 in.) deep. Unlike most dry docks that are made by excavating the land, this one is built into the sea, for which 38 caissons or watertight steel sections drained out seawater before construction could begin.

THE INDIAN NAVY AND ITS INDIGENOUS FLEET

The Indian Navy has a mix of domestic and imported equipment as part of its active fleet. Dedicated efforts towards modernization and self-sufficiency have led to many made-in-India ships and vessels becoming part of the fleet. Here's a look at all the warships commissioned in the last three decades and recently in active duty.

	Year of Commissioning	Name of the Ship/Vessel
1	1990	INS *Ajay;* INS *Kuthar;* INS *Akshay*
2	1991	INS *Kirpan;* INS *Vibhuti;* INS *Khanjar*
3	1992	INS *Vipul*
4	1993	INS *Vinash*
5	1994	INS *Shankul;* INS *Nashak*
6	1995	INS *Vidyut*
7	1997	INS *Prahar;* INS *Gharial;* INS *Delhi*
8	1998	INS *Kora*
9	1999	INS *Mysore*
10	2000	INS *Brahmaputra*
11	2001	INS *Mumbai;* INS *Kirch;* INS *Kulish*
12	2002	INS *Prabal;* INS *Pralaya*
13	2004	INS *Karmuk;* INS *Betwa*
14	2005	INS *Beas*
15	2007	INS *Shardul*
16	2008	INS *Kesari*
17	2009	INS *Airavat*
18	2010	INS *Shivalik*
19	2011	INS *Satpura*
20	2012	INS *Sahyadri*
21	2014	INS *Kolkata;* INS *Kamorta*
22	2015	INS *Kochi*
23	2016	INS *Kadmatt;* INS *Arihant;* INS *Chennai*
24	2017	INS *Kiltan;* INS *Kalvari*
25	2019	INS *Khanderi*
26	2020	INS *Kavaratti*

Largest aircraft carrier

INS *Viraat*, commissioned on 12 May 1987 at Devonport, UK, is the second and largest aircraft carrier of the Indian Navy. The 28,700 tonne INS *Viraat* (R-22), formerly called HMS *Hermes*, was launched in 1953 as the flagship of the South Atlantic Task Force in the Falklands War in 1982. The Indian Navy is among only eight navies in the world to have aircraft carriers.

Record Rewind

Shortest tenure as chief of naval staff

1990

Oscar Stanley Dawson, PVSM, AVSM, ADC, was appointed chief of naval staff on 1 March 1982 and left office on 30 November 1984. He served the office for 2 years and 275 days.

2014

Devendra Kumar Joshi, PVSM, AVSM, YSM, was appointed for the post on 31 August 2012 and left office on 26 February 2014, serving for one year and 180 days.

First 'green' ship

In February 2017, the survey vessel INS *Sarvekshak*, based at the Southern Naval Command in Kochi, Kerala, became India's first naval ship to go green by installing a zero-maintenance solar power system that can generate 5.4 kW of electricity. It replaces the ship's emergency diesel alternator. The customized power-generating system has flexible, razor-thin solar panels on the canopy of the retractable helicopter deck, which use no-fume solid electrolyte batteries and are maintenance-free for 24 years. The solar-power-generating system can be used to run communication equipment and on-board lights, and charge batteries. With an annual carbon emission of 60,225 kg, it will replace about 22,995 litres of diesel.

Longest serving warship/aircraft carrier

INS *Viraat* – the second Centaur-class aircraft carrier in service – served India for 30 years after 27 years of service in the Royal Navy of the UK as HMS *Hermes*. The UK Royal Navy commissioned it in 1959 and it was later sold to the Indian Navy in 1986. It was decommissioned on 6 March 2017.

GENERAL

First modern shipbuilder

In 1736, the East India Company invited Lowji Nusserwanji Wadia to build the first shipyard in Bombay (now Mumbai, Maharashtra). Since then, seven generations of the Wadias have built ships, including HMS *Minden* (the first constructed outside of Great Britain), HMS *Trincomalee* and HMS *Cornwallis*.

First modern shipbuilding yard

Garden Reach Shipbuilders & Engineers (GRSE) Ltd, located on the eastern bank of the River Hooghly in present-day Kolkata, West Bengal, dates to 1884. The company's name was changed to Garden Reach Workshop in 1916 and on 1 April 1960, it was taken over by the Government of India. The name of the company was again changed back to Garden Reach Shipbuilders & Engineers on 1 January 1977. It builds a range of ships from warships to sophisticated commercial vessels, harbour craft to fast, powerful patrol vessels for the Indian Navy and the Indian Coast Guard. It built INS *Ajay*, India's first indigenous patrol boat, in 1960.

First naval dockyard

The Naval Dockyard at Bombay (now Mumbai, Maharashtra) started with the

Colour Awarded to INS *Shivaji*

On 13 February 2020, President Ram Nath Kovind awarded the President's Colour to INS *Shivaji*, Lonavala, the highest honour on a military unit. The establishment, which has served the nation for 75 years, training marine engineers, both officers and sailors of the Indian Navy, the Indian Coast Guard and foreign navies, was commanded by Commodore Ravnish Seth. Through more than 500 courses that include marine engineering, nuclear, biological and chemical defence with damage control and firefighting, among others, it trains more than 2,800 officers and 7,800 sailors annually. Henceforth, the President's Colour will be carried at all ceremonial parades at INS *Shivaji*.

Bunder Pier in 1693. A tiny dry dock was constructed in 1750. The old Bombay Dock and the Duncan Dock were built in 1765 and 1810, respectively. A wet basin was constructed in 1892. The largest naval dockyard today, it is the premier maintenance facility for ships and submarines of the navy.

First naval school
The Signal School on INS *Venduruthy* was established at Mumbai's Carnac Bunder in 1919 in Maharashtra. The next year, it was shifted to the Naval Dockyard, Bombay (now Mumbai, Maharashtra), and in 1941, to HMIS *Talwar*, also in Bombay. In 1946, it finally moved to Kochi, Kerala.

First naval establishment
INS *Circars* was formally commissioned on 12 April 1942, at Visakhapatnam, Andhra Pradesh. Its name comes from the Urdu word for 'His Highness', as the Nizam of Hyderabad was addressed. The districts were known as the 'Circars' even after the Nizam lost them to the French and the British.

First Indian diving school
Since 1954, the naval diving school at INS *Venduruthy* has trained over 6,000 divers from services other than the Indian Coast Guard and Indian Army. The school was started by a Royal Navy officer and became independent in 1972 under Lieutenant Deepak Mohindra.

First naval academy
The first naval academy was established in Kochi, Kerala, in January 1969. The first batch of cadets graduated in December 1970. Commander K. Ramdas was the first officer-in-charge. Earlier, cadets used to be trained in England.

First floating dry dock
The floating dry dock at Port Blair, Andaman and Nicobar Islands, commissioned in 1987, has a lifting capacity of 11,500 tonnes and can accommodate vessels that have a deadweight of up to 30,000 tonnes.

Diamond Jubilee for INAS 310

Indian Naval Air Squadron (INAS) 310, The Cobras, a maritime reconnaissance squadron of the Indian Navy, celebrated its Diamond Jubilee (60 years) on 21 March 2021. Based in Goa, the squadron was commissioned in Hyeres, France, on 21 March 1961 and is the most decorated squadron of the Indian Navy. The squadron has been a part of numerous operations since 1961 and continues to carry out operations along the coastline. They delivered critical medical equipment and transported medical teams, clocking almost 1,000 sorties since the beginning of the COVID-19 pandemic.

First indigenous floating dock
On 20 June 2017, FDN-2, the first indigenously designed and constructed floating dock of the Indian Navy was launched at the Larsen & Toubro Ltd shipyard at Kattupalli in Chennai, Tamil Nadu. The 185 m (607 ft) long and 40 m (131 ft 3 in.) wide platform has best-in-class machinery and control systems. It accommodates up to 8,000-tonne ships with draught up to 7 m (23 ft), including submarines.

First unified theatre command
Vice Admiral Arun Prakash took over as the first commander-in-chief of the Andaman and Nicobar Command in 2001, with operational control of all three services and the Indian Coast Guard in the Andaman and Nicobar theatre.

First all-woman crew to circumnavigate the world
On 21 May 2018, a six-member all-woman crew completed circumnavigating the globe in 254 days on-board INSV *Tarini*, becoming the first Indian all-woman crew to do so. The journey ended at INS *Mandovi* jetty in Panaji, Goa, from where they had set sail on 10 September 2017. The crew included Lieutenant Commanders Vartika Joshi, Pratibha Jamwal, P. Swathi, and Lieutenants S. Vijaya Devi, B. Aishwarya and Payal Gupta. The 17 m (56 ft) sailing vessel was captained by Lieutenant Commander Joshi. The crew was mentored by Commander Dilip Donde, who became India's first solo circumnavigator in 2010.

First helicopter training school
INS *Rajali* at Arakkonam, Tamil Nadu, houses the Indian Naval Air Station (INAS), which is a base for training helicopter pilots.

First Missile Park
On 28 May 2020, the foundation stone was laid at INS *Kalinga* for a Missile Park. Named Agneeprastha, it has been set up with a replica of missiles and ground support equipment showcasing the evolution of missiles the unit has handled. Exhibits have been created from reconditioned scrap and obsolete inventory. The main attraction is the P-70 Ametist, an underwater-launched anti-ship missile

Longest Expedition with a Mixed Crew

INSV *Mhadei* and INSV *Tarini* set sail for the Bay of Bengal Offshore Sailing Expedition on 22 February 2020 from the Indian Naval Ocean Sailing Node in Goa. The crew comprised five naval officers, including two women officers in each boat, covering 6,100 nautical miles over 55 days. Captain Vipul Meherishi, the skipper of INSV *Tarini*, led the expedition. Captain Atool Sinha was the skipper of INSV *Mhadei*. The sailing vessels had scheduled halts at Colombo (Sri Lanka), Yangon (Myanmar), Chittagong (Bangladesh) and Phuket (Thailand).

from the old INS *Chakra* (Charlie-1 submarine) that served the Indian Navy from 1988 to 1991. The Missile Park is dedicated to all officers, sailors and support staff of INS *Kalinga*, who have served at the base since its establishment in 1981. When completed, Agneeprastha will offer glimpses of the missile history of the base.

First deep-sea submarine rescue system

On 12 Dec 2018, the Indian Navy's first flyaway Deep-Sea Submarine Rescue System was inducted by Admiral Sunil Lanba at the Naval Dockyard, Mumbai, Maharashtra. The system has a non-tethered Deep Submergence Rescue Vehicle (DSRV) and associated equipment, which gives the navy the capability to search, locate and rescue crew. The rescue system can be mobilized from the naval base at Mumbai, to the nearest mobilization port by air, land or sea to expedite rescue. On 2 June 2019, the navy conducted the first live 'mating' exercise of the DSRV with a submarine near Visakhapatnam, Andhra Pradesh. On 5 June 2019, an entirely Indian crew conducted its first full submarine rescue drill on the Kilo-class submarine, INS *Sindhudhvaj*, off the eastern coast of India.

First information fusion centre

On 22 December 2018, the first Information Fusion Centre – Indian Ocean Region (IFC–IOR) was inaugurated at the Information Management and Analysis Centre (IMAC), Gurugram, Haryana. The vast Indian Ocean Region needs constant and comprehensive maritime domain awareness and sharing of information on vessels of interest. This collaborative endeavour secures the global commons for a peaceful and stable region.

First combat management system

A combat management system (CMS) for indigenous aircraft carriers has been developed by the Indian Navy with Tata Power Strategic Engineering Division (TPSED), in collaboration with the Weapon and Electronics System Engineering Establishment and MARS, Russia. On 28 March 2019, it was handed over to the navy. All tests and trials conducted on its hardware and software were successful. This is the first CMS developed by a private company for the Indian Navy.

First Light Combat Aircraft Mk-1 Landing on *INS Vikramaditya*

At 10:02 hours on 11 January 2020, an indigenously designed and developed fighter light combat aircraft (LCA) – Tejas (N) Mk-1 – made an arrested landing on INS *Vikramaditya*, India's largest warship. It was piloted by Commodore Jaideep Maolankar. As per protocol, the aircraft was recovered and restrained by high-tensile strength or arrestor wires on the Stobar (short takeoff but arrested recovery).

LCA Tejas on INS *Vikramaditya*

First virtual reality centre

On 12 April 2019, Admiral Sunil Lanba inaugurated the first virtual reality centre (VRC) at the Directorate of Naval Design (Surface Ship Group). This centre boosts the design of indigenous warships, and collaborative design reviews between designers and end-users of warships. It has developed 19 warship designs.

AIR FORCE

PERSONNEL

First Indian pilots

- Lieutenant Indra Lal Roy from Calcutta (now Kolkata, West Bengal) was the first Indian pilot with the Royal Flying Corps and later in the Royal Air Force during the First World War. He claimed 10 victories in air combat, all of them within two weeks in July 1918. He was killed in action when he was only 19 years old and was posthumously awarded the Distinguished Flying Cross.
- The only other Indian pilots known to have flown in the First World War were Sardar Hardit Singh Malik, Lieutenant S.G. Welingkar, Lieutenant Errol Sharat Chandra Sen and Lieutenant Naoroji.

First air chiefs

Air Marshal Subroto Mukerjee became the first Indian chief of air staff when he succeeded Air Marshal Sir G.E. Gibbs on 1 April 1954. However, the IAF chief's rank was only equivalent to that of a lieutenant general of the Indian Army at the time. The IAF got its first air chief marshal only in 1966 when Air Marshal Arjan Singh was promoted to the post in recognition of the IAF's role in the 1965 war with Pakistan.

First Indian station commander

Wing Commander Subroto Mukerjee was given command of the airbase RAF Kohat (now in Pakistan), the first all-Indian station with only Indian Air Force (IAF) squadrons, in 1944.

Longest tenure as air chief

Air Marshal Subroto Mukerjee served the longest tenure as air chief, from 1 April 1954 to 8 November 1960.

First marshal

On 26 January 2002, former chief of the Indian Air Force, Air Chief Marshal Arjan Singh, was given the rank of marshal, equivalent to a field marshal. Arjan Singh was also a recipient of the Distinguished Flying Cross.

First woman flight commander

Wing Commander Shailja Dhami was the first woman to become a flight commander in the IAF. She was commissioned to the position on 26 August 2019 and took command of a Chetak Helicopter Unit at Hindon Airbase, Ghaziabad, Uttar Pradesh. She is also the first woman to be granted a permanent commission and the first to be an authorized instructor for IAF helicopters. She has also flown Cheetah aircraft.

First woman air marshal

Air Marshal Padmavathy Bandopadhyay, AVSM, VSM, (b. 4 November 1944) took over as the director general of medical services (Air) on 1 October 2004. Having joined the IAF in 1968, she was also the first woman to reach the rank of air vice marshal in 2002.

Air Marshal Padmavathy Bandopadhyay: first woman air marshal

First squadron commander

Flight Lieutenant Subroto Mukerjee took over command of 1 Squadron on 3 September 1939 – later becoming the first officer to command a flight, a squadron, a station and finally the IAF.

First commissioned woman pilot by order of merit

Squadron Leader Priya Nalgundwar (b. 28 November 1970) was commissioned in the Indian Air Force in the Flying Branch on 17 December 1994 as part of the first batch of seven women pilots and stood first in the order of merit in her batch. She received her wings from the then chief of air staff Air Chief Marshal S.K. Kaul.

First women combat pilots

In July 2016, for the first time, women combat pilots were inducted into the Indian Air Force with the then defence minister Manohar Parrikar commissioning Mohana Singh, Avani Chaturvedi and Bhawana Kanth.

First woman medical officer

Dr Vijayalakshmi Ramanan (later, wing commander), an army doctor, was inducted into the IAF in 1955.

The Indian Air Force has 7 commands including a training and maintenance command, under which various stations and units are located.

First across sonic barrier

Air Commodore P.C. Lal, Group Captain H. Moolgavkar and Wing Commander Roshan Suri broke through the sonic barrier on 15 October 1954 in a Super Marine Swift aircraft.

First to fly supersonic

Squadron Leader Dilbagh Singh, as the commanding officer (CO) of 1 Squadron, flew a Mystere IV aircraft over Delhi for the first time after it arrived in India on 17 May 1957. He was also the first Indian pilot to fly supersonic in level flight when, as the CO of the newly raised 28 Squadron, he flew a MiG-21F in level flight over Chandigarh in November 1963.

Record Rewind

Flying efforts

2009

During the year 2008-09, the IAF completed 250,306 flying efforts.

2018

During the year 2017-18, the IAF completed 251,405 flying efforts.

First helicopter pilot

On 28 March 1954, Flight Lieutenant A. Neil Todd and his co-pilot Squadron Leader S.K. Majumdar flew the then prime minister, Jawaharlal Nehru, from Palam, Delhi, to Tilpat Range in Faridabad, Haryana, and back.

First technical officer

Harjinder Singh, one of 19 Hawai Sepoys recruited to the IAF in 1931, was promoted to the rank of warrant officer in 1941 and became a flying officer in 1942. He was 41 years old when he learned to fly, earned his wings and became the air officer commander-in-chief of the then newly formed Maintenance Command in Kanpur, Uttar Pradesh, in 1955.

First woman in the Defence Services Staff Course

Padmavathy Bandopadhyay (later air marshal) joined the Indian Air Force as a medical officer. Bandopadhyay was also the first woman to attend the prestigious Defence Services Staff Course (DSSC) in 1978; the first woman in Asia to

TEJAS: BRILLIANT AND POWERFUL

India's premier light combat aircraft (LCA), Tejas, is manufactured by Hindustan Aeronautics Limited (HAL) and developed and designed by HAL, DRDO, the National Aerospace Laboratories (NAL) and the Aeronautical Development Agency (ADA). Living up to its name that translates to 'brightness' and 'power' in Sanskrit/Hindi, it defines speed, sharpness and brilliance, and is the smallest and lightest combat aircraft among its contemporaries.

Developed in the 1980s with an urgent need to replace the ageing MiG-21 aircraft, the LCA programme resulted in the Tejas aircraft. It is remarkable that the Indian Air Force decided to develop an indigenous LCA as early as the 1990s, when major arms equipment was imported. In 1990, its design was finalized, by 1993 it was in its first phase of commencement, and in 1997, after all checks and clearances, the work started. On 4 January 2001, it took its first flight and November 2001 marked the commencement of phase 2 of the Tejas programme. It was introduced in the IAF on 17 January 2015.

Tejas has a tailless, compound, delta-wing configuration. It accommodates technologies such as a fly-by-wire flight control system, multimode radar, digital avionics system and relaxed static stability, among others. The No. 45 Squadron IAF – Flying Daggers – was formed on 1 July 2016 as the first Tejas IAF unit with two aircraft. The second Tejas unit – Flying Bullets – was formed on 27 May 2020. The aircraft serves the IAF and the Indian Navy. Currently in production, 34 aircraft are commissioned in service while 83 are all set to join the IAF by 2026.

LCA Tejas

specialize in aerospace medicine; and the first Indian woman to visit the North Pole (1989–90). In 1995, she was the first serving officer to receive the Indira Gandhi Priyadarshini Award for her work in aerospace, high-altitude medicine and cold physiology.

First chief of foreign air force

Air Commodore K. Jaswant Singh, who was on deputation to Ghana to plan and establish the Ghana Air Force, took charge on 25 March 1959 as its air chief.

First light combat aircraft pilot

Wing Commander Rajiv Kothiyal was shortlisted in 1998 to test-fly light combat aircraft (LCA) in January 2001. He flew about 35 types of aircraft including 20 US aeroplanes while taking a test pilot's course in the USA. On 4 January 2001, he test-flew the LCA and received the Kirti Chakra. He also won the Iven C. Kincheloe Award for the Best Professional Achievement in Flight Testing 2000–01 from the Society of Experimental Test Pilots (SETP), California, USA.

First woman pilot to lead the Republic Day fly-past

Flight Lieutenant Swati Rathore became the first woman pilot to lead the Republic Day fly-past on 26 January 2021. She flew an Mi-17 V5 with the IAF flag in a formation of four choppers. Flight Lieutenant Bhawana Kanth also participated in the Republic Day fly-past. A total of 38 IAF and four Army aircraft were part of the parade.

Rafale Jets Touch Base in India

Five Rafale jets landed in India from France on 29 July 2020 including two twin-seaters and three single seaters. The French-origin aircrafts are part of the 17 Golden Arrows Squadron. The formal induction of the aircrafts would be held on 10 September 2020 at the Ambala air base, Haryana. The French defence minister, Florence Parly, was also invited for the event. India has contracted a deal of 36 Rafales with 31 aircrafts pending delivery.

INDIAN AIR FORCE'S FASTEST FIGHTER AIRCRAFT

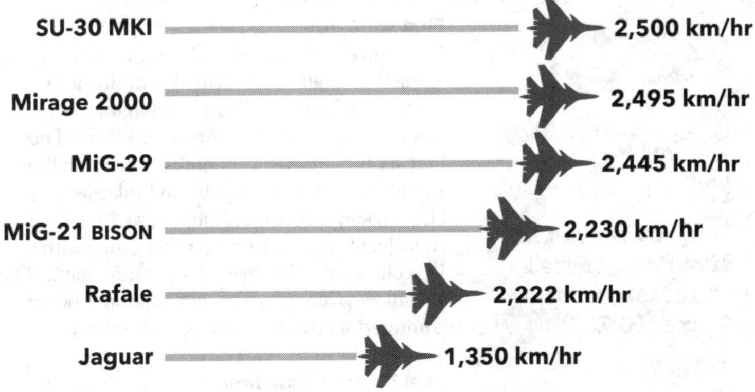

Source: indianairforce.nic.in; and www.dassault-aviation.com; speeds are approximate.

MEDALS AND HONOURS

First couple to be awarded the Vishisht Seva Medals
Flight Lieutenant (Dr) Sati Nath Bandopadhyay and his wife Flight Lieutenant Padmavathy Bandopadhyay were honoured with the Vishisht Seva Medal (VSM) at the same investiture ceremony by Air Chief Marshal O.P. Mehra for their service to the nation in the 1971 Bangladesh operations. They are the only Indian Air Force couple to be awarded such commendation.

First Param Vir Chakra
Flying Officer N.J.S. Sekhon of 18 Squadron is the only IAF officer to have been decorated with the Param Vir Chakra, the highest gallantry award. It was given posthumously after he was killed in an air battle over Srinagar in Jammu and Kashmir on 14 December 1971.

First woman to be awarded the Yudh Seva Medal
Squadron Leader Minty Aggarwal, a woman fighter controller who essayed a stellar role in intercepting retaliatory air attacks by the Pakistan Air Force after the Indian Air Force's Balakot air strikes in February 2019, was awarded the Yudh Seva Medal on 15 August 2019. Aggarwal thereby became the first woman in India's military history to be awarded the medal for distinguished service of a high order during war, conflict or hostilities. Aggarwal was among seven fighter controllers on duty in an underground bunker at the Ambala airbase. She joined the air force in 2011.

First and only Sarvottam Yudh Seva Medal
On 15 August 1999, Air Marshal Vinod Patney was awarded the Sarvottam Yudh Seva Medal (SYSM) for his exemplary leadership during the Kargil conflict in 1999. The award is the highest wartime distinguished service decoration. The medal has been conferred thrice to date and he is the only IAF officer to receive it.

Record Rewind

Longest tenure as director general of Indian Coast Guard (DG ICG)

1990

Vice Admiral H. Johnson served the longest tenure as DG ICG for two years and 353 days. He was appointed to the post on 10 July 1987 and left office on 27 June 1990.

2020

Director General Rajendra Singh served the longest tenure as DG ICG for three years and 122 days. He was appointed to the post on 1 March 2016 and left office on 30 June 2019.

UNITS

First squadron

1 Squadron was formed on 1 April 1933 at Karachi's Drigh Road Airfield with Royal Air Force (RAF) officer Flight Lieutenant C.A. Bouchier as the first commanding officer. The first six Indian officers commissioned into the Indian Air Force were: Subroto Mukerjee, H.C. Sirkar, A.B. Awan, Bhupendra Singh, Amarjeet Singh and J.N. Tandon, along with 19 technicians who formed the complement. The six officers were pilots except Tandon, who was commissioned as first ground duty officer.

First bomber squadron

5 Squadron (Tuskers) was raised on 2 November 1948 on the Consolidated B-24 Liberator bomber. It is now equipped with Jaguar IS and based in Ambala, Haryana.

First transport squadron

The first transport squadron of the IAF was raised with Spitfire fighter aircraft under the command of Squadron Leader S. Sajad Haider at Kohat (now in Pakistan). It moved to Bhopal, Madhya Pradesh, in 1946 and converted to Dakotas, which it flew till 1954, when it converted to Packets, a twin-engine cargo aircraft.

First squadron to have a jet bomber

106 SPR Squadron, though technically tasked with photo reconnaissance work, was the first unit to fly the famous English Electric Canberra in April 1957. The first squadron to have a jet bomber role again was No. 5 Squadron that took charge of the bomber variant of the Canberra in September 1957.

First heavy-lift transport squadron

44 Squadron, known as 'Himalayan Geese', was raised in 1961 and equipped with the An-12 four-engine turboprop transport aircraft. In the 1980s, it was renamed the 'Mighty Jets'.

First foreign base

The IAF base at Ayni in Farkhor, just outside Dushanbe, Tajikistan, had the capacity to station two squadrons. The Indian Army operated a military hospital here since 1997. The base was unused since the mid-1980s and was refurbished by Indian Army engineers to instruct the Tajik Air Force.

First attack helicopter squadron
125 Helicopter Squadron (also known as Gladiators) is a fighter squadron that was formed on 1 November 1983 with the Mil Mi-25 attack gunships. It was re-equipped with Mi-35 helicopters in April 1990. The squadron saw action in Sri Lanka during the operations of the Indian Peacekeeping Force (IPKF) between 1987 and 1990. It is currently based at the Pathankot air force station, Punjab.

EQUIPMENT

First supersonic aircraft
1 Squadron (The Tigers) was equipped with the Dassault MD-452 Mystere Iva in February 1957. The Mystere could break the sound barrier in a dive. However, the first squadron to fly a level-flight–capable supersonic aircraft was the 28 Squadron, raised in October 1963 on the MiG-21F. Aptly christened First Supersonics, 28 Squadron also has the honour of being the first squadron to fly a Mach 2–capable fighter.

First aircraft
The biplane aircraft Westland Wapiti with a maximum speed of 362 km/hr was inducted into the air force on 1 April 1933. Fitted with two machine guns, this aircraft could carry a load of 263 kg. Four Wapitis, which are believed to have been procured for 10 sterling pounds each, formed the A Flight of 1 Squadron, commanded by Flight Lieutenant C.A. Bouchier of the Royal Air Force (RAF).

First jet
The British single-seat Vampire was inducted in 1948, making India the first Asian country with jet fighters. In 1950, India entered into a licence agreement with Havill and Co., UK, and the first HAL-built Vampire flew on 21 February 1952. Vampires were phased out in 1975.

First indigenous aircraft (trainer)
The HT-2-piston-engined elementary trainer was designed at HAL. It made its maiden flight on 5 August 1951 and was in operation from 1953 to 1990. It replaced the Tiger Moth and was used to train over 5,000 Indian and foreign pilots.

First jet bomber
The twin-engine English Electric Canberra, which is a long-range and reconnaissance aircraft, was inducted into the Indian Air Force in 1957. Six IAF Canberras of 5 Squadron served with the UN forces on the Congo peacekeeping assignment in October 1961.

First indigenous fighter aircraft
The single seat Mach-2 combat jet fighter HF (Hindustan Fighter)-24 Mk-1 (Marut Ground Attack Fighter), with two single-shaft turbojet engines, was designed at HAL, Bengaluru. It took its maiden flight on 17 June 1961.

First Gnat
The first Gnat or Ajeet, a single-seat, light fighter bomber, about a third in size and half the weight of a conventional fighter, was inducted into the IAF in 1958.

The first Gnat, made by HAL, flew on 18 November 1959. It won the IAF its only Param Vir Chakra, and was in frontline service for more than three decades.

First indigenous light combat aircraft
Tejas is the first advanced fly-by-wire light combat aircraft (LCA) designed, developed and manufactured indigenously by HAL, DRDO, NAL and ADA. It is a lightweight single-seat multi-role jet fighter, and pegged as the world's smallest and lightest supersonic fighter. It is equipped with satellite-aided inertial navigation system, a digital computer-based attack system and autopilot mode. Tejas can fire air-to-air missiles, and carry bombs and precision-guided ammunition with a reach of over 400 km. It is mainly for use in close air-to-ground operations.

First fly-by-wire
The Mirage 2000 Delta aircraft of the IAF was inducted into the 7 Squadron in June 1985. Nicknamed Vajra by the IAF, it is also operated by the 1 Squadron.

First indigenous advanced light helicopter
The naval version of the advanced light helicopter (ALH), developed by HAL, took its first flight from INS *Viraat* on 8 March 1998. It had an integrated dynamic system, hinge-less main rotor and composite blades, bearing-less tail rotor, advanced cockpit and high-power engines with electronic control. It can exceed a speed of 250 km/hr.

The Chiefs of Air Staff conclave at Aero India 2021 saw the participation of the chiefs of air staff of 24 countries physically and 16 virtually.

First indigenous tandem-seat jet trainer
The intermediate jet trainer (IJT) was designed in India, with the fastest design-to-first-flight time, and flown officially by Squadron Leader Baldev Singh for 20 mins on 21 March 2003. With a 10 m (32 ft 10 in.) wingspan and an overall length of 11 m (36 ft), the 3,500 kg aircraft can touch 750 km/hr. However, the credit of being the first tandem-seat jet trainer used for intermediate flying training in the IAF goes to the Polish PZL TS-11 Iskra.

First biofuel for military aircraft
In December 2018, the IAF flew an An-32 on a biofuel blend made of Jatropha oil and aviation turbine fuel (ATF). This signified that India was one among a small group of nations that had developed, tested and certified a single-step hydro-processed renewable jet (HRJ) process to convert non-edible oil into biofuel for military aircraft. In May 2019, the IAF's workhorse aircraft fleet of An-32 began to use a new fuel. The blend is a biofuel that does far less harm to the environment than conventional fuel. The production of this biofuel from tree-borne oils also creates jobs for tribal people living where it is sourced from.

First indigenous AEW&C class of aircraft
On 14 February 2017, the IAF was given its first indigenous Airborne Early Warning and Control (AEW&C) System class of aircraft in initial operational configuration (IOC) by DRDO, during Aero India 2017, a biennial air show and

aviation exhibition, at the Yelahanka airbase in Bengaluru, Karnataka. It is is built on an Emb-145 platform, and has an air-to-air refuelling capability to enhance surveillance time.

First AESA radar for IAF

The IAF gave the nod in July 2017 for the first Active Electronically Scanned Array (AESA) radar to be integrated into its aircraft. The radar is fitted on to Jaguar fighter aircraft. In conventional radars, the antenna is moved manually to scan enemy targets. The AESA radar moves electronically and rapidly, tracking multiple and long-distance targets, while also jamming enemy communications and radar.

First Apache helicopters

On 3 September 2019, eight Boeing-made Apache Guardian attack helicopters were inducted into service at the Pathankot air force station. The AH-64E (I) Apache helicopter has been built keeping in mind the high mountainous terrain that the IAF operates in. It can also carry out precision attacks. This helicopter can receive and transmit images from the ground to its weapon systems and likewise transmit images from its weapon systems to the ground. The air crew and ground crew were trained to operate the helicopter at the US Army base, Fort Rucker. Twenty-two such helicopters were in service with the IAF by 2020.

First indigenous anti-radiation missile

Rudram-1, a new-generation air-to-surface anti-radiation missile (NGARM), developed by DRDO for the Indian Air Force was test-fired on 9 October 2020 on a radiation target on Wheeler Island off the coast of Odisha. The missile Rudram-1 was fired from a Sukhoi-30 MKI fighter aircraft, the potential launch- source aircraft for the same. With its ability to detect radio sources from 100 km away, the missile can disarm enemy radars and target the range of emitters. Its strike range is between 100 and 250 km.

OPERATIONS

First active operation

In September 1937, the 1 Squadron operated from Miranshah in North Waziristan (now in Pakistan) against hostile tribesmen. The IAF men lived inside a fort for safety and had to wheel in their aircraft into the fort every evening. Flying Officer (later Air Marshal) Aspy Merwan Engineer was the first officer to be Mentioned-in-Dispatches for the operations.

First airlift of Indian troops

During the Kurdish uprising in April 1923, the Royal Air Force flew 280 Sikh troops from Kingarban to Kirkuk, Iraq. Covering the distance that would normally require a five-day march, the flight covered 120.7 km in 10 hours.

Highest helipad operation

In January 2003, the IAF conducted high-altitude trials in the Siachen Glacier area. They airlifted an artillery gun to an elevation of 5,600 m (18,372 ft) and a snow scooter to Point Sonam (6,400 m/21,000 ft). This was the first time a helicopter of this class had operated at such altitudes.

First aircraft lost in conflict
On 30 October 1947, the Indian Air Force lost a Dakota piloted by Flight Lieutenant C.J. Mendoza after the aircraft crashed over the Pir Panjal Range.

Highest landing
Squadron Leader C.S. Raje on 22 July 1962, just before the China Operations, landed a Fairchild C-119 with 32 jawans at Daulat Beg Oldi post in Ladakh at 5,181.6 m (17,000 ft).

First indigenous fighter aircraft
The single seat Mach-2 combat jet fighter HF (Hindustan Fighter)-24 Mk-1 (Marut Ground Attack Fighter), with two single-shaft turbojet engines, was designed at HAL, Bengaluru. It took its maiden flight on 17 June 1961.

First flight to the true North Pole
The IL-76 aircraft of the 44 Squadron, representing the IAF, carried out a flight over the true North Pole in Exercise Cope Thunder-03 in Alaska, USA, with 14 crew members. The mission was launched on 3 June 2003 at 8:15 p.m. IST from USA's Eielson air force base, south-east of Fairbanks, Alaska, and the crew flew over the true North Pole on 20 June 2003 at 00:16 a.m. IST. The aircraft returned to base on 20 June 2003 at 5:51 a.m. IST after a flight lasting 9 hrs 36 mins.

Biggest rapid airlift
On 18 December 2018, the Western Air Command of the IAF airlifted a record 463 tonnes from the Chandigarh airbase and dropped the load in Ladakh. The massive airlift was done in a single wave and proved the IAF's rapid airlift capability. The feat was completed by 16 fixed-wing transport aircraft including C-17 Globemaster, the Ilyushin-76 Gajraj and the medium-lift tactical aircraft, Antonov-32. The airdrop was done in less than six hours.

GENERAL

Only vintage flight
A vintage aircraft flight was raised in Palam, Delhi, in 1988 to house heritage aircraft, such as the Howard, Tiger Moth and Dakota planes.

First Forward Surgical Centre
During an IAF military exercise, Gaganshakti- 2018, from 8 to 22 April 2018, the IAF set up a Forward Surgical Centre (FSC) at Naliya air force station in Gujarat. An FSC can be used for life- and limb-saving surgeries as also to help stabilize a patient with the assistance of a surgical team that can perform 6–8 surgeries a day.

First mobile health app launched by a defence service
MedWatch, a mobile health app, was launched by the IAF on 8 October 2018 for the IAF's 85th anniversary. With content from the Directorate General of Medical Services (Air), it was developed in-house by Directorate of Information Technology (DIT) and is available on the Android platform. It provides health information, reminders and utility tools. The app shares important web links and helpline numbers along with a body mass index (BMI) calculator and health record cards.

COAST GUARD

PERSONNEL

Search and Rescue Data*		
1	Missions	82
2	Lives Saved	123
3	Air Sorties	58
4	Ship Sorties	146
5	Medical Evacuation	10

*1 January–30 November 2020; Source: Press release by the Ministry of Defence, Press Information Bureau

First director general of the Indian Coast Guard
Vice Admiral V.A. Kamath, PVSM, was the first director general of the Indian Coast Guard (ICG) from 19 August 1978 to 31 March 1980.

First woman pilot
Assistant Commandant Monica Seth joined the Indian Coast Guard on 5 June 1998. She flew a total of 1,500 hours during her tenure. She flew on missions during the Kargil conflict in Jammu and Kashmir in 1999 and also for earthquake relief in Gujarat in January 2001.

First woman hovercraft pilot
In 2017, Assistant Commandant Sneha Khatayak became the first woman hovercraft pilot in India.

First and only Integral ICG contingent operating abroad
An ICG Dhruv helicopter – CG853 – has been operating in Maldives along with an ICG contingent. Since its induction, the helicopter has aided in 168 medivac missions, saving 178 lives. In continuance of the same, its stay has been extended till April 2022.

Raising Day Celebrations

On 1 February 2021, The Indian Coast Guard celebrated its 45th Raising Day. Formally established on 1 February 1977 and started with just seven surface platforms, it has grown to a fleet of 156 ships and 62 aircraft. On an average the ICG saves one life every second day at sea. They maintained a constant vigil in the Exclusive Economic Zone even during the COVID-19 restrictions by deploying 12 aircraft and 50 ships daily. The ICG has completed 44 years of glorious service and played a stellar role in pursuing India's interest in maritime zones.

A contingent of the Indian Coast Guard at the Republic Day parade in 2021

First women combatants

In 2017, the Indian Coast Guard became the first Indian armed forces service to deploy women in combat roles on-board ships. Assistant Commandants Anuradha Shukla, Sneha Khatayak, Shirin Chandran and Vasundhara Chouksey were trained at the Indian Coast Guard station at Mandapam, Tamil Nadu.

MEDALS AND HONOURS

First Yudh Seva Medal

Deputy Commandant S.P.S. Basra and Deputy Commandant B.A.S. Bhar were awarded the Yudh Seva Medal (YSM) on 26 January 1989. Commanding the Indian Coast Guard ships ICGS *Ahalya Bai* and ICGS *Tara Bai*, respectively, they prevented the infiltration of the Liberation Tigers of Tamil Eelam (LTTE) in the Palk Bay.

Digital Commissioning for ICGS *Sachet*

On 15 May 2020, Defence Minister Rajnath Singh commissioned ICGS *Sachet* and two interceptor boats (IBs) C-450 and C-451 in Goa. Because of the social distancing norms during the COVID-19 pandemic, the ceremony was held via videoconferencing, the first digital commissioning of a ship. The 105 m (344 ft 6 in.) long ICGS *Sachet* is driven by two 9,100 kW diesel engines, displaces 2,350 tonnes and can notch up a maximum speed of 26 knots with an endurance of 6,000 nautical miles. It can carry a twin-engine helicopter and four high-speed boats apart from an inflatable boat. It is the first in the series of five offshore patrol vessels (OPVs) designed and built indigenously by Goa Shipyard Ltd (GSL) and fitted with state-of-the-art navigation and communication equipment. Its first commander is Deputy Inspector General Rajesh Mittal who presides over 10 other officers and 110 men. The two 30 m (98 ft 5 in.) long IBs (C-450 and C-451) are indigenously designed and built by Larsen & Toubro Shipyard in Hazira, Gujarat, with about 70 per cent indigenous components. They are commanded by Assistant Commandant Gaurav Kumar Gola and Assistant Commandant Akin

ICGS *Sachet*

First to receive President's Tatrakshak Medal
Commandant A.K. Dey received the award for his efforts in firefighting during the construction of an Indian Coast Guard ship, and preventing an oil spill off the coast of Goa in June 1994.

EQUIPMENT

First vessels
ICGS *Kuthar* and ICGS *Kirpan* (formerly of the Indian Navy) were commissioned on 19 August 1978 under Commander N.S. Achreja and Commander V.K. Tuli respectively.

First indigenous offshore patrol vessel
On 21 February 2019, ICGS *Sachet*, the first indigenous offshore patrol vessel (OPV) of the Indian Coast Guard was launched at Goa Shipyard Ltd (GSL). This OPV is part of an indigenous project that was launched on 13 November 2016. Designed in-house, these OPVs will be used for protecting the Exclusive Economic Zone. The vessel weighs 2,400 tonnes and is equipped with features like quick-response boats for rescue and anti-piracy, gunnery simulators and many more advanced features. The hull is considered to be the most efficiently designed yet by GSL, and ensures fuel efficiency and crew comfort.

In two operations, the Indian Coast Guard seized 14.56 kg gold and 400 kg heroin in 2020.

Latest training vessel
On 24 October 2018, ICGS *Varuna*, an indigenously designed training vessel built by Reliance Naval and Engineering Ltd (RNAVAL), was launched at the Pipavav Shipyard, Gujarat. ICGS *Varuna* is a 105 m (344 ft 6 in.) long vessel with a crew of 242 officers and sailors. It is powered by twin diesel engines and can reach a speed of 20 knots. It has ultra-modern navigation and communication systems. This is the largest ship built yet for the Indian Coast Guard.

OPERATIONS

First and longest deep-sea passage by hovercraft
On 13 January 2015, Indian Coast Guard Air Cushion Vehicle (ACV) H-198 undertook area deployment from New Mangaluru, Karnataka, to Androth Island in the Lakshadweep Islands, across the Arabian Sea. The ACV hovercraft, piloted by Commandant Amitabh Banerjee and Deputy Commandant Konark Sharma, covered 142.5 nautical miles (264 km) in five hours. The ACV H-198 is the only hovercraft in India to venture into the lagoon islands of Lakshadweep. The return run of 146 nautical miles (270.39 km) was undertaken on 22 January 2015.

First underwater clean-up
On 5 June 2019, celebrated as World Environment Day, the Indian Coast Guard (Eastern Region) conducted an underwater debris clean-up exercise in the Bay of Bengal near the Chennai (Tamil Nadu) coast, in association with Dive India. The operation lasted two hours during which nearly 500 kg of trash was collected. This

First Affiliation with the Paramilitary

On 22 May 2019, the Indian Coast Guard signed a charter of affiliation with Assam Rifles, the first between an armed force and a paramilitary organization in India, and also a first for any paramilitary force. They may now utilize each other's assets for training, operations and other activities. Through this, ICGS *Shaurya* tied up with 3rd (Naga Hills) Battalion of Assam Rifles, which looks to gain from the Indian Coast Guard's use of technology so that some of its techniques may be used along the Indo-Myanmar border that it guards. The charter also involves the Indian Coast Guard taking five personnel of Assam Rifles on board for international sailing exposure.

was the first underwater clean-up in India to remove debris, nets and plastic from the ocean.

GENERAL

Youngest defence service

The Indian Coast Guard or Sea Police, was constituted as India's fourth defence force under the Coast Guard Act on 18 August 1978, for the preservation and protection of the 2.01 million sq. km Exclusive Economic Zone. The force is under the direction and control of the director general, Indian Coast Guard.

First hovercraft berthing platform

In 2001, the first hovercraft berthing platform was built at Haldia, West Bengal, in eight months by the Military Engineer Services.

Largest integrated shipbuilding facility

Reliance Naval and Engineering Ltd (RNAVAL), known earlier as Reliance Defence and Engineering Ltd and Pipavav Shipyard Ltd, headquartered in Mumbai, Maharashtra, is one of the largest shipbuilding yards of its kind in the world. RNAVAL is the first private sector company in India to earn a licence and contract to construct warships. It has India's largest integrated shipbuilding facility with the shipyard located in Pipavav, Gujarat. Its dry dock measures 662 m x 65 m (2,172 ft x 213 ft). It has the only modular shipbuilding facility in India.

BUSINESS AND ECONOMY

PLANNING

First book on political economy

Written in Sanskrit by Chanakya in the fourth century BCE, the *Arthashastra* is an ancient Indian treatise on statecraft, economic policy and military strategy. It was influential till the 12th century, after which it disappeared. It was rediscovered in 1905 by R. Shamasastry, a Sanskrit scholar, who published it in 1909. Its first English translation was published in 1915. The *Arthashastra* places the knowledge of economics at the heart of a king's education. Its discussion of taxation and expenditure gave expression to three traditional Indian principles: the taxing power of the state is limited, taxation should not be felt to be heavy or exclusive or discriminatory, and tax increases should be graduated.

Architect of planning

Prashanta Chandra Mahalanobis (1893–1972), an Indian scientist and applied statistician, laid down the framework for the formal foundation of economic planning in India. A member of the first Planning Commission of independent India, Mahalanobis was the first to use statistical tools to forecast, plan, analyse and evaluate social and economic welfare activities in India.

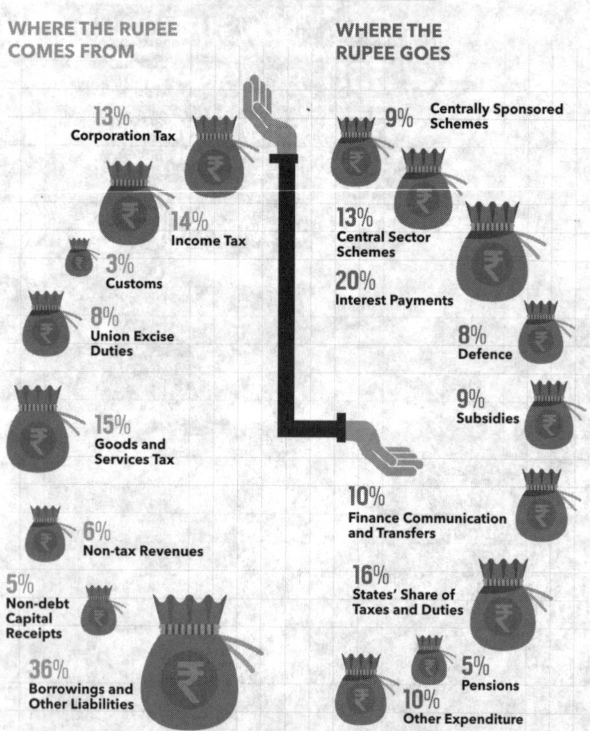

Source: Budget 2021–22, Ministry of Finance, Government of India

First budget

The first Indian budget was presented by James Wilson on 18 February 1869 in colonial India. Wilson, who founded *The Economist* magazine, was a finance member of the Council of India, which advised the Indian viceroy at the time.

First Union budget

The first Union budget of independent India was presented by the then finance minister, R.K. Shanmukham Chetty, on 26 November 1947. This was an economic review without any new taxes levied, as the budget for 1948–49 was 95 days away. After this, a budget for a short period was called an 'interim' budget.

R.K. Shanmukham Chetty, who presented the first Union budget

First interim budget

An interim budget, to enable the government expenditures to continue until the regular budget, was presented first in 1957 by the then finance minister T.T. Krishnamachari.

First Planning Commission

The first Planning Commission was set up in 1951 under the chairmanship of the then prime minister Jawaharlal Nehru, with Gulzari Lal Nanda as the deputy chairman.

First Five Year Plan

The First Five Year Plan of free India was launched in 1951, with a total outlay of ₹2,378 crore (23,780 million).

First Union budget papers in Hindi

While introducing the budget for 1955–56, the then finance minister Sir C.D. Deshmukh circulated the Hindi version of the budget speech for the first time. Hindi versions of the Annual Financial Statement and the Explanatory Memorandum were also circulated from then on.

First annual plans

The first annual plans replaced the full Five Year Plan for an interim period in 1966. These annual plans continued till 1969 and came into force again during 1990–92.

First paperless budget

The Union budget for 2021 was presented on a 'Made-in-India' tablet on 1 February 2021 by Finance Minister Nirmala Sitharaman, doing away with the long-standing tradition of printing the budget papers. The budget was distributed electronically to members of Parliament (MPs).

First paperless budget being presented by Finance Minister Nirmala Sitharaman

Only plan to go through four governments

The initial groundwork for the Eighth Five Year Plan (1992–97) was conducted by the Congress (I) government, the approach paper was finalized during National Front rule, the final document was prepared in the Janata Dal (S) regime and the Congress (I) delivered the revised plan in 1992.

WORKFORCE AND HUMAN RESOURCES

Workers on board

Delhi Cloth Mills (DCM) was the first company to recognize labour rights by inducting a workers' representative into its board in 1938.

Earliest public association

The earliest public association in modern India was the Landholders' Society, an association of the landlords of Bengal, Bihar and Orissa (now Odisha), founded in 1837. It was established to look after the interests of landowners.

Oldest trade unions

- The Madras Labour Union, the first organized trade union, was formed in 1918–19 by labour veterans Annie Besant, B.P. Wadia, Thiruvarur Viruttachala Kalyanasundaram, Sakkarai Chettiar, G. Ramanujalu and G. Selvapathy Chetty.
- The All India Trade Union Congress (AITUC), one of the oldest trade unions, set up in 1920, has a history entwined with that of the organized labour movement and the freedom struggle.

Oldest banking employees' trade union

The All-India Bank Employees Association (AIBEA), founded on 20 April 1946, is the oldest and largest trade union of bank employees.

The last gold coin was issued in 1948 by Nawab Sir Mir Osman Ali Khan Siddiqi Asaf Jah VII, the last nizam of the erstwhile princely state of Hyderabad.

Oldest insurance trade union

The All India Insurance Employees Union (AIIEU), established in January 1951, comprised 80 per cent of the nearly 200,000 employees of the Life Insurance Corporation of India (LIC) and the General Insurance Corporation of India (GIC).

First labour strike

The first labour strike in India was that of the palanquin bearers of Calcutta (now Kolkata, West Bengal) in 1827 in pre-Independence India. They refused to wear badges, and demanded fare on the basis of the distance they covered instead of time.

First Labour Day

The International Workers' Day celebrations were first organized by communist leader Singaravelar or Malayapuram Singaravelu Chettiar (1860–1946) in Madras (now Chennai, Tamil Nadu) on 1 May 1923.

Home: The New Workplace

The COVID-19 pandemic forced many a change in its wake. With lockdowns to begin with and social distancing guidelines to be observed, most workplaces adapted to the 'work from home' (WFH) mode. Several surveys were conducted to understand the impact of the shift. One such survey conducted by Awfis, a co-working space company, reported that the shift to WFH saved an average Indian 1.47 hours of travel time and ₹5,520 per month. TimesJobs reported that 42 per cent of the firms surveyed would continue to work remotely, another 40 per cent stated that they would follow a hybrid structure with WFH and office on alternate days, and 18 per cent sought to revoke WFH from 2021 onwards. It also highlighted the gaps in technology and the need for better infrastructure along with concerns about personal data protection, work–life balance, efficiency and productivity. Meanwhile, India's largest IT service firm Tata Consultancy Services (TCS) in a run-up to 2025, announced that as many as 75 per cent of its more than 4.6 lakh (460,000) employees globally (including 3.5 lakh [360,000] in India) would work from home under an operating model it calls Secure Borderless Work Spaces (SBWS), a huge jump from the industry average of 20 per cent today.

First industrial association
The Industrial Association of Western India was formed in 1890 at the annual conference held at Poona (now Pune, Maharashtra).

First all-India farmers' organization
The All-India Kisan Sabha was formed in 1936 in British India. It was the first pan-India organization of farmers.

First labour legislation
- The Industrial Employment Act of 1946 was followed by protective regulations, such as the Factories Act and the Minimum Wages Act in 1948.
- The first effort to protect unorganized labour was the Coal Mines Provident Fund and Bonus Schemes Bill introduced in 1948, which became an act in the same year.

First organized strike
In 1877, labourers struck work at the Empress Mills in Nagpur, Maharashtra, following a wage cut. In 1884, as many as 5,000 textile workers of Bombay (now Mumbai, Maharashtra) submitted a petition asking for regular payment of wages, a weekly holiday and a midday recess.

Largest strike
On 26 November 2020, over 250 million (25 crore) workers struck work for 24 hours in a nationwide general strike organized by a joint platform of 10 trade unions.

First legislation for women

- The Bombay Maternity Benefit Act was passed in 1929.
- The Equal Remuneration Act was passed in 1976.

First woman chairperson – public sector undertaking

Laxmi Menon, the chief executive of Hindustan Teleprinters Ltd, became its chairperson and managing director in 1989, thereby becoming the first woman chairperson of a public sector undertaking (PSU) in the country.

Longest-serving chairperson

Jehangir Ratanji Dadabhoy Tata, a recipient of the Bharat Ratna in 1992, held the post of chairman of Tata Sons for 53 years (1938–91).

Largest employer

- In the government-controlled sector, the largest employer is Indian Railways with 1,253,592 regular employees as reported on 31 March 2020.
- In the private sector, Tata Consultancy Services continues to be among the biggest employers with 469,261 employees (as reported in December 2020).

Most students recruited by a company from a single institution

A total of 278 students from the 2020 graduation batch of the Vellore Institute of Technology (VIT) in Vellore, Tamil Nadu, were offered jobs by Wipro Technologies for their Turbo Hiring Programme 2020 'dream slot' category In Wipro's campus placement recruitment drive, held during 3–5 September 2019. The students were offered cost to company (CTC) of ₹6.5 lakh (₹650,000) per annum. This offer surpassed the earlier record of 238 job offers by the same company, Wipro Technologies, to VIT students in a placement drive.

First LGBTQIA+ job fair

The RISE (Reimagining Inclusion for Social Equity) job fair organized by the Pride Circle on 12 July 2019 in Bengaluru, Karnataka, was the first job fair exclusively for the LGBTQIA+ community. The fair attracted 450 candidates competing for 250 job opportunities in 35 companies. The employers included Goldman Sachs, Uber, Accenture and Intel, among others.

COINS AND CURRENCY

First lead coins

The first lead coins were found in the Deccan, dating back to the reign of Sri Satai (c. 150 BCE). Most Andhra coins were made of lead or bullion (an alloy of gold or silver with a predominant amount of copper or other base metal). They featured Brahmi legends on both sides. The typical devices featured were the elephant, the bow and the Buddhist chaitya.

Earliest gold coins

The Kushanas (130 BCE–185 CE) issued the earliest gold coins in India. They weighed 121 or 123.1 grains and appear to be based on the auric standard (122.9 grains) of the Romans with whom the Kushanas had regular trade.

Earliest coinage

Ingots of silver, with only three dots as a mark, probably represent the earliest form of coinage on the Indian subcontinent. Following them were heavy silver bars with devices stamped out with a punch on one side of the coin. These two types of coins were in circulation as early as 600 BCE.

Earliest known use of cowries as currency

Cowries were used as legal tender in the Bengal kingdom of Lakhnauti during the reign of Ghiyasuddin Bahadur Shah I (r. 1322–24 CE).

Cowries: one of the earliest 'currencies'

Oldest surviving gold coins

The oldest surviving gold coins are from the reign of Kushana emperor Vima Kadphises (c. 45–78 CE) and they were struck in three denominations – the double stater, the stater or dinara, and the quarter stater. On the obverse of these appears either the king's head or bust, or the king seated cross-legged on a couch, or sitting in a chariot drawn by two horses.

First 2,000-rupee note

The ₹2,000 banknote was released by the Reserve Bank of India (RBI) on 8 November 2016 following the demonetization of ₹1,000 and ₹500 banknotes. In circulation since 10 November 2016, the ₹2,000 banknote is part of the

First Coins for the Visually Impaired

On 7 June 2019, Prime Minister Narendra Modi released a new series of coins, specially conceived to help visually impaired people to identify them, in New Delhi. Designed by the National Institute of Design in Ahmedabad, Gujarat, the series has coins in denominations of ₹1, ₹2, ₹5, ₹10 and ₹20. These coins are characterized by increasing size and weight from lower to higher denominations. The newly included coin of ₹20 was designed as a 12-sided coin with no serrations. The other denominations are circular.

SUPER 30

DHIRUBHAI AMBANI: BUILDING UP A RELIABLE RELIANCE

Dhirubhai Ambani

From working at a petrol station to owning India's largest private sector petrochemical company, the story of Dhirajlal Hirachand Ambani, popularly known as Dhirubhai Ambani, started much before the liberalization of 1991. However, this gave the much needed fillip to Reliance Industries Ltd (RIL), and to Dhirubhai's dream, as it opened the doors for raising resources from global financial markets. By 1992, Dhirubhai had decided to focus on complete backward integration and the building of what finally became India's largest refinery. All these required huge financial resources, and RIL had mastered the art of, first, raising the resources and, second, keeping its shareholders happy.

After liberalization, RIL garnered many firsts to its credit, both at the level of its plants and the raising of resources. In 1992, RIL was the first company to raise money by issuing global depository receipts (GDR), or euro issue, as it was popularly known. In 1996, it was the first Indian company to issue Yankee bonds. These bonds had a maturity period of 50 years. Within months it came out with another Yankee bond issue wherein the maturity period of the bond was 100 years. More than money raised by way of the bond issue, the success of the second issue lay in the assurance that global markets had faith in RIL.

As the legend goes, Dhirubhai Ambani would always focus on the future and one of his favourite question reportedly used to be: Which business would be successful after 15 years? He was among the first in India who thought on a global scale when it came to building capacities for RIL.

Mahatma Gandhi New Series of banknotes with a new design featuring Mangalyaan on the reverse. It is the currency note of the highest denomination in active circulation currently.

Oldest extant mints

Mints were built by the Government of India at Calcutta and at Bombay (now Kolkata and Mumbai respectively) around the same time, and they started operations in 1829. The Calcutta Mint was moved to Strand Road in 1824, while the coins issued there continued to be in the name of the Murshidabad Mint.

First mint

The East India Company started the first mint in India in 1640 at Fort St. George, Madras (now Chennai, Tamil Nadu). In 1671, the first English mint was installed in Bombay (now Mumbai, Maharashtra) through a letter of patent issued by King Charles II of England, but the first coin was minted there only in 1678.

First 200-rupee note

The RBI issued the first-ever currency notes in the denomination of ₹200 on 25 August 2017. This currency note, in the Mahatma Gandhi New Series, carries the motif of the Sanchi stupa on the reverse.

BANKING

First bank

The Bank of Hindustan was established in 1770 by Alexander and Co. of Calcutta (now Kolkata, West Bengal).

First government banking agency

The Imperial Bank of India, which was formed in 1921 by merging the Presidency banks of Bengal, Bombay and Madras, became the State Bank of India (SBI) on 1 July 1955.

Oldest private bank

Punjab National Bank Ltd, the first private bank wholly owned and run by Indians, opened in 1895.

First regional rural banks

The first regional rural banks (RRB) in India were opened in Moradabad and Gorakhpur in Uttar Pradesh, Bhiwani in Haryana, Jaipur in Rajasthan and Malda in West Bengal on 2 October 1975.

30

Record Rewind

Bank with most branches

1991

In January 1990, the State Bank of India had 11,823 branches.

2020

The State Bank of India had 23,694 branches across the country.

First foreign bank

The Chartered Bank, established in 1853 in Madras (now Chennai, Tamil Nadu), was the earliest foreign bank in India. In 1969, it merged with Standard Bank in London, UK, and was incorporated as Standard Chartered Bank.

First cooperative bank

The Greater Bombay Cooperative Bank Ltd was registered on 5 November 1952 under the Bombay State Cooperative Act, with 50 members and an initial capital of ₹21,000.

First bank for housing development

The National Housing Bank (NHB), a subsidiary of the Reserve Bank of India, was established on 9 July 1988.

First Indian bank to open a branch overseas

The Bank of India was the first Indian bank to open a branch outside India in London, UK, in 1946, and also the first to open a branch in Paris, France, in 1974.

First credit card issued by an Indian bank

The Central Bank of India introduced the Central Card in 1980.

First automated teller machine facility

The Hong Kong and Shanghai Banking Corporation (HSBC) started 24-hour banking facilities with automated teller machines (ATM) at its main office in Bombay (now Mumbai), Maharashtra, on 4 September 1987.

First ATMs on wheels

- In December 2002, the Industrial Credit and Investment Corporation of India (ICICI) Bank introduced an ATM on wheels using vans equipped with ATM machines and parked at four locations in Mumbai suburbs (Vile Parle East, Juhu, Andheri West and Kandivali) for fixed hours. The mobile ATM was connected to the central database of the bank through GPRS (General Packet Radio Service) technology for a fixed number of hours.
- The Bank of India was the first government bank to introduce mobile ATMs on 1 January 2003 in Mumbai, Maharashtra.

First floating ATM

The State Bank of India launched a floating ATM installed on a *jhankar* (ferry) plying between Ernakulam and Vypeen in Kerala on 9 February 2004. The ship was owned by the Kerala Shipping and Inland Navigation Corporation.

First Indian bank listed on the New York Stock Exchange

On 22 September 1999, ICICI Bank was listed on the New York Stock Exchange (NYSE), with its American Depository Shares priced at US $9.80. After the Bank of Tokyo-Mitsubishi, it was the second Asian bank to be listed on the NYSE.

First export–import bank

The Government of India set up the Export–Import Bank of India (EXIM Bank) in 1982 as a statutory corporation wholly owned by the Union government, for providing financial assistance to exporters and importers. It acts as the principal financial institution to coordinate the operations of export – import institutions.

First indigenous payment card

The National Payments Corporation of India (NPCI) introduced the RuPay debit card in Mumbai, Maharashtra, on 26 March 2012. The Bank of India, the State Bank of India, the Bank of Baroda and the Union Bank of India were the first banks to offer RuPay debit cards to their customers for domestic payments.

RuPay debit card

First institution for agri loans

On 12 July 1982, the National Bank for Agriculture and Rural Development (NABARD) was established, with its headquarters in Bombay (now Mumbai), Maharashtra, to implement the National Bank for Agricultural and Rural Development Act, 1981. The agricultural credit functions of RBI and refinance functions of the then Agricultural Refinance and Development Cooperation (ARDC) were transferred to NABARD.

First government-owned all-woman bank

Bharatiya Mahila Bank (BMB), India's first government-owned all-woman bank, with the vision of economic empowerment of women, opened its first branch at Nariman Point in Mumbai, Maharashtra, on 19 November 2013. It was incorporated on 5 August 2013 and received a banking licence from the RBI on 25 September 2013. It was merged with the State Bank of India in April 2017.

➘ AT THE RBI

Highest surplus transfer from RBI to the government

On 26 August 2019, the RBI transferred a record sum of ₹123,414 crore (1,234.14 billion) of its surplus to the Government of India for the fiscal year 2018–19, along with ₹52,637 crore (526.37 billion) more of excess provisions. This was recommended by the Bimal Jalan Committee on Economic Capital Framework. The surplus transfer (known as 'dividend' to the government) is nearly double the earlier highest of ₹65,896 crore (658.96 billion) in 2014–15.

First Indian governor of the Reserve Bank of India

Sir Chintaman Dwarakanath Deshmukh, a member of the Indian Civil Service, was the first Indian governor of the Reserve Bank of India (RBI). His association with the bank commenced in 1939, when he was appointed the government's liaison officer. He was appointed governor of RBI in 1943.

The bank with the largest network

The India Post Payments Bank (IPPB), launched in 2018 with 155,000 access points, became the largest banking network in the country. It is also the bank with the largest rural network, with 110,000 access points.

Largest international bank by number of branches

As reported by the Reserve Bank of India, Standard Chartered Bank, with the UK as its country of incorporation, leads the list of international banks in India with the highest number of banking branches, totalling 100. Citibank, incorporated in the USA, comes second with 35 banking branches and HSBC stands third with 26 banking branches.

State/UT with the most ATMs

Maharashtra ranks first in the country as the state with the highest number of ATMs deployed, with 27,274 ATMs as reported in December 2020. Tamil Nadu, with 26,879 ATMs, comes second in the list, followed by Uttar Pradesh, which has 22,059 ATMs.

The Government of India merged 10 nationalized banks into 4 entities in 2019–20.

Bank with most foreign offices

The State Bank of India had 80 foreign offices in 36 countries to service the bank's foreign customers, in addition to retail operations (by July 2020). The focus of these offices is India-related business.

First Indian bank with a merchant banking subsidiary

The State Bank of India was the first bank to set up a wholly owned merchant banking subsidiary when it set up SBI Capital Markets Ltd in April 1986.

Biggest bank fraud

On 14 February 2018, Punjab National Bank (PNB), India's second-largest government-owned lender at the time, declared the largest ever bank fraud in India's financial history. It involved fraudulent letters of undertaking worth around ₹11,400 crore (114 billion) issued by PNB at its Brady House branch in Fort, Mumbai, Maharashtra, to overseas branches of other Indian banks. It was allegedly perpetrated by jeweller–designer Nirav Modi and his uncle and alleged partner Mehul Choksi, among others.

First bank with a satellite network

The State Bank of India installed the first satellite network in September 1988, connecting 134 offices in 64 cities. It facilitated communication by voice, facsimile and message switching via digital electronic exchanges.

First bank to establish a mutual fund

The State Bank of India launched the SBI Mutual Fund in July 1987. Managed by its subsidiary, SBI Capital Markets Ltd, it was established under the amended Banking Regulations Act, 1949, to attract funds from small investors in rural and semi-urban areas.

First woman bank manager

Shanta Kumari became the bank manager of the Syndicate Bank, Seshadripura, Bangalore (now Bengaluru), Karnataka, in 1962.

First woman to head a foreign bank in India

Naina Lal Kidwai was the first Indian woman to lead a foreign bank (ANZ Grindlays, where she worked from 1982 to 1994) in India. She was also the first Indian woman to graduate from Harvard Business School (1982). Her contribution in the areas of trade and industry earned her the Padma Shri in 2007.

First woman managing director and chief financial officer of World Bank Group

Anshula Kant, born in Roorkee (now in Uttarakhand), was appointed as the managing director (MD) and chief financial officer (CFO) of the World Bank on 12 July 2019. Kant is responsible for managing the International Development Association (which offers concessional loans and grants to the world's poorest developing countries), finance and risk management of the Group. Previously a financial officer of the State Bank of India, Kant became the first woman to become MD and CFO of the international financial institution.

With 15,000,000 cards, HDFC Bank is the largest issuer of credit cards in India as reported on 30 September 2020.

First demonetization

In 1946, ₹1,000 and ₹10,000 currency notes were removed from circulation in the first instance of demonetization. Both notes were then reintroduced in 1954, with the introduction of ₹5,000 and ₹500 notes. In 1978, the then prime minister Morarji Desai took ₹1,000, ₹5,000 and ₹10,000 notes out of circulation. On 8 November 2016, Prime Minister Narendra Modi declared ₹500 and ₹1,000 notes invalid. Later, new notes of ₹500, ₹200 and ₹2,000 denominations were introduced.

Most odd amounts deposited

Dr Pramod Agarwal 'Goldiee' (b. 16 January 1962), from Haldwani, Uttarakhand, has been depositing odd amounts in his State Bank of India account at the Mukhani branch in Haldwani. He had opened the account on 29 December 2016. His account statement shows deposits of special amounts such as: ₹11; 111; 1,111; 11,111; 22; 222; 2,222; 22,222; 33; 333; 3,333; 33,333 and so on. The statement showed 4,747 such entries (till 23 May 2019).

INSURANCE

First general insurance company

Triton Insurance Company Ltd, set up by the British in 1850, was the first general insurance company in India.

First life insurance company

The Oriental Life Insurance Company, the first life insurance company in India, started in Calcutta (now Kolkata, West Bengal) in 1818, but served only the Europeans in India then.

First Indian life insurance company
The Bombay Mutual Life Assurance Society was the first Indian life insurance company. It started in 1871.

Largest insurance company
The Life Insurance Corporation of India (LIC) was founded on 1 September 1956. It grew into what is now the biggest public sector insurance company in the country and leads in the insurance sector. It has a total life fund of ₹31,14,496.05 crore (31,144.96 billion), with ₹2.19 crore (21.9 million) new policies, thus garnering 75.9 per cent of the market share in terms of policies and 68.74 per cent of the market share in terms of first-year premiums (31 March 2019–20).

LIC of India: largest insurance company

FINANCIAL INSTRUMENTS

First domestic mutual fund
The Unit Trust of India's (UTI) scheme of 1964 was the first domestic mutual fund in the country.

First offshore mutual fund
Unit Trust of India (UTI) and Merrill Lynch promoted the ₹75 million India Fund in 1986.

First rating agency
Crisil, formed in 1988, was the first rating agency in India. It was set up jointly by the LIC, the Industrial Credit and Investment Corporation of India (lClCl), the General Insurance Corporation (GIC) and various banks.

First woman president of a stock exchange
Forty-five-year-old Omana Abraham became the first woman president of a stock exchange in India, when she was nominated the president of the Cochin Stock Exchange in Kochi, Kerala, in 1991.

First automatic exchange and screen-based trading
The automated Over the Counter Exchange of India (OTCEI), set up in 1992 in Bombay (now Mumbai), Maharashtra, was the ideal avenue for small- and medium-sized companies with an issued capital ranging from ₹30 lakhs (3 million) to ₹25 crore (250 million). This exchange failed to live up to its

KIRAN MAZUMDAR SHAW: BRILLIANCE FROM BREWING TO BIOCON

While there are a few stories of first-time entrepreneurs starting out of garages and making it big in India Inc., when it comes to women entrepreneurs, Kiran Mazumdar Shaw is probably the only one on the list who has achieved this feat.

She wanted to be a doctor but did not make it to medical school. Then she wanted to be a brewer, but could not get a full-time job because in the 1970s, the beer industry was not ready to take on a woman brewer. Finally, in 1978 she started to make enzymes. The first on the list was papain, an enzyme extracted from the raw fruit of the papaya plant. And thus was the foundation of her and her company Biocon's success laid in a small industrial shed with just three employees.

Kiran Mazumdar Shaw

Building a company from scratch, she took it to a level where on the day of its listing on stock exchanges in 2004, valuations exceeded US $1 billion. Biocon became only the second company in India to reach this milestone.

Among other honours, Kiran Mazumdar Shaw has featured in the *Time* magazine list of the top 100 most influential people in the world (2010) and on the Forbes 2020 list of the 100 most powerful women in the world. Today, she heads one of India's largest biopharmaceutical companies. Along with its subsidiaries, Biocon has created a niche for itself with focus on three key therapeutic fields – diabetes, oncology and immunology.

promise and the National Stock Exchange (NSE) came into being in November 1994. It started the first screen-based trading system, in which a network of computers is linked to a central computer located in the stock exchange.

First secured promissory notes

Tata Iron and Steel Company (TISCO), now Tata Steel Ltd, issued promissory notes in June 1992.

First global depository receipts issue

Reliance Industries Ltd issued global depository receipts worth US $150 million in March 1992.

First PSU to go public

Indian Petrochemicals Corporation Ltd (IPCL) went public on 16 November 1992, with a ₹320 crore (3.2 billion) equity issue.

Highest price for stock exchange membership

A broking card for the Bombay Stock Exchange was auctioned for ₹41 million

(₹4.1 crore) to Jardine Fleming Asia, which later shut down. Before that, Baring Securities India Ltd had paid ₹3 crore (30 million) for one in 1995.

India's first depository

The National Securities Depository Limited (NSDL) was jointly promoted by the IDBI, UTI and NSE, and it started operations in August 1996. C.B. Bhave was the first managing director of the NSDL. In September 2016, when the depository completed 20 years of operations, it had 15 million demat accounts.

First woman director of the Bombay Stock Exchange

Forty-year-old Deena Mehta became the first woman director of the Bombay Stock Exchange (BSE), elected by securing 382 of 413 votes in March 1997. This was the first time in 122 years that the BSE elected a woman to its board.

The life insurance sector was nationalized on 19 January 1956.

First private sector mutual fund

Shyam Kothari, head of the H.C. Kothari group of companies, floated the Kothari Pioneer Bluechip Fund in November 1993.

First sectoral fund

The first sector mutual fund called CanExpo was offered by Canara Bank during February–March 1994 as the first emerging industry fund.

Largest mutual fund

HDFC Mutual Fund is the largest mutual fund house in India, with equity and debt assets worth ₹373,000 crore (3.73 trillion) under its management, as reported in March 2020.

FINANCIAL INSTITUTIONS

Oldest stock exchange

The Bombay Stock Exchange (BSE) was born under the shade of a giant banyan tree way back on 9 July 1875. Indian brokers doing business in stocks and shares decided to form an association in Bombay (now Mumbai, Maharashtra) to protect the interests of Indian share brokers and stockbrokers. It was also Asia's first stock exchange.

Stock exchange with most listed companies

The BSE, with 4,722 listed companies, is the largest exchange by the number of listed companies.

Stock exchange with highest membership

With a total of 1,406 members across different segments of financial markets, NSE has the highest number of members in a stock exchange.

Stock exchange with highest volume of derivative contracts

The NSE maintained its position as the world's largest derivatives exchange for a second consecutive year in 2020. It reported a trading volume of 8.85 billion contracts in 2020.

National Stock Exchange, Mumbai, Maharashtra

Stock exchange with highest turnover

The NSE is the stock exchange with the highest turnover, with an average daily turnover of ₹36,432 crore (364.32 billion) in 2019–20. Its average daily turnover for January 2021 stood at ₹72, 472 crore (724.72 billion).

Highest BSE sensitive index level

The BSE sensitive index touched an all-time intra-day high of 62245 on 19 October 2021, the highest ever level since it was formed in 1979

State/UT with the highest contribution to equity trading

Maharashtra leads among states in its contribution to equity trading, with 12,673,663 investors in 2020.

POWER AND ENERGY

First builder of the steam engine

Goluk Chandra, who was a blacksmith in Titigur (now Titagarh), near Barrackpore in West Bengal, indigenously built a steam engine to pump underground water, without any European help, in 1828.

First steam-powered plant

The Calcutta Electric Supply Company (CESC) set up a steam-powered plant in 1899 at Emambagh Lane near Prinsep Ghat in Calcutta (now Kolkata, West Bengal), marking the start of thermal power generation in India.

First commercial use of electricity

Electricity was first introduced commercially on 10 November 1897 at Sidrapong Hydroelectric Power Station in Darjeeling, West Bengal.

First electrification

Calcutta (now Kolkata, West Bengal) was the first city in India to go electric when it received current in 1899.

First private sector power company

Tata Power Company Ltd (TPCL) was the first private sector power company to start operations in 1910 in Bombay (now Mumbai, Maharashtra).

Largest private sector thermal power station

The 4,620 MW Mundra Thermal Power Station at Mundra in the Kachchh

Record Rewind

Highest dividend declared by a company

1991

In 1982, Colgate Palmolive declared a 113 per cent dividend, which was the maximum by a company in India.

2020

The highest dividend declared by an Indian company was 19,480 per cent by software exporter Majesco in 2020.

District of Gujarat is the largest privately operating thermal power plant in India. It is a coal-based power plant, owned and operated by Adani Power. It has nine generating units.

Largest power supplier

The National Thermal Power Corporation (NTPC) Ltd, set up in 1975, is India's largest power company. It has an installed capacity of 63,925 MW (including joint ventures and subsidiaries), 46 NTPC stations, 13 JV stations and 12 renewable energy projects.

First state electricity board

On 1 May 1955, the West Bengal State Electricity Board was the first electricity board in the country to become operational.

First HVDC line project

A high-voltage direct current (HVDC) unit of 28,250 MW was constructed by NTPC Ltd in Madhya Pradesh and commenced operations in 1989. However, India's first commercial HVDC line (1,500 MW) was commissioned in 1991. Extending over 810 km from Dadri to Rihand in Uttar Pradesh, this was also constructed by NTPC.

Most electricity-intensive sector

Of the total consumption of electricity in 2020–21, the industry sector accounted for the largest share (42.7 per cent), followed by the domestic sector (24 per cent), agriculture (17.7 per cent), the commercial sector (8 per cent), traction and railways (1.5 per cent) and others (6.1 per cent).

First nuclear power plant

The Tarapur Atomic Power Station in Palghar, Maharashtra, with an installed capacity of 380 MW, was commissioned in 1969. It had two boiling water reactor units of 210 MW each, fuelled by enriched uranium. It was built by Bechtel Corporation and General Electric Company, USA, under an agreement between the Government of India, the USA and the International Atomic Energy Agency.

First heavy water plant

The first heavy water plant was set up at Nangal in the Rupnagar District of Punjab in 1962. Heavy water or deuterium oxide was the basic fuel used by first-generation nuclear power plants.

First hydropower station

Sidrapong Hydroelectric Power Station in the foothills of Arya Tea Estate near Darjeeling, West Bengal, is the oldest hydroelectric power plant in India. It was

First solar-powered thermal plant
The country's first 50 MW solar-powered thermal power plant, developed by Chhattisgarh-based Godawari Green Energy Ltd (GGEL) in Nokh Village in Jaisalmer District, Rajasthan, went operational in 2013.

Launch of green fuel
On 1 April 2017, Bharat Stage-IV (BS-IV grade) fuel was officially launched across the country to keep carbon emissions in check.

State with highest installed capacity of renewable power
Karnataka has the highest installed capacity of grid-connected renewable power (15,387.98 MW) followed by Tamil Nadu (14,886.32 MW) and Gujarat (12,442.85 MW) as on 31 January 2021.

Largest grid-connected rooftop solar plant
The country's largest grid-connected rooftop solar plant, with a capacity of 7.52 MW, started operations in May 2016 at Dera Beas in Amritsar District, Punjab.

SUPER 30

ECONOMIC REFORMS: MILESTONES

The 1990s are imprinted in Indian history as the decade of economic reforms. In July 1991, India was forced to pledge 47 tonnes of gold to raise foreign exchange and that was probably the moment that changed India forever.

1991: Fundamental changes were introduced in 1991 to liberalize the economy and give a fillip to its rate of growth. The duo of the then prime minister, P.V. Narasimha Rao, and finance minister, Dr Manmohan Singh, was able to initiate unprecedented reforms. The main features included the opening up of the economy for foreign investments, the end of the licence permit raj, and a divestment roadmap for public sector undertakings, to name just a few.

1992: In a year marked by the securities market scam (whose face became Harshad Mehta), the Securities and Exchange Board of India (SEBI) was given statutory powers and the foundation was laid for an equity culture in India. For the first time, millions understood stock markets as being a place where they could invest and earn returns.

1997: Relying on the belief that economic growth will happen when taxes are lower and compliance levels are higher, the budget of 1997 featured lower taxes and freeing companies from the shackles of some outdated laws. It was hailed as a 'dream budget' by the Indian media, with something for everyone.

1999–2003: For the first time, questions were raised about the government's role in running industries such as hotels and airlines. Strategic divestment of public sector undertakings, such as Hindustan Zinc Ltd, was carried out, and the government's stake in Maruti Suzuki Ltd was sold. The formation of an insurance regulator, the Insurance Regulatory and Development Authority of India (IRDAI), in 1999 gave confidence to foreign investors to increase their stake in Indian joint ventures. There was a clearing up of the way for private players to essay pivotal roles in many sectors such as telecom.

2017: The implementation of the goods and services tax (GST) was the highlight among the biggest reforms ever, as it reduced the incidence of indirect taxation. Since India had one of the highest incidences of indirect taxation, the implementation of GST not only reduced this burden but also took steps against tax arbitrage, the primary reason for the generation of black money.

2020: Three farm acts, which allow farmers to sell their produce to anyone they want anywhere in India, met with a mixed response. These laws were repealed in December 2021.

commissioned on 10 November 1897 with a capacity of 2 x 65 kW. This was increased in phases as per rising demands to reach 1,000 kW (1 MW) by 1916.

Longest natural gas pipeline

- The HVJ (Hazira–Vijaipur–Jagdishpur) gas pipeline, owned by Gas Authority of India Ltd (GAIL) and laid during 1986–89, is 2,300 km long.
- Indian Oil Corporation (IOC), Bharat Petroleum Co. Ltd (BPCL) and

Hindustan Petroleum Corporation Ltd (HPCL) announced a joint venture in June 2019 to lay the world's longest (2,757 km) LPG pipeline from Kandla in Gujarat to Gorakhpur in Uttar Pradesh, at a cost of ₹10,000 crore (100 billion).

First oil well

- Oil was first located at Borbil (later Digboi) in Assam in 1890, but systematic drilling for oil had begun in Upper Assam in 1866 and oil was struck at Makum near Margherita at a depth of 36 m (118 ft) on 26 March 1867.
- The first offshore well was sunk in the Bombay High oilfield in 1974.

First pipeline

The Guwahati–Siliguri petroleum product pipeline (between Assam and West Bengal) was commissioned by the Indian Oil Corporation in 1965.

First refinery

The Assam Railways and Trading Co. built a small refinery at Margherita in present-day Tinsukia District, Assam, in 1893 to refine oil from Makum and Digboi areas.

WR **Oldest running refinery**

The Digboi Refinery, under the Indian Oil Corporation, started in 1899 in Assam, is the world's oldest running refinery.

First company to market LPG

The first company to market liquefied petroleum gas (LPG) in India was BPCL in 1955. Now BPCL reaches around 25 million households with 2,137 LPG distributors across the country.

First private branded LPG

Reliance Gas was launched in 1998 by Reliance Petroleum Ltd in collaboration with the local LPG bottlers for the packaging of the product.

First indigenous atomic power plant

Madras Atomic Power Station (MAPS) at Kalpakkam near Chennai, Tamil Nadu, is India's first fully indigenously built nuclear power station under the Indira Gandhi Centre for Atomic Research (IGCAR). Each of its two units generates 220 MW of electricity. The first indigenous 40 MW Fast Breeder Test Reactor (FBTR) was commissioned in August 1985 here.

Record Rewind

Largest thermal power plant

1991

With the commissioning of an additional 500 MW unit at the Korba Thermal Power Station on the River Hasdeo in Korba, Bilaspur District, Madhya Pradesh, on 23 March 1989, the plant achieved its ultimate capacity of 2,100 MW, the highest in India.

2020

Vindhyachal Super Thermal Power Station in Singrauli District, Madhya Pradesh, with an installed capacity of 4,760 MW, is ranked as the biggest thermal power plant in the country. It is a coal-based power plant, owned and operated by NTPC Ltd.

MINING

Largest coal-producing company

Coal India Limited (CIL), a government-owned coal-mining corporate headquartered in Kolkata, West Bengal, came into being in November 1975 when the Government of India took over private coal mines. It is now the single largest coal producer in the world. Operating through 84 mining areas, it has seven wholly owned coal-producing subsidiaries, as well as a mine planning and consultancy company, across eight states in India. CIL reportedly produced 602.13 million tonnes of coal during 2019–20. As per the latest reports, the geological reserves of coal in the country exceed the demand by 326 billion tonnes, which is estimated to be enough to last for several centuries as per the current demands and needs.

A coal mine in operation

State/UT with the most mines

There are 1,303 reporting mines in the country as recorded in 2019–20. Among these, Madhya Pradesh leads in the number of reporting mines (excluding atomic and fuel minerals) with 220 mines, followed by Gujarat (167), Karnataka (140), Odisha (129), Andhra Pradesh (123), Chhattisgarh (92), Telangana (92), Rajasthan (84) and Maharashtra (67). In terms of the value of mineral production, Odisha leads with ₹32,841 crore (328.41 billion), followed by Rajasthan (₹22,776 crore/227.76 billion)) and Andhra Pradesh (₹17,906 crore/179.06 billion).

Oldest gold mine

India's oldest gold mine was located in Kolar, Karnataka. The production here in the mid-1970s was 3,000 kg a year, but was on a decline ever since, and the mines were closed in 2001. The three mines collectively, viz., Champion, Mysore and Nandydroog. at the Kolar goldfields, made it one of the largest and deepest gold mine areas of the world and the only recognized gold mine in the country, known for gold mining for over a century.

First coal mining

The first tonne of coal was struck in Raniganj Coalfield in 1775 by Suetonius Grant Heatly, the then collector of the East India Company for Palamu and Hazaribagh, in present-day Jharkhand. Records have shown that John Summer and Grant Heatly jointly obtained a licence from the then British Governor General Warren Hastings in 1774 to exploit what they then called 'Panchet coal'. They were later joined by another Englishman called Redfern.

 **Coal import for blending purposes reduced by 54 per cent from 2019 to September 2020.**

Only diamond mines

India's only diamond mines are at Panna in Madhya Pradesh and are administered by the government-owned National Mineral Development Corporation (NMDC).

Largest uranium ore deposits

In July 2011, a survey indicated that the Tummalapalle mine near Hyderabad, now in Telangana, could provide up to 150,000 tonnes of low-grade uranium ore.

INDUSTRIES AND COMPANIES

First factory

The first factory in India, which was a dye-manufacturing unit, was set up by the East India Company with the permission of the then Mughal emperor Jahangir in Surat in 1609 CE, marking the beginning of colonialism.

First commercial production of iron and steel

- In 1830, a unit was set up at Porto Novo (now Parangipettai) in Cuddalore District, Tamil Nadu, to produce iron, but it failed.
- In 1853, the East India Iron Company set up two blast furnaces in South Arcot and Coimbatore districts, Tamil Nadu. These closed in 1858.
- In 1875, the Barakar Iron Works, Kulti, Bengal, produced pig iron.
- Steel production began in 1892 at the Metal and Steel Factory at Cossipore (now Kashipur, West Bengal), moving to Ichapore (now Ishapur, West Bengal) in 1905.

First cigarette company

Imperial Tobacco Company (ITC) was established in Calcutta (now Kolkata, West Bengal) in 1910.

First rubber estate and company

The first rubber company, called Malankara Rubber and Produce Company, was started in 1910 by P. John on a 70-acre (28.3 hectares) estate in Thodupuzha, Idukki District, Kerala.

AUTOMOBILE SALE TRENDS (DOMESTIC)*

	Category	Sales Figures
1	Passenger Vehicles	2,711,457
2	Commercial Vehicles	568,559
3	Three-wheelers	216,197
4	Two-wheelers	15,119,387

*2020–21 (till June 2021); Source: Society of Indian Automobile Manufacturers

Decoding Start-ups

While there is no set definition for a start-up, there are some common features that distinguish them. Generally, a start-up is set up by more than one person, so there is usually a founder and a co-founder. It should ideally be bootstrapped. If not, there should be at least one outside investor who has funded the idea of the entrepreneurs. Further, it should have been started to solve a problem, and usually technology is an essential part of such companies. When it comes to technology, the start-up should either be using it to solve a problem, or to scale up the business.

After much deliberation, the Government of India decided that for taxation, a start-up is to be classified separately because it needs to fulfil certain criteria and qualifies for additional benefits in terms of how the money raised by it is to be treated from the perspective of valuing gains and tax rates.

The term start-up started gaining currency during the dotcom boom, but it garnered more pace after app stores came into being because it was mobile apps that changed the landscape of technology. India is said to have the third largest start-up ecosystem in the world. India had about 50,000 start-ups in 2018, of which around 8,900–9,300 were technology-led. As many as 1,300 new technology start-ups came up in 2019 alone, indicating that two to three technology start-ups come up every day in India. While the upward curve of start-ups slowed down during the 2020 COVID-related lockdown, a lot is expected from start-ups in India in the coming years.

First ice-cream company

Joy Ice Creams Pvt. Ltd, which was founded by L.C. Java, was the first company to manufacture and market ice cream. In 1948, Java bought a homogenizer and pasteurizer, and set up a small business that became India's first ice-cream company.

First tea company

- Tea seeds were first imported into India from China in 1774. In 1837, the East India Company set up the first tea estate at Chabua, Dibrugarh District, Assam.
- The Alubari Tea Company, established in 1856 in Darjeeling (now in West Bengal) under the Kurseong and Darjeeling Tea Company, first commercialized tea.

First tyre company

The Dunlop Rubber Company (India) Ltd was established on 19 August 1926, with its registered office in Bombay (now Mumbai, Maharashtra) and an authorized share capital of ₹5 million (50 lakh).

Oldest engineering company

Jessop & Company Ltd, the oldest engineering company in the country, was established in 1788 by two engineers from Britain – Henry and George Jessop.

First scooter manufacturing company

Lambretta, the first scooter introduced by Automobile Products of India (API), was manufactured in 1956.

First cotton textile mill

Though the British had established a cotton textile mill in 1817, the first truly Indian textile mill was set up in July 1854 in Bombay (now Mumbai, Maharashtra) by Cawasji N. Davar. It was called the Bombay Spinning and Weaving Company.

First foreign collaboration

Carr, Tagore and Company was the first Indo-British collaboration under the Charter Act of 1833. There were four partners: W. Carr, Dwarakanath Tagore, D.M. Gordon and William Prinsep. It closed down in 1847.

Oldest jute mill

Wellington Jute Mill in Rishra, near Serampore (now Srirampur, West Bengal), was established by George Auckland in 1855 as the Rishra Twine and Yarn Mills Ltd, with machinery bought from John Kerr of the Douglas Foundry, the leading manufacturers of flax and manufacturing machines in Dundee, Scotland. The mill had an output of eight tonnes a day. It shut down in 1868 and resumed as Calcutta Jute Mills, which later became Wellington Jute Mills. It is now under Ai Champdany Industries Ltd.

First champagne manufacturer

In 1987, its very first year, Shyam Chougule's Champagne India, a subsidiary of Indage in Narayangaon, Pune District, Maharashtra, with a 42-acre (17 hectare) vineyard, entered the export market. Champagne Indage Ltd, as it was renamed after being restructured, was the market leader in wines then, with a production of about 100,000 cases a year.

First five-star hotel

The Taj Mahal Hotel in Mumbai, Maharashtra, said to have been built back to front, was founded by Jamshetji Nusserwanji Tata in 1904. The story goes that in those days there were very few hotels that permitted entry to Indians and Tata himself had been denied admission to Pyrke's Apollo Hotel, close to the present-day Taj Mahal Hotel. This motivated Tata to build the hotel.

First car to be exported

Hindustan Motors Ltd's Ambassador was the first car to be exported in 1975–76 to Guyana in South America.

First plastic factories

- A plastic factory was established in 1926 at Jessore, now in Bangladesh. It manufactured combs, soapboxes, ashtrays and other articles from imported

N.R. NARAYANA MURTHY: THE INFOSYS IMPACT

N.R. Narayana Murthy, Infosys and the growth of the Indian information technology industry are synonymous. Established in 1981, with a capital of reportedly just US $250, Infosys has come a long way. At the end of the second quarter of financial year 2021 the revenue of Infosys stood at around US $12.87 billion with a market capitalization of more than US $6 billion. It took Infosys 23 years to achieve an annual revenue of US $1 billion, but it took them just 23 months to add another billion to their revenue as it reached around US $2 billion in 2006.

There are many firsts to the credit of Infosys co-founder N.R. Narayana Murthy or NRN, as he is popularly known at Infosys. In 1993, Infosys was among the first companies in India to start giving employee stock options (ESOPs). These ESOPs made the company's employees millionaires, a first in India. It also brought on the table a realization among India Inc. that the stock of the company is a currency and that if the value of this currency is taken care of, it can not only attract talent but also help an organization grow organically.

An even more significant revelation was of the fact that for the value of this currency of the company to remain high, the organization needs to follow the highest standard of corporate governance and transparency in dealing with all stakeholders. Infosys under NRN started many practices that were far ahead of the time: communication with minority shareholders every quarter, the concept of earning guidance, announcing major contracts as and when the company acquired them, and sharing information about risks the business might be exposed to due to an event as it unfolded – all added up to a level of transparency much higher than the law of the land required at the time.

All these practices were unheard of in India until the time NRN got Infosys to implement them. A number of them are now part of laws for companies to follow. It is no surprise that NRN was awarded the Padma Shri in 2000 and the Padma Vibhushan in 2008, and is regarded as a living legend in Indian industry.

celluloid sheets and rods.

- In 1933, two units for compression moulding were started with machinery that was imported from Germany.
- The first thermosetting plastic produced in India was phenol formaldehyde moulding, started in 1946.

First retail chain for computers

Computer Point launched India's first retail chain for computers and computer accessories by establishing the first showroom in Bombay (now Mumbai), Maharashtra, on 31 December 1984. It had stores in other cities, like Delhi, too.

First car factory

In 1928, General Motors had commenced the assembly of cars and trucks in Bombay (now Mumbai, Maharashtra) while using imported components. The first indigenous car manufacturing company was the Birlas' Hindustan Motors, which was established at Uttarpara near Calcutta (now Kolkata, West Bengal). The first Indian car, 'Hindustan 10', rolled off the assembly line in 1948.

First power loom

The first power loom for jute cloth was started in 1958 by Henderson and Company, agents of Borneo Jute Company, in present-day Baranagar, Kolkata, in West Bengal. On becoming a limited company, it was named the Baranagore Jute Manufacturing Company and had 512 looms at its peak.

WR **Fastest growing tech-hub**

Bengaluru, Karnataka, was declared the fastest growing tech-hub in the world, based on data analysed for the years 2016–20. The research by London and Partners, UK, released on 14 January 2021, revealed that there was a 5.4 per cent increase in investment during the specified period. Bengaluru was followed by London, Munich, Berlin, Paris and Mumbai.

Highest pharma exports

The Indian pharma industry saw exports of US $20.59 billion (2,059 crore) during the year 2019–20, with the USA being the largest export destination. India is the fourth largest formulations exporter by volume and tenth largest by value. It is also the largest exclusive generic exporter by value.

First batch of microchips

The first microchips rolled out of Semiconductor Ltd, located in Chandigarh, in March 1984.

WR **India leads in the export of measles vaccines**

Ninety per cent of measles vaccines in the world are supplied by India, which also supplies 65 per cent of DPT and BCG vaccines in the world.

First Indian firm to join the World Economic Forum's Global Lighthouse Network

On 3 July 2019, Tata Steel Kalinganagar (TSK) in Kalinganagar, Odisha, was announced as the first and only Indian manufacturing plant to join the World Economic Forum's (WEF) Global Lighthouse Network. This network is a community of manufacturers that lead in the application of the Fourth Industrial Revolution technologies.

First woman chairperson of SAIL

Soma Mondal assumed office as the first ever woman chairperson of the Steel Authority of India Ltd (SAIL) on 1 January 2021. She also holds the distinction of being the first woman director (commercial) of SAIL.

Top IT company

Ranking 38th in *Forbes*' list of the top 100 digital companies in January 2021, Tata Consultancy Services (TCS) is the market leader in the information technology (IT) and IT-enabled services (ITeS) sector. The only other Indian company on the list was Infosys, ranked 71.

HOUSING AND REAL ESTATE

Most household relocations executed in a year

Agarwal Packers and Movers Ltd, headquartered in New Delhi, with 102 branches, carried out services and deliveries for 132,061 household relocations during 2019 –20.

Largest slum

Dharavi in Mumbai, Maharashtra, is India's largest slum with an estimated population of between 300,000 and a million, and spread over 500 acres (202 hectares).

Tamil Nadu: state with the best performance in alleviating poverty

ECONOMY AND GENERAL

Largest share of youth

The share of India's youth in the total population, the highest in the world, is 34.8 per cent (as per the 2011 census) or 42.2 crore (422 million). The National Youth Policy defines 'youth' as persons between 15 and 29 years.

State/UT with the best performance in alleviating poverty

At the end of 2019, Tamil Nadu, with a score of 72, topped the chart of states/UTs on the Sustainable Development Goals (SDG) India Index for the no-poverty goal.

State/UT with the lowest score on the poverty scorecard

Jharkhand, with a score of 28, was the lowest-scoring state on SDG India Index's no-poverty scorecard at the end of 2019.

Gross Domestic Product Drops to a Record Low

The decline of 23.9 per cent in the gross domestic product (GDP) for the first quarter of financial year 2021 over the same quarter in the previous fiscal was the highest ever decline in Indian history. Given the fact that during this period there was a nationwide lockdown due to the COVID-19 pandemic, the decline in GDP was bound to happen, but its extent was not clear. Although the latter part of June 2020 witnessed the end of lockdowns and subsequent opening up, economists opined that reversal of the impact would take time. The results could have been worse but for the part played by the rural sector, which was able to hold ground. Tractor sales, one of the micro-indicators of how rural India is doing, were the first to recover.

Lowest level the rupee touched

The rupee touched an all-time low of ₹77.08 per US dollar (on intraday basis) on 7 March 22.

Forex reserves

The country's foreign exchange reserves touched an all-time high of US $642.453 billion in the week ended 3 September 2021.

First infrastructural index

The Government of India launched a City Liveability Index on 23 June 2017 to measure the quality of life in 116 major cities, based on a set of 79 parameters, such as the availability of roads, education, healthcare, mobility, employment opportunities, emergency response, grievance redressal, pollution, availability of open and green spaces, cultural and entertainment opportunities and so on.

First winner of the Nobel Prize in Economics

- Dr Amartya Kumar Sen (b. 3 November 1933) received the Nobel Prize in economic sciences in 1998, the first Indian and Asian to do so. Born in Santiniketan, West Bengal, he is considered to be a pioneer of welfare economics.
- On 14 October 2019, Indian-origin economist Abhijit Vinayak Banerjee shared the 2019 Nobel Prize in economic sciences with his co-researchers – his wife Esther Duflo, and Michael Kremer – for their work on alleviating global poverty.

Only market run exclusively by women

The 'mother's market' or 'Ima Keithel' in Imphal, the capital of Manipur, is perhaps the only one of its kind in Asia, maybe even the world. Its thousands

Dr Amartya Sen Wins Yet Another Laurel

Economist Dr Amartya Kumar Sen (b. 3 November 1933) won the 2020 Peace Prize of the German Book Trade, announced on 17 June 2020. The 1998 Nobel Prize-winner was awarded for his work addressing global social injustice. The only other Indian to ever win this award was former Indian president, Dr Sarvepalli Radhakrishnan, in 1961.

Dr Amartya Kumar Sen

of stalls are all run by women, selling everything from fruits and vegetables to garments and handmade jewellery. The market has long been a part of Manipuri tradition with evidence suggesting that it dates back to the 16th century.

Equity market
The total market capitalization of the Indian market, based on the companies listed on the Bombay Stock Exchange (BSE), touched an all-time high of ₹20,300,428.17 crore (203 trillion) on 10 February 2021.

RETAIL

Highest number of stores opened in a single day
On 29 October 2018, the Chinese electronics company Xiaomi opened 500 retail stores, called Mi Stores, in rural regions of India, thereby setting a record for the most number of stores opened in a single day. These stores are on the lines of the larger 'Mi Home' stores in metropolitan cities.

First virtual mall
The Digital Mall of Asia is a virtual e-commerce platform, an amalgamation of digital space and real estate, making it the first virtual mall in the country. The mall is open in Delhi, Noida, Pune, Ahmedabad, Bengaluru, Chennai, Gurugram, Hyderabad, Jaipur, Lucknow and Mumbai. Each location has a different digital interface and e-shops can be bought or acquired on rent. The mall works 24 hours a day, seven days a week.

Biggest business deal
In August 2018, Walmart Inc., a US multinational retail corporation, announced the deal agreements that made it the largest shareholder in the Flipkart Group, an e-commerce company founded by Sachin Bansal and Binny Bansal in 2007, and based in Bengaluru, Karnataka. Walmart bought roughly 77 per cent stake in the e-retailer for around US $16 billion (approx. ₹1,000 billion then). This was India's largest acquisition and also the world's biggest purchase of an e-commerce company.

First toy fair online
The country's first toy fair was held virtually from 27 February to 4 March 2021

via videoconferencing. A first-ever event of its kind, this toy fair aimed to boost the Indian toy industry and create linkages between various stakeholders. It was held at *www.indiatoyfair.in*, with more than 1,000 exhibitors from all states and UTs of India showcasing their toys, which were also available for sale online. Panel discussions, seminars and related activities were also held online to provide networking opportunities and exposure to Indian toy manufacturers. The event witnessed a registration of 1.5 million (15 lakh) users.

ADVERTISING

First patented brand

Horlicks, the first patented brand in the country, was launched in the last decade of the 19th century. In the 1940s, Hindustan Thompson Associates (HTA), now J. Walter Thompson India (JWT), coined the 'Balanced Nourishment' concept for the malt-based beverage to make Horlicks more relevant to India.

First known 'advertisements'

- Advertising in India began with the first printed newspaper, which was called *Hicky's Bengal Gazette* and printed from 1780 in Calcutta (now Kolkata, West Bengal). The advertisements consisted of a series of simple messages 'classified' into different categories for easy reference of readers, or they were lists of the latest merchandise from England.
- The first true advertisement was printed in Marathi in the *Bombay Courier* in 1802.

First multinational advertising agencies

- Alliance Advertising was set up during the First World War (1914–18), and other foreign (American) agencies such as L.A. Stronach and D.J. Keymer followed later.
- The first fully multinational agency in the country was Hindustan Thompson Associates (now JWT) in 1926.

First full-service Indian advertising agency

In 1934, Venkatrao Sista opened Sista Advertising and Publicity Services in Bombay (now Mumbai, Maharashtra) as the first Indian agency offering creative work and space selling in the media. Sista, who came to Mumbai as a stenographer of the Great Indian Peninsular Railway, will always be associated with Khatau Voiles, popularized by his agency's campaign.

First ad association

On 21 September 1945, the Advertising Agencies Association of India (AAAI) was registered as a society in Calcutta (now Kolkata, West Bengal). In 1961, its headquarters moved to Bombay (now Mumbai).

Largest billboard

A billboard for Jeep India, erected on the Mumbai–Pune expressway, measured 253 ft (77.1 m) in width and 100 ft (30.48 m) in height. The logo was 164.6 ft (50.17 m) long and 65.8 ft (20.05) high. The total amount of metal used was 80 tonnes and it took 45 days to build the billboard.

Record Rewind

Largest hoarding

1997

Selvel Advertising, Calcutta (now Kolkata), West Bengal, in 1995, put up a hoarding backlit by 735 tube lights and advertising the 555 brand of cigarettes. The hoarding measured 120 ft by 30 ft (3,600 sq. ft).

2020

A hoarding of Mumbai-based Global Advertisers was installed in Bandra in Mumbai, Maharashtra, on 24 January 2014. It measured (in area) 1,560.72 sq. m (16,800 sq. ft), making it the largest in India. The 42.67 m wide and 36.58 m high (140 ft by 120 ft) front-lit hoarding overlooked the Western Express Highway, the Bandra Kala Nagar Junction and other important vantage points. It was visible from a distance of 3 km.

First ad agency abroad
Interads, a Delhi-based ad agency, was the first Indian advertising agency to open a foreign branch in Moscow, Russia, in 1962.

First Indianized foreign brand
Lux toilet soap, sold as the 'favourite beauty soap of film stars', signed on Hindi cinema actor Leela Chitnis as its first Indian model in 1941, in order to Indianize the brand.

First commercials on radio
The first commercial came on Vividh Bharati in 1967.

First ads on TV
The first product to be advertised on TV was Gwalior Suitings in an advertisement that appeared in January 1976.

First colour TV ad
An advertisement made for Bombay Dyeing was the first colour TV ad in 1982, the year that colour TV came to India.

Longest sustained advertising campaign
The Amul 'utterly butterly' topical ad series is the longest sustained campaign, with its tongue-in-cheek, pithy comments on current affairs. The first ad featuring the now iconic 'Amul girl' appeared in March 1966. Started by Sylvester da Cunha in 1966 and run by da Cunha Communications, Mumbai, Maharashtra, the Amul Butter campaign has continued for more than 50 years.

Firsts at Cannes Lions
In 1996, the advertising fraternity bagged three awards at the International Advertising Festival in Cannes, France.

Most at Cannes Lions
In 2017, India won 40 metals including a Grand Prix award.

First agency to handle election campaigns
In 1983, Rediffusion became the first advertising agency to create an advertising and publicity campaign for the Congress party.

SPORTS

GENERAL

Dr Narinder Dhruv Batra: first Indian to head the International Hockey Federation

First Indian to head the international body of an Olympic sport

Hockey India president Dr Narinder Dhruv Batra was the first Indian to head the International Hockey Federation in 2016.

First Indian president of the International Cricket Council

Jagmohan Dalmiya became the first Indian president of the International Cricket Council (ICC) in 1997 and served till 2000.

First Indian chairman of the ICC

N. Srinivasan was the first ICC chairman from India (2014–15).

First Indian independent chairman of the ICC

Shashank Manohar was the first independent chairman of the ICC in 2016 and he was re-elected for another two years.

First Indian president of the World Squash Federation

Indian squash administrator Narayana Ramachandran was president of the World Squash Federation (WSF) for two terms, from 2008 to 2016.

First Indian on the Fédération Internationale de Football Association (FIFA) executive panel

Praful Patel, president, All India Football Federation, and senior vice president,

The Olympic Games 2020

The Olympics Games were postponed from March 2020 to July–August 2021 amid the Covid-19 pandemic. International spectators were not to be allowed at these Games that were still called Tokyo 2020. This was the first time in the history of the Olympics that the Games were postponed and rescheduled, rather than cancelled. The Olympic Games of ancient times were discontinued at the end of the fourth century CE while the modern Olympic Games began in Athens, Greece, in 1896. The Games were cancelled once during the First World War (1916) and twice during the Second World War (1940, 1944). Other disrupted Olympic Games include the 1972 Munich Games in Germany, when Arab attackers gunned down 11 Israeli athletes. In the 1980 Moscow Games, the USA boycotted the Olympics to protest against the Soviet Union's invasion of Afghanistan in the previous year and, in 1984, the Soviet Union boycotted the Los Angeles Games in retaliation of the US snub.

Asian Football Confederation, was the first Indian to be elected to the FIFA Executive Council in April 2019.

First Indian president of the International Kabaddi Federation
Sports administrator Janardan Singh Gehlot was the founder president of the International Kabaddi Federation from 1985 to 2013, and then life president from May 2013.

First Indian to become a FIFA World Cup match commissioner
Former All India Football Federation president Priya Ranjan Dasmunsi was the match commissioner in a FIFA World Cup 2006 game, a group stage match between Australia and Croatia.

First Indian woman to be a member of International Olympic Committee's (IOC) Athletes' Commission
In October 2016, badminton player Saina Nehwal was appointed a member of the IOC's Athletes' Commission.

First sportsman to be nominated to the Rajya Sabha
Wrestler Dara Singh was the first sportsman to be nominated to the Rajya Sabha, the Upper House of the Indian Parliament, in 2003. He was the world champion of a kind of exhibition wrestling.

First sportsperson to be awarded the Padma Shri
Hockey legend and triple Olympian gold medallist, late Balbir Singh (senior) (1924–2020) became the first sportsperson to be awarded the Padma Shri in 1957. The versatile centre forward played a key role in India's victories in 1948 in London, in 1952 in Helsinki and in 1956 in Melbourne.

First woman sportsperson to receive the Padma Vibhushan
M.C. Mary Kom was honoured with the Padma Vibhushan award in 2020. The boxer is the fourth sportsperson in the country to receive the award after chess wizard Viswanathan Anand, mountaineer Edmund Hillary (posthumous) and cricket icon Sachin Tendulkar, who all got the award in 2008.

First Indian to win a world title in motorsport
Aishwarya Pissay from Bengaluru, Karnataka, became the first Indian to win a world title in motorsport. She won the Fédération Internationale de Motocyclisme (FIM) Bajas World Cup (women's category) with 65 points on 13 August 2019 in Varpalota, Hungary. She won the first round in Dubai, UAE, was placed third in Portugal, fifth in Spain and fourth in Hungary.

Aishwarya Pissay: first Indian to win a world title in motorsport

First Indian sportsman to receive an honorary doctorate degree
The Lakshmibai Institute of Physical

Education, Gwalior, Madhya Pradesh, conferred an honorary doctorate degree on former shooter Raja Randhir Singh on 8 September 2000. He represented India in six Olympic Games: in Tokyo (1964), Mexico City (1968), Munich (1972), Montreal (1976), Moscow (1980) and Los Angeles (1984).

First Indian sportswoman to receive an honorary doctorate degree
Kannur University, Kannur, Kerala, conferred an honorary doctorate degree on P.T. Usha on 1 November 2000 for her contribution to athletics. She represented India during 1980–98 in four Olympic Games, five Asian Games and five Asian Championships. She also won the most medals ever by an Indian athlete at the Jakarta Asian Championships in 1985, with five gold medals and a bronze medal.

First Indian sportsman and coach to receive an honorary doctorate degree
The Indian Institute of Technology, Kanpur, Uttar Pradesh, bestowed an honorary doctorate degree on former badminton sports star and chief Indian coach Pullela Gopichand on 28 June 2019 in recognition of his contribution to badminton. The second Indian to win the All England Open Badminton Championships in 2001, he switched to coaching and launched his academy in Hyderabad, Telangana, in 2008.

First fencing title in the senior Commonwealth Championship
Chennai-born fencer C.A. Bhavani Devi made history in November 2018 when she became the first Indian to win the gold medal at the senior Commonwealth Championship.

DOUBLE VICTORY: ARJUNA AWARD-WINNING COUPLES

Kaity Chargeman Khodaiji (1971) and
Farrokh R. Khodaiji (1967) – Both in table tennis

Shiny K. Abraham in athletics (1984) and
Wilson Cherian in swimming (1988)

Bhagyashree (née Sathe) (1987) and
Praveen Thipsay (1984) – Both in chess

Monalisa Baruah Mehta (1987) and
Kamlesh Mehta (1985) – Both in table tennis

Vandana Rao in athletics (1987) and
Joaquim Carvalho in hockey (1986)

Poulomi Ghatak (2009) and
Soumyadeep Roy (2005) – Both in table tennis

Saina Nehwal (2009) and
Parupalli Kashyap (2012) – Both in badminton

Jwala Gutta (2011) and
B. Chetan Anand (2006) – Both in badminton

LARGEST STADIUMS BY CAPACITY		
Stadium	**Capacity**	**City, State**
Narendra Modi Stadium	132,000	Ahmedabad, Gujarat
Buddh International Circuit	110,000	Greater Noida, Uttar Pradesh
Vivekananda Yuba Bharati Krirangan (Salt Lake Stadium)	85,000	Kolkata, West Bengal
Eden Gardens	80,000	Kolkata, West Bengal
Shaheed Veer Narayan Singh International Cricket Stadium	65,000	Raipur, Chhattisgarh

First woman to head a state cricket association

Rupa Gurunath became the first woman president of the Tamil Nadu Cricket Association (TNCA), a BCCI State Association, on 27 September 2019 and will be in office for a term of three years.

First ever international rugby 15s win

The Indian women's rugby team scripted history by clinching their first ever international 15s victory against a higher-ranked Singapore for a bronze medal in the Asian women's Division 1 Rugby 15s Championship 2019.

First book on India's football journey

The first comprehensive book on football in India, *Barefoot to Boots: The Many Lives of Indian Football*, covering the sport from 1888 to 2017, was written by sports writer and broadcaster Novy Kapadia in 2018. The first book on Indian football was *Stories from Indian Football* by Jaydeep Basu in 2003.

First sports magazine

Bengal Sporting was first published in 1837 and edited by British journalist Joachim Hayward Stocqueler.

BBC Indian Sportswoman of the Year

Koneru Humpy won the World Rapid Chess Championship in December 2019 and the Cairns Cup in 2020. She was announced as the Indian sportswoman of the year by BBC on 8 March 2021.

BBC Lifetime Achievement Award

The legendary long jumper and Olympian Anju Bobby George was honoured with the Lifetime Achievement Award by BBC on 8 March 2021.

Youngest sportsperson to receive the Padma Bhushan

Badminton player P.V. Sindhu, at 24 years, became the youngest sportsperson to receive the Padma Bhushan in 2020. Sindhu is the third badminton player to be

THE TRIUMPHANT TRIO

Following the retirement of Sunil Gavaskar, Vijay Amritraj and Prakash Padukone in the late 1980s, the teen-trio of cricketer Sachin Tendulkar, chess player Viswanathan Anand and tennis player Leander Paes caught the imagination of a sports-loving generation. The three lived up to their promise and performed exceptionally, with consistency, to become icons for decades to follow.

Among these three, India saw an Olympic medal, world titles, world records and much more. They scaled new heights in their sporting disciplines, excelled at the biggest stages and inspired more than a generation to turn their passion into a well-paid profession.

Between 1989 and 2013, Tendulkar's stature grew beyond a mere sportsman. A household name in our cricket-crazy nation, Tendulkar was honoured with the Bharat Ratna, India's highest civilian award, in 2014.

Leander, from 1991 to date, continues to inspire a tennis-playing generation. After participating in seven successive Olympic Games, he is three short of 100 Grand Slam appearances.

Anand, after breaking into the world's top10 in July 1991, remains among the elite, active players in chess. At 51, Anand is a hero to many aspirants, inspiring them to the highest achievements in world chess today.

SACHIN TENDULKAR

- Only Bharat Ratna recipient among sportspersons
- Only cricketer in the world to score a hundred international centuries: 51 in Tests and 49 in One-Day Internationals (ODIs)
- Highest number of Tests played: 200
- Highest runs in Tests: 15,921
- Highest runs in ODIs: 18,426
- Highest number of centuries in Tests: 51
- Highest number of centuries outside India: 100
- Longest career in ODIs: 22 years and 91days
- Most runs in the World Cup: 2,278
- Most boundary hits in the World Cup: 241
- Most centuries and half-centuries in the World Cup: Six centuries (a record equalled by Rohit Sharma in 2019) and 15 half-centuries

Sachin Tendulkar

awarded the honour after Pullela Gopichand received it in 2014 and Saina Nehwal in 2016.

Best performance in the Asian Para Games
Indian para athletes won 72 medals in the Asian Para Games 2018 in Jakarta, Indonesia, bagging 15 golds, 24 silvers and 33 bronzes. In 2014, they won 33 medals (three golds, 14 silvers and 16 bronzes).

Best performance in the Asian Games
India participated in the 2018 Asian Games in Jakarta and Palembang, Indonesia

SUPER 30

VISWANATHAN ANAND

- Country's first Grandmaster
- Only five-time world champion from India
- Only undisputed world champion from India
- Held the world no. 1 ranking
- A two-time World Cup winner
- Continues to be the highest-ranked Indian in the world list for over three decades
- Stayed in the world's top-10 ranked players for over 25 years, including over 24 years in succession

Viswanathan Anand

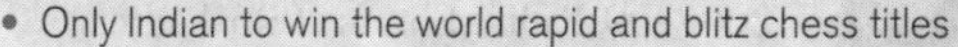

- Only Indian to win the world rapid and blitz chess titles
- Spearheaded the Indian squad that shared the gold medal with Russia in the International Chess Federation or World Chess Federation (FIDE) Online Chess Olympiad in 2020
- Winner of the prestigious Chess Oscar six times between 1997 and 2008

LEANDER PAES

- Winner of Olympic bronze medal in singles in 1996
- Won a rare 'double' at 1999 Wimbledon, by claiming the men's doubles and mixed doubles titles
- Has made the main draw of 97 Grand Slams
- Winner of 18 Grand Slam titles: 10 men's doubles and eight mixed doubles
- Only Indian to appear in seven consecutive Olympic Games from 1992 to 2016
- Most victories in Davis Cup doubles: 45
- In 2010, he became the only player, after Rod Laver, to win a title at Wimbledon in three different decades
- Completed a career 'Grand Slam' in men's doubles in 2012
- Completed a career 'Grand Slam' in mixed doubles in 2016
- Played and won with over 100 different partners in men's doubles and mixed doubles

Leander Paes

(from 18 August to 2 September) and had the best-ever haul with 69 medals, including 15 gold, 24 silver and 30 bronze medals from 465 events. After 67 years, since the inaugural edition of the Games in Delhi in 1951, India matched its best haul of 15 golds.

Most honoured sportsman

The second Indian to win the All England Open Badminton Championships in 2001, Pullela Gopichand was the recipient of the Arjuna Award in 1999, Rajiv Gandhi Khel Ratna Award in 2000–01, Dronacharya Award in 2009, Padma Shri in 2005 and Padma Bhushan in 2014.

First sweep in the Asian Para Games

At the Asian Para Games 2018, Indian para athletes occupied all three positions in high jump when Sharad Kumar (1.90 m), Varun Bhati (1.82 m) and Thangavelu Mariyappa (1.67 m) got the gold, silver and bronze medals, respectively, in the T-42/63 category (lower limb deficiency, leg length difference, impaired muscle power and impaired range of movement).

Most honoured sportswoman

Six-time world champion M.C. Mary Kom was the recipient of the Arjuna Award in 2003, Rajiv Gandhi Khel Ratna Award in 2008–09, Padma Shri in 2006, Padma Bhushan in 2013 and Padma Vibhushan in 2020.

First Indian recipient of the Olympic Order (Gold)

The Olympic Order (Gold), the highest award of the Olympic movement, is given for distinguished contribution to the movement. Former Indian prime minister Indira Gandhi was its first recipient in 1983. The Olympic Order is also awarded in silver and bronze categories.

Reena Raju: first Indian woman to participate in the World Transplant Games

First Indian woman to participate in the World Transplant Games

Reena Raju (b. 4 December 1982) from Bengaluru, Karnataka, was the flag bearer in the opening ceremony at the World Transplant Games 2017 in Malaga, Spain. She represented India in the 100 m sprint and badminton mixed doubles. She was the first Indian to undergo a repeat heart transplant on 22 October 2017 at Frontier Lifeline Hospital, Chennai, for cardiac allograft vasculopathy.

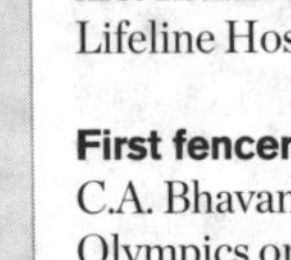

First fencer to qualify for the Olympics

C.A. Bhavani Devi became the first Indian fencer to qualify for the 2020 Tokyo Olympics on 14 March 2021 at the Women's Sabre World Cup in Budapest, Hungary. Chennai-based Bhavani Devi secured her slot through the Asia/Oceania Zone of the Adjusted Official Ranking (AOR).

Best performance in the South Asian Games

India bagged 174 gold, 93 silver and 45 bronze medals in the 13th South Asian Games 2019 in Kathmandu, Nepal.

Youngest Commonwealth Games captain

Seventeen-year-old Prachi Tehlan was the youngest captain representing India in netball at the Commonwealth Games (CWG) 2010, New Delhi.

ARCHERY

NATIONAL SPORTS AWARDS 2020 ARCHERY

Arjuna Award: Atanu Das
Dronacharya Award:
Dharmendra Tiwary (lifetime category)

First Junior World Championships title – men

Palton Hansda won the World Junior Archery Championships (compound – men's) in 2006 at Merida in Mexico.

First to win back-to-back titles

Deepika Kumari became the first Indian archer to win titles back-to-back when she won the cadet individual recurve title in 2009 at Ogden in Utah, USA, and the junior individual recurve gold in 2011 at Legnica, Poland.

First individual international medal

Shyam Lal won a bronze in the 50 m event at the fifth Asia Cup championship in Calcutta (now Kolkata), West Bengal, in January 1988. He represented India in the 1988 Seoul Olympics in South Korea.

First Archery World Cup team gold – women

Rimil Buriuly, Bombayla Devi Laishram and Deepika Kumari toppled Olympic champions South Korea 219–215 to win the first back-to-back World Cup titles at the Archery World Cup (stage 4) at Wroclaw, Poland, on 25 August 2013, after winning the first medal at the World Cup (stage 3) in Medellin, Colombia, in July.

First international gold

In October 1989, India took the gold in the team event at the Asian Archery Championships in Beijing, China, with 1,850 points, while reigning Olympic champion South Korea stood second with 1,842 points. The Indian team comprised Limba Ram, Shyam Lal and Skalzang Dorje.

First international gold – individual

Jayanta Talukdar won an individual gold medal at the Fédération Internationale de Tir à l'Arc (FITA) Meteksan World Cup, in 2006 in Merida, Mexico.

First international gold – women

Dola Banerjee outclassed Tatyana Dorkhova of Ukraine 102–96 in the women's recurve final at the 18th Golden Arrow Grand Prix Championship 2005 at Antalya, Turkey.

Jayanta Talukdar: first international gold in archery – individual

First medal in the Asian Championships – men

Limba Ram became the first Indian archer to win an Asian Archery Championships medal in 1988.

First Olympics representation – men

The Indian national archery team, with Shyam Lal, Limba Ram and Sanjeeva

Singh, participated in the individual and team archery events at the Olympics in 1988 at Seoul, South Korea.

First Olympics representation – women
Dola Banerjee, Reena Kumari and Sumangala Sharma were the first to represent India in archery at the 2004 Olympic Games in Athens, Greece.

First World Championship medal
The Indian men's archery team won a silver medal, behind Korea, at the 43rd World Outdoor Target Archery Championship 2005 in Madrid, Spain. The recurve team comprised Tarundeep Rai, Gautam Singh Sardar, Jayanta Talukdar and Robin Hansda.

Modern Olympic archery came to India in 1970.

First gold medal in a World Cup
Dola Banerjee from West Bengal is the only Indian archer to win gold in a World Cup final, in the women's individual recurve event at the World Cup in Dubai, UAE, in November 2007.

First World Cup compound title – men – individual
Abhishek Verma won an archery World Cup (stage 3) event at Wroclaw, Poland, on 15 August 2015.

First World Cup compound title – men – team
The men's compound archery team of Abhishek Verma, Chinna Raju Srither and Amarjeet Singh bagged the World Cup (stage 1) on 20 May 2017 in Shanghai, China, scoring 226–221 against Colombia.

Abhishek Verma: part of the first World Cup compound title winning team

First Indian compound archery women's team to be ranked world no. 1
The Indian compound archery women's team of V. Jyothi Surekha, P. Lily Chanu, Trisha Deb, Muskan Kirar, Divya Dhayal and Madhumita was the first ever team from India to be ranked world no. 1 in 2018.

First compound para medal
Indian compound mixed pair of Shyam Sundar Swami and Jyoti Bullyan made history with a silver at the World Archery Para Championships 2022 in Dubai.

Best World Championship haul
India won a silver and two bronze medals in the World Archery Championships during 10–15 June 2019 at 's-Hertogenbosch, Netherlands. The men's team of Tarundeep Rai, Atanu Das and Pravin Yadav won silver. The women's compound team of V. Jyothi Surekha, Muskan Kaur and Raj Kaur won the bronze.

Most medals in a World Cup

India won one gold, two silver and two bronze medals in the Archery World Cup (stage 4) at Wroclaw, Poland, in August 2014. The team of Deepika Kumari, Bombayla Devi Laishram and Laxmirani Majhi won the gold in the women's recurve team event. The men's recurve team, with Tarundeep Rai, Jayanta Talukdar and Atanu Das, won a silver medal. Abhishek Verma and Purvasha Shende clinched the silver in the compound mixed pair event. Deepika Kumari bagged two bronze medals in the women's recurve individual event and in the mixed team event with partner Jayanta Talukdar.

Best medal tally in the Asian Championship

Indian recurve archers won one gold, four silver and two bronze medals at the 2021 Asian Archery Championships in Dhaka (Bangladesh). In the last Asian Championships in 2019 too, at Rajamangala National Stadium in Bangkok, Thailand, during 22–28 November 2019, India had won seven medals – one gold, two silver and four bronze medals.

First silver at the Youth Olympics

Fifteen-year-old Akash Malik from Haryana became India's first archery silver medallist at the Youth Olympic Games 2018 in Buenos Aires, Argentina, on 17 October 2018.

Akash Malik: first silver medallist at the Youth Olympic Games

Only siblings to represent India in archery at the Olympics

Archers Dola Banerjee and Rahul Banerjee are the only brother-and-sister pair to represent India at the Olympics.

Hat-trick of bronzes – men

Atanu Das bagged three bronze medals in the Asian Archery Championships 2019 in Bangkok, Thailand. He clinched the men's recurve individual bronze, the recurve mixed team bronze (with Deepika Kumari) and the third bronze with Tarundeep Rai and Jayanta Talukdar in the team recurve event.

Most medals won at the CWG

The Indian team won three gold, a silver and four bronze medals in archery at the 2010 Commonwealth Games in Delhi.

Most gold medals at the World Cup by an individual

India won 3 gold medals in the Archery World Cup (stage 3) 2021 in Paris, France: the individual gold – Deepika Kumari, the mixed team event – Deepika Kumari with her husband Atanu Das, and the women's team event trio of Deepika Kumari, Komalika Bari and Ankita Bhakat.

Deepika Kumari: most gold medals won by an individual

First gold medal in the Asian Para Games

Harvinder Singh won India's maiden archery gold in the Asian Para Games 2018 in the men's individual recurve. He outplayed China's Zhao Lixue 6–0 in the W2/ST category.

ATHLETICS

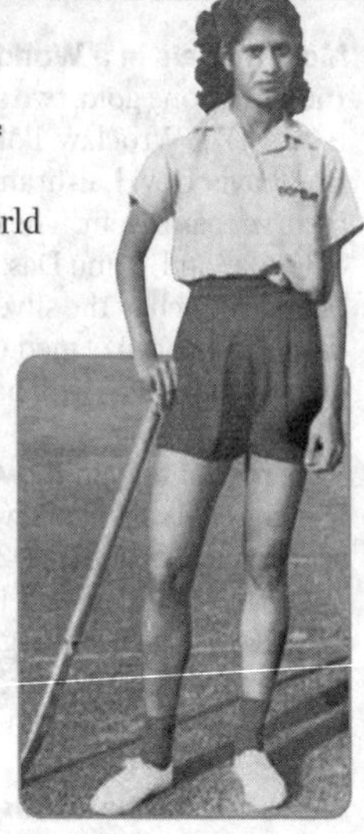
Mary D'Souza: one of the first women at the Olympics

First Indian elected to the International Association of Athletics Federations (IAAF) Council

Adille J. Sumariwalla was elected into the IAAF (now World Athletics) Council at the IAAF Congress in 2015.

First Olympic marathoner

Phadeppa Dareppa Chaugule represented India in the 1920 Antwerp Olympic Games. He finished 19th in 2 hrs 50 mins 45.2 secs.

First women at the Olympics

Mary D'Souza and Nilima Ghose participated in the 1952 Helsinki Olympics. They were both eliminated in the heats of the 100 m and 200 m races, and 80 m and 100 m hurdles, respectively.

First woman captain

Shiny Wilson captained the Indian contingent at the 1992 Olympic Games in Barcelona, Spain.

First international medal in a marathon – women

Asha Agarwal won the Hong Kong Marathon on 27 January 1985. She later won the Asian track and field gold at Jakarta, Indonesia, in 1985, and the Trinidad Marathon in 1986.

First World Championship medal

Anju Bobby George won a bronze in long jump at the 2003 World Championship in Paris, France, in August, with a leap of 6.70 m. She surpassed this at the 2004 Olympics in Athens, Greece, finishing sixth with 6.83 m.

First double gold at the Asian Games

Seven Indian athletes have won two golds in a single Asian Games event so far:

- Lavy Pinto: 100 m and 200 m races in Delhi (1951).
- Parduman Singh Brar: Shot put and discus throw in Manila, Philippines (1954).
- Milkha Singh: 200 m and 400 m in Tokyo, Japan (1958), and the 400 m and 4 x 400 m relay races in Jakarta, Indonesia (1962).
- Hari Chand: 5,000 m and 10,000 m races in Bangkok, Thailand (1978).
- P.T. Usha: Four golds and one silver in Seoul, South Korea (1986).
- Jyotirmoyee Sikdar: Two golds

NATIONAL SPORTS AWARDS 2020 ATHLETICS

Khel Ratna: T. Mariyappan (para athletics)
Dronacharya Award: Purushotham Rai (lifetime category)
Arjuna Award: Dutee Chand, Sandeep (para athletics)
Dhyan Chand Award: Kuldip Singh Bhullar, Jincy Philips, J. Ranjith Kumar (para athletics)

Muhammed Anas Yahiya: A Golden Run

Sprinter Muhammed Anas Yahiya held the national record in the 400 m race with a timing of 45.31 secs set during the 2018 Commonwealth Games in Gold Coast, Australia. On 21 July 2018, he broke his own record with a timing of 45.24 secs at the Cena Noveho Mesta nad Metuji meet in the Czech Republic. He became only the second Indian athlete to enter the finals of the one-lap event at the Games in Gold Coast, after Milkha Singh who won the gold at Cardiff, Wales, in 1958.

Muhammed Anas Yahiya

and a silver in Bangkok, Thailand (1998).

- Ashwini Chidananda Akkunji: Women's 400 m hurdles and 4 x 400 m relay race in Guangzhou, China (2010).

First Asian Games medals – women

In the 1951 Asian Games in Delhi, Roshan Mistry won the silver in the 100 m race, while Mary D'Souza (200 m) won a bronze. The women's 4 x 100 m relay team of Nilima Ghose, Stephie D'Souza, Mary D'Souza and Roshan Mistry also won a silver.

First Asian Games gold – women – individual

Kamaljeet Sandhu won the 400 m race in 57.3 secs at the Asian Games in Bangkok, Thailand, in 1970.

First Asian Games gold – men – individual

Ranjit Singh won a gold in the 800 m marathon on 8 March 1951 at Delhi, clocking 1 hr 59 mins 3 secs. Indian men won 10 golds in this edition of the Asian Games.

First gold medal – women – team

Christine Brown, Stephie D'Souza, Violet Peters and Mary D'Souza won the gold in the 4 x100 m relay, clocking 49.5 secs at the second Asian Games in Manila, Philippines, in 1954.

Only Asian Games gold medal in marathon

Chhota Singh won a gold in the men's marathon in 1951 at Delhi with a timing of 2 hrs 42 mins 58 secs 6 microseconds.

First to win three golds successively in the Asian Games

Manjeet Kaur was the first Indian to win three consecutive golds in the women's 4 x 400 m relay race in the Asian Games (2002, 2006 and 2010).

First gold at World Athletics final

Anju Bobby George was upgraded to a gold, India's first, in January 2014 after Tatyana Kotova of Russia was disqualified for her long-jump win in the World Athletics Championships in Monte Carlo in September 2005, following a failed retest for doping.

Dutee Chand: first gold at the World Universiade

First gold at the World Universiade

Dutee Chand became the first Indian to win the gold at the World Universiade, Naples, Italy, in the 100 m race with a timing of 11.32 secs on 10 July 2019. She is also the first Indian to win a gold in the 100 m race at a global championship. She also won a silver in the 100 m race at the Asian Games in Jakarta in 2018.

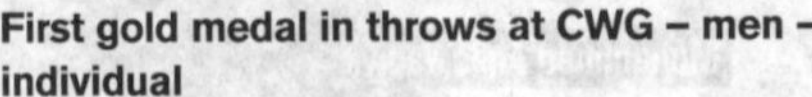

First gold medal in throws at CWG – men – individual

- This feat was achieved by the 6 ft 9 in. tall Vikas Gowda in discus throw. Gowda won this event at the 2014 CWG in Glasgow, Scotland, with a throw of 63.64 m.
- Neeraj Chopra hurled the javelin to a distance of 86.47 m at the 2018 CWG in Gold Coast, Australia, to win the gold medal.

First individual gold medal in track events at the IAAF World U-20 Championships

Hima Das won the gold in the 400 m race in the IAAF (now World Athletics) World U-20 Championships in Tampere, Finland, on 12 July 2018 with a timing of 51.46 secs. She holds the current Indian national record in 400 m with a timing of 50.79 secs set at the 2018 Asian Games in Jakarta, Indonesia.

First medal in CWG – women

Anju Bobby George won the bronze medal in long jump with a best of 6.49 m at the 2002 Commonwealth Games at Manchester, UK, followed by Neelam J. Singh, who won a silver in the women's discus throw.

First clean sweep in a major international meet

Krishna Poonia, Harwant Kaur and Seema Antil bagged the gold, silver and bronze medals respectively in women's discus throw in the 2010 CWG in New Delhi.

Arpinder Singh: first medal at the IAAF Continental Cup

First athlete to win a medal at the IAAF Continental Cup

Arpinder Singh, the 2018 Asian Games gold medallist in triple jump, was the first Indian to win a medal in the prestigious IAAF Continental Cup. He won a bronze medal in triple jump with a distance of 16.59 m.

First Indian to win gold at the IAAF World U-20 Championships

Neeraj Chopra, by clinching the gold on 23 July 2016 at the IAAF (now World Athletics) World U-20 Championships in Bydgoszcz, Poland, with a winning javelin throw of 86.48 m, became the first Indian to win a gold medal at any event in the championships and the first Indian to set a junior world record in athletics. In 2018, he became the second Indian after the legendary runner Milkha Singh to win both Commonwealth and Asian Games gold medals in the same year, breaking the national record on both occasions. At 20 years, he was the youngest ever flagbearer of the Indian contingent at the 2018 Jakarta Asian Games.

Most appearances in marathons
Sunita Godara has completed 85 half- and 69 full marathons in 24 different countries. Starting with the Rath Marathon in 1984, she finished first in 25 marathons, second in 12 and third in 14 of them. She has won 25 gold medals in half-marathons.

Most individual golds in the Asian Games
Two sportspersons have won four gold medals each at the Asian Games:

- Milkha Singh won four golds in two Asian Games in 1958 and 1962.
- P.T. Usha won four golds in the 1986 Asian Games at Seoul, South Korea, in the 200 m, 400 m, 400 m hurdles and the 4 x 400 m relay, and the silver in the 100 m race. In the 1982 Asian Games she won silver in the 100 m and 200 m races.

Best performances in the Olympics
Milkha Singh and P.T. Usha finished fourth in the 400 m and the 400 m hurdles in the 1960 Rome and the 1984 Los Angeles Olympics respectively.

Longest career – men
Bahadur Singh Chouhan who represented India in the inaugural Asian Track and Field (ATF) meet in 1971, also participated in the ninth one at Delhi in 1989. He won gold medals in shot put in the Asian Games in 1978 and 1982, and a silver in 1974.

Bahadur Singh Chouhan: longest career – men

Longest career – women

- P.T. Usha represented India from 1980 to 1998 in four Olympic Games, five Asian Games and five ATF meets.
- Shiny Wilson represented India 72 times in international meets from 1981 to 1995. She won the 800 m in her last major meet – the ATF meet in 1995 in Jakarta, Indonesia.

Best Commonwealth performance
India won 12 medals – two gold, three silver and seven bronze medaks – during the 19th CWG in New Delhi in 2010.

Best performance in the Asian Athletics Championships
India clinched five gold, one silver and three bronze medals in the 2017 Asian

Record Rewind

Oldest gold medallist

2003

Arun Chandra Dutta, at 82 years, won a gold medal in the 10 km Road Race at the 2003 All Assam Amateur Veteran Athletics in Guwahati, Assam.

2020

Man Kaur, at 103 years, won gold in the 200 m dash at the 2019 Asian Masters Athletics Championship for veteran athletes in Sarawak, Malaysia.

Athletics Championships in Bhubaneswar, Odisha, to top the medal tally for the first time in the Championships.

Gold medal in Commonwealth and Asian Games

Milkha Singh won gold in the 440 yards (the quarter-mile dash) race at the 1958 British Empire and Commonwealth Games in Cardiff, Wales, with a timing of 46.6 secs. He also won the 400 m races back to back in the Asian Games at Tokyo, Japan (1958), in 47.0 secs, and Jakarta, Indonesia (1962), in 46.9 secs. He was the first Indian to win individual gold medals in both the Asian Games and the CWG. Milkha Singh was also the first Indian athlete to win a gold medal in the Commonwealth Games.

Best performance in the World Para Athletics Championships

India won two gold, two silver and five bronze medals (a total of nine) at the World Para Athletics Championships 2019 held in Dubai, UAE.

First Commonwealth Games gold medal – women

The first Commonwealth Games gold medal for women came when Krishna Poonia won the discus throw (61.51 m), while the quartet of Sini Jose, Mandeep Kaur, Manjeet Kaur and Ashwini Chidananda Akkunji won the women's 4 x 400 m relay (3 mins 27.77 secs) at the 2010 Delhi Games.

Youngest athletics champion

Henry Rebello won the triple jump at Bangalore (now Bengaluru), Karnataka, in 1946 when he was only 17 years old. He set a record of 50 ft 2 in. at the 1948 National Games, which was surpassed only after a gap of 23 years by Mohinder Singh in 1971.

WR Best performance in the World Transplant Games in ball throw – women

Ankita Shrivastava (b. 8 March 1993) from Bhopal, Madhya Pradesh, set the world record in the World Transplant Games by winning the gold medal (donor class) with a throw of 31.71 m at Newcastle/Gateshead, UK, in August 2019.

WR Best performance in the World Transplant Games in long jump – women

Ankita Shrivastava (b. 8 March 1993) from Bhopal, Madhya Pradesh, set the world record in the World Transplant Games by winning the gold medal (donor

class) with a long jump of 3.61 m at Newcastle/Gateshead, UK, in August 2019.

First to receive IAAF Veteran Pin

Indian track and field legend P.T. Usha was presented the Veteran Pin by the World Athletics governing body – IAAF (now World Athletics), on 24 September 2019.

Varun Kumar Bhati: first bronze in high jump at World Para Athletics Championships

Triple excellence in shot put

Former shot putter Bahadur Singh Chouhan is the only Indian to receive the Arjuna Award, the Dronacharya Award as well as the Padma Shri. Between 1973 and 1985 he won three gold, two silver and three bronze medals at the Asian Games and Asian Championships.

Best throw – discus F-36 (para athletics) – men

Yogesh Kathuniya smashed the world record in men's discus F-36, when he threw 45.18 m to win the gold medal in the World Para Athletics Grand Prix in Berlin, Germany, on 1 July 2018.

First bronze medal at the World Para Athletics Championships

Varun Kumar Bhati won the bronze medal in the men's T-42 category high jump and Karan Jyoti Dalal settled for bronze in the discus throw F-55 at the World Para Athletics Championships in London, UK, in 2017.

BADMINTON

First international doubles title

Sanave Thomas and Rupesh Kumar beat the German duo of Kristof Hopp and Ingo Kindervater 15–7, 15–13, in the final of the 2004 Toulouse Open Championship in France.

First international mixed doubles title

V. Diju and Jwala Gutta won the doubles title at the US $50,000 Bitburger Open in Saarbrücken, Germany, in 2008, beating the eighth-seed Danish pair Joachim Nielsen and Christina Pedersen 8–21, 21–17, 22–20.

First World Championships silver

Saina Nehwal reached the finals of the 2015 World Championships in Jakarta, Indonesia, but lost to Carolina Marin of Spain 16–21, 19–21, thus settling for the silver.

First Asian Games medal – men – individual

Syed Modi won a bronze at the 1982 Delhi Asiad. Leroy D'Sa and Pradeep Gandhe won bronze in the men's doubles while D'Sa won bronze with Kanwal Thakur Singh in the mixed doubles.

First medal at the Asian Games – team
India won the bronze in the team event in 1974 at Tehran, Iran, the country's first medal at the Asian Games.

First World Junior Championship title
Saina Nehwal beat Sayata Sako of Japan 21–19, 21–18 to win India's first World Junior Badminton Championship in Pune, Maharashtra, on 2 November 2008.

First Asian Games medal – women – individual
India reached the finals and won a medal for the first time in badminton in the 2018 Asian Games in Jakarta, Indonesia. Saina Nehwal won a bronze and P.V. Sindhu won a silver.

First Asian Games medal – women – team
The women's team won the bronze medal in the team event in the 2014 Asian Games at Incheon, South Korea.

First Commonwealth Games gold – men – individual
Prakash Padukone won India's first gold medal in badminton at the CWG, at the 1978 Commonwealth Games at Edmonton in Canada, beating Ray Stevens of England.

Gold at the Para-Badminton World Championship
Manasi Joshi won the gold in the women's singles SL3 finals on 25 August 2019 at Basel, Switzerland. She defeated Parul Parmar 21–12, 21–7 to clinch her first title. Manasi had won the silver in the mixed doubles at the Para-Badminton World Championship in Stoke Mandeville, England, in September 2015 and a bronze at the Asian Para Games held in Jakarta, Indonesia, in October 2018.

Manasi Joshi: gold at Para-Badminton World Championship

First Commonwealth Games double gold
At the 2010 CWG in Delhi, Saina Nehwal won the women's singles title, beating Wong Mew Choo (Malaysia) 19–21, 23–21, 21–13 in the final. Jwala Gutta and Ashwini Ponappa won the women's doubles gold medal.

First World Championships medal – men – individual
At the 1983 World Championships in Copenhagen, Denmark, Prakash Padukone won a bronze medal. He also reached the quarter-finals of the Championships four times. After this, only two other Indians, P. Gopichand in 2001 and K. Srikanth in 2017, reached the quarter-finals of the Championships.

First Grand Prix double win
Jwala Gutta achieved a double in a Grand Prix–level tournament, winning the mixed doubles and women's doubles crown at the Bulgarian Open in Sofia on 12 October 2008. In the mixed doubles, Jwala and her partner V. Diju beat Indonesian pair Fran Kurniawan and Shendy Irawati 15–21, 21–18, 21–19. In the

women's doubles, Jwala and Shruti Kurien beat Indonesian pair Shendy Irawati and Meiliana Jauhari 21–11, 21–19.

NATIONAL SPORTS AWARDS 2020 BADMINTON

Dronacharya Award: Gaurav Khanna (para badminton)
Arjuna Award: Satwiksairaj Rankireddy, Chirag Chandrasekhar Shetty
Dhyan Chand Award: Pradeep Shrikrishna Gandhe, Trupti Murgunde, Satyaprakash Tiwari (para badminton)

First Indian men's doubles pair to reach a Super 750 final

Satwiksairaj Rankireddy and Chirag Shetty became the first men's doubles pair to reach a Super 750 final on 27 October 2019 in the French Open Super 750 held in Paris, France. They lost to Indonesia's Marcus Fernaldi Gideon and Kevin Sanjaya Sukamuljo 18-21, 16-21. The Indian duo had won their first Super 500 title at the Thailand Open, Bangkok, in August 2019.

First Commonwealth Games gold – mixed team

India won the gold medal in the mixed team event at the 2018 CWG at Gold Coast, Australia, beating reigning champions Malaysia 3–1 in the final. India's previous best had been a silver medal in the 2010 CWG in New Delhi.

First Super Series title

Saina Nehwal clinched the Indonesia Open title in Jakarta, Indonesia, on 21 June 2009. With 10 Super Series titles to her name, Saina Nehwal also holds the record for the maximum number of wins in Super Series.

First Grand Prix gold

Saina Nehwal became the first Indian woman to clinch a Grand Prix gold when she beat Lydia Cheah of Malaysia 21–8, 21–19 at the Chinese Taipei Grand Prix in Taiwan on 13 September 2008.

First woman to get double gold in the Commonwealth Games

Saina Nehwal is the first Indian woman to win the gold medal in the women's badminton singles event in the Commonwealth Games twice. At the 2018 CWG in Gold Coast, Australia, she beat compatriot P.V. Sindhu 21–18, 23–21 in 56 mins to grab the gold medal, a feat she first achieved at the 2010 Delhi CWG. She was also the first Indian badminton player to win an Olympic medal when she won the bronze at the London Olympics on 4 August 2012, after China's Wang Xin retired following an injury.

Saina Nehwal: first woman to get double gold in the Commonwealth Games

First national champion

Vijay A. Madgavkar (1914–2013) won the inaugural National Championships in 1936.

Most Nationals singles wins

- *Men*: Prakash Padukone won nine successive gold medals from 1971 to 1979.
- *Women*: Aparna Popat won eight successive women's singles from 1998 to 2005.

First Super Series Premier winner – men

K. Srikanth became the first Indian to be ranked world no. 1 on 9 April 2018 for a week. He was the first Indian to win a Super Series Premier Men's title, the China Open in 2014, defeating Olympic Champion Lin Dan. He won six Super Series crowns (2014, 2015 and 2017), with four titles in 2017 itself – the most by an Indian player – the Indonesia Open (2017), Australian Open (2017), Denmark Open (2017) and French Open (2017).

P.V. Sindhu: Super Shuttler

Pusarla Venkata Sindhu has the following records to her credit:

P.V. Sindhu

- **First World Championship gold (women – individual):** She became the first Indian to win the gold at the World Championship, beating Japan's Nozomi Okuhara 21–7, 21–7, on 25 August 2019 in Basel, Switzerland.

- **First Olympic finalist:** P.V. Sindhu won a silver medal in the women's singles event at the 2016 Rio Olympics, after losing to Carolina Marin of Spain 21–19, 12–21, 15–21. She is the youngest Indian Olympic medallist.

- **First World Championship medal**: Sindhu won India's first World Championship medal when she won a bronze at the 2013 World Championship in Guangzhou, China. She has also won the silver twice in the championships – in September 2017 and August 2018.

- **First double silver in World Championships:** She was the first to win silver medals in two back-to-back World Championships in 2017 and 2018.

- **First Indian to win a silver medal at the Asian Games:** Sindhu became the first Indian silver medallist at the Asian Games in 2018, after losing to Tai Tzu Ying of Taiwan 21-13, 21-16.

- **First Indian to win Badminton World Federation World Tour:** P.V. Sindhu became the first Indian to win the season-ending Badminton World Federation (BWF) World Tour Finals tournament in Guangzhou, China, on 16 December 2018. She beat Nozomi Okuhara of Japan 21–19, 21–17 in the final. This was her 11th major title on the international circuit.

Most Nationals singles and doubles wins

Madhumita Bisht, who first participated in the Nationals in 1978, won 29 titles by 2002 – with eight in singles, nine in doubles and 12 in mixed doubles.

Madhumita Bisht: most singles and doubles wins in the Nationals

Longest career

Madhumita Bisht had the longest career among badminton players, representing India for 24 years at the Uber Cup (world championship for women) from 1978 to 2002.

Most Nationals doubles wins

Leroy D'Sa won seven doubles titles in the Nationals and entered 14 finals.

BASKETBALL

NATIONAL SPORTS AWARDS 2020 BASKETBALL

Arjuna Award: Vishesh Bhriguvanshi

First appearance in the Asian Games

India took part in the first Asian Games at New Delhi in 1951, under the captaincy of Ranbir Chand. In its best performance at the Games to date, the team came fourth.

First India-born player in the NBA

Satnam Singh Bhamara set a milestone in the history of Indian basketball when he was drafted into the National Basketball Association (NBA), the premier professional basketball league in the USA, in June 2015. Selected by the Dallas Mavericks, he played his Summer League debut match against the New Orleans Pelicans, scoring four points for his team, on 11 July 2015.

First and only sisters representing the country

Prashanti, Pratima, Priyanka and Divya Singh, four sisters from Varanasi, Uttar Pradesh, have all played basketball for India.

 **22** basketball players have won the Arjuna Award up to September 2019.

Longest sequence of Nationals titles

Services won the men's national title 26 years in a row from 1957 to 1982. Railways won the women's title 17 years in a row from 1986 to 2002.

Most appearances in the Asian Games – women

Prashanti Singh is the only woman basketball player to represent the Indian team in two Asian Games, in 2010 and 2014. She also represented the national team in the 2006 CWG. She has won 22 medals in national championships and federation events.

BOXING

Oldest existing boxing association
The Maharashtra Amateur Boxing Association was formed in 1924.

First Olympic appearance
India entered a boxing team in seven divisions for the first time at the 1948 London Olympics but could not reach the quarter-finals.

First Olympic medal – men
Vijender Singh won a bronze medal (middleweight) in the 2008 Beijing Olympics.

First Olympic medal – women
Six-time women's world champion M.C. Mary Kom won a bronze medal (51 kg) in the 2012 London Olympics.

M.C. Mary Kom: first Olympic boxing medal – women

First medal in the World Boxing Championships – men

- Amit Panghal was the first Indian male boxer to win a silver medal in World Boxing Championship 2019. Seven Indian have won World Championships medals until now: Amit Panghal (2019, silver), Vijender Singh (2009, bronze) Vikas Krishan (2011, bronze), Shiv Thapa (2015, bronze) Gaurav (2017, bronze), Manish Kaushik (2019, bronze) and Akash Kumar (2021, bronze)

- Parveen Kumar won a bronze medal in the lightweight category in the World Junior Championship in Budapest, Hungary, in November 2000.

First World Boxing Championships medal – women

- M.C. Mary Kom from Manipur bagged a silver medal in the 48 kg category in the USA, in December 2001.
- Manju Rani became the second Indian to enter the World Boxing Championships final and won the silver at Ulan-Ude, Russia, in 2019.

NATIONAL SPORTS AWARDS 2020 BOXING

Arjuna Award: Manish Kaushik, Lovlina Borgohain
Dhyan Chand Award: N. Usha, Lakha Singh
Dronacharya Award: Shiv Singh (lifetime category)

First medal at the World Cup
Zoramthanga defeated teammate Dharmender Yadav 17–4 on points to win the light flyweight bronze on 17 November 1990 in Bombay (now Mumbai), Maharashtra.

Most career medals
M.C. Mary Kom has won a record six World Championships, a bronze medal at the 2012 London Olympics, gold medals at five Asian

Championships (2003, 2005, 2010, 2012 and 2017), a gold medal at the 2009 Indoor Asian Games, a bronze medal at the 2010 Asian Games, a gold medal at the 2014 Asian Games and a gold medal at the Commonwealth Games 2018. She won a silver medal and a bronze medal in the 2019 World Championships.

First Asian Games medal
Hari Singh won the silver in the middleweight category at the 1958 Manila Games in the Philippines. Sunder Rao and Ranganathan won the bronze in the lightweight and the welterweight categories, respectively.

First National Championship
The very first National Boxing Championship in the country, organized by the Indian Amateur Boxing Federation, was held in Bombay (now Mumbai), Maharashtra, from 18 to 22 March 1950.

First Asian Games gold – men
Padam Bahadur Mal won the gold medal in the lightweight category in 1962 in the Asian Games held in Jakarta, Indonesia.

First Commonwealth Games gold
Mohammed Ali Qamar won the gold medal in the lightweight category, defeating Darren Langley 27–25 at the Commonwealth Games in Manchester, UK, in 2002.

First medal in the World Championship – senior
Vijender Singh won a bronze medal in the 2009 Milan World Cup in Italy.

Record Rewind

Most medals at the International Boxing Association (AIBA) Women's World Boxing Championships

2001
India had won only one medal, the silver medal won by M.C. Mary Kom in the light flyweight category in Scranton, Pennsylvania, USA.

2019
India has won 37 medals at the AIBA Women's World Boxing Championships. This includes 10 golds, eight silvers and 19 bronzes.

Most medals at the Youth Boxing Championships
The Indian team won five gold, two silver and five bronze medals at the Youth Boxing Championship in November 2019 in Ulaanbaatar, Mongolia.

Most golds in an international meet
India won 10 gold and two silver medals at the 1995 South Asian Games (SAG; formerly SAF) in Chennai, Tamil Nadu. This achievement is second only to South Korea's haul of all 12 gold medals in the 1986 Seoul Asian Games.

Most international titles

- Heavyweight boxer Kaur Singh won gold at four major international events: the Asian Boxing Championship 1980 (Bombay, now Mumbai, Maharashtra) and

Best Performance in the AIBA World Boxing Championships

Amit Panghal

Amit Panghal from Rohtak, Haryana, was the first Indian male boxer to breach the semi-final barrier of the World Championships. On 21 September 2019, he became the first Indian to win a silver medal in the 52 kg category at the AIBA World Boxing Championships 2019, Ekaterinburg, Russia, after losing to Uzbekistan's Shakhobidin Zoirov. Other Indian boxers have won bronze medals in the World Championships – Vijender Singh (2009), Vikas Krishan (2011), Shiva Thapa (2015) and Gaurav Bidhuri (2017), but Panghal was the first to reach the semi-finals. He has also won the gold medal in the light flyweight category in the 2018 Asian Games (Jakarta, Indonesia) and in the 52 kg category of the 2020 Cologne Boxing World Cup (Germany).

1982 (Seoul, South Korea), the 1982 Delhi Asian Games and the 1982 King's Cup in Bangkok, Thailand.

- Super heavyweight boxer Rajkumar Sangwan also won four golds: at the 1991 Asian Invitational Championship in Bangkok, Thailand; the 1993 China Invitational Championship in Beijing, China; the 1993 South Asian Federation (SAF) Games at Dhaka, Bangladesh; and the 1994 Asian Boxing Championship at Tehran, Iran.

Most medals in the Asian Championship – women
M.C. Mary Kom (46 kg), L. Sarita Devi (54 kg), R.L. Jenny (63 kg) and Jyotsna (80 kg and 86 kg) won two golds each at the 2003 and the 2005 Asian Women's Boxing Championship, in Hisar, Haryana, and Kaohsiung, Taiwan, respectively.

Most Asian Games golds
Hawa Singh (heavyweight) won two golds at the 1966 and 1970 Asian Games, both held in Bangkok, Thailand.

Most Commonwealth Championship golds
India won six gold medals and the overall title at the Commonwealth Championship in New Delhi in March 2010. Amandeep Singh (49 kg), Suranjoy Singh (52 kg), Jai Bhagwan (60 kg), Vijender Singh (75 kg), Dinesh Kumar (81 kg) and Paramjeet Samota (+91 kg) won a gold each.

Most medals in the World Cup – men
India won a silver and a bronze medal, and the sixth position overall, in the AIBA Boxing World Cup in October 2019 in Yekaterinburg, Russia.

WR Most medals in the World Boxing Championships
In October 2019, M.C. Mary Kom became the first boxer in the world (male or female) to win eight World Championship medals (six gold, a silver and a bronze).

Best performance in the World Boxing Championships

India won four gold, one silver and three bronze medals in the fourth World Women's Boxing Championship 2006 in New Delhi. M.C. Mary Kom (46 kg), L. Sarita Devi (52 kg), R.L. Jenny (63 kg) and K.C. Lekha (75 kg) won gold medals. N. Usha (57 kg) won a silver. The bronze medal winners were Chhotu Loura (50 kg), Aruna Mishra (60 kg) and Renu (82 kg).

Best performance in the Asian Games

India won two gold, three silver and four bronze medals in the 2010 Asian Games, its best haul at an Asian Games. The gold medallists were Vikas Krishan (60 kg) and Vijender Singh (75 kg). Silver medals were won by V. Santosh Kumar (64 kg), Dinesh Kumar (81 kg) and Manpreet Singh (91 kg). The bronze went to Suranjoy Singh (52 kg), Paramjeet Samota (+91 kg), M.C. Mary Kom (51 kg) and Kavita Goyal (75 kg).

Best performance in Asian Games – women

India won a gold and two bronze medals at the 2014 Incheon Asian Games in South Korea. M.C. Mary Kom won the gold in the women's flyweight (51 kg) event. L. Sarita Devi (lightweight, 60 kg) and Pooja Rani (middleweight, 75 kg) won bronze medals.

Best youth boxer – men

Sachin Siwach was named Asian Boxing Confederation's Best Youth Boxer of 2017.

Sachin Siwach: best Asian youth boxer

Best performance at the Asian Championship

Indian boxers won two gold, four silver and seven bronze medals in Bangkok, Thailand, in April 2019 to finish at the third position with a total of 13 medals. Pooja Rani (81 kg) and Amit Panghal (52 kg) won gold medals; Deepak Singh (49 kg), Kavinder Singh Bisht (56 kg), Ashish Kumar (75 kg) and Simranjit Kaur (64 kg) won silvers; Nikhat Zareen (51 kg), Manisha Moun (54 kg), Sonia Chahal (57 kg), Sarita Devi (60 kg), Shiva Thapa (60 kg), Ashish (69 kg) and Satish Kumar (+91 kg) won bronze medals.

Best performance in the World Youth Women's Boxing Championship

India bagged five golds and two bronzes to take the top spot in the World Youth Women's Boxing Championship 2017 at the N.C. Bordoloi Indoor Stadium, Guwahati, Assam. Nitu (48 kg), Jyoti Gulia (51 kg), Sakshi Chaudhary (54 kg), Shashi Chopra (57 kg) and Ankushita Boro (64 kg) won gold medals. Anupama (81 kg) and Neha Yadav (+81 kg) won bronze medals.

Best performance at the Commonwealth Games

At the 2018 CWG in Gold Coast, Australia, India won three gold, three silver and three bronze medals. M.C. Mary Kom in women's lightweight (48 kg), Gaurav Solanki in flyweight (52 kg) and Vikas Krishan in middleweight (75 kg) won gold medals. Amit Panghal in light flyweight (49 kg), Manish Kaushik in lightweight (60 kg) and Satish Kumar in superweight (+91 kg) won silver medals. Mohammed Hussamuddin in bantamweight (56 kg), Manoj Kumar in welterweight (69 kg) and Naman Talwar in heavyweight (91 kg) won bronze medals.

Vikas Krishan: first to receive AIBA Pro Boxing (APB) best boxing trophy

First Indian male boxer to win the APB Best Boxing trophy

Asian Games gold medallist Vikas Krishan was awarded the APB Best Boxing trophy at AIBA's 70th anniversary in Montreux, Switzerland, 2016.

First Indian woman boxer to receive AIBA Legends award

M.C. Mary Kom received the AIBA Legends Award at AIBA's 70th anniversary gala in Montreux, Switzerland, in 2016.

Most successive professional wins

Vijender Singh demolished former Commonwealth champion Charles Adamu to claim his 12th straight win in November 2019.

First AIBA athletes commission

In November 2019, veteran Indian boxer L. Sarita Devi was elected unopposed to the AIBA's first ever athletes commission to represent the Asian bloc. She is an eight-time Asian Championship medallist, five of them golds.

WR Woman boxer to win most World Championship titles

M.C. Mary Kom is the first female pugilist to win the World Championship crown six times (2002, 2005, 2006, 2008, 2010 and 2018). She also won the most world titles (five) in a row between 2002 and 2010.

World no. 1

- In 2009, AIBA announced Vijender Singh as the top-ranked boxer in the annual middleweight category.
- In January 2019, M.C. Mary Kom (48 kg category) was the top-ranked boxer in the AIBA World Ranking (women) with 1,700 points.

Manish Kaushik: Star Pugilist

A boxer from Bhiwani, Haryana, Manish Kaushik won the bronze medal in the lightweight 63 kg category on 20 September 2019 in the 2019 World Championship in Ekaterinburg, Russia. He lost to Cuba's Andy Gomez Cruz 0–5. He also won a silver in the same weight category in the 2018 Commonwealth Games held in Gold Coast, Australia. The Olympic-bound (Tokyo 2020) boxer also struck gold at the 35th Boxam International Tournament in Castellon, Spain, on 6 March 2021, when he beat Denmark's Nikolai Teteryan by a 3–2 split decision.

Manish Kaushik

CHESS

GENERAL

32 world champions

So far, 32 Indians have won 50 world titles. They are: Viswanathan Anand (world: 2000, 2007, 2008, 2010 and 2012; junior: 1987); P. Harikrishna (boys U-10: 1996; junior: 2004); K. Humpy (girls U-10: 1997; girls U-12: 1998; girls U-14: 2000; junior: 2001); Aarthie Ramaswamy (U-18: 1999); Deep Sengupta (boys U-12: 2000); D. Harika (girls U-14: 2004; girls' U-18: 2006; junior girls: 2008); N. Srinath (boys U-12: 2005); Sahaj Grover (boys U-10: 2005); Girish A. Koushik (boys U-8: 2006); Ivana Furtado (girls U-8: 2006 and 2007); Ch. Mohineesh (boys U-10: 2006); Ch. Sahajasri (boys U-10: 2006); Abhijeet Gupta (boys junior: 2008); Sayantan Das (boys U-12: 2008); Vidit Gujrathi (boys U-14: 2008); Padmini Rout (girls U-14: 2008); B. Adhiban (boys U-16: 2008); Sowmya Swaminathan (girls junior: 2009); M. Karthikeyan (boys U-12: 2011; U-16: 2013); M. Mahalakshmi (girls U-14: 2012; girls U-18: 2015); R. Vaishali (girls U-12: 2012; girls U-14: 2015); N. Priyanka (girls U-10: 2012); Saina Salonika (girls U-10: 2013); R. Praggnanandhaa (boys U-8: 2013; U-10: 2015; U-18: 2019); Divya Deshmukh (girls U-10: 2014; U-14: 2017); Nihal Sarin (boys U-10: 2014); Bharath Subramaniyam (boys U-8: 2015); Rakshitta Ravi (girls U-10: 2015); Aakanksha Hagawane (girls U-16: 2016); D. Jishitha (girls U-14: 2017); D. Gukesh (boys U-12: 2019); and B. Savitha Shri (girls U-12: 2019).

There are 67 Grandmasters from India up to January 2021.

Grandmasters (GMs)

There are 67 Indian Grandmasters. They are: Viswanathan Anand (1987); Dibyendu Barua (1991); Pravin Thipsay (1997); Abhijit Kunte (2000); K. Sasikiran (2000); P. Harikrishna (2001); K. Humpy (2001); Surya Shekhar Ganguly (2002); Sandipan Chanda (2003); R.B. Ramesh (2004); Tejas Bakre (2004); P. Magesh Chandran (2006); Neelotpal Das (2006); Deepan Chakkravarthy (2006); Parimarjan Negi (2006); G.N. Gopal (2007); Abhijeet Gupta (2008); S. Arun Prasad (2008); S. Kidambi (2009); R.R. Laxman (2009); Sriram Jha (2010); Deep Sengupta (2010); B. Adhiban (2010); S.P. Sethuraman (2011); D. Harika (2011); M.R. Lalith Babu (2012); Vaibhav Suri (2012); M.R. Venkatesh (2012); Sahaj Grover (2012); Vidit Gujrathi (2012); M. Shyam Sundar (2012); Akshayraj Kore (2013); Vishnu Prasanna (2013); Saptarshi Roy Chowdhury (2013); Debashis Das (2013); Ankit Rajpara (2014); Aravindh Chithambaram (2015); Murali Karthikeyan (2015); Ashwin Jayaram (2015); Swapnil Dhopade (2015); S.L. Narayanan (2015); Shardul Gagare (2015); Diptayan Ghosh (2016); K. Priyadarshan (2016);

Dibyendu Barua: Grandmaster and recipient of the Arjuna Award

Aryan Chopra (2016); N. Srinath (2017); Himanshu Sharma (2017); Anurag Mhamal (2017); Abhimanyu Puranik (2017); M.S. Thejkumar (2017); Saptarshi Roy (2018); R. Praggnanandhaa (2018); Nihal Sarin (2018); E. Arjun (2018); Karthik Venkatraman (2018); Harsha Bharathakoti (2018); P. Karthikeyan (2018); Stany G.A. (2018); Visakh N.R. (2019); D. Gukesh (2019); P. Iniyan (2019); Swayams Mishra (2019); Girish Koushik (2019); Prithu Gupta (2019); Raunak Sadhwani (2019); G. Akash (2020); and Leon Mendonca (2020).

Arjuna Award winners

Manuel Aaron (1961); Rohini Khadilkar (1980); Dibyendu Barua (1983); Pravin Thipsay (1984); Viswanathan Anand (1985), D.V. Prasad (1987); Bhagyashree Thipsay (1987); Anupama Gokhale (1990); S. Vijayalakshmi (2000); K. Sasikiran (2002); K. Humpy (2003); Surya Shekhar Ganguly (2005); P. Harikrishna (2006); D. Harika (2007); Tania Sachdev (2009); Parimarjan Negi (2010); and Abhijeet Gupta (2013).

Rajiv Gandhi Khel Ratna recipient

Viswanathan Anand received the award in 1991.

Dronacharya Award winners

Raghunandan Gokhale and K. Ashok received the award in 1986 and 2006 respectively.

Padma Shri recipients

Anupama Abhyankar (1986), Viswanathan Anand (1987), Bhagyashree Thipsay (1987) and D. Harika (2019) have been awarded the honour.

Padma Bhushan recipient

Viswanathan Anand received the Padma Bhushan in 1991.

Padma Vibhushan recipient

Viswanathan Anand was awarded the Padma Vibhushan in 2007.

Asian champions – men

Five men have been crowned Asian champions:
K. Sasikiran (2003); Surya Shekhar Ganguly (2009); P. Harikrishna (2011); Parimarjan Negi (2012); and S.P. Sethuraman (2016).

Asian champions – women

Seven Indian women have won the title on nine occasions: Rohini Khadilkar (1981 and 1983); Anupama Gokhale (1985 and 1987); Bhagyashree Thipsay (1991); K. Humpy (2003); Tania Sachdev (2007); D. Harika (2011); and Bhakti Kulkarni (2016).

Asian junior champions – boys

They are: V. Ravi Kumar (1978); Viswanathan Anand (1984 and 1985); Abhijit Kunte (1997); Tejas Bakre (1998); K. Sasikiran (1999); P. Harikrishna (2000); Deepan Chakkravarthy (2002); P. Magesh Chandran (2003); S. Arun Prasad (2004); P. Karthikeyan (2007); Ashwin Jayaram (2008 and 2009); M. Shyam

Sundar (2010 and 2011); N. Srinath (2012, 2013 and 2014); and Aravindh Chithambaram (2016).

Record Rewind

Most world champions

2002

Five Indians had won nine world titles up to 2002.

2019

32 Indians won 50 world titles up to 2019.

Board Prize with a 'perfect' score

Viswanathan Anand scored seven points from seven rounds to win the top Board Prize in the Asian Team Championship in 1989.

Four successive Asian junior titles

Indian boys won from 1997 to 2000 and again from 2007 to 2010, twice winning the title four years in a row.

Golden sweep at Asian Youth Championship

India won 18 medals, including all eight gold medals at stake in the Asian Youth Championship in 2006. Sweety Patel (girls U-8), Sahajasri (girls U-10), Padmini Rout (girls U-12), Bhakti Kulkarni (girls U-14), Prince Bajaj (boys U-8), G.V. Sai Krishna (boys U-10), Vidit Gujrathi (boys U-12) and S. Nitin (boys U-14) won them.

Medal sweep at Asian Junior Championship

India swept all six medals at stake in the Asian Junior Championship in Colombo, Sri Lanka, in 2003. The winners were:

- *Boys*: P. Magesh Chandran (gold), S. Poobesh Anand (silver) and Prathamesh Mokal (bronze);
- *Girls*: Y. Pratibha (gold), J.E. Kavitha (silver) and Saheli Nath (bronze).

India repeated this feat in December 2007. The winners were:

- *Boys*: P. Karthikeyan (gold), Ashwin Jayaram (silver) and Shyam Sundar (bronze);
- *Girls*: Mary Ann Gomes (gold), Padmini Rout (silver) and Kiran Manisha Mohanty (bronze).

Commonwealth champions

Twelve Indians have won the Commonwealth title. They are: Pravin Thipsay (1985); D.V. Prasad (1986); P. Mithrakanth (1996); Atanu Lahiri (1999); K. Sasikiran (2000); P. Harikrishna (2001); Dibyendu Barua (2003); R.B. Ramesh (2007); R.R. Laxman (2010); M.R. Lalith Babu (2012); Abhijeet Gupta (2013, 2015, 2016, 2017 and 2019); and P. Karthikeyan (2018).

Most successful Commonwealth champion

Abhijeet Gupta won the title five times, including three times in a row from 2015 to 2017.

World Railways champions

Indian Railways won the World Railway Chess Championship in Piešťany, Slovakia, in November 2005. The members of the victorious team that scored 37.5 points from a maximum of 42 were P.D.S. Girinath, Vikramaditya Kamble,

Suvrajit Saha, Saptarshi Roy Chowdhury, Nassir Wajih, K. Rathnakaran and Gurpreet Pal Singh.

Oldest to regain world rapid title
Viswanathan Anand, at 48, became the oldest world champion in the rapid format (25-minute time format) in Riyadh, Saudi Arabia, in December 2017. He regained the title won in 2003. Two days later, he also became the oldest medallist in the blitz format (five-minute time format) by claiming the bronze medal.

FIRSTS

First international recognition
Mir Sultan Khan, born in 1905 in Mittha, Punjab, received international recognition at a time when there was no system of Elo ratings. In 1928, he won the all-India title, scoring 8.5 out of 9 points at the British Championship. He won again in 1932 and 1933. He also defeated world champion Jose Casablanca of Cuba at the Hastings tournament. He was considered among the ten best players in the world at the time.

Tejas Bakre: first Asian sub-junior champion

First Asian junior title
V. Ravi Kumar won the first Asian junior title in 1978.

First Asian sub-junior champion
Tejas Bakre won the first Asian sub-junior title in 1998.

First GM norm
Pravin Thipsay was the first to achieve GM norm in London, UK, in 1985.

First medal from Chess Olympiad
India won its maiden medal at the Tromso Chess Olympiad in Norway in 2014. In the open section, India was represented by Parimarjan Negi, K. Sasikiran, S.P. Sethuraman, B. Adhiban and M.R. Lalith Babu, and claimed the bronze medal.

First two-medal win in Chess Olympiad
Abhijeet Gupta (silver) and Tania Sachdev (bronze) helped India win two medals for the first time in the Chess Olympiad in Istanbul, Turkey, in September 2012.

First GM norm in National Championship
P. Konguvel is the first and only player to have gained a nine-game norm from the National 'A' Championship at New Delhi in June 2001.

First International Master – men
Manuel Aaron became an International Master (IM) in 1961.

First International Master – women
Jayshree Khadilkar met the stipulations of the Woman International Master's

(WIM) title in 1978 but was awarded the title in 1978 as per the prevalent FIDE regulations then.

First medal in Asian Games
K. Humpy won the gold medal in the Doha Asian Games, Qatar, in 2006.

First Olympiad medal
Rafiq Khan won a silver in the 1980 Olympiad.

First Olympiad gold
Dibyendu Barua won the gold on the second board of the 1990 Olympiad held in Novi Sad, now in Serbia.

First to win the Asian junior title twice
Viswanathan Anand was the first Indian to win the Asian junior title in 1984 and again in 1985.

First world junior title
Viswanathan Anand was 17 years 225 days old when he won the title on 2 August 1987 at Baguio in the Philippines.

First GM norm in India
Viswanathan Anand was the first to achieve GM norm in New Delhi in 1987.

The 17th Delhi International Chess Open received 2,810 entries across three sections in January 2019.

First Grandmaster
Viswanathan Anand became India's first Grandmaster on 28 December 1987 at the Sakthi Finance Grandmaster Tournament in Coimbatore, Tamil Nadu.

WR **First country to win both world junior titles in a single edition**
India became the first country in the history of the game to win both the world junior titles in a single edition. Abhijeet Gupta and D. Harika won the open and girls' sections. Parimarjan Negi claimed the silver to give India a rare 1–2 finish in the open section.

First Woman Grandmaster norm
Bhagyashree Thipsay was the first to achieve a Woman Grandmaster (WGM) norm in 1986 in the Lloyds Bank Masters tournament when she was 21 years old.

First Woman Grandmaster
S. Vijayalakshmi became the country's first Woman Grandmaster in 2000 at Udaipur, Rajasthan, during the Asian Championship.

First team medal in Asian Games
The trio of K. Sasikiran, P. Harikrishna and K. Humpy won the mixed team gold in Doha, Qatar, in 2006.

First winner at two World Cups
Viswanathan Anand is the first person in the world to successfully defend the men's World Cup title. He did so at Hyderabad (now in Telangana) in October 2002.

First woman to lead a team in the open section
K. Humpy led India 'B' in the open section of the Asian Team Championship at Jodhpur, Rajasthan, in 2003.

First world sub-junior medal
Viswanathan Anand claimed a bronze after sharing the second place in 1984.

First to win the Asian junior girls' title thrice
Mary Ann Gomes won the title in 2006 (New Delhi), 2007 (Mumbai) and 2008 (Chennai).

Mary Ann Gomes: thrice Asian junior girls' champion

First live National Championship on the Internet
Mumbai-based Venus Chess Academy became the first organizer, in any discipline, to cover the matches of the National Championship live on Internet. The unique feat was achieved in the National Chess Championship from Hotel Tulip Star, Mumbai, Maharashtra, in January 2003.

First Online Olympiad
Owing to the Covid-19 pandemic, the Fédération Internationale des Échecs (FIDE), commonly known as the World Chess Federation, organized the inaugural FIDE Chess Online Olympiad in 2020. India shared thc gold medal with Russia.

First FIDE Online World Youth Rapid championship
D. Gukesh (under-14), Rakshitta Ravi (girls under-16) and Nihal Sarin (under-19) won gold medals in December 2020.

Nihal Sarin: U-19 gold medallist at the first FIDE Online World Youth Rapid Championship

MOSTS

Most international age group titles in a year
Tejas Bakre won three gold medals in eight months in the 1998 Asian juniors at Rasht, Iran, in May; the World Youth Games Championship at Moscow in July; and the Asian Sub-junior Championship at Mumbai in December 1998.

Most medals in a continental competition
Indians won 21 medals – seven gold, seven silver and seven bronze – in the 2005 Asian Youth Championship in New Delhi.

Most international titles in a year
Viswanathan Anand won a string of eight titles in the year 2000. Starting with the

World Blitz Cup in Warsaw, Poland, he won the Wydra International at Haifa, Israel; the Advanced Chess title in León, Spain; the Giants Classic in Frankfurt, Germany; the Dortmund International (joint winner) World Cup in Shenyang, China; the Corsica Masters in France; and finally the World Championship title in December 2000 in Tehran, Iran.

Most national titles in a season

P. Harikrishna won five national titles in the 1997–98 season – the 1997 National Sub-juniors held in Aurangabad, Maharashtra; the U-12 at Ahmedabad, Gujarat; the U-18 at Bikaner, Rajasthan; the U-14 rapid title at Guntur, Andhra Pradesh; and the 1998 National Sub-juniors at Aurangabad.

Most titles in the Nationals

- *Men:* Manuel Aaron won nine national titles, five of them in a row during 1969–74.
- *Women:* S. Vijayalakshmi has claimed the national title six times, including five times in a row from 2002.

Hat-trick of titles in Advanced Chess

Viswanathan Anand won a hat-trick of titles in 1999, 2000 and 2001 in León, Spain. In Advanced Chess, players can use database searches on their computers before making a move.

Five Grand Slam victories

Until 2010, the elite tournaments held in Wijk aan Zee (the Netherlands), Linares (Spain) and Dortmund (Germany) formed the equivalent of the Grand Slam. Viswanathan Anand won five times at Wijk aan Zee and three times each at Linares and Dortmund.

City to host most Commonwealth Championships

New Delhi hosted the Commonwealth Championship six times between 2007 and 2019.

Most prize money in an International Open

The 18th edition of the Delhi International Open offered Rs 1.11 crore (US $1.49 million) as prize money across three sections.

FASTEST

Fastest to achieve three International Master norms

P. Harikrishna achieved three International Master norms in less than two months in the Asian Championship held in Udaipur, Rajasthan; the Goodricke tournament held in Kolkata, West Bengal; and the Commonwealth Championship held in Sangli, Maharashtra, in 2000.

YOUNGEST

Youngest International Master

R. Praggnanandhaa, at 10 years and nine months, became the youngest IM in

May 2016, with his third and final IM norm at Bhubaneswar, Odisha.

Youngest to achieve IM norm
R. Praggnanandhaa, at 10 years and six months, became the youngest Indian to make an IM norm in Cannes, France, in February 2016.

Youngest Grandmaster – male
D. Gukesh is the youngest male to become a GM at 12 years, seven months and 17 days.

Youngest Grandmaster – female
K. Humpy is the youngest female to become a GM at 15 years and 58 days.

Youngest Indian in the World Cup and Chess Olympiad
D. Harika competed in the World Cup at 11 years and nine months in Hyderabad in 2002. She was also the youngest to represent India in the Chess Olympiad in Mallorca, Spain, in 2004.

Youngest international title winners
Sanskruti Wankhede and Vallabh Kavi won the Asian Schools chess (U-5) girls' and boys' titles respectively in New Delhi in 2011.

D. Harika: youngest Indian in World Cup and Chess Olympiad

Youngest national champion
At 16 years, G. Akash became the youngest national champion in 2012.

Youngest national junior champion
Abhijeet Gupta from Bhilwara, Rajasthan, became the youngest national junior champion at Nagpur in 2002. He won the U-19 event at the age of 13 years 10 days.

Youngest world champion in any sport
Ivana Furtado became the youngest Indian to win a world title when she claimed the world girls' U-8 crown at the age of seven years and 226 days at Batumi, Georgia, on 29 October 2006.

Youngest to qualify for the National Championship
- Dibyendu Barua remains the youngest to qualify for the National Championship in 1978 when he was 12 years old.
- D. Harika holds the record of being the youngest girl to qualify for the National Women's Championship in 2001 in New Delhi as a 10-year-old. She competed in the 2004 National Championship as a 13-year-old in Visakhapatnam, Andhra Pradesh.

Youngest to beat a Grandmaster

Nine-year-old Hetul Shah defeated Kazakh Nurlan Ibrayev in the first round of the Parsvnath International Open chess tournament in New Delhi on 1 January 2009. He broke the record of Parimarjan Negi, who had achieved the feat at 11 years.

Youngest to win the world junior title

P. Harikrishna won the world junior title in Kochi, Kerala, in November 2004 when he was 18 years 204 days.

Youngest to win the Commonwealth title

P. Harikrishna, then 15 years old, won the gold medal at London, UK, in 2001 after a three-way tie with two British players.

Youngest woman International Master

K. Humpy became the youngest Woman International Master at 12 years, three months and four days.

Youngest winner of the Asian junior (U-20) title

M. Kasturi, at 14 years, won the Asian junior title in Tehran, Iran, in 2001.

BEST

Best performance in the Asian Team Championship

Indian men won the gold medal and women won the silver medal at Esfahan, Iran, in 2006.

Best performance at the World Junior Girls' (U-20) Championship

K. Humpy won the World Junior Girls (U-20) Championship in August 2001 at 14 years.

Best performance – Category 21

Viswanathan Anand beat a field of seven super Grandmasters at Madrid, Spain, between 21 February and 10 March 1998. He beat Alexei Shirov, Peter Svidler, Vassily Ivanchuk and Veselin Topalov 1.5–0.5; lost to Garry Kasparov 0.5–1.5; and drew 1–1 with Vladimir Kramnik.

Best achievement

- Viswanathan Anand's rating of 2817 in March 2011 is the highest by an Indian.
- Among women, K. Humpy's rating of 2623 in July 2009 is the highest in India.

ONLY

First/only winner of Asian junior and sub-junior titles

Tejas Bakre is the only Indian to hold the Asian junior and Asian sub-junior titles at the same time, in 1998.

Only Indian Chess Oscar award winner

Viswanathan Anand is the only Indian to be awarded the Chess Oscar (founded in

1967) by the Russian chess magazine *64 - Chess Review*. He has claimed the Chess Oscar six times: in 1997, 1998, 2003, 2004, 2007 and 2008.

Only Indian woman to reach the final of the World Championship
K. Humpy reached the final of the World Championship in 2011, in which China's Hou Yifan won 5.5–2.5, with two games to spare in their 10-game match.

Only Asian to win at Wijk aan Zee
Viswanathan Anand won the Hoogovens Chess Tournament (Corus Tournament) at Wijk aan Zee, Netherlands, in 1989, though jointly with three others. He won it again, jointly, in 1998, He won the title alone in 2003, 2004 and 2006.

First/only woman to win the World Rapid title
K. Humpy won the Women's World Rapid Chess Championship in Moscow, Russia, in 2019.

Only Indian to win against computers
Viswanathan Anand simultaneously played against six computers and won 4–2 in the Aegon Man versus Computer Chess Event in 1997 at the Hague, Netherlands.

Only Indian to win rapid/blindfold event
Viswanathan Anand won the Melody Amber Blindfold and Rapid Chess Tournament in 1994, 1997 and 2003, and jointly in 2006.

Only semi-finalist of both the World Cup and the World Championship
K. Humpy reached the semi-finals of the World Cup at Hyderabad (now in Telangana) in 2002 and the World Championship at Elista, Russia, in 2004.

Only Indian with three World Championship bronze medals
D. Harika claimed three successive bronze medals at the Women's World Championship in 2012, 2015 and 2017.

Only girl to win National U-12 in the open section
K. Humpy won the National U-12 title in Ahmedabad, Gujarat, in 1999.

Highest cheque received by an Indian sportsperson
Viswanathan Anand won 1.20 million euros for retaining the World Chess title in Sofia, Bulgaria, in May 2010.

CRICKET

WOMEN'S CRICKET

GENERAL

Youngest to debut across all formats
Shafali Verma became the youngest Indian cricketer to make her debut across all three formats of the game when she played her first One-Day International (ODI)

on 27 June 2021, against England in the UK, when she was 17 years and 150 days old. She made her Test debut on 16 June 2021 in Bristol, UK, against England. Her T20I debut came at the age of 15 against South Africa in September 2019 in Surat, Gujarat. She is also the youngest woman ever to play an ODI, and the first Indian and fourth woman to score a half-century in both innings on a Test debut.

Mithali Raj: most career runs in international cricket – women

Most career runs in women's international cricket

Mithali Raj has scored 10,277 runs in her international career, with 669 runs in Tests, 7,244 in ODIs and 2,364 in T20Is.

Longest career

Mithali Raj's cricketing career spans more than 22 years.

Most career wickets across formats

Jhulan Goswami, with 340 wickets in 272 matches, has the most wickets across formats.

Anju Jain: most career dismissals by a wicketkeeper

TESTS

Most career dismissals by a wicketkeeper

Anju Jain has the most career dismissals by a wicketkeeper with 23 dismissals from 1995 to 2003, including 15 caught and eight stumped.

Biggest victory margin

India won by an innings and 34 runs while playing against South Africa in Mysuru, Karnataka, on 16 November 2014.

Narrowest victory margin

India won by 5 wickets against West Indies in Patna, Bihar, on 17 November 1976, and then against England at Taunton, UK, on 1 September 2006.

Lowest total

The lowest total ever was 65 runs for 10 wickets in 46 overs against the West Indies at Jammu, Jammu and Kashmir, on 29 November 1976.

Highest total

The highest total by the women's Test cricket team is 467 in 177.1 overs versus England at Taunton, UK, on 17 August 2002.

First and only double century

Mithali Raj scored 214 runs in 407 balls, against England at Taunton, UK, on 16 August 2002. She also has the best batting average of 51.00 in 10 matches.

Most runs
Sandhya Agarwal has 1,110 runs in 13 matches. She also holds the record for the most centuries, with four in 13 Tests and 23 innings.

Most balls delivered
Former Indian player and left-arm spinner Diana Edulji is the only woman to deliver more than 5,000 balls (5,248) in Test matches.

Mithali Raj has captained India in 124 One-Day Internationals with a win percentage of 60.68.

Most wickets in a Test
Right-arm pacer Jhulan Goswami took 10 wickets in the match against England at Taunton, UK, on 1 September 2006.

Most career wickets in Tests
The record for most wickets in a Test career goes to Diana Edulji, with 63 wickets taken from 1976 to 1991.

Best bowling average
Jhulan Goswami, with an average of 17.36 with 44 wickets in 12 matches, has an unmatched bowling average in women's Test cricket in India.

Best bowling – innings
Neetu David's eight wickets for 53 runs in the India versus England match at Jamshedpur, Jharkhand, on 27 November 1995, makes her the only bowler in women's Test cricket to have claimed eight wickets in an innings.

Most career catches by a fielder
Sudha Shah has taken 21 catches in as many matches, an Indian record for a fielding position.

ONE-DAY INTERNATIONALS

Highest partnership
Deepti Sharma and Poonam Raut made a 320-run stand for the first wicket at the India versus Ireland match at Potchefstroom, South Africa, on 15 May 2017.

Highest individual score
Deepti Sharma was 188 not out at the India versus Ireland match at Potchefstroom, South Africa, on 15 May 2017.

Deepti Sharma: highest individual score

Best bowling average – minimum 50 wickets
Neetu David holds the record with an average of 16.34 (141 wickets in 97 matches).

Clean sweep victories in a bilateral series

The Indian team won all five matches in a bilateral series twice – against England in January 2002, and then against West Indies during February–March 2004.

Century on debut

Mithali Raj scored a century on her debut with 114 runs (not out) versus Ireland at Milton Keynes, UK, on 26 June 1999.

Most runs scored

Mithali Raj has scored 7,391 runs in 220 matches. She is the only woman cricketer to score more than 7,000 runs.

Most career dismissals by a wicketkeeper

Anju Jain has 81 dismissals to her credit, including 30 caught and 51 stumped.

Most career catches by a fielder

Jhulan Goswami has 65 catches in 192 matches.

Most career stumpings by a wicketkeeper

Anju Jain holds a world record with 51 stumpings across her career.

T20 INTERNATIONALS

Largest victory margin

- The largest victory margin in terms of runs is 142 runs versus Malaysia on 3 June 2018 at the Kinrara Academy Oval, Kuala Lumpur, Malaysia.
- In terms of wickets, the largest victory margin has been by 10 wickets against the Australian team on 29 January 2016 at Melbourne, Australia.

Narrowest margin of victory

- By runs, the narrowest margin was 3 runs on two occasions. The first was against the West Indies at North Sound, Antigua, on 19 February 2012, and the second was against New Zealand in Melbourne, Australia, on 27 February 2020.
- By wickets, India's narrowest margin has been against New Zealand, of 3 wickets at Aldershot, England, on 27 June 2011.

Highest partnership

Shafali Verma and Smriti Mandhana put on a 143-run stand for the first wicket versus West Indies at the Darren Sammy National Cricket Stadium, Saint Lucia, on 9 November 2019.

Most career runs

Mithali Raj has scored 2,364 in 89 matches with a batting average of 37.52. The captain of the national Test and ODI teams, she is also the first Indian woman cricketer to reach 2,000 runs during a Women's T20I Asia Cup match versus Sri Lanka in Kuala Lumpur, Malaysia, in 2018.

Highest team total

India's highest team total was 198 for 4 wickets in the third match versus

England at Brabourne Stadium in Mumbai, Maharashtra, in the Tri-Nation Women's T20I Series in March 2018.

Poonam Yadav: most career wickets in T20Is

Lowest team total
India scored only 62 runs in 18.2 overs versus Australia at Billericay, Essex, UK, on 23 June 2011.

Most career wickets
Poonam Yadav has notched up 98 wickets in 72 matches.

Best bowling average (minimum qualification of 30 matches)
Poonam Raut has a record bowling average of 9.66.

Best bowling
Jhulan Goswami took 5 wickets for 11 runs in a T20I match against Australia at Visakhapatnam, Andhra Pradesh, on 23 March 2012.

Most career dismissals by a wicketkeeper
Tania Bhatia has 67 dismissals (23 caught and 44 stumped) in 50 matches.

Most career catches by a fielder
Harmanpreet Kaur holds the record of 47 catches in 121 matches, the highest number of career catches.

MEN'S CRICKET

TESTS

First victory
India, captained by Vijay Hazare, defeated England by an innings and 8 runs on 10 February 1952 at Madras (now Chennai), Tamil Nadu. The victory came in the fifth match of a five-match series and India managed to draw the series 1–1.

Highest team innings score
The highest innings score was 759 runs for 7 wickets against England at Chennai, Tamil Nadu, in 2016.

Highest score on debut (series)
Legendary batsman Sunil Gavaskar scored 774 runs in his very first Test series against West Indies in 1971, a record that remains unbroken.

WR **Most consecutive wins at home (series)**
India recorded their 13th consecutive Test series wins at home when they beat England in a four-match series from 5 February to 8 March 2021, beating Australia to the top spot in the longest winning streak by any team.

Most career wickets
Anil Kumble holds the record with 619 wickets in his Test career spanning 1990–2008.

Highest run chase
India's run chase of 406 runs for 4 wickets against West Indies at Port-of-Spain, Trinidad, in 1976 is its highest successful chase to date.

Most wickets in a debut series
In the India–England Test series from 5 February to 8 March 2021, Axar Patel took 27 wickets in the four-match series. He holds the record jointly with Dilip Doshi, who took the same number of wickets during a six-match home series against Australia in 1979.

First to reach 10,000 runs
Indian cricket legend Sunil Gavaskar first went past the 10,000 mark in 125 matches, reaching 10,122 Test runs in his last series against Pakistan in 1987.

WR **Most career runs**
Sachin Tendulkar's total of 15,921 runs is an unbroken world record for the most career runs in men's Test cricket.

WR **Most individual centuries**
Sachin Tendulkar scored 51 centuries – three versus West Indies in 19 Tests, 11 versus Australia in 35 Tests, two versus Pakistan in 18 Tests, seven versus England in 28 Tests, four in 22 Tests versus New Zealand, nine in 25 Tests versus Sri Lanka, seven in 25 Tests versus South Africa, five in seven Tests versus Bangladesh and three in nine Tests versus Zimbabwe.

Most runs in an over
Hardik Pandya scored 26 runs in an over off Sri Lanka's P.M. Pushpakumara at Pallekele, Sri Lanka, in August 2017. He hit fours off the first two deliveries; the next three balls were hit for sixes. He did not score off the last ball.

Highest individual score in a day
Virender Sehwag, in his knock of 293 against Sri Lanka in Mumbai, Maharashtra, during 2009–10, made 284 runs on the second day of the Test match – the highest individual score in a single day to date.

Anil Kumble: most career wickets in Tests

Sachin Tendulkar: most individual centuries

Virender Sehwag: highest individual score in a day and highest individual innings

Highest individual innings
Virender Sehwag's 319 against South Africa in Chennai, Tamil Nadu, in 2008 is the highest individual score in a Test match.

Lowest team innings score
India recorded an all-time low of 36 runs against Australia in Adelaide in December 2020. It is the fifth lowest in the world.

Highest run aggregate
Sachin Tendulkar's score of 15,921 runs from 1989 to 2013 in 200 Tests is a world record. This score, from 329 innings, amounts to an average of 53.78.

Most 1,000+ runs in a calendar year
Sachin Tendulkar has scored more than 1,000 runs in a calendar year on six occasions. He made 1,000 runs in 12 Tests in 1997; 1,088 runs in 10 Tests in 1999; 1,003 runs in 10 Tests in 2001; 1,392 runs in 16 Tests in 2002; 1,063 runs in 13 Tests in 2008; and 1,562 runs in 11 Tests in 2010.

Highest century partnerships
Rahul Dravid has been part of the most three-figure partnerships, on 88 occasions; thrice for the first wicket, 34 times for the second, 26 times for the third, eight times for the fourth, 12 times for the fifth, thrice for the sixth and twice for the eighth wicket. He partnered with Sachin Tendulkar in 100-plus stands in a world record 20 times and with V.V.S. Laxman 12 times. Dravid's highest stand was with Virender Sehwag in a 410-run stand against Pakistan at Lahore in 2006. Dravid and Tendulkar have added 6,920 partnership runs, the most by any pair in history.

Rahul Dravid: highest century partnerships

Wicket off first ball on debut
Nilesh Kulkarni is the first and only Indian, and the 15th in the world, to capture a wicket off the very first ball on debut, when he bowled out Marvan Atapattu of Sri Lanka in Colombo, Sri Lanka, in 1997.

Wicket off first ball in a match
Syed Abid Ali took the wicket of Roy Fredricks off the very first ball at Port-of-Spain, Trinidad, against the West Indies in 1971. Kapil Dev emulated him twice by dismissing Mohsin Khan at Jalandhar, Punjab, against Pakistan during 1983–84, and Jimmy Cook at Durban versus South Africa in 1992–93.

Best bowling figures on Test debut
Narendra Hirwani took 16 wickets for 136 runs against West Indies at Madras (now Chennai), Tamil Nadu, during 1987–88.

HARD-HITTER

Rohit Sharma

ROHIT SHARMA

Right-handed batsman, prolific run-getter, and the current captains of the Indian national men's cricket team in Tests, ODI and T20 formats, Rohit Sharma has the following achievements to his credit:

ICC World Cup 2019

WR **Most centuries in a single World Cup:** Five centuries, breaking Kumar Sangakkara's record of four centuries.

- **Most centuries in the World Cup:** He equalled Sachin Tendulkar's record of six centuries. Rohit Sharma's six centuries came from 16 innings while Sachin's six centuries came from 44 innings.
- **Most Man of the Match awards in a single World Cup:** Sharma has four Man of the Match awards, jointly held by Aravinda de Silva (Sri Lanka), Lance Klusener (South Africa) and Yuvraj Singh (India).

One-Day Internationals

- **Highest individual innings:** 264 runs versus Sri Lanka on 13 November 2014 at Kolkata, West Bengal.
- **Most sixes in an innings:** 16 sixes in his total of 209 runs against Australia in Bengaluru, Karnataka, on 2 November 2013. This record, at the world level, was broken by England's Eoin Morgan who hit 17 sixes against Afghanistan during the 2019 World Cup.

WR Tests

Most sixes in a series: Sharma scored 17 sixes in the Test series against South Africa on 20 October 2019 in Ranchi, Jharkhand.

Fastest Indian opener to score 1,000 runs

The right-handed batsman achieved the landmark in his 17th innings as the Indian opener against England on 5 March 2021.

T20 Internationals

- **Highest individual innings:** 118 versus Sri Lanka in Indore, Madhya Pradesh, in 2017.

Indian Premier League

- **Player with the most IPL titles:** Six IPL titles; one with the Deccan Chargers, Hyderabad (2009) and five with the Mumbai Indians (2013, 2015, 2017, 2019 and 2020).

Best bowling in an innings
Anil Kumble took 10 wickets for 74 runs against Pakistan at Delhi in one innings during 1998–99.

WR **Best bowling in a match**
Narendra Hirwani took 16 wickets for 136 runs versus West Indies at Madras (now Chennai), Tamil Nadu, during 1987–88.

WR **Most catches in an innings**
The world record of five catches is held by four individuals (along with eight foreign players): Yajurvindra Singh (versus England at Bengaluru, Karnataka, in 1977); Mohammad Azharuddin (versus Pakistan at Karachi, Pakistan, in 1989); K. Srikkanth (versus Australia at Perth, Australia, in 1992); and Ajinkya Rahane (versus Sri Lanka at Galle, Sri Lanka, in 2015).

KING KOHLI

Virat Kohli

VIRAT KOHLI

The former men's national cricket team captain and prolific trailblazer of records, Virat Kohli has many achievements to his credit:

- **First cricketer to win all the three major ICC awards:** Sir Garfield Sobers Trophy for Cricketer of the Year, Test Player of the Year and the ICC Men's ODI Player of the Year in 2018.
- **Only player to touch an average of 50+ across formats:** 54.46 (Test), 58.20 (ODI) and 52.65 (T20I).
- **10 centuries across all formats in a year (2017):** These are the most by a captain, surpassing the record of former Aussie skipper Ricky Ponting and former South Africa captain Graeme Smith, who had nine each.
- **First Indian captain to win a Test series in Australia:** In 2018–19, India won the four-match series 2–1. Virat led India to a record eight consecutive Test series wins.

WR **Six double centuries as skipper:** In December 2017, Kohli overtook former West Indies captain Brian Lara (Kohli took only 48 innings to make the double tons, while Lara took 85).

WR Fastest cricketer to score 23,000 international runs in 490 innings.

TESTS

- **Most wins as captain:** India has won in 40 Test matches out of 68 under Kohli's captaincy. In his seven-year stint as India's Test captain, those 40 wins also made Kohli the 4th most successful captain in Test history, behind only Graeme Smith, Ricky Ponting and Steve Waugh.

Dismissing all 11 batsmen in a match
S. Venkataraghavan dismissed all 11 batsmen in the Delhi Test against New Zealand in 1964–65. His final tally was 12 for 152. He became the second bowler after England's Jim Laker and one among only six bowlers in the world to do this.

WR **Most dismissals by a wicketkeeper in a match**
Rishabh Pant shares the world record with England's Jack Russell (versus South Africa, 1995) and South Africa's A.B. de Villiers (versus Pakistan, 2013), with 11 dismissals in Adelaide, versus Australia, in December 2018.

Most dismissals by a wicketkeeper in an innings
The record for dismissals is six, shared by four players: Syed Kirmani, who caught five and stumped one against New Zealand at Christchurch, New Zealand, in 1975–76; M.S. Dhoni, who caught six against New Zealand at Wellington, New

- After the India–England Test series from 5 February to 8 March 2021, Kohli joined former India skipper M.S. Dhoni with the most number of matches as India's captain in Test cricket, totalling 60.
- Kohli, as captain, also equalled 36 Test wins of Clive Lloyd as captain, behind Graeme Smith of South Africa (with 53) and Ricky Ponting of Australia (with 48). This was also Virat Kohli's 10th successive Test series win at home.

ONE-DAY INTERNATIONALS
- **First to score a century on World Cup debut:** India versus Bangladesh, 2011 World Cup at Mirpur, Bangladesh, on 21 February 2011.
- **Best batting average:** 59.31 in 251 matches.
- **Fastest century:** 100 (not out) in 52 balls against Australia at Jaipur, Rajasthan, on 16 October 2013.

WR **Fastest to score 12,000 runs:** Kohli achieved this in his 242nd innings beating Tendulkar's record of 12,000 runs in 300 innings.
- **Fastest to score 43 centuries:** He achieved this in his 230th innings.
- Won the ICC Men's ODI Player of the Decade award in 2020.
- Won the Sir Garfield Sobers Award for Male Cricketer of the Decade in 2020.

T20 INTERNATIONALS
- **Only player to take a wicket on 0th ball:** Virat Kohli dismissed England's Kevin Pietersen with a wide ball (his first in T20I) in 2011, stumped by Dhoni.

WR **First cricketer to reach 3,000 runs:** Virat Kohli became the first player ever to breach the 3,000 run mark in the T20 International format. He achieved this during his match against England on 14 March 2021 at Ahmedabad, Gujarat.

INDIAN PREMIER LEAGUE
- Most runs in an IPL edition: 973 runs during IPL 2016.

Record Rewind

Most centuries scored in a decade - ODIs

2008

Sachin Tendulkar scored the most centuries in a decade (1990-2000) with 27 centuries.

2010

Virat Kohli became the batsman with the most centuries in a decade (2010-20) with 42 centuries.

Zealand, in 2008–09; Wriddhiman Saha, with five caught and one stumped against West Indies at North Sound, Antigua, in 2016; and Rishabh Pant, with six caught in Adelaide in December 2018 versus Australia.

Most career dismissals by a wicketkeeper
M.S. Dhoni has dismissed 294 batsmen (caught 256 and stumped 38) in 90 Tests.

WR **Most catches in a match**
With eight catches in the match against Sri Lanka at Galle, Sri Lanka, in 2015 (three in the first innings and five in the second), Ajinkya Rahane holds the world record for most catches in a match.

Most dismissals by a wicketkeeper in a series
N.S. Tamhane holds the record with 19 dismissals in five Tests against Pakistan in the 1954–55 series.

WR **Highest score and fastest 100 on debut**
Shikhar Dhawan scored 187 runs in 174 balls (33 fours, two sixes) in his Test debut against Australia at Mohali, Punjab, in 2013. Dhawan reached his 100 in just 85 balls – the fastest by a debutant (where full figures are available).

ONE-DAY INTERNATIONALS

Highest team total
The Indian men's cricket team scored 418 runs for 5 wickets in 50 overs against West Indies at Indore, Madhya Pradesh, on 9 December 2011.

Highest run chase
The Indian team's score of 362 runs for 1 wicket, chasing Australia's 359 runs for 5 wickets in Jaipur, Rajasthan, on 16 October 2013, was the highest run chase.

Highest score on debut
K.L. Rahul scored an unbeaten 100 against Zimbabwe at Harare, Zimbabwe, on 11 June 2016 – the only Indian to make an ODI century on debut.

WR **Fastest 50 runs on debut**
Krunal Pandya became the fastest-scoring debutant to post a half-century in an ODI match in just 26 balls, finishing at 58 not out in 31 balls on 23 March 2021 at the Maharashtra Cricket Association Stadium in Pune, Maharashtra, against England. He became the 15th Indian to score over 50 runs on an ODI debut.

First bowler to take more than three wickets on debut
Prasidh Krishna became the first bowler to take four wickets in an ODI match. He

R. Ashwin: Awesome All-rounder

The India–England Test series during February–March 2021 brought to the fore R. Ashwin's all-rounder skills. He became the first Indian with more than 30 (he took 32) wickets and a century in a four-match Test series, and only the fifth player in the world to do so. He also became the first Indian to take 30 or more wickets in a Test series twice. Ashwin's nine Player of the Series awards in Test cricket are the most won by an Indian, just behind Sri Lankan player Muttiah Muralitharan (11) in this format.

R. Ashwin

finished 4/54 in his debut ODI on 23 March 2021, against England, held at the Maharashtra Cricket Association Stadium in Pune, Maharashtra.

First to score 100 centuries in international cricket
Sachin Tendulkar was the first to score 100 international centuries (51 Test and 49 ODI hundreds). He scored his 100th century at the fourth ODI of the Asia Cup versus Bangladesh on 16 March 2012.

Lowest team total
India scored only 54 runs in 26.3 overs against Sri Lanka at Sharjah, UAE, on 29 October 2000.

WR **Most ODI century partnerships**
Sourav Ganguly and Sachin Tendulkar have 26 century-plus stands as a pair, a world record in ODIs.

Most career wickets
Anil Kumble's ODI record of 337 wickets is the highest.

WR **Most runs in all World Cups**
Sachin Tendulkar scored 2,278 runs in 45 World Cup matches from 1992 to 2011. He also holds the world record for the most centuries in World Cups, with six in 45 World Cup matches; this was equalled by Rohit Sharma in 17 matches.

WR **Most centuries**
Sachin Tendulkar has scored 49 centuries in 463 ODI matches.

WR **Most career Man of the Match awards**
Sachin Tendulkar has won 62 Man of the Match awards in his career. He won the first Man of the Match award in the 1992 World Cup, against Pakistan.

Most career catches
Mohammad Azharuddin took 156 catches in ODIs.

NATIONAL SPORTS AWARDS 2020 CRICKET

Khel Ratna Award: Rohit Sharma
Arjuna Award: Ishant Sharma, Deepti Sharma

Most total career runs
Sachin Tendulkar has made a total of 18,426 runs (including 49 centuries) in his ODI career spanning 463 matches.

Best strike rate
Hardik Pandya has achieved a record strike rate of 115.43 across 57 matches.

Best bowling
Stuart Binny took 6 wickets for 4 runs against Bangladesh at Mirpur, Bangladesh, on 17 June 2014.

Winning four ODI Man of the Match awards in a row
Sourav Ganguly is the only player to have won four consecutive Man of the Match awards in ODIs, a record made against Pakistan at Toronto, Canada, in 1997.

First wins in the World Cup and ICC World Twenty20
India won its first World Cup under the captaincy of Kapil Dev in 1983 and its second World Cup under the leadership of M.S. Dhoni in 2011, thus becoming the third nation after West Indies and Australia to win the World Cup more than once. Dhoni also led India to its first ICC World Twenty20 win in its inaugural 2007 edition.

Unique 100
Shikhar Dhawan scored a century in his 100th ODI, a first-of-a-kind feat in Indian cricket.

Most career catches
Rahul Dravid holds the record with 210 catches in 164 matches (including one catch for the ICC World XI): 47 versus Australia, 30 versus England, 26 versus West Indies, 21 versus South Africa, 21 versus Zimbabwe; 19 versus Pakistan; 17 versus New Zealand; 16 versus Sri Lanka; and 13 versus Bangladesh.

T20 INTERNATIONALS

Highest team total
The highest team total is 260 for 5, for India versus Sri Lanka in Indore, Madhya Pradesh, on 22 December 2017.

Lowest team total
India scored 74 runs in 17.3 overs against Australia at Melbourne on 1 February 2008.

Highest run chase
The Indian team made 211 runs for 4 wickets on 12 December 2009, chasing Sri Lanka's 206 runs for 7 wickets, at Mohali, Punjab.

Most career wickets
Jasprit Bumrah has the most T20I career wickets with 66 in 55 matches.

Best bowling average (minimum 10 wickets)
L. Balaji's bowling average of 12.10 is the best on record for T20I matches.

Best individual bowling
Deepak Chahar took 6 wickets for 7 runs while playing against Bangladesh at Nagpur, Maharashtra, on 10 November 2019.

Most career dismissals as a wicketkeeper
M.S. Dhoni holds the record with 91 dismissals in 98 matches, including 57 caught and 34 stumped.

Best batting average (minimum 50 matches)
Virat Kohli has the best batting average of 52.04 in 95 matches.

Fastest to 50
Yuvraj Singh's 50 runs in 12 balls against England in Durban, South Africa, on 19 September 2007, is the fastest half-century in T20Is.

Only captain to win all three ICC trophies
M.S. Dhoni is the only captain to lead his team to victory in all the three major ICC tournaments: the World T20 in 2007, the Cricket World Cup in 2011 and the Champions Trophy in 2013.

CUE SPORTS

First world billiards team title
India 'B' won a gold while India 'A' bagged a silver in the inaugural World Billiards Team Championship in Glasgow, Scotland, in August 2014. The winning team, with Pankaj Advani, Rupesh Shah, Devender Joshi and Ashok Shandilya, beat India 'A' 5–4.

First Asian Games title
Billiards was introduced at the 1998 Bangkok Asiad. India won two golds, a silver and a bronze. Ashok Shandilya won the gold, beating the world champion Geet Sethi 5–4. In the doubles, Ashok Shandilya and Geet Sethi won a gold, beating Devendra Joshi and Balachandra Bhaskar, who won the bronze.

First Asian snooker title
Yasin Merchant beat Udon Khaimuk of Thailand by eight frames in New Delhi on 15 July 1989 to win the Asian Confederation of Billiard Sports (ACBS) Championship.

Best performance at the Asian Billiards Sports Championship
India won a gold, a silver and three bronze medals in the inaugural Asian Billiards Sports Championship at Al Fujairah, UAE, held from 24 September to 2 October

2016. Siddharth Parikh (billiards 100-up) won the gold medal and Vidya Pillai won the silver (6-red, women). The bronze medallists were Sourav Kothari (billiards 100-up), Kamal Chawla (6-red, men), Amee Kamani and Arantxa Sanchis (6-red, women), Manan Chandra, Sundeep Gulati and Ishpreet Singh Chadha (team snooker).

Best performance in the Asian Games – snooker
At the 2010 Asian Games held in Guangzhou, China, the Indian team won a silver, while Aditya Mehta (individual) and Alok Kumar (8-ball pool) won bronze medals.

First National Championship – billiards
The first National Championship was held in 1931 in Calcutta (now Kolkata), West Bengal, with only eight entries. M.M. Beg won the title.

First National Championship – snooker
The first National Snooker Championship was held in 1939 in Calcutta (now Kolkata, West Bengal). P.K. Deb won the title.

First World Games snooker title
Aditya Mehta won the Quadrennial World Games snooker gold at Cali, Colombia, in July 2013.

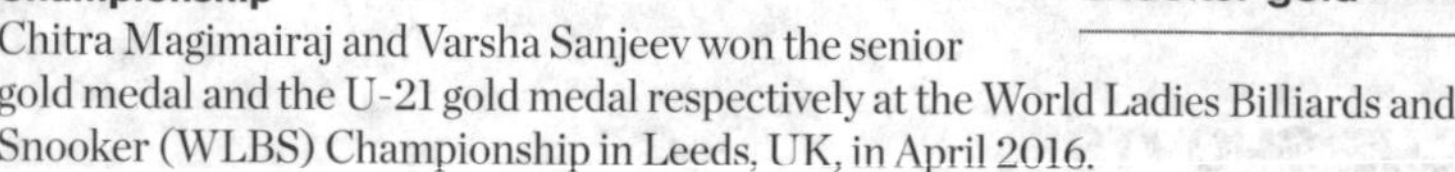

Aditya Mehta: first World Games snooker gold

First win at the World Ladies Billiards and Snooker Championship
Chitra Magimairaj and Varsha Sanjeev won the senior gold medal and the U-21 gold medal respectively at the World Ladies Billiards and Snooker (WLBS) Championship in Leeds, UK, in April 2016.

First World Ladies Billiards and Snooker Association title
R. Umadevi won her maiden, and India's first, World Ladies Billiards and Snooker Association title, beating the then world no. 13, Eva Palmius, 2–0 in the final at Cambridge, England, in April 2012.

First billiards and snooker hat-trick
Geet Sethi achieved a hat-trick of three consecutive National Championship titles in billiards and snooker from 1985 to 1987. He also won the national titles for both sports in 1988.

Most billiards gold medals in the Asian Games
Pankaj Advani won two gold medals in the 2006 Doha Asiad and in the 2010 Asiad at Guangzhou, China.

Most national titles – billiards and snooker
Pankaj Advani has won the national titles for both billiards and snooker a record 32 times.

Most world titles – billiards and snooker
Pankaj Advani has the world champion titles for both billiards as well as snooker

a record 24 times. Pankaj Advani claimed at least one International Billiard and Snooker Federation world title every calendar year.

Pankaj Advani: most national and world titles – billiards and snooker

Highest break in the World Billiards Championship

Geet Sethi had a break of 1,276 over two sessions in 80 mins against Bob Close of England in the quarter-final of the World Professional Championship in Mumbai, Maharashtra, on 1 October 1992.

Highest break under three-pot rule – billiards

Michael Ferreira scored 630 against S.B. Agrawal at the World Championship in Delhi in 1981, a world record for the highest break under the three-pot rule.

First world champion on debut

Geet Sethi became the first person to become a world champion on debut when he beat legendary billiards player Bob Marshall, who was 50 years his senior, to win the 25th World Amateur Billiards Championship in 1985 in Delhi. He was also the first unseeded player to become the world champion.

Highest break – snooker

Geet Sethi had the maximum possible break of 147 against Latif Nazarali at the 54th National Championship in Guntur, Andhra Pradesh, in 1988.

Most billiards grand doubles

Pankaj Advani has won four world doubles in billiards (time and points format) in 2005, 2008, 2014 and 2018.

World 6-red title

Laxman Rawat won the 6-red title versus Muhammad Asif of Pakistan in Mandalay, Myanmar, on 20 September 2019.

Most Asian titles

Pankaj Advani won six Asian billiards titles during 2005–17. In June 2019, he became the only Indian to win the Asian and world titles in both snooker formats.

Oldest woman champion – billiards

Kamala Devi Chandrababu from Tamil Nadu beat Judy Walia from Karnataka 109–63, 65–112, 53–76, 98–72, 95–74 in the 1995 National Championship at Bangalore (now Bengaluru), Karnataka. At 63 years, it was her fourth championship and the second national title after 1991.

Youngest world champion – snooker

Pankaj Advani was 18 years old when he won the amateur World Snooker Championship title in October 2003.

Youngest to win the World Professional title
Pankaj Advani was 24 when he won the World Professional Billiards title at the Northern Snooker Centre, Leeds, England, on 6 September 2009. He outclassed 41-year-old Mike Russell, who has won the World Professional Billiards title a record nine times.

First snooker team World Cup title
Pankaj Advani and Manan Chandra won the inaugural International Billiards and Snooker Federation (IBSF) Snooker Team World Cup 2018 held in Doha, Qatar.

Back-to-back double
Pankaj Advani finished the year 2017 with a back-to-back double in snooker and billiards in the World Championships.

Most competitive 147 breaks in snooker
Aditya Mehta became the first Indian to make 147 maximum breaks in 2014 at the Paul Hunter classic.

Two titles in 6-red snooker
Pankaj Advani was the world's first player to hold both world and continental titles in 6-red snooker at the same time. He is also the only player to win world titles in both 15-red and 6-red snooker.

FOOTBALL

GENERAL

Oldest football tournament
The Durand Football Tournament is the third oldest tournament in the world and the oldest in Asia and India. Started by British diplomat and civil servant Sir Henry Mortimer Durand in 1888 for the British troops in India, it was held in Simla (now Shimla, Himachal Pradesh). In 1940, the tournament was moved to New Delhi. The latest edition, the 129th in the history of the tournament, was held from 2 to 24 August 2019, with Gokulam Kerala winning the tournament.

The Durand Cup: oldest football tournament

First football academy
The Tata Football Academy (TFA) was started at Jamshedpur, Jharkhand, in 1986 with Mohammed Habib and Ranjan Chowdhury as coaches, and Subimal 'Chuni' Goswami as technical director. It has produced over 100 junior and senior international players for India. It was followed by the Williamson Magor Football Academy in Assam and the Chandigarh Football Academy that started in the 1990s.

First Indian to be national coach of a foreign country
Syed Nayeemuddin was appointed national coach of Bangladesh in July 2007. He

was also the first Indian to coach a club side abroad – the Brothers Union of Bangladesh in 2004. In India, he won 33 trophies with Mohammedan Sporting, East Bengal and Mohun Bagan. As national coach, he led India to victory in the 1987 South Asian Federation (SAF) Games in Calcutta (now Kolkata), West Bengal, the 1997 Kathmandu South Asian Football Federation (SAFF) Championship in Nepal and the 2005 Karachi SAFF Championship in Pakistan.

Record Rewind

FIFA rankings

1992
The Indian football team was ranked 143rd in the world.

2020
The Indian football team was ranked 104th in the world.

First Olympic referee

Komaleeswaran Sankar became an Olympic referee when he was selected for the football tournament of the 2000 Sydney Olympics, one among the four match officials chosen from Asia. Sankar, who became a referee in 1988 and a national referee in 1994, retired in 2007 at the age of forty-five, as mandated by FIFA rules.

First World Cup referee

Komaleeswaran Sankar was the first World Cup referee from India when he was chosen to officiate at the 2002 World Cup in South Korea and Japan. His first match was a Group G league match between Mexico and Croatia on 3 June 2002. He officiated in three matches.

First professional coach

Amal Dutta, India's first professional coach, started his career in 1963, coaching East Bengal. He also coached the other two big Kolkata clubs: Mohun Bagan and Mohammedan Sporting.

Most matches officiated

S.S. Hakim officiated in 33 international matches and was a referee in the final of every major domestic tournament including three Nehru Cups. He represented India in the 1960 Rome Olympics and was the team's assistant coach for the 1982 Delhi Asiad. He is the only individual to have played football, coached the national team and functioned as an international referee.

Most appearances as coach in the Olympics

S.A. Rahim from Hyderabad (then in Andhra Pradesh) was the coach of the Indian football team in three consecutive Olympic Games in 1952 (Helsinki), 1956 (Melbourne) and 1960 (Rome).

S.A. Rahim: most appearances as a coach in the Olympics

Most appearances as coach in the Nehru Cup

Syed Nayeemuddin coached the Indian team in the Nehru Cup on four occasions – in 1987 at Kozhikode,

Kerala; in 1988 at Siliguri, West Bengal; in 1989 at Margao, Goa; and in 1997 at Kochi, Kerala.

First foreign coach

English professional footballer Harry Wright was appointed coach of the Indian football team in 1963. He held the position till 1964, leading India to one of its best performances – a runner-up position at the 1964 Asian Football Confederation (AFC) Cup.

First Indian club win

The first win in a major domestic tournament was by Mohun Bagan of Calcutta (now Kolkata, West Bengal), who beat East Yorkshire Regiment of Ghaziabad 2–1 in the Indian Football Association (IFA) Shield tournament final at the Calcutta Football Club Ground on 29 July 1911.

Only Indian coach to gain success with a foreign club

In his eight-year stint in Bangladesh, Syed Nayeemuddin helped his club, Brothers Union of Bangladesh, win three trophies.

Most successful coach at the Asian Games

- S.A. Rahim led as coach on five successful occasions – twice at the Asian Games (1951 and 1962), and thrice at the Quadrangular Tournament (1953, 1954 and 1955).
- The foreign coach with the best record is Bob Houghton of the UK with three trophies: the Nehru Cup (2007 and 2009) and the AFC Challenge Cup in 2008.

Most successful Indian coaches in domestic tournaments

P.K. Banerjee led domestic teams to 53 trophies, Amal Dutta to 35 and Syed Nayeemuddin to 33 of them.

First tiebreaker

The first tiebreaker in a final came when Mohammedan Sporting won the tie 3–1 against Mohun Bagan at the 1983 Peerless Trophy final at Calcutta (now Kolkata, West Bengal). The first tiebreaker match occurred in a third round match of the Durand Tournament played on 17 February 1972 at Delhi. Mohun Bagan beat Indian Navy 5–3.

First international tournament win by a club

East Bengal, coached by Subhash Bhowmick, won the LG ASEAN Club Cup Championship on 26 July 2003 in Jakarta, Indonesia, beating BEC Tero Sasana of Thailand in the final 3–1.

Longest sequence of wins

Mohun Bagan won 42 consecutive matches in the 1994 season till they lost to Dempo SC (Goa) in the Scissors Cup final in November 1994.

First in English professional club

- Mohammed Salim from Calcutta (now Kolkata, West Bengal), was the first from the Indian subcontinent to play for a European club, Celtic FC, in 1936.

- Bhaichung Bhutia was the first Indian footballer to join an English club when he signed a contract to represent second division outfit, Bury FC, from 1999 to 2002.
- Aditi Chauhan was the first Indian woman to play in the English league football on 16 August 2015, as a goalkeeper for West Ham United. She attended Loughborough University, completing an MSc in sports management and represented their football team from 2014–15. Chauhan joined Gokulam Kerala FC for the 2019–20 Indian women's league.

Mohammed Salim (*right*): first in an English professional club

Best record against foreign clubs

East Bengal has the best record against foreign clubs: played 239 matches (both exhibition and tournaments), won 97, drawn 40 and lost 102. They scored 343 goals and conceded 348.

Worst defeats

In international tournaments, India's worst defeats have been 1–10 to Yugoslavia at the 1952 Helsinki Olympics and 1–9 to Burma (now Myanmar) in the 1971 Merdeka Tournament at Kuala Lumpur, Malaysia.

First hat-trick in East Bengal versus Mohun Bagan match

- Amiya Deb scored all four goals for Mohun Bagan against East Bengal in a Darbhanga Shield match on 5 September 1934. Mohun Bagan won 4–1.
- On 13 July 1997, Bhaichung Bhutia scored a hat-trick for East Bengal versus Mohun Bagan in the KBL Federation Cup semi-final, in which East Bengal won 4–1.

First hat-trick

Norman Pritchard scored a hat-trick for St Xavier's College, Calcutta (now Kolkata, West Bengal), against Sovabazar Club in the 1889 Trades Cup.

Most individual goals in an international club match

Bhaichung Bhutia scored six goals, a double hat-trick, for East Bengal against Army FC of the Philippines in the LG ASEAN Cup in Jakarta, Indonesia, on 16 July 2003.

Fastest goal

Midfielder Dipankar Roy scored a goal in 9.33 seconds after kick-off for Bengal versus Karnataka in the 2000 Santosh Trophy held in Thrissur, Kerala.

First woman player to sign a contract with a foreign club

Ngangom Bala Devi made history when she signed a contract with Scottish Giant Rangers FC, a professional football club in Glasgow, UK. She dons a no. 10 jersey for the club and created yet another record on 6 December 2020 when she scored the final goal against Motherwell Women in the Scottish

SUPER 30

OINAM BEMBEM DEVI: FLAGBEARER OF FOOTBALL

Oinam Bembem Devi

A 2017 Arjuna Award recipient, Oinam Bembem Devi began her career in 1988 when she started training at the United Pioneers Club in Imphal, Manipur, and has won 13 senior national women's football championships for Manipur till 2020. Having played for the Indian national team from 1995 to 2016, Oinam Bembem Devi was honoured with the Padma Shri in 2020. Nicknamed the 'Durga of Indian football', she played for India at the Asian Women's Championship in 1995, the Asian Games in 1996, the Asian Football Confederation Cup in 1997 and 2003, as well as the South Asian Games in 2016, where the Indian team won. Under her leadership, India won three SAFF Championship Cup titles in 2010, 2012 and 2014, and South Asian gold medals in 2010 and 2016. She also managed the teams of Eastern Sporting Union in 2017, the Indian Women U-17 team in 2018 (where she was also the assistant coach) and the Manipur Police Sports Club in 2019. The first All India Football Federation (AIFF) Woman Footballer of the Year in 2001, she received the title again in 2013.

Women's Premier League, becoming the first Indian woman to score in a professional European Club.

Fastest international goal
I.M. Vijayan scored against Bhutan within 12 seconds after kick-off in a Group A league match played on 28 September 1999 at the SAF Games at Kathmandu, Nepal.

I.M. Vijayan: fastest international goal

INTERNATIONAL EVENTS

First appearance at the Olympics
With seven barefoot players, India entered the 1948 Olympics under captain Talimeren Ao from Bengal but lost to France 1–2. Sarangapani Raman scored the lone goal. Since then, India has played eight matches in four Olympic Games – 1948, 1952, 1956 and 1960 – won one, drawn one, lost six; scored 10 and conceded 27 goals. After 1960, India has been eliminated in the pre-Olympic stage.

Biggest margin of victory
In the 1963 pre-Olympics, India won 7–0 against Ceylon (now Sri Lanka) at Bangalore (now Bengaluru), Karnataka, and later 7–0 against Bangladesh in the Aga Khan Tournament at Dhaka, Bangladesh, in 1977.

Only hat-trick at the Olympics

Neville D'Souza of Caltex Sports Club, Mumbai, scored a hat-trick against Australia in the 1956 Melbourne Olympics. India won 4–2.

Biggest defeat at the Asian Games

India lost 1–7 to China in 1974 at Tehran in Iran. Magan Singh scored the lone goal.

Football Icons: In Remembrance

Subimal 'Chuni' Goswami

Subimal 'Chuni' Goswami (January 1938–April 2020) was an Indian professional footballer who captained the Indian football team from 1962 to 1964, and led them to victory in the 1962 Asian Games and a silver in the 1964 Asia Cup and in the Merdeka Cup. Popularly known as Chuni Goswami, he also played for the Mohun Bagan Athletic Club, an Indian multi-sport club in Calcutta (now Kolkata), West Bengal, where he was captain during 1960–1964 and scored a record-high of 145 goals in the Calcutta Football League (CFL). Between 1954 and 1968, the club won the CFL Cup for nine years, the IFA Shield for five years, the Durand Cup for five years and the Rovers Cup for three years. A 1963 Arjuna Award recipient, Goswami was honoured with the Padma Shri in 1983 as well as the Mohun Bagan Ratna award in 2005. The only player who led Bengal in the Santosh Trophy for football and the Ranji Trophy for cricket in 2005–06, Goswami was also given the title of sheriff of Kolkata in 2005.

Pradip Kumar Banerjee (23 June 1936–20 March 2020) was an Indian professional footballer who started his career with the Jamshedpur Sports Association in 1952 and played for the Indian national football team from 1955 to 1966. One of the first recipients of the Arjuna Award in 1961, Banerjee played for the Eastern Railway Football Club, a Calcutta Football League club based in Calcutta (now Kolkata), West Bengal, from 1955 to 1968, where he scored 111 goals and won the Santosh Trophy thrice. After making his debut for the Indian national team in 1955 at the Dhaka Quadrangular Football Tournament, Banerjee represented the country in all major international tournaments from 1955 to 1966, such as the 1958 Asian Games (in Tokyo, Japan), the 1962 Asian Games (in Jakarta, Indonesia), where India clinched the gold medal in football, and then the 1966 Asian Games (in Bangkok, Thailand). His total tally of six goals remains the highest by an Indian in the Asian Games. The captain of the team in the 1960 Rome Olympics, he also represented India in the Merdeka Cup in 1959, 1964 and 1965 as well as in the 1964 Asia Cup, where India won the silver.

After playing his last match for India against Malaysia in the 1966 Asian Games, he started his coaching career with the East Bengal Football Club and then the Mohun Bagan Athletic Club. Eventually he became the coach of the Indian football team from 1972 to 1981 and was honoured with the Padma Shri in 1990.

Pradip Kumar Banerjee

The Kolkata Derby: A Legendary Rivalry between East Bengal and Mohun Bagan

The Kolkata Derby (locally known as Boro Match) is the football match played every year in Kolkata, West Bengal, between East Bengal and Mohun Bagan, two professional rival football clubs that were founded in 1920 and 1889 respectively. With 369 matches played between the two clubs since 25 May 1925, East Bengal has won 129, Mohun Bagan has won 119 and 121 were drawn. The first match between The Mariners (Mohun Bagan) and the Red and Gold Brigade (East Bengal) was played on 8 August 1921 in the semi-final of the Cooch Behar Cup. After the first day's play remained goalless, Mohun Bagan beat East Bengal (3-0) in the replayed semi-final match on 10 August 1921. East Bengal beat Mohun Bagan (2-1) for the first time soon after on 26 August 1921 in the knockout phase of Khagendra Shield. On 28 May 1925, Mohun Bagan and East Bengal played their first big match in the Calcutta Football League (CFL), where East Bengal won with Nepal Chakraborty's goal. While East Bengal has more than 150 trophies to its name, Mohun Bagan has 253.

Biggest margin of victory at the Asian Games

India beat Hong Kong 5–2 at the 1958 Asiad in Tokyo, Japan, in its biggest margin of victory at the Asian Games. Mohammad Rahmatullah scored two goals while Subimal 'Chuni' Goswami, D. Damodaran and T. Balaram scored a goal each. India scored three goals in extra time, the first time India played extra time in an international match.

Best performance at the Olympics

India became the first Asian nation to reach the semi-finals of an Olympic football event, beating Australia 4–2 at the 1956 Melbourne Games. India took the lead against Yugoslavia but lost 1–4. In the play-off for the bronze, India lost 0–3 to Bulgaria, ending at fourth position. Samar 'Badru' Banerjee was India's captain and S.A. Rahim was the coach.

Youngest match winner at the Nehru Cup

Bhaichung Bhutia was 19 years old when he scored a goal to beat Uzbekistan 1–0 in 1995 at Calcutta (now Kolkata), West Bengal.

First Indian club to enter the Asian Football Confederation Cup final

- Bengaluru FC was the first Indian club to enter the final of Asia's prestigious club competition, the Asian Football Confederation (AFC) Cup, in October 2016. They lost the final match against Iraq Air Force 0–1 in Doha, Qatar, on

5 November 2016.

• Dempo SC (Goa) was the first club to enter the semi-finals of the Cup in September 2008.

Best performance at pre–World Cup

With three wins, two draws and one defeat (0–1 versus UAE in an away match in Al Ain, UAE), India's performance in the 2001 World Cup qualifiers has been the best yet. It is also the only series of matches where the Indian team scored more goals (11) than they conceded (5).

Biggest margin of victory at pre–World Cup

India beat Brunei 5–0 in Bangalore (now Bengaluru), Karnataka, in a Group 8 qualifier on 20 May 2001. Jules Alberto, I.M. Vijayan, Bhaichung Bhutia, Jo Paul Ancheri and Abdul Hakeem scored for India.

Worst defeat at pre–World Cup

India lost 0–7 to South Korea at Seoul, South Korea, in the 1993 World Cup qualifiers.

Top goal scorers internationally

Sunil Chhetri tops in FIFA-approved tournaments, with 72 goals in 115 matches, followed by Bhaichung Bhutia with 42 goals in 107 matches and I.M. Vijayan with 40 goals in 79 matches.

DOMESTIC EVENTS

First to win three National Football League titles

Mohun Bagan has won three National Football League (NFL) titles: in 1997–98, 1999– 2000 and 2001–02. East Bengal emulated this when they won their third NFL crown in 2003–04. Their earlier wins were in 2000–01 and 2002–03.

Most individual goals in a match in NFL

• Bhaichung Bhutia scored the most goals in an NFL match when he scored five goals playing for JCT against Mahindras in the first NFL in 1997. JCT won the match 6–1.

• In the fourth NFL, Francis Silveira of Churchill Brothers scored four goals in a match against Dempo SC (Goa) for a 5–0 win.

Most successful captain

Bhaichung Bhutia has five tournament wins to his credit as captain: the LG Cup in Vietnam (2002), SAFF Cup in Karachi, Pakistan (2005), Nehru Cup in Delhi (2007 and 2009), and the AFC Challenge Cup in Hyderabad and Delhi in 2008. He is also the second highest international scorer, with 42 goals in 107 matches.

Bhaichung Bhutia: most successful Indian captain

Most goals by a club in the NFL/Indian League (I-League)
East Bengal has scored 690 goals in 460 matches. Other teams to score are Churchill Brothers with 664 goals in 406 matches and Mohun Bagan with 619 goals in 446 matches.

Most individual goals in a match in the I-League
The most goals by a player in an I-League match are seven by Ranti Martins for Dempo SC (Goa) in their 14–0 win versus Air India in Margao, Goa, on 30 May 2011.

Most individual hat-tricks in the NFL and I-League
Nigerian striker Odafa Onyeka Okolie has scored 14 hat-tricks: nine for Churchill Brothers; four for Mohun Bagan; and one for Sporting Clube de Goa.

Top foreign scorers in the Indian Super League (ISL): 2014–18/19
Ferran Corominus (Spain): 34 goals; Iain Hume (Canada): 29 goals.

Winners of the 2018–19 I-League
Chennai City FC beat former champions Minerva Punjab 3–1 to become the 2018-19 I-League champions on 9 March 2019. Chennai City FC joined the I-League in 2016 and won the title for the first time. Spanish-Uruguayan forward Pedro Manzi scored a brace in this match and was the joint top scorer of the league, with 21 goals.

Record Rewind

Top goalscorer

1990

Striker Shabbir Ali scored a record 23 goals since 1974 and was the top goalscorer in India.

2020

Sunil Chhetri, the captain of the Indian national football team, scored a total of 72 goals since 2005. He plays as a striker as well as a winger.

Biggest victory margin in I-League
Dempo SC (Goa) beat Air India 14–0 on 30 May 2011. The next best is Prayag United's 10–1 rout of United Sikkim Football Club on 10 November 2012 in the sixth I-League.

Top Indian scorers in ISL: 2014–18/19
Sunil Chhetri: 30 goals; Jeje Lalpekhlua: 23 goals.

Top Indian scorers in NFL: 1997–2007
Bhaichung Bhutia: 78 goals; R.C. Prakash: 49 goals.

Top foreign scorers in NFL: 1997–2007
Yusif Yakubu: 78 goals; José R. Baretto: 62 goals.

Top Indian scorers in I-League: 2007–2017
Sunil Chhetri: 69 goals; Jeje Lalpekhlua: 39 goals.

Top foreign scorers in I-League: 2007–2017
Ranti Martins: 169 goals; Odafa Onyeka Okolie: 160 goals.

NATIONAL SPORTS AWARDS 2020 FOOTBALL

Arjuna Award: Sandesh Jhingan
Dhyan Chand Award: Sukhvinder Singh Sandhu

First Indian team to win the Durand Cup
Mohammedan Sporting won the Durand Cup in 1940 when it was first moved to Delhi and the final played at Irwin Amphitheatre (now Dhyan Chand National Stadium). Mohammedan Sporting beat Royal Warwickshire Regiment 2–1 in the final.

India's longest unbeaten run in a year
In 2017, India remained unbeaten in nine matches, three away games and six at home:
- 1–0 versus Myanmar; 1–0 versus the Kyrgyz Republic; 2–0 versus Macau; 4–1 versus Macau; and 2–2 versus Myanmar (all Asian Cup qualifiers).
- 3–2 versus Cambodia; 2–0 versus Nepal; 2–1 versus Mauritius; and 1–1 versus St Kitts and Nevis (all friendly matches).

Most wins at the Durand Cup
Mohun Bagan has won the Durand Cup 16 times and finished runner-up 11 times. East Bengal has won 16 times and been runner-up 10 times.

Most individual goals at the Durand Cup
Mohammed Habib scored 12 goals for East Bengal in seven matches (both the semi-finals and the final were replayed) in the 1972 Durand tournament.

Biggest victory margin in an IFA Shield final
Calcutta FC beat Dalhousie 6–0 in the replayed final in 1900. After 1947, the highest victory margin is 5–0 for East Bengal versus Mohun Bagan in 1975.

Only team to beat foreign clubs thrice at the IFA Shields finals
East Bengal beat Pas Club (Iran) 1–0 in 1970, Pyongyang City Club (North Korea) 3–1 in 1973 and Mohammedan Sporting, Dhaka (Bangladesh) 3–1 via penalty shoot-out in 1995 in the IFA Shields finals.

Only club to win both I-League and ISL titles
Bengaluru FC is the only club to win both I-League and ISL titles. They won the seventh I-League in 2014 and the ninth I-League in 2016. On 17 March 2019 they won the ISL title, beating FC Goa 1–0 in the final in Mumbai. Bengaluru FC joined the ISL in 2017.

First team from Kerala to win a national league title – men
Gokulam Kerala won the 2021 I-League, finishing with 29 points from 15 matches, the same as Churchill Brothers (Goa), but Gokulam became champions due to a superior goal difference, becoming the first team from the state of Kerala to win a national league title for men. This is the second time that Churchill

Brothers have come second in the I-League on goal difference. The first was in 2008 when they finished second to Dempo SC (Goa).

GOLF

GENERAL

Padma Shri recipients

Jeev Milkha Singh (2007)

Arjuna Award recipients

P.G. Sethi (1961), A.S. Malik (1963), R.K. Pitamber (1967), Anjali Desai (1972), Vikramjit Singh (1973), S.K. Jamshed (1975), Sita Rawlley (1977), Lakshman Singh (1982), Nonita Lall (1987), Ali Sher (1991), Amit Luthra (1996), Jeev Milkha Singh (1999), Shiv Kapur (2002), Jyoti Randhawa (2004), Arjun Atwal (2007), Gaganjeet Bhullar (2013), Anirban Lahiri (2014), S.S.P. Chawrasia (2017), Shubhankar Sharma (2019) and Aditi Ashok (2020).

Indian Open winners

Nine Indians have won the title spread over 13 times. They are: P.G. Sethi, Kolkata, 1965; Ali Sher, Delhi, 1991 and 1993; Feroze Ali, Kolkata, 1998; Arjun Atwal, Kolkata, 1999; Jyoti Randhawa, Gurgaon (now Gurugram), 2000; Vijay Kumar, Delhi 2002; Jyoti Randhawa, Delhi, 2006 and 2007; C. Muniyappa, Gurgaon (now Gurugram), 2009; Anirban Lahiri, Delhi, 2015; S.S.P. Chawrasia, Delhi, 2016 and 2017.

Jyoti Randhawa: one of the thrice winners of the Indian Open

Most wins in international tournaments – men

So far 25 Indians have won 87 international titles on various tours. Jeev Milkha Singh heads the list with 13 victories, followed by Arjun Atwal with 10, and Jyoti Randhawa and Gaganjeet Bhullar with nine each.

Thrice winner at the Indian Open

Jyoti Randhawa won in October 2007 at the Delhi Golf Club Course for the third time to equal Australian Peter Thomson's record.

Least putts on the European Tour

Jeev Milkha Singh needed just 94 putts for four rounds of the 2001 Desert Classic, with two more than the world record of 92 set by South Africa's David Frost in the 2005 MCI Heritage, Harbour Town, South Carolina, USA.

Indians topping Asian Tour Order of Merit

Jeev Milkha Singh won the Asian Tour Order of Merit in 2006 and 2008. Jyoti Randhawa (2002), Arjun Atwal (2003), Anirban Lahiri (2015) and Shubhankar

Sharma (2018) are the other Indians to top the Order of Merit.

Arjuna Award recipient Jeev Milkha Singh: least putts on the European Tour

Most appearances at the Majors
Eight Indians – Anirban Lahiri (16 times), Jeev Milkha Singh (14 times), Jyoti Randhawa, Arjun Atwal, Shiv Kapur and Shubhankar Sharma (five times each), Gaganjeet Bhullar and Gaurav Ghei (once each) – have appeared in 52 Majors.

Highest prize money across tournaments
A prize fund worth ₹8.80 crore (88 million) spread over 29 tournaments was offered in 2010, the highest in any year on the domestic circuit.

Tournament with highest prize money in a domestic sport
The ₹15 million (1.50 crore) McLeod Russel Tour Championship in 2014 was the first to offer such high prize money in a domestic sport.

Quickest to reach the million mark in prize money
Ashok Kumar won ₹1,00,10,334 in the 2004–05 season of the Indian Tour after just nine events.

Five titles in a season twice on the Indian Tour
Ashok Kumar won five titles in 2004 and repeated the feat in 2007.

Longest representation for India
Gangesh Khaitan (b. 26 September 1953) has been representing India in golf in international championships since 1970 as a junior player, national player and senior player. In August 2019, he was selected in the national team for the 2019 Asia-Pacific Golf Confederation (APGC) Seniors Golf Championship at Sungai Long Golf and Country Club in Kuala Lumpur, Malaysia. With this he completed 50 years of representing India.

NATIONAL SPORTS AWARDS 2020
GOLF

Arjuna Award: Aditi Ashok

Most consecutive medals – specially abled athlete – international tournaments
Ranveer Singh Saini (b. 24 November 2000) from Gurugram, Haryana, won two successive medals at the Special Olympics World Summer Games in golf tournaments in Los Angeles, USA (2015), and Abu Dhabi, UAE (2019).

Most national level gold medals – Special Olympics Bharat
Ranveer Singh Saini (b. 24 November 2000) from Gurugram, Haryana, won 10 gold medals at the Special Olympics Bharat national golf tournaments between 2012 and 2017.

FIRSTS

First sweep of Asian Games golds
Golf first featured in the 1982 Asian Games. Besides the team gold, India won the individual gold and silver medals with champion Lakshman Singh, and runner-up Rajiv Mohta. Two other members of the team were Amit Luthra and Rishi Narain.

First to qualify for the British Open
Gaurav Ghei was the first Indian to qualify for the premier event in 1997.

The All-India Amateur Championship, first held in 1892, is the world's second oldest running golf tournament.

First to qualify for the Professional Golfers' Association European Tour
Jeev Milkha Singh was the first to qualify for the Professional Golfers' Association (PGA) European Tour for the 1998 season.

First European–Asian Tour win
Arjun Atwal is the first Asian to win two co-sanctioned titles on the Tour: the Caltex Singapore Open in February 2002 and the Carlsberg Malaysian Open in February 2003.

First to gain qualification for the PGA Tour
Arjun Atwal became the first Indian to gain qualification for the full US Tour after making it through the Q-school for the year 2004.

First to gain a full 'card' on the PGA Tour
Arjun Atwal was the first to gain a full card (exemption from playing qualifying rounds) after his stupendous show in the 2005 season.

First win on the European Tour in Europe
Jeev Milkha Singh won the Volvo Masters held in Spain in October 2006.

First win on the European Tour
Arjun Atwal won the 2002 Singapore Masters.

First to win on the Japanese PGA Tour
Jyoti Randhawa won the Suntory Open in 2003.

First to play in the US Open
Jeev Milkha Singh was the first to play in the US Open in 2002.

First to play the PGA Championship
Arjun Atwal was the first to play in the PGA Championship in 2005.

First to play the Masters at Augusta
Jeev Milkha Singh played in the Masters at Augusta National Golf Club in Georgia, USA, in 2007.

First international success in U-10
Tanya Wadhwa of Delhi finished third in a U-10 International golf tournament in San Diego, USA, in July 2001.

First to qualify for the Ladies PGA Tour
Aditi Ashok gained the playing rights for the 2017 LPGA Tour via the LPGA Final Q-School.

First to qualify for the Olympic Games
Aditi Ashok was the first woman golfer to qualify for the Rio Olympic Games, Brazil, in 2016.

First to win the Ladies Indian Open
Aditi Ashok became the first to win the Ladies Indian Open in November 2016.

First win on the PGA Tour
Arjun Atwal won the 2010 Wyndham Championship. He was also the first qualifier to win the title in 24 years on the PGA Tour.

First to win on Ladies European Tour
Aditi Ashok was the first to win a title on the Ladies European Tour (LET) by claiming the 2016 Ladies Indian Open. She also won the 2016 Qatar Ladies Open.

First team to qualify for the World Championship
The Indian duo of Gaurav Ghei and Digvijay Singh qualified for the 2003 World Golf Championship at Kiawah Island, USA, after finishing joint second in the Nations Cup.

First to play in a Major
Gaurav Ghei became the first to qualify for a Major when he made it to the 1997 British Open.

First to make the 'cut' in a Major
Jeev Milkha Singh was the first to play all four rounds of the 2002 US Open.

First to represent the country in four multidisciplinary games
Aditi Ashok has participated in the 2013 Asian Youth Games, 2014 Youth Olympic Games, 2014 Asian Games and 2016 Olympic Games.

Aditi Ashok: first to win the Ladies Indian Open

First Olympians
Anirban Lahiri, S.S.P. Chawrasia and Aditi Ashok represented the country in the 2016 Rio Olympics in Brazil.

SHUBHANKAR SHARMA
The twenty-four-year-old holds a unique Indian record of winning two European Tour events in under two months. He won the Joburg Open on 11 December 2017 and the Maybank Open Championship on 4 February 2018. He went on to win the 2018 Asian Tour Order of Merit.

Shubhankar Sharma

First participation in World Cup
Arjun Atwal and Jyoti Randhawa formed the first team to take part in the World Cup in 2005.

First to play in three World Golf Championship events in a year
Jyoti Randhawa was the first to play in three events in the World Golf Championship (WGC) series in 2005.

MOSTS

Most successful rookie of the year
The Rookie Golfer of the Year award was introduced in 1997–98 on the domestic tour. To date, S. Chikkarangappa remains the most successful 'rookie' on the tour. He won ₹32,65,313 and finished second to Rashid Khan on the 2013 Order of Merit.

Most birdies
Jyoti Randhawa broke the course record in Shanghai, China, with a seven-under par 65 that included eight birdies at the Volvo China Open golf tournament in 2000. He finished in a tied fourth place.

Most lucrative season
During the 2017–18 Professional Golfers Association of India (PGAI) Tour 97 golfers earned over ₹1 lakh (0.1 million), with 79 players winning over ₹2 lakh (0.2 million); 67 winning over ₹3 lakh (0.3 million); 51 winning over ₹5 lakh (0.5 million); 29 winning over ₹10 lakh (1 million); 19 winning over ₹15 lakh (1.5 million); 13 winning over ₹21 lakh (2 million); and six players winning over ₹25 lakh (2.5 million).

Most Indian tournaments on the Asian tour
Three tournaments – the Royal Challenge Indian Open, the Hero Honda Masters and the Honda-SIEL tournament figured on the Asian Professional Golf Association Tour in 2002 for the first time.

Most career prize money in the domestic Professional Golf Tour of India
Shamim Khan has earned ₹4.11 crore (41.1 million) from 240 Professional Golf Tour of India (PGTI) tournament appearances, ahead of Mukesh Kumar's total of ₹3.77 crore (37.7 million) from 229 events.

Highest prize money earned in a domestic season
Rashid Khan won two events in 14 tournament appearances in the 2019 season and collected a total of ₹66,27,650 in prize money.

Highest prize money earned in a domestic tournament – women
Aditi Ashok collected US $60,000 as the first to win the Ladies Indian Open title in November 2016.

Most titles on the Asian Tour
Jyoti Randhawa has won eight titles on the Asian Tour: the 1998 and 1999 Hero Honda Masters, the 2000 Indian Open, the 2000 Singapore Open, the 2004 Volvo Masters of Asia, the 2006 Indian Open, the 2007 Indian Open and the 2009 Thailand Open.

Record Rewind

Youngest to win Order of Merit

2002

Jyoti Randhawa was the first and youngest player to win the Asian Tour Order of Merit in 2002 when he was 30 years old.

2018

Shubhankar Sharma became the youngest to win the Asian Tour Order of Merit in December 2018 at 22 years.

Most international titles
Jeev Milkha Singh has won 14 Tour titles spread over three Tours – four on the European Tour, six on the Asian Tour and four on the Japanese Tour.

Most titles in a season on the Indian Tour
Mukesh Kumar won six titles during the 2004–05 season.

BEST

Best finish in the European Tour Order of Merit
Jeev Milkha Singh finished 12th on the 2008 European Tour Order of Merit.

Best finish on the LET Order of Merit
Aditi Ashok finished second on the 2016 LET Order of Merit and also won the Rookie of the Year award.

Best finish in a Major
Anirban Lahiri finished tied fifth in the 2016 PGA Championship.

The Yak Golf Club, situated at an altitude of 3,970 m (13,025 ft) at Kupup, Sikkim, is the highest golf course in the world.

Best world ranking
Jeev Milkha Singh was placed 28th in the world ranking list in 2009.

Best Indian performance on the PGA Tour
In the 2017 season, Anirban Lahiri earned US $1,944,289, the highest by an Indian on the PGA Tour, from 22 events. He had three top-ten finishes.

Best performance based on prize money
Arjun Atwal was the first Indian to win a title on the PGA Tour by claiming the honours in the Wyndham Championship in August 2010. Atwal collected US $918,000 – the highest ever by an Indian golfer.

LOWEST

Lowest winning score on the Asian Tour
Jeev Milkha Singh scored 26-under 262 in the Philip Morris Championship in Seoul, South Korea, winning on the Asian Tour. This is the lowest winning score by an Indian for an international title.

Lowest winning score on European Tour
Arjun Atwal scored a title-winning 24-under 260 in the Carlsberg Malaysian Open in February 2003.

Lowest winning score on the Indian Tour
Mukesh Kumar fired 30-under 250 to win the DDA Open at the Qutab Golf Course, New Delhi, in April 2005.

Lowest round on Indian Tour
Mukesh Kumar carded 11-under 59 in the third round of the DDA Open tournament at the Qutab Golf Course, New Delhi, in 2005.

ONLY

Only Indian to win four European Tour events in India
S.S.P. Chawrasia's all four European Tour titles came in India: the 2008 Emaar MGF Indian Masters in Delhi; the 2011 Avantha Masters at Gurgaon (now Gurugram), Haryana; the 2016 Indian Open in Delhi; and the 2017 Indian Open in Delhi.

S.S.P. Chawrasia: winner of four European Tour events

India's only team title in the USA
Former cricketer Kapil Dev led India to the

TAG Heuer Invitational Golf title in Boston, USA, in September 2004. The team, with Kapil Dev, Nikhil Dewan, Rakesh Rao and Rohit Duggal, shot seven 65-under to win ahead of China, Indonesia, South Africa and two teams from North America, among others.

Kapil Dev: part of India's only team title in the USA

Only Indian to win two European Tour titles in a year

Anirban Lahiri won the Malaysian Open and the Indian Open – both co-sanctioned events on the European Tour – in 2015.

Only Indian to win four titles on the Japanese Tour

Jeev Milkha Singh has won four titles on the Japanese Tour: the 2006 Casio World Open; the 2006 Golf Nippon Series JT Cup, the 2008 Nagashima Shigeo Invitational Sega Sammy Cup, and the 2008 Golf Nippon Series JT Cup.

YOUNGEST

Youngest to win a European Tour title

Shubhankar Sharma, at the age of 21 years and four months, won the 2017 Joburg Open title.

Youngest to win two back-to-back international titles

Shubham Jaglan won the IMG Academy Golf Championship in San Diego and the International Golf Academy titles in Las Vegas – both for children aged 9–10 years – in successive weeks in 2015 in the USA.

Youngest winner on the domestic PGTI Tour

Playing only his second pro event, amateur golfer Karandeep Kochar became the youngest winner on the PGTI Tour in the 2016 Players Championship in Kolkata, West Bengal. At 17 years and five months, he broke Shubhankar Sharma's record of 17 years and eight months, set in 2014.

MISCELLANEOUS

Oldest club

The Royal Calcutta Golf Club set up in 1829 is the oldest club outside the UK. Originally called the Calcutta Golf Club, it was renamed later. The Calcutta Ladies Golf Club was established in 1891.

Longest hole-in-one

Amit Luthra scored a hole-in-one at the second hole of Delhi Golf Club (par 4; 258 yards), using a 5 iron, on 16 March 1998.

Oldest golfer with a hole-in-one

Lieutenant General Ajit Singh, at the age of 90, achieved his first hole-in-one on 18 October 2005 at the Delhi Golf Club on the ninth hole (par 3; 160 yards).

GYMNASTICS

First Olympic appearance
Khushi Ram and Vir Singh were the first gymnasts to represent India at the Olympics, in 1952 at Helsinki.

First appearance in the World Championship
Daljit Inder Singh, Manjit Singh and Vithal Karande participated in the 1970 World Championship held at Ljubljana (in present-day Slovenia).

First medal in the Commonwealth Games – men
Ashish Kumar won the first ever medals (and a rare two at that) in gymnastics: a bronze in the individual floor exercise (score: 14.475) and a silver in the vault (with 15.312 points) at the 2010 CWG, New Delhi.

First medal in the Asian Games – men
With a score of 14.925, Ashish Kumar won a bronze in the floor exercise at the 2010 Guangzhou Asiad in China, India's first and only medal in gymnastics at the Asian Games.

First medal in the Asian Championship
Ashish Kumar won a bronze medal in the floor exercise at the third Senior Asian Gymnastics Championship at Pandit Deen Dayal Upadhyay Indoor Stadium, Surat, Gujarat, on 2 August 2006.

First National Championship
The first National Gymnastics Championship was held in 1952 in Madras (now Chennai, Tamil Nadu) where Khushi Ram emerged as the all-round individual champion and Punjab won the team championship.

Gymnastic Genius

Dipa Karmakar from Agartala, Tripura, won India's first Asian medal (women) when she won the bronze in the table vault by performing the highest-value vault in the sixth Senior Asian ART Gymnastics Championship in Hiroshima, Japan, on 3 August 2015 with a score of 14.725. She won a bronze, the country's first gymnastics medal in the Commonwealth Games, in the artistic women's vault event at the 2014 CWG on 31 July 2014 at Glasgow, Scotland. She was the first Indian woman gymnast to qualify for the Olympics on 14 August 2016 in the Rio Olympics, finally finishing fourth in the women's vault event. She clinched the gold at the World Challenge Cup at Mersin, Turkey, on 8 July 2018. She was named World Class Gymnast by the International Gymnastics Federation on 5 July 2016, becoming the first Indian to earn this honour.

Dipa Karmakar

First National Rhythmic Gymnastics event – women

The first National Rhythmic Gymnastics Championships held in 1989 at Kottayam, Kerala, had an event for women, where Neelamjit Kaur won the rhythmic gymnastics title. She won it again in 1990 at Udaipur, Rajasthan, and in 1991 at Delhi.

Maximum Olympic representations

Anantram Dogra is the only gymnast who has represented India in two Olympic Games – in Melbourne in 1956 and in Tokyo in 1964. He was also selected for the 1960 Rome Olympic Games, but the Indian Army team was called back due to an emergency.

First appearance in the CWG

Manjit Singh, B.S. Nandi and N.B. Bhosle represented India at the 1978 Edmonton CWG in Canada.

Most individual titles in the Nationals

- Kalpana Debnath from Madhya Pradesh won the all-round individual title four years in a row from 1976–77 to 1979–80.
- Rajesh Kumar from Chandigarh won the all-round individual title four times in a row between 1990–91 and 1994–95.

Most successive titles – team

Services won the team National Championship six times in a row between 1954–55 and 1961–62. They won it again six times in a row between 1963–64 and 1971–72. (The tournament was not held for some years.)

First World Cup medal

Aruna Reddy, then 22 years old, from Hyderabad, Telangana, became the first Indian gymnast to win a medal at the Gymnastics World Cup when she won a bronze in vault in Melbourne, Australia, with a score of 13.649 points on 24 February 2018.

HOCKEY

Oldest tournaments

The Beighton Cup was started at Calcutta (now Kolkata, West Bengal) in 1895 and is considered to be the oldest tournament. Presented by T.D. Beighton, legal remembrancer of the Government of Bengal, the Cup was held initially in the form of local matches, evolving into a regular tournament. Its latest edition was held in December 2016, with Indian Oil defeating Bharat Petroleum 5–3.

First women professional players

Penalty corner expert Jasjeet Kaur Handa and Subhadra Pradhan played for HC Den Bosch club in the Dutch League in 2007.

Only captain in successive Olympics

Pargat Singh was the captain first at Barcelona in 1992 and then in 1996 at the Atlanta Olympics, but India did not win a medal at either Games.

First foreign coach

- *Men*: Gerard Rach from Germany, India's first foreign coach, was with the team at the 2004 Athens Olympics, and till January 2005.
- *Women*: Herman Kruis from the Netherlands was the first foreign coach for women's hockey, in charge of the Asia Cup in Hong Kong in September 2007.

The 1952 Helsinki Olympic gold medal-winning hockey team with the then prime minister, Jawaharlal Nehru

Only hat-trick in succession

At the 1952 Helsinki Olympics, centre forward Balbir Singh scored three goals in the semi-final against Great Britain and netted five, including a hat-trick, against the Netherlands in the final.

First international appearance

In 1926, the Indian Army team went to New Zealand to play 21 matches. They won 18, drew two and lost one match. They scored 192 and conceded 24 goals.

First major success by a foreign coach

Australian Terry Walsh was India's coach at the time of the gold medal win at the 2014 Incheon Asian Games in South Korea. In the final, India drew with Pakistan 1–1 but won 4–2 in the penalty shoot-out.

First medal and most successful team in the Olympics

The Indian hockey team won its first Olympic medal in 1928, under the captaincy of Jaipal Singh Munda. From 1928 to 1956, the team was unbeaten, winning six gold medals. Since then, India has been adding medals to its Olympic tally, and currently, with a total of eight gold, one silver and two bronze medals, it is the single most successful team at the Olympic Games.

The victorious Indian hockey team after their debut in the 1928 Olympic match versus Austria

First CWG success – women

At the 2002 Commonwealth Games in Manchester, UK, the Indian women's hockey team won the gold medal, defeating England 3–2. The team was led by Suraj Lata Devi.

Most goals in the Olympics – team

India scored 43 goals in six matches at Moscow in 1980, a record for the

Balbir Singh (Senior): The Hockey Legend

Balbir Singh (Senior) (*centre*)

The winner of a hat-trick of gold medals in the Olympics and one of the greatest hockey players of India, Balbir Singh (Senior) died in May 2020 at the age of 96 years, following a prolonged illness. A mercurial forward, he played for the Indian team in the 1948 Olympic Games and captained the Punjab hockey team in 1949. He was also a member of the Indian team at the 1952 Helsinki Olympics, where he scored three goals in the semi-final against Great Britain and netted five, including a hat-trick, against the Netherlands in the final. By 1956, Singh was the captain of the Indian Olympic team and led them to victory in the Melbourne Games. The first sportsperson to be awarded the Padma Shri (1957), he also won a silver at the 1958 Asian Games. After retiring from active hockey as a player, he was chief selector as well as the coach and manager for the team that won gold at the third World Cup Tournament in Kuala Lumpur, Malaysia, in 1975, thus helping India win the gold medal in hockey after a gap of 11 years. Singh was the manager of the Indian team during 1962–82 and became the director of sports for the Government of Punjab. He authored two books: his autobiography *The Golden Hat-trick: My Hockey Days* (1977) and *The Golden Yardstick: In Quest of Hockey Excellence* (2008).

most goals in an Olympics. In the 1936 Berlin and 1956 Melbourne Olympics, India notched up 38 goals in five matches. It did not concede a single goal in 1928 and 1956.

First Asia Cup win – women

Coached by M.K. Kaushik, the Indian women's hockey team won the Asia Cup for the first time, beating Japan 1–0 in the final at the National Stadium (now Dhyan Chand National Stadium), New Delhi, in February 2004.

First Junior Asia Cup win

India won the fifth Junior Asia Cup in Karachi, Pakistan, in March 2004, beating the hosts 5–2. Tushar Khandekar scored a memorable hat-trick in the final.

First Asian Men's Hockey Champions Trophy

India won the inaugural edition of the tournament held in Ordos City, China, during August–September 2011, by defeating Pakistan 4–2 in the final via penalty strokes.

WR **Most Olympic goals – individual**

Dhyan Chand scored 33 goals in three Olympics – 10 in 1928, 12 in 1932 and 11 in 1936.

Most medals in the Olympics

The world record for the most medals in hockey at the Olympics is held by Leslie Claudius and Udham Singh, who were in four-medal-winning teams – three golds and one silver. Claudius was in the team that won the gold in 1948, 1952 and 1956, and silver in 1960, while Singh played for the gold-winning team in 1952, 1956 and 1964, and the silver-winning team in 1960.

Dhyan Chand: most Olympic golds

Playing for teams with most Olympic golds

The record for playing for teams winning the most Olympic golds – three each – is held by seven Indians: Richard Allen and Dhyan Chand (1928–36); Balbir Singh, R.S. Gentle, Leslie Claudius and R. Francis (1948–56); and Udham Singh (1952, 1956, 1964).

Leslie Claudius: most medals at the Olympics (shared record)

Most goals in a World Cup

In the fifth World Cup in Bombay (now Mumbai), Maharashtra, during 1981–82, India scored 29 goals in seven matches, winning five and losing two.

Biggest victory margin in the Olympics

India created a world record for the biggest victory margin at the Olympics when they beat the USA 24–1 on 11 August 1932 at Los Angeles, USA.

Most appearance in the World Cup

Ashok Kumar of Indian Airlines played in four World Cups from 1971 to 1978, a record for the most appearances at the World Cup.

Best foreign tour

Dhyan Chand, who led the team to New Zealand in 1935, played 48 matches and won them all. India scored 584 goals and conceded 40. Dhyan Chand alone scored 201 goals, his brother Roop Singh scored 187 and F.C. Wells scored 112 goals.

Highest goal scorer at the World Cup

Defender Rajender Singh, who played a solitary World Cup, scored all 12 goals in the 1981–82 tournament in Bombay (now Mumbai), Maharashtra, making him the highest goal scorer at the World Cup.

Best performance in the World Cup – men

India, led by Ajitpal Singh, beat Pakistan 2–1 in the final of the third World Cup at

Kuala Lumpur, Malaysia, in 1975, displaying its best performance at the World Cup.

NATIONAL SPORTS AWARDS 2020 HOCKEY

Khel Ratna Award: Rani Rampal
Dronacharya Award: Romesh Pathania (lifetime category), Jude Felix Sebastian
Arjuna Award: Akashdeep Singh, Deepika Thakur
Dhyan Chand Award: Ajit Singh

Best performance in CWG

Hockey was introduced in the Commonwealth Games in 1998. India's best performances at the Games include silver medals at the 2010 Games in Delhi and the 2014 Games in Glasgow, UK.

Best performances in the Champions Trophy

India reached the final in the 2016 Champions Trophy in London, UK, and the 2018 Champions Trophy in Breda, Netherlands. In both, India lost 1–3 in the penalty shoot-out to Australia.

Biggest victory margin in the Asiad – men

India's biggest victory margin at the Asian Games was 26–0 versus Hong Kong in the League phase of the 2018 Jakarta Asian Games in Indonesia.

Biggest victory margin in the Asiad – women

India's biggest victory margin at the Asiad came in the League phase of the 1998 Bangkok Asiad when it beat Thailand 13–0. Manjinder Kaur and Pritam R. Thakran scored three goals each.

Best recovery in the Men's Hockey Champions Trophy

- India rallied from 0–3 at Amstelveen, Netherlands, to beat Pakistan 5–4 in 1982.
- India trailed West Germany 1–5 in 1985 at Perth, but in the last seven minutes levelled at 5–5. Centre half Joaquim Carvalho scored an equalizing penalty stroke.

Longest winning sequence against Pakistan

From 2016 to 2019, India was unbeaten in 11 successive matches against Pakistan: the 2016 Azlan Shah Trophy: 5–1; the 2016 Asian Champions Trophy: 3–2 in the final; the 2017 World Hockey League semi-final: 7–1; the 2017 World Hockey League placement match: 6–1; the 2017 Asia Cup group match: 3–1; the 2017 Asia Cup Super Four match: 4–0; the 2018 Commonwealth Games group match: 2–2; the 2018 Champions Trophy group match: 4–0; the 2018 Asian Games bronze-winning match: 2–1; the CWG 2018 group match: 2–2; and the 2018 Asian Games bronze winning match: 2–1.

Biggest win in the Asia Cup finals

India beat South Korea 7–2 in the final of the 2007 Asia Cup in Chennai, Tamil Nadu, on 19 September 2007.

Highest goal scorer in Asia Cup

Centre forward Sheikh Mohammed Nayeem scored 11 goals in the second Asia Cup in Dhaka, Bangladesh, in 1985.

Best goalkeeping in the Olympics

Richard J. Allen did not concede a single goal in the five matches in the 1928 Olympics. He let in only two goals in 1932 and one in five games in 1936, conceding only three goals in three successive Olympics – a rare feat.

Fastest goal

Ajit Singh scored within 15 seconds of the start of the League match against Argentina in the 1976 Montreal Olympics – the fastest goal on artificial turf.

Highest goal scorer and double hat-trick in Youth Asia Cup

Defender Jugraj Singh scored 14 goals, including a double hat-trick, in the Youth Asia Cup in Malaysia in June 2001.

Only double hat-trick in the Olympics

Mohammed Shahid scored seven goals, including a double hat-trick, against Thailand (11–0) on 24 September 1986 in the Seoul Olympics.

Only goalkeeper in three finals

Goalkeeper Shankar Laxman played in three Olympic finals – in 1956 at Melbourne, Australia, in 1960 at Rome, Italy, and in 1964 at Tokyo, Japan.

Biggest win over Pakistan

India's 7–1 win over Pakistan on 17 June 2017 in the World Hockey League semi-final in London, UK, is their biggest victory margin over their arch-rivals.

Youngest to win a gold in the Olympics

C. Desamuthu was the youngest player to be in a gold-winning team, aged 19 years and 272 days, when India won in the 1952 Helsinki Olympics.

Oldest players in the Olympics

- Udham Singh (b. 1928) was 36 when he played in the 1964 Tokyo Olympics.
- Prithipal Singh (b. 1932) was also 36 when he was joint captain of the Indian team at the 1968 Mexico Olympics.

Most capped player

Dilip Tirkey is the most capped player in international hockey with 404 matches.

KABADDI

First appearance of kabaddi in the Asian Games

Kabaddi was played for the first time in the 11th Asian Games in 1990 in Beijing, China. Pakistan, Japan, China, Nepal, Bangladesh and India participated, with India winning the gold medal.

First Nationals

- The first kabaddi Nationals for men were held in 1951 in Maharashtra. The host state won the title.
- The first Nationals in kabaddi for women were held in 1955 in Calcutta (now Kolkata), West Bengal. Maharashtra won here too.

• The first championships for junior boys and girls were held in 1974 and 1976 respectively at Asansol, West Bengal.

First demonstration in the Olympics
Kabaddi and other indigenous games were the demonstration games in the 1936 Olympic Games held in Berlin, Germany.

First demonstration at the Asian Games
Kabaddi was an exhibition sport at the 1982 Asian Games held in New Delhi.

NATIONAL SPORTS AWARDS 2020 KABADDI

Dhyan Chand Award: Manpreet Singh
Arjuna Award: Deepak Hooda
Dronacharya Award: Krishan Kumar Hooda (lifetime category)

First Asian Championship
The first Asian Championship for men was held at Calcutta (now Kolkata), West Bengal, in 1980, in which teams from Bangladesh, Nepal and India played. India won the gold medal.

First Pro Kabaddi League
The first Pro Kabaddi League was held in 2014 with eight teams participating. Sixty games were played, with Jaipur Pink Panthers winning the inaugural title, defeating U-Mamba 35–24.

First Pro Kabaddi League

First Asian Junior Championship
The championship was held for the first time at Faridabad, Haryana, in January 2000, with teams from Bangladesh, Nepal, Sri Lanka and Thailand. India won the gold.

Most World Cup wins – men
The Indian team has won all three Kabaddi World Cups, organized by the

International Kabaddi Federation in 2004, 2007 and 2016, beating Iran in the finals of all three.

Record Rewind

Most gold medals in kabaddi in the South Asian Games

1990
India won three gold medals in the South Asian Federation Games (SAF Games).

2020
India won 10 gold medals in 11 editions of the South Asian Games or SAG (formerly SAF Games).

First team to win three consecutive Pro Kabaddi titles
Patna Pirates won three consecutive Pro Kabaddi League titles in 2016–17.

Most Asian Games titles – men
Kabaddi was introduced in the Asian Games in 1990 in Beijing, China, and was open only to men at that time. The Indian team has since won the Asian Games gold seven times – in 1990, 1994, 1998, 2002, 2006, 2010 and 2014. India got a silver medal in the 2018 Asian Games in Jakarta, Indonesia, losing to Iran in the final.

Most Asian Games titles – women
Kabaddi first made an appearance as a competitive sport for women in the 2010 Guangzhou Asian Games in China, 20 years after it was introduced for men. The Indian team won gold in 2010 and 2014, but got a silver in the 2018 Asian Games in Jakarta, Indonesia, losing to Iran in the final.

Most World and Asian Championship medals – women
Sarala Shetty of Bank Sports Board is the only Indian to win the Asian Kabaddi Championship eight times. Captain of the Indian team on eight occasions, she has also won three World Championship medals.

Most expensive non-cricket player
Raider Monu Goyat from Haryana became India's most expensive non-cricket sportsperson when Haryana Steelers bought him at ₹1.51 crore (15.1 million) for season 6 of the Pro Kabaddi League 2018.

New Rules for Modern Kabaddi

Since its inception in 2014, the Pro Kabaddi League has drastically changed the world for those involved with the traditional Indian sport of kabaddi. In its modern avatar, the game has now speeded up with the inclusion of the super tackle, super raid (a raid attempt in which the raider scores three or more points) and do-or-die, keeping viewers on tenterhooks about the match result. While earlier a raid lasted 40-45 seconds, it is now 30 seconds. Also, after two empty raids (raids fetching no points for either team), there is a last raid (do-or-die) where the raiding team must get a point or the raider will be out even if he or she is not tackled.

LUGE

Youngest luge Olympian

WR India's single representative at luge in the Winter Olympics, Shiva Keshavan from Manali, Himachal Pradesh, was the youngest luge Olympian in history, when he participated in the 1998 Nagano Olympics in Japan at the age of 16 years. Keshavan holds the record of having participated in six winter Olympics: 1998 Nagano, Japan; 2002 Salt Lake City, USA; 2006 Turin, Italy; 2010 Vancouver, Canada; 2014 Sochi, Russia; and 2018 Pyeongchang, South Korea. He won the Asian Luge Championships in 2011, 2012, 2016 and 2017.

MARTIAL ARTS: WUSHU

First world wushu champion – men

Praveen Kumar of the Indian Army became the first Indian to win the gold medal on 23 October 2019 in the Sanda 48 kg category of the 15th World Wushu Championship.

First world wushu champion – women

In 2017, Pooja Kadian became the first Indian to be crowned World Champion in the women's Sanda 75 kg category.

POWERLIFTING

Most medals in one edition of the Asian Championship

V.S.N.L. Renuka won four golds in the 48 kg category in squat, bench, deadlift and overall lift of 310 kg at the Asian Powerlifting Championship in Zarafshan, Uzbekistan, in 2000.

Most Commonwealth Championship golds – individual

Sampa Guha won four gold medals in the first Commonwealth Championship at Newcastle, UK, in September 2005.

Best Asian Championship

In its biggest haul at the Asian Championship to date, Indian powerlifters won 49 medals (22 gold, 19 silver and eight bronze medals), besides the Women's Team Championship and overall medals (men and women), at the 18th Asian senior, junior, sub-junior and Masters (men and women) Championship 2006 at Taebaek City, Korea.

Best performance in the World Championship

India won all three medals in the World Championship in Akita, Japan, in November 2000. N. Anbu (52 kg) won gold in the deadlift and an overall silver, while Jentry Francis (56 kg) won the bronze medal.

First father–son duo medallists in international competition

Mukesh Singh Gehlot and his son Vinay Gehlot both competed in the European Championship held from 29 June to 1 July 2018 in Schwetzingen, Germany. Mukesh Singh won two gold medals: 110 kg class (equipped) squat (300 kg), bench press (230 kg) and deadlift (270 kg); and in the same weight category (raw) squat (275 kg), bench press (185 kg) and deadlift (265 kg). Vinay Gehlot won silver and gold medalsin the 100 kg junior category: he got the silver medal in the 100 kg (raw) squat 145 kg, bench press (110 kg) and deadlift (150 kg), and the gold medal in the 100 kg class classic raw deadlift (165 kg).

Best performance in the Asian Junior Championship

At the Asian Junior Championship, Indian boys won the team trophy with four gold, four silver and two bronze medals at New Delhi in May 2001. In the same championship, Indian girls also won the team trophy with three gold, two silver and two bronze medals.

First medal in powerlifting in the Asian Para Games

Farman Basha won India's first medal – a bronze – in the 48 kg category at the inaugural Asian Para Games held in Guangzhou, China, in December 2010.

Best performance in the Commonwealth Championship – men

India bagged a total of five gold, three silver and four bronze medals, and were declared runner-up in the team event, in the second Commonwealth Championship at Christchurch, New Zealand, held from 6 to 9 December 2007.

Best performance in the Asian Sub-junior Championship

The Indian boys' team won the team trophy with five gold and two silver medals at the inaugural Asian Sub-junior Championship held at New Delhi in May 2001. In the same championship, the Indian girls' team bagged four gold and two silver medals.

First medal in CWG in para powerlifting

Sakina Khatun won the bronze medal in the lightweight category at the 2014 Commonwealth Para Games held in Glasgow, Scotland.

Back-to-back Olympia Pro-Powerlifting wins

Mukesh Singh Gehlot from Delhi is the only Indian to win an individual medal in successive IPL Olympia Pro-Powerlifting. He won the gold on his debut in IPL Olympia Pro-Powerlifting 2017 in the 100 kg open category and a bronze in Las Vegas, USA, in 2018.

Double feat

Bhupender Dhawan has been India's coach in two iron sports: powerlifting and bodybuilding. Between 1994 and 2019, he coached the Indian powerlifting team. He has also been the coach of the national bodybuilding squad.

SHOOTING

First Asian Games medals

- *Men:* India's Asian Games medal haul started with Dr Karni Singh winning silver in the trap event in 1974 at Tehran, Iran.
- *Women:* Soma Dutta won a silver in the individual rifle 3-position event and a bronze in air rifle at the 1986 Seoul Games, South Korea.

First Olympic finalist

Anjali Vedpathak-Bhagwat of the Central Industrial Security Force (CISF), Mumbai, Maharashtra, reached the air rifle final in the 2000 Sydney Olympics. She finished eighth with 493.1 points.

Abhinav Bindra: first ever individual Olympic gold medal

First ever individual Olympic gold medal

Abhinav Bindra won India's first individual Olympic gold medal by claiming the honour in the men's air rifle event on 11 August 2008 in Beijing, China.

First World Championship medal

India's first World Championship medal came when Dr Karni Singh from Bikaner, Rajasthan, won a silver medal in the trap event in Cairo, Egypt, in 1962. The gold medal in the event was bagged by Vladimir Zimenko of the USSR.

First World Championship gold

- Ace shooter Abhinav Bindra won India's first gold medal in a World Championship in air rifle at Zagreb, Croatia, on 24 July 2006.
- Manavjit Singh Sandhu won the first shotgun gold medal in a World Championship by beating 124 shooters to the title in the trap event at Zagreb, Croatia, two days after Bindra's effort.

First Asian Games gold

- Randhir Singh won gold in the trap event in the 1978 Games in Bangkok, Thailand, and a bronze in 1982.
- Jaspal Rana won the men's individual 25 m centre-fire pistol event in the 1994 Hiroshima Asiad with 588 points, a new Asian record. It was the only individual gold medal for India that year and the first Asian Games gold in that event.

First CWG gold

- *Men:* Ashok Pandit won the gold in the free pistol event in Auckland, New Zealand, in 1990.
- *Women:* Roopa Unnikrishnan clinched the gold in the rifle prone event in the 1998 Commonwealth Games in Kuala Lumpur, Malaysia. In the 1994 Games at Victoria, Australia, Unnikrishnan won two medals – a silver in the small-bore rifle 3-position and a bronze in the pairs with Kuheli Ganguly.

Rahi Sarnobat: first Asian Games shooting gold medal – women

First woman to win a gold in the Asian Games

Rahi Sarnobat became the first Indian woman to win a gold in the Asian Games (25 m pistol event) in 2018 at Jakarta, Indonesia.

First World Cup silver and gold medals

Anjali Vedpathak-Bhagwat won the gold in the air rifle event in the World Cup at Milan, Italy, in 2003. She had earlier won the silver at Munich, Germany, in 2002.

First World Cup pistol medal

Sonia Rai from Himachal Pradesh won the bronze in the women's air pistol in the World Cup at Resende, Brazil, on 28 April 2006. She shot a 482.2, after 384/400 in the qualification phase.

Saurabh Chaudhary: World Cup gold medallist

WR Gold in the World Cup

Saurabh Chaudhary won the gold medal in the 10 m air pistol event in the World Cup at Munich, Germany, in May 2019. He shot a 246.3 to break his own world record of 245.5 set in the World Championship. He won gold medals in the 2018 Youth Olympics in Buenos Aires, Argentina, and in the 2018 Asian Games in Jakarta, Indonesia.

First gold in the Asian Championship

Dr Karni Singh won an individual gold in the trap event in 1971 at Seoul, South Korea. This was India's first gold in the Asian Championship.

First medals haul in the Asian Championship

India won two gold, one silver and two bronze medals at Jakarta, Indonesia, in 1983, in its first haul in the Asian Championship. Ashok Pandit and Mohinder Lal won the gold in the centre-fire pistol team event with a world record.

First mixed air pistol gold medal in the World Cup – team

Heena Sidhu and Jitu Rai won the gold in the mixed air pistol team event in the World Cup in Delhi in 2017, when it was officially made a medal event.

First team gold in the Asian Clay Championship

Mansher Singh, Moraad Ali Khan and Manavjit Singh won India's first team gold at the Asian Clay Shooting Championship at Chengdu, China, in July 1995 with a tally of 357/ 375, equalling Kuwait's Asian record at the 1994 Hiroshima Asian Games in Japan.

First Nationals

The first shooting national tournament was held in Delhi from 9 to 16 November in 1952.

First to win two golds in a World Cup

Manu Bhaker, then 16 years old, from Jhajjar, Haryana, won the 10 m air pistol gold medal and partnered with Om Prakash Mitharval for the 10 m air pistol mixed team gold in the 2018 World Cup in Mexico.

First ever Olympic medal in shooting
Rajyavardhan Singh Rathore won the silver medal in double-trap shooting, behind Ahmed Al Maktoum of the UAE, in the 2004 Athens Olympics. A year before, Rathore had won gold in the 2003 World Cup in Sydney. Rathore was appointed minister of state for youth affairs and sports in September 2017 and minister of state for information and broadcasting in May 2018.

NATIONAL SPORTS AWARDS 2020 SHOOTING

Dronacharya Award: Jaspal Rana
Arjuna Award: Manu Bhaker, Saurabh Chaudhary, Manish Narwal (para shooting)

World record in skeet in the Asian Championship
Angad Vir Singh Bajwa shot a perfect 60 out of 60 to win the gold in the men's skeet final in the Asian Championship held in Kuwait in November 2018.

Most individual medals in the Asian Shooting Championship
Ronak Pandit won seven golds and a silver in the junior pistol events of the Asian Championship in Kuala Lumpur, Malaysia, in 2004.

World record at the Asian Championship
Suma Shirur shot a perfect 400 out of 400 to win the gold in the women's air rifle in the Asian Championship at Kuala Lumpur, Malaysia, in February 2004. She shares the record with eight others.

Jaspal Rana: most career golds at the South Asian Games

Most career golds at the South Asian Games
Jaspal Rana won 23 golds and a silver in three editions of the SAF Games (now South Asian Games). He won eight golds each at Madras (now Chennai), Tamil Nadu, in 1995 and at Kathmandu, Nepal, in 1999; and seven golds and a silver at Islamabad, Pakistan, in 2004.

Best haul in the Asian Clay Shooting Championship
The best performance at the Asian Clay Shooting Championship was five gold medals at Bangkok, Thailand, in September 2005.

Most CWG medals
Indian shooters bagged a total of 27 medals in the 2006 CWG at Melbourne, Australia, with 16 gold, seven silver and four bronze medals. Gagan Narang bagged four gold medals (a feat he repeated in the 2010 CWG), while Vijay Kumar and Omkar Singh bagged three gold medals each.

Best haul in the World Championship
India bagged 27 medals – 11 gold, nine silver and seven bronze medals – in the World Championship at Changwon, South Korea, in 2018. India finished third behind China and Korea.

Back-to-back gold medals in the Junior World Cups
Elavenil Valarivan (b. 2 August 1999) won gold medals in air rifle in the 2018 Junior World Cups in Sydney, Australia, and Suhl, Germany. She also won the mixed air rifle team gold with Divyansh Singh Panwar in the Junior World Cup in Suhl, with a junior world record of 498.6 in the final.

Best Asian Games haul
Indian shooters won three gold, five silver and six bronze medals in the Asian Games at Doha, Qatar, in 2006, for their best haul of 14 medals in an edition. India had won only 17 medals in all the previous editions put together.

WR **Best performance at the World Cup on debut**
Shahzar Rizvi created a world record at the ISSF World Cup when he scored 242.3 points in the final of the 10 m air pistol event on 3 March 2018 at

INDIA AT ITS FIRING BEST

For long, Indian shooting had to trace Dr Karni Singh's silver medal in the 1962 World Championship as the benchmark for the sport. Over the last three decades, the likes of Jaspal Rana, Anjali Vedpathak-Bhagwat, Abhinav Bindra, Rajyavardhan Singh Rathore, Gagan Narang, Vijay Kumar, Samaresh Jung, Jitu Rai, Tejaswini Sawant, Manavjit Singh Sandhu, Ronjan Sodhi, Heena Sidhu, Anjum Moudgil, Apurvi Chandela, and a bunch of young shooters such as Saurabh Chaudhary and Manu Bhaker have truly made the sport one of the most successful for India in the international arena.

Starting with the Commonwealth Games in Canada and the World Championship in Italy (both in 1994), shooter Jaspal Rana announced his arrival in Indian sports in a resounding manner. The Commonwealth Games, the Asian Games, and the numerous World Cups served as the foundation for the four Olympic medals that have been won so far in the sport for India by Rajyavardhan Singh Rathore, Abhinav Bindra, Vijay Kumar and Gagan Narang. Indian shooting was at its firing best in 2019 when the team topped the medals in all the four World Cups and the World Cup Final for the rifle and pistol events.

Abhinav Bindra: The studious boy from Chandigarh became such a great student of rifle shooting that he became the world champion in Zagreb in 2006 and the Olympic champion in Beijing in 2008. Responsible for winning India's as yet only individual Olympic gold medal, Bindra beat the reigning Olympic champion from China in air rifle in 2008. The foundation for such a phenomenal achievement was made when Abhinav competed in the 2000 Sydney Olympics as the youngest shooter, and later in Athens in 2004, when an unstable wooden flooring robbed him of a medal (when his best shots did not register the best scores). Missing a medal in Rio in 2016 by the slender margin of 0.1, Bindra has experienced the agony and ecstasy of sport at the highest level.

Rajyavardhan Singh Rathore: Rarely has a sportsperson achieved so much so quickly! After winning a World Championship bronze in 2003 to qualify for the

Guadalajara, Mexico. In his debut performance at the World Cup, Rizvi won the gold, beating the reigning Olympic champion Christian Reitz of Germany.

Double world record

- Ronjan Sodhi gained the unique distinction of equalling both the qualifying and final world records in double trap while winning the gold in the World Cup in Belgrade, Serbia, in 2008. He shot 147 in the qualifying phase and ended with 194.
- Gagan Narang won the World Cup final gold in men's air rifle with two world records in Bangkok, Thailand, in November 2008.

Youngest to win a Junior World Championship gold – men

In 2017, Anish Bhanwala (b. 26 September 2002) became the youngest Indian shooter to win a Junior World Championship gold in standard pistol. He won the

SUPER 30

Rajyavardhan Singh Rathore

Olympics, Rathore made his maiden venture in the 2004 Olympic Games in Athens, Greece, merely about six years after he had taken up the sport, and won a silver medal in double trap. The double trap may have gone out of the Olympic schedule, but Rathore has left an indelible impression on Indian sports with his mastery of the event.

Vijay Kumar: An inspiration to the country, Vijay Kumar made shooting five targets in four seconds such a joyto witness. Thanks to a slight tweak in the rules which allowed the six finalists in the 25 m rapid fire pistol event to start the final on par, without the advantage of the qualification scores, Kumar fired at his best to claim the silver in the London Olympics in 2012. Like Rathore, Kumar was also able to win an Olympic medal on his maiden appearance on the world's biggest sporting stage. A versatile shooter with different events including the 10 m air pistol, he won many medals in the Asian Games and the Commonwealth Games.

Gagan Narang: Luck is something that smiled and teased the young man from Hyderabad in the early days, after he capitalized on a slot in the national team for the Afro-Asian Games in 2003.

Part of the Indian team in the 2004 Olympic Games in Athens, Greece, Narang went on to win the World Championship medal in 2010 and the Olympic medal in London, UK, in 2012. He won many gold medals in the Commonwealth Games, and was able to assert his class with medals in the Asian Games as well. In the early format, Narang was able to shoot a perfect 600 out of 600 in the air rifle event that put his name among the best in the world. Even though he continues to shoot, the shooting legend has set up the Gun for Glory Academy with many centres across the country, fast-tracking young shooters to be world no.1.

Apurvi Chandela: The Shooting Star

Ranked world no. 1, with 1,926 points in the 10 m air rifle event, by the International Shooting Sport Federation in May 2019, Apurvi Chandela won a gold medal in the women's 10 m air rifle event (252.9) in the World Cup in New Delhi in February 2019 and a second World Cup gold medal in Munich, Germany, in May 2019. She had earlier won a gold in the 2014 Glasgow Commonwealth Games. She is also an Arjuna Award recipient (2016).

rapid-fire pistol gold in the Junior World Cup in Sydney, Australia, in 2018 and added on the 2018 CWG gold in Gold Coast, Australia. In July 2019, he won the gold in the 25 m rapid pistol event at the ISSF Junior World Cup held at Suhl, Germany.

Best haul in the Olympics
India's win of two medals in the 2012 London Olympics was the best in numbers. Gagan Narang won the air rifle bronze and Vijay Kumar won the rapid-fire pistol silver.

Youngest to win a World Cup gold – women
At Guadalajara, Mexico, in March 2018, Manu Bhaker (b. 18 February 2002) was the youngest to win a gold medal in the women's air pistol and the air pistol mixed gold with Om Prakash Mitharval. She also clinched the gold medals in the Junior World Cups in Sydney, Australia, and Suhl, Germany in 2018. She also won the air pistol gold, ahead of compatriot and former world record holder Heena Sidhu, in the 2018 Commonwealth Games in Gold Coast, Australia.

Manu Bhaker: youngest to win a World Cup gold – women

Most medals in a World Cup
India topped the medals table in the 2019 World Cup in Rio de Janeiro, Brazil, with five gold, two silver and two bronze medals.

Most medals in a Junior World Cup
India topped the medals table in the 2018 Suhl World Cup in Germany with 26 medals: 15 gold, two silver and nine bronze medals. This bettered India's share of 22 out of 66 medals in the 2017 Sydney World Cup, when it won nine golds, five silvers and eight bronzes, to be second behind China (25).

CURRENT RECORDS SET BY INDIAN SHOOTERS				
Shooters	Category	World Record Score	Event	Date
Udhayveer Sidhu, Vijayveer Sidhu, Rajkanwar Singh	25m pistol – junior – men – team	1747	Junior World Cup – Suhl, Germany	June 2018
Manu Bhaker	Air pistol – junior – women	593	Asian Games – Jakarta & Palembang, Indonesia	August 2018
Angad Vir Singh Bajwa	Skeet – men – final	60	Asian Championship – Kuwait, UAE	November 2018
Apurvi Chandela	Air rifle – women – final	252.9	World Cup – Delhi, India	February 2019
Shreya Agarwal	Air rifle – junior – women – final	252.5	Asian Championship – Taoyuan, Taiwan	April 2019
Manu Bhaker, Saurabh Chaudhary	Air pistol – mixed – team	586	World Cup – Munich, Germany	May 2019
Saurabh Chaudhary	Air pistol – junior – final	246.3	World Cup – Munich, Germany	May 2019
Udhayveer Sidhu, Adarsh Singh, Vijayveer Sidhu	Standard pistol – men – team	1707	Junior World Cup –Suhl, Germany	July 2019
Mehuli Ghosh, Elavenil Valarivan, Shreya Agarwal	Air rifle – junior – women – team	1883.3	Junior World Cup – Suhl, Germany	July 2019
Manu Bhaker	Air pistol – junior – women	244.7	World Cup Final – Pultan, China	November 2019
Esha Singh, Priya Raghav, Yuvika Tomar	Air pistol – junior – women – team	1721	Asian Championship – Doha, Qatar	November 2019

Most medals in four consecutive World Cups

India has topped the medals table in four consecutive World Cups in rifle and pistol events. India topped the table in the 2018 Munich World Cup (with five golds and one silver), the 2019 New Delhi World Cup (with three golds), the 2019 Beijing World Cup (with three golds and a silver) and the 2019 Rio de Janeiro World Cup (with five golds, two silver and two bronze medals).

SQUASH

First individual medals in the Asian Championships

- Bhuvaneshwari Kumari won the bronze in the 1990 and 1992 Asian Championships.
- Misha Grewal won a silver in the Asian Championship in 1996 at Amman, Jordan.

First professionals

In the early 1990s, the first pros were Arjun Singh (men) and Misha Grewal (women). The latter became a professional in 1993, and played the women's professional circuit in Asia, Europe and the USA. Her best rankings were second in Asia and 27th in the world.

First silver in the Asian Junior Championship
The Indian girls' squad bagged a silver medal in the Asian Junior Championship at Chennai, Tamil Nadu, in February 2003. They lost 0–3 to Malaysia in the final.

First champion
Rajkumar Narpat Singh won the first squash Nationals in 1953 and made a hat-trick, holding the title for two more years.

First junior and senior nationals title
Anil Nayyar won both junior and senior national titles in 1964, when he was 18 years old.

First junior world no. 1
Saurav Ghosal was the first Indian to be ranked junior world no. 1 when he won the British Junior Open in 2004.

HIGH ON JOSH

JOSHNA CHINAPPA

Joshna Chinappa has the following records to her credit:

- First international success – women: Chinappa became the first Indian woman to claim a Women's International Squash Players Association (WISPA) title, defeating Malaysia's Low Wee Wern 11–8, 11–5, 11–3 in the NSC Super Satellite (no. 3) Squash Tournament final at National Squash Centre, Kuala Lumpur, Malaysia, in November 2008.
- First to win the Asian junior title: She was the first to win the Asian junior title (U-19) in 2003. Later, Dipika Pallikal also won the title in July 2010.
- Most national titles: She won 18 national titles, the most yet by an Indian.
- Youngest national champion – women: She became the youngest national women's champion at 14 years in 2001.

First to win world ranking titles
In August 2003, Ritwik Bhattacharya became the first Indian to win back-to-back international Professional Squash Association (PSA) world ranking tournaments in New Zealand when he won the North Island Championship and the Royal Oak

Joshna Chinappa

Open titles. In 2005, he annexed two more titles – the Esportiu Rocafort Squash Open in Barcelona, Spain, and the Rochester ProAm Squash Championship in New York, USA. So far, he has won four international squash titles.

Saurav Ghosal: India's best performer at the World Championships

First doubles champions

In the first National Doubles Squash Championship held in Chennai, Tamil Nadu, in 2004. Joshna Chinappa and Dipika Pallikal from Tamil Nadu won the women's title and Saurav Ghosal and Harinder Pal Singh Sandhu, also representing Tamil Nadu, won the men's title.

Best performance in the World Championships

Saurav Ghosal was the first Indian to reach the quarter-finals of the World Championships at Manchester, UK, in October 2013. Though he lost to world no. 1 Ramy Ashour in the match, this is India's best performance to date at the World Championships.

Most titles in a row in the Nationals – women

Bhuvaneshwari Kumari was the women's national champion 16 times in a row from 1977 to 1992, a record. Her first national triumph was in 1977 at 16 years. Her record remains unbeaten in the Nationals.

Most titles in a row in the Nationals – men

Major K.S. Jain and Brigadier R.K. Manchanda hold the men's record for the highest number of national titles won, with six wins in a row. Jain won the title from 1958 to 1963, while Manchanda was the champion from 1978 to 1983.

Best in the Asian Games

For the first time, India won the men's team event gold medal in the 2014 Incheon Asian Games in South Korea, beating Malaysia 2–0. Saurav Ghosal, Harinder Pal Singh Sandhu and Mahesh Mangaonkar represented India in this event. The women's team of Dipika Pallikal, Joshna Chinappa and Anaka Alankamony won the silver medal, losing to Malaysia 0–2 in the 2014 Asian Games team event final.

Best performance in the World Team Championships

The Indian men's team led by Saurav Ghosal made a second successive appearance among the top eight in the World Team Championships in June 2013. The women's team also reached the quarter-finals in 2012. This is India's best performance in the World Team Championships.

Youngest to represent India
Saurav Ghosal and Joshna Chinappa were the youngest to represent India in an international event. Ghosal was 16 years old and Chinappa was 15 when they played for India in the 2002 Asian Games in Busan, South Korea.

Best performance in the Asian Juniors
Anaka Alankamony from Chennai, Tamil Nadu, became the youngest winner of the Asian junior title (U-19) at 16 years when she beat Tsz-Wing Tong of Hong Kong 6–11, 11–8, 10–12, 11–7, 11–7 at Amman, Jordan, in June 2011. India enjoyed triple success in this event: Ramit Tandon (U-19 boys) and Saumya Karki (U-17 girls) won silver medals in India's largest haul at the event.

Oldest champion
Brigadier R.K. Manchanda was 37 years old when he won the Nationals title in 1983, thus becoming the oldest national champion in squash. He also became the oldest finalist in 1987 when he was 41 years old. He reached the Nationals final a record 11 times, as did Anil Nayyar, and Manchanda won six of the 11 finals in which he competed.

Highest rankings
- Saurav Ghosal is the first Indian to break into the top 10 in the Professional Squash Association (PSA) world rankings. He was ranked 10th with 6,455 points in April 2019.
- Joshna Chinappa is currently (2021) the highest ranked Indian woman in the 11th position with 5,080 points.
- In 2012, Dipika Pallikal and in 2016, Chinappa were placed 10th in the world rankings.

Youngest champion – men
Adrian Ezra and Ritwik Bhattacharya were both 17 when they won the senior national singles title in 1989 and 1997, respectively, making them the youngest national squash champions to date.

First Commonwealth Games gold
India bagged its first gold medal when Dipika Pallikal and Joshna Chinappa defeated Laura Massaro and Jenny Duncalf of England 11–6, 11–8 to win the women's doubles event in the Commonwealth Games in Glasgow, UK, in 2014.

Dipika Pallikal: member of the team to win first Commonwealth Games gold

SWIMMING

NATIONAL SPORTS AWARDS 2020 SWIMMING

Dhyan Chand Award:
(posthumous) Sachin Nag
Arjuna Award:
Suyash Narayan Jadhav
(para swimming)

First swimmer in the Olympics

D.D. Mulji from Bengal was the first Indian swimmer in the Olympics, taking part in the 1928 Amsterdam Olympics. Indian women participated in the Olympics for the first time at the 1952 Helsinki Olympics, with Dolly Nazir and Arati Saha representing India.

First to participate in the Asian Games

- *Men*: Nine Indian swimmers participated in the inaugural Asian Games held at Delhi in 1951: Sachin Nag, Bimal Chandra, Isaac Mansoor, Santosh Bhattacharjee, Kanti Shaw, Protip Mitra, Shambu Shaw, J.J. Naigamwalla and Bhubaneswar Pandey.
- *Women*: The first Indian woman to participate in Asian Games was Kumari Rima Dutta in the fifth Asian Games held at Bangkok, Thailand, in 1966.

Participation in two consecutive Olympic Games

Sachin Nag represented India in the 1948 London and the 1952 Helsinki Olympics. Sajan Prakash represented the country at the 2016 Rio Olympics and the 2020 Tokyo Olympics.

Participation in two consecutive Paralympics

Suyash Narayan Jadhav represented the country at the Rio Paralympics n 2016 and the 2020 Tokyo Paralympics.

First water polo team in the Asian Games

In 1951, the Indian water polo team first participated in Asian Games and won a gold medal. The team members were Ganesh Das (captain), G. Rattansey, D. Daver, Isaac Mansoor, Jahan Ahir, Robert Dean and Kanti Shaw. The Indian water polo team later participated in the Asian Games in 1970 in Bangkok, Thailand, and won the silver medal. The team then included Pijus Mitra (captain), Samir Kapadia, Tarun Goswami, Abdul Mutlib, Ashok Biswas, Bharat Merchant, Chand Ram, Umed Singh, Avinash Sarang, Pattabhi Raman and Deep Narayan Singh.

2020: The Birth Centenary Year of Sachin Nag (1920–87)

Sachin Nag, born in Varanasi, then in the United Provinces of Agra and Oudh, bagged India's first Asian Games gold with a timing of 1 min. 4.7 secs to win the 100 m freestyle in 1951 in Delhi in the inaugural Asian Games. He also won two bronze medals at the same Asian Games. The recipient of the Dhyan Chand Award posthumously given to him in 2020, Nag had represented India in the 1948 London Olympics in the 100 m freestyle event. He had finished sixth in the first round with a timing of 1 min. 3.8 secs. He was also part of two Olympic water polo squads, in 1948 (London) and in 1952 (Helsinki).

First to participate in the CWG
Divers Dum Bahadur and Vasant Gadge were the first to represent India in the aquatics events in the 1978 Commonwealth Games in Edmonton, Canada. In 1982 for the first time, Indian swimmers participated in the Commonwealth Games at Brisbane, Australia. The team members were Wilson Cherian, Khajan Singh Tokas, T. Thoiba Singh, Sanjeev Chakraborty, Persis Madaan, Geeta Anand and Giselle Bharucha.

First diver in the Asian Games
Three Indian divers participated in the first Asian Games in 1951: K.P. Thakkar, Ashu Dutt and T.T. Dand. Thakkar from Maharashtra won gold medals in the high-board and springboard events, while Dand won a bronze in high-board diving.

First Asian Games gold
India won its first Asian Games gold when Sachin Nag clocked 1 min. 4.7 secs to win the 100 m freestyle in the 1951 Asian Games in Delhi.

Record Rewind

Most national records - men

1990
In the 1980s, Khajan Singh Tokas held eight individual national swimming records in 50 m, 100 m, 200 m and 1,500 m freestyle; 100 m and 200 m butterfly; and 200 m and 400 m individual medley.

2020
Virdhawal Khade holds 11 individual national swimming records.

First to qualify for two Olympic events
Shikha Tandon from Bangalore (Bengaluru), Karnataka, qualified for the 50 m and 100 m freestyle events in the 2004 Athens Olympics, but did not win.

First to reach a CWG final
During CWG 2010 held in Delhi, two Indian men – Virdhawal Khade and Sandeep Sejwal – reached the finals in their best events. Khade was placed seventh in the 50 m butterfly, while Sejwal came eighth in the 50 m breaststroke.

First to win a medal in the Asian Indoor Games
Shikha Tandon won a bronze in the 100 m backstroke event in the Asian Indoor Games in Bangkok, Thailand, in November 2005.

First relay team in a CWG final
The quartet of Virdhawal Khade, Anshul Kothari, Arjun Jayaprakash and Aaron D'Souza qualified for the 4 x 100 m freestyle relay final at the 2010 CWG in Delhi. They clocked 3 mins 27.14 secs to better their qualifying timing, but only finished sixth.

First National Championship
The first National Championship was held in Bombay (now Mumbai), Maharashtra, in 1945.

First Indian para swimmer to qualify for the Paralympic Games
Sharath Gayakwad was the first Indian para

swimmer to qualify for the 2012 London Paralympic Games. He secured the ninth position. He also has a bronze in the 2010 Asian Para Games.

First para swimmer to win a bronze at CWG
Prasanta Karmakar was the first Indian para swimmer to win a bronze medal in the 2010 Delhi Commonwealth Games in the 50 m freestyle in the S-9 category.

Prasanta Karmakar: first para swimmer to win bronze at the Commonwealth Games

First 200 m freestyle in under 2 minutes
J. Abhijit from Karnataka clocked 1 min. 58.68 secs in the 1997 National Games, becoming the first Indian to swim the 200 m freestyle in under 2 mins. Virdhawal Khade from Maharashtra holds the record with 1 min. 49.86 secs.

First 100 m freestyle in under 1 minute
The first Indian swimmer to swim in under 1 min. in the 100 m freestyle category was Basakha Singh, clocking 59.75 secs in 1971. The best performance is by Virdhawal Khade, who clocked 49.47 secs in October 2008. Among women, Shikha Tandon from Karnataka holds the record, with 58.91 secs in 2003.

First visually impaired swimmer to win a gold
Kanchanmala Pande won the gold medal in the 200 m medley event in the S-11 category on 8 December 2017 in the World Para Swimming Championships in Berlin, Germany.

First Indian para swimmer to win gold in the Para Asian games
Suyash Narayan Jadhav won the gold medal in men's 50 m butterfly S-7 (6–7) category in the Para Asian Games held at Jakarta, Indonesia, in 2018. He clocked 32.71 secs.

Manmeet Singh Walia Makes History

A leading representative of Indian table tennis in the 1980s, Manmeet Singh Walia lost his battle to amyotrophic lateral sclerosis, a rare neurodegenerative disease, on 11 May 2020, at the age of 58, in Montreal, Canada. At the top of his game as a sub-junior and junior, he won the Junior National Championship in Allahabad (now Prayagraj), Uttar Pradesh, in 1976, at the age of fourteen. It was in the 1978 Asian Junior Championship (Kuala Lumpur, Malaysia) that he made a name for himself internationally when he won the bronze medal for the country. The national table tennis singles champion for the year 1988–89, Walia was the only Indian to reach the pre-quarter-final stage of the Asian Championship (singles) event in Jakarta in 1988. In 1989, he won the gold medal–winning team in the South Asian Federation Games in Calcutta (now Kolkata), West Bengal. A bronze medallist in the ninth Commonwealth Championship in Wales, UK, Walia also represented India in the World Championship at Tokyo, Japan (1983), in Dortmund, West Germany (now Germany) (1984), at Delhi (1987) and Chiba, Japan (1991).

TABLE TENNIS

NATIONAL SPORTS AWARDS 2020 TABLE TENNIS

Arjuna Award: Madhurika Patkar
Khel Ratna Award: Manika Batra

GENERAL

Arjuna Award recipients

J.C. Vohra (1961), Gautam Divan (1965), Usha Sundararaj (1966), Farrokh R. Khodaiji (1967), Mir Kasim Ali (1969), G. Jagannath (1970), K.F. Khodaiji (1971), Niraj Bajaj (1973), Shailaja Salokhe (1976), Indu Puri (1979), Manjit Dua (1980), V. Chandrashekhar (1982), Kamlesh Mehta (1985), Monalisa Barua (1987), Niyati Shah (1989), M.S. Walia (1990), Chetan Baboor (1997), S. Raman (1998), Mantu Ghosh (2002), A. Sharath Kamal (2004), Soumyadeep Roy (2005), Subhajit Saha (2006), Poulomi Ghatak (2009), Mouma Das (2013), Soumyajit Ghosh (2016), Anthony Amalraj (2017) and Manika Batra (2019).

Only Rajiv Gandhi Khel Ratna recipient

Manika Batra received the award in 2020.

Only Padma Shri award recipient

A. Sharath Kamal received the award in 2019.

No games conceded in Nationals

Farrokh R. Khodaiji won the men's singles title in Guwahati (1967), Kaity Chargeman the women's singles in Kolkata (1970) and Chetan Baboor the men's singles (1999) without dropping a set.

FIRSTS

First national champion

- *Men*: M. Ayub won the men's singles title at Calcutta (now Kolkata, West Bengal) in 1938.
- *Women*: P. Lima won the women's singles in Bombay (now Mumbai) in 1939.

First professional

Chetan Baboor was the first Indian to play as a professional in Europe. He played for Enig Club in Kalmar, Sweden, in 1998.

First gold in the Asian Championship

Gool Nasikwala won the singles, doubles and mixed doubles gold medals in the 1952 Asian Championship in Singapore.

First quarter-finalist in the World Championship

Krishna Nagaraj was the first to reach the men's singles quarter-finals in the 1956 World Championship in Tokyo, Japan.

First doubles pair in the World Championship quarter-finals

Mouma Das and Manika Batra were the first to reach the women's doubles quarter-finals in the 2017 World Championship.

First woman player to play two Olympics
Mouma Das qualified for two Olympic Games: first in 2004 in Athens, Greece, and then in 2016 in Rio de Janeiro, Brazil.

First Commonwealth Championship team title
India won the Commonwealth Championship men's team title in Kuala Lumpur, Malaysia, in 2004.

First CWG doubles gold – men
The duo of A. Sharath Kamal and Subhajit Saha won the men's doubles gold medal in the Commonwealth Games held at Delhi in October 2010.

***Left*: Manika Batra: first CWG singles winner – women**
***Right*: Poulomi Ghatak: first CWG doubles medal – women**

First CWG singles winner – women
Manika Batra won the women's singles gold at Gold Coast, Australia, in 2018.

First CWG doubles medal – women
Poulomi Ghatak and Mouma Das claimed the bronze in the women's doubles in Delhi in October 2010.

First CWG team gold – men
The Indian men's team won the first Commonwealth Games table tennis gold medal in Melbourne, Australia, in 2006.

First International Table Tennis Federation Pro title
A. Sharath Kamal won the International Table Tennis Federation (ITTF) Egypt Open in July 2010 to become the first Indian to win an ITTF Pro Tour event.

First medal in the Asian Games
India's first medal in the Asian Games was the team bronze won in 2018 by A. Sharath Kamal, G. Sathiyan, A. Amalraj and Manav Thakkar, who defeated Japan.

First CWG team gold – women
The Indian women's team won the first CWG team gold at Gold Coast, Australia, in 2018.

First CWG singles winner – men
A. Sharath Kamal won the men's singles gold at Melbourne, Australia, in 2006.

First Indian member of the ITTF's Umpires and Referees Committee
Ganeshan Neelakanta Iyer was inducted as a member of ITTF's Umpires and Referees Committee (URC) in June 2017.

First Indian to be ranked world no. 1 – U-18 – boys
Manav Thakkar was the first Indian to be ranked world no. 1 among boys (U-18) in February 2018.

First medal in the Asian Juniors
India won the bronze medal in the 2006 Asian Junior Championship at Kitakyushu, Japan, by reaching the semi-finals of the girls' event.

Record Rewind

ITTF ranking – men's singles

2001
The highest-ranking Indian player among seniors in January 2001 was Chetan Baboor at no. 83.

2020
The highest-ranking Indian player among seniors in January 2020 was G. Sathiyan at no. 30.

Youngest Indian to qualify for the Olympic Games
Manika Batra became the youngest to play in the Olympic Games in Rio de Janeiro, Brazil, in 2016 at the age of 21 years and two months.

Youngest to win Nationals
Mantu Ghosh was 16 years old when she won the national title at Jaipur, Rajasthan, during the 1990–91 championships.

ITTF Breakthrough Star Award
Manika Batra was given the ITTF Breakthrough Star Award 2018 on 12 December 2018.

First team medal at the World Junior Championship
The boys' team of Soumyajit Ghosh, Harmeet Desai and G. Sathiyan claimed India's first-ever bronze in the 2011 Junior Championship held in Bahrain.

First title in ITTF Junior Tour
Harmeet Desai defeated Soumyajit Ghosh in the 2011 Austrian Open junior boys' final to become the first Indian to win a title on the ITTF Junior Tour.

First international league in India

The first edition of the Ultimate Table Tennis (UTT) was held in July 2017 in Chennai, Delhi and Mumbai. Six teams took part in it. The tournament attracted several international players. Eventually, Falcons Club won the title by beating Shaze Challengers 14–9 in the final.

MOSTS

Longest mixed doubles reign

Farrokh R. and Kaity (Chargeman) Khodaiji from Bombay (now Mumbai), Maharashtra, won the Susan Barna Cup five years in a row (1967–71). They earlier won the title in 1965.

Highest-ranked players

- *Men*: G. Sathiyan was ranked 24th, his career best, by ITTF in April 2019, thus also becoming the highest-ranked Indian table tennis player.
- *Women*: Manika Batra was the first Indian woman to break into the top 50 in the world rankings. She was ranked 47th by ITTF in January 2019.

Most junior/senior titles in a year

Four players have won both titles in one calendar year: Rinku Gupta Acharya (Madhya Pradesh) in 1988; Mantu Ghosh (West Bengal) in 1991; Kasturi Chakraborty (West Bengal) in 1998; and Poulomi Ghatak (West Bengal) during 1998–99.

Most singles titles in a row in the Nationals

- *Men*: A. Sharath Kamal won the title five times between 2006 and 2010.
- *Women*: Indu Puri was champion six times between 1980 and 1985.

Most singles titles in the Nationals

- *Men*: A. Sharath Kamal has won nine men's singles titles in the Nationals.
- *Women*: Indu Puri won the women's singles title eight times – in 1972 and 1975, and from 1979 to 1984.

Most team titles in the Nationals – men/women

Bombay won the title for the Barna Bellack Cup 16 times while Maharashtra won the title for the Corbillon Cup 14 times. The championship was first introduced in 1946 in Madras (now Chennai), Tamil Nadu, where Bombay won the title and remained unbeaten till 1952.

Most World Championship appearances

Mouma Das has played in 16 editions of the World Championship since 1997.

Most medals at CWG

Manika Batra won four medals – the most by an Indian player to date – in the 2018 edition of the Commonwealth Games at Gold Coast, Australia.

Most appearances in National Championships

S. Ramaswamy, who first played in the Nationals in Allahabad (now Prayagraj),

Uttar Pradesh, in 1976, appeared in 30 successive National Championships by February 2006, topping his own record of 29 straight appearances, a record shared with S. Sriram.

Most medals at the CWG and Commonwealth Championships
Mouma Das has 19 team and individual medals at the CWG and the Commonwealth Championships from 2001 to 2018.

Most gold medals in the South Asian Federation Games
A. Sharath Kamal won four gold medals – the men's team event, men's singles, men's doubles and mixed doubles – in the South Asian Federation (SAF, now South Asian) Games in Colombo, Sri Lanka, in August 2006.

Most medals at the CWG
Indians won eight medals, including three golds, in the 2018 Commonwealth Games at Gold Coast, Australia. India claimed gold in the men's team, women's team, women's singles (Manika Batra); silver in men's doubles (A. Sharath Kamal and G. Sathiyan) and women's doubles (Manika Batra and Mouma Das); and bronze in men's singles (A. Sharath Kamal), men's doubles (Harmeet Desai and Sanil Shetty), and mixed doubles (Manika Batra and G. Sathiyan).

Only medallist in four successive Commonwealth Games
A. Sharath Kamal is the only player to win CWG medals in four successive editions: 2006 in Melbourne, Australia; 2010 in Delhi; 2014 in Glasgow, UK; and 2018 at Gold Coast, Australia.

Most participants in a tournament
An unprecedented 4,104 entries were received across 17 categories in the first Indian Table Tennis Marathon 2019, held during 1–5 May 2019 at the Table Tennis Federation TT Hall, Sant Sujan Singh Ji International School, Swaroop Nagar, New Delhi.

Most state/UT representations at the Nationals
N. Ravichandran represented five different units, including three states and a Union Territory at the National Championships. He represented Tamil Nadu, Punjab, Goa and Puducherry as well as the Central Revenue Sports Board at national-level tournaments.

Most players in the world top 100
The year 2018 was a significant one for Indian table tennis. G. Sathiyan (ranked 49th), A. Sharath Kamal (51st), Soumyajit Ghosh (58th), Harmeet Desai (60th), Sanil Shetty (68th) and A. Amalraj (87th) were in the top 100 of world rankings in January 2018. Manika Batra (62nd), Mouma Das (74th) and Madhurika Patkar (81st) also made the grade.

BEST

Best team performance in the World Table Tennis Championships
India finished 10th – its best finish to date – in the men's team events of the 1959

World Championships in Dortmund, Germany. In 2018, India took the 13th place, its second best performance.

Best doubles performance in the Commonwealth Championship

Chetan Baboor and S. Raman won two successive Commonwealth Championship titles in 1997 and 2000.

Best individual performance

A. Sharath Kamal defeated three players from the world's top-20 list in the Asian Cup held in Jaipur, Rajasthan, in March 2015 – world no. 8 Chuang Chih-Yuan (Taipei), world no. 15 Gao Ning (Singapore) and world no. 16 Joo Sae-Hyuk (South Korea).

Best doubles performance at the Commonwealth Games

A. Sharath Kamal holds the distinction of winning the men's doubles medal in three successive CWGs. He partnered Subhajit Saha to win the gold medal in 2010 in Delhi; Anthony Amalraj to win the silver in 2014 in Glasgow, UK; and G. Sathiyan to win the silver in 2018 at Gold Coast, Australia.

A. Sharath Kamal (*left*) and Subhajit Saha: best doubles performance at the Commonwealth Games

Second division titles in World Championship

Indian men beat Brazil 3–2 and the women defeated Luxemburg 3–1 to win the second division titles in the 2016 World Championship in Kuala Lumpur, Malaysia, on 5 March 2016.

TENNIS

GENERAL

First World Deaf Tennis Champion

Unseeded Prithvi Sekhar beat Jaroslav Smedek of the Czech Republic in the men's final of the World Deaf Tennis Championship in Antalya, Turkey, on 19 October 2019, to win the title.

BILLIE JEAN KING (FEDERATION) CUP

First world play-offs qualifying team

Earlier known as the Fed Cup, the Billie Jean King Cup is a team event for women's tennis players who represent their country in singles and doubles matches. The Indian Fed Cup team created history by progressing to the play-offs for the first time ever in March 2020, defeating Indonesia in the Asia-Oceania Group I event in Dubai, UAE, and finishing second behind China. They lost the world group play-off tie against Latvia. The team comprised, Ankita Raina, Rutuja Bhosale, Zeel Desai, Karman Kaur Thandi and Sania Mirza.

ASIAN GAMES

First gold medal in the Asian Games doubles
Leander Paes and Gaurav Natekar won the gold medal in the Hiroshima Asian Games, held in 1994 in Japan – making this the country's first doubles gold medal at the Asian Games. They won by defeating the South Korean duo of Chang Eui-jong and Kim Chi-wan.

First singles gold in Asian Games
Somdev Devvarman won the gold medal at the 2010 Guangzhou Asiad in China, defeating Denis Istomin of Uzbekistan 6–1, 6–2.

First mixed doubles Asian Games gold medallist
India got its first mixed doubles gold at the Asian Games when the team, with Leander Paes and Sania Mirza, won the gold in the Doha Asiad in Qatar in 2006. They defeated the Japanese pair of Satoshi Iwabuchi and Akiko Morigami 7–5, 5–7, 6–2.

DAVIS CUP

WR **Most successful doubles player**
Leander Paes became the most successful doubles player in the history of the Davis Cup with a record 45th victory in March 2020, when he and

Somdev Devvarman: first singles gold in Asian Games – men

Ankita Raina: One to Watch

A tennis player since the age of five, Ankita Raina (b. 11 January 1993) made her first professional appearance at an International Tennis Federation (ITF) tournament in Mumbai, Maharashtra, in 2009. Hailing from Ahmedabad, Gujarat, she represented her state in national tournaments and won her first ITF doubles title in 2011 (with partner Aishwarya Agrawal) and her first ITF singles title in 2012. Raina broke through at the 2017 Mumbai Open when she won one match each against Peangtarn Plipuech of Thailand and Veronika Kudermetova of Russia, and advanced to the quarter-finals.

A key player in the Indian team at the Federation Cup (now the Billie Jean King Cup) from 2014 to 2019, she also secured a bronze medal at the 2018 Asian Games in Indonesia. It was also in 2018 that she won the title at the OEC Taipei WTA Challenger with her partner and fellow countrywoman Karman Kaur Thandi. With an impressive win over Arantxa Rus (from the Netherlands) in the final, Raina won the ITF 25 title in 2019 in Singapore.

Ankita Raina

In 2020, along with winning two back-to-back ITF titles in Nonthaburi, Thailand, with her partner from Netherlands, Bibiane Schoofs, she won two singles titles and helped India make history in the Billie Jean King Cup when it advanced to the Group 2 play-offs for the first time ever, in Dubai. Only the fifth Indian woman to play in the Open Era, Raina made her debut major appearance with an unexpected Grand Slam entry via doubles at the 2021 Australian Open when she partnered with Romanian player Mihaela Buzarnescu to play in the main draw match.

Following a loss in the opening round of the Australian Open, Raina won her first WTA Tour-level singles main draw match when she beat Elizabetta Cocciaretto on 14 February 2021 in Melbourne, Australia, at the Phillip Island Trophy tournament. She went on to win the Phillip Island Trophy (her first Tour level title win for doubles) with her partner, Russian player Kamilla Rakhimova.

With 11 singles and 18 doubles titles on the ITF circuit to her name, Raina has won at least one title every year since she started in 2011 except in 2015. She remains the second Indian, after six-time Grand Slam title winner Sania Mirza, to compete in the women's doubles of a tennis major.

his partner Rohan Bopanna won India's Davis Cup match against Croatia in the do-or-die round of the World Group Qualifiers.

First appearance in the Davis Cup
India played in the Davis Cup for the first time in 1921 against France in Paris and won 4–1. The Indian team comprised S.M. Jacob, Mohammed Sleem, A.A. Fyzee and L.S. Dean.

Leander Paes (*left*) and Mahesh Bhupathi (*right*): first men's doubles title at Wimbledon

Best Davis Cup record in Asia
Though India has never yet won the Davis Cup, they have managed to reach the finals three times (in 1966, 1974 and 1987). Japan is the only other Asian nation to have figured in the Davis Cup finals (once in 1921).

Most appearances in Davis Cup
Leander Paes holds the record of playing the most Davis Cup matches – 128 in 58 ties (as of March 2020). His win/loss records are 48/22 in singles and 45/13 in doubles.

GRAND SLAM TOURNAMENTS

WIMBLEDON

First to play at Wimbledon
Sardar Nihal Singh was the first Indian to play at Wimbledon in 1908. He lost in the first round to Briton Herbert Wilson Fox, who beat him 11–9, 6–2, 6–4.

First junior boys' title
Ramanathan Krishnan won the first junior boy's Wimbledon title in 1954, defeating Ashley Cooper of Australia 6–2, 7–5. Twenty-five years later, Ramanathan's son Ramesh Krishnan won the same title in 1979, creating a unique father-and-son record. Both were recipients of the Padma Shri in 1962 and 1998 respectively. Ramanathan Krishnan was also awarded the Padma Bhushan in 1967.

First seeded at Wimbledon
Dilip Bose was the first seeded Indian player, at no. 15, in Wimbledon singles in 1950. He was a product of Calcutta South Club (now in Kolkata, West Bengal), one of Asia's oldest tennis clubs.

First men's doubles title

The dominant Indian tennis pair of Leander Paes and Mahesh Bhupathi, then popularly known as Lee–Hesh, won India's first men's doubles title at Wimbledon in 1999, defeating Paul Haarhuis (the Netherlands) and Jared Palmer (USA) 6–7, 6–3, 6–4, 7–6.

First mixed doubles title

Leander Paes was the first Indian to win a mixed doubles title when he won it with Lisa Raymond (USA) in 1999. They defeated the pair of Anna Kournikova (Russia) and Jonas Björkman (Sweden) 6–4, 3–6, 6–3. Paes was awarded the Padma Shri in 2001.

First junior girls' doubles title

Indian ace tennis player Sania Mirza and her Russian partner Alisa Kleybanova won the junior girls' doubles title in 2003.

Sania Mirza: first Wimbledon junior girls' doubles title

First Indian woman at Wimbledon

Jenny Sandison was the first woman to represent India in tennis at Wimbledon, way back in 1929. However, she lost in the first round to French player Simone Barbier 6–2, 6–3.

FRENCH OPEN

First mixed doubles title

Mahesh Bhupathi and his Japanese partner Rika Hiraki won the French Open title in 1997, defeating the American team of Lisa Raymond and Patrick Galbraith 6–4, 6–1. With this Bhupathi became the first Indian to win a senior Grand Slam title.

First and only junior champion

Ramesh Krishnan won the juniors title in 1979, the first and only Indian to achieve this feat, and was ranked the world's no. 1 junior player. He became India's Davis Cup captain in 2007.

First all-Indian mixed doubles title

Mahesh Bhupathi and Sania Mirza won India's first ever all-Indian mixed doubles title in 2012, defeating Klaudia Jans-Ignacik (Poland) and Santiago González (Mexico) 7–6 (7-3), 6–1.

Sumit Nagal

Sumit Nagal: Courting Wins

A tennis star in the making, Sumit Nagal (b. 16 August 1997) introduced himself early to the professional arena at the age of seventeen, when he became the sixth Indian player to win a junior Wimbledon Grand Slam title in 2015 (boys' doubles with Vietnam's Ly Hoang Nam). Representing India at the Davis Cup in 2016 and 2019, Nagal won his first Association of Tennis Professionals (ATP) Challenger series title in 2017 in Bengaluru, Karnataka. Reaching the finals in the 2018 Indoor Asian Games (doubles), the right-handed player won his second ATP Challenge series title in 2019 in Buenos Aires, Argentina.

It was in 2019 when Nangal broke through to the US Open main draw and made his debut playing against 20-time Grand Slam champion Roger Federer, grabbing headlines when he took the first set against the tennis icon. In the 2020 US Open, Nagal created history by becoming the first Indian since 2013 to win a match in the main draw of a Grand Slam (singles) when he defeated USA's Bradley Klahn. The Haryana-based player was granted a wild-card entry into the men's singles main draw of the 2021 Australia Open along with seven other athletes from across the world, but he had to bow out after a straight-sets defeat to Lithuania's Ricardas Berankis in their first-round contest.

First all-Indian men's doubles title

Leander Paes and Mahesh Bhupathi won India's first men's doubles title in 1999. The pair defeated Goran Ivanišević (Croatia) and Jeff Tarango (USA) 6–2, 7–5.

US OPEN

First doubles title

Mahesh Bhupathi and his partner Max Mirnyi of Belarus won the US Open doubles title in 2002, defeating the Czech pair of Jiri Novak and Radek Stepanek 6–3, 3–6, 6–4.

First women's doubles title

Sania Mirza was the first Indian to win a women's doubles title in 2015 at the US Open in New York, with Swiss player Martina Hingis. The pair defeated Casey Dellacqua (Australia) and Yaroslava Shvedova (Kazakhstan) 6–3, 6–3.

First mixed doubles title

Mahesh Bhupathi, with his Japanese partner Ai Sugiyama, won the mixed doubles US Open title in 1999, the first Indian to win a mixed doubles title here. The pair defeated Kimberly Po and Donald Johnson of the USA 6–4, 6–4.

First and only junior boys' title

Leander Paes is the first and only Indian to win the junior boy's crown at the US Open in 1991. He beat Karim Alami (Morocco).

AUSTRALIAN OPEN

First men's doubles title

Leander Paes became the first Indian to win a men's doubles title at the Australian Open, along with Radek Stepanek (Czech Republic) in 2012. They defeated Bob Bryan and Mike Bryan of the USA 7–6 (7–1), 6–2.

Record Rewind

Youngest ambassadors of peace

2001

Former Davis Cup captain Vijay Amritraj, then 48 years old, was appointed a United Nations Messenger of Peace in April 2001 by the UN Secretary General Kofi Annan, a unique honour for India and the tennis fraternity.

2020

Twenty-year-old table tennis star Naina Jaiswal was appointed the Official Brand Ambassador of India for World Peace in June 2020 by World Peace Day Berlin, in association with the United Nations World Peace Day.

First mixed doubles title

Leander Paes, with Martina Navratilova of the USA, won the mixed doubles title in 2003, becoming the first Indian to do so. They defeated Eleni Daniilidou (Greece) and Todd Woodbridge (Australia) 6–4, 7–5.

First all-Indian mixed doubles title

Mahesh Bhupathi and Sania Mirza won India's first all-Indian mixed doubles

Australian Open title in 2009, defeating the pair of Nathalie Dechy (France) and Andy Ram (Israel) 6–3, 6–1.

First junior boys' champion

Yuki Bhambri defeated Alexandros-Ferdinandos Georgoudas of Greece 6–3, 6–1 to win the Junior Boys' Championship in 2009.

NATIONALS

First Nationals – grass court

The first tennis Nationals were held in 1946 at the Calcutta South Club lawns in Calcutta (now Kolkata, West Bengal). Sumant Misra beat Manmohan Lal in the final, becoming the first national champion. Khanum Singh (née Haji) was the first women's national champion.

Most Nationals titles

The record for the highest number of National Championship titles belongs to Ramanathan Krishnan, who has won eight grass court titles in 1953, 1956, 1958 to 1960 and 1962 to 1964.

WEIGHTLIFTING

First medals in World Championships

Kunjarani Devi from Manipur bagged three silvers at Manchester, UK, in 1989 in India's debut performance at the World Championships. The Indian squad won seven medals in all at the event. Lalita Polley from West Bengal won two bronzes, and Shyamala Shetty and Chhaya Adak won medals for individual lifts.

Most medals in world and Asian meets

Kunjarani Devi, who holds the record for the highest number of world and Asian meet medals, won 55 medals overall – 21 in six World Championships and the remaining in the Asian Games and in the Asian and Commonwealth Championships.

First gold in the Commonwealth Games – men

E. Karunakaran won gold in the flyweight class in the 1978 Edmonton Games in Canada.

E. Karunakaran: first weightlifting gold in CWG – men

First silver medal at the Olympic Games

Mirabai Chanu scripted a remarkable performance by winning a silver in the 2020 Olympic Games held in Tokyo, Japan, on day one. With an 87 kg lift and a 115 kg lift in the clean and jerk section, Chanu finished with a total of 202 kg.

NATIONAL SPORTS AWARDS 2020 WEIGHTLIFTING

Dhyan Chand Award: Nitten Kirrtane

First Asian Games medals – women

Women's weightlifting was introduced in the 1990 Beijing Asian Games in China, where India won two silvers: Bharati Singh (82 kg category) and Jyotsna Dutta (+82 kg); and two bronzes: Kunjarani Devi (44 kg) and Chhaya Adak (52 kg).

First Asian Games medal

Kamineni Eswara Rao won the silver in the 90 kg category in the 1951 Asian Games held in New Delhi. He was also adjudged the 'Strongest Man of India' at the 1954 senior Nationals.

First gold medal at the Youth Olympic Games

Jeremy Lalrinnunga became the first Indian to win a gold medal at the Youth Olympics Games 2018 held in Buenos Aires, Argentina.

Best performance at an Asian meet

India's weightlifters bagged five gold medals and a bronze at Busan, South Korea, in July 1995. Karnam Malleswari won three gold medals, and Kunjarani Devi bagged two gold medals and the overall title. Arun Murugesan won a bronze in snatch in the 54 kg category for men.

 The Indian Weightlifting Federation was formed in **1935**.

Most gold medals in World Championships

Karnam Malleswari won the gold medal in the World Championships twice – in 1994 (Istanbul, Turkey) and 1995 (Guangzhou, China).

Gold medals in World Championships

On 29 November 2017, Saikhom Mirabai Chanu became the second Indian, after Karnam Malleswari, to win the gold medal at the 2017 World Championships in Anaheim, USA, after a gap of more than two decades. In the women's 48 kg event, she lifted a new world record of 194 kg – with 85 kg in snatch and 109 kg in clean and jerk (also a new national record in clean and jerk).

Most national titles

Balbir Singh Bhatia won 15 national and all-India titles.

Youngest national champion

P.K. Mahanand from Hyderabad won the All-India Championship at Calcutta (now Kolkata), West Bengal, in 1955 at the age of eighteen.

Most medals in CWG

India won five gold, two silver and two bronze medals at the 2018 Gold Coast CWG in Australia, the most at the Commonwealth Games in weightlifting. Saikhom Mirabai Chanu made a record-breaking performance in the clean and jerk event in the 48 kg category. Khumukcham Sanjita Chanu (53 kg) set a Commonwealth Games record in snatch and Punam Yadav won a gold in the 69 kg category. In the men's section, Sathish Sivalingam (77 kg) and Ragala Venkat Rahul (85 kg) won gold medals too. P. Gururaja (56 kg) and Pradeep Singh (105 kg) won silvers, and Vikas Thakur (94 kg) and Deepak Lather (69 kg) won bronzes.

Oldest national champion
Alok Nath Ghosh won the National Championship title in 1974 at 40 years. He had won the first national title in 1958 at Cuttack, Odisha. His first title was for Services and the last one was for the Railways.

Most medals in the Commonwealth Games – women – individual
Yumnam Renu Bala Chanu has won two golds in the CWGs. Her first medal came in the women's 58 kg category at the 2006 CWG in Melbourne, Australia. She repeated this at the 2010 Games in Delhi in the same category.

First Olympic-qualifying gold
Saikhom Mirabai Chanu won the gold medal in the women's 49 kg category at the EGAT Cup international weightlifting championship, an Olympic-qualifying event in Chiang Mai, Thailand, on 7 February 2019. She lifted 82 kg in snatch and 110 kg in clean and jerk to total 192 kg and took gold on her return to international competition after a nine-month lay-off due to an injury. She had won the gold medal on her last appearance in 2018 at the Gold Coast Commonwealth Games in Australia.

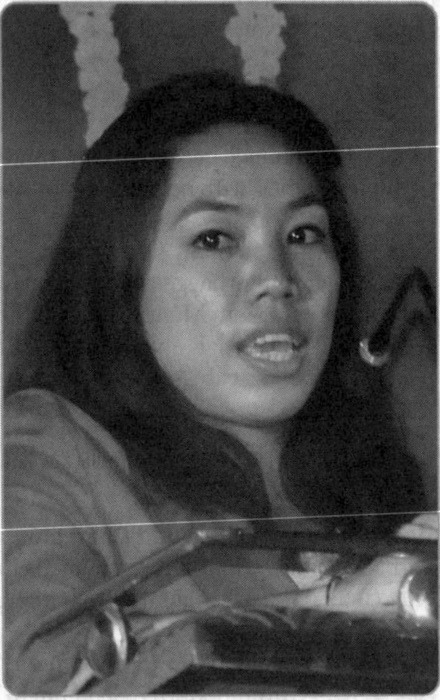

Saikhom Mirabai Chanu: gold at the EGAT Cup

First back-to-back gold medals
Khumukcham Sanjita Chanu made history for the second time when she bagged the gold medal in the women's 53 kg weightlifting event at the 2018 Commonwealth Games at Gold Coast, Australia. Her first gold was at the 2014 Commonwealth Games in the 48 kg category.

Youngest Commonwealth Games medal winner
Eighteen-year-old Deepak Lather (69 kg) from Haryana became the youngest Indian weightlifter to win a medal at the 2018 Commonwealth Games in Glasgow, UK, by clinching a bronze medal.

WRESTLING

First winner of both Olympic and World Championship medals
Sushil Kumar became the first Indian to win medals at both the Olympics and the World Championships. While he won a bronze at the 2008 Beijing Olympics in the 66 kg freestyle category and a silver medal in the same category at the 2012 London Olympics, he also won a gold in the same category at the Moscow World Championship in Russia in 2010.

First woman at the Olympics
Geeta Phogat from Bhiwani, Haryana, was the first Indian woman wrestler to compete at the Olympics during the 2012 London Games. However, she did not advance to the quarter-finals.

First Olympics medal – men
Khashaba Dadasaheb Jadhav from Satara, Maharashtra, won a bronze in the bantamweight category in the 1952 Helsinki Olympics, India's first medal in wrestling at the Olympics.

First at the Olympics
U. Zaw Weik (75 kg), the first to represent India at the Olympics, was placed 15th in the 1936 Olympics at Berlin, Germany.

First medal at the World Championships – men
India's first medal in the World Championship was a bronze in the freestyle category ((67 kg) won by Udey Chand from Hisar, Haryana, in the 1961 World Championships at Yokohama, Japan. He participated in three Olympics: at Rome, Italy, in 1960; at Tokyo, Japan, in 1964; and at Mexico City, Mexico, in 1968.

First medal at the World Championships – women
Alka Tomar of the Noida College of Physical Education won a bronze in the women's 59 kg class at the Senior World Wrestling Championship in Guangzhou, China, during September–October 2006. She was the first Indian woman wrestler to win a World Championship medal after a gap of 39 years.

First World Championship gold medallist
Sushil Kumar from Delhi was the first Indian to win a World Championship gold in the 66 kg freestyle category in Moscow, Russia, in 2010.

Back-to-back World Championship medals
Sajan Bhanwal became the first Indian to win back-to-back medals in the World Championship in the 77 kg category in the Greco-Roman style. He won a silver on 20 August 2019 in Trnava, Slovakia, and a bronze at the Tampere World Championship, Finland, in 2017.

First medal in the Commonwealth Games
• Rashid Anwar won a bronze medal at the 1934 Commonwealth Games held in London, UK, in the 74 kg category,. This was the country's first medal in the Commonwealth Games.

• Lila Ram won the first gold medal in the 1958 Games at Cardiff, Wales, in the heavyweight (100 kg) category.

Most gold medals in the Asian Championship
Sushil Kumar, with three gold medals at the Asian Championship, holds the record for the most wins at the Championship. He won the title in 2003, 2008 and 2010.

Most medals in the Asian Games – men
Kartar Singh won the gold at Bangkok, Thailand, in 1978, a silver in 1982 at Delhi and another gold at the 1986 Seoul Asiad in South Korea. He competed in the 90 kg category in 1978 and 1982, and in 100 kg in 1986 (all in freestyle).

First Olympic medal – women
Sakshi Malik created history as the first Indian woman to win an Olympic medal, a bronze, for wrestling, in the women's freestyle 58 kg category in the Rio Olympics in Brazil on 17 August 2016.

First woman triple winner – World Championships, Asian Games and Commonwealth Games
Vinesh Phogat became the first Indian woman to win medals at the World Championships, Asian Games and Commonwealth Games. While she won bronze at the 2019 World Championships in the 53 kg freestyle and a bronze at the 2014 Incheon Asian Games in the 48 kg category, she was also the first Indian woman to win a gold medal in the 2018 Asian Games in Jakarta and Palembang, Indonesia, in the 50 kg category.

Most medals in the Commonwealth Championships
The Indian contingent, with 42 wrestlers, bagged 40 medals – 15 gold, 20 silver and five bronze – in the 2011 Commonwealth Championships in Melbourne, Australia.

Most individual medals in the Commonwealth Championships – men
Sushil Kumar won the title five times between 2003 and 2017. He won the gold medal in 2003 (London, UK), 2005 (Cape Town, South Africa), 2007 (London, UK), 2009 (Jalandhar, India) and 2017 (Johannesburg, South Africa).

First medal in Asian Games
Vinesh Phogat, competing in the 50 kg freestyle category, bagged India its first gold medal in wrestling in the Asian Games in 2018 in Jakarta, Indonesia. She is the first Indian woman to win a gold medal in wrestling and to win back-to-back Asian Games medals, having won a bronze in 48 kg in Incheon, South Korea, in 2014.

First and only Indian woman wrestler to win the Laureus World Sports Award
Vinesh Phogat is the first and only Indian wrestler to be awarded the Laureus World Sports Award 2019 in the comeback-of-the-year category. Phogat not only returned from her injury but also won the gold medal in both the 2018 Commonwealth Games at Gold Coast, Australia, and the 2018 Asian Games in Jakarta and Palembang, Indonesia.

Vinesh Phogat: first woman to win medals at the World Championships, the Asian Games and the Commonwealth Games

Ranked world no. 2 – women

- In 2018, United World Wrestling (UWW), the international body that governs the sport of amateur wrestling, ranked Asian champion Navjot Kaur as no. 2 in the 65 kg category.
- Vinesh Phogat became no. 2 in the 50 kg category after she won a gold in the 2018 Commonwealth Games and a silver in the Asian Wrestling Championships.

Most individual medals in the World Championship

Bajrang Punia won the World Championship medal three times between 2013 and

Bajrang Punia (*left*): most individual medals in the World Championship

2019. He won the bronze medal in the 60 kg category in 2013, a silver in the 65 kg category in 2018 and a bronze in 2019.

NATIONAL SPORTS AWARDS 2020 WRESTLING

Khel Ratna Award: Vinesh Phogat
Dronacharya Award: Om Prakash Dahiya (lifetime category)
Arjuna Award: Divya Kakran, Rahul Aware
Dhyan Chand Award: Netarpal Hooda

Most medals in the Asian Championship

Between 2013 and 2020, Bajrang Punia won a record seven medals in the 60 kg to 65 kg categories. He won bronze in 60 kg (2013, New Delhi), silver in 61 kg (2014, Astana, Kazakhstan), gold in 65 kg (2017, New Delhi), bronze in 65 kg (2018, Bishkek, Kyrgyzstan), gold in 65 kg (2019, Xian, China) and silver in 65 kg (2020, New Delhi).

Youngest champion in the Asian Games

Malwa Singh won the gold medal in the Greco-Roman style in the light flyweight category at the 1962 Asian Games in Jakarta, Indonesia, at the age of 14 years, thus creating history by becoming the youngest wrestling champion from India.

First Asian Games gold – men

Gold medals were won by Maruti Mane in 90 kg freestyle, Malwa Singh in 52 kg Greco-Roman and Ganpat Andalkar in 100 kg Greco-Roman at the 1962 Asian Games in Jakarta, Indonesia.

Most gold medals in CWGs – men

Sushil Kumar of the Indian Railways and an alumnus of the Noida College of Physical Education, Noida, Uttar Pradesh, won India's first ever men's triple gold in CWGs (Delhi 2010, Glasgow, UK, 2014 and Gold Coast, Australia, 2018).

First Asian Championships gold medal – women

Navjot Kaur from Punjab became the first Indian woman to win the gold at the Senior Asian Wrestling Championships on 2 March 2018, at Bishkek, Kyrgyzstan. She beat Japan's Miya Imai 9–1 to win in the women's 65 kg category.

Two consecutive Commonwealth Games titles – women

Vinesh Phogat won two consecutive Commonwealth Games crowns at Glasgow, UK, in 20142, and Gold Coast, Australia, in 2018.

Most medals in the Commonwealth Games – women

Babita Kumari Phogat won a gold medal (Glasgow, UK, in 2014) and two silvers (Delhi in 2010 and Gold Coast, Australia, in 2018).

First gold medal in the Asian Games

- The first Indian to win a gold medal in the Asian Games was Kartar Singh in the 1986 Seoul Asiad in South Korea in the 100 kg category.
- Yogeshwar Dutt became the first Indian in 28 years to win a gold in the 2014 Incheon Asian Games in the 65 kg freestyle.

INDIAN MEDALLISTS IN THE WORLD WRESTLING CHAMPIONSHIPS (1961–2019) India has won 18 medals in the World Championships					
S. No	Name	Category	City, Country	Year	Medal
1	Udey Chand	67 kg	Yokohama, Japan	1961	Bronze
2	Bishambar Singh	57 kg	New Delhi, India	1967	Silver
3	Alka Tomar (W)	59 kg	Guangzhou, China	2006	Bronze
4	Ramesh Kumar	74 kg	Herning, Denmark	2009	Bronze
5	Sushil Kumar	66 kg	Moscow, Russia	2010	Gold
6	Geeta Phogat (W)	55 kg	Alberta, Canada	2012	Bronze
7	Babita Kumari (W)	51 kg	Alberta, Canada	2012	Bronze
8	Amit Kumar Dahiya	55 kg	Budapest, Hungary	2013	Silver
9	Bajrang Punia	65 kg	Budapest, Hungary	2013	Bronze
10	Sandeep Tulsi Yadav	66 kg	Budapest, Hungary	2013	Bronze
11	Narsingh Yadav	74 kg	Las Vegas, USA	2015	Bronze
12	Bajrang Punia	65 kg	Budapest, Hungary	2018	Bronze
13	Pooja Dhanda (W)	57 kg	Budapest, Hungary	2018	Bronze
14	Deepak Punia	86 kg	Nur-Sultan, Kazakhstan	2019	Silver
15	Vinesh Phogat (W)	53 kg	Nur-Sultan, Kazakhstan	2019	Bronze
16	Bajrang Punia	65 kg	Nur-Sultan, Kazakhstan	2019	Bronze
17	Ravi Dahiya	57 kg	Nur-Sultan, Kazakhstan	2019	Bronze
18	Rahul Aware	61 kg	Nur-Sultan, Kazakhstan	2019	Bronze
19	Anshu Malik	57 kg	Oslo, Norway	2021	Silver
20	Sarita Mor	59 kg	Oslo, Norway	2021	Bronze

Youngest gold medallist at the Commonwealth Games
Ved Prakash was 14 years old when he won the gold medal in the light flyweight class at the 1970 Commonwealth Games at Edinburgh, UK.

First Coach of the Year award
Late Yashvir Singh was the first Indian coach to be recognized as the Coach of the Year in 2010 by the Federation Internationale des Luttes Associées (FILA), the then apex body that governed wrestling.

First Junior Wrestler of the Year award
Deepak Punia (86 kg freestyle) became the first Indian wrestler to get the Junior Wrestler of the Year title in 2019 by the UWW.

First Junior World Champion
Deepak Punia became India's first junior world champion in 18 years after winning a gold medal at the Junior Wrestling World Championship at Tallinn, Estonia, on 14 August 2019. He defeated Russia's Alik Shebzukov in the 86 kg men's freestyle category. The only other Indians to have won the gold in the Junior World Championship are Ramesh Kumar (69 kg) and Palwinder Singh Cheema (130 kg).

Most live wrestling commentaries
Manoj Joshi has worked in print, TV, radio and digital media. His live commentary on wrestling adds up to more than 550 hours for Sony, Doordarshan and various news platforms over three decades.

First gold in Greco-Roman wrestling
- Pappu Yadav was the first grappler to win a gold medal in the 48 kg Greco-Roman category at the 1993 Asian Wrestling Championships held in Ulaanbaatar, Mongolia.
- On 19 February 2020, Sunil Kumar (87 kg) won a gold in Greco-Roman wrestling in the Asian Championships, which came 27 years after the first gold in 1993.

Record Rewind

Most medals at the World Championship

1990
India won two medals in the World Championship - Uday Chand won a bronze medal in the below 68 kg category in the 1961 World Championship at Yokohama, Japan, and Bishamber Singh won a silver in the below 57 kg category in the 1967 World Championship at New Delhi.

2020
India won a total of 18 medals in the World Championship - one gold, four silver and 13 bronze medals.

Best performance in the Greco-Roman event of the Asian Championships
India's best performance in the Greco-Roman category was at the 2020 Asian Championships in New Delhi where Indian grapplers won one gold and four bronze medals. Sunil Kumar (87 kg) won the gold medal while Arjun Halakurki (55 kg), Ashu (67 kg), Aditya Kundu (72 kg) and Hardeep (97 kg) won the bronze medals.

First Indian couple to win silver medals
Sakshi Malik (65 kg) and Satyawart Kadian (97 kg) became the first Indian wrestler couple to win silver medals in the 2020 Asian Championships in New Delhi.

Ranked as world no. 1
In March 2021, the UWW announced Bajrang Punia (65 kg) and Vinesh Phogat (53 kg) as top-ranked wrestlers.

Best performance in the Asian Championship
India won a record haul of 20 medals (five gold, six silver and nine bronze) across formats and genders in the 2020 Asian Championships. The gold medallists were Sunil Kumar (87 kg-Greco-Roman [GR]), Pinki (55 kg women's freestyle [WFS]), Sarita Mor (59 kg WFS), Divya Kakran (68 kg WFS) and Ravi K. Dahiya (57 kg men's freestyle [MFS]). The silver medals were won by Nirmala Devi (50 kg WFS), Sakshi Malik (65 kg WFS), Bajrang Punia (65 kg MFS), Gourav Baliyan (79 kg MFS), Satyawart Kadian (97 kg MFS) and Jitender (74 kg MFS). The bronze went to Arjun Halakurki (57 kg GR), Ashu (67 kg GR), Adity Kundu (72 kg GR), Hardeep (97 kg GR), Vinesh Phogat (53 kg WFS), Anshu Malik (67 kg WFS), Gursharan Preet Kaur (72 kg WFS), Rahul Aware (61 kg MFS) and Deepak Punia (86 kg MFS).

Best performance at the Commonwealth Games – men
At the Commonwealth Games in 2010 in Delhi, the Indian men's team displayed its best performance to date, winning seven gold, three silver and three bronze medals in freestyle and the Greco-Roman style. The gold medals were won by Yogeshwar Dutt (60 kg), Sushil Kumar (66 kg) and Narsingh Panch Yadav (74 kg), all in freestyle wrestling; and Rajender Kumar (55 kg), Ravinder Singh (60 kg), Sanjay Kumar (74 kg) and Anil Kumar (96 kg), all in Greco-Roman wrestling. The silver medals were won by Anuj Kumar (84 kg) and Joginder Kumar (120 kg) in freestyle, and Manoj Kumar (84 kg) in the Greco-Roman style. The bronze medals were bagged by Anil Kumar (55 kg in freestyle), and Sunil Kumar (66 kg) and Dharmender Dalal (120 kg), both in the Greco-Roman style. These wrestlers made history by winning 10 gold medals (in both freestyle and Greco-Roman categories), the highest by any country in the Commonwealth Games.

Best performance at the World Championship
India has a record haul of five medals at the 2019 World Championship held at Nur-Sultan, Kazakhstan. Deepak Punia won a silver in the 86 kg category. Bronze medals were won by Bajrang Punia (65 kg), Rahul Aware (61 kg), Ravi Dahiya (61 kg) and Vinesh Phogat (women, 53 kg).

Best performance in the Commonwealth Games – women
Women's wrestling was introduced in the 2010 Delhi Commonwealth Games, where India bagged three gold medals, two silver medals and one bronze medal in freestyle. Geeta Phogat (55 kg), Alka Tomar (59 kg) and Anita Sheoran (67 kg) won gold medals. The silver medals were won by Nirmala Devi (48 kg) and Babita Phogat (51 kg). Suman Kundu (63 kg) won the bronze medal.

INDIA: 100 YEARS AT THE OLYMPICS

by Gulu Ezekiel

The road from Antwerp, Belgium 1920 to Tokyo, Japan 2020, encompassing 100 years of India's official participation in the Olympic Games has been a rocky one – full of potholes, barriers and diversions – with the occasional smooth stretch. The Tokyo Olympic Games themselves were postponed from 2020 to 2021 on account of the Covid-19 pandemic, but continue to carry the 2020 date.

Yet, India – one of the few nations neither to boycott any Olympic Games nor be banned on political grounds – has today grown into a multisport nation, even though after 70-plus years of Independence it remains some distance from being a sporting superpower.

The roller-coaster journey – with admittedly far more precipitous troughs than crests – shows that India, a country with a population approaching 1.5 billion (second only to China), and one which aspires to be an economic and military powerhouse, remains an enigma on the world sporting map.

It's a question that has been asked countless times and was even once voiced by the late Avery Brundage, who ruled over the International Olympic Committee (IOC) for 20 years, during a meeting with Indian sports journalists at the 1972 Munich Olympics: Why is it that a nation this size has had such little success at the Olympics? Pat came the smart reply (echoing the sentiments of the founder of

The first official Indian Olympic delegation in 1920: ***top row, from left:*** **Dulkar Randhir Shinde, Purna Chandra Bannerjee, Kumar Navale, P.D. Chaugule;** ***middle:*** **Sohrab H. Bhoot (manager), Dr A.H.A Fyzee (medical officer);** ***seated:*** **Sadashiv V. Datar, H.D. Kaikadi**

the modern Olympics, Baron Pierre de Coubertin): 'Maybe because we think the important thing is to take part and not win medals.'

Just eight team golds from a single sport (hockey) and one measly individual gold won by shooter Abhinav Bindra in the 10 m air rifle event at Beijing in 2008 – how could such a dire situation have come about?

The reasons are many—including corruption, nepotism, favouritism and many such ills among India's sports officialdom that clings to power for decades; the lack of proper diets, training and facilities; and most glaring of all, a faulty sporting culture that for so many years placed mere participation as the be-all and end-all of international sports.

So how does one define 'sporting culture'? Bindra, who candidly admitted that he was forced to train in the West as he felt that the necessary support and infrastructure and, yes, culture were lacking back home, felt this 'culture' was multidimensional. Parents who emphasize only academic education, coaches who do not know when to let go of their wards, and society itself that does not lay enough store by sporting excellence – all undermine this sporting culture.

Indeed, the breakthrough – which was as much psychological as anything else – achieved by the then 25-year-old Bindra at Beijing did, however, usher in something of a sporting revolution in India, with corporate funding and private foundations coming in to support sports across the spectrum. The government's role in the form of the Indian Olympic Association (IOA), the Ministry of Youth Affairs and Sports, and the Sports Authority of India (SAI) thus got a much needed boost.

This groundbreaking gold heralded both celebration and reflection on our erratic Olympic past. And each time the Olympic Games come round, a wave of hope rises, echoing decades of dreams of winning, standing at the top of the podium and garnering gold.

Every journey in life starts with baby steps, and India's initial tryst with the Olympics at Antwerp a century back with a five-member contingent in track and field and two wrestlers was no different.

THE BEGINNING

Before we look at that first 'official' contingent, a peep at two curiosities of India's Olympic saga would be apt.

Who was the first Indian-born Olympian, that too at the inaugural Olympics of the modern era at Athens, Greece, in 1896? And, indeed, a competitor in the very first race? And who is the first and still only Indian medal winner in athletics?

The answer to the first question is Charles Henry Stuart Gmelin, son of a missionary, born in Krishnanagar, Nadia District, Bengal, on 28 May 1872. He competed in the colours of Great Britain in the first heat of the 100 m, failing to qualify for the final, but then winning bronze in the 400 m.

Norman Pritchard: athlete par excellence

Then four years later at the chaotic Paris Olympics, another athlete from Bengal, Calcutta (now Kolkata), born Norman Gilbert Pritchard, won silver in both the 200 m and 200 m hurdles. In the latter, he set a world record in the second heat, which was soon eclipsed in the final by American athlete J. Walter Tewksbury.

So who was Pritchard, this mystery man of Indian sport? He was born of English parents in the suburb of Alipore, Calcutta (now Kolkata), on 23 June 1875, but unlike Gmelin, spent his entire youth in Calcutta, studying in St Xavier's School, and excelling in a range of sports including football and rugby.

The two flagbearers of the Indian contingent at the Tokyo Olympics 2020 were six-time world boxing champion M.C. Mary Kom and Manpreet Singh, the captain of the Indian men's hockey team.

One of the many myths surrounding Pritchard is that he was holidaying in Paris in 1900 and just happened to give in his entry for the Olympics! This was proven wrong by the records available of his exploits at athletics events in England where he was invited to compete in the pre-Olympic meets. Indeed, he was one of the world's leading sprinters and his two medals at Paris were not unexpected.

Back then there were no national sports federations and athletes entered on their own accord. But, crucially, the IOC granted his medals to India in the official records and there they have stayed since 1900. That should set the record straight once and for all, even if some British Olympic historians have been attempting in vain to take these away from India.

Pritchard also reached the final of the 110 m hurdles but stumbled and did not gain a place. He ran in but failed to reach the finals of the 60 m and 100 m, a remarkable feat of all-round endurance and excellence attempted never before, nor again, by an Indian at this level.

Pritchard was not only the first from Asia to win an Olympic medal, but he also set the trend for Olympians to enter Hollywood – something that many others would emulate then, and continue to do.

A leading light of the silent era of movies, he acted in 27 films after moving to the USA from England in 1913. He first made a name for himself in Broadway plays under the stage and screen name of Norman Trevor. Sadly, suffering from mental health issues and in penury, he died in Norwalk (now part of Los Angeles), California, on 30 October 1929. However, he had led India's small steps towards the Olympic Games.

THE ANTWERP CONTINGENT

So what was the background to the first contingent sent to Antwerp?

If Jamsetji Tata is known as the father of modern industry in India, his eldest son, Sir Dorabji Tata, took on the mantle of the father of the Olympic movement. Dorabji's passion for sport was kindled during his years studying in England. Back in India in the 1890s, he first turned his attention to cricket in Bombay (now Mumbai), a sport for which his community, of Parsis, is rightly regarded as the pioneers.

It was as the first president of the Deccan

Sir Dorabji Tata, who made India's Olympic dream possible

Gymkhana in Poona (now Pune) that Tata's Olympic dream was born. Impressed by the raw athletic talent on display, he decided to send a team to Antwerp for which selection trials were hastily held in Poona and Bombay in April 1920. Just two months earlier, Tata's appeal to the governor of Bombay, Lloyd George, for help and George's representation to the IOC saw them grant affiliation to India to participate.

Funds were raised by the Gymkhana members, and the government chipped in with ₹6,000. But it was Tata who eventually shelled out nearly half the ₹35,000 budget, and the contingent duly set off from Bombay on 5 June 1920.

In recognition of his efforts, Tata was appointed president of the All India Olympic Committee in 1924, which in 1927 morphed into the Indian Olympic Association, also headed by him.

The IOA continues to be at the helm of Indian sports, though it has had a chequered history including being suspended by the IOC from December 2012 to February 2014 due to its backing of officials tainted by the 2010 New Delhi Commonwealth Games scam.

The Antwerp contingent consisted of Purna Chandra Bannerjee from Calcutta for the 100 m and 400 m, Sadashiv V. Datar of Satara and H.D. Kaikadi of Hubli (now Hubballi) for the marathon, and P.D. Chaugule of Belgaum (now Belagavi) for the 10,000 m and the marathon. The two wrestlers were Dulkar Randhir Shinde (featherweight) and Kumar Navale (middleweight), both from Maharashtra.

While Kaikadi withdrew, Chaugule finished a creditable 19th. But it was wrestler Shinde who came agonizingly close to a medal, losing in the semi-final and finishing fourth after being beaten by Great Britain's Philip Bernand.

This set the trend for our sportspersons over the next century including, most famously, the late Milkha Singh (400 m, 1960) and P.T. Usha (women's 400 m hurdles, 1984), both of whom finished fourth by a whisker. Who knows how India's history at the Olympics may have changed for the better with a medal at the nascent stage?

1924, AND ONWARDS

Things were more organized when it came to selecting the contingent for the 1924 Paris Olympics. India selected a sportswoman for the first time – Nora Margaret Polley (née Fischer). She was born in India in 1894 and competed in tennis in both the women's singles, losing in the third round, and mixed doubles with Sydney Jacob, losing in the second round.

A contingent of 120 Indian athletes participated in the Tokyo Olympics 2020 in archery, athletics, badminton, boxing, equestrian, fencing, field hockey, golf, gymnastics, judo, rowing, sailing, shooting, swimming, table tennis, tennis, weightlifting and wrestling.

It would be 76 years before an Indian woman medalled at the Olympics, when weightlifter Karnam Malleswari won bronze in the 69 kg class at Sydney 2000.

In an aside, Dorabji's wife, Meherbai, was also entered in the tennis mixed doubles. But she and her partner Mohammed Sleem gained a bye in the first round and conceded a walkover in the second, so her

INDIA'S OLYMPIC MEDAL TALLY: AT A GLANCE			
Medallist	**Medal**	**Games**	**Sport**
Norman Pritchard	Silver	Paris, 1900	Athletics
Norman Pritchard	Silver	Paris, 1900	Athletics
National Team	Gold	Amsterdam, 1928	Field hockey
National Team	Gold	Los Angeles, 1932	Field hockey
National Team	Gold	Berlin, 1936	Field hockey
National Team	Gold	London, 1948	Field hockey
National Team	Gold	Helsinki, 1952	Field hockey
Khashaba Dadasaheb Jadhav	Bronze	Helsinki, 1952	Wrestling
National Team	Gold	Melbourne, 1956	Field hockey
National Team	Silver	Rome, 1960	Field hockey
National Team	Gold	Tokyo, 1964	Field hockey
National Team	Bronze	Mexico City, 1968	Field hockey
National Team	Bronze	Munich, 1972	Field hockey
National Team	Gold	Moscow, 1980	Field hockey
Leander Paes	Bronze	Atlanta, 1996	Tennis
Karnam Malleswari	Bronze	Sydney, 2000	Weightlifting
Rajyavardhan Singh Rathore	Silver	Athens, 2004	Shooting
Abhinav Bindra	Gold	Beijing, 2008	Shooting
Vijender Singh	Bronze	Beijing, 2008	Boxing
Sushil Kumar	Bronze	Beijing, 2008	Wrestling
Vijay Kumar	Silver	London, 2012	Shooting
Sushil Kumar	Silver	London, 2012	Wrestling
Saina Nehwal	Bronze	London, 2012	Badminton
M.C. Mary Kom	Bronze	London, 2012	Boxing
Gagan Narang	Bronze	London, 2012	Shooting
Yogeshwar Dutt	Bronze	London, 2012	Wrestling
P.V. Sindhu	Silver	Rio de Janeiro, 2016	Badminton
Sakshi Malik	Bronze	Rio de Janeiro, 2016	Wrestling

participation does not figure in the records.

Amsterdam 1928 was a landmark Olympics for India for two reasons: it was the first in which selections were made by the IOA, which had been formed just a year earlier (though the 1920 and 1924 contingents were also official ones), and it was the first time India was sending a hockey team that wrote the first chapter in the golden saga that would last till the 1960s.

No Olympic team sport has been dominated by one country like India did hockey save perhaps for the mighty Magyars (from Hungary) in water polo and the USA 'dream teams' in basketball.

The opponents were steamrollered as India smashed 29 goals in their five matches without conceding a single one. Britain, which had dominated hockey till then, took the prudent decision not to compete at the Olympics from 1928 to 1936, wary of being humiliated by their colony! Amsterdam also marked the arrival on the world stage of Dhyan Chand Singh Bais, the immortal 'wizard' of hockey who seemed to score goals for fun – 14 of those 29 goals came from his stick that he seemed to wield like a magic wand.

Dhyan Chand won three consecutive golds for India in 1928, 1932 and 1936, as did goalkeeper Richard James Allen, who conceded just three goals in that golden run. Dhyan Chand's birth anniversary (29 August) is celebrated every year as National Sports Day.

Balbir Singh Dosanjh's record in 1952 for the most goals scored by an individual (five) in an Olympic men's hockey final is unbeaten

Western observers had never seen such skills on a sports field and were stunned by the artistry of the Indians. An awestruck Dutch journalist wrote: 'The Indian ball seems ignorant of the laws of gravity. One of those . . . diabolical jugglers stares at the ball intently; it gets upright and remains suspended in the air. This is no longer the game of hockey. It is a juggling turn. It is splendid.'

Admittedly, the opposition was feeble back then, especially at Los Angeles in 1932, with only Japan and the hosts to challenge India. The results were predictable: 11–1 versus Japan and a humiliating 24–1 versus the USA! Dhyan Chand's brother Roop Singh slammed in 10 goals and the 'Wizard' eight in the rout.

Dhyan and Allen were later joined as triple gold medallists by Balbir Singh Dosanjh, Leslie Claudius – independent India's two greatest exponents of hockey – Randhir Singh Gentle and Udham Singh, with Udham and Claudius adding a silver to their three gold medals. In 2018, a movie (*Gold: The Dream That United Our Nation*) starring Akshay Kumar was released, inspired by the life and career of Balbir Singh, who passed away in his mid-nineties in May 2020.

After winning the gold for six straight Olympics from 1928 to 1956 (there were none in 1940 and 1944 due to the Second World War), India were jolted by Pakistan in the final at Rome in 1960 but regained gold four years later at Tokyo, Japan.

We then slipped to bronze in 1968 and 1972, but it was at Montreal 1976 when AstroTurf was introduced that the slide began. Since then, the only time India has medalled was with gold at Moscow 1980, which was devalued due the Western nations' boycott. The fall from grace has been calamitous, the nadir coming when, for the first time, the team failed to even qualify for the 2008 Beijing Olympics.

The first individual medal after Independence was a bronze won by Khashaba Dadasaheb Jadhav in wrestling (bantamweight, 57 kg) at Helsinki 1952. Sadly, his feat received little recognition and it was only in 2001, thirteen years after his death in a road accident, that his widow received a posthumous Arjuna Award on his behalf. The wrestling hall for the 2010 Commonwealth Games in New Delhi was named after this legend.

THE RISE

From 1956 to 1992 – Melbourne to Barcelona – spanning 36 years and 10 Games – India went without an individual medal until tennis star Leander Paes bagged the singles bronze at Atlanta 1996. The senior-most player on the world circuit today, Paes made his Olympic debut in 1992. He holds the Indian record for the most appearances at the Olympics, totalling seven.

Just as the silver won in double trap at Athens in 2004 by shooter Colonel Rajyavardhan Singh Rathore – briefly the minister for sports – went one step further than Paes and Malleswari, Bindra's gold brought so much joy to the nation in 2008. That gold was accompanied by bronze medals by boxer Vijender Singh (middleweight) and wrestler Sushil Kumar (freestyle, 66 kg). Sushil went one better four years later with silver in London 2012 in the same weight class, making him the only two-time individual medallist since 1948.

Though unfortunately tainted by a financial scandal, the 2010 Commonwealth Games in New Delhi helped to bring Olympic sports front and centre, and this resulted in India's best medal haul at London in 2012 – six in all – though a gold proved elusive.

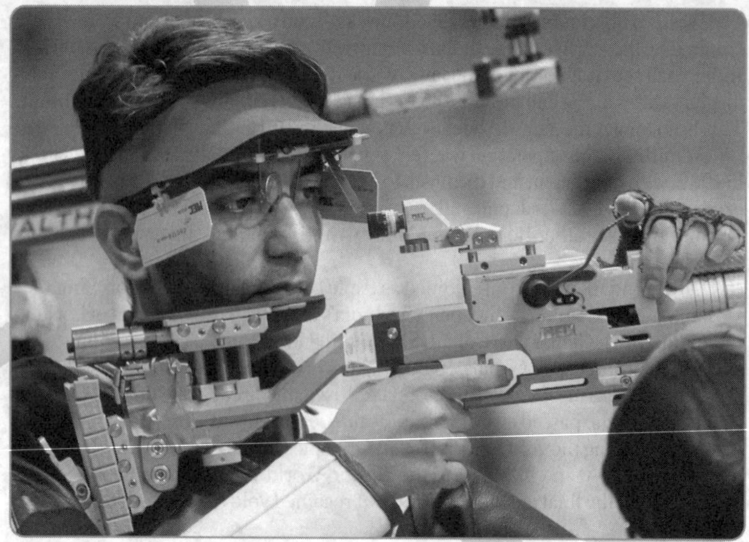

Abhinav Bindra: first Indian individual Olympic gold

Vijay Kumar (25 m rapid fire pistol) and Sushil Kumar won silver while Saina Nehwal (women's badminton), M.C. Mary Kom (women's boxing, flyweight) Gagan Narang (10 m air rifle) and Yogeshwar Dutt (freestyle wrestling, 60 kg) all bagged bronze.

This augured well for the 2016 edition in Rio de Janeiro, but the performance saw a dip with just two medals, silver in badminton by P.V. Sindhu and bronze for woman wrestler Sakshi Malik (freestyle, 58 kg). Gymnast Dipa Karmakar, however, stunned the world with her daring vault routine even though she finished fourth.

Importantly, India has also been competing at the Winter Olympics intermittently since Innsbruck, Austria, in 1964. Though no Indian has come close to a medal, Shiva Keshavan kept the flag flying in men's singles luge for six straight Winter Games till Pyeongchang, South Korea, in 2018.

ON TOWARDS TOKYO

Tokyo is where India briefly regained her hockey glory in 1964. Will the 2020 Olympic Games see more prestige, and perhaps a clutch of gold medals? Just nine gold, seven silver (including Pritchard's two) and 12 bronze medals is slim pickings indeed when compared to the rich haul by the likes of swimmer Michael Phelps and athlete Usain Bolt.

Whether it is giant countries like China, USA and Russia/Soviet Union, who have medals by the truckload, war-torn and impoverished African states like Ethiopia, or a tiny island nation like Jamaica, India has lagged far behind them all. Now in the centenary year, that may well change for the better.

– Gulu Ezekiel has been a sports journalist since 1980. He is the co-author of Great Indian Olympians *and has also written a dozen cricket books including biographies of Sachin Tendulkar, Sourav Ganguly and M.S. Dhoni.*

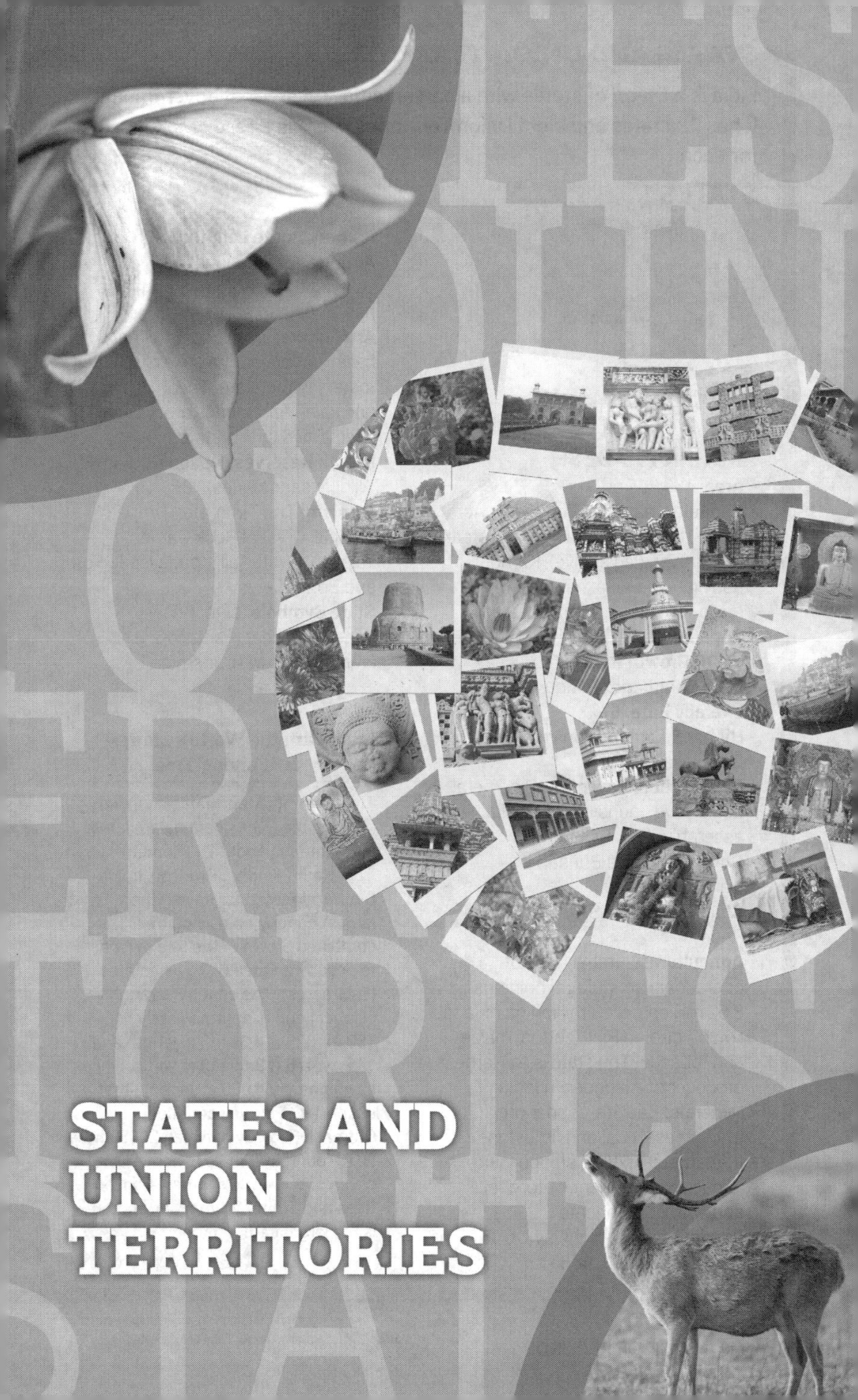

STATES AND UNION TERRITORIES

STATES AND UNION TERRITORIES

India is a Union of states with a parliamentary system of government. It has 28 states and eight Union Territories. Here is a ready reckoner for each.

STATES

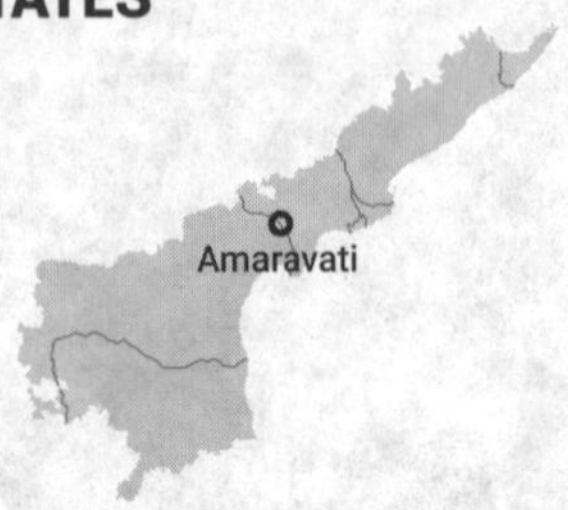

ANDHRA PRADESH

- **Area:** 160,205 sq. km
- **Capital:** Amaravati. The earlier Acts to create three capitals for the state, in Amravati (legislative), Kurnool (judicial) and Visakhapatnam (executive), have been repealed.
- **Population:** 49.67 million
- **GSDP Growth Rate:** 11.2%
- **Main Language:** Telugu
- **Literacy Rate:** 67%
- **Higher Education:** Universities: 41; Colleges: 2,521
- **Constitution/Assembly:** Bicameral. Legislative council: 58; Legislative assembly: 175
- **Governor:** Biswa Bhusan Harichandan
- **Chief Minister:** Y.S. Jagan Mohan Reddy
- **Agriculture:** Number/area of operational agricultural holdings: 8.52 million over 8 million ha of land; MAJOR CROPS: Rice, cotton, maize and tobacco. The state is the largest producer of mangoes in India.
- **Minerals:** Bauxite, copper ore, manganese, coal and limestone
- **Industries:** Textiles, shipbuilding, aquaculture, cement, automobile and auto components
- **Roads:** National highways: 6,467 km; State highways: 6,485 km; Major district roads: 35,471 km
- **Railway Route Length:** 3,703 km
- **Airports:** International: 1; Domestic: 4; Visakhapatnam also has a bustling port.
- **Art/Culture:** Kuchipudi is a near-ballet, dance-drama style that fosters in the state. Theatre and *kalamkari* fabrics are also specialities of this state.
- **Nature Reserves:** National parks: 3; Wildlife sanctuaries: 13
- **Tourism:** The Tirumala–Tirupati Temple, Orvakal Rock Garden, Talakona Waterfall, Kondaveedu Fort and Borra Caves
- **State Symbols:** BIRD: Rose-ringed parakeet (*Psittacula krameri*); FLOWER: Jasmine

State with the World's Largest Canopy on a Living Tree

Thimmamma Marrimanu, an Indian banyan tree (*Ficus benghalensis*) in Anantapur, about 25 kilometres from Kadiri, Andhra Pradesh, holds the world record for having the largest canopy on a living tree. The combined crown of the tree extends to occupy an area of 2.19 hectares (5.41 acres). The canopy is roughly elliptical and is approximately 190 m (623 ft 4.31 in.) in length and 145 m (475 ft 8.66 in.) in width, while having nearly 4,000 prop roots that support it. A survey conducted by Outreach Ecology between 2008 and 2010 found that India is home to seven of the world's largest banyan trees and Thimmamma Marrimamu is the largest among them.

*Gross State Domestic Product; only applicable to certain states; **Does not have an Air Quality Index station

(Genus *Jasminum*); TREE: Neem (*Azadirachta indica*); ANIMAL: Blackbuck (*Antilope cervicapra*)

- **Do Not Miss!** The INS *Kursura*, after being decommissioned, was turned into a submarine museum at Visakhapatnam. This unique museum is open to public to see the weaponry and machinery used on submarines.
- **Swachh Survekshan Ranking**: 6
- **UNESCO Heritage (Intangible cultural, historical or other sites):** None
- **Sustainable Development Index Score:** 67****
- **Smart Cities:** 4
- **Air Pollution Index:** 128 (Moderate)

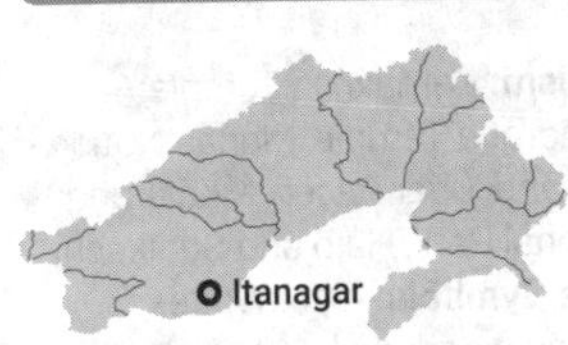

ARUNACHAL PRADESH

- **Area:** 83,743 sq. km
- **Capital:** Itanagar
- **Population:** 1.25 million
- **GSDP Growth Rate:** Not applicable*
- **Main Languages:** Hindi and local languages (Nisi, Dafla, Assamese)
- **Literacy Rate:** 65.4%
- **Higher Education:** Universities: 10; Colleges: 36
- **Constitution/Assembly:** Unicameral. Legislative assembly: 60
- **Governor:** Brigadier Dr B.D. Mishra (Retd)
- **Chief Minister:** Pema Khandu
- **Agriculture:** Number/area of operational agricultural holdings: 0.11 million over 0.38 million ha of land; MAJOR CROPS: Rice, potato, tea, apple and pineapple

Tawang Monastery, Tawang

- **Minerals:** Coal, limestone, dolomites, graphite, lead, quartzite, petroleum, natural gas
- **Industries:** Petrochemicals, textiles and handicrafts
- **Roads:** National highways: 2,513 km; State roads (not classified further): 8,123 km
- **Railway Route Length:** 11.67 km
- **Airports:** Domestic: 2
- **Art/Culture:** Carpet making, wood carving and Apatani tribal dance
- **Nature Reserves:** National parks: 2; Wildlife sanctuaries: 11
- **Tourism:** Tawang Monastery, Parashuram Kund, Malinathan and Itanagar
- **State Symbols:** BIRD: Hornbill (*Buceros bicornis*); FLOWER: Foxtail orchid (*Rynchostylis retusa*); TREE: Hollong (*Dipterocarpus macrocarpus*); ANIMAL: Mithun (*Bos frontalis*)
- **Do Not Miss!** The eco-friendly Ziro Festival of Music in Ziro Valley brings together music and nature.
- **Swachh Survekshan Ranking:** 22
- **UNESCO Heritage (Intangible cultural, historical or other sites):** None
- **Sustainable Development Index Score:** 53
- **Smart Cities:** 2
- **Air Pollution Index:** Not applicable**

***Not part of the survey ****SDI score scale: Achiever: 100; Front Runner: 65-100; Performer: 50-65; Aspirant: <50

ASSAM

- **Area:** 78,438 sq. km
- **Capital:** Dispur
- **Population:** 31.16 million
- **GSDP Growth Rate:** Not applicable*
- **Main Languages:** Assamese and Bengali
- **Literacy Rate:** 72.2%
- **Higher Education:** Universities: 22; Colleges: 526
- **Constitution/Assembly:** Unicameral. Legislative assembly: 126
- **Governor:** Prof. Jagdish Mukhi
- **Chief Minister:** Himanta Biswa Sarma
- **Agriculture:** Number/area of operational agricultural holdings: 2.74 million over 2.97 million ha of land; MAJOR CROPS: Rice, jute, tea, cotton, sugar cane and maize
- **Minerals:** Coal, silica sand, limestone, china clay, iron ore and granite, petroleum and natural gas
- **Industries:** Tea, cement, textiles, sericulture and oil refining
- **Roads:** National highways: 3,844 km; State highways: 2,530 km; Major district roads: 4,379 km
- **Railway Route Length:** 2,442.57 km
- **Airports:** International: 1; Domestic: 5
- **Art/Culture:** Crafts include handloom, sericulture, and bamboo and cane items. Muga silk is produced only here in the world.
- **Nature Reserves:** National parks: 5; Wildlife sanctuaries: 18

Drama in the Forest

'Under the Sal Tree' – an annual theatre festival in Rampur Village of Goalpara District in Assam, is a unique eco-friendly drama fest. Here, a stage made of mud is set up amid towering sal trees and a row of bamboo seats encircles the handmade stage. Founded by Heisnam Kanhailal (1941–2016) and Sukracharjya Rabha in 2008, the festival celebrated its 10th edition in December 2018. No special lighting or acoustic equipment, microphones, drapery or sets a re used in this minimalist festival that encourages sustainability and simplicity.

- **Tourism:** Kamakhya Temple, Navagraha Temple, Manas National Park and Tiger Reserve, Kaziranga National Park, Hajo and Sualkuchi
- **State Symbols:** BIRD: White-winged wood duck (*Asarcornis scutulata*); FLOWER: Foxtail orchid (*Rynchostylis retusa*); TREE: Hollong (*Dipterocarpus macrocarpus*); ANIMAL: One-horned rhinoceros (*Rhinoceros unicornis*)
- **Do Not Miss!** Majuli, the world's largest river island and the Kaziranga National Park, which is home to the famed Indian one-horned rhinoceros
- **Swachh Survekshan Ranking:** 14
- **UNESCO Heritage (Intangible cultural, historical or other sites):** Kaziranga National Park and Manas Wildlife Sanctuary
- **Sustainable Development Index Score:** 55
- **Smart City:** 1
- **Air Pollution Index:** 341 (Very Poor)

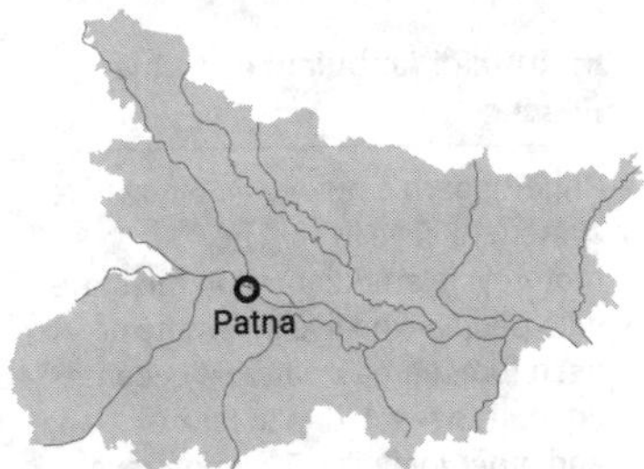

BIHAR

- **Area:** 94,163 sq. km
- **Capital:** Patna
- **Population:** 103.80 million
- **GSDP Growth Rate:** 11.3%
- **Main Language:** Hindi
- **Literacy Rate:** 61.8%
- **Higher Education:** Universities: 33; Colleges: 840
- **Constitution/Assembly:** Bicameral. Legislative council: 75; Legislative assembly: 243
- **Governor:** Phagu Chauhan
- **Chief Minister:** Nitish Kumar
- **Agriculture:** Number/area of operational agricultural holdings: 16.41 million over 6.4 million ha of land; MAJOR CROPS: Rice, wheat, lentils, sugar cane and jute
- **Minerals:** Steatite, pyrites, quartzite, mica and limestone
- **Industries:** Food and beverages, plastic and rubber, tobacco, textiles, leather and dairy
- **Roads:** National highways: 4,839 km; State highways: 4,006 km; Major district roads: 11,145 km
- **Railway Route Length:** 3,730.57 km
- **Airports:** International: 1; Domestic: 1
- **Art/Culture:** Chhat, a festival of sun worship; Madhubani art, a traditional painting made with vegetable dyes
- **Nature Reserves:** National park: 1; Wildlife sanctuaries: 12
- **Tourism:** Rajgir, Nalanda, Bodhgaya, Patna (ancient city of Pataliputra) and Madhubani
- **State Symbols:** BIRD: House sparrow (*Passer domesticus*); FLOWER: Kachnar (*Phanera variegata*); TREE: Peepul (*Ficus religiosa*); ANIMAL: Gaur (*Bos gaurus*)
- **Do Not Miss!** The annual Sonepur Cattle Fair held during November–December is the largest cattle fair in Asia.
- **Swachh Survekshan Ranking:** 24
- **UNESCO Heritage (Intangible cultural, historical or other sites):** The Mahabodhi Temple complex at Bodhgaya and the archaeological site of Nalanda Mahavihara, south-east of Patna
- **Sustainable Development Index Score:** 50
- **Smart Cities:** 4
- **Air Pollution Index:** 292 (Poor)

Mahabodhi Temple, Bodhgaya, Bihar

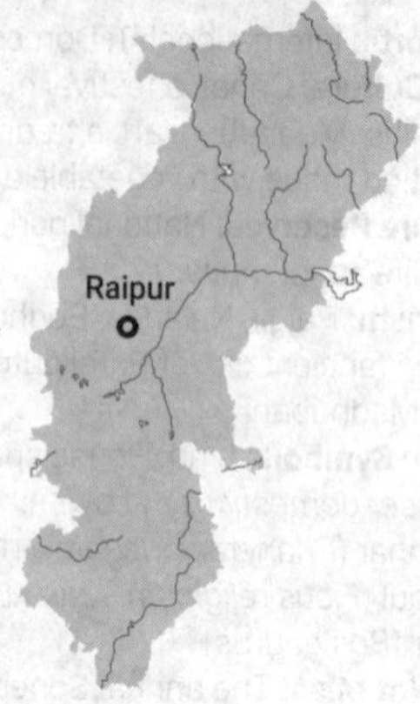

CHHATTISGARH

- **Area:** 135,194 sq. km
- **Capital:** Raipur
- **Population:** 25.54 million
- **GSDP Growth Rate:** 6.7%
- **Main Language:** Hindi
- **Literacy Rate:** 70.3%
- **Higher Education:** Universities: 28; Colleges: 757
- **Constitution/Assembly:** Unicameral. Legislative assembly: 91
- **Governor:** Anusuiya Uikey
- **Chief Minister:** Bhupesh Baghel
- **Agriculture:** Number/area of operational agricultural holdings: 4.01 million over 4.93 million ha of land; MAJOR CROPS: Rice, maize, wheat, niger seed (*ramtil*), groundnut and pulses. The state has one of the biggest collections of rice germ plasm.
- **Minerals:** Coal, iron ore, limestone, bauxite and dolomite
- **Industries:** Cement, mining, steel, aluminium and electricity
- **Roads:** National highways: 3,232 km; State highways: 4,438 km; Major district roads: 11,625 km
- **Railway Route Length:** 1,213 km
- **Airport:** Domestic: 3
- **Art/Culture:** Bamboo art, bell metal (*dhokra*), Kosa silk, wrought iron and terracotta statues

  Nature Reserves: National parks: 3; Wildlife sanctuaries: 11
- **Tourism:** Bastar, Chitrakote Falls, Danteshwari Temple, Kutumsar Cave, Tirathgarh Falls and Kanger Ghati National Park
- **State Symbols:** BIRD: Hill myna (*Gracula religiosa*); TREE: Sal (*Shorea robusta*); ANIMAL: Wild buffalo (*Bubalis bubalis*)
- **Do Not Miss!** The Chitrakote Falls: 29.2 m (96 ft) high waterfalls of the River Indravati, popularly called the 'Niagara Falls of India'
- **Swachh Survekshan Ranking:** 1
- **UNESCO Heritage (Intangible cultural, or historical, or other sites):** None
- **Sustainable Development Index Score:** 56
- **Smart Cities:** 3
- **Air Pollution index:** Not applicable**

Motorbike Ambulances to the Rescue

Chhattisgarh employs an innovative system to save lives. The motorcycle ambulances in the state help people who live in remote or deep forest areas, where it becomes difficult to reach due to lack of roads and other facilities. The motorcycle ambulance is a specially modified bike, with an attached side carrier built keeping the patient's comfort in mind. It has helped numerous pregnant women and other patients receive healthcare in time. The health department of the state government, supported by UNICEF and an NGO Saathi Samaj Sevi Sanstha, set the project in motion.

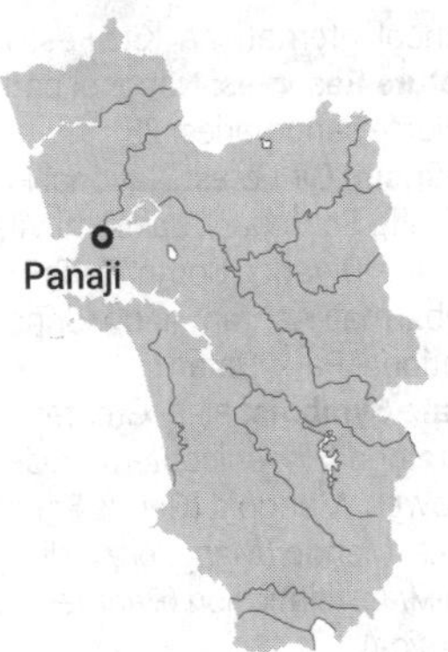

GOA

- **Area:** 3,702 sq. km
- **Capital:** Panaji
- **Population:** 1.45 million
- **GSDP Growth Rate:** Not applicable*
- **Main Language:** Konkani
- **Literacy Rate:** 88.7%
- **Higher Education:** Universities: 3; Colleges: 57
- **Constitution/Assembly:** Unicameral. Legislative assembly: 40
- **Governor:** P.S. Sreedharan Pillai
- **Chief Minister:** Pramod Sawant
- **Agriculture:** Number/area of operational agricultural holdings: 0.07 million over 0.08 million ha of land; MAJOR CROPS: Rice, coconut and cashew nut
- **Minerals:** Iron ore, manganese ore, bauxite and laterite stones
- **Industries:** Agriculture, mining, tourism and hospitality
- **Roads:** National highways: 263 km; State highways: 279 km; Major district roads: 1,173 km
- **Railway Route Length:** 69.3 km
- **Airport:** International: 1
- **Art/Culture:** Bamboo craft, woodcarving, brass metals, seashell craft, papier mâché and wooden lacquered ware
- **Nature Reserves:** National park: 1; Wildlife sanctuaries: 6
- **Tourism:** Baga, Anjuna and Miramar beaches, Basilica of Bom Jesus and Se Cathedral churches in Old Goa, Fort Aguada and Chapora Fort
- **State Symbols:** BIRD: Ruby-throated yellow bulbul (*Pycnonotus gularis*); FLOWER: Red jasmine (*Plumeria rubra)*; TREE: Matti (*Terminalia elliptica*); ANIMAL: Gaur (*Bos gaurus*)

The ruby-throated yellow bulbul: the state bird of Goa

- **Do Not Miss!** The 310 m (1,017 ft) high Dudhsagar Falls on the River Mandovi, overlooking a small railway track section on the Madgaon–Belagavi route
- **Swachh Survekshan Ranking:** 17
- **UNESCO Heritage (Intangible cultural, historical or other sites):** Churches and Convents of Goa, and the Western Ghats (shared)
- **Sustainable Development Index Score:** 65
- **Smart City:** 1
- **Air pollution index:** Not applicable**

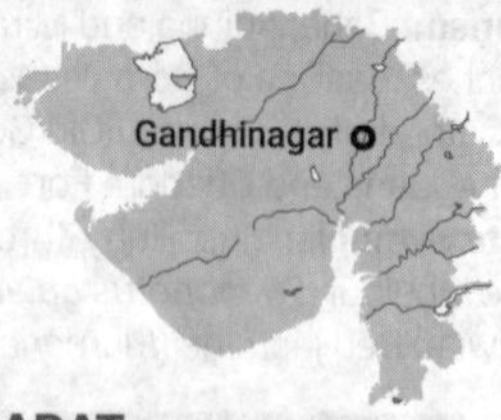

GUJARAT

- **Area:** 196,024 sq. km
- **Capital:** Gandhinagar
- **Population:** 60.38 million
- **GSDP Growth Rate:** 11.1%
- **Main Language:** Gujarati
- **Literacy Rate:** 78%
- **Higher Education:** Universities: 72; Colleges: 2,214
- **Constitution/Assembly:** Unicameral. Legislative assembly: 182
- **Governor:** Acharya Dev Vrat
- **Chief Minister:** Bhupendra Patel
- **Agriculture:** Number/area of operational agricultural holdings: 5.32 million over 9.97 million ha of land; MAJOR CROPS: Cotton, rice, jowar, maize, tobacco and groundnut
- **Minerals:** Lignite, bauxite, manganese, silica and limestone
- **Industries:** Petroleum, diamond, cement, agriculture and textiles. Gujarat is the largest producer of denim in India.
- **Roads:** National highways: 5,017 km; State highways: 17,201 km; Major district roads: 30,809 km
- **Railway Route Length:** 5,258.5 km
- **Airports:** International: 2; Domestic: 7
- **Art/Culture:** Needlework and Kachchhi embroidery, pottery, Patola weaves and furnishings. Ahmedabad hosts the annual International Kite Festival.
- **Nature Reserves:** National parks: 4; Wildlife sanctuaries: 23
- **Tourism:** Gir Forest National Park/ Wildlife Sanctuary, Lakshmi Vilas Palace, Dwarka, Somnath Temple, Sabarmati Ashram and Marine National Park, Patan
- **State Symbols:** BIRD: Greater flamingo (*Phoenicopterus roseus*); FLOWER: Marigold (Genus Tagetes); TREE: Mango (*Mangifera indica*); ANIMAL: Asiatic lion (*Panthera leo persica*)
- **Do Not Miss!** The white sands and salty marshes of Kachchh, nestled between the Arabian Sea and the Thar Desert
- **Swachh Survekshan Ranking:** 5
- **UNESCO Heritage (Intangible cultural, historical or other sites):** Champaner–Pavagadh Archaeological Park, the historic city of Ahmedabad, Western Ghats (shared), Rani Ki Vav (step well) at Patan, and Dholavira
- **Sustainable Development Index Score:** 64
- **Smart Cities:** 6
- **Air Pollution Index:** 108 (Moderate)

The Great Rann of Kachchh

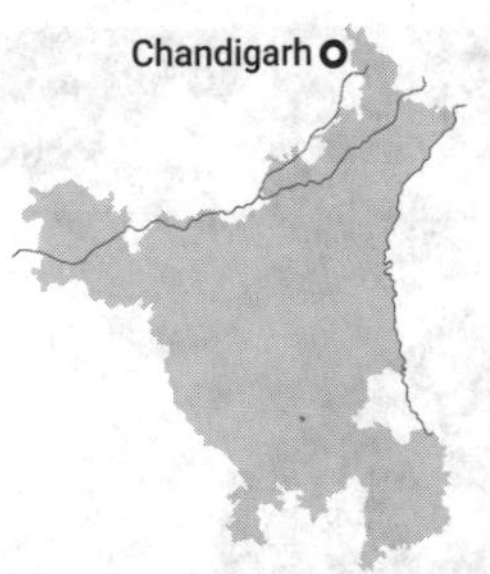

HARYANA

- **Area:** 44,212 sq. km
- **Capital:** Chandigarh
- **Population:** 25.35 million
- **GSDP Growth Rate:** 7.2%
- **Main Language:** Hindi
- **Literacy Rate:** 75.6%
- **Higher Education:** Universities: 48; Colleges: 990
- **Constitution/Assembly:** Unicameral. Legislative assembly: 90
- **Governor:** Satyadeo Narain Arya
- **Chief Minister:** Manohar Lal Khattar
- **Agriculture:** Number/area of operational agricultural holdings: 1.62 million over 3.60 million ha of land; MAJOR CROPS: Wheat, rice, sugar cane, cotton, oilseeds, pulses, mustard and maize
- **Minerals:** Baryte, slate, copper ore, marble, limestone and quartz
- **Industries:** Textiles, agriculture, manufacturing of automobiles and auto components, and information technology
- **Roads:** National highways: 2,623 km; State highways: 1,801 km; Major district roads: 21,948 km
- **Railway Route Length:** 1,710.5 km
- **Airports:** Domestic: 2
- **Art/Culture:** Traditionally rich in folklore, it is the backdrop of The Mahabharata by Vedavyasa. Saangh (folk theatre) and *shisha* embroidery are also popular.
- **Nature Reserves:** National parks: 2; Wildlife sanctuaries: 8
- **Tourism:** Surajkund, Damdama Lake, Kurukshetra and Morni Hills
- **State Symbols**: BIRD: Black francolin (*Francolinus francolinus*); FLOWER: Lotus (*Nelumbo nucifera*); TREE: Peepul (*Ficus religiosa*); ANIMAL: Blackbuck (*Antilope cervicapra*)
- **Do Not Miss!** The National Cactus and Succulent Botanical Garden and Research Centre at Panchkula has more than 3,500 species of endangered and rare cacti. It is considered the biggest such garden in Asia and organizes an annual cactus show in the month of March.
- **Swachh Survekshan Ranking:** 8
- **UNESCO Heritage (Intangible cultural, historical or other sites):** None
- **Sustainable Development Index Score:** 57
- **Smart Cities:** 2
- **Air pollution index:** 343 (Very Poor)

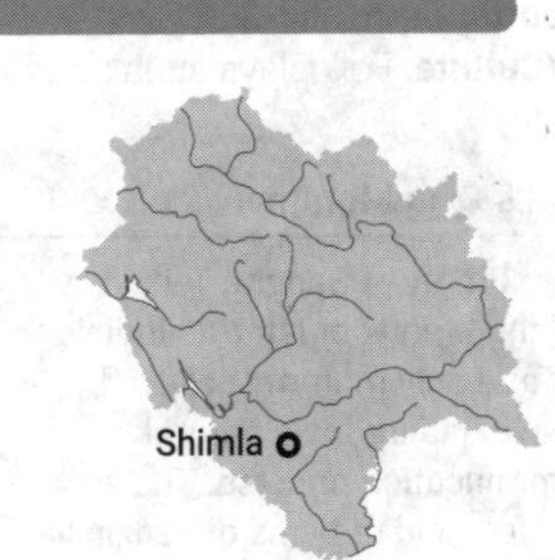

HIMACHAL PRADESH

- **Area:** 55,673 sq. km
- **Capital:** Shimla
- **Population:** 6.86 million
- **GSDP Growth Rate:** Not applicable*
- **Main Languages:** Hindi and Pahari
- **Literacy Rate:** 82.8%
- **Higher Education:** Universities: 26; Colleges: 335
- **Constitution/Assembly:** Unicameral. Legislative assembly: 68

- **Governor:** Rajendra Vishwanath Arlekar
- **Chief Minister:** Jai Ram Thakur
- **Agriculture:** Number/area of operational agricultural holdings: 0.99 million over 0.94 million ha of land; MAJOR CROPS: Rice, wheat, maize, pulses and sugar cane
- **Minerals:** Antimony, gypsum, manganese, limestone, baryte, rock salt and silica sand
- **Industries:** Agriculture, food and beverages, cement, pharmaceuticals and hydroelectricity
- **Roads:** National highways: 2,643 km; State highways: 827 km; Major district roads: 2,832 km
- **Railway Route Length:** 296.26 km
- **Airports:** Domestic: 3
- **Art/Culture:** Folk plays such as Swang, Banthra and Bhagtu, and the ancient architecture across Kullu and Kinnaur districts
- **Nature Reserves:** National parks: 5; Wildlife sanctuaries: 28
- **Tourism:** Shimla, Manali, Lahaul and Spiti, Baspa Valley, Seraj and Tirthan
- **State Symbols:** BIRD: Western tragopan (*Tragopan melanocephalus*); FLOWER: Pink rhododendron (*Rhododendron campanulatum*); TREE: Deodar (*Cedrus deodara*); ANIMAL: Snow leopard (*Uncia uncia*)
- **Do Not Miss!** Chandra Tal or the 'lake of the moon', a high-altitude glacial lake situated at more than 4,267 m (14,000 ft) above the mean sea level in the Lahaul and Spiti District
- **Swachh Survekshan Ranking:** 16
- **UNESCO Heritage (Intangible cultural, or historical, or other sites):** Kalka–Shimla Railway (part of Mountain Railways of India) and Great Himalayan National Park conservation area

The snow leopard: the state animal of Himachal Pradesh

India's Own Mummy

The mummy of Sangha Tenzin, a Buddhist monk or lama, is India's first and only mummy believed to have undergone a natural mummification process. The 500-year-old remains of Tenzin lie behind a glass window in Gue in Lahaul and Spiti District, Himachal Pradesh. The mummy, which was hidden in a tomb in Gue, was discovered only in 1975 after an earthquake destroyed and opened up the tomb. In 2004, the tomb was excavated and the mummy was removed. It is well preserved and has the teeth, hair and skin intact and visible. The mummy is now displayed at a temple in Gue, which is open to the public.

- **Sustainable Development Index Score:** 69
- **Smart Cities:** 2
- **Air Pollution Index:** Not applicable**

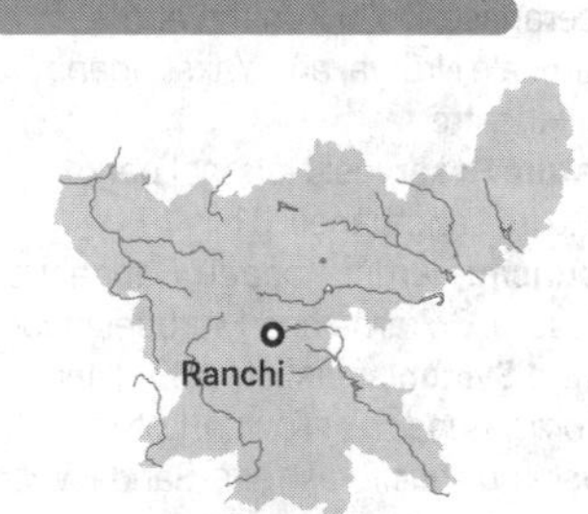

JHARKHAND

- **Area:** 79,714 sq. km
- **Capital:** Ranchi
- **Population:** 32.98 million
- **GSDP Growth Rate:** 4.6%
- **Main Language:** Hindi
- **Literacy Rate:** 66.4%
- **Higher Education:** Universities: 25; Colleges: 308
- **Constitution/Assembly:** Unicameral. Legislative assembly: 81
- **Governor:** Ramesh Bais
- **Chief Minister:** Hemant Soren
- **Agriculture:** Number/area of operational agricultural holdings: 2.8 million over 3.09 million ha of land; MAJOR CROPS: Rice, millet, maize, wheat, pulses, gram and mustard
- **Minerals:** Coal, iron ore, limestone, copper ore, bauxite, pyrite and china clay
- **Industries:** Locomotives, cement, steel, aluminium, mining and quarrying, and sericulture
- **Roads:** National highways: 2,654 km; State highways: 1,339 km; Major district roads: 9,356 km
- **Railway Route Length:** 2,394.5 km
- **Airport:** Domestic: 3
- **Art/Culture:** Santhali dance, wood and bamboo work, Paitkar paintings, tribal ornaments and stone carving
- **Nature Reserves:** National park: 1; Wildlife sanctuaries: 11
- **Tourism:** Ichagarh Bird Sanctuary, Topchanchi Lake, Palna Dam, Dassam Falls, Chachro Crocodile Breeding Centre, Jawaharlal Nehru Zoological Garden and Surya Mandir
- **State Symbols:** BIRD: Koel (*Eudynamys scolopaceus*); FLOWER: Palash (*Butea monosperma*); TREE: Sal (*Shorea robusta*); ANIMAL: Indian elephant (*Elephas maximus indicus*)
- **Do Not Miss!** Experience the Paitkar art form of Amadubi Village, East Singhbhum District: the artists paint on soiled or used papers, and on scrolls made from leaves and bark, applying vermilion and natural dyes with needles or the hairs of a goat.
- **Swachh Survekshan Ranking:** 4
- **UNESCO Heritage (Intangible cultural, historical or other sites):** Chhau dance (shared)
- **Sustainable Development Index Score:** 53
- **Smart City:** 1
- **Air Pollution Index:** 179 (Moderate)

India's Only Underground Power Station

Maithon Dam in Jharkhand is 4,789 m (15,712 ft) long and 50 m (164 ft) high. Built on the River Barakar, the dam is the first of its kind in the country as well as in South-East Asia as it uniquely has an underground power station. The Maithon Hydel Power Station has a total power generation capacity of 60 MW with three units of 20 MW each. It is situated 100 m (328 ft) below the water level.

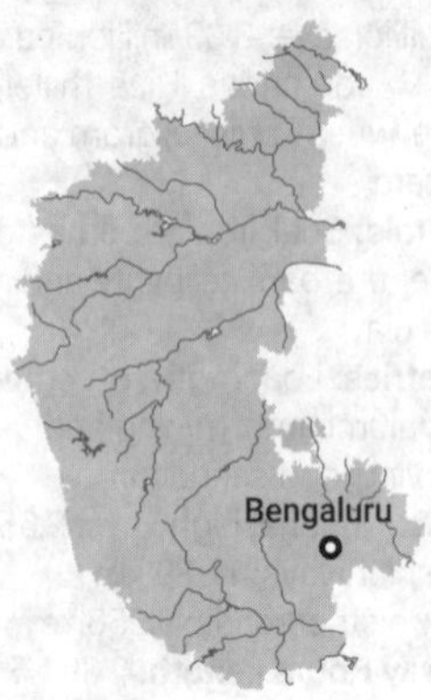

KARNATAKA

- **Area:** 191,791 sq. km
- **Capital:** Bengaluru
- **Population:** 61.13 million
- **GSDP Growth Rate:** 9.3%
- **Main Language:** Kannada
- **Literacy Rate:** 75.4%
- **Higher Education:** Universities: 65; Colleges: 3,594
- **Constitution/Assembly:** Bicameral. Legislative council: 75; Legislative assembly: 224
- **Governor:** Thaawarchand Gehlot
- **Chief Minister:** Basavaraj Bommai
- **Agriculture:** Number/area of operational agricultural holdings: 8.67 million over 11.8 million ha of land; MAJOR CROPS: Rice, ragi, sorghum, pulses, pearl millet and pigeon pea
- **Minerals:** Iron ore, magnesite, dunite, chromite, limestone and china clay
- **Industries:** Automobile, cement, agro-industries, aerospace, information technology, biotech and heavy engineering
- **Roads:** National highways: 6,762 km; State highways: 19,556 km; Major district roads: 49,923 km
- **Railway Route Length:** 3,281.4 km
- **Airports:** International: 2; Domestic: 6
- **Art/Culture:** Dance forms like Veeragase, Dollu Kunitha and Kamsale Nrutya, and Yakshagana folk theatre
- **Nature Reserves:** National parks: 5; Wildlife sanctuaries: 31
- **Tourism:** Hampi, Kodagu, Bengaluru, Mysuru, Gokarna and Murudeshwar
- **State Symbols:** BIRD: Indian roller (*Coracias indica*); FLOWER: Lotus (*Nelumbo nucifera*); TREE: Sandalwood (*Santalum album*); ANIMAL: Indian elephant (*Elephas maximus indicus*)
- **Do Not Miss!** The 643 sq. km Nagarhole National Park, flanking the River Kabini, is a wildlife reserve with many species including tigers and elephants. This protected region includes Bandipur National Park.
- **Swachh Survekshan Ranking:** 21
- **UNESCO Heritage (Intangible cultural, historical or other sites):** Western Ghats (shared), Group of Monuments at Hampi and Group of Monuments at Pattadakal
- **Sustainable Development Index Score:** 66
- **Smart Cities:** 7
- **Air Pollution Index:** 100 (Satisfactory)

Lotus Mahal, Hampi, Karnataka

SUPER 30

TECHNOPARK TURNS THIRTY TOO

India's first information technology (IT) park, the Technopark, located in Trivandrum (now Thiruvananthapuram), Kerala, was registered on 28 July 1990 and celebrated its 30th anniversary in 2020. Inspired by the Apple facility in USA, it was envisioned to create employability, boost infrastructure and provide a harmonious work setting. The largest of its kind in India, it is spread over 662.54 acres and a built-up space of 102.7 million sq. ft, housing around 450 companies including Tata Consultancy Services, Infosys and Nasscom, among others. These companies employ more than 60,000 IT professionals.

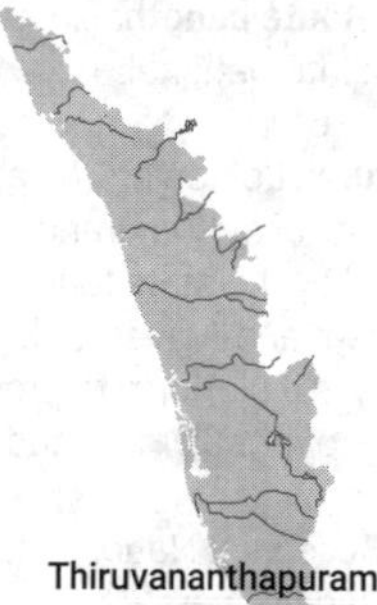

KERALA

- **Area:** 38,863 sq. km
- **Capital:** Thiruvananthapuram
- **Population:** 33.39 million
- **GSDP Growth Rate:** 5.0%
- **Main Language:** Malayalam
- **Literacy Rate:** 94%
- **Higher Education:** Universities: 23; Colleges: 1,280
- **Constitution/Assembly:** Unicameral. Legislative assembly: 141
- **Governor:** Arif Mohammed Khan
- **Chief Minister:** Pinarayi Vijayan
- **Agriculture:** Number/area of operational agricultural holdings: 7.58 million over 1.39 million ha of land; MAJOR CROPS: Natural rubber, pepper, cardamom, nutmeg, cinnamon, coffee and tea
- **Minerals:** China clay (kaolin), limestone, lime shell, silica sand, bauxite and graphite
- **Industries:** Handlooms and textiles, information technology, manufacturing of electronics, tourism and hospitality, agro-based industries and tea production
- **Roads:** National highways: 1,811 km; State highways: 4,342 km; Major district roads: 27,470 km
- **Railway Route Length:** 1,045.36 km
- **Airports:** International: 4
- **Art/Culture:** Classical dance forms like Kathakali, Kutiyattam and Mohiniattam. *Kalamezhuthu* and *kolamezhuthu* (*kolam*) are popular floor decoration art forms.
- **Nature Reserves:** National parks: 6; Wildlife sanctuaries: 17
- **Tourism:** Munnar, Kochi, Jatayu Bird Sculpture, Paradesi Jewish Synagogue, houseboats and backwaters
- **State Symbols:** BIRD: Great hornbill (*Buceros bicornis*); FLOWER: Kanikonna (*Cassia fistula*); TREE: Coconut (*Cocos nucifera*); ANIMAL: Indian elephant (*Elephas maximus indicus*)
- **Do Not Miss!** Boat races are among the grandest traditions of the state. People go to these events in large numbers to watch snake-shaped boats go head to head to the beat of old boat songs.
- **Swachh Survekshan Ranking:** 27
- **UNESCO Heritage (Intangible cultural, or historical, or other sites):** Western Ghats (shared), Kutiyattam (Sanskrit theatre) and Mudiyettu

(ritual theatre and dance drama)
- **Sustainable Development Index Score:** 70
- **Smart Cities:** 2
- **Air Pollution Index:** 50 (Good)

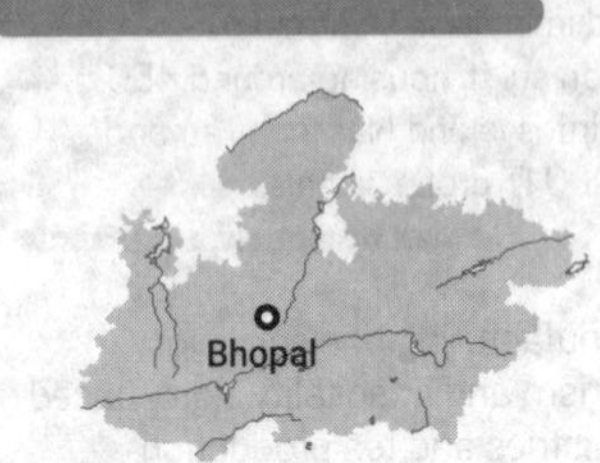

MADHYA PRADESH

- **Area:** 308,245 sq. km
- **Capital:** Bhopal
- **Population:** 72.59 million
- **GSDP Growth Rate:** 7.3%
- **Main Language:** Hindi
- **Literacy Rate:** 69.3%
- **Higher Education:** Universities: 65; Colleges: 1,895
- **Constitution/Assembly:** Unicameral. Legislative assembly: 230
- **Governor:** Mangubhai Chhaganbhai Patel
- **Chief Minister:** Shivraj Singh Chouhan
- **Agriculture:** Number/area of operational agricultural holdings: 10 million over 15.67 million ha of land; MAJOR CROPS: Rice, wheat, jowar, maize, pulses, cotton and sugar cane

A barasingha: the state animal of Madhya Pradesh

- **Minerals:** Diamonds, dolomites, bauxite, coal, limestone and copper
- **Industries:** Automobiles, cement, tourism, electronics and optical fibre, telecommunications and information technology
- **Roads:** National highways: 7,854 km; State highways: 11,389 km; Major district roads: 40,296 km
- **Railway Route Length:** 5,000 km
- **Airports:** International: 1; Domestic: 6
- **Art/Culture:** 'Lokranjan', an annual dance festival at Khajuraho, organized by the state tourism department and Adivasi Lok Kala Academy is a platform to present a number of popular folk and tribal dance forms.
- **Nature Reserves:** National parks: 10; Wildlife sanctuaries: 25
- **Tourism:** Gwalior, Jabalpur, Orchha, Raisen and Bhimbetka
- **State Symbols:** BIRD: Indian paradise flycatcher (*Terpsiphone paradisi*); FLOWER: Madonna lily (*Lilium candidum*); TREE: Banyan (*Ficus benghalensis*); ANIMAL: Swamp deer or barasingha (*Cervus duvaceli*)
- **Do Not Miss!** A ride on the hot-air balloons in Pench National Park over the vast fields encompassed by the River Pench
- **Swachh Survekshan Ranking:** 3
- **UNESCO Heritage (Intangible cultural, historical or other sites):** Khajuraho Group of Monuments, rock shelters of Bhimbetka, Kumbh Mela (shared) at Ujjain and Buddhist monuments at Sanchi
- **Sustainable Development Index Score:** 58
- **Smart Cities:** 7
- **Air Pollution Index:** 117 (Moderate)

MAHARASHTRA

- **Area:** 307,713 sq. km
- **Capital:** Mumbai and Nagpur (Winter)
- **Population:** 112.37 million
- **GSDP Growth Rate:** 7.3%
- **Main Language:** Marathi
- **Literacy Rate:** 82.3%
- **Higher Education:** Universities: 62; Colleges: 4,340
- **Constitution Assembly:** Bicameral. Legislative council: 78; Legislative assembly: 288
- **Governor:** Bhagat Singh Koshyari
- **Chief Minister:** Uddhav Thackeray
- **Agriculture:** Number/area of operational agricultural holdings: 15.28 million over 20.50 million ha of land; MAJOR CROPS: Rice, jowar, bajra, moong, tur and gram
- **Minerals:** Coal, limestone, manganese, iron ore, bauxite, silica sand and sea sand
- **Industries:** Food products, breweries, tobacco and related products, textile products, cinema, printing and publishing, cement, rubber and plastic
- **Roads:** National highways: 15,437 km; State highways: 39,000 km; Major district roads: 109,530 km
- **Railway Route Length:** 5,745.5 km
- **Airports:** International: 3; Domestic: 10
- **Art/Culture:** Festivals such as Ganesh Chaturthi and Gudi Padwa. *Mashru* and *himroo* fabrics are part of the woven art forms.
- **Nature Reserves:** National parks: 6; Wildlife sanctuaries: 48
- **Tourism:** Mumbai, Ajanta, Ellora, Elephanta, Mahabaleshwar, Matheran and Panchgani
- **State Symbols:** BIRD: Yellow-footed green pigeon *(Treron phoenicoptera)*; FLOWER: Jarul (*Lagerstroemia speciosa*); TREE: Mango (*Mangifera indica*); ANIMAL: Indian giant squirrel (*Ratufa indica*)
- **Do Not Miss!** Taraporewala Aquarium in Mumbai, India's oldest aquarium, houses a multitude of freshwater and marine fishes.
- **Swachh Survekshan Ranking:** 2
- **UNESCO Heritage (Intangible cultural, historical or other sites):** Ajanta, Ellora and Elephanta caves, Chhatrapati Shivaji Maharaj Terminus, Western Ghats (shared), Kumbh Mela (shared) at Nashik, and the Victorian and Art Deco ensembles of Mumbai
- **Sustainable Development Index Score:** 64
- **Smart Cities:** 8
- **Air Pollution Index:** 198 (Moderate)

Chhatrapati Shivaji Maharaj Terminus, Mumbai

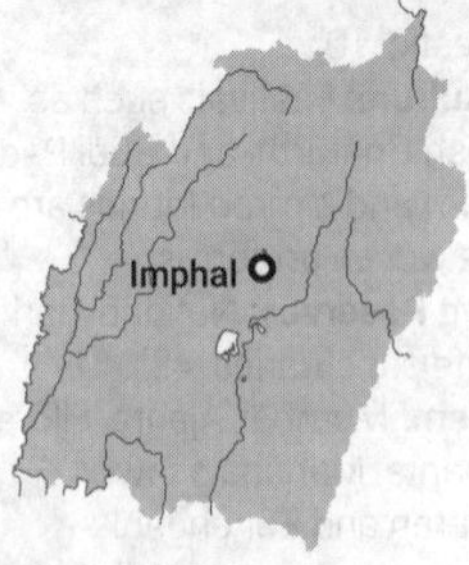

Siroi or shirui lily: the state flower of Manipur

MANIPUR

- **Area:** 22,327 sq. km
- **Capital:** Imphal
- **Population:** 2.85 million
- **GSDP Growth Rate:** Not applicable*
- **Main Languages:** Manipuri, Tangkhul
- **Literacy Rate:** 76.9%
- **Higher Education:** Universities: 6; Colleges: 91
- **Constitution/Assembly:** Unicameral. Legislative assembly: 60
- **Governor:** La. Ganesan
- **Chief Minister:** N. Biren Singh
- **Agriculture:** Number/area of operational agricultural holdings: 0.15 million over 0.17 million ha of land; MAJOR CROPS: Potato, mustard, sugar cane, tobacco, rice, maize and pulses
- **Minerals:** Chromite, limestone and serpentinite, china clay, idocrase and rock salt
- **Industries:** Handloom, agriculture and tourism
- **Roads:** National highways: 1,745 km; State highways: 715 km; Major district roads: 9,467 km
- **Railway Route Length:** 13 km
- **Airport:** International: 1
- **Art/Culture:** Cane and bamboo basketry, pottery, and Manipuri dance
- **Nature Reserves:** National park: 1; Wildlife sanctuaries: 2
- **Tourism:** Shree Govindajee Temple, Moirang, Khwairamband Bazar (Ima Keithel, entirely a women's market), Nupi Lan (Women's War) Memorial Complex and Khonghampat Orchidarium
- **State Symbols:** BIRD: Nongyeen (*Syrmaticus humiae*); FLOWER: Siroi/shirui lily (*Lilium mackliniae*); TREE: Uningthou (*Phoebe hainesiana*); ANIMAL: Sangai deer (*Rucervus eldii eldii*)
- **Do Not Miss!** Loktak Lake, which is known for *phumdi*, a floating mass of vegetation, soil and organic matter that has solidified over time (people can even build houses on it), and the habitat of Sangai deer
- **Swachh Survekshan Ranking:** 20
- **UNESCO Heritage (Intangible cultural, historical or other sites):** Sankirtana, ritual singing, drumming and dancing
- **Sustainable Development Index Score:** 60
- **Smart City:** 1
- **Air Pollution Index:** Not applicable**

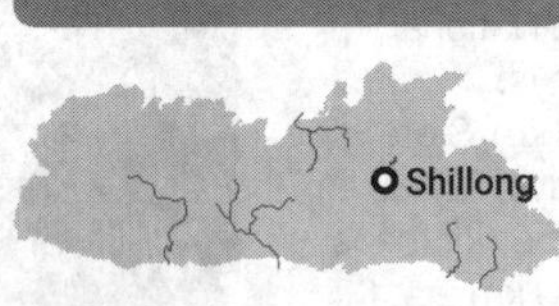

MEGHALAYA

- **Area:** 22,429 sq. km
- **Capital:** Shillong

- **Population:** 2.97 million
- **GSDP Growth Rate:** Not applicable*
- **Main Languages:** Khasi, Pnar, Garo, Bengali, Assamese and English
- **Literacy Rate:** 74.4%
- **Higher Education:** Universities: 10; Colleges: 51
- **Constitution/Assembly:** Unicameral. Legislative assembly: 60
- **Governor:** Satya Pal Malik
- **Chief Minister:** Conrad Kongkal Sangma
- **Agriculture:** Number/area of operational agricultural holdings: 0.23 million over 0.3 million ha of land; MAJOR CROPS: Rice, maize, oranges (Khasi mandarin), pineapple, plums and peaches
- **Minerals:** Limestone, coal, clay (lithomargic), granite, copper ore, silica sand, sillimanite and quartz
- **Industries:** Agriculture and food processing, horticulture, tourism, hydroelectricity, handlooms, cement, handicrafts and sericulture
- **Roads:** National highways: 1,203 km; State highways: 772 km; Major district roads: 5,095 km
- **Railway Route Length:** 8.76 km
- **Airport:** Domestic: 1
- **Art/Culture:** Behdienkhlam is the most important festival and Phawar is a form of Khasi music.
- **Nature Reserves:** National parks: 2; Wildlife sanctuaries: 4
- **Tourism:** Sohra, Shillong, Mawsynram, Mawlynnong, Nohwet, Garo Hills, East Khasi Hills, Mawsmai Falls and Cave
- **State Symbols:** BIRD: Hill myna (*Gracula religiosa*); FLOWER: Lady's slipper orchid (*Paphiopedilum insigne*); TREE: White teak (*Gmelina arborea*); ANIMAL: Clouded leopard (*Neofelis nebulosa*)
- **Do Not Miss!** The Nohkalikai Falls, the highest plunge waterfall in India, falling from a height of 340 m (1,115 ft)
- **Swachh Survekshan Ranking:** 26
- **UNESCO Heritage (Intangible cultural, historical or other sites):** None
- **Sustainable Development Index Score:** 54
- **Smart City:** 1
- **Air Pollution Index:** 58 (Satisfactory)

Living-root Bridges

The living-root bridges, also known locally as *jing kieng jri,* are an indigenous way devised by the Khasi tribe of Meghalaya to cross the turbulent streams in Sohra (earlier Cherrapunji). These bridges are not built, but grown! They are made of thick tangled roots and can support up to 35 people at a time. The bridges are built by planting rubber fig trees (*Ficus elastica*) on both banks of a stream or river, and over a course of 15–30 years, the Khasi people join the elastic roots using a temporary bamboo structure. The bridges can be 45–76 m (147–250 ft) long. Some of the ancient root bridges are believed to be more than 500 years old.

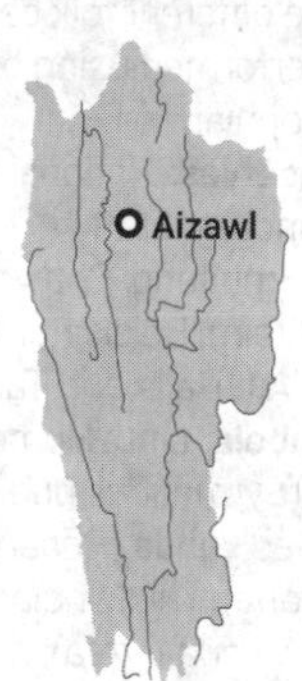

MIZORAM

- **Area:** 21,087 sq. km
- **Capital:** Aizawl
- **Population:** 1.092 million

- **GSDP Growth Rate:** Not applicable*
- **Main Languages:** Mizo and English
- **Literacy Rate:** 91.3%
- **Higher Education:** Universities: 3; Colleges: 32
- **Constitution/Assembly:** Unicameral. Legislative assembly: 40
- **Governor:** Dr Kambhampati Haribabu
- **Chief Minister:** Pu Zoramthanga
- **Agriculture:** Number/area of operational agricultural holdings: 0.09 million over 0.11 million ha of land; MAJOR CROPS: Maize, rice, sugar cane, tapioca, ginger and cotton
- **Minerals:** Sandstone, clay, lignites and pyrites
- **Industries:** Bamboo, sericulture, tourism, agro-products and agro-processing industries
- **Roads:** National highways: 1,382 km; State highways: 170 km; Major district roads: 1,750 km
- **Railway Route Length:** 1.5 km
- **Airport:** Domestic: 1
- **Art/Culture:** Often called the 'songbird of the East', Mizoram resonates with vibrant music, songs and beautiful energetic dances. Among the different folk dances, Cheraw, performed using bamboo poles, is popular.
- **Nature Reserves:** National parks: 2; Wildlife sanctuaries: 9
- **Tourism:** Hmuifang, Phawngpui (the Blue Mountain), Reiek, Palak Lake, Tuirihiau Waterfalls and Tamdil
- **State Symbols:** BIRD: Hume's pheasant (*Syrmaticus humiae*); FLOWER: Red vanda (*Renanthera imschootiana*); TREE: Indian rose chestnut (*Mesua ferrea*); ANIMAL: Saza/serow (*Capricornis thar*)
- **Do Not Miss!** The Mizo Heritage Museum in the capital city
- **Swachh Survekshan Ranking:** 25
- **UNESCO Heritage (Intangible cultural, historical or other sites):** None
- **Sustainable Development Index Score:** 56
- **Smart City:** 1
- **Air Pollution Index:** 150 (Moderate)

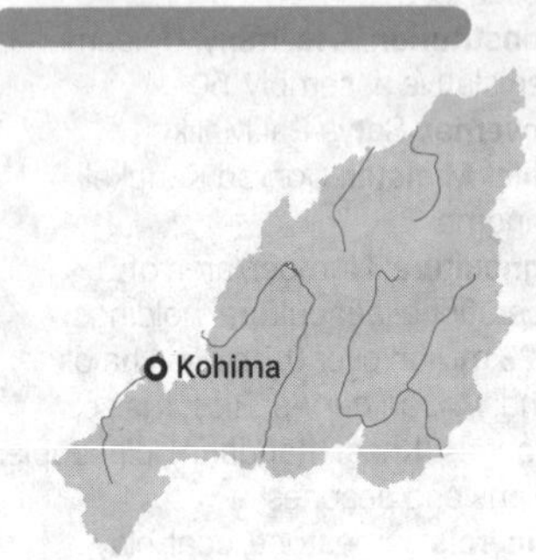

NAGALAND

- **Area:** 16,579 sq. km
- **Capital:** Kohima
- **Population:** 1.99 million
- **GSDP Growth Rate:** Not applicable*
- **Main Languages:** English and Nagamese
- **Literacy Rate:** 79.6%
- **Higher Education:** Universities: 5; Colleges: 66
- **Constitution /Assembly:** Unicameral. Legislative assembly: 60
- **Governor:** Prof. Jagdish Mukhi
- **Chief Minister:** Neiphiu Rio
- **Agriculture:** Number/area of operational agricultural holdings: 0.19 million over 0.95 million ha of land; MAJOR CROP: Rice
- **Minerals:** Coal, limestone, nickel, cobalt, copper, dunite, petroleum and natural gas
- **Industries:** Bamboo processing, agro-based and forest-based industries, food processing, mining, horticulture, tourism, sericulture, handloom and handicrafts
- **Roads:** National highways: 1,173 km; State highways: 722 km; Major

A performance at the Hornbill Festival, Nagaland

district roads: 6,467 km

- **Railway Route Length:** 11.2 km
- **Airport:** Domestic: 1
- **Art/Culture:** The state is linguistically rich with each tribe having its own language. The tribes also celebrate festivals all the year round, earning the state its popular title, 'The Land of Festivals'.
- **Nature Reserves:** National park: 1; Wildlife sanctuaries: 3
- **Tourism:** Kohima (including the War Cemetery), Khonoma, Dimapur, Mokokchung, Diezephe craft village, Kachari ruins, Diphupar and Chumukedima village
- **State Symbols:** BIRD: Blyth's tragopan (*Tragopan blythii*); FLOWER: Rhododendron (*Rhododendron arboreum*); TREE: Alder (*Alnus nepalensis*); ANIMAL: Mithun (*Bos frontalis*)
- **Do Not Miss!** The Hornbill festival, conceived by the state's tourism department and held in the first week of December, is an annual event where all tribes come together to celebrate, exhibit and sell their traditional wares, food and crafts.
- **Swachh Survekshan Ranking:** 19
- **UNESCO Heritage (Intangible cultural, historical or other sites):** None
- **Sustainable Development Index Score:** 57
- **Smart City:** 1
- **Air Pollution Index:** 133 (Moderate)

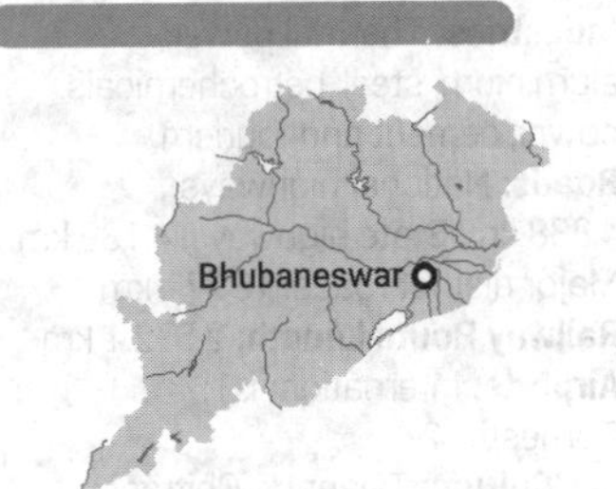

ODISHA

- **Area:** 155,707 sq. km
- **Capital:** Bhubaneswar
- **Population:** 41.98 million
- **GSDP Growth Rate:** 7.1%
- **Main Language:** Odia
- **Literacy Rate:** 72.9%
- **Higher Education:** Universities: 28; Colleges: 1,052
- **Constitution/Assembly:** Unicameral. Legislative assembly: 147

WHAT'S IN A NAME?

In the last three decades, three states had their names changed.

September 2006: Pondicherry to Puducherry. The new name is closer to the original Putucerri (meaning 'new village' in Tamil). Its French colonizers had changed the name to Pondichéry.

January 2007: Uttaranchal to Uttarakhand (meaning 'northern region). The name was given to honour those who had fought for this state in the name of the 'Uttarakhand Andolan'.

September 2011: Orissa to Odisha. The change of name was effected to correct its long-standing Anglicized pronunciation and spelling.

- **Governor:** Prof. Ganeshi Lal
- **Chief Minister:** Naveen Patnaik
- **Agriculture:** Number/area of operational agricultural holdings: 4.86 million over 4.61 million ha of land; MAJOR CROPS: Rice, pulses, oilseeds, jute, coconut, tea, cotton and rubber
- **Minerals:** Iron ore, manganese, coal, bauxite, dolomite and limestone
- **Industries:** Thermal power, aluminium, steel, petrochemicals, power, cement and tourism
- **Roads:** National highways: 4,838 km; State highways: 4,139 km; Major district roads: 16,271 km
- **Railway Route Length:** 2,572.1 km
- **Airports:** International: 1; Domestic: 2
- **Art/Culture:** Talapatra Chitras, an ancient craft – etchings and paintings on palm leaf
- **Nature Reserves:** National parks: 2; Wildlife sanctuaries: 19
- **Tourism:** Puri, Konark, Cuttack, Chandaneswar, Gopalpur, Udayagiri and Khandagiri. Chilika Lake is the largest brackish-water lake in Asia.
- **State Symbols:** BIRD: Indian roller (*Coracias benghalensis*); FLOWER: Ashoka (*Saraca asoca*); TREE: Fig (*Ficus carica*); ANIMAL: Sambar deer (*Rusa unicolor*)
- **Swachh Survekshan Ranking:** 10
- **UNESCO Heritage (Intangible cultural, historical or other sites):** The Sun Temple at Konark and Chhau dance (shared)
- **Sustainable Development Index Score:** 58
- **Smart Cities:** 2
- **Air Pollution Index:** 167 (Moderate)

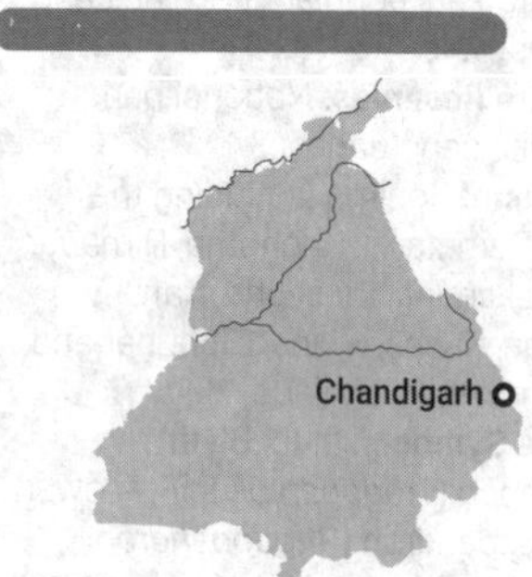

PUNJAB

- **Area:** 50,362 sq. km
- **Capital:** Chandigarh
- **Population:** 27.74 million
- **GSDP Growth Rate:** 6.2%
- **Main Language:** Punjabi
- **Literacy Rate:** 75.8%
- **Higher Education:** Universities: 32;

Colleges: 1,008

- **Constitution/Assembly:** Unicameral. Legislative assembly: 117
- **Governor:** Banwarilal Purohit
- **Chief Minister:** Bhagwant Singh Mann
- **Agriculture:** Number/area of operational agricultural holdings: 1.09 million over 3.95 million ha of land; MAJOR CROPS: Wheat, rice, cotton, sugar cane, yellow mustard, maize, barley and fruits
- **Minerals:** Quartz, silica sand, quartzite and sulphur
- **Industries:** Dairy, agriculture, logistics, handloom and handicraft, food and beverages, real estate and information technology
- **Roads:** National highways: 2,769 km; State highways: 1,103 km; Major district roads: 6,980 km
- **Railway Route Length:** 2,269.3 km
- **Airports:** International: 1; Domestic: 5
- **Art/Culture:** Gatka, Kikli, Jaago, Dhamal, Sammi, Dankara, Julli, Luddi, Jhumar, Giddha and Bhangra are popular folk dance forms.
- **Nature Reserves:** National parks: None ; Wildlife sanctuaries: 13
- **Tourism:** Golden Temple, Jallianwala Bagh and the Wagah border in Amritsar, Bhakra Dam, Qila Androon, Moti Bagh Palace and Chhatbir Zoo in Patiala
- **State Symbols:** BIRD: Northern goshawk (*Accipiter gentilis*); FLOWER: Gladiolus (*Gladiolus grandiflorus*); TREE: Sheesham (*Dalbergia sissoo*); ANIMAL: Blackbuck *(Antilope cervicapra)*
- **Do Not Miss!** Punjabi cuisine: *sarson da saag* with *makke di roti* is famous all over the country.
- **Swachh Survekshan Ranking:** 9
- **UNESCO Heritage (Intangible cultural, historical or other sites):** Traditional craft of making utensils using copper and brass among the Thathera community of Jandiala
- **Sustainable Development Index Score:** 62
- **Smart Cities:** 3
- **Air Pollution Index:** 92 (Satisfactory)

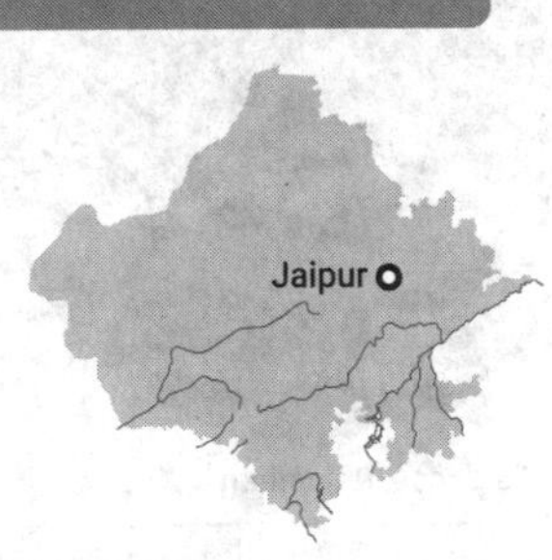

RAJASTHAN

- **Area:** 342,239 sq. km
- **Capital:** Jaipur
- **Population:** 68.548 million
- **GSDP Growth Rate:** 7.2%
- **Main Languages:** Hindi and Rajasthani
- **Literacy Rate:** 66.1%
- **Higher Education:** Universities: 83; Colleges: 2,876
- **Constitution/Assembly:** Unicameral. Legislative assembly: 200
- **Governor:** Kalraj Mishra
- **Chief Minister:** Ashok Gehlot
- **Agriculture:** Number/area of operational agricultural holdings: 7.65 million over 20.87 million ha of land; MAJOR CROPS: Wheat, rice, jowar, bajra, maize, pulses, small millets and mustard
- **Minerals:** Lead, zinc, silver, soapstone, gypsum, limestone, ball clay and jasper
- **Industries:** Mineral processing, tourism and hospitality, agriculture, handicrafts, chemicals, cement and textiles

Roads: National highways: 7,906 km; State highways: 15,019 km; Major district roads: 23,445 km

Kalbelia dance, Rajasthan

- **Railway Route Length:** 5,893 km
- **Airports:** International: 1; Domestic: 5
- **Art/Culture:** Ghoomar, Gair, Chari, Terathali and Kalbelia dance forms, and Kathputli theatre are famous.
- **Nature Reserves:** National parks: 5; Wildlife sanctuaries: 25
- **Tourism:** Jaipur, Jodhpur, Udaipur, Bikaner, Mount Abu (Sirohi) and Ranthambore National Park (Tiger Reserve) in Sawai Madhopur
- **State Symbols:** BIRD: Indian bustard (*Ardeotis nigriceps*); FLOWER: Rohida (*Tecomella undulata*); TREE: Khejri (*Prosopis cineraria*); ANIMAL: Camel (*Camelus dromedarius*) and Chinkara (*Gazella bennettii*)
- **Do Not Miss!** Golden sand dunes in the Thar Desert
- **Swachh Survekshan Ranking:** 11
- **UNESCO Heritage (Intangible cultural, historical or other sites):** Hill forts, Jaipur city, Jantar Mantar, Keoladeo Ghana National Park, Kalbelia folk songs and dances
- **Sustainable Development Index Score:** 57
- **Smart Cities:** 4
- **Air Pollution Index:** 116 (Moderate)

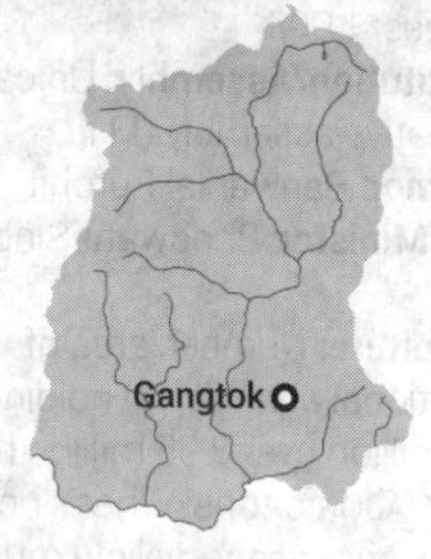

SIKKIM

- **Area:** 7,096 sq. km
- **Capital:** Gangtok
- **Population:** 0.68 million
- **GSDP Growth Rate:** Not applicable*
- **Main Languages:** English; Bhutia, Lepcha and other local languages
- **Literacy Rate:** 81.4%
- **Higher Education:** Universities: 7; Colleges: 16
- **Constitution/Assembly:** Unicameral. Legislative assembly: 32
- **Governor:** Ganga Prasad
- **Chief Minister:** Prem Singh Tamang
- **Agriculture:** Number/area of operational agricultural holdings: 0.07 million over 0.09 million ha of land; MAJOR CROPS: Oranges, large cardamom, ginger, turmeric, cherry, pepper and baby corn
- **Minerals:** Copper, lead, zinc, silver, dolomite, quartzite and talc/steatite/soapstone
- **Industries:** Tourism, agriculture, floriculture, agro-processing, hydroelectric power, tea, electronics and pharmaceuticals
- **Road:** National highways: 463 km; State highways: 663 km; Major district roads: 1,415 km
- **Railway Route Length:** None
- **Airport:** Domestic: 1
- **Art/Culture:** Singhi Chham masked/costumed dance is performed on ceremonial and festive occasions. *Thangka* art, displaying elaborate hand-painting on scrolls, also

flourishes in the region.
- **Nature Reserves:** National park: 1; Wildlife sanctuaries: 7
- **Tourism:** Gangtok, Pelling, Zuluk, Nathu La and Tsomgo Lake
- **State Symbols:** BIRD: Blood pheasant (*Ithaginis cruentus*); FLOWER: Noble dendrobium (*Dendrobium nobile*); TREE: Rhododendron (*Rhododendron arboreum*); ANIMAL: Red panda (*Ailurus fulgens*)
- **Do Not Miss!** Gurudongmar Lake, at more than 5,182 m (17,000 ft) above the mean sea level, is the second highest glacial lake in India.
- **Swachh Survekshan Ranking:** 13
- **UNESCO Heritage (Intangible cultural, historical or other sites):** Khangchendzonga (Kangchenjunga) National Park
- **Sustainable Development Index Score:** 65
- **Smart Cities:** 2
- **Air Pollution Index:** Not applicable**

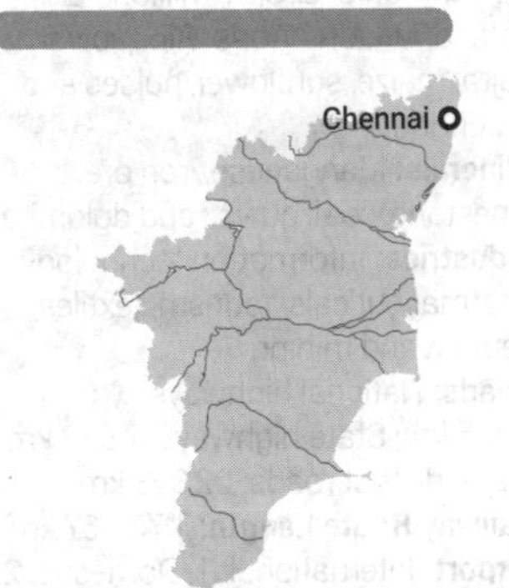

TAMIL NADU

- **Area:** 130,058 sq. km
- **Capital:** Chennai
- **Population:** 72.14 million
- **GSDP Growth Rate:** 8.1%
- **Main Language:** Tamil
- **Literacy Rate:** 80.1%
- **Higher Education:** Universities: 59; Colleges: 2,462
- **Constitution/Assembly:** Unicameral. Legislative assembly: 234
- **Governor:** R.N. Ravi
- **Chief Minister:** M.K. Stalin
- **Agriculture:** Number/area of operational agricultural holdings: 7.93 million over 5.97 million ha of land; MAJOR CROPS: Rice, millets, pulses, sugar cane, cotton, sunflower, coconut and cashew nuts
- **Minerals:** Granite, lignite, graphite, bauxite, magnesite and limestone
- **Industries:** Textiles, heavy commercial vehicles, engineering, information technology, leather tanning industries, cement, electronic hardware and tourism
- **Roads:** National highways: 4,946 km; State highways: 12,095 km; Major district roads: 45,379 km
- **Railway Route Length:** 4,027 km
- **Airports:** International: 4; Domestic: 2
- **Art/Culture:** Pongal is the harvest festival celebrated by farmers in January. Bharatanatyam is a classical dance from the state. At the Natyanjali Dance Festival, the temple city of Chidambaram pays special tribute to Lord Nataraja, the 'Cosmic Dancer'.
- **Nature Reserves:** National parks: 5; Wildlife sanctuaries: 29
- **Tourism:** Chennai, Mamallapuram, Chidambaram, Thanjavur, Srirangam, Madurai and Rameswaram
- **State Symbols:** BIRD: Emerald dove (*Chalcophaps indica*); FLOWER: Gloriosa lily (Kandhal) (*Gloriosa superba*); TREE: Palm tree (*Borassus flabellifer*); ANIMAL: Nilgiri tahr (*Nilgiritragus hylocrius*)
- **Do Not Miss!** The Nilgiri Mountain Railway at Udhagamandalam (part of Mountain Railways of India).
- **Swachh Survekshan Ranking:** 15
- **UNESCO Heritage (Intangible cultural, historical or other sites):**

Entrance of Brihadisvara Temple, Thanjavur, Tamil Nadu

The Great Living Chola Temples, Nilgiri Railway (part of Mountain Railways of India), Group of Monuments at Mamallapuram and the Western Ghats (shared)
- **Sustainable Development Index Score:** 67
- **Smart Cities:** 11
- **Air Pollution Index:** 78 (Satisfactory)

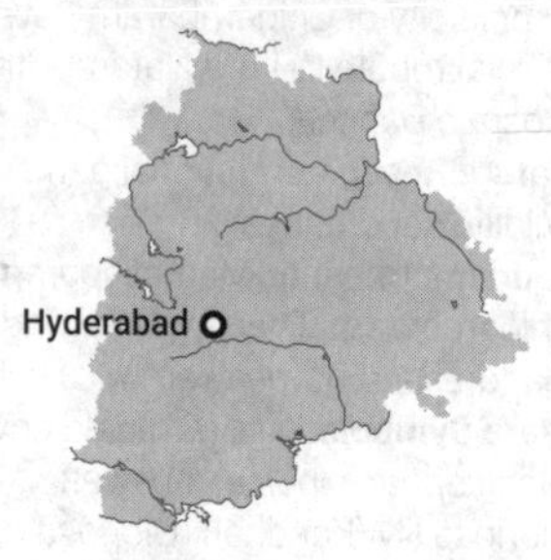

TELANGANA

- **Area:** 112,077 sq. km
- **Capital:** Hyderabad
- **Population:** 35.04 million
- **GSDP Growth Rate:** 10.4%
- **Main Language:** Telugu
- **Literacy Rate:** 66.5%
- **Higher Education:** Universities: 24; Colleges: 1,976
- **Constitution/Assembly:** Bicameral. Legislative council: 40; Legislative assembly: 119
- **Governor:** Dr Tamilisai Soundararajan
- **Chief Minister:** K. Chandrashekar Rao
- **Agriculture:** Number/area of operational agricultural holdings: 5.94 million over 5.97 million ha of land; MAJOR CROPS: Rice, jowar, bajra, maize, sunflower, pulses and groundnut
- **Minerals:** Manganese, iron ore, limestone, coal, quartz and dolomite
- **Industries:** Information technology, pharmaceuticals, tourism, textiles, cement and mining
- **Roads:** National highways: 3,455 km; State highways: 2,553 km; Major district roads: 22,303 km
- **Railway Route Length:** 1,736.67 km
- **Airport:** International: 1; Domestic: 2
- **Art/Culture:** Perini Sivatandavam or the 'dance of warriors'; traditions of storytelling such as Golla Suddulu, Oggu Kathalu and Gotralu
- **Nature Reserves:** National parks: 3; Wildlife sanctuaries: 9
- **Tourism:** Hyderabad, Warangal, Alampur, Adilabad and Nalgonda
- **State Symbols:** BIRD: Palapitta (*Coracias indica*); FLOWER: Tangedu

Puvvu (*Senna auriculata*); TREE: Jammi Chettu (*Prosopis cineraria*); ANIMAL: Jinka (*Axis axis*)
- **Do Not Miss!** The famed Salar Jung Museum in Hyderabad
- **Swachh Survekshan Ranking:** 18
- **UNESCO Heritage (Intangible cultural, historical or other sites):** Kakatiya Rudreshwara (Ramappa) Temple
- **Sustainable Development Index Score:** 67
- **Smart Cities:** 2
- **Air Pollution Index:** 105 (Moderate)

TRIPURA

- **Area:** 10,492 sq. km
- **Capital:** Agartala
- **Population:** 3.68 million
- **GSDP Growth Rate:** Not applicable*
- **Main Languages:** Bengali, Kokborok and English
- **Literacy Rate:** 87.2%
- **Higher Education:** Universities: 4; Colleges: 52
- **Constitution/Assembly:** Unicameral. Legislative assembly: 60
- **Governor:** Satyadeo Narain Arya
- **Chief Minister:** Biplab Kumar Deb
- **Agriculture:** Number/area of operational agricultural holdings: 0.57 million over 0.28 million ha of land; MAJOR CROPS: Pineapple, orange, cashew nut, jackfruit, coconut, tea, rice and rubber
- **Minerals:** Natural gas, glass sands, fireclay, shale and silica sand
- **Industries:** Natural gas, food processing, rubber, tea, bamboo, handloom and handicrafts, sericulture and tourism
- **Roads:** National highways: 806 km; State highways: 329 km; Major district roads: 1,189 km
- **Railway Route Length:** 192.5 km
- **Airport:** Domestic: 1
- **Art/Culture:** Hoza Giri dance of the Reang tribesmen, Garia tribal dance, Dhamail dance and musical duels

Ujjayanta Palace, Agartala, Tripura

(Kabi Gaan)

- **Nature Reserves:** National parks: 2; Wildlife sanctuaries: 4
- **Tourism:** Ujjayanta Palace, Kunjaban Palace, Lake Palace, Unakoti near Kailashahar, Tripura Sundari/ Tripureswari Temple in Udaipur, Dumboor Lake, Rudrasagar, Amarsagar, Jagannath Dighi and Kalyan Sagar
- **State Symbols:** BIRD: Green imperial pigeon (*Ducula aenea*); FLOWER: Indian rose chestnut (*Mesua ferrea*); TREE: Agarwood (*Aquilaria malaccensis*); ANIMAL: Phayre's leaf monkey (*Trachypithecus phayrei*)
- **Do Not Miss!** The Poush Sankranti Fair held every year in January at Tirthamukh to mark the beginning of the sun's northern course
- **Swachh Survekshan Ranking:** 23
- **UNESCO Heritage (Intangible cultural, historical or other sites):** None
- **Sustainable Development Index Score:** 58
- **Smart City:** 1
- **Air Pollution Index:** 163 (Moderate)

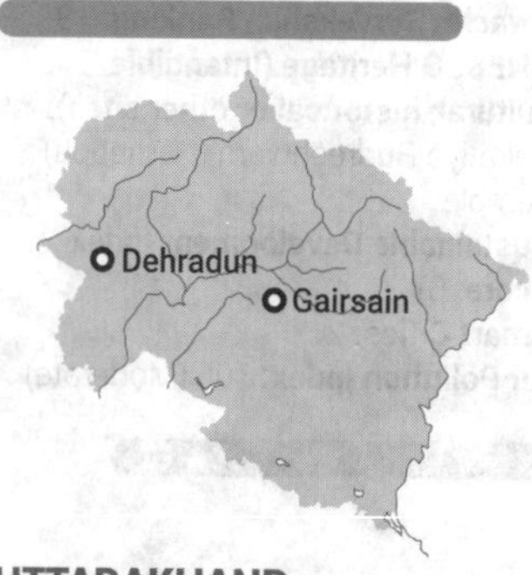

UTTARAKHAND

- **Area:** 53,483 sq. km
- **Capital:** Dehradun; and Gairsain (summer)
- **Population:** 10.17 million
- **GSDP Growth Rate:** Not applicable*

The Valley of Flowers, Uttarakhand

- **Main Languages:** Hindi, Garhwali and Kumaoni
- **Literacy Rate:** 78.8%
- **Higher Education:** Universities: 36; Colleges: 395
- **Constitution/Assembly:** Unicameral. Legislative assembly: 70
- **Governor:** Lt Gen. Gurmit Singh (Retd)
- **Chief Minister:** Pushkar Singh Dhami
- **Agriculture:** Number/area of operational agricultural holdings: 0.88 million over 0.74 million ha of land; MAJOR CROPS: Rice, wheat, soyabean, groundnuts, coarse cereals and pulses
- **Minerals:** Limestone, marble, rock phosphate, dolomite, magnesite and gypsum
- **Industries:** Hydroelectricity, tourism and hospitality, automobile components, agro-based industries and textiles
- **Roads:** National highways: 2,713 km; State highways: 4,329 km; Major district roads: 4,967 km
- **Railway Route Length:** 339.9 km
- **Airports:** Domestic: 3
- **Art/Culture:** Several fairs and festivals celebrated by tribes such as the Bhotias (Shaukas), Tharus, Buxas and Jaunsaris
- **Nature Reserves:** National parks: 6; Wildlife sanctuaries: 7
- **Tourism:** Dehradun, Mussoorie, Jageshwar, Baijnath, Sat Tal, Bhimtal, Harshil, Dhanaulti and Dayara meadow
- **State Symbols:** BIRD: Himalayan monal (*Lophophorus impejanus*); FLOWER: Brahma kamal (*Saussurea obvallata*); TREE: Burans (*Rhododendron arboreum*); ANIMAL: Alpine musk deer (*Moschus chrysogaster*)
- **Do Not Miss!** Maha Ganga *aarti* or the worship of the River Ganga at Triveni Ghat in Rishikesh or Har Ki Pauri in Haridwar
- **Swachh Survekshan Ranking:** 12
- **UNESCO Heritage (Intangible cultural, historical or other sites):** Nanda Devi and Valley of Flowers National Parks, Ramman – ritual theatre of the Garhwal and Kumbh Mela (shared) in Haridwar
- **Sustainable Development Index Score:** 64
- **Smart City:** 1
- **Air Pollution Index:** Not applicable**

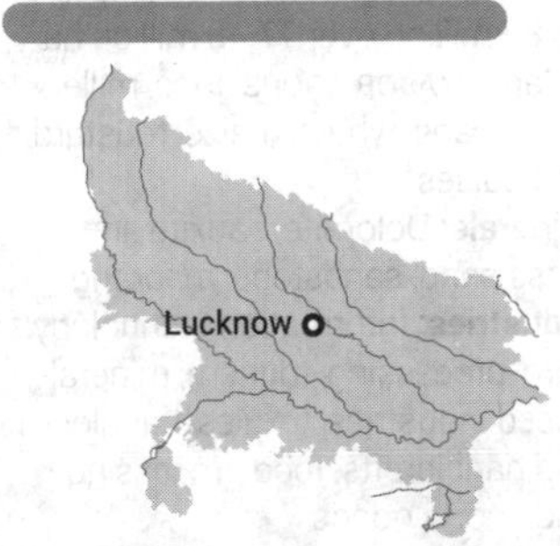

UTTAR PRADESH

- **Area:** 240,928 sq. km
- **Capital:** Lucknow

CHANGING NAMES IN UP

Uttar Pradesh, India's most populous state, saw a few name changes for cities, districts and other areas from 1990 to 2020:

1. Kanpur Dehat to Ramabai Nagar (1 July 2010) and back to Kanpur Dehat (30 July 2012)

2. Allahabad to Prayagraj (16 October 2018)

3. Faizabad District to Ayodhya District (November 2018)

4. Mughalsarai to Pandit Deen Dayal Upadhyaya Nagar (2018)

- **Population:** 199.59 million
- **GSDP Growth Rate:** 6.4%
- **Main Languages:** Hindi and Urdu
- **Literacy Rate:** 67.7%
- **Higher Education:** Universities: 79; Colleges: 6,447
- **Constitution/Assembly:** Bicameral. Legislative council: 100; Legislative assembly: 403
- **Governor:** Anandiben Patel
- **Chief Minister:** Yogi Adityanath
- **Agriculture:** Number/area of operational agricultural holdings: 23.82 million over 17.45 million ha of land; MAJOR CROPS: Rice, millet, sugar cane, wheat, maize, mustard and pulses
- **Minerals:** Dolomite, bauxite and glass sand, sandstone, *maurang*
- **Industries:** Information technology, agro-processing, tourism, mineral-based industries, textiles, handloom and handicrafts, food processing and sports goods
- **Roads:** National highways: 8,712 km; State highways: 7,201 km; Major district roads: 55,061 km
- **Railway Route Length:** 9,077.5 km
- **Airports:** International: 2; Domestic: 5
- **Art/Culture:** Chikankari – traditional, delicate hand embroidery on chiffon, muslin, organza, organdie and silk
- **Nature Reserves:** National park: 1; Wildlife sanctuaries: 26
- **Tourism:** Mathura, Vrindavan, Kanpur, Prayagraj, Varanasi, Agra and Ayodhya
- **State Symbols:** BIRD: Sarus crane (*Grus antigone*); FLOWER: Palash (*Butea monosperma*); TREE: Ashoka (*Saraca asoca*); ANIMAL: Barasingha (*Rucervus duvaucelii*)
- **Do Not Miss!** Varanasi, located on the banks of the River Ganga, is a holy city for Hindus.
- **Swachh Survekshan Ranking:** 7
- **UNESCO Heritage (intangible cultural, historical or other sites):** Taj Mahal, Fatehpur Sikri and Agra Fort, and Kumbh Mela (shared) in Prayagraj
- **Sustainable Development Index Score:** 55
- **Smart Cities:** 10
- **Air Pollution Index:** 302 (Very Poor)

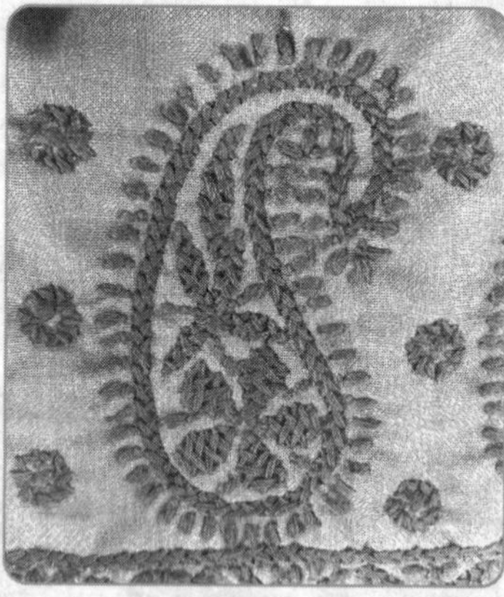

Chikankari embroidery, a traditional hand embroidery form of Uttar Pradesh

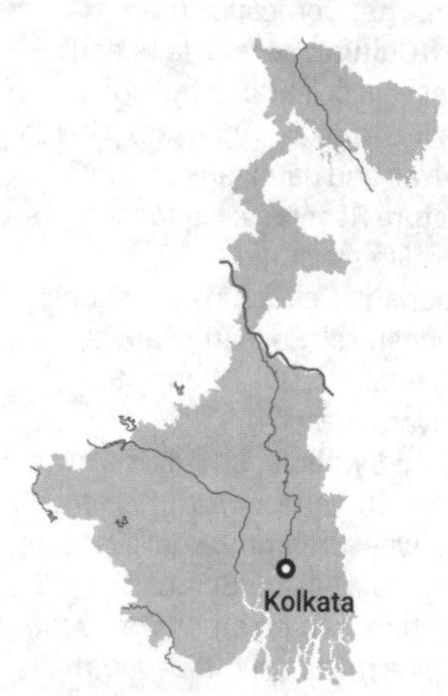

WEST BENGAL

- **Area:** 88,752 sq. km
- **Capital:** Kolkata

- **Population:** 91.28 million
- **GSDP Growth Rate:** 9.1%
- **Main Language:** Bengali
- **Literacy Rate:** 76.3%
- **Higher Education:** Universities: 45; Colleges: 1,370
- **Constitution/Assembly:** Unicameral. Legislative assembly: 294
- **Governor:** Jagdeep Dhankhar
- **Chief Minister:** Mamata Banerjee
- **Agriculture:** Number/area of operational agricultural holdings: 7.24 million over 5.48 million ha of land; MAJOR CROPS: Jute, rice, tea, maize and sugar cane
- **Minerals:** China clay resources, dolomite, coal and fireclay
- **Industries:** Electronics and information technology, iron and steel, metallurgy, engineering, textiles, leather products and aquaculture
- **Roads:** National highways: 2,956 km; State highways: 3,262 km; Major district roads: 10,449 km
- **Railway Route Length:** 4,135.2 km
- **Airports:** International: 2; Domestic: 5
- **Art/Culture:** Baul singing is an ancient tradition, besides Patachitra art, *dhokra* metal casting, Bankura terracotta horses and Kantha embroidery.
- **Nature Reserves:** National parks: 6; Wildlife sanctuaries: 16
- **Tourism:** Darjeeling, Santiniketan, Digha, Shankarpur, Kolkata, Purulia, Howrah and Dakshineswar
- **State Symbols:** BIRD: White-throated kingfisher (*Halcyon smyrnensis*); FLOWER: Night-flowering jasmine (*Nyctanthes arbortristis*); TREE: Chhatim tree (*Alstonia scholaris*); ANIMAL: Fishing cat (*Prionailurus viverrinus*)
- **Do Not Miss!** A ride on the city tram and India's first subway rail. Kolkata is considered to be the only city in India with all modes of transportation – land, water and air.
- **Swachh Survekshan Ranking:** Not applicable***
- **UNESCO Heritage (Intangible cultural, historical or other sites):** Darjeeling Himalayan Railway (part of Mountain Railways of India), Chhau dance (shared), Sunderbans National Park and Durga Puja
- **Sustainable Development Index Score:** 60
- **Smart City:** 1
- **Air Pollution Index:** 317 (Very Poor)

UNION TERRITORIES

ANDAMAN AND NICOBAR ISLANDS

- **Area:** 8,249 sq. km
- **Capital:** Port Blair
- **Population:** 0.43 million
- **Main Languages:** Hindi, Nicobarese, Bengali, Tamil, Malayalam, Telugu
- **Literacy Rate:** 86.6%
- **Higher Education:** Universities: None; Colleges: 8
- **Constitution/Assembly:** The Union Territory is governed by the Central government. A lieutenant governor appointed by the president of India presides over the territory.
- **Lt Governor:** Admiral Devendra Kumar Joshi (Retd)
- **Agriculture:** Number/area of operational agricultural holdings: 0.012 million over 0.021 million ha of

Glass-bottomed boats moored at Jolly Buoy Island, Andaman and Nicobar Islands

land; MAJOR CROPS: Rice, coconut, areca nut, pulses and oilseeds

- **Minerals:** Subeconomic concentrations
- **Industries:** Small-scale village and handicraft industries, fish processing, production of polythene bags, steel furniture, mild steel barrels, aluminium doors and windows
- **Roads:** National highways: 330 km; State highways: 266 km; Major district roads: 139 km
- **Railway Route Length:** None
- **Airport:** International: 1
- **Art/Culture:** The indigenous peoples of the islands belong to four major tribes: The Great Andamanese, the Onge, the Jarawa and the Sentinelese. They are tribes of hunter-gatherers.
- **Nature Reserves:** National parks: 6; Wildlife sanctuaries: 96
- **Tourism:** Cellular Jail, National Memorial, Marine Museum, Water Sports Complex, Mahatma Gandhi Marine National Park, islands such as Ross, Viper, Havelock and Neil
- **Official Symbols**: BIRD: Andaman wood pigeon (*Columba palumboides*); FLOWER: Andaman pyinma (*Lagerstroemia hypoleuca*); TREE: Andaman padauk (*Pterocarpus dalbergioides*); ANIMAL: Dugong or sea cow (*Dugong dugon*)
- **Do Not Miss!** The glass-bottomed boat ride at Jolly Buoy Island
- **Swachh Survekshan Ranking:** Not applicable***
- **UNESCO Heritage (Intangible cultural, historical or other sites):** None
- **Sustainable Development Index Score:** 61
- **Smart City:** 1
- **Air Pollution Index:** Not applicable**

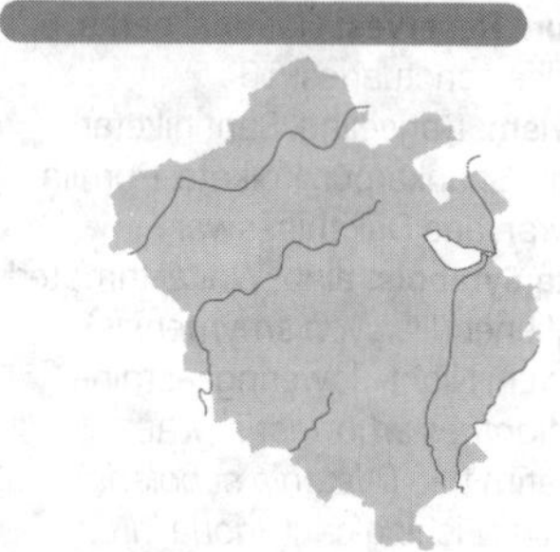

CHANDIGARH

- **Area:** 114 sq. km
- **Population:** 1.05 million

Nek Chand's marvellous Rock Garden, Chandigarh

- **Main Languages:** Hindi, Punjabi and English
- **Literacy Rate:** 86%
- **Higher Education:** Universities: 3; Colleges: 25
- **Constitution/Assembly:** It has only one parliamentary constituency.
- **Administrator:** Banwarilal Purohit
- **Agriculture:** Number/area of operational agricultural holdings: 0.001 million over 0.001 million ha of land; MAJOR CROPS: Rice, wheat and maize
- **Minerals:** None
- **Industries:** Light engineering industry, industrial fasteners, electrical/ electronic items, machine tools, pharmaceuticals, plastic goods, sanitary fittings, steel/ wooden furniture and food products
- **Roads:** National highways: 15 km; State highways: 200 km; Major district roads: 83 km
- **Railway Route Length:** 15.7 km
- **Airport:** International: 1
- **Art/Culture:** Chandigarh shares the cultural aspects of both Haryana and Punjab, and hosts cultural festivals annually, such as the Festival of Gardens and the Annual Chandigarh Carnival.
- **Nature Reserves**: National parks: None; Wildlife sanctuaries: 2
- **Tourism:** Sukhna Lake, Rock Garden, International Dolls Museum and Sector-17 Plaza
- **Official Symbols:** BIRD: Indian grey hornbill (*Ocyceros birostris*); FLOWER: Dhak (*Butea monosperma*); TREE: Mango (*Mangifera indica*); ANIMAL: Grey mongoose (*Herpestes edwardsii*)

- **Do Not Miss!** Chandigarh War Memorial, which is located in a bougainvillea garden
- **Swachh Survekshan Ranking:** Not applicable***
- **UNESCO Heritage (Intangible cultural, historical or other sites):** The architectural work of Le Corbusier
- **Sustainable Development Index Score:** 70
- **Smart City:** 1
- **Air Pollution Index:** 98 (Satisfactory)

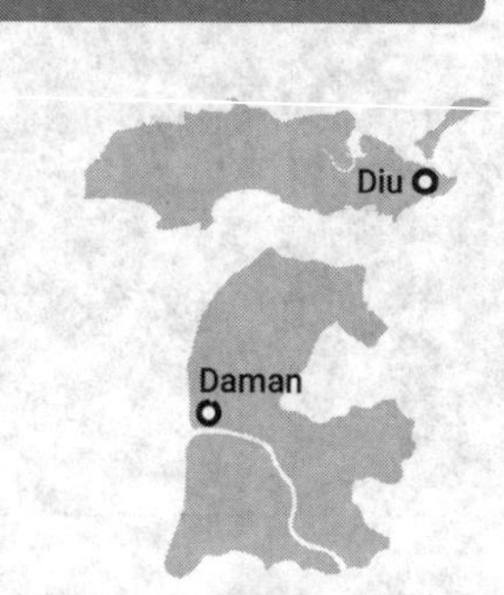

DADRA AND NAGAR HAVELI AND DAMAN AND DIU

- **Area:** 603 sq. km
- **Capital:** Daman
- **Population:** 0.58 million
- **Main Languages:** Gujarati and Hindi
- **Literacy Rate:** 81.65% (average of the two)
- **Higher Education:** Universities: None; Colleges: 18
- **Constitution/Assembly:** The territory has only one parliamentary constituency.
- **Administrator:** Praful Patel
- **Agriculture:** Number/area of operational agricultural holdings: 0.023 million over 0.024 million ha of land; MAJOR CROPS: Rice, bajra, mangoes and sapota (*Manilkara zapota*)
- **Minerals:** Limestone (marginal)
- **Industries:** Textiles and yarns, plastic, rubber, chemical material production and metal-based units
- **Roads:** National highways: 53 km; State highways: 52 km; Major district roads: 289 km
- **Railway Route Length:** None
- **Airports:** Domestic: 1
- **Art/Culture:** Tribal festivals such as Kanseri festival, Divaso festival, Garba festival, folk-dance festival and Vagh Baras
- **Nature Reserves:** National parks: None; Wildlife sanctuaries: 2
- **Tourism:** Tadkeshwar Mahadev Mandir, Deer Park at Khanvel, Dudhni Lake, Forts of Moti Daman and Nani Daman, Basilica of Bom Jesus, Dadra, and Hirwa Van Garden at Silvassa
- **Official Symbols**: Not designated
- **Do Not Miss!** The Tribal Museum in Silvassa is a tribute to and an effort to safeguard and depict the rich legacy of tribal culture and society in its untouched form. The museum also showcases puppets and dolls depicting a unique way of life.
- **Swachh Survekshan Ranking:** Not applicable***
- **UNESCO Heritage (Intangible cultural, historical or other sites):** None

Asia's Longest Beach Festival

Festa de Diu, hosted in Daman and Diu, is a festival that goes on for the longest duration reportedly in all of Asia. Starting at the beginning of December and concluding in mid-February, it caters to music, art, adventure, entertainment and culture enthusiasts in a beautiful location. The festival schedules events based on a theme every week.

SUPER 30

ONLY MERGER IN 30 YEARS!

The Union Territories of Dadra and Nagar Haveli, and Daman and Diu were combined as one on 26 January 2020. This is the first time in the last three decades that two UTs have been merged into one. The reason for the move was to ensure efficient administration and to prevent duplication of work. Located along the western coast near Gujarat, both UTs were liberated from Portuguese rule in December 1961.

- **Sustainable Development Index Score:** 63; 61
- **Smart Cities:** 2
- **Air Pollution Index:** Not applicable**

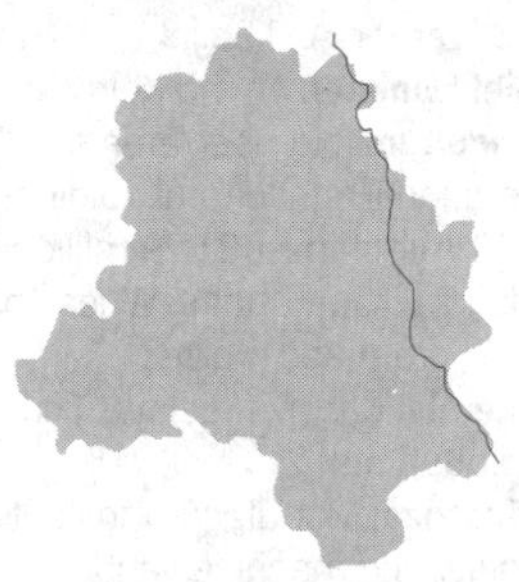

NATIONAL CAPITAL TERRITORY OF DELHI

- **Area:** 1,484 sq. km
- **Population:** 16.75 million
- **Main Languages:** Hindi, Punjabi, Urdu and English
- **Literacy Rate:** 86.2%
- **Higher Education:** Universities: 27; Colleges: 178
- **Constitution/Assembly:** Unicameral. Legislative assembly: 70

Lotus Temple, Delhi

- **Lt Governor:** Anil Baijal
- **Chief Minister:** Arvind Kejriwal
- **Agriculture:** Number/area of operational agricultural holdings: 0.021 million over 0.029 million ha of land; MAJOR CROPS: Wheat, bajra, jowar, gram and maize
- **Minerals:** Kaolin, fireclay, silica sand and quartzite
- **Industries:** Manufacturing light engineering machines and automobile parts, sports goods, bicycles, footwear, textiles and leather goods
- **Roads:** National highways: 69 km; Major district roads: 2,462 km (state highways not classified)
- **Railway Route Length:** 183.3 km
- **Airport:** International: 1
- **Art/Culture:** The Tourism and Transportation Development Corporation organizes events such as the Roshanara Festival, Shalimar Festival, Qutub Festival, Winter Carnival, Garden Tourism Festival, Jahan-e-Khusrau Festival and Mango Festival every year.
- **Nature Reserves:** National parks: None; Wildlife sanctuary: 1
- **Tourism:** Rashtrapati Bhavan, Lal Qila (Red Fort), Jama Masjid, Qutub Minar, India Gate, Humayun's Tomb, National Museum and Lotus Temple
- **Official Symbols**: BIRD: House sparrow (*Passer domesticus*); ANIMAL: Nilgai (*Boselaphus tragocamelus*)
- **Do Not Miss!** The Sulabh International Museum of Toilets in Mahavir Enclave is the only such museum in the world.
- **Swachh Survekshan Ranking:** Not applicable***
- **UNESCO Heritage (Intangible cultural, historical or other sites):** Humayun's Tomb, Qutub Minar complex and Red Fort complex
- **Sustainable Development Index Score:** 61
- **Smart City:** 1
- **Air Pollution Index:** 334 (Very Poor)

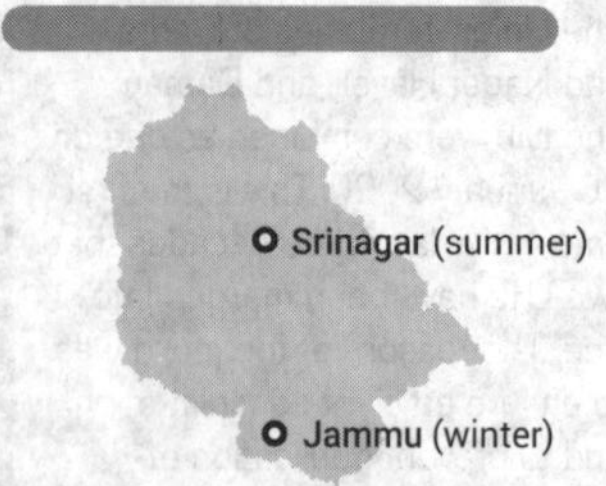

JAMMU AND KASHMIR

- **Area:** 42,241 sq. km
- **Capital:** Srinagar (summer); Jammu (winter)
- **Population:** 12.2 million
- **Main Languages:** Urdu, Kashmiri and Dogri
- **Literacy Rate:** 67.2% (before the division)
- **Higher Education:** Universities: 13; Colleges: 291
- **Constitution/Assembly:** Unicameral. Legislative assembly: to be announced
- **Lt Governor:** Manoj Sinha
- **Agriculture:** Number/area of operational agricultural holdings: Not announced; MAJOR CROPS: Apples, rice, wheat, saffron and cumin
- **Minerals:** Limestone, chromite, bauxite, coal and lignite
- **Industries:** Machinery, sericulture, horticulture and handicrafts
- **Roads:** National highways: 2,601 km; State highways: 130 km; Major district roads: 11,272 km (all prior to the division)
- **Railway Route Length:** 298.2 km
- **Airports:** International: 1; Domestic: 1
- **Art/Culture:** Woodcarving, papier mâché, hand embroidery, carpet-weaving, and musical traditions employing the *rabab* and the santoor

SUPER 30

REORGANIZING THE MAP

The following states have been divided up to make new states and Union Territories in the last 30 years.

	Date	Split from	New State/Union Territories
1	1 November 2000	Madhya Pradesh	Chhattisgarh
2	9 November 2000	Uttar Pradesh	Uttaranchal was renamed Uttarakhand on 1 January 2007
3	15 November 2000	Bihar	Jharkhand
4	31 October 2019	Jammu and Kashmir	Divided into two Union Territories: Jammu and Kashmir, and Ladakh

- **Nature Reserves:** National parks: 3; Wildlife sanctuaries: 13
- **Tourism:** Kashmir Valley, Dal Lake, Gulmarg, Pahalgam and Shri Vaishno Devi shrine
- **Official Symbols:** BIRD: Black-necked crane (*Grus nigricollis*); FLOWER: Lotus (*Nelumbo nicifera*); TREE: Chinar tree (*Planatus orientalis*); ANIMAL: Hangul (*Cervus elaphus hanglu*)
- **Do not miss!** Carved walnut wood is a local speciality. Walnut trees locally called 'doon kul' are traditionally cut only on maturation after hundreds of years.
- **Swachh Survekshan Ranking:** Not Applicable***
- **UNESCO Heritage (Intangible

A chinar garden in autumn in the Kashmir Valley

cultural, or historical, or other sites): None
- **Sustainable Development Index Score:** 59
- **Smart Cities**: 2
- **Air Pollution Index:** Not applicable*

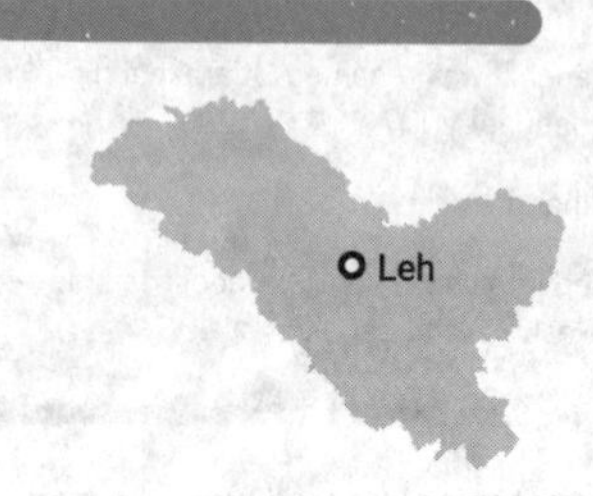

LADAKH

- **Area:** 59,146 sq. km
- **Capital:** Leh, Kargil
- **Population:** 0.27 million
- **Main Languages:** Ladakhi (Bhoti), Tibetan, Urdu and Hindi
- **Literacy Rate:** Leh: 62%
- **Higher Education:** Universities: 1; Colleges: 3
- **Constitution/Assembly:** The territory is represented by a single constituency in the Parliament.
- **Lt Governor:** Radha Krishna Mathur
- **Agriculture:** Number/area of operational agricultural holdings: Not announced; MAJOR CROPS: Wheat, barley, pulses, fruits, oilseeds
- **Minerals:** Borax, potash, sulphur and pyrites
- **Industries:** Tourism, mountaineering and agriculture
- **Roads:** National highways, state highways and major district roads: Data unavailable
- **Railway Route Length:** None
- **Airport:** Domestic: 1
- **Art/Culture:** Woodcarving, papier mâché and *thangka* art
- **Nature Reserves:** National park: 1; Wildlife sanctuaries: 2
- **Tourism:** Leh, Pangong Tso, Nubra Valley, Shanti Stupa, Alchi Monastery and Thikse Monastery
- **Official Symbols:** Not announced
- **Do Not Miss!** The Indian Astronomical Observatory at Hanle is one of the world's highest sites for optical, infrared and gamma-ray telescopes.
- **Swachh Survekshan Ranking:** Not Applicable***

Thikse Monastery, Leh, Ladakh

- **UNESCO Heritage (Intangible cultural, historical or other sites):** Buddhist chanting of Ladakh: recitation of sacred Buddhist texts in the trans-Himalayan Ladakh region.
- **Sustainable Development Index Score:** 59
- **Smart Cities:** None
- **Air Pollution Index:** Not applicable*

LAKSHADWEEP

- **Area:** 32 sq. km
- **Capital:** Kavaratti
- **Population:** 0.064 million
- **Main Languages:** Malayalam, Jeseri (Dweep Bhasha) and Mahal
- **Literacy Rate:** 91.8%
- **Higher Education:** Universities: None; Colleges: None
- **Constitution/Assembly:** It is represented by one constituency in the Parliament.
- **Administrator:** Praful Patel
- **Agriculture:** Number/area of operational agricultural holdings: 0.010 million over 0.003 million ha of land; MAJOR CROP: Coconut
- **Minerals:** Limestone/lime shell
- **Industries:** Coconut fibre extraction and conversion into fibre products, coir fibre factories and tourism
- **Roads:** Not recorded
- **Railway Route Length:** None
- **Airport:** Domestic: 1
- **Art/Culture:** Kolkali and Parichakali are the two popular folk-art forms, and Lava is the most popular local dance form.
- **Nature Reserves:** National parks: None; Wildlife sanctuary: 1
- **Tourism:** Agatti, Bangaram, Kalpeni, Kadmat, Kavaratti and Minicoy
- **Official Symbols**: BIRD: Noddy tern (*Anous stolidus*); TREE: Breadfruit (*Artocarpus altilis*); ANIMAL: Butterfly fish (*Chaetodon falcula*)
- **Do Not Miss!** An open-sea dive at Minicoy Island.
- **Swachh Survekshan Ranking:** Not applicable***
- **UNESCO Heritage (Intangible cultural, historical or other sites):** None
- **Sustainable Development Index**

Minicoy Island, Lakshadweep

- **Score:** 63
- **Smart City:** 1
- **Air Pollution Index:** Not applicable**

PUDUCHERRY

- **Area:** 479 sq. km
- **Capital:** Puducherry
- **Population:** 1.24 million
- **Main Languages:** Tamil, Telugu, Malayalam, English and French
- **Literacy Rate:** 85.8%
  Higher Education: Universities: 4; Colleges: 74
- **Constitution/Assembly:** Unicameral. Legislative assembly: 33
- **Lt Governor:** Dr Tamilisai Soundararajan
- **Chief Minister:** N. Rangaswamy
- **Agriculture:** Number/area of operational agricultural holdings: 0.034 million over 0.021 million ha of land; MAJOR CROPS: Rice, pulses, coconut, areca nut and spices
- **Minerals:** Limestone, kaolin and lignite
- **Industries:** Food and beverages, pharmaceuticals, mechanical and chemical industries
- **Roads:** National highways: 64 km; Major district roads: 397 km
- **Railway Route Length:** 22.16 km
- **Airport/Port:** Domestic: 1
- **Art/Culture:** Korai mats and handmade Bommai dolls made of terracotta, papier mâché and plaster
- **Nature Reserves:** National parks: None; Wildlife sanctuary: 1
- **Tourism:** Backwaters, rivers, beaches and other areas developed as sustainable eco-tourist facilities.
- **Official Symbols:** BIRD: Koel (*Eudynamys scolopaceus*); FLOWER: Cannonball (*Couroupita guianensis*); TREE: Bael (*Aegle marmelos*); ANIMAL: Indian palm squirrel (*Funambulus palmarum*)
- **Do Not Miss!** A guided tour on vintage bicycles through the classical French colonies and traditional Tamil settlements.
- **Swachh Survekshan Ranking:** Not applicable***
- **UNESCO Heritage (Intangible cultural, historical or other sites):** None
- **Sustainable Development Index Score:** 66
- **Smart City:** 1
- **Air Pollution Index:** Not applicable**

Bommai – traditional dolls made by hand, using terracotta, in Puducherry

Compiled by ***Jatin Ahuja,*** *@wildernama (Instagram)*

NOTE: CCA-SA refers to the Creative Commons Attribution-Share Alike Wikimedia Commons/International Wikimedia Commons licences; Public Domain/PD: All public domain photographs have been sourced from: Wikimedia Commons/Public Domain; PIB: Press Information Bureau; GoI: Government of India.

THE HUMAN STORY 1–76

Images are by courtesy of the record holders; **13: bottom:** Shakuntala Devi: Hindustan Times; **22: top:** Vanitha Balasubramaniyan Iyer: by courtesy of N.V. Balasubramanian; **29: bottom:** Baby: Shutterstock.com; **69: top:** Khushi: by courtesy of Abhimanyu Kumar; **73: top:** Vikas Khanna: Hindustan Times; **76: top:** Chekutty dolls: by courtesy of chekutty.in.

THRILLING 30s 77–80

Images are by courtesy of the record holders.

STRUCTURES 81–112

Opener pic, 81: Shutterstock.com; **85: middle:** Longest corridor: CRS PHOTO/ Shutterstock.com; **86–87: bottom:** Bharatpur palace: poojam7/Shutterstok.com; **90: top right:** Lepakshi Temple: Shutterstock.com; **91: middle:** Nataraja temple: Shutterstock.com; **92: bottom:** Akshardham temple: Shutterstock.com; **96: background:** by courtesy of Jatayu Earth Center; **98: top:** B.V. Doshi: by courtesy of Sanyam Bahga; **99: top:** Krushi Bhawan: by courtesy of Andre J Fanthome/Studio Lotus; **101: top:** Chenab bridge: by courtesy of Bhisham Pratap Padha; **102: middle:** Indira Gandhi canal: Shutterstock.com; **104: left:** Lighthouse: Shutterstock.com; **106: top left:** The Light Box: by courtesy of RC Architects; **110: middle:** Lamo centre: by courtesy of Thomas Kelly/ LAMO Trust, Leh; **111: middle:** Floating cottages: by courtesy of Poovar Island Resort; **112: middle:** Gulmarg Gondola: Public Domain/Vikas Yadav.

EDUCATION 113–148

Opener pic, 113: CRS PHOTO/ Shutterstock.com; **114: bottom:** The Akshar Foundation School: by courtesy of The Akshar Foundation; **118: bottom:** Digital Education: bodom/Shutterstock.com; **119: top:** Happiness Classes: Hindustan Times; **120: top:** Computer classrooms: by courtesy of Edimpact; **123: top:** IIT Roorkee: Shutterstock.com; **126: bottom:** Abhyas Gali: Hindustan Times; **127: bottom:** IIM Calcutta: Hindustan Times; **128: top:** Ranjitsinh Disale: by courtesy of Varkey Foundation; **130: top:** Kadambini Ganguly: Public domain-India; **134: middle:** Dr Manabi Bandyopadhyay: Hindustan Times; **135: background**: Shutterstock.com; **142: middle:** Partition Museum: Shutterstock.com; **145: top:** Indian Museum: Public Domain; **147: top:** Avi Gupta: by courtesy of Jeopardy Productions, Inc.

MEDIA AND COMMUNICATIONS 149–184

Opener pic, 149: Geralt/Pixabay.com; **151: middle:** French Alps: Shutterstock.com; **153: middle:** *The Hindu:* by courtesy of Bilal Ahmad; **155: bottom right:** *Chandamama*: by courtesy of Sree Ganesh Thottempudi; **163: top:** Ravish Kumar: Government Open Data License–India (GODL)/Vice President's Secretariat; **173: bottom right:** Dakshin Gangotri: Tristan tan/Shutterstock.com; **172: top:** Mumbai post office: Snehal Jeevan Pailkar/Shutterstock.com; **173: middle right:** Raja Rammohun Roy: brandonht/Shutterstock.com; **174: top right:** Henry Dunant: rook76/ Shutterstock.com; **177: background:** Telephone: Shutterstock.com; **178: top:** BSNL: lakshmiprasada S/

Shutterstock.com; **182: top right:** WeChat: Ju Jae-young/ Shutterstock.com.

AGRICULTURE 185–204

Opener pic, 185: Sarangib/Pixabay. com; **187: top:** Locust: Hindustan Times; **188: middle:** Tocklai: Daniel J. Rao/Shutterstock.com; **190: top:** Farmers' protest: CCO 1.0 Universal Public Domain Dedication/Randeep Maddoke; **192: bottom:** Araku coffee: by courtesy of Nevin John; **196: top:** Asafoetida: Shutterstock.com; **198: top:** Amrita Patel: Government Open Data License–India (GODL)/Prime Minister's Office; **202: top:** K.C. Rekha: Vivek R Nair/Hindustan Times; **204: top:** Steam tractor: Shutterstock.com.

TRANSPORT 205–228

Opener pic, 205: Shutterstock.com; **206: bottom left:** S.V. Setty: Public Domain; **208: bottom:** Air India: Komenton/Shutterstock.com; **210: bottom:** Boeing 787 Dreamliner: vaalaa/Shutterstock.com; **211: background:** Captain Indraani Singh: by courtesy of Captain Indraani Singh; **214: top left:** Restaurant on Wheels: by courtesy of https://indiarailinfo.com; **219: bottom right:** Nitin Gadkari: Government Open Data License–India (GODL)/Ministry of Water Resources; **220: top right:** Gendered lights: by courtesy of Satvik Tejasvi; **222: top:** Hop-on Toilets: by courtesy of SaraPlast Pvt. Ltd; **223: bottom:** Highest filling station: touringdiaries/Shutterstock.com; **228: bottom:** Shipping Corporation of India: pjhpix/Shutterstock.com.

THE NATURAL WORLD 229–252

Opener pic, 229: Shutterstock.com; **231: top right:** Caving expedition: Amitrane /Shutterstock.com; **232: top left:** Aghanashini: Shutterstock.com; **234: top left:** Blackbuck: Shutterstock. com; **235: top left:** Elephant Hospital: by courtesy of Wildlife SOS India; **236: top right:** Snow leopard: Shutterstock.com; **237: top:** Peregrine falcon: Shutterstock. com; **bottom:** Vijay Cavale: by courtesy of Shashank Dalvi; **238: top:** Blue Indian Roller: by courtesy of Bahar Nature Foundation; **bottom right:** Bird atlas: Hindustan Times; **240: bottom right:** *Raorchestes chalazodes*: by courtesy of Dr Seshadri K.S.; **242: bottom:** Gharial: Shutterstock.com; **243: bottom right:** Romulus Whitaker: Hindustan Times; **244: bottom right:** Star tortoise: Shutterstock.com; **246: bottom:** Eucalyptus trees: Shutterstock.com; **251: bottom:** Orchids: by courtesy of the record holder; **252: middle:** Mango leaf: by courtesy of the record holder.

ENVIRONMENT AND SUSTAINABILITY 253–268

Opener pic, 253, from top, clockwise: Shutterstock.com; by courtesy of the record holders; Kaboompics.com/ pexels.com; **254: bottom:** Reverse vending machine: by courtesy of GEM Enviro Management; **255: top:** *Kulhad*: Shutterstock.com; **middle:** Bamboo toothbrush: by courtesy of the record holder; **256: top:** B.Y.O.C. grocery store: by courtesy of Bittu John; **257: bottom:** Chandrabhaga beach: Shutterstock. com; **258: top:** Car dustbins: by courtesy of the record holder; **260: bottom:** Neem celebration: courtesy of the record holder; **261: top right:** Elephant: Shutterstock.com; **262: top:** Aarey forest: Hindustan Times; **263: bottom:** Robin: Shutterstock.com; **264: top:** Kaziranga: Anwesha Langthasa/ Shutterstock.com; **266: bottom:** Udit Singhal: by courtesy of Udit Singhal; **267: top:** Green leaves: ismanoor/ Pixabay.com; **268: background:** Cyclone Amphan: Shutterstock.com.

PERFORMING ARTS 269-298

Opener pic, 269: Shutterstock.com; **271: top right:** *Boogie Woogie:* Hindustan Times; **273: top right:** Narthaki Nataraj: by courtesy of Dr Narthaki Nataraj; **274: top right:** V. Unbeatable: by courtesy of V. Unbeatable Dance Group; **277: middle:** Margamkali: by courtesy of the record holder; **283: background:** Gramophone: Shutterstock.com; **284: top right:** Lydian Nadhaswaram: levradin/Shutterstock.com; **285: top right:** Sharan Rani Backliwal: Public Domain-Iran; **286: top right:** M.S. Subbulakshmi: Chandraprabha Cinetone/Public Domain – India; **287: bottom right:** Gaana app: FaizalRamli/Shutterstock.com; **290: middle right:** Sajna Sudheer: by courtesy of the record holder; **292: bottom right:** Girish Karnad: Hindustan Times; **294: middle:** *Nukkad Natak:* by courtesy of the record holder; **296: top right:** Theatre: Shutterstock.com.

VISUAL ARTS 299–332

Opener pic, 299: Manju Mandavya/Shutterstock.com; **300:** Raja Harishchandra: Flickr's' The Commons'/no known copyright restrictions/New York Public Library; **301: from top, clockwise:** Rajinikanth: Government Open Data License–India (GODL)/Government of India.; Kamal Haasan: CCA 3.0 Unported/Bollywood Hungama – http://www.bollywoodhungama.com/more/photos/view/stills/parties/id/1659181/; Amitabh Bachchan: CCA 3.0 Unported/Bollywood Hungama – *http://www.bollywoodhungama.com/moviemicro/images/id/531746/type/view/imageid/1186119/category/parties*; S. Shankar: Hindustan Times; Dhanush: CCA 3.0 Unported/Bollywood Hungama – *http://www.bollywoodhungama.com/more/photos/view/stills/parties-and-events/id/1927451*; K. Balachander: Sai Sen/Mint; **302: bottom:** Gulzar: Government Open Data License–India (GODL)/Ministry of Information and Broadcasting; **304:** A. Sreekar Prasad: by courtesy of the record holder; ; **bottom:** Sushant Singh Rajput: Suhail Suri/Shutterstock.com; **307: top:** Soumitra Chatterjee: Hindustan Times; **308: top:** *Hunterwali* poster: Public Domain – India; **bottom:** Shefali Shah: Hindustan Times; **310: from left:** Shah Rukh Khan: Denis Makarenko/Shutterstock.com; Salman Khan: CCA 3.0 Unported/Bollywood Hungama – *http://www.bollywoodhungama.com/more/photos/view/stills/parties/id/1561508*; Aamir Khan: Denis Makarenko/Shutterstock.com; **311: middle:** Irrfan Khan: CCA 3.0 Unported/Bollywood Hungama – *http://www.bollywoodhungama.com/more/photos/view/stills/parties-and-events/id/6043458*; **313: bottom:** S.P. Balasubrahmanyam: Government Open Data License–India (GODL)/Ministry of Information and Broadcasting; **314: top:** BookMyShow: FOOTAGE VECTOR PHOTO/Shutterstock.com; **317: bottom:** Homai Vyarawalla: Government Open Data License–India (GODL)/Ministry of Information and Broadcasting; **319: middle:** Ebrahim Alkazi: Hindustan Times; **321: top:** Space exhibition: by courtesy of the record holder; **324: middle:** Kajal Singh: by courtesy of Kajal Singh aka Dizy; **325: background:** Telleas Reveals: by courtesy of Pranav Gohil/St+Art India Foundation; **inset:** Vishwaroopa: by courtesy of AkshatNauriyal/St+Art India Foundation; Katha crazy twins: by courtesy of Harsh Raman/St+Art India Foundation; **326: top:** Largest Zentangle Art: by courtesy of the record holder; **bottom:** Largest pencil drawing: by courtesy of the record holder; **327: middle:** Largest Warli painting: by courtesy of the record holder; **328: middle:** Longest cartoon strip: by courtesy of the record holder; **329: top to bottom:** by courtesy of Sudarsan Pattnaik; **330: top:** largest oil painting: by courtesy of the record holder; **bottom:** Largest acrylic painting: by courtesy of the record holder; **331: left:** Sand paintings: courtesy of the record holder; **332: top:** Largest traditional floor art: by courtesy of the record holders.

GOVERNMENT 333–360

Opener pic, 333: Shutterstock.com; **336: top:** A.O. Hume: Public Domain–USA; **339: background:** Elections: David Talukdar/Shutterstock.com; **340: top:** EVM machine: Government Open Data License–India (GODL); **341: bottom:** Security Council: lev radin/ Shutterstock.com; **343: top:** Dr Zakir Hussain: Public domain–India/Nation Museum Government of India; **345: bottom:** Lalthiamuani: by courtesy of Lalthiamuani; **347: top:** Kamala Harris: Public Domain–USA; **349: bottom:** First cabinet: Public Domain–India; **352: top:** S.P. Sinha: Public Domain –UK/Bassano Ltd; **355: top:** K. Prithika: by courtesy of Ashok Kumar; **357: bottom:** Indira Banerjee: Arvind Yadav/Hindustan Times.

LITERATURE 361–376

Opener pic, 361: Ricardo Esquivel/ Pexels.com; **363: top:** Sahitya Akademi: Hindustan Times; **364: top:** Madhuri Vijay: by courtesy of HarperCollins India; **365: middle:** Thickest book: by courtesy of the record holder; **366: top right:** Vikram Seth: by courtesy of Aradhana Seth; **367: bottom:** Sign language dictionary: by courtesy of PIB; **368: bottom:** Book village: Hindustan Times; **370: top:** *Wild Embers* cover: by courtesy of Hachette India; **371: background:** Kim Van Vuuren/ Pexels.com; **374: top:** Amitav Ghosh: Hindustan Times; **375: bottom:** Titanium manuscript: by courtesy of the record holder; **376: bottom:** Mita Kapur: by courtesy of Urvi Bhuwania.

SCIENCE AND TECHNOLOGY 377–404

Opener pic, 377: Shutterstock.com; **378: bottom right:** S. Ramanujan: Public Domain–UK; **380: top right:** Kilogram weights: Shutterstock.com; **383: middle:** M.P. Birla Planetarium: **385: top right:** Vigyan Samagam: by courtesy of Vigyan Samagam; **388: middle:** Fusion reactor: Shutterstock. com; **389: top:** Lab glassware: Shutterstock.com; **390: bottom right:** Sudipta Sengupta: by courtesy of Sudipta Sengupta; **391: middle:** Vanadium ore: Shutterstock.com; **393: bottom left:** MANAV healthcare: Shutterstock.com; **395: top right:** Lalji Singh: Government Open Data License–India (GODL)/Ministry of Science & Technology; **397: background:** Shutterstock.com; **398: middle:** Computers: Shutterstock.com; **401: top right:** CARTOSAT-3: Government Open Data License– India (GODL)/Indian Space Research Organization; **402: bottom:** Vyommitra: Government Open Data License–India (GODL)/Indian Space Research Organization; **403: top:** Chandrayaan-2: by courtesy of Indian Space Research Organization; **404: bottom right:** Kalamsat-V2: by courtesy of Space Kidz India.

ADVENTURE 405–444

Opener pic, 405: Shutterstock.com; **407: middle:** Major D.P. Singh by courtesy of the record holder; **408: top right:** Harshil V. Mane: by courtesy of the record holder; **409: middle:** Lt Col Dharamdatt Goel by courtesy of the record holder; **410: top right:** Mayank Nagpal: by courtesy of the record holder; **411: top right:** Skydiving: Shutterstock.com; **413: middle:** Eric Paul: by courtesy of the record holder;

414: top and bottom: by courtesy of the record holders; **416: bottom right:** Pallavi Fauzdar: by courtesy of the record holder; **417: middle:** Rally: by courtesy of the record holder; **418: middle:** Motorcycle ride: by courtesy of the record holders; **419: middle:** Biking expedition: Shutterstock.com; **420: middle:** Saurabh Bharat Zagade: by courtesy of the record holder; **421: top:** Soyab Ansari: by courtesy of the record holder; **bottom:** Vedangi Kulkarni: by courtesy of Vedangi Kulkarni; **423: middle:** Sailing expedition: by courtesy of the record holder; **425: background:** Shutterstock.com; **426: top:** Tandem skydiving by courtesy of Mandip Singh Soin; **427: top:** Monch summit: by courtesy of Mandeep Singh Soin; **428: middle:** Alok Yadav: by courtesy of the record holder; **429: bottom:** Police: ArnavIG/Shutterstock.com; **430: middle:** Srikaanth: by courtesy of the record holders; **431: bottom:** Expedition on River Beas: by courtesy of the record holder; **434: bottom left:** Praveen Kumar: by courtesy of the record holder; **435: bottom:** Gaurav Makkar: by courtesy of the record holder; **437: top right:** Trishul Peak: Shutterstock.com; **bottom:** Mt Everest: Shutterstock.com; **439: top:** Ajeet and Deeya Bajaj: by courtesy of Ajeet Bajaj; **bottom:** Satyarup Siddhanta: by courtesy of the record holder; **440: top:** Vikas Shukla: by courtesy of the record holder; **bottom:** Bachendri Pal: Government Open Data License–India (GODL)/President's Secretariat; **441: bottom:** Sangeeta Sindhi: by courtesy of the record holder; **443: top right:** trekking: Shutterstock.com; **444: top:** Col J.K. Bajaj: by courtesy of the record holder.

MEDICAL SCIENCES 445–466

Opener pic, 445: Shutterstock.com; **448: bottom right:** Upendranath Brahmachari: Public Domain-India; **450: top right:** Lifeline Express: Government Open Data License–India (GODL)/ Ministry of Railways; **454: middle right:** Dr S.I. Padmavati: Hindustan Times; **455: top right:** Screening: Prosun Paul/ Shutterstock.com; **458: middle and bottom:** Craniopagus surgery twins: by courtesy of the record holder; **459: top right:** LASIK: Shutterstock.com; **460: top right:** Dr Kaliki Hymavathi: by courtesy of the record holder; **462: middle right:** Dr Karthik Babu: by courtesy of the record holder; **463: top left:** Mohalla clinics: Virendra Singh Gosain/Hindustan Times; **464: middle right:** Urethral calculus: by courtesy of the record holder; **466: top:** NHS: Shutterstock.com.

COMBATING COVID-19 467–482

Opener pic, 467: from top, clockwise: Shutterstock.com; Manoej Paateel/Shutterstock.com; sdx15/Shutterstock.com; **468–469: background:** Shutterstock.com; **470–471: background:** Shutterstock.com; **insets:** Pool testing: Hindustan Times; Vande Bharat: Hindustan Times; **472: background:** Shutterstock; **inset:** Lockdown: Dinesh Hukmani/ Shutterstock.com; **473 background:** Shutterstock.com; **474–475: top background:** Shutterstock.com; **bottom background:** Shutterstock.com; **insets, clockwise:** V310: by courtesy of Noccarc Robotics; AgVa: Hindustan Times; **476–477: background:** Shutterstock.com; **insets, clockwise:** Airlens Corona: by courtesy of Persapien Innovations; Aarogya Setu: sdx15/Shutterstock.com; Mobile booths: Hindustan Times; **478–479: backgrounds:** Shutterstock.com; **insets:** Robot: Shutterstock.com; Drone: Shutterstock.com; **right background:** Shutterstock.com, **inset:** vaccine export:

Manoej Paateel/Shutterstock.com; **480–481: background:** Shutterstock.com; **481: inset:** vials: Shutterstock.com; **482: background:** Shutterstock.com; **inset:** Bird feeders: by courtesy of Sunny Shah.

DEFENCE 483–522

Opener pic, 483: Manish Jaisi/Shutterstock.com; **484: bottom:** Medals: RAMNIKLAL MODI/Shutterstock.com; **485: middle:** Lieutenant Bhavana Kasturi: Ajay Aggarwal/Hindustan Times; **486: bottom:** Dogs gifted: by courtesy of PIB; **488: top:** Indo-Korean Friendship Park: by courtesy of PIB; **490: top:** Shankhnaad: Shutterstock.com; **bottom:** E-cars: by courtesy of Indian Army; **494: top:** Mudhol hound: by courtesy of the record holder; **496: top:** Wreckage: by courtesy of PIB; **501: middle:** INS *Kora:* Government Open Data License–India (GODL)/Indian Navy; **502: bottom:** Dry Dock: by courtesy of PIB; **505: top:** INS *Shivaji:* by courtesy of Indian Navy; **506: top:** Diamond Jubilee: by courtesy of PIB; **507: top:** INSV *Tarini:* Government Open Data License–India (GODL)/Indian Navy; **508: top:** LCA on Vikramaditya: Hindustan Times; **509: bottom:** Padmavathy Bandhopadhyay: Hindustan Times; **511: bottom:** Tejas: Government Open Data License–India (GODL)/Indian Navy; **512: bottom:** Rafale: CCO 1.0 Universal Public Domain Dedication/Dylan Agbagni; **519: bottom:** ICG parade: by courtesy of PIB; **520: bottom:** ICGS *Sachet:* by courtesy of Indian Coast Guard; **522: top:** Affiliation: by courtesy of PIB.

BUSINESS AND ECONOMY 523–554

Opener pic, 523: Shutterstock.com; **525:** R.K. Shanmukham Chetty: Public domain–India/Government of India work; **525: bottom right:** Paperless budget: by courtesy of PIB; **527: top:** Work from home: Shutterstock.com; **529: top: Cowries:** Shutterstock.com; **bottom:** Coins for visually impaired: by courtesy of PM india website; **530: top right:** Dhirubhai Ambani: Hindustan Times; **532: bottom right:** RuPay: lakshmiprasada S/Shutterstock.com; **533: background:** Jayant Bahel/Shutterstock.com; **536: top right:** LIC: PhotographerIncognito/Shutterstock.com; **537: top right:** Kiran Mazumdar Shaw: Hindustan Times; **539: top right:** National Stock Exchange: Public Domain–International; **541: background:** Shutterstock.com; **544: middle:** Coal mine: Dr Arpan Chatterjee/Shutterstock.com; **546: top right:** Startup: Shutterstock.com; **550: middle:** Tamil Nadu: Jayakumar/Shutterstock.com; **551: top right:** GDP: Shutterstock.com; **552: top right:** Amartya Sen: Government Open Data License– India (GODL)/Prime Minister's Office.

SPORTS 555–678

Opener pic, 555: Shutterstock.com; **556: top right:** Dr Narinder Dhruv Batra: Sonu Mehta/Hindustan Times; **bottom right:** Olympic: ROMAN DZIUBALO/Shutterstock.com; **557: bottom right:** Aishwarya Pissay: by courtesy of the record holder; **560: middle:** Sachin Tendulkar: Santosh Harare/Hindustan Times; **561: top:** Viswanathan Anand: Pratham Gokhale/Hindustan Times; **bottom:** Leander Paes: RomainBiard/Shutterstock.com; **562: top:** Reena Raju: by courtesy of record holder; **563: bottom right:** Jayanta Talukdar: Government Open Data License–India (GODL)/President's Secretariat; **564: middle:** Abhishek Verma: Government Open Data License–India (GODL)/President's Secretariat; **565: top right:** Akash Malik: Raj K. Raj/Hindustan Times; **bottom:** Deepika Kumari: Rajnish Katyal/Hindustan Times; **566: top right:**

Mary D'Souza: Public Domain; **567: top right:** Muhammed Anas Yahiya: Government Open Data License–India (GODL)/Indian Navy; **568: top right:** Dutee Chand: Subhankar Chakraborty/ Hindustan Times; **bottom:** Arpinder Singh: Virendra Singh Gosain/Hindustan Times; **569: bottom:** Bahadur Singh: Public Domain; **571: top:** Varun Kumar Bhati: Government Open Data License–India (GODL)/Prime Minister's Office, Government of India; **572: middle:** Manasi Joshi: by courtesy of Manasi Joshi; **573: bottom:** Saina Nehwal: Government Open Data License–India (GODL)/Ministry of Youth Affairs and Sports; **574: middle:** P.V. Sindhu: Kunal Patil/Hindustan Times; **575: top right:** Madhumita Bisht: Government Open Data License–India (GODL)/President's Secretariat; **576: top right:** M.C. Mary Kom: Sanjeev Verma/Hindustan Times; **578: top right:** Amit Panghal: Vipin Kumar/Hindustan Times; **579: middle:** Sachin Siwach: Anmol Wahi/Hindustan Times; **580: top right:** Vikas Krishan: Pradeep Gaur/Mint; **bottom:** Manish Kaushik: Shankar Narayan/Hindustan Times; **581: bottom right:** Dibyendu Barua: by courtesy of the record holder; **584: middle right:** Tejas Bakre: by courtesy of the record holder; **586: top right:** Mary Ann Gomes: Public Domain/Frank Hoppe; **middle:** Nihal Sarin: by courtesy of Nihal Sarin; **588: middle right:** D. Harika: by courtesy of the record holder; **591: top right:** Mithali Raj: Ravi Choudhary/Hindustan Times; **middle:** Anju Jain: Government Open Data License–India (GODL)/ President's Secretariat; **592: bottom right:** Deepti Sharma: Satish Bate/ Hindustan Times; **594: top right:** Poonam Yadav: Government Open Data License–India (GODL)/President's Secretariat; **595: top right:** Anil Kumble: Government Open Data License–India (GODL)/Prime Minister's Office; **middle:** Sachin Tendulkar: CCA 3.0 Unported/Bollywood Hungama – http://www.bollywoodhungama.com/more/photos/view/stills/parties-and-events/id/4628555; **bottom:** Virender Sehwag: Government Open Data License–India (GODL)/President's Secretariat; **596: middle:** Rahul Dravid: Santosh Harhare/ Hindustan Times; **597: top right:** Rohit Sharma: Mitch Gunn/Shutterstock.com; **598: middle right:** Virat Kohli: Shutterstock.com; **601: top:** R. Ashwin: Hindustan Times; **604: middle right:** Aditya Mehta: by courtesy of the record holder; **605: top right:** Pankaj Advani: Hindustan Times; **606: middle right:** Durand Cup: Hindustan Times; **607: bottom right:** S.A. Rahim: PD/The Hindu; **609: top:** Mohammed Salim: PD/ Unknown; **610: top:** Oinam Bembem Devi: Government Open Data License–India (GODL)/President's Secretariat; **bottom:** I.M. Vijayan: Hindustan Times; **611: top right:** Subimal 'Chuni' Goswami: Public Domain/The Hindu; **bottom:** Pradip Kumar Banerjee: Public Domain/Unknown; **612:** Kolkata Derby: sup10mah/Shutterstock.com; **613: bottom right:** Bhaichung Bhutia: Hindustan Times; **616: bottom:** Jyoti Randhawa: mooinblack/Shutterstock.com; **617: top:** Jeev Milkha Singh: mooinblack/Shutterstock.com; **619: bottom right:** Aditi Ashok: pendakisolo/Shutterstock.com; **620: top right:** Shubhankar Sharma: masuti/ Shutterstock.com; **622: bottom right:** S.S.P. Chawrasia: Yu Chun Christopher Wong/Shutterstock.com; **623: top right:** Kapil Dev: Hindustan Times; **624: bottom left:** Dipa Karmakar: Ravi Choudhary/Hindustan Times; **626: top and middle:** PD; Hockey team/PD Bharatiya;; **627:** Balbir Singh (Senior): PD/Balbir Singh (Senior); **628: top right:** Dhyan Chand: PD/Unknown; **middle:** Leslie Claudius: Ramakrishna Samanta/Hindustan Times; **631: bottom:** Pro Kabaddi League: Hindustan Times; **635: top right:** Abhinav Bindra:

Open Government Licence version 1.0/British High Commission, India; **bottom:** Rahi Sarnobat: Government Open Data License–India (GODL)/ Ministry of Youth Affairs and Sports; **636: top right:** Saurabh Chaudhary: BurhaanKinu/Hindustan Times; **637: bottom:** Jaspal Rana: Virendra Singh Gossain/Hindustan Times; **639: middle:** Rajyavardhan Singh Rathore: Government Open Data License–India (GODL)/Ministry of Information and Broadcasting; **640: top left:** Apurvi Chandela: BurhaanKinu/Hindustan Times; **bottom:** Manu Bhaker: Government Open Data License–India (GODL)/Rajya Sabha TV; **642: bottom:** Joshna Chinappa: Santosh Harhare/ Hindustan Times; **643: top right:** Saurav Ghosal: Kunal Patil/Hindustan Times; **644: bottom:** Dipika Pallikal: CHEN WS /Shutterstock.com; **647: top right:** Prasanta Karmakar: Hindustan Times; **649: middle left:** Manika Batra: Stefan Holm/Shutterstock.com; **middle right:** Poulomi Ghatak: Government Open Data License–India (GODL)/ Ministry of Youth Affairs and Sports; **653: middle:** A. Sharath Kamal and Subhajit Saha: Government Open Data License–India (GODL)/Ministry of Youth Affairs and Sports; **654: left:** Somdev Devvarman: Rena Schild/Shutterstock.com; **655:** Ankita Raina: Teo Wei Keong/ Shutterstock.com; **656: top:** Mahesh Bhupathi and Leander Paes: by courtesy of PIB; **657: top:** Sania Mirza: Mai Groves/Shutterstock.com; **658: top:** Sumit Nagal: lev radin/Shutterstock.com; **660: bottom right:** E. Karunakaran: PD/T.N Raghu; **662: middle right:** Saikhom Mirabai Chanu: Sunny Shende/ Hindustan Times; **665:** Vinesh Phogat: Azamat Mukanov/Shutterstock.com; **666: bottom:** Bajrang Punia: Sanjeev Verma/Hindustan Times; **671: bottom:** First Indian Olympic delegation: CCA-SA 3.0/Undetermined (Photo uploaded by Dmuc (talk) (Uploads); **672: bottom right:** Norman Pritchard: PD/Unknown; User de:User: FreeMO on de.wikipedia; **673: bottom right:** Sir Dorabji Tata: PD/ Unknown; **676: bottom:** Balbir Singh: Rajnish Katyal/Hindustan Times; **678: top:** Abhinav Bindra: Sanjeev Verma/ Hindustan Times.

STATES AND UNION TERRITORIES 679–716

Opener pic, 679: from top, clockwise: Shutterstock.com; **681: top right:** Tawang Monastery: Shutterstock.com; **683: middle:** Mahabodhi Temple: Shutterstock.com; **685: middle:** Bulbul: Shutterstock.com; **686: bottom right:** Rann of Kachchh: Shutterstock.com; **688: top right:** Snow leopard: Shutterstock.com; **690: bottom right:** Lotus Mahal: Shutterstock.com; **692: bottom left:** Barasingha: Shutterstock.com; **693: bottom right:** Chhatrapati Shivaji Maharaj Terminus: Shutterstock.com; **694: top right:** Shirui lily: Shutterstock.com; **697: top:** Hornbill Festival: VikramjitK/ Shutterstock.com; **700: top left:** Kalbelia dance: AbhishekMittal/ Shutterstock.com; **702: top:** Brihadisvara temple: Shutterstock.com; **703: bottom:** Ujjayanta Palace: Shutterstock.com; **704: bottom:** Valley of Flowers: hutterstock.com; **706: bottom left:** Chikankari: by courtesy of Shubhali Chopra; **708: top:** Glass-bottomed boats: Shutterstock.com; **709: top:** Rock garden: Shutterstock.com; **711: bottom:** Lotus Temple: Shutterstock.com; **713: bottom:** Chinar: MusaibMushtaq/ Shutterstock.com; **714: bottom:** Thikse Monastery: Shutterstock.com; **715: bottom:** Minicoy Island: Shutterstock.com; **716: bottom right:** Minicoy Island: Bommai: Shutterstock.com.

A

B

C

D

E

F

G

H

I

J

K

L

M

N

O

P

Q

R

S

T

U

V

W

X

Y

Z

ABBREVIATIONS USED IN THE BOOK

b. = born on
in. = inch/inches
ft = feet
cm = centimetre/centimetres
m = metre/metres
g = gram/grams
kg = kilogram/kilograms
hr = hour/hours
min./mins = minute/minutes
sec./secs = second/seconds
Mt = Mount

PREAMBLE

Limca Book of Records ('*LBR*'), as a record-keeping publication, has been compiling records since 1987 and has seen over 30 editions. It is India's first and longest continuously published book of records.

It is, however, a private book, run and managed by a private organization with no public funding whatsoever. The retail price is also subsidized by the owner Coca-Cola India Private Limited ('CCIPL'). The *LBR* also accepts absolutely no funding or payment or any other charges from record applicants or record holders for entries or for processing or for publication acceptance.

Consequently, it is important to understand that all decisions are taken by applying a set of standards that are specific and stringent, but equally are subjective, and based on what the editors and staff of *LBR* and Consultants ('*LBR* Team') think are most suitable for the book. And that decision is solely *LBR*'s and not answerable to or affected by any other individual, entity or by what another entity may do or accept.

I. INTRODUCTION

1. *LBR* is a catalogue of achievements made by Indians. It catalogues unique milestones and landmarks including, but not limited to, firsts, bests, mosts, inventions, discoveries, and honours and awards received, by Indians at home or abroad in all fields – both human and natural – that can be qualified in superlatives and that conform to the prevailing editorial policy in force during any year.

While this is primarily a catalogue of superlatives and achievements, it is also a book of records, and a work of reference, and therefore in the spirit of empirical record-keeping, will record other milestones that may be negative or not celebratory or laudatory but are notable, such as 'longest trial in a court of law' or records pertaining to disasters or crime. Any such record is a statement of fact on record, and is not meant to downplay any entity nor encourage anyone to attempt to beat such records.

LBR encompasses an extensive range of information and is thus divided into several chapters and record categories. Prospective entries under these chapters and categories may include, but are not limited to, any of the following headings: a record, a quantifiable skill, a superlative or historical landmark/phenomenon/man-made or natural event/process/structure considered as remarkable as a record by the *LBR* Team.

2. Anyone with a reasonable claim for a record may write to *LBR* for possible inclusion (subject to acceptance by *LBR* criteria).

3. Entry into *LBR* and attempt of any record are subject to compliance with the general Terms and Conditions (the 'Terms') as well as the specific rules and guidelines applicable to each type of record attempt or claim (the 'Attempt'). Where there are no pre-existing terms to cover a particular record or Claim, a relevant policy shall be decided by the *LBR* Team and that shall be binding. Earlier policies and parameters go under continuous review and modifications, and the *LBR* Team is not bound to any previously existing parameters.

4. Individuals or groups interested in attempting to set or break a record must understand and accept general policy and study the Terms and the specific rules and guidelines applicable to the Attempt, and sign the Disclaimer and Indemnity Form (available before the commencement of any Attempt) in order to be considered for inclusion in *LBR*. Records already set and sent for inclusion post facto are also bound by all the rules and guidelines; and acceptance of all Terms and Conditions is a necessary qualifier to any record being accepted.

5. All Terms, rules and guidelines apply to a person/persons making a record Attempt ('Applicant'/'Applicants') who sends an Application to *LBR* as well as any and every person/persons ('Participant'/'Participants') part of such an Attempt (for example, in an Attempt by a group or organization).

6. *LBR* is owned by CCIPL, which reserves the right to modify these Terms and any other rules and guidelines established in relation to an Attempt or general policy. CCIPL does not implement or involve itself in editorial policy and does not process submissions. *LBR* is collated and published by publishers Hachette Book Publishing India Pvt. Ltd/Hachette India, who will process the entries, make all decisions on acceptance and inclusion, and publish the book autonomously as is required for an independent book of records. Publication dates and content design are decided and implemented in conjunction with CCIPL.

All such modifications of Terms and Conditions and policy will be updated on the website: *https://www.coca-colaindia.com/limca-book-of-records* and anyone attempting to enter their record in *LBR* must review the Terms and the corresponding rules for each Attempt regularly to remain informed of any changes or modifications therein.

7. *LBR* and its representatives do NOT charge any fee or accept any money for the application, review, processing or acceptance of records [*please see clauses III(17) and III(18) of 'General Guidelines' pertaining to certificates and discount on sale of copies to Applicants*].

II. ELIGIBILITY CRITERIA

1. To be eligible for consideration by the *LBR* Team for a successful Attempt, the 'Applicant' must fulfil the following conditions:

a. The Applicant should be a resident Indian, an NRI (Non-Resident Indian) or an OCI (Overseas Citizen of India), and must submit ID and residence proofs and other documents as required by law to establish this.
b. The Applicant must have read and consented to the Terms, the specific rules and guidelines applicable to the Attempt, and must have signed and submitted the Disclaimer and Indemnity Form before undertaking the Attempt.
c. *LBR* does not accept applications of children below 13 years except in certain memory-related categories, select skill and art-based categories, and those under certain national and international sports categories as decided by the *LBR* Team, and as per certification by relevant national and international sports organizations and authorities. The Applicant must fall in one of the two age groups, as specified below, and must adhere to the eligibility criteria of that age group.

2. The Attempt must be corroborated by a valid proof of age:

a. Age Group I – Between 13 years and up to 18 years
b. Age Group II – Above 18 years

3. Age Group I:

a. An Applicant undertaking an Attempt under this age group must be older than thirteen (13) years and younger than or up to eighteen (18) years at the time of the Attempt.
b. Consent from a parent or legal guardian must be submitted, after such parent or legal guardian has read the Terms as provided and consented to the same. The parent or legal guardian is also required to have read and consented to the Disclaimer and Indemnity Form, and provided a Certificate of Medical Fitness, signed and stamped by a certified doctor, in certain Attempts as decided and indicated by the *LBR* Team, and any other rules specified in relation to the category of the Attempt, before undertaking the Attempt.
c. Certain categories of records may not be permitted for Applicants from this age group, as may be notified by CCIPL and/or *LBR* from time to time. Any record in this age group must be cleared with *LBR* before it occurs, to see if it will be considered suitable as a record entry and *LBR*'s decision shall be final regarding its own criteria for inclusion and safety.
d. Attempts that are detrimental to the health of such persons, or that are potentially dangerous, or that are in violation of any law in force will not be accepted for entry in *LBR*.
e. Any Attempt by minors beyond 15 minutes will be considered as endurance and would lead to the rejection of the claim. Any record attempt below that time duration (or even if the activity is strenuous within that time frame) that the *LBR* team deems as stressful or strenuous for a minor, or as dangerous, harmful or injurious in any other way, may also be rejected at the discretion of the *LBR* team.
f. Guardians/parents must sign a Disclaimer and Indemnity Form assuring against any exertion, stress or harm caused to the minor record applicant and indemnifying *LBR* and CCIPL against any such occurrence.
g. Memory records are available to this age group and subject to the decision of the *LBR* Team and representatives of *LBR*.
h. Certain records, such as the lightest/heaviest baby born or a medical feat performed on a child below 13 years may be accepted at the discretion of the *LBR* Team under the Medical Sciences chapter, wherein the child/baby itself is not an active actor/participant in the record.

4. Age Group II:
  a. The Applicant must be above eighteen (18) years of age.
  b. The Applicant must have carefully read and consented to the Terms, and the specific rules and guidelines set down for the Attempt, and submitted the Disclaimer and Indemnity Form before engaging in the Attempt as well as a Certificate of Medical Fitness (with the medical practitioner's registration number mentioned on it) to attempt any physical feat or one involving mental exertion, or one deemed so by the *LBR* Team.

III. GENERAL GUIDELINES

1. Standard norms and rules should be adhered to while setting national and world records. In some cases there may be additional event-specific norms that need to be observed.

2. The onus of proving a record claim rests on the Applicant. The claim, signed by the Applicant, should be backed by adequate and satisfactory documents without which it will not be accepted. Materials submitted as supporting evidence, like press clippings, audio/videotapes, flash/pen drives, CDs and photographs, become the property of the publisher Hachette Book Publishing India Pvt Ltd/Hachette India and the Copyright Owner, but only copies should be submitted with the originals kept safe by the claimant for Life after the claim has been accepted [*see also Section V* (*Evidence*)]. Forms such as the Application Form duly signed by the Applicant and validating/witnessing authorities as indicated by the representatives of *LBR* and/or the rules and guidelines need to be submitted in original (hard copy) and a copy retained by the Applicant/Applicants for Life after the claim has been accepted. *LBR* does not take any responsibility for lost material/s if the record is questioned or objected to by any person. In case of a query or objection raised, the responsibility of providing the evidence again for reverification [*see also Reverification of Evidence clause V(15)*] and all expenditures therein lies with the Applicant.

3. It is not necessary or binding for someone from *LBR* to be present at the record-making event, but proper authentication of the same must be ensured. Authentication should be by someone who is competent and in a responsible position, such as a Gazetted Officer, District Magistrate or Principal of a school/college, unless specified otherwise.

4. Applicants must update themselves with the latest record before any Attempt to break it. Potential record-breakers should inform *LBR* at least 30 days in advance about the record Attempt details and procedure in order to avoid disqualification on technicalities.

5. While breaking an existing record, the rules, technical specifications and set precedents should be followed. For example, the needle-threading record specifies a no. 13 needle. No other needle should be used.

6. Records should be absolute and not technical offshoots. For example, if one is setting a typing record, it is assumed that it is normal typing. One-finger or two-finger typing will not be registered as separate records. Records have to be quantifiable and comparable, and overly specific variables may not be considered.

7. While *LBR* does accept new categories, these will have to be of high interest value and have definable and comparable parameters, and these are entirely subject to the *LBR* Team's decision. For example, even if no record exists, a two-hour marathon for guitar playing will not be accepted.

8. Not every record set by women is eligible for entry as the subcategory 'First woman to…'

9. Collections should have a basic 'standard'. Limited numbers of obscure articles may not be accepted unless of exceptional interest value, and that shall be decided upon by the *LBR* Team.

10. For distance records, only basic types of vehicles are recognized: four-wheelers and plus, two-wheelers, geared bicycles, gearless bicycles, tandem bicycles and electric vehicles. In terms of endurance, for instance, if the category is Four Corners of India by a two-wheeler, then motorcycles of any cubic capacity (cc) and scooters are considered under the same category. To ensure measurability, distance against time will be the criterion. Cross-country or intra-country motoring/cycling or other vehicular records must get prior clearance from us for inclusion. Vehicles may be categorized according to engine capacity: up to 150 cc, 151–450 cc and above 450 cc.

11. Before attempting any driving record, Applicants have to submit a copy of the following document/documents, as applicable, attested by a Gazetted Officer, Notary Public: their valid driving licence/earlier experience certificate in case of motor sport or bicycling record; pilot's licence/aero sports course certificate/earlier experience certificate in case of aero sports record; mountaineering/mountain sports course certificate/earlier experience certificate in case of a mountain sports record; and water sports course certificate/earlier experience certificate in case of a water sports record to the *LBR* office for prior approval.

12. The *LBR* Team would like all claimants to send in supporting photographs. In physical evidence with documents or photographs, they should not be stapled to the entry. Detachable clips should be used in such cases. In cases where applicable and as indicated by the *LBR* Team, time- and date-stamped video recordings of the Attempt must be provided.

13. Attempts that may result in physical harm, such as 'hitting head against a wall' or mental/emotional duress for the Applicant, such as 'isolating oneself for 100 days' will not be considered and are entirely the decision of the *LBR* team.

14. Any record in the book may be reconsidered or dropped without prior intimation.

15. Certificates issued are valid only for the date or period specified and will be considered ended if surpassed by a new record, and/or change in criteria, measuring methods, or if disputed and found to be erroneous on reverification [*see clause V(15)*].

16. For reasons of space or any other reasons, a confirmed entry may be dropped at the time of going to press. The *LBR* Team may inform the Applicant of the change in status but is not bound to do so.

17. Record holders within India are entitled to ONE complimentary copy of their certificate and its postage, if eligible, and further copies need to be ordered by writing to the *LBR* Team and on payment (including GST) as indicated. Record holders outside India are entitled to ONE complimentary copy of their certificate but will need to pay courier and/or postal charges (including applicable taxes/surcharges). Requests for the reissue of older certificates issued in previous years are considered on a case-by-case basis and such certificates reissued on payment within reasonable time as per printing schedules provided the record is accessible in our archived editions.

18. Record holders are not entitled to any remuneration or free copies of *Limca Book of Records*. They may, however, avail a 30 per cent discount on the cover price of the book by writing to *the LBR* Team and following the payment process.

19. If new record holders do not receive their certificate within two months after the release of the book, they may contact the *LBR* office.

20. The *LBR* Team reserves the sole right to decide on the suitability of all records for inclusion in the book. The Team's decision on all such matters is final. Any attempt to browbeat or threaten the *LBR* Team or representatives shall result in instant disqualification.

21. ATTEMPTS BY MINORS: Records by minors below 13 years are not accepted, except under certain memory-related categories, select skill and art-based categories, and certain recognized national and international tournament categories as decided by the respective Consultants for specific sports.

22. Records that are against the law (e.g. driving at an age not qualified for licence) or those that require excessive physical exertion (like a marathon) detrimental to a minor's health will not be accepted.

23. OBJECTIONS/DISCREPANCIES: Objections raised by any person regarding any published entry shall be entertained only within a period of three (3) years from the date of publication or acceptance/certification of a record/entry. However, discrepancies identified by the *LBR* team *suo motu* shall be addressed regardless of passage of time. Applicants must note that, in accordance with the prevailing laws, there is no limitation in respect of criminal liability should it arise.

A. CHAPTERS AND CATEGORIES

LBR reserves the right to include or exclude any chapter or category, or section or record category as otherwise listed below and is under no obligation to publish all or any of the listed chapters or categories in *LBR* or any of its publications.

The list provided here is only for illustrative and explanatory reasons, and for the clarity of persons seeking to engage in an Attempt. Further, the following list only consists of chapters and categories that have been published in previous editions and is non-exhaustive. *LBR* may, at its sole discretion, include additional chapters or categories, delete a chapter or category, or even merge two or more chapters or categories as the *LBR* Team deems appropriate. Any such addition, deletion or merging of chapters or categories creates no obligation on the *LBR* Team's and/or CCIPL's part to inform any person making an Attempt of such addition, deletion or merger. Records after acceptance may also be changed or deleted if suitable circumstances warrant it, and this also shall be the sole decision of the *LBR* Team.

1. THE HUMAN STORY

This chapter contains records, talents and information, and includes, but is not limited to, unique achievements, uncommon talents, collections, community development initiatives and other human feats. Applicants under this category are required to not break any laws, and must sign and submit the Disclaimer and Indemnity Form, Self-Declaration of Medical Fitness and Certificate of Medical Fitness, as applicable, at least one fortnight (based on working days) prior to the Attempt. *LBR* prohibits and will not accept any Attempt that is likely to cause harm or be of nuisance to the general public, or is likely to cause unnecessary waste of essential goods or resources such as food items, or is likely to harm the environment; and of course, possible physical, mental or emotional harm to oneself.

a. Records involving alcohol consumption as an event or performance measure will not be considered.
b. Yoga or endurance, or speed or strength records are only for Age Group II unless specifically permitted otherwise in writing.
c. Applicants from Age Group I can perform for a maximum of 15 minutes in mass participation records involving strength, speed or performance. Any Attempt longer than that will be considered endurance on the part of minors and rejected. In such records attempting mosts in terms of numbers, minors will not be counted, such as in a two-hour-long dance performance. The allowance may depend upon the nature of the Attempt. For example, minor Applicants/Participants might participate in an Attempt involving reading for more than 15 minutes but will not be allowed at any claim of a mass physical feat for more than that time period – such as most Participants performing the plank together. Such applications, if accepted by the *LBR* Team, will need a Medical Fitness Certificate confirming that no harm will be caused to the Applicant/Participant by such an Attempt.
d. A new section for virtual records has been added from this edition onwards. The current categories are for single sessions conducted on a single platform.
e. We do not have categories related to religious traditions and ceremonies, unless they form general records.
f. Records indicating or involving harm to physical or mental health will not be considered, such as 'most blood donated in a day'.

2. STRUCTURES

This chapter contains records related to general, modern, residential, religious, mechanical and historical structures, bridges, dams, flyovers, and various other specialized structures.

a. There are no set parameters of the claim regarding fastest construction as each construction would have multiple aspects of difference and the *LBR* Team does not wish to encourage the fastest construction of public services or private buildings.

3. EDUCATION

This chapter contains records and information related to literacy, schools, higher education, archives, libraries, museums and quizzes. *LBR* has discontinued the 'youngest' category as a record claim. Record claims with qualifications beyond postgraduation are considered. Record claims pertaining to online courses or UGC's NET-based qualifications or publication of research papers will not be considered.

4. MEDIA AND COMMUNICATIONS

This chapter contains records and information related to the broad fields of (a) media and (b) communications, and may be divided into six sections: (i) print, (ii) radio, (iii) television, (iv) post and philately, (v) telecom, and (vi) Internet, social media and apps (applications). Applicants wishing to undertake an Attempt under this chapter must ensure compliance with the specific guidelines provided by the *LBR* Team.

5. AGRICULTURE

This chapter contains records and information, and may include, but shall not be limited to, topics such as agricultural crops, farm machinery, milk and milk products, poultry, animal sciences, fisheries, agricultural research and awards. Specific rules are to be complied with for Attempts under this chapter.

6. DEFENCE

This chapter contains records and information pertaining to all the branches of the armed or para-military forces and related military records. This chapter does not accept entries unless routed through the appropriate defence authority/organization with the understanding that no official secrets, or confidential information, are being revealed in the process. An independent entry by current or former defence personnel should be accompanied with a self-declaration that no official secrets or confidential information is being revealed. The chapter is otherwise compiled by the *LBR* Team from news sources originating with government ministries and information sources such as the official websites of the Indian Navy, Army, Air Force and Coast Guard as well as the Press Information Bureau, Government of India.

7. TRANSPORT

This chapter contains records and information, and the sections under this chapter include road, rail, water and air transport. Applicants who claim records under any of these sections shall provide evidence of the same, including authentication documents as required by the *LBR* Team.

8. SCIENCE AND TECHNOLOGY

This chapter contains absolute records like oldest planetarium and first nuclear reactor along with discoveries and records in, but not limited to, mathematics, physics, chemistry, biology, engineering, environmental sciences, computers, information technology and space technology. All Attempts under this chapter are required to follow the specific rules for both types of events as provided by the *LBR* Team. For a new invention to be considered as a record, it must be patented with a recognized national/international body. This chapter also includes records and relevant information compiled by the *LBR* Team.

9. VISUAL ARTS

This chapter contains records and information related to cinema, photography, painting and some categories of drawing and cartooning. The records related to national and regional commercial and art cinema is based on information collected from the National Film Archive of India (NFAI), public domain, magazines and national newspapers. The records about box-office collection are obtained from the website *www.boxofficeindia.com,* the standard source in India for collecting such details, or similar sources.

a. Individual record claims may be submitted for consideration under this chapter, subject to compliance with the basic criteria laid down:
   i. The film should have been cleared by the Central Board for Film Certification (CBFC) and given a censor certificate.
   ii. Certification requirements for OTT content/films/drama series will be decided on a case-by-case basis and as per the laws of the land and relevant authorities/organizations.
   iii. The film should be screened at film festivals or at public theatres/auditoriums.

b. Information related to painting and photography is collected from newspapers, magazines, the Internet and any other verified source. Individual record claims may be submitted for consideration under this chapter, subject to compliance with the basic criteria laid down:
   i. No miniature paintings in any medium are considered in this chapter currently. They may be eligible for entry in the chapter titled 'The Human Story' depending on parameters.
   ii. All rangoli, *alpana* and *kolam* records have been categorized under one category of 'Traditional floor art'.

iii. Considering that art is a subjective concept, the *LBR* Team reserves the final decision regarding the artwork so produced. Random repetition of patterns, block colour patches, strokes of paint, or smearing paint randomly on the canvas would lead to the rejection of the claim. Similarly, geometric shapes, haphazard lines and arbitrary usage of colour would also lead to rejection. The artwork so produced should have a coherent sense of pattern, colour and tone. It should depict a certain level of skill and creation of aesthetics. For photography claims, repetitive, fragmented and haphazard images would not be considered. The images should have a coherent sense of posture, alignment and lighting.

iv. The largest art competition would be a single-day category following the rules of continuous events and being of a maximum of 12 hours' duration.

v. Portrait categories: A portrait should have only a single person in the painting/mosaic. A portrait is considered to be a drawing/painting of the head and shoulder of a person for the purposes of record claims.

vi. Origami claims have been sorted into the following categories:
   1. Largest origami mosaic – solo/group
   2. Single-item origami (single sheet, single item): A) Tallest/Longest; B) Widest
   3. Multiple-item origami (multiple sheets, multiple items): A) Tallest – solo/group; B) Widest – solo/ group
   4. Marathon origami (single day, single venue) – solo
   5. Most towel origami made - solo/group – in 1 hour

vii. Claims regarding pencil carvings (graphite) have been sorted into the following categories:
   1. Largest collection of carved pencils
   2. Most pencil carvings done – single day
   3. Most pencil carvings done – 1 hour
   4. Smallest pencil carving

10. PERFORMING ARTS

This chapter contains records related to talent and information in the fields of dance, music and theatre (including but not limited to puppetry and other local theatre types depending on parameters), and dance drama and dance-martial arts crossovers. The records are further divided into marathon events or group events. All Attempts under this chapter are required to follow the specific rules for both types of events as provided by the *LBR* Team. Record claims pertaining to fastest performances will not be considered.

11. ADVENTURE

This chapter may be divided into various sections, including but not limited to, aero sports, mountaineering, road expeditions, water sports, marathons (those not classified internationally as athletics track and field events) and other adventure activities. A person undertaking an Attempt under this category may seek the *LBR* Team's guidance for specific guidelines. Potential Applicants are advised to note that such guidelines or safety advice provided by the *LBR* Team shall merely be explanatory and non-exhaustive, and shall not create any responsibilities or liabilities whatsoever on behalf of the *LBR* Team and/or CCIPL, whatsoever.

a. For all Ironman triathlon related claims, we refer to the International Triathlon Union and the Indian Triathlon Federation.

b. For swimming records, only solo as well as up to three-person relay crossings (each covering at least 10 km) are considered. Exceptions may be made for para swimmers or extremely remarkable records, subject to the discretion and decision of the *LBR* Team and Consultants.

c. A minimum altitude of 6,000 m is required to review any mountaineering claim. Claims regarding Mt Kilimanjaro (5,895 m) will not be considered in accordance with the same. All mountaineering claims must be verified by the Indian Mountaineering Foundation or a similar credible international body.

d. For road expeditions, there are separate categories for women in solo attempts and group attempts where Applicants and, if present, Participants are women.

e. **Adventure/Marathon and Endurance Claims:**

i. A detailed **logbook** must be maintained with entries in chronological order. All entries in this logbook must be witnessed and authenticated by reputed individuals/competent authorities (a Gazetted Officer, District Magistrate or Principal of a school/college, unless specified otherwise). A sample sheet will be given by the *LBR* Team on request. Emphasis will be on events that highlight special skills.

ii. In cases where applicable and as indicated by the *LBR* team, time- and date-stamped videos of the Attempt must be provided.

iii. All adventure/endurance events come under five categories. Special instructions on rest breaks for each of them follow:
    1. **Marathon (non-stop)**: A five-minute break for rest after every completed hour is allowed as per prevailing international norms. These breaks may be accumulated (e.g., a 15-minute break may be taken after 3 hours of non-stop action) but not added to the tally. The logbook must clearly indicate the rest breaks.
    2. **Virtually non-stop**: Minimal breaks permitted for medical/toilet purposes but no rest breaks. Breaks are to be indicated in the logbook.
    3. **Continuous**: Performed on a rotating or relay basis.
    4. **Normal**: Breaks permitted as and when necessary.
    5. **Absolute non-stop**: No breaks at all.

iv. Attempts jeopardizing individual or public safety and public property are not encouraged.

v. All adventure feats, stunts, sports, etc., require prior written approval from the authorities concerned.

12. GOVERNMENT

This chapter contains information and records. This category may include, but shall not be limited to, such subjects as nationhood, parties, elections, the Parliament, states, administration, government officials, civics, judiciary, and law and order.

13. MEDICAL SCIENCES

This chapter contains records and information from the field of medical sciences such as medical breakthroughs, medical camps, firsts and mosts in selective medical procedures, mass participations, medical tests, medical devices and equipment. Claims are acceptable only from registered medical practitioners and related to government-approved medical practices and institutions, such as those affiliated to the Indian Medical Association, the Ministry of Health and Family Welfare, and any others as deemed eligible by the *LBR* Team.

The *LBR* Team will reject any Attempts that may potentially or otherwise harm or endanger persons/patients, e.g., 'speed' related records such as 'most kidneys transplanted in a day' or 'most LASIK surgeries performed in a day' whether at a medical centre or in camps – charitable or otherwise.

LBR may accept camp-related statistics that turn out to be records, but may not process or encourage any camps set up to create records, especially speed-related medical science Attempts because such attempts may jeopardize patient safety.

14. THE NATURAL WORLD

This chapter contains information and records, and the entries are compiled from multiple and deemed verified reports in magazines, newspapers and Internet resources available to *LBR* on topics including, but not limited to, geographical features, flora, fauna, environment and conservation. Information related to flora and fauna is verified with nature conservation authorities, well-known wildlife institutions, government websites and relevant international websites. All claims related to rainwater harvesting and pollution control are counterchecked with government sources and/or authoritative expert bodies. Gardening records relate to non-agricultural production, and claims, such as largest pumpkin, will require scale-comparative photographs as well as other indicated documentation.

15. LITERATURE

This chapter contains records and information from the field of literature. Applicants willing to undertake an Attempt under this chapter must ensure compliance with the basic criteria laid down as under:

a. Only published works will be considered unless the work created is an art installation, or superlative or artefact.

b. No long ghazals/poems, rewriting of religious texts, or anthologies will be considered.

c. A work infringing copyright or violative of any other prevailing laws will not be considered.

d. General category claims – book(s) self-published or published by a publishing house – should be available for purchase online and/or at bookshops. Sales records must be certified by publishers who have audited accounts or Nielsen BookScan.

16. BUSINESS AND ECONOMY

This chapter contains records and information, and the sections under this chapter may include, but shall not be limited to, the economy, financial institutions, financial instruments, banking, industries and companies, workforce, housing and real estate, and advertising. Applicants who claim records under any of these sections shall provide proof of the same, including authentication letters from independent observers including at least one expert in the field. Industry company data must be from authentic authorized bodies such as the Registrar of Companies and SEBI, or in the case of own company figures, audited figures must be submitted.

17. SPORTS

The Sports chapter of the *LBR* primarily contains records, sports-related statistics and information. It is prepared by independent Consultants, who are well-established journalists and/or authorities in particular sports. The Consultants in conjunction with the *LBR* Team are the final authority on all records under this chapter. In cases where an uncommon sport is involved, the decisions will be made in consultation with an expert in the field.

IV. PROCEDURE FOR ATTEMPT

1. *LBR* recognizes two types of Attempts:

a. an Attempt to break a previously existing record; and
b. an Attempt to set a new record.

2. The following procedure must be followed by any person willing to undertake an Attempt to be considered for entry in *LBR*. An application by the person attempting the record should be either emailed to ***lbr.entries@hachetteindia.com*** or couriered/mailed by registered post [*see clause IV(3.): Application Procedure*]:

a. Such application should contain details regarding the unique achievement or proposal to set a record for the consideration of the *LBR* Team, along with the complete address and contact number of the person attempting the same, at least one (1) month before the Attempt in order to avoid disqualification on technicalities. For specific requirements in the procedure for an Attempt please refer to Section III of these Terms.
b. The person undertaking the Attempt must approach the *LBR* Team regarding the proper procedure and information or documents required for consideration of a successful Attempt.
c. On completion of an Attempt, the Applicant must provide the *LBR* Team detailed and accurate documentation, as required by the *LBR* Team, and these will then be scrutinized by the *LBR* Team.
d. All entries to an edition are confirmed only after the deadline, i.e., the last date for submission of entries. Any Application made after such a date may be considered for a subsequent edition of *LBR*.
e. On confirmation of an entry, a certificate shall be mailed to the Applicant who carried out the successful Attempt. Such certificates shall be sent after the particular edition for which the Attempt has been considered, is printed or released.
f. For all Attempts to be undertaken, the person undertaking such an Attempt must sign and submit the Disclaimer and Indemnity Form and Certificate of Medical Fitness (in hard copy), as and when required, to the *LBR* Team, prior to the Attempt. The acceptance of any application for entry in *LBR* shall be conditional on the signing of and adherence to the Disclaimer and Indemnity Form, the Terms, and any other specific rules and guidelines established by *LBR* in relation to a particular category of Attempt.

3. APPLICATION PROCEDURE

a. All applications must be sent to the following addresses:
Limca Book of Records (Editorial)
Hachette Book Publishing India Pvt. Ltd
4th/5th Floors, Corporate Centre
Plot No. 94, Sector 44
Gurugram 122003, Haryana, India
Ph: (Board) +91-124-4195000; Fax: +91-124-4148900

Email: *lbr.entries@hachetteindia.com*
Hachette Book Publishing India Pvt. Ltd is a company incorporated under the Indian Companies Act, 1956, with CIN U22222DL2007PTC164081

b. *LBR*'s primary mode of communication is email (and only via its formal email IDs), which is both retrievable and transparent as well as formal record. No Attempt should be made based on phone or other verbal conversations, or communication on social media/ messaging platforms.
c. There is no need for personal visits to the *LBR* office to hand over record-related applications, documentation or evidence, and in case the Applicant does visit personally, the application and requisite documents may be handed over at the Reception. Since all claim formats devised are such that they need written submission, everything should be clear from written communication.
d. Submissions must be in English since *LBR* is currently published in the English language (submissions in other languages shall be accepted, but they should be accompanied with an English translation).
e. The primary application shall consist of the following:
   i. Name of the Applicant;
   ii. Complete postal address of the Applicant;
   iii. Contact details of the Applicant;
   iv. Description of the record the Applicant wishes to apply for, and event plan; and
   v. Confirmation of acceptance of *LBR* procedures, Terms and guidelines via a formal statement on email or signed hard copy.
f. These applications shall be perused by the *LBR* Team, and further correspondence shall take place between the Applicant and the *LBR* Team member concerned, from the assigned chapter/section.
g. On acceptance of the initial application, the general guidelines and record-specific guidelines shall be emailed or couriered to the Applicant by the *LBR* Team along with the procedure and documentation required.
h. On receipt of the correspondence from a member of the *LBR* Team, the Applicant shall send the following documents (in both soft and hard copy) to the postal address mentioned in clause IV3.(a) above:
   i. A covering letter stating the Attempt details;
   ii. A signed copy of the Disclaimer and Indemnity Form sent to the Applicant;
   iii. A self-attested copy of the Applicant's government-approved identity proof (such as passport, voter ID card, PAN card, Aadhaar, etc.);
   iv. A self-attested copy of the Applicant's government- approved age proof (such as passport, birth certificate, ration card, etc.) together with the 'Required Documents'.
i. On authentication and verification of the Required Documents, the Applicant shall obtain a confirmation from the *LBR* Team to proceed with the Attempt.
j. After completing the Attempt in accordance with the provisions of Sections III and IV, and collecting evidence of the Attempt in accordance with the provisions of Section V, the Applicant shall send the following to claim a record (the 'Claim'):
   i. Details of the supposed record, duly authenticated by Gazetted Officers, or relevant public authorities, or relevant authorities in charge or other competent authorities. Such authentication must be on the basis of personal verification of every detail of the Claim.
   ii. Material evidence of the event, consisting of all the evidence collected by the Applicant during the Attempt. All CDs/DVDs, flash/pen drives and other data storage media/devices sent to the *LBR* Team, as part of the application process, should have the Applicant's name and the record category written legibly on it.
k. A Claim that is successfully submitted shall be considered for entry in the *LBR*.
l. The application procedure should be completed within the last date of submission. Entries submitted after the deadline may not be considered for the subsequent edition unless extension was granted in writing or on email for extenuating circumstances.
m. In addition to the aforementioned rules, specific requirements provided under the relevant categories must be fulfilled.

V. EVIDENCE

1. The onus of proving a record is on the Applicant. The Claim, signed by the Applicant, should be backed by adequate and satisfactory documentation without which it will not be accepted by the *LBR* Team.

2. The Applicant must, as part of the verification process, submit all supporting documents including at least two authentication letters (originals) on stamp paper, photographs (or CD/DVD/flash drive containing still photos), personal details of the Applicant, including residential address and contact details, along with a covering letter, without which the Claim will not be considered for entry.

3. Outside of moral and creative ownership rights, which will vest with the creator/artist/author, etc., the assigned copyright/publishing rights and any other intellectual property rights in and to any such material evidence shall, to the extent permitted by law, be waived unconditionally by the Applicant and transferred to *LBR* and CCIPL by the submission.

4. The evidence must only be sent after the Required Documents have been verified and the primary application has been duly confirmed and evidence asked for.

5. Only the Claim may be supplemented by evidence of the record with the following to be submitted on the currently prevailing and commonly available and accessible data storage media from where it is easily retrievable, such as a flash/pen drive or hard drive, with the onus of providing a backup copy/original being on the applicant:

a. Press clippings of local, national or international newspapers, or press cuttings, or news reports in an electronic form, furnishing direct evidence of the record; or
b. Audio recordings from radio, or any such fact of record which could be heard, furnishing direct evidence of the record; or
c. Direct evidence/audio-visual recording of the record; or
d. Any other fact of record that may be in audio, visual or audio-visual format, furnishing direct evidence of the record; or
e. Photographs of any such fact of record documented by photographs furnishing direct evidence of the record. (It is advisable to submit high-resolution photographs only that are pictures 1,500 pixels wide for horizontal images and 1,500 pixels high for vertical images, of 1 MB or more.)

6. If any of the above-mentioned evidence is in a local language, it must be sent along with an attested copy of an English translation of the said document.

7. The evidence must be clear, distinct and unambiguous.

8. *LBR* reserves the right to refuse the Claim if evidence sufficient to prove the record act beyond reasonable doubt is not furnished, or for any other reason whatsoever at *LBR*'s discretion.

9. For categories where specific evidence is required, a reference is invited to the respective category, mentioned in this Rules and Guidelines document, for the requirements.

10. The material evidence provided by the Applicant shall not be returned. The Applicant is advised to keep all original evidence along with copies.

11. Wherever possible, a person from the *LBR* Team may also visit for verification. In such cases also, the evidence shall be sent along with the Claim.

12. In case of records where giant structures are put in place or supersize objects are involved, the measurements shall be taken in the presence of appropriate observers and authenticators, such as Gazetted Officers, Principal of a school/college, an engineering expert, or others as approved by the *LBR* Team.

13. Originals must not be sent, unless specifically requested by *LBR* for scrutiny. *LBR* will not keep copies longer than twelve (12) months after acceptance of the Claim, but record holders should keep their evidence to be produced for disputes for Life [*see below – Reverification of Evidence clause V.(15)*]. Evidence and documents of rejected records will be destroyed immediately after informing the Applicant of the decision.

14. All records and evidence are accepted in good faith and normal deep scrutiny. Any submission of fake evidence shall be met with a charge of cheating and other offences as mentioned in the Indian Penal Code and other applicable laws.

15. REVERIFICATION OF EVIDENCE:

a. In case a discrepancy in the record comes to light, as pointed out by any person or independently detected by the *LBR* Team, the onus of providing the evidence again for reverification of the record entry lies entirely with the record holder. If, in the opinion of the *LBR* Team, the discrepancy for whatsoever reason that has come to light is genuine, the same shall be communicated to the record holder and evidence sought for reverification; in the meantime, the record will be frozen/suspended and the certificate considered withdrawn until the evidence is reverified by a panel consisting of an *LBR* Team member and a legal consultant. Announcement of such a suspended/frozen record will appear only on the *LBR* website publicly and nowhere else. Subsequent to reverification, the record may either be restored, or amended or struck off completely.

b. *LBR* will not keep any data or records longer than one year [12 months] from acceptance in writing. In the event of any objection or discrepancy needing reverification [*see clause V.(15) above*], the record holder must keep all supporting evidence safe and readily accessible.

VI. ACCEPTANCE CRITERIA

1. Each Attempt must be categorized within one of the chapters or categories listed under Section II and III.A. However, *LBR* reserves the right, to be exercised at its sole and absolute discretion, to accept applications for Attempts.

2. Records must be absolute and not technical offshoots and they must be quantifiable, comparable and measurable.

3. No Claim shall be considered valid unless it is sent, along with the required evidence, in the manner prescribed in Sections IV and V.

4. *LBR* reserves the right to publish or delete any chapter, section, category or record in the present or any future edition of *LBR*, without any notice to the Applicants. *LBR* is under no obligation to inform record holders when a record may be dropped. Such decisions shall be the sole prerogative of the *LBR* Team in the larger continuing interests of the book.

5. Records shall be considered for publishing only on the grounds of their interest value and general public acceptance.

6. *LBR* will not consider potentially dangerous Attempts by Applicants, particularly those belonging to Age Group I, being up to thirteen (13) years of age.

7. Further, no entries in violation of any law, rule, regulation, guideline or any other statutory instrument shall be accepted.

8. Entries for the new edition of *LBR* will be confirmed only after the annual deadline, which is usually 31 May.

9. In all matters pertaining to the *Limca Book of Records*, the *LBR* Team and/or CCIPL's decision shall be final and binding.

10. Record claims are accepted in good faith and may be considered records and published in the book as such unless disproved with appropriate evidence.

11. It should be borne in mind, that *LBR* by its rejecting a Claim is not stating that the Claim may not be a record, or that the achievement, if any, is belittled. It is merely stating that for its purposes and within the framework of the book as run by its editorial policy it does not think the Claim suitable to feature.

12. Harassment of staff, including overt or covert threats, including threats of legal process, for rejecting a Claim, or for any other reason whatsoever, or defaming *LBR* or the *LBR* Team on public platforms will not be acceptable and will be met with all the measures under law. Any such behaviour will also result in automatic disqualification of the Claim.

VII. STATUTORY COMPLIANCE

1. It is mandatory for Applicants to abide by all local, state and national laws, rules and regulations applicable in relation to the Attempt. *LBR* expressly prohibits any Attempt that involves violation of any local, state or national laws, rules or regulations. Applicants are under an obligation to ensure that all activities related to the Attempt are neither unlawful, nor against public decency and morality. Applicants must note that *LBR* strongly discourages Attempts that are likely to offend the sentiments of any community. *LBR* also discourages Attempts that may cause harm to the public or animals, or cause any damage to the environment, and Applicants are requested to refrain from such Attempts. Applicants shall bear sole responsibility for any consequences arising out of any non-compliance with any applicable laws, rules or regulations insofar as they relate to the Attempt. *LBR* shall not be liable for any harm caused to the public or the environment in the course of the Attempt, and *LBR* shall not be responsible for any non-compliance with any applicable local, state or national or international laws, rules and regulations insofar as they relate to the Attempt.

2. With the submission of any Claim a record holder agrees to abide by the Terms and conditions in full and is thereby covenanting that the submission is true with no falsification of evidence or no mala fide intent of any sort whatsoever.

VIII. SAFETY PRECAUTIONS

1. The Applicant is requested to take all reasonable safety precautions prior to the Attempt including, but not limited to, the testing of all equipment used for the Attempt, the utilization of prescribed safety equipment in relation to the Attempt, the presence of requisite medical personnel and treatment facilities, and any applicable safety permits required under local, state or national laws, rules and regulations.

2. The Applicant understands that the Attempt may be dangerous to them, other Participants and spectators, and that they must identify such risks, with the help of professional advice, such as the risk of accident, illness, paralysis, injury, loss or death that may be caused by negligence, forces of nature, or other agencies, known and unknown. The Applicant knowingly and freely assumes all such risks, both known and unknown, and assumes full personal responsibility for the Attempt and its consequences.

3. The Applicant shall bear sole responsibility for taking all such safety precautions and acknowledge that CCIPL, the *LBR* Team and/or their respective directors, publishers, editors, officers, appointed representatives, Consultants, or agents shall not, in any manner whatsoever, be responsible for making any safety arrangements for the Attempt.

IX. PUBLICITY

1. The Applicant undertakes and irrevocably and unconditionally permits CCIPL and *LBR* to cover any Attempt through various media including newspapers, radio, television (news and other channels), Internet, mobile apps, social media, etc., and shall not raise any objection, protest or demur whatsoever to such coverage or in this regard. Whilst *LBR* shall make all reasonable efforts, there is no obligation on the part of *LBR* to air or otherwise engage in publicizing any Attempt. The Applicants must, at the request of CCIPL/*LBR*, participate in all promotional activity (such as publicity and photography) in relation to a successful Attempt, free of charge, and consent to CCIPL and *LBR* using their name and image in all promotional materials, free of charge, should CCIPL/*LBR* Team wish to do so as mentioned under Clause X below.

2. In case of publicity-related interview and other opportunities and/or events where the participation or presence of the Applicant may be required, the *LBR*/CCIPL Team will contact the Applicant in writing/on email for their consent and willingness for such an interview and/or event.

X. LICENCE TO USE NAME, IMAGE, LIKENESS, RECORD

Applicants hereby grant in perpetuity to CCIPL and *LBR*, its authorized agents, successors and assigns, the worldwide licence to use the name, image, likeness, pictures, video recordings, audio recordings, etc., of the Applicants in relation to any Attempts undertaken by the Applicants (the 'Licensed Property'). Applicants agree and grant to CCIPL and Hachette Book Publishing India Pvt. Ltd/Hachette India a waiver of their privacy and personality rights, and grant the right to use any element of the Licensed Property for any purpose in connection with *LBR* including, but not limited to, the publication and distribution of *LBR*, the promotion of *LBR*, CCIPL, and any of its divisions or products, and the filing of copyright, trademark and other similar registrations in relation to *LBR* that involve the Licensed Property. All material submitted in connection with a potential entry in *LBR* (whether in written, audio, electronic or visual form, or a combination of any or all of those) or any photographs, video and/or film footage and/or audio recording taken of Applicants are assigned to *LBR* and CCIPL upon submission and become the property of *LBR* and CCIPL exclusively. *LBR* and CCIPL may use the material in any medium in any reasonable manner it deems fit. Copyright in any such material remains the sole property of *LBR* and CCIPL.

XI. INTELLECTUAL PROPERTY RIGHTS

The name 'Limca' and the 'Limca' logo are registered trademarks of The Coca-Cola Company, USA, and should not be used for any publicity in relation to an Attempt, or after a Claim has been accepted, without the expressed permission of CCIPL. All right, title and interest including, but not limited to, the Intellectual Property Rights, in *LBR* and in any and all entries received shall vest solely and exclusively with CCIPL at all times. CCIPL or any person or entity permitted by CCIPL in this regard shall be entitled to use any information in connection with the entry in any media for future promotional, marketing, publicity and any other purpose, without any permission and/or payment to the Applicant.

XII. RESPONSIBILITY FOR ALL ASSOCIATED COSTS AND INSURANCE

The Applicant understands and acknowledges that all expenses incurred in relation to the Attempt shall be borne solely by the Applicant. CCIPL and/or *LBR* Team shall in no manner be responsible for reimbursing any expenses incurred in the course of the Attempt, or even in the event that the Applicant is successful at the Attempt. CCIPL/*LBR* shall not be responsible for providing any kind of insurance in relation to any Attempt, and shall not be responsible for any emergency medical expenses or any subsequent medical expenses in the event of any incident/accident, illness or incapacity arising out of the Attempt.

XIII. WAIVER OF CLAIMS AND INDEMNITY

1. Applicants acknowledge and consent on behalf of themselves, their heirs, successors, assigns, personal representatives and next of kin, to WAIVE ALL CLAIMS AND RELEASE AND HOLD HARMLESS the *LBR* Team, Hachette Book Publishing India Pvt. Ltd/Hachette India and all its employees, directors, parent or affiliate organizations, Consultants, representatives, partners, CCIPL, its directors, publishers, editors, officers, employees and representatives, and its partners, affiliates, subsidiaries, advertising agencies, agents and their respective directors, officers, employees and representatives (the 'Released Parties'), with respect to any and all injury, disability, paralysis, death, or loss or damage to person, property or reputations, arising out of the Attempt, to the fullest extent permitted by law. The Applicants agree to indemnify and hold the Released Parties harmless from all losses, liabilities, damages, costs or expenses (including but not limited to reasonable legal fees and other litigation costs and expenses) incurred by any of the Released Parties as a result of any claims or suits that the Applicant (or anyone claiming by, under or through the Applicant) may bring against any of the Released Parties to recover any losses, liabilities, costs, damages or expenses that arise during or result from the Attempt.

2. Further,

a. *LBR* retains an indemnity for human error or typographical error, and the right to revise a record because of that; and the right to withdraw or modify a certificate because of such error lies with the *LBR* Team.

b. The right to suspend records/certification on receipt of disputes or objections lies with the *LBR* editorial team. In such cases the record verification will be revisited, and the claimant must provide reverification [*see clause V.(15)*] and if necessary further detailing to answer such objections. If the Applicant is not able to furnish a copy of the evidence as per the original claim, the record and certification may be cancelled.

c. The principle of acceptance is basic verification and acceptance in good faith, so records should be clear and detailed. *LBR* reserves the right to do forensic examination or reopen a record case later if found to be suspect.

d. Faking of records and evidence is a criminal offence and shall be dealt with strictly under the prevailing laws. The application/Claim/record shall be cancelled and the Applicant/record holder shall be immediately blacklisted and no further applications/claims from them shall be entertained; and the rights to legal prosecution shall be reserved.

e. For records involving mass participation/huge numbers, for example, 'most people at a concert' or 'most vehicles in a rally', the simple principle of sequentially numbered badges should be there with a logbook of a unique identifier (licence/registration number, individual ID card or any similar clearly visible device).

f. *LBR* is a private body and its editorial criteria solely belong to it alone and its decisions shall be the ones solely binding on any record.

XIV. SEVERABILITY

Each of the provisions contained in these Rules and Guidelines/Terms is considered to be reasonable by CCIPL, *LBR* and the Applicants, and each clause, subclause, paragraph and sub-paragraph shall be construed as independent of any other provision. If any provision of these Rules and Guidelines/Terms proves to be invalid, void or illegal it shall not in any way affect, impair or invalidate any other provision and the remaining provisions shall remain in full force and effect.

XV. DISPUTE

The courts of competent jurisdiction at Delhi shall have exclusive jurisdiction to determine any and all disputes arising out of, or in connection with, any Attempt undertaken or entry made for the purpose of *LBR*. Further, all issues and questions concerning the construction, validity, interpretation and enforceability of these Rules and Guidelines/Terms, or the rights and obligations of the Applicants and/or CCIPL and/or partners of *LBR*, shall be governed and construed in accordance with the laws of the Republic of India.

Note: For specific guidelines all Applicants are requested to contact the *LBR* Team by email at lbr.entries@hachetteindia.com

APPENDIX 1

The clauses below are subject to ongoing review and modifications, and applicants may check this appendix from time to time to update themselves on categories that may have been discontinued, modified or changed.

1. SPECIAL NOTE FOR PROSPECTIVE ATTEMPTS

a. For young children: No marathon records or dangerous records will be considered for children. They can attempt records in mental mathematics, collections and Rubik's cube. The pre-approved categories are as follows:

Major categories:

i. Mental Mathematics (without using pen and paper)

ii. Calculation (using pen and paper)

Spoken or visual or flashing numbers (for calculation purposes) will be considered as mental mathematics. Both the major categories have the following subcategories for attempting records:

- Five-minute event: The Applicant will be given 5 minutes to attempt the event. The time will be the major benchmark for making and breaking records.
- Marathon event: The Applicant sets the quantum of calculations for attempting the record. The time will not be considered for attempting a new record. However, for breaking the record in this category both time and the quantum will be considered as parameters.
- Sprint event: The Applicant will be given one (1) minute to attempt a record. Time cut-off will be the major benchmark for breaking records. The Attempt must be made in the approved categories only. The age criteria are U-18 and above 18 only. The documents submitted/record attempted will not be considered on their face value and will be only considered for review after the *LBR* Team approves it. Calculations with or without decimals will be considered as the same.
- The following events will not be considered for records:
  - i. Multiplication and division by a single digit;
  - ii. Writing/speaking of multiplication tables;
  - iii. Squaring of 1-, 2- and 3-digit numbers;
  - iv. Multiplication of 2-digit numbers;
  - v. Any record Attempt with even a single error; and
  - vi. Multiple claims under the same category.

b. There are categories in the book, marked to indicate that they are one-time categories. These categories will not be carried forward into our subsequent editions and are not contestable.

c. Certain categories in the book are marked to indicate that the age group(s) of Participants in the record have been modified. These entries too shall not be carried into subsequent editions and are not contestable. Applicants may, on a case-to-case basis, undertake an Attempt in the category under the modified specific rules and guidelines as informed by the *LBR* Team.

d. Additional pointers to remember before sending the documentation or claims:
   - i. Do not send any documents unless requested by the *LBR* Team, post-approval.
   - ii. Do not send any documentation if your event has not been approved for consideration by the *LBR* Team.
   - iii. Documents received by *LBR* for events that are not pre-approved through email will not be reviewed by the *LBR* Team.

2. A NOTE FOR PAST, PRESENT AND POTENTIAL RECORD HOLDERS

a. The name *Limca* and the *Limca* logo are registered trademarks of The Coca-Cola Company, USA, and should not be used for publicity when a record is being attempted or after the Claim has been accepted, without written permission of the publisher.

b. When records are being attempted, it is not obligatory for the *LBR* Team to provide invigilators. However, where possible they may do so.

c. All Attempts at breaking old records and setting new ones are undertaken entirely at the risk of the Applicant. Neither the *LBR* Team nor CCIPL can be held responsible by the Applicant/person undertaking an Attempt or third party for any liability that may arise out of such an Attempt.

d. Applicants may use the name 'Limca Book of Records' while attempting the record as long as
   - i. they do not use the logo of the *Limca Book of Records* or Limca brand or any Licensed Property of CCIPL;
   - ii. they do not receive or give money in the execution of such an Attempt using *LBR* as a party or implied party or endorser; and
   - iii. they do not offer Participants/partners any kind of inducement using *LBR* as a party. **This is strictly prohibited and will result in the Applicant's name being blacklisted and rejected for any future application/Attempts.**

e. The *LBR* Team reserves the complete and incontestable right to decide which chapters, sections, photographs, categories and records to publish or delete in future editions. *LBR* will not consider potentially dangerous record Attempts by minors or any Attempt that violates a law.

f. *LBR* strives to be completely authentic. However, it sometimes happens that an earlier record may come to light or be applied for after the book is released. In such cases corrections/updates will be carried out in the next edition or as deemed fit by the *LBR* Team.

g Records that are 'firsts' are not entitled to perpetuity and can be dropped from the book without any prior intimation. For reasons of space or any other reasons whatsoever, a confirmed Claim may also be dropped. *LBR* Team members may inform the Applicant of the change in status but are not bound to do so. Such decisions are the sole prerogative of the *LBR* Team in the larger continuing interest of the book.

h. The record holders are not entitled to any prize money, gift(s) or free copies of *LBR*.

i In all matters pertaining to *Limca Book of Records*, the *LBR* Team's decision is final.

3. DISCONTINUED CATEGORIES

a. A few categories have been discontinued and will not be featured in any subsequent editions. The website is updated regularly regarding such categories.

b. Youngest category: The youngest category has been dropped. The only exceptional cases are sports, art and creative skills and any other reputed competitions where there is a quantifiable group. The age categories are specified only to ensure that no records are created against the law (for example, driving at an age not legally permissible) and to ensure that minors do not try to attempt records that require excessive physical exertion (like marathon events or climbing high mountains) and/or those that may be detrimental to their physical, mental or emotional well-being.

c. Most surgeries/medical procedures within a time duration: The category for most surgeries/ medical procedures has been discontinued as the quality of the procedure may be compromised during such claims.

d. Tractor service camps: The category for most tractors serviced has been discontinued as such claims are difficult to monitor and make it an industry-specific claim.

e. Largest blood/organ donation drives

f. Wrist cracking/wrist rotation

g. Most couplets written

h. Holding most burning candles in the mouth

i. Fastest construction of structures

j. Fastest yoga asanas

k. Collection of error coins

l. Longest interview

m. Limbo skating

n. Most one-hand claps

o. Most postcards sent in a day – solo/group, single/multiple venues

p. Largest packers and movers of household goods

q. Most people screened/diagnosed – single/multiple venues

4. WHY WAS YOUR RECORD REJECTED?

Unfortunately, many applications are rejected. The following are the general reasons that lead to rejection of applications:

a. Not accepted Terms and conditions and/or incomplete Application Form.

b. Insufficient documentation: The details provided do not suffice for verification purposes.

c. Not met criteria: For record purposes, we have certain criteria and set categories. For instance, in physical feats we only have categories for 1 minute or 1 hour claims. Any claim that does not follow the format (e.g., most push-ups in 40 seconds instead of 30 seconds) is not accepted.

d. Specific titles: Generally, we measure our record titles by one single parameter so that anybody can attempt and break/surpass that record. If the record claim is too specific or has multiple variables, we would not be considering such claims. For example, 'most push-ups in one minute' would be considered whereas 'most push-ups done in 1 minute by a teacher', would not be accepted.

e. Inappropriate/Offensive: *LBR* does not accept or encourage inappropriate or offensive claims.

f. Claims involving alcohol/smoking/substance usage: *LBR* does not encourage or accept claims involving alcohol, smoking or substance use.

g. Animal welfare: Any claim that is not in accordance with animal rights laws or involves any mistreatment of animals is neither encouraged nor accepted in *LBR*.

h. Personality related claims: Claims related to famous personalities, such as 'most people dressed as' or 'most times performing as' will only be considered for internationally recognized, iconic and universally acknowledged personalities. The *LBR* Team reserves the right of discretion in any such claim.

i. Record claims involving wastage of food/medical supplies, e.g., artworks made with fresh food materials would not be considered.

j. Environmentally harmful claims: *LBR* does not support any claim that may have any sort of adverse effect on the environment.

k. Fastest musicians: *LBR* does not consider claims such as fastest guitarist, fastest piano player, etc., as it is not possible to judge the quality of music produced in such claims.

l. Firsts: The firsts in a field are generally not accepted unless they mark change in trend, beginning of a new era or change the traditional way for the matter. The *LBR* Team reserves the right to accept or reject any such claim.

m. Poetry: *LBR* does not accept claims pertaining to poetry due to its subjective nature.

n. Originality/Uniqueness-based claims: Uniqueness/originality cannot be a parameter of competence for a record. The *LBR* Team reserves the right of discretion in any such claim.

o. Sports achievements: For records directly involving performance in sports, *LBR* only accepts those which occur at a top-level professional, international, or pre-eminent amateur levels, or as per the decision of the relevant Consultant in specific cases.

p. *LBR* does not have categories for largest anthology and longest preservation of food items/articles.

q. Claims relating to number of research papers written or published will not be accepted.

Assuming no disruptions, the next edition of *LBR* is planned for publication in end-2022. The last date for new entries and applications (complete with relevant documentation) for the *Limca Book of Records* 2023 edition: 31 May 2022

Please address all correspondence to:

Limca Book of Records (Editorial)
Hachette Book Publishing India Pvt. Ltd
4th/5th Floors, Corporate Centre
Plot No. 94, Sector 44
Gurugram 122003, Haryana, India

Phone: (Board) +91-124-4195000

Fax: +91-124-4148900

Email: lbr.entries@hachetteindia.com

Rules and Guidelines:
https://www.hachetteindia.com/limca-book-of-records/rules-and-guidelines.aspx

Website: www.coca-colaindia.com/limca-book-of-records

Note: In order to have an accessible, credible and reproducible record of interactions with Applicants, email (and where it is unavailable, postal mail – registered or courier) is the preferred form of communication and correspondence.

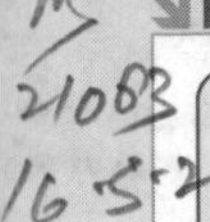

NEW CATEGORIES OPEN FOR APPLICATION

LBR welcomes participation in setting fresh records in the new categories being introduced:

VIRTUAL SESSIONS: We will review applications for single sessions conducted online on a single platform. The parameters would be based on the number of Participants and the duration of the Attempt.

TEDX TALKS (parameter – number of TEDx Talks)

- Most **TEDx Talks** delivered in a year by an individual
- Most **TEDx Talks** delivered in a day

General Guidelines

i. The event should be a proper licensed event. The organizer should hold a valid TEDx licence and a copy of the same is to be shared for verification.
ii. The event may include talks, demonstrations and performances.
iii. The talk cannot exceed 18 minutes as per TEDx rules.
iv. Ideally, there should be a different talk for each event.
v. Videos of the talks given should be uploaded on the official TEDx YouTube channel to be considered for the category.
vi. The claim so submitted should be in accordance with all TEDx rules.

FLASH MOBS: (parameter – number of Participants in the Attempt)

- Most in a Flash Mob

General Guidelines

i. The gathering for the performance of the flash mob should be sudden, as is the general understanding of a flash mob.
ii. Only single-venue claims will be considered.
iii. The flash mob has to perform for a minimum of 10 minutes in order to be considered.
iv. All Participants and the Applicant need to be a part of the performance for the entire duration of the Attempt.
v. All Participants must perform simultaneously. The Participants cannot be divided into separate groups that perform at different times.

Note: Such records involving crowds and people in proximity may be attempted only after the full official relaxation of the pandemic-related advisory and regulations.

SOCIAL MEDIA: (parameter – number of likes on a single post)

- Most liked Instagram image/post – lifetime (for both verified and non-verified accounts)

General Guidelines

i. The claim so submitted should be in accordance with all Instagram rules.
ii. Likes from 'fake accounts' or the Applicant's other accounts will not be considered.

Rules and Guidelines Version 2020–21